بسم الله الرحمن الرحيم

"The house of al-Arqam is the house of Islām"

Al-Ḥākim (d.405 h.) in *al-Mustadrak ʿala al-Ṣaḥiḥayn* (6185)

An Introduction to the

Ḥanbali Madhhab

المدخل

إلى مذهب الإمام أحمد بن حنبل

ʿAbd al-Qādir Ibn Badrān al-Dimashqī (d.1346/1927)

Translated by Amr Abu Ayyub

دار الأرقم
DAR AL-ARQAM

ISBN: 978 1 8384897 1 7

British Library Cataloguing in Publishing Data
A catalogue record for this book is available from the British Library

First edition, 2021

Prepared and published by Dar al-Arqam Publishing
Birmingham, United Kingdom

www.daralarqam.bigcartel.com
Email: daralarqam@hotmail.co.uk

Translated by Amr Abu Ayyub

He is a student of Islamic knowledge based in the United States. He has a number of *ijāzāt* in ḥadīth and Qurʾān, and has been engaged in the study of Islamic law for a decade. His interests include Islamic legal theory, objectives of the Sharīʿah, development of Islamic legal systems, exegesis of the Qurʾān, and theology.

Edited by Adnan Karim

Head of translation at Dar al-Arqam. He has translated and edited a number of works for Dar al-Arqam.

If you would like to support our work, donations can be made via:

- www.daralarqam.bigcartel.com/product/donate
- www.patreon.com/daralarqam
- www.paypal.me/daralarqam

Printed in Turkey by Mega | export@mega.com.tr

AN INTRODUCTION TO THE

ḤANBALĪ MADHHAB

ʿAbd al-Qādir Ibn Badrān al-Dimashqī (d. 1346/1927)

DAR AL-ARQAM

الفهرس

Contents

تقديم الناشر
Publisher's Foreword

We would like to thank our team who persevered through this lengthy journey, endured the toil of long days and nights, and remained steadfast until reaching its end. Before the reader is the end result of our efforts, and all praise is to Allah for its facilitation.

May Allah make it a means of reward for us, bless it and allow us to remain sincere.

Dar al-Arqam Publishing
Birmingham, UK
2nd April 2021

مقدمة المترجم

Translator's Introduction

In the Name of Allah, the Most Merciful, the Giver of Mercy

When I was approached by Shaykh ʿAdnan Karim, of Dar al-Arqam Publishing, in the summer of 2019 to translate al-Shaykh ʿAbd al-Qādir ibn Badrān's *al-Madkhal ilā Madhhab al-Imām Aḥmad ibn Ḥanbal*, I was ecstatic. As a person who loved al-Imam Aḥmad ibn Ḥanbal ﵀ his *madhhab*, and his ways, no book would have satisfied me more. Unfortunately, I would only begin working on this marvellous volume in the winter of 2019.

As I worked on *al-Madkhal*, my love for this work, its author and its subject matter only grew. From the cheerful, spirited temperament of Ibn Badrān ﵀ to the rich, robust content of this volume, the work, to me, was indispensable. If Jerusalem is the heart of the Levant, Damascus is its spirit and soul. Mention of its gardens and greenery evokes nostalgia in even the most hardened of hearts. When that sentimentality is infused with discussions on religion, law, theology, and history, it brightens every chapter, enriches every discussion, and enlivens every sentence. Indeed, one feels the glee of Ibn Badrān in his words; he references the words of al-Imam Aḥmad as being gardens, making him the one basking in said gardens, enjoying their sunlight and inhaling their fresh air.

Born in Douma, Syria, in the year 1280 *hijri*, corresponding to 1863 C.E., the great scholar, polymath, jurist, and scholar of hadith, ʿAbd al-Qādir ibn Badrān[1] was just one of the offspring in a long line of remarkable scholars, all known as Ibn Badrān. He learned to read and write with his teacher, al-Shaykh ʿAdnān ibn Muḥammad ʿAds. As he grew older, he began learning religious sciences with his grandfather, al-Shaykh Muṣṭafā, as well as al-Shaykh Muḥammad ibn ʿUthmān al-Ḥanbalī, known better as "The Ora-

---

1 Mentioned by Muḥammad ibn Nāṣir al-ʿAjamī in his book, *ʿAllāmat al-Shām ʿAbd al-Qādir ibn Badrān al-Dimashqī: Ḥayātuhu wa Āthāruhu* (p. 16). Note that this biographical information was adapted from al- ʿAjamī's book, as well as Dr. ʿAbdullāh al-Turkī's book, *al-Madhhab al-Ḥanbalī: Dirāsat fī Tārīkhī wa Simātihi wa Ashhari Aʿlāmihi wa Muʾallafātih*.

tor of Douma."

After studying with the scholars of his locality, he moved to Damascus and learned from al-Shaykh Salīm ibn Yāsīn al-ʿAṭṭār al-Shāfiʿī, a scholar of ḥadīth from Damascus, as well as al-Shaykh Muḥammad ibn Muṣṭafā al-Ṭanṭāwī al-Azharī, a scholar specialised in astronomy, mathematics, and other rational sciences. Lastly, he learned from the Muftī of the Ḥanbalīs in his era, al-Shaykh Aḥmad ibn Ḥasan al-Shaṭṭī. Al-Shaykh Aḥmad ibn Ḥasan al-Shaṭṭī was the son of the great Ḥanbalī scholar, al-Shaykh Ḥasan al-Shaṭṭī. He also learned ḥadīth from al-Shaykh Badr al-Dīn al-Ḥasanī. With that said, al-Shaykh Ibn Badrān remarks, "I only studied under scholars for five years. I do not mention this boastfully nor pridefully, but rather I mentioned it to show thankfulness to Allah for what He has given me."

Al-Shaykh Ibn Badrān authored many works on various sciences, but mainly on law and legal theory. Some of his works include:

One. *Ādāb al-Muṭālaʿah*: On how to read a book.

Two. *Ḥāshiyat ʿAlā Akhṣar al-Mukhtaṣarāt*: A commentary on one of the introductory works on Ḥanbalī substantive law, known as *Akhṣar al-Mukhtaṣarāt*, authored by al-Shaykh Muḥammad ibn Badr al-Dīn ibn Balbān al-Dimashqī. This book has been printed in Arabic, and his comments are of great value.

Three. *Sharḥ Thulāthiyyāt al-Imām Aḥmad*: A commentary on the narrations from the *Musnad* of al-Imām Aḥmad that contain only three reporters in the chain of narration.

Four. *Nuzhat al-Khāṭir al-ʿĀṭir Sharḥ Kitāb Rawḍat al-Naẓir wa Junnat al-Munāẓir*: A book on Ḥanbalī legal theory. It is an explanation of al-Imām al-Muwaffaq ibn Qudāmah's book, *Rawḍat al-Naẓir*, which itself is a summation of *al-Mustaṣfā fī ʿIlm al-Uṣūl*, authored by al-Imām Ḥujjat al-Islām al-Ghazālī.

Five. *Al-Manhal al-Ṣāfī Sharḥ al-Kāfī fī ʿIlmay al-ʿArūḍ wa ʾl-Qawāfī*: On poetic meters in the Arabic Language.

As can be seen, al-Shaykh Ibn Badrān authored books on various topics, from literature, to law, to legal theories, to language, to ḥadīth, thus cementing himself as one of the polymaths of his era.

Al-Shaykh Ibn Badran became ill with hemiplegia at the end of his life and one of its symptoms was paralysis on the right side of his body. After many months of enduring the pains of this disease, he passed away in the year 1346 *hijri*, coinciding with September 25th 1927 C.E. May Allah have mercy on him and bestow on him an abundance of rewards for the services he rendered for the Ummah.

Often times, mention of al-Ṣāliḥiyyah district is made by Ibn Badrān. This district was a well-known hub of Ḥanbalī scholars and teachers. Some of the greatest Ḥanbalī scholars passed through this area. To fully understand the significance of this district, the families who resided there must be identified, and the reasons for their mass migration into Damascus must be clarified.

Indeed, the Ḥanbalī Madhhab did not have much of a presence in the Levant; the predominant schools of law were that of the Shāfiʿī and Ḥanafī schools. In his discussions on al-Ṣāliḥiyyah, Dr. ʿAbdullāh al-Shamrānī mentions that the Ḥanbalī school had no presence in the Levant until al-Imām Abu ʿl-Faraj ʿAbd al-Wāḥid al-Shīrāzī ﵀ migrated to Jerusalem from Baghdad. One of his students was a man by the name of Qudāmah ibn Miqdām al-ʿUmarī ﵀ a descendent of ʿUmar ibn al-Khaṭṭāb ﵁. Al-Shaykh Qudāmah was a resident of Jammāʿīl, a district of Nablus, Palestine. Al-Imām Abu ʿl-Faraj ﵀ supplicated for Qudāmah that his offspring be blessed. Qudāmah's offspring would become known as 'Āl Qudāmah,' or, 'the Family of Qudāmah.' His offspring include such names as Muwaffaq al-Dīn ibn Qudāmah, the author of *al-Mughnī, al-Kāfī, al-Muqniʿ*, and other works on substantive law and jurisprudence. Al-Muwaffaq used to say, "We are all blessings of Abu ʿl-Faraj."

Later, al-Shaykh Qudāmah ﵀ undertook giving sermons in his town Jammāʿīl, and that position would be held by his son and his grandson. His grandson, al-Shaykh Aḥmad ibn Muḥammad ibn Qudāmah, a celebrated scholar, orator, and jurist, was the first to migrate from Jerusalem to Damascus. After he settled in the Damascus district, he wrote to his family in Jammāʿīl to join him. Of the names of those who migrated were his two sons, Abu ʿUmar al-Maqdisī and al-Muwaffaq ibn Qudāmah, among others.

Soon, Damascus would be unsuitable for the Qudāmah family. They decided it was time to leave the central location of Damascus and reside in one of its surrounding areas. Al-Shaykh Aḥmad ibn Qudāmah and others looked for an area that was suitable for their farming, as they were farmers in their hometown of Jammāʿīl. They found an area near Mount Qasyun, north of Damascus, that was abandoned. As such, they settled there in the year

554 *hijri*. The Qudāmah family could not afford to build homes for each family, nor did they have expertise to do so themselves. They hired a worker to build three homes for them all. At this time, the area because known as, al-Ṣāliḥiyyah, which is an ascription to righteousness, since its residents were righteous. A mosque was erected carrying the name of al-Imam Aḥmad ibn Ḥanbal. It became known as Jāmiʿ al-Ḥanābilah, or, the Gathering Place of the Ḥanābilah, shown in figure 2, below.

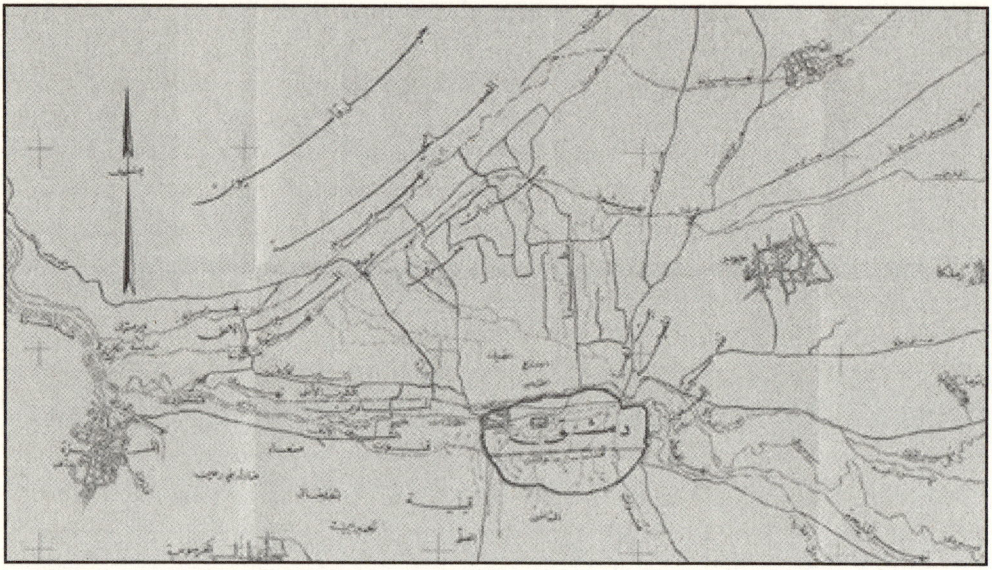

Figure 1 A map of Damascus showing Salihiyyah District in the north.

Figure 2 An image of the Ḥanbali Mosque in Salihiyyah

Some of the famous families that you will find biographed in *al-Madkhal* are:

- The Family of Qudāmah.
- The Family of Mufliḥ.
- The Family of ʿAbd al-Hādī.
- The Family of Qāḍī al-Jabal.

Just these four families produced hundreds of scholars and possibly thousands of volumes of authorships on Islamic law, creed, ḥadīth, exegesis, and other sciences.

Some notable figures are:

- Al-Shaykh Aḥmad ibn Qudāmah: He originally settled in al-Ṣāliḥiyyah with the Qudāmah family.
- Al-Shaykh Abu ʿUmar ibn Qudāmah: He was the brother of al-Imām al-Muwaffaq and the father of al-Imām Shams al-Dīn ibn Qudāmah, known better as Ibn Abī ʿUmar, the author of *al-Sharḥ al-Kabīr*.
- Muwaffaq al-Dīn ʿAbdullāh ibn Aḥmad ibn Qudāmah: He was the greatest Ḥanbalī scholar of his time and one of the main pillars of the Ḥanbalī Madhhab. He codified the *madhhab* to a large extent. Every Ḥanbalī who came after him studied his books; tens of books have emanated from just one of his works: *al-Muqniʿ*. It has been explained tens of times, summarised, and its summary has been explained, and so forth. His book *al-Mughnī* is one of the masterpieces of Islamic law, to the extent that the Sultan of Scholars, al-ʿIzz ibn ʿAbd al-Salām, the famous Shafiʿī scholar and *mujtahid*, said, "I have never seen a book authored by a Muslim quite like *al-Muḥallā* by Ibn Ḥazm, and *al-Mughnī* by Ibn Qudāmah." He also said, "My heart did not feel at ease giving *fatwa* until I purchased two books: *al-Mughnī* and *al-Muḥallā*."
- Ibn Abī ʿUmar: He was the nephew of al-Muwaffaq and his most outstanding student. He authored *al-Sharḥ al-Kabīr*, which is an explanation of *al-Muqniʿ*. He taught a number of the great scholars of Islam, among them al-Nawawī and Shaykh al-Islām Ibn Taymiyyah.
- Shams al-Dīn ibn ʿAbd al-Hādī: He was a great scholar of ḥadīth and one of the foremost students of al-Shaykh Taqī al-Dīn ibn Taymiyyah.
- Sharaf al-Dīn ibn Qāḍī al-Jabal: He was a great scholar and great-grandson

of al-Shaykh Ibn Abī ʿUmar. He was a student of al-Shaykh al-Islām Ibn Taymiyyah and authored *al-Fāʾiq*, on the Ḥanbalī *madhhab*.

• Shams al-Dīn ibn Mufliḥ: The great Ḥanbalī jurist and student of Shaykh al-Islām Aḥmad ibn Taymiyyah. He was the scholar of the Ḥanbalī *madhhab* of his time. He authored *al-Furūʿ* and *al-Adāb al-Sharʿiyyah*, two books that are often read by Ḥanbalī students today.

• Burhān al-Dīn ibn Mufliḥ: He was also a great scholar of *fiqh*, and the grandson of al-Imām Shams al-Dīn. He authored *al-Mubdiʿ*, an explanation of *al-Muqniʿ*, and other works.

• ʿAlāʾ al-Dīn al-Mardāwī: The greatest of the latter-day scholars. He authored many books in service to the *madhhab*, including *al-Inṣāf*, which is an explanation and appendix to *al-Muqniʿ*, and *al-Tanqīḥ al-Mushbiʿ*, which is a summation of *al-Inṣāf*.

• Mūsā ibn Aḥmad al-Ḥajjāwī: The author of *al-Iqnāʿ* and other important works referred to by latter-day Ḥanbalīs.

The Ḥanbalī mosque in al-Ṣāliḥiyyah was an oft-visited place of knowledge. Scholars such as al-Shaykh Taqī al-Dīn ibn Taymiyyah, al-Dhahabī, Ibn Kathīr, al-ʿIrāqī, and Ibn Ḥajar travelled there to learn ḥadith, in particular. The number of blessings that emanated from just one mosque is almost unfathomable. May Allah have mercy on all of the scholars of Islam, and may He show mercy to the great scholars of al-Ṣāliḥiyyah for all that they did for Islam and Muslims.

Working on *al-Madkhal* has been a pleasurable experience. Apart from Ibn Badrān's tone, his place amongst the scholarly has been solidified. He studied the traditional Islamic sciences and was proficient in many of them. Indeed, his discussions on jurisprudence and legal theory show a wide readership of the *uṣūl* literature. As I rendered his words into English, I found myself cross-referencing his quotations, only to notice that he quoted quite literally tens of sources.

As is the case with every book other than the Book of Allah the Exalted, there will be room for improvement, even if subtle. As such, I decided to outline my work on this book in the following points:

1) I have in my possession the print of *al-Madkhal* that was published by Dr. ʿAbdullāh al-Turkī, printed by *Muʾassasat al-Risālah*. It consists of 520 pages. In the introduction, Dr. ʿAbdullāh mentioned that he could not find

a manuscript of *al-Madkhal*, instead relying on a very early print found in Damascus. His work consisted of cross-referencing Ibn Badrān's quotations and attempting to fix any errors he found in the original print and he also referenced any ahadith he found to their original sources.

2) However, reading through *al-Madkhal*, I found that there were still typographical errors. Most of these errors can be attributed to Dr. ʿAbdullāh never finding a manuscript of the original work. By the Mercy and Grace of Allah, I was able to find the manuscript, written in the author's own handwriting. This allowed me to correct the errors I could find in Dr. ʿAbdullāh's work and render the text as Ibn Badrān wrote it. Where there are corrections, I have noted them in the footnotes.

3) Because most English-speaking readers will not have had access to see how our traditional manuscripts look nor how they are cross-referenced in publications, I decided to place images of the manuscript where there were errors. I wanted the English reading world to see the efforts put by Muslims at preserving our tradition and heritage. I have also placed the first and last page of the manuscript in this very introduction for those curious.

4) One of my contributions to the work itself, I believe, is my referencing of quotes mentioned by Ibn Badrān. I referenced almost every discernible quote back to its original source, and where there were lapses in accuracy, I corrected them based on the words of the one quoted. As such, a student or reader would find names of books in the footnotes that they might otherwise have not heard of nor knew their worth. This, of course, is when I could find the reference.

5) Lastly, and what I believe to be my most time-consuming contribution, I added explanatory notes where I felt there was a need. Sometimes, the works of great scholars contain phrases that require further inspection and explanation. Where I have added a comment, I have signified it by using [t]. Where there is no such marking, it is a footnote added by Dr. ʿAbdullāh al-Turkī ﷺ.

This book also offered a number of challenges. When the project was first specified and delegated to me, there were discussions on whether to omit the fifth chapter, on Legal Theory. However, Shaykh ʿAdnan made the prudent decision that the book should appear in English in full, as it is in Arabic. The legal theories section was challenging in the sense that, despite one's studies on the subject, explaining the topic is another journey altogether. I found myself sometimes consulting tens of books on *Uṣūl al-Fiqh* just to translate a single phrase. Sometimes, *al-Burhān* by Imām al-Ḥaramayn al-Juwaynī would have the answer. At other times, it was *al-Mustaṣfā* by al-Imām al-Ghazālī, or *al-Baḥr al-Muḥīṭ* by al-Imam Badr al-Dīn al-Zarkashī. At other times, the commentaries contained the subtle detail I looked for; al-Shaykh al-ʿAṭṭār's commentaries on al-Imām al-Maḥallī's explanation of *Jamʿ al-Jawāmiʿ* was very useful. The following *uṣūl* books of our *aṣḥāb* were instrumental:

• *Sharḥ Mukhtaṣar al-Rawḍah* by al-Imām Najm al-Dīn al-Ṭūfī.

• *Al-Taḥbīr Sharḥ al-Taḥrīr* by al-Qāḍī 'Alā' al-Dīn 'Alī ibn Ismāʿīl al-Mardāwī.

• *Uṣūl al-Fiqh* by al-Imām Shams al-Dīn ibn Mufliḥ.

• *Sharḥ al-Kawkab al-Munīr* by al-Imām Ibn al-Najjār al-Futuhi.

• *Al-Musawwadah*, by the family of Taymiyyah: Al-Imām Majd al-Dīn Abu 'l-Barakāt 'Abd al-Salām ibn 'Abdullāh ibn Taymiyyah, his son, al-Imām 'Abd al-Ḥalīm, and his grandson, Shaykh al-Islām Taqī al-Dīn Aḥmad ibn 'Abd al-Ḥalīm ibn 'Abd al-Salām ibn Taymiyyah.

• *Rawḍat al-Nāẓir wa Junnat al-Munāẓir* by al-Imām Muwaffaq al-Dīn ibn Qudāmah al-Maqdisī.

May Allah have mercy on them and all scholars of Islam.

This journey was worthwhile, beneficial, and enriching. I am forever indebted to al-Shaykh 'Abd al-Qādir ibn Badrān for authoring this book. Little did he know that it would be translated into the English language and be the cause for so much benefit in the Ummah.

Works such as this do not just appear in a vacuum. There are a number of people I need to acknowledge, whose contributions to the field of *uṣūl al-fiqh* have been instrumental to me. I also must thank my teachers and mentors with whom I would discuss these various topics and attempt to come to conclusions. Last, but not least, I must thank my family for their continued support. May Allah the Exalted reward them all individually on my behalf.

If I have made any errors in this work, it is my own flaw; Allah and His Messenger, peace and blessings of Allah be on him, are absolved of any blame. However, if any portion of this work is beneficial, it is of the favours and blessings of Allah the Exalted. I am truly indebted to al-Imām Aḥmad ibn

Ḥanbal and carry the utmost love for him in my heart, and I hope that this contribution to his way of thought weighs heavily on my scale of deeds on the Day of Judgement.

Amr Abu Ayyub
December 30, 2020

First Page of the Arabic Manuscript

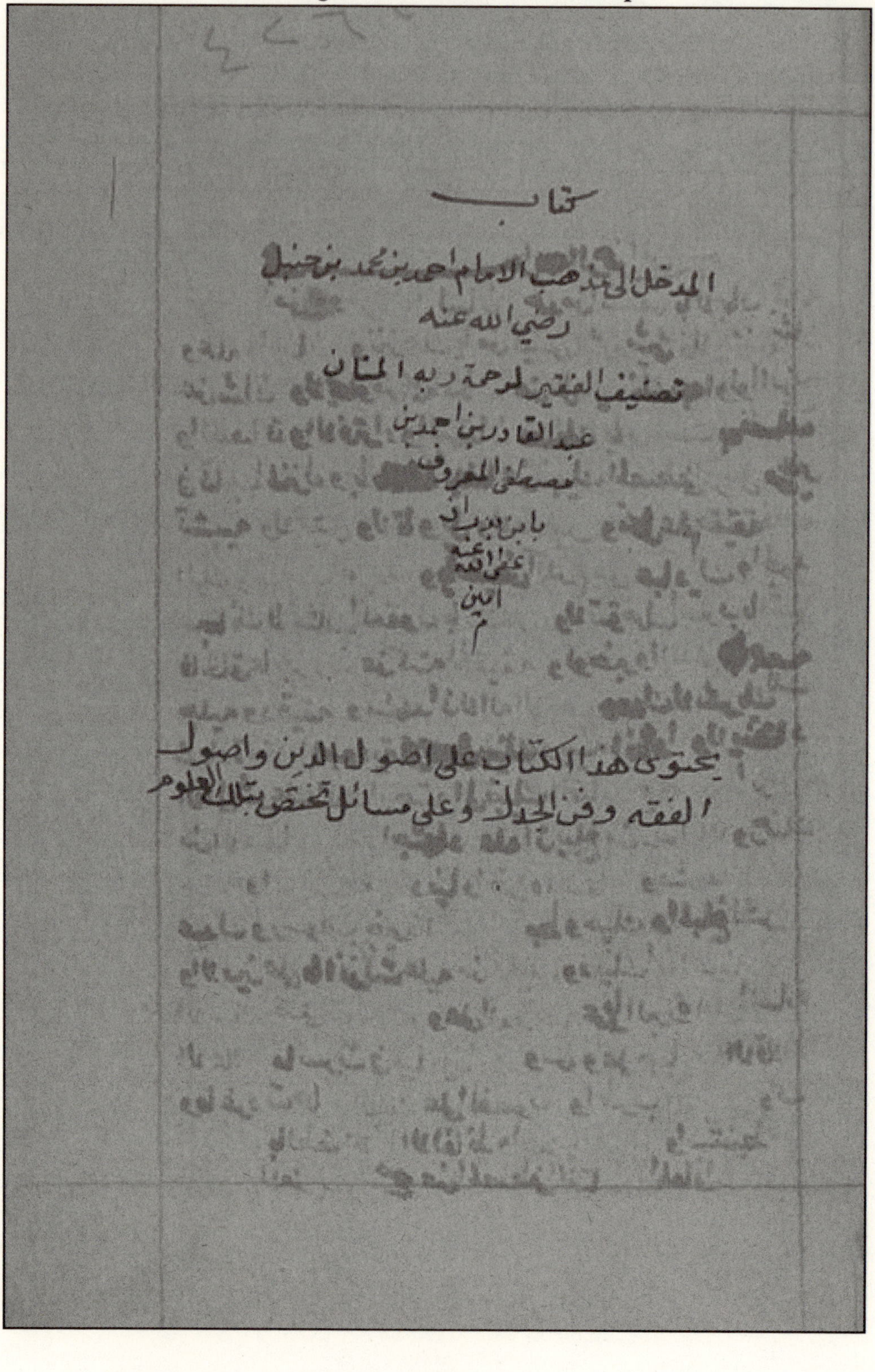

كتاب

المدخل الى مذهب الامام احمد بن محمد بن حنبل

رضي الله عنه

تصنيف الفقير لرحمة ربه المنان

عبد القادر بن احمد بن

مصطفى المعروف

بابن بدران

عفى الله عنه

امين

يحتوى هذا الكتاب على اصول الدين واصول

الفقه وفن الجدل وعلى مسائل تختص بتلك العلوم

Last Page of the Arabic Manuscript

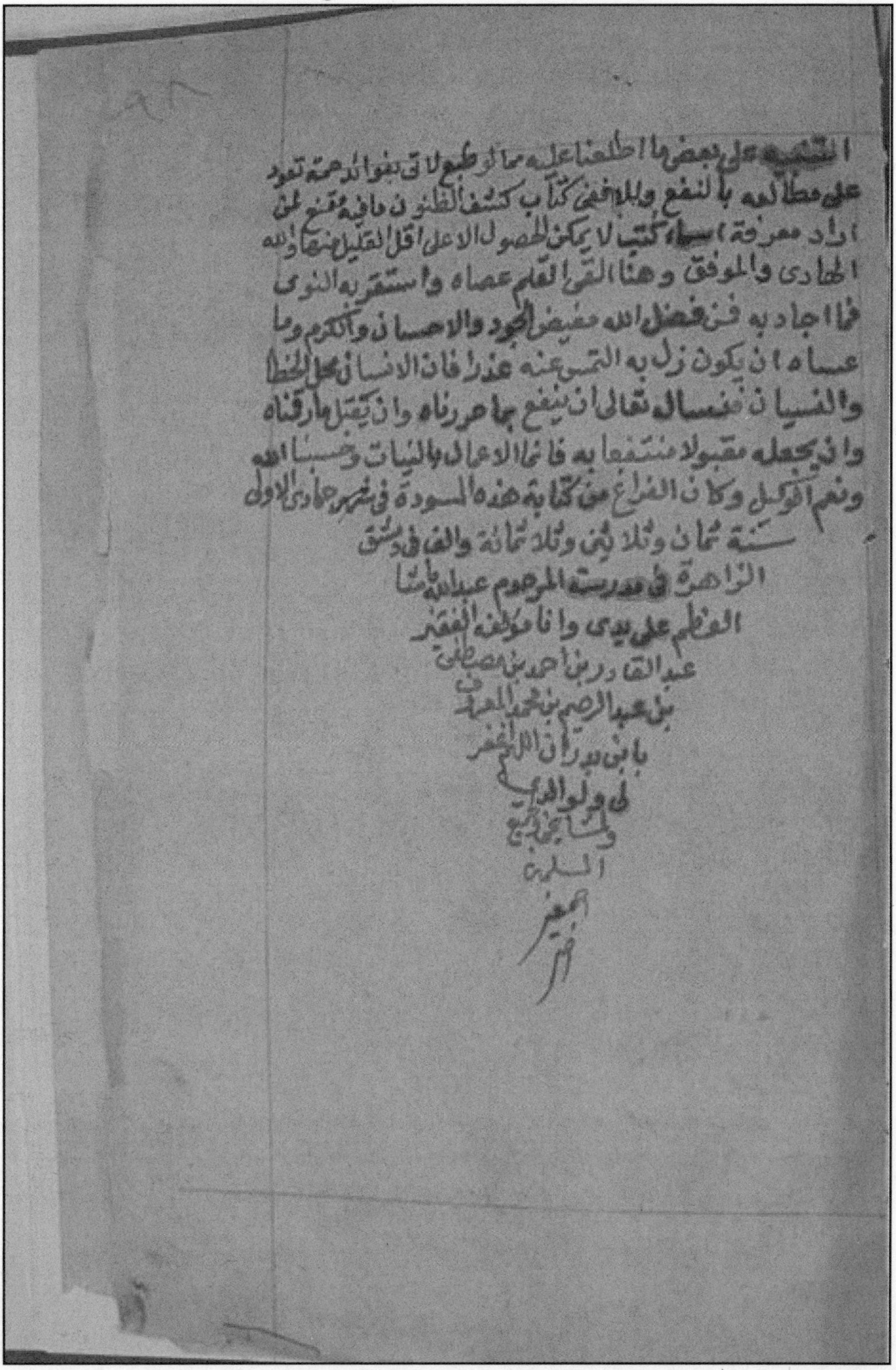
التنبيه على بعض ما اطلعنا عليه مما لو طبع لاتى بفوائد جمة تعود
على مطالعه بالنفع ولا يخفى كتاب كشف الظنون وما فيه مقنع لمن
اراد معرفة اسماء كتب لا يمكن الحصول الا على اقل القليل منها والله
الهادي والموفق وهنا القى القلم عصاه واستقر به النوى
فما اجاد به فمن فضل الله مفيض الجود والاحسان والكرم وما
عساه ان يكون زل به التمس عنه عذرا فان الانسان محل الخطا
والنسيان فنسأله تعالى ان ينفع بما حررناه وان يتقبل ما رقمناه
وان يجعله مقبولا منتفعا به فانما الاعمال بالنيات وحسبنا الله
ونعم الوكيل وكان الفراغ من كتابة هذه المسودة في شهر جمادى الاولى
سنة ثمان وثلاثين وثلاثمائة والف في دمشق
الزاهرة في مدرسة المرحوم عبدالله باشا
العظم على يدي وانا مؤلفه الفقير
عبد القادر بن احمد بن مصطفى
بن عبد الرحيم بن محمد المعروف
بابن بدران اللهم اغفر
لي ولوالدي
ولمشايخي ولجميع
المسلمين

ترجمة الإمام أحمد

A Brief Biography of al-Imām Aḥmad

I would be remiss if I did not begin this work introducing the school of thought of al-Imām Aḥmad ibn Muḥammad ibn Ḥanbal by first introducing you to al-Imām Aḥmad himself. Indeed, a man of such stature in the eyes of Muslims is hardly done justice by even the most intensive biographical account of his ventures, humble asceticism, and brave forbearance. While there are many accounts of al-Imām Aḥmad's greatness, there would be no justice given to his person nor his feats by someone of my rank. Instead, I chose to evoke the most poignant memories, as written by some of the great scholars who adhered to his *madhhab*. I have decided to translate portions of al-Qāḍī Abu Ya'lā's biographical account of al-Imām Aḥmad ﷺ. The information you will read was authored in *Ṭabaqāt al-Ḥanābilah* (1/2-45), which can be loosely described as Abu Ya'lā's *Histories of the Ḥanbalī Madhhab*, as well as *Manāqib al-Imām Aḥmad*, an entire volume dedicated to the life and times of al-Imām Aḥmad ibn Ḥanbal ﷺ, authored by al-Imām Abu 'l-Faraj ibn al-Jawzī ﷺ.

His Birth, Name, and Lineage

Al-Imām Aḥmad ﷺ was born in the month of Rabī' al-Awwal in the year 164, according to his own testimony. He was born in the city of Baghdad, after his mother travelled there from Khurasan while still pregnant with him. Though he was from Basra, his father's residence was in Marw. He never met his father or his grandfather. His mother's name was Ṣafīyyah bint Maymūnah bint 'Abd al-Mālik al-Shaybānī, from the tribe of 'Āmir.

His name was Aḥmad ibn Muḥammad ibn Ḥanbal ibn Hilāl ibn Asad ibn Idrīs ibn 'Abdullāh ibn Ḥayyān ibn 'Abdullāh ibn Anas ibn 'Awf ibn Qasit ibn Māzin ibn Dhuhl ibn Shaybān ibn Tha'labah ibn 'Ukkābah ibn Sa'b ibn 'Alī ibn Bakr ibn Wā'il ibn Qasit ibn Hunb ibn Afsa ibn Ḍu'mī ibn Jādilah ibn Asad ibn Rabī'ah ibn Nizār ibn Mȧd ibn 'Adnān ibn Ud ibn al-Humaysa ibn Hamal ibn al-Nabt ibn Qaydar ibn Ismā'īl ibn Ibrāhīm, peace and blessings of Allah be on him and all prophets.

His lineage coincides with that of our Messenger Muḥammad ﷺ in Nizār. Nizār had two sons, the first being Muḍar, from whom the Prophet ﷺ descends, and the other being Rabīʿah, from whom al-Imām Aḥmad ibn Ḥanbal descends.

His Early Years

As mentioned previously, al-Imām Aḥmad رحمه الله was born and raised in Baghdad. In Baghdad, he learned knowledge and ḥadīth from its scholars. Afterwards, he left Baghdad to seek knowledge elsewhere. From an early age, al-Imām Aḥmad رحمه الله was seen to be virtuous, studious, and intelligent. Whilst still young, when he was in the presence of women, he would constantly look down. Abu Sirāj ibn Khuzaymah رحمه الله remarked, "My father said to me, 'I spend money to bring teachers and tutors to my children to teach them manners, and they do not succeed! However, this boy, Aḥmad ibn Ḥanbal, is an orphan, and look how he is!"

His Search for Knowledge

Al-Imām Aḥmad رحمه الله said, "The first person I learned ḥadīth from was Abu Yūsuf." He was referring to al-Imām Abu Yūsuf al-Qāḍī, one of two most important students of al-Imām Abu Ḥanīfah رحمه الله. He began studying ḥadīth at the age of sixteen. In that same year, al-Imām Mālik ibn Anas رحمه الله passed away. He keenly pursued knowledge, traveling to great distances to learn and seek knowledge. As a matter of fact, he did not busy himself with marriage or earnings until he felt he had a sufficient amount of knowledge. According to al-Imām Abu Bakr ibn al-Marrūdhī, al-Imām Aḥmad رحمه الله said, "I married after I turned forty."

His Rank and Status

Al-Rabʿī ibn Sulaymān said, "Al-Shafiʿī said to us, 'Aḥmad is an *imām* in eight characteristics: He is an *imām* in ḥadīth, an *imām* in jurisprudence, an *imām* in language, an *imām* in Qurʾān, an *imām* in poverty, an *imām* in asceticism, an *imām* in abstinence, and an *imām* in Sunnah.'"

An *Imām* in Ḥadīth

No two people disagree that al-Imām Aḥmad رحمه الله was of the utmost quality of scholarship in ḥadīth. He authored his compendious corpus of ḥadīth, was a skilled and erudite ḥadīth critic, knew the statuses of narrators of ḥadīth, and knew the interpretations of ḥadīth. Abu ʿUbayd al-Qāsim ibn Sallām said, "Knowledge concluded with four individuals: Aḥmad ibn Ḥanbal, ʿAlī ibn al-Madīnī, Yaḥyā ibn Maʿīn, and Abu Bakr ibn Abī Shaybah. Of them, Aḥmad ibn Ḥanbal was the greatest jurist."

Once, al-Shāfiʿī ﷺ said to al-Imām Aḥmad ﷺ, "Abu ʿAbdullāh! Today, I was discussing such-and-such issue with the people of Iraq. If only I knew of a ḥadīth from Allah's Messenger ﷺ." Al-Imām Aḥmad proceeded to narrate three aḥādīth to him, to which he responded, "May Allah reward you." Once, he said to al-Imām Aḥmad ﷺ, "You are more knowledgeable of ḥadīth and its men. If a ḥadīth is authentic, tell me; it can consist of Kūfan or Shāmī narrators, I will still follow it if it is authentic."

Abu Zurʿah al-Rāzī stated, "We used to guess that Aḥmad ibn Ḥanbal knew 700,000 narrations." In another instance, he said, "Aḥmad used to memorise a million narrations." It was said to him, "How do you know?" He replied, "I studied with him, and we studied the various chapters [of ḥadīth] together."

Indeed, this testimony is corroborated by another narration, where Ṣāliḥ, the son of al-Imām Aḥmad, said, "I heard my father say, 'I wrote a million narrations with my own handwriting. This is not counting the narrations that were written for me.'"

An *Imām* in Jurisprudence

The truth found in this proposition is quite evident and manifest. The foundational sources of law are the Qur'an, the Sunnah of the Messenger ﷺ, and the views of his companions. After these three sources comes juristic analogy. Most early scholars did not author works on law; their jurisprudence emanated from the narrations they memorised and learned.

With that said, there are a number of scholars that transmitted and quoted the jurisprudence of al-Imām Aḥmad, including his two sons, ʿAbdullāh and Ṣāliḥ, his cousin, Ḥanbal, and others, including Isḥāq al-Kawsaj, Abu Dāwūd al-Sijistānī (the author of the famous *Sunan* work), Abu Bakr al-Athram, Abu Bakr al-Marrūdhī, Abu Ḥātim al-Rāzī, Abu Zurʿah al-Rāzī (the two famous ḥadīth critics), and others. A number of scholars also narrated ḥadīth from him. Al-Athram ﷺ said, "Once, while in the gathering of Abu ʿUbayd al-Qāsim ibn Sallām, I uttered a view on a topic. One of the attendees stated, 'Whose view is that?' I said, 'The one who is unmatched in the East and West: Aḥmad ibn Ḥanbal.' Abu 'Ubayd said, 'He has told the truth.'"

Isḥāq ibn Rāhawayh ﷺ said, "I heard Yaḥyā ibn Ādam say, 'Aḥmad ibn Ḥanbal is our *imām*.'" Abu Thawr said, "Aḥmad ibn Ḥanbal was more knowledgeable and possessed more of a legal mind than al-Thawrī."

An *Imām* in Language

Al-Marrūdhī said, "Abu 'Abdullāh (Aḥmad ibn Ḥanbal) used to never make grammatical mistakes when speaking." Al-Imām Aḥmad also said of himself, "I studied more of the Arabic Language than Abu 'Amr ibn al-'Alā'[2] did." Indeed, he would be questioned about vague or obscure words in the Arabic language in the context of the Divine Revelation. 'Abdullāh ibn Aḥmad said, "I asked my father about when the Prophet ﷺ forbade selling *al-mujr*, and he responded, 'Meaning, what is still in the womb.'" He also said, "I asked my father about the ḥadīth of Ibn Mas'ūd ﷺ, '*Al-ma'k* is sufficient of injustice.' He said, '*Al-ma'k* means procrastination.'"

If one were to peruse the questions posed to al-Imām Aḥmad ﷺ and his answers, one would find many such examples. Al-Qaḍī Abu Ya'lā ﷺ mentioned a number of examples in his book *al-Ṭabaqāt*.

An *Imām* in Qur'ān

After one learns the efforts and breadth of knowledge of al-Imām Aḥmad regarding the Qur'ān, this fact becomes evident. Abu 'l-Ḥusayn ibn al-Munādī ﷺ said, "Aḥmad authored an exegesis of the Qur'ān comprising of 120,000 aḥādīth." He also authored a book on abrogating verses, the chronology of the Qur'ān, the answers of the Qur'ān, and so forth. 'Abdullāh ibn Aḥmad said, "My father used to complete the Qur'ān twice a week: one at night, and one during the day."

An *Imām* in Poverty

This is truly a praiseworthy characteristic and is a station held by the prophets and the pious. Abu Barzah al-Aslamī ﷺ reported that Allah's Messenger ﷺ said, "Muslim paupers will enter paradise before the rich Muslims by forty years, to the point that the rich Muslims will wish, on the Day of Resurrection, that they were poor." Also, Abu Sa'īd ﷺ reported that he heard

2 He is referring to the great scholar of Qur'ān and the Arabic Language.

the Prophet ﷺ say, "Allah, allow me to die poor, and do not take my life while I am rich."

Al-Imām Abu Bakr al-Marrūdhī said, "Abu 'Abdullāh used to love paupers. I have never seen the poor more honoured in any gathering than they were in his." In another showing of his love, he was once told of a poor sick person, and said to Abu Bakr al-Marrūdhī, "Go visit him and say, 'What would you like, so that I can do it for you?'" He then handed him some perfume and said, "Apply some perfume on him."

An *Imām* in Asceticism

The asceticism of al-Imām Aḥmad is one of his most defining qualities. Indeed, he had the choice to be a wealthy person and earn of the worldly life, but he refused it. He was offered posts and positions but refused them. He was offered wealth, authority, and power, but rejected it all, saying, "Minimalism in worldly matters is sufficient; abundance of worldly matters does not suffice." He would also say, "I become happy when I have nothing." He also said, "Some food is less than others, some clothes are worse than others. These are mere days."

Isḥāq ibn Hāni' reported that he once visited al-Imām Aḥmad at early hours in order to read *Kitāb al-Zuhd* to him, one of al-Imām Aḥmad's own authorships. He said, "I spread a mat and pillow for him, to which he said, 'What is this?' I replied, 'I have placed them for you to sit on them.' He replied, 'Remove them. *Al-Zuhd* can only be read with asceticism.' I removed them, and he sat on the dirt."

Once, Abu 'Umayr 'Īsā ibn Muḥammad ibn 'Īsā al-Naḥḥās heard someone mention al-Imām Aḥmad, and he said, "May Allah have mercy on him. He was so abstinent from the worldly life, so resembling to the predecessors, and so adherent to the pious. The world was presented to him, yet he rejected it; innovations were shown to him, and he refuted them." Sulaymān ibn al-Ash'ath once said, "I never heard Aḥmad ibn Ḥanbal mention the worldly life." As a matter of fact, he once said, "My happiest days are when I wake with nothing."

An *Imām* in Abstinence

Abu 'Abdullāh al-Simsār reported, "The mother of 'Abdullāh ibn Aḥmad (meaning, al-Imām Aḥmad's deceased wife) used to own a house, and

Aḥmad would receive a share of its rent proportional to the inheritance he was due from his wife. The houses needed some repairs, and his son ʿAbdullāh paid for those repairs. Abu ʿAbdullāh (Aḥmad ibn Ḥanbal) later refused the money he was receiving from that house, saying, 'He ruined it for me.'"

The reason why he refused to take the money was that he feared that money given to his son from the Caliph was used to repair the house. He did not want to receive any dividends on anything paid for by the Caliph. He prohibited his two sons and his uncle from taking stipends from the Caliph, but they resisted on the basis of their dire need. Al-Imām Aḥmad ﵀ boycotted them for a month for taking the money.

When al-Imām Aḥmad ﵀ was sick, the Caliph, al-Mutawakkil, sent him Ibn Māsūyah, a doctor, who would administer medicines for the *imām*. However, even after taking the medicines, he would not get better. Ibn Māsūyah entered the quarters of al-Mutawakkil, who said, "Woe to you! Did no medicines work on Ibn Ḥanbal?" Ibn Māsūyah said, "Commander of the Believers, Aḥmad ibn Ḥanbal is not sick in his body. His illness is due to his lack of food intake and his constant fasting and worship." At that, the Caliph al-Mutawakkil remained silent. Al-Marrūdhī ﵀ said, "I heard Aḥmad say, 'Fear has prevented me from eating and drinking; I no longer desire it.'"

Isḥāq, the uncle of al-Imām Aḥmad, said, "I entered the quarters of Aḥmad, and his hand was under his pillow. I said to him, 'My nephew, what is this sadness?' He lifted his head and said, 'Glad tidings to the one whom Allah has made obscure and unknown.'" His son Ṣāliḥ said, "My father would not even let anyone bring him water to perform ablution."

An *Imām* in Sunnah

No two scholars differ that, in the sciences of the Sunnah, he is the great, erudite scholar and the vast, abundant ocean. He was harmed in the path of Allah, but remained patient, further aiding the Book of Allah the Exalted and the Sunnah of Muhammad ﷺ. To the Sunnah, he is similar to when Allah the Exalted said: **{And He will give you something else that will really please you: His help and an imminent breakthrough. So, give the faithful the good news.}** [Qur'ān: 61:13].

ʿAlī ibn al-Madīnī ﵀ once said, "Allah aided this religion through two men,

Abu Bakr al-Ṣiddīq ﷺ during the wars of apostasy, and Aḥmad ibn Ḥanbal during his inquisition."

Once, al-Rabīʿ ibn Sulaymān ﷺ said, "Al-Shāfiʿī ﷺ said, 'Only a disbeliever hates Aḥmad.' I replied, 'You refer to him as a disbeliever?' He said, 'Yes, whoever hates Aḥmad ibn Ḥanbal opposes the Sunnah, whoever opposes the Sunnah intends the Companions, whoever intends the Companions hates the Prophet ﷺ, and whoever hates the Prophet ﷺ has disbelieved in Allah the Exalted.'"

Aḥmad, the son of al-Imām Isḥaq ibn Rāhawayh ﷺ said, "I heard my father say, 'Had it not been for Aḥmad ibn Ḥanbal and his sacrifices, Islam would have disappeared.'" ʿAbbās al-Dūrī ﷺ once said, "I heard Yaḥyā ibn Maʿīn say, 'People wanted me to be like Aḥmad ibn Ḥanbal. No, by Allah, we cannot possibly be Aḥmad nor even tread the same path Aḥmad trod.'"

The Recognition of his Peers

Al-Imām Aḥmad ﷺ was widely recognised by his peers and elders. Previously, we quoted the statement of al-Shāfiʿī ﷺ, who acknowledged al-Imām Aḥmad's scholarly capabilities in eight different aspects of the religion and knowledge. In another statement, he said, "When I left Baghdad, I left behind no one more abstinent, pious, possessing of juristic capabilities, or knowledgeable than Aḥmad ibn Ḥanbal." In another testimony, showing his amazement with the great *imām*, Aḥmad ibn Ḥanbal, al-Shāfiʿī ﷺ said, "I have never seen anymore more intelligent than two men: Aḥmad ibn Ḥanbal and Sulaymān ibn Dāwūd al-Ḥāshimī."

While al-Shāfiʿī ﷺ is possibly the most recognisable name mentioned in the midst of discussions on the recognition al-Imām Aḥmad ﷺ received, there were other generational scholars who expressed similar astonishment and praise of al-Imām Aḥmad. Take, for one, ʿAlī ibn al-Madīnī ﷺ the great critic of ḥadīth. Once, al-Imām al-Bukhārī ﷺ said, "I have never thought myself to be so small as I did when I compared myself to ʿAlī ibn al-Madīnī." Al-Imām ʿAlī ibn al-Madīnī once said, "I have taken Aḥmad ibn Ḥanbal as an *imām*, to stand before me and Allah. Who can achieve the things done by Abu ʿAbdullāh?" In another statement, he said, "Imām Aḥmad is my sire." In another testament to the reliance al-Imām ʿAlī ibn al-Madīnī had on al-Imām Aḥmad, he said, "It is more beloved to me to ask Aḥmad ibn Ḥanbal about the answer to an issue than it is to ask Abu ʿĀṣim and ʿAbdullāh ibn Dāwūd. Truly, knowledge is not synonymous with age."

Another great scholar whose recognition of al-Imām Aḥmad's juristic abilities needs mention is Abu ʿUbayd al-Qāsim bin Sallām. He once said, "Knowledge [of ḥadīth] ultimately resides with four individuals: Aḥmad ibn Ḥanbal—who is the most possessing of juristic capabilities among them, Ibn Abī Shaybah—who has the strongest memory among them, ʿAlī ibn al-Madīnī—who has the vastest knowledge among them, and Yaḥyā ibn Maʿīn, who was the most proficient at documenting among them." In another instance, he said, "Aḥmad ibn Ḥanbal is our *imām*. Indeed, I adorn myself by mentioning him." Once, two men debated in his presence, and one stated a view, to which his interlocutor responded, "Whose view is that?" The first man said, "A man who has no peer in the East nor the West." He said, "Whom are you referring to?" The man said, "Aḥmad ibn Ḥanbal." Abu ʿUbayd then interjected, "He is telling the truth. There is no one in the East nor the West matching him. I have never seen a man more knowledgeable of the Sunnah than him."

Not only did the jurists and ḥadīth critics acknowledge his virtue and worth, but the ascetics and those close to Allah the Exalted also did the same. Here, we have Bishr al-Ḥāfī, the famous ascetic, being asked about Aḥmad ibn Ḥanbal ﵀ and him responding, "Am I truly being asked about Aḥmad? Ibn Ḥanbal was put into the bellows, and when he emerged, he was pure gold." When al-Imām Aḥmad ﵀ was informed about this statement, he said, "Praise belongs to Allah who allowed Bishr to be pleased with what I did." Referring, of course, to his inquisition. Once, when al-Imām Bishr was asked to utter words of support for al-Imām Aḥmad, he replied, "Am I to undertake the work of the prophets? Indeed, Aḥmad ibn Ḥanbal has undertaken the work of the prophets."

If we were to mention all of the scholars' praise and recognition of al-Imām Aḥmad ﵀ it could suffice as an independent work.

His Dislike of Writing His Statements

One of the main reasons that the *madhhab* of al-Imām Aḥmad ﵀ almost died out was his fervent dislike of people authoring books that were not comprised of textual evidences, be they verses of the Qurʾān or aḥādīth from the Prophet ﷺ. Ḥanbal ibn Isḥāq said, "I found that Abu ʿAbdullāh dislikes that any of his views or *fatāwā* are written."

However, al-Imām Ibn al-Jawzī remarked, "Such was al-Imām Aḥmad ﵀. He would prohibit others from writing his words, out of his own humility.

Allah then destined that his views would be gathered, organised, and popularised."

His Humility

Al-Imām Aḥmad ﵀ was a man of great consciousness of Allah the Exalted. Although he holds such a lofty place in this Ummah, he severely disliked his name being mentioned or being famous. Once, his uncle entered his quarters and found him laying with his hand under his pillow. He said, "My nephew, why such sorrow? Why such sadness?" Al-Imām Aḥmad replied, "My uncle: Glad tidings to the one whose name Allah the Exalted has made obscure and unknown." His advice to others was, "Keep yourself unknown and obscure. By Allah, I have been tested with famousness."

His wish was to remain unknown and obscure, outside of the public eye. He once remarked, "By Allah, if I had any way of doing so, I would not reside in this city; I would leave it, so that I am not mentioned nor remembered by anyone." He would dislike for anyone to follow him, so as to not appear to have a large following. He would walk alone, humble. If anyone followed him, he would stop in his tracks and wait for them to pass along.

Yaḥyā ibn Maʿīn once said, "I have never seen anyone like Aḥmad ibn Ḥanbal. I befriended him for fifty years, and he never boasted about his own piety or any goodness he had." His humility and humbleness would even prevent him from wishing to be shown respect he did not feel he deserved. Once, he was approached by Ismaʿīl ibn Isḥāq al-Thaqafī ﵀ who said, "The first time I saw him, I said to Abu ʿAbdullāh, 'Allow me to kiss your head.' To which he replied, 'I have not reached a level to be deserving of such behaviour.'"

His Sickness and Subsequent Death

His son, ʿAbdullāh, said, "My father said to me, 'I have just completed my seventy-seventh year. I have now entered my seventy-eighth year.' He became ill with a fever that night." Abu Bakr al-Marrūdhī ﵀ mentioned that he became ill two nights before the end of Rabīʿ al-Awwal in the year 241 *hijri*. He was ill for nine days, and when he became extremely sick, people heard of his sickness and rushed to visit him. Due to the sheer number of visitors, the sultan placed guards at his doorstep. When Abu ʿAbdullah Aḥmad ibn Ḥanbal ﵀ would allow, people would enter in hordes to greet him, and he would respond to them by gesturing with his hand. When the guards came, his door was locked and guarded, and people remained outdoors, even to the extent that some stores had to close down. People tried to enter his home through windows and even the ceiling.

People would enter and supplicate for him in particular, and he would respond, "And for all Muslims." An elderly man entered and said, "Remember standing in front of Allah." At that, Abu ʿAbdullāh ﷺ sobbed, and tears flowed down his cheeks. A couple of days before he passed away, he said, "Bring the children in," and the children rushed to him. He hugged them, rubbed their heads with his hand, smelled them, and his eyes welled with tears. A man said, "Do not be sad for them," and he gestured with his hand, so as to say, "That is not why I am crying."

On the night of Friday, he became very slow-moving. His family thought he passed away. When they went to outstretch his legs, he pulled them back in. They then began to make him say, "There is no God but Allah (*lā ilāha illa 'llāh*)," and he would repeat after them. He turned to the *qiblah* and faced it with his feet. On Friday morning, people gathered and filled the streets and pathways. At the outset of the day, he passed away. People screamed and their cries were loud; it was as though the entire world had been shaken.

Ḥanbal ﷺ said, "While he was in jail, three hairs of the Prophet ﷺ were given to Abu ʿAbdullāh by one of the sons of al-Faḍl ibn al-Rabīʿ. Abu ʿAbdullāh stated in his final will and testament that a hair should be placed on each eye and the last hair should be placed on his tongue. His wish was fulfilled when he died.

Abu ʿAbdullāh Aḥmad ibn Ḥanbal passed onto his Lord on Friday the 28th of Rabīʿ al-Awwal, 241 *hijri* at the age of seventy-seven. Al-Haytham ibn Khalaf ﷺ said, "We buried Aḥmad ibn Ḥanbal on Friday after *ʿaṣr* in the year 241, and I have never seen a larger gathering." Similarly, Abu Ṣāliḥ al-Qanṭarī ﷺ said, "I have witnessed events for forty years. I have never seen a gathering quite like this one." The caliph of the time sent twenty estimators to see how many people prayed on Aḥmad ibn Ḥanbal, and they estimated 1.3 million people, not counting those on ships.

His Final Will and Testament

In the Name of Allah, the Most Merciful, the Giver of Mercy. This is the final will and testament of Aḥmad ibn Muḥammad ibn Ḥanbal. His will is to testify that there is no God but Allah, alone and without any partners, and that Muhammad is His slave and messenger. He was sent with guidance and the true religion in order to make it supersede over all other religions, even if the polytheists dislike it.

He also wills that those who obey him, such as his family and relatives, worship Allah the Exalted among the worshippers, and praise Him among those who praise Him. They must remain sincere to the Muslim congregation.

I will that I am pleased with Allah the Exalted as a Lord, Islam as a religion, and Muhammad ﷺ as a prophet.

I also state that I owe ʿAbdullāh ibn Muḥammad, known as Fūrān, approximately fifty dinars. He is truthful in his claim to that money. As such, it should be paid to him from the returns on the house, if Allah wills. If it is enough, the children of Ṣāliḥ and ʿAbdullah, the two sons of Aḥmad bin Ḥanbal should be given: each boy and girl should be given ten dirhams, after the wealth of Abu Muḥammad is paid to him.

Abu Yūsuf, as well as Ṣāliḥ, and ʿAbdullah, the two sons of Aḥmad ibn Muḥammad ibn Ḥanbal, testify to this will.

The Effect His Death Had on People

Al-Warkānī ؒ the neighbour of al-Imām Aḥmad ؒ said, "The day Aḥmad ibn Ḥanbal died, memorials and wailing occurred among four types of people: Muslims, Jews, Christians, and Magians. The day he died, 20,000 Jews, Christians, and Magians accepted Islam."

The effect of al-Imām Aḥmad ibn Ḥanbal is still felt today. Millions of individuals read his *Musnad*, benefit and learn from his *fiqh*, and study his ways. To Allah we belong, and to Him we shall return. May Allah grant al-Imām Aḥmad the highest levels of paradise, allow us to unite with him there, and grant us the capability to follow his righteous footsteps.

المدخل

إِلَىٰ مَذهَبِ الإِمَامِ أَحْمَدَ بنِ حَنْبَل

[المقدمة المؤلف]

Author's Introduction

بِسْمِ اللَّهِ الرَّحْمَٰنِ الرَّحِيمِ

In the Name of Allah, the Most Merciful, the Giver of Mercy

نحمدك يَا من هُوَ مَحْمُود بِكُل لِسَان حمد من اتّصف بِالْإِيمَان بقوله وَعَمله والجنان، وننزهك يَا من لَيْسَ كمثله شَيْء فَلَا يشْغلهُ شَأْن عَن شَأن، وَلَا يَخْلُو من علمه مَكَان، عَن كل مَا يصفك بِهِ أولو الزيغ والطغيان، والافتراء والبهتان. نصفك بِمَا وصفت بِهِ نَفسك فِي كتابك الْمنزل، وَبِمَا بلغنَا عَن نبيك الْمُصْطَفى الْمُرْسل، من غير تَشْبِيه وَلَا تَمْثِيل، وَلَا تَأْوِيل وَلَا تَعْطِيل، وَنكل علم حَقِيقَة ذَلِك إِلَيْك يَا وَاجِب الْوُجُود، وَيَا مفيض الْكَرم على عِبَادك والجود سُبْحَانَكَ لَا تمثلك الْعُقُول بالتفكير، وَلَا تتوهمك الْقُلُوب بالتصوير، فالخلق عاجزون عَن كنه الْحَقِيقَة، وَلَو خبروا الْعلم بأجمعه جليه ودقيقه.

We praise You, O You who are praised in every tongue, in a manner befitting those who espouse faith in their statements, actions, and hearts. O One who has nothing like unto Him, who no matter distracts Him from another, and whose knowledge leaves no place untouched and unaffected, we declare You transcendent above every way You are described by people of deviation, transgression, fabrication, and falsehood. We describe You as You have described Yourself in Your revealed scripture, and as has reached us from Your chosen prophet who was sent, without likening or comparing You to creation, and without reinterpreting or negating Your attributes. We consign the realities of that to You, O the One whose existence is necessary, and whose generosity and bounties have overflown to Your slaves. Intellects cannot compare You to anything with their thoughts, and hearts cannot imagine any image to assign to You. Creation is wholly incapable of understanding the essence of the truth, even if they were told of all knowledge, both its apparent and its minute parts.

ونشهد أَن لَا إِلَه إِلَّا أَنْت وَحدك لَا شريك لَك شَهَادَة مقرّ بالعبودية لَا يَجْعَل بَيْنك وَبَينه أندادا، وَلَا ينقاد إِلَّا إِلَى شرعك الَّذِي أوحيته إِلَى نبيك انقيادا، ويجتهد فِيمَا يرضيك من الِاعْتِقَاد وَالْعَمَل اجْتِهَادًا، عله أَن يبلغ من رضاك ورحمتك مرَادا، وَأَن ترزقه فِي دُنْيَاهُ وأخراه إسعادا.

We testify that there is no God but you, alone and without partners. It is a testimony of one who acknowledges servitude, does not associate partners with You, only submits to Your religion which You sent to Your messenger, and exerts his full effort in pleasing You, by espousing the correct beliefs and striving in worship. Hopefully, it leads to Your pleasure and mercy, which is the ultimate goal, and acts as a cause for sustenance in this life and happiness in the hereafter.

ونشهد أَن مُحَمَّدًا عَبدك وَرَسُولك خير خلقك ومهبط وحيك والمبلغ لشرعك والأمين على مَا أنزلت عَلَيْهِ من كتابك وَدينك ﴿إِنَّ الدِّينَ عِنْدَ اللهِ الْأِسْلَامُ﴾ [آل عمرَان: ١٩]

We also testify that Muḥammad is Your slave and messenger. He is the greatest of Your creation, the one to whom revelation descended, and the conveyor of Your religion. He was entrusted with Your scripture and religion, which You have revealed to him. **{The true religion, in Allah's eyes, is Islam.}** [Qur'ān 3:19]

صلى الله عَلَيْهِ وعَلى آله وَصَحبه عُمُوما البررة الْكِرَام، السَّادة الْأَعْلَام، مَا سرت فِي ميادين الطروس وعَلى جباهها الأقلام وَمَا غردت حمائم الأيك على الغصون وأطرب العيس حادي العيس بألطف الْأَلْفَاظ، وأعذب اللحون واستنبط من الْكتاب الْعَزِيز وَمَا صَحَّ عَن الْمُصْطَفى الْمُخْتَار أدق الْمعَانِي المستنبطون، وَسلم تَسْلِيمًا.

May Allah send encompassing blessings on him, his righteous and noble family and companions—all of whom were masters and authorities, so long as pens are put to paper in authoring works, so long as doves in jungles sing from their branches, so long as camels sway their necks when listening to beautiful words and tunes sung by their herders, and so long as those with depth in understanding are able to extract from the Noble Book and the authentic reports from the Prophet, and may He send everlasting peace on them.

أما بعد:

As to the discussion at hand:

فَيَقُول الْفَقِير لعفو ربه المنان، عبد الْقَادِر بن أَحْمد بن مصطفى بن عبد الرَّحِيم بن مُحَمَّد الْمَشْهُور كأسلافه بِابْن بدران:

I, the one who is in dire need of the forgiveness of His Lord the Benevolent, ʿAbd al-Qādir, son of Aḥmad, son of Muṣṭafā, son of ʿAbd al-Raḥīm, son of Muḥammad, and who is known, as were his predecessors, as "Ibn Badrān", proclaim:

أنني لما من الله عَليّ بِطَلَب الْعلم، هجرت لَهُ الوطن والوسن وَكنت أبكر فِيهِ بكور الْغُرَاب، وأطوف الْمعَاهد لتحصيله، وأذهب فِيهِ كل مَذْهَب، وأتبع فِيهِ كل شعب وَلَو كَانَ عسرا، أشرف على كل يفاع، وأتأمل كل غور، فَتَارَة أطوح بنفسي فِيمَا سلكه ابْن سينا فِي (الشفا) و(الإشارات) وَتارَة أتلقف مَا سبكه أَبُو نصر الفارابي من صناعَة الْمنطق وَتلك الْعبارَات، وَتارَة أجول فِي مَوَاقِف (الْمَقَاصِد) و(المواقف) وَأَحْيَانا أطلب الْهِدَايَة ظنا مني أَنَّهَا تهدي إِلَى رشد.

When Allah the Exalted blessed me with the yearning to seek knowledge, I forsook for it my land and my sleep. I would wake at early hours for it, resembling a crow, and would go from one institute to the next to attain it. During my pursuit I went in every direction, delved into every pass—even if it were difficult, ascended every mountaintop, and descended into every depth. Sometimes, I would cast myself into the topics discussed by Avicenna in his *Kitāb al-Shifā* (*The Book of Healing*) and his book, *al-Ishārāt wa al-Tanbīhāt* (*The Book of Directives and Remarks*), and at other times, I would grasp at the concepts formulated by Abu Naṣr al-Fārābī when he undertook the development of formal logic and its expressions. At other times, I would stroll by the undertakings of *al-Maqāṣid* (*The Objectives*), [by Saʿd al-Dīn al-Taftāzānī] and *al-Mawāqif fī ʿIlm al-Kalām* (*Posits on Kalām*), [by ʿAḍud al-Dīn al-Ījī] and at times seek guidance therein, thinking that they lead to some sort of guidance.

فأضم إِلَيْهَا مَا سلكه ابْن رشد، ثمَّ أردد فِي الطبيعي والإلهي نظرا، وَفِي تشريح الأفلاك أتطلب خبرا أَو خَبرا، ثمَّ أجول فِي ميادين الْعُلُوم مُدَّة كعدد السَّبع الْبَقَرَات الْعِجَاف، فأرتد إِلَيّ الطّرف خاسئا وَهُوَ حسير، وَلم أحصل من معرفَة الله جلّ جَلَاله إِلَّا على أَوْهَام وخطرات وساوس وأشكال نشأ من الْبَحْث والتدقيق، فأدفعه بِمَا أقنع نَفسِي بنفسي، فَلَمَّا همت فِي تِلْكَ الْبَيْدَاء الَّتِي هِيَ على حد قَول أبي الطّيب:

I would add to those books the writings of Ibn Rushd (Averroes) and would pause and think about nature and divinity, causing me to reflect. I would look at the anatomy of the stars, seeking knowledge or information. Then, I would stroll in the domains and fields of various sciences for periods of time extending as long as the years spent as prophesied by the dream of the seven skinny cows,[3] until my sight returned to me, defeated and weary. I gained nothing of knowledge about Allah the Exalted but that it was based on delusions, whisperings, and contentions that emanated from research and scrutinising texts , which I would ward off by providing rationalisations that only served to convince myself. I wandered into that desolate wilderness, which is reminiscent of the statement of Abu 'l-Ṭayyib [al-Mutanabbī], who said:

يَتلون الخريت من خوف التوى فِيهَا كَمَا تلون الحرباء

A skillful guide would turn from fear of dying,
In that dreadful land as chameleons change how they appear.

ناداني مُنَادِي الْهدى الْحَقِيقِيّ: هَلُمَّ إِلَى الشّرف والكمال، ودع نجاة ابْن سينا

3 [T] This is a reference to when Allah the Exalted said, **{The king said, 'I dreamed about seven fat cows being eaten by seven lean ones; seven green ears of corn and [seven] others withered. Counsellors, if you can interpret dreams, tell me the meaning of my dream.'}** [Qur'ān 12:43] Prophet Yūsuf ﷺ interpreted this dream to mean, **{You will sow for seven consecutive years as usual. Store all that you reap, left in the ear, apart from the little you eat. After that will come seven years of hardship which will consume all but a little of what you stored up for them; after that will come a year when the people will have abundant rain and will press grapes.'}** [Qur'ān 12: 47-49]

الموهومة إِلَى النجاة الْحَقِيقِيَّة، وَمَا ذَلِك إِلَّا بِأَن تكون على مَا كَانَ عَلَيْهِ السّلف الْكِرَام من الصَّحَابَة وَالتَّابِعين وَالتَّابِعين لَهُم بِإِحْسَان، فَإِن الْأَمر لَيْسَ على مَا تتوهم، وَحَقِيقَة الرب لَا يُمكن أَن يُدْرِكهَا المربوب، وَمَا السَّلامَة إِلَّا بِالتَّسْلِيمِ، وَكتاب الله حق، وَلَيْسَ بعد الْحق إِلَّا الضلال.

I was called by a herald to true guidance, who said, "Come forth to true honour and completeness; leave the illusion of Avicenna's salvation and come to true salvation, by following what the pious predecessors taught, including the companions, their successors, and their students who followed them in guidance. It is not as you think; the reality of the Lord cannot be encompassed and grasped by one under His control. Safety is only through submission. The Book of Allah the Exalted is the truth, and after truth, there is nothing but falsehood."

فهنالك هدأ روعي، وَجعلت عقيدتي كتاب الله أكل علم صِفَاته إِلَيْهِ بِلَا تجسيم وَلَا تَأْوِيل وَلَا تَشْبِيه وَلَا تَعْطِيل، وانجلى مَا كَانَ على قلبِي من رين أورثته قَوَاعِد أرسطوطاليس، وَقلت: مَا كَانَ إِلَّا من النّظر فِي تِلْكَ الوساوس والبدع والدسائس، فَمن أَيْن لعباد الْكَوَاكِب أَن يرشدونا إِلَى الصِّرَاط الْمُسْتَقيم وَمَا كَانُوا مهتدين؟ وَمن أَيْن لأَصْحَاب المقالات أَن يعلمُوا حَقِيقَة قيوم الأَرْض وَالسَّمَوَات؟ وَلَو كَانَت حَقِيقَة صِفَات الله تَعَالَى تدْرك بالعقول، لوصل أَصْحَاب رسائل إخْوَان الصفاء إِلَى الصَّفَا، ولوصل صَاحب النَّجَاة والشفا إِلَى النجَاة وغليل لبه وشفا، وَلَكِن **﴿وَلَا يحيطون بِشَيْء من علمه إِلَّا بِمَا شَاءَ﴾** [البقرة: ٢٥٥]، **﴿وَمَا أُوتِيتُمْ من الْعلم إِلَّا قَلِيلا﴾** [الإسراء: ٨٥].

At that moment, my dismay subsided. I made my creed that of the Book of Allah the Exalted; I consign knowledge of His Attributes to Him, without anthropomorphism, reinterpretation, likening, or negation. I found that the stain that enveloped my heart, a byproduct of studying the authorships of Aristotle, had vanished. I remarked to myself that [the stain on my heart] only occurred due to reading books encompassing such whisperings, heresies, and machinations, for how can it be conceived that worshippers of planets are to guide us to the upright path, when they themselves were not rightly guided? And how can the author of *"The Categories,"* learn the realities of the Eternal Maintainer of the earth and the heavens? Had the realities of the Attributes of Allah the Exalted been comprehensible by nothing more than intellects, the authors of the *Epistles of the Brethren of Purity* would have reached the pinnacle, and Avicenna, the author of the *Book of Healing* and the *Book of Salvation*, would have reached salvation and would have quenched his thirst, thereby healing himself. However, Allah said: **{But they do not comprehend any of His knowledge except what He wills.}** [Qur'ān 2:255] And: **{You have only been given a little knowledge.}** [Qur'ān 17:85]

وَأَيْنَ هم من قَوْله صلى الله عَلَيْهِ وَسلم: **((عَلَيْكُم بِسنتي وَسنة الْخُلَفَاء الرَّاشِدين المهديين من بعدِي عضوا عَلَيْهَا بالنواجذ، وَإِيَّاكُم ومحدثات الْأُمُور، فَإِن كل محدثة بِدعَة، وكل بِدعَة ضَلَالَة))** لَكِن من اتبع هَوَاهُ هام فِي كل وَاد، وَلم يبال بِأَيّ شعب سلك، وَلَا بِأَيّ طَرِيق هلك.

Where are such people when juxtaposed with the ḥadīth of the Prophet ﷺ, where he said, **"Adhere to my Sunnah and the Sunnah of the Rightly Guided Caliphs after me. Hold fast to it with the molar teeth. Beware of newly-invented matters, for every newly-invented matter is an innovation, and every innovation is misguidance."**[4] However, those who follow their desires wander and roam in every valley, caring not for which path they tread nor which road will inevitably lead to their own destruction.

فَمن ثمَّ جعلت شغلي كتاب الله تدريسا وتفسيرا، وسنة نبيه الْمُخْتَار قِرَاءَة أَيْضا وشرحا وتحريرا، فَللَّه الْحَمد على هَذِه الْمِنَّة، وأسأله الثَّبَات على ذَلِك وازدياد النِّعْمَة.

Consequently, I directed my efforts towards the Book of Allah; teaching it and studying its meanings, and the Sunnah of His Chosen Prophet; which I read, explained, and closely analysed its wordings. Praise belongs to Allah for this blessing. I ask Him to keep me steadfast in my endeavors and to increase the blessing which He has already bestowed.

ثمَّ إِنِّي زجرت نَفسِي فِي بحار الْأُصُول وَالْفُرُوع، والبحث عَن الْأَدِلَّة حَتَّى لَا

4 Reported by Aḥmad (127) and Abu Dāwūd (4607).

أكون منقادا لكل قائِد، وَلَا مُقلدًا تقليدا أعمى لمن يَقُودهُ، فَإِن هَذِه حَالَة لَا يرضى بهَا الصّبيان فضلا عَمَّن أُوتِيَ شَيْئا من الْعقل، ثمَّ سبرت الْمذَاهب المتبوعة الْآن وَكثِيرًا من غير المتبوعة، فَوجدت كلا مِنْهُم، قدس الله أسرارهم، وَجعل فِي عليين مَنَازِلهمْ، قد اجْتهد فِي طلب الْحق، وَلم يأل جهدا فِي طلبه، وَلَا قصر فِي اجْتِهَاده بل قَامَ بِمَا عهد إِلَيْهِ حق الْقيام، ونصح الْأمة واجتنب كل مَا يشين.

I cast myself into the seas of legal theories, subsidiary matters of law, and the search for evidence, so as to not be subject to being led by just any leader, nor a blind follower of whoever steers me. Such a state is displeasing to children, let alone those who have been given some portion of intellect. I explored the schools of law that are followed nowadays, and even perused many of those that are not as popularly followed. I found them, may Allah sanctify their secrets and raise their levels in paradise, to have exerted their efforts in seeking the truth, never failing to strive in its pursuit; nay, they never so much as acted neglectfully in their quests. Rather, they upheld their responsibilities to the utmost fashion, advising the followers of Muḥammad ﷺ sincerely and avoiding all things that discredit them.

غير أَن الإِمَام أَحْمد بن مُحَمَّد بن حَنْبَل رَضِي الله عَنهُ كَانَ أوسعهم معرفَة بِحَدِيث رَسُول الله صلى الله عَلَيْهِ وَسلم كَمَا يعلم ذلك من اطلع على مُسْنده الْمَشْهُور، وَأَكْثَرهم تتبعا لمذاهب الصَّحَابَة وَالتَّابِعِينَ.

With that said, al-Imām Aḥmad ibn Muḥammad ibn Ḥanbal ؓ had the vastest knowledge of the ḥadīth of Allah's Messenger ﷺ as is plainly obvious to anyone that has familiarised themselves with his famous corpus, and was also most keen on acquiring information of the views and ways of thought of the companions and their successors.

فلذَلِك كَانَ مذْهبه مؤيدا بالأدلة السمعية، حَتَّى كَأَنَّهُ ظهر فِي الْقرن الأول لشدَّة اتِّبَاعه لِلْقُرْآنِ وَالسّنة، إِلَّا أَنه كَانَ رَحمَه الله تَعَالَى لشدَّة ورعه ينْهَى عَن كِتَابَة كَلَامه ليبقي بَاب الِاجْتِهَاد لمن هُوَ أهل لَهُ مَفْتُوحًا، وليعلم الْقَوْم أَن فضل الله لَا يَنْقَطِع، وَأَن خزائنه لم تنفد، على عكس مَا يَدعِيهِ القاصرون، وينتحله المبطلون، ولحسن نِيَّته قيض الله من دون فتَاوَاهُ وَجَمعهَا ورتبها حَتَّى صَار لَهُ مَذْهَب مُسْتَقل

مَعْدُود بَين الْأَئِمَّة الَّذين دونوا وألفوا.

Based on those facts, his school of thought is mainly supported by textual evidences; one would think he was born in the first generation of Islam by how closely he adhered to the Qur'ān and the Sunnah. Nevertheless, due to his stringent and exorbitant abstention, he forbade others from writing his statements, so as to keep the doors of exercising legal thought open to those qualified, and so that people could know that the favours of Allah the Exalted never cease and that His repositories are never expended, contrary to the claims of those whose intellects are limited and the views professed by liars. Due to his sincerity, Allah the Exalted sent someone who would inscribe his verdicts, gathering and organising them into what would become an independent school of thought with its rightful weight and recognition among scholars who wrote and authored.

ثمَّ هيأ الله لَهُ أتباعا وأصحابا سلكوا فِي رواياته مَسْلَك الِاجْتِهَاد كَمَا تعلمه مِمَّا سَيَأْتِي وألفوا فِي ذَلِك المطولات والمتوسطات والمختصرات، فجزاهم الله خيرا، غير أَنهم تركُوا اصْطِلَاحَات مُتَفَرِّقَة فِي غُضُون الْكتب لَا يعلمهَا إِلَّا المتقنون، وسلكوا مسالك لَا يُدْرِكهَا إِلَّا المحصلون.

Then, Allah the Exalted destined that he have followers and disciples who studied his narrations and exerted scholarly effort—as you will see later— in writing compendiums, intermediate books, and compendious works, may Allah reward them with good. However, they used verbiage and terminology in their books that are unknown to non-specialists, and their methodologies in authoring are only known to the knowledgeable.

وَأصَاب هَذَا الْمَذْهَب مَا أصَاب غَيره من تشتت كتبه حَتَّى آلت إِلَى الاندراس، وأكب النَّاس على الدُّنْيَا فنظروا إِلَيْهِ، فَإِذا هُوَ منهل سنة وَفقه صَحِيح. لَا مورد مَال، فهجره كثير مِمَّن كَانَ مُتبعا لَهُ رَجَاء طلب قَضَاء أَو وَظِيفَة، فَمن ثمَّ تقلص ظله من بِلَادنَا السورية وخصوصا فِي دمشق إِلَّا قَلِيلا، وأشرق نوره فِي الْبِلَاد النجدية من جَزِيرَة الْعَرَب، وهب قوم كرام مِنْهُم لطبع كتبه، وأنفقوا الْأَمْوَال الطائلة لإحياء هَذَا الْمَذْهَب لَا يطْلبُونَ بذلك إِلَّا وَجه الله تَعَالَى، وَلَا يقصدون إِلَّا إحْيَاء مَذْهَب السّلف وَمَا كَانَ عَلَيْهِ الصَّحَابَة والتابعون. فجزاهم الله خيرا

وَأحسن إِلَيْهِم.

The Ḥanbalī school of thought was afflicted with the same ailment that affected other schools of thought, namely, its books became so dispersed that the entire school almost disappeared. People became so infatuated with the worldly life, but then looked to the [Ḥanbalī school] and found it to be a fountain of Sunnah and valid Islamic law, and not a good source of money. As such, many who previously followed the school abandoned it to seek other work as judges or to receive positions. Consequently, its shade dwindled in our land of Syria, and especially in Damascus; only a few adhered to it. Its light shone once again in Najd, in the Arabian Peninsula, at the hands of noble individuals who printed versions of its books, spending hordes of money to revive this school of thought, and when doing so, sought nothing but the Face of Allah, and to revive the school of thought of the pious predecessors, and the teachings of the companions and their successors. As such, may Allah reward them and treat them kindly.

على أَن قوما من أولي التَّقْلِيد الْأَعْمَى، أسراء الْوَهم والخيالات الْفَاسِدَة وَالْجهل الْمركب، يطعنون فِي أُولَئِكَ، وينفرون النَّاس مِنْهُم، وَمَا ذَلِك إِلَّا أَن الله أَرَادَ بأولئك الْقَوْم خيرا، فاظهر لَهُم أَعدَاء لينشروا فَضلهمْ من حَيْثُ لَا يعلمُونَ ﴿وَسَيَعْلَمُ الَّذِينَ ظَلَمُوا أَيَّ مُنْقَلَبٍ يَنْقَلِبُونَ﴾ [الشُّعَرَاء: ٢٢٧]

With that said, adherents to blind following and captives of delusions, false imaginations, and compounded ignorance, disparaged them and sought to drive others away from them. They only did so because Allah the Exalted intended for those individuals to achieve something good. As such, He exposed enemies of theirs who would spread their virtues from whence they did not know. Allah the Exalted said, **{The evildoers will find out what they will return to.}** [Qur'ān 26:227]

وَمَا هَؤُلَاءِ إِلَّا على حد مَا حَكَاهُ الْحَافِظ أَبُو الْقَاسِم عَليّ بن عَسَاكِر الدِّمَشْقِي فِي أَوَائِل (تَارِيخه) عَن أبي يحيى السكرِي قَالَ:

Such individuals are reminiscent of what al-Ḥāfiẓ Abu 'l-Qāsim 'Alī bin 'Asākir al-Dimashqī stated in the outset of his *Histories* (*Tārīkh ibn 'Asākir*), where he reported that Abu Yaḥyā al-Sukkarī said:

دخلت مَسْجِد دمشق، فَرَأَيْت بِهِ حلقا، فَقلت: هَذَا بلد دخله جمَاعَة من الصَّحَابَة، فملت إِلَى حَلقَة فِي صدرها شيخ جَالس، فَجَلَست إِلَيْهِ، فَقَالَ لَهُ رجل أَمَامه: من عَليّ بن أبي طَالب؟ فَقَالَ: خفاق - يَعْنِي ضَعِيفا - كَانَ بالعراق، اجْتمعت عَلَيْهِ جمَاعَة، فقصد أَمِير الْمُؤمنِينَ أَن يحاربه، فنصره الله عَلَيْهِ، قَالَ: فاستعظمت ذَلِك، وَقمت.

I entered the mosque of Damascus and found gatherings therein. I said, "This is a land which was entered by a group of companions." I attended one of those gatherings where an old man was teaching while sitting down. I sat with him, and a man in front of him said, "Who was ʿAlī ibn Abī Ṭālib?" He replied, "A weak man residing in Iraq who gathered some adherents and sought to wage war against the Commander of the Faithful (intending Muʿāwiyah ﵁) but Allah aided [Muʿāwiyah] over him." I regarded his statement as grave, so I stood, and left the gathering.

فَرَأَيْت فِي جَانب الْمَسْجِد شَيخا يُصَلِّي إِلَى سَارِيَة، حسن السمت وَالصَّلَاة والهيئة، فَقلت لَهُ: يَا شيخ أَنا رجل من أهل الْعرَاق، جَلَست إِلَى تِلْكَ الْحلقَة، وقصصت عَلَيْهِ الْقِصَّة، فَقَالَ: فِي هَذَا الْمَسْجِد عجائب، بَلغنِي أَن بَعضهم يطعن على أبي مُحَمَّد الْحجَّاج بن يُوسُف، فعلي بن أبي طَالب من هُوَ ثمَّ جعل يبكي انْتهى.

Then, around the side of the mosque, I saw an old man praying behind a pillar. He looked amiable, prayed beautifully, and his outward appearance was pleasant. I said to him, "O *shaykh*, I am from Iraq. I sat in that gathering," and proceeded to mention the story to him. He said, "Wonders happen in this mosque. I was informed that some curse Abu Muḥammad al-Ḥajjāj ibn Yūsuf, so who is ʿAlī ibn Abī Ṭālib?" Then he began to weep.[5] **[End.]**

فَهَؤُلَاءِ مَا عرفُوا إِلَّا عليا المركون فِي مخيلتهم، وَلم يعلمُوا عليا الْحَقِيقِيّ، وَكَذَلِكَ الَّذين يطعنون على المتبعين لمَذْهَب السّلف يطعنون على قوم لَا وجود لَهُم إِلَّا فِي مخيلتهم الْفَاسِدَة وتصوراتهم المختلة، وَلَو فَهموا حَقِيقَة الْقَوْم، لانقادوا

5 *Tārīkh Dimashq* by Ibn ʿAsākir (1/365).

إِلَيْهِم، وجعلوهم أَئِمَّة هدَاهُم، وَلذَلِك وضعت كتابي خدمَة لهَذَا الْمَذْهَب الْحق ومشاركة لَهُم فِي إحيائه، عله ينالني من الْأجر مَا ينالون، وَمن الْخَيْر وَالْبركَة مَا يؤملون.

Such people only knew the 'Alī that was embedded in their imaginations; they did not know the true 'Alī. Likewise, the ones who disparage those who follow the way of the pious predecessors disparage people that exist only in their corrupted imaginations and wrongly conceived perceptions. If they understood their realities, they would have followed them, making them into leaders of guidance. I partly wrote this book to serve this veracious school of thought and to participate with them in reviving it. Hopefully, I can garner the same rewards as them and the goodness and blessings that they hope for.

وَلما رتبته وأتممته وسميته بـ(المدخل إِلَى مَذْهَب الإِمَام أَحْمد بن مُحَمَّد بن حَنْبَل)، وضمنته جلّ مَا يحْتَاج إِلَى مَعْرفَته المشتغل بِهَذَا الْمَذْهَب، وسلكت بِهِ مسلكا لم أجد غَيْرِي سلكه حَتَّى صَار بحيث يسْتَحق أَن يكون مدخلًا لسَائِر الْمذَاهب، وَلَيْسَ على المخترع أَن يَسْتَوْفِي جَمِيع الْأَقْسَام، بل عَلَيْهِ أَن يفتح الْبَاب، ثمَّ لَا يَخْلُو فِيمَا بعد من مستحسن لَهُ يقف عِنْد مَا دونه، أَو مُسْتَدْرك عَلَيْهِ يذكر مَا أخل بِهِ، أَو مُخْتَصر لَهُ يحذف مَا يرَاهُ من الزِّيَادَات يزعمه، على أَنه لَا يُمكن الْإِنْسَان أَن يَأْتِي بِمَا يستحسنه جَمِيع الْبشر، فَإِن هَذَا شَأْن الْعلي الْأَعْلَى جلّ وَعلا.

After I organised this book, I called it, *"The Introduction to the School of Thought of al-Imām Aḥmad ibn Ḥanbal,"* and I comprised it of most of the information needed by those who busy themselves with the study of this school of thought. I wrote my book in a way that I have never seen anyone else write in, making it eligible to be a framework to introduce the rest of the schools of thought. When someone is creative, they do not need to have met every requirement, but they simply need to open the door. Afterwards, there will be some readers who highly appraise their work, others who viewed it to have some deficiencies and intend on supplementing them, and others who summarise it, removing any information they thought was too exhaustive. A human cannot perform an action that all of humanity approves at the same time, that is the sole domain of Allah, the High, the Highest, the Exalted.

ورتبت هَذَا الْمدْخل على ثَمَانِيَة عُقُود عدد أَبْوَاب الْجنان، رَجَاء أَن يدخلنا الله يَوْم الْقِيَامَة مِنْهَا كلهَا: وَهَذِه فهرست تِلْكَ الْعُقُود:

I arranged this introduction into eight chapters, mimicking the doors of paradise. I did this with hope that Allah will allow us to enter into paradise from all eight of its doors. The following is the arrangement of these chapters:

العقد الأول: فِي العقائد الَّتِي نقلت عَن الإِمَام المبجل أَحْمد بن مُحَمَّد بن حَنْبَل.

The First Chapter: On the beliefs that have been reported from the esteemed *imām*, Aḥmad ibn Muḥammad ibn Ḥanbal.

العقد الثَّانِي: فِي السَّبَب الَّذِي لأَجله اخْتَار كثير من كبار الْعلمَاء مَذْهَب الإِمَام أَحْمد على مَذْهَب غيره.

The Second Chapter: On the reasons many major scholars chose the school of law of al-Imām Aḥmad over other schools of law.

العقد الثَّالِث: فِي ذكر أصُول مذْهبه فِي استنباط الْفُرُوع وَبَيَان طَرِيقَته.

The Third Chapter: On the fundamentals and methods of his legal theory of deriving subsidiary rulings.

العقد الرَّابِع: فِي مَسْلَك كبار أَصْحَابه فِي تَرْتِيب مذْهبه واستنباطه من فتياه وَالرِّوَايَات عَنهُ، وتصرفهم فِي ذَلِك الْإِرْث المحمدي الأحمدي.

The Fourth Chapter: On the manner in which the major students [of al-Imām Aḥmad] codified his school of thought, deriving it from his verdicts and statements, and their treatment of the inheritance of Muḥammad and then Aḥmad.

العقد الْخَامِس: فِي الأُصُول الْفِقْهِيَّة الَّتِي دونهَا الْأَصْحَاب، وَفِي فن الجدل.

The Fifth Chapter: On the legal theories codified by the *aṣḥāb*[6] and their contributions to the science of disputation.

العقد السَّادِس: فِيمَا اصْطلحَ عَلَيْهِ المؤلفون فِي فقه الإِمَام أَحْمد مِمَّا يحْتَاج إِلَيْهِ المبتدئ.

The Sixth Chapter: On the basic terminologies used by the authors who wrote about the jurisprudence of al-Imām Aḥmad.

العقد السَّابِع: فِي ذكر الْكتب الْمَشْهُورَة فِي الْمَذْهَب، وَبَيَان طَرِيقَة بَعْضهَا وَمَا عَلَيْهِ من التعليقات والحواشي حسب الْإِمْكَان.

The Seventh Chapter: On the important and famous books within the school of thought, defining some of them and listing the commentaries on them, to the extent possible.

العقد الثَّامِن: فِي أَقسَام الْفِقْه عِنْد أَصْحَابنَا، وَمَا ألف فِي هَذَا النَّوْع، وَفِي هَذَا العقد دُرَر، ورد الْعَجز على الصَّدْر.

The Eighth Chapter: On the categories of jurisprudence according to our *aṣḥāb* and authorships about this topic. Note that this chapter has many gems and even rectifies the deficiency of the early chapters [on creed].

وَهَذِه طلائع تِلْكَ الْعُقُود وَمَا أودع فِيهَا من الْفقر والدرر وَالله الْمعِين.

These are the headings of the chapters and their contents, which comprise of various sections and gems. Allah the Exalted is the Helper.

6 [T] The term *aṣḥāb* is used here, and throughout this work and other works by Ḥanbalī scholars, to refer to adherents to the Ḥanbalī *madhhab*, and especially its scholars.

العقد الأول

Chapter One

فِي العقائد الَّتِي نقلت عَن الإِمَام المبجل أَحْمد بن مُحَمَّد بن حَنْبَل

On the Beliefs That Have Been Reported from the Esteemed Imām, Aḥmad ibn Muḥammad ibn Ḥanbal

اعْلَم أننا ذاكرون - إِن شَاءَ الله - مَا كَانَ عَلَيْهِ الإِمَام أَحْمد من الِاعْتِقَاد الَّذِي هُوَ مَذْهَب الصَّحَابَة وَالتَّابِعِينَ، وَالْأَئِمَّة الْمُجْتَهدين، والسادة الْمُحدثين رضوَان الله عَلَيْهِم، ولسنا نذْكر إِلَّا مَا نَقله لنا الثِّقَات من كَلَامه فِي هَذَا النَّوْع، ليستغني بذلك أَتْبَاعه عَمَّا ألف فِي علم العقائد عُمُوما مِمَّا دخله التَّأْوِيل والتعطيل والتشبيه والتمثيل، أَو حام حول الْحُلُول والاتحاد، أَو كَانَ من قبيل مغالطة الْخصم فِي الجدل، فَظَنهُ الغبي مذهبا لقائله، فقلده بِهِ تقليدا أعمى، فضل وأضل، حَيْثُ إِن مسالك الجدل غير مسالك الِاعْتِقَاد.

Be aware that we shall mention, by the Will of Allah, the beliefs held by al-Imām Aḥmad, which were representative of the beliefs of the companions, their successors, the *mujtahid*[7] *imāms*, and the scholars of ḥadīth, may Allah be pleased with them. We shall not mention any of his quotes except that it was narrated to us by trustworthy reporters. This way, his followers can do without the generality of books authored about beliefs, some of which were infested with reinterpretation, negation, likening Allah [to His creation] and declaring a resemblance to Allah [for creation], others hovered around pantheism, and some others were mere works of sophistic argumentation against adversaries and foes, but some fools thought they were the positions held by their authors and began to blindly follow them, thereby becoming misguided and misguiding others. When a book is authored in the modality

7 [T] Meaning, the scholars who have reached the rank of *ijtihād*. In religious terminology, *ijtihād* refers to exertion of the fullest effort in seeking probability in a conclusion regarding a religious ruling.

of argumentation, it differs from a book authored to authoritatively establish creed.

وَأَنت إِذا طرحت التعصب، وَنظرت فِي كتب عُلَمَاء الْكَلَام الموثوق بهم بإنصاف، وسبرت غورهم فِي عقائدهم، تجدها رَاجِعَة إِلَى عقيدة السّلف إِمَّا بالاضطرار وَإِمَّا بِصَرِيح التَّصْرِيح أَو التَّلْوِيح، كَمَا جرى لأبي الْحسن الْأَشْعَرِيّ، فَإِنَّهُ لما ألف الْكتب فِي الرَّد على الْمُعْتَزلَة على طَرِيقَة فن الجدل، أعلن أخيرا بِبَيَان عقيدته فِي كِتَابه الْمُسَمّى ب(الإنابة) عَن مَذْهَب أهل الْحق وَصرح فِيهِ بِأَن مذْهبه مَذْهَب الصَّحَابَة وتابعيهم بِإِحْسَان، فَمن فهم مقاصده، أصبح سلفيا بحتا، وَمن لم يفهم موارده الْتقط مسَائِل كتبه الَّتِي رد بهَا على الْمُعْتَزلَة على علاتها، وَجعلهَا مذهبا لَهُ، ونسبها إِلَى الْأَشْعَرِيّ.

If you were to abandon bigotry and were to read the works of trustworthy scholars of Islamic philosophy with precision and levelheadedness, and were to explore them in depth, you would find that they emanate from the beliefs of the Salaf, either by their logical and necessary conclusions, or by their explicit adoption [of the creed of the Salaf], or by allusion to their beliefs in an indirect fashion. This is what happened with Abu 'l-Ḥasan al-Ashʿarī, who, when he authored his books in response to the Muʿtazilites and used a polemic style of writing, eventually declared his creed in his book, *al-Ibānah ʿan Uṣūl al-Diyānah* (*Clarifying the Foundations of Religion*). In there, he declared his beliefs to be those of the people of truth, and explicitly said that his way of thought is that of the companions and their successors in goodness. Anyone who understands his intents would inevitably become a pure follower of the Salaf. However, some did not understand the issues mentioned in his books, which he authored to refute the defective beliefs of the Muʿtazilites, and took those beliefs as their creed, then ascribed them to al-Ashʿarī.

وَمَا رَأَيْت أحدا من الأشاعرة كشف هَذَا الْمَعْنى، ونادى بِالصَّوَابِ سوى الشَّيْخ مُحَمَّد بن يُوسُف السنوسي، فَإِنَّهُ قَالَ فِي شرح لَهُ صَغِير على عقيدته الْمَشْهُورَة الْمُسَمَّاة ب(أم الْبَرَاهِين) عِنْد الْكَلَام على صفة الْكَلَام مَا نَصه:

I have yet to see a follower of the Ashʿarī belief clarify this ambiguity and espouse the truth, apart from al-Shaykh Muḥammad ibn Yūsuf al-Sanūsī, who said in his small explanation of his famous creedal work called *Umm al-Barāhīn*, when speaking about the attribute of the speech of Allah:

وكنه هَذِه الصّفة - يَعْنِي صفة الْكَلَام وَسَائِر صِفَات الله جلّ وَعز - مَحْجُوب عَن الْعقل كالذات الْعلية، فَلَيْسَ لأحد أَن يَخُوض فِي الكنه بعد مَا يجب لذاته سُبْحَانَهُ أَو لصفاته، وَمَا يُوجد فِي الْكتب من التَّمْثِيل بالكلام النَّفْسِيّ إِنَّمَا هُوَ للرَّدّ على الْمُعْتَزلَة حَيْثُ قَالُوا إِن الْكَلَام لَا يُوجد من غير حرف وَلَا صَوت. فَقَالَ أهل السّنة: إِنَّا نجد لنا كَلَاما نفسيا بِلَا حرف وَلَا صَوت، وَفِيه من كَلَام الفصحاء:

The essence of this attribute (meaning, the attribute of speech and the rest of Allah's attributes) is hidden from intellects, just as His lofty essence is hidden. After knowledge of what is necessary of His essence or attributes, none can delve further into His essence or His attributes. Also, the discussions in the books about "internal speech" only occurred in response to the Mu'tazilites who claimed that speech cannot occur without a letter and sound. Ahl al-Sunnah responded by saying, "We speak internally without a letter or sound," about which the eloquent said:

إِن الْكَلَام لفي الْفُؤَاد وَإِنَّمَا   جعل اللِّسَان على الْفُؤَاد دَلِيلا

Speech resides in the heart,
Tongues show what hearts entail.[8]

وَمَا قصدُوا إِلَّا التَّمْثِيل من حَيْثُ الْحَرْف وَالصَّوْت فَقَط، أما الْحَقِيقَة فَجلت صِفَات الله أَن يماثلها شَيْء من صِفَات خلقه، فَإِن كلامنا النَّفْسِيّ فِيهِ حُرُوف متعاقبة تنعدم وتحدث، وَيُوجد فِيهِ تَقْدِيم وَتَأْخِير وترتيب وَغير ذَلِك، فاعرف هَذَا فقد زلت هُنَا أَقْدَام لم تؤيد بِنور من الْملك العلام. هَذَا كَلَامه.

They only intended to give an example of [the concept of speech occurring without] letters and sounds. As for the reality, Allah's attributes far transcend anyone likening them to attributes of His creation. Our internal speech contains successive letters which are not in existence, but then exist.

8 This monostich is attributed to al-Akhṭal, but it is not in his collection of poetry. The likelier explanation is that it is not his utterance. Perhaps it is invented.

Also, our speech has usual order, and so forth. Therefore, know these facts, for they have been the cause for the slippage of many a foot of those who were not aided with a light from the King and the Knowledgeable. **[End]**

فقد صرح بِالْحَقِّ، وَلم يخْش فِيهِ لومة لائم.

As can be seen, he explicitly stated the truth, fearing not the blame or critique of anyone.

ولي فِي هَذَا مَسْلَك آخر وَهُوَ أَن الْأَعْيَان إِمَّا جَوَاهِر وَإِمَّا أَعْرَاض، وَالْكَلَام لَا شكّ فِي أَنه عرض يحْتَاج إِلَى مَحل يقوم بِهِ، وَهُوَ الْجَوْهَر، وَهُوَ يَقْتَضِي أَن وجود الْجَوْهَر سَابق على وجود الْعرض، فَإِذا قُلْنَا بِالْكَلَام النَّفْسِيّ، لزم أَن يكون ذَلِك الْعرض قَائِما بالجوهر وَهُوَ النَّفس، وَلزِمَ مِنْهُ إِثْبَات النَّفس لله تَعَالَى، وحدوث الْكَلَام ضَرُورَة أَن الْعرض حَادث لَا محَالة.

Personally, I view the issue differently, which is that an individual instance of something can either be a substance or an accident. Speech, undoubtedly, is an accident, requiring a receptacle or substrate, namely, a substance. This necessitates that the existence of the substance precedes the existence of the accident. If we were to espouse the belief of "internal speech" as it pertains to Allah, it would necessitate the existence of the accident in the substance, which is the soul, and it necessitates that we ascribe a soul to Allah the Exalted. Speech is temporal, by logical necessity, because accidents are undoubtedly temporal [and speech is an accident].

وَحِينَئِذٍ فإمَّا أَن نبقي الْكَلَام على ظَاهره وندعي حُدُوث كَلَامه تَعَالَى، وَثُبُوت النفسية لَهُ تَعَالَى وَهُوَ خلاف الْمَطْلُوب، لأَن المطلوب تنزيهه تَعَالَى عَن سمات الْحَوَادِث، وَيلْزم مِنْهُ أَن الْكَلَام صفة لله تَعَالَى قَائِمَة بِذَاتِهِ هُوَ حَادث، والمركب من الْحَادِث وَالْقَدِيم حَادث.

As such, we either keep the speech as it is literally and claim that Allah's speech is temporal, thereby necessitating that we affirm a soul for Allah the Exalted, which is contrary to the requirement of declaring Allah the Exalted transcendent above the attributes of temporally existing things. This would also logically necessitate that speech is an attribute of Allah the Exalted which exists as a consequent of the existence of His essence, which is eternal. However, something temporal combined with something eternal is still temporal.

وينتج الدَّلِيل أَنه تَعَالَى حَادث وَهُوَ خلاف الْمُدعى، لِأَنَّهُ إِقَامَة الدَّلِيل على قدم الصِّفَات والذات مَعًا.

The summation of this argument would lead to believing Allah the Exalted is temporal, which is contrary to the Islamic claim, as its evidence is overwhelming in support of the eternal nature of Allah's essence and attributes.

وَإِمَّا أَن نجنح إِلَى التَّأْوِيل فَنَقُول: كَلَام نَفسِي يَلِيق بِذَاتِهِ، فَيُقَال لَهُ حِينَئِذٍ: قل من أول الْأَمر وكلم الله مُوسَى تكليما بِكَلَام يَلِيق بِذَاتِهِ تَعَالَى، وَاقْتصر على هَذَا، ودع عَنْك ذَلِك التَّطْوِيل الَّذِي لَيْسَ هُوَ من شَأْن البلغاء والعقلاء.

The other option is to resort to reinterpreting the attribute altogether, claiming that the speech is internal, befitting His essence. At that, we say: State that Allah spoke to Mūsā with true speech that befits His essence, and limit yourself to that claim, avoiding your verboseness, which is not a characteristic of the eloquent or the intellectual.

وَمثل هَذَا يُقَال فِي تَأْوِيل الْيَد بِالْقُدْرَةِ، والاستواء بِالِاسْتِيلَاءِ، فَإِن الْقُدْرَة صفة مُشْتَركَة بَين الْخَالِق والمخلوق، فَإِذا قلت بهَا لزمك أَن تَقول: قدرَة تلِيق بِذَاتِهِ تَعَالَى. فاطرح هَذَا وَقل: يَد تلِيق بِذَاتِهِ تَعَالَى، وَأَيْضًا فالقدرة عرض تحْتَاج إِلَى أَن تقوم بالجوهر، وَيلْزم فِي ذَلِك مَا لزم فِي صفة الْكَلَام من الْحُدُوث لله تَعَالَى.

The same can be said about reinterpreting the hand, and claiming it is His ability, and claiming that the ascension is only to capture and control. Ability is an attribute which applies to both the Creator and the creation. If one espouses that ability is an attribute of Allah, the qualification of, "As befits His essence," is necessary. This can be applied to the hand as well, by saying, "The hand of Allah the Exalted befits His essence." Further, ability is an accident that must exist in the substance, but that would necessitate the same consequence as when discussing the attribute of speech, which is that Allah the Exalted is temporal.

وَأما الِاسْتِيلَاء فَإِن مادته تَقْتَضِي سبق مستول سَابق، وَأَن الثَّانِي قهر الأول

وَاسْتولى على مَا كَانَ مستوليا عَلَيْهِ، فليت شعري من كَانَ المستولي أَولا على الْعَرْش حَتَّى إِن الله تَعَالَى قهره وَاسْتولى عَلَيْهِ؟! أَلا يرى أَن قَوْلهم:

As for reinterpreting ascension as "conquering," the word "conquer" necessitates that there was a previous conqueror, and that the second conqueror overcame the first and conquered what was previously under their dominion. If only I knew who was the first to conquer the throne before Allah the Exalted overcame them and conquered it? However, they use the monostich:

قد اسْتَوَى بشر على الْعِرَاق.

Bishr has conquered Iraq.

يُنَادي على أَن الْعِرَاق لم يكن بيد بشر، بل كَانَ فِي يَد غَيره، ثمَّ إِن بشرا غلب ذَلِك المستولي وَضم الْعِرَاق إِلَيْهِ، أفيليق بشأن عَاقل أَن يصف ربه بِتِلْكَ الصِّفَات؟ تَعَالَى الله عَن ذَلِك علوا كَبِيرا.

But they fail to realise that Iraq was not under the dominion of Bishr; it was conquered by someone else. Then, Bishr overcame that first conqueror and took Iraq into his possession. Is it befitting for a man of sound intellect to ascribe such attributes to Allah the Exalted? Truly, Allah the Exalted is far transcendent above such claims.

وَحَيْثُ تبين أَن الْحق الصراح هُوَ مَذْهَب السّلف، وَأَن هَذَا الْمَذْهَب ظهر على لِسَان الْأَئِمَّة وأخصهم بذلك الإِمَام أَحْمد بن حَنْبَل، وَجب علينا أَن ننقل لطلاب الْيَقِين كَلَامه بنصه ليهتدوا بِهِ إِلَى الصِّرَاط الْمُسْتَقيم فَنَقُول:

As such, it becomes clear that the absolute and unadulterated truth lies in the way of the Salaf, and that their way of thought has been espoused by the great scholars of Islam, and more specifically, by al-Imām Aḥmad ibn Ḥanbal. It becomes incumbent on us to transmit his speech to the seekers of certainty, verbatim and unaltered, so that they may benefit from it in guiding them to the upright path. As such, we say:

روى الْقَاضِي أَبُو يعلى مُحَمَّد بن الْحُسَيْن بن خلف الْفراء فِي

(الطَّبَقَات) والحافظ أَبُو الْفرج عبد الرَّحْمَن بن عَليّ بن الْجَوْزِيّ الْحَنْبَلِيّ فِي كِتَابه (مَنَاقِب الإِمَام أَحْمد) وَذكر القَاضِي برهَان الدّين إِبْرَاهِيم بن مُفْلِح فِي كِتَابه (الْمَقْصد الأرشد) أَن أَبَا بكر أَحْمد بن مُحَمَّد البردعي التَّمِيمِي قَالَ:

Al-Qāḍī Abu Yaʿlā Muḥammad ibn Muḥammad ibn al-Ḥusayn ibn Khalaf al-Farrā said in his book *al-Ṭabaqāt*[9], al-Ḥāfiẓ Abu ʻl-Faraj ʻAbd al-Raḥmān ibn ʻAlī ibn al-Jawzī al-Ḥanbalī reported in his book *Manāqib al-Imām Aḥmad*[10] (*The Virtues of al-Imām Aḥmad*) and al-Qāḍī Burhān al-Dīn Ibrāḥīm ibn Mufliḥ reported in his book *al-Maqṣad al-Arshad* (*The Guided Objective*) that Abu Bakr Aḥmad ibn Muḥammad al-Bardaʿi al-Tamīmī said:

لما أشكل على مُسَدّد بن مسرهد أَمر الْفِتْنَة - يَعْنِي فِي القَوْل بِخلق الْقُرْآن وَمَا وَقع فِيهِ النَّاس من الِاخْتِلَاف فِي الْقدر والرفض والاعتزال وَخلق الْقُرْآن والإرجاء - كتب إِلَى أَحْمد بن حَنْبَل: أَن اكتب إِلَيّ سنة رَسُول الله صلى الله عَلَيْهِ وَسلم، فَلَمَّا ورد الْكتاب على أَحْمد بن حَنْبَل بَكَى وَقَالَ: إِنَّا لله وَإِنَّا إِلَيْهِ رَاجِعُون، يزْعم هَذَا الْبَصْرِيّ أَنه قد أنْفق على الْعلم مَالا عَظِيما وَهُوَ لَا يَهْتَدِي إِلَيّ سنة رَسُول الله صلى الله عَلَيْهِ وَسلم، فَكتب إِلَيْهِ:

When Musaddad ibn Musarhad became confused by the topic of "the tribulation" (referring to the view of the Qurʾān being created and the differences people had in predestination, following the Shiite beliefs, Muʿtazilī beliefs, creation of the Qurʾān, and *irja*ʿ[11]) he wrote to Aḥmad ibn Ḥanbal, saying, "Write to me, explaining the Sunnah of Allah's Messenger ﷺ." When the writing reached Aḥmad ibn Ḥanbal, he wept, and said, "To Allah we belong, and to Him we shall return; this man from Basrah alleges that he has spent so much wealth in the pursuit of knowledge, but he was not guided to the Sunnah of Allah's Messenger ﷺ." He then wrote to him, saying:

بِسم الله الرَّحْمَن الرَّحِيم

In the Name of Allah, the Most Merciful, the Giver of Mercy

---

9 *Al-Ṭabaqāt* (1/342).
10 *Al-Manāqib* (217).
11 [T] *Irjā*ʿ means to exclude actions from faith.

الْحَمد لله الَّذِي جعل فِي كل زمَان بقايا من أهل الْعلم يدعونَ من ضل إِلَى الْهدى، وَينْهَوْنَ عَن الردى، ويحيون بِكِتَاب الله الْمَوْتَى، وبسنة رَسُول الله صلى الله عَلَيْهِ وَسلم أهل الْجَهَالَة والردى. فكم من قتيل لإبليس قد أحيوه، وَكم من ضال تائه قد هدوه، فَمَا أحسن آثَارهم على النَّاس، ينفون عَن دين الله تَحْرِيف الغالين، وانتحال المبطلين، وَتَأْوِيل الضَّالّين الَّذين عقدوا أولوية الْبدع، وأطلقوا عنان الْفِتْنَة مخالفين فِي الْكتاب، يَقُولُونَ على الله وَفِي الله - تَعَالَى عَمَّا يَقُول الظالمون علوا كَبِيرا - فِي كِتَابه بِغَيْر علم، فنعوذ بِاللَّه من كل فتْنَة مضلة، وَصلى الله على مُحَمَّد النَّبِي وَآله وَسلم تَسْلِيمًا.

All praise belongs to Allah the Exalted who designated, in each era, a small number of people of knowledge who call those who have lost their way back to guidance and prohibit people from things that lead to their destruction. They bring life to the dead with the Book of Allah the Exalted, and bring life to the people of ignorance and destruction with the Sunnah of Allah's Messenger ﷺ. How many a person killed by Iblīs did they revive, and how many a misguided person did they guide. What a great impact they have on people: They refute the distortions of the extreme and the misinterpretations of the falsifiers, distancing such falsehoods from the religion. Also, they refute the false interpretations of the misguided, who have raised the banners of innovations and have given full reign to tribulations, thereby contradicting the Book. They say about Allah and of Allah, but Allah the Exalted is far transcendent above the claims of the unjust. They speak about His Book without knowledge. We seek refuge in Allah the Exalted from every misguiding tribulation, and may Allah the Exalted send blessings on Muḥammad, the Prophet, as well as his family, and may He send encompassing salutations.

أما بعد: وفقنا الله وَإِيَّاكُم لكل مَا فِيهِ رِضَاهُ وطاعته، وجنبنا وَإِيَّاكُم مَا فِيهِ سخطه، واستعملنا وَإِيَّاكُم عمل الخاشعين لَهُ، العارفين بِهِ، الْخَائِفِينَ مِنْهُ، فَإِنَّهُ المسؤول ذَلِك.

As to what follows: may Allah the Exalted grant us and you divine aid in achieving everything that results in obedience and pleasure to Allah the Exalted, and may He deliver us and you from anything that angers Him. May

He use us and you in doing actions of those who are submissive to Him, know Him, and fear Him. Surely, He is to be asked for such things.

وأوصيكم وَنَفْسِي بتقوى الله الْعَظِيم، وَلُزُوم السّنة وَالْجَمَاعَة، فقد علمْتُم مَا حل بِمن خالفها وَمَا جَاءَ فِيمَن أتبعهَا، فَإِنَّهُ بلغنَا عَن النَّبِي صلى الله عَلَيْهِ وَسلم أَنه قَالَ **((إِن الله ليدْخل العَبْد الْجنَّة بِالسنةِ يتَمَسَّك بهَا)).**

I advise you and I advise myself to fear and obey Allah the Exalted and to hold fast to the Sunnah and the congregation. You have become aware of what has befallen those who contradict it and those who follow it. It has been reported to us that the Prophet ﷺ said, **"Allah the Exalted will enter a slave into paradise due to the Sunnah that he holds fast to."**[12]

وآمركم أَن لَا تؤثروا على الْقُرْآن شَيْئا، فَإِنَّهُ كَلَام الله، وَمَا تكلم الله بِهِ فَلَيْسَ بمخلوق، وَمَا أخبر بِهِ عَن الْقُرُون الْمَاضِيَة فَلَيْسَ بمخلوق، وَمَا فِي اللَّوْح الْمَحْفُوظ وَمَا فِي الْمُصحف وتلاوة النَّاس وكيفما قرىء وكيفما وصف، فَهُوَ كَلَام الله غير مَخْلُوق. فَمن قَالَ مَخْلُوق، فَهُوَ كَافِر بِاللَّه الْعَظِيم، وَمن لم يكفره فَهُوَ كَافِر.

I command you to not prefer anything over the Qur'ān, for it is the speech of Allah. Anything Allah utters is not created; anything He informed us of regarding the previous generation is not created; anything in the Preserved Tablet, in the *muṣḥaf*[13] and the recitations of people, no matter how they recite or how the Qur'ān is described is not created. Anyone who says the Qur'ān is created is a disbeliever in Allah the Exalted, and anyone who does not believe they are a disbeliever is also a disbeliever.

ثمَّ من بعد كتاب الله سنة نبيه صلى الله عَلَيْهِ وَسلم والْحَدِيث عَنهُ، وَعَن المهديين من أَصْحَاب النَّبِي صلى الله عَلَيْهِ وَسلم وَالتَّابِعِينَ من بعدهمْ، والتصديق بِمَا جَاءَت بِهِ الرُّسُل، وَاتِّبَاع السّنة نجاة، وَهِي الَّتِي نقلهَا أهل الْعلم كَابِرًا عَن كَابر.

After the Book of Allah comes the Sunnah of His Prophet ﷺ and ḥadīths from him and the rightly guided people, namely, the companions of the

12 Reported by al-Dāraquṭnī in *al-Afrād*, as reported in *Kanz al-'Ummāl* (1/184), from 'Ā'ishah with the wording, **"Whoever holds fast to the Sunnah will enter paradise."** I did not come across a chain of narration in order to judge it.

13 [T] A *muṣḥaf* is a written copy of the Qur'ān.

Prophet ﷺ and their successors. Also, one must affirm what the messengers have taught. Following the Sunnah is salvation, and the Sunnah is what has been transmitted by major scholars from major scholars.

واحذروا رَأْي جهم فَإِنَّهُ صَاحب رَأْي وَكَلَام وخصومات.

Further, beware of the view of Jahm [ibn Safwān], for he was a person who used his rational abilities and philosophy to determine creed and to argue [against orthodoxy].

وَأما الْجَهْمِية، فقد أجمع من أدركنا من أهل الْعلم أَنهم قَالُوا: إِن الْجَهْمِية افْتَرَقت ثَلَاث فرق، فَقَالَت طَائِفَة مِنْهُم: الْقُرْآن كَلَام الله وَهُوَ مَخْلُوق، وَقَالَت طَائِفَة: الْقُرْآن كَلَام الله وسكتت، وَهِي الواقفة الملعونة، وَقَالَت طَائِفَة مِنْهُم: ألفاظنا بِالْقُرْآنِ مخلوقة، فَهَؤُلَاءِ كلهم جهمية كفار يستتابون فَإِن تَابُوا وَإِلَّا قتلوا.

As far as the Jahmite sect goes: the scholars we have met have unanimously agreed that the Jahmites are of three groups: (i) a group of them stated that the Qur'ān is the speech of Allah but is created, (ii) another group said that the Qur'ān is the speech of Allah, and left it at that, and they are called *al-Wāqifah* (those who desist), and they are accursed, and (iii) a group said that our utterances of the words of the Qur'ān are created. All three groups are Jahmites and are disbelievers. They are to be asked to repent; if they do not, they are to be executed.

وَأجْمع من أدركنا من أهل الْعلم على أَن من هَذِه مقَالَته إِن لم يتب لم يناكح وَلَا يجوز قَضَاؤُهُ، وَلَا تُؤْكَل ذَبِيحَته.

The scholars we have met have unanimously agreed that if someone who espouses such a view does not repent, they are not to be married, are not to judge, and their slaughtered meat is not to be eaten.

وَالْإِيمَان قَول وَعمل، يزِيد وَينْقص، زِيَادَته إِذا أَحْسَنت، ونقصانه إِذا أسأت.

Further, faith is statement and action. It increases and decreases. It increases when you do good, and it decreases if you do bad.

وَيخرج الرجل من الْإِيمَان إِلَى الْإِسْلَام، فَإِن تَابَ رَجَعَ إِلَى الْإِيمَان، وَلَا يُخرجهُ

من الْإِسْلَام إِلَّا الشّرك بِاللَّه الْعَظِيم، أَو برد فَرِيضَة من فَرَائِض الله جاحدا لَهَا، فَإِن تَركهَا كسلا أَو تهاونا بهَا، كَانَ فِي مَشِيئَة الله إِن شَاءَ عذبه وَإِن شَاءَ عَفا عَنهُ.

A person leaves faith to Islam.[14] If they repent, they return to faith. Nothing removes one from Islam but associating a partner in worship with Allah the Exalted or rejecting an obligatory action that Allah has obligated, while also denying its obligation. If a person abandons an obligation out of laziness or negligence, they are subject to the will of Allah: if He so wishes, He will punish them, and if He so wishes, He will pardon them.

وَأما الْمُعْتَزلَة فقد أجمع من أدركنا من أهل الْعلم أَنهم يكفرون بالذنب، وَمن كَانَ مِنْهُم كَذَلِك، فقد زعم أَن آدم كَانَ كَافِرًا، وَأَن إخْوَة يُوسُف حِين كذبُوا أباهم عَلَيْهِ السَّلَام كَانُوا كفَّارًا.

As for the Muʿtazilite sect: The scholars we have met have unanimously agreed that they judge people as disbelievers due to sins. Those who have such a view allege that Ādam was a disbeliever and that the brothers of Yūsuf, when they lied to their father, were also disbelievers.

وأجمعت الْمُعْتَزلَة على أَن من سرق حَبَّة، فَهُوَ كَافِر، وَفِي لفظ فِي النَّار تبين مِنْهُ امْرَأَته، ويستأنف الْحَج إِن كَانَ حج. فَهَؤُلَاءِ الَّذين يَقُولُونَ بِهَذِهِ الْمقَالة كفَّار، وحكمهم أَلا يكلموا وَلَا يناكحوا، وَلَا تُؤْكَل ذَبَائِحهم، وَلَا تقبل شَهَادَتهم حَتَّى يتوبوا.

Adherents to the Muʿtazilite sect unanimously agree that if someone steals a seed, they are a disbeliever, or, put another way, are in the hellfire. As such, their wife should be separated from them, and they must do their Ḥajj over if they performed Ḥajj. Anyone who espouses such views is a disbeliever.

---

14 [T] To clarify this concept, consider the narration ʿAbdullāh ibn Aḥmad reported from his father, al-Imām Aḥmad ibn Ḥanbal, who, through his chain of narration, reported that Muḥammad ibn ʿAlī said, "This is Islam," after which he drew a large circle. He then drew a smaller circle inside of it, and said, "This is faith. Therefore, when the Messenger ﷺ says, 'A fornicator, when fornicating, is not a person of faith; a thief, when stealing, is not a person of faith, and a drinker of alcohol, while drinking, is not a person of faith,' it means that one leaves from faith to Islam, but does not leave Islam altogether. If they repent, Allah will forgive them, and they return to the [circle of] faith." Refer to *al-Sunnah* by ʿAbdullāh ibn Aḥmad (1/352).

They are not to be spoken to nor are they to be married; their slaughtered meat is also not to be eaten, and their testimonies must not be accepted until they repent.

وَأما الرافضة: فقد أجمع من أدركنا من أهل الْعلم أَنهم قَالُوا: إِن علي بن أبي طَالب أفضل من أبي بكر الصّديق، وَإِن إِسْلَام عَليّ كَانَ أقدم من إِسْلَام أبي بكر، فَمن زعم أَن عليا بن أبي طَالب أفضل من أبي بكر فقد رد الْكتاب وَالسّنة، يَقُول الله تَعَالَى: ﴿**مُحَمَّدٌ رَسُولُ اللهِ وَالَّذِينَ مَعَهُ**﴾ [الْفَتْح: ٢٩] فَقدم الله أَبَا بكر بعد النَّبِي وَلم يقدم عليا. وَقَالَ النَّبِي صلى الله عَلَيْهِ وَسلم: **((لَو كنت متخذا خَلِيلًا لاتخذت أَبَا بكر خَلِيلًا، وَلَكِن الله قد اتخذ صَاحبكُم خَلِيلًا - يَعْنِي نَفسه - وَلَا نَبِي بعدِي))**.

As for the Rafiḍite sect, the scholars we have met have unanimously agreed that they believe that ʿAlī ibn Abi Ṭālib is more virtuous than Abu Bakr al-Ṣiddīq, and that ʿAlī accepted Islam prior to Abu Bakr. With that said, whoever alleges that ʿAlī ibn Abi Ṭālib is more virtuous than Abu Bakr has indeed rejected the Qurʾān and Sunnah. Allah the Exalted said: **{Muḥammad is the Messenger of God and those with him.}** [Qurʾān 48:29] Allah the Exalted gave preference to Abu Bakr ﵁ after the Prophet ﷺ, and did not give preference to ʿAlī ﵁. Also, the Prophet ﷺ said, **"If I were to take a close friend, it would be Abu Bakr. However, Allah the Exalted has taken me as a close friend, and there is no prophet after me."**[15]

وَمن زعم أَن إِسْلَام عَليّ كَانَ أقدم من إِسْلَام أبي بكر، فقد أَخطَأ لِأَن أَبَا بكر أسلم وَهُوَ يَوْمئِذٍ ابْن خمس وَثَلَاثِينَ سنة وَعلي يَوْمئِذٍ ابْن سبع سِنِين لم تجر عَلَيْهِ الْأَحْكَام وَالْحُدُود والفرائض.

Further, anyone who claims that ʿAlī accepted Islam before Abu Bakr has erred, for Abu Bakr accepted Islam at the age of thirty-five, while ʿAlī accepted Islam at the age of seven, an age where rulings, punishments, and obligations are not yet applicable.

---

15 Reported by Muslim (2383) from the report of Ibn Masʿūd with the wording, **"If I were to take anyone as a close friend, it would be Abu Bakr. However, he is my brother and my companion, and Allah the Exalted has taken me as His close friend."**

ونؤمن بِالْقضَاءِ وَالْقدر خَيره وشره وحلوه ومره من الله، وَأَن الله خلق الْجنَّة قبل خلق الْخلق، وَخلق لَهَا أهلا، وَنَعِيمهَا دَائِم، فَمن زعم أَنه يبيد من الْجنَّة شَيْء فَهُوَ كَافِر. وَخلق النَّار قبل خلق الْخلق، وَخلق لَهَا أَهلا، وعذابها دَائِم، وَأَن الله يخرج أَقْوَامًا من النَّار بشفاعة النَّبِي مُحَمَّد صلى الله عَلَيْهِ وَسلم.

To continue, we believe the Divine Will and in predestination: its good parts, bad parts, sweet parts, and bitter parts, are all from Allah. We also believe that Allah created heaven before He created creation, and that He created people to inhabit it. Its bliss is eternal. Whoever claims that any part of paradise will ever vanish is a disbeliever. Also, He created hellfire before the rest of creation, and created its inhabitants. Its torment is eternal. We also believe that Allah will extract some people from hellfire due to the intercession of the Prophet ﷺ.

وَأَن أهل الْجنَّة يرَوْنَ رَبهم بِأَبْصَارِهِمْ لَا محَالة.

We also believe that the inhabitants of paradise will see their Lord with their eyes, without a doubt.

وَأَن الله كلم مُوسَى تكليما وَاتخذ إِبْرَاهِيم خَلِيلًا.

And that Allah spoke to Mūsā with true speech and took Ibrāḥīm as a close friend.

وَالْمِيزَان حق، والصراط حق، والأنبياء حق، وَعِيسَى ابْن مَرْيَم عبد الله وَرَسُوله وكلمته.

Further, the scale is true, the bridge [over hellfire, which each person will cross over] is true, and ʿĪsā the son of Maryam is the slave of Allah, His messenger, and the product of His Word.

وَالْإِيمَان بالحوض والشفاعة، وَالْإِيمَان بالعرش والكرسي، وَالْإِيمَان بِملك الْمَوْت وَأَنه يقبض الْأَرْوَاح ثمَّ ترد إِلَى الأجساد فِي الْقُبُور، ويسألون عَن الْإِيمَان والتوحيد وَالرسل، وَالْإِيمَان بمنكر وَنَكِير وَعَذَاب الْقَبْر، وَالْإِيمَان بالنفخ فِي الصُّور، والصور قرن ينْفخ فِيهِ إِسْرَافيل.

Also, we have faith in the pool [of the Messenger ﷺ,] intercession, the throne and the footstool, and the Angel of Death—who we believe captures the souls and then returns them to the bodies when they are in the grave where people will be asked about faith, monotheism, and the Messenger. We also have faith in Munkar and Nakīr and punishment in the grave, blowing in the horn [which will cause people to all die at the first blowing, and then come back to life at the second one], and that the horn will be blown by Angel Isrāfīl.

وَأَن الْقَبْر الَّذِي هُوَ بِالْمَدِينَةِ قبر النَّبِي صلى الله عَلَيْهِ وَسلم، مَعَه أَبُو بكر وَعمر، وَقُلُوب الْعباد بَين إِصْبَعَيْنِ من أَصَابِع الرَّحْمَن عز وَجل، والدجال خَارج فِي هَذِه الْأمة لَا محَالة، وَينزل عِيسَى ابْن مَرْيَم إِلَى الأَرْض فيقتله بِبَاب لد، وَمَا أنكرته الْعلمَاء من أهل السّنة من الشُّبْهَة، فَهُوَ مُنكر.

We also believe that the grave in Madīnah is that of the Prophet ﷺ, and that Abu Bakr and ʿUmar are buried beside him. [We also believe] the hearts of the slaves are between two Fingers of al-Raḥmān (Allah) the Exalted and that the Anti-Christ will emerge in this nation, without any doubt. We also believe that ʿĪsā, the son of Maryam, will descend to earth to kill him at the Door of Ludd. Further, any dubious matter the scholars of Ahl al-Sunnah reject is reprehensible.

واحذروا الْبدع كلهَا، وَلَا عين تطرف بعد النَّبِي صلى الله عَلَيْهِ وَسلم أفضل من أبي بكر، وَلَا عين تطرف بعد أبي بكر أفضل من عمر، وَلَا بعد عمر عين تطرف أفضل من عُثْمَان، وَلَا بعد عُثْمَان بن عَفَّان عين تطرف أفضل من عَليّ بن أبي طَالب. قَالَ أَحْمد: كُنَّا نقُول: أَبُو بكر وَعمر وَعُثْمَان ونسكت عَن عَليّ حَتَّى صَحَّ لنا حَدِيث ابْن عمر بالتفضيل.

Beware of all innovation. No eye that batted after the Prophet ﷺ was more virtuous than that of Abu Bakr, no eye that batted after Abu Bakr was more virtuous than that of ʿUmar, no eye that batted after ʿUmar was more virtuous than that of ʿUthmān and no eye that batted after the death of ʿUthmān was more virtuous than that of ʿAlī ibn Abi Ṭālib. Aḥmad said, "We would say, 'Abu Bakr, 'Umar and 'Uthmān' and would remain silent without mentioning 'Alī, until we found authentic the ḥadīth of Ibn 'Umar which mentions his virtue (as the fourth best Muslim)."

قَالَ أَحْمد هم وَالله الْخُلَفَاء الراشدون المهديون.

Aḥmad said: By Allah, they are the Rightly-Guided Caliphs.

وَأن نشْهد للعشرة أَنهم فِي الْجنَّة: أَبُو بكر، وَعمر، وَعُثْمَان، وَعلي، وَطَلْحَة، وَالزُّبَيْر وَسعد، وَسَعِيد، وَعبد الرَّحْمَن بن عَوْف، وَأَبُو عُبَيْدَة بن الْجراح. فَمن شهد لَهُ النَّبِي صلى الله عَلَيْهِ وَسلم بِالْجنَّةِ شَهِدنَا لَهُ بهَا.

We testify that the ten are in paradise, namely: Abu Bakr, 'Umar, 'Uthmān, 'Alī, Ṭalḥah, al-Zubayr, Ṣa'd, Sa'īd, 'Abd al-Raḥmān ibn 'Awf, and Abu 'Ubaydah ibn al-Jarrāḥ. Anyone whom the Prophet ﷺ testified is in paradise, we also testify to their entrance into paradise.

وَرفع الْيَدَيْنِ فِي الصَّلَاة زِيَادَة فِي الْحَسَنَات، والجهر بآمين عِنْد قَول الإِمَام: وَلَا الضَّالّين، وَالصَّلَاة على من مَاتَ من أهل هَذِه الْقبْلَة وحسابهم على الله عز وَجل، وَالْخُرُوج مَعَ كل إِمَام خرج فِي غَزْوَة وَحجَّة، وَالصَّلَاة خلف كل بر وَفَاجِر صَلَاة الْجُمُعَة وَالْعِيدَيْنِ، وَالدُّعَاء لأئمة الْمُسلمين بالصلاح، وَلَا نخرج عَلَيْهِم بِالسَّيْفِ، وَلَا نُقَاتِل فِي الْفِتْنَة، وَلَا نتألى على أحد من الْمُسلمين أَن يَقُول: فلَان فِي الْجنَّة وَفُلَان فِي النَّار إِلَّا الْعشْرَة الَّذين شهد لَهُم النَّبِي صلى الله عَلَيْهِ وَسلم بِالْجنَّةِ. والكف عَن مساوىء أَصْحَاب رَسُول الله صلى الله عَلَيْهِ وَسلم، تحدثُوا بفضائلهم وأمسكوا عَمَّا شجر بَينهم.

Raising the hands in prayer is an increase in good deeds. We view that one should utter "*Amīn* (O Allah, accept)" after the *imām* says, "*Wa la 'l-ḍālīn*". We offer funeral prayers for those of this Qiblah, but we acknowledge that their accounting is with Allah. We proceed with every ruler to war and to Ḥajj, if they engage in those activities, and we pray behind every righteous and sinful person during Friday prayers and the two Eids. We supplicate for righteousness for the rulers, and we do not rebel against them with weapons. We also do not fight during times of tribulation. We do not take an oath that any Muslim is definitively in paradise or hellfire, except for the ten that Allah's Messenger ﷺ testified are in paradise. We also refrain from mentioning anything wrong that the companions of Allah's Messenger ﷺ might have done. Instead, mention their virtues, and abstain from discussing the quarrels that occurred between them.

وَلَا تشَاور أهل الْبدع فِي دينك، وَلَا ترافق أحدا مِنْهُم فِي سفرك وصفوا الله بِمَا وصف بِهِ نَفسه، وانفوا عَن الله مَا نَفَاهُ عَن نَفسه. واحذروا الْجِدَال مَعَ أَصْحَاب الْأَهْوَاء.

Never seek counsel from a person of innovation in matters pertaining to your religion, and do not ever accompany one in your travels. Describe Allah the Exalted as He has described Himself, and negate what He has negated for Himself. Beware of debating people of vain desires.

وَلَا نِكَاح إِلَّا بولِي وخاطب وشاهدي عدل. والمتعة حرَام إِلَى يَوْم الْقِيَامَة، وَالتَّكْبِير على الْجَنَائِز أَربع، فَإِن كبر الإِمَام خمْسا فكبر مَعَه كَفعل عَليّ بن أبي طَالب، قَالَ عبد الله بن مَسْعُود: كبر مَا كبر إمامك. قَالَ أَحْمد: خالفني الشَّافِعِي فَقَالَ: إِن زَاد على أَربع تَكْبِيرَات تُعَاد الصَّلَاة، وَاحْتج عَليّ بِحَدِيث النَّبِي صلى الله عَلَيْهِ وَسلم **((أَنه صلى على جَنَازَة فَكبر أَرْبعا))** وَفِي رِوَايَة **((صلى على النَّجَاشِيّ فَكبر أَرْبعا))**.

There is no marriage except with a guardian, a proposer, and two honest witnesses. Temporary marriages are disallowed until the Day of Resurrection, and during funeral prayers, there are four *takbīrs*. If the *imām* says a fifth *takbīr*, say it with him, just as ʿAlī ibn Abi Ṭālib did.[16] ʿAbdullāh ibn Masʿūd said, "Make the *takbīr* along with your *imām*."[17] Aḥmad said, "Al-Shāfiʿī contradicted me, saying, 'If the *imām* utters more than four *takbīrs*, the prayer must be redone.' He invoked, as evidence in response to me, the ḥadīth of the Prophet ﷺ that he uttered four *takbīrs* when he led a funeral

16 Al-Ṭaḥāwī (1/287), al-Dāraquṭnī (1/191) and al-Bayhaqī (4/37).

17 Reported by ʿAbd al-Razzaq in his *Musannaf* (6403), al-Bayhaqī (4/37) and Ibn Ḥazm in *al-Muḥallā* (5/126), and it has an authentic chain of narration.

prayer. In another narration, 'He led al-Najāshī's funeral prayer, and he uttered four *takbīrs*.'"[18]

وَزَاد ابْن مُفْلِح فِي (الْمَقْصد الأرشد): وَمن طلق ثَلَاثًا فِي لفظ وَاحِد، فقد جهل، وَحرمت عَلَيْهِ زَوجته. وَلم أجد هَذِه الزِّيَادَة فِي رِوَايَة الْحَافِظ ابْن الْجَوْزِيّ. وَالْمسح على الْخُفَّيْنِ للْمُسَافِر ثَلَاثَة أَيَّام ولياليهن، وللمقيم يَوْم وَلَيْلَة.

Ibn Mufliḥ added in *al-Maqṣad al-Arshad* that Aḥmad said, "Whoever utters three divorces in one statement has acted ignorantly, but his wife is forbidden for him."[19] However, I did not find that addition in the report of Ibn al-Jawzī. He continued: Wiping on leather socks is permissible for a person traveling for three days and three nights, and only one day and one night for the person in residence.

وَصَلَاة اللَّيْل وَالنَّهَار مثنى مثنى، وَلَا صَلَاة قبل الْعِيد، وَإِذا دخلت الْمَسْجِد، فَلَا تجْلِس حَتَّى تصلي رَكْعَتَيْنِ تَحِيَّة الْمَسْجِد. وَالْوتر رَكْعَة، وَالْإِقَامَة فُرَادَى. أَحبُّوا أهل السّنة على مَا كَانَ مِنْهُم. أماتنا الله وَإِيَّاكُم على الْإِسْلَام وَالسّنة، ورزقنا وَإِيَّاكُم الْعلم، ووفقنا وَإِيَّاكُم لما يحب ويرضى.

Prayer at night is two by two. There is no prayer before Eid. If you enter the mosque, do not sit until you offer two units of prayer, as a greeting to the mosque. The *witr* prayer is one unit, and each statement in the *iqāmah* is to be uttered only once (except *"qad qāmat al-ṣalāt"*). Love the people of Sunnah, despite their flaws. May Allah the Exalted allow us and you to die on Islam and the Sunnah, and may he grant us knowledge. May He also grant us and you divine aid in achieving what He loves and is pleased with.

هَذَا آخر مَا اتَّصل بِنَا مِمَّا كتبه الإِمَام إِلَى مُسَدّد رحمهمَا الله تَعَالَ.

This is the last portion of what has been narrated to us from the letter of the *imām* to Musaddad ﷺ.

---

18 Reported by Mālik (1/266) and al-Bukhārī (3/163) from the ḥadīth of Abu Hurayrah who reported that Allah's Messenger ﷺ announced the death of al-Najāshī during the day in which he died, and he went with them to an open prayer area, lined them up, and uttered four *takbīrs*.

19 [T] *Al-Maqṣad al-Arshad* (3/28).

وَفِي الْأُصُول الَّتِي نقلنا عَنْهَا خلاف فِي بعض الْمسَائِل بِحَيْثُ تُوجد الْمَسْأَلَة فِي رِوَايَة ابْن الْجَوْزِيّ وَلم تُوجد فِيمَا نَقله صَاحب (الْمَقْصد) وَقد ضممنا زِيَادَة بعض إِلَى بعض.

The manuscripts that we have quoted from have some variations in some of the issues, where one issue is present in the narration of Ibn al-Jawzī and not present in what was reported by the author of *al-Maqṣad*. We have combined those additions into one.

وَأما التَّصْرِيح باللعن فَلم نجده إِلَّا فِيمَا نَقله الْبُرْهَان ابن مُفْلِح وَلَعَلَّه من زِيَادَة الرواة، فَإِن ورع وزهده يَأْبَى لَهُ ذَلِك. وَبَقِي فِي هَذِه الرسَالَة مَوَاضِع تحْتَاج إِلَى بَيَان لَا بَأْس بإيراده فلنذكره على شريطة التَّلْخِيص فَنَقُول:

As for an explicit curse, we could not find it anywhere except in what was reported by al-Burhān ibn Mufliḥ and it might be an addition of a narrator, because the abstinence and cautiousness of the *imām* would prevent him from ever saying such a thing. The letter that al-Imām Aḥmad wrote to Musaddad has some areas that require some clarification. There is no harm in discussing these points now, in summary:

الْموضع الأول: قَول الإِمَام فِي قدم الْقُرْآن وَمَا فِي الْمُصحف وتلاوة النَّاس غير مَخْلُوق مَعْنَاهُ: أَن الْقُرْآن مهما تكيف بكيفية، فَهُوَ كَلَام الله، وَكَلَامه تَعَالَى غير مَخْلُوق، سَوَاء كتب فِي الْمَصَاحِف أَو تكلم بِهِ التَّالِي، فَإِنَّهُ لَا يخرج عَن كَونه كَلَام الله تَعَالَى. وَإِيَّاك أَن تذْهب فِي كَلَامه مَذْهَب سعد الدّين مَسْعُود التَّفْتَازَانِيّ فِي شَرحه لعقائد النَّسَفِيّ، حَيْثُ نسب إِلَى بعض الْأَصْحَاب أَنهم يَقُولُونَ بقدم جلد الْمُصحف والكاغد والحبر الَّذِي كتب بِهِ الكاغد، فَتكون قد أعظمت الافتراء على الْقَوْم، ونسبت إِلَيْهِم مَا لم يقل بِهِ عَاقل فضلا عَن أَئِمَّة أَعْلَام، وَلم تدر أَن مُرَادهم تَنْزِيه كَلَام الله تَعَالَى عَن أَن ينْسب إِلَيْهِ كَونه مخلوقا، فَإِنَّهُ مهما قرىء أَو كتب، فَلَا يخرج عَن كَونه كَلَام الله تَعَالَى، وَلَا يَلِيق بِأحد أَن يدعِي أَن كَلَامه تَعَالَى مَخْلُوق. فحقق هَذَا الْمقَام، واطرح التعصب ينور الله قَلْبك بِنور الْإِيمَان والعرفان.

The first instance: The statement of the *imām* that the Qur'ān is eternal, and that what is in the *muṣḥaf* and the recitation of people is not created means that the Qur'ān, no matter how it is transcribed or uttered, remains the speech of Allah, and the speech of Allah the Exalted is not created, regardless if it is written in a *muṣḥaf* or if a reciter utters it; it remains the speech of Allah the Exalted. Beware of interpreting his words in the way of Ṣa'd al-Dīn Mas'ūd al-Taftāzānī. In his explanation of the *Creed of al-Nasafī*, he claimed that some of the *aṣḥāb* believe in the eternal nature of the binding, paper, and ink that is used to write on the paper. Truly, this is a major distortion and false claim against them; the view that was ascribed to them would never be uttered by a sane human, let alone major scholars. He was unaware that their intent was to declare Allah the Exalted transcendent above having created speech. Therefore, however it is read or written, it is still the speech of Allah the Exalted. It is not appropriate for anyone to claim that His speech is created. Be very precise in this instance, and reject bigotry, and as such, Allah the Exalted will enlighten your heart with the light of faith and knowledge.

الْموضع الثَّانِي: قَوْله: واحذروا رَأْي جهم أَرَادَ بِهِ جهم بن صَفْوَان، وَهُوَ من الجبرية الْخَالِصَة، ظَهرت بدعته بترمذ، وَقَتله سالم ابن أحوز المازني بمرو فِي آخر ملك بني أُميَّة، وَوَافَقَ الْمُعْتَزلَة فِي نفي الصِّفَات الأزلية، وَزَاد عَلَيْهِم بأَشْيَاء.

The second instance: When he said, "Beware of the view of Jahm," he meant Jahm ibn Ṣafwān, who was an unadulterated Jabrite (meaning that he did not believe in predestination). His heresy appeared in Tirmidh, and he was killed by Sālim ibn Aḥwaz al-Māzinī in Marw, during the ending of the era of the Umayyads. His views concurred with the Mu'tazilites in that he rejected eternal attributes. However, he had additional heresies that the Mu'tazilites did not.

مِنْهَا قَوْله: لَا يجوز أَن يُوصف الْبَارِي تَعَالَى بِصفة تكون مُشْتَركَة بَينه وَبَين خلقه، لِأَن ذَلِك يَقْتَضِي تَشْبِيها فَقَالَ: لَا يجوز أَن يُوصف تَعَالَى بِكَوْنِهِ حَيا عَالما، وَأثبت كَونه قَادِرًا فَاعِلا، لِأَنَّهُ لَا يُوصف شَيْء من خلقه بِالْقُدْرَةِ وَالْفِعْل والخلق.

One of these views is that it is not permissible to describe Allah the Exalted by using any attributes shared with the creation, because that necessitates likening creation to Allah. He opined that it is not permissible to describe

Allah the Exalted as being alive and knowing. However, he affirmed ability and action for Allah the Exalted, but none of creation should be described as having ability, action, or creation.

وَمِنْهَا أَنه أثبت لله تَعَالَى علوما حَادِثَة لَا فِي مَحل، قَالَ: لَا يجوز أَن يعلم الشَّيْء قبل خلقه، لِأَنَّهُ لَو علم ثمَّ خلق أفيبقى علمه على مَا كَانَ أَو لم يبْق؟ فَإِن بَقِي، فَهُوَ جهل، فَإِن الْعلم بِأَن سيوجد غير الْعلم بِأَن قد وجد، وَإِن لم يبْق، فقد تغير، والمتغير مَخْلُوق لَيْسَ بقديم. وَوَافَقَ فِي هَذَا مَذْهَب هِشَام بن الحكم قَالَ: وَإِذا ثَبت حُدُوث الْعلم، فَلَيْسَ يَخْلُو إِمَّا أَن يحدث فِي ذَاته تَعَالَى، وَذَلِكَ يُؤَدِّي إِلَى التَّغَيُّر فِي ذَاته، وَأَن يكون محلا للحوادث، وَإِمَّا أَن يحدث فِي مَحل، فَيكون الْمحل مَوْصُوفا بِهِ لَا الْبَارِي تَعَالَى، فتعين أَنه لَا مَحل لَهُ، فَأثْبت علوما حَادِثَة بِعَدَد المعلومات الْمَوْجُودَة.

Jahm also ascribed to Allah the Exalted knowledge that is temporal without a receptacle. He said that it is not possible for Him to know of anything before He creates it, because if He were to know, then create, would His knowledge be exactly as it was before the creation, or not? If it is the same, then it means He is ignorant of the new creation, because knowledge of what will happen is different than knowledge of what already existed. If His knowledge is no longer the same, it means that it has changed, and anything that can change is created, not eternal. In this aspect, his views coincide with those of Hishām ibn al-Ḥakam, who said, "If we acknowledge the temporal nature of knowledge, then the possibilities are either (i) that it comes temporally into existence in His essence, and this means that His essence changes and is a receptacle of temporal changes, or (ii) that it comes into existence temporally in a receptacle, and as such, the receptacle is described as knowledgeable, not Allah the Exalted. Therefore, the only logical conclusion is that there is no receptacle of knowledge." As such, he opined that there are temporal pieces of knowledge in the same number as there are available pieces of information.

وَمِنْهَا: قَوْله فِي الْقُدْرَة الْحَادِثَة: إِن الْإِنْسَان لَيْسَ يقدر على شَيْء وَلَا يُوصف بالاستطاعة، وَإِنَّمَا هُوَ مجبور فِي أَفعاله لَا قدرَة لَهُ وَلَا إِرَادَة وَلَا اخْتِيَار، وَإِنَّمَا

يخلق الله تَعَالَى الْأَفْعَال فِيهِ على حسب مَا يخلق فِي سَائِر الجمادات، وينسب إِلَيْهِ الْأَفْعَال مجَازًا كَمَا ينسب إِلَى الجمادات كَمَا يَقُول: أثمرت الشَّجَرَة، وجري المَاء، وتحرك الْحجر، وطلعت الشَّمْس وغربت، وتغيمت السَّمَاء وأمطرت، وأزهرت الأَرْض وأنبتت، إِلَى غير ذَلِك. وَالثَّوَاب وَالْعِقَاب جبر، كَمَا أَن الْأَفْعَال جبر، قَالَ: وَإِذا ثَبت الْجَبْر، فالتكليف أَيْضا كَانَ جبرا.

Further, in describing temporal abilities, he stated that humans are incapable of doing anything and should not be described as "able." Humans, in his view, are forced into their action; they have no will, choice, or wishes of their own. Allah the Exalted creates the actions of slaves just as He creates the actions of inanimate objects. Actions are ascribed to Allah metaphorically, just as they are ascribed to inanimate objects when one says, "The tree produced fruit," "The water flowed," "The rock moved," "The sun rose or set," "The sky is cloudy and it rained," "The earth produced vegetation and flowers," and so forth. Rewards and punishment are forced on a person, just as actions are forced on them. Since people are forced into things, they are also forced into responsibility.

وَمِنْهَا: قَوْله: إِن حركات أهل الْجنَّة وَالنَّار تَنْقَطِع، وَالْجنَّة وَالنَّار تفنيان بعد دُخُول أَهلهَا فِيهِمَا، وتلذذ أهل الْجنَّة بنعيمها، وتألم أهل النَّار بجحيمها، إِذْ لَا يتَصَوَّر حركات لَا تتناهى آخرا كَمَا لَا تتَصَوَّر حركات لَا تتناهى أَولا، وَحمل قَوْله تَعَالَى ﴿خَالِدِينَ فِيهَا﴾ [هود: ١٠٧] على التَّأْكِيد وَالْمُبَالغَة دون الْحَقِيقَة فِي التخليد كَمَا يُقَال: خلد الله ملك فلَان، وَاسْتشْهدَ على الِانْقِطَاع بقوله تَعَالَى ﴿خَالِدِينَ فِيهَا مَا دَامَتِ السَّمَاوَاتُ وَالْأَرْضُ إِلَّا مَا شَاءَ رَبُّكَ﴾ [هود: ١٠٧] فالآية اشْتَملت على شَرْطِيَّة واستثناء، وَالْخُلُود والتأبيد لَا شَرط فِيهِ وَلَا اسْتِثْنَاء.

Another of his views is that the movements of the people of paradise and hellfire cease, and that paradise and hellfire both will eventually vanish after its residents enter them and after the people of paradise enjoy its pleasures and the people of hellfire feel the pain of its torment. The reason he had this belief was due to his opinion that just as infinite regression is impossible, so is infinite progression. When Allah the Exalted said: **{There you will remain for eternity.}** [Qur'ān 39:72] Jahm commented that Allah the Exalted said that as meaning a mere emphasis on the length of time, as opposed to declaring heaven or hellfire to be for the remainder of eternity, just as it is said in Arabic, "Allah the Exalted gave so-and-so an eternal kingdom." Then, to prove that heaven and hellfire perish eventually, he quoted the verse when Allah the Exalted said: **{There to remain for as long as the heavens and earth endure, unless your Lord wills otherwise.}** [Qur'ān 11:107] He stated that the verse contains a condition and an exception, both of which cannot exist in the case of eternal things.

وَمِنْهَا: قَوْله: من أَتَى بالمعرفة ثمَّ جحد بِلِسَانِهِ لم يكفر بجحده، لِأَن الْعلم والمعرفة لَا يزولان بالجحد، فَهُوَ مُؤمن. قَالَ وَالْإِيمَان لَا يَتَبَعَّض أَي: لَا يَنْقَسِم إِلَى عقد وَقَول وَعمل، قَالَ: وَلَا يتفاضل أَهله فِيهِ، فإيمان الْأَنْبِيَاء وإيمان الْأمة على نمط وَاحِد، إِذْ المعارف لَا تتفاضل.

Moreover, he opined that if someone acknowledges Allah but then utters words of rejection of the faith, they do not leave the fold of Islam, despite their rejection, because, as he claimed, knowledge and acknowledgement are not nullified by rejection. As such, the person is a believer. He also said that faith cannot be divided, which means that it is not divided into beliefs, speech, and actions. He also believed that people are not on varying levels of faith; the faith of prophets, to him, is tantamount to the faith of any other Muslim. As such, he claimed that all Muslims are equal in their faith in Allah, since knowledge cannot be of varying degrees.

وَكَانَ السّلف كلهم من أَشد الرادين على جهم، ونسبته إِلَى التعطيل الْمَحْض، وَهُوَ أَيْضا مُوَافق للمعتزلة فِي نفي رُؤْيَة الْمُؤمنِينَ لرَبهم يَوْم الْقِيَامَة، وَفِي إِثْبَات خلق الْكَلَام وَإِيجَاب المعارف بِالْعقلِ قبل وُرُود الشَّرْع.

The pious predecessors were of the fiercest degree in responding to al-Jahm, going so far as to ascribe him to making absolute rejection of the attributes of Allah. Jahm also agreed with the Muʿtazilites in that he negated that believers will see Allah the Exalted on the Day of Resurrection, that Allah's speech is created, and that things must be recognised as good or evil through only the intellect before revelation can be sent [to confirm what the intellect has already given a value judgement on].[20]

وَقد شن الْغَارة على جهم وَأَتْبَاعه وإخوانه من المبتدعة أساطين الْعلمَاء. وردوا استدلالهم، وَأَكْثر من نصب نَفسه لبَيَان الْحق وَالرَّدّ عَلَيْهِم من طريقي الْعقل وَالنَّقْل الإِمَام أَبُو مُحَمَّد عَليّ بن أَحْمد بن حزم الظَّاهِرِيّ، ثمَّ شيخ الْإِسْلَام أَحْمد بن تَيْمِية الْحَرَّانِي، ثمَّ صَاحبه شمس الدّين مُحَمَّد بن قيم الجوزية قدس الله أسرارهم. فَمن أَرَادَ الِاطِّلَاع على كسر جيوشهم، وغلبتهم فِي ميدان الِاسْتِدْلَال، فعَلَيهِ بكتب هَؤُلَاءِ الْأَعْلَام، وَلَو أننا اشترطنا فِي كتابنَا هَذَا الِاخْتِصَار، لاقتفينا أثر أُولَئِكَ النُّجُوم، فاهتدينا بهم، وعسانا إِن شرعنا بشرح نونية ابْن الْقيم أَن نأتي بِمَا يَكْفِي ويشفي.

The great and luminous scholars waged a proverbial war against Jahm, his followers, and his associates in innovation by refuting their evidences. The person who most frequently put himself to the task of clarifying the truth and refuting them—both from textual and logical standpoints—was al-Imām Abu Muḥammad ʿAlī ibn Aḥmad ibn Ḥazm al-Ẓāhirī, and then Shaykh al-Islām Aḥmad ibn Taymiyyah al-Ḥarrānī and his disciple Shams al-Dīn Muḥammad ibn Qayyim al-Jawzīyyah, may Allah sanctify their secrets. Whoever wishes to see their armies destroyed and defeated in the battlefield of evidences, they must read the books of such authorities. Had it not been that I made a condition that we would be concise in this book, I would have trodden the traditions of such stars and would have sought guidance in my work from them. Perhaps, if I explain the *Nūniyyah* of Ibn al-Qayyim, I will mention information that will both suffice and cure [of any doubts or deviations].

الْموضع الثَّالِث: ذكر الإِمَام رَضِي الله عَنهُ الْمُعْتَزلَة، وهم طوائف كَثِيرَة استوفى أقسامها من ألف فِي الْملَل والنحل كَأبي مَنْصُور الْبَغْدَادِيّ، وَأبي الْفَتْح مُحَمَّد بن عبد الْكَرِيم الشهرستاني، وَلَكنهُمْ على كثرتهم يعمهم القَوْل بأصول اتَّخذُوهَا

20 [T] Al-Shahrastānī quoted al-Jahm ibn Ṣafwān as saying, "Unadulterated rationality dictates virtue or vice in things prior to revelation. Then, revelation descends confirming the virtues and vices recognised by intellection." Refer to *al-Milal wa 'l-Niḥal* (1/88).

أساسا لمداركهم ونحلتهم وَهِي قَوْلهم إِن الله تَعَالَى قديم، والقدم أخص وصف ذَاته، وَنفَوْا الصِّفَات الْقَدِيمَة أصلا فَقَالُوا: هُوَ عَالم بِذَاتِهِ، قَادر بِذَاتِهِ، حي بِذَاتِهِ، لَا بِعلم وَلَا قدرَة وحياة، هِيَ صِفَات قديمَة وَمَعَان قَائِمَة بِهِ، لِأَنَّهُ لَو شاركته الصِّفَات فِي الْقدَم الَّذِي هُوَ أخص الْوَصْف لشاركته فِي الإلهية.

The third instance: The *imām* ﷺ mentioned the Muʿtazilites, who are many sects within themselves, as mentioned by the authors of books detailing the beliefs of various sects and religions, such as Abu Manṣūr al-Baghdādī and Abu ʿl-Fatḥ Muḥammad ibn ʿAbd al-Karīm al-Shahrastānī. However, despite the number of sub-sects that fall under the umbrella of the Muʿtazilites, they all share foundational views that are fundamental to their perception of the faith and creed. These foundational views are: Allah is eternal, and eternal is the most descriptive attribute of His essence. They rejected eternal attributes, claiming that He is knowledgeable, able, and alive in His essence, but He possesses no knowledge, ability or life. They claimed they are eternal attributes and meanings that are in and of His essence. To them, had the attributes shared in their eternal nature, which is the most descriptive attribute of Allah, they would be described as independent gods.

وَاتَّفَقُوا على أَن كَلَامه مُحدث مَخْلُوق فِي مَحل، وَهُوَ حرف وَصَوت كتب أَمْثَاله فِي الْمَصَاحِف حكايات عَنهُ، فأينما وجد فِي الْمحل عرض، فقد فني فِي الْحَال.

The various Muʿtazilite sects unanimously agreed that the speech of Allah is temporal and created in a receptacle. They said that the Qurʾān consists of letters and sounds, and what has been written in its copies represents its contents. Anything that exists in a receptacle is an accident that ceases to exist in that moment[21].

وَاتَّفَقُوا على أَن الْإِرَادَة والسمع وَالْبَصَر لَيست مَعَاني قَائِمَة بذاته، لَكِن اخْتلفُوا فِي وُجُوه وجودهَا ومحامل مَعَانِيهَا. وَاتَّفَقُوا على رُؤْيَة الله تَعَالَى بالأبصار فِي دَار الْقَرار، وَنفي التَّشْبِيه عَنهُ من كل وَجه: جِهَة، ومكانا، وَصُورَة، وجسما وتحيزا، وانتقالا، وزوالا، وتغيرا، وتأثرا، وأوجبوا تَأْوِيل الْآيَات المتشابهة الَّتِي يشْتَبه فِيهَا،

21 [T] Meaning, the moment they are uttered, they cease to exist, since they are accidents and if its receptacle is nonexistent so is it.

وَسموا هَذَا النمط توحيدا.

They also agreed that Allah's will, hearing, and sight are not concepts that exist within His essence. They disagreed in the nature of their existences and how to understand the underlying concepts intended by those individual words. They agreed in negating that Allah the Exalted will be seen with eyesight in paradise,[22] and agreed that all likenesses to Him must be negated in all ways: In direction, place, image, body, occupying a space, movement, disappearance, change, and effects. They obligated reinterpreting the verses that are ambiguous that might be understood to define a likeness to Him, and they stated that the culmination of these beliefs is tantamount to monotheism, calling it, "*tawhīd*."

وَاتَّفقُوا على أَن العَبْد قَادر، خَالق لأفعاله: خَيرهَا وشرها، مُسْتَحق على مَا يَفْعَله ثَوَابًا وعقابا فِي الدَّار الْآخِرَة، والرب منزه أَن يُضَاف إِلَيْهِ شَرّ وظلم وَفعل هُوَ كفر ومعصية. لِأَنَّهُ لَو خلق الظُّلم، كَانَ ظَالِما، كَمَا لَو خلق الْعدْل، كَانَ عادلا.

They agreed that the slave is able and creates both their good and evil actions. As such, they deserve reward or punishment in the hereafter. The Lord is transcendent above being attached to any evil, injustice, or actions of disbelief. To them, had Allah the Exalted created injustice, He would be described as unjust, just as if He created justice, He would be described as just.

وَاتَّفقُوا على أَن الْحَكِيم لَا يفعل إِلَّا الصّلاح وَالْخَيْر، وَيجب من حَيْثُ الْحِكْمَة رِعَايَة مصَالح الْعباد، وَأما الْأَصْلَح والألطف، فَفِي وُجُوبه خلاف عِنْدهم، وَسموا هَذَا النمط عدلا.

Further, they agreed that the Wise must only do what is upright and righteous. It is an obligation, inasmuch as Allah the Exalted is Wise, that He caters to whatever benefits humankind. They differ, however, on whether it is obligatory on Allah to do what is best and kindest to His creation. They

22 [T] The printed version says "Will be seen," but the translation of the accurate quote is what I placed in the text (i.e. the word "*nafī*" (negate) was missing).

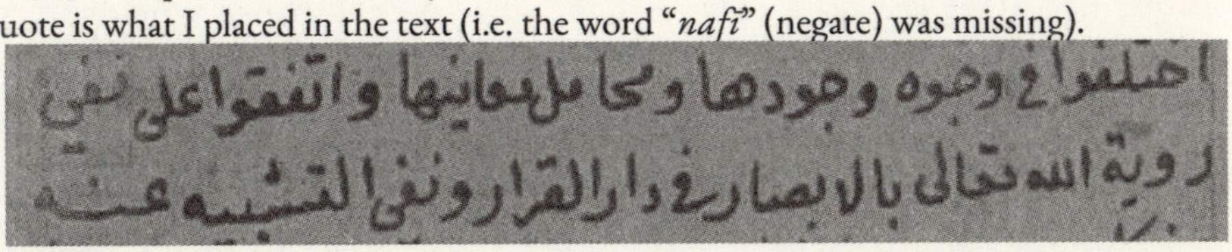
اختلفوا في وجوه وجودها ومحامل معانيها واتفقوا على نفي
رؤية الله تعالى بالابصار في دار القرار ونفي التشبيه عنه

called the culmination of these beliefs *"al-'adl"*, which means their conceptualisation of justice.

وَاتَّفَقُوا على أَن الْمُؤمن إِذا خرج من الدُّنْيَا على طَاعَة وتوبة، اسْتحق الثَّوَاب والعوض، والتفضيل معنى آخر وَرَاء الثَّوَاب، وَإِذا خرج من غير تَوْبَة عَن كَبِيرَة ارتكبها، اسْتحق الخلود فِي النَّار، وَلَكِن يكون عِقَابه أخف من عِقَاب الْكفَّار، وَسموا هَذَا النمط وَعدا ووعيدا.

They also agreed that if the believer leaves this world in a state of obedience and repentance, they deserve reward and recompense. Favours of Allah are a concept beyond rewards. However, if a believer leaves this world without having repented from a major sin that they committed, they deserve to spend eternity in hellfire. However, their punishment will be less severe than that of the disbelievers. They described this particular belief as *"al-wa'd wa 'l-wa'īd,"* which means, promise of reward and promise of punishment.

وَاتَّفَقُوا على أَن أُصُول الْمعرفَة وشكر النِّعْمَة وَاجِب قبل وُرُود السّمع، وَالْحسن والقبيح يجب معرفتهما بِالْعقلِ، واعتناق الْحسن، وَاجْتنَاب الْقَبِيح وَاجِب كَذَلِك، وورود التكاليف أَلْطَاف للباري تَعَالَى أرسلها إِلَى الْعباد بتوسط الْأَنْبِيَاء عَلَيْهِم السَّلَام امتحانا واختبارا ﴿**ليهلك من هلك عَن بَيِّنَة وَيحيى من حيّ عَن بَيِّنَة**﴾ [الأنفال: ٤٢]، وَاخْتلفُوا فِي الْإِمَامَة وَالْقَوْل فِيهَا نصا واختيارا، فَهَذِهِ أصُول مذاهبهم، وَأما الْفُرُوع فللطوائف فِيهَا اخْتِلَاف يطول بَيَانه.

They also agreed that the fundamentals of knowledge and thankfulness for blessings are obligatory even before hearing revelation. They believed that noble and ignoble things are known through ration. They stated that doing noble actions and avoiding distasteful ones is an obligation. Their belief was that the requirements were acts of kindness from Allah the Exalted which He sent to His slaves via the Prophets ﷺ as a test and examination for mankind. As Allah the Exalted said, **{So that those who were to die might die after seeing a clear proof, and so that those who were to live might live after seeing a clear proof.}** [Qur'ān 8:42] They disagreed about the concept of choosing leadership and whether it must be through textual evidence from revelation or through a selection process. These are the foundations of their way of thought. As for the subsidiary matters, there are various points of view within the Muʿtazilite tradition making the discussion too lengthy for the purposes of this book.

الْموضع الرَّابِع: ذكر الإِمَام رَضِي الله عَنهُ الرافضة، وهم أَيْضا فرق، ويجمعهم الْقَوْل بِوُجُوب التَّعْيِين والتخصيص، فَإِنَّهُم شايعوا عليا عَلَيْهِ السَّلَام على الْخُصُوص، وَقَالُوا بإمامته وخلافته نصا ووصاية إِمَّا جليا وَإِمَّا خفِيا، واعتقدوا أَن الْإِمَامَة لَا تخرج من أَوْلَاده، وَإِن خرجت، فبظلم يكون من غَيره، أَو بتقية من عِنْده، قَالُوا: وَلَيْسَت الْإِمَامَة قَضِيَّة مصلحية تناط بِاخْتِيَار الْعَامَّة، وينتصب الإِمَام بنصبهم، بل هِيَ قَضِيَّة أصولية، هِيَ ركن الدّين لَا يجوز للرسول عَلَيْهِ الصَّلَاة وَالسَّلَام إغفاله وإهماله وَلَا تفويضه إِلَى الْعَامَّة وإرساله.

The fourth instance: The *imām* ﷺ mentioned the Rāfiḍite sect, who are also split into various factions. They are all united in the concept that leadership must be supported by texts. They supported ʿAlī ﷺ in particular and stated that he was the leader and caliph as per the texts or advices of the Prophet ﷺ, be they apparent or vague. They believed that leadership must never leave the progeny of ʿAlī, and if it does, it is merely due to the transgressions of others or due to a deception (*taqiyyah*) that they are engaging in. They stated that leadership does not fall under the concept of the public domain, and as such, is not chosen by the masses; civilians cannot choose or anoint a leader. Rather it is a matter of core religious principle to them, of which the Messenger ﷺ could not forget, neglect, or entrust to the public.

وَقَالُوا بِثُبُوت عصمَة الْأَئِمَّة وجوبا عَن الْكَبَائِر والصغائر، وَالْقَوْل بالتولي والتبري قولا وفعلا وعقدا إِلَّا فِي حَال التقية، ويخالفهم بعض الزيدية فِي ذَلِك.

They espoused the belief that their *imāms* are infallible and cannot fall into major or lesser sins. They considered this point central to their belief system. They also believed in alliance and disavowal in action, statement, and belief (to Allah, His Messenger and their *imāms*) except when in the case of *taqiyyah* (hiding one's belief out of protection), while some of the Zaydī iterations of Shiʿism disagree on this concept.

وَالْإِمَام رَضِي الله عَنهُ رد على المفضلة فَقَط، وترفع عَن أَن يذكر مِنْهُم من يسب

الشَّيْخَيْنِ للاتفاق على قَبِيح مقاصدهم. وَلقد أحسن ابْن حزم حَيْثُ قَالَ فِي كِتَابه (الْفِصَل فِي الْملَل والأهواء والنحل) بعد أَن أتم الْكَلَام على المرجئة:

Al-Imām Aḥmad ﷺ only responded to those who give preference to ʿAlī. He was far above mentioning those who curse the two *shaykhs*, because all agree that their intents behind doing so are evil. Ibn Ḥazm excellently stated in his book, *al-Fiṣal fī 'l-Milal wa 'l-Ahwā' wa 'l-Niḥal*, after speaking about the Murjiʿite sect:

وَالْأَصْل فِي أَكثر خُرُوج هَذِه الطوائف عَن ديانَة الْإِسْلَام أَن الْفرس كَانُوا من سَعَة الْملك، وعلو الْيَد على جَمِيع الْأُمَم، وجلالة الخطير فِي أنفسهم حَتَّى إِنَّهُم كَانُوا يسمون أنفسهم الْأَحْرَار وَالْأَبْنَاء، وَكَانُوا يعدون سَائِر النَّاس عبيدا لَهُم.

Generally, the reason the majority of these sects have abandoned true Islam is that the Persian Empire had a vast kingdom and superiority over all other nations. They were extremely prideful of themselves, and would even call themselves, "The sons of the free." They believed the rest of people were to be their slaves.

فَلَمَّا امتحنوا بزَوَال الدولة عَنْهُم على أَيدي الْعَرَب، وَكَانَت الْعَرَب أقل الْأُمَم عِنْد الْفرس خطرا، تعاظمهم الْأَمر، وتضاعفت لديهم الْمُصِيبَة، وراموا كيد الْإِسْلَام بالمحاربة فِي أَوْقَات شَتَّى، وَفِي كل ذَلِك يظْهر الله سُبْحَانَهُ وَتَعَالَى الْحق، وَكَانَ من قائمتهم ستقادة واستاسيس وَالْمقنع وبابك وَغَيرهم، وَقبل هَؤُلَاءِ رام ذَلِك عمار الملقب بخداش وَأَبُو سلم السراج، فَرَأَوْا أَن كيد الْإِسْلَام على الْحِيلَة أنجع، فأظهر قوم مِنْهُم الْإِسْلَام، واستمالوا أهل التَّشَيُّع بِإِظْهَار محبَّة أهل بَيت رَسُول الله صلى الله عَلَيْهِ وَسلم واستشناع ظلم عَليّ رَضِي الله عَنهُ، ثمَّ سلكوا بهم مسالك شَتَّى حَتَّى أخرجوهم عَن الْإِسْلَام.

When they were tested with the fall of their empire at the hands of the Arabs, who were considered by the Persians to be the least possible threat to their empire, they were gravely stricken, making the calamity exponentially worse. They tried to resist Islam by fighting back at various times. However, in every instance, Allah the Exalted made the truth prevail. Of their leaders were Satqādah, Istāsīs, Muqannaʿ, Bābāk, and others. Before them, this idea was the objective of ʿAmmār, who was nicknamed Khidāsh, and Abu Salam al-Sirāj, both of whom thought that fighting Islam through deception was more effective. As such, some of them started to act as though they were Muslims, and they enticed the supporters of ʿAlī by feigning love for the family of the Prophet ﷺ and declaring that ʿAlī was supremely wronged, convincing some supporters of ʿAlī ؓ of various beliefs, some of which led to their leaving Islam altogether.

فقوم مِنْهُم أدخلوهم إِلَى الْقَوْل بِأَن رجلا يَنْتَظر يدعى الْمهْدي، عِنْده حَقِيقَة الدّين، إِذْ لَا يجوز أَن يُؤْخَذ الدّين من هَؤُلَاءِ الْكفَّار، إِذا نسبوا أَصْحَاب رَسُول الله صلى الله عَلَيْهِ وَسلم إِلَى الْكفْر.

The outcome was that some began to espouse the view that there would be an awaited man named al-Mahdī, and that he possessed knowledge of the realities of the religion. Religion cannot be learned from such disbelievers, since they said the companions of the Prophet ﷺ were disbelievers.

وَقوم خَرجُوا إِلَى نبوة من ادعوا لَهُ النُّبُوَّة، وَقوم سلكوا بهم المسلك الْقَائِل صَاحبه بالحلول وَسُقُوط الشَّرَائِع، وَآخَرُونَ تلاعبوا فأوجبوا عَلَيْهِم خمسين صَلَاة فِي كل يَوْم وَلَيْلَة. وَآخَرُونَ قَالُوا: بل هِيَ سبع عشرَة صَلَاة، فِي كل صَلَاة خمس عشرَة رَكْعَة، وَهَذَا قَول عبد الله بن عمر بن الْحَارِث الْكِنْدِيّ قبل أَن يصير خارجيا صفريا.

Others left the faith and followed prophesies of whomever they claimed was a prophet. Others took the route of believing in pantheism and that all religious rites were not incumbent. Others took the religion as a plaything and obligated fifty prayers during the day and night, while others obligated only seventeen prayers, but with fifteen units in each prayer, as was the view of ʿAbdullāh ibn ʿUmar ibn al-Ḥārith al-Kindī, before he became a Kharijite.

وَقد سلك هَذَا المسلك أَيْضا عبد الله بن سبأ الْحِمْيَرِي الْيَهُودِيّ، فَإِنَّهُ - لَعنه الله - أظهر الْإِسْلَام لكيد أَهله، فَهُوَ كَانَ أصل إثارة النَّاس على عُثْمَان رَضِي الله عَنهُ، وأحرق عَليّ بن أبي طَالب رَضِي الله عَنهُ مِنْهُم طوائف أعلنوا لَهُ بالإلهية.

Another person who took this route was ʿAbdullāh ibn Sabaʾ al-Ḥimyarī, who was a Jewish man. He, may Allah curse him, feigned Islam in order to plot against its adherents. He was the root of the unrest against ʿUthmān ﷺ. A portion of them claimed ʿAlī ﷺ was a god, and so he burned them at the stake.

وَمن هَذِه الْأُصُول الملعونة حدثت الإسماعيلية والقرامطة وهما طَائِفَتَانِ مجاهرتان بترك الْإِسْلَام جملَة، قائلتان بالمجوسية الْمَحْضَة. ثمَّ مَذْهَب مزدك الموبذ الَّذِي كَانَ على عهد أنوشروان ابْن قيماذ ملك الْفرس، وَكَانَ يَقُول بِوُجُوب تأسي النَّاس فِي النِّسَاء وَالْأَمْوَال.

From these accursed foundations emerged the Ismaʿilites and the Qarāmiṭah sects, both of which openly proclaim that they have left Islam altogether and believe in outright Zoroastrianism. There also was the ideology of Mazdak the Younger, who lived during the era of Anushirvan, son of Kavad I the king of Persia. He believed in the sharing of both women and wealth." **[End.]**

قَالَ ابْن حزم: فَإِذا بلغ النَّاس إِلَى هذَيْن الشعبين أَخْرجُوهُ عَن الْإِسْلَام كَيفَ شاؤوا، إِذْ هَذَا هُوَ غرضهم فَقَط، فَالله الله عباد الله، اتَّقوا الله فِي أَنفسكُم، وَلَا يَغُرنكُمْ أهل الْكفْر والإلحاد. وَمن موه كَلَامه بِغَيْر برهَان، لَكِن تمويهات، وَوعظ على خلاف مَا أَتَاكُم بِهِ كتاب ربكُم وَكَلَام نَبِيكُم صلى الله عَلَيْهِ وَسلم فَلَا خير فِيمَا سواهُمَا.

Ibn Ḥazm said, "If people reach either of these two sects, they will cause them to leave Islam in any possible way; indeed, that is their only goal. Therefore, be conscious of Allah, slaves of Allah, and fear Him in yourselves. Do not be deceived by people of disbelief and heresy. Anyone who coats their speech with adornments without providing evidences but only conceal their true intentions with falsified words, and admonishes you in ways you do not know to have emanated from the Book of your Lord and the speech of your Prophet ﷺ, [avoid them] for there is no goodness in anything but those two (i.e. the Qur'ān and the Sunnah).

وَاعْلَمُوا أَن دين الله ظَاهر لَا بَاطِن فِيهِ، وجهر لَا سر تَحْتَهُ، كُله برهَان وَلَا

مُسَامَحَة فِيهِ، واتهموا كل من يَدْعُو أَن يتبع بِلَا برهَان، وكل من ادّعى للديانة سرا وَبَاطنا فَهِيَ دعاوي ومخارق.

Know, too, that the religion of Allah the Exalted is apparent; there are no hidden realities. It is open, not secretive. It is all based on evidences, and there is no room for changes. Asperse against (lit. accuse) anyone who calls to following something without providing evidence for it, as well as everyone who claims religiosity in secret and within themselves: both claims are false.

وَاعْلَمُوا أَن رَسُول الله صلى الله عَلَيْهِ وَسلم لم يكتم من الشَّرِيعَة كلمة فَمَا فَوْقهَا، وَلَا اطلع أخص النَّاس بِهِ من زَوْجَة، أَو ابْنة، أَو عَم، أَو ابْن عَم، أَو صَاحب على شَيْء من الشَّرِيعَة كتمه عَن الْأَحْمَر وَالْأسود ورعاة الْغنم. وَلَا كَانَ عِنْده عَلَيْهِ الصَّلَاة وَالسَّلَام سر وَلَا رمز وَلَا بَاطِن غير مَا دعى النَّاس كلهم إِلَيْهِ، وَلَو كتمهم شَيْئا لما بلغ كَمَا أَمر. وَمن قَالَ هَذَا فَهُوَ كَافِر.

Also know that Allah's Messenger ﷺ did not conceal a single word of the legislation, let alone more. Nor was he selective in sharing certain information about legislation with those closest to him, such as his wives, daughters, uncles, cousins, or any companions, and then refrained from sharing that same information with a red or black person, or a shepherd. Nor did he have any secrets, hidden symbols, or a secretive interior that conflicted with what he called people to. If he were to hide anything, it would mean that he had not fulfilled his obligation to convey the message, and if anyone makes such a claim, they are disbelievers.

فإياكم وكل قَول لم يبن سَبيله، وَلَا وضح دَلِيله، وَلَا تعوجا عَن مَا مضى عَلَيْهِ نَبِيكُم صلى الله عَلَيْهِ وَسلم وَأَصْحَابه رَضِي الله عَنهُم. قَالَ: وَجُمْلَة الْخَيْر كُله أَن تلتزموا مَا قصّ عَلَيْكُم ربكُم تَعَالَى فِي الْقُرْآن بِلِسَان عَرَبِيّ مُبين لم يفرط فِيهِ من شَيْء تبيانا لكل شَيْء، وَمَا صَحَّ عَن نَبِيكُم صلى الله عَلَيْهِ وَسلم بِرِوَايَة الثِّقَات من أَئِمَّة أَصْحَاب الحَدِيث رَضِي الله عَنْهُم مُسْندًا إِلَيْهِ صلى الله عَلَيْهِ وَسلم، فهما طريقتان يوصلانكم إِلَى رِضَى ربكُم عز وَجل. هَذَا كَلَامه فقد نَادَى بِالْحَقِّ علنا، وَأَبَان عَن عقيدة الْفرْقَة النَّاجِية فرحمه الله تَعَالَى.

Therefore, beware of words that have no evidence showing their veracity or whose evidence has simply not been clarified. Do not deviate from what the Prophet ﷺ and his companions ؓ taught." He said, "Goodness in its entirety is in adhering to what Allah the Exalted has told us in the Qur'ān, which He revealed in clear Arabic language, and did not neglect to clarify anything, as well as what has been authentically reported from your Prophet ﷺ via trustworthy narrators from the ḥadīth masters ؓ, and which have connected chains of narrations."[23] That is what he said. He has called to the truth publicly and has openly clarified the beliefs of the Saved Sect. May Allah the Exalted have mercy on him.

الْموضع الْخَامِس: قَول الإِمَام رَضِي الله عَنهُ: كُنَّا نقُول: أَبُو بكر وَعمر وَعُثْمَان ونسكت عَن عَليّ حَتَّى صَحَّ لنا حَدِيث ابْن عمر بالتفضيل، يُشِير إِلَى أَنه رَضِي الله عَنهُ كَانَ يَدُور مَعَ الدَّلِيل الصَّحِيح كَيْفَمَا دَار، فَإِذا أشكل عَلَيْهِ، سكت إِلَى أَن يتجلى لَهُ الْحق، وَلما كَانَ عِنْده تردد فِي حَدِيث ابْن عمر من حَيْثُ الصِّحَّة وَعدمهَا أطرح الْميل القلبي وَلم يعبأ بِهِ، فَلَمَّا تبين لَهُ صِحَّته باح بمضمونه، وَلَيْسَ سُكُوته أَيْضا إِلَّا عَن دَلِيل، فقد قَالَ فِي مُسْنده: حَدثنَا أَبُو مُعَاوِيَة، حَدثنَا سُهَيْل بن أبي صَالح عَن أَبِيه، عَن ابْن عمر قَالَ: كُنَّا نعد، وَرَسُول الله صلى الله عَلَيْهِ وَسلم حَيّ وَأَصْحَابه متوافرون: أَبُو بكر وَعمر وَعُثْمَان ثمَّ نسكت.

The fifth instance: The *imām* ؓ said, "We would say: Abu Bakr, 'Umar, and 'Uthmān, and would remain silent without mentioning 'Alī, until we found authentic the ḥadīth of Ibn 'Umar which mentions his virtue (as the fourth best Muslim)." He is referring to the fact that he would follow authentic evidences wherever they went. If something was unclear to him, he would remain silent until the truth was made apparent to him. When he had some hesitation regarding the ḥadīth of Ibn 'Umar from the perspective of its authenticity, or lack thereof, he refused to follow the inclination of his heart, paying no heed to it. When he was convinced of its authenticity, he openly proclaimed its contents. His silence, therefore, was also due to evidence. He said in his *Musnad*, "It was narrated to us by Abu Mu'āwiyah—Suhayl ibn Abī Ṣāliḥ—his father—Ibn 'Umar, who said: 'We would consider—when the Prophet ﷺ was alive and his companions were in abundance: Abu Bakr,

23 [T] *al-Fiṣal fi 'l-Milal wa 'l-Ahwā' wa 'l-Niḥal* (2/91-92).

'Umar, and 'Uthmān, then we would remain silent.'"[24]

وَرَوَاهُ التِّرْمِذِيّ وَقَالَ: هَذَا حَدِيث حسن صَحِيح، غَرِيب من هَذَا الْوَجْه، يستغرب من حَدِيث عبيد الله بن عمر، وَقد رُوِيَ هَذَا الحَدِيث من غير وَجه عَن ابْن عمر انْتهى.

This ḥadīth was reported by al-Tirmidhī, who said, "This ḥadīth is of the grade *ḥasan ṣaḥīḥ*, but is singularly reported through this chain of narration; it is singular from 'Ubaydullāh ibn 'Umar. This narration has been reported from Ibn 'Umar via other narrations."

وَقَوله (من غير وَجه) أَشَارَ بِهِ إِلَى مَا رَوَاهُ الإِمَام، فَإِنِّي كشفت عَلَيْهِ فِي (الْمسند) فَلم أَجِدهُ، وَلست أَدْرِي هَل هُوَ فِيهِ فزاغ عَنهُ الْبَصَر، أم هُوَ مَفْقُود مِنْهُ، وَكَذَلِكَ فتشت عَلَيْهِ فِي الْكتب السِّتَّة فَلم أَجِدهُ، لكنني وجدت أَن الْحَافِظ أَبَا الْقَاسِم عَليّ بن عَسَاكِر الدِّمَشْقِي رَوَاهُ فِي تَرْجَمَة أبي بكر الصّديق رَضِي الله عَنهُ من تَارِيخه الْكَبِير عَن ابْن عمر، قَالَ: كُنَّا نقُول وَرَسُول الله حَيّ: أفضل الْأمة بعد رَسُول الله صلى الله عَلَيْهِ وَسلم أَبُو بكر ثمَّ عمر، ثمَّ عُثْمَان ثمَّ عَليّ، فيبلغ ذَلِك رَسُول الله صلى الله عَلَيْهِ وَسلم وَلَا يُنكره. وَفِي لفظ: ثمَّ نَدع أَصْحَاب رَسُول الله صلى الله عَلَيْهِ وَسلم فَلَا نفاضل بَينهم. وَحَيْثُ إِن الإِمَام أَشَارَ إِلَى صِحَة هَذَا الحَدِيث تركنَا الْكَلَام عَلَيْهِ اكْتِفَاء بتوثيق إِمَام الْمُحدثين.

When he said, "Via other narrations," he is referring to what the *imām* reported. I tried to find it in the *Musnad*, but alas, could not. I do not know if it is present in the *Musnad* but that my eyes drifted away from finding it, or if it is missing from there. I also searched for it in the other six books of ḥadīth, but could not find it. However, I found that al-Ḥāfiẓ Abu 'l-Qāsim ibn 'Asākir al-Dimashqī in his *Major Histories* reported it in the biography of Abu Bakr al-Ṣiddīq from Ibn 'Umar, who said, "When the Messenger of Allah the Exalted was alive, we would say, 'The noblest of this nation after Allah's Messenger ﷺ are Abu Bakr, then 'Umar, then 'Uthmān, and then 'Alī. That was told to Allah's Messenger ﷺ and he did not object.'" And in another narration, "Then, [after those four,] we would not rank the

24 Reported by Aḥmad (2/14) and al-Bukhārī (7/14).

companions of Allah's Messenger." Since the *imām* [Aḥmad] indicated this ḥadīth is authentic, we will not discuss it in detail, since it was declared as authentic by the leader of the ḥadīth masters.

وَقد أخرج ابْن عَسَاكِر رَضِي الله عَنهُ أَنه قَالَ: من فضلني على أبي بكر وَعمر جلدته جلد المفتري، وَهل أَنا إِلَّا حَسَنَة من حَسَنَات أبي بكر وَعمر؟! وَله كَلَام غير هَذَا ذكرته فِي كتابي (تَهْذِيب تَارِيخ ابْن عَسَاكِر).

Ibn ʿAsākir ﷺ also reported that ʿAlī ﷺ said, "Whoever ranks me above Abu Bakr and ʿUmar will be whipped as liars. What am I but a single good deed of Abu Bakr and ʿUmar?"[25] He has other similar quotations that I mentioned in my summary of Ibn ʿAsākir's *Tārīkh*.

وروى الْحَافِظ ابْن الْجَوْزِيّ، وَالْقَاضِي أَبُو يعلى فِي (طبقاته)، وبرهان الدّين بن مُفْلِح فِي (الْمَقْصد الأرشد) عَن مُحَمَّد بن حميد الأندراني عَن الإِمَام أَحْمد أَنه قَالَ:

Al-Ḥāfiẓ Ibn al-Jawzī, al-Qāḍī Abu Yaʿlā in his *Ṭabaqāt*, and Burhān al-Dīn ibn Mufliḥ in *al-Maqṣad al-Arshad* all reported from Muḥammad ibn Ḥumayd al-Andarānī, that al-Imām Aḥmad said:

صفة الْمُؤمن من أهل السّنة وَالْجَمَاعَة من شهد أَن لَا إِلَه إِلَّا الله وَحده لَا شريك لَهُ، وَأَن مُحَمَّدًا عَبده وَرَسُوله، وَأقر بِجَمِيعِ مَا أَتَت بِهِ الْأَنْبِيَاء وَالرسل، وَعقد قلبه على مَا ظهر من لِسَانه، وَلم يشك فِي إيمَانه، وَلم يكفر أحدا من أهل التَّوْحِيد بذنب، وأرجأ مَا غَابَ عَنهُ من الْأُمُور إِلَى الله عز وَجل، وفوض أمره إِلَى الله، وَلم يقطع بِالذنُوبِ، الْعِصْمَة من عِنْد الله.

The description of a believer who belongs to Ahl al-Sunnah wa 'l-Jamāʿah is that they testify that there is no deity [worthy of worship] but Allah, alone and without partners, and that Muḥammad is His slave and messenger, and affirms all that the messengers and prophets taught. Further, their heart firmly believes in what their tongue proclaims and they have no doubts in their heart. They also do not excommunicate any people of monotheism due to a sin they committed, and defer matters of the unseen to Allah the

25 *Tārīkh Dimashq* (30/369).

Exalted. They also defer all of their matters to Allah the Exalted and do not believe that, due to their sins, their protection from Allah the Exalted ceases.

وَعلم أَن كل شَيْء بِقَضَاء الله وَقدره، الْخَيْر وَالشَّر جَمِيعًا، وَرَجا لمحسن أمة مُحَمَّد، وتخوف على مسيئتهم، وَلم ينزل أحدا من أمة مُحَمَّد الْجنَّة بِالْإِحْسَانِ، وَلَا النَّار بذنب اكْتَسبهُ حَتَّى يكون الله الَّذِي ينزل بخلقه كَيفَ يَشَاء.

Further, they know that everything is according to the predestination and destiny set by Allah the Exalted. That includes the good and the bad. They hope good for the people of the nation of Muḥammad, and are fearful for those that do evil actions. They do not declare any single individual from the nation of Muḥammad as being definitely a person of paradise simply due to their good actions, nor do they declare an individual a person of hellfire due to sins that they have committed, unless Allah, who judges His creation as He Wills, judges [that the person is a person of paradise or hellfire].

وَعرف حق السّلف الَّذين اخْتَارَهُمْ الله لصحبة نبيه، وَقدم أَبَا بكر وَعمر وَعُثْمَان، وَعرف حق عَليّ بن أبي طَالب، وَطَلْحَة، وَالزُّبَيْر، وَعبد الرَّحْمَن بن عَوْف، وَسعد بن أبي وَقاص، وَسَعِيد بن زيد بن عَمْرو بن نفَيْل على سَائِر الصَّحَابَة، فَإِن هَؤُلَاءِ التِّسْعَة الَّذين كَانُوا مَعَ النَّبِي صلى الله عَلَيْهِ وَسلم على جبل حراء، فَقَالَ النَّبِي صلى الله عَلَيْهِ وَسلم: **((اسكن حراء فَمَا عَلَيْك إِلَّا نَبِي أَو صديق أَو شَهِيد))** وَالنَّبِيّ صلى الله عَلَيْهِ وَسلم عاشرهم، وترحم على جَمِيع أَصْحَاب مُحَمَّد صَغِيرهمْ وَكَبِيرهمْ، وَحدث بفضائلهم، وَأمْسك عَمَّا شجر بَينهم.

Also, one must know the rights of the pious predecessors that Allah has chosen to accompany the Prophet ﷺ. They give precedence to Abu Bakr, ʿUmar, and ʿUthmān, and understand the rights of ʿAlī ibn Abī Ṭālib, Ṭalḥah, al-Zubayr, ʿAbd al-Raḥmān ibn ʿAwf, Ṣaʿd ibn Abī Waqqāṣ, and Saʿīd ibn Zayd ibn ʿAmr ibn Nufayl, giving them precedence over all other companions. Those nine individuals were with the Prophet ﷺ on Mount Ḥirā, and the Prophet ﷺ said, **'Be still, Ḥirā, for standing on you is none other than a prophet, an honest trustworthy person, or a martyr.'**[26] The Prophet ﷺ lived with them. Also, they ask Allah to have mercy on all of the companions of Muḥammad—both the young and the old, inform others

26 Reported by Muslim (2417).

of their virtues, and refrain from speaking about disputes that occurred between them.

وَصَلَاة الْعِيدَيْنِ والخسوف وَالْجُمُعَة وَالْجَمَاعَات مَعَ كل أَمِير بر أَو فَاجر، وَالْمسح على الْخُفَّيْنِ فِي السّفر والحضر، وَالْقصر فِي السفير.

The two Eid prayers, eclipse prayers, Jumuʿah, and congregational prayers should be performed with every leader, the righteous or sinful. Wiping on the leather socks whilst travelling or as a resident is also legislated, as is shortening the prayers during travels.

وَالْقُرْآن كَلَام الله وتنزيله وَلَيْسَ بمخلوق.

The Qur'ān is the speech of Allah the Exalted and His revelation. It is not created.

وَالْإِيمَان قَول وَعمل يزِيد وَينْقص. وَالْجِهَاد مَاض مُنْذُ بعث الله مُحَمَّدًا صلى الله عَلَيْهِ وَسلم إِلَى آخر عِصَابَة يُقَاتلُون الدَّجَّال لَا يضرهم جور جَائِر.

Faith is speech and action, and it increases and decreases. *Jihad* is continuous from the moment Allah the Exalted sent Muḥammad ﷺ until the last group of individuals who fight the Dajjāl, who are not harmed by the injustice of despots.

وَالشِّرَاء وَالْبيع حَلَال إِلَى يَوْم الْقِيَامَة على حكم الْكتاب وَالسّنة.

Buying and selling are lawful until the Day of Resurrection, according to the judgement passed in the Qur'ān and Sunnah.

وَالتَّكْبِير على الْجَنَائِز أَرْبعا

There are four *takbīrs* during funeral prayers.

وَالدُّعَاء لأئمة الْمُسلمين بالصلاح، وَلَا تخرج عَلَيْهِم بسيفك، وَلَا تقَاتل فِي فتْنَة، والزم بَيْتك.

One must supplicate for leaders of the Muslims, that they be righteous. Do not rebel against them with weapons, and do not fight in civil wars; stay in your home.

وَالْإِيمَان بِعَذَاب الْقَبْر، وَالْإِيمَان بمنكر وَنَكِير، وَالْإِيمَان بالحوض والشفاعة، وَالْإِيمَان بِأَن أهل الْجنَّة يرَوْنَ رَبهم تبَارك وَتَعَالَى. وَالْإِيمَان بِأَن الْمُوَحِّدين يخرجُون من النَّار بَعْدَمَا امتحشوا، كَمَا جَاءَت الْأَحَادِيث فِي هَذِه الْأَشْيَاء عَن النَّبِي صلى الله عَلَيْهِ وَسلم، نؤمن بتصديقها، وَلَا نضرب لَهَا الْأَمْثَال. هَذَا مَا اجْتمع عَلَيْهِ الْعلمَاء فِي جَمِيع الْآفَاق.

One must believe in the punishment of the grave, Munkir and Nakīr, the pool and the intercession, and that the people of paradise will see their Lord the Exalted. One must have faith in monotheists leaving hellfire after being burned in there, as the aḥadīth reported from the Prophet ﷺ have clarified. We believe by attesting to them, without giving similitudes to reject them. These are the beliefs that scholars of all regions have unanimously agreed upon."

انْتَهَت رِوَايَة الأندراني وتليها رِوَايَة عَبدُوس

That is the end of the quotation from the narration of al-Andarānī. Next is the narration of ʿAbdūs.

روى أَبُو يعلى فِي (الطَّبَقَات) والخلال والحافظ ابْن الْجَوْزِيّ فِي (المناقب) عَن عَبدُوس بن مَالك أَبُو مُحَمَّد الْعَطَّار قَالَ: سَمِعت أَبَا عبد الله أَحْمد بن مُحَمَّد بن حَنْبَل يَقُول:

Abu Yaʿlā in his *Ṭabaqāt*, al-Khallāl, and al-Ḥāfiẓ Ibn al-Jawzī in his *Manāqib* all reported that ʿAbdūs ibn Mālik Abu Muḥammad al-ʿAṭṭār said, "I heard Abu ʿAbdullāh Aḥmad ibn Muḥammad ibn Ḥanbal say:

أُصُول السّنة عندنَا التَّمَسُّك بِمَا كَانَ عَلَيْهِ أَصْحَاب رَسُول الله صلى الله عَلَيْهِ وَسلم والاقتداء بهم وَترك الْبدع - **((وكل بِدعَة فَهِيَ ضَلَالَة))** وَترك المراء والجدال والخصومات فِي الدّين.

The foundations of the Sunnah to us are: Holding fast to what the companions of Allah's Messenger ﷺ taught, following them, and avoiding innovations. '**Every innovation is misguidance.**' Also, avoiding disputation and argumentation about religion.

وَالسّنة عندنَا آثَار رَسُول الله صلى الله عَلَيْهِ وَسلم، وَالسّنة تفسر الْقُرْآن، وَهِي دَلَائِل الْقُرْآن، وَلَيْسَ فِي السّنة قِيَاس، وَلَا تضرب لَهَا الْأَمْثَال، وَلَا تدْرك بالعقول وَلَا الْأَهْوَاء، وَإِنَّمَا هُوَ الِاتِّبَاع وَترك الْهوى.

The Sunnah, to us, refers to the narrations from Allah's Messenger ﷺ. The Sunnah explains the Qur'ān and gives directions concerning it. There is no analogy in the Sunnah, and the Sunnah should not be rejected by giving similitudes. It is not achieved through intellect nor through following of desires. It is to follow and to abandon one's desires.

وَمن السّنة اللَّازِمَة الَّتِي من ترك مِنْهَا خصْلَة لم يقبلهَا ويؤمن بهَا، لم يكن من أَهلهَا.

From the important parts of the Sunnah, which, if someone forsakes just one aspect of them by not accepting or believing in them, it makes them not from the people of Sunnah:

الْإِيمَان بِالْقدرِ خَيره وشره، والتصديق بالأحاديث فِيهِ، وَالْإِيمَان بهَا، وَلَا يُقَال: لم وَلَا كَيفَ؟ إِنَّمَا هُوَ التَّصْدِيق وَالْإِيمَان بهَا، وَمن لم يعرف تَفْسِير الحَدِيث ويبلغه عقله، فقد كفي ذَلِك واحكم لَهُ، فَعَلَيهِ الْإِيمَان بِهِ، وَالتَّسْلِيم لَهُ، مثل حَدِيث الصَّادِق المصدوق، وَمثل مَا كَانَ مثله فِي الْقَضَاء وَالْقدر، وَمثل أَحَادِيث الرُّؤْيَة كلهَا، وَإِن نبت عَن الأسماع، واستوحش مِنْهَا المستمع، فَإِنَّمَا عَلَيْهِ الْإِيمَان بهَا.

Faith in predestination, both its good parts and bad parts. As well as attesting to and believing in aḥadīth relating to it. "Why," or "how" are questions that should not be asked. We are tasked with merely believing it. If someone hears the aḥadīth on the topic and their minds are finding difficulty understanding them, they are not obliged to continue to search, because it has been sufficiently explained already. Therefore, they must merely believe in and submit to it. An example is the ḥadīth of the truthful person who is also believed,[27] as well as other reports about predestination and destiny. Another example are all of the aḥadīth about seeing Allah the Exalted. Even if people who hear these narrations are averse to them and desert them, they still must believe in them.

وَأَن لَا يرد فِيهَا حرفا وَاحِدًا، وَغَيرهَا من الْأَحَادِيث المأثورات عَن الثِّقَات، وَأَن لَا يُخَاصم أحدا، وَلَا يناظره، وَلَا يتعَلَّم الْجِدَال، فَإِن الْكَلَام فِي الْقدر، والرؤية، وَالْقُرْآن، وَغَيرهَا من السّنَن، مَكْرُوه مَنْهِيّ عَنهُ، لَا يكون صَاحبه - وَإِن أصَاب بِكَلَامِهِ السّنة - من أهل السّنة حَتَّى يدع الْجِدَال وَيسلم ويؤمن بالآثار.

One must not reject a single letter, let alone more, of the aḥadīth that have been reported from trustworthy narrators. One must not be argumentative on matters of the religion nor debate anyone; one should not learn the art of rhetoric and debate. Debating about predestination, seeing Allah, the Qur'ān, and other parts of the Sunnah is disliked and forbidden. A person who engages in such things, even if their speech is in agreement with the Sunnah, is not of Ahl al-Sunnah until they avoid arguing and instead submit and believe in the narrations.

وَالْقُرْآن كَلَام الله، وَلَيْسَ بمخلوق، وَلَا يضعف أَن يَقُول الْقُرْآن لَيْسَ بمخلوق، فَإِن كَلَام الله لَيْسَ ببائن مِنْهُ، وَلَيْسَ مِنْهُ شَيْء مَخْلُوق. وَإِيَّاك ومناظرة من أحدث فِيهِ، وَمن قَالَ بِاللَّفْظِ وَغَيره، وَمن وقف فِيهِ، فَقَالَ: لَا أَدْرِي أمخلوق أَو لَيْسَ بمخلوق؟

27 Reported by al-Bukhārī (11/417) in the outset of the Chapter on Predestination, as well as Muslim (2643) in the Chapter of Predestination, from Ibn Mas'ūd, who said, "Allah's Messenger ﷺ the truthful one who is also believed, said, 'The creation of each one of you is brought together in their mother's womb for forty days in the form of a drop, then they become a clot of blood for a similar period, then a morsel of flesh for a similar period, then there is sent to him the angel who blows his soul into him and who is commanded with four matters: The angel is ordered to write their sustenance, lifespan, their actions, and if they will be happy or miserable. By the One who there is no deity worthy of worship but Him, one of you would do the actions of the people of paradise until there is merely a hand span between them and paradise, but what was predestined overtakes them, causing them to do actions of the people of hellfire, and they enter hellfire. Also, one of you would do the actions of the people of hellfire until they are merely a hand span away from hellfire, but what was predestined overtakes them, causing them to do actions of the people of paradise, and they enter paradise.'" Ibn Rajab has explained this ḥadīth beautifully in his book, *Jāmi' al-'Ulūm wa 'l-Ḥikam*.

وَإِنَّمَا هُوَ كَلَام الله، فَهَذَا صَاحب بِدعَة، مثل من قَال: هُوَ مَخْلُوق. وَإِنَّمَا هُوَ كَلَام الله وَلَيْسَ بمخلوق

The Qur'ān is the speech of Allah. It is not created. One should not be too weak to say, "The Qur'ān is uncreated." The speech of Allah is not distinct from Him, and none of Allah is created. Beware of debating people who innovate in these matters, those who claim that the pronunciation of the Qur'ān is created, and those who hesitate to take a position, instead saying, "I do not know if it is created or uncreated; it is just the speech of Allah." Such a person is a person of innovation, similar to those who say it is created. The Qur'ān, therefore, is the speech of Allah, uncreated.

وَالْإِيمَان بِالرُّؤْيَةِ يَوْم الْقِيَامَة كَمَا رُوِيَ عَن النَّبِي صلى الله عَلَيْهِ وَسلم من الْأَحَادِيث الصِّحَاح، وَأَن النَّبِي صلى الله عَلَيْهِ وَسلم قد رأى ربه، فَإِنَّهُ مأثور عَن رَسُول الله صلى الله عَلَيْهِ وَسلم صَحِيح، رَوَاهُ قَتَادَة، عَن عِكْرِمَة، عَن ابْن عَبَّاس. وَرَوَاهُ الْحَاكِم بن أبان، عَن عِكْرِمَة عَن ابْن عَبَّاس. وَرَوَاهُ عَليّ بن زيد، عَن يُوسُف بن مهْرَان، عَن ابْن عَبَّاس. والْحَدِيث عندنَا على ظَاهره، كَمَا جَاءَ عَن النَّبِي صلى الله عَلَيْهِ وَسلم، وَالْكَلَام فِيهِ بِدعَة، وَلَكِن نؤمن بِهِ على ظَاهره، وَلَا نناظر فِيهِ أحدا.

One must believe that believers will see Allah on the Day of Resurrection, as has been reported from the Prophet ﷺ in authentic narrations. Further, that the Prophet ﷺ saw his Lord, as has been reported in an authentic narration from Qatādah, who reported from 'Ikrimah, who heard it from Ibn 'Abbās. Al-Ḥakam ibn Abān reported from 'Ikrimah, who reported from Ibn 'Abbās. 'Alī ibn Zayd also reported it from Yūsuf ibn Mahrān, from Ibn 'Abbās. The ḥadīth, to us, should be understood as being apparent, as it was reported from the Prophet ﷺ. Speaking about such matters is an innovation. We believe the ḥadīth is apparent and do not debate anyone on the topic.

وَالْإِيمَان بالميزان يَوْم الْقِيَامَة كَمَا جَاءَ **((يُوزن العَبْد يَوْم الْقِيَامَة فَلَا يزن جنَاح بعوضة))** وتوزن أَعمال الْعباد كَمَا جَاءَ فِي الْأَثر، والتصديق بِهِ، والأعراض عَمَّن رد ذَلِك، وَترك مجادلته. وَإِن الله يكلم الْعباد يَوْم الْقِيَامَة لَيْسَ بَينه وَبينهمْ ترجمان

وَالْإِيمَان بِهِ والتصديق.

One must also believe in the scale on the Day of Resurrection. The Prophet ﷺ said, **"A slave will be weighed on the Day of Resurrection and will not even weigh the wing of a mosquito."**[28] The actions of the slaves will also be weighed, as the ḥadīth states. As such, we must attest to this fact and should turn a blind eye to those who reject it; they should not be engaged on such matters. And Allah the Exalted speaks to His slaves on the Day of Resurrection without an interpreter. One must believe in this and attest to it.

وَالْإِيمَان بالحوض وَأَن لرَسُول الله صلى الله عَلَيْهِ وَسلم حوضا يَوْم الْقِيَامَة، ترد عَلَيْهِ أمته، عرضه مثل طوله مسيرَة شهر، آنيته كعدد نُجُوم السَّمَاء على مَا صحت بِهِ الْأَخْبَار من غير وَجه.

Continuing, one must believe in the pool and that Allah's Messenger ﷺ has a pool on the Day of Resurrection, which his nation will drink from. It is as wide as the distance of a month's travel, and its cups are as numerous as the stars in the sky, as has been authentically reported through various chains of narration.

وَالْإِيمَان بِعَذَاب الْقَبْر، وَأَن هَذِه الْأمة تفتن فِي قبورها، وتسأل عَن الْإِيمَان، وَالْإِسْلَام، وَمن ربه، وَمن نبيه، ويأتيه مُنكر وَنَكِير كَيفَ شَاءَ الله وَكَيف أَرَادَ، وَالْإِيمَان بِهِ والتصديق بِهِ.

One must also believe in punishment of the grave, and that this nation is tested in their graves. They will be asked about faith and Islam; they will be asked who their lord is, and who their prophet is. Munkir and Nakīr will appear as Allah wills and however Allah wishes. We must believe in this concept and attest to it.

وَالْإِيمَان بشفاعة النَّبِي صلى الله عَلَيْهِ وَسلم، وبقوم يخرجُون من النَّار بعد مَا احترقوا وصاروا فحما، فَيُؤْمَر بهم إِلَى نهر على بَاب الْجنَّة كَمَا جَاءَ الْأَثر، كَيفَ شَاء وكما يشَاء، إِنَّمَا هُوَ الْإِيمَان بِهِ والتصديق بِهِ.

Further, one must believe in the intercession of the Prophet ﷺ and in the

28 Reported by al-Bukhārī (4729) and Muslim (2785).

fact that some people will leave hellfire after being burnt to coal. It will be commanded that they be taken to a river at the door of paradise, as the ḥadīth states. This will occur however Allah wills and in whatever fashion He decides. Our obligation is to believe in it and attest to it.

وَالْإِيمَان بِأَن الْمَسِيح الدَّجَّال خَارج، مَكْتُوب بَين عَيْنَيْهِ: كَافِر. وَالْأَحَادِيث الَّتِي جَاءَت فِيهِ، وَالْإِيمَان بِأَن ذَلِك كَائِن، وَأَن عِيسَى ابْن مَرْيَم عَلَيْهِ السَّلَام ينزل فيقتله بِبَاب لد.

We also believe that al-Masīḥ al-Dajjāl (the False Messiah) will emerge. Between his eyes will be written "*kāfir* (disbeliever)." We believe in the aḥadīth reported about the topic, and believe that it will occur. We also believe that ʿĪsā the son of Maryam ﷺ will descend and kill him at the Door of Ludd.

وَالْإِيمَان قَول وَعمل، يزِيد وَينْقص، كَمَا جَاءَ فِي الْخَبَر: **((أكمل الْمُؤمنِينَ إِيمَانًا أَحْسنهم خلقا))** وَمن ترك الصَّلَاة، فقد كفر وَلَيْسَ من الْأَعْمَال شَيْء تَركه كفر إِلَّا الصَّلَاة، من تَركهَا فَهُوَ كَافِر، وَقد أحل الله قَتله. والنفاق: هُوَ الْكفْر أَن يكفر بِاللَّه ويعبد غَيره، وَيظْهر الْإِسْلَام فِي الْعَلَانِيَة، مثل الْمُنَافِقين الَّذين كَانُوا على عهد رَسُول الله صلى الله عَلَيْهِ وَسلم **((ثَلَاث من كن فِيهِ فَهُوَ مُنَافِق))** على التَّغْلِيظ يروونها كَمَا جَاءَت وَلَا نفسرها. وَقَوله: **((لَا ترجعوا بعدِي كفَّارًا ضلالا يضْرب بَعْضكُم رِقَاب بعض))**. وَمثل: **((إِذا التقى المسلمان بسيفهما فالقاتل والمقتول فِي النَّار))** وَمثل: **((سباب الْمُؤمن فسوق، وقتاله كفر))** وَمثل: **((من قَالَ لِأَخِيهِ: يَا كَافِر فقد بَاء بهَا أَحدهمَا))** وَمثل: **((كفر بِاللَّه تَعَالَى من تبرأ من نسب وَإِن دق))** وَنَحْو هَذِه الْأَحَادِيث مِمَّا قد صَحَّ وَحفظ، وَإِنَّا نسلم لَهُ وَإِن لم نعلم تَفْسِيرهَا، وَلَا نتكلم فِيهِ، وَلَا نجادل فِيهِ، وَلَا نفسر هَذِه الْأَحَادِيث إِلَّا بِمثل مَا جَاءَت، لَا نردها إِلَّا بِأَحَق مِنْهَا.

Faith comprises of statements and actions. It increases and decreases. The ḥadīth states, **"The believers with the most complete faith are those**

who have the best manners."[29] If someone abandons prayer, they have disbelieved. There is only one action that its abandonment causes one to disbelieve, and that action is prayer. Those who abandon prayer are disbelievers, and Allah has allowed for them to receive capital punishment. Hypocrisy is disbelief; it means to disbelieve in Allah and worship something other than Allah, but to publicly act as though one is Muslim, similar to the hypocrites during the time of Allah's Messenger ﷺ. When the Prophet ﷺ said, **"There are three qualities, if a person has them, they are a hypocrite,"**[30] it is meant to show the graveness of the action. The scholars, however, report it as is, without explaining it. The Prophet ﷺ also said, **"Do not go back, after me, to becoming disbelievers and misguided, where you strike the necks of one another."**[31] Also, he said, **'When two Muslims meet to fight one another with swords, the killer and the killed are both in hellfire."**[32] Also, the Prophet ﷺ said, **"Cursing a Muslim is sinfulness, and fighting them is disbelief."**[33] Also, he said, **"Whoever says to their brother [in faith], 'You disbeliever!' Then it will fall on one of them."**[34] Also he said, **"He has disbelieved in Allah, the one who absolves himself of his lineage, even in the most minute way."**[35] These, and other similar aḥadīth that have been authentically reported and preserved [are approached in the same way]: We submit to them even if we are unaware of their explanations. We do not speak about nor debate their interpretations. We do not interpret these aḥadīth with anything but other textual sources, and we do not reject any ḥadīth unless there is one that is more authentic.

وَالرَّجم حق على من زنى وَقد أحصن، إِذا اعْترف أَو قَامَت عَلَيْهِ الْبَيِّنَة، قد رجم رَسُول الله صلى الله عَلَيْهِ وَسلم ورجمت الْخُلَفَاء الراشدون.

Stoning is truth, and the person who deserves the punishment is a person who commits adultery after having been married, and then later admits to it or it is proven against them. The Prophet ﷺ stoned adulterers and so did the Rightly-Guided Caliphs.

---

29 Reported by Aḥmad (2/250) and Abu Dāwūd (4682).
30 Reported by Muslim (59).
31 Reported by al-Bukhārī.
32 Reported by al-Bukhārī (1/81), and Muslim (2888).
33 Reported by al-Bukhārī (10/387).
34 Reported by al-Bukhārī (10/428).
35 Reported by Abu Bakr al-Marwazī in *al-Musnad*.

قَالَ: وَلَا نشْهد على أحد من أهل الْقبْلَة بِعَمَل يعمله بجنة وَلَا نَار، نرجو للصالح، ونخاف على الْمُسِيء المذنب، وَنَرْجُو لَهُ رَحْمَة الله. وَمن لَقِي الله بذنب تجب لَهُ بِهِ النَّار تَائِبًا غير مصر عَلَيْهِ فَإِن الله يَتُوب عَلَيْهِ **﴿وهو الذي يَقْبَلُ التَّوبَةَ عَنْ عِبَادِهِ وَيَعْفُو عَنِ السَّيِّئَاتِ﴾** [الشورى: ٢٥] وَمن لقِيه، وَقد أقيم عَلَيْهِ حد ذَلِك فِي الدُّنْيَا من الذُّنُوب الَّتِي قد اسْتوْجبَ بهَا الْعقُوبَة، فَأمره إِلَى الله، إِن شَاءَ عذبه، وَإِن شَاءَ غفر لَهُ.

We do not testify that any member of Ahl al-Qiblah[36] will enter paradise or hellfire on account of a deed they do. We hope for the righteous and fear for the sinful evildoers, but we still hope that Allah shows them mercy. Anyone who meets Allah with a sin that should otherwise make fire incumbent for him, but the person has repented to Allah and is not persisting on that sin, Allah will forgive him. He states: **{It is He who accepts repentance from His servants and pardons bad deeds.}** [Qur'ān 42:25] Also, if someone meets Allah having received a penalty in this life for a sin they committed that requires a penalty, their matter is to Allah: if He so wishes, He will punish them, but if He so wishes, He will forgive them.

قَالَ: وَمن الْإِيمَان الِاعْتِقَاد بِأَن الْجنَّة وَالنَّار مخلوقتان، قد خلقتا كَمَا جَاءَ عَن رَسُول الله صلى الله عَلَيْهِ وَسلم: **((دخلت الْجنَّة فَرَأَيْت قصرا، وَرَأَيْت فِيهَا الْكَوْثَر، واطلعت فِي الْجنَّة فَرَأَيْت أَكثر أَهلهَا كَذَا، وأطلعت فِي النَّار فَرَأَيْت أَكثر أَهلهَا كَذَا وَكَذَا))** فَمن زعم أَنَّهُمَا لم يخلقا، فَهُوَ مكذب بِالْقُرْآنِ وَأَحَادِيث رَسُول الله، وَلَا أَحْسبهُ يُؤمن بِالْجنَّةِ وَالنَّار.

A part of faith is to believe that paradise and hellfire are both created, as it was reported from the Messenger of Allah ﷺ, **"I entered paradise and saw a palace, and I found the *Kawthar* in there."**[37] He also said that he entered paradise and saw its people and that he saw the people of hellfire.[38] Anyone who claims it is not yet created has belied the Qur'ān and the aḥadīth of Allah's Messenger ﷺ and I do not think it is likely that they believe in paradise or the hellfire.

---

36 [T] This literally means "people of the direction of prayer," and means a Muslim.
37 Reported by al-Bukhārī (11/412).
38 Reported by al-Bukhārī (12/366) and Muslim (2737).

وَمن مَاتَ من أهل الْقبْلَة موحدا، نصلي عَلَيْهِ، ونستغفر لَهُ، وَلَا يحجب عَنهُ الاسْتِغْفَار، وَلَا نَترُك الصَّلَاة عَلَيْهِ لذنب أذنبه، صَغِيرا كَانَ أَو كَبِيرا، ونفوض أمره إِلَى الله عز وَجل.

We pray the funeral prayer on any person of Ahl al-Qiblah that passes away as a monotheist. We also ask Allah to forgive them. Seeking forgiveness for them is not prohibited. We do not refrain from praying on them due to a sin they committed, regardless if it was a major or lesser sin. We entrust their matters to Allah the Exalted.

وقتال اللُّصُوص والخوارج جَائِز، إِذا عرضوا للرجل فِي نَفسه وَمَاله، فَلهُ أَن يُقَاتل عَن نَفسه وَمَاله، وَيدْفَع عَنهُمَا بِكُل مَا يقدر، وَلَيْسَ لَهُ إِذا فارقوه أَو تَركُوهُ أَن يطلبهم، وَلَا يتتبع آثَارهم، لَيْسَ لأحد إِلَّا للْإِمَام أَو وُلَاة الْمُسلمين، إِنَّمَا لَهُ أَن يدْفع عَن نَفسه فِي مقَامه، وَيَنْوِي بِجهْدِهِ أَن لَا يقتل أحدا، فَإِن أَتَى على بدنه فِي دَفعه عَن نَفسه فِي المعركة، فأبعد الله الْمَقْتُول، وَإِن قتل هَذَا فِي تِلْكَ الْحَال وَهُوَ يدْفع عَن نَفسه وَمَاله رَجَوْت لَهُ الشَّهَادَة، كَمَا جَاءَ فِي الْأَحَادِيث، وَجَمِيع الْآثَار فِي هَذَا إِنَّمَا أَمر بقتاله، وَلم يُؤمر بقتْله، وَلَا اتِّبَاعه، وَلَا يُجهز عَلَيْهِ إِن صرع، وَإِن كَانَ طريحا، وَإِن أَخذه أَسِيرًا، فَلَيْسَ لَهُ أَن يقْتله، وَلَا أَن يُقيم عَلَيْهِ الْحَد، وَلَكِن يرفع أمره إِلَى من ولاه الله، فَيحكم فِيهِ.

Fighting highway robbers and the Kharijites is permissible if they attack a person's self or wealth. One can fight to defend themselves and their wealth to the best of their abilities. However, if they leave one alone, they cannot be sought or followed. That right belongs only to the supreme leader or leaders of the Muslims. One may only defend themselves in the moment they are attached, and should try their best to not kill anyone. If they kill the [robber or Kharijite] while defending themselves, may Allah cause the one killed to be distant from His mercy. If they are killed, however, in that situation when they are defending themselves and their wealth, I hope that they have earned martyrdom, as in the aḥadīth. All narrations on this topic command one to fight back, not to kill or follow them. One should not kill the person if they overcome them or if they lie on the ground after the fight. If they take [the robber or Kharijite] as a captive, they may not kill them or establish any [state ordained] penalty against them. They should press charges in the presence of those whom Allah has made in charge, and that person should judge in the matter.

والسمع وَالطَّاعَة للأئمة، وأمير الْمُؤمنِينَ: الْبر والفاجر، وَمن ولي الْخلَافَة: من اجْتمع النَّاس عَلَيْهِ ورضوه، وَمن غلبهم بِالسَّيْفِ حَتَّى صَار خَليفَة، وَيُسمى أَمِير الْمُؤمنِينَ.

One must hear and obey the rulers and the Commander of the Faithful, no matter if the leaders are righteous or evil. Also included are those who are chosen for the caliphate by popular vote or who took the caliphate with the sword and made themselves the caliph. [Both] should still be given the title, 'The Commander of the Faithful.'

والغزو مَاض مَعَ الْأُمَرَاء إِلَى يَوْم الْقِيَامَة الْبر والفاجر، لَا يتْرك وَقِسْمَة الْفَيْء وَإِقَامَة الْحُدُود إِلَى الْأَئِمَّة مَاض، لَيْسَ لأحد أَن يطعن عَلَيْهِم، وَلَا ينازعهم، وَدفع الصَّدقَات إِلَيْهِم جَائِزَة نَافِذَة، من دَفعهَا إِلَيْهِم أَجْزَأت عَنهُ برا كَانَ أَو فَاجِرًا.

War is ordained with the commanders until the Day of Resurrection, regardless if the commander is righteous or sinful; it is not to be abandoned. The division of war spoils and establishment of [Allah's ordained] penalties are continuous responsibilities of the leaders. None can attack them or dispute with them. Paying charity to them [to disperse] is permissible and valid. If someone pays their charity to them, it is valid, irrespective of whether the leader was righteous or a sinner.

وَصَلَاة الْجُمُعَة خَلفه وَخلف من ولي جَائِزَة إِمَامَته رَكْعَتَيْنِ، من أعادهما فَهُوَ مُبْتَدع، تَارِك للآثار، مُخَالف للسّنة، لَيْسَ لَهُ من فضل الْجُمُعَة شَيْء إِذا لم ير الصَّلَاة خلف الْأَئِمَّة كائنين من كَانُوا: برهم وفاجرهم، فَالسنة أَن تصلي مَعَهم رَكْعَتَيْنِ، وَتَدين بِأَنَّهَا تَامَّة، لَا يكن فِي صدرك شكّ.

Friday prayers behind them and any other leader are also permissible, he leads two units. Whoever repeats them [after having prayed with the leader] is an innovator who has abandoned the narrations and contradicted the Sunnah; they earn nothing of the virtues of Friday if they do not believe in praying behind the leaders, irrespective of whom they may be and irrespective of whether they are righteous or sinful. The Sunnah is to pray two units with them and to believe that they are valid and complete, without any doubts in one's chest.

وَمن خرج على إِمَام من أَئِمَّة الْمُسلمين، وَقد كَانُوا اجْتَمعُوا عَلَيْهِ، وأقروا لَهُ بالخلافة بِأَيّ وَجه كَانَ، بِالرِّضَى أَو بالغلبة، فقد شقّ هَذَا الْخَارِج عَصا الْمُسلمين، وَخَالف الْآثَار عَن رَسُول الله، فَإِن مَاتَ الْخَارِج عَلَيْهِ، مَاتَ ميتَة جَاهِلِيَّة. وَلَا يحل قتال السُّلْطَان، وَلَا الْخُرُوج عَلَيْهِ لأحد من النَّاس، فَمن فعل ذَلِك، فَهُوَ مُبْتَدع على غير السّنة وَالطَّرِيق. انْتَهَت رِوَايَة عَبدُوس وَإِلَيْك غيرهَا.

Whoever rebels against a leader of the Muslims while the Muslims were previously united under them and agreed that they are rightful caliphs—irrespective of how they came into power and whether they had people's approval or if they simply dominated and overcame them—the rebel has disunited the Muslims and has contradicted the narrations from the Prophet. If the rebel dies upon it, he dies a death of pre-Islamic ignorance. It is not permissible for anyone to fight against the sultan or to rebel against him. Whoever does that is an innovator who is not following the Sunnah or the [correct] path." This is the conclusion of the report of ʿAbdus. Still to be mentioned is another narration.

أخرج أَبُو يعلى فِي (الطَّبَقَات) والحافظ ابْن الْجَوْزِيّ فِي (المناقب)، وَذكر الْبُرْهَان ابْن مُفْلِح فِي (الطَّبَقَات) عَن الْحسن بن إِسْمَاعِيل الربعِي أنه قَالَ:

Abu Yaʿlā in his *Ṭabaqāt*, al-Ḥāfiẓ Ibn al-Jawzī in his *Manāqib*, and al-Burhān ibn Mufliḥ in his *Ṭabaqāt* reported that al-Ḥasan ibn Ismāʿīl al-Rabʿī said:

قَالَ لي أَحْمد بن حَنْبَل إِمَام أهل السّنة، والصابر لله عز وَجل تَحت المحنة:

Aḥmad ibn Ḥanbal, the *imām* of Ahl al-Sunnah, and the patient one for the sake of Allah in the wake of his trial, said:

اجْمَعْ تسعون رجلا من التَّابِعين، وأئمة الْمُسلمين، وأئمة السّلف، وفقهاء الْأَمْصَار على أَن السّنة الَّتِي توفّي عَلَيْهَا رَسُول الله صلى الله عَلَيْهِ وَسلم، أَولهَا الرضى

بِقضَاء الله تَعَالَى، وَالتَّسْلِيم لأَمره، وَالصَّبْر تحت حكمه، وَالْأَخْذ بِمَا أَمر الله بِهِ، وَالنَّهْي عَمَّا نهى الله عَنهُ، وإخلاص الْعَمَل لله.

Ninety men of the successors of the companions, the *imāms* of the Muslims, the *imāms* of the pious predecessors, and the legists of the various lands, have all agreed that the Sunnah which Allah's Messenger ﷺ died having taught comprises of, firstly, contentment with the predestination of Allah the Exalted, submitting to His commands, patience under His judgements, doing what He has commanded to do, avoiding what He has forbidden from doing, and sincerity in action to Allah.

وَالْإِيمَان بِالْقدرِ: خَيره وشره، وَترك المراء والجدال والخصومات فِي الدّين وَالْمسح على الْخُفَّيْنِ، وَالْجهَاد مَعَ كل خَليفَة: بر وَفَاجِر، وَالصَّلَاة على من تَابَ من أهل الْقبْلَة.

Also, faith in predestination, both its good parts and bad parts, avoiding argumentation and disputing about the religion, wiping on the leather socks, *jihād* with every caliph, regardless whether they are righteous or evil, and offering the funeral prayers for members of Ahl al-Qiblah who repent.

وَالْإِيمَان قَول وَعمل، يزِيد الطَّاعَة، وَينْقص بالمعصية، وَالْقُرْآن كَلَام الله، منزل على قلب نبيه صلى الله عَلَيْهِ وَسلم، غير مَخْلُوق من حَيْثُ تلى.

Faith is speech and action; it increases with obedience and decreases with disobedience. The Qur'ān is the speech of Allah the Exalted which was sent to the heart of His Prophet ﷺ. It is not created, even when recited.

وَالصَّبْر تَحت لِوَاء السلطان على ما كان منه من عدل أو جور، ولا نخرج على الأمراء بِالسَّيْفِ، وَإِن جاروا، وَلَا نكفر أحدا من أهل التَّوْحِيد وَإِن عمِلُوا بالكبائر، والكف عَمَّا شجر بَين أَصْحَاب رَسُول الله صلى الله عَلَيْهِ وَسلم.

Also, patience under the flag of the sultan, irrespective of their justice or injustice. We do not rebel against leaders with the sword, even if they are unjust. We do not excommunicate any person of monotheism, even if they commit major sins. We avoid speaking about the disputes that occurred between the companions of the Prophet ﷺ.

وَأفضل النَّاس بعد رَسُول الله أَبُو بكر، وَعمر، وَعُثْمَان، وَعلي ابْن عَم رَسُول الله، والترحم على جَمِيع أَصْحَاب النَّبِي صلى الله عَلَيْهِ وَسلم، وأزواجه، وَأَوْلَاده، وأصهاره رضوَان الله عَلَيْهِم أَجْمَعِينَ.

The best people after Allah's Messenger ﷺ are Abu Bakr, 'Umar, 'Uthmān, and 'Alī, the cousin of Allah's Messenger. We ask Allah to have mercy on all the companions of the Prophet ﷺ, as well as his wives, children, and in-laws. May Allah be pleased with them all.

فَهَذِهِ هِيَ السّنة الزموها تسلموا، أَخذهَا بركَة، وَتركهَا ضَلَالَة.

This is the Sunnah. Hold fast to it, and you will be safe. Adhering to it is a blessing, and abandoning it is misguidance.

رَوْضَة فِي كَلِمَات للْإِمَام فِي مسَائِل من أصُول الدّين

A Garden of al-Imām Aḥmad's Speech About Issues Pertaining to Principles of the Religion

روى عَنهُ أَبُو دَاوُد صَاحب السّنَن أَنه قَالَ: الْإِيمَان: قَول وَعمل، وَيزِيد وَينْقص، الْبر كُله من الْإِيمَان، والمعاصي تنقص الْإِيمَان.

Abu Dāwūd, the author of the *Sunan*, reported that he said, "Faith is speech and action. It increases and decreases. All actions of righteousness are from faith, and sins decrease faith."

وروى الْحَافِظ ابْن الْجَوْزِيّ، عَن صَالح بن الإِمَام أَحْمد قَالَ:

Al-Ḥāfiẓ Ibn al-Jawzī reported that Ṣāliḥ, the son of al-Imām Aḥmad said:

تناهى إِلَيّ أَن أَبَا طَالب يَحْكِي عَن أبي أَنه يَقُول: لَفْظِي بالقرآن غير مَخْلُوق فَأَخْبَرت أبي بذلك، فَقَالَ: من أخْبرك؟ فَقلت: فلَان، فَقَالَ: ابْعَثْ إِلَى أبي طَالب، فوجهت إِلَيْهِ، فجَاء، وَجَاء بوران، فَقَالَ لَهُ: إِنِّي أنا قلت لَك: لَفْظِي بِالْقُرْآنِ غير مَخْلُوق؟ وَغَضب وَجعل يرعد.

It reached me that Abu Ṭālib narrated from my father that he would say, "My utterance of the Qur'ān is uncreated." I told that to my father, and he said, "Who told you that?" I replied, "So-and-so." He said, "Send for Abu Ṭālib," which I did, and he came, along with Būrān. [My father] said to [Abu Ṭālib], "Have I told you that my utterance of the Qur'ān is uncreated?" And he became extremely angry and was making [Abu Ṭālib] tremble.

فَقَالَ: قَرَأت (قل هُوَ الله أحد) فَقلت: هَذَا لَيْسَ بمخلوق، فَقَالَ لَهُ: لم حكيت عني أَنِّي قلت لَك: لَفْظِي بِالْقُرْآنِ غير مَخْلُوق؟! وَبَلغنِي أَنَّك وضعت ذَلِك فِي كتاب، وكتبت بِهِ إِلَى قوم، فَإِن كَانَ فِي كتابك، فامحه أَشد المحو، واكتب إِلَى

الْقَوْم الَّذين كتبت إِلَيْهِم: إِنَّنِي لم أقل ذَلِك. فَجعل بوران يعْتَذر لَهُ، وَانْصَرف أَبُو طَالب، فَذكر أَنه قد كَانَ حك ذَلِك من كِتَابه، وَأَنه قد كتب إِلَى الْقَوْم يُخْبِرهُمْ أَنه وهم على أبي فِي الْحِكَايَة هَذَا.

He then said, "I read, **{Say, "He is Allah the One."}** [Qur'ān 112:1] and I said, 'This is not created.' Why did you say that I said, 'My utterance of the Qur'ān is uncreated? I have been told that you wrote that in a book and wrote it to others in letters. If it is in your book, erase it at once and completely, and write to those you previously wrote to and tell them that I said no such thing." Būrān began apologising to him, and Abu Ṭālib left. It was mentioned later that he erased that sentence from his book and that he wrote to the people he had previously informed, telling them that he erroneously attributed the statement to my father.

قلت: وَلَقَد وهم أَبُو طَالب حَقًا، فَإِن قَول الإِمَام: هَذَا لَيْسَ بمخلوق، أَشَارَ بِهِ إِلَى المقروء، وَأَبُو طَالب فهم أَنه أَشَارَ بِهِ إِلَى أَلْفَاظ القارىء، وَهَذَا أَشد الْغَلَط، وحاشا أَن يَجْعَل لَفظه بِالْقُرْآنِ غير مَخْلُوق فليفهم.

I say: Truly, Abu Ṭālib erred. When the *imām* said, "This is not created," he was referring to what is being read. However, Abu Ṭālib inferred that he was referencing the utterances of the reciter. This is a major mistake. Far be it from al-Imām Aḥmad ﷺ to state that his utterance of the Qur'ān is uncreated. Therefore, pay keen attention to understand this issue.

وَكَانَ يَقُول فِي أَحَادِيث الصِّفَات: نرويها كَمَا جَاءَت. وَكَانَ يَقُول: عُلَمَاء الْمُعْتَزلَة زنادقة. وَقَالَ لِابْنِهِ عبد الله: لَا تصل خلف من قَالَ: الْقُرْآن مَخْلُوق، فَإِن صلى رجل خَلفه، أَعَاد الصَّلَاة. وَقَالَ للميموني: يَا أَبَا الْحسن! إِذا رَأَيْت رجلا يذكر أحدا من أَصْحَاب رَسُول الله صلى الله عَلَيْهِ وَسلم بِسوء فاتهمه على الْإِسْلَام. وَقَالَ: لما مرض رَسُول الله صلى الله عَلَيْهِ وَسلم قدم أَبَا بكر ليُصَلِّي بِالنَّاسِ، وَقد كَانَ فِي الْقَوْم من هُوَ أَقرَأ مِنْهُ، وَإِنَّمَا أَرَادَ الْخلَافَة.

The position of Aḥmad regarding the aḥadīth of the attributes was that he would say, "We report them as they came." He would also say, "The scholars of the Muʿtazilites are heretics." He once said to his son, ʿAbdullāh, "Do not pray behind those who claim the Qur'ān is created. If one were to pray behind someone with such a view, he should repeat his prayer." He also said to al-Maymūnī, "Abu 'l-Ḥasan, if you see someone disparaging the companions of Allah's Messenger ﷺ, accuse his Islam." He also said, "When Allah's Messenger ﷺ became ill, he commanded Abu Bakr to lead the people in prayer, although there were others present who had memorised more of the Qur'ān than he did. He intended [to appoint Abu Bakr to] the caliphate."

وَأخرج ابْن الْجَوْزِيّ فِي (المناقب) وَأَبُو يعلى فِي (طبقاته) عَن عَبدُوس بن مَالك الْعَطَّار قَالَ: سَمِعت أَبَا عبد الله أَحْمد بن مُحَمَّد بن حَنْبَل يَقُول:

Further, Ibn al-Jawzī reported in his book *al-Manāqib*, and Abu Ya'lā reported in his book *al-Ṭabaqāt*, that 'Abdus ibn Mālik al-'Aṭṭār said: I heard Abu 'Abdullāh Aḥmad ibn Muḥammad ibn Ḥanbal say:

خير هَذِه الْأمة بعد نبيها أَبُو بكر الصّديق، ثمَّ عمر بن الْخطاب، ثمَّ عُثْمَان بن عفَّان، نقدم هَؤُلَاءِ الثَّلَاثَة كَمَا قدمهم أَصْحَاب رَسُول الله صلى الله عَلَيْهِ وَسلم، لم يَخْتَلِفُوا فِي ذَلِك، ثمَّ من بعد هَؤُلَاءِ الثَّلَاثَة أَصْحَاب الشورى الْخَمْسَة: عَليّ، وَالزُّبَيْر، وَطَلْحَة، وَعبد الرَّحْمَن بن عَوْف، وَسعد وَكلهمْ يصلح للخلافة، وَكلهمْ إِمَام.

The best of this nation after its prophet is Abu Bakr al-Ṣiddīq, then 'Umar ibn al-Khaṭṭāb, then 'Uthmān ibn 'Affān. We give precedence to those three as the companions of Allah's Messenger ﷺ did. They did not differ among those three. After them are the five individuals who were men of council and consultation, and they are, 'Alī, al-Zubayr, Ṭalḥah, 'Abd al-Raḥmān ibn 'Awf, and Ṣa'd. All of them were fit to be caliphs, and they were all *imāms*.

نذْهب فِي ذَلِك إِلَى حَدِيث ابْن عمر (كُنَّا نعد وَرَسُول الله حَيّ، وَأَصْحَابه متوافرون: أَبُو بكر، ثمَّ عمر، ثمَّ عُثْمَان، ونسكت.

To prove this, we cite the ḥadīth of Ibn 'Umar, "We would consider, when the Prophet ﷺ was alive and his companions were in abundance: Abu Bakr, 'Umar, and 'Uthmān, then we would remain silent.'[39]

---

39 Reported by Aḥmad (2/14) and al-Bukhārī (7/14).

ثمَّ نعد أَصْحَاب الشورى، أهل بدر من الْمُهَاجِرين، وَأهل بدر من الْأَنْصَار من أَصْحَاب رَسُول الله على قدر الْهِجْرَة والسابقة أَولا فأولا.

Then, we consider the people of sound council, the veterans of Badr who migrated [to Madīnah], and the veterans of Badr who were residents of Madīnah (Anṣār), among the companions of Allah's Messenger ﷺ, and would favour them based on migration and how early they entered into Islam.

ثمَّ أفضل النَّاس بعد هَؤُلَاءِ أَصْحَاب رَسُول الله صلى الله عَلَيْهِ وَسلم، الْقرن الَّذِي بعث فيهم كل من صَحبه سنة، أَو شهرا، أَو يَوْمًا، أَو سَاعَة، أَو رَآهُ، فَهُوَ من أَصْحَابه، لهُ من الصُّحْبَة على قدر مَا صَحبه، وَكَانَت سابقته مَعَه، وَسمع مِنْهُ، وَنظر إِلَيْهِ نظرة.

After those individuals, the best people are the companions of Allah's Messenger ﷺ, and this is inclusive to everyone who lived during the generation that the Prophet ﷺ was sent in. Anyone who accompanied the Prophet ﷺ be it for a year, a month, a day, an hour, or merely momentarily saw him, is a companion inasmuch as they accompanied him, had an earlier relationship with him, heard from him, or even looked at him once.

فأدناهم صُحْبَة هُوَ أفضل من الْقرن الَّذين لم يروه، وَلَو لقوا الله بِجَمِيعِ الْأَعْمَال، كَانَ هَؤُلَاءِ الَّذين صحبوا النَّبِي صلى الله عَلَيْهِ وَسلم، ورأوه، وسمعوا مِنْهُ، وَرَآهُ بِعَيْنِه، وآمن بِهِ، وَلَو سَاعَة، أفضل لصحبتهم من التَّابِعين، وَلَو عمِلُوا كل أَعمال الْخَيْر.

The lowest level of companions is still better than the generation that did not see the Prophet ﷺ, even if [the latter] met Allah having done all righteous deeds. Those that accompanied the Prophet ﷺ and saw him, heard from him, looked at him with their own eyes, and believed in him, even if [they accompanied him] for a mere hour, are greater than the Tābiʿīn simply due to their companionship. This is even if they (the Tābiʿīn) did all good actions.

وَمن انْتقصَ أحدا من أَصْحَاب رَسُول الله، وأبغضه لحَدث كَانَ مِنْهُ، أَو ذكر

مساويه، كَانَ مبتدعا حَتَّى يترحم عَلَيْهِم جَمِيعًا، وَيكون قلبه سليما.

Anyone who criticises a companion of Allah's Messenger, hates him due to something he did, or mentions his faults is an innovator, until he asks Allah to have mercy on them all, and finds no ill-will in his heart against them.

تَنْبِيه: أدرج أَبُو يعلى هَذِه الرِّوَايَة فِي رِوَايَة عَبدُوس السَّابِقَة، وأفردها ابْن الْجَوْزِيّ، وَنحن تبِعْنَاهُ فِي إفرادها.

Note that Abu Ya'lā included this report with the previously mentioned report of 'Abdus, but Ibn al-Jawzī mentioned it on its own. I followed Ibn al-Jawzī in that I consider it a narration on its own.

وَكَانَ يَقُول: قدمُوا عُثْمَان على عَليّ، وَقَالَ: من قدم عليا على أبي بكر أزرى بأصحاب الشورى. وَقَالَ أَيْضا: من فضل عليا على أبي بكر، فقد طعن على رَسُول الله، وَمن قدم عليا على عمر، فقد طعن على رَسُول الله، وعَلى أبي بكر، وَمن قدم عليا على عُثْمَان فقد طعن على رَسُول الله، وَأبي بكر، وَعمر، وعَلى الْمُهَاجِرين، وَلَا أَحسب يصلح لَهُ عمل.

Al-Imām Aḥmad used to also say, "Prefer 'Uthmān over 'Alī." He also said, "Whoever considers 'Alī to be preferred over Abu Bakr has disparaged the people of council." He also said, "Whoever considers 'Alī to be preferred over Abu Bakr has disparaged Allah's Messenger. Whoever considers 'Alī to be preferred over 'Umar has disparaged Allah's Messenger. Whoever considers 'Alī to be preferred over 'Uthmān has disparaged Allah's Messenger, Abu Bakr, 'Umar, and all of the migrants. I do not think their actions will be valid."

روى ابْن الْجَوْزِيّ ذَلِك عَن مُحَمَّد بن عَوْف، عَن أَحْمد.

This was reported by Ibn al-Jawzī from Muḥammad ibn 'Awf, who reported from Aḥmad.

وروى أَيْضا عَن عبد الله بن الإِمَام أَحْمد قَالَ:

He also reported from 'Abdullāh, the son of al-Imām Aḥmad, who said:

كنت بَين يَدي أبي جَالِسا ذَات يَوْم فَجَاءَت طَائِفَة من الكرخية، فَذكرُوا خلَافَة أبي بكر، وَخِلَافَة عمر، وَخِلَافَة عُثْمَان، فَأَكْثرُوا، وَذكروا خلَافَة عَليّ بن أبي طَالب، فزادوا، وأطالوا، فَرفع أبي رَأسه إِلَيْهِم فَقَالَ: يَا هَؤُلَاءِ، قد أَكثرْتُم القَوْل فِي عَليّ والخلافة، إِن الْخلَافَة لَا تزين عليا، بل عَليّ يزينها.

I was with my father when a group came from Karkh and mentioned the caliphate of Abu Bakr, then that of ʿUmar, then that of ʿUthmān, and said many things. Then, they mentioned the caliphate of ʿAlī ibn Abī Ṭālib and said many things, speaking for a very long time. My father raised his head to them and said, "People, you have spoken a lot about ʿAlī and his caliphate. The caliphate does not adorn ʿAlī; ʿAlī adorns the caliphate."

قَالَ البشاري: فَحدثت بِهَذَا بعض الشِّيعَة فَقَالَ لي: قد أخرجت نصف مَا كَانَ فِي قلبِي على أَحْمد بن حَنْبَل من البغض.

Al-Bishārī said, "I mentioned this quote to a Shiite and he said, 'You have erased half of the hatred I have for Aḥmad ibn Ḥanbal from my heart.'"

وَكَانَ الإِمَام أَحْمد يَقُول: مَا لأحد من الصَّحَابَة من الْفَضَائِل بِالْأَسَانِيدِ الصِّحَاح مَا لعَلي رَضِي الله عَنهُ، وَقَالَ: من لم يثبت الْإِمَامَة لعَلي، فَهُوَ أضلّ من حمَار أَهله.

Al-Imām Aḥmad would say, "There is no companion with as many virtues narrated in authentic chains of narration as ʿAlī." He also said, "Whoever does not affirm that ʿAlī was an *imām* is more misguided than the donkey of their family."

وروى ابْن الْجَوْزِيّ عَن حَنْبَل قَالَ:

Ibn al-Jawzī reported that Ḥanbal said:

قلت لأبي عبد الله أَحْمد بن حَنْبَل: هَل خلَافَة عَليّ ثَابِتَة؟ فَقَالَ: سُبْحَانَ الله! يُقيم علي الْحُدُود، وَيقطع، وَيَأْخُذ الصَّدَقَة، ويقسمها بِلَا حق وَجب لَهُ؟! أعوذ بِاللَّه من هَذِه الْمقَالة! نعم هُوَ خَليفَة، رضية أَصْحَاب رَسُول الله، وصلوا خَلفه،

وغزوا مَعَه، وَجَاهدُوا، وحجوا، وَكَانُوا يسمونه أمير المؤمنين، راضين بذلك غير منكرين، فنحن تبع لهم.

I said to Abu ʿAbdullāh, Aḥmad ibn Ḥanbal, "Is the caliphate of ʿAlī established?" He said, "Transcendent is Allah! He established penalties, he cut [the hands of thieves], he took [obligatory] alms and dispersed it without due right? I seek refuge in Allah from such a statement! Yes, he was a caliph. The companions of Allah's Messenger ﷺ were pleased with him; they prayed behind him, went to war with him, fought, made Ḥajj, and referred to him as the Commander of the Faithful, with pleasure, never rejecting him. We follow them."[40]

وقال له رسول الخليفة: ما تقول فيما كان من علي ومعاوية؟ فقال: لا أقوم إلا الحسني.

The messenger of the caliph of his time said to him, "What are your thoughts on what transpired between ʿAlī and Muʿāwiyah?" He responded, "I only say good things."

وسأله رجل من بني هاشم عن مثل ذلك، فقرأ قوله تعالى ﴿تِلْكَ أُمَّةٌ قَدْ خَلَتْ لَهَا مَا كَسَبَتْ وَلَكُم مَّا كَسَبْتُمْ وَلَا تُسْأَلُونَ عَمَّا كَانُوا يَعْمَلُونَ﴾ [البقرة: ١٤١]، وقال له ابنه عبد الله: من الرافضي؟ فقال: الذي يشتم، ويسب أبا بكر وعمر. وقال عبد الله: سألت أبي عن رجل شتم رجلا من أَصْحَاب رَسُول الله، فَقَالَ: مَا أَرَاهُ على الْإِسْلَام.

Also, a man from the Banū Hāshim asked him a similar question, and he responded by reciting: **{That community passed away: what they earned belongs to them, and what you earn belongs to you. You will not be answerable for their deeds.}** [Qur'ān 2:141] His son, ʿAbdullāh, said to him, "Who can be described as a Rāfiḍite (Shiite)?" He responded, "Anyone who curses and disparages Abu Bakr and ʿUmar." ʿAbdullāh said, "I asked my father about someone who curses one of the companions of Allah's Messenger, and he responded, 'I do not think they are Muslim.'"[41]

---

40 *Manāqib al-Imām Aḥmad* (p. 220).
41 Ibid.

شذرة أيْضا فِي كَلَامه فِي الْأُصُول

Golden Discussions on Fundamentals

أخرج ابْن الْجَوْزِيّ، عَن أَحْمد بن مُحَمَّد بن هاني الطَّائِي الْمَعْرُوف بالأثرم قَالَ: سَمِعت أَبَا عبد الله أَحْمد بن حَنْبَل يَقُول: إِنَّمَا هُوَ السّنة والاتباع، وَإِنَّمَا الْقيَاس: يقيس على أصل، ثمَّ يَجِيء إِلَى الأَصْل فيهدمه، ثمَّ يَقُول: هَذَا قِيَاس، فعلى أَي شَيْء كَانَ هَذَا الْقيَاس؟! وَقيل لَهُ: لَا يَنْبَغِي أَن يقيس إِلَّا رجل عَالم كَبِير، يعرف نِسْبَة الشَّيْء بالشَّيْء معرفَة كَثِيرَة، فَقَالَ أجل لَا يَنْبَغِ.

Ibn al-Jawzī reported that Aḥmad ibn Muḥammad ibn Ḥānī al-Ṭā'ī, widely known as al-Athram said, "I heard Abu 'Abdullāh Aḥmad ibn Ḥanbal say, 'We must follow the Sunnah. Analogy [when falsely used] means to analogise based on a foundational text, then dismantle the foundational text, then claim this is analogy. What thing was the analogy based on?' It was also said to him, 'Only a great scholar can perform analogy; it must be done by someone who understands the relations between things to a large extent.' He responded, 'Indeed; it is not appropriate [for anyone else].'"[42]

قَالَ الْأَثْرَم:

Al-Athram said:

وَسمعت أَبَا عبد الله يَقُول: إِذا كَانَ فِي الْمَسْأَلَة عَن النَّبِي صلى الله عَلَيْهِ وَسلم حَدِيث لم نَأْخُذ فِيهَا بقول أحد من الصَّحَابَة، وَلَا بقول من بعدهمْ، وَإِذا كَانَ فِي الْمَسْأَلَة عَن أَصْحَاب رَسُول الله صلى الله عَلَيْهِ وَسلم قَول مُخْتَلف، نتخير من أقاويلهم، وَلَا نَأْخُذ بقول من بعدهمْ، وَإِذا لم يكن فِيهَا حَدِيث، وَلَا قَول لأحد من الصَّحَابَة، نتخير من أَقْوَال التَّابِعين، وَرُبمَا كَانَ الحَدِيث عَن النَّبِي صلى الله عَلَيْهِ وَسلم وَفِي إِسْنَاده شَيْء، فنأخذ بِهِ إِذا لم يجىء خِلَافه قَالَ: وربما أَخذنَا

42 Ibid. (p. 244).

بِالْحَدِيثِ الْمُرْسَل إِذا لم يجيء خِلَافه.

I heard Abu ʿAbdullāh say, "If a ḥadīth from Allah's Messenger ﷺ discusses some matter, we do not accept the statements of the companions afterwards, nor those after them. Further, if the companions of Allah's Messenger have varying opinions, we choose from among those opinions, and do not espouse views of those after them. If there is no ḥadīth or opinion of the companions on a subject, we choose one of the views of the successors of the companions. Sometimes, a ḥadīth of the Prophet ﷺ would have some discrepancies in the chain of transmission. If that is the case, we accept it so long as there is nothing [textual] that contradicts it. Sometimes, we accept the *mursal*[43] reports, if nothing else contradicts it."[44]

وروى مُحَمَّد بن عَوْف بن سُفْيَان الطَّائِي الْحِمصِي عَن الإِمَام أَحْمد مقَالَة طَوِيلَة فِي الِاعْتِقَاد، حَكَاهَا عَنهُ أَبُو يعلى فِي (الطَّبَقَات) لَكِنَّهَا لما كَانَت مسائلها قد تضمنتها رسالتا مُسَدّد، وعبدوس، أضربنا عَن ذكرهَا خوف التَّطْوِيل.

Muḥammad ibn ʿAwf ibn Sufyān al-Ṭāʾī al-Ḥimṣī reported a long statement from al-Imām Aḥmad pertaining to beliefs, and Abu Yaʿlā mentioned it from him in his *Ṭabaqāt*. However, since its contents were already discussed in the two reports of Musaddad and ʿAbdus, I refrained from quoting it, out of fear of prolongation.

وروى أَبُو يعلى فِي تَرْجَمَة أَحْمد بن جعفر بن يَعْقُوب الْفَارِسِ الأصطخري عَنهُ رِسَالَة مُطَوَّلَة عَن الإِمَام أَحْمد، وَنحن ننقلها هُنَا وَإِن كَانَ فِيهَا تكْرير لما مضى، فَإِن المكرر أحلى.

Abu Yaʿlā reported a long quotation from al-Imām Aḥmad in his biography of Aḥmad ibn Jaʿfar ibn Yaʿqūb al-Fārisī al-Iṣṭakhrī.[45] I will mention it here.

---

43 [T] A *mursal* narration is one where a successor of the companions says, "Allah's Messenger said." Refer to *ʿUlum al-Ḥadīth* by Ibn al-Ṣalāḥ (p. 47).

44 [T] Reported by al-Khaṭīb al-Baghdādī in *al-Faqīh wa ʾl-Mutafaqqih* (1/534).

45 [T] It should be noted that many parts of this letter are disputed by other Ḥanbalī scholars, and as such, the portions mentioning things that contradict the verbiage used by the Salaf are doubtful, at best. Ibn Rajab and al-Dhahabī both were quite explicit in denying the authenticity of parts of this letter that are not corroborated by other supporting narrations with similar wordings. The fact that al-Iṣṭakhrī mentioned them singularly is indicative of some tampering, as al-Dhahabī suggests, although he does

If it repeats something previously mentioned, what will be repeated will be even sweeter [the second time].

قَالَ الأصطخري:

Al-Iṣṭakhrī said:

قَالَ أَبُو عبد الله أَحْمد بن مُحَمَّد بن حَنْبَل هَذِه مَذَاهِب أهل الْعلم، وَأَصْحَاب الْأَثر، وَأهل السّنة المتمسكين بعروقها، المعروفين بهَا، المقتدى بهم فِيهَا، من لدن أَصْحَاب النَّبِي صلى الله عَلَيْهِ وَسلم إِلَى يَوْمنَا هَذَا، وَأدْركت من أدْركْت من عُلَمَاء أهل الْحجاز وَالشَّام وَغَيرهم عَلَيْهَا، فَمن خَالف شَيْئا من هَذِه الْمذَاهب، أَو طعن فِيهَا، أَو عاب قَائِلهَا فَهُوَ مُبْتَدع، خَارج من الْجَمَاعَة، زائل عَن مَنْهَج السّنة وسبيل الْحق.

Abu ʿAbdullāh Aḥmad ibn Muḥammad ibn Ḥanbal said, "These are the beliefs of the people of knowledge, the carriers of tradition, and the people of Sunnah who hold fast to its roots and are known to [do so] and who are followed in such matters. [These beliefs] extend to the time of the companions of the Prophet ﷺ until this very day. I met many scholars from the Hejaz, the Levant, and other areas, all espousing these same beliefs. Therefore, if anyone were to oppose any part of these beliefs, disparage them, or dispraise its adherents, they are innovators and have left the congregation, deviating from the methodology of the Sunnah and the path of truth.

وَكَانَ قَوْلهم: إِن الْإِيمَان قَول، وَعمل، وَنِيَّة، وَتمسك بِالسنةِ، وَالْإِيمَان يزِيد وَينْقص، وَيسْتَثْنى فِي الْإِيمَان غير أَن لَا يكون الِاسْتِثْنَاء شكا، إِنَّمَا هِيَ سنة عِنْد الْعلمَاء مَاضِيَة.

Their beliefs were: Faith is statement, action, intention, and adherence to the Sunnah. Faith increases and decreases. It is permissible to say, "I am a believer if Allah wills," so long as it does not indicate doubt. The statement is a long-practiced *sunnah* according to the scholars.

---

not go as far as to say al-Iṣṭakhrī was the one fabricating these statements. The areas of contention are clarified by myself in the footnotes.

قَالَ: وَإِذا سُئِلَ رجل أمؤمن أَنْت؟ فَإِنَّهُ يَقُول: أَنا مُؤمن إِن شَاءَ الله، أَو، مُؤمن أَرْجُو، أَو يَقُول: آمَنت بِاللَّه وَمَلَائِكَته وَكتبه وَرُسُله

If a person is asked, "Are you a believer?" They should respond, "I am a believer, if Allah wills," or, "I hope that I am a believer," or, "I believe in Allah, His angels, His books, and His messengers."

وَمن زعم أَن الْإِيمَان قَول بِلَا عمل، فَهُوَ مرجىء، وَمن زعم أَن الْإِيمَان هُوَ الْقَوْل، وَالْأَعْمَال شرائع، فَهُوَ مرجىء، وَمن زعم أَن الْإِيمَان لَا يزِيد وَلَا ينقص، فقد قَالَ بقول المرجئة، وَمن لم ير الِاسْتِثْنَاء فِي الْإِيمَان، فَهُوَ مرجىء، وَمن زعم أَن إيمَانه كَإِيمَانِ جِبْرِيل وَالْمَلَائِكَة، فَهُوَ مرجىء، قَالَ: وَمن زعم أَن الْمعرفَة تَنْفَع فِي الْقلب لَا يتَكَلَّم بهَا، فَهُوَ مرجىء.

Whoever alleges that faith is statement without action is a Murjiʿite. Whoever alleges that faith is statements, and that actions are simply legislations, he is a Murjiʿite. Whoever claims that faith does not increase or decrease has espoused the view of the Murjiʿite sect. Whoever does not believe one can say "If Allah wills" when referring to his faith is a Murjiʿite. Whoever claims that their faith is of the same level as that of Gabriel and the angels is a Murjiʿite. Likewise, whoever believes knowledge benefits in the heart and that one does not need to utter [any statements of faith], he is a Murjiʿite.

قَالَ: وَالْقدر خَيره وشره، وقليله وَكَثِيره، وَظَاهره وباطنه، وحلوه ومره، ومحبوبه ومكروهه، وَحسنه وقبيحه، وأوله وَآخره، من الله قَضَاء قَضَاهُ، وَقدرا قدره عَلَيْهِم، لَا يعدو أحد مِنْهُم مَشِيئَة الله عز وَجل، وَلَا يُجَاوز قَضَاءَهُ، بل هم كلهم صائرون إِلَى مَا خلقهمْ لَهُ واقعون فِيمَا قدر عَلَيْهِم لأفعاله، وَهُوَ عدل مِنْهُ عز وَجل.

We believe in predestination, the good parts and the bad parts, the parts that result in abundance and the parts that result in meagreness, the apparent and the hidden, the sweet and the bitter, the liked and the disliked, the nice and the bad, and the first and the last. All of them are predestination that Allah has destined for people. None are exempt from the will of Allah the Exalted and none can bypass His destiny for them. All people will eventually do what they were created to do, and will unavoidably[46] experience whatever

46 [T] I have corrected this sentence based on the printed edition of *Ijmāʿ al-Salaf fi*

was destined for them. It is justice on the part of Allah the Exalted.

وَالزِّنَا، وَالسَّرِقَة، وَشرب الْخمر، وَقتل النَّفس، وَأكل المَال الْحَرَام، والشرك بِاللَّه، والمعاصي كلهَا بِقَضَاء وَقدر من غير أَن يكون لأحد من الْخلق على الله حجَّة، بل لله الْحجَّة الْبَالِغَة على خلقه ﴿لَا يُسْأَلُ عَمَّا يَفْعَلُ وَهُمْ يُسْأَلُونَ﴾ [الْأَنْبِيَاء: ٢٣]

Fornication, thievery, drinking alcohol, murder, consuming unlawful wealth, polytheism, and sins all occur by the predestination of Allah, however, none of creation can use [predestination] as an excuse against Allah. Rather, Allah has the conclusive case against His creation: **{He cannot be called to account for anything He does, whereas they will be called to account.}** [Qur'ān 21:23]

علم الله تَعَالَى مَاض فِي خلقه بِمَشِيئَة مِنْهُ، قد علم - من إِبْلِيس وَمن غَيره مِمَّن عَصَاهُ، من لدن أَن عصي تبَارك وَتَعَالَى إِلَى أَن تقوم السَّاعَة - الْمعْصِيَة، وخلقهم لَهَا، وَعلم الطَّاعَة من أهل الطَّاعَة، وخلقهم لَهَا، وكل يعْمل لما خلق لَهُ، وصائر إِلَى مَا قضى عَلَيْهِ، وَعلم مِنْهُ، لَا يعدو أحد مِنْهُم قدر الله ومشيئته.

Allah's knowledge is thoroughly encompassing of His creation, by His will. He knew that Iblīs and other disobedient individuals would disobey Him, and He will continue to know, from the moment He was first disobeyed until the hour begins. He knows that people will sin, and He created them to actualise those sins. He also knows the actions of obedience that people of obedience will do, and created them to actualise those actions. Everyone does what they were created for and will inevitably face what was destined for them, and Allah the Exalted knew what they would do and what they would face. None can absolve themselves of the predestination and will of Allah.

وَالله الْفَاعِل لما يُرِيد، الفعال لما يَشَاء، وَمن زعم أَن الله شَاءَ لِعِبَادِهِ الَّذين عصوه الْخَيْر وَالطَّاعَة، وَأَن الْعباد شَاؤُوا لأَنْفُسِهِمْ الشَّرّ وَالْمَعْصِيَة، فعملوا على مشيئتهم، فقد زعم أَن مَشِيئَة الْعباد أغْلظ من مَشِيئَة الله تبَارك وَتَعَالَى، فَأَي افتراء أكبر على

'l-I'tiqād (p. 40), which is al-Imām Ḥarb al-Kirmānī's account of this monologue of al-Imām Aḥmad.

الله عز وَجل من هَذَا؟!

Allah does what He wishes and wants. What graver allegation against Allah the Exalted is there than that of someone who claims that, if Allah the Exalted wished goodness and obedience for a disobedient slave, and that the slave wished evil and disobedience for himself, that the will of the slave would overpower the will of Allah the Exalted?

وَمن زعم أَن الزِّنَا لَيْسَ بِقدر، قيل لَهُ: أَرَأَيْت هَذِه الْمَرْأَة إِن حملت من الزِّنَا وَجَاءَت بِولد، هَل شَاءَ الله عز وَجل أَن يخلق هَذَا الْوَلَد، وَهل مضى فِي سَابق علمه؟ فَإِن قَالَ: لَا، فقد زعم أَن مَعَ الله خَالِقًا، وَهَذَا هُوَ الشّرك صراحا.

To those who believe that fornication does not occur by predestination, we say, think of a woman who fornicates and becomes pregnant. Did Allah the Exalted will to create that child? Was the creation of that child in Allah's previous knowledge? If they say, "No," they have claimed that there is a creator alongside Allah, and this is explicit polytheism.

وَمن زعم أَن السّرقَة، وَشرب الْخمر، وَأكل المَال الْحَرَام لَيْسَ بِقَضَاء وَقدر، فقد زعم أَن هَذَا الْإِنْسَان قَادر على أَن يَأْكُل رزق غَيره. وَهَذَا صراح قَول الْمَجُوسِيَّة، بل أكل رزقه، وَقضى الله أَن يَأْكُلهُ من الْوَجْه الَّذِي أكله.

Whoever claims that thievery, drinking alcohol, and consuming unlawful wealth are not a part of predestination has claimed that a person is able to consume the provisions of others. This is explicitly the belief of the Zoroastrians. The correct belief would be, they consumed their wealth, but Allah was the One that predestined that they would consume the wealth in whichever way or manner it was done.

وَمن زعم أَن قتل النَّفس لَيْسَ بِقدر من الله عز وَجل، فقد زعم أَن الْمَقْتُول مَاتَ بِغَيْر أَجله، وَأي كفر أوضح من هَذَا؟ بل ذَلِك بِقَضَاء الله عز وَجل، وَذَلِك بمشيئته فِي خلقه، وتدبيره فيهم، وَمَا جرى من سَابق علمه فيهم، وَهُوَ الْعدْل، الْحق، الَّذِي يفعل مَا يُرِيد وَمن أقرّ بِالْعلمِ لزمَه الْإِقْرَار بِالْقُدْرَةِ، والمشيئة على الصغر والقمأ.

Further, whoever claims that murder does not occur by the predestination of Allah has claimed that the murdered person died without reaching their due time [which Allah ordains.] What disbelief is clearer than such a claim? Rather, the truth is that [murder] occurs by the predestination of Allah the Exalted, by His will which manifests in His creation, and it is His plan for them as has occurred in His previous Knowledge about them. He is the just and the truth; He does as He wants. And if one attests to Allah's omnipotent knowledge, it is binding that he attests to His omnipotent capability, and that His will encompasses even the small and insignificant.

وَلَا نشْهد على أحد من أهل الْقبْلَة أنه فِي النَّار لذنب عمله، وَلَا لكبيرة أَتَاهَا إِلَّا أَن يكون فِي ذَلِك حديث، كَمَا جَاءَ، على مَا رُوِيَ بِصَدقه، ونعلم أَنه كَمَا جَاءَ، وَلَا ننص الشَّهَادَة.

We do not testify that any member of Ahl al-Qiblah is definitively going to hellfire due to a sin or major sin that they perpetrated, unless there is a specific ḥadīth stating such. If there is, we take it as is and believe in it. We do not definitively say that a person is a martyr, either.

والخلافة فِي قُرَيْش مَا بَقِي من النَّاس اثْنَان لَيْسَ لأحد من النَّاس أَن ينازعهم فِيهَا، وَلَا يخرج عَلَيْهِم، وَلَا يقر لغيرهم بهَا إِلَى قيام السَّاعَة.

The caliphate must remain the realm of the Quraysh, so long as there are two people existing on earth. None can dispute with them in [the caliphate] and none should rebel against them or acknowledge the legitimacy of a caliphate that is not headed by someone from the Quraysh, until the Day of Resurrection.

وَالْجهَاد مَاض، قَائِم مَعَ الْأَئِمَّة بروا أَو فجروا، لَا يُبطلهُ جور جَائِر، وَلَا عدل عَادل، وَالْجُمُعَة وَالْعِيدَيْنِ، وَالْحج مَعَ السُّلْطَان، وَإِن لم يَكُونُوا بررة، وَلَا أتقياء، وَلَا عُدولًا. وَدفع الصَّدقَات، وَالْخَرَاج، والأعشار، والفيء، والغنائم إِلَى الْأُمَرَاء، عدلوا فِيهَا أم جاروا. والانقياد إِلَى من ولاه الله أَمركُم، لَا تنْزع يدا من طَاعَته، وَلَا تخرج عَلَيْهِ بسيفك حَتَّى يَجْعَل الله لَك فرجا ومخرجا، وَلَا تخرج على السلطان، وتسمع وتطيع، وَلَا تنكث بيعَة، فَمن فعل ذَلِك، فَهُوَ مُبْتَدع، مُخَالف، مفارق

لِلْجَمَاعَة. وَإِن أَمرك السُّلْطَان بِأَمْر هُوَ لله مَعْصِيّة، فَلَيْسَ لَك أَن تُطِيعهُ أَلْبَتَّة، وَلَيْسَ لَك أَن تخرج عَلَيْهِ، وَلَا تَمنعهُ حَقه.

Jihad will also continue under the leadership of the leader [of the Muslims], irrespective if [the leader] is righteous or sinful. It is not nullified by oppression perpetrated by an oppressor or justice enacted by a just person. Jumuʿah, the two Eids, and Ḥajj are all valid and legitimate under the Muslim leader, even if they were not righteous, pious, or conscious of Allah. Likewise, payment of alms, land tax, tithe, booty, and spoils are to the leaders, irrespective of whether they are just or unjust in dispersing that wealth. One must obey those whom Allah has made in charge of your matters. Do not revoke allegiance to them by disobeying them, and do not rebel against them violently until Allah the Exalted grants you ease and a way out [of the difficulties presented by an unjust ruler]. Do not rebel against the sultan; hear and obey, and do not revoke your pledge of allegiance. Whoever does so is an innovator, contrarian, and deserter of the congregation. If the sultan commands you to do something that is disobedience to Allah, you may not obey him whatsoever, but you still cannot rebel against him or deprive him of his rights.

والإمساك فِي الْفِتْنَة سنة مَاضِيَة، وَاجِب لُزُومهَا، فَإِن ابْتليت، فَقدم نَفسك دون دينك، وَلَا تعن على الْفِتْنَة وَلَا بِلِسَان، وَلَكِن اكفف يدك، وَلِسَانك وهواك، وَالله الْمعِين.

Neutrality during unrest is a practice for which there is precedent amongst scholars. It is an obligation to adhere to it. If you are tested, give precedence to [sacrificing] your body before your religion. Do not aid in unrest, even through speaking. Restrain your hands, tongue, and vain desires. Allah is the assister.

والكف عَن أهل الْقبْلَة، وَلَا تكفر أحدا مِنْهُم بذنب، وَلَا تخرجه من الْإِسْلَام بِعَمَل، إِلَّا أَن يكون فِي ذَلِك حَدِيث، فيروى الحَدِيث كَمَا جَاءَ، وكما رُوِيَ، ونصدقه، ونقبله، ونعلم أَنه كَمَا رُوِيَ، نَحْو ترك الصَّلَاة، وَشرب الْخمر، وَمَا أشبه ذَلِك. أَو يبتدع بِدعَة ينْسب صَاحبهَا إِلَى الْكفْر، وَالْخُرُوج من الْإِسْلَام، فَاتبع الْأَثر فِي ذَلِك وَلَا تجاوزه.

Refrain from people of the Qiblah. Do not excommunicate any of them on account of a sin, and do not declare them outside the fold of Islam on account of an action. Unless, of course, there is a ḥadīth on the topic, and in that case, the ḥadīth is to be reported as is and should be both believed in and accepted; we know that [the reality] is as has been reported. Examples of this are abandonment of prayer, drinking alcohol, and so forth, or if a person invents something in the religion that causes them to fall into disbelief and exit Islam. Therefore, follow narrations in such matters and do not overstep its boundaries.

والأعور الدَّجَّال خَارج لَا شكّ فِي ذَلِك وَلَا ارتياب، وَهُوَ أكذب الْكَاذِبين.

Without any doubt or uncertainty, the one-eyed antichrist will emerge. He is the most heinous of all liars.

وَعَذَاب الْقَبْر حق، يسْأَل العَبْد عَن دينه، وَعَن ربه، وَعَن الْجنَّة، وَعَن النَّار. ومنكر وَنَكِير حق، وهما فتانا الْقَبْر، فنسأل الله الثَّبَات.

The punishment in the grave is truth. The slave will be asked about their religion, lord, paradise, and hellfire. Munkir and Nakīr are truth, and they are the two examiners that come to the grave [to ask people these questions]. We pray to Allah to give us steadfastness.

وحوض مُحَمَّد صلى الله عَلَيْهِ وَسلم حق، ترده أمته، وَله آنِية يشربون بهَا مِنْهُ.

The pool of Muḥammad ﷺ is also truth. His nation will drink from it, and they will have cups there to drink from.

والصراط حق، وضع على سَوَاء جَهَنَّم، ويمر النَّاس عَلَيْهِ، وَالْجنَّة من وَرَاء ذَلِك. نسْأَل الله السَّلامَة.

The bridge over hellfire is truth and people will pass over it. Paradise lies on the other side of said bridge. We pray to Allah for safety.

وَالْمِيزَان حق، توزن بِهِ الْحَسَنَات والسيئات كَمَا شَاءَ الله أَن توزن.

The scale is truth. The good deeds and the bad will be measured in a manner that Allah wills.

والصور حق، ينْفخ فِيهِ إسْرَافيل فَيَمُوت الْخلق، ثمَّ ينْفخ فِيهِ الْأُخْرَى فَيقومُونَ لرب الْعَالمين.

The horn is truth. Isrāfīl will blow into it, and all creation will die, and then he will blow into it again and they will stand before the Lord of all that exists.

والحساب، وَالْقَضَاء، وَالثَّوَاب، وَالْعِقَاب، وَالْجنَّة وَالنَّار، واللوح الْمَحْفُوظ تستنسخ مِنْهُ أَعمال الْعباد لما سبق فِيهِ من الْمَقَادِير وَالْقَضَاء. والقلم حق، كتب الله بِهِ مقادير كل شَيْء، وأحصاه فِي الذّكر تبارك وَتَعَالَى.

Accounting, judgement, reward, punishment, paradise, and hellfire [are the truth]. Actions of the slaves are copied and written based on the Preserved Tablet, as it contains a prior mention of all proportions and predestination. The Pen is the truth. Allah the Exalted wrote with it the proportions of everything and mentioned all things.

والشفاعة يَوْم الْقِيَامَة حق، يشفع قوم فِي قوم فَلَا يصيرون إِلَى النَّار، وَيخرج قوم من النَّار بعد مَا دخلوها بشفاعة الشافعين، وَيخرج قوم من النَّار بعدمَا دخلوها وَلَبِثُوا فِيهَا مَا شَاءَ الله، ثمَّ يخرجهم من النَّار، وَقوم يخلدُونَ فِيهَا أبدا أبدا، وهم أهل الشّرك والتكذيب والجحود وَالْكفْر بِاللَّه عز وَجل، ويذبح الْمَوْت يَوْم الْقِيَامَة بَين الْجنَّة وَالنَّار. وَقد خلقت الْجنَّة وَمَا فِيهَا، وَالنَّار وَمَا فِيهَا، خلقهما الله عز وَجل وَخلق الْخلق لَهما، وَلَا يفنيان، وَلَا يفنى مَا فيهمَا أبدا. فَإِن احْتج مُبْتَدع أَو زنديق بقول الله عز وَجل ﴿كُلُّ شَيْءٍ هَالِكٌ إِلَّا وَجْهَهُ﴾ [الْقَصَص: ٨٨] وَنَحْو هَذَا من متشابه الْقُرْآن؛ قيل لَهُ: كل شَيْء مِمَّا كتب الله عَلَيْهِ الفناء والهلاك هَالك، وَالْجنَّة وَالنَّار خلقا للبقاء لَا للفناء وَلَا للهلاك، وهما من الْآخِرَة لَا من الدُّنْيَا.

Intercession on the Day of Resurrection is true. A people will be interceded for and they will not go to the hellfire, and a group will be removed from the fire after entering it due to the intercession of the intercessors.[47] Likewise, Allah will extract people from hellfire who spent time there for as long as Allah willed, and then He will remove them from the hellfire. Another

47 This is referring to Muslims who were meant to not spend eternity in hellfire.

group of individuals will remain in hellfire for absolute eternity, and they are people of polytheism, belying, denying, and disbelief in Allah the Exalted. Death will be slaughtered on the Day of Resurrection in the area between paradise and hellfire. Paradise and all of its contents, and hellfire and all of its contents have both been created. Allah the Exalted created them and created creation to inhabit them. They will never cease to exist, and none in them will cease to exist. Some innovators or heretics will attempt to use the following verse to contend this belief: **{Everything will perish except His Face.}** [Qur'ān: 28:88] They will also attempt to use other ambiguous verses of the Qur'ān. The response to them would be: Everything that Allah wrote to perish and cease to exist will perish. Paradise and hellfire, however, were created for eternal existence, not to perish or cease to exist. Also, they are of the realm of the hereafter, not of the realm of the worldly life.

والحور الْعين لَا يمتن عِنْد قيام السَّاعَة، وَلَا عِنْد النفخة، وَلَا أبدا، لِأَن الله عز وَجل خَلقهنَّ للبقاء لَا للفناء، وَلم يكْتب عَلَيْهِنَّ الْمَوْت، فَمن قَالَ خلاف هَذَا، فَهُوَ مُبْتَدع، وَقد ضل عَن سَوَاء السَّبِيل.

The Hūri women will not die at the time of the Hour, nor will they die when the horn is blown or ever, because Allah the Exalted created them for eternal existence, not to perish; He did not write that they will die. Anyone who says otherwise is an innovator and has deviated from the Straight Path.

وَخلق سبع سموات بَعْضهَا فَوق بعض، وَسبع أَرضين بَعْضهَا أَسْفَل من بعض، وَبَين الأَرْض العلياء وَالسَّمَاء الدُّنْيَا مسيرَة خَمْس مئة عَام، وَبَين كل سَمَاء إِلَى سَمَاء مسيرَة خَمْس مئة عَام، وَالْمَاء فَوق السَّمَاء الْعليا السَّابِعَة، وعرش الرَّحْمَن عز وَجل فَوق المَاء، وَالله عز وَجل على الْعَرْش، والكرسي مَوضِع قَدَمَيْهِ، وَهُوَ يعلم مَا فِي السَّمَوَات وَالْأَرضين السَّبع، وَمَا بَينهمَا، وَمَا تَحت الثرى، وَمَا فِي قَعْر الْبحار، ومنبت كل شَعْرَة وشجرة، وكل زرع، وكل نَبَات، ومسقط كل ورقة، وَعدد كل كلمة، وَعدد الْحَصَى والرمل وَالتُّرَاب، وَمَثَاقِيل الْجبَال، وأعمال الْعباد، وآثارهم، وَكَلَامهم، وأنفاسهم وَيعلم كل شَيْء لَا يخفى عَلَيْهِ من ذَلِك شَيْء، وَهُوَ على الْعَرْش فَوق السَّمَاء السَّابِعَة، ودونه حجب من نَار وظلمة، وَمَا هُوَ أعلم بهَا.

Allah created seven heavens in levels, one above the other. He also created seven worlds in layers, one below the other. Between the highest world and the lowest heaven is the distance of travel for five hundred years. Between each heaven is the distance of travel for five hundred years. Water resides above the seventh heaven, and the Throne of Allah the Exalted is above the water. Allah the Exalted is above the throne. The footstool is the area of His two feet. He knows what is in the seven heavens and seven worlds, as well as everything in between, including whatever is under the earth, whatever is in the depths of the oceans, whatever hair or tree that has taken root, every vegetation and plant, the place where each and every leaf falls, the amounts of all words, the amount of pebbles and specks of sand and dirt, the weight of the mountains, the actions of the slaves and the effects those actions had, their speech, their breaths, and everything else. None of those things are hidden to Him, whilst He is above the throne, above the seventh heaven. Beneath Him are barriers of fire, light, and darkness, and other things that only He knows of.

فَإِن احْتج مُبْتَدع ومخالف بقول الله عز وَجل ﴿وَهُوَ مَعَكُمْ أَيْنَ مَا كُنتُمْ﴾ [الْحَدِيد: ٤] وَبِقَوْلِهِ ﴿مَا يَكُونُ مِن نَّجْوَىٰ ثَلَاثَةٍ إِلَّا هُوَ رَابِعُهُمْ﴾ [المجادلة: ٧] وَنَحْو هَذَا من متشابه الْقُرْآن، فَقل: إِنَّمَا يَعْنِي بذلك الْعلم، لِأَن الله تَعَالَى على الْعَرْش، فَوق السَّمَاء السَّابِعَة الْعليا، يعلم ذَلِك كُله، وَهُوَ بَائِن من خلقه، لَا يَخْلُو من علمه مَكَان، وَللَّه عز وَجل عرش، وللعرش حَملَة يحملونه، وَالله عز وَجل على عَرْشه، وَلَيْسَ لَهُ حد، وَالله أعلم بحده، وَالله عز وَجل سميع لَا يشك، بَصِير لَا يرتاب، عليم لَا يجهل، جواد لَا يبخل، حَلِيم لَا يعجل، حفيظ لَا ينسى، يقظان لَا يسهو، قريب لَا يغْفل، يَتَحَرَّك، وَيتَكَلَّم، وَينظر، ويبسط، ويضحك، ويفرح، وَيُحب، وَيكره، وَيبغض، ويرضى، ويغضب، ويسخط، وَيرْحَم، وَيَعْفُو، ويغفر، وَيُعْطِي، ويمْنَع، وَينزل كل لَيْلَة إِلَى سَمَاء الدُّنْيَا كَيفَ يَشَاء: ﴿لَيْسَ كَمِثْلِهِ شَيْءٌ وَهُوَ السَّمِيعُ الْبَصِيرُ﴾ [الشورى: ١١]، وَقُلُوب الْعباد بَين أصْبعَيْنِ من أَصَابِع الرَّحْمَن، يقلبها كَيفَ يَشَاء، ويوعيها مَا أَرَادَ، وَخلق آدم بِيَدِهِ على صورته، وَالسَّمَوَات وَالْأَرْض يَوْم الْقِيَامَة فِي كَفه، وَيَضَع قدمه فِي النَّار فتنزوى، وَيخرج قوما من النَّار بِيَدِهِ.

Innovators and the wayward may quote the verse where Allah the Exalted said: **{He is with you wherever you are.}** [Qur'ān: 57:4] Or where Allah said: **{There is no secret conversation between three people where He is not the fourth, nor between five where He is not the sixth, nor between less or more than that without Him being with them, wherever they may be.}** [Qur'ān 58:7] They quote these and other ambiguous verses of the Qur'ān. Respond to them by saying that these verses are referring to His knowledge, because Allah the Exalted is above the throne, above the highest heavens, but still knows all of those things. He is separate from His creation, but His knowledge never is nonexistent in a single place. Allah the Exalted has a throne, and the throne has carriers. Allah the Exalted is above His throne. He has no limits, but if He does, only He knows of them. Allah the Exalted is hearing, without doubt, seeing, without uncertainty. He is knowledgeable, never unaware of anything, generous, never stingy, forbearing, never impatient, observant, never forgetful, awake, never inattentive, and close, never heedless. He moves,[48] speaks, sees, extends, laughs, becomes happy, loves, dislikes, hates, is pleased, is angered, is discontent, shows mercy, pardons, forgives, gives, deprives, and descends every night to the lowest heavens, however He wishes. Allah the Exalted states: **{There is nothing like Him: He is the All Hearing, the All Seeing.}** [Qur'ān 42:11] The hearts of the slaves are between two fingers of Allah the Exalted, and he turns them as He wishes, and allows them to understand as much as He wants. He created Adam in his shape, and the heavens and the earth will be, on the Day of Resurrection, in His hand. He will place His foot into the hellfire and it will be filled. He will also remove some people from hellfire with His hand.

وَينظر إِلَى وَجهه أهل الْجنَّة، يرونه فيكرمهم، ويتجلى لَهُم فيعطيهم، وَتعرض عَلَيْهِ الْعباد يَوْم الْقِيَامَة، ويتولى حسابهم بِنَفسِهِ، لَا يَلِي ذَلِك غَيره عز وَجل.

The inhabitants of paradise will look at His Countenance. They will see Him, and He will honor them. He will present Himself to them, and He will give them. Slaves will be presented to Him on the Day of Resurrection,

48 [T] According to al-Ḥāfiẓ Ibn Rajab, al-Imām Aḥmad never ascribed movement to Allah the Exalted, and mentioned that all of the narrations that quote the *imām* saying so are weak. Refer to his explanation of *Ṣaḥīḥ al-Bukhārī*, named, *Fatḥ al-Bārī* (6/533), as well as his addendum to al-Qāḍī Abu 'l-Ḥusayn ibn Abī Ya'lā's book, *Ṭabaqāt al-Ḥanābilah*, which is a chronologically ordered compendium detailing the lives of various Ḥanbalī scholars, called, *Dhayl Ṭabaqāt al-Ḥanābilah* (3/509).

and He will account them Himself. None but Allah the Exalted will undertake accounting.

وَالْقُرْآن كَلَام الله، تكلم بِهِ، لَيْسَ بمخلوق، وَمن زعم أَن الْقُرْآن مَخْلُوق فَهُوَ جهمي كَافِر، وَمن زعم أَن الْقُرْآن كَلَام الله ووقف وَلم يقل: لَيْسَ بمخلوق، فَهُوَ أخبث من قَول الأول، وَمن زعم أَن ألفاظنا بِهِ، وتلاوتنا لَهُ مخلوقة، وَالْقُرْآن كَلَام الله، فَهُوَ جهمي، وَمن لم يكفر هَؤُلَاءِ الْقَوْم كلهم، فَهُوَ مثلهم.

The Qur'ān is the Speech of Allah. He spoke it. It is not created. Whoever alleges that the Qur'ān is created is a Jahmite and a disbeliever. Also, whoever claims that the Qur'ān is the speech of Allah the Exalted but stops there and does not say "uncreated," he is worse than the claimant of the first view. Whoever claims that our utterance of it or recitation of it is created, although the speech of Allah is uncreated, he is a Jahmite. Whoever does not declare those people as disbelievers is like them.

وَكَلَّمَ اللَّهُ مُوسَى تَكْلِيماً من فِيهِ، وناوله التَّوْرَاة من يَده إِلَى يَده، وَلم يزل الله عز وَجل متكلما ﴿فَتَبَارَكَ اللهُ أَحْسَنُ الْخَالِقِينَ﴾ [الْمُؤْمِنُونَ: ١٤].

Allah the Exalted Spoke to Mūsā truly, from His mouth[49] and handed him the Torah hand to hand. Allah the Exalted has eternally been speaking, **{So glorified is Allah, the best of Creators.}** [al-Mu'minūn: 14]

والرؤيا من الله عز وَجل، وَهِي حق، إِذا رأى صَاحبهَا شَيْئا فِي مَنَامه مَا لَيْسَ هُوَ ضغث، فقصَّهَا على عَالم، وَصدق فِيهَا، وأولها الْعَالم على أصل تَأْوِيلهَا الصَّحِيح، وَلم يحرف، فالرؤيا تَأْوِيلهَا حِينَئِذٍ حق. وَقد كَانَت الرُّؤْيَا من الْأَنْبِيَاء عَلَيْهِم السَّلَام وَحيا، فَأَي جَاهِل أَجْهَل مِمَّن يطعن فِي الرُّؤْيَا، وَيَزْعُم أَنَّهَا لَيست بِشَيْء؟! وَبَلغنِي أَن من قَالَ هَذَا الْقَوْل لَا يرى الِاغْتِسَال من الِاحْتِلَام، وَقد رُوِيَ

49 [T] This is another instance where the narrator has not accurately quoted al-Imām Aḥmad. Al-Imām al-Dhahabi has declared this to be inauthentic. He said in his book, *Siyar A'lām al-Nubalā*, "Pay no heed to the treatise mentioned by al-Iṣṭakhrī." (11/286) He also said, "He mentioned [that al-Imām Aḥmad said], 'Allah spoke with His mouth,' and other reprehensible quotations, things that, by Allah, the *imām* never said. May Allah fight the one who fabricated these statements." (11/303)

عَن النَّبِي صلى الله عَلَيْهِ وَسلم **((أَن رُؤْيا الْمُؤمن كَلَام يكلم الرب عَبده))** وَقَالَ: إِن الرُّؤْيَا من الله عز وَجل وَبِاللَّهِ التَّوْفِيق.

Good dreams are from Allah the Exalted and contain the truth. If a person sees a dream that is not muddled and they tell it truthfully to a knowledgeable person who interprets it correctly without fabricating anything, the interpretation becomes truth at that point. If the dream occurs to a Prophet ﷺ, it is revelation. Who, then, is more ignorant than the one who disparages dreams, claiming they mean nothing? I was told that some who take this view do not view that baths are taken after wet dreams. The Prophet ﷺ said, **"The dreams of believers contain speech which Allah wishes to convey to His slave."**[50] Dreams are from Allah, and divine aid comes from Him.

وَمن الْحجَّة الْوَاضِحَة الثَّابِتَة الْبَيِّنَة الْمَعْرُوفَة ذكر محَاسِن أَصْحَاب رَسُول الله صلى الله عَلَيْهِ وَسلم كلهم أَجْمَعِينَ، والكف عَن ذكر مساويهم الَّتِي شجرت بَينهم، فَمن سبّ أَصْحَاب رَسُول الله صلى الله عَلَيْهِ وَسلم أَو وَاحِدًا مِنْهُم، أَو تنقص، أَو طعن عَلَيْهِم، أَو عرض بعيبهم، أَو عَاب وَاحِدًا مِنْهُم، فَهُوَ مُبْتَدع، رَافِضِي، خَبِيث، مُخَالف، لَا يقبل الله مِنْهُ صرفا وَلَا عدلا، بل حبهم سنة، وَالدُّعَاء لَهُم قربَة، والاقتداء بهم وَسِيلَة، وَالْأَخْذ بآثارهم فَضِيلَة.

In clear, authentic, well-known and manifest evidences, there is mention of the virtues of all of the companions of Allah's Messenger ﷺ and [an injunction] to refrain from mentioning the flaws that emanated in their internal disputes. Therefore, whoever curses even one of the companions of Allah's Messenger ﷺ or belittles them, disparages them, flaunts their flaws, or shames a single one of them is an innovator, a Rafiḍite, an evil person, and a contrarian. Allah will not accept any of their voluntary or obligatory actions. Rather, loving [the companions] is the Sunnah, supplicating for them garners closeness [to Allah], imitating them is a medium [to paradise], and holding fast to their narrations is a virtue.

وَخير الْأمة بعد النَّبِي صلى الله عَلَيْهِ وَسلم أَبُو بكر، وَعمر بعد أبي بكر، وَعُثْمَان بعد عمر، وَعلي بعد عُثْمَان، ووقف قوم على عُثْمَان. وهم خلفاء راشدون

50 Reported by al-Ḥakīm al-Tirmidhī (p. 118).

مهديون، ثمَّ أَصْحَاب رَسُول الله صلى الله عَلَيْهِ وَسلم بعد هَؤُلَاءِ الْأَرْبَعَة خير النَّاس، لَا يجوز لأحد أَن يذكر شَيْئا من مساويهم، وَلَا يطعن على أحد مِنْهُم بِعَيْب وَلَا بنقص، فَمن فعل ذَلِك، فقد وَجب على السُّلْطَان تأديبه وعقوبته، لَيْسَ لَهُ أَن يعْفُو عَنهُ، بل يُعَاقِبهُ ويستتيبه، فَإِن تَابَ قبل مِنْهُ، وَإِن ثَبت، أعَاد عَلَيْهِ الْعُقُوبَة، وخلده فِي الْحَبْس حَتَّى يَمُوت أَو يُرَاجع.

The best of the Ummah after the Prophet ﷺ is Abu Bakr, then ʿUmar is after Abu Bakr, then ʿUthmān is after ʿUmar, and then ʿAlī after ʿUthmān. Some [scholars] stopped at ʿUthmān. They are the [four] righteous and rightly-guided caliphs. Then, after those four, the companions of Allah's Messenger ﷺ are the best of people. It is not permissible for anyone to mention their flaws, disparage them, or dispraise them by mentioning their deficiencies. If anyone does that, the ruler of the lands must punish them to teach them manners; they may not be pardoned, but rather, they must be punished and told to repent. If they repent, it is accepted, but if they persist, they should be punished again, and they should be held in prison until they either die or desist.

ونعرف للْعَرَب حَقّهَا، وفضلها، وسابقتها، ونحبهم لحَدِيث النَّبِي صلى الله عَلَيْهِ وَسلم ((**فَإِن حبهم إِيمَان، وبغضهم نفاق**)) وَلَا نقُول بقول الشعوبية وأراذل الموَالِي الَّذين لَا يحبونَ الْعَرَب وَلَا يقرونَ لَهَا بِفضل، فَإِن لَهُم بِدعَة ونفاقا وَخِلَافًا.

We acknowledge the rights of the Arabs, as well as their virtues and their early support [of the Prophet ﷺ]. We love them, due to the ḥadīth where the Prophet ﷺ said, **"Love of them is faith, and hating them is hypocrisy."**[51] We do not take the views of the Shuʿūbiyyah and the non-Arab new Muslims who do not love Arabs or acknowledge any of their virtues. They are engaged in innovation, hypocrisy, and contrarianism.

وَمن حرم من المكاسب، والتجارات، وَطيب المَال من وَجهه، فقد جهل، وَأَخْطَأ، وَخَالف، بل المكاسب من وَجههَا حَلَال، قد أحلهَا الله عز وَجل، وَرَسُول الله صلى الله عَلَيْهِ وَسلم. وَالرجل يَنْبَغِي لَهُ أَن يسْعَى على نَفسه وَعِيَاله من فضل ربه، فَإِن ترك ذَلِك على أَنه لَا يرى الْكسْب، فَهُوَ مُخَالف. وكل أحد

51 Reported by al-Ḥākim (4/87).

أَحق بِمَالِه الَّذِي وَرثهُ واستفاده، أَو أوصى بِهِ أَو كَسبه، لَا كَمَا يَقُول المتكلمون المخالفون.

Whoever prohibits earning, trading, or lawful wealth has acted ignorantly, erred, and has contradicted [the religion]. Rather, earning in lawful ways is permissible; Allah the Exalted has allowed it, and Allah's Messenger ﷺ allowed it. A man should strive to earn for themselves and their families of Allah's bounties. If a person avoids working out of believing that earning is unlawful, they have contradicted [the religion]. Everyone has the most right to their own wealth which they inherited and earned, or were given in a will, contrary to the false view that scholars of *kalām* hold.

وَالدّين إِنَّمَا هُوَ كتاب الله عز وَجل، وآثار، وَسنَن، وَرِوَايَات صِحَاح عَن الثِّقَات بالأخبار الصَّحِيحَة القوية الْمَعْرُوفَة يصدق بَعْضهَا بَعْضًا حَتَّى يَنْتَهِي ذَلِك إِلَى رَسُول الله صلى الله عَلَيْهِ وَسلم، وَأَصْحَابه رضوَان الله عَلَيْهِم، وَالتَّابِعِينَ وتابع التَّابِعين أَو من بعدهمْ من الْأَئِمَّة المعروفين، المقتدى بهم، المتمسكين بِالسنةِ، والمتعلقين بالآثار، لَا يعْرفُونَ بِدعَة، وَلَا يطعن فيهم بكذب، وَلَا يرْمونَ بِخِلَاف، وَلَيْسوا أَصْحَاب قِيَاس وَلَا رَأْي، لِأَن الْقيَاس فِي الدّين بَاطِل، والرأي كَذَلِك وأبطل مِنْهُ، وَأَصْحَاب الرَّأْي وَالْقِيَاس فِي الدّين مبتدعة ضلال، إِلَّا أَن يكون فِي ذَلِك أثر عَمَّن سلف من الْأَئِمَّة الثِّقَات.

The religion comprises of the Book of Allah the Exalted, the narrations, the Sunnah, and the authentic narrations through trustworthy narrators providing authentic, cogent meanings that solidify one another, until the chain of transmission reaches Allah's Messenger ﷺ, the companions, their successors, their successors or the known scholars after them who are followed. They hold fast to the Sunnah and stick to the narrations. They do not acknowledge or adhere to innovations, and none can accuse them of lying or being contrarian. They are not people of analogy or rhetoric, because analogy in [the fundamentals of] the religion is falsehood, and rhetoric is even falser. People of analogy and rhetoric in the [fundamentals of] the religion are innovators and misguided, unless they follow a narration of the trustworthy pious predecessors.

وَمن زعم أنه لَا يرى التَّقْلِيد، وَلَا يُقَلّد دينه أحدا، فَهُوَ قول فَاسق عِنْد الله وَرَسُوله صلى الله عَلَيْهِ وَسلم إِنَّمَا يُرِيد بذلك إِبْطَال الْأَثر، وتعطيل الْعلم وَالسّنة، والتفرد بِالرَّأْيِ وَالْكَلَام، والبدعة، وَالْخلاف.

Anyone who believes that *taqlīd*[52] is not permissible and that they do not follow anyone in their religion has uttered a sinful statement in the sight of Allah the Exalted and His Messenger ﷺ; intending through this to nullify narrations and destroy knowledge and the sunnah. They intend to make unilateral claims based on their own machinations and philosophies, innovations and contrarian views.

وَهَذِه الْمذَاهب والأقاويل الَّتِي وصفت مَذَاهِب أهل السّنة وَالْجَمَاعَة والْآثَار وَأَصْحَاب الرِّوَايَات وَحَملَة الْعلم الَّذين أدركناهم، وأخذنا عَنْهُم الحَدِيث، وتعلمنا مِنْهُم السّنَن، وَكَانُوا أَئِمَّة معروفين ثِقَات، أَصْحَاب صدق، يقْتَدى بهم، وَيُؤْخَذ عَنْهُم، وَلم يَكُونُوا أَصْحَاب بِدعَة، وَلَا خلاف، وَلَا تَخْلِيط، وَهُوَ قَول أئمتهم وعلمائهم الَّذين كَانُوا قبلهم، فَتمسكُوا بذلك - رحمكم الله - وتعلموه، وعلموه، وَبِاللَّهِ التَّوْفِيق.

The aforementioned views are the ways of thought of Ahl al-Sunnah wa 'l-Jamā'ah wa 'l-Athār (the People of the Sunnah and Narrations). They are the views of those who narrate and the carriers of knowledge we have met, and learned ḥadīth and the Sunnah from. They were the renowned masters and were trustworthy and truthful; they were deserving of being followed and studied from. They were not people of innovations, contradictions, or confusion. These views are also shared by those whom were before them. Hold fast to those views, may Allah have mercy on you. Learn them and teach them. Divine aid comes from Allah the Exalted.

ولأصحاب الْبدع ألقاب وَأَسْمَاء، لَا تشبه أَسمَاء الصَّالِحين، وَلَا الْعلمَاء من أمة مُحَمَّد صلى الله عَلَيْهِ وَسلم. وَمن أسمائهم:

The people of innovation have titles and nicknames, unlike the names of the righteous or the scholars of the Ummah of Muḥammad ﷺ. Of these names are:

52 [T] Meaning, following a scholar.

المرجئة: وهم الَّذين يَزْعمُونَ أَن الْإِيمَان قول وَلَا عمل، وَأَن الْإِيمَان قول والأعمال شرائع، وَأَن الْإِيمَان مُجَرّد، وَأَن النَّاس لَا يتفاضلون فِي إِيمَانهم، وَأَن إِيمَان الْمَلَائِكَة والأنبياء وَاحِد، وَأَن الْإِيمَان لَا يزِيد وَلَا ينقص، وَأَن الْإِيمَان لَيْسَ فِيهِ اسْتِثْنَاء، وَأَن من آمن بِلِسَانِهِ وَلم يعْمل، فَهُوَ مُؤمن حَقًا. هَذَا قَول المرجئة، وَهُوَ أَخبث الْأَقَاوِيل، وأضلها، وأبعدها من الْهدى.

The Murji'ites: They are people who claim that faith is statements without actions, and that faith consists of statements while the actions are just legislated. They also claim that faith is devoid of any additional factors and that people are not of varying levels in their faith. They believe that the faith of the angels and prophets are of the same level and that faith does not increase or decrease. They also say it is impermissible to say, "I am a believer, if Allah wills,' and claim if someone utters the statement of faith with their tongues without doing any actions, they are still true believers. These are the beliefs of the Murji'ites, and they are the evilest, most misguided, and furthest from guidance of all ideologies.

والقدرية: وهم الَّذين يَزْعمُونَ أَن إِلَيْهِم الاستطالة والمشيئة وَالْقُدْرَة، وَأَنَّهُمْ يملكُونَ لأَنْفُسِهِمْ الْخَيْر وَالشَّر، والضر والنفع، وَالطَّاعَة وَالْمَعْصِيَة، وَالْهدى والضلالة، وَأَن الْعباد يعلمُونَ بدءا من غير أَن يكون سبق لَهُم ذَلِك من الله عز وَجل، أَو فِي علمه، وَقَوْلهمْ يضارع الْمَجُوسِيَّة والنصرانية، وَهُوَ أصل الزندقة.

The Qadarites: They claim that they have full autonomous abilities, will, and capabilities. They believe that they possess the capabilities to bring benefit or harm to themselves, as well as harm and benefit, and can bring about obedience or disobedience, and guidance or misguidance, by their own power and will. They also believe that worshippers initiate[53] their own actions without Allah the Exalted having previously predestined or known about it. Their position is parallel to that of the Zoroastrians and the Christians. It is the root of heresy.

والمعتزلة: وهم يَقُولُونَ قَول الْقَدَرِيَّة، ويدينون بدينهم، ويكذبون بِعَذَاب الْقَبْر،

53 [T] The printed copy states "they learn (يعلمون)," or "they know," while the printed edition of *Ṭabaqāt al-Ḥanābilah* (1/32) states, "initiates (يعملون بدءاً)."

والشفاعة، والحوض. وَلَا يرَوْنَ الصَّلَاة خلف أحد من أهل الْقبْلَة وَلَا الْجُمُعَة إِلَّا من كَانَ على هواهم، ويزعمون أَن أَعمال الْعباد لَيست فِي اللَّوْح الْمَحْفُوظ.

The Muʿtazilites: They have similar views to the Qadarites and follow their ideology. They also deny the punishment of the grave, intercession, and the pool. They do not believe one may pray in congregation or the Friday prayer behind just any Muslim, unless that Muslim happens to follow the same misguidance as them. They believe the actions of the slaves are not written in the Preserved Tablet.

والنصيرية: وهم قدرية، وهم أَصْحَاب الْجبة والقيراط، وَالَّذين يَزْعمُونَ أَن من أَخذ حَبَّة أَو قيراطا أَو دانقا حَرَامًا، فَهُوَ كَافِر، وَقَوْلهمْ يضاهي قَول الْخَوَارِج.

The Nuṣayrites: They are also Qadarites, and they believe whoever takes a grain, a carat, or a *dāniq* of gold unlawfully is a disbeliever. Their view parallels that of the Kharijites.

والجهمية أَعدَاء الله: وهم الَّذين يَزْعمُونَ أَن الْقُرْآن مَخْلُوق، وَأَن الله لم يكلم مُوسَى، وَأَن الله لَيْسَ بمتكلم، وَلَا يتَكَلَّم، وَلَا ينْطق، وكلاما كثيرا أكره حكايته، وهم كفار، زنادقة، أَعدَاء الله.

The Jahmites: They are enemies of Allah. They claim the Qurʾān is created and that Allah never spoke to Mūsā. They claim that Allah cannot speak, does not speak, and cannot utter anything. They have many other views, which I dislike mentioning here. They are disbelievers and are heretics; they are enemies of Allah the Exalted.

والواقفة: يَزْعمُونَ أَن الْقُرْآن كَلَام الله، وَلَكِن ألفاظنا بِالْقُرْآنِ، وقرائتنا لَهُ مخلوقة، وهم جهمية فساق.

The Wāqifites: They claim that the Qurʾān is the speech of Allah but our utterances and recitation of the Qurʾān are created. They are Jahmites and are sinners.

والرافضة: وهم الَّذين يتبرأون من أَصْحَاب مُحَمَّد صلى الله عَلَيْهِ وَسلم، ويسبونهم، وينتقصونهم، ويكفرون الْأَئِمَّة إلا الْأَرْبَعَة: عَليّ، وعمار، والمقداد، وَسليمَان.

وَلَيْسَت الرافضة من الْإِسْلَام فِي شَيْء.

The Rāfiḍites: They absolve themselves from the companions of Muḥammad ﷺ. They curse them, belittle them, and declare great leaders amongst them to be disbelievers. However, they make an exception for four of the leaders: ʿAlī, ʿAmmār, al-Miqdād and Salmān. The Rāfiḍites have nothing to do with Islam.

والمنصورية: وهم رافضة أَخبث من الروافض، وهم الَّذين يَقُولُونَ: من قتل أَرْبَعِينَ نفسا مِمَّن خَالف هواهم دخل الْجنَّة، وهم الَّذين يخيفون النَّاس، ويستحلون أَمْوَالهم، وهم الَّذين يَقُولُونَ: أَخطَأ جِبْرِيل عَلَيْهِ السَّلَام بالرسالة، وَهَذَا هُوَ الْكفْر الْوَاضِح الَّذِي لَا يشوبه إِيمَان. فنعوذ بِاللَّه مِنْهُ.

The Manṣūrites: They are a more extreme and viler version of the Rāfiḍites. They say that whoever kills forty people that disagree with their ideology will enter paradise. They frighten people and declare their wealth as lawful. They say that Jibrīl ﷺ was mistaken in whom he delivered the message to, a belief which is clear disbelief that has no semblance of faith attached to it. We seek refuge in Allah the Exalted from it.

والسبائية: وهم رافضة، وهم قريب مِمَّن ذكرت، يخالفون الْأَئِمَّة، كذابون، وصنف مِنْهُم يَقُولُونَ: عَليّ فِي السَّحَاب، وَعلي يبْعَث قبل يَوْم الْقِيَامَة، وَهَذَا كذب وزور وبهتان.

The Sabāʾites: They are a category of the Rāfiḍites, and they are similar to those previously mentioned. They contradict the *imāms* and are liars. Some of them claim that ʿAlī is in the clouds and that he will be resurrected before the Day of Resurrection, both of which are lies, fabrications, and untruths.

والزيدية وهم رافضة، وهم الَّذين يتبرؤون من عُثْمَان، وَطَلْحَة، وَالزُّبَيْر، وَعَائِشَة، ويرون الْقِتَال مَعَ كل من خرج من ولد عَليّ رَضِي الله عَنهُ، برا كَانَ أَو فَاجِرًا، حَتَّى يغلب أَو يقتل.

The Zaydites: They are Rāfiḍites as well, and they absolve themselves of ʿUthmān, Ṭalḥah, al-Zubayr and ʿĀʾishah. They believe in fighting alongside all offspring of ʿAlī, irrespective if they are righteous or evil, until they are victorious or are killed.

والخشبية: وهم يَقُولُونَ بقول الزيدية، وهم فِيمَا يَزْعمُونَ ينتحلون آل مُحَمَّد صلى الله عَلَيْهِ وَسلم وكذبوا، بل هم المبغضون لآل مُحَمَّد صلى الله عَلَيْهِ وَسلم دون النَّاس، إِنَّمَا الشِّيعَة لآل مُحَمَّد المتقون، أهل السّنة والأثر، من كَانُوا وَحَيْثُ كَانُوا، الَّذين يحبونَ آل مُحَمَّد صلى الله عَلَيْهِ وَسلم وَجَمِيع أَصْحَاب مُحَمَّد، لَا يذكرُونَ أحدا مِنْهُم بِسوء، وَلَا عيب، وَلَا منقصة. فَمن ذكر أحدا من أَصْحَاب مُحَمَّد صلى الله عَلَيْهِ وَسلم بِسوء، أَو طعن عَلَيْهِم، أَو تبرأ من أحد مِنْهُم، أَو سبهم، أَو عرض بشتمهم، فَهُوَ رَافِضِي خَبِيث مخبث.

The Khashabites: They have the same views as the Zaydites, but they try to impersonate people who love the family of Muḥammad ﷺ, although they are lying in their claim. In reality, of all people, they hate the family of Muḥammad ﷺ. Rather, the group of the family of Muḥammad ﷺ are the pious, namely, the people of the Sunnah and narrations, whoever they are and wherever they reside, the ones who love the family of Muḥammad ﷺ as well as all of the companions of Muḥammad ﷺ. They do not mention any of them disparagingly, nor do they mention their flaws or deficiencies. Anyone who mentions the companions of Muḥammad ﷺ in a disparaging manner, dispraises them, absolves themselves of them, or curses them openly is an evil Rāfiḍite.

وَأما الْخَوَارِج: فمرقوا من الدّين، وفارقوا الْملَّة، وشردوا عَن الْإِسْلَام، وشذوا عَن الْجَمَاعَة، فضلوا عَن السَّبِيل وَالْهدى، وَخَرجُوا على السُّلْطَان، وسلوا السَّيْف على الْأَئِمَّة، وَاسْتَحَلُّوا دِمَاءَهُمْ وَأَمْوَالهمْ، وأبعدوا من خالفهم إِلَّا من قَالَ بقَوْلهمْ، وَكَانَ على مثل قَوْلهم ورأيهم، وَثَبت مَعَهم فِي بَث ضلالتهم، وهم يشتمون أَصْحَاب مُحَمَّد صلى الله عَلَيْهِ وَسلم وأصهاره وأختانه، ويتبرأون مِنْهُم، ويرمونهم بالْكفْر والعظائم، ويرون خلافهم فِي شرائع الْإِسْلَام، وَلَا يُؤمنُونَ بِعَذَاب الْقَبْر، وَلَا الْحَوْض، وَلَا الشَّفَاعَة، وَلَا خُرُوج أحد من النَّار.

The Khārijites: They have renounced and left the religion. They have strayed from Islam and have deviated from the congregation. They have abandoned the path and guidance. They rebel against rulers and unsheathe their swords against leaders, declaring their blood and wealth lawful. They excommunicate all those who do not hold their views and support them in propagating them. They curse the companions and in-laws of the Prophet ﷺ and absolve themselves of them, and accuse them of disbelief and major sins. Their perspective on the legislations of Islam do not coincide with that of the companions. They do not believe in the punishment of the grave, the pool, intercession, or that anyone will leave hellfire.

وَيقُولُونَ من كذب كذبة، أَو أَتَى صَغِيرَة أَو كَبِيرَة من الذُّنُوب، فَمَاتَ من غير تَوْبَة، فَهُوَ فِي النَّار خَالِدا مخلدا أبدا. وهم يَقُولُونَ بقول البكرية فِي الْحبَّة والقيراط، وهم قدرية، جهمية، مرجئة، رافضة، لَا يرَوْنَ الْجَمَاعَة إِلَّا خلف إمَامهمْ، وهم يرَوْنَ الصَّوْم قبل رُؤْيَة الْهلَال، وَالْفطر قبل رُؤْيَته، وهم يرَوْنَ النِّكَاح بِغَيْر ولي وَلَا سُلْطَان، ويرون الْمُتْعَة دينهم، ويرون الدِّرْهَم بِدِرْهَمَيْنِ يدا بيد، وَلَا يرَوْنَ الصَّلَاة فِي الأخفاف، وَلَا الْمسْح عَلَيْهَا، وَلَا يرَوْنَ للسُّلْطَان عَلَيْهِم طَاعَة، وَلَا لقرشي عَلَيْهِم خلَافَة، وَأَشْيَاء كَثِيرَة يخالفون عَلَيْهَا الْإِسْلَام وَأَهله، وَكفى بِقوم ضَلَالَة يكون هَذَا رَأْيهمْ ومذهبهم وَدينهمْ، وَلَيْسوا من الْإِسْلَام فِي شَيْء.

They claim that anyone who simply lies or does a lesser or major sin and dies without having repented from that error will remain in the hellfire forever. They take the same view as the [Nusayrites] in regards to grains and coins. They are also Qadarites, Jahmites, Murjiʿites, and Rāfiḍites. They do not view that the congregation is valid unless it is behind their leader, and they view that one must begin fasting before even seeing the moon and must end the month of Ramadan before seeing the moon. They believe that a woman can marry without the guardian and leader, and they believe that temporary marriages are lawful. They believe [that usury is allowed,] where a dirham is given for two, hand to hand. They do not believe that one may pray in or wipe on leather socks. They do not believe they must obey rulers, and that no person from the Quraysh has any right to the caliphate over them. There are many other issues they contradict Islam and the Muslims on. The views previously mentioned are sufficient to show their misguidance. They have no connection to Islam.

وَمن أَسمَاء الْخَوَارِج:

From the names of the Khārijites are:

الحرورية: وهم أَصْحَاب حرروا.

The Ḥarūrites, who originated from an area called Ḥarūrā.

والأزارقة: وهم أَصْحَاب نَافِع بن الْأَزْرَق، وَقَوْلهمْ أَخبث الْأَقَاوِيل، وأبعده من الْإِسْلَام وَالسّنة.

The Azāriqites, who were followers of Nāfiʿ ibn al-Azraq. Their views are the worst of them all, and the furthest from Islam and the Sunnah.

والنجدية: وهم أَصْحَاب نجدة بن عَامر الحروري.

The Najdites, who were followers of Najdah ibn ʿĀmir al-Ḥarūrī.

والأباضية: وهم أَصْحَاب عبد الله بن إباض.

The Ibāḍites, who were followers of ʿAbdullāh ibn Ibāḍ.

والصفرية: وهم أَصْحَاب دَاوُد بن النُّعْمَان.

The Ṣifriyyah, who were followers of Dāwūd ibn al-Nuʿmān.

والمهلبية والحارثية والحارمية: كل هَؤُلَاءِ خوارج فساق مخالفون للسّنة، خارجون من الْملَّة أهل بِدعَة وضلالة.

Other names are the Muhallabites, the Ḥārithites, and the Khārmites. They are all Khārijites and sinners, contradictory to the Sunnah and have left the correct understanding of the religion; they are people of innovation and misguidance.

والشعبية أَو الشعوبية: وهم أَصْحَاب بِدعَة وضلالة، وهم يَقُولُونَ: إن الْعَرَب والموالي عندنَا وَاحِد، لَا يرَوْنَ للْعَرَب حَقًا، وَلَا يعْرفُونَ لَهُم فضلا، وَلَا يحبونهم، بل يبغضون الْعَرَب، ويظهرون لَهُم الغل والحسد والبغضة فِي قُلُوبهم وَهَذَا قول قَبِيح، ابتدعه رجل من أهل الْعرَاق، فتابعه يسير، فَقتل عَلَيْهِ.

The Shaʿbites or Shuʿubites: They are people of innovation and misguidance. They say that Arabs and non-Arabs are the same, and do not believe Arabs have any rights or virtues. They do not love Arabs; rather, they hate them. They show malice, envy, and hatred in their hearts towards Arabs. Their views are heinous. Their views were innovated by a man from Iraq, and a small number of people followed him. He was executed.[54]

وَأَصْحَاب الرَّأْي: وهم مبتدعة، ضلال، أَعدَاء السّنة والأثر، يبطلون الحَدِيث، ويردون على الرَّسُول صلى الله عَلَيْهِ وَسلم، ويتخذون صَاحب الرَّأْي، وَمن قَالَ بقوله إِمَامًا، ويتدينون بدينهم، وَأي ضَلَالَة أبين مِمَّن قَالَ بِهَذَا، وَترك قَول الرَّسُول وَأَصْحَابه، وَيتبع صَاحب الرَّأْي وَأَصْحَابه؟! فكفى بِهَذَا غيا مرديا وطغيانا.

The people of rational discretion: They are innovators and misguided. They are enemies of the Sunnah and narrations. They reject aḥadīth and contend with Allah's Messenger ﷺ. They take to people who prefer using rational discretion and take them as leaders, following them in religion. What deviance is more severe than one who calls to this; to abandon the statements of the Prophet ﷺ and his companions, and to instead follow an adherent of rational discretion and his associates? This is sufficient to prove they are misguided, destroyed, and transgressive.

وَالْوَلَايَة بِدعَة، والبراءة بِدعَة، وهم الَّذين يَقُولُونَ: نتولى فلَانا، ونتبرأ من فلَان، وَهَذَا القَوْل بِدعَة فَاحْذَرُوهُ، فَمن قَالَ بِشَيْء من هَذِه الْأَقَاوِيل، أَو رَآهَا، أَو صوبها، أَو رضيها، أَو أحبها، فقد خَالف السّنة، وَخرج من الْجَمَاعَة، وَترك الْأَثر، وَقَالَ بالْخِلَافِ، وَدخل فِي الْبِدْعَة، وَزَل عَن الطَّرِيق، وَمَا توفيقنا إِلَّا بِاللَّه.

Showing enmity to some companions while showing alliance to other companions is an innovation, so beware of doing so. Anyone who takes any of the aforementioned beliefs as their ideology, or even approves, loves, or is pleased with them has contradicted the Sunnah, exited from the congregation, left the narrations, stated something contrary, fallen into innovations, and deviated from the path. Our divine aid is only from Allah.

وَقد رَأَيْت لأهل الْبدع والأهواء وَالْخلاف أَسمَاء مشنعة قبيحة، يسمون بهَا أهل

54 It states in the marginalia on Abu Yaʿlā's book *al-Ṭabaqāt*, "It is thought that the individual's name was Abu ʿUbaydah Maʿmar ibn al-Muthannā. However, he was not killed. So Allah knows best."

السّنة، يُرِيدُونَ بذلك عيبهم، والطعن عَلَيْهِم، والوقعية فيهم، والإزراء بهم عِنْد السُّفَهَاء والجهال.

I have found that the people of innovations, desires, and contrarianism use very crude words to describe Ahl al-Sunnah, in order to shame them, disparage them, speak ill of them, and belittle them in front of the foolish people and ignoramuses.

فَأَما المرجئة: فَإِنَّهُم يسمون أهل السّنة شكاكا. وكذبت المرجئة، بل هم بِالشَّكِّ أولى، وبالتكذيب أشبه.

The Murji'ites refer to Ahl al-Sunnah as "doubters." They have lied. Rather. they are more susceptible to falling into doubt and are closer to belying the religion.

وَأما الْقَدَرِيَّة: فَإِنَّهُم يسمون أهل السّنة وَالْإِيمَان مجبرة. وكذبت الْقَدَرِيَّة، بل هم أولى بالتكذيب وَالْخلاف، ألغوا قدر الله عز وَجل عَن خلقه، وَقَالُوا: لَيْسَ لَهُ بِأَهْل تبَارك وَتَعَالَ.

As for the Qadarites, they refer to the people of Sunnah and faith as not believing in freewill. They have lied, rather they are closer to belying and contradicting the truth. They nullified Allah's predestination which He set for His creation. They said that predestination is not befitting of Allah the Exalted.

وَأما الْجَهْمِية: فَإِنَّهُم يسمون أهل السّنة المشبهة. وكذبت الْجَهْمِية أَعدَاء الله، بل هم أولى بِالنِّسْبَةِ والتكذيب، افتروا على الله عز وَجل الْكَذِب، وَقَالُوا الْإِفْك والزور، وَكَفرُوا بقَوْلهمْ.

Jahmites refer to Ahl al-Sunnah as being people who liken Allah to His creation. The Jahmites, the enemies of Allah, have lied. Rather, they are closer to likening Allah to His creation as well as to belying. They have fabricated lies against Allah the Exalted and have made fallacious and false accusations. They have disbelieved due to their views.

وَأما الرافضة: فَإِنَّهُم يسمون أهل السّنة الناصبة. وكذبت، بل هم أولى بِهَذَا

لإنصابهم أَصْحَاب رَسُول الله صلى الله عَلَيْهِ وَسلم بالسب والشتم، وَقَالُوا فيهم بِغَيْر الْحق، ونسبوهم إِلَى غير الْعدْل كفرا وظلما وجرأة على الله تَعَالَى، واستخفافا بِحَق الرَّسُول صلى الله عَلَيْهِ وَسلم، - وَالله - أولى بالتعيير والانتقام مِنْهُم.

As for the Rāfiḍites, they refer to Ahl al-Sunnah as being haters of the family of the Prophet ﷺ. They are liars however, and they are more rightful to this name due to their hate of the companions of Allah's Messenger ﷺ, their cursing and disparaging of them. They claim untrue things about the companions. They ascribe them to injustice out of their disbelief, injustice, and audacity against Allah the Exalted, as well as their lack of respect for the rights of the Messenger ﷺ. They, by Allah, are more worthy of being disparaged and being shown vengeance.

وَأما الْخَوَارِج: فَإِنَّهُم يسمون أهل السّنة وَالْجَمَاعَة مرجئة. وكذبت الْخَوَارِج فِي قَوْلهم، بل هم المرجئة يَزْعُمُونَ أَنهم على إِيمَان وَحق دون النَّاس، وَمن خالفهم كَافِر.

As for the Khārijites, they refer to Ahl al-Sunnah wa 'l-Jamā'ah as being Murji'ites. The Khārijites have lied in their claim, however. They are the true Murji'ites. They claim that they have faith and the truth apart from all others, and that anyone who disagrees with them is a disbeliever.

وَأما أَصْحَاب الرَّأْي: فَإِنَّهُم يسمون أصحاب السّنة ثابتية وحشوية. وَكذب أَصْحَاب الرَّأْي أَعدَاء الله، بل هم الثابتية والحشوية، تركُوا آثَار الرَّسُول وَحَدِيثه، وَقَالُوا بِالرَّأْيِ، وقاسوا الدّين بالاستحسان، وحكموا خلاف الْكتاب وَالسّنة، وهم أَصْحَاب بِدعَة، جهلة، ضلال، وطلاب دنيا بِالْكَذِبِ والبهتان.

As for the people of rational discretion, they refer to the people of the Sunnah by using derogatory words that disparage their constant relaying of aḥadīth. They have lied, however, and are enemies of Allah. They are the ones who constantly fill domains of knowledge with verbosity. They have abandoned the aḥadīth and narrations of the Messenger and have instead resorted to their own intellects. They perform analogies through rational approval of matters, judging in contradiction to the Qur'ān and the Sunnah. They are people of innovation and are ignorant, misguided and seekers of the worldly life through lying and fabricating.

رحم الله عبدا قَالَ بِالْحَقِّ، وَاتبع الْأَثر، وَتمسك بِالسنةِ، واقتدى بالصالحين. اللَّهُمَّ ادحض بَاطِل المرجئة، وأوهن كيد الْقَدَرِيَّة، وأزل دولة الرافضة، وامحق شبه أَصْحَاب الرَّأْي، واكفنا مُؤنَة الخارجية، وَعجل الانتقام من الْجَهْمِية.

May Allah have mercy on a slave who utters the truth, follows narrations, holds fast to the Sunnah, and emulates the righteous. O Allah, invalidate the falsehoods of the Murji'ites, weaken the plots of the Qadarites, obliterate the nation of the Rāfiḍites, crush the doubts of the people of rational discretion, suffice us with the materials [used to fight] the Khārijites, and hastily take vengeance from the Jahmites.

انتهى ما رواه أبو يعلى في (طبقاته) عن الاصطخري، ولم أجد هذه الرسالة في (المناقب) لابن الجوزي، وذكر البرهان ابن مفلح صدرها في (طبقاته) وفي هذه الرسالة حط على بعض الأئمة، ولم يقصد بذلك تنقيصهم، ولكن سبيله في ذلك على ما قاله الحافظ ابن الجوزي:

That is the end of the quotation that Abu Yaʿlā mentioned in his book *al-Ṭabaqāt* as reported by al-Isṭakhrī. I did not find this letter in Ibn al-Jawzī's book *al-Manāqib*, although Burhān al-Dīn ibn Mufliḥ mentioned its beginning in his book *al-Ṭabaqāt*. This letter contains some harsh words against some great scholars. [Al-Imām Aḥmad] did not intend to belittle them, but rather, his reason for doing so was clarified by al-Ḥāfiẓ Ibn al-Jawzī, who said:

وَقد كَانَ الإِمَام أَحْمد لشدَّة تمسكه بِالسنةِ، وَنَهْيه عَن الْبِدْعَة - يتَكَلَّم فِي جمَاعَة من الأخيار إِذا صدر مِنْهُم مَا يُخَالف السّنة، وَكَلَامه فِي ذَلِك مَحْمُول على النَّصِيحَة فِي الدّين، ثمَّ روى عَنهُ أَنه طلب من إِسْمَاعِيل بن إِسْحَاق السراج أَن يسمعهُ كَلَام الْحَارِث المحاسبي، فأحضر إِسْمَاعِيل بشرا، وَأَجْلسهُ فِي مَكَان مَعَ أَصْحَابه بِحَيْثُ يسمعهُ الإِمَام أَحْمد، وَكَانَ ذَلِك لَيْلًا، فَتكلم من نصف اللَّيْل إِلَى الصَّباح، فَلَمَّا انْقَضى كَلَامه، قَالَ لَهُ إِسْمَاعِيل: كَيفَ رَأَيْت هَؤُلَاءِ يَا أَبَا عبد الله؟ فَقَالَ: مَا أعلم أَنِّي رَأَيْت مثل هَؤُلَاءِ فِي عُلُوم الْحَقَائِق، وَلَا سَمِعت مثل كَلَام هَذَا الرجل، وعَلى مَا وصفت من أَحْوَالهم، وَلَا أرى لَك صحبتهم.

Due to al-Imām Aḥmad's intense adherence to the Sunnah and strict opposition to innovation, he spoke about a group of righteous individuals due to a contradiction of the Sunnah emanating from them. His speech should be understood as advice in the religion. It is narrated that he asked Ismāʿīl ibn Isḥāq al-Sarrāj to relay some of what al-Ḥārith al-Muḥāsibī said. Ismāʿīl brought Bishr and sat him with his companions so that al-Imām Aḥmad could hear him. That was at night. He spoke from the middle of the night until morning. When he finished his speech, Ismāʿīl said to him, "What did you think of them O Abā ʿAbdillāh [Aḥmad ibn Ḥanbal]?" He said, "I do not think I have seen anyone resemble these people in their understandings of realities, nor have I heard speech resembling the speech of this man. Despite your description of their circumstances, I do not think you should accompany them."[55]

وروى عَنهُ ابْن الْجَوْزِيّ أَنه قَالَ: من رد حَدِيث رَسُول الله، فَهُوَ على شفا هلكة وَإِنَّمَا كَانَ ينْهَى عَن الرَّأْي ليتوفر النَّاس على النَّقْل.

Ibn al-Jawzī also reported that he said, "Whoever rejects a ḥadīth of Allah's Messenger ﷺ is on the verge of destruction." He would prevent people from engaging in rational discretion in order to have people resort to reported narrations.

وَقَالَ لعُثْمَان بن سعيد: لَا تنظر فِي كتب أبي عبيد، وَلَا فِيمَا وضع إِسْحَاق، وَلا سُفْيَان، وَلَا الشَّافِعِي، وَلَا مَالك، وَعَلَيْك بِالْأَصْلِ.

He once said to ʿUthmān ibn Saʿīd, "Do not look into the books of Abu ʿUbayd, or the authorships of Isḥāq, Sufyān, al-Shāfiʿī, or Mālik. Take from the source."[56]

وَقَالَ إِسْحَاق بن إِبْرَاهِيم بن هانئ: سَأَلته عَن كتب أبي ثَوْر فَقَالَ: كتاب ابتدع فهو بِدعَة، عَلَيْكُم بِالْحَدِيثِ. وَقَالَ لَهُ رجل: اكتب كتب الرَّأْي؟ فَقَالَ: لَا، قَالَ: فَابْن الْمُبَارك قد كتبهَا؟ فَقَالَ: إِن ابْن الْمُبَارك لم ينزل من السَّمَاء، إِنَّمَا أمرنَا أَن نَأْخُذ الْعلم من فَوق.

Isḥāq ibn Ibrahīm ibn Hāniʾ said, "I asked him about the books of Abu

55 [T] *Manāqib al-Imām Aḥmad* (p. 253).
56 [T] Ibid (p. 263).

Thawr, and he replied, 'A new book, therefore an invention. Follow the ḥadīth.' A man said to him, 'Should I transcribe the books of rational discretion?' He responded, 'No, you should not.' The man responded, 'But Ibn al-Mubārak did so.' He responded, 'Ibn al-Mubārak did not descend from the heavens. We were told to take knowledge from above.'"[57]

قَالَ ابْن الْجَوْزِيّ: وَكَانَ ينْهى عَن كِتَابَة كَلَامه، فنظر الله إِلَى حسن قَصده، فنقلت أَلْفَاظه وحفظت، فَقل أَن تقع مَسْأَلَة إِلَّا وَله فِيهَا نَص من الْفُرُوع وَالْأُصُول، وَرُبمَا عدمت فِي تِلْكَ الْمَسْأَلَة نُصُوص الْفُقَهَاء الَّذين صنفوا وجمعوا. فَرضِي الله عَنهُ وأرضاه آمين.

Ibn al-Jawzī said: "Therefore, he would prohibit people from writing what he said. Allah looked at his pure intentions, and caused his words to be transmitted and preserved. It is quite rare to find an issue without also finding commentary [of al-Imām Aḥmad], be it in subsidiary matters or foundational matters that perhaps no other jurists have commented on, although the [other jurists] wrote and gathered [many more words.] May Allah be pleased with him and please him. Allah, accept our supplication."[58]

---

57 [T] Ibid (p. 264).
58 [T] Ibid (p. 261).

العقد الثَّانِي

Chapter Two

فِي السَّبَب الَّذِي لأَجله اخْتَار كثير من كبار الْعلمَاء مَذْهَب الإِمَام أَحْمد على مَذْهَب غَيره

On the Reasons Many Major Scholars Chose the School of Law of al-Imām Aḥmad Over Other Schools of Law

هَذَا العقد لَهُ مدْخل عَظِيم لمن يُرِيد التمذهب بِمذهب أَحْمد، وَمَا ذَلِك إِلَّا لِأَن الدَّاخِل على بَصِيرَة فِي شَيْء أَعقل من الدَّاخِل فِيهِ على غير بَصِيرَة، وَأبْعد عَن التعصب والتقليد الْمَحْض، وكل إِنْسَان يخْتَار لمطعمه وملبسه وحوائجه الضرورية، فلِأن يخْتَار ويحتاط لدينِهِ أولى.

This chapter contains a greatly important introduction for anyone who wishes to embrace the *madhhab* of al-Imām Aḥmad, because someone who embraces and adopts something after learning about it is smarter than the one who does so without insight into its specifics. Also, learning about why to choose al-Imām Aḥmad's school of law [before adopting it] means one is less likely to become a zealot and engage in absolute blind following. Everyone chooses what to eat, wear, and how to fulfill their necessary needs, and so choosing and being cautious in religion is more befitting.

وَلما كَانَ الْمُقَلّد لَا رَأْي لَهُ وَلَا تَرْجِيح، وَإِنَّمَا نصِيبه من الْعلم أَن يَقُول: قَالُوا فقُلْنَا، أثبتنا لَهُ هَذَا العقد ليتزين بِهِ، ونصبنا لَهُ هَذَا السّلم أملا بِأَنَّهُ إِن ترك التعصب الذميم، وَالْجهل الْمركب، ارْتقى قَلِيلا إِلَى دَرَجَات أَوَائِل الْعلم، ولاح لَهُ لمعان من نور الْهدى، فيجره اخْتِيَار الْمَذْهَب إِلَى اخْتِيَار بعض الْفُرُوع بِالدَّلِيلِ والبرهان، فَيكون حِينَئِذٍ من المفلحين، ويتزحزح عَن نَار الْغَفْلَة والتقليد الْأَعْمَى المذموم على لِسَان كل عَاقل لَهُ قلب، أَو أَلْقى السّمع وَهُوَ شَهِيد. وَإِلَيْك بَيَان مَا نوهنا

بِهِ، وأشرنا إِلَيْهِ.

Since a *muqallid* does not have his own individual views nor does he weigh opinions and choose what he thinks is best, his portion of knowledge is to say, "[The scholars] said such-and-such, so we say the same," we have included this chapter in order for [the *muqallids*] to adorn themselves with its contents and we have erected this ladder out of hope that one forsakes dispraised zealousness and compounded ignorance. We hope that one can ascend in the levels of beginner knowledge and so the light of guidance can beam, coming into light, so that if they choose the *madhhab*, they choose to follow its subsidiary matters with evidence and proof, making themselves of the successful, and distancing themselves from the fire of heedlessness and blind-following which is censured by every intellectual with a heart or who pays heed whilst testifying to the truth. Here is the clarification of what we have alluded to and made mention of:

قَالَ الإِمَام الْحَافِظ أَبُو الْفرج عبد الرَّحْمَن ابْن الْجَوْزِيّ، أحد الْمُجْتَهدين فِي مَذْهَب أَحْمد فِي كتاب (المناقب) فِي الْبَاب الثامن وَالتسْعين مِنْهُ:

Al-Imām al-Ḥāfiẓ Abu 'l-Faraj 'Abd al-Raḥmān ibn al-Jawzī, one of the *mujtahid imāms* of the Ḥanbalī Madhhab, said in his book, *Manāqib al-Imām Aḥmad*, in the eighty-ninth chapter:

اعْلَم - وفقك الله - أنه مِمَّا يتَبَيَّن الصَّوَاب فِي الْأُمُور المشتبهة لمن أعرض عَن الْهوى، والتفت عَن العصبية، وَقصد الْحق بطريقه، وَلم ينظر فِي أَسمَاء الرِّجَال وَلَا فِي صيتهم، فَذَلِك الَّذِي ينجلي لَهُ غامض المشتبه. فَأَما من مَال بِهِ الْهوى، فعسير تقويمه.

Know, may Allah grant you aid, that the reasons whereby people reach correct conclusions on contentious matters include shunning one's desires, turning away from zealousness, and seeking the truth through its path, not by [taking views] merely by looking at the names and famousness of some individuals. For such people, difficult, contentious matters become clear. As for one whose desires cause him to divert from the truth, it is difficult for him to be rectified.

وَاعْلَم أننا نَظرنَا فِي أَدِلَّة الشَّرْع، وأصول الْفِقْه، وسبرنا أَحْوَال الْأَعْلَام الْمُجْتَهدين،

فَرَأَيْنَا هَذَا الرجل - يَعْنِي الإِمَام أَحْمد - أوفرهم حظا من تِلْكَ الْعُلُوم، فَإِنَّهُ كَانَ من الحافظين لكتاب الله عز وَجل، وقرأه على أساطين أهل زَمَانه، وَكَانَ لَا يمِيل شَيْئا فِي الْقُرْآن، ويروي قَوْله صلى الله عَلَيْهِ وَسلم **((أنزل الْقُرْآن فخما ففخموه))** وَكَانَ لَا يدغم شَيْئا فِي الْقُرْآن إِلَّا اتخذتم وبابه، كَأبي بكر، ويمد مدا متوسطا.

Know, too, that we have looked at the evidences of the religion, including legal theory, and have explored the circumstances of the great *mujtahid imāms*. Our conclusion was that this man (i.e. al-Imām Aḥmad) had the biggest share in those sciences. He memorised the Book of Allah the Exalted and read it to the great authorities of his time. He did not perform *imālah*[59] when reciting the Qur'ān. He would narrate the ḥadīth of the Prophet ﷺ, **"The Qur'ān was revealed with emphasised letters, so emphasise them."**[60] [61] He also would not merge two letters, except for in two words, the first being *ittakhadhtum*[62] and other similar words, similar to Abu Bakr,[63] and would elongate the letters only moderately.[64]

وَكَانَ رَضِي الله عَنهُ من المصنفين فِي فنون عُلُوم الْقُرْآن، من التَّفْسِير والناسخ والمنسوخ، والمقدم والمؤخر فِي الْقُرْآن، وجوابات الْقُرْآن، والمسند وَهُوَ ثَلَاثُونَ ألف حَدِيث. وَكَانَ يَقُول لِابْنِهِ عبد الله: احتفظ بِهَذَا الْمسند، فَإِنَّهُ سَيكون للنَّاس إِمَامًا. والتاريخ، وَحَدِيث شُعْبَة، والمناسك الْكَبِير وَالصَّغِير، وَأَشْيَاء أخر. وَقَالَ عبد الله: قَرَأَ علينا أبي الْمسند، وَمَا سَمعه مِنْهُ غيرنَا، وَقَالَ لنا: هَذَا كتاب قد جمعته وانتقيته من أَكثر من سَبْع مئة ألف حَدِيث، فَمَا اخْتلف الْمُسلمُونَ فِيهِ

59 [T] *Imālah* means to make the *alif* (ا) letter sound between a *yā* (ي) and an *alif* (ا).
60 [T] The word used was *tafkhim*, which is a term used in *tajwīd* sciences to make the *alif* (ا) letter pronounced slightly closer to a *waw* (و) letter.
61 Reported by Ibn al-Anbārī and al-Ḥākim (2/231). Al-Dhahabī said, "This ḥadīth is weak and contradicts authentic narrations."
62 [T] He would merge the *dhāl* (ذ) and the *tā* (ت), making it sound like, *ittakhattum*.
63 [T] He means here, Abu Bakr ibn 'Ayyāsh. Refer to the editor's comments on *Manāqib al-Imām Aḥmad* (p. 66) printed by Dār Hajar.
64 [T] This refers to the various types of elongation of the three letters of elongation, which are *alif* (ا), *yā* (ي) and *wāw* (و). The long elongation (*al-madd al-mushbi'*) means to elongate the character six times, the moderate elongation (*al-madd al-mutawassiṭ*) means to elongate the character four times, and the short elongation (*madd al-qaṣr*) means to elongate the character to the length of just two.

من حَدِيث رَسُول الله فَارْجِعُوا إِلَيْهِ، فَإِن وجدتموه فِيهِ وَإِلَّا فَلَيْسَ بِحجَّة.

He ﷺ also authored in the various sciences of the Qur'ān, such as exegesis, abrogation, word placement in the Qur'ān, and the Qur'ān's responses to questions. His corpus of ḥadīth, the *Musnad*, contains thirty-thousand aḥadīth. He would say to his son, 'Abdullāh, "Preserve this *Musnad*, because it will be a source of reference (lit. an *imām*) for the people." He also wrote on history, the narrations of Shu'bah, and wrote both a large and a small book on pilgrimage rituals, as well as other authorships. 'Abdullāh said, "My father read his *Musnad* to us, and none but us heard it from him. He said, 'This book is one I have gathered and have chosen these aḥadīth from seven-hundred thousand aḥadīth. If Muslims differ about the aḥadīth of Allah's Messenger ﷺ refer to it. If you find the [differed on] ḥadīth in [the *Musnad*], use it as evidence; otherwise, it is not evidence.'" **[End]**[65]

قَالَ ابْن الْجَوْزِيّ:

Ibn al-Jawzī said:

وَأما النَّقْل، فقد سلم الْكل لَهُ بِانْفِرَادِهِ فِيهِ، بِمَا لم يَنْفَرد بِهِ سواهُ من الْأَئِمَّة، من كَثْرَة محفوظه مِنْهُ، وَمَعْرِفَة صَحِيحه من سقيمه، وفنون علومه، وَقد ثَبت أَنه لَيْسَ فِي الْأَئِمَّة الْأَعْلَام قبله من لَهُ حَظّ فِي الحَدِيث كحظ مَالك، وَمن أَرَادَ مقَام معرفَة أَحْمد فِي ذَلِك من مقَام مَالك، فَلْيَنْظر فرق مَا بَين الْمسند والموطأ.

As for his knowledge of transmitted sciences, all have succumbed to acknowledge that he stands alone, unparalleled by any other masters, due to the amount he memorised, his knowledge of discernment between authentic and inauthentic narrations, and the various categories pertaining to knowledge [of ḥadīth]. It is established that, prior to al-Imām Aḥmad, none had such a large impact on ḥadīth as Mālik. Whoever wants to know Aḥmad's level of knowledge in comparison to Mālik's should look at the disparity between the *Musnad* and the *Muwaṭṭa'*.

وَقَالَ ابْنه عبد الله: سَمِعت أَبَا زرْعَة يَقُول: كَانَ أَحْمد بن حَنْبَل يحفظ ألف ألف حَدِيث (بتكرير الْألف مرَّتَيْنِ) فَقيل لَهُ: وَمَا يدْريك؟ قَالَ: ذاكرته، فَأخذت عَلَيْهِ

65 [T] *Manāqib al-Imām Aḥmad* (p. 261).

الْأَبْوَاب. وَقيل لأبي زرْعَة: من رَأَيْت من الْمَشَايِخ الْمُحدثين أحفظ؟ فَقَالَ: أَحْمد بن حَنْبَل، حزرت كتبه فِي الْيَوْم الَّذِي مَاتَ فِيهِ، فبلغت اثْنَي عشر حملا، وعدلا مَا كَانَ على ظهر كتاب مِنْهَا حَدِيث فلَان وَلَا فِي بَطنه حَدثنَا فلَان، وكل ذَلِك كَانَ يحفظه أَحْمد عَن ظهر قلبه.

His son 'Abdullāh said, "I heard Abu Zur'ah say, 'Aḥmad ibn Ḥanbal memorised one million aḥadīth.' It was said to him, 'How do you know that?' He responded, 'I studied with him, and tested him in the various chapters.' It was said to Abu Zur'ah, 'Which scholar amongst the ḥadīth masters is the greatest in memorisation?' He responded, 'Aḥmad ibn Ḥanbal. His books were appraised on the day he passed away, and they equalled twelve loads. None of them mentioned, 'This is the ḥadīth narrated by so-and-so.' He memorised all of his books by heart.'" **[End]**[66]

قَالَ ابْن الْجَوْزِي: وَقد كَانَ أَحْمد يذكر الْجرْح وَالتَّعْدِيل من حفظه إِذا سُئِلَ عَنهُ، كَمَا يقْرَأ الْفَاتِحَة، وَمن نظر فِي كتاب (الْعِلَل) لأبي بكر الْخلال عرف ذَلِك، وَلم يكن هَذَا لأحد من بَقِيَّة الْأَئِمَّة.

Ibn al-Jawzī said: Aḥmad used to recollect his critiques of narrators from memory when asked. He knew them as well as he knew al-Fātiḥah. Anyone who reads the book called *al-'Ilal* by Abu Bakr al-Khallāl is aware of this fact. None of the other *imāms* had this unique quality.

وَكَذَلِكَ انْفِرَاده فِي علم النَّقْل بفتاوى الصَّحَابَة، وقضاياهم، وإجماعهم، وَاخْتِلَافهمْ، لَا تنَازع فِي ذَلِك.

Likewise, he stood alone in the breadth of his knowledge of transmitted judgements, rulings, consensuses, and disagreements of the companions. None doubt this fact.

وَأما علم الْعَرَبيَّة: فقد قَالَ أَحْمد: كتب من الْعَرَبيَّة أَكثر مِمَّا كتب أَبُو عَمْرو الشَّيْبَانِيّ.

As for his knowledge of the Arabic Language, al-Imām Aḥmad said [of himself], "I studied more of the Arabic Language than Abu 'Amr al-Shaybānī."

66 [T] Ibid (p. 662).

وَأما الْقيَاس: فَلهُ من الاستنباط مَا يطول شَرحه. قَالَ أَبُو الْقَاسِم ابْن الْجبلي: أَكثر النَّاس يظنون أَن أَحْمد إِنَّمَا كَانَ أَكثر ذكره لموْضِع الْمحنة وَلَيْس هُوَ كَذَلِك، كَانَ أَحْمد بن حَنْبَل إِذا سُئِلَ عَن الْمَسْأَلَة كَأَن علم الدُّنْيَا بَين عَيْنَيْهِ.

As far as his knowledge of analogies, he has many instances of deriving [from the texts], the discussion of which would be extremely lengthy. Abu 'l-Qāsim ibn al-Jabbulī said, "Most people think that Aḥmad was mainly well-known due to his inquisition,[67] but that is not true. When Aḥmad ibn Ḥanbal was asked about an issue, it was as though the entirety of knowledge in this world presented itself before his eyes."[68]

وَقَالَ إِبْرَاهِيم الْحَرْبِيّ: أدْركْت ثَلَاثَة لن يرى النَّاس مثلهم أبدا، وتعجز النِّسَاء أَن يلدن مثلهم: رَأَيْت أَبَا عبيد الْقَاسِم بن سَلام، فَمَا مثلته إِلَّا بجبل نفخ فِيهِ روح، وَرَأَيْت بشر بن الْحَارِث، فَمَا شبهته إِلَّا بِرَجُل عجن من قرنه إِلَى قدمه عقلا، وَرَأَيْت أَحْمد بن حَنْبَل فرأيته كَأَن الله جمع لَهُ علم الْأَوَّلين والآخرين من كل صنف، يَقُول مَا شَاءَ، ويمسك مَا شَاءَ.

Ibrāḥīm al-Ḥarbī said, "I met three individuals the likes of whom the world will never see again, and women will be forever incapable of birthing anyone similar to them: I met Abu 'Ubayd al-Qāsim ibn Sallam. The only comparison I can make of him is a mountain that had a soul breathed into it. I also met Bishr ibn al-Ḥārith. The only comparison I can make of him is a man who had intellect kneaded into his person from head to toe. I also met Aḥmad ibn Ḥanbal, and I found that it was as though Allah had gathered all types of knowledge of the previous and later generations into him. He would say what he wanted and would withhold whatever he wanted."

وَقَالَ أَحْمد بن سعيد الرَّازِيّ: مَا رَأَيْت أسود رَأس أحفظ لحَدِيث رَسُول الله، وَلَا أعلم بفقهه ومعانيه من أَحْمد. قَالَ الْخلال: كَانَ أَحْمد قد كتب كتب الرَّأْي، وحفظها، ثمَّ لم يلْتَفت إِلَيْهَا وَكَانَ إِذا تكلم فِي الْفِقْه تكلم كَلَام رجل قد انتقد الْعُلُوم، فَتكلم عَن معرفَة.

---

67 [T] This refers to the inquisition of al-Imām Aḥmad on the issue of the createdness of the Qur'ān.

68 [T] *Manāqib al-Imām Aḥmad* (p. 662).

Aḥmad ibn Sa'īd al-Rāzī said, "I have never met a man with black hair who memorised more of the ḥadīth of Allah's Messenger or had a greater understanding of its legal implications and meanings than Aḥmad." Al-Khallāl said, "Aḥmad transcribed and memorised the books of rational deduction in religion, but then never paid heed to them. When he would speak on the law, he would speak as a man who was a critique in all sciences. As such, he spoke from a place of knowledge."

قَالَ الإِمَام أَبُو الْوَفَاء عَلِيّ بن عقيل الْحَنْبَلِيّ الْبَغْدَادِي: وَمن عَجِيب مَا نَسْمَعهُ عَن هَؤُلَاءِ الْجُهَّال أَنهم يَقُولُونَ: أَحْمد لَيْسَ بفقيه لكنه مُحدث، وَهَذَا غَايَة الْجَهْل، لِأَنَّهُ قد خرج عَنهُ اختيارات بناها على الْأَحَادِيث بِنَاء لَا يعرفهُ أَكْثَرهم، وَخرج عَنهُ من دَقِيق الْفِقْه مَا لَيْسَ نرَاهُ لأحد مِنْهُم، وَانْفَرَدَ بِمَا سلموه لَهُ من الْحِفْظ، وشاركهم وَرُبمَا زَاد على كبارهم.

Al-Imām Abu 'l-Wafā' 'Alī ibn 'Aqīl al-Ḥanbalī al-Baghdādī said, "One of the strangest things we hear ignoramuses say is, 'Aḥmad was not a jurist, he was just a scholar of ḥadīth.' This is utter ignorance, because there are narrations [from al-Imām Aḥmad] where he deduces based on the aḥadīth in ways many of them cannot fathom, and other narrations where he speaks in minute matters of law in a way that we do not see others doing. Further, in the aspect that they agree he is a scholar in, which is memorisation of ḥadīth, he stands alone, while he is at least equal to or greater than their senior scholars [in his knowledge of *fiqh*.]"[69]

ثم ذكر ابن عقيل مسائل دقيقة مما استنطبه الإمام، ثم قال: ومما وجدنا من فقه الإمام أحمد، ودقة علمه، أنه سئل عن رجل نذر أن يطوف بالبيت على أربع؟ قال: يطوف طوافين، ولا يطوف على أربع. فانظروا إِلَى هَذَا الْفِقْه، كَأَنَّهُ نظر إِلَى الْمَشْي على أَربع فَرَآهُ مثله وخروجا عَن صُورَة الْحَيَوَان النَّاطِق إِلَى التَّشْبِيه بالبهائم، فصانه، وصان الْبَيْت وَالْمَسْجِد عَن الشُّهْرَة، وَلم يبطل حكم الْقَضِيَّة فِي الْمَشْي على الْيَدَيْنِ، بل أبدلها بِالرجلَيْنِ اللَّتَين هما آلَة الْمَشْي.

Ibn 'Aqīl then went on to mention some of the minute aspects of law that the *imām* deduced, and then continued to say, "One of the issues where we

69 [T] Quoted in *Manāqib al-Imām Aḥmad* (p. 80).

find the understanding al-Imām Aḥmad had of the law, as well as his precision in his knowledge, is that he was once asked about a man who made an oath to circle the Kaʿbah on all fours. He responded, 'He should circle the Kaʿbah twice and should not circle on all fours.' Look at his understanding. He viewed walking on all fours as humiliating and outside of the nature of human beings, instead resembling livestock. As such, he protected [the man] and protected the Kaʿbah from being disrespected. He did not nullify the ruling of the matter of walking on the two hands, but rather, he substituted the two hands with the two feet, which are the original instruments of walking." **[End]**[70]

ثمَّ ذكر مسَائِل من هَذَا الْقَبِيل، ثمَّ قَالَ، وَلَقَد كَانَت نَوَادِر أَحْمد نَوَادِر بَالِغَة فِي الْفَهم إِلَى أقْصَى طبقَة. قَالَ: وَمن هَذَا فقهه واختياراته، لَا يحسن بالمنصف أَن يغض مِنْهُ فِي هَذَا الْعلم، وَمَا يقْصد هَذَا إِلَّا مُبْتَدع قد تمزق فُؤَاده من خمول كَلمته. وانتشار علم أَحْمد، حَتَّى إِن أَكثر الْعلمَاء يَقُولُونَ: أُصَلِّي أصل أَحْمد، وفرعي فرع فلَان. فحسبك مِمَّن يرضى بِهِ فِي الْأُصُول قدوة.

Then, he continued to mention other similar matters, and said, "The discussions Aḥmad had on rarities show his exemplary level of understanding, reaching the highest level. [...] This is shown in his understanding of the law and his opinions. It is not correct for a just person to detract from [his skill] in the knowledge of jurisprudence. Only an innovator whose heart has been ripped apart by obscurity would take such an endeavour. The knowledge of Aḥmad has become widespread, to the point that most scholars say, 'My foundations are those of Aḥmad, and my views in subsidiary matters are those of so-and-so.' Therefore, those who are pleased with him in the foundations are sufficient for you to follow in their footsteps."

قَالَ ابْن الْجَوْزِي: إِن أَحْمد ضم إِلَى مَا لَدَيْهِ من الْعلم مَا عجز عَنهُ الْقَوْم من الزّهْد فِي الدُّنْيَا، وَقُوَّة الْورع، وَلم ينْقل عَن أحد من الْأَئِمَّة أَنه امْتنع من قبُول أوقاف السلاطين، وهدايا الإخوان كامتناعه، وَلَوْلَا خدش وُجُوه فضائلهم - رَضِي الله عَنْهُم - لذكرنا عَنْهُم مَا قبلوا ورخصوا بِأَخْذِهِ.

Ibn al-Jawzī said: Aḥmad also added to his knowledge something many

70 [T] Ibid.

were unable to do, which is being ascetic and cautious in the worldly life. It was not reported that any of the *imāms* refrained from taking endowments from the rulers and gifts from friends as much as Aḥmad refrained. Had it not been that it would likely disparage them—may Allah be pleased with them—we would have mentioned some of what they accepted and allowed others to accept.

وَقد عقد ابْن الْجَوْزِيّ فِي مناقبه بَابا خَاصّا فِي بَيَان زهده فِي الْمُبَاحَات، ثمَّ إِنَّه ضم إِلَى ذَلِك الصَّبْر على الامتحان، وبذل المهجة فِي نصْرَة الْحق، وَلم يكن ذَلِك لغيره.

Ibn al-Jawzī authored an entire chapter in *al-Manāqib* to mention the asceticism of al-Imām Aḥmad in avoiding things that were lawful. He added [to asceticism:] patience in the midst of tribulations and sacrificing his soul in supporting the truth. That was a unique quality to al-Imām Aḥmad.

وَقد أخرج أَبُو نعيم الْحَافِظ، عَن الشَّافِعِي رَضِي الله عَنهُ أَنه قَالَ:

Al-Ḥāfiẓ Abu Nu'aym reported that al-Shāfi'ī ﷺ said:

قَالَ لي مُحَمَّد بن الْحسن: صاحبنا أعلم أم صَاحبكُم؟ قلت: تُرِيدُ المكابرة أم الْإِنْصَاف؟ قَالَ: بل الْإِنْصَاف، فَقلت لَهُ: فَمَا الْحجَّة عنْدكُمْ، قَالَ الْكتاب وَالسّنة وَالْإِجْمَاع وَالْقِيَاس، قَالَ: قلت: أنْشدك الله، صاحبنا أعلم بِكِتَاب الله أم صَاحبكُم، فَقَالَ، إِذا أنشدتني بِاللَّه فصاحبكم، قلت: فصاحبنا أعلم بِسنة رَسُول الله صلى الله عَلَيْهِ وَسلم أم صَاحبكُم؟ قَالَ صَاحبكُم، قلت: فصاحبكم أعلم بأقاويل أَصْحَاب رَسُول الله أم صَاحبكُم؟ قَالَ: صَاحبكُم، قلت: فَبَقيَ شَيْء غير الْقيَاس؟ قَالَ: لَا، قلت: فَنحْن ندعي الْقيَاس أَكثر مِمَّا تدعُونَهُ، وَإِنَّمَا يُقَاس على الْأُصُول فيعرف الْقيَاس، قَالَ: وَيُرِيد بصاحبكم مَالِكًا.

Muḥammad ibn al-Ḥasan said to me, "Is our fellow more knowledgeable, or is yours?" I responded, "Do you wish to engage in stubborn contentiousness or would you like an impartial answer?" He replied, "I wish to have an impartial answer." I replied, "What does evidence consist of to you?" He replied, "The Qur'ān, the Sunnah, consensus, and analogy." I said, "I ask you by Allah, is our fellow more knowledgeable in the Book of Allah, or is yours?' He replied, "Since you asked me by Allah, I must admit that it is your fellow." I said, "Is our fellow more knowledgeable about the Sunnah of Allah's Messenger ﷺ or is your fellow?" He said, "Your fellow." I said, "Is our fellow more knowledgeable about the views of the companions of Allah's Messenger or is your fellow?" He said, "Your fellow is." I said, "So is there anything remaining except for analogy?" He replied, "No, there is nothing else." I said, "We have more of a right to claim knowledge in analogies, because analogy must be based on a text to deduce from." [Abu Nuʿaym] said, "By, 'Your fellow,' he was referring to Mālik."[71]

قَالَ ابْن الْجَوْزِي: فقد كفانا الشَّافِعِي رَضِي الله عَنهُ بِهَذِهِ الْحِكَايَة المناظرة لأَصْحَاب أبي حنيفَة، وَقد عرف فضل صاحبنا على مَالك، فَإِنَّهُ حصل مَا حصله مَالك، وَزَاد عَلَيْهِ كثيرا، وَقد ذكرنَا شاهد هَذَا بِاعْتِبَار الْمسند مَعَ الْمُوَطَّأ.

Ibn al-Jawzī said, "Al-Shāfiʿī ﷺ has provided sufficient questioning in this short debate with a student of Abu Ḥanīfah. By his debate, we now know that our fellow [al-Imām Aḥmad] is superior to Mālik, since he had everything Mālik had and more. We have mentioned an example of this when we compared *al-Musnad* to *al-Muwaṭṭa*."

وَقد كَانَ الشَّافِعِي عَالما بفنون الْعُلُوم، إِلَّا أَنه سلم لِأَحْمَد علم النَّقْل الَّذِي عَلَيْهِ مدَار الْفِقْه.

Al-Shāfiʿī was versed in all sciences. However, he admitted that Aḥmad was more knowledgeable in narrations, which is the basis of jurisprudence.

وَقد روى ابْن الْجَوْزِيّ عَن عبد الله بن أَحْمد قَالَ: سَمِعت أبي يَقُول: قَالَ لي الشَّافِعِي: أَنْتُم أعلم بِالْحَدِيثِ منا، فَإِذا صَحَّ الحَدِيث، فَقولُوا لنا حَتَّى نَذْهَب إِلَيْهِ. وَأخرج هَذِه الْحِكَايَة الطَّبَرَانِيّ، وَأَبُو نعيم الْحَافِظ.

Ibn al-Jawzī reported that ʿAbdullāh ibn Aḥmad said, "I heard my father say, 'Al-Shāfiʿī said to me, 'You are more knowledgeable about ḥadīth than I am. If you are aware that a ḥadīth is authentic, tell me, so that I can take that ḥadīth and espouse it.'" This story was reported by al-Ṭabarānī and al-Ḥāfiẓ Abu Nuʿaym.

71 [T] Ibid (p. 663).

وروى الطَّبَرَانِي أَن أَحْمد كَانَ يَقُول: اسْتَفَادَ منا الشَّافِعِي مَا لم نستفد مِنْهُ. وَأخرج الْحَافِظ ابْن عَسَاكِر عَن الْحسن بن الرّبيع أَنه قَالَ: أَحْمد إِمَام الدُّنْيَا، وَقَالَ: لَوْلَا أَحْمد لأحدثوا فِي الدّين. وَقَالَ: إِن لِأَحْمَد أعظم منَّة على جَمِيع الْمُسلمين، وَحق على كل مُسلم أَن يسْتَغْفر لَهُ.

Further, al-Ṭabarānī reported that Aḥmad said, "Al-Shāfiʿī benefited more from me than I did from him."[72] Al-Ḥāfiẓ Ibn ʿAsākir reported that al-Ḥasan ibn al-Rabīʿ said, "Aḥmad is the *imām* of the world," and also, "Had it not been for Aḥmad, people would have innovated in the religion." In another instance, he said, "Aḥmad has the greatest favour on all Muslims and his right on all Muslims is that they ask Allah the Exalted to forgive him."

قلت: وَقد ذكرنَا كثيرا من مناقبه فِي كتابنَا (تَهْذِيب تَارِيخ ابْن عَسَاكِر) قَالَ ابْن الْجَوْزِيّ:

I have mentioned many of his virtues in my book *Tahdhīb Tārīkh Ibn ʿAsākir*. Ibn al-Jawzī said:

قلت: فَهَذَا بَيَان طَرِيق الْمُجْتَهدين من أَصْحَاب أَحْمد، لقُوَّة علمه، وفضله الَّذِي حث على اتِّبَاعه عَامَّة المتبعين، يَعْنِي - بِفَتْح الْبَاء الْمُوَحدَة - فَأَما الْمُجْتَهد من أَصْحَابه، فَإِنَّهُ تتبع دَلِيله من غير تَقْلِيد لَهُ، وَلِهَذَا يمِيل إِلَى إِحْدَى الرِّوَايَتَيْنِ عَنهُ دون الْأُخْرَى، وَرُبمَا اخْتَار مَا لَيْسَ فِي الْمَذْهَب أصلا، لِأَنَّهُ تَابع للدليل، وَإِنَّمَا ينْسب هَذَا إِلَى مذْهبه لميله لعُمُوم أَقْوَاله.

This clarifies the ways of the *mujtahid* scholars who were also students of Aḥmad. They were his students due to the strength of his knowledge and his virtues, which caused many to urge the masses of laypeople to follow his rulings. As for the *mujtahid imāms* who also were his students, they would follow evidences, without blindly following him, which is why sometimes, if Aḥmad has two views on an issue [the *mujtahid* student of Aḥmad] would incline to one view in favour of another. Sometimes, they choose views that were not a part of his body of judicial rulings, but would follow the evidence and ascribe the opinion to his school of law due to the general statements [al-Imām Aḥmad made about following evidences].

72 [T] Ibid (p. 664).

ثم قَالَ: فَإِن قَالَ أَصْحَاب أبي حنيفَة: إِن أَبَا حنيفَة قد لَقِي الصَّحَابَة فَالْجَوَاب من وَجْهَيْن: أَحدهمَا: أن الدَّارَقُطْنِيّ قَالَ: لم يلق أَبُو حنيفَة أحدا من الصَّحَابَة. وَقَالَ أَبُو بكر الْخَطِيب: رأى أنس بن مَالك. وَالثَّانِي: أن سعيد بن الْمسيب وَغيره من التَّابِعين لقوا الصَّحَابَة، فَإِن كَانَ الْفضل باللقي فَلم لم يقدموهم عَلَيْهِ؟

If disciples of Abu Ḥanīfah say, "Abu Ḥanīfah met some of the companions." The answer is twofold: (i) Al-Dāraquṭnī states that Abu Ḥanīfah did not meet any of the companions. However, Abu Bakr al-Khaṭīb said, "He saw Anas ibn Mālik." (ii) Sa'īd ibn al-Musayyib and other Tābi'īn also met the companions. If virtue was garnered by simply meeting the companions, why do they not prefer them over him?

وَإِن قَالَ أَصْحَاب مَالك: إِن مَالِكًا لَقِي التَّابِعين، قُلْنَا: هَذَا يُوجب تَقْدِيم التَّابِعين لرؤيتهم الصَّحَابَة.

If the disciples of Mālik state, "Mālik met the Tābi'īn." The response is, this necessitates that we prefer the Tābi'īn, as they saw the companions.

وَإِن قَالَ الشَّافِعِيَّة: إِن الشَّافِعِي نسبه أقرب إِلَى رَسُول الله صلى الله عَلَيْهِ وَسلم من غَيره قُلْنَا: النّسَب لَا يُوجب التَّقْدِيم فِي الْعلم، فَإِن عُمُوم عُلَمَاء التابعين كالْحسن وَابْن سِيرِين وَعَطَاء وَطَاوُوس وَعِكْرِمَة وَمَكْحُول وَغيرهم كَانُوا من الموَالِي، وتقدموا على خلق كثير من أهل الشّرف بِالنّسَبِ، لِأَن تقدمهم كَانَ بِكَثْرَة الْعلم لَا بِقرب النّسَب. وَقد أَخذ النَّاس بقول ابْن مَسْعُود وَزيد مَا لم يَأْخُذُوا بقول ابْن عَبَّاس. قلت: وَهَذَا بَاب وَاسع جدا.

If the Shāfi'īs state, "Al-Shāfi'ī is closer in lineage to Allah's Messenger ﷺ than others." The response is that lineage does not necessitate superiority in knowledge. The majority of the scholars of the Tābi'īn, such as al-Ḥasan, Ibn Sīrīn, 'Aṭā', Ṭāwūs, 'Ikrimah, Makḥūl and others were freed slaves, and they were superior to many people of honourable lineages, as their superiority was based on their knowledge, not their lineage. People have taken the views of Ibn Mas'ūd and Zayd at times in issues where Ibn 'Abbās has a differing view. I say: This is a very vast subject.

وَذكر ابْن الْجَوْزِيّ من هَذَا كثيرا ثمَّ قَالَ: هَذَا قدر الِانْتِصَار لاختيارنا لمَذْهَب أَحْمد. وَرَحْمَة الله على الْكل، وَلِلنَّاسِ فِيمَا يعشقون مَذَاهِب.

Ibn al-Jawzī mentioned much of this, and then he said: This is the summation of why we chose the school of law of al-Imām Aḥmad. May Allah have mercy on all. People have ways of thought in what they love, as well.

وَكَانَ الإِمَام أَبُو الْوَفَاء عَليّ بن عقيل الْبَغْدَادِيّ يَقُول:

Al-Imām Abu 'l-Wafa' 'Alī ibn 'Aqīl al-Baghdādī once said:

هَذَا الْمَذْهَب - يَعْنِي مَذْهَب أَحْمد - إِنَّمَا ظلمه أَصْحَابه، لِأَن أَصْحَاب أبي حنيفَة وَالشَّافِعِيّ، إِذا برع أحد مِنْهُم فِي الْعلم تولى الْقَضَاء وَغَيره من الولايات، فَكَانَت الْولَايَة سَببا لتدريسه واشتغاله بِالْعلمِ. فَأَما أَصْحَاب أَحْمد: فَإِنَّهُ قل فيهم من يعلم بِطرف من الْعلم إِلَّا ويخرجه ذَلِك إِلَى التَّعَبُّد والتزهد لغَلَبَة الْخَيْر على الْقَوْم، فينقطعون عَن التشاغل بِالْعلمِ. انْتهى.

This school of law (i.e. that of Aḥmad) was wronged by its adherents. The students of Abu Ḥanīfah and al-Shāfi'ī would, when distinguishing themselves with their knowledge, take up positions as judges and other state vacancies, which were causes for them to teach and busy themselves with knowledge. As for the disciples of Aḥmad, whenever one of them learned some knowledge, it would cause them to worship more and become ascetics due to the general goodness that was a distinguishing characteristic of theirs. At that, they would stop busying themselves with knowledge.[73] **[End.]**

وَهَذَا غَايَة مَا وَقع اختيارنا عَلَيْهِ من القَوْل فِي هَذَا الْمَوْضُوع، ليعلم المتبع لمَذْهَب مَا لأي معنى اتبعهُ، ولأي برهَان اخْتَارَهُ دون غَيره، فَلَا يكون مُتبعا للهوى والتقليد الْأَعْمَى الضار، والتعصب الذميم. وَالله الْمُسْتَعَان.

This is all we thought to mention on this topic, so that a person that undertakes adhering to a school of law understands why they did so and based on which evidences they chose one school over another. This is so that they do not follow their desires or engage in harmful blind following and distasteful zealousness. Divine aid is sought from Allah.

73 [T] *Manāqib al-Imām Aḥmad* (p. 673).

تَنْبِيه: لَا يذهب بك الْوَهم مِمَّا قدمنَا إِلَى أَن الَّذين اخْتَارُوا مَذْهَب أَحْمد، وقدموه على غَيره من الْأَئِمَّة - وهم من كبار أَصْحَابه - أَنهم اخْتَارُوا تَقْلِيده على تَقْلِيد غَيره فِي الْفُرُوع، فَإِن مثل هَؤُلَاءِ يَأْبَى ذَلِك مسلكهم فِي كتبهمْ ومصنفاتهم، بل المُرَاد بِاخْتِيَار مذْهبه، إِنَّمَا هُوَ السلوك على طَرِيقَة أُصُوله فِي استنباط الْأَحْكَام، وَإِن شِئْت قل: السلوك فِي طَرِيق الِاجْتِهَاد مسلكه دون مَسْلَك غَيره على الطَّرِيقَة الَّتِي سنبينها فِيمَا بعد إِن شَاءَ الله.

One more thing to note is that one should not mistakenly assume, based on the previous quotations, that the great scholars and disciples of al-Imām Aḥmad chose the school of Aḥmad and preferred him as their *imām* over others only to blindly follow him in subsidiary matters. Such great scholars are far above such a concept, as shown by their books and authorships. The meaning is that they chose his legal theories in deducing rulings. In other words, they treaded his path of performing *ijtihād* in favour of other paths. The way they did so will be clarified in a following chapter.

وَأما التَّقْلِيد فِي الْفُرُوع: فَإِنَّهُ يترفع عَنهُ كل من لَهُ ذكاء وفطنة، وقدرة على تأليف الدَّلِيل، ومعرفته، وَمَا التَّقْلِيد إِلَّا للضعفاء الجامدين، الَّذين لَا يفرقون بَين الغث والسمين. وَكَيف يظنّ بِمثل أَحْمد بن جَعْفَر ابْن الْمُنَادِي وَأبي بكر النجاد وَمُحَمّد بن الْحسن أَبي بكر الْآجُرِيّ وَالْحسن بن حَامِد وَالْقَاضِي أبي يعلى مُحَمَّد بن الْحُسَيْن بن مُحَمَّد بن خلف ابن الفراء وَأبي الْوَفَاء عَليّ بن عقيل الْبَغْدَادِيّ وَأبي الْخطاب مَحْفُوظ بن أَحْمد الكلوذاني وَعلي بن عبيد الله الزاغواني وموفق الدّين عبد الله بن قدامَة الْمَقْدِسِي وَشيخ الْإِسْلَام الْمجد ابْن تَيْمِية وحفيده الإِمَام تَقِيّ الدّين أَحْمد بن عبد الْحَلِيم بن عبد السَّلَام ابن تَيْمِية والمحقق شمس الدّين مُحَمَّد ابن الْقيم وَغَيرهم: أَنهم مقلدون فِي الْفُرُوع، وكتبهم الممتلئة بالأدلة طبقت الْآفَاق، ومداركهم ومسالكهم سَارَتْ بمدحها الرُّكْبَان، وكتبهم مَلَأت قلب كل منصف من الْإِيمَان والإيقان. فتنبه أَيهَا الألمعي، وَلَا تكن من المقلدين الغافلين.

As for blindly following in subsidiary matters, everyone with intelligence, intellect, and the ability to understand and know the evidences is far above such a thing. Blind following is for the weak minded and inflexible person who cannot differentiate between the meagre and the fleshy. How can one think that people such as Aḥmad ibn Jaʿfar ibn al-Munādī, Abu Bakr al-Najjād, Muḥammad ibn al-Ḥasan Abu Bakr al-Ājurrī, al-Ḥasan ibn Ḥāmid, al-Qāḍī Abu Yaʿlā Muḥammad ibn al-Ḥusayn ibn Muḥammad ibn Khalaf ibn al-Farrā, Abu ʿl-Wafā ʿAlī ibn ʿAqīl al-Baghdādī, Abu ʿl-Khaṭṭāb Maḥfūẓ ibn Aḥmad al-Kalwadhānī, ʿAlī ibn ʿUbayd al-Zāghūnī, Muwaffaq al-Dīn ʿAbdullāh ibn Qudāmah al-Maqdisī, Shaykh al-Islam al-Majd ibn Taymiyyah, as well as his grandson al-Imām Taqī al-Dīn Aḥmad ibn ʿAbd al-Ḥalīm ibn ʿAbd al-Salām ibn Taymiyyah, the great researcher Shams al-Dīn Muḥammad ibn al-Qayyim, and others, were blindly following in the subsidiary matters, when their books, which are filled with evidences, filled the horizon, and their ways and knowledge have been praised by all, filling the hearts of all impartial people with faith and certainty? Be very aware, then, you brilliant individual, and do not be a heedless blind follower.[74]

---

74 [T] In addition to the compelling and interesting things mentioned by al-Shaykh ʿAbd al-Qādir ibn Badrān, there is another quotation from Shaykh al-Islam Taqī al-Dīn Aḥmad ibn Taymiyyah who said, after surveying the views of the scholars on an issue in his *Majmūʿ al-Fatāwā* (25/232-233):

> This is the view of Isḥāq ibn Rāhawayh, a contemporary of Aḥmad ibn Ḥanbal who was of the same way of thought of Aḥmad, both in its legal theories and its subsidiary deductions. Many times, their views on issues are exactly the same. Al-Kawsaj asked questions of Aḥmad, as well as of Isḥāq, and Harb al-Kirmānī asked questions of both Aḥmad and Isḥāq, as did others. This is the reason al-Tirmidhī couples the views of Aḥmad with those of Isḥāq, as he reported their views from the questions of al-Kawsaj. Likewise, Abu Zurʿah, Abu Ḥātim, Ibn Qutaybah, and other pious predecessors who were scholars of Sunnah and ḥadīth used to learn jurisprudence in accordance with the *madhhab* of Aḥmad and Isḥāq, preferring their views over those of others. Further, the scholars of ḥadīth, such as al-Bukhārī, Muslim, al-Tirmidhī, al-Nasāʾī, and others, were also followers of [Aḥmad and Isḥāq], and would learn knowledge of jurisprudence from them. Dāwūd was also a student of Isḥāq.
>
> When Aḥmad ibn Ḥanbal would be asked about Isḥāq, he would respond, "Am I to be asked about Isḥāq? Nay, Isḥāq should be asked about me." Further, al-Shāfiʿī, Aḥmad ibn Ḥanbal, Isḥāq, Abu ʿUbayd, Abu Thawr, Muḥammad ibn Nasr al-Marwazī, Dāwūd ibn ʿAlī, as well as others, were all jurists who understood ḥadīth. May Allah have mercy on them all.

العقد الثَّالِث
Chapter Three

فِي ذكر أُصُول مذْهبه فِي استنباط الْفُرُوع وَبَيَان طَرِيقَته فِي ذَلِك
On the Fundamentals and Methods of His Legal Theory of Deriving Subsidiary Rulings

أما طَرِيقَة الإِمَام فِي الْأُصُول الْفِقْهِيَّة: فقد كَانَت طَرِيقَة الصَّحَابَة وَالتَّابِعِينَ لَهُم بِإِحْسَان، لَا يتَعَدى طريقتهم، وَلَا يتجاوزها إِلَى غَيرهَا، كَمَا هِيَ عَادَته فِي مسالكه فِي التَّوْحِيد، والفتيا فِي الْفِقْه، وَفِي جَمِيع حركاته وسكناته، وكما تقدم لَك آنِفا مَا كَانَ عَلَيْهِ من الِاعْتِقَاد، وكما سنبينه من مسالكه فِي الِاجْتِهَاد.

The methods of the *imām* in his fundamental legal theories were those of the companions and those who followed them in righteousness. He would never overstep their ways in favour of other methods. This was his habit in matters pertaining to faith, law, and even his behavior in his movements and moments of stillness. It has been previously proven that he followed [the companions] in creed, but it remains to be seen how he followed them in using deductive interpretation to derive law.

وَحَيْثُ علمت ذَلِك فَاعْلَم أَنه قد صرح المجتهدون من أهل مذْهبه التَّابِعين لَهُ فِي الْأُصُول أَن فتاوَاهُ - رَضِي الله عَنهُ - مَبْنِيَّة على خَمْسَة أصُول.

As that is now understood, one must understand that the *mujtahid imāms* who followed his *madhhab*, and who, by extension, also followed his legal theories, explicitly stated that his rulings were based on five foundational evidences:

الأَصْل الأول النَّص: كَانَ إِذا وجد النَّص، أفتى بِمُوجبِه، وَلم يلْتَفت إِلَى مَا خَالفه، لَا إِلَى من خَالفه كَائِنا من كَانَ.

The First Evidence: Divine Texts: Whenever he found textual evidence supporting a view, he would give a judgement predicated on that text, disregarding all other sources of law and the individuals who may happen to embrace other views, regardless who they were.

وَلِهَذَا لم يلْتفت إِلَى خلاف عمر فِي المبتوتة، لحَدِيث فَاطِمَة بنت قيس.

Due to this factor, he did not pay heed to the difference of opinion expressed by ʿUmar on the topic of whether a divorced woman has the right to financial support after being divorced three times, because he followed the ḥadīth of Fāṭimah bint Qays,[75] [wherein she stated that Allah's Messenger ﷺ did not designate any provision of a house or alimony].

وَلَا إِلَى خِلَافه فِي التَّيَمُّم للْجنب، لحَدِيث عمار بن يَاسر الْمُصَرّح بِصِحَّة تيَمّم الْجنب.

He also did not take his differing view on the topic of dry ablution for major ritual impurity into consideration, because he was aware of the ḥadīth of ʿAmmār ibn Yāsir which explicitly validates use of dry ablution for a person in a state of major ritual impurity.

وَكَذَلِكَ لم يلْتفت إِلَى قَول عَليّ وَعُثْمَان وَطَلْحَة وَأبي أَيُّوب وَأبي بن كَعْب فِي ترك الْغسْل من الإكسال، لصِحَّة حَدِيث عَائِشَة أَنَّهَا فعلته هِيَ وَرَسُول الله صلى الله عَلَيْهِ وَسلم فاغتسلا، إِلَى غير ذَلِك مِمَّا هُوَ كثير جدا.

Further, he did not take into consideration the views of ʿAlī, ʿUthmān, Ṭalḥah, Abu Ayyūb, or Ubayy ibn Kaʿb on the topic of whether a man who had intercourse with his wife must perform a bath if he did not ejaculate, and his evidence was the authentic ḥadīth of ʿĀ'ishah who reported that it happened with her and Allah's Messenger ﷺ, and that they both bathed afterwards.[76] There are many other examples of this concept.

وَلم يكن يقدم على الحَدِيث الصَّحِيح عملا، وَلَا رَأيا، وَلَا قِيَاسا، وَلَا قَول صَاحب، وَلَا عدم علمه بالمخالف الَّذِي يُسَمِّيه كثير من النَّاس بِالْإِجْمَاع،

75 Reported by Muslim (1480) (46) in the Book of Divorce.
76 Reported by al-Bukhārī (1/375, 376) and Muslim (368) and (112).

ويقدمونه على الحَدِيث الصَّحِيح. وَقَالَ الإِمَام ابْن الْقيم وَغَيره من عُلَمَاء الْأُصُول: قد كذب أَحْمد من ادّعى هَذَا الْإِجْمَاع، وَلم يسغ تَقْدِيمه على الحَدِيث الثَّابِت، وَكَذَلِكَ الشَّافِعِي أَيْضا نَص فِي رِسَالَته الجديدة على أَن مَا لم يعلم فِيهِ خلاف لَا يُقَال لَهُ: إِجْمَاع، وَلَفظة: مَا لَا يعلم فِيهِ خلاف فَلَيْسَ إِجْمَاعًا.

[Al-Imām Aḥmad] never gave priority to anything over the authentic ḥadīth, irrespective if it was a common practice, deductive reasoning, analogy, view of the companions, or lack of awareness that someone differed—which is termed by many as the concept of "consensus" and which they place above authentic aḥadīth. Al-Imām Ibn al-Qayyim, and other scholars of legal theory, have stated that Aḥmad belies those who claim consensus on matters, and also does not allow for anyone to give preference to it over the authentic ḥadīth. Likewise, al-Shāfiʿī, in his *Risālah*[77]—which outlines his later way of thought—states that if someone does not know of differences of opinion, they may not claim consensus on the matter. He said, "Lack of awareness of differing views does not constitute consensus."

وَقَالَ عبد الله ابْن الإِمَام أَحْمد:

ʿAbdullāh ibn al-Imām Aḥmad said:

سَمِعت أبي يَقُول: مَا يَدعِي فِيهِ الرجل الْإِجْمَاع، فَهُوَ كذب، وَمن ادّعى الْإِجْمَاع، فَهُوَ كَاذِب، لَعَلَّ النَّاس اخْتلفُوا، مَا يدريه وَلم ينْتَه إِلَيْهِ؟ فَلْيقل: لَا نعلم النَّاس اخْتلفُوا. هَذِه دَعْوَى بشر المريسي وَالأَصَم، وَلكنه يَقُول: لَا نعلم النَّاس اخْتلفُوا، أَو لم يبلغنِي ذَلِك. هَذَا لَفظه.

I heard my father say, "Whenever a person claims consensus on a matter, it is a lie, and whoever claims consensus has lied. Perhaps people have differed and he was not aware of it or it did not reach him. He should instead say, 'We do not know if any scholars differed on this matter.' This is the claim of Bishr al-Marrīsī and al-Aṣam. However, one should say, 'I am unaware of scholars differing on this matter,' or, 'I was not informed of differences of opinion.'"[78]

---

77 [T] In reality this discussion occurred in a different book, also authored by al-Shāfiʿī, known as *Jimaʿ al-ʿIlm*.

78 [T] *Masāʾil al-Imām Aḥmad*, the version of ʿAbdullāh ibn Aḥmad (p. 439).

ونصوص رَسُول الله أجل عِنْد الإِمَام أَحْمد، وَسَائِر أَئِمَّة الحَدِيث من أَن يقدموا عَلَيْهَا توهم إِجْمَاع مضمونه عدم الْعلم بالمخالف، وَلَو سَاغ، لتعطلت النُّصُوص، وساغ لكل من لم يعلم مُخَالفا فِي حكم مَسْأَلَة، أَن يقدم جَهله بالمخالف على النُّصُوص، فَهَذَا هُوَ الَّذِي أنكرهُ الإِمَام أَحْمد وَالشَّافِعِيّ من دَعْوَى الْإِجْمَاع، لَا مَا يَظُنّهُ بعض النَّاس أَنه استبعاد لوُجُوده.

The texts of Allah's Messenger ﷺ were honoured by al-Imām Aḥmad and all ḥadīth masters, and as such, they would not have given preference to an alleged consensus over a ḥadīth, when the alleged consensus was based on lack of awareness of contrary views on the issue. If this were justifiable, it would cancel the texts and license every individual who lacked knowledge of variance in a matter's ruling to give precedence to his ignorance of a variance over the texts. This is the exact concept rejected by al-Imām Aḥmad and al-Shāfiʿī when they discussed [dubious] claims to consensus. However, people mistakenly think that [Aḥmad and al-Shāfiʿī] were rejecting the concept of consensus altogether.

الأَصْل الثَّانِي من أصُول فتاوى الإِمَام أَحْمد: مَا أفتى بِهِ الصَّحَابَة، فَكَانَ رَضِي الله عَنهُ إِذا وجد لبَعْضِهِم فَتْوَى لَا يعرف لَهُ مُخَالف مِنْهُم فِيهَا لم يتجاوزها إِلَى غَيرهَا وَلم يقل: إِن ذَلِك إِجْمَاع، بل من ورعه فِي الْعبارَة يَقُول: لَا أعلم شَيْئا يَدْفَعهُ، أَو نَحْو هَذَا.

The Second Evidence: Rulings of the Companions: This is the second evidence used by al-Imām Aḥmad when giving rulings. If Aḥmad ﷺ was aware of a *fatwā* of one or some of the companions, and did not know of any conflicting views of other companions, he would not bypass their views in favour of anything else. He would not claim consensus, but, out of carefulness in wording, he would say, "I am not aware of anything that would falsify this view," or some similar phrase.

وَكَانَ إِذا وجد هَذَا النَّوْع عَن الصَّحَابَة لم يقدم عَلَيْهِ عملا، وَلَا رَأيا، وَلَا قِيَاسا، فَكَانَت فَتَاوَاهُ لذَلِك من تأملها، وَتَأمل فَتَاوَى الصَّحَابَة؛ رأى مُطَابقَة كل مِنْهُمَا على الْأُخْرَى، وَرَأى الْجَمِيع كَأَنَّهَا تخرج من مشكاة وَاحِدَة، حَتَّى إِن الصَّحَابَة

إذا اخْتلفُوا على قَوْلَيْنِ جَاءَ عَنهُ فِي الْمَسْأَلَة رِوَايَتَانِ، وَكَانَ تحريه لفتاوى الصَّحَابَة كتحري أَصْحَابه لفتاواه ونصوصه، بل أعظم.

Further, if he found this type of evidence reported from some of the companions, he would not prefer customary actions, rational views, or analogies. Because of this fact, if one were to juxtapose the rulings of Aḥmad with those of the companions, they would find them in harmony and consistent with one another, as though they emanate from a single niche. This is to the extent that where the companions differed, resulting in two distinct views, Aḥmad would have two reported responses on the issue. He was extremely keen in his inquiries into and search of the rulings of the companions, even more so than his students were keen on researching his rulings and texts.

حَتَّى إِنَّه ليقدم فتاواهم على الحَدِيث الْمُرْسل. قَالَ إِسْحَاق بن إِبْرَاهِيم بن هانئ فِي (مسَائِله) قلت لأبي عبد الله: حَدِيث عَن رَسُول الله مُرْسل بِرِجَال ثَبت أحب إِلَيْك، أَو حَدِيث عَن الصَّحَابَة وَالتَّابِعِينَ مُتَّصِل بِرِجَال ثَبت؟ قَالَ أَبُو عبد الله - رَحمَه الله -: عَن الصَّحَابَة أعجب إِلَى، وَمن ثمَّ صَارَت فتَاوَاهُ إِمَامًا وقدوة لأهل السّنة على اخْتِلَاف طبقاتهم، حَتَّى إِن الْمُخَالفين لمذهبه فِي الِاجْتِهَاد، والمقلدين لغيره، ليعظمون نصوصه وفتاواه، ويعرفون لَهَا حَقّهَا وقربها من النُّصُوص وفتاوى الصَّحَابَة.

This was so much so that he would give preference to their edicts over *mursal* narrations. Isḥāq ibn Ibrāḥīm ibn Hāni' said, in his *Masā'il*, "I said to Abu 'Abdullāh, 'Which is more preferred to you: (i) a *mursal* Prophetic ḥadīth with trustworthy narrators, or (ii) a report from the companions and followers which has a connected chain of trustworthy narrators?' Abu 'Abdullāh replied, 'The statement of the companion, in that case, would be preferable to me.'"[79] Because of this attitude, his edicts became sources of knowledge and leadership to the people of Sunnah, irrespective of generation or scholarly levels. Even those who differ with his school of law in their *ijtihād* or blindly follow someone else respect his rulings and texts and give them their due respect, acknowledging their closeness to the texts and rulings of the companions.

79 [T] *Masā'il al-Imām Aḥmad*, the version of Isḥāq ibn Ibrāḥīm ibn Hāni' (2/165).

الأَصْل الثَّالِث من أُصُوله: إِذا اخْتلف الصَّحَابَة، تخير من أَقْوَالهم مَا كَانَ أقربها إِلَى الْكتاب وَالسّنة، وَلم يخرج عَن أَقْوَالهم. فَإِن لم يتَبَيَّن لَهُ مُوَافقَة أحد الْأَقْوَال حكى الْخلاف فِيهَا، وَلم يجْزم بقول. قَالَ إِسْحَاق بن إِبْرَاهِيم بن هانئ فِي (مسَائِله):

The Third Evidence: When the companions differed, he would choose whichever of their views he felt was closer to the Qur'ān and Sunnah, but would not espouse a view that was not held by one of the companions. If he was unsure of which opinion of the companions [was closer to the Sunnah], he would say, "This issue is one of difference of opinion," and would not definitively state his view. Isḥāq ibn Ibrāḥīm ibn Hāni' said in his *Masā'il*:

قيل لأبي عبد الله: يكون الرجل فِي قومه، فيسْأَل عَن الشَّيْء فِيهِ اخْتِلَاف؟ قَالَ: يُفْتِي بِمَا وَافق الْكتاب وَالسّنة، وَمَا لم يُوَافق الْكتاب وَالسّنة أمسك عَنهُ، قيل لَهُ: أفيجاب عَلَيْهِ؟ قَالَ: لَا.

It was said to Abu 'Abdullah, "What if a person is in his community and is asked about some issue wherein there is a difference of opinion?" He replied, "He should give a ruling in accordance to the Qur'ān and Sunnah. If he cannot determine a view that is in agreement with the Qur'ān and Sunnah, he should refrain." It was then said, "Should he answer the question?" He replied, "No."[80]

الأَصْل الرَّابِع: الْأَخْذ بالمرسل والْحَدِيث الضَّعِيف إِذا لم يكن فِي الْبَاب شَيْء يَدْفَعهُ، وَهُوَ الَّذِي رَجحه على الْقيَاس، وَلَيْسَ المُرَاد بالضعيف عِنْده الْبَاطِل وَلَا الْمُنكر، وَلَا مَا فِي رِوَايَته مُتَّهم بِحَيْثُ لَا يسوغ الذّهاب إِلَيْهِ، فَالْعَمَل بِهِ، بل الحَدِيث الضَّعِيف عِنْده قسيم الصَّحِيح، وَقسم من أَقسَام الْحسن: وَلم يكن يقسم الحَدِيث إِلَى صَحِيح وَحسن وَضَعِيف، بل إِلَى صَحِيح وَضَعِيف. وللضعيف عِنْده مَرَاتِب، فَإِذا لم يجد فِي الْبَاب أثرا يَدْفَعهُ، وَلَا قَول صَحَابِيّ، وَلَا إِجْمَاعا على خِلَافه كَانَ الْعَمَل بِهِ عِنْده أولى من الْقيَاس.

The Fourth Evidence: *Mursal* and Weak Narrations if Nothing Con-

80 [T] Ibid. (2/167).

tradicts Them: He would prefer [this category of evidence] over analogies. The meaning of "weak narrations," in this context, is not false or extremely weak narrations, or narrations reported by a person who is accused [of being weak or untrustworthy] wherein his narration is unusable in proving a ruling, and by extension, acting on it. The weak narration to [Aḥmad] is actually a category of authentic narrations, as [in his terminology], a weak ḥadīth is considered *ḥasan*[81] [in later day nomenclature]. He did not categorise ḥadīth into authentic, acceptable, and weak, but rather, to just authentic and weak. Weak narrations, to him, varied in their levels, as well. Therefore, if there was nothing that contradicted [the weak ḥadīth], such as another narration, a statement of the companions, or a consensus, he would act on it, and would prefer it over analogies.

وَلَيْسَ أحد من الْأَئِمَّة إِلَّا وَهُوَ مُوَافق لَهُ على هَذَا الأَصْل من حَيْثُ الْجُمْلَة، فَإِنَّهُ مَا مِنْهُم أحد إِلَّا وَقد قدم الحَدِيث الضَّعِيف على الْقيَاس، فَأَبُو حنيفَة قدم حَدِيث القهقهة فِي الصَّلَاة على مَحْض الْقيَاس على مَا فِيهِ من الْمقَال بِحَيْثُ إِنَّه أجمع أهل الحَدِيث على ضعفه.

All scholars, in principle, agree with this concept; all scholars prefer mildly weak aḥadīth over analogies. Abu Ḥanīfah gave preference to the ḥadīth of laughing in the prayer[82] over an analogy, although the ḥadīth itself has been judged as weak by the consensus of all scholars of ḥadīth. Likewise, he gave preference to the ḥadīth of ablution with a fermented date drink[83] over analogies, and most ḥadīth masters also declare that ḥadīth to be weak.

---

81 [T] A *ḥasan* ḥadīth is one that is accepted, between an authentic narration and a weak one.

82 The ḥadīth is reported by ʿAbd al-Razzaq in his, *Musannaf* (3761), from Abu 'l-ʿĀlīyah al-Riyāḥī who reported that a blind man tripped into a well while the Prophet ﷺ was leading his companions in prayer, and some of the people praying laughed. The Prophet ﷺ them commanded those who laughed to perform ablution over and to pray again. The narrators of the ḥadīth are all trustworthy, but it is a *mursal* report.

83 This ḥadīth was reported by Aḥmad (1/450), al-Tirmidhī (88) and Abu Dāwūd (84) from the ḥadīth of Ibn Masʿūd, who said, "The Prophet ﷺ asked me on the night when the jinn heard the Qur'ān, 'What is in your flask?' I replied, 'A fermented date drink,' to which the Prophet ﷺ said, **'It consists of pure dates and purifying water.'** Afterwards, he performed ablution using it." It has been graded as weak by al-Ṭaḥāwī in *Sharḥ Maʿānī al-Āthār* (1/57-58).

وَقدم حَدِيث ((**أكثر الْحيض عشرَة أَيَّام**))، وَهُوَ ضَعِيف باتفاقهم، على مَحْض الْقيَاس، فَإِن الَّذِي ترَاهُ فِي الْيَوْم الثَّالِث عشر مساوٍ فِي الْحَد والحقيقة وَالصّفة لدم الْيَوْم الْعَاشِر.

Further, he preferred the ḥadīth of, "The longest menstruation can last is ten days,"[84] which is weak according to the agreement of ḥadīth masters, over an analogy. Analogy would dictate that what a woman sees on the thirteenth day is analogous, both in definition, reality, and description, to the blood she sees on the tenth day.

وَقدم حَدِيث ((**لَا مهر أقل من عشرَة دَرَاهِم**))، وَأَجْمعُوا على ضعفه بل بُطْلَانه، على مَحْض الْقيَاس، فَإِن بذل الصَدَاق مُعَاوضَة فِي مُقَابلَة بذل الْبضْع، فَمَا تراضيا عَلَيْهِ جَازَ، قَلِيلا كَانَ أَو كثيرا.

Lastly, he prefers the ḥadīth of, "**No wedding gift may be less than ten dirhams,**"[85] although the scholars unanimously agree that it is not only weak, but outright rejected. Still, he preferred it to an outright analogy, which would go that giving the wedding gift is in exchange for the woman giving her private areas to [her husband], and as such, whatever they agree on should be permissible, irrespective of amount.

وَقدم الشَّافِعِي خبر تَحْرِيم صيد وج - مَعَ ضعفه - على الْقيَاس. وَقدم خبر جَوَاز الصَّلَاة بِمَكَّة فِي وَقت النَّهْي، مَعَ ضعفه ومخالفته لقياس غَيرهَا من الْبِلَاد. وَقدم فِي أحد قوليه حَدِيث ((**من قاء أَو رعف فَلْيَتَوَضَّأ أَو ليبن على صلَاته**)) على الْقيَاس مَعَ ضعف الْخَبَر وإرساله.

Al-Shāfiʿī preferred the ḥadīth prohibiting game of the valley of Wajj[86], although it is weak, to an analogy. Likewise, he gave preference to the ḥadīth of praying in Makkah during the time of prohibition[87], although it is weak,

84 Reported by al-Dāraquṭnī (p. 80).

85 Reported by al-Dāraquṭnī (p. 392) and al-Bayhaqi (7/133).

86 Aḥmad (1416) and Abu Dāwūd (2032) reported that al-Zubayr reported that Allah's Messenger ﷺ said, "**The game of Wajj, as well as its thorny trees, are unlawful: Allah made them unlawful.**" Wajj is a valley near Taif.

87 This ḥadīth was reported by Aḥmad (5/165) and al-Dāraquṭnī (2/274) from Abu Dharr, who said that he heard Allah's Messenger say, "**One may not pray after *'asr***

and although Makkah is analogous to other cities. Also, although he has two opinions on the matters, one of them is to prefer the ḥadīth of, "**Whoever vomits or has a nosebleed should perform ablution and then[88] should resume their prayer from wherever they left,**"[89] over the analogy, although the ḥadīth is weak due to being *mursal*.

وَأما مَالك: فَإِنَّهُ يقدم الحَدِيث الْمُرْسل، والمنقطع، والبلاغات، وَقَول الصَّحَابِيّ على الْقيَاس.

As for al-Imām Mālik, he would prefer *mursal* narrations, narrations with a missing narrator, narrations reported without a chain of narration, and the views of the companions over analogies.

فَإِذا لم يكن عِنْد الإِمَام أَحْمد فِي الْمَسْأَلَة نَص وَلَا قَول الصَّحَابَة أَو وَاحِد مِنْهُم وَلَا أثر مُرْسل أَو ضَعِيف، عدل إِلَى الأَصْل الْخَامِس الَّذِي سَنذكرُهُ

If al-Imām Aḥmad did not find a divine text detailing the ruling on an issue, did not find views of at least one of the companions, and did not find a *mursal* or weak narration, he would resort to the fifth evidence.

الأَصْل الْخَامِس: الْقيَاس: كَانَ الإِمَام أَحْمد يَسْتَعْمِلهُ للضَّرُورَة، على مَا علمت مِمَّا سبق، فَفِي كتاب الْخلال عَن أَحْمد قَالَ: سَأَلت الشَّافِعِي عَن الْقيَاس، فَقَالَ: إِنَّمَا يُصَار إِلَيْهِ عِنْد الضَّرُورَة أَو مَا هَذَا مَعْنَاهُ، فَهَذِهِ الأُصُول الْخَمْسَة من أُصُول فَتَاوَى الإِمَام أَحْمد، وَعَلَيْهَا مدارها.

The Fifth Evidence: Analogy: Based on what has previously been clarified, al-Imām Aḥmad would use analogies out of necessity. In the book of al-Khallāl, he reported that Aḥmad said, "I asked al-Shāfiʿī about analogy, and he replied, 'It should be used out of necessity.'"[90] As such, those are the five evidences that al-Imām Aḥmad would use to pass rulings, and upon them they revolved.

---

until the sun sets, nor after *fajr* until the sun rises, except when in Makkah; except when in Makkah."

88 [T] The text says, "Or should continue their prayer," but the original narrations state what I have placed.

89 Reported by Ibn Mājah (1221).

90 [T] *Al-ʿUddah* (4/1336).

وَكَانَ - رَضِي الله عَنهُ - يتوَقَّف أَحْيَانًا فِي الْفَتْوَى لتعارض الْأَدِلَّة عِنْده، أَو لاخْتِلَاف الصَّحَابَة فِيهَا، أَو لعدم اطِّلَاعه فِيهَا على أثر، أَو قَول أحد من الصَّحَابَة وَالتَّابِعِينَ. وَكَانَ شَدِيد الْكَرَاهَة وَالْمَنْع للإفتاء بِمَسْأَلَة لَيْسَ فِيهَا أثر عَن السّلف، كَمَا قَالَ لبَعض أَصْحَابه: إياك أَن تَتَكَلَّم فِي مَسْأَلَة لَيْسَ لَك فِيهَا إِمَام.

Sometimes, Aḥmad ﷺ would abstain from giving a ruling, because of the conflicted evidences he was aware of, or because the companions themselves had differences of opinions. Sometimes, he would not pass a ruling because he was unaware of a narration, or a statement from the companions or the Tābiʿīn. He was very strict in forbidding giving rulings that did not coincide with a narration from the pious predecessors. He once said to his students, "Beware of promoting a view that has no precedence."

وَكَانَ يسوغ استفتاء فُقَهَاء الحَدِيث وَأَصْحَاب مَالك، وَيدل عَلَيْهِم، وَيمْنَع من استفتاء من يعرض عَن الحَدِيث، وَلَا يَبْنِي مذْهبه عَلَيْهِ، وَلَا يسوغ الْعَمَل بفتواه، قَالَ ابْن هانئ:

He would allow people to ask jurists who were scholars of ḥadīth, and would allow them to ask the disciples of Mālik. He would actually direct people to them. He would forbid asking those who turn a blind eye to aḥadīth and do not base their opinions on them. He would not permit acting on the rulings of such individuals. Ibn Hāni' said:

سَأَلت أَبَا عبد الله عَن الَّذِي جَاءَ فِي الحَدِيث **((أجرؤكم على الْفتيا أجرؤكم على النَّار))**. قَالَ أَبُو عبد الله: يُفْتِي بِمَا لم يسمع. قَالَ: وَسَأَلته عَمَّن أفتى يفتيا يَعْنِي فِيهَا؟ قَالَ: فإثمها على من أفتاها، قلت: على أَي وَجه يُفْتِي حَتَّى يعلم مَا فِيهَا؟ قَالَ: يُفْتِي بالبحث، لَا يدْرِي إِيش أَصْلهَا.

I asked Abu ʿAbdullah about the one mentioned in the ḥadīth, **"Those of you most audacious in giving rulings are the ones most audacious in making themselves susceptible to the hellfire,"**[91] and he replied, "This pertains to those who give rulings without basing [the rulings] on [narrations] they heard."[92] I also asked him about a person who gives a ruling

91 Reported by al-Dārimī (1/57).
92 [T] *Masā'il al-Imām Aḥmad*, the version of Isḥāq ibn Ibrāhīm ibn Hāni' (2/165).

about something they are unaware of the correct answer to, and he responded, "The one who gave the ruling incurs a sin." I replied, "How can one gain awareness to the level where they can give rulings?" He said, "He can do so by researching; how else could he pass rulings, considering they do not know the evidence that affects a ruling in the issue?"[93]

وَقَالَ أَبُو دَاوُد فِي مسَائِله: مَا أحصي مَا سَمِعت أَحْمد سُئِلَ عَن كثير مِمَّا فِيهِ الِاخْتِلَاف فِي الْعلم فَيَقُول: لَا أَدْرِي. قَالَ: وسمعته يَقُول: مَا رَأَيْت مثل ابْن عُيَيْنَة فِي الْفَتْوَى أحسن فتيا مِنْهُ، كَانَ أَهْون عَلَيْهِ أَن يَقُول لَا أَدْرِي.

Abu Dāwūd said, in his *Masā'il*, "I cannot count the amount of times Aḥmad was asked about many issues in knowledge where there is a difference of opinion, and he would say, 'I do not know.' I also heard him say, 'I have not seen a person give better rulings than Ibn 'Uyaynah. It was extremely easy for him to say, 'I do not know.''"[94]

وَقَالَ عبد الله ابْنه فِي مسَائِله: سَمِعت أبي يَقُول: وَقَالَ عبد الرَّحْمَن بن مهْدي: سَأَلَ رجل من أهل الغرب مَالك بن أنس عَن مَسْأَلَة، فَقَالَ: لَا أَدْرِي، فَقَالَ: يَا أَبَا عبد الله! تقول لَا أَدْرِي؟ قَالَ: نعم فأبلغ من ورائك أَنِّي لَا أَدْرِي.

'Abdullāh ibn Aḥmad said, in his *Masā'il*, "I heard my father say, "Abd al-Raḥmān ibn Mahdī said, 'A man from the west asked Mālik ibn Anas about an issue, and he replied, 'I do not know.' The man said, 'O Abā 'Abdillāh! You say: I do not know?' [Mālik] responded, 'Yes, so tell those in your lands that I do not know.'"[95]

وَقَالَ عبد الله: كنت أسمع أبي كثيرا يسْأَل عَن الْمسَائِل، فَيَقُول: لَا أَدْرِي، وَيقف إِذا كَانَت مَسْأَلَة فِيهَا اخْتِلَاف، وَكَثِيرًا مَا كَانَ يَقُول: سل غَيْرِي، فَإِن قيل لَهُ: من نسْأَل؟ قَالَ: سلوا الْعلمَاء، وَلَا يكَاد يُسَمِّي رجلا بِعَيْنِه.

'Abdullah said: I often would hear my father asked about an issue and respond, "I do not know," and would also abstain from giving an answer if

93 [T] Ibid.

94 [T] *Masā'il al-Imām Aḥmad*, the version of Abu Dāwūd al-Sijistānī (question 1782; 1787).

95 [T] *Al-Jāmi' li 'Ulūm al-Imām Aḥmad* (5/131).

the question was pertaining to an issue where there is much difference of opinion. He would also often say, "Ask someone else." If it were said to him, "Whom should we ask?" He would say, "Ask the scholars," but would rarely name anyone in particular.

قَالَ: وَسمعت أبي يَقُول: كَانَ ابْن عُيَيْنَة لَا يُفْتِي فِي الطَّلَاق وَيَقُول: من يحسن هَذَا؟!

He said: I heard my father say, "Ibn 'Uyaynah would never give rulings in matters of divorce; he would say, 'Who is capable of such a thing?'"

قَالَ ابْن الْقيم: قلت: الجراة على الْفتيا تكون من قلَّة الْعلم، وَمن غزارته وسعته، فَإِذا قل علمه أفتى عَن كل مَا يسْأَل عَنهُ بِغَيْر علم، وَإِذا اتَّسع علمه اتسعت فتياه، وَلِهَذَا كَانَ ابْن عَبَّاس من أوسع الصَّحَابَة فتيا، فقد جمع أَبُو بكر مُحَمَّد بن مُوسَى بن يَعْقُوب ابْن أَمِير الْمُؤمنِينَ الْمَأْمُون فتيا ابْن عَبَّاس فِي عشْرين كتابا وَأَبُو بكر مُحَمَّد الْمَذْكُور أحد أَئِمَّة الْعلم.

Ibn al-Qayyim said: Audaciousness and propensity to give rulings stems from a lack of knowledge, but it is also a staple indicator of abundance and breadth of knowledge. When a person has little knowledge, they pass rulings on everything they are asked about, without knowledge. In contrast, when one has vast knowledge, they also answer more questions. Due to this reason, Ibn 'Abbās was from the most vast in edicts amongst the companions. As a matter of fact, Abu Bakr Muḥammad ibn Mūsā ibn Ya'qūb, one of the *imāms* of knowledge and the son of the caliph al-Ma'mūn, gathered the rulings of Ibn 'Abbās into twenty volumes.

وَكَانَ سعيد بن الْمسيب وَاسع الْفتيا، وَمَعَ ذَلِك كَانُوا يسمونه الجريء.

Further, Sa'īd ibn al-Musayyib had many edicts, and they would refer to him as being audacious.

هَذَا مُجمل مسالك الإِمَام أَحْمد فِي الْفتيا وَالِاجْتِهَاد واستنباط الْكَلَام.

Therefore, the previously mentioned facts are the general approach al-Imām Aḥmad took in regards to passing rulings, exerting effort in determining rulings, and deriving rulings from the texts.

تَتِمَّة: وَرَأَيْت لِلْحَافِظِ عبد الرَّحْمَن بن رَجَب الْحَنْبَلِيّ مُحدث الشَّام كلَاما حسنا فِي هَذَا الْمَوْضُوع فِي كِتَابه (جَامع الْعُلُوم وَالْحكم) عِنْد كَلَامه على الحَدِيث التَّاسِع من الْأَرْبَعين النواوية قَالَ:

In conclusion, I came across some useful information presented by al-Ḥāfiẓ ʿAbd al-Raḥmān ibn Rajab al-Ḥanbalī, the ḥadīth master of the Levant, in his book *Jāmiʿ al-ʿUlūm wa ʾl-Ḥikam*, when he commented on the ninth ḥadīth of *al-Nawawi's Forty Aḥadīth*. He said:

قَالَ الْمَيْمُونِي: سَمِعت أَبَا عبد الله - يَعْنِي أَحْمد - يسْأَل عَن مَسْأَلَة فَقَالَ: وَقعت هَذِه الْمَسْأَلَة، بليتم بهَا بعد؟! قَالَ ابْن رَجَب: وَقد انقسم النَّاس فِي هَذَا أقساما، فَمن أَتبَاع أهل الحَدِيث من سد بَاب الْمسَائِل حَتَّى قل فقهه وَعلمه بحدود مَا أنزل الله على رَسُوله، وَصَارَ حَامِل فقه غير فَقِيه.

Al-Maymūnī said, "I heard Abu ʿAbdullah (meaning, Aḥmad) being asked about an issue, and he responded, 'Has this issue occurred? Were you tested with this?'" [Ibn Rajab said:] In this issue, people differ. Some followers of Ahl al-Ḥadīth close the door entirely to issues, to the point that their knowledge of the law and their knowledge of the restrictions Allah the Exalted sent to His Messenger is deficient, making them carriers of rulings without understanding them.

وَمن فُقَهَاء أهل الرَّأْي من توسع فِي توليد الْمسَائِل قبل وُقُوعهَا، مَا يَقع فِي الْعَادة مِنْهَا وَمَا لَا يَقع، وَاشْتَغلُوا بتكليف الْجَواب عَن ذَلِك، وَكَثْرَة الْخُصُومَات فِيهِ، والجدال عَلَيْهِ، حَتَّى يتَوَلَّد من ذَلِك افْتِرَاق الْقُلُوب، ويستقر فِيهَا بِسَبَبِهِ الْأَهْوَاء والشحناء، والعداوة والبغضاء، ويقترن ذَلِك كثيرا بنية المغالبة، وَطلب الْعُلُوّ والمباهاة، وَصرف وُجُوه النَّاس، وَهَذَا مِمَّا ذمه الْعلمَاء الربانيون، ودلت السّنة على قبحه وتحريمه.

Other jurists of Ahl al-Raʾy often discussed hypothetical issues before they would even happen. They would discuss things that could happen per normal scenarios and things that are very unlikely to happen. They busied themselves with finding answers to those hypothetical questions, often spending much energy and time debating them. This resulted in disunity in their hearts. Due to this, desires, rancour, enmity, and hatred settle in the hearts. Often times, [these feelings] are coupled with the intention of winning a debate and seeking to overcome their interlocutor, all to boast and garner the attention of people. This is what the *rabbānī*[96] scholars forbade and what the Sunnah has indicated to as being an ugly, forbidden action.

وَأما فُقَهَاء أهل الحَدِيث الْعَامِلُونَ بِهِ فَإِن مُعظم هممهم الْبَحْث عَن مَعَانِي كتاب الله عز وَجل، وَمَا يفسره من السّنَن الصَّحِيحَة، وَكَلَام الصَّحَابَة وَالتَّابِعِين لَهُم بِإِحْسَان، وَعَن سنة رَسُول الله صلى الله عَلَيْهِ وَسلم، وصحيحها وسقيمها، ثمَّ التفقه فِيهَا وفهمها، وَالْوُقُوف على مَعَانِيهَا، ثمَّ معرفَة كَلَام الصَّحَابَة وَالتَّابِعِين لَهُم بِإِحْسَان فِي أَنْوَاع الْعُلُوم من التَّفْسِير والْحَدِيث ومسائل الْحَلَال وَالْحرَام وأصول السّنة والزهد وَالرَّقَائِق وَغير ذَلِك، وَهَذَا هُوَ طَرِيقَة الإِمَام أَحْمد، وَمن وَافقه من أهل الحَدِيث الربانيين.

As for the jurists of Ahl al-Ḥadīth who act on [the ḥadīth], the majority of their efforts are spent in searching for the meanings of the Book of Allah the Exalted, the authentic narrations that explain [the Qur'ān], and the speech of the companions and their followers in righteousness. Further, they search for the Sunnah of Allah's Messenger ﷺ and try to discern between the authentic and weak narrations. After they do so, they attempt to derive law from them and understand them, pausing to deduce meanings. Then, they try to learn the statements of the companions and their followers in goodness on all topics and sciences, including exegesis of the Qur'ān, ḥadīth, the lawful and the unlawful, the foundations of the Sunnah, asceticism, heart-softening statements, and so forth. This was the way of al-Imām Aḥmad and the *rabbānī* scholars of ḥadīth who concurred with his method.

وَفِي معرفَة هَذَا شغل شاغل عَن التشاغل بِمَا أحدث من الرَّأْي مِمَّا لَا ينْتَفع بِهِ، وَلَا يقع وَإِنَّمَا يُورث التجادل فِيهِ الْخُصُومَات، والجدال، وَكَثْرَة القيل والقال. وَكَانَ الإِمَام أَحْمد كثيرا إِذا سُئِلَ عَن شَيْء من الْمسَائِل المولدات الَّتِي لَا تقع يَقُول: دعونَا من هَذِه الْمسَائِل المحدثة.

96 [T] A *rabbānī* scholar has many definitions, from the wise scholar to "The one who teaches people the minor issues before the major issues." (*Tāj al-'Arūs* 2/461) Refer also to al-Ṭabarī's discussions on these interpretations under Sūrat Āli 'Imrān, verse 79.

Learning such things busies one from having to busy themselves with the discussions that scholars of Raʾy conceive, some of which is not beneficial, but rather results in debates, causing disputes, arguments, and much gossip. In contrast, when al-Imām Aḥmad would be asked about a hypothetical scenario, he would often say, "Let us not partake in made-up scenarios."

قَالَ ابْن رَجَب: وَمن سلك طَرِيقَة لطلب الْعلم على مَا ذَكرْنَاهُ، تمكن من فهم جَوَاب الْحَوَادِث الْوَاقِعَة غَالِبا، لِأَن أُصُولهَا تُوجد فِي تِلْكَ الْأُصُول الْمشار إِلَيْهَا، وَلَا بُد أَن يكون سلوك هَذَا الطَّرِيق خلف أَئِمَّة أَهل الدين الْمجمع على هدايتهم ودرايتهم كالشافعي، وَأحمد، وَإِسْحَاق، وَأبي عبيد، وَمن سلك مسلكهم، فَإِن من ادّعى سلوك هَذَا الطَّرِيق على غير طريقهم وَقع فِي مفاوز ومهالك، وَأخذ بِمَا لَا يجوز الْأَخْذ بِهِ، وَترك مَا يجب الْعَمَل بِهِ. انْتهى.

Ibn Rajab said: Those who learn knowledge in the way we previously outlined are usually able to answer questions to new scenarios, since the evidences used to derive from would be similar to these foundations mentioned above. One must follow this path behind the masters of the religion whose guidance and knowledge all agree on, such as al-Shāfiʿī, Aḥmad, Isḥāq, Abu ʿUbayd, and others who trod their path. Whoever claims to follow this path without following that of those scholars will fall into disasters and destruction, taking views that are not permissible to take, and abandoning things they must act on.[97]

وَمن هُنَا تزداد علما بمسالك الإِمَام أَحْمد رَضِي الله عَنهُ.

Therefore, [Ibn Rajab's] comments add more knowledge to the ways and methods of al-Imām Aḥmad ﷺ.

97 *Jāmiʿ al-ʿUlūm wa ʾl-Ḥikam* (1/201-203).

العقد الرَّابع

Chapter Four

فِي مسالك كبار أَصْحَابه فِي تَرْتِيب مذْهبه واستنباطه من فتياه وَالرِّوَايَات عَنهُ وتصرفهم فِي ذَلِك الْإِرْث المحمدي الأحمدي

On the Manner in Which His Major Disciples Codified His School of Thought, Deriving It from His Verdicts and Statements, and Their Treatment of the Inheritance of Muḥammad ﷺ, as Interpreted by Aḥmad

اعْلَم أَن الإِمَام أَحْمد رَضِي الله عَنهُ كَانَ يكره وضع الْكتب الَّتِي تشْتَمل على التَّفْرِيع والرأي، وَمَا ذَلِك إِلَّا ليتوفر الِالْتِفَات إِلَى النَّقْل، ويزرع فِي الْقُلُوب التَّمَسُّك بالأثر، وَقَالَ يَوْمًا لعُثْمَان بن سعيد: لَا تنظر فِي كتب أبي عبيد، وَلَا فِيمَا وضع إِسْحَاق وَلَا سُفْيَان وَلَا الشَّافِعِي وَلَا مَالك، وَعَلَيْك بِالْأَصْلِ.

Al-Imām Aḥmad used to dislike authoring books that comprise of branching and investigating subsidiary matters by way of rational discretion. His reason for disliking such a concept was to turn people's attention to textual evidences and to plant the concept of holding fast to narrations in the hearts. He once said to 'Uthmān ibn Sa'īd, "Do not lay eyes on the books of Abu 'Ubayd nor the compilations of Isḥāq, Sufyan, al-Shāfi'ī, or Mālik. Busy yourself with the divine texts."[98]

وَقَالَ إِسْحَاق بن إِبْرَاهِيم بن هانئ: سَأَلت أَحْمد عَن كتب أبي ثَوْر فَقَالَ: كتاب ابتدع فِيهِ بِدعَة، وَلم يُعجبهُ وضع الْكتب. وَكَذَلِكَ كَانَ يكره أَن يكْتب شَيْء من رَأْيه وفتواه. وروى الْحَافِظ ابْن الْجَوْزِيّ فِي مناقبه عَن أَحْمد أَنه قَالَ القلانس من السَّمَاء، تنزل على رُؤُوس قوم يَقُولُونَ برؤوسهم هَكَذَا وَهَكَذَا. قَالَ ابْن الْجَوْزِيّ:

Isḥāq ibn Ibrāhīm ibn Hāni' said, "I asked [Aḥmad] about the books of

---

98 [T] *Manāqib al-Imām Aḥmad* (p. 263).

Abu Thawr, and he said, '[Abu Thawr] invented a new innovation by simply authoring it.' He did not like that books were authored. He also disliked that any of his own views or rulings were written."[99] Further, al-Ḥāfiẓ Ibn al-Jawzī said in his *Manāqib* that al-Imām Aḥmad said, "*Qalānis*[100] descend from the heavens on the heads of people who [do] such-and-such with their heads."[101] Ibn al-Jawzī commented:

الْمَعْنى لَا يريدها، وَقَوله: هَكَذَا وَهَكَذَا: أَي يميلون رؤوسهم عَن أَن تتمكن مِنْهَا، وَمعنى الْكَلَام: أنهم لَا يُرِيدُونَ الرياسة وَهِي تقع عَلَيْهِم، وَيحْتَمل أَن يُرِيد أَنهم يطأطؤن رؤوسهم تواضعا، فَلذَلِك كَانَ أَحْمد ينْهَى عَن كتب كَلَامه تواضعا، فَقدر الله لَهُ أَن دون ورتب وشاع. انْتهى.

He means that they descend on people who do not desire it. When he said, "Such-and-such," he referred to people who move their heads to avoid the hat descending onto their heads. In summary, the meaning of what Aḥmad said is that such people do not desire leadership, but it simply happens to them outside of their will. It is possible that when he said, 'Such-and-such,' he was referring to people who lower their heads in humbleness. Due to this reason, Aḥmad used to prohibit people from writing his speech out of humbleness. Allah destined, however, that it would be written, codified, and popularised.[102] **[End]**

قلت: وَالْمعْنَى الثَّانِي هُوَ الْأَقْرَب، فقد رُوِيَ عَنهُ أَنه كَانَ يَقُول: طُوبَى لمن أخمل الله عز وَجل ذكره، وَكَانَ لَا يدع أحدا يتبعهُ فِي مَشْيه، وَرُبمَا كَانَ مَاشِيا، فيتبعه أحد من النَّاس، فيقف حَتَّى ينْصَرف الَّذِي يتبعهُ. وَكَانَ يمشي وَحده متواضعا.

In my view, the second view is closer [to the true intent of Aḥmad]. It was reported that he would say, "Glad tidings to the one whom Allah the Exalted has made obscure, to the point that no one follows them even when they walk. Sometimes, they might walk and notice a follower, and then stop so that the person who was following them departs, and then continue walk-

99 [T] Ibid (p. 264).
100 [T] This refers to what is known in modern days as a "*Kufi*." It is the plural of the word *qalansuwah*. In this context, al-Imām Aḥmad is referring to a type of hat worn by scholars or judges during his time.
101 [T] Ibid (p. 266).
102 [T] Ibid.

ing alone, humble."[103]

وَحَيْثُ إن الإِمَام أَحْمد كَانَ يحب توفر الِالْتِفَات إِلَى النَّقْل، ويختار التَّوَاضُع، أشغل أوقاته فِي جمع السّنة والأثر، وَتَفْسِير كتاب الله تَعَالَى، وَلم يؤلف كتابا فِي الْفِقْه، وَكَانَ غَايَة مَا كتب فِيهِ رِسَالَة فِي الصَّلَاة، كتبهَا إِلَى إِمَام صلى وَرَاءه، فأساء فِي صلَاته، وَهِي رِسَالَة قد طبعت ونشرت فِي أيامنا.

Since al-Imām Aḥmad loved constant reviewing of the textual evidences and chose humbleness, he busied himself with gathering the Sunnah and narrations and explaining the Book of Allah. He never wrote a book on law. The most he did was write a letter about prayer to the *imām* of a mosque whom he prayed behind, and the *imām* prayed poorly. This letter has been reproduced and distributed during these times.

فَعلم الله من حسن نِيَّته وقصده، فَكتب عَنهُ أَصْحَابه من كَلَامه وفتواه أَكثر من ثَلَاثِينَ سفرا انتشرت كلهَا فِي الْآفَاق، ثمَّ جَاءَ أَحْمد بن مُحَمَّد بن هَارُون أَبُو بكر الْخلال، فصرف عنايته إِلَى جمع عُلُوم أَحْمد بن حَنْبَل، وَإِلَى كِتَابَة مَا رُوِيَ عَنهُ، وَطَاف لأجل ذَلِك الْبِلَاد، وسافر للاجتماع بأصحاب أَحْمد، وَكتب مَا رُوِيَ عَنهُ بِالْإِسْنَادِ، وَتبع فِي ذَلِك طرفه من الْعُلُوّ وَالنُّزُول، وصنف كتبا فِي ذَلِك. مِنْهَا: كتاب (الْجَامِع) وَهُوَ فِي نَحْو مِائَتي جُزْء، وَلم يقاربه أحد من أَصْحَاب الإِمَام أَحْمد فِي ذَلِك.

Allah the Exalted knows of his good intentions and goals, and so his disciples wrote over thirty volumes of just his speech and edicts, all of which spread across the various lands. Afterwards, Aḥmad ibn Muḥammad ibn Hārūn, also known as Abu Bakr al-Khallāl, came along and dedicated his time to gathering Aḥmad's knowledge of various sciences and writing whatever was reported from him. He travelled the lands in order to accomplish this goal. He travelled to meet the disciples of Aḥmad, and wrote the statements that were attributed to him, along with the chains of narrations. He sought corroborating narrations, as well, consisting of narrations that consisted of few people between him and Aḥmad and the narrations that had more people between him and Aḥmad. He wrote books on this, including his book *al-*

103 [T] Ibid (p. 376).

Jāmiʿ, which is about two-hundred volumes. None of the disciples of al-Imām Aḥmad came close to writing anything as large or comprehensive.

وَكَانَت وَفَاته سنة إِحْدَى عشرَة وثلاث مئة. هَذَا مَا ذكره ابْن الْجَوْزِيّ فِي (المناقب) من أَن جَامع الْخلال فِي نَحْو من مِائَتي جُزْء. وَقَالَ ابْن الْقيم فِي (إِعْلَام الموقعين): وَجمع الْخلال نصوصه فِي (الْجَامِع الْكَبِير) فَبلغ نَحْو عشْرين سفرا أَو أَكثر. انْتهى. وَلَا مُعَارضَة بَين قوليهما، لِأَن الْمُتَقَدِّمين كَانُوا يطلقون على الكراس وعَلى مَا يقرب من الكراسين جُزْءا، وَأما السّفر: فَهُوَ مَا جمع أَجزَاء، فتنبه.

He died in the year 311, as mentioned by Ibn al-Jawzī in his book *al-Manāqib*, the same book wherein he mentioned that *al-Jāmiʿ* was approximately two-hundred volumes. Ibn al-Qayyim said in *Iʿlām al-Muwaqqiʿīn*, "Al-Khallāl gathered the texts of al-Imām Aḥmad in his large compendium, and it was approximately twenty tomes, or more."[104] There is no conflict between the two statements, as the earlier scholars would refer to smaller works as volumes (*juzʾ*), and those volumes, when gathered into a single work, is referred to as a tome (*sifr*).

وَمن ثمَّ كَانَ جَامع الْخلال هُوَ الأَصْل لمَذْهَب أَحْمد، فَنظر الْأَصْحَاب فِيهِ، وألفوا كتب الْفِقْه مِنْهُ، وَكَانَ من جملَة من سلك فِي مذْهبه مسالك الِاجْتِهَاد - فِي تَرْجِيح الرِّوَايَات المنقولة عَنهُ بَعْضهَا على بعض - عمر بن الْحُسَيْن بن عبد الله بن أَحْمد أَبُو الْقَاسِم الخرقِيّ، فَإِنَّهُ صنف فِي مَذْهَب أَحْمد (مُخْتَصره) الْمَشْهُور الَّذِي شَرحه القَاضِي أَبُو يعلى وَشَيْخه ابْن حَامِد، وموفق الدّين الْمَقْدِسِي فِي كِتَابه (الْمُغنِي) وَغَيرهم. وَقَالَ أَبُو إِسْحَاق الْبَرْمَكِي: عدد مسَائِل الخرقِيّ أَلفَانِ وثلاث مئة مَسْأَلَة.

Continuing, *Jāmiʿ al-Khallāl* became the point of reference for Aḥmad's school of law. The disciples read it and authored other works on law based off it. One of the said disciples who wrote on the school of law of Aḥmad while also using scholarly discretion in choosing the most likely of his narrations was ʿUmar ibn al-Ḥusayn ibn ʿAbdullah ibn Aḥmad Abu ʾl-Qāsim

104 [T] *Iʿlām al-Muwaqqiʿīn ʿan Rabb al-ʿĀlamīn* (1/23).

al-Khiraqī. He wrote his summation, entitled *al-Mukhtaṣar*. It gained fame and has a commentary written by al-Qāḍī Abu Ya'lā as well as his teacher Ibn Ḥāmid, Muwaffaq al-Dīn ibn Qudāmah in his book *al-Mughnī*, and others. Abu Isḥāq al-Barmakī said, "The number of issues discussed by al-Khiraqī reaches two thousand three hundred."[105]

وَكتب أَبُو بكر عبد الْعَزِيز على نُسْخَة مُخْتَصر الْخرقِيّ: خالفني الْخرقِيّ - فِي مُخْتَصره - فِي سِتِّينَ مَسْأَلَة، وَلم يسمهَا. قَالَ القَاضِي أَبُو الْحُسَيْن: فتتبعتها، فَوَجَدتهَا ثَمَانِيَة وَتِسْعين مَسْأَلَة. وَكَانَت وَفَاة الْخرقِيّ فِي دمشق سنة أَربع وَثَلَاثِين وثلاث مئة.

Abu Bakr 'Abd al-'Azīz wrote on his copy of al-Khiraqī's *Mukhtaṣar*, "Al-Khiraqī and I disagree on approximately sixty issues in his *Mukhtaṣar*."[106] However, he did not elaborate on which issues those were. Al-Qāḍī Abu 'l-Ḥusayn said, "I searched for those issues, and I found that there were actually ninety-eight issues."[107] Al-Khiraqī passed away in Damascus in the year 334.

وَأما أَبُو بكر: فَهُوَ عبد الْعَزِيز بن جَعْفَر بن أَحْمد بن دَارا، كَانَ يعرف بِغُلَام الْخلال، فَهُوَ صَاحب كتابي (الشافي) و(التنبيه) فِي فقه الْمَذْهَب الأحمدي، وَصَاحب الْخلاف مَعَ الشَّافِعِي، وَكَانَت وَفَاته سنة ثَلَاث وَسِتِّينَ وثلاث مئة.

The person "Abu Bakr" referenced is 'Abd al-'Azīz ibn Ja'far ibn Aḥmad ibn Dārā. He was known as Ghulām al-Khallāl (the boy of al-Khallāl). He wrote two books on the school of law of Aḥmad, one was called *al-Shāfī* and the other was *al-Tanbīh*.[108] He wrote a third book known as *al-Khilāf ma' 'l-Shāfi'ī*, which details al-Imām Aḥmad's disagreements with al-Shāfi'ī. He passed in the year 363.

وعَلى الْجُمْلَة: فَإِن الْخلال لما جمع الرِّوَايَات عَن أَحْمد ومهدها فِي كتبه، أَخذ الْأَصْحَاب فِي الْجمع وَتَدْوِين الْمَذْهَب وتأليف كتب الْفِقْه. فجزاهم الله خيرا.

---

105 *Ṭabaqāt al-Ḥanābilah* (2/76).
106 [T] Ibid.
107 [T] Ibid.
108 [T] He also wrote *Zād al-Musāfir* which has been printed in 2019.

To summarise, al-Khallāl gathered the narrations of Aḥmad and placed them in his books. From there, the followers of al-Imām Aḥmad began to compile and codify the *madhhab*, and write books on law. May Allah reward them with good.

شذرة

Gems

فِي بَيَان طَرِيقَة الْأَصْحَاب فِي فهم كَلَام الإِمَام أَحْمد وَطَرِيق تصرفهم فِي الرِّوَايَات عَنهُ

In Detailing How the Disciples of al-Imām Aḥmad Understood His Quotes and How They Treated His Narrations

أَظُنك أَيهَا السَّامع لما علمت أَن فتَاوَى الإِمَام أَحْمد كَانَت هِيَ وفتاوى الصَّحَابَة كَأَنَّهَا تخرج من مشكاة وَاحِدَة، حَتَّى إِن الصَّحَابَة إِذا اخْتلفُوا على قَوْلَيْنِ جَاءَ عَنهُ فِي الْمَسْأَلَة رِوَايَتَانِ، وَقد يكون لَهُ فِي الْمَسْأَلَة الْوَاحِدَة رِوَايَات، ثمَّ إِنَّك تنظر فِي كتب الْأَصْحَاب، فتجد غالبها مَبْنِيا على قَول وَاحِد، وَرِوَايَة وَاحِدَة، أخذك الشوق إِلَى أَن تعلم كَيفَ كَانَ تصرف الْأَصْحَاب فِي ذَلِك، وَمَا هِيَ طَرِيقَة المرجحين لإحدى الرِّوَايَات على الْأُخْرَى، وَكَيف كَانَت طريقتهم فِي الْمسَائِل الَّتِي لَيْسَ فِيهَا رِوَايَة عَن الإِمَام، فَإِذا سما بك الشوق إِلَى هَذَا، فاستمع لما أتلو عَلَيْك لتتجلى لَك الْحَقَائِق، ولتكون من أَمرك على يَقِين.

I think you, the reader, have learned that the edicts of al-Imām Aḥmad and the rulings of the companions emanate from the same niche, to the point that even if the companions differed amongst one another and that resulted in two varying views, two views on the issue would be quoted from him. Further he might have multiple narrations on a single issue, and after viewing the books of the adherents of the *madhhab* you find that they are often times based off one view. After learning these facts, you, I am sure, are yearning to know how the *aṣḥāb* understood those various quotes and chose one over the other. Further, you must yearn to learn how they understood issues that may not have had a direct quotation from the Imām explaining it. If your eagerness has reached such a high level, read what I will tell you so that the realities become clear to you and so that you can attain certainty.

لَا يخفاك أَن الْأَصْحَاب أخذُوا مَذْهَب أَحْمد من أَقْوَاله وأفعاله وأجوبته وَغير ذَلِك، فَكَانُوا إِذا وجدوا عَن الإِمَام فِي مَسْأَلَة قَوْلَيْنِ، عدلوا أَولا إِلَى الْجمع بَينهمَا بطرِيقَة من طرق الْأُصُول، إِمَّا بِحمل عَام على خَاص، أَو مُطلق على مُقَيّد، فَإِذا أمكن ذَلِك، كَانَ الْقَوْلَانِ مذْهبه.

It is no secret that the adherents to the *madhhab* of Aḥmad learned it from his statements, actions, answers and other avenues. When they found that the *imām* has two views on a topic, they would first attempt to reconcile the two views by use of the legal theory framework. So sometimes, they would interpret a general statement in light of a more specific statement on the topic. Other times, they would interpret an unconditional statement in light of a conditional statement. If they were successful in doing so, both views would be considered his *madhhab*.

وَإِن تعذر الْجمع بَينهمَا وَعلم التَّارِيخ، فَاخْتلف الْأَصْحَاب، فَقَالَ قوم: الثَّانِي مَذْهَب، وَقَالَ آخَرُونَ: الثَّانِي وَالْأول، وَقَالَت طَائِفَة: الأول وَلَو رَجَعَ عَنهُ. وَصحح القَوْل الأول الشَّيْخ عَلَاء الدّين المرداوي فِي كِتَابه (تَصْحِيح الْفُرُوع) وَتبع غَيره فِي ذَلِك.

However, if they could not reconcile the views but they knew the respective dates of the statements, the *aṣḥāb* differed on how to treat the views. Some said that the second (later) view would be his *madhhab*, others said that both would be his views, and others said that the first view would be considered his *madhhab*, even if he withdrew that opinion. The first view [that the later view is considered his *madhhab*] was declared as the truest by al-Shaykh 'Alā' al-Dīn al-Mardāwī in his book *Taṣḥīḥ al-Furū'*, following the views of other scholars who stated this position.

فَإِن جهل التَّارِيخ، فمذهبه أقرب الْأَقْوَال من الْأَدِلَّة أَو قَوَاعِد مذْهبه، ويخص عَام كَلَامه بِخَاصَّة فِي مَسْأَلَة وَاحِدَة.

Lastly, if the date is unknown, his *madhhab* is the view that is most corroborated by the evidences or the maxims of his *madhhab*. His general statements should be understood in light of his specific ones on the same topic.

قَالَ ابْن مُفْلِح:

Ibn Mufliḥ said:

فِي الْأَصَح والمقيس على كَلَامه مذْهبه فِي الْأَشْهر، فَإِن أفتى فِي مَسْأَلَتَيْنِ متشابهتين بحكمين مُخْتَلفين فِي وَقْتَيْنِ قَالَ بَعضهم وَبعد الزَّمن فَفِي جَوَاز النَّقْل والتخريج وَلَا مَانع وَجْهَان.

If his two views conflict on a single issue, the more general statements are qualified by the more specific ones,[109] according to the stronger view. Also, according to the more popular view, if a view emerges as a deduction of analogies from his words, it is, too, considered his *madhhab*. If he gave two distinct rulings to two similar questions at two different times, and as some said, a long time elapsed between the two rulings; if there is no impediment[110], there are two views on whether it is permissible to quote and extrapolate [from the earlier view].

وَقَوله: لَا يَنْبَغِي، وَلَا يصلح، أَو استقبحه، أَو هُوَ قَبِيح أَو لَا أرَاهُ، يحملهُ الْأَصْحَاب على التَّحْرِيم، قَالَه ابْن مُفْلِح فِي (فروعه) ثمَّ قَالَ: وَقد ذكرُوا أَنه يسْتَحبّ فِرَاق غير القفيفة، وَاحْتَجُّوا بقول أَحْمد: لَا يَنْبَغِي أَن يمْسِكهَا. وَسَأَلَهُ أَبُو طَالب عَن الرجل يُصَلِّي إِلَى الْقَبْر وَالْحمام والحش؟ فَقَالَ: لَا يَنْبَغِي أَن يكون، لَا يُصَلِّي إِلَيْهِ. قَالَ أَبُو طَالب: قلت: فَإِن كَانَ؟ قَالَ: يجْزِيه. وَنقل عَنهُ أَبُو طَالب فِيمَن يقْرَأ فِي الْأَرْبَع كلهَا بِالْحَمْد وَسورَة: أَنه قَالَ: لَا يَنْبَغِي أَن يفعل، وَقَالَ فِي رِوَايَة الْحُسَيْن بن حسان فِي الإِمَام يقصر فِي الأولى، وَيطول فِي الثَّانِيَة: لَا يَنْبَغِي هَذَا. قَالَ القَاضِي أَبُو يعلى: كره ذَلِك لمُخَالفَة السّنة انْتهى.

---

109 [T] In the printed copy of *al-Madkhal*, this portion is considered a part of the words of Ibn Badrān. However, they are actually the beginning part of the quote from Ibn Mufliḥ that was provided. I have quoted Ibn Mufliḥ's discussion in full. His discussion occurs in his book, *al-Furūʿ*. Refer to *al-Furūʿ* along with *Taṣḥiḥ al-Furūʿ* (1/42).

110 [T] According to al-Imām al-Mardāwī who commented on this quote of Ibn Mufliḥ in his book *Taṣḥīḥ al-Furūʿ* (1/43), this means, "If the quotation [of the words of Aḥmad] or extrapolation leads to violating consensus, nullifying what multitudes of scholars have agreed on, or conflicts with an explicitly worded divine text from the Qur'ān or Sunnah, it is not allowed to quote or extrapolate from [Aḥmad's words]. This was stated in *Adab al-Muftī* [by Ibn Ḥamdān]."

When [Aḥmad] says, "It is not appropriate", "It is not virtuous," "It is disgraceful," or, "I do not view [its permissibility]," it means he views [the thing he is commenting on] as being forbidden. On this note, [the *aṣḥāb*] mention that it is recommended to separate between [a man] and an unchaste woman, citing Aḥmad's statement, "It is not appropriate for him to stay married to her." Further, Abu Ṭālib asked him about a person who prays towards a grave, bathhouse, or designated shrubbery meant for relieving oneself. He replied, "It is not appropriate for that to occur; they should not pray towards those things." Abu Ṭālib asked, "What if a person does so?" Aḥmad said, "It fulfills the obligation of prayer." Abu Ṭālib also transmitted that he was asked about a four-unit prayer wherein Sūrat al-Fātiḥah and another *sūrah* were recited in every unit, and he replied, "It is not appropriate to do so." Likewise, al-Ḥusayn ibn Ḥassān reported that he was asked about an *imām* that reads a short *sūrah* in the first unit and a long one in the second unit, to which he replied, "It is not appropriate to do so." Abu Ya'lā said, "He disliked that practice because it contradicts the Sunnah."[111] **[End.]**

هَذَا يدل على أنه لَيْسَ جَمِيع الْأَصْحَاب يحملون قَول الإِمَام: لَا يَنْبَغِي، وَنَحْوه على التَّحْرِيم، بل فِي ذَلِك الْحمل خلاف، فَإِن بَعضهم حمل قَوْله: لَا يَنْبَغِي - فِي مَوَاضِع من كَلَامه - على الْكَرَاهَة كَمَا رَأَيْته آنفا.

The final statement [of Abu Ya'lā] shows that not all of the *aṣḥāb* view that when the *imām* says, "It is not appropriate to do so," and similar statements, that it refers to prohibition. The scholars differ on interpreting those phrases. As you previously saw, some scholars held his statement, "It is not appropriate," to refer to something being *makrūh*.

وَقدم فِي (الرِّعَايَة) أَن قَوْله: لَا يَنْبَغِي يحمل على الْكَرَاهَة، وَقَوله: أكره أَو لَا يُعجبنِي، أَو لَا أحبه أَو لَا أستحسنه، للنَّدْب. وَاخْتَارَ هَذَا المسلك شيخ الْإِسْلَام أَحْمد ابن تَيْمِية الْحَرَّانِي، وَجعل غيرهمَا فِي ذَلِك وَجْهَان، وَجعلُوا قَوْله للسَّائِل، يفعل كَذَا احْتِيَاطًا للْوُجُوب، قدمه فِي (الرِّعَايَة) وَ(الْحَاوِي الْكَبِير).

The author of *al-Ri'āyah* (Ibn Ḥamdān) held that when the *imām* says, "I dislike", "It does not delight me", "I do not love it", or, "I do not like it," it

111 [T] *Al-Furū'* along with *Taṣḥīḥ al-Furū'* (1/42).

refers to the action being voluntary. This was also the view of Shaykh al-Islam Aḥmad ibn Taymiyyah al-Ḥarrānī. Other scholars mentioned a contrary view to [that of Ibn Ḥamdān and Ibn Taymiyyah], and considered his answer to the questioner, "One should do this out of caution," to mean it is obligatory, as stated in *al-Riʿāyah* and *al-Ḥāwī al-Kabīr* (by Abu Ṭālib).

وَقَالَ فِي (الرِّعَايَتَيْنِ) وَ(الْحَاوِي الْكَبِيرِ) و(آداب المستفتي) الأولى النّظر إِلَى الْقَرَائِنِ فِي الْكل، فَإِن دلّت على وجوب أَو ندب أَو تَحْرِيم أَو كَرَاهَة أَو إِبَاحَة حمل قَوْله عَلَيْهِ سَوَاء تقدّمت أَو تَأَخَّرت أَو توسطت. قَالَ فِي (تَصْحِيح الْفُرُوع): وَهُوَ الصَّوَاب، وَكَلَام أَحْمد يدل على ذَلِك انْتهى.

[Ibn Ḥamdān stated] in his two *al-Riʿāyah*,[112] [Abu Ṭālib stated] in al-Ḥāwī al-Kabīr, and [Ibn Ḥamdān] mentioned in *Ādāb al-Mustaftī*:[113] "It is more ideal to look at the context. If the context indicates it is forbidden, voluntary, prohibited, disliked, or lawful, the statement should be understood [in light of the contextual cues], regardless if they occur before, during, or after the quote."[114] [Al-Mardāwī] said in *Taṣḥīḥ al-Furūʿ*, "This is the correct view, and Aḥmad's statements indicate that."[115]

وَقَالَ الإِمَام ابْن الْقيم فِي كِتَابه إعْلَام الموقعين:

Al-Imām Ibn al-Qayyim said in his book *Iʿlām al-Muwaqqiʿīn*:

قد غلط كثير من الْمُتَأَخِّرين من أَتبَاع الْأَئِمَّة على أئمتهم، حَيْثُ تورع الْأَئِمَّة من إِطْلَاق لفظ التَّحْرِيم، وأطلقوا لفظ الْكَرَاهَة، فنفى الْمُتَأَخّرُونَ التَّحْرِيم عَمَّا أطلق عَلَيْهِ الْأَئِمَّة الْكَرَاهَة، ثمَّ سهل عَلَيْهِم لفظ الْكَرَاهَة، وَخفت مُؤْنَته عَلَيْهِم، فَحَمله بَعضهم على التَّنْزِيه، وَتجَاوز بِهِ آخَرُونَ إِلَى كَرَاهَة ترك الأولى، وَهَذَا كثير جدا فِي تصرفاتهم، فَحصل بِسَبَبِهِ غلط عَظِيم على الشَّرِيعَة وعَلى الْأَئِمَّة.

Many latter-day followers mistakenly understood the *imāms* they follow, since many [early scholars] were hesitant to declare things "forbidden" out of humility, and instead chose to refer to them as "disliked." This led to the

112 [T] He has the large *Riʿāyah* and the smaller *Riʿāyah*.
113 [T] The title of the book is *Ṣifat al-Muftī wa 'l-Mustaftī*, and it has been printed.
114 *Ṣifat al-Fatwā* (pp. 93-94).
115 [T] *Al-Furūʿ wa Taṣḥīḥ al-Furūʿ* (1/45).

later scholars to deny prohibition of the things the [early] *imāms* declared as disliked. This facilitated using the word "disliked," and made it much easier for them. Some understood this word to mean that one must hold themselves above doing such a thing, while others held it to mean that it is simply not ideal. This occurs often in their works, and it results in massive misunderstandings of the religion and of the *imāms*.

وَقد قَالَ الإِمَام أَحْمد فِي الْجمع بَين الْأُخْتَيْنِ بِملك الْيَمين: أكرهه وَلَا أَقُول: هُوَ حرَام، ومذهبه تَحْرِيمه، وَإِنَّمَا تورع عَن إِطْلَاق لفظ التَّحْرِيم لأجل قَول عُثْمَان، يَعْنِي بِجَوَازِهِ.

Al-Imām Aḥmad said, when speaking about whether two sisters could both be subject to concubinage, "I dislike it, but I do not claim it is forbidden." However, his view is that it is forbidden. He was cautious in not saying it was forbidden due to the view of 'Uthmān, which was that it was lawful.

وَقَالَ أَبُو الْقَاسِم الْخرقِيّ فِيمَا نَقله عَن الإِمَام أَحْمد: وَيكرهُ أَن يتَوَضَّأ فِي آنِية الذَّهَب وَالْفِضَّة، ومذهبه أَنه لَا يجوز.

Abu 'l-Qāsim al-Khiraqī transmitted from al-Imām Aḥmad, "It is disliked to perform ablution out of utensils of gold and silver." However, his view was that it was forbidden.

وَقَالَ فِي رِوَايَة أبي دَاوُد: يسْتَحبّ أَن لَا يدْخل الْحمام إِلَّا بمئزر، وَهَذَا اسْتِحْبَاب وجوب. وَقَالَ فِي رِوَايَة إِسْحَاق بن مَنْصُور: إِذا كَانَ أَكثر مَال الرجل حَرَامًا فَلَا يُعجبنِي أَن يُؤْكَل مَاله، وَهَذَا على سَبِيل التَّحْرِيم.

Further, in the report of Abu Dāwūd it states: "It is recommended that one not enter the bathhouse except with a bottom cover." This recommendation was actually an obligation [to Aḥmad.] In the narration of Isḥāq ibn Manṣūr, he said, "If the majority of the wealth of a man is unlawful, it is disliked to me to eat of his wealth." This meant a prohibition to Aḥmad.[116] **[End]**

ثمَّ إِن ابْن الْقيم أَطَالَ النَّفس فِي هَذَا الْمَوْضُوع، فَنقل رِوَايَات كَثِيرَة عَن الإِمَام

116 [T] *I'lām al-Muwaqqi'īn* (1/32).

أَحْمد جَاءَت بِلَفْظ الْكَرَاهَة، وَالْمَقْصُود التَّحْرِيم، ثمَّ حُكيَ عَن مُحَمَّد بن الْحسن أَنه قَالَ: إِن كل مَكْرُوه فَهُوَ حرَام، إِلَّا أَنه لما لم يجد فِيهِ نصا قَاطعا، لم يُطلق عَلَيْهِ لفظ الْحَرَام. وروى مُحَمَّد أَيْضا عَن أبي حنيفَة وَأبي يُوسُف أَنه إِلَى الْحَرَام أقرب انْتهى.

Ibn al-Qayyim continued and mentioned many more examples of this concept. He reported many more narrations from al-Imām Aḥmad with the wording "It is disliked," while he intended that it is forbidden. Then, he quoted Muḥammad ibn al-Ḥasan as saying, "Everything referred to with the term disliked is forbidden." However, when [Muḥammad ibn al-Ḥasan] did not find an explicit text [forbidding something], he would not use the word "forbidden" when discussing its ruling. Muḥammad also reported that Abu Ḥanīfah and Abu Yūsuf's usage of the term "disliked" is closer to meaning, "forbidden."

قلت: وَمرَاده بذلك مَا وَقع فِي كَلَام الْأَئِمَّة من أَن هَذَا مَكْرُوه لَا بِالنّظرِ إِلَى مَا اصْطَلح عَلَيْهِ من بعدهمْ من التقسيمات الَّتِي يذكرونها فِي كتب الْأُصُول وَالْفُرُوع، فَإِن هَذَا اصْطِلَاح حَادث لَا ينزل عَلَيْهِ كَلَام الْأَئِمَّة.

The point of [Ibn al-Qayyim's] digression into the topic was to show that when the early scholars used the term "disliked" it was not in accordance with the terminology codified by the later scholars or the categories of each terminology mentioned in the books of legal theory and subsidiary rulings. The latter is a new nomenclature that cannot be used to interpret the words of the early scholars.

وَأما الْمَالِكِيَّة: فقد حملُوا قول مَالك: أكره كَذَا، وَشبهه، على جعله مرتبَة متوسطة بَين الْحَرَام والمباح، وَلَا يطلقون عَلَيْهِ اسْم الْجَوَاز، على أَن مَالِكًا قَالَ فِي كثير من أجوبته، أكره كَذَا وَهُوَ حرَام.

As far as the Mālikis go, they held the statements of Mālik where he says "I dislike such-and-such thing" to mean something between a lawful thing and a forbidden thing. So, they do not declare it lawful altogether. With that said, there are many instances where Mālik said, in response to questions, "I dislike such-and-such," and it is forbidden [in his view.]

فَمِنْهَا: أَن مَالِكًا نَص على كَرَاهَة الشطرنج، وَهَذَا عِنْد أَكثر أَصْحَابه على التَّحْرِيم، وَحمله بَعضهم على الْكَرَاهَة الَّتِي هِيَ دون التَّحْرِيم.

For example, Mālik was explicit in his dislike of chess. This, according to the majority of his adherents, means it was forbidden. Some, though, have held his statement to mean it was disliked, which is lesser than prohibition.

وَأما الشَّافِعِي: فَإِنَّهُ قَالَ فِي اللّعب بالشطرنج: إِنَّه لَهو شبه الْبَاطِل، أكرهه وَلَا يتَبَيَّن لي تَحْرِيمه. فقد نَص على كَرَاهَته، وَتوقف فِي تَحْرِيمه، فَلَا يجوز أَن ينْسب إِلَيْهِ - وَلَا إِلَى مذْهبه - أَن اللّعب به جَائِز، وَأَنه مُبَاح، فَإِنَّهُ لم يقل هَذَا وَلَا مَا يدل عَلَيْهِ. وَالْحق أَن يُقَال: إِنَّه كرهه وَتوقف فِي تَحْرِيمه، فَأَيْنَ هَذَا من أَن يُقَال: إِن مذْهبه جَوَاز اللّعب بهَا وإباحته.

As for al-Shāfiʿī, he said, when discussing chess, “It is a game of falsehood. I dislike it, but it is not clear to me that it is forbidden.” Therefore, he explicitly stated that it is disliked, stopping short of forbidding it. As such, it is not permissible to ascribe a view to him, or his school of law, that playing chess is lawful, since he never said or indicated such a thing. The truth is that he disliked it but stopped short of forbidding it. How, then, can one say that his view was that it was permissible and lawful to play chess?

وَمن هَذَا أَيْضا أَنه نَص على كَرَاهَة تزوج الرجل ابْنَته من مَاء الزِّنَا، وَلم يقل قطّ: إِنَّه مُبَاح وَلَا جَائِز. وَالَّذِي يَلِيق بجلالته وإمامته ومنصبه الَّذِي أحله الله بِهِ من الدّين أن هَذِه الْكَرَاهَة مِنْهُ على وَجه التَّحْرِيم، وَأطلق لفظ الْكَرَاهَة لِأَن الْحَرَام يكرههُ الله وَرَسُوله، وَقَالَ تَعَالَى ﴿**كُلُّ ذَٰلِكَ كَانَ سَيِّئُهُ عِندَ رَبِّكَ مَكْرُوهًا**﴾ [الإِسْرَاء: ٣٨]

A similar example is that [al-Shāfiʿī] explicitly stated that it is disliked for a man to marry his illegitimate daughter. He never absolutely stated that it was allowed or lawful. The only way to interpret his statement, which is in a manner that befits his great knowledge, nobility, and high rank that Allah gave him in this religion, is that he meant that it was forbidden, and that he merely stated it was disliked because it is a reprehensible thing to Allah and His Messenger. Allah the Exalted said: **{The evil of all these actions is**

disliked to your Lord.} [Qur'ān 17:38]

وَفِي الصَّحِيح ((إن الله عز وَجل كره لكم قيل وَقَالَ، وَكَثْرَة السُّؤَال، وإضاعة المَال)) فالسلف كَانُوا يستعملون الْكَرَاهَة فِي مَعْنَاهَا الَّذِي اسْتعْملت فِيهِ فِي كَلَام الله تَعَالَى وَرَسُوله، وَلَكِن الْمُتَأَخِّرُونَ اصْطَلحُوا على تَخْصِيص الْكَرَاهَة بِمَا لَيْسَ بِمحرم وَتَركه أرجح من فعله، ثمَّ حمل من حمل كَلَام الْأَئِمَّة على الِاصْطِلَاح الْحَادِث، فغلط.

Also, the Prophet ﷺ said in the authentic narration, **"Allah dislikes for you: Spreading of gossip, asking too many questions, and wasting money."**[117] The Salaf would use the term "disliked" in the same manner it was used in the speech of Allah and the speech of His Messenger ﷺ. However, latter-day scholars canonised the term "disliked (*makrūh*)" as referring to something that is not forbidden but is best not to be done. After the canonisation, some scholars back-projected the new canonised terminology and used it to interpret the words of the early scholars, falling into mistakes while doing so.

وأقبح غلطا من حمل لفظ الْكَرَاهَة أَو لفظ ((لَا يَنْبَغِي)) فِي كَلَام الله وَرَسُوله على الْمَعْنى الاصطلاحي الْحَادِث، وَقد اطرد فِي كَلَام الله وَرَسُوله اسْتِعْمَال ((لَا يَنْبَغِي)) فِي الْمَحْظُور شرعا أَو قدرا، وَفِي المستحيل الْمُمْتَنع كَقَوْلِه تَعَالَى ﴿وَمَا يَنْبَغِي لِلرَّحْمَنِ أَنْ يَتَّخِذَ وَلَدًا﴾ [مَرْيَم: ٩٢] وَقَوله ﴿وَمَا عَلَّمْنَاهُ الشِّعْرَ وَمَا يَنْبَغِي لَهُ﴾ [يس: ٦٩] وَقَوله ﴿وَمَا تَنَزَّلَتْ بِهِ الشَّيَاطِينُ وَمَا يَنْبَغِي لَهُمْ﴾ [الشُّعَرَاء: ٢١١]

Even worse, some interpret the word "disliked" or "inappropriate" in the Qur'ān and Sunnah according to the canonised latter-day terminology. In the speech of Allah and the speech of the Messenger ﷺ the phrase, "not befitting" is consistently used for something that is either religiously forbidden, never destined, or simply a logical impossibility. For example, Allah's statement: **{It does not befit the Lord of Mercy [to have offspring]}** [Qur'ān 19:92] Also, Allah states: **{We have not taught him poetry, nor is it fitting for him.}** [Qur'ān 36:69] Also, He states: **{It was not the jinn who brought down this Qur'ān: it is not fit for them to do so, nor can they.}** [Qur'ān 26: 210-211]

117 Reported by al-Bukhārī (3/270) and Muslim (3/1341).

وَقوله على لِسَان نبيه ((**كَذبَنِي ابْن آدم وَمَا يَنْبَغِي لَهُ، وَشَتَمَنِي ابْن آدم وَمَا يَنْبَغِي لَهُ**)) وَقَوله صلى الله عَلَيْهِ وَسلم ((**إِن الله لَا ينَام وَلَا يَنْبَغِي لَهُ أَن ينَام**)) وَقَوله فِي لِبَاس الْحَرِير: ((**لَا يَنْبَغِي هَذَا لِلْمُتقين**)) وأمثال ذَلِك.

Further, Allah the Exalted said—as reported in the *ḥadīth qudsī*, **"The son of Adam belied me, and it was not appropriate for him to do so, and he cursed me, and it was not appropriate for him to do so."**[118] Also, the Prophet ﷺ said, **"Allah does not sleep, nor is it appropriate for Him to sleep."**[119] Also, he said regarding [men] wearing silk, **"This is not appropriate for the pious."**[120] There are also other examples.

وَالْمَقْصُود من ذَلِك أَن الْمُجْتَهد إِذا رأى دَلِيلا قَطْعِيا، بِحل أَو حُرْمَة، صرح بِلَفْظ الْحل أَو التَّحْرِيم، وَإِذا لم يجد نصا قَاطعا، فاجتهد واستفرغ وَسعه فِي معرفَة الْحق، فأداه اجْتِهَاده إِلَى استنباط حكم تحاشى إِطْلَاق لفظ التَّحْرِيم، وأبدله بقوله: أكره وَنَحْوه، ويقصد بذلك مَعْنَاهُ الْمَفْهُوم من الْكتاب وَالسّنة، لَا مَعْنَاهُ الَّذِي اصْطلحَ عَلَيْهِ الْمُتَأَخّرُونَ. وَكَذَلِكَ لَا يجوز تَنْزِيل كَلَام الله وَرَسُوله على الاصطلاحات الْحَادِثَة، وَإِنَّمَا تنزل على مُقْتَضى مَا كَانَ يفهمهُ الصَّحَابَة من الْمَعْنى اللّغَوِيّ لَا غير، وعَلى الْحَقِيقَة الشَّرْعِيَّة.

The point is that when a *mujtahid* scholar comes to know of a conclusive evidence that would make something lawful or unlawful, they would explicitly state it as being permitted or forbidden. However, if they did not find a conclusive proof, they would use their scholastic abilities to acquire the truth on that issue and come to a conclusion to derive a ruling and after coming to that conclusion, they would be cautious in not using the word "forbidden" and instead use the phrase "I dislike it" etc. By using such phrases and words, they intend their meanings as used in the Qur'ān and the Sunnah, not the later canonised terminology. Likewise, it is not permissible to understand those terms in the Qur'ān and Sunnah according to the later canonised definitions. They should be understood as the companions understood them, which is to say, understand them according to their linguistic meanings and the religious terminology.

---

118 Reported by al-Bukhārī (8/128).

119 Reported by Muslim (179).

120 Reported by al-Bukhārī (1/408) and Muslim (2075).

فَافْهَم هَذَا، فَإِنَّهُ هِدَايَة واستبصار، وَبَيَان لمن كَانَ لَهُ قلب أَو أَلْقى السّمع وَهُوَ شَهِيد. وروى أَبُو عمر بن عبد الْبر أَن مَالِكًا كَانَ إِذا اجْتهد فِي مَسْأَلَة، واستنبط لَهَا حكما يَقُول: إِن نظن إِلَّا ظنا وَمَا نَحن بمستيقنين.

Therefore, one must understand this point, because it is guidance and insight; it clarifies for whoever has a heart and listens attentively. Abu 'Umar ibn 'Abd al-Barr reported that when Mālik would come to a conclusion on an issue and derive a ruling, he would say, "We only use conjecture [for this;] we are not certain."[121]

121 [T] *Jāmi' Bayān al-'Ilm wa Faḍlih* (2/32).

فصل

Section

وَإذا قَالَ الإِمَام: أحب كَذَا أَو يُعجبنِي أَو أعجب إِلَيّ، فَعِنْدَ الْأَكْثَر يحمل على النّدب، وَقدمه فِي (الْفُرُوع) وَغَيره، وَقيل: يحمل على الْوُجُوب.

When the *imām* says, "I love this," "This pleases me," or "This is more pleasing to me," the majority held it to mean that he views the action he is commenting on as recommended. This is what the author of *al-Furūʿ* (Ibn Mufliḥ), amongst others, thought was the preferred view. Others said it should be held to mean it is obligatory to him.

قيل: وَكَذَا إِذا قَالَ: هَذَا حسن أَو أحسن، وَقَوله: أَخْشَى، أَو أَخَاف أَن يكون، أَو إِلا يكون كيجوز، أَو لَا يجوز، وأجبن عَنهُ، فَقيل: يحمل على التَّوَقُّف لتعارض الْأَدِلَّة، وَقيل: هُوَ على ظَاهره.

Likewise, when he says, "This is good," "This is better." As for when he says, "I fear," "I am afraid it is such-and-such," or, "Unless it is such-and-such," it means it is permissible. When he says, "It is not permissible," or, "I am fearful of passing a ruling," some said it means he is not definitively taking a position due to the conflicting evidences. Others said that it should be understood apparently.

وَإِن أجَاب عَن شَيْء ثمَّ قَالَ عَن غَيره: أَهْون أَو أَشد أَو أشنع فَقيل: هما سَوَاء، وَقيل بِالْفرقِ، قَالَه فِي (الْفُرُوع).

Likewise, if he gave an answer about something, and then said about something else, "It is less severe," "It is more severe," or, "It is more heinous," some interpreted it to mean that [both things being asked about] have the same ruling, and others, such as the author of *al-Furūʿ*, said there is a difference.

وَقَالَ الشَّيْخ عبد الْحَلِيم بن تَيْمِية وَالِد شيخ الإِسلام فِي (مسودة الْأُصُول):

Al-Shaykh ʿAbd al-Halim ibn Taymiyyah, the father of Shaykh al-Islam [Ibn Taymiyyah], said in *Musawwadat al-Uṣūl*:

إِذا سُئِلَ الإِمَام أَحْمد عَن مَسْأَلَة فَأجَاب فِيهَا بحظر أَو إِبَاحَة، ثمَّ سُئِلَ عَن غَيرهَا فَقَالَ: ذَلِك أسهل، أَو ذَلِك أَشد، أَو قَالَ: كَذَا أسهل من كَذَا، فَهَل يتَضَمَّن ذَلِك الْمُسَاوَاة بَينهمَا فِي الحكم أم لَا؟ اخْتلف فِي ذَلِك الْأَصْحَاب، فَذهب أَبُو بكر غُلَام الْخلال إِلَى الْمُسَاوَاة بَينهمَا فِي الحكم، وَقَالَ أَبُو عبد الله بن حَامِد: يَقْتَضِي ذَلِك الِاخْتِلَاف. انْتهى.

When al-Imām Aḥmad is asked about an issue, and he judges it as permissible or impermissible, then he is asked about something else, and he says, "It is better," or, "It is worse," or, if he says, 'Such-and-such is better than such-and-such,' does it mean the two things [he comments on] have the same ruling, or not? The *aṣḥāb* have differed: Abu Bakr Ghulām al-Khallāl opined that they are equivalent in ruling. Abu ʿAbdullah ibn Ḥāmid opined that they have different rulings altogether.[122] **[End]**

وَإِذا قَالَ أَحْمد: أجبن عَنهُ، فَفِيهِ خلاف، ذهب فِيهِ صَاحب (الرِّعَايَة) إِلَى الْجَوَاز، وَجعله فِي (الْفُرُوع) فِي الْقُوَّة كقوة كَلَام لم يُعَارضهُ أقوى مِنْهُ، وَذهب بعض الْأَصْحَاب بِهِ إِلَى الْكَرَاهَة.

There is a difference of opinion on when Aḥmad says, "I am fearful of passing a ruling." The author of *al-Riʿāyah* interpreted it as permissibility. In *al-Furūʿ*, the author stated that its definitiveness is only inasmuch as there is no view that is stronger than it.[123] [124] Other adherents took the view that it means it is disliked.

وَقَول أحد من أَصْحَاب الإِمَام أَحْمد فِي تَفْسِير مذْهبه، وإخباره عَن رَأْيه، وَمَفْهُوم

122 [T] *Al-Musawwadah* (p. 5).

123 [T] *Al-Furūʿ wa Taṣḥīḥ al-Furūʿ* (1/46).

124 [T] This phrase has been mentioned with more details by Ibn Ḥāmid in his, *Tahdhīb al-Ajwibah*, where he said, "When he says, 'I am fearful of passing a ruling,' it is his view, but that it is weak enough where he cannot definitively say it is a stronger view to him, but also not weak enough to necessitate rejection altogether." (p. 679)

كَلَامه وَفعله: ينزل منزلة مذْهبه فِي الْأَصَح كإجابته فِي شَيْء بِدَلِيل. وَالْأَشْهر أَنه كإجابته يَقُول صَحَابِيّ. وَاخْتَارَ ابْن حَامِد أَنه كَقَوْل فَقِيه، يَعْنِي مُجْتَهدا، قَالَ فِي (تَصْحِيح الْفُرُوع): وَهُوَ أقرب إِلَى الصَّوَاب، ويعضده منع الإِمَام أَحْمد من اتِّبَاع آراء الرِّجَال.

When one of the *aṣḥāb* interprets his *madhhab*, informs of his view, or explains the connotations within his words and actions, it is to be held as part of his *madhhab*, according to the more correct view. The position would resemble [Aḥmad] answering a question while also providing evidence. The more popular view is that it has the same strength as if he were giving an answer by providing the view of a companion. Ibn Ḥāmid also argued that if he responded with the view of a *mujtahid* jurist [it was also his *madhhab*].[125] The author of *Taṣḥīḥ al-Furūʿ* (i.e., al-Mardāwī) said, "This view is closest to the truth, and is supported by al-Imām Aḥmad's prohibition of following the opinions of men."[126]

وَإِن أَجَاب الإِمَام بقول فَقِيه فَفِيهِ وَجْهَان: أَحدهمَا: أَنه مذْهبه، وَالثَّانِي: لَا.

The other view is that it is not his *madhhab*.

وَمَا انْفَرد بِهِ وَاحِد وَقوي دَلِيله، أَو صحّح الإِمَام خَبرا أَو حسنه أَو دونه وَلم يردهُ، فَفِي كَونه مذْهبه وَجْهَان.

If a singular narrator reports the view of Aḥmad, and that view is supported by convincing evidence, and the *imām* authenticated it or viewed it as good, recorded it and it was not rejected, there are two views as to whether it should be attributed to his *madhhab*:

قَالَ فِي (الرِّعَايَة): وَمَا انْفَرد بِهِ بعض الرواة عَنهُ، وَقوي دَلِيله، فَهُوَ مذْهبه، وَقيل: بل مَا رَوَاهُ جمَاعَة بِخِلَافِهِ.

[Ibn Ḥāmid] said in *al-Riʿāyah*, "What a narrator from [Aḥmad] singularly

125 [T] *Ṣifat al-Fatwā* (p. 348).

126 [T] *Al-Furūʿ wa Taṣḥīḥ al-Furūʿ* (1/46). The reasoning is that if he were to offer the view of another *mujtahid* scholar, one can safely presume that al-Imām Aḥmad was aware of the evidences of that scholar and also espouses that evidence as a basis for the view.

reports and is supported by convincing evidence, it is his *madhhab*. The other view is that if a group of narrators narrate something from Aḥmad, the narration of the group is his *madhhab*."

وَإِن ذكر قَوْلَيْنِ، وَحسن أَحدهمَا، أَو علله، فَفِيهِ خلاف، فَقَالَ فِي (الرَّوْضَة الْأُصُولِيَّة)، و(مختصرها) للطوفي، و(مختصر التَّحْرِير): إِن الحكم يتبع الْعلَّة، فَمَا وجدت فِيهِ الْعلَّة، فَهُوَ قَوْله، سَوَاء قيل بتخصيص الْعلَّة، أَو لم يقل. وَقيل: لَا يكون ذَلِك مذهبا لَهُ.

If he mentions two opinions and says one is accurate or preferred, or provides reasoning for one view, there is a difference of opinion on whether it is his *madhhab*. It states in *al-Rawḍah* [by Ibn Qudāmah], its summation by al-Ṭūfī, and *Mukhtaṣar al-Taḥrir* [by Ibn al-Najjār al-Futūḥī]: The ruling follows from the cause of the ruling; if the cause exists in some other [unmentioned] issue, it is considered his opinion, irrespective if he considers the *ratio legis* to be specific or not. Others opined that it is not a part of his *madhhab*.

وَإِن ذكر قَوْلَيْنِ، وَفرع على أَحدهمَا، فَقيل: هُوَ مذْهبه لتحسينه إِيَّاه أَو تَعْلِيله، وَقدم هَذَا فِي (الرِّعَايَتَيْنِ) وَ(الْحَاوِي) وَغَيرهم، وَهُوَ مَذْهَب الْأَثْرَم والخرقي وَغَيرهمَا. قَالَه ابْن حَامِد فِي (تَهْذِيب الْأَجْوِبَة) وَقيل: لَا يكون مذْهبه، وَاخْتَارَهُ جمَاعَة.

If he mentions two views, and then ramifies one of them, it was said that it is his *madhhab*, because he approves of it or provides rationalisation for it. This is the view preferred in the two *al-Riʿāyahs*, as well as al-Ḥāwī and other books. It is the view of al-Athram and al-Khiraqī, as stated by Ibn Ḥāmid in *Tahdhīb al-Ajwibah*. The other view is that it is not his *madhhab*, and this choice was the preferred view of a group of scholars.

قَالَ ابْن حَامِد: وَالْأَفْضَل أَن يفصل، فَمَا كَانَ من جَوَاب لَهُ فِي أصل يحتوي مسَائِل خرج جَوَابه على بَعْضهَا، فَإِنَّهُ جَائِز أَن ينْسب إِلَيْهِ نَفسه ذَلِك الأَصْل من حَيْثُ الْقيَاس.

Ibn Ḥāmid said, "It is best to treat each case individually. If his answer is about some maxim that entails various underlying issues, but his answer does not directly provide an answer to some of those issues, it is possible to attribute the rest of the issues under the maxim to [his *madhhab*] via analogy."[127]

وَمن ثمَّ قَالَ فِي (التَّحْرِير) مفرعا على هَذَا:

For that reason, the author of *[Mukhtaṣar] al-Taḥrīr* stated, while ramifying [Ibn Ḥāmid's] position:

فَلَو أفتى فِي مَسْأَلَتَيْنِ متشابهتين بحكمين مُخْتَلفين فِي وقت لم يجز نقل الحكم من كل مِنْهُمَا إِلَى الْأُخْرَى، وَلَو نَص على حكم مَسْأَلَة ثمَّ قَالَ: لَو قَالَ قَائِل بِكَذَا؛ أَو ذهب ذَاهِب إِلَيْهِ - يُرِيد خِلَافه - كَانَ مذهبا لم يكن ذَلِك مذهبا لَهُ، وَإِذا سُئِلَ عَن مَسْأَلَة فتوقف فِيهَا كَانَ مذْهبه فِيهَا الْوَقْف. انْتهى.

Therefore, if [Aḥmad] judged in two similar cases but gave two different rulings in a single moment, it is not possible to extend the ruling of each ruling to the other. If he states a ruling in an issue, then says, "If someone else took such-and-such view," or, "If this were espoused by someone," meaning something contrary to the view he explicitly stated, it would be considered a valid approach by [the one who espoused the other view], but would not be the *madhhab* of [Aḥmad]. Further, if he were asked about an issue and refused to give an answer, his *madhhab* would be to refrain from answering.[128] **[End]**

وَقَالَ فِي (تَصْحِيح الْفُرُوع) فِيمَا لَو ذكر قَوْلَيْنِ وَفرع على أَحدهمَا الْمَذْهَب لَا يكون بِالِاحْتِمَالِ، وَإِلَّا فمذهبه أقربهما من الدَّلِيل، وَإِذا أفتى بِحكم فَسكت وَنَحْوه، لم يكن رُجُوعا. قدمه ابْن حَامِد فِي (تَهْذِيب الْأَجْوِبَة) وَتَابعه الشَّيْخ تَقِيّ الدّين أَحْمد بن تَيْمِية.

The author of *Taṣḥīḥ al-Furū*ʿ mentioned the case when Aḥmad would mention two views and would ramify one of them, whether it is considered the *madhhab*. He stated, "The *madhhab* is not established through sim-

---

127 [T] The printed version of *al-Madkhal* stated, "It is possible to attribute it to the maxim via analogy." However, what I have placed in the main text is more accurate, as reflected by the two published editions of *Tahdhīb al-Ajwibah*, the first by ʿAlām al-Kutub (p. 37) and the second by Maktabat al-ʿUlūm wa ʾl-Ḥikam (pp. 385-386).
128 [T] *Al-Kawkab al-Munīr* (4/500).

ple probability." In that case, he says, the *madhhab* should be the closest in alignment of the two views [mentioned by Aḥmad] to the evidence.[129] Likewise, if [Aḥmad] gives a ruling and then remains silent,[130] it is not considered a retraction, as preferred by Ibn Ḥāmid in his *Tahdhīb al-Ajwibah*, and as chosen by al-Shaykh Taqī al-Dīn Aḥmad ibn Taymiyyah."[131]

قَالَ المرداوي فِي (تَصْحِيح الْفُرُوع): وَهُوَ أولى. وَقَالَ فِي (الْفُرُوع): وَفِي سُكُوته رُجُوعا وَجْهَان.

Al-Mardāwī said in *Taṣḥīḥ al-Furūʿ*, "This is the more preferred view." And in *al-Furūʿ* he mentioned that there are two views on his silence.

وَمَا علله بعلة تُوجد فِي مسَائِل، فالأكثر أَن مذْهبه فِيهَا كالمعللة، وَقيل: لَا، وَيلْحق مَا توقف فِيهِ بِمَا يُشبههُ.

If Aḥmad gives a cause for his judgement of a ruling, and the *ratio legis* he mentions is present in some other rulings, the majority [of the *aṣḥāb*] opine that his view in [the similar] issues is that of the one where he mentioned the *ratio legis*. Some, however, disagreed.

وَإِن اشتبهت مَسْأَلَتَانِ أَو أَكثر مُخْتَلفَة بالخفة والثقل، فَقَالَ فِي (الرِّعَايَة الْكُبْرى) وَتبعهُ فِي (الْحَاوِي الْكَبِير): الأولى الْعَمَل بِكُل مِنْهُمَا كمن هُوَ أصلح لَهُ، وَالْأَظْهَر

129 [T] This quotation is not exactly in the order mentioned by al-Mardāwī, and the statement, "In that case, he says, the *madhhab* should be the closest in alignment of the two views [mentioned by al-Imām Aḥmad] to the evidence," is not a quote from al-Mardāwī at all, but rather, from Ibn Mufliḥ. For completeness, I will mention what al-Mardāwī said, "The first view is that [if al-Imām Aḥmad ramifies a view], it is not his *madhhab* unless he explicitly prefers it or gives a ruling based on it. My comment is: this is the correct view, and was chosen by Ibn Ḥamdān in *Adab al-Muftī*. The second view is that it is his *madhhab*. This view was mentioned first in sequence [by Ibn Ḥamdān] in *Ṣifat al-Muftī* and *al-Riʿāyah al-Kubrā*, and was the view of al-Shaykh Taqī al-Dīn in *al-Musawwadah*. My comment is: It is a weak view; the *madhhab* cannot be established through simple probability." (1/49)

130 [T] According to al-Mardāwī this means, "If he gives a ruling, and then someone objects, and he remains silent [without providing a response to the objection], is his silence a sign that he recanted his original ruling?" (1/50)

131 [T] *Al-Furūʿ wa Taṣḥīḥ al-Furūʿ* (1/50).

عَنهُ هُنَا التَّخْيير.

When [al-Imām Aḥmad] remains silent on an issue, the ruling [of that issue] should be that of the scenario and issue it most resembles. If two or more issues are similar but differ in volume and weight,[132] then each should do what is best for them, and the more apparent ruling [relayed from Aḥmad] is that one has the choice. This was stated in *al-Riʿāyat al-Kubrā*, and the author of *al-Ḥāwī al-Kabīr* followed that view, as well.

وَقَالَ نجم الدّين الطوفي فِي (مُخْتَصر الرَّوْضَة الأُصُوليَّة):

Najm al-Dīn al-Ṭūfī stated in his summation of *al-Rawḍah*:

إِذا نَص الْمُجْتَهد على حكم فِي مَسْأَلَة لعِلَّة، فبينها، فمذهبه فِي كل مَسْأَلَة وجدت فِيهَا تِلْكَ الْعلَّة كمذهبه فِيهَا، إِذْ الحكم يتبع الْعلَّة. وَإِن لم يبين الْعلَّة، فَلَا - وَإِن اشتبهتا - إِذْ هُوَ إِثْبَات مَذْهَب بِالْقِيَاسِ، ولجواز ظُهُور الْفرق لَهُ لَو عرضت عَلَيْهِ.

If a *mujtahid* scholar states the ruling of an issue by mention of its rationale and cause which he clarifies, his *madhhab* in every issue encompassed by the same rationale and cause is that of the ruling he explicitly stated, since rulings are predicated on their causes and rationales. If, however, [the *mujtahid* scholar] does not clarify the cause and rationale, then the same cannot be said, even if they are quite similar, since that would be affirming a position based on analogy in a case where there still remains the possibility that there are differences [between the two issues] that he would be aware of if the two issues were presented to him.

وَلَو نَص فِي مَسْأَلَتَيْنِ مشتبهتين على حكمين مُخْتَلفين، لم يجز أَن يَجْعَل فيهمَا رِوَايَتَانِ بِالنَّقْلِ والتخريج، كَمَا لَو سكت عَن إِحْدَاهمَا وَأولى، وَالْأولَى جَوَاز ذَلِك بعد الْجد والبحث من أَهله، إِذْ خَفَاء الْفرق مَعَ ذَلِك - وَإِن دق - مُمْتَنع عَادَة.

If he gives two different rulings on two similar issues, [some opined] it is not

132 [T] Such as a product being a certain price if it is weighed, and another price if the seller goes by volume instead of just weight.

permissible to state they are two different opinions [on the same issue] by extending and extrapolating [his words].[133] This is similar to if he [was asked about two issues but] did not comment on one of them; rather, it is even more worthy of this approach. With that said, it is best to consider [extrapolating one of the two similar issues to be a variant of the other similar issue, and vice versa] possible after strenuous research by capable scholars, since even if the differences [between the two issues] are quite subtle, it is usually impossible for them to be wholly in-discoverable.

وَقد وَقع فِي مَذْهَبنَا، فَقَالَ فِي (الْمُحَرر): وَمن لم يجد إِلَّا ثَوابًا نجسا صلى فِيهِ وَأعَاد، نَص عَلَيْهِ، وَنَصّ فِيمَن حبس فِي مَوضِع نجس فصلى أَنه لَا يُعِيد، فيتخرج فيهمَا رِوَايَتَانِ. وَذكر مثل ذَلِك فِي الْوَصَايَا وَالْقَذْف، وَمثله فِي مَذْهَب الشَّافِعِي كثير. ثمَّ التَّخْرِيج قد يقبل تقريرا لنصين، وَقد لَا يقبل.

This has occurred in our *madhhab*: in *al-Muḥarrar* [by al-Majd ibn Taymiyyah] it states, "If someone can only find an impure garment, they should pray in it, but then repeat [the prayer, once they have a clean garment]. This was explicitly stated [by Aḥmad]. Likewise, he explicitly stated that if someone is imprisoned in an impure area and prayed there, he should not repeat the prayer. This results in two separate narrations.[134] He mentioned the same about wills and defamation.[135] There are also many examples of this

133 [T] Al-Imām Najm al-Dīn al-Ṭūfī clarifies, saying, "This means, if he explicitly gives two different rulings on two different issues, it is not permissible to take one of those two rulings and apply it to the other by claiming it is a second opinion on the issue, making [the *mujtahid imām*] have two views on the topic." (*Sharh Mukhtaṣar al-Rawḍah*, 3/640)

134 [T] Al-Ṭūfī says : This is because the purity of the garment and the place of prayer are both conditions for the prayer. This is the similarity between the two issues. On the issue of the impure garment, he stated that the prayer does have to be repeated. As such, that ruling can be applied to the [impure] place, resulting in the same view. On the topic of the impure place, he stated that one does not have to repeat the prayer, and that view can be applied to the impure garment, resulting in the same view. There is no doubt that each of the two issues has two different opinions: one occurred through an explicit text and the other through extrapolation. (*Sharh Mukhtaṣar al-Rawḍah*, 3/641).

135 [T] Al-Ṭūfī stated: On wills: if a will is found for an individual in their own handwriting, it should be applied, as explicitly stated [by Aḥmad]. Likewise, he also explicitly stated that if a testator writes a will and then seals it and says, "Testify to what is in it," that it is not applicable. The issue results in two different opinions. The point of similarity between the two is that there is a will that is authored with the handwriting

in the Shāfiʿī *madhhab*. With that said, the extrapolation is also subject to critique [by showing relevant differences between the two issues].

وَإِذا نَص على حكمين مُخْتَلفين فِي مَسْأَلَة، فمذهبه آخرهما إِن علم التَّارِيخ، كتناسخ أَخْبَار الشَّارِع، وَإِلَّا فأشبههما بأصوله وقواعد مذْهبه، وأقربهما إِلَى الدَّلِيل الشَّرْعِيّ، وَقيل: كِلَاهُمَا مَذْهَب لَهُ، إِذْ لَا ينْقض الِاجْتِهَاد بِالِاجْتِهَادِ، فَإِن أُرِيد ظَاهره، فَمَمْنُوع، وَإِن أُرِيد أَن مَا عمل بِالْأولِ لَا ينْقض، فَلَيْسَ مِمَّا نَحن فِيهِ. ثمَّ يبطل بِمَا لَو صرح بِرُجُوعِهِ عَنهُ، فَكيف يَجْعَل مذهبا لَهُ مَعَ تصريحه باعتقاد بُطْلَانه؟

If [a *mujtahid* scholar] gives two different rulings on a single issue, his *madhhab* should be considered the later of the two views, if the chronology is known, just as the rulings of the legislation are abrogated. If [the date is not known], the view that is most aligned with [the scholar's] legal theory, the maxims of his *madhhab*, and the closest to the religious evidence [should be considered his *madhhab*]. It was stated that both should be considered the *madhhab* [of the scholar], since one *ijtihād* is not nullified by another. If the apparent implication of that position is intended, it is impossible to agree to such a view. However, if what is meant is if someone acted on the first view, their actions are not null, the response is: that is not the point of discussion

---

of [the testator], but there are two explicitly different rulings in each case. This variance results in each being extrapolated to the other [resulting in two views], as has preceded.

On slander: if a man says to his wife, "You are a fornicator," and she replies, "I have fornicated with you," her right to have him punished for defamation is waived by acknowledging what he stated about her, and she also cannot be accused of defaming him. This has been explicitly stated [by Aḥmad]. He also explicitly stated that if a man says to his wife, "You and so-and-so committed fornication together," he has defamed them both. As such, this resulted in two different opinions. The similarity between them is that when she said, "I fornicated with you," she has defamed him by indirect implication, and when he says to her, "You have fornicated with so-and-so," it is a defamation of that "so-and-so" by indirect implication. His explicit texts have differed on these two issues, and as such, it results in differences of opinion." (*Sharh Mukhtaṣar al-Rawḍah*, 3/642)

The important factor for why the first case is not considered a defamation and the second is was mentioned by al-Shaykh Manṣūr al-Buhūtī, who said, "Acknowledging fornication while attributing it to have been with a particular individual is not defamation, such as when someone says, 'I fornicated with so-and-so,' it is not defamation of [the woman accused]." (*Sharḥ Muntahā al-Irādāt*, 3/359)

in this instance. In continuation, their position is further nullified by the case where [a *mujtahid*] explicitly retracts the first view. How can it still be claimed to be a part of his *madhhab* when he explicitly states that he believes otherwise?

وَلَو خَالع مُجْتَهد زَوجته ثَلَاث مَرَّات يعْتَقد الْخلْع فسخا، ثمَّ تغير اجْتِهَاده، فاعتقده طَلَاقا، لزمَه فراقها.

If a *mujtahid* does a *khul'*[136] with his wife thrice, while believing that a *khul'* is an annulment, and then changes his view, considering [*khul'* to be] a divorce, it is incumbent on him to part with his wife.

وَلَو حكم بِصِحَّة نِكَاح مُخْتَلف فِيهِ حَاكم، ثمَّ تغير اجْتِهَاده، لم ينْتَقض للُزُوم التسلسل بِنَقْض النَّقْض، واضطراب الْأَحْكَام.

However, if a judge rules valid a marriage [the validity of which] is differed on, and then he changes his view, [the marriage] does not become nullified, lest he falls into an infinite regress of nullifications and confusion of rulings.[137]

وَلَو نكح مقلد بفتوى مُجْتَهد، ثمَّ تغير اجْتِهَاده، فَالظَّاهِر لَا يلْزمه فراقها، إِذْ عمله بالفتوى جرى حكم الْحَاكِم.

Further, if a *muqallid* marries based on the *fatwā* of a *mujtahid*, and then [the *mujtahid*] changes his view, the apparent view is that [the one who married] does not have to leave [his wife], since his acting on a *fatwā* is considered the ruling of the judge.[138] **[End]**

هَذَا كَلَامه، وَبسطه تكفل بِهِ الْعَلامَة نجم الدّين الطوفي فِي شَرحه فَلَا نطيل بِهِ.

136 [T] A *khul'* divorce is, "When a man separates from his wife with specific phrases for compensation." (*Muntahā al-Irādāt*, 2/131)

137 [T] Al-Ṭūfī states: Technically, by use of analogy, the judgement should be nullified because of the contradictory *ijtihād* done afterwards, just as *ijtihād* that is not done in a judicial setting nullifies the previous ruling, as mentioned in the issue of [the *mujtahid* and] the *khul'*. However, this analogy was disregarded in favor of *istiḥsān* (which is "to forgo judging an issue on the precedent of its analogues because of the presence of a specific religious evidence;" refer to *Sharh Mukhtaṣar al-Rawḍah*, 3/190), in order to correctly regulate matters and to prevent things from becoming confused." (*Sharh Mukhtaṣar al-Rawḍah*, 3/649)

138 [T] *Sharh Mukhtaṣar al-Rawḍah* (3/638).

This is what [al-Ṭūfī] stated. Al-ʿAllāmah Najm al-Dīn al-Ṭūfī also took it on himself to expound on these issues in his explanation, so we will not elongate this section with doing so.

وَحَاصِل مَا تقدم أَن نُصُوص الْأَئِمَّة بِالْإِضَافَة إِلَى مقلديهم كنصوص الشَّارِع بِالْإِضَافَة إِلَى الْأَئِمَّة.

The summary of what preceded, however, is that the texts of the *imāms* are to their followers what the divine texts are to the scholars.

وَاعْلَم أَيْضا أَن بَين التَّخْرِيج وَالنَّقْل فرقا من حَيْثُ إِن الأول أَعم من الثَّانِي، لِأَن التَّخْرِيج يكون من الْقَوَاعِد الْكُلية للْإِمَام، أَو الشَّرْع أَو الْعقل، لِأَن حَاصِل مَعْنَاهُ بِنَاء فرع على أصل بِجَامِع مُشْتَرك، كتخريجنا على تَفْرِيق الصَّفْقَة فروعا كَثِيرَة، وعَلى قَاعِدَة تَكْلِيف مَا لَا يُطَاق أَيْضا فروعا كَثِيرَة فِي أُصُول الْفِقْه وفروعه، وَقد جعل فقهاؤنا ذَلِك كَأَنَّهُ فن مُسْتَقل، فألف فِيهِ الْحَافِظ ابن رجب كِتَابه الْمُسَمّى بـ(القواعد الْفِقْهِيَّة) وَألف بعده فِي ذَلِك ابْن اللحام، كَمَا ستعلمه فِيمَا سَيَأْتِي إِن شَاءَ الله تَعَالَى، لكنهما لم يتجاوزا فِي التَّخْرِيج الْقَوَاعِد الْكُلية الْأُصُولِيَّة.

Also know that the terms "extrapolating" and "extending" in the above text have subtle differences, as the first is more general than the second. Extrapolation occurs based on the general maxims that the *imām* adheres to, or based on the legislation, or based on the intellect, since its resulting outcome is to base a subsidiary matter on a foundational ruling due to a commonality between the two rulings. This is similar to our extrapolation of many rulings based on the discussion on separation between items sold in a single transaction,[139] and extrapolating of many subsidiary topics in legal theory and in judicial law from the maxim of "Not holding people responsible for things they cannot bear." Our jurists have considered such topics a separate science in and of itself, which made al-Ḥāfiẓ Ibn Rajab write his book *al-Qawāʿid al-Fiqhiyyah*, and after him, Ibn al-Laḥḥām authored a book, as you will soon learn, Allah willing. However, they did not go beyond extrapolating from the universal legal maxims.

139 [T] In *Muntahā al-Irādāt*, it states, "It means to combine between something that can validly be sold and something that cannot [in one transaction]." Refer to *Sharh Muntahā al-Irādāt* by al-Shaykh Manṣūr al-Buhūtī (2/20) for more information.

وَأما النَّقْل فَهُوَ أَن ينْقل النَّص عَن الإِمَام ثمَّ يخرج عَلَيْهِ فروعا فَيجْعَل كَلَام الإِمَام أصلا وَمَا يُخرجهُ فرعا وَذَلِكَ الأَصْل مُخْتَصّ بنصوص الإِمَام فَظهر الْفرق بَينهمَا

As for extending, it is when a text is reported from the *imām* and is then used to extrapolate rulings, making the text of the *imām* the foundation, and whatever is extrapolated as the subsidiary. Extending, therefore, is specific to the texts of the *imām*. That is the difference between the two.

فصل

Section

أراك أيها الناظر وقد علمت مما رقمناه آنفا مسالك تصرف الْأَصْحَاب فِي رِوَايَات الإِمَام، وَأَنَّهُمْ أثبتوا لَهَا أصولا كَمَا أثبت الْأَئِمَّة أصولا لمسالك الِاجْتِهَاد الْمُطلق، وَأن ذَلِك التَّصَرُّف مُفَرع على أصُول الْفِقْه عَامَّة، وَعلمت أن هَذِه التَّصَرُّفَات لَا تخْتَص بِمذهب بِعَيْنِه، بِالْإِضَافَة إِلَى التَّصَرُّف فِي كَلَام الْأَئِمَّة، وَأن المتبع لِلْأُصُولِ الْمُطلقَة يُقَال لَهُ: مُجْتَهد مُطلق. والمتبع لِلْأُصُولِ الْخَاصَّة بِكَلَام الإِمَام يُقَال له: مُجْتَهد الْمَذْهَب.

I see that you, the reader, have witnessed and learned—from what we previously wrote—the methods of the *aṣḥāb* in treating the narrations of the Imām, and that they codified some theories on how to interpret them, just as the scholars codified legal theories to engage in absolute *ijtihād*. Further, you have learned that their treatment [of his statements] branches from the general legal theories. You have also learned that these approaches are not unique to just one *madhhab*, but can also be used to understand the words of other scholars. You have learned that when a scholar follows the general legal theories [as it pertains to the divine texts], they are known as a *mujtahid muṭlaq* (absolute *mujtahid*). And when a scholar follows the specific theories of interpreting the words of individual *imāms*, they are called the *mujtahid al-madhhab* (*mujtahid* within a *madhhab*).

سما بك الشوق للنفع أَن نذْكر جملا من كَلَام الباحثين فِي تِلْكَ الْأُصُول الْخَاصَّة، لتَكون كالإثبات لما تقدم، وكالتفصيل، وَلَا تسأم مِمَّا وَقع فِيهِ مكررا،

فَإِن المكرر أحلى، وَإِلَيْك الْمَوْعُود بِهِ منثورا.

After learning these facts, you must be yearning for us to mention some texts that researchers have presented on the topic of those specific theories, so that they can solidify and explain what was previously mentioned. Do not be weary of any repetitious information, for what is repeated is sweeter. Alas, I present to you what I have promised, written in prose.

مَذْهَب الْإِنْسَان: مَا قَالَه أَو دلّ عَلَيْهِ، بِمَا يجْرِي مجْرى القَوْل من تَنْبِيه أَو غَيره، فَإِن عدم ذَلِك، لم تجز إِضَافَته إِلَيْهِ. ذكره أَبُو الْخطاب. وَقَالَ أَيْضا: مذْهبه مَا نَص أَو نبه عَلَيْهِ، أَو شملته علته الَّتِي علل بهَا. وَقَالَ الشَّيْخ عبد الحليم وَالِد شيخ الْإِسْلَام ابْن تَيْمِية: اخْتلف أَصْحَابنَا فِي إِضَافَة الْمَذْهَب إِلَيْهِ من جِهَة الْقيَاس على قَوْله، فَذهب الْخلال وَأَبُو بكر عبد العزيز إِلَى أَنه لَا يجوز ذَلِك، وَنَصره الْحلْوانِي، وَذهب الْأَثْرَم والخرقي وَابْن حَامِد إِلَى جَوَاز ذَلِك.

A person's *madhhab* is what they say or indicate in ways that resemble speech, such as notifying of something, and so forth. If [those two methods of instruction] are unavailable, it is not permissible to ascribe [the *madhhab*] to the person, as Abu 'l-Khaṭṭāb [al-Kalwādhānī] mentioned. He also said, "A person's *madhhab* is what they explicitly state or point out, or is encompassed by the same cause of a ruling that he judged by."[140] Al-Shaykh 'Abd al-Ḥalīm, the father of Shaykh al-Islam Ibn Taymiyyah, said, "Our *aṣḥāb* have differed on whether to ascribe as the *madhhab* of a person an analogy which uses his speech as the basis. Al-Khallāl and Abu Bakr 'Abd al-'Azīz opined it is not allowed, and al-Halwānī supported their view. However, al-Athram, al-Khiraqī, and Ibn Ḥāmid allowed it."[141]

وَقَالَ الشَّيْخ مجد الدين ابن تَيْمِية:

Al-Shaykh Majd al-Dīn ibn Taymiyyah said:

إِذا نَص الإِمَام على مَسْأَلَة، وَكَانَت الْأُخْرَى تشبهها شبها يجوز أَن يخفى على مُجْتَهد، لم يجز أَن تجْعَل الْأُخْرَى مذْهبه بذلك. هَذَا قَول أبي الْخطاب، فَأَما لَا

140 [T] *Al-Tamhīd fī Uṣūl al-Fiqh* by al-Imām Abu 'l-Khaṭṭāb [al-Kalwādhānī] (4/372).

141 [T] *Al-Musawwadah* (p. 524).

يخفى على بعض الْمُجْتَهدين، فَلَا يفرق الإِمَام بَينهمَا، وَهَذَا فِي ظَاهره متناقض، فَيحمل على مَسْأَلَتَيْنِ يتَرَدَّد فيهمَا: هَل هما مِمَّا يخفى الشّبَه بَينهمَا على بعض الْمُجْتَهدين أَو لَا يخفى؟ وَقد ذكر فِي الْمَسْأَلَة بعد هَذِه: أَنه لَو قَالَ: الشُّفْعَة لِجَار الدَّار وَلَا شُفْعَة فِي الدّكان، فَلَا ينْقل حكم إحدهمَا إِلَى الْأُخْرَى.

If the *imām* explicitly states his view on an issue, and there is another issue that resembles it subtly enough that it could be obscure to some *mujtahid*, it is not permissible to claim [the ruling on the second issue] is the *madhhab* [of the *imām*] because of that resemblance. This was the view of Abu 'l-Khaṭṭāb. As for if the differences are not hidden to some *mujtahids*, the *imām* would not have differentiated between them. This is apparently contradictory.[142] To resolve the contradiction, his view would be applied to an issue that is unclear in the sense that one cannot discern if it is a case that would be hidden to some *mujtahids*, or would not be hidden. To illustrate further, [Abu 'l-Khaṭṭāb] mentioned if [a scholar] were to explicitly say that the right of pre-emption[143] belongs to the owner of the neighbouring house, but not to the neighbour of a store-front, neither of those two rulings can be applied to the other.

فَأَما إِذا لم يُصَرح فِي الْأُخْرَى بِحكم، فَالظَّاهِر حملهَا على نظيرتها، وَهَذَا يَقْتَضِي الْقيَاس على قَوْله إِذا لم يُصَرح بالمعرفة، وَإِنَّمَا تكون هَذِه فِيمَا يخفى على بعض الْمُجْتَهدين، وَإِذا لم يُصَرح فِي الأخرى بِحكم، فَالظَّاهِر حملهَا على نظيرتها. وَقَالَ ابْن حمدَان: مَا قيس على كَلَامه، فَهُوَ مذْهبه، وَقيل: لَا، وَقيل: إِن جَازَ تَخْصِيص الْعلَّة وَإِلَّا فَهُوَ مذْهبه. وَقَالَ أَيْضا - وَهُوَ من عِنْده - إِن نص عَلَيْهَا، أَو أَوْمأ إِلَيْهَا، أَو علل الأَصْل بهَا، فَهُوَ مذْهبه، وَإِلَّا فَلَا، إِلَّا أَن تشهد أَقْوَاله، أَو أَفعاله، أَو أَحْوَاله لِلعِلَّةِ المستنبطة بِالصِّحَّةِ وَالتَّعْيِين.

142 [T] The reason why it is contradictory is that if it is obscure to some *mujtahid*, it is not obscure to others, and if it is not obscure to some scholars, it might be obscure to others. As such, both qualifications eliminate the same set of scholars.

143[T] This is known as the issue of *al-shuf'ah*, which is when one of two partners in a business wishes to sell their share of the business, the other partner can force a purchase of it to own the entire business. The issue mentioned by al-Majd here is referring to a person who wishes to sell their home. The scholars differ on whether the neighbour has the first right to purchase the home.

As for if [the *imām*] does not explicitly mention a ruling on either of the two cases, the apparent view [as mentioned by Abu 'l-Khaṭṭāb] is to extrapolate [the explicit ruling] to its analogues and parallels. This necessitates using [the view of the *imām*] in an analogy if it is an issue that some *mujtahids* would possibly be unaware of, and this rule applies with two preconditions: (i) it must be a case where [the difference] is not perceivable by some *mujtahid* scholars, and (ii) it must be one where [the *imām*] did not explicitly state a ruling in [its analogue]. Ibn Ḥamdān said, "Anything that is analogous to his words is his *madhhab*," but others said that it is not. It was stated that if the *ratio legis* of the ruling is particular to the ruling that the *imām* offered the judgement on, extending the *ratio legis* is not his *madhhab*, but if otherwise, it is. [Ibn Ḥamdān] also stated, 'If [the *mujtahid imām*] explicitly states the cause, indicates it, or rationalises the foundational ruling by use of the cause, it (the subsidiary) is a part of his *madhhab*. Otherwise, it is not, unless his statements, actions, and behaviour testify to the deduced cause [of the ruling] by validating or specifying it.'

قَالَ ابْن حمدَان: فعلى قَوْله: إِن مَا قيس على كَلَامه مذْهبه. وَقَالَ من عِنْده أَيْضا: إِن أفتى فِي مَسْأَلَتَيْنِ متشابهتين بحكمين مُخْتَلفين فِي وَقْتَيْنِ، جَازَ نقل الحكم وتخريجه من كل وَاحِدَة إِلَى الْأُخْرَى، وَقيل: لَا يجوز، كَمَا لَو فرق هُوَ بَينهمَا أَو قرب الزَّمن. وَاخْتَارَ أَيْضا إِن علم التَّارِيخ، وَلم يَجْعَل أول قوليه فِي مَسْأَلَة وَاحِدَة مذهبا لَهُ جَازَ نقل الثَّانِيَة إِلَى الأولى فِي الأقيس، وَلَا عكس إِلَّا أَن يَجْعَل أول قوليه فِي مَسْأَلَة وَاحِدَة مذهبا لَهُ مَعَ معرفَة التَّارِيخ، وَإِن جهل التَّارِيخ، جَازَ نقل أقربهما من كتاب، أَو سنة أَو إِجْمَاع أَو أثر أَو قَوَاعِد الإِمَام وَنَحْو ذَلِك إِلَى الْأُخْرَى فِي الأقيس، وَلَا عكس إِلَّا أَن يَجْعَل أول قوليه فِي مَسْأَلَة وَاحِدَة مذهبا لَهُ مَعَ معرفَة التَّارِيخ، وَأولى لجَوَاز كَونهَا الْأَخِيرَة دون الراجحة.

Ibn Ḥamdān also said, "Based on our statement, 'Anything that is analogous to his words is his *madhhab*,' we can say that if a person gives a ruling in two separate issues with two different answers at two different times, it is permissible to extend and extrapolate each ruling to the other. Some said it is not possible, just as it would not be possible to do so if he differentiated between the two within a short time-frame.[144] If the chronology is known, and the

144 [T] Ibn Ḥamdān said, "Because it would be assumed that he remembered [his

first of his two views is not considered his final *madhhab*, it is possible to extrapolate his second view to the first if it is the more veracious analogy, but not [the first view stated to the second one stated], unless if his first view is considered a part of his *madhhab*, then it is allowed [to extrapolate the first view to the second view], as long as the date is known. If the dates [of the rulings] are unknown, it is allowed to extend a ruling closest to the Qur'ān, Sunnah, consensus, narration, or the general legal theories of the *imām* to the other, if it is the more veracious analogy, but not the opposite.[145] However, if his first view in a single issue is considered his *madhhab*, and its date is known, it can be done, and is preferable, since it is possible that [the other view] is his last stated view, but not necessarily the stronger view.[146] **[End]**

فصل

Section

قَالَ الإِمَام شيخ الْإِسْلَام أَحْمد بن تَيْمِية - قدس الله روحه - فِي (مسودة الْأُصُول):

Shaykh al-Islam Aḥmad bin Taymiyyah, may Allah sanctify his soul, said in his book, *Musawwadat al-Uṣūl*:

الرِّوَايَات الْمُطلقَة نُصُوص الإِمَام أَحْمد. وَكَذَا قَوْلنَا: وَعنهُ: وَأما التَّنْبِيهَات بِلَفْظِهِ، فقولنا: أَوْمَأ إِلَيْهِ أَحْمد، أَو أَشَارَ إِلَيْهِ، أَو دلّ كَلَامه عَلَيْهِ، أَو توقف.

Anytime a "narration," without any other qualifier, is mentioned, it is a text of al-Imām Aḥmad. Likewise, when we say, "It is also reported from him." As for his textual indications of things, we refer to them by saying, "Aḥmad alluded to it," or, "Aḥmad referred to it," or, "Aḥmad's speech indicated it," or, "Aḥmad abstained."

---

ruling] on the first case when he offered his ruling on the second one." Refer to *Ṣifat al-Muftī* (p. 316).

145 [T] The opposite being extending the ruling that is perceived as further from the Qur'ān, Sunnah, consensus, narration, or the general legal theories of the *imām* to the other, closer view.

146 [T] *Al-Musawwadah* (pp. 525-526).

وَأما الْأَوْجه: فأقوال الْأَصْحَاب وتخريجهم إِن كَانَت مَأْخُوذَة من كَلَام الإِمَام أَحْمد أَو إيمائه أَو دَلِيله أَو تَعْلِيله أَو سِيَاق كَلَامه وقوته.

The term "variances (*awjuh*)" refers to the views of the *aṣḥāb* and their extrapolations if they are taken from the speech of al-Imām Aḥmad, his indications, evidences, causes for rulings, and the contextual setting and emphasis of his speech.

وَإِن كَانَت مَأْخُوذَة من نُصُوص الإِمَام ومخرجه مِنْهَا - فَهِيَ رِوَايَات مخرجة لَهُ، أَو منقولة من نصوصه إِلَى مَا يشبهها من الْمسَائِل، إِن قُلْنَا: مَا قيس على كَلَامه مَذْهَب لَهُ. وَإِن قُلْنَا: لَا، فَهِيَ أوجه لمن خرجها وقاسها.

If [the variances] are taken from the texts of the *imām* and extrapolated from them, they are considered extrapolated or extended from his [explicit] texts to encompass similar issues. That is, of course, if we opine that analogues to his speech are considered his *madhhab*, based on what has previously been mentioned. If [analogues] are not [considered the *madhhab*], then they are variances belonging to whoever extrapolated and analogised them.

فَإِن خرج من نَص وَنقل إِلَى مَسْأَلَة فِيهَا نَص يُخَالف مَا خرج فِيهَا، صَار فِيهَا رِوَايَة منصوصة، وَرِوَايَة مخرجة.

If, however, it is extrapolated from a text and applied to another issue, and that issue has an explicit text [of Aḥmad] which contradicts the extrapolation, it results in two narrations: the first is a textual narration, and the other is an extrapolated narration based on his texts. [That is, of course, if we claim that views extrapolated from his texts are his *madhhab*.If we opine that extrapolated views are not the *madhhab* of the *imām*, then the issue has two views, one being a narration from al-Imām Aḥmad and a variant perspective belonging to the scholar who extracted it.][147]

وَإِن لم يكن فِيهَا مَا يُخَالف النَّص الْمخْرج فِيهَا من نَصه فِي غَيرهَا، فَهُوَ وَجه لمن خرجه.

If there is no text from al-Imām Aḥmad contradicting the extrapolated

147 [T] The text between the brackets has been added for context from al-Qāḍī 'Alā' al-Dīn al-Mardāwī's discussions in *al-Insāf fī Ma'rifah al-Rājiḥ min al-Khilāf* (12/256).

opinion that is extracted from his textual rulings in other issues: it is a *wajh* belonging to whoever extracted it.

فَإِن خَالفه غَيره من الْأَصْحَاب فِي الحكم دون طَرِيق التَّخْرِيج فَفِيهَا لَهما وَجْهَان.

If another member of the *aṣḥāb* contradicts [the one who extrapolated it] in the ruling, not in the method of extrapolation, there becomes two variances belonging to each of them.

وَيُمكن جعلهَا مذهبا لِأَحْمَد بالتخريج دون النَّقْل لعدم أخذهما من نَصه.

[In *Al-Riʿāyah*, it states, 'Both can be considered the *madhhab* of al-Imām Aḥmad via extrapolation, not through extension [of Aḥmad's view], because [those rulings] were not taken from his [explicit] texts.'][148]

وَإِن جهلنا مستندهما، فَلَيْسَ أَحدهمَا قولا مخرجا للْإِمَام، وَلَا مذهبا لَهُ بِحَال.

If we are unaware of where they drew their conclusions from, neither opinions are to be considered extrapolated from al-Imām Aḥmad and neither can be attributed to him as being a part of his *madhhab*.

فَمن قَالَ من الْأَصْحَاب هُنَا: هَذِه الْمَسْأَلَة رِوَايَة وَاحِدَة، أَرَادَ نَصه.

When one of the *aṣḥāb* says, "This issue has one narration," they mean a text [from Aḥmad].

وَمن قَالَ: فِيهَا رِوَايَتَانِ، فإحداهما بنَص وَالْأُخْرَى بإيماء، أَو تَخْرِيج من نَص آخر لَهُ، أَو بِنَصّ جَهله منكره.

When one of the *aṣḥāb* says, "There are two narrations,' he means that one is textually reported from Aḥmad and the other is merely indicated, or is extrapolated from another text, or is a text unknown to the one rejecting it."

وَمن قَالَ: فِيهَا وَجْهَان، أَرَادَ عدم نَصه عَلَيْهِمَا، سَوَاء جهل مُسْتَنده أم لَا، وَلم يَجعله مذهبا لِأَحْمَد، فَلَا يعْمل إِلَّا بأصح الْوَجْهَيْنِ وأرجحهما، سَوَاء وَقعا مَعًا أَو لَا، من وَاحِد أَو أَكثر، وسَوَاء علم التَّارِيخ أَو جهل.

148 [T] This paragraph was taken from *al-Inṣāf* (12/257).

When one of them says, 'There are two variances,' they mean [Aḥmad] did not give a direct ruling on the issue, regardless if they are unaware of the source or are aware of it. They do not claim it is the *madhhab* of Aḥmad and because of that, only the stronger and more veracious of the two variances should be acted on, regardless if they occur at the same time, if they occur from a single person or many, or if the date is known.

وَأما الْقَوْلَانِ هُنَا: فقد يكون الإِمَام نَص عَلَيْهِمَا كَمَا ذكره أَبُو بكر عبد العزيز فِي (زَاد الْمُسَافِر) أَو نَص على أَحْدَهما، وَأَوْمَأَ إِلَى الآخر، وَقد يكون مَعَ أَحدهمَا وَجه أَو تَخْرِيج أَو احْتِمَال بِخِلَافِهِ.

When one of them says, "There are two opinions," they could mean that Aḥmad has texts that apply to both, as Abu Bakr 'Abd al-'Azīz mentioned in [*al-Shāfī*.][149] It could also mean that one is a text and the other is indicated by [Aḥmad]. It could also mean that one is a variance, extrapolation, or a possibility which is contrary to the other view.

وَأما الِاحْتِمَال، فقد يكون الدَّلِيل مرجوحا بِالنِّسْبَةِ إِلَى مَا خَالفه، أَو لدَلِيل مسَاوٍ لَهُ.

As for "possibilities" mentioned by the *aṣḥāb*, they could refer to some opinion that has evidence that is outweighed when compared to the contrary opinion, or the evidence could be equal [to the other view]. [Some of the *aṣḥāb* might select this view, making it remain as a variance in the *madhhab*].[150]

وَأما التَّخْرِيج: فَهُوَ نقل حكم مَسْأَلَة إِلَى مَا يشبهها، والتسوية بَينهمَا فِيهِ.

As for the term "extrapolation (*takhrīj*),"[151] it means to assign the ruling of

149 [T] Here and in *al-Musawwadah*, it states, "In *Zād al-Musāfir*." Both were authored by Abu Bakr ibn 'Abd al-'Azīz, also known as Ghulām al-Khallāl. I went with, *al-Shāfi*, as that is what is mentioned by al-Mardāwī in *al-Inṣāf* (12/257).

150 [T] The text found between the brackets has been added by the translator as extra benefit, from *al-Insāf fī Ma'rifah al-Rājiḥ min al-Khilāf* by al-Qāḍī 'Alā' al-Dīn al-Mardāwī (12/257).

151 [T] Therefore, there are two terminologies that are similar. The first is "*al-naql wa 'l-takhrīj*," which means, "to extend and extrapolate," and the other is "*al-takhrīj*," which means to extrapolate. The difference was mentioned by Najm al-Dīn al-Ṭūfī who said, "*Al-naql wa 'l-takhrīj* refers to extrapolating from the texts of the *imām*

an issue to another issue that resembles it and to consider them tantamount to one another. That has been previously explained.

وَأما التَّوَقُّف: فَهُوَ ترك الْعَمَل بِالْأولِ وَالثَّانِي، وَالنَّفْي وَالْإِثْبَات إِن لم يكن فِيهَا قَول، لتعارض الْأَدِلَّة وتعادلها عِنْده، فَلهُ حكم مَا قبل الشَّرْع من حظر وَإِبَاحَة ووقف.

As for the term, "abstention (*al-waqf*)," it refers to acting on neither the first nor second [opinion], and to avoid affirming nor negating any particular ruling if there is no opinion on the matter, because of the seemingly conflicting or equal evidences to them. Such things are given the same rulings they would have before legislation was revealed: if it was unlawful [before legislation], it would continue to be unlawful, if it was lawful [before legislation], it would continue to be lawful, and if no ruling was given, the ruling of abstention remains.[152] **[End]**

۞۞۞

فصل

Section

فِي قَول الشَّافِعِي رَضِي الله عَنهُ: إِذا وجدْتُم فِي كتابي خلاف سنة رَسُول الله، فَقولُوا بسنته ودعوا مَا قلت. اخْتلف الْعلمَاء فِي تَفْسِيره، والإنصاف فِيهِ، مَا قَالَه أَبُو عَمْرو ابْن الصّلاح، مَعْنَاهُ:

Al-Shāfiʿī ﷺ said, "If you find anything in my book contradicting the Sunnah of Allah's Messenger ﷺ, you should espouse what is in his Sunnah and abandon what I have said." Scholars differed on how to interpret his words. The nuanced explanation was given by Abu ʿAmr ibn al-Ṣalāḥ, who said:

من وجد من الشَّافِعِيَّة حَدِيثا يُخَالف مذْهبه، فَإِن كملت فِيهِ آلَات الِاجْتِهَاد مُطلقًا أَو فِي ذَلِك الْبَاب، أَو فِي تِلْكَ الْمَسْأَلَة، كَانَ لَهُ الِاسْتِقْلَال بِالْعَمَلِ بذلك

---

by extending [a ruling] from one to another on account of the similarities between the two rulings. *Takhrīj* means to extrapolate based on the universal maxims." (*Sharḥ Mukhtaṣar al-Rawḍah* 3/644).

152 [T] *Al-Musawwadah* (pp. 532-533).

الحَدِيث، وَإِن لم تكمل آلته، وَوجد فِي قلبه حزازة من مُخَالفَة الحَدِيث - بعد أَن بحث، فَلم يجد لمُخَالفَته عَنهُ جَوَابا شافيا - فَإِن كَانَ قد عمل بذلك الحَدِيث إِمَام مُسْتَقل، فَلَهُ أَن يتمذهب بمذهبه فِي الْعَمَل بذلك الحَدِيث، وَيكون ذَلِك عذرا لَهُ فِي ترك مَذْهَب إِمَامه فِي ذَلِك. هَذَا كَلَامه.

If an adherent to the Shāfiʿī *madhhab* finds a ḥadīth that contradicts their *madhhab*, if they have the tools making them eligible for either absolute *ijtihād* or *ijtihād* in that specific chapter or topic, it is allowed for them to act independently on that ḥadīth. However, if someone does not have those necessary tools and finds discomfort in contradicting a ḥadīth after researching and not finding a sufficient reason as to why they should not act on that ḥadīth, they may follow the *madhhab* of an independent scholar in acting on that ḥadīth, if, after researching, they found that an independent scholar had indeed acted on that ḥadīth. That would be a sufficient cause for them to not follow the *madhhab* of their *imām* in that issue.[153] **[End.]**

قلت: وَيجوز أَن يسْلك هَذَا المسلك فِي مَذْهَب أَحْمد أَيْض.

I say: This is a valid approach in the *madhhab* of Aḥmad as well.

153 [T] Refer to *Adab al-Muftī wa 'l-Mustaftī* by al-Ḥāfiẓ Ibn al-Ṣalāḥ (p. 121).

العقد الْخَامِس

Chapter Five

فِي الْأُصُول الْفِقْهِيَّة الَّتِي دونهَا الْأَصْحَاب

On the Legal Theories Codified by the *Aṣḥāb*

لَعَلَّك إِذا اطَّلَعت على مَا رقمناه سَابِقًا من الْأُصُول الْكُلية الَّتِي تَدور عَلَيْهَا فتَاوَى الإِمَام أَحْمد وَلَا تتعداها، حداك الشوق إِلَى زِيَادَة بَيَان عَن تفصيلها، مِمَّا أسسه فطاحل الْأَصْحَاب ونظارهم، فبنوا بهَا الْفُرُوع على أساس متين، وَجعلُوا مَا أَصله الإِمَام أصلا لقواعدهم، وَمَا كنى بِهِ تَصْرِيحًا بعوائدهم، فها أَنا أشفي مِنْك غلَّة الصدي، وأريحك من التَّعَب فِي تنقيب الْأَسْفَار.

After reading what was previously written, namely, the universal rules that the rulings of al-Imām Aḥmad revolve around, never overstepping them, you must have a deep yearning to know more about their details as explained by the great scholars and researchers who were adherents to the *madhhab* of Aḥmad. Through these theories, they based the subsidiary matters on a firm basis and made the fundamental rules set by the *imām* the foundations for their maxims; they made what he referred to as the explicit framework of their yields. I will quench your extreme thirst and will relieve you of the labour of exploring the books.

وأقدم لديك اعتذاري بِأَن كتب الْأُصُول قد دونت فَنًّا مُسْتقِلًّا بنت قَوَاعِده على الدَّلِيل، وسلكت بهَا مسالك الْخلاف والجدل، وناقش الْوَاحِد مِنْهُم من خَالف مسالكه الْحساب، وَأظْهر كل مؤلف مِنْهُم مَا لَدَيْهِ من البراعة ودقة الْفَهم، فَمن مسهب جعل كِتَابه أسفارا، وَمن متوسط غيث فَوَائده أصبح مدرارا، من موجز كَادَت كَلِمَاته أَن تعد، يحْتَاج متفهمها إِلَى إِعْمَال الْفِكر، والتوغل فِي الْجد.

I first present you with an apology. The books of legal theory were written as an independent science which based its foundations on the evidences and they often are filled with disputation and contentions. An author will discuss the views of those who disagree with their methods of consideration. Each author would manifest their proficiency and preciseness in understanding. Some elaborated at lengths, rendering their books into large volumes. Some wrote medium sized works in which their hearts poured with abundant rain. Some wrote compendious authorships where the words are almost countable. All of those books require a person to really use their minds and to immerse themselves in deep study.

وَأَكْثر هَذِه قد كثر ظُهُورهَا طبعا، وَعم نوالها، فَأخذ حبها من المغرمين بهَا قلبا وسمعا وَإِنِّي وَإِن كنت تعرضت لهَذَا الْبَحْر الزاخر، ونصبت نَفسِي هُنَا خَادِمًا لتِلْك المآثر والمفاخر، إِلَّا أَنِّي لست الْآن بصدد تأليف مُسْتَقل، أَقُول فِي خطبَته: هَذَا جهد الْمقل، لكنني رمت بَيَان قَوَاعِد مُجَرّدَة عَن دليلها، وفوائد لَا أصحبها بتعليلها، أمليتها تذكرة وتذكارا، وهذبتها جاعلا لَهَا التَّصْحِيح مسبارا، وَقد وفق الله أَن ابتدأت بشرح (رَوْضَة النَّاظر وجنة المناظر) لموفق الدّين الْمَقْدِسِي، فبينت اخْتِيَار مَا هُوَ الْمُخْتَار، وناقشت فِي الدَّلِيل حَسْبَمَا سلكه النظار.

The majority of these works have been published and their gifts continuously keep giving. Love of these sciences snatched the hearts and ears of those deeply infatuated with them. Although I have embarked on this copious ocean, and here I appoint myself a servant of those remarkable feats and boast-worthy deeds, I am not in the midst of authoring an independent work where I start by saying, "I say this is the effort of a poor man." I merely sought to clarify principles without mentioning their evidences and beneficial points without coupling them with their justifications. I wrote it as a reminder and a memento, and I refined it, making authenticity and veraciousness its resounding theme. Allah has given me divine aid to start explaining *Rawḍat al-Nāẓir wa Junnat al-Munāẓir* by Muwaffaq al-Dīn al-Maqdisī, where I clarified what the chosen position is and discussed the evidences as done by previous researchers.

وَحَيْثُ ظَنَنْت أَن عُذْرِي وَقع موقع الْقبُول، سَاغَ لي أَن أتجاسر فَأَقُول.

Since I now think that my apology has been accepted, I feel it is now appropriate to venture along. So, without further ado:

مُقَدّمَة

Introduction

اعْلَم أَن أصُول الْفِقْه وأدلة الشَّرْع ثَلَاثَة أضْرب: أصل، وَمَفْهُوم أصل، واستصحاب حَال.

Know that legal theories and evidences of legislation are of three types: The foundation, referents of the foundation and the presumption of continuity.

وَالْأَصْل: ثَلَاثَة أضْرب: الْكتاب وَالسّنة وَإِجْمَاع الْأمة. وَالْكتاب ضَرْبَان: مُجمل ومفصل. وَالسّنة ضَرْبَان: مسموع من النَّبِي صلى الله عَلَيْهِ وَسلم ومنقول عَنهُ، وَالْكَلَام فِي الْمَنْقُول فِي سَنَده من حَيْثُ التَّوَاتُر والآحاد، وَفِي مَتنه من حَيْثُ هُوَ قَول أَو فعل. وَالْإِقْرَار قسم من أَقسَام الْفِعْل وَالْقَوْل، لِأَنَّهُ إِقْرَار على وَاحِد مِنْهُمَا. وَالْإِجْمَاع سكوتي وَقَوْلي.

Foundations consist of three types: **(1)** The Qur'ān, which is of two categories: (i) Ambiguous and (ii) Unambiguous. **(2)** The Sunnah, which is of two types: (i) Heard from the Prophet ﷺ and (ii) reported from the Prophet ﷺ which has further discussions: (i) When discussing its chain of narration, it is of two types: (a) Recurrent narrations and (b) solitary narrations. (ii) When discussing what the text is reporting, it is of two types: (a) Statements, (b) actions, and (c) acknowledgements of the Prophet, which is a category of both statements and actions, as it indicates acknowledgement of either. **(3)** Consensus of the Ummah, which is of two types: (i) Silent consensus and (ii) proclaimed consensus.

وَمَفْهُوم الأَصْل ثَلَاثَة أضْرب: مَفْهُوم الْخطاب، وَدَلِيله، وَمَعْنَاهُ.

Referents of the foundations are of three types: (i) The referent of the speech. (ii) The evidence of the speech. (iii) The meaning of the speech.

واستصحاب الْحَال ضَرْبَان. أَحدهمَا: اسْتِصْحَاب بَرَاءَة الذِّمَّة، وَالثَّانِي:

اسْتِصْحَاب حكم الْإِجْمَاع بعد الْخلاف.

The presumption of continuity is of two types: (i) Presuming the continuity of default legality, and (ii) presuming the continuity of a consensus occurring after previous disagreement.

وَلَك إِجْمَال آخر يمكنك مَعَه أَن تَقول: إِن أُصُول الْفِقْه وأدلة الشَّرْع على ضَرْبَيْنِ: أَحدهمَا: مَا طَرِيقَة الْأَقْوَال. وَالثَّانِي: الاستخراج.

Another way of concisely explaining the above concepts is to say that Islamic legal theories and evidences of legislation are of two types: (i) speech related and (ii) deductions or extrapolations.

فَأَما الْأَقْوَال فَهِيَ النَّص والعموم وَالظَّاهِر وَمَفْهُوم الْخطاب وفحواه وَالْإِجْمَاع. وَأما الاستخراج فَهُوَ الْقيَاس.

As for statements, they are divided into: (i) Explicit and unequivocal, (ii) general, (iii) apparent, (iv) referents of speech, (v) consequents of speech and (vi) consensus. As for deductions and extrapolations, it refers to analogy.

والإجمال الأول أصح، لِأَنَّهُ أعم لوُجُود دَلِيل الْخطاب واستصحاب الْحَال، وَذَلِكَ حجَّة عِنْد أَصْحَاب أَحْمد. وَأما قَول الصَّحَابِيّ إِذا لم يُخَالف غَيره، فمختلف فِيهِ عِنْد أَحْمد، وَهَذَا الضَّبْط تقريبي حدانا إِلَيْهِ الِاخْتِصَار.

The first summation is more veracious, because it is more encompassing of the presence of the evidence of speech and the presumption of continuity, both of which are evidences to the *aṣḥāb* of Aḥmad. Aḥmad considered the statements of the companions that are unchallenged by other views a point of difference of opinion. With that said, what has been mentioned is a rough overview prompted by my intention of summarising.

بسط هَذَا الإجْمَال

Expounding on This Summation

اعْلَم أَن الْمركب لَا تمكن مَعْرفَته إِلَّا بعد معرفَة مفرداته، وَلما كَانَ أُصُول الْفِقْه مركبا من كَلِمَتَيْنِ: مُضَاف مُضَاف إِلَيْهِ، كَانَ لأصول الْفِقْه تعريفان، لِأَنَّهُ إِن نظر إِلَيْهِ من حَيْثُ اعْتِبَار مَجْمُوع لَفظه الَّذِي تركب مِنْهُ سمي فِي الِاصْطِلَاح إجماليا لقبيا، وَكَانَ تَعْرِيفه: الْعلم بالقواعد الَّتِي يتَوَصَّل بهَا إِلَى استنباط الْأَحْكَام الشَّرْعِيَّة الفرعية من أدلتها التفصيلية، وَإِن نظر إِلَيْهِ بِاعْتِبَار كل وَاحِد من مفرداته الْأُصُول، كَانَ تَعْرِيفه بِأَنَّهُ الْأَدِلَّة، لِأَن الْمَادَّة الَّتِي تركب مِنْهَا لفظا أُصُول الْفِقْه هِيَ الْأُصُول، وَالْفِقْه فِيهَا مُفْرد ذَلِك الْمركب، فَيحْتَاج فِي تَعْرِيفه التفصيلي إِلَى تَعْرِيف كل وَاحِد مِنْهَا على حِدته. فالأصول الْأَدِلَّة الْآتِي ذكرهَا يَعْنِي: الْكتاب وَالسّنة وَالْإِجْمَاع وَالْقِيَاس، وَمَا فِي خلال ذَلِك من الْقَوَاعِد.

Know that a composite phrase cannot be understood without understanding the basic significations of which it is composed. The term *uṣūl al-fiqh* is composed of two words: an adjunct and a governed noun. As such, the term *uṣūl al-fiqh* has two definitions. If the term is approached as being a composite of the nouns it comprises of, the definition is: knowledge on the principles used to deduce religious rulings in subsidiary matters from their particularised evidences. However, if the term is approached by analysing each of the two nouns, the definition [of *uṣūl al-fiqh*] is merely evidences. The reason is that the term is composed of *uṣūl* and *fiqh*, and both need to be defined individually. The *uṣūl* are those which are forthcoming, namely, the Qur'ān, the Sunnah, consensus, and analogy, as well as the maxims pertaining to [those principles].

وَالْأُصُول: جمع أصل، وأصل الشَّيْء مَا يسْتَند تحقق ذَلِك الشَّيْء إِلَيْهِ تَأْثِيرا، وَإِنَّمَا زدنا (تَأْثِيرا) احْتِرَازًا من اسْتِنَاد الْمُمكن إِلَى الْمُؤثر مَعَ أَنه لَيْسَ أصلا لَهُ. وَلَا

شكّ أَن الْفِقْه مُسْتَند فِي تحقق وجوده إِلَى الْأَدِلَّة، فَهُوَ كالغصن من الشَّجَرَة.

The word *al-uṣūl* is the plural form of the word *aṣl*, which refers to an essential item for the realisation of a thing, in that the essential item has a direct cause and effect relationship to the thing. I used the term "cause" in order to distinguish between a contingency relationship, where realisation of a thing is a possible effect but is not reliant on the cause. There is no doubt that jurisprudence is reliant on evidences, just as the existence of a branch is reliant on the existence of the tree itself.

وَالْفِقْه فِي اللُّغَة: الْفَهم، وَاصْطِلَاحا قيل: الْعلم بِالْأَحْكَام الشَّرْعِيَّة الفرعية عَن أدلتها التفصيلية بالاستدلال، وَقيل: ظن جملَة من الْأَحْكَام الشَّرْعِيَّة الفرعية باستنباطها من أَدِلَّة تفصيلية. وعَلى كل من التعريفين مؤاخذات، وَلَكِن القَوْل الثَّانِي أخف إشْكَالا.

The word *fiqh* linguistically, refers to understanding. In religious terminology, it refers to knowledge about subsidiary religious rulings gained from deduction from their particular evidences. Another definition provided was: having probability in a set of subsidiary religious rulings deduced from particular evidences. Both definitions are contentious, but the second view has less objections.

فصل فِي التَّكْلِيف

Section [One:] On Responsibilities

هُوَ لُغَة: إِلْزَام مَا فِيهِ كلفة: أَي مشقة. وَشرعا: إِلْزَام مُقْتَضى خطاب الشَّرْع. وعَلى هَذَا تكون الْإِبَاحَة تكليفا لِأَنَّهَا من مقتضيات الْخطاب الْمَذْكُور. وَمن قَالَ: إِن الْإِبَاحَة لَيست تكليفا يَقُول: التَّكْلِيف هُوَ الْخطاب بِأَمْر أَو نهي.

The term *al-taklīf* linguistically, means to make something difficult binding. In religious terminology, it refers to the implications of religious instructions being binding. As such, the lawfulness (*ibāhah*) of a thing is considered a part of responsibilities, as it is an implication of the religious instructions. Those that say that lawfulness is not a part of the religious responsivities define *al-taklīf* as religious instructions containing commandments or prohibitions.

وَله شُرُوط يتَعَلَّق بَعْضهَا بالمكلف، وَبَعضهَا بالمكلف بِهِ، فَأَما الَّذِي يتَعَلَّق بالمكلف فالعقل، وَفهم الْخطاب، فَلَا تَكْلِيف على صبي وَلَا مَجْنُون، لعدم الْمُصَحح للامتثال مِنْهُمَا، وَهُوَ قصد الطَّاعَة. والمميز مثل الصَّبِي فِي عدم التَّكْلِيف.

Some of its conditions pertain to the cognisant person responsible for fulfilling the commandments of the religion (*mukallaf*), and some of them pertain to the thing one is tasked to do. The conditions pertaining to the *mukallaf* are: (i) Intellect. (ii) Understanding the instruction. As such, neither a child nor clinically insane person is responsible, because of their lack of ability to perform what validates their obedience, namely, intent of worship [when obeying the religious instruction.] A *mumayyiz* (a child above the age of seven) resembles the child in that they are not responsible.

فَإِن قيل: كَيفَ أوجبتم الزَّكَاة والغرامات فِي مَال الصَّبِي وَالْمَجْنُون، ونفيتم عَنْهُمَا التَّكْلِيف؟ قُلْنَا: الْوُجُوب لَيْسَ على نفسهما، بل هُوَ ربط الْأَحْكَام بالمسببات

لوُجُود الضَّمَان بِبَعْض أَفعَال الْبَهَائِم.

With that said, a question arises, which is: how can we obligate *zakāt* and fines from the wealth of the child and the clinically insane person, although they are not responsible under the law? The answer is: The obligation [of paying *zakāt* and fines] is not pertinent to their selves, but rather, they are rulings connected to effects of their actions, similar to how liability is established even through the actions of livestock.

وَلَا تَكْلِيف على النَّائِم وَالنَّاسِي والسكران الَّذِي لَا يعقل لعَدَمِ الْفَهم. وَالْحق أَن الْمُكره إِذا بلغ بِهِ الْإِكراه إِلَى حد الإلجاء، سقط عَنهُ التَّكْلِيف. وَالْكفَّار مخاطبون بِفُرُوع الْإِسْلَام على أصح الْقَوْلَيْنِ.

A sleeping person, someone who forgot, and a drunkard who loses cognition are not responsible, because they lack understanding. Also, the truth is that if a person is coerced to the extent that they are forcibly made to do something, they also are not responsible. Further, disbelievers are addressed with instructions to perform the subsidiary matters of Islam, according to the more correct of the two views on the topic.

وَأما مَا يتَعَلَّق بالمكلف بِهِ فَهُوَ:

As for things that pertain to the thing that one is tasked with doing:

أَن يكون الْمُكَلف بِهِ مَعْلُوم الْحَقِيقَة للمكلف، وَإِلَّا لم يتَوَجَّه قَصده إِلَيْهِ.

Its reality should be known to the *mukallaf*, otherwise, they cannot direct their intention to performing that action.

وَأَن يكون مَعْلُوما كَونه مَأْمُورا بِهِ، وَإِلَّا لم يتَصَوَّر مِنْهُ قصد الطَّاعَة، والامتثال.

It should be known to be a commandment, otherwise, it cannot be conceived that they intend obedience and adherence.

[وأن يكون] مَعْدُوما، إِذْ إِيجَاد الْمَوْجُود محَال.

It must already be non-existent, since bringing something existent into being is an impossibility.

وَيَنْقَطِع التَّكْلِيف حَال حُدُوث الْفِعْل.

Responsibility ends during the action.

وَأَن يكون الْمُكَلف بِهِ مُمكنا لِأَن الْمُكَلف بِهِ يَسْتَدْعِي حُصُوله، وَذَلِكَ يسْتَلْزم تصور وُقُوعه، والمحال لَا يتَصَوَّر وُقُوعه، فَلَا يَسْتَدْعِي حُصُوله، فَلَا تَكْلِيف بِهِ.

The thing one is tasked with doing must be possible, because an action that is commanded elicits its actualisation, but that also necessitates that its occurrence can be conceptualised. The occurrence of impossibilities cannot be conceptualised, and as such, they are not elicited, and by extension, they are not responsibilities that one must fulfil.

وَلَا تَكْلِيف إِلَّا بِفعل، لِأَن مُتَعَلق التَّكْلِيف الْأَمر وَالنَّهْي، وَكِلَاهُمَا لَا يكون إِلَّا فعلا. أما فِي الْأَمر، فَظَاهر لِأَن مُقْتَضَاهُ إِيجَاد فعل مَأْمُور بِهِ كَالصَّلَاةِ وَالصِّيَام، وَأما فِي النَّهْي، فمتعلق التَّكْلِيف فِيهِ كف النَّفس عَن الْمنْهِي عَنهُ كَالْكَفِّ عَن الزِّنَى، وَهُوَ أَيْضا فعل.

There is no responsibility without involvement of an action, since responsibilities are contingent on commandments and prohibitions, and neither can be achieved without an action. As for commandments, it is quite obvious: it implies producing something one is commanded to do, such as prayer or fasting. As for prohibitions: the responsibility is dependent on restraining oneself from doing things that are prohibited, such as avoiding fornication, which is also an action.

فصل فِي أحكَام التّكْلِيف

On the Ruling Types

الحكم فِي اللُّغَة: الْمَنْع. وَفِي اصْطِلَاح الْأُصُولِيِّينَ: مُقْتَضى خطاب الشَّرْع الْمُتَعَلّق بِأَفْعَال الْمُكَلّفين اقْتِضَاء أَو تخييرا. ثمَّ إِن ذَلِك الْخطاب إِمَّا أَن يرد باقتضاء الْفِعْل مَعَ الْجَزْم، وَهُوَ الْوُجُوب، أَو يرد باقتضاء الْفِعْل، لَكِن لَيْسَ مَعَ الْجَزْم، وَهُوَ النّدب، أَو باقتضاء التّرْك مَعَ الْجَزْم، وَهُوَ التَّحْرِيم، أَولا مَعَ الْجَزْم، وَهُوَ الْكَرَاهَة، أَو التَّخْيِير، وَهِي الْإِبَاحَة. وَعِنْدنَا: أَن الْإِبَاحَة من خطاب الشَّرْع، فَهِيَ حكم شَرْعِي، خلافًا للمعتزلة.

The term *ḥukm* (ruling) literally refers to obstruct something. In the nomenclature of the legists, it means the implications of the instructions of legislation that pertain to the actions of responsible, cognisant humans, either by demanding something or giving free choice in something. This instruction either: (i) Implies performing an action and does so imperatively, it is called *wājib* (obligatory). (ii) Implies performing an action and does not do so imperatively, it is called *mandūb*[154] (recommended). (iii) If the instruction implies abstaining from something and does so imperatively, it is called *ḥarām* (forbidden). (iv) If the instruction implies abstaining from something and does not do so imperatively, it is called *makrūh* (undesirable). (v) Lastly, if the instruction gives one the free choice in something, it is known as *mubāḥ*[155] (lawful). To us (the Ḥanbalīs), the *mubāḥ* is a part of the instructions of legislation, and as such, a religious ruling, contrary to the Muʿtazilites.

۞۞۞

[فصل]

[Subsection One]

154 [T] A more common term is *mustaḥabbb*.
155 [T] Another term used is *ḥalāl*.

[*Al-Wājib* (Obligatory)][156]

فَالْوَاجِب: مَا ذمّ شرعا تَاركه مُطلقًا، أَي: فِي كل الْأَزْمَان، فقولنا: مُطلقًا احْتِرَاز من الْوَاجِب الموسع، والمخير، وَفرض الْكِفَايَة، فَإِن التّرْك يلْحقهَا فِي الْجُمْلَة، وَهُوَ ترك الموسع فِي بعض أَجزَاء وقته، وَترك بعض أَعْيَان الْمُخَير، وَترك بعض الْمُكَلّفين لفرض الْكِفَايَة.

Al-Wājib: Something that, if abandoned absolutely, its abandoner is censured in legislation. Meaning, at all times. When we say, "absolutely," it is to avoid inclusion of obligations with latitude, obligations that are subject to one's choice,[157] and communal obligations, all of which have some measure of abandonment. In the case of the obligation that has latitude, it is abandoned during some portion of its allotted and allowed time. As it pertains to obligations that are subject to one's choice, some of the other choices will undoubtedly be overlooked. Lastly, as it pertains to communal obligations, some *mukallaf* individuals will simply not do the action.

لَكِن ذَلِك لَيْسَ تركا مُطلقًا إِذْ الموسع إِن ترك فِي بعض أَجزَاء وقته، فعل فِي الْبَعْض الآخر، والمخير إِن ترك بعض أعيانه، فعل الْبَعْض الآخر، وَفرض الْكِفَايَة إِن تَركه بعض الْمُكَلّفين، فعله الْبَعْض الآخر، وَكلهمْ فِيهِ كالشخص الْوَاحِد، فَلَا يتَعَلَّق بِهَذَا التّرْك ذمّ، لِأَنهُ لَيْسَ تركا مُطلقًا بِمَعْنى خلو مَحل التَّكْلِيف عَن إِيقَاع الْمُكَلف بِهِ.

However, any of [the previously mentioned types of abandonment] will not reach the level of absolute abandonment, since the obligation that has latitude will only be abandoned for a portion of its specified time, and will be done at other times. Obligations that are subject to one's choice will only be abandoned inasmuch as the other options are chosen, since some other

156 [T] This heading has been added by the translator for clarity in organising the book and is not from the words of al-Shaykh Ibn Badrān.

157 [T] Ibn Badrān is referring to when Allah the Exalted said, **{The atonement for breaking an oath is to feed ten poor people with food equivalent to what you would normally give your own families, or to clothe them, or to set free a slave - if a person cannot find the means, he should fast for three days.}** [Qur'ān 5:89] One can choose any of those qualities mentioned in the verse of expiating broken oaths, and by doing so, they would abandon the other unchosen qualities.

choices will be done. Likewise, if the communal obligation is abandoned by some *mukallaf* individuals, others will fulfill the obligation, and they, as a community, are considered to be equivalent to one person. As such, that abandonment is not censured, because it is not absolute abandonment, where the time of obligation lacks the *mukallaf* actualising it.

وَالْوَاجِب: مرادف للْفَرض عندنَا على الْأَصَح من أَقْوَال الْأُصُولِيِّين.

Wājib, according to us, is synonymous to *farḍ*, according to the more correct of the two views presented by the legists.

ثم اعلم أن الواجب الشامل للْفَرض يَنْقَسِم إِلَى معِين وَإِلَى مُبْهَم فِي أَقسَام محصورة. وتلخيص القَوْل فِيهِ: أَن الْوَاجِب إِمَّا أَن يكون معينا كَأَن ينذر عتق هَذَا العَبْد الْمعِين، أَو عتق سَالم من عبيده، فَيكون مُخَاطبا بِعِتْقِهِ على التَّعْيِين، وَكَذَا لَو نذر الصَّدَقَة بِمَال بِعَيْنِه كهذه الدَّنَانِير أَو الْإِبِل وَنَحْو ذَلِك.

Further, know that the *wājib*, which includes the *farḍ*, comprises of specific obligations and unclarified obligations. To summarise, obligations are either specific, such as "Free this particular slave," such as when one makes an oath to free a specific slave, or to free any of their slaves named "Sālim." In such a case, one is instructed to free that slave in specific. Likewise is the case if someone makes an oath to give a specific portion of their wealth in charity, such as by saying, 'I will give these specific dinars, camels, etc. in charity.'

وَإِمَّا أَن يكون مُبْهما فِي أَقسَام محصورة كإحدى خِصَال الْكَفَّارَة، ككفارة الْيَمين الْمَذْكُورَة فِي قَوْله تَعَالَى ﴿**فَكَفَّارَتُهُ إِطْعَامُ عَشَرَةِ مَسَاكِينَ مِنْ أَوْسَطِ مَا تُطْعِمُونَ أَهْلِيكُمْ أَوْ كِسْوَتُهُمْ أَوْ تَحْرِيرُ رَقَبَةٍ**﴾ [الْمَائِدَة: ٨٩]، وَهَذِه الْمَسْأَلَة تعرف بِمَسْأَلَة الْوَاجِب الْمُخَير.

Or, [the obligation] could be unclarified, but limited to a specific set of categories. For example, when expiating, one is obligated to do one of the things mentioned in the verse of expiating an oath: **{The atonement for breaking an oath is to feed ten poor people with food equivalent to what you would normally give your own families, or to clothe them, or to set free a slave - if a person cannot find the means, he should fast for three days.}** [Qur'ān 5:89] This is the obligation with a choice.

وَأما وَقت الْوُجُوب: فإمَّا أَن يكون مُقَدرا بِقدر الْفِعْل. بِحَيْثُ ضيق على الْمُكَلف فِيهِ حَتَّى لَا يجد سَعَة يُؤَخر فِيهَا الْفِعْل، أَو بعضه، ثمَّ يتداركه إِذن، بل من ترك شَيْئا مِنْهُ، لم يُمكن تَدَارُكه إِلَّا قَضَاء، وَذَلِكَ كَالْيَوْمِ بِالنِّسْبَةِ إِلَى الصَّوْم. وَيُسمى هَذَا بِالْوَاجِبِ الْمضيق.

As for the time of obligation: sometimes it is limited to the time needed to complete the action, where a *mukallaf* would find no time to delay the action, or a part of the action. If they delay it, they must make it up, since anything missed in its allotted time can only be rectified by making it up. An example is a day as it pertains to fasting.[158] This is known as "a narrow obligation (*al-wājib al-muḍayyaq*)."

وَإِمَّا أَن يكون وَقت الْوُجُوب أقل من قدر فعله، كَإِيجَاب عشْرين رَكْعَة فِي زمن لَا يسع أَكثر من رَكْعَتَيْنِ. وَهَذَا فرد من أَفْرَاد التَّكْلِيف بالمحال الْمُسَمّى بتكليف مَا لَا يُطَاق، وَفِي جَوَازه خلاف بَين الْعلمَاء، وَالصَّحِيح مَنعه.

Or, the time of obligation is less than the time it takes to complete the action, such as obligating twenty units of prayer in a time that only would physically allow for two units. This is a type of tasking an impossible responsibility, known [to jurists] as, "the obligation of something impossible." The scholars differed on its possibility, but the correct view is that it is not possible.

وَإما أَن يكون وَقت الْوَاجِب أَكثر من وَقت فعله، وَهَذَا يُقَال لَهُ: الْوَاجِب الموسع، وَذَلِكَ كأوقات الصَّلَوَات، وَهَذَا فِيهِ خلاف، فعندنا وَعند الْمَالِكِيَّة وَالشَّافِعِيَّة وَالْأَكْثَر: للمكلف فعل الْوَاجِب من الصَّلَوَات فِي أَي أَجزَاء الْوَقْت شَاءَ فِي أَوله، أَو آخِره، أَو وَسطه، وَمَا بَين ذَلِك مِنْهُ. وَأوجب أَكثر أَصْحَابنَا والمالكية الْعَزْم على الْفِعْل إِذا أخر إِلَى آخر الْوَقْت، وَيتَعَيَّن آخِره، وَهُوَ قَول الأشعرية، والجبائي وَابْنه من الْمُعْتَزلَة، وَلم يُوجِبهُ من أَصْحَابنَا أَبُو الْخطاب ومجد الدّين ابن تَيْمِية وَجمع، وَمن الْمُعْتَزلَة أَبُو الْحُسَيْن.

158 [T] Meaning, an example of a narrow obligation is the day as it pertains to fasting. The allotted time for the fast is the day, and one cannot delay the action beyond the day, and also cannot delay a part of the action past the day. If someone begins their fast at noon, they must make the day up.

The obligation could allot more time than needed for its completion. This is known as an "expanded obligation (*al-wājib al-muwassa'*)." Examples are the times of the prayers, although there is a difference of opinion [on whether the times of prayers are included in this category]. According to us [the Ḥanbalīs], the Mālikis, the Shāfi'īs, and the majority, a *mukallaf* may offer their obligatory prayers during any portion of its beginning, middle, or ending times, or anything in between. Many of our *aṣḥāb* and the Mālikis stipulated that one must have firm intention [at the time of the outset of the obligation] to delay the prayer to the latest allotted time. At the end of the allotted time, it becomes incumbent. This is also the view of the Ash'arītes, and al-Jubbā'ī and his son from the Mu'tazilites. Of our *aṣḥāb*, Abu 'l-Khaṭṭāb, Majd al-Dīn ibn Taymiyyah, and a group of scholars did not obligate [intending to delay]. Abu 'l-Ḥusayn of the Mu'tazilites also took [the latter] view.

وَأنكر أَكثر الْحَنَفِيَّة الْوَاجِب الموسع، وَقَالُوا: وَقت الْوُجُوب: هُوَ آخر الْوَقْت، وَإِذا فعل قبل الآخر، فَقَالَ بَعضهم: هُوَ نفل يسْقط بِهِ الْفَرْض، وَتردد الْكَرْخِي مِنْهُم، فَتَارَة قَالَ: يتَعَيَّن الْوَاجِب فِي أَي أَجزَاء الْوَقْت كَانَ، وَتارَة قَالَ: إِن بَقِي الْفَاعِل مُكَلفا إِلَى آخر الْوَقْت، كَانَ مَا فعله قبل ذَلِك وَاجِبا، وَإِلَّا فَهُوَ نفل. انْتهى.

The majority of Ḥanafī scholars rejected the existence of expanded obligations, saying that the time of obligation is the last possible portion of the allotted time, and some said that if one does the action before the ending of its specified time, it is a voluntary action that absolves one of the obligation. Among Ḥanafī scholars, al-Karkhī hesitated; at times he said that the obligation becomes incumbent at any portion of the allotted time, and at other times, said that if a person remains *mukallaf* until the allotted time ends, their prayer beforehand is considered obligatory, and otherwise,[159] it is voluntary.

قلت: وَالْمُخْتَار قَول الْجُمْهُور الْمُتَقَدّم، وَهُوَ الَّذِي تدل عَلَيْهِ السّنة. وَإِذا مَاتَ الْمُكَلف فِي أَثْنَاء وَقت الْوَاجِب الموسع قبل فعله، وضيق وقته، مثل أَن مَاتَ بعد زَوَال الشَّمْس، وَقد بَقِي من وَقت الظهْر مَا يَتَّسِع لفعلها، وَلم يصلها، لم يمت

159 [T] Meaning, if they cease being *mukallaf* by losing one of the qualifications of a *mukallaf* (such as becoming clinically insane).

عَاصِيا لِأَنهُ فعل مُبَاحا، وَهُوَ التَّأْخِير الْجَائِز بِحكم توسيع الْوَقْت. أما لَو أَخّرهُ حَتَّى ضَاقَ الْوَقْت عَن فعله، مثل أَن مَاتَ وَلم يبْق مَا يَتَّسِع إِلَّا لأَقل من أَربع رَكْعَات فَإِنَّهُ يَمُوت عَاصِيا، هَذَا مَا قَالَه الْأَكْثَر. وَالتَّحْقِيق: أَن عصيانه يكون مُقَدرا بِقدر مَا أَخّرهُ حَتَّى ضَاقَ الْوَقْت عَنهُ، فَإِن ضَاقَ عَن رَكْعَة أَو رَكْعَتَيْنِ أَو ثَلَاث كَانَ عَاصِيا بِحَسب ذَلِك، وَلَا يَجْعَل فِي مَعْصِيَته كمن أخر الْوَاجِب كُله.

My view is: The chosen position is that of the majority of scholars, and that is indicated by the Sunnah. If a *mukallaf* person dies during the time of an extended obligation before performing the obligation and before the allotted time is close to ending (such as one dying right after the sun passes the zenith, but there is still enough time to perform the *ẓuhr* prayer), but did not pray, they do not die in a state of sinfulness, because they did something lawful by delaying within the allotted time. However, if a person delays the prayer until there does not remain enough time to perform the action, such as dying and leaving time to perform less than four units of prayer, they die in a state of sinfulness. This is the view of the majority. After scrutiny, it becomes clear that one's sinfulness is inasmuch as their delay of the prayer until the time became too short. If the remaining time allows for the completion of one, two, or three units during the allotted time, their sinfulness is inasmuch as they can do. Their sin is not tantamount to the one who delays the obligatory prayer altogether.

فصل فِي مسألة مَا لَا يتم الْوَاجِب إِلَّا بِهِ

A Subsection on Ancillaries to Obligatory Actions

اعْلَم أَن هَذِه الْمَسْأَلَة لَهَا ملحظان:

This topic has two points of consideration:

أولهمَا: مَا يتَوَقَّف على وجوب الْوَاجِب وَهَذَا لَا يجب إِجْمَاعًا، سَوَاء كَانَ سَببا أَو شرطا أَو انْتِفَاء مَانع:

First: The prerequisite for an obligatory action becoming obligatory on a particular individual is not obligatory in and of itself, according to the consensus of the scholars, irrespective if it is a reason (*sabab*), condition (*sharṭ*), or lack of an impediment (*mani'*).[160]

فالسبب كالنصاب، يتَوَقَّف عَلَيْهِ وجوب الزَّكَاة، فَلَا يجب تَحْصِيله على الْمُكَلف لتجب عَلَيْهِ الزَّكَاة.

An example of a reason is the minimum acquired wealth necessary before *zakāt* becomes obligatory. The obligation of *zakāt* is dependent on owning the necessary amount of wealth. One, however, is not obligated to earn that amount of wealth just so that they can earn the obligation of paying *zakāt*.

وَالشَّرط كالإقامة فِي الْبَلَد، إِذْ هِيَ شَرط لوُجُوب أَدَاء الصَّوْم، فَلَا يجب تَحْصِيلهَا إِذا عرض مُقْتَضى السّفر ليجب عَلَيْهِ فعل الصَّوْم.

An example of a condition is residence in a town. The obligation of fasting is dependent on the condition of residing in the town one is currently in. If one has a cause for travel, they are not obligated to gain residence in a town just to be tasked with the obligation of fasting.

وَالْمَانِع كَالدّين، فَلَا يجب نَفْيه لتجب الزَّكَاة.

An example of a lack of impediment is debt [which is an impediment to the obligation of *zakāt*]. One is not obligated to eliminate their debt just so that they earn the obligation of *zakāt*.

وَثَانِيهمَا: مَا يتَوَقَّف عَلَيْهِ إِيقَاع الْوَاجِب أَي: الَّذِي لَا يتم الْوَاجِب إِلَّا بِهِ، وَهُوَ نَوْعَانِ:

Second: Something that an obligatory action is predicated on. Meaning, it is a necessary ancillary to the obligatory action. This is of two types:

أَحدهمَا: مَا لَيْسَ فِي قدرَة الْمُكَلف ووسعه وطاقته تَحْصِيله، وَلَا هُوَ إِلَيْهِ، كالقدرة وَالْيَد فِي الْكِتَابَة، فَإِنَّهُمَا شَرط فِيهَا، وهما مخلوقتان لله فِي الْمُكَلف، لَا قدرَة لَهُ على إيجادهما، وكحضور الإِمَام وَالْعدَد الْمُشْتَرط فِي الْجُمُعَة للْجُمُعَة، فَإِنَّهُمَا

160 [T] For example, a prerequisite for the obligation of *zakāt* is owning the *niṣāb*, however, it is not obligatory on a person to go earn the *niṣāb* in order to fulfill the obligation of *zakāt*. The obligation of *zakāt* is consequential.

شرط لَهَا، وَلَيْسَ إِلَى آحاد الْمُكَلفين بِالْجمعَةِ إِحْضَار الْخَطِيب لِيُصَلي الْجُمُعَة، وَلَا إِحْضَار آحَاد النَّاس ليتم بهم الْعدَد، فَهَذَا النَّوْع غير وَاجِب إِلَّا على القَوْل بتكليف الْمحَال.

One. Things that the provision of which are outside of the abilities and capacities of the *mukallaf*, and it is not within their facilities in the first place. Examples are ability and a hand in terms of writing,[161] both of which are conditions to writing, and both of which are created by Allah the Exalted for the *mukallaf*; one has no ability to procure those things on their own. Another example is the presence of the *imām* and the prerequisite number of people for Friday prayers, both of which are conditions for [Friday prayers.] Individual *mukallaf* attendees of Friday prayers are unable to procure and bring forth an *imām* to lead in it, and are unable to bring into existence further individuals to complete the prerequisite number of people. This category is not obligatory, unless one takes the view that Allah tasks humans with impossibilities.

ثَانِيهمَا: مَا هُوَ مَقْدُور للمكلف، وَهُوَ إِمَّا أَن يكون شرطا لوُقُوع الْفِعْل، أَو غير شَرط. فَإِن كَانَ شرطا كالطهارة وَسَائِر الشُّرُوط للصَّلَاة، وكالسعي إِلَى الْجُمُعَة، فَإِن صرح بِعَدَمِ إيجَابه كَقَوْلِه: صل وَلَا أوجب عَلَيْك الْوضُوء، لم يجب، عملا بِمُوجب التَّصْرِيح، وَإِن صرح بإيجابه، وَجب لذَلِك، وَإِن لم يُصَرح بإيجَاب وَلَا عَدمه، بل أطلق، وَجب أَيْضا عندنَا. وَهُوَ قَول الأشعرية والمعتزلة. وَقيل: لَا يجب، وَإِن لم يكن الَّذِي لَا يتم الْوَاجِب إِلَّا بِهِ شرطا كمسح جُزْء من الرَّأْس فِي غسل الْوَجْه فِي الْوضُوء، وإمساك جُزْء من اللَّيْل مَعَ النَّهَار فِي الصَّوْم، فَمثل هَذَا لَا يجب خلافًا للأكثرين حَيْثُ قَالُوا بِوُجُوبِهِ.

Two. Things that the *mukallaf* is able to achieve. This is either a precondition or not a precondition. If it is a precondition for the existence and achievement of the action, for example, purification and all other preconditions of prayer, as well as going to the Friday prayer, [it is of three types:] (i) If [the Legislator] explicitly states it is not an obligation, such as by saying,

161 [T] Meaning, one cannot write without ability to write and a hand to write with. No human that is stripped of ability is able to garner that ability on their own, nor is someone without a hand able to procure one in order to write again.

"Pray, but *wuḍū* is not an obligation," it is not an obligation, because of the ramifications of the explicit statement. (ii) If [the Legislator] explicitly states it is an obligation, it is also an obligation. (iii) If [the Legislator] does not explicitly state it is an obligation or a non-obligation, but rather, leaves it unrestricted, it is also an obligation according to [the Ḥanbalīs]. This is also the view of the Ashʿarītes and the Muʿtazilites. It was also said that it is not an obligation. The second is something that an obligation cannot be achieved without, but is not a precondition, such as wiping a part of the head in order to wipe the entirety of the head during *wuḍū*, and such as avoiding eating for a small portion of the night before dawn when fasting. This is not an obligation, contrary to many [scholars] who said that it is an obligation.

قلت: الْمُخْتَار الْوُجُوب لِأَن مَا لَا بُد مِنْهُ فِي الْوَاجِب هُوَ من لوازمه، وَالْأَمر بالملزوم أَمر باللازم.

My view though is that it is an obligation, because it is a necessary condition to the completion of the obligation. It is a consequent, and a commandment to complete the antecedent is a commandment to complete the consequent.

وَيتَفَرَّع على هَذِه الْمَسْأَلَة فرعان:

This issue leads to two subsidiary issues:

أَحدهمَا: إِذا اشتبهت أُخْته أَو زَوجته بأجنبية، أَو ميتَة بمذكاة حرمتا، إِحْدَاهمَا بِالْأَصَالَةِ وَالْأُخْرَى بِعَارِض الِاشْتِبَاه.

One. If a person confuses his sister or wife with a non-related woman, or is confused between whether some meat is correctly slaughtered or not, both are unlawful [in both cases]. One [of the two choices] is unlawful because of the original ruling, and the other because of the resemblance that occurred.

ثَانِيهمَا: الزِّيَادَة على الْوَاجِب: إِمَّا أَن تكون متميزة عَنهُ، أَو لَا. فَإِن تميزت عَنهُ، كَصَلَاة التَّطَوُّع بِالنِّسْبَةِ إِلَى المكتوبات، فَتلك الزِّيَادَة ندب اتِّفَاقًا، وَإِن لم تتَمَيَّز عَن الْوَاجِب بِأَن لَا تنفصل حَقِيقَتهَا من حَقِيقَته حسا كالزيادة فِي الطُّمَأْنِينَة وَالرُّكُوع وَالسُّجُود وَمُدَّة الْقيام وَالْقعُود، على أقل الْوَاجِب، وَهُوَ مَا لَا يُطلق عَلَيْهِ اسْم هَذِه الْأَفْعَال، فَتلك الزِّيَادَة الَّتِي هَذَا شَأْنهَا وَاجِبَة عِنْد القَاضِي أبي يعلى،

ندب عِنْد أبي الْخطاب، وَهُوَ الصَّوَاب.

Two. Increasing in the obligation. This is of two categories: Either it is distinct from the obligation or not. As for the distinct, e.g. voluntary prayers in relation to obligatory ones, the increase is voluntary, according to the agreement of all scholars. However, if the action shares the same name and is not distinct, in that it is not different in nature from the obligatory action as it is manifested by the action of the person, such as extending beyond the minimal obligation in tranquility, elongating the prostration, bowing, standing, and sitting, the increase is obligatory to al-Qāḍī Abu Ya'lā, and voluntary to Abu 'l-Khaṭṭāb, and the latter is the correct view.[162]

تَنْبيه: الْوَاجِب: هُوَ الْمَأْمُور بِهِ جزما، وَشرط ترتّب الثَّوَاب عَلَيْهِ نِيَّة التَّقَرُّب بِفعْلِهِ. وَالْحرَام: هُوَ الْمنْهِي عَنهُ جزما، وَشرط ترتّب الثَّوَاب على تَركه نِيَّة التَّقرُّب بِهِ، فترتب الثَّوَاب وَعَدَمه فِي فعل الْوَاجِب وَترك الْحَرَام. وعدمهما رَاجع إِلَى وجود شَرط الثَّوَاب وَعَدَمه، وَهُوَ النِّيَّة، لَا إِلَى انقسام الْوَاجِب وَالْحرَام فِي نفسهما.

Note: An obligatory action is one that is instructed with an imperative tone. The condition for earning rewards is that one must have the intention of garnering closeness [to Allah] by doing so. A forbidden action is one that is prohibited with an imperative tone. The condition for earning rewards for avoiding it is doing so with the intention of garnering closeness [to Allah]. Therefore, the reward is earned or lost due to the condition of reward or the lack thereof, which is the intention, not the categorisation of the obligation or prohibition in and of themselves.

فصل

Subsection [Two]

[*Mandūb* (Recommended)][163]

162 [T] To give a tangible example, suppose that the minimum time for sitting is x number of seconds. If a person sits for that number of time, and adds a tiny additional amount of time, that additional amount of time would be considered obligatory according to al-Qāḍī Abu Ya'lā and voluntary to Abu 'l-Khaṭṭāb.

163 [T] This heading has been added by the translator for clarity in organising the book and is not from the words of al-Shaykh Ibn Badrān.

وَأما النّدب فَهُوَ لُغَة: الدُّعَاء إِلَى الْفِعْل، وَقيل: الدعاء إِلَى أَمر مُبْهَم، وَشرعا: مَا أثيب فَاعله، وَلم يُعَاقب تَاركه مُطلقًا، سَوَاء تَركه إِلَى بدل أَو لَا، وَهُوَ مرادف للسّنة وَالْمُسْتَحب، فالسواك وَالْمُبَالغَة فِي الْمَضْمَضَة وَالِاسْتِنْشَاق وتخليل الْأَصَابِع وَنَحْو هَذَا يُقَال لَهُ: مَنْدُوب، وَسنة، ومستحب. وَالْمَنْدُوب مَأْمُور بِهِ لقَوْله صلى الله عَلَيْهِ وَسلم **((لَوْلَا أَن أشق على أمتِي لأمرتهم بِالسِّوَاكِ))**.

As for the term *"al-nadb"*, it refers, linguistically, to an encouragement to perform an action. It was said that it means an encouragement to do an unspecified action. In the nomenclature of legislation, it refers to something a person earns reward for doing, and does not earn punishment for abstaining from it absolutely, irrespective if they replace it with another action or not. This term (*al-nadb*) is synonymous to the two terms *sunnah* and *mustaḥabb*. The *siwāk* toothbrush, emphasis in gargling and snuffing [in ablution], washing between the fingers [in ablution], and other similar actions are called *mandūb*, *sunnah*, or *mustaḥabb*. A *mandūb* action is one that is instructed to do, because the Prophet ﷺ said, **"Had it not been that I did not wish to create hardship for my nation, I would have commanded them to use the *siwāk*."**[164]

تَنْبِيه: توسع أَصْحَابنَا فِي أَلْفَاظ الْمَنْدُوب، فَالْمَشْهُور مَا تقدم من أَنه يُسمى سنة ومستحبا، وَقَالَ ابْن حمدَان فِي (الْمقنع) وَيُسمى تَطَوّعا وَطَاعَة ونفلا وقربة، إِجْمَاعًا. وَقَالَ ابْن قَاضِي الجبل: وَيُسمى أَيْضا مرغبا فِيهِ، وإحسانا. وَقَالَ مدرس المستنصرية فِي (الْحَاوِي): أَعْلَاهُ سنة، ثمَّ فَضِيلَة، ثمَّ نَافِلَة.

Note: Our *aṣḥāb* have been liberal in using the various terms that refer to the *mandūb*. The most popular usage, though, is what was previously mentioned, namely, that it is referred to as *sunnah*, and *mustaḥabb*. Ibn Ḥamdān said his book *al-Muqni'*, "It is also referred to as volunteering (*taṭawwu'*), obedience (*ṭā'ah*), voluntary (*nafl*), and a means of garnering closeness (*qurbah*), by consensus." Ibn Qāḍī al-Jabal said, "It is also referred to as being encouraged (*muraghaban fīhi*), and good conduct (*iḥsān*)." The teacher of al-Mustanṣiriyyah[165] said in *al-Ḥāwī*, "The highest level is a *sunnah*, then a

164 Reported by Mālik (1/66) and al-Shāfi'ī (1/27), as well as al-Bukhārī (2/311-312).
165 [T] This title was given to Nūr al-Dīn Abu Ṭālib, 'Abd al-Raḥmān ibn 'Umar ibn Abi 'l-Qāsim al-Baṣrī, one of the great *imāms* of the Ḥanābilah. Refer to *Shadharāt*

virtue (*faḍīlah*), then a voluntary action (*nafl*)."

وَقَالَ أَصْحَابنَا والمالكية وَالشَّافِعِيَّة: الْعِبَادَة الطَّاعَة، وَقَالَ بذلك الْحَنفِيَّة وَلَكِن اشترطوا النِّيَّة. وَالطَّاعَة مُوَافقَة الْأَمر. وَالْمَعْصِيَة عِنْد الْفُقَهَاء مُخَالفَة الْأَمر، وَعند الْمُعْتَزلَة مُخَالفَة الْإِرَادَة. وكل قربَة طَاعَة وَلَا عكس.

Our *aṣḥāb*, the Mālikis, and the Shāfiʿīs all stated that worship is obedience. The same was stated by the Ḥanafī scholars, but they stipulated the intention. Obedience is to conform to a commandment, and disobedience is, according to the jurists, to contradict a commandment. According to the Muʿtazilah, [disobedience is] to contradict the Will. Every action that garners closeness to Allah is obedience, but the opposite is not true.[166]

✡✡✡

فصل

Subsection [Three]

[*Ḥarām* (Forbidden)][167]

الْحَرَام ضد الْوَاجِب، مَأْخُوذ من الْحُرْمَة، وَهِي: مَا لَا يحل انتهاكه. وَشرعا: مَا ذمّ فَاعله وَلَو قولا، أَو عمل قلب. وَيُسمى مَحْظُورًا وممنوعا ومزجورا ومعصية وذنبا وقبيحا وسيئة وفاحشة وإثما.

Ḥarām is the opposite of the *wājib*. It comes from the Arabic word *al-ḥurmah*, which means something that cannot be transgressed. In the terminology of the religion, it refers to something that, if done, the one doing the action is censured, even if the action is a statement or an action of the heart.

al-Dhahab (3/386-387).

166 [T] Al-Imām Ibn al-Najjār al-Futūḥī said, "This is because, in order to refer to an action as garnering closeness to Allah, the intention is a precondition. However, the same is not said of actions of obedience. As such, an action that garners closeness to Allah the Exalted is more unique than an action of obedience." (*Sharḥ al-Kawkab al-Munīr*, 3/385). This means that one can do an action of obedience, such as prayer, without the correct intention, and as such, not gain any closeness to Allah the Exalted by doing so.

167 [T] This heading has been added by the translator for clarity in organising the book and is not from the words of al-Shaykh Ibn Badrān.

Other words that refer to [*al-ḥarām*] are: *maḥẓūr* (banned), *mamnūʿ* (un-permitted), *mazjūr* (censured), *maʿṣiyah* (disobedience), *dhanb* (sin), *qabīḥ* (repulsive), *sayyiʾah* (vice), *fāḥishah* (immorality), and *ithm* (wrongdoing).

وَمن الْحَرَام نوع يُقَال لَهُ: الْمُخير، ومثاله أَن يُقَال للمكلف: لَا تنْكح هَذِه الْمَرْأَة أَو أُخْتهَا أَو بنت أُخْتهَا أَو بنت أَخِيهَا، فَيكون مَنْهِيّا عَنْهُمَا على التَّخْيِير، فأيتهما شَاءَ اجْتنب ونكح الْأُخْرَى. كَمَا أَنه إِذا أسلم عَلَيْهِمَا قيل لَهُ: طلق إِحْدَاهمَا، وَأمْسك الْأُخْرَى أيتها شِئْت.

There is also a type of *ḥarām* which is called *mukhayyar* (choice). An example is if it is told to a *mukallaf*, "Do not marry this woman along with her sister, her sister's daughter, or her brother's daughter." As such, they are forbidden from those actions, but it is by choice; he can avoid any of the women and marry any of the others [so long as he does not marry two or more of those mentioned]. Likewise, if a person has [married a woman and her sister or niece], he is told, 'Divorce one of them, and keep the other. You can choose between the two.'

وَاعْلَم أَن الْفِعْل الْوَاحِد الْمنْهِي عَنهُ إِمَّا أَن يُلَاحظ من حَيْثُ كَونه جِنْسا، أَو يُلَاحظ من حَيْثُ كَونه نوعا. فَإِن لوحظ من حَيْثُ الجنسية، جَازَ أَن يكون موردا لِلْأَمْرِ وللنهي، وَأَن يتَوَجَّه كل مِنْهُمَا إِلَيْهِ بِاعْتِبَار أَنْوَاعه، وَإِن لوحظ من حَيْثُ النوعية، جَازَ أَن يتَوَجَّه الْأَمر إِلَيْهِ بِاعْتِبَار شخص من أَفْرَاده، وَالنَّهْي إِلَيْهِ بِاعْتِبَار شخص آخر. فمثال الأول الْعِبَادَة، وتحتها نَوْعَانِ: عبَادَة لله، وَعبادَة لغيره، وَقد تعلق الْأَمر بالنوع الأول، وَتعلق النَّهْي بِالثَّانِي.

A single forbidden action can be a genus or can be a type. If it is a genus, it can be either a commandment or a prohibition, and can take those rulings based on the type that falls under the genus. However, if it is a type, it can be a commandment to one person and a prohibition to another. An example of genus is worship. There are two types of worship: (i) worship of Allah, and (ii) worship of something other than Allah. Commandments pertain to the first, and prohibitions pertain to the second.

ثمَّ إِن عبَادَة الله تَعَالَى تصير جِنْسا بِاعْتِبَار مَا تحتهَا من الْأَنْوَاع كَالصَّلَاةِ وَالزَّكَاة

وَغيرهمَا، فَالْأَمْر يتَعَلَّق بِالصَّلَاةِ، وَالنَّهْي تعلق بهَا من جِهَة إيقاعها فِي مَكَان مَغْصُوب، أَو من جِهَة إيقاعها بِلَا طَهَارَة. وحاصله أَن الْأَمر وَالنَّهْي يتوجهان إِلَى الْجِنْس بِاعْتِبَار تعداد أَنْوَاعه، وَإِلَى النَّوْع بِاعْتِبَار تعداد أشخاصه.

Worship of Allah can be considered a genus when considering its subsidiary types, such as prayer, *zakāt*, and so forth. Commandments pertain to prayer, and prohibitions pertain to performing the prayer in a usurped area or without being in a state of purity. Therefore, a commandment and a prohibition can pertain to a genus inasmuch as we consider its types, and can pertain to a type inasmuch as we consider its manifestations.

وَأما الْفِعْل الْوَاحِد بالشخص، فَلهُ جِهَة وَاحِدَة، إِذْ يَسْتَحِيل كَونه وَاجِبا حَرَامًا كَمَا لَو قَالَ: صل هَذِه الظّهْر، لا تصل هَذِه الظّهْر. وتمثيلنا بإيقاع الصَّلَاة فِي مَكَان مَغْصُوب مَبْنِيّ على القَوْل بِأَنَّهَا لَا تصح فِيهِ، وَلَا يسْقط الطّلب بهَا، وَلَا عِنْدهَا، وَإِلَيْهِ ذهب أَحْمد وَأَكْثر أَصْحَابه والظاهرية، والزيدية والجبائية. وَقيل: يسْقط الْفَرْض عِنْدهَا، لَا بهَا، وَهَذَا قَول الباقلاني والرازي. وَذهب أَحْمد فِي رِوَايَة عَنهُ وَمَالك وَالشَّافِعِيّ والخلال وَابْن عقيل والطوفي إِلَى أَنَّهَا تحرم وَتَصِح، وَمَعْنَاهُ: أَنَّهَا تصح بِمَعْنى تسْقط الطّلب، لَكِن لَا ثَوَاب بهَا، وَإِلَى هَذَا صَار الْأَكْثَر، وَقيل: إِن لفاعلها ثَوابًا. وَقَالَت الْحَنَفِيَّة: تكره. قَالَ نجم الدّين الطوفي: مَذْهَب الْحَنَفِيَّة فِي هَذَا الأَصْل، أَدخل فِي التدقيق، وأشبه بالتحقيق.

As for a single action pertaining to a single person, it can only be one thing, since it is impossible for an action to be both an obligation and a prohibition. An example would be to say, "Pray this particular *ẓuhr* prayer, but do not pray this particular *ẓuhr* prayer." The previous example mentioned, regarding prayer in a usurped area is not similar, as the prayer is not valid, nor does it waive one's obligation, neither by doing it nor does it indicate its completion.[168] This was the view taken by Aḥmad, the majority of his *aṣḥāb*,

---

168 [T] This terminology used by the legists is, "It does not waive the responsibility with it nor at it (لا تسقط بها ولا عندها)." The meaning is that they mean it is similar to a *wadh*ʿ ruling, which is just a sign that a ruling is activated or not. Al-Imām Badr al-Dīn al-Zarkashī stated, "Abu Bakr [al-Bāqillānī] stated, 'It does not occur as commanded, but the responsibility of redoing the prayer is waved at completion, but not through the prayer itself, just as responsibilities are waived by unforeseen valid excuses, such

the Ẓāhiris, the Zaydīs, and the Jubbā'īs. It was stated that the obligation is waived as an indication of its completion, but not because of the prayer that was offered. This view was that of al-Bāqillānī and al-Rāzī. Aḥmad, in another narration, Mālik, al-Shāfi'ī, al-Khallāl, Ibn 'Aqīl and al-Ṭūfī took the view that [the prayer] is forbidden, but that it is valid. This means that it is valid in that it waives the responsibility, but that one earns no rewards for it. This was the view of the majority. It was also stated that the one doing the prayer earns rewards. The Ḥanafīs stated it is *makrūh*, and Najm al-Dīn al-Ṭūfī stated, "The position of the Ḥanafī scholars in this theory is closer to precision and most resembling adequacy."[169]

فصل

Subsection [Four]

[*Makrūh* (Undesirable)][170]

الْمَكْرُوه ضد الْمَنْدُوب، إِذْ الْمَنْدُوب الْمَأْمُور بِهِ غير الْجَازِم، وَالْمَكْرُوه الْمنهِي عَنهُ غير الْجَازِم. فالمندوب قسيم الْوَاجِب فِي الْأَمر، وَالْمَكْرُوه قسيم الْحَرَام فِي النَّهْي. وَشرعا: مَا مدح تَارِكه وَلم يذم فَاعله، وَهُوَ دَاخل تَحت النَّهْي فَيُقَال: إِنَّه مَنْهِيّ عَنهُ، وَلَا يتَنَاوَلهُ الْأَمر الْمُطلق إِذْ الْأَمر الْمُطلق بِالصَّلَاةِ لَا يتَنَاول الصَّلَاة الْمُشْتَملَة على السدل والتحضر وَرفع الْبَصَر إِلَى السَّمَاء واشتمال الصماء والالتفات، وَنَحْو ذَلِك من المكروهات فِيهَا.

Al-makrūh is the opposite of *al-mandūb*, since a *mandūb* action is one that is instructed but is not done so imperatively. A *makrūh* action is one that is forbidden, but not done so imperatively. The *mandūb* shares with the *wājib* in that it is a commandment and instruction, and the *makrūh* shares with the *ḥarām* in that it is a prohibition. In religious terminology, it refers

as insanity, and so forth.' It is as though he considered it a cause for the obligation to be waived, or a sign that it has been waved, as a *wadh'* ruling, but not a cause for its absolute completion, as that is predicated on its validity." (*Al-Baḥr al-Muḥīṭ*, 1/347)

169 [T] *Sharḥ Mukhtaṣar al-Rawḍah* (1/379).

170 [T] This heading has been added by the translator for clarity in organising the book and is not from the words of al-Shaykh Ibn Badrān.

to something that, if a person does not do it, they are praiseworthy, but if they do it, they incur no censure. It falls under prohibitions, however, so it is said to be forbidden. It cannot fall within the boundaries of an outright command, since an outright command does not comprise of lowering the hands to the side, placing the hands on the hips, looking to the sky, to wrap oneself in a garment while constricting the arms, looking around, and other such undesirable actions in the prayer.

وَأطلق بعض أَصْحَابنَا الْمَكْرُوه على الْحَرَام، فقد قَالَ الْخرقِيّ فِي (مُخْتَصره) وَيكرهُ أَن يتَوَضَّأ فِي آنِية الذَّهَب وَالْفِضَّة. انْتهى. مَعَ أَن التَّوَضُّؤ فيهمَا حرَام بِلَا خلاف فِي ذَلِك فِي الْمَذْهَب.

Some of our *aṣḥāb* used the term *makrūh* to refer to *ḥarām*. Al-Khiraqī said in his *Mukhtaṣar*, "It is undesirable *(makrūh)* to perform ablution using water stored in a golden or silver utensil."[171] Though he used the term *makrūh*, it is forbidden to do so, without any disagreement within the *madhhab*.

وَقد تطلق على ترك الأولى كَقَوْل الْخرقِيّ أَيْضا: وَمن صلى بِلَا أَذَان وَلَا إِقَامَة، كرهنا لَهُ ذَلِك وَلَا يُعِيد. وَأَرَادَ أَن الأولى أن يُصَلِّي بِأَذَان وَإِقَامَة أَو بِأَحَدِهِمَا، وَإِن أخل بهما ترك ذَلِك الأولى. وَقَالَ الْآمِدِيّ: قد يُطلق الْمَكْرُوه على الْحَرَام، وعَلى مَا فِيهِ شُبْهَة وَتردد، وعَلى ترك مَا فعله رَاجِح وَإِن لم يكن مَنْهِيّا عَنهُ. انْتهى.

The term is also sometimes used to refer to undesirability, such as when al-Khiraqī says, "Whoever prays without the *adhān* or *iqāmah*, we find that an undesirable action for them to do, but they do not have to repeat the prayer."[172] He means it is best for one to pray after having done an *adhān* and *iqāmah*, or at least with one of them, and that if one does not, they have done a less ideal action. Al-Āmidī stated, "*Makrūh* sometimes is used to refer to the *ḥarām*, things that are doubtful or that cause one to have second thoughts, and not doing something that is more preferable, even if it is not prohibited."[173]

قلت: أما إِطْلَاقه على الْحَرَام، فقد سبق لَك بَيَانه فِي أَن الْإِمَامَيْنِ أَحْمد ومالكا

---

171 [T] *Mukhtaṣar al-Khiraqī* (p. 12).
172 [T] Ibid (p. 20).
173 [T] *Al-Iḥkām fī Uṣūl al-Aḥkām* (1/122).

يطلقانه على الْحَرَام الَّذِي يكون دَلِيله ظنيا تورعا مِنْهُمَا. وَأما الْبَاقِي فَهُوَ بِمَعْنى ترك الأولى.

My comment: As for its usage to refer to the *ḥarām*, I have previously explained how the two *imāms*, Aḥmad and Mālik, use this term for the *ḥarām* to refer to things that are presumptive in their evidence, and they do so to err on the side of caution. As for the rest, they use it to refer to not doing the more ideal option.

قَالَ الطوفي فِي (مُخْتَصر الرَّوْضَة): وَإِطْلَاق الْكَرَاهَة ينْصَرف إِلَى التَّنْزِيه.

Al-Ṭūfī said in *Mukhtaṣar al-Rawḍah*, "The term *makrūh* is used to refer to something that a person should be above doing."[174]

وَقَالَ المرداوي فِي (التَّحْرِير) الْمَكْرُوه إِلَى الْحَرَام أقرب، وَهُوَ فِي عرف الْمُتَأَخِّرين للتنزيه، وَيُقَال لفَاعِله: مُخَالف وَغير ممتثل ومسيء، نصا. وَقيل: يخْتَص الْحَرَام. وَقَالَ القَاضِي أَبُو يعلى وَابْن عقيل: يَأْثَم بترك السّنَن أَكثر عمره. قَالَ الإِمَام أَحْمد: من ترك الْوتر، فَهُوَ رجل سوء.

Al-Mardāwī stated in his book *al-Taḥrīr*: *Makrūh* is closest to *ḥarām*, and in the nomenclature of the later-day scholars, it refers to something that one should transcend above doing. The one who does it is referred to as being "contradictory," "not adherent," and "has done something bad," as explicitly stated [by Aḥmad.] Some said [those terms] are used only for *ḥarām* actions. Al-Qāḍī Abu Ya'lā and Ibn 'Aqīl both said that a person is sinful for abandoning voluntary actions for the majority of their life. Al-Imām Aḥmad said, "Whoever abandons the *witr* prayer is a man of evil."[175]

فصل

Subsection [Five]

[*Mubāḥ* (Lawful)][176]

174 [T] *Sharh Mukhtaṣar al-Rawḍah*, 1/382.

175 [T] *Taḥrīr al-Manqūl* (p. 117).

176 [T] This heading has been added by the translator for clarity in organising the

الْمُبَاح، هُوَ لُغَة: الْمُعْلن والمأذون، وَشرعا: مَا اقْتضى خطاب الشَّرْع التَّسْوِيَة بَين فعله وَتَركه، من غير مدح يَتَرَتَّب على فعله وَلَا ذمّ يَتَرَتَّب على تَركه. والمباح غير مَأْمُور بِهِ عِنْد الْجُمْهُور.

The term *mubāḥ* linguistically refers to something that is announced and allowed. In religious terminology, it is a religious instruction that implies that doing the action and abstaining from the action are equal. No praise is attached to doing the action, and no censure is attached to abandoning it. *Mubāḥ* actions are not commandments, according to the majority.

وَقَالَ الكعبي المعتزلي وَأَتْبَاعه: هُوَ مَأْمُور بِهِ، وَلَيْسَ مِنْهُ فعل غير مُكَلّف، وَيُسمى طلقا وحلالا، وَيُطلق هُوَ والحلال على غير الْحَرَام. وَلَيْسَ بتكليف عِنْد الْأَئِمَّة الْأَرْبَعَة.

Al-Kaʿbī, the Muʿtazilite, and his followers claimed that they are commandments, and that the actions of those who are not responsible are not considered *mubāḥ*. Other terminologies used to refer to it are: *ṭalq*, and *ḥalāl*. It (i.e. the term *mubāḥ*) and *ḥalāl* are used to refer to things that are not forbidden. It is not a responsibility according to the four *imāms*.

وَقَالَ مجد الدّين ابن تَيْمِية: الْإِبَاحَة تَكْلِيف. وَقصد بذلك أَنَّهَا مُخْتَصَّة بالمكلف.

Majd al-Dīn ibn Taymiyyah said, "Lawfulness is a responsibility," and he meant that it pertains to responsible persons.

تَتِمَّة: اخْتلف الْعلمَاء فِي الْأَعْيَان المنتفع بهَا قبل وُرُود الشَّرْع، فَقَالَ أَبُو الْحسن التَّمِيمِي، وَأَبُو الْخطاب - وَكِلَاهُمَا من الْحَنَابِلَة - وَالْحَنَفِيَّة - هِيَ على الْإِبَاحَة، فَمَا جَاءَ فِي الشَّرْع الحكم عَلَيْهِ بِشَيْء عَملنَا، وَمَا لم يرد، فَهُوَ بَاقٍ على إِبَاحَته.

A Continuation: Scholars differ on individual substances that are used prior to the coming of legislation. Abu 'l-Ḥasan al-Tamīmī and Abu 'l-Khaṭṭāb—both of whom are from the Ḥanābilah—and the Ḥanafī [scholars] stated that they are lawful. As such, [according to them], anything that is given a ruling in legislation must be adhered to, but if nothing is mentioned, the item remains lawful by default.

---

book and is not from the words of al-Shaykh Ibn Badrān.

وَقَالَ ابْن حَامِد، وَالْقَاضِي أَبُو يعلى، وَبَعض الْمُعْتَزلَة: إِنَّهَا على الْحَظْر، أَي: الْمَنْع. فَمَا لم يرد شرع بالحكم عَلَيْهِ فَهُوَ مَحْظُور.

Ibn Ḥāmid, al-Qāḍī Abu Ya'lā, and some Mu'tazilites, however, stated that they are unlawful. As such, [according to them], anytime legislation has not given a ruling on an item or thing, it is unlawful.

وَقَالَ أَبُو الْحسن الخرزي من الْحَنَابِلَة، والواقفية - وهم الَّذين يقفون فِي الْأَحْكَام عِنْد تجاذب الْأَدِلَّة لَهَا - إِنَّهَا على الْوَقْف أَي: لَا يدرى: هَل هِيَ مُبَاحَة أَو محظورة.

Abu 'l-Ḥasan al-Kharzī of the Ḥanābilah, and the scholars who tend to abstain (i.e. those who abstained from taking a view due to the strength of the evidences) said that the ruling is abstention, namely, that it cannot be definitively said that it is lawful nor unlawful.

وَأما الْمُعْتَزلَة: فقد قسموا الْأَفْعَال الاختيارية إِلَى مَا حسنه الْعقل: فَمِنْهُ وَاجِب، وَمِنْه مَنْدُوب، وَمِنْه مُبَاح، وَإِلَى مَا قبحه الْعقل: فَمِنْهُ حرَام، وَمِنْه مَكْرُوه، وَإِلَى مَا لم يقْض الْعقل فِيهِ بِحسن وَلَا بقبح فَهَذَا اخْتلفُوا فِيهِ، فَمنهمْ من قَالَ: إِنَّه وَاجِب. وَمِنْهُم من قَالَ: إِنَّه محرم. وَمِنْهُم من توقف فِيهِ، هَذَا مَا حَقَّقَهُ عَنْهُم الْآمِدِيّ. وَالْمُخْتَار الْإِبَاحَة. وَفَائِدَة هَذَا الْخلاف اسْتِصْحَاب كل وَاحِد من الْقَائِلين حَال أَصله قبل الشَّرْع فِيمَا جهل دَلِيله سمعا بعد وُرُود الشَّرْع.

As for the Mu'tazilites, they categorised optional actions into three: (i) Things that are rationally commendable, and they consist of: Obligations, recommended actions and lawful actions. (ii) Things that are rationally reprehensible, and they consist of: Unlawful actions and undesirable actions (iii) Things that are neither rationally commendable nor reprehensible. In this case, they have differed into three groups: Some said they are obligatory, some said they are forbidden and some abstained. This is what al-Āmidī has verified as their position, however, the chosen view is that they are lawful. The point behind this disagreement is that each person who has a view should keep in mind the case of the item's ruling before legislation if they are unaware of its evidence after legislation has arrived.

فَائِدَة: الْجَائِز لُغَة: العابر، بِالْعينِ الْمُهْملَة، وَاصْطِلَاحا: يُطلق على الْمُبَاح وعَلى مَا لَا يمْتَنع شرعا، فيعم غير الْحَرَام، أَو عقلا، فيعم الْوَاجِب وَالرَّاجِح والمساوي والمرجوح، وعَلى مَا اسْتَوَى فِيهِ الْأَمْرَانِ شرعا كالمباح، أَو عقلا كفعل الصَّغِير، وعَلى الْمَشْكُوك فِيهِ بِاعْتِبَار الشَّرْع أَو الْعقل. وَأما الْمُمكن: فَهُوَ مَا جَازَ وُقُوعه حسا، أَو وهما، أَو شرعا.

It is useful to note here that the term *jā'iz* (with an un-dotted letter *'ayn*) means something passing. In religious terminology, it refers to something that is lawful and permissible, without any religious restraints, thereby encompassing things that are not unlawful in religion. The term also refers to things that have no rational restraints. In culmination, therefore, it encompasses things such as obligations, more likely actions, equal actions, and less likely actions. It also refers to things that are equal on both sides in the religious sense, making it similar to a *mubāḥ* action, or in the rational sense, such as the action of a young person. It also refers to things that are doubtful in religious or rational terms. As for the term *mumkin* (possible), it refers to something that can possibly happen perceptibly, imaginatively, or religiously.

تَنْبِيه: إِذا نسخ الْوُجُوب بَقِي الْجَوَاز، وَقَالَ الْمجد، وَالْأَكْثَر، وَحكي عَن أَصْحَابنَا: أَن الْبَاقِي مُشْتَرك بَين النّدب وَالْإِبَاحَة. وَقَالَ أَبُو يعلى وَأَبُو الْخطاب وَابْن عقيل وَابْن حمدَان: بَقِي النّدب. وَقيل: تبقى الْإِبَاحَة، وَهُوَ مثل القَوْل بِالْجَوَازِ، وَهُوَ الْمُخْتَار. وَقَالَ الْحَنَفِيَّة والتميمي وَالْغَزالِيّ: يعود الْبَاقِي إِلَى أَصله قبل وُرُود الشَّرْع، وَهَذَا نَظِير قَول الْفُقَهَاء: إِذا بَطل الْخُصُوص بَقِي الْعُمُوم. وَلَو صرف النَّهْي عَن التَّحْرِيم بقيت الْكَرَاهَة، قَالَ ابْن عقيل وَغَيره.

Note: If an obligation becomes abrogated, it remains a lawful action to do. Al-Majd, and the majority, as well as our *aṣḥāb*, stated that [after abrogation] the remaining action is either recommended or simply lawful. Abu Ya'lā, Abu 'l-Khaṭṭāb, Ibn 'Aqīl, and Ibn Ḥamdān stated that it remains recommended. Some stated that it remains permissible, which is similar to the first view [of being lawful]. It is the chosen view. The Ḥanafī scholars, al-Tamīmī, and al-Ghazālī stated that the action takes its original ruling prior to legislation. This is similar to when jurists say, "If the particularisation is nullified, the generality remains." If a prohibition no longer carries the ruling of unlawfulness, it keeps the ruling of being undesirable, as stated by Ibn ʿAqīl and others.

فصل فِي خطاب الْوَضع

Section on the Declaratory Instructions

خطاب الْوَضع: هُوَ مَا اسْتُفِيدَ بِوَاسِطَة نصب الشَّارِع علما مُعَرفا لحكمه لتعذر معرفَة خطابه فِي كل حَال. هَكَذَا عرفه أَكثر عُلَمَاء الْأُصُول.

The term *khiṭāb al-waḍʿ* refers to a ruling learned by the legislation placing some signal which indicates a ruling, since His instructions cannot be known at all times and situations. That is how most scholars of legal theory defined it.

وَلما كَانَ هَذَا الْحَد فِيهِ غموض يعسر حلّه على كثير من المطالعين لهَذَا الْكتاب قربنا مَعْنَاهُ بقولنَا: مَعْنَاهُ أن الشَّرْع وضع أَي: شرع أمورا سميت أسبابا وشروطا وموانع تعرف عِنْد وجودهَا أَحْكَام الشَّرْع من إِثْبَات أَو نفي فالأحكام تُوجد بِوُجُود الْأَسْبَاب والشروط، وتنتفي بِوُجُود الْمَانِع وَانْتِفَاء الْأَسْبَاب والشروط.

This definition, however, is obscure; it is difficult for most readers of this book to understand. Therefore, I have attempted to facilitate its meaning. It means that the legislation has placed (*waḍaʿ*) i.e., declared certain things that are considered causes, preconditions, and impediments, and at the existence of those things, the existence or nonexistence of religious rulings are known. The existence of rulings, therefore, is predicated on the existence of the causes and preconditions, and the nonexistence of rulings is predicated on the presence of an impediment or the nonexistence of the causes or preconditions.

ثمَّ إِن الشَّرْع بِوَضْع هَذِه الْأُمُور أخبرنَا بِوُجُود أَحْكَامه وانتفائها عِنْد وجود تِلْكَ الْأُمور أَو انتفائها، فَكَأَنَّهُ قَالَ مثلا: إِذا وجد النّصاب الَّذِي هُوَ سَبَب وجوب الزَّكَاة والحول الَّذِي هُوَ شَرطه، فاعلموا أني أوجبت عَلَيْكُم أَدَاء الزَّكَاة، وَإِن وجد الدّين الَّذِي هُوَ مَانع وُجُوبهَا، أَو انْتَفى السوم الَّذِي هُوَ شَرط الْوُجُوب فِي

السَّائِمَة، فاعلموا أَنِّي لم أوجب عَلَيْكُم الزَّكَاة. وَكَذَا الْكَلَام فِي الْقصاص، وَالسَّرِقَة، وَالزِّنَى، وَكثير من الْأَحْكَام بِالنّظرِ إِلَى وجود أَسبَابهَا وشروطها وَانْتِفَاء موانعها وَعكس ذَلِك. وَبِهَذَا الْبَيَان فهم الْمَقْصُود من خطاب الْوَضع، وتخلص النَّاظر من حل التعقيد الَّذِي تضمنه التَّعْرِيف، وَحَيْثُ علمت ذَلِك فَاعْلَم أَن هَذَا الْعلم الْمَنْصُوب أَصْنَاف.

By placing these parameters, the religion has also told us of the existence or nonexistence of the rulings when those things exist or do not exist. As an example, it is as though the religion is saying, "When the minimum amount of wealth is present—which is the cause for the obligation of *zakāt*, and when a year passes—which is its condition, know that I have made *zakāt* obligatory on you. However, if one has debt—which is an impediment to the obligation, or livestock stop grazing—which is a precondition for paying *zakāt* on grazing livestock, know that *zakāt* is no longer obligatory on you." The same can be said about retribution, stealing, fornication, and many other rulings that are predicated on causes, preconditions, and the nonexistence of impediment, and vice versa. With this explanation, the meaning of "declaratory instructions" becomes clear, and the reader rids themselves of the obscurity contained in its definition. As you have learned this, be aware that this knowledge is of categories:

أَحدهَا: الْعلَّة:

First: The cause (*al-ʿillah*):

وَهِي فِي أصل الْوَضع: الْعرض الْمُوجب لخُرُوج الْبدن الحيواني عَن الِاعْتِدَال الطبيعي، ثمَّ استعيرت عقلا لما أوجب الحكم الْعقلِيّ لذاته كالكسر للانكسار، والتسويد للسواد وَنَحْوه ثمَّ استعيرت شرعا لمعان ثَلَاثَة:

Linguistically, the term *ʿillah* refers to an accident necessitating a departure of an animal body from its natural state of balance (health). Then, it was used as a metaphor to refer to what necessitates a rational consequence in and of itself, such as the action of breakage for something breaking, blackening for something becoming black, and so forth. Then, it was used metaphorically to refer to three meanings in the religious nomenclature:

أَحدهَا: مَا أوجب الحكم الشَّرْعِيّ لَا محَالة، وَهُوَ الْمَجْمُوع الْمركب من مُقْتَضى الحكم وَشَرطه وَمحله وَأَهله، تَشْبِيها بأجزاء الْعلَّة الْعَقْلِيَّة، وَذَلِكَ كَمَا يُقَال: وجوب الصَّلَاة حكم شَرْعِي، ومقتضاه أَمر الشَّارِع بِالصَّلَاةِ، وَشَرطه أَهْلِيَّة الْمُصَلِّي لتوجه الْخطاب إِلَيْهِ بِأَن يكون بَالغا عَاقِلا، وَمحله الصَّلَاة، وَأَهله الْمصلي. فالعلة هُنَا الْمَجْمُوع الْمركب من هَذِه الْأُمُور. والأهل وَالْمحل ركنان من أَرْكَانهَا. وَبِالْجُمْلَةِ فَهَذِهِ الْأَشْيَاء الْأَرْبَعَة تسمى عِلّة، وَمُقْتَضى الحكم: هُوَ الْمَعْنى الطَّالِب لَهُ، وَشَرطه يَأْتِي بَيَانه، وَأَهله: هُوَ الْمُخَاطب بِهِ، وَمحله: مَا تعلق بِهِ.

One. Something that necessitates a religious ruling, without a doubt. It is compounded, comprising of the necessitation of the ruling, the precondition of the ruling, the receptacle, and the actualiser. It is similar to the parts of a rational cause, which is why we say: The obligation of prayer is a religious ruling, its necessitation is that the Legislator commanded that prayer be done, its precondition is the legal capacity of the one praying in order for the religious instruction to pertain to them—and legal capacity is achieved with puberty and sound mind, its receptacle is the actual prayer, and its actualiser is the one who is praying. As such, the cause is compounded of these things. The actualisers and the receptacles are both two of its pillars. Generally speaking, these four things [when compounded] are referred to as a "cause": (i) The necessitation of the ruling, which is the thing or action the instruction necessitates. (ii) The preconditions, which will be clarified at a later time. (iii) The actualiser, which is the person instructed by the ruling. (iv) The receptacle, which is what the ruling relies on for completion.

ثَانِيهَا: مُقْتَضى الحكم وَإِن تخلف لفَوَات شَرط، أَو وجود مَانع. وَبَيَانه: أَن الْيَمين هُوَ الْمُقْتَضِي لوُجُوب الْكَفَّارَة، فيسمى عِلّة لَهُ، وَإِن كَانَ وجوب الْكَفَّارَة إِنَّمَا يتَحَقَّق بِمَجْمُوع أَمريْن: الْحلف الَّذِي هُوَ الْيَمين، والحنث فِيهَا، لَكِن الْحِنْث شَرط فِي الْوُجُوب، وَالْحلف هُوَ السَّبَب الْمُقْتَضِي لَهُ. فَقَالُوا: هُوَ عِلّة، فَإِذا حلف الْإِنْسَان على فعل شَيْء أَو تَركه، قيل: قد وجدت مِنْهُ عِلّة وجوب الْكَفَّارَة، وَإِن كَانَ الْوُجُوب لا يُوجد حَتَّى يَحْنَث، وَإِنَّمَا هُوَ بِمُجَرَّد الْحلف انْعَقد سَبَبه.

Two. The implications of the ruling, even if they are not applicable due to the non-existence of a precondition or the existence of an impediment. To clarify, breaking a right-hand oath implies that offering the expiation is an obligation. As such, [breaking the oath] is its cause, although the obligation of offering the expiation happened with the combination of two things: (i) The oath, which is the reason that necessitated [the obligation of offering the expiation]. (ii) Breaking that oath, which is the precondition to the obligation [of offering the expiation.] As such, they stated that it is its cause, and if a person gives an oath to do or not do something, they stated that the cause for the obligation of the expiation is now present, although the obligation does not become enacted until the person breaks the oath; with the existence of the oath, the cause is effectuated.

ثَالِثِهَا: حِكْمَة الحكم، وَهِي الْمَعْنى الْمُنَاسب الَّذِي ينشأ عَنهُ الحكم، كمشقة السّفر للقصر وَالْفطر، وَالدّين لمنع الزَّكَاة، والأبوة لمنع الْقصاص، فَيُقَال: مشقة السّفر هِيَ عِلّة استباحة الْقصر وَالْفطر للْمُسَافِر، وَالدّين فِي ذمَّة مَالك النّصاب عِلّة لمنع وجوب الزَّكَاة، وَكَون الْقَاتِل أَبَا عِلّة لمنع وجوب الْقصاص. وَالْمعْنَى الْمُنَاسب هُوَ كَون حُصُول الْمَشَقَّة على الْمُسَافِر معنى مُنَاسِب لتخفيف الصَّلَاة بقصرها، وَالتَّخْفِيف عَنهُ بِالْفطرِ، وانقهار مَالك النّصاب بِالدّينِ عَلَيْهِ معنى مُنَاسِب لإِسْقَاط وجوب الزَّكَاة عَنهُ، وَكَون الْأَب سَبَب وجود الْوَلَد معنى مُنَاسِب لسُقُوط الْقصاص، لِأَنهُ لما كَانَ سَبَب إيجاده لم تقتض الْحِكْمَة أَن يكون الْوَلَد سَبَب إعدامه وهلاكه لمحض حَقه.

Three. The wisdom of the ruling, which is an attribute that has a reasonable relationship, from which the ruling emanates. As examples, difficulty [is an attribute with a reasonable relationship] to travel, resulting in one shortening their prayers and breaking their fast. Other examples are debt and its effect of impeding the obligation of *zakāt* and fatherhood and its effect on impeding retribution [if he kills his son.] In such scenarios, it is stated that the difficulties of travel were the cause for the permissibility of shortening the prayer and breaking the fast for the traveller, the debt being a financial obligation on the one who has the minimum *zakāt* eligible amount of wealth is a cause for preventing the obligation of *zakāt*, and the fact a murderer fathered the one he murdered is a cause for preventing the obligation of retribution. The attribute which has a reasonable relationship is as follows: (i) The existence of difficulty for the one traveling has a reasonable relationship so as to ease the prayers via shortening and ease fasting via allowing its breaking. (ii) The overbearing weight of debt felt by a person, even with the minimum amount for *zakāt* to be obligatory has a reasonable relationship so as to suspend the obligation of *zakāt* on that person. (iii) The fact that the father is the reason for the existence of the son has a reasonable relationship so as to suspend retribution, because, since he is the reason for [the son's] existence, wisdom does not dictate that the son be the reason for the father's ceasing to exist simply to fulfill his (the son's) rights.

وَاعْلَم بِأَن الْفُقَهَاء كثيرا مَا يذكرُونَ فِي كتبهمْ مثل هَذِه الْعِلَل، وَمن هُنَا نشأت الفروق بِحَيْثُ صَارَت كَأَنَّهَا فن مُسْتَقل، كَمَا سنبينه فِيمَا بعد إِن شَاءَ الله تَعَالَى، فَيُقَال: مَا الْفرق بَين أَن لَا يقتل الْأَب بِابْنِهِ إِذا قَتله وَبَين وجوب رجمه إِذا زنى بابنته؟ فيجاب بِالْفرقِ بَين الأول بِكَوْنِهِ سَبَب إيجاده، وَبَين الثَّانِي من حَيْثُ إِن الرَّجْم إِنَّمَا هُوَ لمحض حق الله تَعَالَى، وَالْأول لمحض حق الْوَلَد.

Know, too, that the jurists often mention such causes in their books, and for this reason discussions on differentia began, to the point that [discussions on differentia] became an independent science [known as The Science of Differentia (*ʿilm al-furūq*)], as we will clarify later, Allah willing. The question is asked: What difference exists between a father not receiving capital punishment in retribution for killing his son, yet it is obligatory to stone the father if he commits fornication with his daughter? Answer: The difference between the two cases is that in the first, the father is the reason for the son's existence, and in the second, stoning of the father would occur purely to fulfil the right of Allah, while the first scenario is purely due to the right of the child.

ثَانِيهَا: السَّبَب: وَهُوَ لُغَة: مَا توصل بِهِ إِلَى الْغَرَض الْمَقْصُود. وَشرعا: مَا يلْزم من وجوده الْوُجُود، وَمن عَدمه الْعَدَم لذاته، فيوجد الحكم عِنْده لَا بِهِ، وَذَلِكَ لِأَنَّهُ لَيْسَ مؤثرا فِي الْوُجُود، بل هُوَ وصلَة ووسيلة إِلَيْهِ كالحبل مثلا فَإِنَّهُ يتَوَصَّل بِهِ إِلَى إِخْرَاج المَاء من الْبِئْر، وَلَيْسَ هُوَ الْمُؤثر فِي الْإِخْرَاج، وَإِنَّمَا الْمُؤثر حَرَكَة المستقي لِلْمَاءِ. ثمَّ استعير السَّبَب شرعا لمعان.

The second declaratory instruction: The medium (*al-sabab*): Linguistically, it refers to something used to achieve an intended goal. In legal terminology, it refers to something that, if it is exists, it necessitates the existence of something else, and if it does not exist, it necessitates the nonexistence of something in and of itself. The ruling exists when it exists, not because it exists, since it does not play a part in bringing it into existence. Rather, it is a medium and means to it, such as a rope: A rope is used to pull water out of a well, but is not the cause for the extraction of the water. The cause of the extraction of the water is the action of the one attempting to get the water. Then, the word was used metaphorically to refer to a number of meanings in the religious nomenclature:

أَحدهَا: مَا يُقَابل الْمُبَاشرَة، كحفر الْبِئْر مَعَ التردية فِيهَا، فَإِذا حفر شخص بِئْرا، وَدفع آخر إنْسَانا، فتردى فِيهَا، فَهَلَك، فَالْأول - وَهُوَ الْحَافِر - متسبب إِلَى هَلَاكه، وَالثَّانِي - وَهُوَ الدَّافِع - مبَاشر لَهُ. فَأطلق الْفُقَهَاء السَّبَب على مَا يُقَابل الْمُبَاشرَة، فَقَالُوا: إِذا اجْتمع المتسبب والمباشر، غلبت الْمُبَاشرَة، وَوَجَب الضَّمَان على الْمُبَاشر، وَانْقطع حكم التَّسَبُّب. وَله أَمْثِلَة أُخْرَى محلهَا كتب الْفُرُوع.

One. The opposite of a direct action. For example, if someone digs a well and someone is pushed into it, falls, and dies. The first person [who dug the well] is the medium to and an accessory of the death, but the second person who actually did the pushing is the one who committed the direct action. Therefore, the jurists use the term '*sabab*' to contrast with direct action. They said that if direct and indirect actioners conflict, the direct actioner is responsible and must pay liability, and the ruling of the indirect actioner ceases. There are other examples mentioned in the books of substantive law.

الثَّانِي: عِلّة الْعلَّة، كالرمي سمي سَببا للْقَتْل، وَهُوَ عِلّة الْإِصَابَة، والإصابة عِلّة لزهوق النَّفس الَّذِي هُوَ الْقَتْل، فالرمي هُوَ عِلّة عِلّة الْقَتْل، وَقد سموهُ سَببا.

Two. The cause of the cause. For example, shooting was called the cause for killing, but shooting is the cause of the injury, and the injury is the cause of the death. As such, shooting is the cause of the cause, and as such, they refer to it as a medium (*sabab*).

الثَّالِث: الْعلَّة بِدُونِ شَرطهَا، كالنصاب بِدُونِ حولان الْحول، سمي سَببا لوُجُوب الزَّكَاة.

Three. A cause without its precondition. For example, owning the minimum *zakāt* eligible wealth without having completed a year with that wealth was called a *sabab* for the obligation of *zakāt*.

الرَّابِع الْعلَّة: الشَّرْعِيَّة كَامِلَة، وَهِي الْمَجْمُوع الْمركب من الْمُقْتَضى وَالشّرط، وَانْتِفَاء الْمَانِع، وَوُجُود الْأَهْل وَالْمحل، يُسمى سَببا، ثمَّ إِن هَذِه الْعلَّة قد تكون وقتا كالزوال لِلظهْرِ، وَقد تكون معنى يسْتَلْزم حِكْمَة باعثة كالإسكار للتَّحْرِيم وَنَحْوه.

Four. A complete religious cause, which is compounded of: The necessitation of the ruling, the preconditions, lack of impediments, the presence of the actualizer and the receptacle, which are termed as 'mediums'. Furthermore, this cause could be: A time, such as the sun reaching the zenith to indicate *ẓuhr* prayer, in which case, it is called a *sabab*. It could be a property that necessitates some wisdom, such as the property of intoxication being the reason behind prohibition, and so forth.

وَسميت هَذِه الْعلَّة سَببا فرقا بَينهَا وَبَين الْعلَّة الْعَقْلِيَّة، لِأَن الْعَقْلِيَّة مُوجبَة لوُجُود معلولها كالكسر للانكسار، وَسَائِر الْأَفْعَال مَعَ الانفعالات، فَإِنَّهُ مَتى وجد الْفِعْل الْقَابِل، وانتفى الْمَانِع وجد الانفعال، بِخِلَاف الْأَسْبَاب، فَإِنَّهُ لَا يلْزم من وجودهَا وجود مسبباتها. وَأما الْعلَّة الشَّرْعِيَّة الْكَامِلَة، فَإِنَّهَا وَإِن كَانَ يلْزم من وجودهَا وجود معلولها سَببا مَعَ أَن السَّبَب لَا يلْزم من وجوده وجود مسببه، لَكِن لما كَانَ تأثيرها لَيْسَ لذاتها، بل بِوَاسِطَة نصب الشَّارِع لَهَا ضعفت لذَلِك عَن الْعلَّة الْعَقْلِيَّة، فَأَشْبَهت السَّبَب الَّذِي حكمه أَن يحصل عِنْده لَا بِهِ، فَلذَلِك سميت سَببا.

These things (i.e., the fourth group) are referred to as "mediums" to differentiate between them and the term "cause" as it is used in formal logic. The cause, in formal logic, necessitates the existence of the effect, such as breaking necessitating a breakage, and all other actions that produce effects. In these cases, whenever there is a receptive action, and no impediments exist, the effect is produced. This is contrary to a medium, because a medium does not necessitate its effect. As for complete religious causes, although their existence necessitates the existence of their effects as a medium (although mediums do not necessitate the existence of their effects), since their effects are not in and of themselves, but rather, by means of the Legislator erecting those [rules], they are weaker than the causes referred to in formal logic. As such, they are closer to being mediums, and their rulings occur when they exist, not because they exist. As such, they were referred to as *sabab*.

ثَالِثهَا: الشَّرْط: وَهُوَ فِي اللُّغَة الْعَلامَة، وَمِنْه قَوْله تَعَالَى ﴿فَقَدْ جَاءَ أَشْرَاطُهَا﴾ [مُحَمَّد: ١٨] أَي: علاماتها. وَفِي الشَّرْع مَا يلْزم من عَدمه الْعَدَم، وَلَا يلْزم من وجوده وجود وَلَا عدم لذاته، وَذَلِكَ كالإحصان الَّذِي هُوَ شَرط وجوب رجم الزَّانِي، فَإِن وجوب الرَّجْم يَنْتَفِي بِانْتِفَاء الْإِحْصَان، فَلَا يرْجم إِلَّا مُحصن. وكالحول الَّذِي هُوَ شَرط وجوب الزَّكَاة، يَنْتَفِي وُجُوبهَا لانتفائه، فَلَا تجب إِلَّا بعد تَمام الْحول.

The third declaratory instruction: Preconditions (*sharṭ*): Linguistically, the word *sharṭ* refers to a sign, such as when Allah the Exalted said: **{Its signs** *(ashraṭ* pl. *sharṭ)* **are already here.}** [Qur'ān 47:18] In religious terminology, it refers to something that, if it does not exist, something else does not exist, but if it does exist, it does not necessitate existence or nonexistence of another thing without exterior factors. For example, prior marriage is a precondition for the obligation of stoning the adulterer. The obligation of stoning disappears with the nonexistence of a prior marriage, and as such, only a married person receives the punishment of stoning. Further, passage of a full lunar year is a precondition to the obligation of *zakāt*, and the obligation ceases so long as the year is not completed. Therefore, only after the completion of the year is *zakāt* obligatory.

ثمَّ إِن الشَّرْط إِن أخل عَدمه بحكمة السَّبَب، فَهُوَ شَرط السَّبَب، وَذَلِكَ كالقدرة على تَسْلِيم الْمَبِيع، فَإِن تِلْكَ الْقُدْرَة شَرط لصِحَّة البيع الَّذِي هُوَ سَبَب ثُبُوت الْملك الْمُشْتَمل على مصلحَة، وَهُوَ حَاجَة الابتياع لِعلة الِانْتِفَاع بِالْمَبِيعِ، وَهِي متوقفة على الْقُدْرَة على التَّسْلِيم، فَكَانَ عَدمه مخلا بحكمة الْمصلحَة الَّتِي شرع لَهَا البيع.

Further, if the lack of a precondition breaches the wisdom of the *sabab*, it becomes known as "the precondition of the medium (*sharṭ al-sabab*)." An example is the ability to hand over merchandise, on which the validity of a transaction is predicated. The transaction is the medium through which ownership of the item, which is comprised of its utility, is transferred. The utility is the need to barter and transact to benefit from various products. Those concepts are all reliant on the ability to hand over merchandise. As such, lack of [ability to hand over merchandise] breaches the wisdom of the utility for which transactions were legislated.

وَإِن استلزم عدم الشَّرْط حِكْمَة تَقْتَضِي نقيض الحكم، فَهُوَ شَرط الحكم، كالطهارة للصَّلَاة، فَإِن عدم الطَّهَارة حَال الْقُدْرة عَلَيْهَا مَعَ الْإِتْيَان بِالصَّلَاةِ يَقْتَضِي نقيض حِكْمَة الصَّلَاة، وَهُوَ الْعقَاب، فَإِنَّهُ نقيض وُصُول الثَّوَاب.

In contrast, if the lack of a precondition necessitates the opposite of a ruling, it becomes "the precondition of the ruling (*sharṭ al-ḥukm*)." For example, consider purity and its relationship to prayer: Praying without ritual purity, while able [to purify themselves], necessitates the opposite of the wisdom of the prayer, which is punishment. Therefore, it is the opposite of [the true wisdom of prayer, which is] earning rewards.

وَاعْلَم أَن الشَّرْط منحصر فِي أَرْبَعَة أَنْوَاع:

Know, too, that preconditions are limited to four categories:

الأول: عَقْلِي؛ كالحياة للْعلم، فَإِنَّهُ إِذا انْتَفَت الْحَيَاة، انْتَفَى الْعلم، وَلَا يلْزم من وجودهَا وجوده.

One. Rational: Such as life [being a precondition] to knowledge. If life ceases, so does knowledge. However, if life exists, it does not necessitate the existence of knowledge.

الثَّانِي: شَرْعِي، كالطهارة للصَّلَاة.

Two. Religious: Such as ritual purity [being a precondition] to prayer.

الثَّالِث: لغَوِيّ، كعبدي حر إِن قُمْت. وَهَذَا النَّوْع كالسبب، فَإِنَّهُ يلْزم من وجود الْقيام وجود الْعتْق، وَمن عدم الْقيام عدم الْعتْق الْمُعَلق عَلَيْهِ.

Three. Linguistic: Such as saying, "My slave is free if I stand." This resembles a medium, because it necessitates that when standing exists, so does freeing of the slave, and necessitates that when standing does not exist, the consequent, which is freeing of the slave, does not exist.

الرَّابِع: عادي، كالغذاء للحيوان، إِذْ الْعَادة الْغَالِبَة أَنه يلْزم من انْتِفَاء الْغذَاء انْتِفَاء الْحَيَاة، وَمن وجوده وجودهَا، إِذْ لَا يتغذى إِلَّا الْحَيّ، فعلى هَذَا يكون الشَّرْط العادي مطردا منعكسا كالشرط اللّغَوِيّ، ويكونان من قبيل الْأَسْبَاب لَا من قبيل الشُّرُوط.

Four. Customary: Such as nourishment [being a precondition] to [the life of] animals. Customarily, the lack of nourishment necessitates the lack of life, and the presence of nourishment necessitates the presence of life. Only living organisms can be nourished. Based on this, a customary precondition has the quality of coexistence and coexclusion (*al-ṭard wa al-ʿaks*), just like the linguistic precondition. As such, they are mediums, not true preconditions.

وَمَا جعل قيدا لشَيْء فِي معنى كالشرط فِي العقد، فَالْأَصَح أَنه كالشرط الشَّرْعِيّ، وَقيل: كاللغوي.

Further, it is more veracious to view anything that is considered a stipulation for something else, such as conditions in contracts, to be similar to religious preconditions, though others said it should be considered a linguistic precondition.

واللغوي أغلب اسْتِعْمَاله فِي السَّبَبِيَّة الْعَقْلِيَّة، كَقَوْلِك: إِذا طلعت الشَّمْس، فالعالم مضيء، وَفِي الشَّرْعِيَّة كَقَوْلِه تَعَالَى ﴿وَإِنْ كُنْتُمْ جُنُباً فَاطَّهَّرُوا﴾ [الْمَائِدَة: ٦] وَاسْتعْمل اللّغَوِيّ لُغَة فِي شَرط لم يبْق للمسبب شَرط سواهُ، نَحْو: إِن تأتني أكرمك، فَإِن الْإِتْيَان شَرط لم يبْق للإكرام سواهُ، لِأَنهُ إِذا دخل الشَّرْط اللّغَوِيّ عَلَيْهِ، علم أَن أَسبَاب الْإِكْرَام حَاصِلَة، لَكِن متوقفة على حُصُول الْإِتْيَان.

The linguistic preconditions are usually used to refer to causes in rational sciences, such as when one says, "If the sun rises, the world becomes light," as well as for the religious precondition, such as when Allah the Exalted states: **{And if you are in a state of sexual impurity, then perform a ritual bath.}** [Qurʾān 5:6] The linguistic one is used linguistically to refer to the final preconditions of the effect, such as saying, "If you visit me, I will honor you." Visiting is the final precondition of being honoured. If the linguistic precondition occurs, it becomes known that honouring will occur, but it is contingent on visitation happening.

رَابِعهَا: الْمَانِع: وَهُوَ مَا يلْزم من وجوده الْعَدَم، وَلَا يلْزم من عَدمه وجود وَلَا عدم لذاته، فَهُوَ عكس الشَّرْط.

The fourth declaratory instruction: Impediments (*māniʿ*): Linguistically, the term *māniʿ* refers to something that, if it exists, something else does not exist, but if it does not exist, it does not necessitate existence or nonexistence of another thing without external factors. Therefore, it is the opposite of a precondition.

وَهُوَ إِمَّا للْحكم، كالأبوة فِي الْقصاص مَعَ الْقَتْل الْعمد، وَيعرف بِأَنَّهُ وصف وجودي ظَاهر منضبط مُسْتَلْزم لحكمة تَقْتَضِي نقيض حكم السَّبَب مَعَ بَقَاء حكم الْمُسَبّب. وَإِمَّا لسَبَب الحكم، كَالدّين لِلزَّكَاةِ مَعَ ملك نِصَاب، وَيعرف بِأَنَّهُ وصف يخل وجوده بِحكم السَّبَب.

Impediments sometimes belong to the ruling, such as fatherhood impeding the ruling of retribution as a punishment for murder [of one's own son]. It is defined as: An attribute that is apparent, consistent, and externally existing, which necessitates some wisdom that implies the opposite of the ruling of the cause although the ruling of the effect still exists.[177] It could also impede the cause for a ruling, such as debt impeding [the obligation of] *zakāt* when one owns the minimum eligible amount of wealth. This is known as an attribute that, when present, breaches the ruling of the cause.

وَنصب الْعلَّة، وَالسَّبَب، وَالشَّرط، وَالْمَانِع لتفيد مَا اقتضته من الْأَحْكَام حكم شَرْعِي، فَجعل الزِّنَا سَببا لوُجُوب الْحَد حكم شَرْعِي. وَهَكَذَا يُقَال فِي نَظَائِره.

Legislating the cause, the medium, the precondition, and the impediment to indicate the implications of rulings is a religious ruling. For example, stating that fornication is the cause that obligates the penalty is a religious rul-

177 [T] When he says, "Necessitates some wisdom," the wisdom was previously defined, which is that the father is the one who caused the son to come into life, and as such, the son should not be the cause for the father's departure from life.

When he says, "That implies the opposite of the ruling of the cause," the opposite of the ruling is that the father is not punished with the death penalty.

When he says, "Although the ruling of the effect still exists," i.e., the murder.

ing. The same can be said about all other examples.

تَنْبِيه: اعْلَم أَن مَا ذكرْنَاهُ هُنَا من انقسام خطاب الْوَضع إِلَى الْأَنْوَاع الْأَرْبَعَة إِنَّمَا هُوَ تَقْسِيم لكلياته، وَبَقِي لَهُ أَقسَام جزئية تعد كاللواحق لَهُ، وَإِلَيْك بَيَانهَا.

Note: When we define declaratory rulings as being of four categories, it is a categorisation of its universals. It still has individual instances that can be considered ancillaries, and they are:

أَحدهَا: الصِّحَّة: وَعرفهَا الْفُقَهَاء بِأَنَّهَا وُقُوع الْفِعْل كَافِيا فِي سُقُوط الْقَضَاء، كَالصَّلَاةِ الْوَاقِعَة بشروطها وأركانها مَعَ انْتِفَاء موانعها، فَإِذا وَقعت كَذَلِك، سقط الطّلب بقضائها:

First: Validity (*ṣiḥḥah*): The jurists define it as the action being sufficient to not require the action be repeated. An example is a prayer that occurs with all of its preconditions and pillars done correctly, and without any impediments. If it occurs as such, the instruction to repeat the prayer [due to invalidity] is no longer applicable.

وَقَالَ المتكلمون: الصِّحَّة مُوَافقَة الْأَمر، فَكل من أَمر بِعبَادة، فَوَافَقَ الْأَمر بِفعْلِهَا، كَانَ قد أَتَى بهَا صَحِيحَة، وَإِن اخْتَلَّ شَرط من شُرُوطهَا أَو وجد مَانع. وَهَذَا أَعم من قَول الْفُقَهَاء، لِأَن كل صِحَة، فَهِيَ مُوَافقَة الْأَمر عِنْد الْمُتَكَلِّمين، وَلَيْسَ كل مُوَافقَة الْأَمر صِحَة عِنْد الْفُقَهَاء.

Scholars of *kalām* stated that validity is to coincide with the commandment. As such, everyone that is commanded to do some action of worship and adheres to the commandment by doing the action, they have done the action in a valid form, even if they lack one of its preconditions or have an impediment. This is more general than what the jurists state. According to the scholars of *kalām*, every valid action is adherence to the commandment, but according to jurists, not every adherence to the commandment necessitates validity.

فَصَلَاة الْمُحدث وَهُوَ يظنّ الطَّهَارَة صَحِيحَة على قَول الْمُتَكَلِّمين دون الْفُقَهَاء، وَالْقَضَاء وَاجِب على الْقَوْلَيْنِ، وَمن هُنَا تعلم أَن الْخلاف بَينهمَا لَفْظِي حَقِيقِيّ،

والبطلان يُقَابل الصِّحَّة على الرأيين، فعلى قَول الْفُقَهَاء الْبطلَان وَهُوَ وُقُوع الْفِعْل غير كَاف فِي سُقُوط الْقَضَاء، وعَلى قول الْمُتَكَلّمين هُوَ مُخَالفَة الْأَمر.

For example, when a person prays in a state of minor ritual impurity whilst thinking they are ritually pure, it is valid according to the scholars of *kalām*, but not according to the jurists. However, both [the scholars of *kalām* and the jurists] state that they must redo the prayer. This shows that the disagreement they have is mere semantics. The jurists state that it is an invalid prayer because the action that occurred is not sufficient to not require the action to be repeated, whilst the scholars of *kalām* will argue that the person has contradicted the commandment.

وَأما الصِّحَّة فِي الْمُعَامَلَات كعقد البيع وَالرَّهْن وَالنكَاح وَنَحْوهَا فَهِيَ ترَتّب أَحْكَامهَا الْمَقْصُودَة بهَا عَلَيْهَا.

Validity, as it pertains to transactions, such as sales contracts, mortgages, marriages, and so forth, means that the consequent rulings intended by those actions are enacted.

قَالَ الْآمِدِيّ: وَلَا بَأْس بتفسير الصِّحَّة فِي الْعِبَادَات بِهَذَا، وَمَعْنَاهُ: أَن مَقْصُود الْعِبَادَة إِقَامَة رسم التَّعَبُّد، وَبَرَاءَة ذمَّة العَبْد مِنْهَا، فَإِذا أفادت ذَلِك، كَانَ هُوَ معنى أَنَّهَا كَافِيَة فِي سُقُوط الْقَضَاء، فتكون صحيحة.

Al-Āmidī stated: "There is no problem with defining validity in worship in the same way."[178] It means that the intent behind worship is to establish the description of servitude and to acquit oneself of the action. If it fulfils [those two intents], the meaning is that [the worship] sufficiently abated the need for redoing it, rendering it valid.

والبطلان وَالْفساد مُتَرَادِفَانِ عِنْد أَصْحَابنَا وَالْجُمْهُور، فَيُقَال: صَحِيح وفاسد، كَمَا يُقَال: صَحِيح وباطل. وَأثبت أَبُو حنيفَة قسما متوسطا بَين الصَّحِيح وَالْبَاطِل،

178 [T] *Al-Iḥkām* (1/131). However, the exact wording of al-Āmidī is, "There is nothing wrong with one stating that worship is 'valid,' intending this meaning." When he says, "intending this meaning," or as Ibn Badrān quoted above, "in the same way," he is referring to validity in worship being described in the same way as the term, 'validity,' is used to describe transactions.

سَمَّاهُ الْفَاسِد، وَقَالَ: هُوَ مَا كَانَ مَشْرُوعا بِأَصْلِهِ دون وَصفه.

According to our *aṣḥāb* and the majority, nullity and invalidity are synonymous. As such, either can be used as antonyms of "validity." Abu Ḥanīfah, though, stated there is a category that is between valid and invalid, which he referred to as "null (*fāsid*)." He said, "It is something permissible in its default scenario, but not with its specific descriptions."[179]

على أَن أَصْحَاب أَحْمد، وَأَصْحَاب الشَّافِعِي فرقوا بَين الْفَاسِد وَالْبَاطِل فِي الْفِقْه فِي مسَائِل كَثِيرَة، وَقَالَ فِي (شرح التَّحْرِير) لعلاء الدّين عَليّ المرداوي: غَالب الْمسَائِل الَّتِي حكمُوا عَلَيْهَا بِالْفَسَادِ هِيَ مَا إِذا كَانَ مُخْتَلفا فِيهَا بَين الْعلمَاء، وَالَّتِي حكمُوا عَلَيْهَا بِالْبُطْلَانِ هِيَ مَا إِذا كَانَ مجمعا على بُطْلَانهَا، أَو الْخلاف فِيهَا شَاذ، قَالَ: ثمَّ وجدت بعض أَصْحَابنَا قَالَ: الْفَاسِد من النِّكَاح: مَا يسوغ فِيهِ الِاجْتِهَاد، وَالْبَاطِل: مَا كَانَ مجمعا على بُطْلَانه. هَذَا كَلَامه.

The *aṣḥāb* of Aḥmad and the followers of al-Shāfiʿī have differentiated between invalidity and nullity in various matters of law. ʿAlā al-Dīn al-Mardāwī stated in his *Sharḥ al-Taḥrīr*, "The majority of issues where they rule that [the action] is invalid are those that are differed on amongst scholars, and when they rule it is null, it is because there is unanimous agreement that the action is null and void, or the difference of opinion is a very unpopular view. I have found some of our *aṣḥāb* say, 'An invalid marriage is one where [the specifics of the marriage are subject to] *ijtihād*, and null marriages are ones where all scholars agree it is null.'"[180]

ثَانِيهَا: الْأَدَاء: وَهُوَ فعل الْمَأْمُور بِهِ فِي وقته الْمُقدر لَهُ شرعا، كَفعل الْمغرب مَا بَين غرُوب الشَّمْس وغروب الشَّفق، وَيدخل فِي ذَلِك مَا كَانَ مضيقا كَالصَّوْمِ، وموسعا محدودا كوقت الصَّلَوَات، أَو غير مَحْدُود كَالْحَجِّ، فَإِن وقته الْعُمر. وتحديده بِالْمَوْتِ ضَرُورِيّ لَيْسَ كتحديد أَوْقَات الصَّلَوَات.

Second: Fulfilment (*adāʾ*): *Adāʾ* means to perform a commandment during

179 [T] For example, the default ruling of selling something is that it is permissible. However, the specifics of the sale could be prohibited, such as someone selling something prohibited.
180 [T] *Al-Taḥbīr Sharḥ al-Taḥrīr* (3/1111).

its legally stipulated time-frame, such as performing the *maghrib* prayer between the time the sun sets and before the twilight disappears. This includes commandments that are narrow in time-frame, such as fasting, and others that have expanded time-frames (to a degree), such as the timings of prayers. Others have no time-frame, such as the Ḥajj; the time-frame wherein Ḥajj must be performed is the entire lifespan [of the *mukallaf* person]. Limiting it by death is by necessity, not similar to the limitations of the timings of prayers.

ثَالِثهَا: الْإِعَادَة: وَهِي فعل الْمَأْمُور بِهِ فِي وقته الْمُقدر لَهُ شرعا، لخلل فِي الأول سَوَاء كَانَ الْخلَل فِي الْأَجْزَاء - كمن صلى بِدُونِ شَرط أَو ركن - أَو فِي الْكَمَال - كمن صلى مُنْفَردا - فيعيدها جمَاعَة فِي الْوَقْت. هَكَذَا قَالَ الأصوليون.

Third: Repetition (*I'ādah*): This refers to repeating an action during its legally allotted time, due to some deficiency in the first iteration. This is equally true for when the deficiency was in one of its parts, such as a person praying without achieving a precondition or fulfilling a pillar, or in its completeness, such as a person praying alone, and then repeating the prayer in congregation within the allotted time of the prayer, as has been stated by legal theorists.

وَقَالَ موفق الدّين الْمَقْدِسِي، فِي (الرَّوْضَة) الْإِعَادَة فعل الشَّيْء مرة بعد أُخْرَى، وَهَذَا التَّعْرِيف أوفق من الأول، وموافق لقَوْل الْأَصْحَاب: من صلى ثمَّ حضر جمَاعَة، سنّ لَهُ أَن يُعِيدهَا مَعَهم، إِلَّا الْمغرب على خلاف هَذَا. ويشمل قَوْلهم: من صلى مَا إِذا صلى الأولى مُنْفَردا أَو فِي جمَاعَة، فأثبتوا الْإِعَادَة مَعَ عدم الْخلَل فِي الأولى. وَفِي مَذْهَب مَالك: لَا تخْتَص الْإِعَادَة بِالْوَقْتِ، بل هِيَ فِيهِ لاستدراك المندوبات، وَبعد الْوَقْت لاستدراك الْوَاجِبَات.

Muwaffaq al-Dīn al-Maqdisī stated in his *al-Rawḍah*, "Repetition is to do an action another time."[181] [182] This definition is more suitable than the first one and is more in line with what the *aṣḥāb* state in the matter of a person who prays and then attends the congregation: It is the Sunnah for them to

181 [T] Ibn Badrān quoted it as, "To do an action time after time." However, what I have placed is found in the printed copies of *Rawḍat al-Nāẓir wa Junnat al-Munāẓir*.
182 [T] *Rawḍat al-Nāẓir wa Junnat al-Munāẓir* (1/184).

repeat the prayer with [the congregation], unless it is the *maghrib* prayer, for it has a different ruling. When the *aṣḥāb* say, "A person who prays," it includes those who offered their first prayer alone or in congregation. They affirmed the repetition though the first prayer did not have a deficiency. In the *madhhab* of Mālik, it states that repetition is not restricted to a time, rather, if one wishes to make up missed recommended actions [in the worship], they may do so within the time [of the action of worship], but after the time is over, they may repeat the worship to make up for missed obligations of the prayer.

رَابِعهَا: الْقَضَاء: وَهُوَ فعل الْمَأْمُور بِهِ خَارج الْوَقْت أَي: بعد خُرُوجه لفَوَات الْفِعْل فِيهِ لعذر أَو غَيره، بِأَن أخر الْمَأْمُور بِهِ عمدا حَتَّى خرج وقته، ثمَّ فعله. وَالْأَحْسَن من هَذَا أَن يُقَال فِي تَعْرِيف الْقَضَاء: إنه إِيقَاع الْعِبَادَة خَارج وَقتهَا الَّذِي عينه الشَّرْع لمصْلحَة فِيهِ.

Fourth: Compensation *(al-qaḍā')*: Compensatory worship is when a person performs a commandment outside of its allotted time, because they did not perform it during the allotted time, whether for a valid reason or not. [An example of an invalid reason is] delaying a commandment purposely until the time-frame ended, then performing the action. A better definition is to state it is to perform an action of worship outside of its religiously allotted time, a time which has been set for certain benefits.

فَائِدَة: الْعِبَادَة قد تُوصَف بِالْأَدَاءِ وَالْقَضَاء كالصلوات الْخمس، وَقد لَا تُوصَف بهما كالنوافل لعدم تَقْدِير وَقتهَا، وَقد تُوصَف بِالْأَدَاءِ وَحده كَالْجُمُعَةِ وَالْعِيدَيْنِ، وَعدم الْقَضَاء فيهمَا للتوقيف أَو الْإِجْمَاع، لَا لامتناعه عقلا وَلَا شرعا.

At this point, it is useful to note that an action of worship can be described as fulfilled or compensatory, such as the five daily prayers, and might not be described as such, such as the voluntary actions, since they have no allotted time. Also, some actions can only be described as being "fulfilled," and cannot be compensated, such as Jumu'ah and the two 'Eid prayers. The lack of ability to compensate for their nonperformance is either due to religion not prescribing anything or there being unanimous agreement that no compensation exists. However, the presence of [the description of being "compensatory"] is neither a rational nor a religious impossibility.[183]

(الْإِجْزَاء) يخْتَص بِالْعبَادَة سَوَاء كَانَت وَاجِبَة أَو مُسْتَحبَّة. وَقَالَ المتكلمون: إجْزَاء الْعِبَادَة كفايتها فِي سُقُوط التَّعَبُّد، وَالْقَوْل مثل الصِّحَّة، فَلَا يفارقها فِي إِثْبَات وَلَا نفي، فَإِذا وجد أَحدهمَا وجد الآخر، وَإِذا انْتَفَى انتفي. والنفوذ: تصرف لَا يقدر فَاعله على رَفعه، كالعقود اللَّازِمَة من البيع وَالْإِجَارة وَالْوَقْف وَغيرهَا إِذا اجْتمعت شُرُوطهَا، وانتفت موانعها.

The concept of sufficiency (*ijzā'*) is one that pertains to worship, regardless if it is obligatory or voluntary. Scholars of *kalām* opined that sufficiency means that it sufficiently abated the action of worship. Acceptance is the same as validity; it does not vary, neither in affirmation [of the attribute] nor negation. That is to say, if either [acceptance or validity] is present, the other is also present, and vice versa. The concept of something being binding is one where its actioner cannot nullify or invalidate it. Examples are contracts that require fulfilment, such as in sales transactions, leases, or when declaring something an endowment, and so forth, if their conditions are met and their impediments do not exist.

خَامِسهَا الْعَزِيمَة والرخصة: الْعَزِيمَة لُغَة: الْقَصْد الْمُؤَكّد، وَشرعا: هِيَ الحكم الثَّابِت بِدَلِيل شَرْعِي خَال عَن معَارض رَاجِح. فقولنا: الحكم الثَّابِت بِدَلِيل شَرْعِي، يتَنَاوَل الْوَاجِب، وَالْمَنْدُوب، وَتَحْرِيم الْحَرَام، وَكَرَاهَة الْمَكْرُوه. فالعزيمة وَاقعَة فِي جَمِيع هَذِه الْأَحْكَام، وَلِهَذَا قَالَ أَصْحَابنَا: إِن سَجْدَة (ص) هَل هِيَ من عزائم السُّجُود أَو لَا؟ مَعَ أَن سَجدَات الْقُرْآن كلهَا عِنْدهم ندب.

Fifth [and sixth] of the ancillaries: The concession (*rukhṣah*) and regularity (*ʿazīmah*): In the Arabic language, an *ʿazīmah* refers to a solid, firm resolve. In religious nomenclature, it refers to a ruling that is established through a religious evidence and which is lacking any outbalancing conflicting [evidence]. Therefore, when we state it is "a ruling established through religious evidence," it encompasses obligations, recommendations, forbiddances, and undesirables. Regularity affects all of these rulings, which is why our *aṣḥāb*

183 [T] This means that if Allah were to prescribe compensation of *Jumuʿah* and the two ʿEid prayers, it does not result in a rationally impossible outcome, nor does it result in a religiously forbidden outcome. It is simply that Allah did not prescribe it.

have questioned whether the prostration in Sūrat Ṣād (38) is an *ʿazīmah* or not, though all prostrations of recitation of the Qurʾān are considered recommended to [the Ḥanbalī scholars].

وَقَوْلنَا: بِدَلِيل شَرْعِي، احْتِرَاز عَمَّا ثَبت بِدَلِيل عَقْلِي، فَإِن ذَلِك لَا تسْتَعْمل فِيهِ الْعَزِيمَة والرخصة.

When we state, 'through religious evidence,' it is to avoid including rulings that are established through rational evidences, where the concepts of concession and regularity are not applicable.

وَقَوْلنَا: خَال من معَارض رَاجِح، احْتِرَاز عَمَّا ثَبت بِدَلِيل شَرْعِي، لَكِن لذَلِك الدَّلِيل معَارض مسَاوٍ أَو رَاجِح، كتحريم الْميتَة عِنْد عدم المخمصة، هُوَ عَزِيمَة لِأَنَّهُ حكم ثَابت بِدَلِيل خلا من معَارض، فَإِذا وجدت المخمصة، حصل الْمعَارض لدَلِيل التَّحْرِيم، وَهُوَ رَاجِح عَلَيْهِ حفظا للنَّفس، فَجَاز الْأكل، وحصلت الرُّخْصَة.

When we state, "Lacking any outbalancing conflicting [evidence]," it is to avoid including things that are established via religious evidences, but those conflicting evidences are either equal [in strength of indication of a ruling], or are outbalancing [the other evidence, making them the weightier and more veracious claim]. For example, when it comes to eating a carcass when a person is not in fear of starvation, it is a regular ruling, since it is a ruling that has been established with [religious] evidence and does not have any conflicting evidences [that would suggest it is normally allowed to eat the carcass.] However, when one fears starvation, there emerges a conflict with the evidence cited to prove its [default] prohibition. Further, [the evidence that states one must eat the carcass to avoid dying] is outbalancing of [the evidence of prohibition of eating a carcass], because of preservation of oneself. As such, eating it becomes permissible, and one engages in the concession.

والرخصة لُغَة: السهولة، وَشرعا: مَا ثَبت على خلاف دَلِيل شَرْعِي لمعارض رَاجِح. وَقَالَ الْعَسْقَلَانِي فِي شرح (مُخْتَصر الطوفي): أَجود مَا يُقَال فِي الرُّخْصَة ثُبُوت حكم لحالة تَقْتَضِيه مُخَالفَة مُقْتَضى دَلِيل يعمها. وَذكر ابْن حمدَان هَذَا الْحَد فِي (مقنعه): وَمن الرُّخْصَة مَا هُوَ وَاجِب كَأَكْل الْميتَة للْمُضْطَر، ووجوبه

على الصَّحِيح الَّذِي عَلَيْهِ الْأَكْثَر. وَمِنْهَا مَا هُوَ مَنْدُوب، كقصر الْمُسَافِر الصَّلَاة إِذا اجْتمعت الشُّرُوط، وانتفت الْمَوَانِع. وَمِنْهَا مَا هُوَ مُبَاح. كالجمع بَين الصَّلَاتَيْنِ فِي غير عَرَفَة ومزدلفة، وَكَذَا بيع الْعَرَايَا.

In the Arabic language, a *rukhṣah* refers to something easy. In religious terminology, though, it refers to a ruling that is established in contradiction to the religious evidences, because of an outbalancing conflicting [evidence]. Al-ʿAsqalānī stated in his explanation of al-Ṭūfī's *Mukhtaṣar Rawḍat al-Nāẓir*, "The best definition of a *rukhṣah* is the establishment of a ruling for some extenuating situation that contradicts the implication of another evidence that normally would have encompassed it."[184] Ibn Ḥamdān mentioned the following definition in his *Muqniʿ*, "Some concessions are obligatory, such as eating a carcass if one is in dire necessity; it is obligatory, according to the veracious view that the majority hold. Some are recommended, such as shortening the prayer for a traveller, if they meet the criteria and do not have any impediments. Some are lawful, such as combining the prayers without being in ʿArafah or Muzdalifah, and engaging in selling of *ʿarāyā*.[185]

وَهنا أَربع تَنْبِيهَات:

Here, there are four things worth noting:

التَّنْبِيه الأول: أن الْعَزِيمَة والرخصة وصفان للْحكم لَا للْفِعْل، فَتكون الْعَزِيمَة بِمَعْنى التَّأْكِيد فِي طلب الشَّيْء، وَتَكون الرُّخْصَة بِمَعْنى الترخيص، وَمِنْه حَدِيث **((فاقبلوا رخصَة الله))** وَقَول أم عَطِيَّة: نهينَا عَن اتِّبَاع الْجَنَائِز وَلم يعزم علينا.

First: Concession and regularity are descriptions of the rulings [of the actions], not of the actions themselves. As such, a regular ruling means that there is imperativeness in demanding something, whilst a concession means that there is some sort of easing [of restrictions]. An example [of a concession], is when the Prophet ﷺ said, **"So accept the concession Allah has given you."**[186] And Umm ʿAṭiyyah stated, "We were prohibited from fol-

184 [T] *Sharḥ Mukhtaṣar al-Rawḍah* (p. 38 of the manuscript).
185 [T] The concept of selling of *ʿarāyā* is when someone sells fresh dates that are still on their date-palm trees by estimating their worth as dried dates. Refer to *Kashāf al-Qināʿ* (3/258).
186 Reported by al-Nasāʾī (4/176). Jābir ibn ʿAbdullah reported that Allah's Messen-

lowing funeral processions, though the prohibition was not done imperatively."[187]

التَّنْبِيه الثَّانِي: اخْتلف فِي الْعَزِيمَة والرخصة أَيهمَا أفضل؟ فَقيل: فِي مثل أكل الْميتَة: الْإِجَابَة أفضل حفظا للنَّفس، وَاسْتِيفَاء لحق الله فِيهَا، وَقيل: الِامْتِنَاع أفضل. وَقد نَص أَحْمد فِي رِوَايَة جَعْفَر بن مُحَمَّد فِي الْأَسير يُخَيّر بَين الْقَتْل وَشرب الْخمر فَقَالَ: إِن صَبر، فَلهُ الشّرف، وَإِن لم يصبر، فَلهُ الرُّخْصَة.

Second: There has been a disagreement on whether the concession or the regular ruling is better. In matters such as eating a carcass, it was stated that eating it is better, to protect the soul and to fulfill Allah's rights towards it. It was also stated that avoiding the food is better. In the narration of Ja'far ibn Muḥammad, Aḥmad opined in the case where a prisoner is given the choice between being killed or drinking alcohol, and stated, "If he is patient, he earns honour. If he is not patient, he can resort to the concession."[188]

وَقَالَ الْقَاضِي أَبُو يعلى فِي (أَحْكَام الْقُرْآن) الْأَفْضَل أَن لَا يُعْطي التقية، وَلَا يظْهر الْكفْر حَتَّى يقتل. وَاحْتج بِقصَّة عمار وخبيب بن عدي حَيْثُ لم يُعْط أهل مَكَّة التقية حَتَّى قتل، فَكَانَ عِنْد الْمُسلمين أفضل من عمار.

Al-Qāḍī Abu Ya'lā stated in his book *Aḥkām al-Qur'ān* that it is best for a person to not lie and give the coercer what they seek, and not apparently show they are disbelievers; [they should remain firm] until killed. He used the stories of 'Ammār and Khubayb ibn 'Adī as evidence. The latter did not give the People of Makkah what they wanted to hear, and because of that, was killed, and was considered more virtuous to the Muslims than 'Ammār.

قَالَ نجم الدّين سُلَيْمَان الطوفي فِي شرح (مختصرة) فِي الْأُصُول عقيب أَن نقل

---

ger ﷺ passed by a man who was sitting in the shade of a tree, spraying some water on his head. The Prophet ﷺ said, **"What is the matter with your fellow?"** They responded, "O Messenger of Allah, he is fasting." He replied, **"It is not of righteousness for you to fast during travel. Adhere to the concession that Allah gave you and accept it."**

187 Reported by al-Bukhārī (3/115).

188 [T] I could not find a reference to a book called *al-Muqni'* written by Ibn Ḥamdān.

كَلَام القَاضِي : قلت : الْعجب من أَصْحَابنَا يرجحون الأخْذ بِالرُّخْصَةِ فِي الْفطر، وَقصر الصَّلَاة فِي السّفر مَعَ يسَارة الْخطب فيهمَا، ويرجحون الْعَزِيمَة فِيمَا يَأْتِي على النَّفس كالإكراه على الْكفْر، وَشرب الْخمر، فإمَّا أَن يرجحوا الرُّخْصَة مُطلقًا، أَو الْعَزِيمَة مُطلقًا، أما الْفرق، فَلَا يظْهر لَهُ كَبِير فَائِدَة.

Najm al-Dīn Sulaymān al-Ṭūfī stated in his explanation of his summation on legal theories, after quoting al-Qāḍī, "I find it odd that our *aṣḥāb* prefer taking the concession in breaking the fast and shortening the prayer when travelling, though both [fasting and praying the full units of prayer] pose no serious trouble, but at the same time, they prefer the regular ruling when it comes to one's life when they are coerced into disbelief and drinking alcohol. They should either prefer the concession in all cases or prefer the regular ruling in all cases. There appears to not be much benefit in differentiating between the two cases."[189]

التَّنْبِيه الثَّالِث : قد يكون سَبَب الرُّخْصَة اختياريا، كالسفر، واضطراريا كالاغتصاص باللقمة الْمُبِيح لشرب الْخمر. فَليعلم هَذَا الأَصْل وَمَا قبله لِكَثْرَة مَنَافِع هَذِه المباحث فِي كتب الْفِقْه.

Third: The reason for the [legality of engaging in the] concession could be choice-based, such as travel, and could be necessity-based, such as choking on a bite of food, which would allow for the concession of drinking alcohol [to avoid choking to death.] This principle, as well as the previously mentioned one, should be known, because they have much benefit in discussions in books of law.

التَّنْبِيه الرَّابِع : قد يشْتَمل الْفِعْل الْوَاحِد على الْوَصْف بِالرُّخْصَةِ من جِهَة، وبالعزيمة من جِهَة ثَانِيَة، وَذَلِكَ فِيمَا إِذا تعلق بِفعل الْمُكَلف حقان، فَكل تَخْفِيف تعلق بِحَق الله تَعَالَى وبحق العَبْد، فَهُوَ بِالْإِضَافَة إِلَى حق الله تَعَالَى عَزِيمَة، وبالإضافة إِلَى حق الْمُكَلف رخصَة، فالتيمم مثلا هُوَ رخصَة من حَيْثُ إِن الله تَعَالَى يسر على الْمُكَلف، وَسَهل عَلَيْهِ، وسامحه فِي أَدَاء الْعِبَادَة مَعَ الْحَدث الْمَانِع، وَلم يشق عَلَيْهِ بِطَلَب المَاء حَيْثُ يتَعَذَّر أَو يشق، وَلم يَأْمُرهُ بِإِعَادَة الصَّلَاة إِذا صلاهَا

189 [T] *Sharḥ Mukhtaṣar al-Rawḍah* (1/466).

بِالتَّيَمُّمِ. وَهُوَ أَيْضا عَزِيمَة بِالنِّسْبَةِ إِلَى حق الله تَعَالَى حَيْثُ لَا بُد من الْإِتْيَان بِهِ للقادر عَلَيْهِ، وَقس عَلَيْهِ نَظَائِره.

Fourth: A single action could be described as a concession from one perspective and a regularity from another, and this occurs in matters where there are two rights attached to the action of the *mukallaf*. Every easing [of rulings] pertains to the rights of Allah the Exalted as well as those of the slaves. When describing an ease as it pertains to Allah the Exalted, it is still considered a regular ruling, but when describing [an ease] as it pertains to a *mukallaf*, it is a concession. For example, dry ablution is a concession inasmuch as Allah the Exalted has facilitated and eased for the *mukallaf*, allowing them to perform the action of worship although they have a ritual impurity that would otherwise prevent them from doing so. Allah the Exalted did not make things difficult on the person by ordering them to find water in cases when it is impossible or difficult, and He also did not command the one who prayed with *tayammum* to redo their prayer. When considering the rights of Allah the Exalted, it is a regular ruling inasmuch as the person must [perform *tayammum*] if they are capable of doing so. This rule applies to other similar scenarios, as well.

فصل فِي اللُّغَات

Section [Four:] On Languages

من عَادَة الْأُصُولِيِّينَ التَّعَرُّض لمباحث اللُّغَات فِي كتبهمْ، وَذَلِكَ لِأَن هَذِه المباحث هِيَ كالمدخل إِلَى أصُول الْفِقْه من جِهَة أنه أحد مُفْرَدَات مادته، وَهِي الْكَلَام، والعربية، وتصور الْأَحْكَام الشَّرْعِيَّة، وَذَلِكَ أَن لمباحث اللُّغَات مدخلًا كَبِيرا لمن يُرِيد دُخُول أَبْوَاب الْفِقْه والاطلاع على حقائقها، فأصول الْفِقْه متوقفة على معرفَة اللغَة لوُرُود الْكتاب وَالسّنة بهَا اللذين هما أصُول الْفِقْه وأدلته. فَمن لَا يعرف اللُّغَة لَا يُمكنهُ اسْتِخْرَاج الْأَحْكَام من الْكتاب وَالسّنة.

Generally speaking, it is the practice of legal theorists to discuss languages in their books. The reason they do this is because these discussions are introductions to legal theory, since language is one of its subject matters. *Uṣūl al-fiqh* discusses speech, the Arabic language, and conceptualisation of religious rulings. Therefore, discussions on language play a major role for those wishing to enter the chapters of law and read its realities. Legal theory is contingent on knowledge of language, since the Qur'ān and Sunnah were revealed in it, and since they are the foundations of all legal theories. If someone does not know language, therefore, they cannot extract rulings from the Qur'ān and Sunnah.

إِذا علمت هَذَا فَاعْلَم أَن اللُّغَة إِنَّمَا هِيَ الْأَلْفَاظ الدَّالَّة على الْمعَانِي النفسية. يَعْنِي: أَن الْمُتَكَلّم يتَصَوَّر فِي نَفسه نِسْبَة شَيْء لشَيْء بعد تصور مُفْرَدَات مركب يدل على النِّسْبَة بَينهمَا، كَمَا يتَصَوَّر الْعلم، ثمَّ يتَصَوَّر نفعه، ثمَّ يضم إِلَى ذَلِك نِسْبَة الْمَوْضُوع إِلَى الْمَحْمُول، أَو نِسْبَة الْمسند إِلَى الْمسند إِلَيْهِ، ثمَّ يعبر عَن تِلْكَ النِّسْبَة بِلِسَانِهِ فَيَقُول: الْعلم نَافِع، فَتلك الْأَلْفَاظ الدَّالَّة على هَذَا الْمَعْنى هِيَ اللُّغَة.

After knowing that, be aware that language is defined as words that indicate meanings one holds within themselves. Meaning, a speaker conceptualises the relation of something to another thing, and then conceptualises individual words belonging to a compound expression that can indicate said relation. For example, one can conceptualise knowledge and then can conceptualise its benefit, and then add to that the relation between a subject and a predicate. Then, they can express that relation with their tongue, by stating, "Knowledge is beneficial." Those words that indicate the meaning of the sentence are "the language."

وَأنت خَبِير بِأَن التَّصَوُّر لَا يخْتَلف حَتَّى يُقَال لَهُ: تصور هندي، أَو عَرَبِيّ، أَو فَارسي، وَإِنَّمَا الَّذِي يخْتَلف، وَيُسمى بأسماء هُوَ اللَّفْظ الْمعبر بِهِ عَمَّا فِي الضَّمِير والتصور.

Most know that conceptualisation does not change to the point where we can define specific Indian, Arab, or Persian conceptualisations. The thing that changes in name, though, are the words used to express what is in one's conscience and their conceptualisations [of ideas].

وَسبب ذَلِك الِاخْتِلَاف إِنَّمَا هُوَ اخْتِلَاف أمزجة الْأَلْسِنَة، وَعلة اخْتِلَاف أمزجة الْأَلْسِنَة وَسَببه، اخْتِلَاف الأهوية وطبائع الْأَمْكِنَة، فَإِذا غلب الْبرد مثلا على مَكَان برد هواؤه، وطبع الْبرد التكثيف والتثقيل، لِأَن العنصرين الباردين - وهما المَاء وَالْأَرْض - ثقيلان كثيفان، وَالْمَاء أشدهما بردا، وَالْأَرْض أشدهما كَثَافَة، فيغلب الثقل على أَلْسِنَة أهل ذَلِك الْقطر، فيثقل النُّطْق على ألسنتهم، ثمَّ يضعون الْأَلْفَاظ الْمَخْصُوصَة للمعاني الْمَخْصُوصَة، فَيَجِيء النُّطْق بهَا ثقيلا كالعجمي والتركي وَغَيرهمَا.

The reason for such differences is due to the differences in temperament of the tongues. The reason for the differing temperaments of tongues is the differences in atmospheres and the nature of various locations on earth. For example, cold is very thick and heavy, since the two cold substances, water and earth, are heavy and thick. Water is the colder of the two, and earth is the denser of the two. If a place is very cold, then, heaviness of language becomes the norm of residents of that region. Their pronunciations become heavy, and when they adhere to certain words to indicate certain meanings, it results in their words becoming heavy, such as what happens with non-Arabs and Turks, as well as others.

وَإذا غلب الحر على مَكَان، سخن هواؤه، وطبع الْحَرَارَة التجفيف والتحليل والتلطف، فتغلب الخفة على أَلْسِنَة أهل ذَلِك الْمَكَان، فيخف النُّطْق على ألسنتهم، ثمَّ يضعون الْأَلْفَاظ الْمَخْصُوصَة للمعاني الْمَخْصُوصَة، فَيَجِيء النُّطْق بهَا خَفِيفا سَمحا سهلا كاللغة الْعَرَبيَّة، فَلهَذَا كَانَت أفْصح اللُّغَات، وأحسنها، وَأَشْرَفهَا، وَحصل الإعجاز والتحدي بِكَلَام الله تَعَالَى النَّازِل بهَا دون كَلَامه النَّازِل بغَيْرهَا، مَعَ أَنه قد كَانَ فِي قدرَة الله سُبْحَانَهُ أَن يعجز أهل كل لِسَان بِمَا نزله من كَلَامه بذلك اللِّسَان، وَقد أَشَارَ إِلَى هَذَا المتقدمون من الْأَطِبَّاء فِي فلسفة الطِّبّ.

Further, when heat is the predominant atmosphere of a region, its air becomes hot. The nature of heat is dryness, permissiveness, and ease. As such, ease becomes the predominant nature of the tongues of that area. Pronunciation, too, becomes easy. Then, they adhere to certain words to indicate certain meanings, and when they pronounce those words, it results in easy, light, forgiving words, such as those of the Arabic language. This is why [the Arabic Language] is the most eloquent, best, and most noble of all languages. The miraculousness and challenge [of replicating] the Speech of Allah the Exalted was pertaining to the [Qurʾān] which was revealed [in Arabic], not any of His Speech revealed in other languages. It was possible for Allah the Exalted to challenge the speakers of each language to [produce something similar to] His Speech which He sent in that language. This was alluded to by the early physicians and philosophers of medicine.

وَاعْلَم أَن الْمُخْتَار أَن اللُّغَة بَعْضهَا حَاصِل بالتوقيف والتعليم، وَبَعضهَا حَاصِل بالاصطلاح. وَقَوله تَعَالَى ﴿وَعَلَّمَ آدَمَ الْأَسْمَاءَ كُلَّهَا﴾ [الْبَقَرَة: ٣١]، مَعْنَاهُ وَالله أعلم: أَنه علمه مَا احْتَاجَ مِنْهَا، بِدَلِيل قَوْله تَعَالَى: ﴿ثُمَّ عَرَضَهُمْ عَلَى الْمَلَائِكَةِ فَقَالَ أَنْبِئُونِي بِأَسْمَاءِ هَؤُلَاءِ﴾ [الْبَقَرَة: ٣١]، وَهُوَ إِشَارَة إِلَى مُسَمّى محسوس، وَهَذَا يَقْتَضِي أَنه كَانَ ثمَّ أَشْيَاء محسوسة، علم الله تَعَالَى آدم، أَي: أَلهمه أسمائها وَلم يلهمها الْمَلَائِكَة، وَهَذَا لَا يَقْتَضِي أَن يكون آدم تعلم جَمِيع لُغَات الْبشر من عَهده إِلَى آخر الدوران.

Know, too, that the chosen view is that some parts of language are taught, and others are conventions humans invented to communicate. Allah the

Exalted states: **{He taught Adam the names of all things.}** [Qur'ān 2: 31] This means—and Allah the Exalted knows best, that He taught [Adam] the vocabulary that he would need. The evidence is the completion of the verse, where Allah the Exalted states: **{Then He presented them to the angels and said, "Tell Me the names of these."}** [Qur'ān 2: 31] This is a reference to sensible and perceivable things being dubbed a certain name. This necessitates that there were some things that were sensory and observable. Allah the Exalted taught Adam by inspiring in him the names of those things, but did not inspire the angels or reveal to them the same information. This does not necessitate that Adam had knowledge of all languages of humankind from his time until the earth stops revolving.

وتنقسم اللُّغَة إِلَى أَسمَاء الْأَعْلَام كزيد وخَالِد، وَإِلَى أَسمَاء الصِّفَات كعالم وقادر. وَهَذِه لاتثبت بِالْقِيَاسِ اتِّفَاقًا، وَإِلَى أَسمَاء الْأَجْنَاس والأنواع الَّتِي وضعت لمعان فِي مسمياتها. تَدور مَعهَا وجودا وعدما، وَهَذَا النَّوْع من اللغة يَصح الْقيَاس عَلَيْهِ، وَذَلِكَ كَالْخمرِ، فَإِن اسْمه يَدُور مَعَ التخمير وجودا وعدما، فَإِنَّهُ يَصح إِطْلَاق اسْمه على كل مَا خامر الْعقل قِيَاسا بعلة المخامرة، فَحَيْثُ فهم الْجَامِع بَين شَيْئَيْنِ جَازَ تَسْمِيَة الْفَرْع باسم الأَصْل قِيَاسا.

In continuation, language comprises of proper nouns, such as Zayd and Khālid, and adjectives, such as knowledgeable and able. Nouns and adjectives cannot be established through syllogisms, by agreement [of the scholars]. Then, there are generic nouns which were conventionally used because of some meaning that is indicated by the terms, and which are consistent; when the meaning is present, so too is the noun, and vice versa, and when the meaning is not present, the noun, too, is not present, and vice versa. Syllogisms apply to generic nouns. For example, the term "*al-khamr* (alcohol)": its name is contingent on its meaning, which is intoxication. When this meaning is present, so too is the term "*khamr*," and when it is not present, the item cannot be described as "*khamr*." Further, anything that preoccupies and intoxicates the mind can be described as "*khamr*," since they share a relevant commonality, which is the intoxication. When a commonality between two things is understood, it is permissible to refer to the subsidiary matter by using the same term used to refer to its premise.

وَمن هُنَا أَخذ الْفُقَهَاء أصلا فرعوا عَلَيْهِ فروعا مِنْهَا: أَن اللائط يحد قِيَاسا على

الزَّانِي بِجَامِعِ الْإِيلَاجِ الْمحرم، وشارب النَّبِيذ يحد قِيَاسا على شَارِب الْخمر بِجَامِعِ السكر والتخمير، ونباش الْقُبُور يحد قِيَاسا على سَارِق أَمْوَال الْأَحْيَاء بِجَامِع أَخذ الْمَال خُفْيَة عِنْد من يَقُول بذلك. وَهَذَا كُله مَبْنِيّ على قَاعِدَة إِثْبَات اللُّغَة بِالْقِيَاسِ، وَالَّذين قَالُوا: لَا قِيَاس فِي اللُّغَة كبعض الْحَنَفِيَّة قَالُوا: لَا حد فِي ذَلِك.

From this, jurists extracted a foundational maxim on which they based many aspects of substantive law. For example, they stated that a person who engages in homosexuality should be given a penalty similar to a fornicator, and the relevant commonality between [a fornicator and a person engaging in sodomy] is unlawful penetration. Also, a person who drinks *nabīdh* should be penalised the same way a drinker of alcohol should be, since they both engaged in an action that preoccupies and intoxicates the mind. Also, a grave-looter should be penalised similar to how a thief of the goods of living beings is, since they share the commonality of taking wealth secretly, according to those who take that view. All of these rulings are based on the maxim of establishing terminologies based on syllogisms. Those who said that terminologies cannot be established via syllogisms, such as some Ḥanafī scholars, opined that none of the previous cases are deserving of a penalty.

فَائِدَة: أولع كثير من أهل عصرنا بسؤال حَاصله: أَن من تقدم على نبينا مُحَمَّد صلى الله عَلَيْهِ وَسلم من الْأَنْبِيَاء الْمُرْسلين إِنَّمَا كَانَ مَبْعُوثًا لِقَوْمِهِ خَاصَّة، فَلذَلِك بعث بلسانهم، وَنَبينَا مُحَمَّد صلى الله عَلَيْهِ وَسلم مَبْعُوث لجَمِيع الْخلق، فَلم لم يبْعَث بِجَمِيعِ الْأَلْسِنَة، وَلم يبْعَث إِلَّا بِلِسَان بَعضهم وهم الْعَرَب؟ وَالْجَوَاب: أَنه لَو بعث بِلِسَان جَمِيعهم، وَأنزل الْقُرْآن عَلَيْهِ كَذَلِك لَكَانَ كلَاما خَارِجا عَن الْمَعْهُود، وَيبعد بل يَسْتَحِيل أَن ترد كل كلمة من الْقُرْآن مكررة بِكُل الْأَلْسِنَة، مَعَ أَنَّهَا لَا تنضبط، وتتجدد مَعَ تجدّد الْأَزْمَان كَمَا تَجَدَّدَتْ اللُّغَة الفرنسوية والإنكليزية وَغَيرهمَا. وَإِذا كَانَ الْأَمر كَذَلِك تعين الْبَعْض، وَكَانَ لِسَان الْعَرَب أَحَق، لِأَنَّهُ أوسع وأفصح، وَلِأَنهُ لِسَان المخاطبين وَإِن كَانَ الحكم عَلَيْهِم وعَلى غَيرهم.

It is beneficial to note here that many people during my era are enamored with the question which goes: The prophets sent before our Prophet Muḥammad ﷺ were sent to their own people, and because of that, they were sent with the tongues of their people. Our Prophet Muḥammad ﷺ

however, was sent to all of creation. Why, then, was he not sent in all languages, but was only sent in a language of some of them, namely the Arabs? The answer is that if he were sent in all languages, and the Qur'ān were sent in such a manner, the speech would contradict the conventions of people, and it would be difficult, nay, impossible, for each and every word in the Qur'ān to be repeated in every language. Also, there would be no mechanism of regulation, and languages evolve over time, just as French, English, and other languages have evolved. As that is the case, it must be sent in the language of some, and the language of the Arabs is most worthy, since it is the vastest, most eloquent, and the language of the spoken-to, irrespective if the judgement pertains to them or to others.

وَأَيْضًا فَإِن الدول من قبل وَإِلَى عهدنا اصْطَلحُوا على جعل اللُّغَة الرسمية فِيمَا بَينهم لُغَة وَاحِدَة، ليسهل التخاطب بهَا فِيمَا بَينهم، واختاروا أَن تكون أخف من غَيرهَا على لسانهم، كَمَا جعل دوَل زمننا اللُّغَة الفرنسوية هِيَ اللُّغَة الرسمية فِيمَا بَينهم، وكل دولة حكمت بلدا ذَا ألسن مُخْتَلفَة تجْعَل لغتها رسمية فِيمَا بَينهم، وَهَذَا قانون طبيعي فِي الْعمرَان.

Further, previous nations—up until our own times, have adopted certain languages which are considered "official languages," which they use amongst themselves. They use a single language, so as to facilitate mutual conversation and interaction between them. They choose languages that are most easily pronounced to them. For example, contemporary nations make French the official language for dealings between them. Every nation that has colonised lands of varying tongues and languages creates an official language to use among them. This is a natural and standard practice in ekistics.

وَلما بعث الله مُحَمَّدًا صلى الله عَلَيْهِ وَسلم إِلَى جَمِيع الْأُمَم على اخْتِلَاف ألسنتهم اقْتَضَت حكمته أَن يعلم الْخلق ذَلِك القانون الطبيعي، فَأنْزل كِتَابه بلغَة نبيه الَّتِي هِيَ أفْصح اللُّغَات وأوسعها وأدخلها فِي الإعجاز، ليجعل اللُّغَة الْعَرَبيَّة لُغَة رسمية لجَمِيع الْأُمَم الَّتِي أوجب عَلَيْهَا الْإِيمَان بذلك النَّبِي الْكَرِيم، وليحصل الْوِفَاق لأمة مُحَمَّد صلى الله عَلَيْهِ وَسلم فِي اللِّسَان كَمَا وَجب عَلَيْهِم الْوِفَاق فِي القلوب، وَفِي التَّوْحِيد، وَفِي جَمِيع المعتقدات، فَليعلم ذَلِك وَالله الْمُوفق.

When Allah sent Muḥammad ﷺ to all nations, irrespective of their different languages, His wisdom dictated that creation know that standard practice. To illustrate this, He sent His Book in the language of His Prophet, which is the most eloquent, vast, and most apt to do with miraculousness. He made the Arabic language the official language of all nations that were obligated to believe in that noble Prophet. In this way, the Ummah of Muḥammad ﷺ could be in unison in their language and tongue, just as He obligated unison and unity in their hearts, in monotheism, and in all beliefs. Be keen to know these facts. May Allah the Exalted grant success.

فصل

Subsection [One]

اعْلَم أَن الْأَسْمَاء على أَرْبَعَة أضْرب: وضيعية، وعرفية، وشرعية، ومجاز مُطلق.

Nouns are of four types: Conventional, customary, religious and metaphorical.

فَأَما الوضعية: فَهِيَ الثَّابِتَة بِالْوَضْعِ، وَهُوَ تَخْصِيص الْوَاضِع لفظا باسم بِحَيْثُ إِذا أطلق ذَلِك اللَّفْظ، فهم مِنْهُ ذَلِك الْمُسَمّى، كَمَا أَنه مَتى أطلق لفظ الْأسد، فهم مِنْهُ حد الْحَيَوَان الْخَاص المفترس.

Conventional nouns are those established by conventions of people, in the sense that a person has designated a term and given it a name, and whenever that term is uttered, the meaning that it entails is understood. For example, whenever the term "lion" is uttered, people understand its definition, being a specific predatory animal.

والعرفي: مَا خص عرفا بِبَعْض مسمياته الَّتِي وضع لَهَا فِي أصل اللُّغَة عِنْد ابْتِدَاء وَضعهَا، كَلَفْظِ الدَّابَّة الَّذِي هُوَ فِي أصل الْوَضع لكل مَا دب لاشتقاقه من الدبيب، ثمَّ خص فِي عرف الِاسْتِعْمَال بذوات الْأَرْبَع، وَإِن كَانَ بِاعْتِبَار الأَصْل يتَنَاوَل الطَّائِر لوُجُود الدبيب مِنْهُ.

Customary nouns are terms that are specified by custom to refer to some of its definitions that have been designated by its original usage in language when the word was first developed. For example, the word *"dābbah"* literally means something that crawls on the earth. However, then it was used within various customs to refer to four-legged animals. However, according to its original meaning, the word encompasses birds, since some birds crawl or walk on land.

وَمِنْه مَا شاع أَي: اشْتهر اسْتِعْمَاله فِي غير مَا وضع لَهُ فِي الأَصْل، كالغائط، فَهُوَ فِي أصل الْوَضع اسْم للمطمئن، أَي: المنخفض من الأَرْض، ثمَّ اشْتهر اسْتِعْمَاله عرفا فِي الْخَارِج المستقذر من الْإِنْسَان.

Some have also become famously used to refer to something other than its original usage. For example, *al-ghā'iṭ* was used to refer to a depressed or sinking area of land. However, it is famously used to refer to human excretion.[190]

وكالرواية الَّتِي هِيَ فِي الأَصْل: اسْم للبعير الَّذِي يستقى عَلَيْهِ، ثمَّ اشْتهر اسْتِعْمَالهَا فِي المزادة التِي هِيَ وعَاء المَاء، وَهَذَا اللَّفْظ الْعرفِيّ هُوَ مجَاز بِالنِّسْبَةِ إِلَى الوضعي الَّذِي هُوَ الْمَوْضُوع الأول، وَحَقِيقَة فِيمَا خص بِهِ فِي الْعرف لاشتهاره فِيهِ.

Another example is the term *riwāyah*, which originally refers to livestock used to seek water. Then, it was used to refer to the container which holds water. This customary usage is a type of metaphor when juxtaposed with its original usage, and a literal meaning when referring to its customary usage, since it is popularly used in that way.

والشرعية: مَا نَقله الشَّرْع أَي: خرج بهَا الشَّارِع عَن وضع أهل اللُّغَة، ثمَّ وَضعهَا بِإِزَاءِ معنى شَرْعِي كَالصَّلَاةِ وَالصِّيَام. وَقيل: إِن الشَّارِع أبقى فِي الصَّلَاة معنى الدُّعَاء. ثمَّ ضم إِلَيْهِ شُرُوطًا كَالْوضُوءِ، وَالْوَقْت، والسترة، وَغير ذَلِك.

Religious: This consists of terms where the religion has changed their usage. Meaning, the term is used in a conventional linguistic manner, and then the religion uses the terminology, and it is used to refer to a religious concept. Such terms include *ṣalāt* and *ṣiyām*. [Since prayer refers to supplication linguistically,] some have said that the religion has kept the meaning

190 [T] This is because before the invention of bathrooms, Arabs would go to lower areas of land to relieve themselves.

of supplication in the prayer, and then added some preconditions, such as ablution, entrance of the time, a *sutrah* (something placed in front of the one praying), and so forth.

وَهَذِه الْأَلْفَاظ عِنْد إِطْلَاقهَا تصرف إِلَى مَعْنَاهَا الشَّرْعِيّ، لِأَن الشَّارِع مُبين للشَّرْع لَا للغة، وَكَذَا فِي كَلَام الْفُقَهَاء، وَمَتى ورد اللَّفْظ، وَجب حمله على الْحَقِيقَة فِي بَابه: لُغَة، أَو شرعا، أَو عرفا، وَلَا يحمل على الْمجَاز إِلَّا بِدَلِيل يمْنَع حمله على الْحَقِيقَة من معَارض قَاطع، أَو عرف مَشْهُور، كمن قَالَ: رَأَيْت راوية، فَإِن إِرَادَة المزادة مِنْهُ ظَاهِرَة بِالْعرْفِ الْمَشْهُور.

When these terms are used, the meaning is the religious definition, because the Legislator defines the religion, not language. Likewise, the same applies to when jurists use these terms. Whenever these terms are used, they must refer to their real meanings in their respective contexts: [when referring to these terms in the] linguistic sense, religious, or customary. These terms should not be held to refer to metaphors without evidence that prevents accepting their real, literal meanings. Evidences include some clear-cut contradictory [premise] or a well-known custom. For example, if someone says, "I saw the *rāwiyah*," it is clear they are referring to the flask of water, according to the customary usage.

وَأما الْمجَاز الْمُطلق: فَهُوَ اللَّفْظ الْمُسْتَعْمل فِي غير مَوْضُوع أول على وَجه يَصح، فاللفظ الْمُسْتَعْمل جنس يعم الْحَقِيقَة وَالْمجَاز، وَفِي غير مَوْضُوع أول فصل مخرج للْحَقِيقَة، وَذَلِكَ كاستعمال لفظ الْأسد فِي الرجل الشجاع، فَإِنَّهُ غير مَوْضُوع للأسد الأول، إِذْ مَوْضُوعه الأول هُوَ السَّبع.

Metaphorical: Metaphors are words utilised in other than their original usage in a correct way. When I said, "words utilised," I was referring to words as a genus that encompass literal and figurative meanings. When I said, "other than their original usage," I was referring to a differentia that excludes literal usages. For example, the term lion can be used to refer to a brave man. That is not the original usage of the word lion though; originally, it refers to a predatory animal.

وَقَوْلنَا: على وَجه يَصح، نُرِيد بِهِ شَرط الْمجَاز، وَهُوَ أَنه لَا بُد لَهُ من علاقَة مَعَ قرينَة

مَانِعَة من إِرَادَة الْمَعْنى الْحَقِيقِيّ. والعلاقة - بِكَسْر العين - هِيَ مَا ينْتَقل الذِّهْن بواسطته عَن محل الْمجَاز إِلَى الْحَقِيقَة، وَذَلِكَ كالشجاعة الَّتِي ينْتَقل الذِّهْن بواسطتها عَن الرجل الشجاع إِذا أطلقنا عَلَيْهِ لفظ أَسد إِلَى السَّبع المفترس، إِذْ لَوْلَا هَذِه العلاقة - وَهِي صفة الشجَاعَة - لما صَحَّ التَّجَوُّز، وَلما انْتقل الذِّهْن إِلَى السَّبع المفترس عِنْد إِطْلَاق لفظ الْأسد على الرجل الشجاع، وَلَكَانَ [إطلاق لفظ الْأسد عَلَيْهِ علمية ارتجالا.

When I said, "in a correct way," I was referring to the condition of using metaphors, which is that there must be some associated commonality [between the metaphorical and real usages], as well as some indication preventing it from being intended in its real sense. The associated commonality is the medium by which the mind connects between the metaphor and the real sense. For example, bravery is a medium by which the mind goes from thinking of a brave man, when referred to as a lion, and makes the connection with the predatory animal. Without this commonality, namely, the description of bravery, there would be no way to establish the metaphor, and the mind would not think of a predatory animal when the term "lion" is used for a brave man. As such, the usage of the term "lion" to describe is an improvisation.

وَالْمُعْتَبر فِي العلاقة أَن تكون ظَاهِرَة يسْرع الْفَهم إِلَيْهَا عِنْد إِطْلَاق لفظ الْمجَاز، حرصا على سرعَة التفاهم، وحذرا من إبطائه، لِأَن ذَلِك عكس مَقْصُود الْوَاضِع والمتجوز والمخاطبين فِيمَا بينهم، كإطلاق لفظ الْأسد على الشجاع بِجَامِع الشجَاعَة، وَهِي صفة ظَاهِرَة، لَا كإطلاق لفظ الْأسد على الْحَيَوَان الأبخر لخفاء صفة البخر فِي الْأسد، فَإِنَّهُ لَا يكَاد يعلمهَا فِيهِ إِلَّا الْقَلِيل من النَّاس، بِخِلَاف الشجَاعَة، فَإِنَّهُ لَا يجهلها إِلَّا الْقَلِيل النَّادِر.

It is important for a commonality to be apparent, so that one quickly understands it when the metaphorical usage of the word is uttered. This is to ensure that mutual understanding is created quickly and to protect against delays in two parties speaking to one another, which defeats the purpose of both the one using the term conventionally, the one using it metaphorically, and the purposes for which people converse with one another. For example, one could use the term lion to refer to a brave person, considering that the commonality between a real lion and a brave person is bravery. Bravery, in this case, is an apparent attribute. However, using the term lion to refer to another animal that has bad breath [is not apparent], because bad breath is not an apparent attribute of a lion. Actually, only a few people might actually be aware of that fact. This is not the case with bravery, for only few are unaware of this.

وَاعْلَم أَنِ للمجاز علاقات كَثِيرة، وَهِي - وَإِن كَانَ اسْتِيفَاء الْكَلَام عَلَيْهَا مَحله علم الْبَيَان، وَذَلِكَ الْعلم مَشْهُور بَين أهل الْعلم فِي زمننا أَكثر من شهرة علم الْأُصُول - إِلَّا أننا لَا بُد لنا من ذكر جمل مِنْهَا لاستدعاء الْمقَام لَهَا، فَنَقُول:

Metaphorical language has many such commonalities. However, discussions on these topics are more appropriate in books on rhetorical devices and language. These topics are very well-known to scholars of our age, even more than legal theories are known. With that said, I shall mention some discussions, since the situation calls for that.

يتجوز بِالسَّبَبِ عَن الْمُسَبّب، نَحْو قَول الْقَائِل: فعلت هَذَا لأبلو مَا فِي ضميرك، أَي: أعرفهُ. تجوز بالابتلاء عَن الْعرْفَان، لِأَن الِابْتِلَاء سَببه، إِذْ من ابتلى شَيْئا عرفه.

[The first type:] One can use the medium metaphorically to refer to the effect, by saying, "I did this to test what is within you," but actually meaning, "to know what is within you." The person uses "test" metaphorically to refer to "know" since testing a person is the means by which one can know what is within a person.

وأصناف السَّبَب أَرْبَعَة: قابلي، وصوري، وفاعلي، وغائي، وكل وَاحِد مِنْهُمَا يتجوز بِهِ عَن سَببه:

There are four types of causes: Material, formal, efficient and final, and each is valid to be used for its cause:

مِثَال الأول: - وَهُوَ تَسْمِيَة الشَّيْء باسم قابله - قَوْلهم: سَالَ الْوَادي، وَالْأَصْل سَالَ المَاء فِي الْوَادي، لَكِن لما كَانَ الْوَادي سَببا قَابلا لسيلان المَاء فِيهِ صَار المَاء

من حَيْثُ القابلية كالسبب لَهُ، فوضع الْوَادي مَوضع.

Material: Which is to call something by the name of its facilitator or the thing that receives it. For example, one can say, "The valley flowed," though they would normally say, "The water flowed in the valley." However, being that the valley is a medium that can allow for flowing of water, making it a facilitator of the water, the word "valley" is placed in its stead.

وَمِثَال الثَّانِي: - وَهُوَ تَسْمِيَة الشَّيْء باسم صورته - هَذِه صُورَة الْأَمر وَالْحَال، أي حَقِيقَته.

Formal: Which is to refer to something by its manifestation, such as by saying, "This is the manifestation of the situation," meaning, the reality of the situation.[191]

وَمِثَال الثَّالِث: - وَهُوَ تَسْمِيَة الشَّيْء باسم فَاعله حَقِيقَة أَو ظنا - قَوْلهم فِي الْكتاب الْجَامِع لنَوْع علمه: هُوَ شيخ جَالس على الْكُرْسِيّ، أَو على الرف، لِأَن الشَّيْخ، أَعنِي الْمُصَنّف، هُوَ فَاعل الْكتاب. وَقَوْلهمْ للمطر: سَمَاء، لِأَن السَّمَاء فَاعل مجازي للمطر، بِدَلِيل إِسْنَاد الْفِعْل إِلَيْهَا فِي قَوْلهم: أمْطرت السَّمَاء.

Efficient: Which is to name something by the one who did it, whether in reality or by supposition. For example, a book that comprehensively collects knowledge on its subject matter is referred to as, "a teacher sitting on a chair," or, "on a shelf," since a teacher, meaning the author, is the one who brought about the book. Also, when referring to rain, they call it, "the sky," since the sky is a metaphorical cause of rain, as evinced by when they ascribe rain to the sky, by saying, "the sky has produced rain."

وَمِثَال الرَّابِع: - وَهُوَ تَسْمِيَة الشَّيْء باسم غَايَته - تَسْمِيَة الْعِنَب خمرًا، وَالْعقد نِكَاحا، لِأَنهُ غَايَته ويؤول إِلَيْهِ.

Final: Which is to call something by its end, such as calling grapes *khamr* (wine), or calling a marriage contract *nikāḥ* (sexual intercourse), because that is the end or finality achieved by those things, respectively.

191 [T] Another example mentioned by al-Imām Najm al-Dīn al-Ṭūfī is, "Also, such as when they refer to a hand by saying 'power' as though they make power a form or description of the hand." (*Sharḥ Mukhtaṣar al-Rawḍah* 1/508)

الْقسم الثَّانِي: التَّجَوُّز بِالْعِلَّةِ عَن الْمَعْلُول، كالتجوز بِلَفْظ الْإِرَادَة عَن الْمُرَاد، لِأنهَا عِلّة كَقَوْلِه تَعَالَى: ﴿وَيُرِيدُونَ أَنْ يُفَرِّقُوا بَيْنَ اللهِ وَرُسُلِهِ﴾ [النِّسَاء ١٥٠] أي: يفرقون بِدَلِيل أَنه قوبل بقوله عز وَجل ﴿وَالَّذِينَ آمَنُوا بِاللهِ وَرُسُلِهِ وَلَمْ يُفَرِّقُوا﴾ [النِّسَاء: ١٥٢] وَلم يقل: وَلم يُرِيدُوا أَن يفرقُوا.

The second type: Metaphorically using the cause to refer to the effect. For example, one can refer to the intended outcome by using intent metaphorically. For example, Allah the Exalted said: **{And they wish to make a distinction between Allah and His messengers.}** [Qur'ān 4:150] Meaning, they do actually differentiate, due to the comparison with Allah's statement: **{But Allah will give [due] rewards to those who believe in Him and His messengers and make no distinction between any of them.}** [Qur'ān 4:152] In this second verse, He did not say, "They wish to differentiate."

وَكَذَلِكَ قَول الْقَائِل: رَأَيْت الله فِي كل شَيْء، لِأَن الله سُبْحَانَهُ وَتَعَالَى هُوَ موجد كل شَيْء وعلته، فَأطلق لَفظه عَلَيْهِ، وَمَعْنَاهُ: رَأَيْت كل شَيْء، فاستدللت بِهِ على وجود الله سُبْحَانَهُ، لظُهُور آثار الْقُدْرَة والإلهية فِيهِ، فَدلَّ عَلَيْهِ - سُبْحَانَهُ - دلَالَة الْعلَّة على معلولها، وَالْمَفْعُول على فَاعله.

Also, this occurs when one says, "I saw Allah the Exalted in everything," because Allah the Exalted is the cause and creator of everything. As such, they refer to the effect by referring to the case. The meaning of the sentence is, "I saw everything, and used that as evidence that Allah the Exalted exists, since the effects of His Divine Powers are manifested." In that case, the person refers to Allah the Exalted in the sense that Allah is the cause for those effects.

الْقسم الثَّالِث: التَّجَوُّز باللازم عَن الْمَلْزُوم، كتسمية السّقف جدارا، لِأَن الْجِدَار لَازم لَهُ، وَتَسْمِيَة الْإِنْسَان حَيَوَانا، لِأَن الْحَيَوَان لَازم لَهُ.

The third type: Metaphorically using the consequent to refer to the antecedent. For example, one can refer to a ceiling as being a "wall," because a wall is an antecedent to the presence of the ceiling. One can also refer to humans as "animals," since being an animal is an antecedent to being a human.[192]

192 [T] This is referring to the species coming in a later category than the genus in

الْقسم الرَّابِع: التَّجَوُّز بِلَفْظ الْأَثر عَن الْمُؤثر، كتسميتهم ملك الْمَوْت موتا لِأَن الْمَوْت أثر لَهُ، وَقَول الشَّاعِر يصف ظَبْيَة:

The fourth type: Metaphorically using the effect to refer to the affecter. For example, they refer to the Angel of Death as "death" itself since death is an effect of [the Angel of Death]. Also, the poet described a doe by saying:

فَإِنَّمَا هِيَ إقبال وإدبار

Truly, it is coming and going.[193]

لِأَن الإقبال والإدبار من أفعالها، وَهِي آثار لَهَا، وَكَذَلِكَ قَوْلهم: زيد عدل، أَو صَوْم، أَو كرم، أَو خير، أَو بر، وكقولهم: الطَّرِيق جور، أَي: مائل، فَهُوَ وصف للطريق، فَينزل منزلَة الْأَثر، وَزيد عدل وَنَحْوه سمي باسم فعل من أَفعاله.

The reason is that coming and going are actions and effects of the doe. They also say, "Zayd is justice/fasting/generosity/goodness/piousness." Likewise, their statement, "The path is difficult," when it is sloped. It is a description of the path but the difficulty is the effect of it being sloped. Likewise, Zayd being described as justice etc. is him being described by one of his actions.

الْقسم الْخَامِس: التَّجَوُّز بِلَفْظ الْمحل عَن الْحَال فِيهِ، كتسمية المَال كيسا، فِي قَوْلهم: هَات الْكيس، وَالْمرَاد المَال الَّذِي فِيهِ، لِأَنهُ حَال فِي الْكيس. وَكَذَلِكَ تَسْمِيَة الْخمر كأسا أَو زجاجة، وَالطَّعَام مائدة أَو خوانًا، وَالْمَيِّت جَنَازَة، والمكتوب ورقة كتابا وبطاقة، لِأَن هَذِه الْأَشْيَاء حَالَة فِي الْمحَال الْمَذْكُورَة.

The fifth type: Metaphorically using the receptacle to refer to the thing that

Porphyry's Five Predicables in his *Isagoge*, which is an introduction to Aristotle's Categories. The animal is a genus, and the human is a species of that genus. Therefore, an organism can be an animal without being a human, but the opposite is not true. A species is defined by mentioning the genus and the differentia. In the case of a human, he is defined as, "an animal that can engage in rational thought." The first, "animal," is the genus, while the second, "that can engage in rational speech," is the differentia, as it differentiates between the species of humans from other species, such as a horse, which is defined as, "an animal with the ability to neigh."

193 This is the second hemistich of a line uttered by al-Khansā'. However, in this line, she was describing a camel, not a doe. It is a part of a longer poem eulogising her brother Ṣakhr. Refer to *Khazānat al-Adab* (1/207 onwards) by al-Baghdādī.

it receives. For example, money can be referred to as a bag, such as when someone says, "Pass me the bag," meaning, "pass me the money in the bag," as it resides in the bag. Likewise, wine can be referred to as "the glass," food as "the table," the dead as "a funeral," a written thing as "a paper," "a book," or "a card." These things all reside in their respective receptacles.

فَهَذِهِ خَمْسَة أَقسَام، وَإِذا قابلتها بعكسها، حصل لَك خَمْسَة أَقسَام أُخْرى، وَإِلَيْك بَيَانهَا:

Therefore, these are the five types. When contrasted with their opposites, we are presented with another five types. Therefore:

السَّادِس: التَّجَوُّز بِلَفْظ الْمُسَبّب عَن السَّبَب، كَقَوْلِه تَعَالَى: ﴿يَا أَيهَا الذِينَ آمَنُوا لَا تَأْكُلُوا أَمْوَالَكُم بَيْنَكُم بِالْبَاطِلِ﴾ [النساء: ٢٩] أَي: لَا تأخذوها، فَتجوز بِالْأَكْلِ عَن الْأَخْذ، لِأَنهُ مسبب عَن الْأَخْذ إِذْ الْإِنْسَان يَأْخُذ فيأكل.

The sixth type: Using the effect to refer to the medium. For example, when Allah the Exalted said: **{O believers! Do not devour one another's wealth illegally.}** [Qur'ān 4:29] Meaning, do not take it. Allah used the term "devour" to refer to taking, because it is an effect of taking; as in, one will take the money and will use it for consumption.

السَّابِع: التَّجَوُّز بِلَفْظ الْمَعْلُول عَن الْعلَّة، كالتجوز بِلَفْظ المُرَاد عَن الْإِرَادَة، كَقَوْلِه تَعَالَى ﴿إِذا قَضَى أَمْراً﴾ [مريم: ٣٥]، أَي إِذا أَرَادَ أَن يقْضِي، فالقضاء مَعْلُول الْإِرَادَة، فتجوز بِهِ عَنْهَا، وَكَقَوْلِه تَعَالَى: ﴿وَإِنْ حَكَمْتَ فَاحْكُمْ﴾ [الْمَائِدَة: ٤٢] أَي: إِذا أردْت أَن تحكم.

The seventh type: Using the effect to refer to the cause. For example, one could use the intended action to refer to the intent. Such as when Allah states: **{When He decrees something, He says only, "Be," and it is.}** [Qur'ān 19:35] Meaning, when He wishes to decree something. "Decrees" therefore is the effect of His Will to do it. Because of that, He used [the effect] to refer to it. In another verse, Allah the Exalted said: **{But if you judge between them, then do so with justice.}** [Qur'ān 5:42] Meaning, if you intend on judging, do so with justice.

الثَّامِن: التَّجوُّز بالملزوم عَن اللَّازِم، كتسمية الْعلم حَيَاة، لِأَنَّهُ ملزوم الْحَيَاة، إِذْ الْحَيَاة شَرط للْعلم، والمشروط ملزوم للشّرط، فَكَذَلِك التَّجوُّز بِكُل مَشْرُوط عَن شَرطه هُوَ تجوز بالملزوم عَن اللَّازِم لَهُ.

The eighth type: Metaphorically using the antecedent to refer to the consequent. For example, knowledge can be called "life," since it is a consequent of life, since life is the antecedent of knowledge, and knowledge cannot exist without life. The conditional is contingent on the condition, and therefore, using the conditional to refer to its condition is also a type of using the antecedent to refer to the consequent.

التَّاسِع: التَّجوُّز بِلَفْظ الْمُؤثر عَن الْأَثر، كَقَوْل الْقَائِل: «رَأَيْت الله وَمَا أرى فِي الْوُجُود إِلَّا الله» يُرِيد آثاره الدَّالَّة عَلَيْهِ فِي الْعَالم وكقولهم فِي الْأَمر المهم وَغَيره: هَذِه إِرَادَة الله، أَي: مُرَاده، فَأطلق لفظ الْإِرَادَة على الْمُرَاد إطلاقا لاسم الْمُؤثر على الْأَثر، لِأَن الْإِرَادَة مُؤثرَة فِي الْمُرَاد.

The ninth type: Metaphorically using the affecter to refer to the effect. For example, one could say, "I saw Allah, and I only see Allah in existence." Meaning, one sees the effects of Allah the Exalted in the world. Also, it could be stated in important matters, "This is the will of Allah," meaning, what He wanted. In this case, the term "will" was used to refer to the effect, and this is a form of using the affecter to refer to the effect, since where there is a will, there is a willed thing.

الْعَاشِر: التَّجوُّز بِلَفْظ الْحَال عَن الْمحل، كتسمية الْكيس مَالا، والكاس خمرًا، والمائدة طَعَاما، والجنازة مَيتا، والورقة مَكْتُوبًا.

The tenth type: Metaphorically using something that is received to refer to the receptacle. For example, a bag can be called "money," a glass can be referred to as "wine," a meal can be referred to as "the table," a funeral procession can be referred to as "the dead," and a paper can be referred to as "the written thing."

فَهَذِهِ الْخَمْسَة عكس الَّتِي قبلهَا، وَبهَا صَار الْكل عشرَة.

These last five are the opposites of the first given. As such, we currently have discussed ten types.

الْحَادِي عشر: تَسْمِيَة الشَّيْء بِاعْتِبَارِهِ وصف زائل، أَي: كَانَ بِهِ وَزَالَ عَنهُ، كإطلاق العَبْد على الْعَتِيق بِاعْتِبَار وصف الْعُبُودِيَّة الَّذِي كَانَ قَائِما بِهِ فَزَالَ عَنهُ، وَكَذَا تَسْمِيَة الْخمر عصيرا، والعصير عنبا بِاعْتِبَار مَا كَانَ.

The eleventh type: Referring to something considering a description it previously had, but no longer. Meaning, it had this quality, but does not anymore. For example, one can refer to a freed slave as being a slave, considering that they previously had the quality of being a slave, though it is not the case any longer. Also, one can refer to wine as juice, and can refer to juice as grapes, considering that the juice was previously in the form of the grapes.

الثَّانِي عشر: تَسْمِيَة الشَّيْء بِاعْتِبَار وصف يؤول وَيصير إِلَيْهِ، كإطلاق الْخمر على الْعصير فِي قَوْله تَعَالَى حِكَايَة: ﴿إِنِّي أَرَانِي أَعْصِرُ خَمْرًا﴾ [يُوسُف: ٣٦]، وَإِنَّمَا كَانَ يعصر عنبا، فَيحصل مِنْهُ عصير، لَكِن لما كَانَ الْعصير يؤول إِلَى وصف الْخمر بِهِ أطلق عَلَيْهِ لفظ الْخمر.

The twelfth type: Referring to something by what it will eventually become. For example, the term "wine" can be used to refer to juice, such as when Allah said—relaying what the man said to Prophet Yūsuf: **{I dreamt I was pressing wine.}** [Qur'ān 12:36] What he indeed saw was himself juicing some grapes. That juice would later be fermented and would lead to it becoming wine. As such, the term wine was used.

الثَّالِث عشر: إِطْلَاق مَا بِالْقُوَّةِ على مَا بِالْفِعْلِ كتسمية الْخمر فِي الدن مُسكرا لِأَن فِيهِ قُوَّة الْإِسْكَار، وَتَسْمِيَة النُّطْفَة إنْسَانا لِأَن الْإِنْسَان فِيهِ بِالْقُوَّةِ، أَي: قَابل لصيرورته إنْسَانا.

The thirteenth type: Referring to a thing's proximate power to the thing that possesses the power. For example, one can refer to wine in a vessel as being an intoxicant, since wine has the ability to intoxicate. One can also refer to sperm as human, since it has the ability to possibly form into a human.

الرَّابِع عشر: عكس الَّذِي قبله، وَهُوَ إِطْلَاق مَا بِالْفِعْلِ على مَا بِالْقُوَّةِ، كتسمية

الْإِنْسَان الْحَقِيقِيّ نُطْفَة أَو مَاء مهينا وَهُوَ أَيْضا من بَاب التَّسْمِيَة بِاعْتِبَار وصف زائل.

The fourteenth type: Using the thing that possesses power to refer to what is in its proximate power. For example, one can refer to an actual human as being sperm or "contemptible droplet." This can also be considered [of the eleventh type] as a description of a previous description that has now gone away.

الْخَامِس عشر: التَّجَوُّز بِالزِّيَادَةِ كَقَوْلِه تَعَالَى ﴿لَيْسَ كَمِثْلِهِ شَيْءٌ﴾ [الشورى: ١١]، أَي لَيْسَ مثله، وَالْكَاف زَائِدَة على رَأْي من ذهب إِلَى هَذَا، وَالتَّحْقِيق أَن لَا زِيَادَة فِي الْآيَة، وَأَن الْمَعْنى: لَو فَرضنَا أَن لَهُ مثلا فَلَيْسَ لمثله مثل، فانتفت الْمُمَاثلَة عَنهُ تَعَالَى بطرِيق الْأَوْلَوِيَّة، لِأَن انْتِفَاء مثل الْمثل يُوجب انْتِفَاء الْمثل. والمثال الْجيد أَن يُقَال: لَيْسَ كزيد إِنْسَانا.

The fifteenth type: Using an additional letter, such as when Allah the Exalted said: **{There is nothing like Him: He is the All Hearing, the All Seeing.}** [Qur'ān 42:11] According to some scholars, the letter *kāf* (ك) in the word *ka-milthlihi* is superfluous. However, the truth is that the addition is not superfluous and that the meaning is, "If we were to suppose that He has some likeness, His likeness has no likeness." Therefore, the concept of likeness is *a fortiori* negated from Allah the Exalted, since the negation of a likeness of the likeness is a negation of the likeness altogether. A better example would be to state, "Zayd is not human."[194]

السَّادِس عشر: التَّجَوُّز بِالنَّقْصِ: كَقَوْلِه تَعَالَى حِكَايَة ﴿واسأل الْقَرْيَة﴾ [يُوسُف: ٨٢]، أَي: أهل الْقَرْيَة. ﴿وَأُشْرِبُوا فِي قُلُوبِهِمُ الْعِجْلَ﴾ [الْبَقَرَة: ٩٣] أَي: حب الْعجل. ﴿فَذَلِكُنَّ الَّذِي لُمْتُنَّنِي فِيهِ﴾ [يُوسُف: ٣٢] أَي: فِي حبه.

The sixteenth type: Omitting a word, such as when Allah the Exalted said: **{Ask the town where we have been.}** [Qur'ān 12:82] This means, "Ask the residents of the town." Allah the Exalted also states: **{The calf was root-**

194 [T] The meaning by stating this would be either to insult or praise a person, even if one were to believe that the person is of the genus of 'humans.' Refer to *Sharḥ Kitāb Sībawayh* by Abu Sa'īd al-Sirāfī (1/319). The *kāf* (ك) in the sentence is superfluous. That is the point of al-Shaykh Ibn Badrān.

ed in their hearts because of their disbelief.} [Qur'ān 2:93] Meaning, love of the calf. Allah the Exalted also states: **{She said, "This is the one you blamed me for."}** [Qur'ān 12:32] Meaning, love of [Prophet Yūsuf].

السَّابِع عشر: تَسْمِيَة الشَّيْء باسم مَا يشابهه، وَهُوَ الْمُسَمّى بالاستعارة بالِاتِّفَاقِ، كَقَوْلِك: رَأَيْت أسدا فِي الْحمام، تُرِيدُ رجلا شجاعا، وَكلمت حمارا، تُرِيدُ بِهِ رجلا بليدا. وَهَذَا النَّوْع يحْتَاج إِلَى شرح وَبَيَان، وَمحله كتب الْبَيَان، وَاسْتِيفَاء بَحثه هُنَا يخرجنا عَن الْمَقْصُود.

The seventeenth type: Giving something the name of another thing it resembles. This is known as a metaphor. For example, one can say, "I saw a lion in the bathhouse," and mean a brave man. Or, they could say, "I spoke to a donkey," and intend a dimwitted individual. This type of metaphor requires more explanation and clarification, but its discussions occur in books on rhetoric. If I were to engage fully in this topic, it would take me outside of the purpose [of this book].

الثَّامِن عشر: تَسْمِيَة الشَّيْء باسم ضِدّه، كَقَوْلِه تَعَالَى: ﴿وَجَزَاءُ سَيِّئَةٍ سَيِّئَةٌ مثلهَا﴾ [الشورى: ٤٠] ﴿فَمن اعْتدى عَلَيْكُم فاعتدوا عَلَيْهِ﴾ [الْبَقَرَة: ١٩٤]، حَيْثُ سمى الْجَزَاء سَيِّئَة وعدوانا، وَيجوز أَن يَجْعَل من بَاب الْمجَاز للمشابهة، لِأَن جَزَاء السَّيئَة يشبهها فِي صُورَة الْفِعْل، وَفِي كَونهَا تسوء من وصلت إِلَيْهِ، وَكَذَلِكَ جَزَاء الْعدوان، وَيجوز أن يكون هَذَا من بَاب التَّجَوُّز بِلَفْظ السَّبَب عَن الْمُسَبّب، حَيْثُ يُسمى عُقُوبَة السَّيئَة والاعتداء سَيِّئَة واعتداء، لِأَن الْعقُوبَة مسببة عَن السَّبَب والاعتداء.

The eighteenth type: Giving something the name of its opposite. For example, Allah the Exalted states: **{The reward of an evil deed is an equivalent evil deed.}** [Qur'ān 42:40] Also: **{So, if anyone commits aggression against you, commit aggression back against them.}** [Qur'ān 2:194] Allah referred to the recompense as being an evil deed, and aggression. This is a common usage when done metaphorically in order to liken the action. The recompense of an evil action resembles [the evil action] in manner and method, in the sense that it harms the one being shown the recompense. The same goes for the recompense of aggression. This could also be considered an example of the first type; in that it is use of the medium metaphorically to refer to the effect. The punishment of an evil deed and the aggression are called "an evil deed" and aggression, since they are punishments that are the result of the medium of an evil deed and aggression.

التَّاسِع عشر: تَسْمِيَة الْجُزْء باسم الْكل، كإطلاق لفظ الْعَام وَالْمرَاد الْخَاص، كَقَوْلِه تَعَالَى ﴿الَّذِينَ قَالَ لَهُمُ النَّاسُ﴾ [آل عمرَان: ١٧٣]، وَالْمرَاد وَاحِد معِين، وَقَوْلنَا: قام الرِّجَال، وَالْمرَاد بَعضهم، وَرَأَيْت زيدا، وَإِنَّمَا رَأَيْت بعضه.

The nineteenth type: A part can be given the name of the whole. For example, a general wording could be used to refer to a specific subset of that generality. Allah the Exalted states: **{Those whose faith only increased when the people said, "Fear your enemy: they have amassed a great army against you," and who replied, "Allah is enough for us: He is the best protector."}** [Qur'ān 3:173] When Allah said "the people," he was referring to a particular person. Likewise would be the case if we were to say, "The people stood," and mean only a subset of that population, or if we were to say, "I saw Zayd," when in fact they only saw a part of Zayd.

الْعشْرُونَ: عكس ذَلِك، كتسمية الْكل باسم الْجُزْء، كَقَوْلِهِم للزنجي: أسود، وَإِن كَانَ الْأسود إِنَّمَا هُوَ جزئه وَهُوَ أَكْثَره، فَأطلق الْأسود على جَمِيعه، وَإِن كَانَ أَسْنَانه وأخمصه أسودين، لَكِن هَذَا الْمِثَال لَيْسَ بجيد، وَإِن ذكره صَاحب (الْمَحْصُول)، والمثال الْجيد قَوْله صلى الله عَلَيْهِ وَسلم «**الْمُسلمُونَ تتَكَافَأ دِمَاؤُهُمْ، وهم يَد على من سواهم**» فَسمى الْمُسلمين باسم جُزْء يسير مِنْهُم، وَهُوَ الْيَد، إِشَارَة إِلَى أَنه يَنْبَغِي لَهُم أَن يَكُونُوا فِي الائتلاف والاجتماع كيد وَاحِدَة.

The twentieth type: The opposite of [the nineteenth type], which is to refer to the whole by mentioning its part. For example, people refer to Africans as being "black," while their blackness is just a part of them, though the most prominent part. Therefore, "black" was used to refer to their whole, even if their teeth and soles are not black. This example, though, is not a good example, even though it was mentioned by the author of *al-Maḥṣūl* [whose name was Fakhr al-Dīn al-Rāzī]. A better example is when the Prophet ﷺ said, **"The blood of Muslims is equal, and they are like a single hand**

against others."[195] Here, the Prophet ﷺ referred to Muslims with just a part of them, which was the hand, indicating that they must be, in their unity and cohesion, like a single hand.

الْحَادِي وَالْعِشْرُونَ: إِطْلَاق اللَّفْظ الْمُشْتَقّ بعد زَوَال الْمُشْتَقّ مِنْهُ، كَقَوْلِنَا لِلْإِنْسَان بعد فَرَاغه من الضَّرْب: ضَارب. وَهَذَا مَحل خلاف.

The twenty-first type: Using the derived noun after the derivative has ceased. For example, one can refer to someone, after they have hit something, as being "a hitter." This type has been contended, though.

الثَّانِي وَالْعِشْرُونَ: الْمجَاز بالمجاورة، كتسمية مزادة المَاء راوية.

The twenty-second type: Metaphors based on proximity. For example, one can refer to a water flask as being an irrigation or water source.

الثَّالِث وَالْعِشْرُونَ: الْمجَاز الْعرفِيّ، كاستعمال الدَّابَّة فِي الْحمار وَنَحْوه.

The twenty-third type: A customary metaphor. For example, one can refer to a donkey, and other such animals, as being "walking beasts."

الرَّابِع وَالْعِشْرُونَ: تَسْمِيَة الْمُتَعَلّق - بِفَتْح اللَّام - باسم الْمُتَعَلّق - بِكَسْرِهَا - كتسمية الْمَعْلُوم علما والمقدور وَقدره، كَقَوْلِه تَعَالَى ﴿**وَلَا يُحِيطُونَ بِشَيْءٍ مِنْ عِلْمِهِ إِلَّا بِمَا شَاءَ**﴾ [الْبَقَرَة: ٢٥٥] أَي معلومه، وَقَوْلهمْ: رَأينَا قدرَة الله، أَي: مقدوره.

The twenty-fourth type: Referring to the noun by using its infinitive. For example, one can refer to something known as being knowledge, and something able as being ability. Allah the Exalted states: **{But they do not comprehend any of His knowledge except what He wills.}** [Qur'ān 2:255] When He said, "His knowledge," He was referring to the things He knows. Also when one says, "I have seen the ability of Allah," meaning the things He was able to do.

وَقد يتجوز بِلَفْظ الْمَعْلُوم عَن الْعلم، والمقدور عَن الْقُدْرَة، عكس الأول، كَمَا لَو حلف حَالف بِمَعْلُوم الله ومقدوره وَأَرَادَ الْعلم وَالْقُدْرَة، جَازَ، وانعقدت يَمِينه.

[The twenty-fifth type:] The opposite can also occur. One can refer to

195 Reported by Abu Dāwūd (4530) and al-Nasā'ī (8/24).

knowledge by mentioning "the things one knows," or refer to ability as, "the things one is able to do." For example, one can swear by the things Allah knows or by the things Allah can do, and mean to swear by His knowledge or His ability. This is permissible, and if one were to do so, it would be considered a right-hand oath.

وَاعْلَم أَن وُجُوه الْمجَاز أَكثر مِمَّا ذَكرْنَاهُ هُنَا، وَكلهَا ناشئة عَن تعدد أَصْنَاف العلاقة الرابطة بَين مَحل الْمجَاز والحقيقة، فَكل مسميين بَينهمَا علاقَة رابطة جَازَ التَّجَوُّز باسم أَحدهمَا عَن الآخر، سَوَاء نقل ذَلِك التَّجَوُّز الْخَاص عَن الْعَرَب أَو لم ينْقل، كَمَا هُوَ الْأَصَح عِنْد البلغاء.

Moving on, there are many different types of metaphors that were not mentioned here. All of them emanate from the multiplicity of the types of relationships between the metaphorical and the literal usages of the words. Every two things that have some sort of relationship can be used metaphorically to refer to the other, regardless if that metaphorical usage was done by the Arabs or not, as is the correct view according to linguists.

نعم يتَفَاوَت الْمجَاز قُوَّة وضعفا بِحَسب تفَاوت ربط العلاقة بَين الْحَقِيقَة وَالْمجَاز، وَذَلِكَ التَّفَاوُت قد يكون بِدَرَجَة وَاحِدَة كَمَا ذكر فِي الراوية بِالنِّسْبَةِ إِلَى الْجمل، وَقد يكون بدرجتين كَقَوْل الشَّاعِر:

True, metaphors vary in their strength or weakness proportionally to the strength or weakness of the relationship between the literal and the metaphorical words. Variance can be of a single level, such as referring to a camel by calling it "*rāwiyah*,"[196] and could be on two levels, such as when the poet said:

إِذا نزل السَّمَاء بِأَرْض قوم   وَعَيناهُ وَإِن كَانُوا غضابا

If the sky descends in the lands of a people, we graze of it even to the owner's upheaval.[197]

---

196 [T] The root word is, "*rawiy*," which means to quench thirst. As such, when the term *rāwiyah* is used metaphorically to refer to a camel, it is due to this usage. Refer to *Gharīb al-Ḥadīth* by Ibrāḥīm al-Ḥarbī (2/781), and *Tahdhīb al-Lughah* by al-Azharī (2/68).

197 This monostich belongs to Muʿāwiyah ibn Mālik al-Āmirī, from the *Mifḍaliyyah*

فَفِيهِ مجَاز إفرادي: من جِهَة أَنه سمى الْغَيْث سَمَاء لحصوله عَن المَاء النَّازِل من السحَاب المجاور للسماء وَهُوَ الْعُلُوّ. ومجاز إسنادي: وَهُوَ وَصفه العشب بالنزول لحصوله عَن المَاء المتصف بالنزول من الْغَمَام إِلَى غير ذَلِك مِمَّا لَا يخفى على المتأمل.

Here, he uses a singular metaphor by referring to rain as "the sky," since rain descends from clouds, which are close in proximity to "the sky," in the sense that they are high in the air. There is also a metaphor by attribution created, in that the vegetation is referred to as "the descended," [when he says, "we graze of it,"] because the vegetation receives the water which descends from the clouds [and its growth is attributed to the rain]. This is not unclear to the one who thinks deeply.

وَيَنْبَغِي لمن حاول علم الشَّرِيعَة النّظر والارتياض فِي هَذِه الْأَنْوَاع المجازية، ليعرف مواقع أَلْفَاظ الْكتاب وَالسّنة. وَقد صنف فِيهِ الْعلمَاء كتبا كَثِيرَة، كـ(الإيجاز فِي الْمجَاز) لِلْحَافِظِ ابْن الْقيم، و(إعجاز الْقُرْآن) للخطابي، وللرماني، وَلابْن سراقَة، وَلأبي بكر الباقلاني، ولعَبْد القاهر الْجرْجَانِيّ، وللفخر الرَّازِيّ، وَلابْن أبي الْأَصْبع واسْمه (الْبُرْهَان) وَغير ذَلِك مِمَّا يطول ذكره.

It is appropriate for a person who wishes to try to learn legislative knowledge to research and practice these types of metaphors, so that they may understand the contexts of the words in the Qur'ān and the Sunnah. The scholars have authored many books on the topic. For example, *al-Ījāz fi 'l-Majāz* was written by al-Ḥāfiẓ Ibn al-Qayyim, *Ījāz al-Qur'ān* was written by al-Khaṭṭābi, [and other authorships on this are by] al-Rummānī, Ibn Surāqah, Abu Bakr al-Bāqillānī, ʿAbd al-Qāhir al-Jurjānī, al-Fakhr al-Rāzī, Ibn Abi 'l-Uṣbuʿ—named *al-Burhān*, and many others, whose mention will be quite lengthy.

وَقَالَ نجم الدّين سُلَيْمَان الطوفي: كتاب (الْمجَاز) للشَّيْخ عز الدين بن عبد السَّلَام: أَجود مَا رَأَيْت فِي هَذَا الْفَنّ، وَلَقَد أحسن فِيهِ غَايَة الْإِحْسَان، وَضمنَهُ من ذَلِك النكت البديعة، والفرائد الحسان، فجزاه الله وَسَائِر الْعلمَاء عَمَّا أفادوا

poem number 105.

بِهِ جزيل الْإِحْسَان. انْتهى.

Najm al-Dīn Sulaymān al-Ṭūfī stated, "*Al-Majāz* by al-Shaykh 'Izz al-Dīn ibn 'Abd al-Salām is the best book on the topic. He wrote excellently and filled it with useful, unique points. May Allah the Exalted reward him and all other scholars for the benefit they provided, and give them the best treatment."[198]

وَحكى السُّيُوطِيّ فِي (الإتقان) أَنه لخص هَذَا الْكتاب، وَضم إِلَيْهِ زيادات كَثِيرَة، وسمى ملخصه (مجَاز الفرسان إِلَى مجَاز الْقُرْآن) ثمَّ لخصه أَيْضا فِي كِتَابه (الإتقان)، وللطوفي كتاب (فواصل الْآيَات). وَأقرب مَا ذكر تناولا ووجودا كتاب (الإيجاز فِي الْمجَاز) لِابْنِ الْقيم، فَإِنَّهُ الضَّالة المنشودة، وَقد طبع فِي مصر، فسهل تناوله، وجنى جنته لمتناوله دَان، فجزاه الله خيرا.

In his book, *al-Itqān*, al-Suyūṭī stated that he summarised and made additions to [*al-Majāz* by al-'Izz ibn 'Abd al-Salām], and called his summation *Majāz al-Fursān ilā Majāz al-Qur'ān*. He also summarised it in his book, *al-Itqān*. Al-Ṭūfī wrote *Fawāṣil al-Āyāt*. The most popular book, both in the amount of people who have studied it and its popularity in the market, is *al-Ījāz fi 'l-Majāz* by Ibn al-Qayyim. It is the lost treasure that so many have sought. It was published in Egypt, making it easy to find and making the fruit of its gardens easy for picking, for those who seek to do so. Therefore, may Allah reward him.

تَنْبِيه: اخْتلف الْعلمَاء فِي وُقُوع الْمجَاز فِي الْقُرْآن، فَذهب الْجُمْهُور إِلَى وُقُوعه فِيهِ، وَأنْكرهُ جمَاعَة: مِنْهُم الظَّاهِرِيَّة، وَابْن الْقَاص من الشَّافِعِيَّة، وَابْن خويزمنداد من الْمَالِكِيَّة، وَاسْتَدَلُّوا لمذهبهم بِأَن الْمجَاز أَخُو الْكَذِب، وَالْقُرْآن منزه عَنهُ، وَأَن الْمُتَكَلّم لَا يعدل إِلَيْهِ إِلَّا إِذا ضَاقَتْ بِهِ الْحَقِيقَة فيستعير، وَذَلِكَ محَال على الله تَعَالَى.

Note: The scholars have disagreed on whether the Qur'ān uses metaphors. The majority stated that it does, and a group, including adherents to the Ẓāhirī *madhhab*, Ibn al-Qāṣ of the Shāfi'ī school, and Ibn Khuwayzmindād of the Māliki school claimed that it did not. As evidence for their view, they

---

198 [T] *Sharḥ Mukhtaṣar al-Rawḍah* (1/516).

claimed that metaphors are siblings of lies, and the Qurʾān transcends such things. They stated that a speaker only uses metaphors when the literal usage constricts their ability to express themselves, so in that case, they use metaphors, and it is impossible for Allah the Exalted to have such a limitation.

ورد عَلَيْهِم المثبتون بِأَنَّهُ لَو سقط الْمجَاز من الْقُرْآن، لسقط مِنْهُ شطر الْحسن، فقد اتّفق البلغاء على أَن الْمجَاز أبلغ من الْحَقِيقَة، وَلَو وَجب خلو الْقُرْآن من الْمجَاز وَجب خلوه من الْحَذف، والتوكيد، وتثنية الْقَصَص وَغَيرهَا.

Those who affirmed the existence of metaphors responded by saying: If metaphors were removed from the Qurʾān, half of its beauty would be stripped, for scholars of rhetoric have agreed that metaphors are more eloquent than literal expressions. If we were to state it to be incumbent for the Qurʾān to not have metaphors, then we would state the same for omissions, emphasis, repetition of stories, and so forth.

وَمِمَّنْ منع أَن فِي الْقُرْآن مجَازًا من أَصْحَاب أَحْمد أَبُو الْحسن الخرزي، وَابْن حَامِد، وَأَبُو الْفضل التَّمِيمِي ابْن أبي الْحسن التَّمِيمِي، وَللْإِمَام أَحْمد ابْن تَيْمِية بحث طَوِيل فِي الْحَقِيقَة وَالْمجَاز فِي كتاب الْإِيمَان تنبغي مُرَاجعَته، وَنَقله هُنَا يخرجنا عَن الْمَقْصُود. وَبِكُل حَال فَالْمَسْأَلَة لَيست بِذِي بَال.

Of the *aṣḥāb* of Aḥmad who denied the existence of metaphors in the Qurʾān were: Abu ʿl-Ḥasan al-Kharzī, Ibn Ḥāmid, Abu ʿl-Faḍl al-Tamīmī ibn Abi ʿl-Ḥasan al-Tamīmī, and al-Imām Aḥmad ibn Taymiyyah, who has lengthy discussions on literal meanings and metaphors in his book *Kitāb al-Īmān*. His discussions should be read, though mentioning them here would go outside of our topic. All in all, though, the issue is not one of particular importance.

إِذا تقرر هَذَا، فَاعْلَم أَن الْحَقِيقَة تعرف بمبادرتها إِلَى الْفَهم بِدُونِ قرينَة، وَبِأَن يكون اللَّفْظ مِمَّا يَصح الِاشْتِقَاق مِنْهُ، والتصريف إِلَى الْمَاضِي والمستقبل، وَاسم الْفَاعِل وَالْمَفْعُول، وَبِأَن يكون أحد اللَّفْظَيْنِ يسْتَعْمل وَحده من غير مُقَابل، وَالْآخر لَا يسْتَعْمل إِلَّا فِي الْمُقَابلَة، كالمكر فِي حق الله تَعَالَى، فَإِنَّهُ يَصح أَن يُقَال: مكر زيد بعمرو، وَلَا يَصح ذَلِك فِي حق الله تَعَالَى إِلَّا مُقَابلَة لمكر الْمَخْلُوق

نَحْو ﴿ومكروا ومكر الله﴾ [آل عمران: ٥٤]، وَكَقَوْلِه تَعَالَى: ﴿نسوا الله فنسيهم﴾ [التوبة: ٦٧]، وتعرف أَيْضا بِأَن اسْتِحَالَة نفي اللَّفْظ يدل عَلَيْهَا بِخِلَاف الْمجَاز، فَإِنَّهُ يجوز نَفْيه، وَذَلِكَ لِأَنهُ يَسْتَحِيل أَن تَقول للْإنْسَان البليد: لَيْسَ بإنْسَان، وَيجوز أَن تَقول عَنهُ: لَيْسَ بِحِمَار.

It is important to know that a literal meaning is one that quickly crosses one's mind without any context needed. Further, it must be a term that can be derived from and inflected into a past tense, future tense, a subject or object noun. Also, the case must be that one of the two [usages of the word] can be used without indicating reciprocity, and the other must be used with reciprocity, such as plotting when it comes to Allah. It is possible to say, "Zayd plotted against 'Amr," but it cannot be said about Allah the Exalted [that He plotted against something] without the quality of reciprocating the plots of creation. For example, Allah the Exalted states: **{The [disbelievers] schemed but Allah also schemed; Allah is the best of schemers.}** [Qur'ān 3:54] Also, His statement: **{They neglected Allah, so He neglected them.}** [Qur'ān 9:67] A literal word is also defined as being one that cannot be negated, contrary to a metaphor, which can be negated. It is not possible to state that an unintelligent human is simply not a human [as they literally are a human], but it can be said, "He is not a donkey," [in order to negate stupidity, making the donkey the metaphorical usage of the term.]

وتعرف الْحَقِيقَة أَيْضا بِصِحَّة الِاسْتِعَارَة من لَفظهَا، فَلَمَّا صَحَّ اسْتِعَارَة لفظ الْأسد للرجل الشجاع، علم أَن لفظ الْأسد حَقِيقَة فِي الْحَيَوَان المفترس، مجَاز فِي الرجل الشجاع.

A literal word can also be known because it can be used for a metaphor. Since the term "lion" can be used to metaphorically refer to a brave man, it follows that the term "lion," literally refers to a predatory animal and metaphorically is used to refer to a brave man.

وَاعْلَم أَنه لَا يلْزم أَن يكون لكل حَقِيقَة مجَاز عقلا، وَالصَّحِيح أَنه يلْزم كل مجَاز أَن تكون لَهُ حَقِيقَة، وَلَا تتَوَقَّف صِحَة الْمجَاز على نقل اسْتِعْمَاله فِي مَحَله عَن الْعَرَب على الْأَظْهر اكْتِفَاء بالعلاقة المجوزة كَمَا بَيناهُ سَابِقًا، كَمَا أَن الِاشْتِقَاق

وَالْقِيَاس الشَّرْعِيّ واللغوي لَا يسْتَلْزم ذَلِك.

Know, too, that it is not necessarily the case that every literal word has a metaphorical counterpart, though the opposite is true. Also, the correct view is that a valid use of a metaphor is not contingent on the Arabs having used it in that exact way. Rather, the clearer view is that if there is a common relevance between the two words that allows for the passage into a metaphor, it may be used, as previously outlined. The same applies to religious and linguistic analogies and syllogisms.

وَالْحق أَن أصل الْمجَاز ثَابت مُطلقًا، مُفردا ومركبا، فِي عُمُوم اللُّغَة وخصوص الْقُرْآن، وَأَنه ثَابت أَيْضا فِي الْمُفْرد والمركب على الْأَظْهر فِيهِ، وَذَلِكَ أَنَّك ترى الْعَرَب يستعملون لفظ الأسد فِي الشجاع، وَأَنت خَبِير بِأَن الْأسد لفظ مُفْرد دلّ على مُسَمّى مُفْرد، والشجاع كَذَلِك. فَهَذَا يُسمى مجَازًا إفراديا ومجازا فِي الْمُفْردَات.

The truth is that the metaphor as a foundational aspect of speech is established without restriction: Both in singular and in compounded ways, used in the general language and the specific usages of the Qur'ān. Metaphors exist in singular words and in compounded words. The Arabs use the term "lion" to refer to a brave person, and you know that a lion is a singular noun referring to a singular designation, as does the term "brave." This is known as a singular metaphor, and a metaphor used in singulars.

وَالْمجَاز التركيبي: هُوَ الْوَاقِع فِي الْأَلْفَاظ المركبة نَحْو قَول الشَّاعِر:

A compounded metaphor is one used in compounded phrases, such as when the poet said:

أشاب الصَّغِير وأفنى الْكَبِير   كرّ الْغَدَاة وَمر الْعشي

The young have become grey haired, and the old have died, because of the recurrence of the early mornings and the passage of eves.

فَلفظ الزَّمَان الَّذِي هُوَ مُرُور اللَّيْل وَالنَّهَار حَقِيقَة فِي مَدْلُوله، وَلَفظ الإشابة حَقِيقَة فِي مَدْلُوله أَيْضا، وَهُوَ تبييض الشّعْر لنَقص الْحَرَارَة الغريزية لِضَعْفِهَا بِالْكبرِ. لَكِن

إِسْنَاد الإشابة إِلَى الزَّمَان مجَاز. إِذْ المشيب للنَّاس فِي الْحَقِيقَة هُوَ الله تَعَالَى، فَهَذَا مجَاز فِي التَّرْكِيب أَي: فِي إِسْنَاد الْألفَاظ بَعْضهَا إِلَى بعض لَا فِي نفس مدلولات الْألفَاظ، وَهَكَذَا كل لفظ كَانَ مَوْضُوعا فِي اللغَة ليسند إِلَى لفظ آخر أسْند إِلَى غير ذَلِك من اللَّفْظ، فإسناده مجَاز تركيبي، وَهَذَا النَّوْع من الْمجَاز يُسَمِّيه عُلَمَاء فن الْمعَانِي بالمجاز الْعقلِيّ، وَحده عِنْدهم: إِسْنَاد الْفِعْل أَو مَعْنَاهُ إِلَى ملابس لَهُ غير مَا هُوَ لَهُ بتأول.

The term "time," which refers to the passage of night and day, refers to those meanings literally. Likewise, the phrase, "becoming grey haired," is literally referring to one's hair becoming white because of the natural weakening of one's natural heat due to old age.[199] However, attributing greying of the hair to the passage of time is a metaphor, since the real cause of greying of the hair is Allah the Exalted. This is a compounded metaphor, because

---

199 [T] With respect to this statement, it was a common belief among pre-modern physicians to think that grey hairs emanated from what was referred to as a decrease of natural heat. It stems from Greek medicine, which was the predominant trend until modern times. For example, Aristotle states:

> But the greyness of hair which is due to age results from weakness and deficiency of heat. For as the body declines in vigour we tend to get cold at every time of life, and especially in old age, this age being cold and dry. We must remember that the nutriment coming to each part of the body is concocted by the heat appropriate to the part; if the heat is inadequate the part loses its efficiency, and destruction or disease results [...] A proof that this is so is this: Grey hairs have often grown on men in consequence of disease, and later on dark hairs instead of them after restoration to health. The reason is that in sickness the whole body is deficient in natural heat and so the parts besides, even the very small ones, participate in this weakness; and again, much residual matter is formed in the body and all its parts in illness, wherefore the incapacity in the flesh to concoct the nutriment causes the grey hairs. But when men have recovered health and strength again they change, becoming as it were young again instead of old; in consequence the states change also. Indeed, we may rightly call disease an acquired old age, old age a natural disease; at any rate, some diseases produce the same effects as old age." (*On the Generation of Animals*, Book V, Chapter 4)

Though the ideas he mentioned vis-à-vis disease and greying of hair are astute, his theories regarding the natural heat are not backed by modern scientific discoveries. This, of course, diminishes nothing from the stature of Ibn Badrān, for he was a product of his times. If anything, it shows his broad education, as he was aware of the strand of medicine that was practiced in his time.

the words come together in a compounded state to create this imagery and meaning that does not exist in the individual words. This extends to any word in language that is attributed to a word that itself is attributed to some other concept; it is called a compounded metaphor. Scholars of rhetoric refer to this type as a rational metaphor, and they define it as: Attributing an action, or its meaning, to some closely related word to refer to a meaning outside of its normal usage with interpretation.

وَحَاصِل قَوْله بتأول: أَن ينصب الْمُتَكَلّم قرينَة صارفة عَن أَن يكون الْإِسْنَاد إِلَى مَا هُوَ لَهُ. ثمَّ اعْلَم أَن التَّحْقِيق أَن الْخلاف لَيْسَ فِي جَوَاز الْمجَاز مُطلقًا، وَلَا فِي وُقُوعه، وَإِنَّمَا الْخلاف فِي أَن الْمَنْقُول فِي هَذَا الْمجَاز هَل هُوَ حكم عَقْلِي أَو لفظ وضعي؟ وَأَنت إِذا حققت ذَلِك وجدت الْخلاف لفظيا.

To summarise in explanation of "with interpretation", it is for the speaker to do so with some measure of a contextual clue that allows for one to not understand it according to its normal usage.[200] Further, be aware that the reality of the difference is not whether metaphors are absolutely possible nor whether they have occurred, but rather, whether it becomes a rational ruling or a conventional ruling once it occurs. If you were to look deeply at this, you would find that the difference of opinion in this matter is mere semantics.

وَحَيْثُ انْتهى تَقْسِيم الْكَلَام إِلَى الْحَقِيقَة وَالْمجَاز فلنتكلم على انقسامه من جِهَة ثَانِيَة هِيَ أمس بِمَا نَحن بصدده فَنَقُول:

Since we are done discussing the categorisation of speech into literal and metaphorical, we should now speak about a different categorisation which is more relevant to our current discussions:

لَا يخفى أَن الصَّوْت عرض مسموع، وَاللَّفْظ صَوت مُعْتَمد على مخرج من مخارج الْحُرُوف، والكلمة لفظ وضع لِمَعْنى مُفْرد، وَجمع الْكَلِمَة كلم مُفِيدا كَانَ أَو غير مُفِيد، وَهِي جنس، أَنْوَاعه ثَلَاثَة: اسْم وَفعل وحرف.

It is not unknown that sounds are accidents that can be heard. An utterance is a sound that relies on one of the exit points of letters. A word is an

200 [T] Refer to *Mukhtaṣar al-Ma'ānī* by al-Imām Ṣa'd al-Dīn al-Taftāzānī (1/38).

utterance that has conventionally been used for a singular meaning, and its plural is *kalim*, regardless if it gives information or not. Words are a genus, and under them are three types: (i) Nouns (*ism*), (ii) verbs (*fi'l*) and (iii) particles (*ḥarf*).

وَالْكَلَام مَا تضمن كَلِمَتَيْنِ بِالْإِسْنَادِ، وَهُوَ نِسْبَة أحد الجزئين إِلَى الآخر لإِفَادَة الْمُخَاطب، وَشَرطه الإفادة، وَلَا يتألف إِلا من اسْمَيْنِ نَحْو: زيد قَائِم، أَو فعل وَاسم نَحْو: قَامَ زيد، فَالْأولى جملَة إسمية، وَالثَّانِيَة جملَة فعلية، وَنَحْو قَوْلك: يَا زيد، وَإِن يقم زيد أقِم فعليتان.

"Speech" is defined as something that comprises of two or more words in relation to one another to give some meaning to the one being spoken to. Its condition is that it expresses some discernible meaning. It can only comprise of two *isms*, such as, "Zayd is standing,"[201] or an *ism* and a verb, such as, "Zayd stood." The first is a noun-based sentence, while the second is a verb-based sentence. When one says, "O Zayd," or, "If Zayd stands, I too shall stand,' they are using verb-based sentences.

هَذَا مَا اتّفق ذكره من كليات مبَاحث الْعَرَبيَّة ومقدماتها، وَله محَال مُخْتَصَّة بِهِ، فَلَا نطيل بِهِ، وَلَا بالمناقشة فِيهِ، ولننقل الْكَلَام فِيهِ إِلَى مبَاحث شَأْنهَا أَن تذكر فِي فن الْأُصُول وَإِن كَانَ موضوعها الْألفَاظ فَهِيَ كَأَنَّهَا ذَات وَجْهَيْنِ: من جِهَة الْعَادة أصولية، وَمن جِهَة التَّحْقِيق لغوية، فَنَقُول:

These are the universals and basic premises of the Arabic Language. They have their own domains which discuss them, so we will not speak at length nor discuss these matters here. I wish to segue into discussions that are relevant and worthy of mention when discussing the science of legal theories. Since the discussions are on utterances, they have two contexts: a customary usage in law, and a customary usage in language. So we say:

اعْلَم أَن اللَّفْظ إِمَّا أَن يحْتَمل معنى وَاحِدًا فَقَط، أَو يحْتَمل أَكثر من معنى وَاحِد، وَالْأول النَّص، وَالثَّانِي إِمَّا أَن يتَرَجَّح فِي أحد معنييه أَو مَعَانِيه وَهُوَ الظَّاهِر، أَو لَا

201 [T] Here, standing is an adjective. Note that in Arabic, nouns, pronouns, adjectives, and adverbs are all considered '*ism*.'

يترَجَّح وَهُوَ الْمُجمل.

Note that an expression can either have: [...] (i) A single possible meaning. This is referred to as a *nass*, which is explicit, unequivocal, univocal. (ii) Multiple possible meanings. This also has two categories: (a) If one of the meanings carries more weight and likeliness, it is *ẓāhir*, which means apparent. (b) If no meaning is likelier, and all are equal possibilities, it is *mujmal*, which means obscure.

الأول: النَّص، وَهُوَ لُغَة: الْكَشْف والظهور، وَمِنْه: نصت الظبية رَأسهَا: إِذا رفعته وأظهرته. وَاصْطِلَاحا: مَا أَفَادَ بِنَفسِهِ من غير احْتِمَال. وَذهب بعض الْعلمَاء إِلَى أن النَّص مَا دلّ على معنى قطعا، وَلَا يحْتَمل غَيره قطعا كأسماء الْأَعْدَاد نَحْو وَاحِد، اثْنَيْنِ، ثَلَاثَة، وَهَذَا التَّعْرِيف أشبه باللغة، وَهُوَ مُرَاد الإِمَام أَحْمد بقَوْلهمْ: نَص عَلَيْهِ أَحْمد، أَو هُوَ مَنْصُوص أَحْمد.

First. *Naṣṣ*: Linguistically, it refers to something obvious and apparent. They say, a doe has made her head apparent (*naṣṣat*), if she raises her head. In legal terminologies, it refers to something that gives a meaning in and of itself, without the possibility of another meaning. Some scholars opined that a *naṣṣ* is something that has one meaning only, and does not possibly encompass another meaning. Examples are the names of numbers, such as one, two, three, and so forth. The latter definition is more in line with language, and it is intended when [the *aṣḥāb*] state, "This is Aḥmad's *naṣṣ/manṣūṣ*."

وَقَالَ الأصوليون: هُوَ مَا دلّ على معنى كَيفَمَا كَانَ، وَهَذَا هُوَ الْغَالِب فِي كَلَام الْفُقَهَاء فِي الِاسْتِدْلَال حَيْثُ يَقُولُونَ: لنا النَّص وَالْمعْنَى، وَدلّ النَّص على هَذَا الحكم، وَقَضَاء الشَّرْع فِي النَّص أَن لَا يتْرك إِلَّا بنسخ.

Legal theorists stated that a *naṣṣ* refers to a text with a meaning, irrespective of how it is used. This is the predominant usage of the jurists when they attempt to prove their positions by saying things like, "We have the text (*naṣṣ*) and the meaning," "the text indicates this ruling," or, "the judgement of the religion on texts is that they should not be abandoned unless they are abrogated."

وَقد يُطلق على مَا تطرق إِلَيْهِ احْتِمَال يعضده دَلِيل، لِأَنَّهُ بذلك الِاحْتِمَال يصير

كَالظَّاهِرِ، وَالظَّاهِر يُطلق عَلَيْهِ لفظ النَّص، ومثاله قَوْله تَعَالَى ﴿وَامْسَحُوا بِرُؤُوسِكُمْ وَأَرْجُلَكُمْ﴾ [الْمَائِدَة: ٦] بِكَسْر اللَّام، وَهُوَ ظَاهر فِي أَن فرض الرجلَيْن الْمسْح مَعَ احْتِمَال الْغسْل، فاحتمال الْغسْل مَعَ الدَّلِيل الدَّال عَلَيْهِ يُسمى أَيْضا، لِأَنهُ صَار مُسَاوِيا للظَّاهِر فِي الْمسْح، وراجحا عَلَيْهِ حَتَّى إِنه يجوز لنا أَن نقُول: ثَبت غسل الرجلَيْن بِالنَّصِّ، وَيُطلق النَّص على الظَّاهِر أَيْضا لتلاقيهما فِي الِاشْتِقَاق، إِذْ النَّص وَالظَّاهِر مأخذهما من الِارْتفَاع والظهور.

Further, the word *naṣṣ* sometimes refers to a text wherein there is a possibility of a meaning that is strengthened by an external evidence. With that external evidence, the text becomes similar to the *ẓāhir* level of texts. Sometimes, an apparent text is referred to by calling it a *naṣṣ*. An example is when Allah the Exalted states: **{Wipe your heads and wash your feet up to the ankles.}** [Qur'ān 5: 6] If one reads this verse with a *kasra* mark on the *lām* (ل), making it *wa arjulikum*, it is joined with the heads in that it should be wiped, but it is possible to mean washed. The possibility of this verse indicating the obligation of washing the feet, along with the evidence that supports that possibility, is called a *naṣṣ*, since it is now equal to the apparent meaning of wiping. Actually, it is a likelier and more veracious possibility, where we could state that washing the feet is proven via a *naṣṣ*. Another reason why *naṣṣ* and *ẓāhir* are used interchangeably is that both are taken from the same root meaning, which is elevation and apparency.

الثَّانِي: الظَّاهِر: وَهُوَ فِي الْحَقِيقَة وَنَفس الْأَمر الشاخص الْمُرْتَفع، وَمِنْه قيل لأشراف الأَرْض: ظواهر؛ وَالظَّاهِر خلاف الْبَاطِن، وكما أَن الْمُرْتَفع من الْأَشْخَاص هُوَ الظَّاهِر الَّذِي تتبادر إِلَيْهِ الْأَبْصَار، فَكَذَلِك الْمَعْنى الْمُتَبَادر من اللَّفْظ هُوَ الظَّاهِر الَّذِي تتبادر إِلَيْهِ البصائر والأفهام.

Second: *Ẓāhir*: Its literal meaning is something that is apparent and elevated. Elevations of land are called *ẓāhir*. Similarly, a person that is elevated is *ẓāhir*, as the eyes are quickly drawn to them in that elevated state, and it is the opposite of *bāṭin* (hidden). Therefore, a meaning that quickly comes to one's mind and catches one's attention when reading an expression is the apparent (*ẓāhir*) meaning of that expression.

وَأما إِطْلَاق الظَّاهِر على اللَّفْظ الْمُحْتَمل أمورا هُوَ فِي أَحدهَا أرجح، فَهُوَ اصْطِلَاح لَا حَقِيقَة، وَإِنَّمَا هُوَ فِي اسْتِعْمَال الْفُقَهَاء، ويعرفونه، بِأَنَّهُ اللَّفْظ الْمُحْتَمل لمعنيين هُوَ فِي أَحدهمَا أرجح دلَالَة.

As for using the term *ẓāhir* to refer to an expression that could have a number of possibilities, but one is likeliest, it is just a terminology, not its literal usage. This is the usage of the jurists, and they define it as being: An utterance that can possibly have two meanings, but one is likelier of a meaning.

وَحكمه أَنه لَا يعدل عَنهُ إِلَّا بتأويل، وَهُوَ صرف اللَّفْظ عَن ظَاهره لدَلِيل يصير بِهِ الْمَرْجُوح راجحا.

The ruling of a *ẓāhir* text is that it should not be forwent without a valid reinterpretation, which is to divert the expression from its apparent meaning due to an evidence, making the less likely meaning [at first glance] the likelier one [when considering the supporting evidence].

وَمِثَال ذَلِك - ليتضح المرام - قَوْله صلى الله عَلَيْهِ وَسلم **«الْجَار أَحَق بصقبه»** رَوَاهُ البُخَارِيّ وَالتِّرْمِذِيّ وَصَححهُ. والصقب: الْقرب والملاصقة، وَالْمرَاد بِهِ الشُّفْعَة. فَهَذَا الحَدِيث ظَاهر فِي ثُبُوت الشُّفْعَة للْجَار الملاصق والمقابل أَيْضا، مَعَ احْتِمَال أَن المُرَاد بالجار: الشَّرِيك المخالط، إِمَّا حَقِيقَة أَو مجَازًا، لَكِن هَذَا الِاحْتِمَال ضَعِيف بِالنِّسْبَةِ إِلَى الظَّاهِر، فَلَمَّا نظرنَا إِلَى قَوْله عَلَيْهِ الصَّلَاة وَالسَّلَام: **«إِذا وَقعت الْحُدُود وصرفت الطّرق، فَلَا شُفْعَة»** رَوَاهُ البُخَارِيّ وَأَبُو دَاوُد وَالتِّرْمِذِيّ وَصَححهُ، صَار هَذَا الحَدِيث مقويا لذَلِك الِاحْتِمَال الضَّعِيف فِي الحَدِيث الْمُتَقَدّم حَتَّى ترجحا على ظَاهره، فقدمناهما وَقُلْنَا: لَا شُفْعَة إِلَّا للشَّرِيك المقاسم، وحملنا عَلَيْهِ الْجَار فِي الحَدِيث الأول، وَهُوَ حمل سَائِغ فِي اللُّغَة.

An example to clarify the point is when the Prophet ﷺ said, **"The neighbour is more deserving of the right of closeness."**[202] It was reported by al-Bukhārī and al-Tirmidhī—who deemed it as authentic. The Prophet ﷺ referred to it as closeness, but this ḥadīth is pertaining to the right of

202 Reported by al-Bukhārī (4/361).

preemption.[203] This ḥadīth apparently indicates that both the adjacent and facing neighbour have the right of preemption. There is also the possibility that when the ḥadīth says, **"neighbour,"** it is referring to a partner, either literally or metaphorically. However, this possibility is quite weak when juxtaposed with the apparent indication of the text. With that said, if we examine the statement of the Prophet ﷺ where he said, **"If the boundaries of the property are demarcated or the ways and streets are fixed, then there is no preemption."**[204] This ḥadīth strengthens the previously weak possibility in the first ḥadīth, actually making [the previously weak possibility] stronger and more veracious than the apparent meaning [on its own]. As such, we (the Ḥanbalīs) give preference to this ḥadīth and state that the right of preemption belongs only to the partner and shareholder. We used the second ḥadīth to interpret the neighbour mentioned in the first ḥadīth to mean a partner, and this is a valid linguistic interpretation of the word.

ثمَّ إن الِاحْتِمَال الْمَرْجُوح الْمُقَابل للراجح الظَّاهِر قد يكون بَعيدا عَن الْإِرَادَة، وَقد يكون قَرِيبا مِنْهَا، وَقد يكون متوسطا بَين الطَّرفَيْنِ. فالاحتمال الْبعيد يحْتَاج فِي حمل اللَّفْظ عَلَيْهِ إِلَى دَلِيل قوي لتجبر قُوَّة الدَّلِيل ضعف الِاحْتِمَال، فيقويان على الِاسْتِيلَاء على الظاهِر، وَالِاحْتِمَال الْقَرِيب يَكْفِيهِ فِي ذَلِك أدنى دَلِيل، وَالِاحْتِمَال الْمُتَوَسّط يَكْفِيهِ دَلِيل متوسط بَين الدَّلِيلَيْنِ قُوَّة وضعفا. وَبِالْجُمْلَةِ فالغرض من دَلِيل التَّأْوِيل أَن يكون بِحَيْثُ إِذا انْضَمَّ إِلَى احْتِمَال اللَّفْظ المؤول، اعتضد أَحدهمَا بِالْآخرِ، واستوليا على الظاهِر، وقدما عَلَيْهِ، فَمَا كَانَ فِي احْتِمَال اللَّفْظ من ضعف جبر بِاعْتِبَار قُوَّة فِي الدَّلِيل، وَمَا كَانَ فِيهِ من قُوَّة سومح بِقَدرِهِ من الدَّلِيل، وَالْمُعْتَمد قبالة المعتدل، فهما يحصلان الْغَرَض.

To continue, the weak possibility—which is obverse to the likely, apparent possibility—might be far-fetched, could be conceivable, and could also be somewhere in the middle of that spectrum. A far-fetched possibility requires, when understanding the text in light of that [far-fetched meaning], a very strong evidence that compensates for the weakness of that possibility. Together, they possess the ability to overcome the apparent meaning. A conceivable possibility requires the least supporting evidence. A middling

203 [T] This issue was explained previously.

204 Reported by al-Bukhārī (4/339), Abu Dāwūd (3514), and al-Tirmidhī (1370), who judged it as authentic.

possibility requires a reasonable evidence, lying on the spectrum between the weak evidence and the strong evidence. Generally speaking, the point behind the evidence for a reinterpretation is that, when it is coupled with the possibility of the interpretation of the word being reinterpreted, they assist one another, and they overcome the strength of the more apparent interpretation, thereby earning preference over it. If the wording itself is unlikely, it is strengthened by its supporting evidence, and if the wording is more likely, the strength of its supporting evidence can be given an equal share of leeway [in its strength] in relation to the possibility of reinterpretation. As such, these two things,[205] when coupled, serve the purpose [of giving preference to a reinterpretation over the apparent indication of the text].

ثمَّ إِن هَذَا الدَّلِيل الْمُرَجح إِمَّا أَن يكون قرينَة، أَو ظَاهرا، أَو قِيَاسا، فَأَما الْقَرِينَة، فإمَّا أَن تكون مُتَّصِلَة، أَو مُنْفَصِلَة، فمثال الْمُتَّصِلَة: مَا رَوَاهُ صَالح وحنبل عَن أَحْمد قَالَ: كلمت الشَّافِعِي فِي مَسْأَلَة الْهِبَة، فَقلت: إِن الْوَاهِب لَيْسَ لَهُ الرُّجُوع فِيمَا وهب، لقَوْله صلى الله عَلَيْهِ وَسلم: «**الْعَائِد فِي هِبته كَالْكَلْب يعود فِي قيئه**» وَكَانَ الشَّافِعِي يرى أَن لَهُ الرُّجُوع، فَقَالَ: لَيْسَ بِمحرم على الْكَلْب أَن يعود فِي قيئه، قَالَ أَحْمد: فَقلت لَهُ: فقد قَالَ النَّبِي صلى الله عَلَيْهِ وَسلم فِي صدر الحَدِيث الْمَذْكُور «**لَيْسَ لنا مثل السوء**» فَسكت الشَّافِعِي.

Further, the strengthening evidence could be: (i) Contextual, which could be: (a) conjunctive or (b) disjunctive, (ii) an apparent text or (iii) an analogy. An example of a conjunctive contextual evidence is what Ṣāliḥ and Ḥanbal reported from Aḥmad, who said, "I spoke to al-Shāfiʿī about the issue of gifting, and said, 'A person who gives a gift has no right to go back on the gift because the Prophet ﷺ said, **'A person who takes back their gift is similar to a dog who eats its own vomit.'**"[206] Note that al-Shāfiʿī used to opine that a person who gave a gift has the right to ask for it to be returned. [Aḥmad said,] "Al-Shāfiʿī said, 'It is not impossible for a dog to eat his own vomit.' I replied, 'The Prophet ﷺ said, in the outset of the ḥadīth I mentioned, **'An evil example does not apply to us.'** Afterwards, al-Shāfiʿī did not respond."

205 [T] Meaning, the possibility of reinterpretation and the evidence of reinterpretation.

206 Reported by al-Bukhārī (12/304) and Muslim (7).

وَمِثَال الْقَرِينَة الْمُنْفَصِلَة: مَا ذكره الْفُقَهَاء فِيمَن جَاءَ من أهل الْجِهَاد بمشرك، فَادّعى أَنه أَمنه، وَأنْكرهُ الْمُسلم، فَادّعى أسره، فَفِيهِ أَقْوَال، ثَالِثهَا: القَوْل قَول من ظَاهر الْحَال صدقه، فَلَو كَانَ الْكَافِر أظهر قُوَّة وبطشا وشهامة من الْمُسلم جعل ذَلِك قرينَة فِي تَقْدِيم قَوْله، مَعَ أَن قَول الْمُسلم لإسلامه وعدالته أرجح، وَقَول الْكَافِر مَرْجُوح، لَكِن الْقَرِينَة الْمُنْفَصِلَة عضدته حَتَّى صَار قَوْله أقوى من الْمُسلم الرَّاجِح.

An example of a disjunctive contextual evidence is what the jurists mention pertaining to when a soldier brings a polytheist during war, and the polytheist claims that the soldier granted him a promise of safety, but the Muslim denies it, claiming he took the polytheist as a prisoner. There are numerous views on the topic, and the third of them is that the one whose apparent state is honesty should be believed. If the disbeliever shows to have more strength, courage, and chivalry than the Muslim, that is an inference used to give preference to his statement, even though the statement of the Muslim, because of his Islam and his uprightness, is stronger and the statement of a disbeliever is weaker. However, the inferred disjunctive contextual clue strengthens the disbeliever, making his statement more believable than that of the Muslim, who otherwise, is more believable.

وَأما الظَّاهِر فَمن أمثلته قَوْله تَعَالَى ﴿حُرِّمَتْ عَلَيْكُمُ الْمَيْتَةُ﴾ [الْمَائِدَة: ٣]، فَإِنَّهُ ظَاهر فِي تَحْرِيم جلدهَا، دبغ أَو لم يدبغ، مَعَ احْتِمَال أَن الْجلد غير مُرَاد بالمعوم احْتِمَالا مترددا لَهُ، من جِهَة أَن إِضَافَة التَّحْرِيم إِلَى الْميتَة يَقْتَضِي تَحْرِيم الْأكل، وَالْجلد غير مَأْكُول يَقْتَضِي عدم تنَاول الْجلد، وَمن جِهَة أَن عُمُوم اللَّفْظ قوي متناول لجَمِيع أَجْزَائِهَا يَقْتَضِي تنَاول الْجلد، ثمَّ نظرنَا فِي قَوْله عَلَيْهِ السَّلَام: **«أَيّمَا إيهَاب دبغ فقد طهر»** فَهُوَ عُمُوم وَظَاهر بتناول إهَاب الْميتَة، فَكَانَ هَذَا الظَّاهِر مقويا لاحْتِمَال عدم إِرَادَة جلد الْميتَة من الْآيَة الْمَذْكُورَة فِي التَّحْرِيم.

An example of an apparent text used as an evidence is where Allah the Exalted states: **{Forbidden to you are carrion.}** [Qur'ān 5:3] This verse apparently prohibits the use of the hide of the dead animal, regardless if it were tanned or not. However, it is possible that the hide is not intended by the generality of the wording, because when the prohibition is ascribed to the dead carcass, it necessitates the prohibition of eating it, and hides are not eaten. If these two premises are true, then the verse does not include the use of the hide. In contrast, the generality of the wording quite strongly indicates inclusion of all of its parts, necessitating inclusion of its hide, as well. Then, we find the statement of the Prophet ﷺ, "**Any hide that has been tanned has indeed become purified.**"[207] This ḥadīth is also general and inclusive of the hides of carcasses. This apparent text strengthens the possibility that hides of carcasses were not intended by the aforementioned verse that discussed the prohibition [of dead carcasses].

وَمِثَال النَّص قَوْله عَلَيْهِ السَّلَام فِي شَاة مَيْمُونَة: **«أَلا أَخَذْتُم إهابها فدبغتموه فانتفعتم بِهِ** فَقَالُوا: إِنَّهَا ميتَة، **قَالَ: إِنَّمَا حرم من الْميتَة أكلهَا»**، فَهَذَا نَص فِي طَهَارَة جلد الْميتَة.

An example of a univocal text in this regard is what the Prophet ﷺ said regarding the ewe of Maymūnah, **"Why did you not take off its skin? You could put it to use, after tanning it."** The Companions responded, "It was dead." The Prophet replied, **"Eating the carcass is what was prohibited."**[208] This ḥadīth univocally states the purity of the hide of a dead carcass [after it is tanned].[209]

وَمِثَال الْقيَاس: إِن تَركه تَعَالَى ذكر الْإِطْعَام فِي كَفَّارَة الْقَتْل ظَاهر فِي عدم وُجُوبه، إِذْ لَو وَجب لذكره كَمَا ذكر التَّحْرِير وَالصِّيَام، هَذَا مَعَ احْتِمَال أَن يكون وَاجِبا

207 [T] Reported by Mālik (1/498), Muslim (366), and al-Shāfiʿī (1/23).

208 Reported by al-Bukhārī (3/281) and Muslim (363).

209 [T] While the example al-Shaykh Ibn Badrān mentioned to illustrate an apparent or univocal ḥadīth to strengthen a possible interpretation of a divine text is accurate and quite splendid, note that the position of al-Imām Aḥmad was that the two ḥadīths mentioned by Ibn Badrān are actually abrogated. His evidence was the ḥadīth of ʿAbdullah ibn Ḥakīm, who said, "The letter of Allah's Messenger ﷺ came to us, a month or two before he died, and it stated, **'Do not utilise parts of a dead carcass: neither its hide nor its ligaments.'**" This was reported by Aḥmad, Abu Dāwūd, al-Nasāʾī, al-Tirmidhī, and Ibn Mājah. Mention of the timing of the letter was only made in the narrations of Abu Dāwūd and Aḥmad, the latter of whom said, "How authentic is this chain of narration!" He also said, "The ḥadīth of Ibn Ḥakīm is the most authentic one." Refer to *Kashāf al-Qināʿ ʿan Matn al-Iqnāʿ* by al-Shaykh Manṣūr ibn Yūnus al-Buhūtī (1/54). This issue is one of the unique rulings that al-Imām Aḥmad had and the other three great *imāms*, Abu Ḥanīfah, Mālik, and al-Shāfiʿī did not espouse. The *aṣḥāb* refer to these opinions as "*mufradāt*", or, singular views of Aḥmad.

مسكوتا عَنهُ يَسْتَخْرِجهُ المجتهدون، ثمَّ رَأينَا إِثْبات الْإِطْعَام فِي كَفَّارَة الْقَتْل بِالْقِيَاسِ إثْبَاته فِي كَفَّارَة الظِّهَار وَالصِّيَام وَالْيَمِين متجها، لِأَن الْكَفَّارَات حُقُوق لله تَعَالَى، وَحكم الِامْتِثَال وَاحِد، فثبوت الْإِطْعَام فِي تِلْكَ الْكَفَّارَات تَنْبِيه على ثُبُوته فِي كَفَّارَة الْقَتْل.

An example of an analogy is that Allah the Exalted did not mention feeding in the midst of mentioning the expiation of manslaughter, apparently indicating that it is not obligatory, since if it were obligatory Allah would have mentioned it, just as He mentioned the freeing of slaves and fasting. Of course, the possibility remains that it is an unmentioned obligation that the *mujtahid* scholars would extract. We found, though, that obligating feeding of the poor is a likely ruling for this case based on analogy, for feeding the poor is found in the expiations of *ẓihār,*[210] fasting, and breaking the right-hand oath. Expiations are the rights of Allah the Exalted, and the ruling of adhering to them is one. Therefore, the fact that feeding the poor is an obligatory expiation of those other indiscretions shows that it is an obligation in the expiation of manslaughter, as well.

ثمَّ اعْلَم أَن كل من أَرَادَ تَأْوِيل ظَاهر من الظَّوَاهِر، فَعَلَيهِ أَمْرَانِ:

Continuing, if one wishes to reinterpret an apparent text, they must do two things:

أَحدهمَا: بَيَان الِاحْتِمَال الْمَرْجُوح مَعَ الظَّاهِر.

(i) They must show how the less likely interpretation is still a possibility in the apparent text.

الثَّانِي: بَيَان عاضد الِاحْتِمَال الْمَرْجُوح أَي الدَّلِيل الَّذِي يعضده ويقويه حَتَّى يقدم على الظَّاهِر.

(ii) They must show strengthening evidence that supports the less likely possibility. Meaning, they must show the supporting evidence to strengthen the less likely possibility and cause it to be a more preferable interpretation than the apparent meaning of the text.

---

210 [T] The concept of *ẓihār* is when a person says to his wife, "You, to me, are similar to the back of my mother." Meaning, he likens intercourse with his wife to intercourse with his mother in prohibition. Refer to *Sharḥ Muntahā al-Irādāt* (3/165).

ثمَّ إِن الظَّاهِر وَالاحْتِمَال الْمَرْجُوح إِذا تقابلا فقد تحتف بِالظَّاهِرِ قَرَائِن ترفع ذَلِك الِاحْتِمَال وتبطله، ثمَّ قد تكون كل وَاحِدَة من الْقَرَائِن دافعة للاحتمال وَحدهَا، وَقد لَا تنْدَفع إِلَّا بِمَجْمُوع تِلْكَ الْقَرَائِن، وَذَلِكَ بِحَسب قُوَّة الْقَرَائِن، وظهورها، ومقاومتها لذَلِك الِاحْتِمَال، وقصورها عَنهُ، فقد تقاومه قرينَة وَاحِدَة أَو قرينتان فتدفعه، وَقد لَا تقاومه إِلَّا جَمِيعهَا فَلَا تنْدَفع بِدُونِهِ.

Sometimes, when the apparent meaning of the text and the less likely possible interpretation are at odds, other evidences used in conjunction can be made to support the apparent reading of the text and nullify other possibilities. Sometimes, a single supporting evidence can be used to nullify and repudiate the other possibilities, and sometimes, there are multiple evidences that, when aggregated, work to nullify other possibilities. That, of course, is contingent on the strength and apparency of those collective evidences and how well they stand in comparison to the other possibilities. One or two supporting evidences may nullify the other possibility, or combining all possible supporting evidences is the only way to nullify the other inference and possible interpretation, and without all of those supporting evidences acting in aggregation, the other possibility remains legitimate.

فمثال رفع الِاحْتِمَال الْمَرْجُوح بالقرائن المحتفة بِالظَّاهِرِ: «أَن غيلَان بن سَلمَة الثَّقَفِيّ رَضِي الله عَنهُ أسلم وَله عشر نسْوَة فِي الْجَاهِلِيَّة فأسلمن مَعَه، فَأمره النَّبِي صلى الله عَلَيْهِ وَسلم أَن يتَخَيَّر أَرْبعا مِنْهُنَّ» رَوَاهُ ابْن مَاجَه وَالتِّرْمِذِيّ. وَفِيمَا يتداوله الْفُقَهَاء: «أمسك مِنْهُنَّ أَرْبعا، وَفَارق سائرهن» وَعَلِيهِ اتجه النزاع:

An example of nullifying the less likely possible interpretation by other evidences that support the apparent interpretation is that Ghaylān ibn Salamah al-Thaqafī accepted Islam while being married to ten women during the pre-Islamic times of ignorance. All of his wives accepted Islam with him. The Prophet ﷺ commanded him to choose just four of them.[211] This was reported by Ibn Mājah and al-Tirmidhī. A discussion that jurists have on this topic is on the end of the ḥadīth, where the Prophet ﷺ told him to choose just four of them, meaning, and divorce the rest. This is the focal point of the difference of opinion.

---

211 Reported by al-Shāfiʿī (2/351), Aḥmad (4609) and (4631), al-Tirmidhī (1128), and Ibn Mājah (1953).

فالحنفية قَالُوا: إِن من أسلم وَتَحْته أَكثر من أَربع نسْوَة فَإِن كَانَ تزوجهن فِي عقد وَاحِد، بَطل نِكَاحهنَّ، وَلم يجز أَن يخْتَار مِنْهُنَّ شَيْئا، وَإِن تزَوَّجن متعاقبات اخْتَار من الأول أَرْبعا وَترك الْبَاقِي. وَالْأَئِمَّة الثَّلَاثَة على أَنه يخْتَار مِنْهُنَّ أَرْبعا مُطلقًا. وَلما كَانَ مَا ذهب إِلَيْهِ الْحَنَفِيَّة مُخَالفا لظَاهِر الحَدِيث، إِذْ ظَاهر الْإِمْسَاك فِيهِ اسْتِدَامَة نِكَاح أَربع، وَظَاهر الْمُفَارقَة تَسْرِيح الْبَاقِيَات - احتاجوا إِلَى تَأْوِيله.

Ḥanafī scholars argued that if someone accepts Islam while being married to more than four wives, if they married them with a single contract, the marriage contract is invalidated, and they may not choose any of the wives. However, if he marries them one after the other, he must choose the first four, and divorce the rest. The three other *imāms* opined that he may choose any four wives. Since the Ḥanafī view is contradictory to the apparent signification of the text, which otherwise states that the marriage to any four is considered valid, and that the others are divorced, they (the Ḥanafī scholars) needed to prove their view by reinterpreting the ḥadīth.

فحملوا الْإِمْسَاك على ابْتِدَاء النِّكَاح، كَأَنَّهُ قَالَ: أمسك أَرْبعا بِأَن تبتدىء نِكَاحهنَّ، وَفَارق سائرهن بِأَن لَا تبتدىء العقد عَلَيْهِنَّ. وعضدوا هَذَا التَّأْوِيل بِالْقِيَاسِ، وَهُوَ أَن بعض النسْوَة لَيْسَ بِأولى الْإِمْسَاك من بعض، إِذْ هُوَ تَرْجِيح من غير مُرَجّح، ورد بَقِيَّة الْأَئِمَّة هَذَا التَّأْوِيل بِأَن السَّابِق إِلَى فهمنا وَفهم الصَّحَابَة من الْإِمْسَاك الاستدامة لَا ابْتِدَاء النِّكَاح، وَمن الْمُفَارقَة التسريح لَا ترك النكَاح، فَيكون هَذَا مَدْلُول اللَّفْظ وَمُقْتَضَاهُ، وَبِأَن النَّبِي صلى الله عَلَيْهِ وَسلم فوض الْإِمْسَاك والفراق إِلَى غيلَان مُسْتقِلّا بِهِ حَيْثُ قَالَ: أمسك وَفَارق، لَو كَانَ المُرَاد بِهِ ابْتِدَاء النكَاح لما اسْتَقل بِهِ بالِاتِّفَاقِ، إِذْ لابد من رضى الزَّوْجَة وَمن الْوَلِيّ عندنَا، فَكَانَ يجب أَن يَقُول: أمسك أَرْبعا مِنْهُنَّ إِن رضين، وَيبين لَهُ شَرَائِط النكَاح، لِأَن ذَلِك بَيَان فِي وَقت الْحَاجة إِلَيْهِ، فَلَا يجوز تَأْخِيره إِلَى غير ذَلِك من الْأَجْوِبَة الَّتِي محلهَا الْكتب المطولة فِي هَذَا الْفَنّ.

They claimed that when the Prophet ﷺ said to keep just four, he meant that he should remarry just four and should divorce the others by not initiating a marriage contract with them. Their evidence to support this reinterpretation is an analogy. They said, none of the wives are more worthy of being kept in their marriage than the rest. Choosing any four is giving preponderance without any justifiable reason. The rest of the *imāms* rejected this reinterpretation, claiming that the meaning that comes quickly to one's mind, and to the minds of the companions, is that when the Prophet ﷺ said to choose four, that those four marriage contracts remain established, not that he must remarry them, and when he said to divorce the rest, he did not mean to simply not remarry them. This is the implication and signification of the apparent text. The Prophet ﷺ also gave Ghaylān full autonomy in keeping and leaving his wives, saying, **"Choose,"** and, **"Divorce."** Had the meaning been to remarry them, he would not have an autonomous choice to do so, by agreement of all scholars, since the wife must also agree to remarry, and, according to the Ḥanbalī scholars, approval must be sought of her guardian. As such, the Prophet ﷺ would have had to say, "Keep four of your wives if they wish to remain with you," and then clarify the conditions of marriage, since that would be the time of need, and the Prophet ﷺ cannot delay clarification of rulings beyond their time of need. There are other responses to the Ḥanafī view that are mentioned in other, longer works that deal with this science.

فَهَذِهِ قَرَائِن تدفع تأويلهم، على أَن الإِمَام الْغَزالِيّ أنصف فِي هَذَا الْمقَام فَقَالَ: والإنصاف أَن تَأْوِيل الظوَاهِر يخْتَلف باخْتلَاف أَحْوَال الْمُجْتَهدين، وَإِلا فلسنا نقطع بِبُطْلَان تَأْوِيل أبي حنيفَة - رَحمَه الله تَعَالَى - مَعَ هَذِه الْقَرَائِن، وَإِنَّمَا الْمَقْصُود تذليل الطَّرِيق للمجتهدين، وَالله سُبْحَانَهُ وَتَعَالَى أعلم.

These supporting evidences I mentioned nullify their reinterpretation. Al-Imām al-Ghazālī was quite fair in this issue and stated, "In fairness, reinterpreting apparent texts varies in proportion to the statuses of the *mujtahid* scholars. As such, we cannot state with full certainty that the interpretation of Abu Ḥanīfah was invalid by use of these supporting evidences. The point, though, is to facilitate the path for the *mujtahid* scholars."[212] And Allah the Exalted knows best.

وَنحن نقُول: إِنَّمَا قصدنا فِي هَذَا الْكتاب وَغَيره من كتبنَا الْمُشْتَملَة على الأَدِلَّة

212 [T] Refer to *al-Mustaṣfā* by al-Imām al-Ghazālī (p. 197). He mentions six ways to negate the view of al-Imām Abu Ḥanīfah ﵀ and concludes with the beautiful remark mentioned by Ibn Badrān.

بيَان الْإِيضَاح بالأمثلة، واستنباط الْفَوَائِد من كتاب الله وَمن كَلَام رَسُوله، مَعَ احترام الْعلمَاء وَحفظ مقامهم، حشرنا الله فِي زمرة المهديين مِنْهُم.

In this book, and other books I wrote that mention evidences, I seek to clarify by mentioning examples and by deducing useful points from the Book of Allah the Exalted and the speech of His Messenger ﷺ, while still respecting the scholars and preserving their status. May Allah the Exalted resurrect us amongst the guided of them.

وَهنا قد انْتهى مَا توخيناه من الْكَلَام على النَّص وَالظَّاهِر، وذكرناهما هُنَا لقرب مباحثهما من مبَاحث مبادي اللُّغَة، وأخرنا الْكَلَام على الْمُجْمل إِلَى مَا بعد الْمُطلق والمقيد لِأَنهُ أشبه بهما. وَهنا قد انْتهى الْكَلَام على مَا هُوَ مُقَدّمَة فِي هَذَا الْفَنّ، ولنشرع إِن شَاءَ الله تَعَالَى على الْأُصُول، وَإِلَيْك الْبَيَان.

This concludes what we intended to clarify regarding univocal and apparent texts. I mentioned them here because they are of the same genre of the discussions on the origins of language. I delayed speaking about *mujmal* (obscure) texts and will discuss them after mentioning *muṭlaq* (unqualified) and *muqayyad* (qualified) texts, because [discussions on obscure texts] are more resembling those discussions. Here, we end the discussions on the introduction to this science, and let us now, Allah willing, discuss legal theories and foundations.

فصل في الأصول

Section [Five:] On Legal Theories

اعْلَم أَن الْمُحَقِّقين من عُلَمَاء هَذَا الشَّأْن عرفُوا تِلْكَ الْأُصُول بالضوابط، وَهَذِه الطَّرِيقَة وَإِن كَانَ التَّعْرِيف بها ضَعِيفا إِلَّا أننا نسلكها هُنَا، ثمَّ نورد تَعْرِيف كل قسم عِنْد ذكره لأننا أردنَا الضَّبْط هُنَا وَلم نرد الْحُدُود، وَإِن كَانَت تَأتي عرضا، واخترنا هُنَا طَرِيقَة الْآمِدِيّ، فَإِنَّهُ قَالَ مَا مَعْنَاهُ: إِن الدَّلِيل الشَّرْعِيّ أَي: الَّذِي طَرِيق مَعْرفَته الشَّرْع إِمَّا أَن يرد من جِهَة الرَّسُول أَو لَا من جِهَته، فَإِن ورد من جِهَة الرَّسُول، فَهُوَ إِمَّا من قبيل مَا يُتْلَى - وَهُوَ الْكتاب - أَو لَا وَهُوَ السّنة. وَإِن ورد لَا من جِهَة الرَّسُول، فإمَّا أَن تشْتَرط فِيهِ عصمَة من صدر عَنهُ أَو لَا، وَالْأول الْإِجْمَاع، وَالثَّانِي إِن كَانَ حمل مَعْلُوم على مَعْلُوم بِجَامِع مُشْتَرك، فَهُوَ الْقيَاس، وَإِلَّا فَهُوَ الِاسْتِدْلَال.

Know that the scholars of this science who engaged in deep research defined these theories by their maxims. That way—though defining something in that way is not the best—is what we will take here. Then, we will define each subsection when the times comes, because here, we want to understand the maxims, not necessarily definitions, though the definitions will undoubtedly be mentioned incidentally. Here, we have chosen to use the way of al-Āmidī, who essentially stated that a religious evidence, i.e., an evidence that is known through legislation, can either be: (i) From the Messenger ﷺ or not. If the Messenger taught it, it is either: (a) Recited scripture; namely, the Qur'ān. (b) Not recited; namely, the Sunnah. (ii) If it is not from the Messenger: (a) If it was conditioned on infallibility, it is known as consensus. (b) If it was not conditioned on infallibility, there are two cases: (b.1) If it were to extend some known ruling to some known case due to a commonality between the two, it is analogy (*qiyās*). (b.2) If it were not, it is known as inferences.

فالثلاثة الأول - وَهِي الْكتاب وَالسّنة وَالْإِجْمَاع - نقلية، والآخران معنويان، والنقلي أصل للمعنوي، وَالْكتاب أصل للْكُل.

The first three mentioned above, i.e. the Qur'ān, the Sunnah, and consensus, are textual evidences. The other two are abstract, though the textual evidences are the root bases for the abstract ones. The Qur'ān is the source and authority of all other categories.

فالأدلة إِذن خَمْسَة: الْكتاب وَالسّنة وَالْإِجْمَاع وَالْقِيَاس وَالِاسْتِدْلَال. وعرفه الْآمِدِيّ بِأنهُ دَلِيل ليس بِنَصّ وَلَا إِجْمَاع وَلَا قِيَاس.

Therefore, there are five evidences: The Qur'ān, Sunnah, consensus, analogy and inferences. Al-Āmidī defined inferences as being evidences that are neither divine texts, consensus, nor analogies.[213]

ومصدر هَذِه الْأُصُول هُوَ الله تَعَالَى، إِذْ الْكتاب قَوْله، وَالسّنة بَيَانه، وَالْإِجْمَاع دَال على النَّص، ومدركها الرَّسُول عَلَيْهِ السَّلَام، لِأَنهُ لَا سَماع لنا من الله تَعَالَى، وَلَا من جِبْرِيل، فَلم يبْق لنا مدرك لهَذِهِ الْأُصُول إِلَّا الرَّسُول. فالكتاب سمع مِنْهُ تبليغا، وسنة تصدر عَنهُ تبيينا، وَالْإِجْمَاع وَالْقِيَاس مستندان فِي إثباتهما إِلَى الْكتاب وَالسّنة.

The source and authority of all of these principles is Allah the Exalted, since the Qur'ān is His speech, the Sunnah is its clarification, and consensus indicates the existence of a text. The one who received the Qur'ān is the Messenger ﷺ since we do not hear directly from Allah nor from Jibrīl. Therefore, the only remaining option is that the Messenger ﷺ is the recipient of these foundations. The Qur'ān was heard from him in the sense that he delivered it, the Sunnah emanated from him via his explanations [of the Qur'ān,] and consensus and analogy owe their legitimacy to the Qur'ān and Sunnah.

وَاعْلَم أَن هَذِه الْأُصُول هِيَ الْمُتَّفق عَلَيْهَا بَين الْجُمْهُور، وَثمّ أَرْبَعَة أُخْرَى هِيَ مَحل خلاف: شرع من قبلنَا، وَقَول الصَّحَابِيّ الَّذِي لَا مُخَالف لَهُ، وَالِاسْتِحْسَان،

213 [T] I could not find a reference for al-Āmidī's statement. However, this definition is commonly referenced in Shāfiʿī works. Refer to al-ʿAṭṭār's commentaries on al-Maḥallī's explanation of *Jamʿ al-Jawāmiʿ* (2/382).

والاستصلاح. وستمر بك هَذِهِ الْأُصُول التِّسْعَة مبينَة حسب الْإِمْكَان إِن شَاءَ الله تَعَالَى.

Know, too, that these evidences are ones that the majority agree are legitimate. There are four other evidences that not all scholars accept, namely: (i) The legislations given to nations before ours. (ii) The statement of the companion, if there is no known varying view. (iii) Juristic discretion. (iv) Public interests and utility. All nine of these foundational principles will be discussed at a later time, to the best of my ability, Allah willing.

الْكتاب الْعَزِيز الَّذِي هُوَ أصل الأصُول

The Noble Qur'ān: The Foundation of all Principles

كتاب الله: كَلَامه الْمنزل للإعجاز بِسُورَة مِنْهُ، وَهُوَ الْقُرْآن، وَفِيه مسَائِل:

The Book of Allah refers to His Speech which was revealed to prove miraculous inimitability through just one of its chapters. It is called the Qur'ān. There are a number of important things to discuss about the Qur'ān:

الأولى: الْقرَاءَات السَّبع متواترة، وَهُوَ الْمَشْهُور. وَقَالَ ابْن الْحَاجِب: هِيَ متواترة فِيمَا لَيْسَ من قبيل الآدَاء، كالمد والإمالة وَتَخْفِيف الْهمزَة وَنَحْوهَا، وَهَذَا خلاف الْمَشْهُور. وَذهب الطوفي إِلَى أَن الْقرَاءَات متواترة عَن الْأَئِمَّة السَّبْعَة، أما تواترها عَن النَّبِي صلى الله عَلَيْهِ وَسلم إِلَى الْأَئِمَّة السَّبْعَة فَهُوَ مَحل نظر، فَإِن أَسَانِيد الْأَئِمَّة السَّبْعَة بِهَذِهِ الْقرَاءَات السَّبْعَة إِلَى النَّبِي صلى الله عَلَيْهِ وَسلم مَوْجُودَة فِي كتب الْقرَاءَات، وَهِي نقل الْوَاحِد عَن الْوَاحِد، لم تستكمل شُرُوط التَّوَاتُر، قَالَ: وأبلغ من هَذَا أَنَّهَا لم تتواتر بَين الصَّحَابَة.

The First Discussion: The Seven Modes of Recitation are recurrent (*mutawātir*). That is the popular view. Ibn al-Ḥājib stated, "They are recurrent, but that does not encompass styles of recitation, such as elongation, *imālah,*[214] softening of *hamzah* (ء) letters, and so forth."[215] This is contrary to the popular view. Al-Ṭūfī took the view that the modes of recitation are recurrent in respect to their transmission from the Seven Imāms.[216] As for their recurrence from the Prophet ﷺ reaching the Seven Imāms, it is contentious, since the chains of narration of the Seven Imāms that contain these recitations to the Prophet ﷺ are mentioned in the books on modes of rec-

214 [T] *Imālah* means to make the *alif* (ا) letter sound between a *yā* (ي) and an *alif* (ا).

215 [T] Refer to *Bayān al-Mukhtaṣar Sharḥ Mukhtaṣar Ibn al-Ḥājib* (1/462).

216 [T] The Seven Reciters are: ʿAbdullah ibn Kathīr al-Dārī al-Makkī, ʿAbdullah ibn ʿĀmir al-Yaḥṣabī al-Shāmī, ʿĀṣim ibn Abi ʾl-Nujūd al-Asadī al-Kūfī, Abu ʿAmr ibn al-ʿAlā al-Baṣrī, Ḥamzah ibn al-Zayyāt al-Kūfī, Nāfiʿ al-Madinī, and ʿAlī ibn Ḥamzah al-Kisāʾī.

itation, and they contain cases where singular individuals report from other singular individuals, thereby not fulfilling the conditions of recurrence. He also said, "More indicative of this point is that they were not recurrent among the companions."

قَالَ: وَاعْلَم أَن بعض من لَا تَحْقِيق عِنْده ينفر من الْقَوْل بِعَدَمِ تَوَاتر الْقرَاءَات ظنا مِنْهُ أَن ذَلِك يسْتَلْزم عدم تَوَاتر الْقُرْآن، وَلَيْسَ ذَلِك بِلَازِم، لِأَنهُ فرق بَين مَاهِيَّة الْقُرْآن، والقراءات، وَالْإِجْمَاع على تَوَاتر الْقُرْآن.

In another instance, he stated, "Know that some who have not engaged in precise research flee from the view that the modes of recitation are not recurrent, thinking that this necessitates that the Qur'ān is not recurrent. This is not a consequent [of the non-recurrence of the modes of recitation,] since there is a difference between the essence of the Qur'ān and the modes of recitation. There is consensus that the Qur'ān is recurrent."[217]

الثَّانِيَة: الْمَنْقُول أحادا نَحْو (فَصِيَامُ ثَلاثَةِ أَيَّامٍ مُتَتَابعَاتٍ) وَهِي قِرَاءَة ابْن مَسْعُود حجَّة عندنَا وَعند أبي حنيفَة خلافًا للباقين.

The Second Discussion: Recitations that are reported through singular chains of narration, such as, "Then they must fast three days consecutively."[218] This was a recitation of Ibn Mas'ūd, and it is evidence to us (the Ḥanābilah) and the adherents to Abu Ḥanīfah's school, contrary to the other schools of law.

الثَّالِثَة: الْقُرْآن مُشْتَمل على الْحَقِيقَة وَالْمجَاز، خلافًا لقوم - وهم الظَّاهِرِيَّة والرافضة - فَإِنَّهُم منعُوا جَوَاز وُقُوع الْمجَاز فِي الْقُرْآن، وَقد مر بك هَذَا الْبَحْث.

The Third Discussion: The Qur'ān comprises of literal and metaphorical words. This fact was denied by some, namely, the Ẓāhirītes and the Rāfiḍites, who denied the plausibility of metaphors occurring in the Qur'ān. This has

217 [T] *Sharḥ Mukhtaṣar al-Rawḍah* (2/24).

218 [T] This singular report of Ibn Mas'ūd is appended to the end of the verse where Allah states: **{Allah does not take you [to task] for what is thoughtless in your oaths, only for your binding oaths: the atonement for breaking an oath is to feed ten poor people with food equivalent to what you would normally give your own families, or to clothe them, or to set free a slave - if a person cannot find the means, he should fast for three days.}** [Qur'ān 5:89]

already been discussed.

الرَّابِعَة: قَالُوا: المعرب مَوْجُود فِي الْقُرْآن، وَهُوَ بتَشْديد الرَّاء وفتحهَا. وَهُوَ مَا أَصله أعجمي ثمَّ عرب، أَي: استعملته الْعَرَب على نَحْو اسْتِعْمَالهَا لكلامها، فَقيل لَهُ مُعرب توسطا بَين العجمي والعربي. وَأَقُول الْحق أَن الْمُدَّعِي أَنه مُعرب إِن كَانَ من الْأَعْلَام كإبراهيم وَإِسْحَاق وَيَعْقُوب فَهَذَا لَيْسَ بعربي وَلَا يضر، وَإِن كَانَ من غير الْأَعْلَام فَهُوَ من توَافق اللغَات قطعا.

The Fourth Discussion: Arabised words exist in the Qur'ān. This means that there are words that were originally not Arabic but were then Arabised, meaning, the Arabs used them in ways they used their own original [Arabic] words. It was referred to as "Arabised," to show that they lie in between non-Arabic words and Arabic words. My view is that the claim that there are Arabised words applies to proper nouns, such as Ibrāḥīm, Isḥāq, and Ya'qūb. These names are not Arab names, and there is no harm there. However, if the [so-called] Arabised word is not a proper noun, it is simply that the two languages (Arabic and the other language) coincide in using a single word in each respective language.

وَنقل ابْن إِسْحَاق فِي (الْمَغَازِي) وَابْن فَارس فِي (فقه اللُّغَة) عَن أبي عبيد كَلَاما حَاصله: أَن فِي اللغَة ألفاظا أَصْلهَا أعجمي كَمَا قَالَ الْفُقَهَاء، لَكِن استعملتها الْعَرَب فعربتها بألسنتها، وحولتها عَن أَلْفَاظ الْعَجم إِلَى ألفاظها، فَصَارَت عَرَبِيَّة. ثمَّ نزل الْقُرْآن وَقد اخْتلطت بِكَلَام الْعَرَب، فَمن قَالَ إِنَّهَا عَرَبِيَّة فَهُوَ صَادِق، يَعْنِي بِاعْتِبَار التعريب الطارئ، وَمن قَالَ إِنَّهَا أَعْجَمِيَّة فَهُوَ صَادِق، يَعْنِي بِاعْتِبَار أَصْلهَا، قَالَ أَبُو عبيد: وَإِنَّمَا سلكنا هَذَا الطَّرِيق لِئَلَّا يظنّ بالفقهاء الْجَهْل بِكِتَاب الله تَعَالَى، وهم كَانُوا أعلم بالتأويل، وَأَشد تَعْظِيمًا لِلْقُرْآنِ. انْتهى. قلت وَمِنْه تعلم أَن النزاع فِي الْمَسْأَلَة لَفْظِي.

Ibn Isḥāq reported in *al-Maghāzī*, and Ibn Fāris mentioned in *Fiqh al-Lughah* that Abu 'Ubayd mentioned something that, in essence, states that: In the Arabic language, there are words that are originally non-Arab, as the jurists stated. Then, the Arabs used them and Arabised them, making them consistent with their language, and used Arabic letters to replace the non-Arabic ones, making the words Arabic. Then, the Qur'ān was revealed, and those words were already intermixed with the speech of the Arabs. Those who claimed they are Arabic words have told the truth when considering Arabization happened to those words, and those who said they are non-Arabic words have also told the truth when considering their roots. Abu 'Ubayd stated, "I took this route so that none thinks that the jurists are ignorant of the Book of Allah. Actually, they were more knowledgeable of interpretation [of the Qur'ān] and honoured the Qur'ān more." I say: This shows that the dispute on this issue is mere semantics.

الْخَامِسَة: فِيهِ الْمُحكم والمتشابه، فَأَما الْمُحكم فَهُوَ لُغَة: مفعل من أحكمت الشَّيْء أحكمه أحكاما: إِذا أثْبته فكَانَ على غَايَة مَا يَنْبَغِي من الْحِكْمَة. والمتشابه: مَا بَينه وَبَين غَيره أَمر مُشْتَرك، فيشبهه ويلتبس بِهِ.

The Fifth Discussion: The Qur'ān has unequivocal (*muḥkam*) and ambiguous (*mutashābih*) verses: First, *muḥkam*, [...] linguistically, means to do something to the utmost level of precision. *Mutashābih* refers to something that shares some commonality with something else, causing them to be confused for one another.

وَأما معنى الْمُحكم، فأجود مَا قيل فِيهِ: إنه المتضح الْمَعْنى، كالنصوص والظواهر، لِأَنَّهُ من الْبَيَان فِي غَايَة الْإِحْكَام والإتقان.

With regards to the technical definitions, the best definition of *muḥkam* is something clear, such as univocal and apparent texts, since it is of the utmost level of precision in conveying a meaning.

والمتشابه مُقَابل لَهُ، وَهُوَ غير متضح الْمَعْنى، فتشتبه بعض محتملاته بِبَعْض، وَذَلِكَ التشابه وَعدم الاتضاح إِمَّا الِاشْتِرَاك كلفظي الْعين والقرء، أَو لإجمال، وَهُوَ إِطْلَاق اللَّفْظ بِدُونِ المُرَاد مِنْهُ نَحْو قَوْله تَعَالَى ﴿وَآتُوا حَقَّهُ يَوْمَ حَصَادِهِ﴾ [الْأَنْعَام: ١٤١]، فَلم يبين مِقْدَار الْحق. أَو لظُهُور تَشْبِيه فِي صِفَات الله تَعَالَى كآيات الصِّفَات وأخبارها، فَإِن المُرَاد مِنْهَا اشْتبهَ على النَّاس، فَقَالَ قوم بظاهرها، فجسموا وشبهوا، وفر قوم من التَّشْبِيه، فتأولوا وحرفوا فعطلوا، وتوسط قوم فَسَلمُوا، وأمروه كَمَا جَاءَ مَعَ اعْتِقَاد التَّنْزِيه فَسَلمُوا، وهم أهل السّنة.

In contrast, *mutashābih* refers to something that does not have a clear meaning, where its significations could be confused for others. The ambiguity could emanate from the word being a homonym, such as the words, *al-ʿayn*[219] and *al-qurʾ*,[220] or could be due to the Qurʾān outlining a ruling without giving specifics. For example, Allah the Exalted states: **{Pay the dues at harvest.}** [Qurʾān 6:141] The verse does not clarify what the dues are. Another reason for ambiguity is that there are some descriptions of Allah the Exalted, such as in the verses and aḥadīth that detail the Attributes of Allah the Exalted. The meanings and intents of those texts are ambiguous to people. Some accepted their literal interpretations, thereby falling into anthropomorphism and likening Allah to His creation. Others fled from anthropomorphism and reinterpreted those texts, falling into distortion which led to negation of [those texts and Attributes]. Lastly, a group of scholars took the moderate route and submitted to them, leaving them as is, while believing that Allah the Exalted is transcendent. As such, they were safe [from falling into error]. Indeed, they are the People of the Sunnah.

وَجعل كثير من الْعلمَاء من الْمُتَشَابه الْحُرُوف الَّتِي فِي فواتح السُّور، فَإِنَّهُ لَا شكّ أَن لَهَا معنى لم تبلغ أفهامنا إِلَى مَعْرفَته، فَهِيَ مِمَّا اسْتَأْثر الله بِعِلْمِهِ، وَلم يصب من تمحل لتفسيرها، فَإِن ذَلِك من النقول على الله بِمَا لم يقل، وَمن تَفْسِير كَلَام الله بمحض الرَّأْي.

Many considered the letters that begin many chapters of the Qurʾān[221] to be considered ambiguous. Undoubtedly, they have meanings, but our intellects have not reached a level to be able to understand them. The meaning of those letters are the sole domain and knowledge of Allah. Those who sought to interpret them have erred, since they are fabrications against Allah the Exalted by ascribing to Him things that He did not say and explaining the speech of Allah with mere intellect.

وَحكم الْمُحكم هُوَ وجوب الْعَمَل بِهِ، وَالْحق أَن حكم الْمُتَشَابه هُوَ عدم جَوَاز الْعَمَل بِهِ لقَوْله تَعَالَى ﴿فَأَمَّا الَّذِينَ فِي قُلُوبِهِمْ زَيْغٌ فَيَتَّبِعُونَ مَا تَشَابَهَ مِنْهُ ابْتِغَاءَ الْفِتْنَةِ

219 [T] In Arabic, an *ʿayn* can refer to an eye, a spy, a spring, a letter, and so forth.
220 [T] In Arabic, *qurʾ* can refer to a menstrual period, or could mean the pure state after completion of a menstrual period.
221 [T] Such as *alif-lām-mīm*, etc.

وَابْتِغَاءَ تَأْوِيلِهِ وَمَا يَعْلَمُ تَأْوِيلَهُ إِلَّا اللهُ﴾ [آل عمرَان: ٧] وَهنا الْوَقْف وَاجِب نقلا وعقلا وَالله الْهَادِي.

The ruling of the unequivocal texts is that they must be implemented, and the truth is that the ambiguous verses may not be acted on [without further clarification]. Allah the Exalted states: **{Those with deviant hearts follow the elusive verses seeking doubt through their interpretations—but none grasps their meaning except Allah.}** [Qur'ān 3:7] In ambiguous matters, abstention is an obligation, as dictated by textual and rational evidences. Allah is the Guider.

الأَصْل الثَّانِي السّنة

The Second Foundational Principle: The Sunnah

السنة في اللغة: الطريقة والسيرة، وَفِي اصْطِلَاح الشَّرْع: مَا نقل عَن النَّبِي صلى الله عَلَيْهِ وَسلم قولا أَو فعلا أَو إِقْرَارا على فعل، وَهَذَا مَعْنَاهَا بِاعْتِبَار الْعرف الْخَاص باصطلاح الْعلمَاء. وَأما مَعْنَاهَا بِاعْتِبَار الْعرف الْعَام، فَهُوَ: مَا نقل عَن النَّبِي صلى الله عَلَيْهِ وَسلم أَو عَن السّلف من الصَّحَابَة وَالتَّابِعِينَ وَغَيرهم من الْأَئِمَّة المقتدى بهم.

Linguistically, *al-Sunnah* refers to one's way and behaviour. In religious nomenclature, it refers to things that are reported from the Prophet ﷺ, be they statements, actions, or sanctioning of some actions. This is the meaning when considering the conventional usage specifically used by scholars. As for the convention used generally, it refers to anything reported from the Prophet ﷺ or the pious predecessors, such as the companions, their successors, and other scholars of guidance who are followed.

ثمَّ اعْلَم أَن قَول النَّبِي صلى الله عَلَيْهِ وَسلم إِمَّا أَن يكون مسموعا مِنْهُ لغيره بِلَا وَاسِطَة، أَو مَنْقُولًا إِلَيْهِ بِوَاسِطَة الروَاة، فَإِن كَانَ مسموعا مِنْهُ فَهُوَ حجَّة قَاطِعَة على من سَمعه، كالصحابة الَّذين سمعُوا مِنْهُ الْأَحْكَام لَا يسوغ خلَافهَا بِوَجْه من الْوُجُوه إِلَّا بنسخ أَو جمع بَين متعارض بالتأويل، وَذَلِكَ فِي التَّحْقِيق لَا يعد خلافًا.

The statement of the Prophet ﷺ could either be heard by others without an intermediary, or could be transmitted to one by way of narrators. If the statement is heard directly from the Prophet ﷺ, it is definitive evidence for the one who heard it. For example, the companions who heard the rulings from the Prophet ﷺ cannot contradict them in any way or fashion, unless it were abrogated, or one statement is preferred over another conflicting statement by way of valid interpretation. That, in reality, is not considered a difference of opinion.

وَإِن كَانَ مَنْقُولًا إِلَى الْغَيْر، فَذَلِك النَّقل إِمَّا أَن يكون تواترا أَو آحادا، فَإِن كَانَ تواترا فَهُوَ أَيْضا حجَّة قَاطِعَة، كالمسموع مِنْهُ عَلَيْهِ السَّلَام، لِأَن التَّوَاتُر يُفِيد الْعلم، فَصَارَ كالمسموع شفاها مِنْهُ فِي إِفَادَة الْعلم، غير أَن مدرك الْعلم فِي المسموع الْحس، وَفِي التَّوَاتُر الْمركب من السّمع وَالْعقل.

If the statement of the Prophet ﷺ is transmitted to others, the narration could either be: (i) Recurrent (*mutawātir*) or (ii) singular *(āḥād)*. If the narration is recurrent, it too is decisive evidence, similar to one hearing directly from the Prophet ﷺ, as recurrence provides definitive knowledge. As such, it is similar to a statement heard directly from the mouth of the Prophet ﷺ in that it provides definitive knowledge, although when someone hears something directly using their sense of hearing, it is an additional factor that establishes knowledges. The establishment of knowledge in recurrence is compounded, comprising of hearing and rational inference.

وَإِن كَانَ آحادا، وَجب الْعَمَل بِمُقْتَضَاهُ - كَمَا سَيَأْتِي - مَا لم يكن مُجْتَهدا يصرفهُ عَن مُقْتَضى مَا سمع أَو نقل إِلَيْهِ دَلِيل، فَيجب عَلَيْهِ مُتَابعَة الدَّلِيل، وَذَلِكَ كَتَرْكِ الْعَام إِلَى الْخَاص، وَالْمُطلق إِلَى الْمُقيد، والمرجوح إِلَى الرَّاجِح، وَغير ذَلِك.

If the narration is singular—it is still an obligation to act on it—as will be mentioned, so long as no *mujtahid* diverts one from the implications of the ḥadīth they heard, or there is some other evidence reported to them. One is obligated to follow the evidence. For example, one may be diverted from following a general text to following a specific one. Or, one can be diverted from following an unrestricted text to following a restricted one. Lastly, one can be diverted from a less weighty and veracious view to instead following the weightier and more veracious view, and so forth.

تَنْبِيه: قد اتّفق من يعْتد بِهِ من أهل الْعلم على أن السّنة المطهرة مُسْتَقلَّة بتشريع الْأَحْكَام، وَأَنَّهَا كالقرآن فِي تَحْلِيل الْحَلَال، وَتَحْرِيم الْحَرَام، وَقد ثَبت عَنهُ صلى الله عَلَيْهِ وَسلم أنه قَالَ: **«أَلا وَإِنِّي أُوتيت الْقُرْآن وَمثله مَعَه»** أَي: من السّنَن الَّتِي لم ينْطق بهَا الْقُرْآن، وَذَلِكَ كتحريم لُحُوم الْحمر الْأَهْلِيَّة، وَتَحْرِيم كل ذِي نَاب من السبَاع، ومخلب من الطير، وَغير ذَلِك مِمَّا لم يَأْتِ عَلَيْهِ الْحصْر، وَمَا

ورد من طَرِيق ثَوْبَان بِعرْض الْأَحَادِيث على الْقُرْآن فَقَالَ يحيى بن معِين: إِنَّه مَوْضُوع، وَضعته الزَّنَادِقَة، وَقَالَ عبد الرَّحْمَن بن مهْدي: الْخَوَارِج وضعُوا حَدِيث «مَا أَتَاكُم عني، فاعرضوه على كتاب الله» إِلَى آخِره، وَقد عَارض حَدِيث الْعرض قوم فَقَالُوا: عرضنَا هَذَا الحَدِيث على كتاب الله فخالفه لأَنا وجدنَا فِيهِ: ﴿وَمَا آتَاكُمُ الرَّسُول فَخُذُوهُ وَمَا نهاكم عَنهُ فَانْتَهوا﴾ [الْحَشْر: ٧]

Note: Reputable scholars have agreed that the pure Sunnah can independently legislate rulings and that, in legalising lawful things or forbidding prohibited things, it holds the same weight as the Qur'ān. The Prophet ﷺ said, **"Truly, I have been given the Qur'ān and its likeness along with it."**[222] He meant the traditions that the Qur'ān did not teach. Examples are the prohibition of the meat of donkey, prohibition of eating any predatory animals with canines and birds with claws, as well as other rulings that are almost innumerable. As for the narration that has been reported from Thawbān where the Prophet ﷺ said to compare the aḥadīth to the Qur'ān [and if they conflict, reject the aḥadīth], Yaḥyā ibn Ma'īn stated that it was fabricated by heretics. 'Abd al-Raḥmān ibn Mahdī said, "The Kharijites fabricated the ḥadīth, **'Anything that reaches you and is attributed to me, compare it to the Book of Allah.'**" Some have stated that they compared this ḥadīth to the Book of Allah the Exalted and have found it to contradict the Qur'ān itself, for Allah states: **{Whatever the Messenger gives you, take it. And whatever he forbids you from, leave it.}** [Qur'ān 59:7]

قَالَ الْأَوْزَاعِيّ: الْكتاب أحْوج إِلَى السّنة من السّنة إِلَى الْكتاب. قَالَ ابْن عبد الْبر: يُرِيد أَنَّهَا تقضي عَلَيْهِ، وَتبين الْمُرَاد مِنْهُ. وَقَالَ يحيى بن أبي كثير: السّنة قاضية على الْكتاب. انْتهى.

Al-Awzā'ī stated, "The Qur'ān is more in need of the Sunnah than the Sunnah is of the Qur'ān." Ibn 'Abd al-Barr stated, "He means that the Sunnah presides over the Qur'ān, clarifying its meanings. Yaḥyā ibn Abi Kathīr said, 'The Sunnah presides over the Qur'ān.'"[223]

وكل من لَهُ إِلْمَام بِالْعلمِ يعلم أَن ثُبُوت حجية السّنة المطهرة، واستقلالها بتشريع

222 Reported by Aḥmad (4/130-131), al-Darimi (1/144), Abu Dāwūd (4604), al-Tirmidhī (2660), and Ibn Mājah (12).
223 [T] Reported by al-Dārimī (1/145) and al-Marwazī in *al-Sunnah* (p. 28).

الْأَحْكَام ضَرُورِيَّة دينية، وَلَا يُخَالف فِي ذَلِك إِلَّا من لَا حَظّ لَهُ فِي دين الْإِسْلَام.

Anyone with the slightest amount of knowledge knows that the pure Sunnah is evidence and that it acts independently in legislation; indeed, this is a necessary belief of the religion, and only those with no share of Islam would dispute this fact.

فصل فِي شذرات من مباحث السّنة

A Section on Some Golden Discussions on the Sunnah

الأولى: الْخَبَر: مَا صَحَّ أَن يُقَال فِي جَوَابه صدق أَو كذب، فَيخرج مِنْهُ الْأَمر، وَالنَّهْي، والاستفهام، وَالتَّمَنِّي، وَالدعَاء، وَهُوَ قِسْمَانِ: متواتر وآحاد.

The First Discussion: A *khabar* (report) is something that can be declared true or false as a reply. As such, it does not include commandments, prohibitions, questions, wishes, and supplications. Reports are of two types: (i) Recurrent and (ii) singular.

فالتواتر لُغَة: التَّتَابُع، وَاصْطِلَاحا: إِخْبَار قوم يمْتَنع تواطؤهم على الْكَذِب بِشُرُوط تذكر، وَهُوَ يُفِيد الْعلم، وَذَلِكَ الْعلم الْحَاصِل بِهِ ضَرُورِيّ عِنْد القَاضِي أبي يعلى، وَوَافَقَهُ الْجُمْهُور، وَيحصل بِالنّظرِ، ويتوقف عَلَيْهِ عِنْد أبي الْخطاب، وَوَافَقَهُ الكعبي، وَأَبُو الْحُسَيْن الْبَصْرِيّ من الْمُعْتَزلَة، وَإِمَام الْحَرَمَيْنِ، وَالْغَزالِيّ، والدقاق من أَصْحَاب الشَّافِعِي، وَالْخلاف لَفْظِي لِأَن الْقَائِل بِأَنهُ ضَرُورِيّ لَا يُنَازع فِي توقفه على النّظر فِي الْمُقدمَات، وَالْقَائِل بِأَنهُ نَظَرِي لَا يُنَازع فِي أَن الْعقل يضْطَر إِلَى التَّصْدِيق بِهِ. وَإِذا وَافق كل وَاحِد من الْفَرِيقَيْنِ صَاحبه على مَا يَقُوله فِي حكم هَذَا الْعلم وَصفته، لم يبْق النزاع بَينهمَا إِلَّا فِي اللَّفْظ.

Mutawātir (Recurrent): Linguistically, it refers to continuity. In religious terminology, it refers to a report emanating from so many people that they cannot all possibly be lying. It has some other conditions. It provides knowledge, and according to al-Qāḍī Abu Yaʿlā and the majority, that knowledge is necessary. It occurs by way of inference and deliberation, and it is contingent on inference according to Abu ʿl-Khaṭṭāb, al-Kaʿbi, Abu ʿl-Ḥusayn al-Baṣrī from the Muʿtazilites, al-Imām al-Ḥarāmayn [al-Juwaynī], al-Ghazālī, and al-Daqqāq from the disciples of al-Shāfiʿī. And the difference of opinion is semantics, because those who claim it is necessary knowledge do not deny it is contingent on inference and deliberation in respect to its original premises. And those who claim it is speculative do not deny that the intellect must necessarily believe its truth. Therefore, when both parties agree on the judgements and descriptions of this knowledge, the only remaining difference is in semantics.

وَمَا أَفَادَ الْعلم من الْأَخْبَار فِي وَاقعَة مُعينَة وَجب أَن يفِيدهُ فِي كل وَاقعَة غَيرهَا، وَمَا أَفَادَ الْعَالم شخصا من النَّاس وَجب أَن يفِيدهُ لكل شخص غَيره إِذا شَاركهُ فِي سَماع ذَلِك الْخَبَر، بِحَيْثُ لَا يجوز أَن يخْتَلف الْخَبَر فيُفِيد الْعلم فِي وَاقعَة دون أُخْرَى، وَلَا شخص دون آخر، مَا لم يكن هُنَاكَ قرينَة تدل على الِاخْتِصَاص.

To continue, any report that provides knowledge on a particular happening must also provide knowledge on all other happenings. Also, anything that provides knowledge to one person must, by necessity, establish knowledge for all others, if they heard the same report. As such, a single report in a single circumstance cannot provide knowledge in one situation or to one person, and not apply to its equivalents. Unless, of course, there is some additional evidence that would indicate an exception to the rule.

وَيجوز حُصُول الْعلم بِخَبَر الْوَاحِد مَعَ الْقَرَائِن، لقِيَام الْقَرِينَة مقَام المخبرين فِي إِفَادَة الظَّن وتزايده، حَتَّى يجْزم بِهِ، كمن أخبرهُ وَاحِد بِمَوْت مَرِيض مشرف على الْمَوْت، ثمَّ مر ببابِهِ فَرَأى تابوتا على بَاب دَاره وصراخا وعويلا وانتهاك حَرِيم، فإننا نجزم بِمَوْت الشَّخْص الَّذِي أخبرنَا بِمَوْتِهِ، وَلَوْلَا إِخْبَار الْمخبر لجوزنا موت شخص آخر.

Knowledge can be gained with singular reports, as long as they have supporting evidences, since a supporting evidence can take the place of reporters in providing knowledge that borders on certainty, and could even go beyond simply bordering certainty, making it certain and factual. For example, one can be informed of the death of someone who was on the verge of dying, then, [the one informed] can pass by their house and see a coffin at the doorstep, and women wailing or screaming inside the house. As such, we can claim with certainty that the person who was said to be dead has, indeed died. Had one not been told of the death of that particular individual, we could have made a plausible assumption that some other resident of that household had died.

الثَّانِيَة: للتواتر ثَلَاثَة شُرُوط:

The second discussion: Recurrence has three conditions:

أولهَا: أَن يكون مُسْتَندا إِلَى مُشَاهدَة حس، بِأَن يُقَال: رَأينَا مَكَّة وبغداد، وَلَا يَصح التَّوَاتُر عَن مَعْقُول لاشتراك المعقولات فِي إِدْرَاك الْعُقَلَاء لَهَا.

First: It must be information of something proven by the senses. For example, one can say, "We saw Makkah and Baghdad." Recurrence does not apply to rational things, since all rational things share the commonality in being able to understand and infer that rational thing.[224]

ثَانِيهَا: اسْتِوَاء الطَّرفَيْنِ والواسطة فِي كَمَال الْعدَد، بِأَن يكون عدد التَّوَاتُر مَوْجُودا فِي الطَّبَقَة الْمُشَاهدَة، وَفِي الطَّبَقَة المخبرة، وَفِي الَّتِي بَينهمَا، بِحَيْثُ تكون كل وَاحِدَة من هَذِه الطَّبَقَات مستكملة لعدد التَّوَاتُر، فَلَو نقص بَعْضهَا عَن عدد التَّوَاتُر، خرج الْخَبَر عَن كَونه متواترا، والتحق بالآحاد.

Second: The beginning, end, and middle must all collectively meet the necessary number of people. Meaning, the group of people who saw or heard the initial report must have reached the requisite number to consider it a valid recurrent narration. Then, the group of people reporting must also fulfill the required number of people. Lastly, everyone in between [the original witnesses and the reporting group] must also fulfill the requisite number of people. If any of these groups do not reach the requisite number, it is no longer *mutawātir*, and it is then considered to be singular.

ثَالِثهَا: الْعدَد، وَقد اخْتلف الْعلمَاء فِي تَعْيِينه اخْتِلَافا كثيرا، وَالْحق إِن المخبرين يلْزم أَن يكون عددهمْ بَالغا مبلغا يمْتَنع فِي الْعَادة تواطؤهم على الْكَذِب، وَلَا يُقيد ذَلِك بِعَدَد معِين، بل ضابطه: حُصُول الْعلم الضَّرُورِيّ بِهِ. وَلَا تشْتَرط عَدَالَة المخبرين، وَلَا إسْلَامهمْ، وَلَا عدم انحصارهم فِي بلد أَو عدد، وَلَا عدم اتِّحَاد الدّين وَالنّسب، وَلَا عدم اعْتِقَاد نقيض الْمخبر بِهِ، وكتمان أهل التَّوَاتُر مَا يحْتَاج

224 [T] For example, two being half of four is not something subject to discussions on *tawātur*, as that rational judgement is not one specific only to specialists. Refer to *Sharḥ Mukhtaṣar al-Rawḍah* (2/87).

إِلَى نَقله مُمْتَنع وَفِي جَوَاز الْكَذِب على عدد التَّوَاتُر خلاف الْأَظْهر الْمَنْع.

Third: The scholars have a multiplicity of views when it comes to determining the exact number of people required for the report to be considered *mutawātir*. The truth is that those informing must reach such a high number which usually means they cannot all be telling a lie. This is not restricted to a particular number. The only maxim that can be used to determine a *mutawātir* narration is that it results in necessary knowledge. Also, the uprightness and righteousness of the narrators is not a precondition, nor is them being Muslim. Them all being from different places and of different religions and lineages are not preconditions. Also, it is not a precondition for them to not believe in the opposite of the report. It is impossible for people who report on a recurrent basis to all collude in hiding it. There is a difference of opinion on whether a number of people reaching the *mutawātir* level can all collectively lie, and the view which stands out as being correct is that it is impossible.

الثَّالِثَة: الْآحَاد، وَهُوَ مَا عدم شُرُوط التَّوَاتُر، أَو بَعْضهَا. وَعَن الإِمَام أَحْمد فِي حُصُول الْعلم بِخَبَر الْوَاحِد قولَانِ:

The third discussion: Singular reports are those that do not fit the conditions of *mutawātir* ones, or at least some of the conditions. There are two reports from al-Imām Aḥmad pertaining to whether or not singular narrations provide certain knowledge:

أَحدهمَا: لَا يحصل الْعلم بِهِ، وَهُوَ قول الْأَكْثَرين والمتأخرين من أَصْحَابه، قَالَ الطوفي: وَهُوَ الْأَظْهر من الْقَوْلَيْنِ.

First: They do not provide necessary knowledge. This is the view of the majority, as well as the later-day Ḥanbalī scholars. Al-Ṭūfī stated, "It is apparently the more veracious of the two views."[225]

وَالثَّانِي: يحصل بِهِ الْعلم، وَهُوَ قَول جمَاعَة من الْمُحدثين، قَالَ الْآمِدِيّ: وَهُوَ قَول بعض أهل الظَاهِر، وَحمل بعض الْعلمَاء قَول الإِمَام أَحْمد الثَّانِي على أَخْبَار مَخْصُوصَة كثرت رواتها، وتلقتها الْأمة بِالْقبُولِ، ودلت الْقَرَائِن على صدق ناقلها

225 [T] *Sharḥ Mukhtaṣar al-Rawḍah* (2/103).

فَيكون إِذن من الْمُتَوَاتر.

Second: It does provide necessary knowledge. This is the view of a group of ḥadīth scholars. Al-Āmidī stated, "This is the view of some adherents to the Ẓāhirī school." Some scholars interpreted this supposed second view of al-Imām Aḥmad to refer to specific narrations that have many narrators and all Muslims accept, and are shown to have supporting evidences indicating the truthfulness of the reporters. Therefore, they reach the level of *mutawātir*.

الرَّابِعَة: قسم المحدثون أَخْبَار الْآحَاد الصَّحِيحَة إِلَى سَبْعَة أَقسَام:

The fourth discussion: The scholars of ḥadīth have categorised the authentic singular reports into seven categories:

أَحدهَا: أَحَادِيث البُخَارِيّ وَمُسلم، وَهُوَ الْمعبر عَنهُ فِي عرفهم بالمتفق عَلَيْهِ، وَقد أفرد الْحَافِظ عبد الْغَنِيّ الْمَقْدِسِي أَحَادِيث الْأَحْكَام من هَذَا النَّوْع فِي كتاب سَمَّاهُ (عُمْدَة الْأَحْكَام) وَقد شرحته فِي مجلدين.

First: The aḥadīth of al-Bukhārī and Muslim. To refer to these aḥadīth, they say, "*Muttafaqun 'alayh* (agreed upon)." Al-Ḥāfiẓ 'Abd al-Ghani al-Maqdisī has authored a book called *'Umdat al-Aḥkām*, where he took aḥadīth from [al-Bukhārī and Muslim] pertaining to rulings. I have personally explained his book in two volumes.

وَثَانِيها: مَا انْفَرد بِهِ البُخَارِيّ عَن مُسلم.

Second: Aḥadīth that al-Bukhārī has reported and Muslim has not.

وَثَالِثهَا: مَا انْفَرد بِهِ مُسلم عَن البُخَارِيّ.

Third: Aḥadīth that Muslim has reported, but al-Bukhārī did not.

وَرَابِعهَا: مَا أخرجه الْأَئِمَّة بعدهمَا على شَرطهمَا.

Fourth: Aḥadīth that are reported by scholars after [al-Bukhārī and Muslim] upon their conditions of authenticity.

وخامسها: مَا خرج على شَرط البُخَارِيّ وَحده.

Fifth: Aḥadīth that have been reported and rely only on the conditions set by al-Bukhārī.

وسادسها: مَا خرج على شَرط مُسلم وَحده.

Sixth: Aḥadīth that have been reported that only rely on the conditions set by Muslim.

وَذَلِكَ كَمَا فِي (الْمُسْتَدْرك) على (الصَّحِيحَيْنِ) لأبي عبد الله الْحَاكِم وَغَيره.

An example of the last two categories is *al-Mustadrak 'ala al-Ṣaḥīḥayn*, by Abu 'Abdullah al-Ḥākim, and other books, as well.

وَمعنى التَّخْرِيج على شَرط الشَّيْخَيْنِ أَو شَرط أَحدهمَا أَنَّهُمَا اخْتلفَا فِي رُوَاة الحَدِيث لاخْتِلَاف صفاتهم الْمُعْتَبرَة عِنْدهمَا، فاتفقا على الْإِخْرَاج عَن طَائِفَة من الروَاة، وَانْفَرَدَ البُخَارِيّ بالرواية عَن طَائِفَة مِنْهُم، وَانْفَرَدَ مُسلم بالرواية عَن طَائِفَة، فَزعم المستدركون عَلَيْهِمَا أَنهم قد وجدوا أَحَادِيث قد رَوَاهَا من خرجا عَنهُ اتِّفَاقًا وانفرادا، وَمن سَاوَى من خرجا عَنهُ فخرجوها وَقَالُوا: هَذَا اسْتِدْرَاك عَلَيْهِمَا على شَرطهمَا أَو شَرط وَاحِد ومنهما.

The meaning of reporting according to the conditions of the two *shaykhs* (al-Bukhārī and Muslim), or according to the conditions of just one of them is that the two *shaykhs* differed in respect to the narrators of aḥadīth, because they differed on the qualities the narrator must have that affect their transmission of reports. They agreed on some narrators, al-Bukhārī held some others in high regard and reported from them individually, and Muslim held some others in high regard, and reported from them individually. Those that came later claimed that they found aḥadīth that were reported by the narrators that they agreed upon, the narrators that they individually reported from, or those who are of the same stature and level as those [previous two categories of narrators]. They essentially stated, "We are completing and correcting their works, based on the conditions they agreed on, or at least based on the conditions of either of them."

وسابعها: مَا أخرجه بَقِيَّة الْأَئِمَّة كَأبي دَاوُد، وَالتِّرْمِذِيّ، وَالنَّسَائِيّ وَغَيرهم من أَئِمَّة الحَدِيث. وَأَعْلَى هَذِه الْأَقْسَام الأول، وَهُوَ الْمُتَّفق عَلَيْهِ.

Seventh: Aḥadīth reported by the other scholars, such as Abu Dāwūd, al-Tirmidhī, al-Nasā'ī, and other scholars of ḥadīth. The highest category is the first one, namely, the aḥadīth agreed upon by al-Bukhārī and Muslim.

وَالتَّحْقِيق فِي أَحَادِيث (الصَّحِيحَيْنِ) أَنَّهَا مفيدة للظن الْقوي الْغَالِب، لما حصل فِيهَا من اجْتِهَاد الشَّيْخَيْنِ فِي نقد رجالها، وَتَحْقِيق أحوالها، أما حُصُول الْعلم بهَا، فَلَا مطمع فِيهِ، وَذَلِكَ فِي غَيرهَا من الْأَقْسَام الْأُخر أولى.

Also, the veracious view is that the aḥadīth of the two *Ṣaḥīḥ* collections provide knowledge that borders on certainty, since the two *shaykhs* have worked extensively and diligently to critique their narrators and ascertain their statuses in reporting. As for these aḥadīth providing necessary knowledge, there is no point in arguing that case [for al-Bukhārī and Muslim's aḥadīth], let alone the other categories.

الْخَامِسَة: يجوز التَّعَبُّد بِخَبَر الْوَاحِد وَالْعَمَل بِهِ، وَعَلِيهِ دلّ الْعقل والسمع، وَقد عمل كثير من الصَّحَابَة بِخَبَر الْوَاحِد، وَقد رَجَعَ الْكل إِلَى خبر عَائِشَة فِي الْغسْل بالتقاء الختانين، وَفِي كتب الحَدِيث كثير من ذَلِك.

The fifth discussion: It is permissible to base worship and act upon singular narrations, as indicated to by rational and textual arguments. Many of the companions acted on singular reports, and they all acted on the ḥadīth of 'Ā'ishah which states that one must perform purification from major ritual impurity if the two private areas touch. There are many instances of this in the books of ḥadīth.

السَّادِسَة: يعْتَبر فِي الرَّاوِي المقبول الشَّهَادَة شُرُوط وَهِي:

The sixth discussion: A number of conditions are considered with regards to the narrator whose narrations are accepted.[226]

الْإِسْلَام، وَاخْتلف فِي صِحَة الرِّوَايَة عَن المبتدعة، فَاخْتَارَ أَبُو الْخطاب قبُولهَا من

226 [T] Dr. 'Abdullah al-Turkī stated, "In the printed edition, it states, 'narrator whose testimony is accepted,' but what I have placed in the text is mentioned in other books of legal theory, and is more in line with the context." What he said is correct, and the manuscript also mentions "a number of conditions are considered with regards to the narrator whose testimony is accepted."

الْفَاسِق المتأول لحُصُول الْوَازِع أَي: الْكَاف لَهُ عَن الْكَذِب، وَهُوَ قَول الشَّافِعِي، وَقَالَ الطوفي من أَصْحَابنَا: الْمُحدث إِذا كَانَ ناقدا بَصيرًا جَازَ أَن يروي عَن جمَاعَة من المبتدعة الَّذين يفسقون ببدعتهم، كعباد بن يَعْقُوب الروَاجِنِي - بِالْجِيم وَالنُّون - وَكَانَ غاليا فِي التَّشَيُّع، وَجَرِير بن عُثْمَان، وَكَانَ يبغض عليا كرم الله وَجهه، وَفِي الحَدِيث: **«لَا يحبك إِلا مُؤمن وَلَا يبغضك إِلَّا مُنَافِق»**.

First: Islam. Also, scholars have differed if one can accept the reports of innovators. Abu 'l-Khaṭṭāb took the view that reports are accepted from sinful people who have some misinterpretation if the person has restraint, in the sense that he would not lie. This is the view of al-Shāfiʿī. Al-Ṭūfī, one of our *aṣḥāb*, stated, "If the scholar of ḥadīth is a critic and is versed, they may report from a group of innovators that are considered sinners due to the severity of their innovations, such as ʿAbbād ibn Yaʿqūb al-Rawājinī—who was an extreme Shiite, and Hurayz ibn ʿUthmān—who hated ʿAlī, may Allah honour his face. In the ḥadīth, it states, **'Only a believer loves you, and only a hypocrite hates you.'**"[227]

وَالثَّانِي الْعَدَالَة: وَهِي اعْتِدَال الْمُكَلف فِي سيرته شرعا بِحَيْثُ لَا يظْهر مِنْهُ مَا يشْعر بالجرأة على الْكَذِب، وتحصل بأَدَاء الْوَاجِبَات، وَاجْتنَاب الْمَحْظُورَات ولواحقها.

Second: The uprightness of the cognisant, legally responsible adult in their behavior in respect to their adherence to religious injunctions. No action should emanate from the reporter that would indicate they have a propensity to lie. The uprightness described is attained when one completes their obligations and avoids the prohibitions, and their concomitant actions.

وتعرف عَدَالَة الشَّخْص بِأُمُور:

The uprightness of a person can be realised via a number of ways:

أَحدهَا: الْمُعَامَلَة والمخالطة الْمُطلعة فِي الْعَادة على خبايا النُّفُوس ودسائسها.

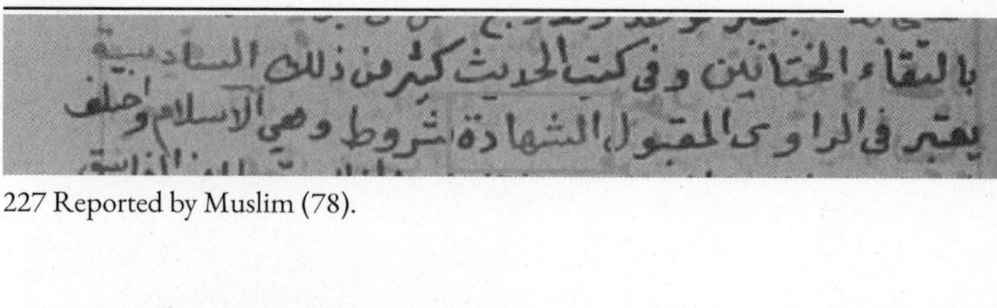
بالتقاء الختانين وفى كتب الحديث كثير من ذلك السادسة
يعتبر فى الراوى المقبول الشهادة شروط وهي الاسلام والحلف

227 Reported by Muslim (78).

One. By dealing with them and mixing with them to an extent where—normally—one would have enough information to know the secrets of their selves and their vices.

الثَّانِي: التَّزْكِيَة: وَهِي ثَنَاء من تثبت عَدَالَته عَلَيْهِ، وشهادته لَهُ بِالْعَدَالَةِ.

Two. Praise of others. Someone who is themselves upright can testify to their uprightness.

الثَّالِث: السمعة الجميلة المتواترة أَو المستفيضة، وبمثلها عرف عَدَالَة كثير من أَئِمَّة السّلف.

Three. A good reputation known by so many individuals that it becomes a recurrent theme. Many of the scholars of the Salaf are known to be upright through this way.

وَالثَّالِث: التَّكْلِيف، بِأَن يكون عَاقِلا بَالغا، إِذْ لَا مَانع للصَّبِيّ وَالْمَجْنُون عَن الْكَذِب، وَلَا عبَادَة لَهما، فَإِن سمع الرَّاوِي فِي حَال صغره، وروى بعد بُلُوغه، قبل قَوْله.

Third: They must be *mukallaf*; they must be cognisant and have reached the age of puberty, since there is no preventing of an insane person or child from lying, and since they are not tasked with any actions of worship. If a reporter heard something when he was still a child and then narrates it to others after becoming a pubescent, his statement is accepted.

الرَّابِع: أَن يكون ضابطا لما سَمعه حَالَة السماع، إِذْ لَا وثوق بقول من لَا ضبط لَهُ، فَأَما رِوَايَة مَجْهُول الْعَدَالَة، فروِيَ عَن أَحْمد - فِي أحد الْقَوْلَيْنِ عَنهُ - أَنَّهَا لَا تقبل، وَهُوَ قَول الشَّافِعِي. وَرُوِيَ عَنهُ أَنَّهَا تقبل، وَهُوَ قَول أبي حنيفَة. وَاتَّفَقُوا على أَنه لَا تقبل رِوَايَة مَجْهُول الإِسْلَام، والتكليف، والضبط.

Fourth: They must accurately and precisely recall what they heard when hearing narrations, since one cannot trust a person who has no accuracy in their reports. As for reports from those whose uprightness is unverified, it was reported that Aḥmad—in one of the two views reported from him—stated that the reports should not be accepted, thereby agreeing with al-

Shāfiʿī. It was also reported from Aḥmad that it should be accepted, which is coincidentally the view of Abu Ḥanīfah. They all agreed, though, that the reports from a person whose Islam, puberty, or accuracy are unverified are not accepted.

السَّابِعَة: لَا تشْترَط ذكورية الرَّاوِي وَلَا رُؤْيَته، لقبُول الصَّحَابَة خبر عَائِشَة من وَرَاء الْحجاب، وَلَا فقهه، وَلَا معرفَة نسبه، وَلَا يشْترَط أَن لَا يكون عدوا وَلَا قَرِيبا لمن رُوِيَ فِي حَقه خَبرا، وَمن اشْتبهَ اسْمه باسم مَجْرُوح، رد خَبره حَتَّى يعرف حَاله.

The seventh discussion: Maleness is not a condition for the narrator, nor is seeing the one reported from. The reason is that the companions accepted the reports of ʿĀʾishah when she reported from behind a curtain. Further, the narrator does not need to be a jurist, their lineage does not need to be known, and there is no condition stating they must not be either an enemy to or a friend of the one they are reporting about. If someone's namesake is a person who has been critiqued, their reports should be rejected until their individual status is known and verified.

الثَّامِنَة: الْجرْح - بِفَتْح الْجِيم - أَن ينْسب إِلَى الشَّخْص مَا يرد قَوْله لأَجله أَي: من قبيل مَعْصِيّة صَغِيرَة أَو كَبِيرَة، أَو ارْتِكَاب دنيئة، وَبِالْجُمْلَةِ أَن ينْسب إِلَيْهِ مَا يخل بِالْعَدَالَةِ الَّتِي هِيَ شَرط قبُول الرِّوَايَة.

The eighth discussion: The term *jarḥ* (critique) refers to ascribing to a person something that would cause their narrations to be rejected. This could include a lesser or major sin or doing some lowly action. Generally, it refers to a person being ascribed to anything that would cause their uprightness—which is a condition for the acceptance of their narrations—to be in question.

وَالتَّعْدِيل بِخِلَافِهِ، وَهُوَ: أَن ينْسب إِلَى الرَّاوِي من الْخَيْر والعفة والصيانة والمروءة والتدين بِفعل الْوَاجِبَات وَترك الْمُحرمَات مَا يسوغ قبُول قَوْله شرعا لدلَالَة هَذِه الْأَحْوَال على تحري الصدْق ومجانبة الْكَذِب، وَلَا خَفَاء فِي مَسِيس الْحَاجة إِلَى الْجرْح وَالتَّعْدِيل فِي هَذَا الْبَاب ليعلم من يَنْبَغِي الْأَخْذ عَنهُ من غَيره.

The opposite [of a *jarḥ*] is a *taʿdīl* (praise), which is to ascribe to a narrator some goodness, modesty, preservation of their religion, chivalry, and religiosity by doing the obligations and avoiding the prohibitions, where their report can be religiously accepted, since these actions indicate that a person is actively seeking to be truthful and avoid lying. The importance of *jarḥ* and *taʿdīl* in these matters is extremely important, so that one can know whom to accept from and whom not to.

وَمذهب الإِمَام أَحْمد أَن التَّعْدِيل لَا يشْترط بَيَان سَببه استصحابا لحَال الْعَدَالَة، وَبه قَالَ الشَّافِعِي، بِخِلَاف سَبَب الْجرْح، فَإِنَّهُ يشْترط بَيَانه فِي أحد الْقَوْلَيْنِ عَن أَحْمد، وَهُوَ القَوْل الْمَنْصُور عندنَا، وَذَلِك لاخْتِلَاف النَّاس فِي سَبَب الْجرْح واعتقاد بَعضهم مَا لَا يصلح أَن يكون سَبَب الْجرْح جارحا، كشرب النَّبِيذ متأولا، فَإِنَّهُ يقْدَح فِي الْعَدَالَة عِنْد مَالك دون غَيره، وَكَمن يرى إنْسَانا يَبُول قَائِما، فيبادر لجرحه بذلك، وأمثال هَذَا، فَيَنْبَغِي بَيَان سَبَب الْجرْح ليَكُون على ثِقَة واحتراز من الْخَطَأ والغلو فِيهِ.

The position of al-Imām Aḥmad is that the reason for praise of a person does not need to be clarified, due to the presumption of default uprightness [of the Muslim]. This view was also that of al-Shāfiʿī. However, as it pertains to critique, its reason must be clarified, according to one of the two views reported from Aḥmad and which has been supported by [Ḥanbalī scholars]. The reason why it must be clarified is that people differ in reasons for critiquing others, and some might consider something a reason to be a valid critique, while in reality it is not. An example is drinking *nabīdh* while believing it is allowed due to a misinterpretation. Al-Imām Mālik considered drinking *nabīdh* to malign one's uprightness, though others did not. Another example is if someone sees a person urinating while standing and hastily passes a judgement against him, and so forth. Therefore, the reason for critique must be clarified so that one is cautious and prudent, so as to not fall into mistakes or extremism in such matters.

وَيَنْبَغِي أَن يكون الْجَارِح عَالما باخْتلَاف الْمذَاهب فِي الْجرْح وَالتَّعْدِيل. وَإِذا تعَارض الْجرْح وَالتَّعْدِيل فالجرح مقدم، وَإِن زَاد عدد المعدلين لتَضَمّنه زِيَادَة خفيت على الْمعدل، وَهَذَا فِيمَا أمكن اطلَاع الْجَارِح على زِيَادَة، أما إِذا اسْتَحَالَ ذَلِك، مثل أَن قَالَ الْجَارِح: رَأَيْت هَذَا قد قتل زيدا فِي وَقت كَذَا، وَقَالَ الْمعدل:

رَأَيْت زيدا حَيا بعد ذَلِك الْوَقْت، فهاهنا يتعارضان فيتساقطان، وَيبقى أصل الْعَدَالَة ثَابتا.

The one critiquing must be aware of the varying schools and opinions in praise and criticism whilst critiquing. If a criticism and a praise conflict, the criticism should be given preference, even if the number of people who praised is more, because the one critic might have some additional information that was unknown to those praising. This, of course, is contingent on the one offering the critique being capable of knowing that additional information. As for if it is impossible for them to know such a thing, such as saying, "I saw this person kill Zayd at such-and-such time," and the one praising says, "I saw Zayd alive after the time you said he was killed," at this point, they are mutually exclusive, and cancel each other out. What remains, in that scenario, is the default status of being upright.

والمحدود فِي الْقَذْف إِن كَانَ الْقَذْف صدر مِنْهُ بِلَفْظ الشَّهَادَة بِأَن شهد عَلَيْهِ بِالزِّنَا مثلا وَردت شَهَادَته، قبلت رِوَايَته، وَلم يرد خَبره، وَإِن كَانَ بِغَيْر لفظ الشَّهَادَة، ردَّتْ رِوَايَته حَتَّى يَتُوب.

If someone is penalised due to slandering a person and accusing them of fornication, there are two cases. If the slander occurred via a wording of testimony [in front of a judge], by saying, "I saw this person committing fornication," and their testimony is rejected, their narrations are still acceptable and their reports are not rejected. However, if they do not do so with a wording of testimony, their narrations are rejected until they repent.

التَّاسِعَة: مَا يحصل بِهِ التَّعْدِيل ثَلَاثَة أَشْيَاء:

The ninth discussion: There are three ways a person can be declared credible:

أَحدهَا: صَرِيح القَوْل بِأَن يَقُول: هُوَ عدل رَضِي، مَعَ بَيَان السَّبَب.

One. They are explicitly stated to be credible, by saying, "This person is praiseworthy and acceptable," while also clarifying why.

الثَّانِي: الحكم بِشَهَادَتِهِ.

Two. Their testimonies are accepted.

الثَّالِث: الْعَمَل بِخَبَر الرَّاوِي بِشَرْط أَن يعلم أَن لَا مُسْتَند للْعَمَل غير رِوَايَته، وَإِلَّا لم يكن تعديلا، لاحْتِمَال أنه عمل بِدَلِيل آخر، وَافق رِوَايَة الرَّاوِي، وَكَانَت هِيَ زَائِدَة لَا حَاجَة إِلَيْهَا وَلَا معول عَلَيْهَا.

Three. [A scholar] acts on the reports of the narrator, so long as it is known that there is no evidence for the action other than this report. Otherwise, it is not a praise, because [the scholar] might have acted on another evidence that coincides with the report of the person in question. If that were the case, the [narration of the one in question] is superfluous and unneeded; it is not relied on.

الْعَاشِرَة: إن عرف من مَذْهَب الرَّاوِي، أَو عَادَته، أَو صَرِيح قَوْله أَنه لَا يرى الرِّوَايَة، أَو لَا يروي إِلا عَن عدل، كَانَت رِوَايَته تعديلا لمن روى عَنهُ، وَإِن لم يعلم ذَلِك، لم تكن رِوَايَته عَنهُ تعديلا لَهُ، إِذْ قد يروي الشَّخْص عَمَّن لَو سُئِلَ عَنهُ لسكت.

The tenth discussion: If the practice or explicit remark of a narrator shows that they only report from upright individuals or do not believe in narrating from non-credible sources, when they do narrate from someone, that is considered a praise and acknowledgement of that person's uprightness. If that is not known, their narration is not considered a praise, because a person could narrate from someone who, if he was asked about him he would remain silent [without offering praise].

الْحَادِيَة عشر: قَالَ أَصْحَابنَا وَالْجُمْهُور: الصَّحَابَة كلهم عدُول، لَا حَاجَة إِلَى الْبَحْث عَن عدالتهم، ومرادهم من لم يعرف بقدح، ذكره علاء الدين عَلي بن سُلَيْمَان المرداوي فِي (التَّحْرِير) وَقيل: لم يزَالُوا عُدُولًا حَتَّى وَقع الْخلاف بَينهم واقتتلوا، وَهَذَا القَوْل ينْسب إِلَى وَاصل بن عَطاء وَأَصْحَابه الواصلية. وَقيل: هم كغيرهم من رُوَاة الْأمة، فيبحث عَن عدالتهم.

The eleventh discussion: Our *aṣḥāb* and the majority stated that all of the companions are upright. There is no need to ascertain their uprightness. They mean, of course, those that are not known to have been criticised. This was mentioned by ʿAlā al-Dīn ʿAlī ibn Sulaymān al-Mardāwī in *al-Taḥrīr*. It was stated that they were upright until their differences and infighting. This was opined by Wāṣil ibn ʿAṭā' and his disciples. Others stated that they are similar to other narrators in the Ummah, and their uprightness should be ascertained.

والصحابي من لَقِي النَّبِي صلى الله عَلَيْهِ وَسلم، أَو رَآهُ يقظة حَيا عِنْد الإِمَام أَحْمد وَأَصْحَابه وَالْبُخَارِيّ وَالْأَكْثَر، مُسلما، وَلَو ارْتَدَّ ثمَّ أسلم وَلم يره، وَمَات عَلَيْهِ وَلَو جنيا فِي الْأَظْهر. وَقيل: من طَالَتْ صحبته عرفا، وَحكي عَن الْأَكْثَر، وَقيل: من صَحبه سنة، أَو غزا مَعَه، أَو روى عَنهُ، وَالْقَوْل الأول أولى.

A companion is defined as someone who met the Prophet ﷺ or saw him while awake, and while the Prophet ﷺ was alive. This was the view of al-Imām Aḥmad and his disciples, al-Bukhārī, and the majority. Another condition is that he must have been Muslim, even if [the companion] who saw him later apostatised, but then returned to Islam and did not see him a second time, and then died as a Muslim. The companion can be of the *jinn*, as well, according to the more apparent view. Some said that [a companion is] someone who accompanied the Prophet ﷺ for an extended period that is usually considered lengthy. This was stated to be the majority view. Some said that the companion is someone who accompanied the Prophet ﷺ for a year, went to war with him, or reported from him. The first view is most ideal.

وَيعلم كَونه صحابيا بأخبار غَيره بِأَنَّهُ صَحَابِيّ اتِّفَاقًا، فَلَو أخبر عَن نَفسه بِأَنَّهُ صَحَابِيّ فَقَالَ أَصْحَابنَا، وَالْأَكْثَر: يقبل قَوْله، وَقَالَ جمع: لَا يقبل.

A person is known to be a companion by the reports of others, where they state they were a companion, according to the view agreed on by most scholars. Or, they can claim to be companions themselves. Our *aṣḥāb* and the majority stated that their claim should be accepted, while others said it should not.

وَالْقَوْل فِي التَّابِعِيّ مثل القَوْل فِي الصَّحَابِيّ، إِلَّا فِي إِثْبَات الْعَدَالَة. وَشرط ابْن حبَان كَونه فِي سنّ يحفظ فِيهِ عَن الصَّحَابِيّ، وَاشْترط الْخَطِيب الْبَغْدَادِيّ وَجمع الصُّحْبَة.

The same can be said about the successors of the companions (*Tābiʿīn*), except in ascertaining their uprightness. Ibn Ḥibbān stated that, to be considered a successor of the companions, one must have been of an age where they can memorise things the companions said. Al-Khaṭīb al-Baghdādī and a group of scholars stated that it is a condition for them to have accompanied the companions for a while.

الثَّانِيَة عشرَة: الرَّاوِي إِمَّا أَن يكون صحابيا أَو غير صَحَابِيّ، فالصحابي لألفاظ رِوَايَته مَرَاتِب:

The twelfth discussion: A reporter could either be a companion or could not be a companion. When a companion narrates, the way they express their narration is of varying levels:

أقواها: أَن يَقُول: سَمِعت رَسُول الله صلى الله عَلَيْهِ وَسلم يَقُول، أَو حَدثنِي، أَو أَخْبرنِي، أَو نَبأَنِي، أَو شافهني، وَهُوَ الأَصْل فِي الرِّوَايَة.

The strongest level is when they say, "I heard Allah's Messenger ﷺ say," or, "Allah's Messenger ﷺ informed me," "Told me," "Stated to me," or "Spoke to me, [directly.]" This is the default in respect to narrations.

ثمَّ بعد هَذَا قَالَ رَسُول الله صلى الله عَلَيْهِ وَسلم، لكنه دون سَمِعت فِي الْقُوَّة، لاحْتِمَال الْوَاسِطَة فِي قَوْله: قَالَ.

The next level is when they say, "Allah's Messenger ﷺ said." It is lesser in strength than when the companion says, "I heard," since there is a possibility of a medium between them and the Prophet ﷺ when they merely say, "He said."

ثمَّ بعده أَمر رَسُول الله بِكَذَا، وَنهى عَن كَذَا، أَو أمرنَا بِكَذَا، ونهينا عَن كَذَا، أَو رخص لنا أَو حرم علينا، وَهَذَا كُله حجَّة عندنَا وَعند الشَّافِعِي، وَالْأَكْثَر. وَمثله قَوْله: من السّنة كَذَا، وَكُنَّا نَفْعل، وَنَحْوه على عهد النَّبِي صلى الله عَلَيْهِ وَسلم كَذَا، وَكَانُوا يَفْعَلُونَ كَذَا، لَكِن قَوْله: كَانُوا يَفْعَلُونَ، إِن أضيف إِلَى عهد النبوَّة كَانَ حجَّة إقرارية، وَإِن لم يضف إِلَى عهد النبوَّة، لم يكن حجَّة إقرارية، بل يكون إِجْمَاعًا ظنيا لَا قَطْعِيا. قَالَ أَبُو الْخطاب: وَيقبل قَول الصَّحَابِيّ: هَذَا الْخَبَر

مَنْسُوخ، وَيرجع فِي تَفْسِير الْخَبَر إِلَيْهِ.

The next level is when the companion says, "Allah's Messenger ﷺ commanded such-and-such," "Allah's Messenger ﷺ forbade such-and-such," "We were commanded to such-and-such," "We were forbidden from such-and-such," "We were granted a dispensation," "Made forbidden to us was," and so forth. All of these ways of expressing reporting from the Prophet ﷺ are evidences, according to [Ḥanbalī scholars], al-Shāfiʿī, and the majority. Of this level is when the companion says, "It is the Sunnah to do such-and-such," "We used to do such-and-such," and others, when they mention that they used to do those things during the time of the Prophet ﷺ. However, when they say, "We used to do such-and-such," if it is mentioned that they were doing these things during the time of the Prophet ﷺ then it is evidence in the sense that the Prophet ﷺ confirmed their actions. However, if it is not stated they did those things during the time of the Prophet ﷺ, it is not considered evidence of approval, but rather, it is considered a speculative consensus, not a definitive one. Abu 'l-Khaṭṭāb stated, "The statement of the companion is accepted when they say, 'This report is abrogated.' To understand reports, one must refer to the companions."[228]

الثَّالِثَة عشر: الرِّوَايَة عَن غير الصَّحَابِيّ لَهَا مَرَاتِب:

The thirteenth discussion: The narrations of non-companions are of varying levels:

إحداهَا: سَمَاعه قِرَاءَة الشَّيْخ لِلْحَدِيث على جِهَة إِخْبَاره للراوي أَنه من رِوَايَته لِيروي الرَّاوِي عَنهُ، فللراوي حِينَئِذٍ أَن يَقُول: سَمِعت فلَانا - يَعْنِي شَيْخه - يَقُول كَذَا، وَله أَن يَقُول: قَالَ فلَان، وحَدثنِي فلَان، وَأَخْبرنِي فلَان.

First: Hearing the teacher recite the ḥadīth by informing the narrator that they reported it from the one they heard from, allowing the listener to then repeat the narration to others. The narrator can then say, "I heard so-and-so

228 [T] *Sharḥ Mukhtaṣar al-Rawḍah* (2/196). This quote was provided by al-Ṭūfī. According to al-Ṭūfī, "Because the companion is most aware of what he heard. Their explanations could be either statement-based or action-based. For example, Ibn 'Umar ﷺ understood the ḥadīth of, **"The two sellers have the opt-out option, so long as they do not part,"** to mean parting in body. As such, after buying or selling something, he would walk a few paces, so as to effectuate the transaction." Refer to *Sharḥ Mukhtaṣar al-Rawḍah* (2/200-201).

(i.e. his teacher) say," or can say, "So-and-so said," "informed me," or, "told me."

الثَّانِيَة: أَن يقْرَأ الرَّاوِي على الشَّيْخ فَيَقُول الشَّيْخ: نعم، أَو يسكت، فَلهُ الرِّوَايَة عَنهُ بذلك، لظُهُور الصِّحَّة، والإجابة، ثمَّ لَهُ أَن يَقُول: أخبرنَا، وَحدثنَا فلَان، قِرَاءَة عَلَيْهِ.

Second: The narrator can recite to the teacher, and the *shaykh* can approve or remain silent. In that case, the narrator can narrate from the teacher, since the correctness of the report is shown or the teacher approved of it. Then, the narrator can say, "I was told by," or, "I was informed by," because they recited to them.

الثَّالِثَة: الْإِجَازَة، نَحْو: أجزت لَك أَن تروي عني الْكتاب الْفُلَانِيّ، أَو مَا صَحَّ عنْدك من مسموعاتي.

Third: Permission to narrate (*ijāzah*). For example, the teacher could say, "I have authorised you to report such-and-such book from me," or, "reports that I have narrated that are authentic to you."

والمناولة، نَحْو: خُذ هَذَا الْكتاب، فاروه عني، وَيَكْفِي مُجَرّد اللَّفْظ دون المناولة، فَيَقُول فِيهِمَا: حَدثنِي أَو أَخْبرنِي إجَازَة، فَإِن لم يقل ذَلِك، بل اقْتصر على قَوْله: حَدثنِي أَو أَخْبرنِي، فقد أجَازه قوم. وَالْحق أَنه لَا يجوز لإشعاره بِالسَّمَاعِ مِنْهُ، وَهُوَ كذب، وَلَو قَالَ: خُذ هَذَا الْكتاب، أَو هُوَ سَمَاعي، وَلم يقل: اروه عني، لم تجز رِوَايَته.

There is also a concept known as *munāwalah*, e.g., when the teacher gives a book to the student, allowing them to report it on their authority. It is enough to authorise them without saying the word "*munāwalah*." The reporter then can say, "I was told (or informed) through authority to report." Some have stated that it is allowed for the narrator to say, "I was informed (or told)," without explicitly stating that they received it via *ijāzah*. However, the correct view is that they may not do so, because it gives the impression that they heard the report directly, which is a lie. If the teacher says, "Take this book," or, "This book contains narrations that I heard," and did not say, "I authorise you to report from me," it is not permissible to narrate the reports in the books to others.

وَلَا يروي عَنهُ مَا وجده بِخَطِّهِ، لَكِن يَقُول: وجدت بِخَط فلَان وَتسَمى الوجادة. وَلَو قَالَ: هَذِه نُسْخَة صَحِيحَة من كتاب البُخَارِيّ وَنَحْوه، لم يجز رِوَايَتهَا عَنهُ مُطلقًا، وَلَا الْعَمَل بهَا إِن كَانَ مُقلدًا، إِذْ فَرْضه تَقْلِيد الْمُجْتَهد، وَإِن كَانَ مُجْتَهدا فَقَوْلَانِ: الْأَصَح الْجَوَاز.

The student also may not narrate the reports they find in the handwriting of the teacher. They may say, however, "I found in the handwriting of so-and-so," and this is known as the concept of *wijādah*. If they say, "This is an authentic copy of al-Bukhārī's book etc.," the student may not report from it nor act on it if they are blind-followers, since their obligation is to follow a *mujtahid* scholar. If they are a *mujtahid* scholar, there are two views, and the more correct view is that they may follow them.

وَلَا يروي عَن شَيْخه مَا شكّ فِي سَمَاعه مِنْهُ، فَلَو شاع الحَدِيث الْمَشْكُوك فِي سَمَاعه فِي مسموعات الرَّاوِي، وَلم يتَمَيَّز، فَلم يعلم: هَل هُوَ هَذَا الحَدِيث أَو هَذَا، أَو هَل هُوَ هَذَا الْكتاب أَو هَذَا، لم يرو شَيْئا من مسموعاته، فَإِن ظن أَنه وَاحِد مِنْهَا بِعَيْنِه، أَو أَن هَذَا الحَدِيث مسموع لَهُ، فَفِي جَوَاز الرِّوَايَة اعْتِمَادًا على الظَّن خلاف.

One should not report things from their teacher that they doubt they heard. If the ḥadīth wherein they are doubtful of its hearing is confused with one that they truly heard, and they cannot differentiate between them (or between books) and do not know which is which, they should not report any of their narrations. If they have probable belief that it is a particular ḥadīth, or that the ḥadīth they are about to narrate is one they heard directly, the scholars have differed on whether they can narrate based on their probable belief.

وإنكار الشَّيْخ الحَدِيث غير قَادِح فِي رِوَايَة الْفَرْع لَهُ، وَيحمل إِنْكَار الشَّيْخ على نسيانه جمعا بَينهمَا، وَإِذا وجد سَمَاعه بِخَط يثق بِهِ، وَغلب على ظَنه أَنه سَمعه، جَازَ أَن يرويهِ، وَإِن لم يذكر السماع.

If a teacher denies teaching a ḥadīth, it does not affect the truthfulness of the student narrating from them, and the rejection of the teacher is interpreted as the teacher simply being forgetful, so that neither are belied. If someone finds aḥadīth they heard in their own handwriting and they trust it is theirs, and they have probable belief that they heard those narrations, they can narrate them, even if it is not explicitly mentioned in their handwriting that they heard those narrations.

الرَّابِعَة عشرَة: الزِّيَادَة من الثِّقَة مَقْبُولَة، لفظية كَانَت أَو معنوية، كالحديث التَّام وَأولى.

The fourteenth discussion: Additions to a narration, if done by a trustworthy narrator, are accepted, irrespective if they are verbal or simply adding meanings. It resembles a full ḥadīth, and *a fortiori* it is accepted.[229]

الْخَامِسَة عشرة: الْجُمْهُور على قبُول مُرْسل الصَّحَابِيّ، أما مُرْسل غير الصَّحَابِيّ كَقَوْل من لم يعاصر النَّبِي صلى الله عَلَيْهِ وَسلم: قَالَ النَّبِي صلى الله عَلَيْهِ وَسلم وَمن لم يعاصر أَبَا هُرَيْرَة: قَالَ أَبُو هُرَيْرَة، فَفِيهِ قَولَانِ: الْقبُول: وَهُوَ مَذْهَب مَالك وَأبي حنيفَة، وَاخْتَارَهُ القَاضِي وَجَمَاعَة من الْمُتَكَلِّمين. وَالْمَنْع: وَهُوَ قَول الشَّافِعِي وَبَعض الْمُحدثين.

The fifteenth discussion: The majority of scholars accept the *mursal* reports of companions. As for *mursal* narrations belonging to non-companions, such as those not contemporaneous with the Prophet ﷺ saying, "The Prophet ﷺ said," or someone not contemporaneous with Abu Hurayrah saying, "Abu Hurayrah said," the scholars have two views on whether it should be accepted. The first view states that it should be accepted, and that

229 [T] The argument here, as quoted by al-Imām Najm al-Dīn al-Ṭūfī, is twofold. The first is, "It is analogous to a full ḥadīth that a trustworthy reporter individually narrates. An addendum is *a fortiori* worthier of acceptance, since it is not an independent narration, but rather, is appended to another narration. If a full ḥadīth reported independently is to be accepted, *a fortiori* one that is not independent should be accepted." This is as it pertains to what al-Shaykh Ibn Badrān mentioned. As for the second argument for accepting the additions of trustworthy narrators, he said, "The second perspective is that a trustworthy narrator adding to the wording is possible, and in this case, the narrator has informed of the addition [that they heard]. Everything that is a possibility and also told of by a trustworthy person must be accepted." Refer to *Sharḥ Mukhtaṣar al-Rawḍah* (2/221).

was the view of Mālik, Abu Ḥanīfah, al-Qāḍī, and a group of scholars of *kalām*. Others stated that it is not permissible, and that is the view of al-Shāfiʿī and some ḥadīth masters.

السَّادِسَة عشرة: الْجُمْهُور يقبل خبر الْوَاحِد فِيمَا تعم بِهِ الْبلوى، كرفع الْيَدَيْنِ فِي الصَّلَاة، وَنقض الْوضُوء بِمَسّ الذّكر، وَنَحْوهمَا، وَالْمرَاد مِمَّا تعم بِهِ الْبلوى مَا يكثر التَّكْلِيف بِهِ.

The sixteenth discussion: The majority accept singular reports in matters that are considered generally popular occurrences among people (*ʿumam al-balwā*), such as raising the hands in prayer, invalidating purification by touching the privates, and so forth. When I refer to popular occurrences among people, I mean that people are often tasked with the responsibility of performing those things.

وَيقبل أَيْضا فِيمَا يسْقط بِالشُّبُهَاتِ كالحدود، وَفِيمَا يُخَالف الْقيَاس، وَفِيمَا يُخَالف الْأُصُول أَو معنى الْأُصُول. وَالْفرق بَين الْمَسْأَلَتَيْنِ أَن الْقيَاس أخص من الْأُصُول، إِذْ كل قِيَاس أصل، وَلَيْسَ كل أصل قِيَاسا. فَمَا خَالف الْقيَاس قد خَالف أصلا خَاصًّا، وَمَا خَالف الْأُصُول يجوز أَن يكون مُخَالفا لقياس، أَو نَص، أَو إِجْمَاع، أَو استِدْلَال، أَو اسْتِصْحَاب، أَو اسْتِحْسَان، أَو غير ذَلِك. فقد يكون الْخَبَر مُخَالفا لِلْقِيَاسِ مُوَافقا لبَعض الْأُصُول.

Singular reports are also accepted in things that waive with doubts, such as the penalties of Islam. They are also accepted when they contradict analogies and when they contradict legal principles or the ramifications of principles. The difference between the two cases is that analogy is more specific than the concept of legal principles, since every analogy is a foundational legal principle, but not every legal principle is an analogy. Therefore, anything that contradicts analogies has contradicted just one fundamental legal principle, but if some report contradicts "legal principles," as a broad terminology, it might contradict an analogy, a divine text, a consensus, an inference, a presumption of continuity, or due to favouring another evidence etc. A report could contradict analogy but could coincide with other legal principles.

وَقد يكون بِالْعَكْس، كانتقاض الْوضُوء بِالنَّوْمِ مُوَافق للْقِيَاس من أنه تَعْلِيق الحكم بمظنته كَسَائِر الْأَحْكَام الْمُعَلقَة بمظانها، وَهُوَ مُخَالف لبَعض الْأُصُول - وَهُوَ الِاسْتِصْحَاب - إِذْ الأَصْل عدم خُرُوج الْحَدث.

The opposite could also be true. For example, the nullification of ablution that occurs when one sleeps is in line with analogy, because it connects a ruling to its likely cause, such as other rulings that are tied to their likely cause. However, this ruling contradicts other legal principles, i.e. presumption of continuity, when considering that by default, one has not nullified their ablution.

وَقد يكون مُخَالفا لَهما جَمِيعًا كَخَبَر الْمُصراة، فَإِن الْقيَاس كَمَا دلّ على ضَمَان الشَّيْء بِمثلِهِ، كَذَلِك النَّص وَالْإِجْمَاع دَلا على ذَلِك، وَقد يكون مُوَافقا لَهما كالآثار الْوَارِدَة فِي تَحْرِيم النَّبِيذ، مُوَافقَة لقياسه على الْخمر، وَالنَّص وَالْإِجْمَاع على تَحْرِيمهَا، وَالنَّص على تَحْرِيم كل مُسكر، وأصحابنا لم يتْركُوا حَدِيث القهقهة لمُخَالفته الْقيَاس، بل لعدم صِحَّته عِنْدهم.

And the ruling could contradict both cases together, such as the ḥadīth reported on tying the udders of livestock. Analogy would dictate that liability is equal to the item, as have divine texts and consensus.[230] A ruling could also be in agreement with both, such as the narrations about prohibiting *nabīdh*, which is analogous to wine, and wine is prohibited by divine texts and consensus. The texts state that every intoxicant is unlawful. As for the ḥadīth of laughing,[231] our *aṣḥāb* did not abandon that ḥadīth due to its con-

230 [T] The Prophet ﷺ said, **"Do not tie the udders of camel and goats [to give the false impression that they have large amounts of milk]. Whoever buys such an animal has two options: they may choose to keep [the animal], or, they can return [the animal] and supplement [the return] with a *sā*ʿ of dates."** Reported by al-Bukhārī (4/361) and Muslim (5/165-167) Note that a *sā*ʿ is an old measurement, and its equivalent in modern standards of weight is 2036 grams, or 2.036 kilograms (refer to *Naẓm al-Maqādir al-Sharʿiyyah* by Dr. ʿĀmir Bahjat). The summary of this issue is that, if we were to use analogy, the person would only have to return the amount of milk they used, since that would be equivalent to the milk they took from the udder of the livestock. However, contrary to that analogy is this text, which states that if they return the animal, they must also return a *sā*ʿ of dates.

231 The ḥadīth is reported by ʿAbd al-Razzaq in his *Musannaf* (3761), from Abu 'l-ʿĀlīyah al-Riyāḥayy who reported that a blind man tripped into a well while the

tradiction to analogy, but rather because they did not consider it authentic.

السَّابِعَة عشرة: تجوز رِوَايَة الحَدِيث بِالْمَعْنَى المطابق للفظ للعارف بمقتضيات الْأَلْفَاظ الْفَارِق بَينهَا. قَالَ الْقَرَافِيّ: يجوز بِثَلَاثَة شُرُوط: أَن لَا يزِيد فِي التَّرْجَمَة، وَلَا ينقص، وَلَا يكون أخْفى من لفظ الشَّارِع.

The seventeenth discussion: It is permissible to report a ḥadīth by conveying its meaning using equivalent terms [as in the original ḥadīth]. This is contingent on a person being aware of the connotations of words and able to differentiate between them. Al-Qarāfī stated, "It is permissible with three conditions: (i) They must not add to the translation, (ii) they must not subtract from the narration, and (iii) they must not use verbiage that is less clear than the terms used by the legislator."[232]

تَتِمَّة: ذهب الإِمَام أَحْمد، وَتَبعهُ موفق الدّين الْمَقْدِسِي، وَالْأَكْثَر إِلَى أَنه يعْمل بِالْحَدِيثِ الضَّعِيف فِي الْفَضَائِل، وَقَالَ شيخ الْإِسْلَام أَحْمد ابن تَيْمِية: يعْمل بِهِ فِي التَّرْغِيب والترهيب، لَا فِي إِثْبَات مُسْتَحبّ وَغَيره. وَرُوِيَ الْمَنْع عَن أَحْمد أيضا، وَكَانَ يكْتب حَدِيث الرجل الضَّعِيف للاعتبار وَالِاسْتِدْلَال بِهِ مَعَ غَيره. وَقَالَ الْخلال فِي (الْجَامِع): لَا يحْتَج بِحَدِيث ضَعِيف فِي المأثم. وَقَالَ: مَذْهَب أَحْمد القَوْل بِالْحَدِيثِ الضَّعِيف أَو المضطرب إِذا لم يكن لَهُ معَارض. وَقد تقدم مثل ذَلِك عِنْد الْكَلَام على أصُول الإِمَام أَحْمد فَلْيُرَاجع.

In conclusion, it was held by al-Imām Aḥmad—and Muwaffaq al-Dīn al-Maqdisī followed him in this—and the majority that weak aḥadīth may be implemented in matters pertaining to virtuous actions. Shaykh al-Islam Aḥmad ibn Taymiyyah stated, "It is permissible to act on [weak aḥadīth] in matters pertaining to encouragement and warning, not in establishing some action to be recommended or anything else."[233] The prohibition [of using weak aḥadīth] has also been reported from Aḥmad, and he would record the

---

Prophet ﷺ was leading his companions in prayer, and some of the people praying laughed. The Prophet ﷺ them commanded those who laughed to perform ablution over and to pray again. The narrators of the ḥadīth are all trustworthy, but it is a *mursal* report.

232 [T] *Sharḥ Tanqīḥ al-Fuṣūl* (p. 380).

233 [T] *Majmūʿ al-Fatāwā* (18/68).

aḥadīth of weak narrators just to use them as supplementary evidences to be used with other evidences. Al-Khallāl said in *al-Jāmi'*, "Weak aḥadīth are not used to establish prohibition." He also said, "The *madhhab* of Aḥmad is that he would adhere to weak or unsound aḥadīth if there were no contradictions to [those narrations]." This has previously been discussed when I mentioned the foundations of al-Imām Aḥmad, so refer to that section.

وَلما كَانَ النّسخ لاحقا للْكتاب وَالسّنة مَعًا عقبناهما بقولنا.

Since abrogation has a subsequent relationship to the Qur'ān and Sunnah, the next chapter will discuss it:

بَاب النّسخ

A Chapter on Abrogation

هُوَ فِي اللُّغَة: الرّفْع والإزالة. وَقد يُرَاد بِهِ مَا يشبه النَّقْل نَحْو: نسخت الْكتاب.

In Arabic, the word *naskh* refers to lifting and removing something. It can also be used in a way to refer to the transfer of something, such as when one says, "I copied (did *naskh* of) the book."

وَفِي اصْطِلَاح الْأُصُولِيِّينَ: هُوَ رفع الحكم الثَّابِت بطرِيق شَرْعِي بِمثلِهِ متراخ عَنهُ، فَيدْخل مَا ثَبت بِالْخِطَابِ، أَو مَا قَامَ مقَامه من إِشَارَة أَو إِقْرَار فِي النَّاسِخ والمنسوخ، وَهُوَ جَائِز عقلا، وواقع سمعا فِي الْكتاب وَالسّنة بِلَا خلاف فِي ذَلِك بَين الْمُسلمين.

And in the terminology of the legists, it refers to abrogation of an established ruling in a legal way by replacing it with another religious ruling that is implemented at a later time. Therefore, abrogation is inclusive of rulings established via direct instructions, or anything that has the same legal weight, such as by indication, or affirmation. Abrogation is rationally conceivable and has occurred in the Qur'ān and Sunnah. No Muslims have disagreed on this fact.

وَفَائِدَته: أَن الله تَعَالَى علم الْمصلحَة فِي الحكم تَارَة، فأثبته بِالشَّرْع، وَعلم الْمفْسدَة فِيهِ تَارَة، فنفاه بالنسخ، وَهَذَا لَا بداء فِيهِ، لأننا نقطع بِكَمَال علم الله تَعَالَى، والبداء يُنَافِي كَمَال الْعلم.

The point of abrogation is that Allah the Exalted knows that a ruling has the general and overall benefit of humanity in a moment, and therefore, establishes that ruling in the legislation. Then, He knows that it is harmful to society and humanity in another instance, so He nullifies it through abrogation. This does not indicate a change in Allah's Divine Knowledge or that He learned something He was previously unaware of, since we can conclusively state that the knowledge of Allah the Exalted is complete, and the concept of change in Allah's divine knowledge is irreconcilable with the completeness of Allah's knowledge.

وللنسخ فَائِدَتَانِ:

Abrogation has two benefits:

أحدهمَا: رِعَايَة الْأَصْلَح للمكلفين تفضلا من الله تَعَالَى لَا وجوبا.

First: It caters to what is best for responsible individuals. It is a favour from Allah the Exalted, and it is not obligatory on Allah to provide it.

ثَانِيهمَا: امتحان الْمُكَلّفين بامتثالهم الْأَوَامِر والنواهي، خُصُوصا فِي أمرهم بِمَا كَانُوا منهيين عَنهُ، ونهيهم عَمَّا كَانُوا مأمورين بِهِ، فَإِن الانقياد لَهُ أدل على الْإِيمَان وَالطَّاعَة، وَفِي هَذَا الْبَاب شذرات:

Second: It tests responsible people in their adherence to commandments and abstention from prohibitions, especially in matters that they were previously forbidden from doing, and forbidding them from doing previously allowed actions. Submission in such cases is evidence of one's faith and obedience. There are a number of useful discussions to be had on this topic:

الأولى: يجوز نسخ التِّلَاوَة وَالْحكم، وإحكامهما - بِكَسْر الْهمزة - أَي: إبقائهما محكمين غير منسوخين، وَيجوز نسخ اللَّفْظ فَقَط دون الْمَعْنى، وَنسخ الْمَعْنى دون اللَّفْظ، وَأَنت إِذا تَأَمَّلت هَذَا الْمقَام وجدته سِتَّة أَقسَام:

The first discussion: Abrogation could be of a recitation and of a ruling. The opposite of abrogation is establishment, which is to state the ruling or recitation's continuity, thereby denying their abrogation. Further, it is possible that a word is abrogated, but its meaning is not, and it is possible that a meaning is abrogated, but its wording is not. If you were to closely consider this discussion, you would realise there are six types:

الأول: مَا نسخ حكمه وَبَقِي رسمه، كنسخ آيَة ﴿الْوَصِيَّةُ لِلْوَالِدَيْنِ وَالْأَقْرَبِينَ﴾ [الْبَقَرَة: ١٨٠]، بِآيَة الْمَوَارِيث، وَنسخ الْعدة حولا بالعدة أَرْبَعَة أشهر وَعشرا.

One. Abrogation of a ruling but continuity of the text. For example, the following verse was abrogated: **{It is prescribed that when death approaches any of you—if they leave something of value—a will should be made in favour of parents and immediate family with fairness. This is an obligation on those who are mindful of Allah.}** [Qur'ān 2:180] This was abrogated by the verse of heirs[: **{Concerning your children, Allah commands you that a son should have the equivalent share of two daughters. If there are only daughters, two or more should share two-thirds of the inheritance, if one, she should have half. Parents inherit a sixth each if the deceased leaves children; if he leaves no children and his parents are his sole heirs, his mother has a third, unless he has brothers, in which case she has a sixth. [In all cases, the distribution comes] after payment of any bequests or debts. You cannot know which of your parents or your children is more beneficial to you: this is a law from Allah, and He is all knowing, all wise.}** [Qur'ān 4:11]] Another example is the waiting period for a woman, which was abrogated from one year to four months and ten days.

الثَّانِي: مَا نسخ حكمه ورسمه، وَثَبت حكم النَّاسِخ ورسمه، كنسخ اسْتِقْبَال بَيت الْمُقَدّس باستقبال الْكَعْبَة.

Two. Abrogation of a ruling and the text, while the abrogating ruling and text remains. For example, facing Jerusalem was abrogated and replaced with facing the Kaʿbah.

الثَّالِث: مَا نسخ حكمه وَبَقِي رسمه، وَرفع رسم النَّاسِخ وَبَقِي حكمه، كَقَوْلِه تَعَالَى ﴿فَأَمْسِكُوهُنَّ فِي الْبُيُوتِ حَتَّى يَتَوَفَّاهُنَّ الْمَوْتُ﴾ [النِّسَاء: ١٥]، الْآيَة نسخت بقوله تَعَالَى: «الشَّيْخ وَالشَّيْخَة إِذا زَنَيَا فَارْجُمُوهُمَا أَلْبَتَّة نكالا من الله». وَقد ثَبت فِي الصَّحِيح أن هَذَا كَانَ قُرْآنا يُتْلَى ثمَّ نسخ لَفظه وَبَقِي حكمه.

Three. Abrogation of a ruling while the text remains, and abrogation of the text of the abrogating text while the ruling remains. For example, Allah the Exalted states: **{If any of your women commit a lewd act, call four witnesses from among you, then, if they testify to their guilt, keep the women at home until death comes to them or until Allah shows them another way.}** [Qur'ān 4:15] This verse was abrogated by another verse, which states, "An elder man and woman, if they commit fornication, stone them, absolutely, as a cautionary punishment from Allah." This has been authentically reported in the *Ṣaḥīḥ* as being a part of the Qur'ān, but then the text was abrogated, though the ruling remained.[234]

الرَّابِع: مَا نسخ حكمه ورسمه، وَنسخ رسم النَّاسِخ وَبَقِي حكمه، كَمَا ثَبت فِي الصَّحِيح. عَن عَائِشَة أَنَّهَا قَالَت: كَانَ فِيمَا أنزل: عشر رَضعَات مُتَتَابِعَات يحرمن، فنسخت بِخمْس رَضعَات، فتوفي رَسُول الله وَهن فِيمَا يُتْلَى من الْقُرْآن.

Four. Abrogation of a ruling and a text, and abrogation of the text of the abrogating text but its ruling remaining. For example, it is authentically reported in the *Ṣaḥīḥ* that 'Ā'ishah stated, "One of the verses revealed was, 'Nursing ten times makes one forbidden for marriage,' but the verse was abrogated, and the ruling was made to five times. Allah's Messenger ﷺ passed away while that was recited in the Qur'ān."[235]

قَالَ الْبَيْهَقِيّ: فالعشر مِمَّا نسخ رسمه وَحكمه، وَالْخمس نسخ رسمه وَبَقِي حكمه، بِدَلِيل أَن الصَّحَابَة حِين جمعُوا الْقُرْآن لم يثبتوها رسما، وَحكمهَا بَاقٍ عِنْدهم.

Al-Bayhaqī stated, "Therefore, the ruling on nursing ten times was abrogated as was its text, and the text of nursing five times was abrogated, though its ruling remained. The evidence is that when the companions gathered the Qur'ān into a single corpus, they did not write that verse. However, its

234 Reported by al-Bukhārī (12/128-131) from 'Abdullah ibn 'Abbās, who said that 'Umar ibn al-Khaṭṭāb stated, while sitting on the pulpit of Allah's Messenger ﷺ, "Allah has sent Muḥammad ﷺ with the truth and has sent to him the Book. One of the verses revealed was the verse on stoning. I fear that, over the course of time, someone will say, 'We do not find stoning in the Book of Allah,' and thereby become misguided by abandoning an obligation that Allah the Exalted has revealed. Truly, stoning is in the Book of Allah; that it is incumbent that if a man or woman marry and then commit adultery, they must be stoned, if the proof is established, pregnancy occurs, or either of them admit to it."

235 Reported by Mālik (2/608). The meaning is that the abrogation that occurred via nursing five times was one of the latest verses revealed to the Prophet ﷺ, to the point that when he passed away, some were still reciting it as part of the Qur'ān, because they were not aware that it was abrogated. When it became common knowledge, those who initially took that view ceased and they unanimously attested to it not being recited as part of the Qur'ān.

ruling remained intact."[236]

قَالَ ابْن السَّمْعَانِيّ: معنى قَوْلهَا: وَهِي فِيمَا يُتْلَى من الْقُرْآن، أَنه يُتْلَى حكمهَا دون لَفظهَا، وَقَالَ الْبَيْهَقِيّ: الْمَعْنى أَنه يتلوه من لم يبلغهُ نسخ تِلَاوَته.

Ibn al-Samʿānī stated, "The meaning of her statement, 'that was recited in the Qur'ān,' is that its ruling was recited, though its wording was not."[237] Al-Bayhaqī also said, "It means that those who were unaware of the abrogation of the textual part were still reciting it."

الْخَامِس: مَا زَالَ رسمه لَا حكمه، وَلَا يعلم النَّاسِخ لَهُ، كَمَا فِي الصَّحِيح **«لَو كَانَ لِابْنِ آدم واديان من ذهب لتمنى لَهما ثَالِثا لَا يمْلَأ جَوف ابْن آدم إِلَّا التُّرَاب وَيَتُوب الله على من تَابَ»** فَإِن هَذَا كَانَ قُرْآنا ثمَّ نسخ رسمه.

Five. Removal of the text, but not the ruling, and there is no known abrogator of the text. For example, in the *Ṣaḥīḥ*, it is reported, **"Had a child of Ādam had two valleys of gold, they would wish for a third one. Surely, only dirt shall fill the belly of the child of Ādam, and Allah the Exalted will forgive those who repent."**[238] This was originally a part of the Qur'ān, but then its text was abrogated and no longer recited as part of the Qur'ān.

السَّادِس: نَاسخ صَار مَنْسُوخا، وَلَيْسَ بَينهمَا لفظ متلو، كالمواريث بِالْحلف والنصرة، فَإِنَّهُ نسخ بالتوارث بِالْإِسْلَامِ وَالْهجْرَة، ونسخه بِآيَة الْمَوَارِيث.

Six. An abrogating verse becoming abrogated, while between the two, there is no text that is recited. For example, it used to be that inheritance was based on treaties and support, but then was abrogated with inheritance being based on Islam and migration, which was then replaced with the verse on inheritance.

الثَّانِيَة: نسخ الْأَمر قبل امتثاله جَائِز، نَحْو أَن يَقُول الشَّارِع فِي رَمَضَان مثلا: حجُّوا فِي هَذِه السّنة، ثمَّ يَقُول فِي يَوْم عَرَفَة أَو قبله: لَا تَحُجُّوا، وَهَذِه الْمَسْأَلَة

236 [T] Mentioned by al-Zarkashi in *al-Bahr al-Muḥīṭ* (5/254).
237 [T] *Qawāṭiʿ al-Adillah fi 'l-Uṣūl* (1/427).
238 Reported by al-Bukhārī (11/216-217) and Muslim (1049).

ذكرتها تبعا للروضة وَغيرهَا، وَلَا فَائِدَة لَهَا إِلَّا المناقشة.

The second discussion: Abrogating a commandment before it is adhered to is possible. For example, the Legislator can say during Ramadan, "Perform Ḥajj during this year," but then, on the day of ʿArafah, or before it, He can say, "Do not perform Ḥajj." I mentioned this issue because it was mentioned in *al-Rawḍah* and other texts. However, there is no benefit to it, other than pontification.

الثَّالِثَة: الزِّيَادَة على النَّص إِمَّا أَن لَا تتعَلَّق بِحكم النَّص أصلا، أَو تتعَلَّق بِهِ، فَإِن لم تتعَلَّق بِهِ، فَلَيْسَتْ نسخا لَهُ إِجْمَاعًا، وَذَلِكَ كزيادة إِيجَاب الصَّوْم بعد إِيجَاب الصَّلَاة، فَإِنَّهُ لَيْسَ نسخا لإِيجَاب الصَّلَاة بِالْإِجْمَاع، وَإِن تعلّقت الزِّيَادَة بِحكم النَّص الْمَزِيد عَلَيْهِ، فَتلك الزِّيَادَة إِمَّا جُزْء لَهُ، أَو شَرط، أَو لَا جُزْء، وَلَا شَرط، مِثَال كَونهَا جُزْءا لَهُ زِيَادَة رَكْعَة فِي الصُّبْح، أَو عشْرين سَوْطًا فِي حد الْقَذْف، فَتَصِير الصُّبْح ثَلَاث رَكْعَات، وَالثَّالِثَة جُزْء مِنْهَا، وحد الْقَذْف مئة سَوط، وَالْعشْرُون الزَّائِدَة جُزْء مِنْهَا.

The third discussion: When there is an addition to a textual evidence, if it does not deal with the ruling in the textual evidence, it does not abrogate the previous text—according to consensus. An example includes adding the obligation of fasting after the obligation of praying. Obligating fasting does not abrogate the obligation of the prayer, by consensus. However, if it does relate to the ruling at hand, the addition could either be a part or condition of the ruling, or could not be a part or condition of the ruling. An example of it being a part of the ruling is adding a unit of prayer in *fajr*, or adding another twenty lashes in the penalty of slander, thus making *fajr* three units—the last one being a part of the original ruling, and making the flogging consist of one hundred lashes—with the additional twenty being a part of the original ruling.

وَمِثَال كَونهَا شرطا: نِيَّة الطَّهَارَة هِيَ شَرط لَهَا، وَقد زيدت فِي حَدِيث **«إِنَّمَا الْأَعْمَال بِالنياتِ»** وَغَيره على مَا فِي آيَة الْوضُوء بِنَاء على أَن النِّيَّة لَيست مستفادة من الْآيَة، على خلاف بَين الْعلمَاء.

An example of it being a condition is the intention of purification being a condition for it, and it was added in the ḥadīth of, **"Actions are but by intentions,"**[239] and other aḥadīth. This addition was made to the verse that describes the rulings of ablution, since the intention is not taken directly from the verse. This, however, is a point of difference among scholars.

وَمِثَال كَون الزِّيَادَة لَيست جُزْءا وَلَا شرطا التَّغْرِيب على الْجلد فِي زنا الْبكر، إِذْ الْجلد لَا يتَوَقَّف على التَّغْرِيب توقف الْكل على جزئه، وَلَا توقف الْمَشْرُوط على شَرطه، وَلَيْسَ شَيْء من ذَلِك نسخا عندنَا، خلافًا للحنفية، وَحكى الْآمِدِيّ عَن القَاضِي عبد الْجَبَّار وَالْغزالِيّ فِي المثالين الْأَوَّلين أَنَّهُمَا وافقا الْحَنَفِيَّة فِي أَنه نسخ. وَقد أَطَالَ الأصوليون ذيول هَذِه الْمَسْأَلَة. وفائدتها على مَا فِي (الْبَحْر) للزركشي: أَن مَا ثَبت أَنه من بَاب النّسخ، وَكَانَ مَقْطُوعًا بِهِ، فَلَا ينْسَخ إِلا بقاطع كالتغريب. وَالله الْمُوفق.

An example of it not being a part or condition is the ruling of banishment over lashing as a penalty for a virgin who fornicates. Lashing is not reliant on banishment in the sense that a complete action relies on the sum of its parts, nor is it an action relying on its condition. This to us is not considered abrogation. This is contrary to the Ḥanafī scholars. Al-Āmidī also stated that al-Qāḍī ʿAbd al-Jabbār and al-Ghazālī agreed with the Ḥanafī scholars in the first two cases, stating that they were abrogation. Legal theorists have extensively studied this issue. According to al-Zarkashī in *al-Baḥr al-Muḥīṭ*, its benefit is, "Anything that is a definitive abrogation cannot be abrogated without a definitive text, such as the ruling on banishment."[240] And Allah is the granter of success.

الرَّابِعَة: يجوز نسخ الْعِبَادَة إِلَى غير بدل، كنسخ وجوب الْإِمْسَاك بعد النّوم فِي اللَّيْل، وَذَلِكَ أَنهم كَانُوا فِي صدر الْإِسْلَام مَتى نَام أحدهم قبل أَن يفْطر من صَوْمه، حرم عَلَيْهِ الْأكل حَتَّى اللَّيْلَة الثَّانِيَة، فَخفف ذَلِك عَنْهُم بنسخه بِإِبَاحَة الْأكل إِلَى طُلُوع الْفجْر من غير بدل. وَمن ذَلِك نسخ اعْتِدَاد الْمُتَوفَّى عَنْهَا حولا باعتدادها أَرْبَعَة أشهر وَعشرا فتمام الْحول نسخ لَا إِلَى بدل.

239 Reported by al-Bukhārī (1/9,18) and Muslim (1907).
240 [T] *Al-Baḥr al-Muḥīṭ* (5/310).

The fourth discussion: An action of worship can be abrogated without a replacement. For example, the obligation of ceasing to eat after sleeping at night [in Ramadan] was abrogated. In the early stages of Islam, when one would sleep before breaking their fast, it was forbidden for them to eat again until the next night. Allah lessened the burden of that ruling by allowing eating until *fajr*, without replacing the original ruling. Another example is that initially, when a woman's husband passed away, she was obligated to remain in a mourning period for a year, but that was abrogated and made into four months and ten days. Therefore, completion of a year was abrogated without a replacement.

الْخَامِسَة: يجوز نسخ كل من الْكتاب ومتواتر السّنة وآحادها بِمثلِهِ، وَهَذَا اتِّفَاق لَا اخْتِلَاف فِيهِ، وَيجوز نسخ السّنة بِالْكتاب خلافًا للشَّافِعِيّ، واستنكر جمَاعَة من الْعلمَاء مِنْهُ ذَلِك.

The fifth discussion: The Qur'ān, recurrent Sunnah, and singular Sunnah can be abrogated with their similar texts. This is a point of agreement without any difference of opinion. It is possible for the Qur'ān to abrogate the Sunnah, contrary to al-Shāfiʿī's view, which was to the dismay of a group of scholars.

تَنْبِيه: الْأَدِلَّة النقلية الَّتِي يتَطَرق النّسخ إِلَيْهَا وَبهَا هِيَ: الْكتاب، ومتواتر السّنة، وآحادها، وكل وَاحِد مِنْهَا إِمَّا أَن ينْسَخ بِمثلِهِ من جنسه أَو بالآخرين مَعَه، فَيحصل من ذَلِك تسع صور:

Note: The textual evidences that are susceptible to abrogation are: The Qur'ān, recurrent Sunnah, and singular Sunnah. Each of these can be abrogated by its equivalent in the same category or by other categories. Therefore, there are nine cases:

الأولى: نسخ الْكتاب بِالْكتاب.

One. Abrogating Qur'ān via Qur'ān.

الثَّانِيَة: نسخ الْكتاب بمتواتر السّنة.

Two. Abrogating Qur'ān via recurrent Sunnah.

الثَّالِثَة: نسخ الْكتاب بآحاد السّنة.

Three. Abrogating Qurʾān via singular Sunnah.

الرَّابِعَة: نسخ متواتر السّنة بمتواتر السّنة.

Four. Abrogating recurrent Sunnah via recurrent Sunnah.

الْخَامِسَة: نسخ متواتر السّنة بِالْكتاب.

Five. Abrogating recurrent Sunnah via Qurʾān.

السَّادِسَة: نسخ متواتر السّنة بالآحاد.

Six. Abrogating recurrent Sunnah via singular Sunnah.

السَّابِعَة: نسخ الْآحَاد بالآحاد.

Seven. Abrogating singular Sunnah via singular Sunnah.

الثَّامِنَة: نسخ الْآحَاد بِالْكتاب.

Eight. Abrogating singular Sunnah via Qurʾān.

التَّاسِعَة: نسخ الْآحَاد بالمتواتر.

Nine. Abrogating singular Sunnah via recurrent Sunnah.

وَالضَّابِط فِي ذَلِك على الْمَشْهُور بَينهم أَن النَّص ينْسَخ بأقوى مِنْهُ، وَلَا ينْسَخ بأضعف مِنْهُ، فيسْقط بِمُقْتَضى هَذَا الضَّابِط من الصُّور التسع صُورَتَانِ: نسخ الْكتاب بالآحاد، وَنسخ الْمُتَوَاتر بالآحاد. وعَلى قَول الْبَاجِيّ، وَبَعض الظَّاهِرِيَّة: يَصح النّسخ فِي الصُّور التسع.

The popular rule that scholars use is that a text can be abrogated by a text of [the same or] greater strength, and cannot be abrogated by something weaker than it. As such, two cases from the nine are not applicable to abrogation, namely: (i) Abrogating Qurʾān via singular Sunnah. (ii) Abrogating recurrent Sunnah via singular Sunnah. According to al-Bājī and some adherents to the Ẓāhirī school, all nine cases are applicable.

السَّادِسَة: الْإِجْمَاع لَا ينْسَخ، وَلَا ينْسَخ بِهِ، وَلَا بِالْقِيَاسِ، وَأما الْقيَاس فَلَا ينْسَخ.

The sixth discussion: Neither consensus nor analogies can be abrogated or used to abrogate.

فَائِدَتَانِ:

There are also two useful beneficial points to mention here:

إِحْدَاهمَا: الطَّرِيق الَّذِي يعرف بِهِ كَون النَّاسِخ نَاسِخا إِنَّمَا هُوَ أُمُور:

First: There are a number of ways to determine that a text is abrogating:

أولهمَا: أَن يكون فِيهِ مَا يدل على تقدم أَحدهمَا، وَتَأَخر الآخر فِي النُّزُول لَا التِّلَاوَة، فَإِن الْعدة بأَرْبعَة أشهر وَعشر سَابِقَة على الْعدة فِي الْحول، فِي التِّلَاوَة، مَعَ أَنَّهَا ناسخة لَهَا، وَمن ذَلِك التَّصْرِيح فِي اللَّفْظ بِمَا يدل على النّسخ، كَقَوْلِه تَعَالَى: ﴿**الْآنَ خَفَّفَ اللهُ عَنكُمْ**﴾ [الْأَنفَال: ٦٦] وَكَقَوْلِه: ﴿**أَأَشْفَقْتُمْ أَنْ تُقَدِّمُوا بَيْنَ يَدَيْ نَجْوَاكُمْ صَدَقَاتٍ**﴾ [المجادلة: ١٣]

The first way: There is something to indicate that one precedes the other and one was revealed later. The point is not to see which is recited first and which is recited last (rather, the point of revelation is looked at), because the verse about the mourning period of the woman being four months and ten days is earlier in the *muṣḥaf* than the verse about the waiting period being a year. However, the former abrogated the latter. Another example of an indication is that the text itself shows abrogation. For example, Allah the Exalted states: **{Now Allah has lightened your burden.}** [Qur'ān 8:66] Also, He states: **{Were you afraid to give charity before consulting the Prophet?}** [Qur'ān 58:13]

ثَانِيهَا: أَن يعرف ذَلِك من قَوْله عَلَيْهِ السَّلَام، كَأَن يَقُول: هَذَا نَاسخ لهَذَا، أَو مَا فِي مَعْنَاهُ، كَقَوْلِه «**كنت نَهَيْتُكُمْ عَن زِيَارَة الْقُبُور أَلا فزوروها**».

The second way: The Prophet ﷺ states explicitly that something is abrogated, or alludes to it. For example, the Prophet ﷺ stated, **"I previously forbade you from visiting graves; now, I state to visit them."**[241]

241 Reported by Muslim (977).

وَثَالِثهَا: أَن يعرف ذَلِك بِفِعْلِهِ عَلَيْهِ السَّلَام، كرجمه لماعز وَلم يجلده.

The third way: To observe abrogation from the actions of the Prophet ﷺ. For example, the Prophet ﷺ stoned Mā'iz instead of lashing him.

رَابِعهَا: إِجْمَاع الصَّحَابَة على أَن هَذَا نَاسخ، وَهَذَا مَنْسُوخ، كنسخ الْحُقُوق الْمُتَعَلّقَة بِالْمَالِ بِالزَّكَاةِ.

The fourth way: The consensus of the companions that something is an abrogation and something is abrogated. For example, the abrogation of financial rights when it comes to paying *zakāt*.

خَامِسهَا: نقل الصَّحَابِيّ لتقدم أحد الْحكمَيْنِ وَتَأَخر الآخر، إِذْ لَا مدْخل لِلِاجْتِهَاد فِيهِ.

The fifth way: A companion could transmit that some ruling was earlier and another was later, since this is not something up to their legal and juristic discretion.

سادسها: كَون أحد الْحكمَيْنِ شَرْعِيًّا، وَالْآخر مُوَافقا للْعَادَة، فَيكون الشَّرْعِيّ نَاسِخا.

The sixth way: One of the two rulings is religious and the other is customary, making the religious one abrogating of the customary one.

وَأما حَدَاثَة الصَّحَابِيّ وَتَأَخر إِسْلَامه، فَلَيْسَ ذَلِك من دَلَائِل النّسخ وَإِذا لم يعلم النَّاسِخ من الْمَنْسُوخ بِوَجْه من الْوُجُوه، فرجح ابْن الْحَاجِب الْوَقْف وَقَالَ الْآمِدِيّ: إِن علم افتراقهما مَعَ تعذر الْجمع بَينهمَا فعندي أَن ذَلِك غير مُتَصَوّر الْوُقُوع، وَبِتَقْدِير وُقُوعه فَالْوَاجِب إِمَّا الْوَقْف عَن الْعَمَل بِأَحَدِهِمَا، أَو التَّخْيِير بَينهمَا إِن أمكن، وَكَذَلِكَ الحكم فِيمَا إِذا لم يعلم شَيْء من ذَلِك. انْتهى. وَزَاد فِي (الرَّوْضَة) أَن النّسخ يعرف بالتاريخ، نَحْو: قَالَ سنة خمس كَذَا، وعام الْفَتْح كَذَا، وَيكون رَاوِي أحد الْخَبَرَيْنِ مَاتَ قبل إِسْلَام رَاوِي الثَّانِي.

If a companion reports and he accepted Islam late, it is not evidence of abrogation. If one cannot differentiate between the abrogating and the abrogated text in any way, Ibn al-Ḥājib stated that they should abstain. Al-Āmidī stated, "If one knows that they are contradictory and cannot reconcile them, I think that is not a conceivable situation. However, if we were to assume for the sake of argument that it does occur, the obligation becomes that they should abstain from acting on either of them, or should choose between one of them if they can. Likewise, the same applies if one cannot determine any of those things.[242] In *al-Rawḍah*, [Ibn Qudāmah] added that abrogation can be known via the date, such as, "It was said in such-and-such year," or, "During the year of the conquest of Makkah," and that a narrator of one of the two narrations died before the Islam of the second reporter.

ثَانِيهِمَا: للنسخ شُرُوط:

Second:[243] The conditions of abrogation:

الأول: أَن يكون الْمَنْسُوخ شَرْعِيًّا لَا عقليا.

One. The abrogation must be of some religious aspect, not something rational.[244]

الثَّانِي: أَن يكون النَّاسِخ مُنْفَصِلا عَن الْمَنْسُوخ، مُتَأَخِّرًا عَنهُ، فَإِن المقترن كالشرط وَالصّفة وَالِاسْتِثْنَاء لَا يُسمى نسخا بل تَخْصِيصًا.

Two. The abrogating text must be separate from the abrogated one and must be after it chronologically. If a text is coupled with another, such as a condition, description, or an exception, it is not referred to as abrogation. Rather, it is referred to as "particularising the text."

الثَّالِث: أَن يكون النّسخ بشرع، فَلَا يكون ارْتِفَاع الحكم بِالْمَوْتِ نسخا بل سُقُوط تَكْلِيف.

Third. The abrogation must emanate from the religion. When one is no longer responsible for carrying out religious duties because of death, it is not called abrogation, but rather, abatement of duties.

---

242 [T] *Al-Iḥkām fī Uṣūl al-Aḥkām* by al-Imām Sayf al-Dīn al-Āmidī (3/182).
243 [T] Meaning, the second beneficial point.
244 [T] For example, an objective rational truth cannot be abrogated. It cannot be the case that x + 2 = 4, x is 2, and then x becomes abrogated and becomes 3.

الرَّابِع: أَن لا يكون الْمَنْسُوخ مُقَيّدا بِوَقْت، وَإِلَّا فَلَا يكون انْقِضَاء ذَلِك الْوَقْت نسخا لَه.

Four. The abrogation must not be contingent on any particular timeframe. If a ruling is tied to the time, the ending of the time-frame is not considered abrogation of that ruling.[245]

الْخَامِس: أَن يكون النَّاسِخ مثل الْمَنْسُوخ فِي الْقُوَّة أَو أقوى مِنْهُ.

Five. The abrogating text must be either equal to or stronger than the abrogated text.

السَّادِس: أَن يكون الْمُقْتَضِي للمنسوخ غير الْمُقْتَضِي للناسخ حَتَّى لَا يلْزم الْبداء.

Six. The abrogation should not be on the same grounds as the abrogated text, so as not to insinuate that Allah regrets His initial ruling.[246]

السَّابِع: أَن يكون مِمَّا يجوز نسخه، فَلَا يدْخل النّسخ أصل التَّوْحِيد لِأَن الله - تَعَالَى بأسمائه وَصِفَاته - لم يزل وَلَا يزَال. وَمثل ذَلِك مَا علم بِالنَّصِّ أَنه يتأبد وَلَا يتأقت.

Seven. It must be something that can be abrogated. For example, the foundation of monotheism cannot be abrogated, because Allah the Exalted with His Names and Attributes is Eternal. Other examples are those known in texts that they will be rulings forever and not for just a period of time.

ثمَّ لما كَانَ الْكتاب وَالسّنة تلحقهما أَحْكَام لفظية ومعنوية، كالأمر وَالنَّهْي، والعموم وَالْخُصُوص، لَا جرم عقبناهما بقولنَا.

Since the Qur'ān and Sunnah are supplemented with rulings pertaining to their texts and the meanings they entail, such as the commandment, prohibition, generality, particularisation, and so forth, the next chapter will dis-

245 [T] For example, when the Ḥajj time ends, it does not mean that Ḥajj has been abrogated.

246 [T] For example, assume Allah has obligated something by saying, "Do this, as it is a righteous action," and then later abrogates the obligation by saying, "Do not do this, for it is not righteousness." In this case, the obligation and its subsequent abrogation occurred on the same grounds of righteousness.

cuss these matters.

الْأوامِر والنواهي

On Commandments and Prohibitions

أما الْأَمر فَاخْتلف فِي تَعْرِيفه، وَالْأولَى أَن يُقَال فِيهِ: اقْتِضَاء فعل غير كف على جِهَة الاستعلاء، فالاقتضاء جنس، وَغير كف يخرج النَّهْي، لِأَنَّهُ يَقْتَضِي الْكَفّ وَهُوَ فعل، وعَلى سَبِيل الاستعلاء، يخرج مَا إِذا كَانَ على سَبِيل التسفل، وَهُوَ الدُّعَاء، وَمَا كَانَ على سَبِيل التَّسَاوِي، وَهُوَ الالتماس.

Scholars have differed in defining commandments. The best definition is to state that a commandment is to demand performing an action, not an abstention, and to do so from a position of authority. Therefore, demands are a genus, and when I said, "not an abstention," it was to avoid including prohibitions, which imply abstaining from something, which is itself an action. When I said, "from a position of authority," it was to not include demands made from a position of humility, as that would be called a supplication, and also does not include something done from a position of equality, as that is referred to as a request.

وللأمر صِيغَة مَوْضُوعَة لَهُ، تدل عَلَيْهِ حَقِيقَة، كدلالة سَائِر الْأَلْفَاظ الْحَقِيقِيَّة على موضوعها، وَتلك الصِّيغَة حَقِيقَة فِي الطّلب الْجَازِم، مجَاز فِي غَيره مِمَّا وَردت فِيهِ، وَذَلِكَ أَن صِيغَة الْأَمر، وَهِي لفظ افْعَل، نَحْو اعْلَم، وَاضْرِبْ، ودحرج، وَانْطَلق، واستخرج، أطلقت فِي الِاسْتِعْمَال اللّغَوِيّ لمعان:

Commandments have particular wordings that indicate them literally, just as all other significations that indicate their true and literal nature when the word is uttered. The wording of the commandment is, in its true nature, an imperative demand. If the wording is not used [as an imperative command], it is being used metaphorically. Expressions that indicate commandments are on the *if'al* structure ("do"), such as, "learn," "hit," "flip," "go," and "extract." However, in its linguistic usage, wordings that indicate commandments have various possible meanings:

أَحدهَا: الطّلب الْجَازِم نَحْو: ﴿أَقِيمُوا الصَّلَاة﴾ [البقرة: ٤٣]

One. Demanding imperatively, such as when Allah the Exalted states: **{Establish prayer.}** [Qur'ān 2:43]

وَثَانِيها: النّدب، كَقَوْلِه تَعَالَى فِي حق الأرقاء الطالبين للكتابة ﴿فَكَاتِبُوهُمْ﴾ [النُّور: ٣٣] وَالْكِتَابَة مَنْدُوبَة عِنْد الْأَكْثَرين.

Two. Recommending, such as when Allah the Exalted states: **{If any of your slaves wish to pay for their freedom, <u>make a contract with them</u> accordingly, if you know they have good in them, and give them some of the wealth Allah has given you.}** [Qur'ān 24:33] According to the majority, giving them a contract is recommended.

وَثَالِثهَا: الْإِبَاحَة، نَحْو قَوْله تَعَالَى: ﴿وَإِذَا حَلَلْتُمْ فَاصْطَادُوا﴾ [المائدة: ٢]، ﴿فامشوا فِي مناكبها وكلوا من رزقه﴾ [الْملك: ١٥]

Three. Allowing, such as when Allah the Exalted states: **{When you have completed the rites of pilgrimage, hunt.}** [Qur'ān 5:2] Also, when He states: **{Move about in its regions and eat from His provisions.}** [Qur'ān 67:15]

وَرَابِعهَا: التَّعْجِيز، نَحْو قَوْله عز وَجل: ﴿كُونُوا حِجَارَةً أَوْ حَدِيداً﴾ [الْإِسْرَاء: ٥٠]، أَي: فَلَنْ تعجزني إعادتكم

Four. Defeating and showing powerlessness, such as when Allah the Exalted states: **{Be stone, or iron, or whatever you think is harder to bring to life!}** [Qur'ān 17:50] Meaning, you would not defeat My ability to bring you back to life.

وخامسها: التسخير: نَحْو قَوْله تَعَالَى: ﴿فَقُلْنَا لَهُمْ كُونُوا قِرَدَةً خَاسِئِينَ﴾ [الْبَقَرَة: ٦٥]، أَي: مسخت مواد أجسامهم لانقلابها عَن الإنسانية إِلَى القردية بِالْأَمر الإلهي.

Five. Subjugating, such as when Allah the Exalted states: **{We said to them, "Be disgraced apes!"}** [Qur'ān 2:65] Meaning, the material makeup of their bodies was changed because they turned from humans to monkeys, by the Divine Commandment.

وسادسها: التَّسْوِيَة، نَحْو قَوْله تَعَالَى: ﴿فَاصْبِرُوا أَوْ لَا تَصْبِرُوا سَوَاءٌ عَلَيْكُمْ﴾ [الطّور: ١٦] أي: الصَّبْر وَعَدَمه متساويان.

Six. Equating, such as when Allah the Exalted states: **{Be patient or not - it makes no difference for you.}** [Qur'ān 52:16] Meaning, patience, or the lack thereof, are equals.

وسابعها: الإهانة، نَحْو قَوْله عز وَجل: ﴿ذُقْ إِنَّكَ أَنْتَ الْعَزِيزُ الْكَرِيمُ﴾ [الدُّخان: ٤٩]، على جِهَة الإهانة لَهُ، وَقَوله تَعَالَى: ﴿ذُوقُوا مَسَّ سَقَرَ﴾ [الْقَمَر: ٤٨]، ﴿وَذُوقُوا عَذَابَ الْحَرِيقِ﴾ [الأنفال: ٥٠] ﴿ذُوقُوا مَا كُنْتُمْ تَكْسِبُونَ﴾ [الزمر: ٢٤].

Seven. Humiliating, such as when Allah the Exalted states: **{Taste this, you powerful, respected man!}** [Qur'ān 44:49] This, although it is a commandment, is meant to humiliate the person being spoken to, [in hellfire]. Allah the Exalted also states: **{Feel the touch of Hell.}** [Qur'ān 54:48] Also, Allah the Exalted states: **{Taste the torment of burning!}** [Qur'ān 8:50] Lastly, Allah the Exalted states: **{Taste what you have earned.}** [Qur'ān 39:24]

وثامنها: الْإِكْرَام، نَحْو قَوْله تَعَالَى: ﴿ادْخُلُوهَا بِسَلَامٍ آمِنِينَ﴾ [الْحجر: ٤٦]

Eight. Honouring, such as when Allah the Exalted states: **{Enter them in peace and safety.}** [Qur'ān 15:46]

وتاسعها: التهديد، نَحْو قَوْله تَعَالَى: ﴿اعْمَلُوا مَا شِئْتُمْ﴾ [فصلت: ٤٠] ﴿لِيَكْفُرُوا بِمَا آتَيْنَاهُمْ وَلِيَتَمَتَّعُوا﴾ [العنكبوت: ٦٦]، فَهَذَا أَمر يلازم الْأَمر.

Nine. Threatening, such as when Allah the Exalted states: **{Do whatever you want.}** [Qur'ān 41:40] Also, He states: **{Let them show their ingratitude for what We have given them; let them take their enjoyment-soon they will know.}** [Qur'ān 29:66] This commandment begins with the letter *lām* (ل).[247]

---

247 [T] In the printed copy of *al-Madkhal*, it states, "This is a commandment necessitating commandment," but that is a mistake, and what I have placed is correct.

وعاشرها: الدُّعاء نَحو اللَّهُمَّ اغفِر لي، ﴿رَبنَا أَفْرِغْ عَلَيْنَا صَبْراً وَتَوَفَّنَا مُسْلِمِينَ﴾ [الْأَعْرَاف: ١٢٦]

Ten. Supplication, such as when one says, "O Allah, forgive me." Or, as Allah the Exalted stated that the believers state: **{Our Lord, pour steadfastness upon us and let us die in devotion to You.}** [Qur'ān 7:126]

وحادي عشرهَا: الْخَبَر كَحَدِيث «**إِذا أَنْت لم تَسْتَحي فَاصْنَعْ مَا شِئْت**».

Eleven. A declarative sentence, such as when the Prophet ﷺ said, **"If you are not shameful, you shall do as you will."**[248]

وَثَانِي عشرهَا: التَّمَنِّي، كَقَوْل امرئ الْقَيْس:

Twelve. Wishing for something, such as when Imru' 'l-Qays said:

أَلا أَيهَا اللَّيْل الطَّوِيل أَلا انجلي.

Alas, long night, begone![249]

أَي: أَتَمَنَّى انجلاءك عني.

He meant that he had wished for the long night to end.

وثالث عشرهَا: الْإِرْشَاد إِلَى مصلحَة دنيوية أَو غيرهَا، نَحْو ﴿**وَأَشْهِدُوا إِذَا تَبَايَعْتُمْ**﴾ [الْبَقَرَة: ٢٨٢]، ﴿**قوا أَنفسكُم وأهليكم نَارا**﴾ [التَّحْرِيم: ٦]، يَعْنِي بالتأديب والتعليم.

Thirteen. Guiding to some worldly benefit, or any other benefit. For example, Allah the Exalted states: **{Have witnesses present whenever you trade with one another.}** [Qur'ān 2:282] Also, Allah the Exalted states: **{Believers, guard yourselves and your families against a Fire ...}**

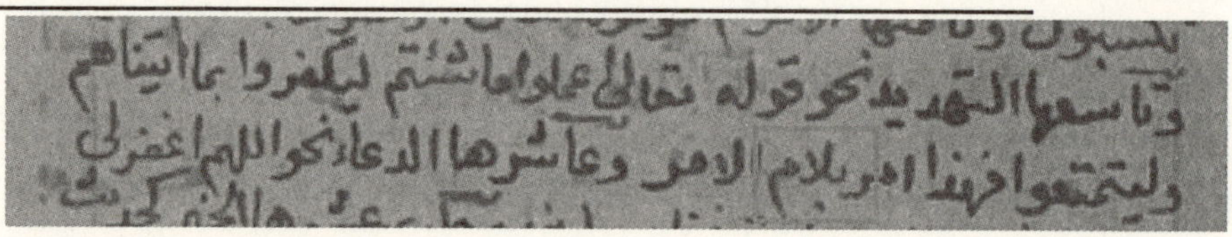
وتاسعها التهديد نحو قوله تعالى اعملوا ما شئتم ليكفروا بما آتيناهم
وليتمتعوا فهذا امر بلام الامر وعاشرها الدعاء نحو اللهم اغفر لي

248 Reported by al-Bukhārī (10/434).
249 This line is from the *Hanging Ode* (*Mu'allaqah*) of Imru' 'l-Qays.

[Qur'ān 66:6] I.e. via nurturing and teaching.

ورابع عشرهَا: الامتنان، نَحْو ﴿كُلُوا مِنْ طَيِّبَاتِ مَا رَزَقْنَاكُمْ﴾ [الْبَقَرة: ٥٧] ﴿وَكُلُوا مِنْ رِزْقِهِ﴾ [الْملك: ١٥]

Bestowing of favours, such as when Allah the Exalted states: **{Eat from the good things We have provided for you.}** [Qur'ān 2:57] Also, Allah stated: **{Eat from His provision.}** [Qur'ān 67:15]

وخامس عشرهَا: الْإِنْذَار، نَحْو ﴿خُذُوا حِذْرَكُمْ﴾ [النِّسَاء: ٧١]

Fifteen. Warning, such as when Allah the Exalted states: **{Be on your guard.}** [Qur'ān 4:71]

وسادس عشرهَا: الاحتقار، نَحْو ﴿أَلْقُوا مَا أَنْتُمْ مُلْقُونَ﴾ [يُونُس: ٨٠]

Sixteen. Degrading, such as when Allah the Exalted states: **{Throw down whatever you have.}** [Qur'ān 10:80]

وسابع عشرهَا: التَّفْوِيض، نَحْو ﴿فَاقْضِ مَا أَنْتَ قَاضٍ﴾ [طه: ٧٢]

Seventeen. Entrusting something to someone else, such as: **{So decide whatever you will.}** [Qur'ān 20:72]

وثامن عشرهَا: الْمشورة، نَحْو ﴿فَانْظُرْ مَاذَا تَرَى﴾ [الصافات: ١٠٢]

Eighteen. Consulting, such as in the Qur'ān: **{What do you think?}** [Qur'ān 37:102]

وتاسع عشرهَا: الِاعْتِبَار، نَحْو ﴿انْظُرُوا إِلَى ثَمَرِهِ إِذَا أَثْمَرَ﴾ [الْأَنْعَام: ٩٩]

Nineteen. Reflecting, such as when Allah the Exalted states: **{Watch their fruits as they grow and ripen!}** [Qur'ān 6:99]

وَالْعشْرُونَ: التَّكْذِيب، نَحْو ﴿قُلْ هَاتُوا بُرْهَانَكُمْ﴾ [الْبَقَرة: ١١١]

Twenty. Belying, such as when Allah the Exalted states: **{Say, "Produce your evidence."}** [Qur'ān 2:111]

وَالْحَادِي وَالْعشْرُونَ: الالتماس، كَقَوْلِك لنظيرك: افْعَل.

Twenty one. Requesting, such as when one says to his peer, "Do such-and-such action."

وَالثَّانِي وَالْعشْرُونَ: التلهيف، نَحْو ﴿مُوتُوا بِغَيْظِكُمْ﴾ [آل عمرَان: ١١٩].

Twenty two. Bemoaning, such as when Allah the Exalted states: **{Die of rage.}** [Qur'ān 3:119]

هَذَا وَلَا يشْتَرط فِي كَون الْأَمر أمرا إِرَادَته. ثمَّ إِن هَاهُنَا مسَائِل:

Note, too, that for an order to be an order, one does not have to intend it. There are a number of important discussions to be had in this regard:

الأولى: الْأَمر الْمُطلق يدل على الْوُجُوب مَا لم تكن قرينَة تصرفه إِلَى أحد الْمعَانِي السَّابِقَة، أَو غَيرهَا مِمَّا لم نذكرهُ.

First: An absolute commandment indicates obligation, so long as there is no evidence to divert the meaning to one of the [twenty-two] previously mentioned significations [of a wording indicating a commandment], or any other signification that was not mentioned.

الثَّانِيَة: صِيغَة الْأَمر الْوَارِدَة بعد الْحَظْر للْإِبَاحَة كَقَوْلِه صلى الله عَلَيْهِ وَسلم **«كنت نَهَيْتُكُمْ عَن زِيَارَة الْقُبُور أَلا فزوروها»**، وَكَقَوْلِه تَعَالَى ﴿**وَإِذَا حَلَلْتُمْ فَاصْطَادُوا**﴾ [الْمَائِدَة: ٢]، وَهل النَّهْي بعد الْأَمر يَقْتَضِي التَّحْرِيم أَو الْكَرَاهَة؟ خلاف، وَالأشبه أَنه يَقْتَضِي التَّحْرِيم.

Second: A commandment occurring after a prohibition indicates that the commanded action has become lawful. For example, the Prophet ﷺ said, **"I previously forbade you from visiting graves; now, I state to visit them."**[250] Also, Allah the Exalted said: **{When you have completed the rites of pilgrimage, hunt.}** [Qur'ān 5:2] There is a difference of opinion on whether a prohibition occurring after a commandment indicates prohibition or undesirability. The most veracious view is that it signifies prohibition.

الثَّالِثَة: الْأَمر الْمُطلق لَا يَقْتَضِي التّكْرَار، وَهَذَا هُوَ الْحق، وَذَلِكَ لِأَنَّهُ لَا دلَالَة

250 Reported by Muslim (977).

لصيغة الْأَمر إِلَّا على مُجَرّد إِدْخَال مَاهِيَّة الْفِعْل فِي الْوُجُود، لَا على كمية الْفِعْل، فَلَو دلّ على الْمرة كَالْحَجِّ، أَو على التّكْرَار كَالصَّلَاةِ وَالصَّوْم المفردين، فَإِن تِلْكَ الدّلَالَة لَيست من حَيْثُ الْقَرَائِن الدَّالَّة على الْمرة أَو على التّكْرَار.

Third: An absolute commandment does not indicate repetition. This is the truth. The reason is that the wording of a commandment only signifies bringing the action into material existence. It does not indicate a quantity of the action. If it were to indicate a single time, such as al-Ḥajj, or multiple iterations, such as prayer and fasting as individual instances, the indication is not inferred from the wording of the commandment, but rather, from other contextual evidences that indicate that the action is meant to be performed once or to be repeated numerous times.[251]

الرَّابِعَة: الْأَمر بالشَّيْء نهي عَن أضداده، وَالنَّهْي عَنهُ أَمر بِأحد أضداده من حَيْثُ الْمَعْنى لَا الصِّيغَة، أي: بطرِيق الاستلزام. فَالْأَمْر بِالْإِيمَان - مثلا - نهي عَن الْكفْر، وَالْأَمر بِالْقيامِ نهي عَن جَمِيع أضداده كالقعود، والاضطجاع، وَالسُّجُود، وَغير ذَلِك، وَالنَّهْي عَن الْقيام أَمر بِوَاحِد من أضداده لَا بجميعها.

Fourth: A commandment is, by extension of its meaning and not its wording, prohibitive of all of its opposites, by implication. A commandment to adhere to faith, for example, is a prohibition of disbelief. An order to stand is a prohibition of all of its opposites, such as sitting, lying, prostrating, and so forth. Prohibition of standing is a commandment to do one of its opposites, not all of its opposites.[252]

---

251 [T] The printed version states, "It is not due to the contextual evidences that indicate the action is meant to be performed once or to be repeated numerous times." However, as Dr. al-Turkī points out in the footnotes, this cannot be true as it conflicts with his main proposition in this paragraph. Indeed, his intuition was correct, as indicated by the manuscript.

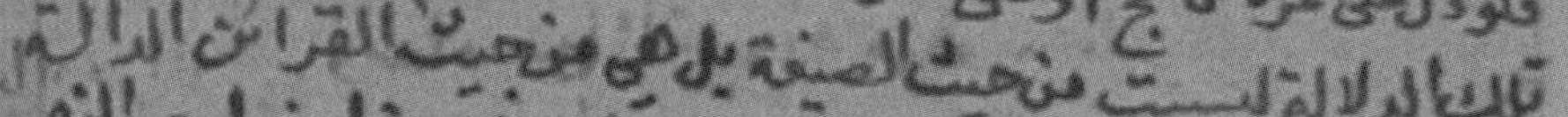
لصيغة الامر الا على مجرد ادخال
فلو دل على المرة كالحج او على التكرار كالصلاة والصوم المفردين فان
تلك الدلالة ليست من حيث الصيغة بل هي من حيث القرائن الدالة

252 [T] Meaning, one can sit, lie down, recline, and so forth. It does not mean one has to do all of these actions to adhere to the prohibition.

الْخَامِسَة: الْأَمر إِذا اقترنت بِهِ قرينَة فَوْرًا وتراخ: عمل بمقتضاها فِي ذَلِك، وَإِن كَانَ مُطلقًا أَي: مُجَردا عَن قرينَة، فَهُوَ للفور فِي ظَاهر الْمَذْهَب. وَمعنى الْفَوْر: الشُّرُوع فِي الِامْتِثَال عقب الْأَمر من غير فصل. والتراخي: تَأْخِير الِامْتِثَال عَن الْأَمر زمنا يُمكن إِيقَاع الْفِعْل فِيهِ فَصَاعِدا.

Fifth: If a commandment is coupled with some other evidence or contextual point that would indicate performing the action immediately or would give latitude in performing the action, the [additional contextual evidence] should be implemented and regarded. If it has no such thing and is mentioned as an absolute, it is meant to be done immediately, according to the *madhhab*. The meaning of "immediately" is that one should embark on adhering directly after the commandment, without any delay. The meaning of an action with latitude is that one can delay adhering to the commandment for a period of time, or more, where the action can be performed.

السَّادِسَة: الْوَاجِب الْمُؤَقت لَا يسْقط بِفَوَات الْوَقْت، وَلَا يفْتَقر قَضَاؤُهُ إِلَى أَمر جَدِيد، فَإِذا أَمر بِصَلَاة الْفجْر - مثلا - فِي وَقتهَا الْمعِين لَهَا، فَلم يصلها حَتَّى طلعت الشَّمْس، كَانَ وجوب قَضَائهَا الأول، وَلَا يحْتَاج إِلَى أَمر جَدِيد، وَذَلِكَ لِأَن الشَّرْع لما عهد مِنْهُ إِيثَار اسْتِدْرَاك عُمُوم الْمصَالح الْفَائِتَة، علمنَا من عَادَته بذلك أَنه يُؤثر اسْتِدْرَاك الْوَاجِب الْفَائِت فِي الزَّمن الأول بِقَضَائِهِ فِي الزَّمن الثَّانِي، فَكَانَ ذَلِك ضربا من الْقيَاس.

Sixth: One is not absolved from performing an obligatory action confined to a time-frame if they miss the allotted time-frame. Also, making up the action does not require another commandment. For example, if one is commanded to offer the *fajr* prayer during its allotted time, and only does so after the sun has risen, the obligation of making up the missed prayer is based on the initial commandment; no new commandment [to make up the prayer] is needed. The reason is that generally, the religion gives preference to rectifying all benefits that have been missed, and we also know that the religion wishes that an obligation that is missed in its initial time-frame is made up in its second time-frame. Therefore, this is a type of syllogism [to show this point].

السَّابِعَة: مُقْتَضى الْأَمر حُصُول الْإِجْزَاء بِفعل الْمَأْمُور بِهِ إِذا أَتَى بِجَمِيعِ مصححاته من ركن وَشرط، فَفعل صَلَاة الظّهْر - وَنَحْوهَا من الصَّلَوَات - بِجَمِيعِ مصححاتها يَقْتَضِي حُصُول الْأَجْزَاء بِحَيْثُ لَا يجب قَضَاؤُهَا فِيمَا بعد.

Seventh: The implication of a commandment signifies that one has sufficiently complied with the commandment when they have performed the action along with all of its ancillaries that render it valid, such as its pillars and its preconditions. For example, performing the *ẓuhr* prayer or any other prayer along with its ancillaries that render it valid implies that one has sufficiently adhered to that commandment and does not need to redo the action.

الثَّامِنَة: الْأَمر المتوجه إِلَى جمَاعَة إِمَّا أَن يكون بِلَفْظ يَقْتَضِي تعميمهم بِهِ، أَو لَا يكون، فَإِن كَانَ بِلَفْظ يَقْتَضِي تعميمهم نَحْو قَوْله تَعَالَى ﴿**وَأَقِيمُوا الصَّلَاةَ وَآتُوا الزَّكَاةَ**﴾ [الْبَقَرَة: ٤٣]، فإمَّا أَن لَا يعْتَرض عَلَيْهِ دَلِيل يدل على اخْتِصَاص الْخطاب ببعضهم؛ أَو يعْتَرض دَلِيل على ذَلِك، فَإِن لم يعْتَرض على الْعُمُوم دَلِيل اقْتضى وُجُوبه على كل وَاحِد مِنْهُم، وَإِن اعْترض على الْعُمُوم دَلِيل يَقْتَضِي اخْتِصَاصه ببعضهم، فالبعض إِمَّا معِين، فَإِن كَانَ معينا، فَذَلِك هُوَ الْعَام لمخصوص، سَوَاء كَانَ التَّعْيِين باسم كَقَوْلِه تَعَالَى ﴿**إِنَّا أُرْسِلْنَا إِلَىٰ قَوْمٍ مُّجْرِمِينَ إِلَّا آلَ لُوطٍ إِنَّا لَمُنَجُّوهُمْ أَجْمَعِينَ**﴾ [الْحجر: ٥٨-٥٩] وَقَول الْقَائِل: قَامَ الْقَوْم إِلَّا زيدا. أَو بِصفة كَقَوْلِه تَعَالَى: ﴿**الْأَخِلَّاءُ يَوْمَئِذٍ بَعْضُهُمْ لِبَعْضٍ عَدُوٌّ إِلَّا الْمُتَّقِينَ**﴾ [الزخرف: ٦٧]

Eighth: Sometimes, a commandment uses verbiage that indicates it is inclusive, and at other times, it does not. If the wording indicates it is all-inclusive, such as when Allah the Exalted states: **{Keep up the prayer, pay the prescribed alms.}** [Qur'ān 2:43] This evidence could either have no evidence to indicate that the instruction is directed to only a few of them, or could have such evidence. If there is no evidence that would contend with the generality of the wording, the obligation becomes directed at each and every person. However, if there is evidence to indicate it is instructing only a subset of the generality, and if the subset is defined, it is known as "a particularized generality (*al-ʿām al-makhṣūṣ*)." Particularization can occur via a noun, such as when Allah the Exalted states: **{They replied, 'We have**

been sent to a people who are guilty.' But We shall save the household of Lot.} [Qur'ān 15:58-59] Another example is when one says, "The people stood, except for Zayd." The particularization can also occur via a description, such as when Allah the Exalted states: **{Close friends will be enemies to one another on that Day, except the righteous.}** [Qur'ān 43:67]

وَإِن كَانَ ذَلِك الْبَعْض غير معِين، أَو كَانَ الْخطاب بِلَفْظ لَا يعم الْجَمِيع كَقَوْلِه تَعَالَى ﴿وَلْتَكُن مِنْكُمْ أُمَّةٌ يَدْعُونَ إِلَى الْخَيْرِ وَيَأْمُرُونَ بِالْمَعْرُوفِ﴾ [آل عمرَان: ١٠٤]، فَهَذَا هُوَ الْمُسَمّى بِفَرْض الْكِفَايَة، وَهُوَ مَا مَقْصُود الشَّرْع فعله، لتَضَمّنه مصلحَة لَا تعبد أَعْيَان الْمُكَلّفين بِهِ كَصَلَاة الْجِنَازَة وَالْجهَاد، فَإِن مَقْصُود الشَّرْع فعلهمَا لما تضمناه من مصلحَة الشَّفَاعَة للْمَيت، وحماية بِلَاد الْإِسْلَام من استِبَاحَة الْعَدو لَهَا، وَلم يرد بهما تعبد أَعْيَان الْمُكَلّفين، كَمَا أَرَادَ ذَلِك بِالْجمعَةِ وَالْحج.

If the subset is not particularized, or the wording does not indicate generality, such as when Allah states: **{Be a community that calls for what is good, urges what is right, and forbids what is wrong: those who do this are the successful ones.}** [Qur'ān 3:104] This is what is known as a communal obligation (*farḍ al-kifāyah*). The goal of the religion as it pertains to communal obligations is that they are achieved [by someone, but no one in specific], since they contain benefit. It does not mean that each individual responsible Muslim must perform them. Two examples are the funeral prayer and *jihād*: the goal of the religion is that they are performed, since they contain benefits. For the funeral, the benefit is intercession on behalf of the dead, and for *jihād*, the benefit is protection of Muslim lands from being violated by enemies. The goal of the religion was not to task individual *mukallaf* persons, in contrast to the obligations of Friday prayers and Ḥajj [which are obligations on each and every *mukallaf* person who fits the criteria of obligation].

فَفرض الْكِفَايَة وَفرض الْعين مشتركان فِي التَّعَبُّد، والمصلحة، وَالْفرق بَينهمَا أَن الْمَقْصُود فِي فرض الْكِفَايَة تَحْصِيل الْمصلحَة الَّتِي تضمنها، فَمن أَي شخص حصلت، كَانَ هُوَ الْمَطْلُوب، وَفِي فرض الْعين تعبد الْأَعْيَان بِفِعْلِهِ، وَالْفرق الْعَام

بَينهمَا هُوَ أَن فرض الْكِفَايَة مَا وَجب على الْجَمِيع وَسقط بِفعل الْبَعْض، وَفرض الْعين مَا وَجب على الْجَمِيع وَلم يسْقط إِلَّا بِفعل كل وَاحِد مِمَّن وَجب عَلَيْهِ، وَهَذَا الْفرق حكمي.

Communal obligations and individual obligations share in that they are actions of worship and contain inherent utility and benefit. Where they differ, though, is that the goal of the communal obligations is to attain some benefit inherent to the obligation itself. Therefore, regardless of who does the obligation, if it is done, the point of the instruction has been achieved. In individual obligations, each particular person is instructed to perform them. The general differentiation between the two is that the communal obligations are obligations on the whole body [of Muslims] and the rest are absolved [if the few achieve it]. As for individual obligations, they are obligatory on each, and one is not absolved until they perform what is obligated on them. This is the difference in the rulings pertaining to the two.

فَوَائِد تتَعَلَّق بِفَرْض الْكِفَايَة:

There are some useful benefits that pertain to communal obligations.

إِحْدَاهُنَّ: لَا يشْتَرط فِي الْخُرُوج من عُهْدَة فرض الْكِفَايَة تحقق وُقُوعه من بعض الطوائف، بل أَي طَائِفَة غلب على ظَنّهَا أَن غَيرهَا قَامَ بِهِ سقط، وَإِن غلب على ظن كل من الطَّائِفَتَيْنِ أَو الطوائف أَن الْأُخْرَى قَامَت بِهِ سقط بِهِ عَن الْجَمِيع، عملا بِمُوجب الظَّن، لِأَنهُ كَمَا صلح الظَّن مثبتا للتكاليف، صلح مسْقطًا لَهَا.

First: In order for one to absolve themselves of the communal obligation, it is not a condition that they have full certainty that some did it. Rather, if someone believes it is probable that someone else has done it, they are absolved. If both parties have probable belief that the other has performed it, all are absolved, since probable belief establishes rulings, and it also absolves from rulings.

الثَّانِيَة: الْقَائِم بِفَرْض الْكِفَايَة أفضل من غير الْقَائِم بِهِ، ضَرُورَة أَنه حصل مصْلحَته دون غَيره.

Second: The one who performs the communal obligation is better than the one who does not. This is necessarily known, because the one who has done the obligation, and none else, has established its benefit.

الثَّالِثَة: اخْتلفُوا أَيهمَا أفضل: فَاعل فرض الْعين، أم فَاعل فرض الْكِفَايَة؟ فَقيل: فَاعل فرض الْعين أفضل لِأَنَّهُ فَرْضه أهم، وَقيل: فَاعل فرض الْكِفَايَة أفضل إِذْ هُوَ أسقط الْفَرْض عَن نَفسه وَعَن غَيره، وَنسب هَذَا إِلَى إِمَام الْحَرَمَيْنِ.

Third: The scholars have differed on who is more virtuous: Is it the one who does the individual obligation—since that is more important, or is it the one who does the communal obligation—since they have absolved both themselves and others from having to perform the obligation? The second view was ascribed to Imām al-Ḥaramayn [al-Juwaynī].

الرَّابِعَة: هَل يتَعَيَّن فرض الْكِفَايَة، وَيجب إِتْمَامه على من تلبس بِهِ أم لَا؟ قَالَ الطوفي: الْأَشْبَه أنه يتَعَيَّن، كالمجاهد يحضر الصَّفّ، وطالب الْعلم يشرع فِي الِاشْتِغَال بِهِ، وَنَحْو هَذَا من صوره.

Fourth: If someone is performing a communal obligation, does it become individualised, and they are obligated to see it to completion? Al-Ṭūfī stated, "The more veracious view is that it does become individualised. Examples include a soldier standing in rank, and a student of knowledge who has begun learning. These are two examples."[253]

الخامسة: مَا ثَبت فِي حَقه صلى الله عَلَيْهِ وَسلم من الْأَحْكَام. أَو خُوطِبَ بِهِ من الْكَلَام نَحْو: ﴿يَا أَيُّهَا الْمُزَّمِّلُ﴾ [المزمل: ١]، ﴿يَا أَيُّهَا الْمُدَّثِّرُ﴾ [المدثر: ١]، يتناول أمته؛ وَيثبت فِي حَقهم مثل مَا يثبت فِي حَقه، وَكَذَلِكَ مَا توجه إِلَى صَحَابِيّ من الْخطاب، يتَنَاوَل غَيره من الْمُكَلّفين الصَّحَابَة وَغَيرهم، حَتَّى إِنَّه يتَنَاوَل النَّبِي صلى الله عَلَيْهِ وَسلم مَا لم يقم دَلِيل مُخَصص لَهُ بِمَا ثَبت فِي حَقه، كوجوب السِّوَاك، والأضحى، وَالْوتر، أَو بِمَا خُوطِبَ بِهِ نَحْو: ﴿يَا أَيُّهَا النَّبِيُّ إِنَّا أَحْلَلْنَا لَكَ أَزْوَاجَكَ﴾ [الأحزاب: ٥٠]، إِلَى قَوْله: ﴿خَالِصَةً لَكَ مِنْ دُونِ الْمُؤْمِنِينَ﴾، أَو للصحابي مَا توجه إِلَيْهِ دون غَيره، كَقَوْلِه عَلَيْهِ السَّلَام لأبي بردة

253 [T] *Sharḥ Mukhtaṣar al-Rawḍah* (2/410).

«تجزيك وَلَا تجزي أحدا بعْدك»

Fifth: In regards to any rulings established for the Prophet ﷺ, or anytime he was addressed, such as: **{O you wrapped.}** [Qur'ān 73:1] Also: **{You, wrapped in your cloak.}** [Qur'ān 74:1] These commandments include his Ummah, and any ruling established for the Prophet ﷺ is also addressed to his Ummah. The same applies to instructions addressed to a particular companion: It applies to other *mukallaf* individuals, including other companions, and other Muslims [who came later]. It even includes the Prophet ﷺ, as long as there is no evidence to show that it does not apply to him. Examples are the obligation of the *siwāk*, the *aḍḥā* prayer, and offering *witr* prayer [all of which were obligations on the Prophet ﷺ, but not on others]. Other examples are when the Prophet ﷺ is addressed: **{Prophet, We have made lawful for you the wives whose bride gift you have paid, [...] [to the statement] this is only for you [O, Prophet] and not the rest of the believers.}** [Qur'ān 33:50] Also, if a companion is addressed with some commandment and [there is evidence to suggest] it does not apply to anyone else, such as the Prophet's ﷺ statement to Abu Burdah, **"It is sufficient for you, but not for anyone after you."**[254]

السَّادِسَة: تعلق الْأَمر إِلَى الْمَعْدُوم إن كَانَ بِمَعْنى طلب إِيقَاع الْفِعْل مِنْهُ حَال عَدمه فَهُوَ محَال بَاطِل بِالْإِجْمَاع لِأَن الْمَعْدُوم لَا يفهم الْخطاب فضلا عَن أَن يعْمل بِمُقْتَضَاهُ، وَإِن كَانَ بِمَعْنى الْخطاب لَهُ إِذا وجد وَوجدت فِيهِ شُرُوط التَّكْلِيف، فَهُوَ جَائِز عندنَا وَعند الأشعرية خلافًا للمعتزلة وَبَعض الْحَنَفِيَّة.

Sixth: A commandment pertaining to a nonexistent thing: If the meaning of this expression is that there is an instruction to perform an action, and that instruction is addressed to a person in a state of nonexistence, such a concept is impossible and false by consensus. A nonexistent thing cannot understand an instruction, let alone act on its implications. If it means that some instruction is addressed to a nonexistent person posited on when they gain the conditions of responsibility, this is a possibility to us and to the Ash'arītes, contrary to the Mu'tazilites and some Ḥanafī scholars.

السابعة: الْأَمر بِمَا علم الْآمِر انْتِفَاء شَرط وُقُوعه صَحِيح عندنَا، خلافًا للمعتزلة وَإِمَام الْحَرَمَيْنِ، وَهَذَا مُقَيّد بِمَا إِذا كَانَ الْآمِر عَالما بِانْتِفَاء شَرط الْوُقُوع، كالباري

254 Reported by al-Bukhārī (2/380).

عز وَجل مَعَ عَبده فِيمَا إِذا أمره بِصَوْم رَمَضَان - مثلا - وَهُوَ يعلم أَنه يَمُوت فِي شعْبَان، أما إِذا كَانَ الْآمِر والمأمور جاهلين بذلك، كالسيد مَعَ عَبده، فَلَا بُد من علم الْمُكَلف بتحقيق الشَّرْط، وَقد وَقع الأول، فَإِن الله أَمر الْخَلِيل عَلَيْهِ السَّلَام بِذبح وَلَده مَعَ علمه أَنه لَا يُمكنهُ من ذبحه، والتمكن من ذبحه شَرط لَهُ، وَقد علم الله انتفاءه.

Seventh: If a person giving a command knows that the condition for the occurrence is nonexistent, the commandment is still valid to [the Ḥanbalī scholars,] contrary to the Muʿtazilites and Imām al-Ḥaramayn. This is contingent on the commanding person knowing that the condition for occurrence is nonexistent. An example is Allah the Exalted obligating His slave to fast Ramadan, for example, while knowing that the person will die in Shaʿbān. However, if the one giving the command and the one being ordered do not know of such a restriction—such as a master commanding his slave—the one being instructed must be aware of the condition being a possibility. This has occurred, for when Allah the Exalted commanded Ibrāḥīm to slaughter his son, He knew that He would not enable Ibrāḥīm to complete the task. Enablement is a condition to slaughtering, and Allah the Exalted knew He was unable.

من فروع هَذِه الْقَاعِدَة أَن من أفسد صَوْم رَمَضَان بِمَا يُوجب الْكَفَّارَة، ثمَّ مَاتَ أَو جن، لم تسْقط عَنهُ الْكَفَّارَة، لِأَنَّهُ قد بَان عصيانه بإقدامه على الْإِفْسَاد فحصلت فَائِدَة التَّكْلِيف، فَلَا يقْدَح فِيهِ انْتِفَاء شَرط صِحَة صَوْم الْيَوْم بِمَوْتِهِ قبل إكماله.

An issue that relates to this one is that if one invalidates their fasting in Ramadan by doing something that requires them to pay an expiation, but then they die or go insane, they are not absolved of the expiation, because their indiscretion occurred when they invalidated their fast. As such, the consequence of responsibility occurred at that time. The fact that the condition for the validity of fasting is nonexistent, due to death, before they paid the expiation does not affect [the obligation of the expiation].

وَكَذَلِكَ من مرض أَو سَافر فِي يَوْم قد وطئ فِيهِ، لم تسْقط عَنهُ الْكَفَّارَة، لِأَن عصيانه اسْتَقر قبل وجود الْمُبِيح للإفطار.

Likewise, if a person becomes sick or travels on a day of Ramadan in which they also had intercourse, they are not absolved of the expiation, since their indiscretion occurred before the cause for allowing breaking the fast occurred.

وَمن فروعها أَيْضا أَن الْمَرْأَة يجب عَلَيْهَا الشُّرُوع فِي صَوْم يَوْم علم الله أَن تحيض فِيهِ، لِأَن حَقِيقَة الصَّوْم بِكَمَالِهِ، وَإِن فَاتَت بطريان الْحيض، لَكِن طاعتها بالعزم على امْتِثَال الْأَمر بِالصَّوْمِ بِتَقْدِير عدم الْحيض، أَو معصيتها لعدم الْعَزْم لم يفت.

Another issue relating to this one is that although Allah the Exalted knows that a woman will menstruate on a particular day [in Ramadan], she must still initiate her fast. The reality of fasting is completing the day, even if she later loses the ability to do so because of her menstruation. However, her obedience lies in her firm resolve and intention to fast had she not menstruated, and she is sinful if she did not have that intention.

فصل

Section [on Prohibitions]

وأما النهي: فَهُوَ القَوْل الإنشائي الدَّال على طلب كف عَن فعل على جِهَة الاستعلاء، فَخرج الْأَمر لِأَنهُ طلب فعل غير كف، وَخرج الالتماس وَالدُّعَاء، لِأَنهُ لَا استعلاء فيهمَا، وَقد اتَّضح فِي الْأَوَامِر أَكثر أَحْكَامه، إِذْ لكل حكم مِنْهُ وزان من الْأَمر، أَي: حكم يوازنه على الْعَكْس، مِثَاله فِي حدهما أَن الْأَمر اقْتِضَاء فعل، وَالنَّهْي اقْتِضَاء كف عَن فعل، وَالْأَمر ظَاهر فِي الْوُجُوب، وَاحْتِمَال النّدب وَالنَّهْي ظَاهر فِي التَّحْرِيم مَعَ احْتِمَال الْكَرَاهَة. وَصِيغَة الْأَمر افْعَل، وَصِيغَة النَّهْي لَا تفعل.

A prohibition is a statement used as origination (*inshā'*)[255] that indicates instruction to abstain from doing something, and it is done from a position of authority. This excludes commandments, since they are instructions to do something, but do not include abstention. Also, requests and supplications are excluded [by this definition], since neither are done from a position of authority. The majority of the exclusions mentioned in the commandments section are pertinent here, since both have an inverse relationship, meaning that a commandment is to imply an action, while a prohibition is to imply abstaining from an action. A commandment apparently indicates obligation, but carries the possibility of referring to a recommendation, while a prohibition apparently indicates a prohibition, but carries the possibility of undesirability. The expression of a commandment is "do" while the expression of the prohibition is "do not do."

وَالنَّهْي يلْزمه التّكْرَار والفور، وَالْأَمر يلزمانه على الْخلاف فِيهِ وَالْأَمر يَقْتَضِي صِحَة

---

255 [T] In the Arabic Language, a statement is either a declaratory statement (*khabar*) or an origination (*inshā'*). A *khabar* is one where it can be said that the one who uttered it is truthful or lying. For example, "Muḥammad has traveled," or, "'Alī is home." An *inshā'* is one where the utterer cannot be called a liar or truthful. For example, "Muḥammad, travel," or, "Stay home, 'Alī." Refer to *al-Balāghah al-Wāḍiḥah* (p. 144 and 169).

الْمَأْمُور بِهِ، وَالنَّهْي يَقْتَضِي فَسَاد الْمنْهِي عَنهُ، وكما يخرج عَن عُهْدَة الْمَأْمُور بِهِ بِفِعْلِهِ، كَذَلِك يخرج عَن عُهْدَة الْمنْهِي عَنهُ بِتَرْكِهِ، فَهَذَا معنى الموازنة بَين الْأَمر وَالنَّهْي.

A prohibition indicates repetition and urgency, while a commandment indicates the opposite. A commandment necessitates validity of the action while a prohibition necessitates invalidity of the prohibited thing. One absolves themselves of the commandment by performing it, and one absolves themselves of the responsibility of the prohibition by avoiding it. This is what is meant by the inverse relationship between commandments and prohibitions.

وَمن مباحثه أَن النَّهْي إِذا ورد عَن السَّبَب الَّذِي يُفِيد حكما اقْتضى فَسَاده، سَوَاء كَانَ النَّهْي عَنهُ لعَينه أَو لغيره، فِي الْعِبَادَات، أَو فِي الْمُعَامَلَات، وَذَلِكَ كالنهي عَن بيع الْغرَر وَعَن البيع وَقت النداء وَفِي الْمَسْجِد كَبيع الْمُزَابَنَة وكالنهي عَن نِكَاح الْمُتْعَة والشغار، وَنِكَاح الْإِمَاء لمن لَا يحن لَهُ، فَإِنَّهُ يَقْتَضِي الْفساد فِي ذَلِك كُله، على خلاف فِي بعضه.

A discussion to be had in this regard is that if a prohibition pertains to a cause that would result in a ruling, it necessitates invalidity, irrespective if the prohibition pertains to the cause in and of itself, or pertains to some external factor. This is true in matters of worship and in matters of transactions. Examples are the prohibition of aleatory contracts, selling during the prayer's call or within the mosque, *muzābanah* contracts,[256] temporary marriages, *shighār* marriages,[257] and marrying slave-girls if they are not lawful for them.[258] In all of the previous cases, the prohibition necessitates they

256 [T] A *muzābanah* contract is where there is an exchange, where one of the parties sells dried dates in exchange for dates that are still on the date palm trees. The only exception is the *arāyā* transaction, which has previously been explained. Refer to *Sharḥ Muntahā al-Irādāt* (2/68).

257 [T] A *shighār* marriage is defined as, "A man marrying a girl under his custodianship (such as his daughter, sister, etc.) to another man, in exchange for the other man marrying a girl under his own custodianship to the first man, without any dowry between the two." Refer to *Sharḥ Muntahā al-Irādāt* (2/666).

258 [T] Meaning, the man is free, has sufficient money [to afford marrying a free woman], or does not fear falling into fornication. Refer to *Sharḥ Muntahā al-Irādāt* (2/670).

are invalid, though there are differences of opinion on some of them.

إِلَّا لدَلِيل يدل على أَنه لَا يَقْتَضِي الْفساد، بل الْإِثْم بِفعل السَّبَب أَو كَرَاهَته، وَذَلِكَ كَبيع الْحَاضِر للبادي، وتلقي الركْبَان، أَو النجش وَنَحْوهَا، فَإِن النَّهْي ورد عَنْهَا، لَكِن دل الدَّلِيل على أَن النَّهْي الْمَذْكُور لَا يَقْتَضِي فَسَادهَا على الْأَظْهر، لَكِن يحرم تواطئها أَو يكره لأجل النَّهْي.

This, of course, is all if there is no evidence to show that the prohibition does not necessitate invalidation, but only causes one to incur a sin or to have fallen into an undesirable action. Examples are selling of a towns-person to a nomad, setting up outside of town to meet newcomers and sell to them, manipulating the buyers by false bidding on the product, and so forth. All of these are prohibited, but there is evidence to show that the sales are not invalidated in and of themselves. However, it is forbidden to engage in them, or they are disliked because of the prohibition.

وَقَالَ الطوفي فِي (مُخْتَصر الرَّوْضَة): وَالْمُخْتَار أَن النَّهْي عَن الشَّيْء لذاته أَو وصف لَهُ لَازم مُبْطل، ولخارج عَنهُ غير مُبْطل، وَفِيه لوصف غير لَازم تردد، وَالْأولَى الصِّحَّة. هَذَا كَلَامه.

Al-Ṭūfī stated in *Mukhtaṣar al-Rawḍah*, "The view I choose is that the prohibition of something in and of itself, or a prohibition of an inseparable quality [of the prohibited thing], necessitates that it is invalid. However, a prohibition for some external factor does not nullify the transaction. As for if the quality is separable, there is a difference of opinion, though the more correct view is that it is valid.[259]

فمثال النَّهْي عَنهُ لذاته الْكفْر، وَالْكذب، وَالظُّلم، والجور، وَنَحْوهَا من المستقبح لذاته عقلا. وَمِثَال النَّهْي عَن الْفِعْل لوصف لَازم لَهُ نِكَاح الْكَافِر الْمسلمَة، وَبيع العَبْد الْمُسلم من كَافِر، فَإِن ذَلِك يلْزم مِنْهُ إِثْبَات الْقيام والاستيلاء، والسبيل للْكَافِرِ على الْمُسلم، فَيبْطل هَذَا الْوَصْف اللَّازِم لَهُ.

Examples of things prohibited in and of themselves are: Disbelief, lying, oppression, transgression, and other things that are rationally reprehensible.

259 [T] *Sharḥ Mukhtaṣar al-Rawḍah* (2/429).

Examples of things that are prohibited due to an inseparable quality are: A non-believing male marrying a Muslim woman, and selling a Muslim slave to a non-Muslim—which would dictate the non-Muslim having reign and authority over the Muslim. As such, both are prohibited due to this inseparable quality.

وَمِثَال النَّهْي عَن الْفِعْل لأمر خَارج عَنهُ لَا تعلق بِهِ عقلا، مَا لَو نهي عَن الصَّلَاة فِي دَار، لِأَن فِيهَا صنما مَدْفُونا.

An example of things that are prohibited for external factors that have no rational connection with the action is if one is forbidden from praying in a house because there is a buried idol.

أَو شرعا، مَا لَو نهى عَن بيع الْجَوْز وَالْبيض خشيَة أَن يقامر بِهِ، أَو عَن بيع السِّلَاح من الْمُسلمين خشيَة أَن يقطعوا بِهِ الطَّرِيق، أَو عَن غرس الْعِنَب أَو بَيْعه خشيَة أَن يعصر خمرًا، وَنَحْوه، لم يكن ذَلِك النَّهْي مُبْطلًا وَلَا مَانِعا، لِأَن هَذِه الْمَفَاسِد - وَإِن تعلّقت بِهَذِهِ الْأَفْعَال تعلقا عقليا بِمَعْنى أَن هَذِه الْأَفْعَال تصلح أَن تكون سَببا لتِلْك الْمَفَاسِد - لَكِنَّهَا غير مُتَعَلقَة بهَا شرعا، لِأَن الشَّرْع لم يعْهَد مِنْهُ الِالْتِفَات فِي الْمَنْع إِلَى هَذَا التَّعَلُّق الْعقلِيّ الْبعيد.

An example of having no religious connection is someone being prohibited from selling nuts or eggs because they fear [the buyer] will gamble with them. Or, one is prohibited from selling weapons to Muslims for fear that they might become highway robbers. Another example is prohibition from planting or selling grapes out of fear that it might be juiced and made into wine. Such things never invalidate nor impede a transaction. Although there is some rational connection between these things—in the sense that any of these items could rationally be causes for those harms—the harms have no religious connection to the items, as the legislation has not been known to forbid things based on some far-fetched rational connection.

وَمِثَال مَا كَانَ النَّهْي فِيهِ لوصف غير لَازم النَّهْي عَن البيع وَمَا فِي مَعْنَاهُ من الْعُقُود وَقت النداء، وَإِنَّمَا نهي عَنهُ لكَونه بِالْجُمْلَةِ متصفا بِكَوْنِهِ مفوتا للْجُمُعَة، أَو مفضيا إِلَى التفويت بالتشاغل بِالْبيعِ، لَكِن هَذَا الْوَصْف غير لَازم للْبيع، لجَوَاز أَن يعْقد

مئة عقد مَا بَين النداء إِلَى الصَّلَاة، ثمَّ يُدْرِكهَا، فَلَا تفوت، فَالْأولى فِي هَذَا العقد الصِّحَّة.

An example of something prohibited due to some separable quality is the prohibition of sales and other contractual agreements during the call to prayer. The prohibition is because, generally speaking, they will miss the Friday prayer or it would lead to missing the prayer due to busying themselves with selling. However, this quality is not a necessary quality of selling, since it is possible for a person to complete a hundred sales between the call to prayer and the prayer itself, and then catch the prayer, thereby not missing it. As such, the correct view is that this type of contractual agreement is valid.

۞۞۞

فَوَائِد

Some Useful Benefits

الأولى: مَا علق عَلَيْهِ الْأَمر من شَرط، كَقَوْلِه: إِذا زَالَت الشَّمْس فصلوا، أَو صفة، كَقَوْلِه تَعَالَى ﴿الزَّانِيَةُ وَالزَّانِي فَاجْلِدُوا﴾ [النُّور: ٢]، إِن ثَبت أَنه عِلّة للْفِعْل، فَلَا خلاف فِي تكرره بتكرره، وَإِن لم يكن عِلّة فَإِن قيل: الْأَمر الْمُطلق للتكرار، فهاهنا أولى. وَإِن قيل لَيْسَ للتكرار، اخْتلفُوا هَاهُنَا وَاخْتَارَ الْآمِدِيّ عَدمه.

First: If a commandment hinges on some precondition, such as the religion teaching, "If the sun sets, pray," or an attribute, such as Allah the Exalted saying: **{Strike the adulteress and the adulterer one hundred times.}** [Qur'ān 24:2] If the [condition or attribute] is established as a cause for the action, none disagree that so long as it is repeated, the commandment [pertaining to the action] is repeated. However, if it is not a cause, some said that the absolute commandment indicates repetition, and in this case, it is more deserving of repetition. However, if one takes the view that absolute commandments do not indicate repetition, the scholars have differed. Al-Āmidī opined that [it does not indicate repetition].

وَأما النَّهْي الْمُعَلق بِمَا يتَكَرَّر، فَمن قَالَ: مُطلق النَّهْي يَقْتَضِي التّكْرَار، أثبت التّكْرَار هَاهُنَا بطرِيق الأولى، وَمن قَالَ: لَا يَقْتَضِي التكْرَار، اخْتلفُوا هَل يَقْتَضِيهِ أم

لَا؟ وَالْأَظْهَر أنه يَقْتَضِيهِ بِخِلَاف الْأَمر.

As for a prohibition pertaining to something that is repeated, some scholars viewed that prohibitions indicate repetition, and as such, it is more worthy of being repeated [as the prohibition hinges on a condition or attribute]. However, others took the view that prohibitions do not indicate repetition, and they differed on whether a prohibition that is contingent on a condition or an attribute necessitates repetition. The correct view is that it does, indeed, indicate repetition, contrary to the commandment.

الثَّانِيَة: ترد صِيغَة النهي للتَّحْرِيم، نَحْو: لَا تقتلُوا، وللكراهة، نَحْو: لَا يمسك ذكره بيمينه وَهُوَ يَبُول، وللتحقير، نَحْو: ﴿**وَلَا تَمُدَّنَّ عَيْنَيْكَ**﴾ [طه: ١٣١]، ولبيان الْعَاقِبَة ﴿**وَلَا تحسبن الله غافلا**﴾ [إبْرَاهِيم: ٤٢] وللدعاء ﴿**لَا تُؤَاخِذْنَا**﴾ [الْبَقَرَة: ٢٨٦] ولليأس ﴿**لَا تَعْتَذِرُوا**﴾ [التَّوْبَة: ٩٤] وللإرشاد ﴿**لَا تَسْأَلُوا عَنْ أَشْيَاءَ**﴾ [الْمَائِدَة: ١٠١]، وللأدب ﴿**وَلَا تَنْسَوُا الْفَضْلَ بَيْنَكُمْ**﴾ [الْبَقَرَة: ٢٣٧]، وللتهديد: لَا تمتثل أَمْرِي، ولإباحة التّرْك: كالنهي بعد الإيجَاب على رَأْي، وللالتماس: كَقَوْلِك لنظيرك: لَا تفعل، وللتصبر ﴿**لَا تحزن**﴾ [التوبة: ٤٠] ولإيقاع الأمن ﴿**ولا تتخف**﴾ [القصص: ٣١]، وللتسوية ﴿**فاصبرو أو لا تصبروا**﴾ [الطور: ١٦] فإن تجردت صيغة النهي عن ذلك فالمختار أنها للتحريم.

Second: Prohibitive expressions could mean: (i) [Legal] forbiddance (*taḥrīm*), such as when the legislation states, "Do not kill." (ii) Undesirability, such as, "Do not hold your privates with your right hand when urinating." (iii) Disparagement, such as when Allah states: **{Do not let your eyes crave what We have allowed some of the disbelievers to enjoy.}** [Qur'ān 20:131] (iv) Showing outcomes, such as: **{Do not think [O Prophet] that Allah is unaware of what the disbelievers do.}** [Qur'ān 14:42] (v) Supplication, such as: **{Lord, do not burden us.}** [Qur'ān 2:286] (vi) Instilling hopelessness, such as: **{"Do not make excuses."}** [Qur'ān 9:94] (vi) Guidance, such as: **{Do not ask about matters.}** [Qur'ān 5:101] (vii) Teaching morals, such as: **{And do not forget kindness among yourselves.}** [Qur'ān 2:237] (viii) Threatening, such as saying, "If you do not obey my commandment!" (ix) Allowing the action to be forsaken, such as when some previously obligated matter is forbidden, according to a view. (x) Requesting, such as saying to one's peer, "Do not do that." (xi) Instilling forbearance, such as: **{Do not worry.}** [Qur'ān 9:40] (xii) Instilling a sense of safety, such as: **{And have no fear.}** [Qur'ān 28:31]

فَإِن تجردت صِيغَة النْهي عَن ذَلِك فالمختار أَنَّهَا للتَّحْرِيم.

If the prohibitive expression does not have any of the previously mentioned contexts, the chosen view is that the expression indicates legal forbiddance (i.e. that the action is *ḥarām*).

الثَّالثة: النَّهْي يَقْتَضِي الْفَوْر والدوام عِنْد أَصْحَابنَا، وَالْأَكْثَر، وَخَالف الباقلاني والرازي. وَيكون النَّهْي عَن وَاحِد ومتعدد، جمعا، وفرقا، وجميعا.

Third: Prohibitions indicate urgency and continuance according to our *aṣḥāb* and according to the majority. Al-Bāqillānī and al-Rāzī took different views. A prohibition can be of a single thing, multiple things, a group, separate things, or a whole of something.

الْعُمُوم وَالْخُصُوص

On Generality and Specificity

أما الْعَام: فَاعْلَم أَن اللَّفْظ إِمَّا أَن يدل على مَاهِيَّة مَدْلُوله من حَيْثُ هِيَ هِيَ، أَو لَا، فَإِن دلّ على الْمَاهِيّة من حَيْثُ هِيَ هِيَ، أَي: مَعَ قطع النّظر عَن جَمِيع مَا يعرض لَهَا من وحدة، وَكَثْرَة، وحدوث، وَقدم، وَطول، وقصر، وَسَوَاد، وَبَيَاض، فَهَذَا هُوَ الْمُطلق، وَذَلِكَ لِأَن الْإِنْسَان مثلا من حَيْثُ هُوَ إِنْسَان إِنَّمَا يدل على حَيَوَان نَاطِق، لَا على وَاحِد، وَلَا على حَادث، وَلَا طَوِيل، وَلَا أسود، وَلَا على ضد شَيْء من ذَلِك. وَإِن كُنَّا نعلم أَنه لَا يَنْفَكّ عَن بعض تِلْكَ.

As for generality, you must know that a term either refers to the essence of its signification as it is, or does not. If the term refers to an essence as it is—meaning, without taking into account anything that occurs to it, such as it being singular, plural, temporal, eternal, long, short, black, white, and so forth—it is referred to as an absolute and unrestricted term. An example is that a human, inasmuch as he is a human, refers to a rational speaking animal. It does not refer to any particular individual; it does not refer to temporality, length, blackness, nor any opposites of those descriptions. Though, we do know that [for an instance of a human to exist], some of those descriptions are bound to occur.

وَإِن لم يدل على الْمَاهِية من حَيْثُ هِيَ، فإمَّا أَن يدل على وحدة أَو وحدات، فَإِن دلّ على وحدة، فَهِيَ إِمَّا مُعينَة، كزيد وَعَمْرو، وَهُوَ الْعلم، أَو غير مُعينَة، كَرجل وَفرس، وَهُوَ النكرة، وَإِن دلّ على وحدات مُتعَدِّدَة، وَهِي الْكَثْرَة، فَتلك الْكَثْرَة، إِمَّا بعض وحدات الْمَاهِيّة أَو جميعها، فَإِن كَانَت بَعْضهَا فَهو اسم الْعَدَد كعشرين وَثَلَاثِين وَنَحْوهَا، وَإِن كَانَت جَمِيع وحدات الْمَاهِيّة فَهُوَ الْعَام. وعَلى هَذَا فالعام: هُوَ اللَّفْظ الدَّال على جَمِيع أَجزَاء مَاهِيَّة مَدْلُوله.

If a term does not refer to an essence as it is, it can either refer to an instantiation, or multiples. If it refers to an instantiation, it can either refer to a particular, such as Zayd or ʿAmr, and that is known as a proper noun. If it does not refer to a particular, such as "man," or "horse," it is a common noun. If, however, it refers to multiple instances, that is a multitude. The multitude can either be individual instances of the essence or could be the entirety of the essence. If they are individual instances, they are known as numbers, such as twenty, thirty, and so forth. If they refer to the entirety of the essence of the multitude, it is known as "general." As such, "generality (*ʿām*)" is defined as: A term that indicates all particulars of the essence of what it is referring to.

وَقد اسْتُفِيدَ من هَذَا التَّقْسِيم معرفَة حُدُود مَا تضمنه من الْحَقَائِق، وَهُوَ الْمُطلق، وَالْعلم، والنكرة، وَاسم الْعدَد. فالمطلق: هُوَ اللَّفْظ الدَّال على الْمَاهِيّة الْمُجَرَّدَة عَن وصف زَائِد. وَالْعلم: هُوَ اللَّفْظ الدَّال على وحدة مُعينَة. وَاسم الْعدَد: هُوَ اللَّفْظ الدَّال على بعض ماهيات مَدْلُوله.

The previous categorisation helps to understand the definitions of the concepts being described, namely: absolutes, proper nouns, common nouns, and numbers. Therefore, 'absolute' (*muṭlaq*) is term that refers to an essence stripped of any additional factors and descriptors. A proper noun is a term that refers to a particular thing. A number is a term referring to a part of the essences of what it is referring to.

وَالْفرق بَين الْخَاص وَاسم الْعدَد أَن دلَالَة الْخَاص إِنَّمَا هِيَ على وحدة وَاحِدَة معينَة أَو مَخْصُوصَة، وَاسم الْعدَد يدل على وحدات مُتعَدِّدَة غير مستغرقة.

The difference between a particularization and a number is that the signification of the particularized item is a reference to a single or specific unit. As for numbers, they refer to various units without denoting any particular.[260]

ثمَّ اعْلَم أَن اللَّفْظ يَنْقَسِم إِلَى مَا لَا أَعم مِنْهُ، وَذَلِكَ كالمعلوم أَو الشَّيْء، لِأَن

260 [T] This means, when one says, "I want twenty out of one hundred horses," it can be any of those twenty, and that term "twenty" does not denote any specific twenty. However, when one says, "I want twenty horses, but make sure they are Arabian," they have particularized Arabian horses. That, in essence, is the difference al-Shaykh Ibn Badrān is communicating.

الْمَعْلُوم يتَنَاوَل جَمِيع الْأَشْيَاء قديمها ومحدثها، ومعدومها، وموجودها، لتَعلق الْعلم بذلك كُله، وَالشَّيْء يتَنَاوَل الْقَدِيم، والمحدث، والجوهر، وَالْعرض، وَسَائِر الموجودات، فالشيء أخص من الْمَعْلُوم، لِأَن كل شَيْء مَعْلُوم، وَلَيْسَ كل مَعْلُوم شَيْئا. وَهَذَا النَّوْع يُسمى الْعَام الْمُطلق.

Further, a term can be described as the utmost generality. Examples include two words, namely, "known," and "thing." A "known" thing includes all things, whether they are eternal, temporal, nonexistent, or existent, since knowledge encompasses all of those things. As for "thing," it includes things that are eternal, temporal, substances, accidents, and all other existing things. The term "thing" is more particularized than the term "known", since every "thing" can be described as "known," but not every "known" thing can be described as a "thing." This category of terms is known as absolute generality.

وينقسم اللَّفْظ إِلَى مَا لَا أخص مِنْهُ، وَيُسمى الْخَاص الْمُطلق، وَذَلِكَ كزيد وَعَمْرو وَنَحْوهمَا، إِذْ لَا يُوجد أخص من ذَلِك يعرف بِهِ، وَلِهَذَا كَانَت الْأَعْلَام أعرف المعارف عِنْد بعض النُّحَاة.

Terms can also be described as the utmost particular, which is also known as absolute particularization. Examples are ʿAmr, Zayd and so forth, since there is no more particular way to refer to that person. Due to this reason, proper nouns are seen as the most definite of nouns according to some of the grammarians.

وينقسم إِلَى مَا بَينهمَا، وَيُقَال لَهُ: الْعَام أَو الْخَاص الإضافي، فَإِن الْحَيَوَان - مثلا - خَاص بِالنِّسْبَةِ إِلَى مَا فَوْقه، وَهُوَ الْجِسْم الْمُطلق، عَام بِالنِّسْبَةِ إِلَى مَا تَحْتَهُ من أَنْوَاعه كالإنسان وَالْفرس وَنَحْوهمَا، وكالموجود فَإِنَّهُ خَاص بِالنِّسْبَةِ إِلَى الْمَعْلُوم، عَام بِالنِّسْبَةِ إِلَى الْجَوْهَر، فَتَقول: كل إِنْسَان حَيَوَان، وَلَيْسَ كل جسم حَيَوَانا.

Next, terms can be described as being between the utmost particular and the utmost general. They can be referred to as general or particular relatively. An animal, for example, is a particular relative to the category above it, namely, a body, but is a general relative to the species it encompasses, such as a human, horse, and so forth. Further, the same can be said about things that are "existent," for they are particular when relative to things that are "known," but general when relative to a substance. One can say, "Every human is an animal, but not every body is an animal."

وَالضَّابِط فِي الْعَام وَالْخَاص أَن كل شَيْئَيْنِ انقسم أَحدهمَا إِلَى الآخر وَغَيره، فالمنقسم أَعم من المنقسم إِلَيْهِ، فالموجود يَنْقَسِم إِلَى جَوْهَر وَغَيره كالعرض. والجوهر يَنْقَسِم إِلَى نَام وَغَيره كالجماد، والنامي يَنْقَسِم إِلَى حَيَوَان وَغَيره كالنبات، وَالْحَيَوَان يَنْقَسِم إِلَى إِنْسَان وَغَيره كالفرس.

The maxim to consider in respect to generality and particularization is: Anything that can be categorised into two or more things, the more encompassing category is relatively general when considering the less encompassing category. For example, existent things are categorised into: substances, and non-substances. A substance can be categorised into animate and inanimate. Animate can be categorised into animals and non-animals, such as plants. Animals can also be categorised into humans and non-humans, such as horses.

إِذا علم هَذَا فَليعلم أَن الْأَلْفَاظ الَّتِي يُسْتَفَاد مِنْهَا الْعُمُوم خَمْسَة:

Since that is now known, you must know that there are five terms that indicate generality:

أَحدهمَا: مَا عرف بأل الَّتِي لَيست للْعهد، وَهُوَ إِمَّا لفظ وَاحِد كالسارق والسارقة، أَو جمع، ثمَّ الْجمع إِمَّا أَن يكون لَهُ وَاحِد من لَفظه كالمسلمين وَالْمُشْرِكين، وَالَّذين جمع الَّذِي، أَو لَا يكون لَهُ وَاحِد من لَفظه كالناس وَالْحَيَوَان وَالْمَاء وَالتُّرَاب، إِذْ لَا يُقَال فِيهِ: ناسة وَلَا حيوانة، لِأَن هَذِه الْأَلْفَاظ وضعت لتدل على جنس مدلولها لَا على آحاده مُنْفَرِدَة، والمعرف بِاللَّامِ العهدية لَا يكون عَاما لدلالته على ذَات مُعينَة نَحْو لقِيت رجلا، فَقلت للرجل.

First: Anything designated with "the (أل)" which is not definite.[261] It can

261 [T] The word "the (أل)" to the Arabs, when in the definite sense, means to use "the" to refer to something newly present within one's knowledge, a sort of contextual clue that allows one to understand what "the" is referring to. It is of three types:

First: Explicitly mentioned information that is present within one's knowledge. For

either be a single word, such as "the thief," or, "the female thief," or could refer to something plural. If it refers to a plural word, sometimes that word can have a singular form, such as *muslim*, which is the singular form of *muslimīn* or *mushrik*, which is the singular form of *mushrikīn*. Other times, it does not have a singular form, such as [the Arabic forms of] "people," "animals", "water" and "dirt." One cannot refer to "people" or a spec of "dirt" with a singular form. These terms were used to refer to a genus, not to individual instances. A definite "the," by nature, cannot be used in the general sense, because it is used to define a single instance of a thing. For example, one can say, "I saw a man, and I said to the man."

الثَّانِي: مَا أضيف من أَلْفَاظ الْعُمُوم إِلَى معرفَة كعبيد زيد وَمَال عَمْرو، فَالْأول لَفظه جمع، وَالثَّانِي اسْم جنس، فَلَو قلت: رَأَيْت عبيد زيد وَمَال عَمْرو، اقْتضى ذَلِك أَن الرُّؤْيَة كَانَت لجَمِيع ذَلِك.

Second: When a general term is used in the genitive case of possession, and attributed to a proper noun. For example, one can say, "the slaves of Zayd" or, "the wealth of 'Amr." The first example contains a plural word (slaves), while the second example contains a genus (wealth). Therefore, if you were to say, "I saw Zayd's slaves and 'Amr's wealth," that would necessitate that you saw all of those things.

الثَّالِث: أدوات الشَّرْط نَحْو: (من) - بِفَتْح الْمِيم - فِيمَا يعقل وَ(مَا) فِيمَا لَا يعقل. وَقيل: إِن (مَا) فِي الْخَبَر والاستفهام تكون للعاقل وَغَيره، و(أَيْن) و(أنى) وَ(حَيْثُ)

example, Allah the Exalted states: **{We have sent a messenger to you [people] to be your witness, just as We sent a messenger to Pharaoh, but Pharaoh disobeyed the messenger, so We seized him with a stern grip.}** [Qur'ān 73:15-16]

In this case, we know who "the Messenger," is, since he has previously been mentioned. The verse means, "Pharaoh disobeyed the messenger sent to him."

Second: A known place or thing that does not need additional recognition nor definition. For example, Allah the Exalted states: **{Even if you do not help the Prophet, Allah helped him when the disbelievers drove him out: When the two of them were in the cave.}** [Qur'ān 9:40] The term "the cave," refers to a specific mountain that we know, which is Mount Thawr.

Third: When the thing referred to as "the" is present and witnessable. For example, Allah the Exalted states: **{Today I have perfected your religion for you, completed My blessing upon you, and chosen as your religion Islam.}** [Qur'ān 5:3] In this verse, Allah the Exalted is referring to the Day of 'Arafah, and this verse was revealed on that day. Refer to *Awḍaḥ al-Masālik 'alā Alfiyyat Ibn Mālik* by Ibn Hishām (1/181).

للمكان، وَ(مَتى) للزمان الْمُبْهم وَ(أي) لِلْكُلّ، وتعم (من) وَ(أي) المضافة إِلَى الشَّخْص ضميرهما، فَاعِلا كَانَ أَو مَفْعُولا.

Third: Conditional particles, such as "whoever" for an animate being, and "whatever" for an inanimate thing. It was said that "whatever" can be used in declarative and interrogative sentences to refer to animate beings as well as others. Other examples are, "wherever," "anywhere," and, "whence," when referring to a place, "whenever," for an indefinite time, and "any," for everything. The two terms, "whoever" and "anyone," imply generality when compounded to refer to an individual with a pronoun, regardless if the pronoun refers to the subject or the object.[262]

الرَّابِع: (كل) وَ(جَمِيع) وَنَحْوهمَا، و(معشر) و(معاشر) وَ(عَامة)، و(كافة)، و(قاطبة)، وَمَا أشبه هَذِه الْأَلْفَاظ.

Fourth: "All," "every," and so forth. "Folks," "the populace," "the masses," and "all together, without exception," etc. all refer to generality.

الْخَامِس: النكرة فِي سِيَاق النَّفْي أَو الْأَمر نَحْو قَوْله تَعَالَى: ﴿وَلَمْ تَكُن لَّهُ صَاحِبَةٌ﴾ [الْأَنْعَام: ١٠١]، ﴿وَلَمْ يَكُن لَّهُ شَرِيكٌ فِي الْمُلْكِ﴾ [الْإِسْرَاء: ١١١] ﴿وَلَمْ يَكُن لَّهُ كُفُوًا أَحَدٌ﴾ [الصمد: ٤] وَنَحْو أعتق رَقَبَة. وَحكم النكرة الْوَاقِعَة فِي سِيَاق النَّهْي حكم النكرَة الْوَاقِعَة فِي سِيَاق النَّفْي نَحْو: لَا تخاصم أحدا

Fifth: An indefinite noun in the context of a negation or commandment indicates generality. For example, Allah the Exalted states: **{He has no spouse.}** [Qur'ān 6:101] He also states: **{He has no partner in His rule.}** [Qur'ān 17:111] Lastly, He states: **{Nor is there ever anyone equal or similar to Him.}** [Qur'ān 112:4] Also, "Free a slave." And the ruling of the indefinite in the context of prohibition is that of an indefinite noun in the context of a negation, e.g. "Do not fight anyone."

تَتِمَّة: معيار الْعُمُوم صِحَة الِاسْتِثْنَاء من غير عدد.

Addition: The standard by which we can know what is general is if it can

262 [T] Examples of it being the subject, "Whoever of you stands," and an example of it being an object is, "Whoever of you I stand up." Refer to *Uṣūl al-Fiqh* by Ibn Mufliḥ (2/767).

receive an exception without specifying a number.

تَنْبِيه: أَقسَام أَلْفَاظ الْعُمُوم الْمَذْكُورَة تَقْتَضِي الْعُمُوم عندنَا، بِقصد وَاضع اللُّغَة إفادتها الْعُمُوم مَا لم يقم دَلِيل أَو قرينَة تدل على أَن المُرَاد بهَا الْخُصُوص، فَيكون من بَاب إِطْلَاق الْعَام وَإِرَادَة الْخَاص، وَلما كَانَ مَا تقدم إِنَّمَا هُوَ كالقواعد الْكُلية، وَكَانَت الْمسَائِل الَّتِي بعده كالجزئيات، أخرناها عَنهُ فَقُلْنَا: وَهَاهُنَا مسَائِل:

Note, too, that the categories of the terms that indicate generality that were mentioned, necessitate generality according to [Ḥanbalī scholars]. The reason is that the one who formulated that usage of language intended such things. This, however, is not the case if there is an evidence or contextual clue that would indicate some particular meaning or thing, making it a general statement which was intended for a particular usage. The previously mentioned facts were universal principles, and what is to follow are subsidiary matters, and due to that, I have delayed speaking about them until now. However, without further ado, I say that there are a number of issues:

الأولى: أقل الْجمع ثَلَاثَة عِنْد الْأَكْثَرين، وَمِنْهُم أَبُو حنيفَة وَالشَّافِعِيّ وَأحمد، وَحكي عَن الْمَالِكِيَّة وَابْن دَاوُد الظَّاهِرِيّ وَبَعض الشَّافِعِيَّة والنحاة أَنه اثْنَان. وَحَكَاهُ أَيْضا فِي (الْمَحْصُول) عَن القَاضِي أبي بكر والأستاذ أبي إِسْحَاق وَجمع من الصَّحَابَة وَالتَّابِعِينَ. وَحكى الْآمِدِيّ القَوْل بِالْأولِ عَن ابْن عَبَّاس وَأبي حنيفَة وَالشَّافِعِيّ وَبَعض أَصْحَابه ومشايخ الْمُعْتَزلَة. وَالثَّانِي عَن عمر وَزيد بن ثَابت وَمَالك وَدَاوُد وَالْقَاضِي أبي بكر وَأبي إِسْحَاق وَالْغَزالِيّ وَبَعض الشَّافِعِيَّة.

First: The least number of things that can be considered plural is three, according to the majority, including Abu Ḥanīfah, al-Shāfiʿī, and Aḥmad. It was reported from Māliki scholars, Ibn Dāwūd al-Ẓāhirī, some grammarians and Shāfiʿī scholars that it is two. In *al-Maḥṣūl*, [al-Rāzī] mentions it as a view of al-Qāḍī Abu Bakr, al-Ustādh Abu Isḥāq, and a number of companions and Tābiʿīn. Al-Āmidī claimed that the first view belonged to Ibn ʿAbbās, Abu Ḥanīfah, al-Shāfiʿī and some of his disciples, and the *shaykhs* of the Muʿtazilites. The second view was attributed to ʿUmar, Zayd ibn Thābit, Mālik, Dāwūd, al-Qāḍī Abu Bakr, Abu Isḥāq, al-Ghazālī, and some Shāfiʿī scholars.

وَفَائِدَة هَذَا الْخلاف: أَنه إِذا علق حكم على جمع - كَأَن يَقُول: لله عَليّ أَن أتصدق بِدَرَاهِم، أَو أَصوم أَيَّامًا وَنَحْوه - وتعذر الْبَيَان، فعلى القَوْل الأول: يلْزمه التَّصَدُّق بِثَلَاثَة دَرَاهِم، وَصَوْم ثَلَاثَة أَيَّام، مَا لم يدل دَلِيل من الْخَارِج على مِقْدَار من الْعدَد معِين. وعَلى القَوْل الثَّانِي: يَكْفِيهِ اثْنَان.

The importance of this difference of opinion shows that when a ruling is contingent on a plural noun, such as saying, "I vow to Allah the Exalted to give dirhams in charity," or, "I vow to Allah the Exalted to fast some days," and so forth, and they do not clarify how many dirhams or how many days. The first view dictates that the person must give at least three dirhams and fast at least three days, so long as there is no external evidence to show that [the one giving the vow] intended another set number of days. According to the scholars who held the second view, the person must give at least two dirhams [and fast only two days].

وَمحل الْخلاف فِي غير لفظ جمع وَنحن وَقُلْنَا وقلوبكما، مِمَّا فِي الْإِنْسَان مِنْهُ شَيْء وَاحِد فَإِنَّهُ وفَاق.

Note that this disagreement is not regarding words used in the plural sense which a person only has one of, such as, "we said," the royal "we," and, "my hearts." All scholars agree on this point.

الثَّانِيَة: الِاعْتِبَار فِيمَا ورد على سَبَب خَاص بِعُمُومِهِ لَا بِخُصُوص السَّبَب، خلافًا لمَالِك وَبَعض الشَّافِعِيَّة.

Second: Consideration must be given to the generality of the wording of text, not the particular instance that elicited the text.[263] This is contrary to Mālik and some Shāfiʿī scholars.

الثَّالِثَة: قَول الرَّاوِي: نهى رَسُول الله صلى الله عَلَيْهِ وَسلم عَن الْمُزَابَنَة، وَقضى بِالشُّفْعَة، وَنَحْوه، يَصح التَّمَسُّك بِهِ فِي الْعُمُوم فِي أَمْثَال تلك الْقَضِيَّة المحكية.

Third: The statement of the narrator: "The Prophet ﷺ forbade *muzābanah*

263 [T] This means, if the Prophet ﷺ gave a ruling in a particular case, and used general wording, should we consider the generality of the wording to encompass all Muslims after? Or, should we consider only the specific instance to refer to that person, and then, use that instance for an analogy?

transactions,"[264] or, "The Prophet ﷺ judged that the preemption is valid," and other such statements, it is valid to adhere to the generality of these wordings and apply them to identical situations.

الرَّابِعَة: الْخطاب الْوَارِد مُضَافا إِلَى النَّاس وَالْمُؤمنِينَ، وَالْأمة والمكلفين، نَحْو يَا أَيُّهَا النَّاسُ ﴿وَتُوبُوا إِلَى اللهِ جَمِيعاً أَيُّهَا الْمُؤْمِنُونَ﴾ [النُّور: ٣١]، و﴿كُنتُمْ خَيْرَ أُمَّةٍ أُخْرِجَتْ لِلنَّاسِ﴾ [آل عمرَان: ١١٠]، وَنَحْو ذَلِك يتَنَاوَل العَبْد لِأَنَّهُ من النَّاس، وَالْمُؤمنِينَ، وَالْأمة والمكلفين. وَخُرُوجه عَن بعض الْأَحْكَام، كوجوب الْحَج، وَالْجهَاد، وَالْجُمُعَة إِنَّمَا هُوَ لأمر عَارض، وَهُوَ فقره، واشتغاله بِخِدْمَة سَيّده، وَنَحْو ذَلِك، كَالْمَرِيضِ وَالْمُسَافر وَالْحَائِض يتناولهم الْخطاب الْمَذْكُور، وَيخرجُونَ عَن بعض الْأَحْكَام، كوجوب الصَّوْم وَالصَّلَاة على الْحَائِض، وَوُجُوب الصَّوْم وإتمام الصَّلَاة على الْمُسَافِر، وَوُجُوب الصَّوْم على الْمَرِيض لأمر عَارض، وَهُوَ الْمَرَض وَالسّفر وَالْحيض.

Fourth: When an expression in a text addresses people, believers, the Ummah, or *mukallaf* people, such as: "O people," or: **{Turn to Allah in repentance all together, O believers.}** [Qur'ān 24:31] Also: **{You are the best community ever raised for humanity.}** [Qur'ān 3:110] Such expressions are inclusive of slaves, since they are amongst the people, the believers, the Ummah, and *mukallaf* people. The fact that some rulings do not apply to them, such as the obligation of Ḥajj, warfare and the Friday prayer, is due to an extrinsic factor; it could be due to poverty, or being busy with one's serving of their master. Also, sick and travelling people, and menstruating women are included within such general addresses. They are excluded from some rulings, however; fasting and prayer are not obligatory on the menstruating woman, fasting and completion of the prayer [as four units] are not obligatory on travellers, and fasting is not an obligation on the sick person. This is all due to an extrinsic quality, namely, sickness, travel, and menstruation.

وَيدخل النِّسَاء فِي خطاب النَّاس، وَالَّذِي لَا تَخْصِيص فِيهِ بِالرِّجَالِ وَالنِّسَاء

---

264 [T] A *muzābanah* contract is where there is an exchange, where one of the parties sells dried dates in exchange for dates that are still on the date palm trees. Refer to *Sharḥ Muntahā al-Irādāt* (2/68).

كأدوات الشَّرْط نَحْو: من رَأَيْت فَأكْرمه، فَإِنَّهُ يتَنَاوَل النِّسَاء أَيْضا. وَأما الَّذِي يخص غَيْرهنَّ كالرجال والذكور، فَإِنَّهُ لَا يتناولهن. وَنَحْو: الْمُسلمين وَالْمُؤمنِينَ، ﴿وكلوا وَاشْرَبُوا﴾ [البقرة: ١٨٧]، مِمَّا هُوَ لجمع الذُّكُور، فَفِيهِ خلاف: فَذهب أَبُو الْخطاب وَالْأَكْثَر إِلَى أَنَّهُنَّ يدخلن فِيهِ.

Furthermore, women are included when the phrase, "O people," is used. Women are also not excluded in conditional statements, such as, "If you see a person, honour them." It includes women, as well. As for things that are specific to men and males, they are not included. As for when Allah the Exalted refers to "believers," and "Muslims," such as when He states: **{Eat and drink...}** [Qur'ān 2:187] I.e. wherein a masculine plural word is used, scholars have differed. Abu 'l-Khaṭṭāb and the majority opined that women are included.

وتلخيص مَحل النزاع أَن مَا اخْتصَّ بِأحد القبيلين من الْأَلْفَاظ لَا يتَنَاوَل الآخر كالرجال والذكور والفتيان والكهول والشيوخ، فَهَذَا مُخْتَصّ بِالرِّجَالِ، وَلَفظ النِّسَاء وَالْإِنَاث والفتيات والعجائز لَا يتَنَاوَل الرِّجَال.

To summarise the difference of opinion on this, when a word is used that is not gender inclusive, such as, "men," "males," "young men," "old men," and so forth, such expressions are addressed only to men. For women, words such as, "women," "females," "young women," or, "old women," do not include men.

وَمَا وضع لعُمُوم الرِّجَال، وَالنِّسَاء نَحْو: النَّاس، والبشر، وَالْإِنْسَان إِن أُرِيد بِهِ النَّوْع كالحيوان النَّاطِق، أَو الشَّخْص كفرد من أَفْرَاده، وَولد ادم وَذريته، وأدوات الشَّرْط، فَالْحق أَنه يتَنَاوَل القبيلين: النِّسَاء وَالرِّجَال، فَيدْخل النِّسَاء فِي نَحْو: ﴿يَا بني آدم﴾ [الأعراف: ٣١] بالتغليب عَادَة، وَكَذَا فِي نحو: بني تميم ونحوها من القبائل بخلاف بني زيد وعمرو ممن ليس أبا لقبيلة. ويدخلن أيضا في مثل قوله عليه السلام «**يا معشر الشباب من استطاع منكم الباءة فليتزوج**» بعموم العلة، وهو أن شهودة النكاح غريزة في القبيلين، وكل منهما محتاج إلى قضائها.

However, terms that are used to include men and women, include: "People," "humankind," and "mankind," if the genus of humans are intended as animals capable of rational speech, or if a particular instance of that genus is intended. Other examples are, "the child/descendants of Adam," and conditional particles. All of these things include men and women. To illustrate, when Allah the Exalted states: **{O sons of Adam!}** [Qur'ān 7:31] The term, *banī* (sons) was used generically. The same applies to things such as Banī Tamīm etc. when referring to tribes, contrary to saying, "The boys of Zayd or 'Amr" if they are not the forefather of the tribe. Women are also included in statements of the Prophet ﷺ such as, **"Young men, whoever among you can afford to marry should do so."**[265] The reason is that women are included in the cause of the ruling, since desires are shared inhibitions between men and women, and both are in need of fulfilling those desires.

وأما جمع المذكر السالم، وضمير الجمع المتصل بالفعل نحو: المسلمين، وكلوا واشربوا، فقال الأكثر: يعم الرجال والنساء، وهو الحق. وقيل: لا يعمهما.

As for masculine plurals or plural words attributed to verbs, such as, "Muslimīn (Muslims)," "You all eat," and "You all drink," the majority have stated that it includes men and women. This is the truth. However, others took the view that they do not include women.

الْخَامِسَة: اللَّفْظ الْعَام إِذا خص بِصُورَة مثل مَا لَو قَالَ: **﴿فاقْتُلوا الْمُشركين﴾** [التوبة: ٥] ثمَّ قَالَ: لَا تقتلُوا أهل الذِّمَّة إِذا أَدّوا الْجِزْيَة، وَكَقَوْلِه تَعَالَى **﴿حُرِّمَتْ عَلَيْكُمُ الْمَيْتَةُ وَالدَّمُ﴾** [الْمَائِدَة: ٣]، مَعَ قَوْله عَلَيْهِ السَّلَام: **«أحلّت لنا ميتَتَانِ وَدَمَانِ السّمك وَالْجَرَاد»** كَانَ مَا بَقِي غير مَخْصُوص حجَّة مُطلقًا، وَهُوَ مَذْهَب عَامَّة الْفُقَهَاء، وَمِنْهُم أَحْمد وَأَصْحَابه، وَالْبَاقِي بعد التَّخْصِيص حَقِيقَة أَيْضا.

Fifth: When a general expression is particularized, such as when Allah the Exalted states: **{... Wherever you encounter the idolaters, kill them ...}** [Qur'ān 9:5] Then, we find that the religion teaches not to kill people of covenant if they pay the *jizyah*. Another example is when Allah the Exalted states: **{You are forbidden to eat carrion; blood.}** [Qur'ān 5:3] And then we combine that with the statement of the Prophet ﷺ who said, **"There are two things that are lawful to be eaten without being slaughtered:**

265 Reported by al-Bukhārī (9/92) and Muslim (1400).

fish, and locusts."[266] In such cases, these general texts can be cited to present a ruling on the items that fit the generality and have not been specifically given a different ruling. This is the view of the majority of jurists, including Aḥmad and his disciples. The remnants after the particularization are still considered the real, literal meaning of the verse.

السَّادِسَة: الْمُتَكَلّم بِكَلَام عَام يدْخل تَحت عُمُوم كَلَامه فِي الْأَمر وَغَيره، وَمن أمثلته قَوْله صلى الله عَلَيْهِ وَسلم «**من قَالَ لَا إِلَه إِلا الله خَالِصا من قلبه دخل الْجنَّة**» وَكَقَوْلِه: «**صلوا خمسكم، وصوموا شهركم، تدْخلُوا جنَّة ربكُم**» مَا لم تدل قرينَة على عدم دُخُوله كَمَا لَو قَالَ لغلامه: من رَأَيْت فَأكْرمه، وَيكون حِينَئِذٍ من الْعَام الْمُخَصّص.

Sixth: When a speaker uses general wording, those addressed are included within the generality of their statement, whether it is a commandment or a prohibition. An example is the Prophet ﷺ saying, **"Whoever says 'there is no God but Allah (*lā ilāha illa 'llāh*) sincerely from their heart will enter paradise."**[267] Also, the Prophet ﷺ said, **"Pray your five, fast your month, and you will enter the paradise of your Lord."**[268] This is the case so long as there is no evidence to indicate that others are not included. For example, one could say to their servant, 'Whomever you see, honour them.' In such a case, the statement would be a general one, but a specific person is intended.

وَإِذا ورد اللَّفْظ، وَجب اعْتِقَاد كَونه عَاما، وَأَن يعْمل بِهِ قبل الْبَحْث عَن الْمُخَصّص، ثمَّ إِن وجد مَا يخصصه عمل بِهِ، وَإِلَّا بَقِي على عُمُومه.

When a word is mentioned in a text, one must believe it is general and must act on it before looking for some other text to particularize it. Then, if they find a text that particularizes it, they act on [the second text]. Otherwise, it

---

266 Reported by al-Shāfiʿī (2/425), Aḥmad (2/97), and Ibn Mājah (3314).
267 Reported by Abu Nuʿaym (7/312) and al-Bazzār (7). Similar wordings have been reported by al-Bukhārī (99) and Muslim (31).
268 [T] Dr. ʿAbdullah al-Turkī could not find a reference for this ḥadīth. However, after searching, I was able to find that it was reported by Aḥmad (22161), with the wording, **"Worship your Lord, pray your five, fast your month, give the charity of your wealth, and obey your commanding leaders to enter the paradise of your Lord."**

remains general.

ثمَّ هَل يشْتَرط حُصُول اعْتِقَاد جازم بِأَن لَا مُخَصص أَو تكْفِي غَلَبَة الظَّن بِعَدَمِهِ؟ فَذهب إِلَى الأول القَاضِي أَبُو بكر، وَإِلَى الثَّانِي الْأَكْثَرُونَ، وَمِنْهُم ابْن سُرَيج، وَإِمَام الْحَرَمَيْن وَالْغزالِيّ، وَهُوَ الْحق، لِأَن الأول يُفْضِي إِلَى تَعْطِيل العمومات، إِذْ لَا طَرِيق إِلَى الْقطع بِانْتِفَاء الْمُخَصّص، لِأَن مدركه الْبَحْث النظري، وَهُوَ إِنَّمَا يُفِيد غَلَبَة الظَّن.

However, is it a condition that one has firm belief that there is nothing to particularize the [general] text, or is it sufficient to believe it likely and probable that there is no particularizing text? Al-Qāḍī Abu Bakr took the former view, while the majority took the latter view, including Ibn Surayj, Imām al-Ḥaramayn, and al-Ghazālī. Indeed, the latter view is the truth. The first view leads to negation and nonacceptance of many generalities, since there is no way to have firm, absolute belief that there is no particular text on the subject, as the discovery of texts is a speculative and theoretical practice, and it only results in likeliness and high probability.

وَيجوز تَخْصِيص الْعُمُوم إِلَى أَن يبْقى وَاحِد، فَإِذا قَالَ: أكْرم أهل بلد كَذَا، يجوز أن يخصص حَتَّى لَا يبْقى مَأْمُورا بإكرامه إِلَّا شخص وَاحِد.

It is possible to particularize a general text until only one person remains addressed by the generality. If one says, “Honour the people of such-and-such town,” they can continue to particularize the statement until only one person is applicable.

والمخصص هُوَ الْمُتَكَلّم بالخاص، وموجوده، واستعماله فِي الدَّلِيل الْمُخَصّص مجَاز.

The one who particularizes a generality is the speaker. Using “particularizing” to refer to a text is a metaphorical usage of the word.

السَّابِعَة: أن الْعَام عُمُومه شمولي، وَعُمُوم الْمُطلق بدلي، فَمن أطلق على الْمُطلق اسْم الْعُمُوم، فَهُوَ بِاعْتِبَار أَن موارده غير منحصرة، وَالْفرق بَينهمَا أَن عُمُوم الشُّمُول كلي، يحكم فِيهِ على كل فَرد فَرد، وَعُمُوم الْبَدَل كلي من حَيْثُ إِنَّه لَا يمْنَع نفس

تصور مَفْهُومه من وُقُوع الشّركَة فِيهِ، وَلَكِن لَا يحكم فِيهِ على كل فَرد، بل على فَرد شَائِع فِي أَفْرَاده، يَتَنَاوَلهَا على سَبِيل الْبَدَل، وَلَا يتَنَاوَل أَكثر من وَاحِد مِنْهَا دفْعَة.

Seventh: A general (*ʿām*) statement is all-inclusive, while an unrestricted (*muṭlaq*) statement is appositive. Those who refer to absolute statements as being general have done so in the sense that both can result in an innumerable number of instances. However, the difference between the two is that generality (*ʿām*) is all-inclusive; generality applies to each individual instance. However, appositive generality is universal in the sense that conceptualising its meaning does not prevent from its application to multiple instances.[269] However, in an unrestricted statement, one does not cast a ruling on each and every instance, but rather, a prevailing attribute of its instances. Each person is included, therefore, as an appositive to its counterpart. In one moment, the unrestricted statement can only be applicable to just one instance.[270]

الثَّامِنَة: الْمَفْهُوم مُطلقًا عَام فِيمَا سوى الْمَنْطُوق، ويخصص كالعام، وَرفع كل تَخْصِيص أَيْضا عِنْد أَكثر أَصْحَابنَا وَغَيرهم، وَقَالَ ابْن عقيل، وموفق الدّين الْمَقْدِسِي، وَشَيخ الْإِسْلَام ابْن تَيْمِية، وَغَيرهم: لَا يعم. وَالْحق الأول.

Eighth: Referents and implications of speech are considered general language, without restriction. These are contrasted with pronounced meanings. They can also be particularized, just as any general statement. Particularizing an implication of a statement can occur until it applies to no instances,[271] according to the majority of our *aṣḥāb*, and others. Ibn ʿAqīl,

---

269 [T] For example, if one were to say, "Free a slave," conceptualizing a "slave" in and of itself does not prevent that multiple instances share in the meaning of slavery. As such, this is an unrestricted statement, as it can refer to any slave, not one in particular.

270 [T] To explain further, if one were to say, "Free the slaves," it would be general, as its signification indicates inclusiveness of each and every slave. However, if one were to say, "Free a slave," freeing any slave would fulfil the commandment. In the latter case, when one frees "a" slave, only one slave is being freed in that moment, though conceptualizing "slaves" as having an innumerable number of instances is rationally a possibility. Therefore, "all" is general, and "any," is unrestricted.

271 [T] This is contrary to when the generality is pronounced. When the generality is pronounced, the furthest it can be particularized is until one remains. As such, one cannot say, 'I give you all of my wealth, except all of my wealth.' The same does not apply to a referent or implication of a text, which can be particularized until no instances that it applies to remain.

Muwaffaq al-Dīn al-Maqdisī, Shaykh al-Islam Ibn Taymiyyah, and others, stated that it is not general language. The truth is the first view.

التَّاسِعَة: قَالَ الشَّافِعِي: ترك الاستفصال فِي حِكَايَة الْحَال مَعَ قيام الِاحْتِمَال ينزل منزلَة الْعُمُوم فِي الْمقَال، مِثَاله أَن ابْن غيلَان أسلم عَن عشر نسْوَة، فَقَالَ النَّبِي صلى الله عَلَيْهِ وَسلم **«أمسك أَرْبعا مِنْهُنَّ وَفَارق سائرهن»** وَلم يسْأَل عَن كَيْفيَّة وُرُود عقده عَلَيْهِنَّ فِي الْجمع، وَالتَّرْتِيب، فَكَانَ إِطْلَاقه القَوْل دَالا على أَنه لَا فرق بَين أَن تتفق تِلْكَ الْعُقُود مَعًا، أَو على التَّرْتِيب.

Ninth: Al-Shāfiʿī stated that in a situation where one could ask for further clarity but does not, the ruling is general. For example, Ibn Ghaylān accepted Islam and had ten wives. The Prophet ﷺ said to him, **"Keep four of them and leave the rest."** [Ibn Ghaylān] did not ask on how to re-initiate the contract or the order of whom he should keep. As such, his silence indicated that there is no difference in how those contracts are initiated: they can be all together or can be done one at a time.

الْعَاشِرَة: ذكر عُلَمَاء الْبَيَان أَن حذف الْمُتَعَلّق يشْعر بالتعميم، نَحْو: زيد يُعْطي وَيمْنَع بِحَذْف المفعولين، وَنَحْو: قَوْله تَعَالَى **﴿وَلَسَوْفَ يُعْطِيكَ رَبُّكَ فَتَرْضَى﴾** [الضحَى: ٥] بِحَذْف الْمَفْعُول الثَّانِي، وَكَقَوْلِه تَعَالَى: **﴿فَأَما من أعْطى وَاتَّقى﴾** [اللَّيْل: ٥]. **﴿وَاللهُ يَدْعُو إِلَى دَارِ السَّلَامِ﴾** [يُونُس: ٢٥]

Tenth: Scholars of rhetoric have stated that omitting an object indicates generality. For example, one could say, "Zayd gives and withholds." Another example is when Allah the Exalted states: **{Your Lord is sure to give you so much that you will be well satisfied.}** [Qurʾān 93:5] The second object was omitted. Allah the Exalted also states: **{There is the one who gives, who is mindful...}** [Qurʾān 92:5] Also, He states: **{But Allah invites to the Home of Peace.}** [Qurʾān 10:25]

فَيَنْبَغِي أَن يكون ذَلِك من أَقسَام الْعُمُوم، وَإِن لم يذكرهُ المتقدمون من أهل الْأُصُول، وَذكر مَعْنَاهُ القَاضِي عَلَاء الدّين المرداوي الْحَنْبَلِيّ فِي (التَّحْرِير) فَقَالَ:

This can be considered appropriately as a category of generality in speech, even if the early scholars of legal theory did not mention it. Its meaning was mentioned, though, by al-Qāḍī ʿAlā' al-Dīn al-Mardāwī al-Ḥanbalī in *al-Taḥrīr*, where he said:

مثل لَا آكل أَو إِن أكلت، فَعَبْدي حر، يعم مفعولاته، فَيقبل تَخْصِيصه، فَلَو نوى مَأْكُولا معينا قبل بَاطِنا عِنْد أَصْحَابنَا والمالكية وَالشَّافِعِيَّة، وَعند ابْن الْبَنَّا وَالْحَنَفِيَّة لَا، وَيقبل أَيْضا حكما عِنْد أَحْمد وَمَالك وَأبي يُوسُف وَمُحَمّد، وَعنهُ: لَا كالشافعية.

One can say, "I will not eat," or, "if I eat, my slave is free," by generalising the objects. Such statements can be particularized. If the person intends some specific food, it is accepted as a personal ruling according to our *aṣḥāb*, the Māliki scholars, and the Shāfiʿī scholars. Ibn al-Bannā' and the Ḥanafī scholars said it is not accepted. It is also accepted in judicial settings according to Aḥmad, Mālik, Abu Yūsuf, and Muḥammad. Another view of his (Aḥmad) is that it is not accepted in judicial settings, thereby agreeing with the Shāfiʿī scholars.

ويعم الزَّمَان وَالْمَكَان عندنَا وَعند الْمَالِكِيَّة، وَعند الشَّافِعِيَّة والآمدي لَا، فَلَو زَاد فَقَالَ: لَحْمًا وَنوى معينا، قبل عندنَا وَعند الْحَنَفِيَّة، وَحكي اتِّفَاقًا.

It is also inclusive of time and place according to us and the Māliki scholars. According to the Shāfiʿī scholars and al-Āmidī, it does not. Therefore, if the person says, "I will not eat meat," and intended a particular type of meat, it is accepted by us and the Ḥanafī scholars. It was stated to be a matter of agreement.

ثمَّ قَالَ فِي (التَّحْرِير) تَنْبِيه: علم من ذَلِك أَن الْعَام فِي شَيْء عَام فِي متعلقاته، وَقَالَه الْعلمَاء إِلَّا من شَذ. انْتهى.

Therefore, a general statement is also general when applied to its objects, as stated by the scholars. Some scholars took an irregular view and said otherwise. **[End]**[272]

وَمِنْه تعلم أَن هَذِه الْقَاعِدَة مُعْتَبرَة عِنْد الْعلمَاء، لَكِن يَنْبَغِي أَن يعلم أَن الْعُمُوم فِيمَا ذكر إِنَّمَا هُوَ دلَالَة الْقَرِينَة على أَن الْمُقدر عَام، والحذف إِنَّمَا هُوَ لمُجَرّد

272 [T] *Taḥrīr al-Manqūl wa Tahdhīb ʿIlm al-Uṣūl* (pp. 214-215).

الِاخْتِصَار لَا للتعميم.

From al-Mardāwī's words, you learn that this principle is accepted by scholars. However, it must be known that generality of the mentioned items is due to contextual inferences showing that the omitted item is general. Omission in and of itself is meant for brevity, not necessarily for generality.

الْحَادِيَة عشرة: الْكَلَام الْعَام الْخَارِج على طَرِيقَة الْمَدْح أَو الذَّم نَحْو: ﴿**إِنَّ الْأَبْرَارَ لَفِي نَعِيمٍ وَإِنَّ الْفُجَّارَ لَفِي جَحِيمٍ**﴾ [الانفطار: ١٣-١٤]، هُوَ عَام عِنْد الْجُمْهُور.

Eleventh: General speech that is in the context of praise or dispraise is considered general according to the scholars. An example is when Allah the Exalted said: **{Indeed, the virtuous will be in bliss, and the wicked will be in Hell.}** [Qur'ān 82:13-14]

الثَّانِيَة عشرة: ذكر بعض أَفْرَاد الْعَام الْمُوَافق لَهُ فِي الحكم لَا يَقْتَضِي التَّخْصِيص عِنْد الْجُمْهُور، كَقَوْلِه عَلَيْهِ الصَّلَاة وَالسَّلَام «**أَيّمَا إهاب دبغ فقد طهر**» مَعَ قَوْله فِي حَدِيث آخر فِي شَاة مَيْمُونَة «**دباغها طهورها**» فالتنصيص على الشَّاة فِي الحَدِيث الآخر لَا يَقْتَضِي تخصيص عُمُوم «**أَيمَا إهاب دبغ فقد طهر**» لِأَنَّهُ تنصيص على بعض أَفْرَاد الْعَام بِلَفْظ لَا مَفْهُوم لَهُ إِلَّا مُجَرّد مَفْهُوم اللقب، فَمن أَخذ بِهِ، خصص بِهِ، وَمن لم يَأْخُذ بِهِ، لم يخصص بِهِ، وَلَا متمسك لمن قَالَ بِالْأَخْذِ بِهِ.

Twelfth: Mention of some instances of the generality that have the same ruling is not particularization according to the majority of scholars. For example, the Prophet ﷺ said, **"Any hide that has been tanned has indeed become pure."**[273] He also said about the goat of Maymūnah, **"By tanning it, it becomes purified."**[274] Mention of the goat in this context does not indicate that the first ruling has been particularized to only be referring to the hides of goats. Indeed, it is mere illustration of an instance of the general ruling; it carries no other indication except serving as a proper noun. Those who believe proper nouns carry independent indications have used this text to particularize the ḥadīth, and those who do not, did not. There is no jus-

---

273 [T] Reported by Aḥmad (1895) and Ibn Mājah (4/602).
274 Reported by al-Bukhārī (3/281) and Muslim (363).

tification for those who take the view that proper nouns carry any sort of particularization.

الثَّالِث عشرة: إِذا علق الشَّارِع حكما على عِلّة، عَم الحكم تِلْكَ الْعلَّة حَتَّى يُوجد بوجودها فِي كل صُورة، وَذَلِكَ الْعُمُوم بِالشَّرْعِ لَا باللغة، لَكِن بِشَرْط أَن يكون الْقيَاس الَّذِي اقتضته الْعلَّة من الأقيسة الَّتِي ثبتَتْ بِدَلِيل نقل أَو عقل، لَا بِمُجَرَّد مَحْض الرَّأي والخيال المختل.

Thirteenth: If the religion ties a ruling to a cause, the ruling encompasses the cause, existing where the cause exists, in every situation. This generality is instated by the religion, not the language. However, it is conditional on the analogy used to extend the ruling to the cause in other situations being a valid analogy that is established via a textual or rational evidence. It must not have occurred simply through one's unadulterated opinion nor through their flawed imagination.

الرَّابِع عشرة: الْفرق بَين العَام الْمَخْصُوص، وَالْعَام الَّذِي أُرِيد بِهِ الْخُصُوص، وَذَلِكَ أَن الذِي أُرِيد بِهِ الْخُصُوص: مَا كَانَ المُرَاد أقل، وَمَا لَيْسَ بِمُرَاد هُوَ الْأَكْثَر، وَبَيَانه أَن الْعَام الْمَخْصُوص كَقَوْلِه تَعَالَى ﴿إِنَّ الْإِنْسَانَ لَفِي خُسْرٍ﴾ [الْعَصْر: ٢]، وَالْعَام الَّذِي أُرِيد بِهِ الْخُصُوص كلي اسْتعْمل فِي جزئي، وَهُوَ مجَاز، وقرينته عقيلة لَا تنفك عَنهُ، وَالْأول أَعم مِنْهُ.

Fourteenth: There is a difference between a general statement that has been particularized, and a general statement uttered to intend some particular instance, which is used to intend the minority, not the majority, of the instances of the general statement. An example of a general statement that has been particularized is when Allah the Exalted states: **{Surely humanity is in loss.}** [Qur'ān 103:2] [Then, to particularize and limit its inclusiveness, Allah the Exalted states: **{Except those who have faith, do good, and urge each other to the truth, and urge each other to perseverance.}** [Qur'ān 103:3]] A general statement uttered to intend some particular instance is a universal used to refer to a particular. It is a metaphorical usage of [the universal word]. The evidence [indicating it is intending some particular] is rational and is inseparable. The first (a general statement that has been particularized) is more general.

فصل

Section [on Particularization]

وَأما الْخُصُوص فقد تقدّمت الْإِشَارَة إِلَى تَعْرِيفه، ونقول هُنَا: الْخَاص هُوَ اللَّفْظ الدَّال على شَيْء بِعَيْنِه، لِأَنَّهُ مُقَابل الْعَام، فَكَمَا أَن الْعَام يدل على أَشْيَاء من غير تعْيين، وَجب أن يكون الْخَاص مَا ذكرْنَاهُ. فالعام كالرجال، وَالْخَاص كزيد وَعَمْرو، وَهَذَا الرجل.

We have previously alluded to the definition of particularization. To state it again here: A particularized term is one that refers to something in specific, and nothing but that thing. It is contrasted with generality. The definition of a general term is one that refers to things without specifying any one instance of that thing, so in contrast, the definition of a particularized term is as I mentioned. An example of a general term is "men" while an example of a specific one is, "'Amr," "Zayd," or, "This particular man."

والتخصيص: بَيَان المُرَاد بِاللَّفْظِ، أَو يُقَال: بَيَان أَن بعض مَدْلُول اللَّفْظ غير مُرَاد بالحكم، فَقَوله تَعَالَى: ﴿**وَالْمُحْصَنَاتُ مِنَ الَّذِينَ أُوتُوا الْكِتَابَ مِنْ قَبْلِكُمْ**﴾ [الْمَائِدَة: ٥] مُخَصص لقَوْله تَعَالَى: ﴿**وَلا تَنْكِحُوا الْمُشْرِكَاتِ**﴾ [الْبَقَرَة: ٢٢١]، ومبين أَن المُرَاد بالمشركات مَا عدا الكتابيات على التَّعْرِيف الأول، أَو يُقَال: إِن بعض مَدْلُول المشركات غير مُرَاد بِالتَّحْرِيمِ، وَهن الكتابيات على الثَّانِي، والمخصص بِكَسْر الصَّاد الأولى مُشَدّدَة يُطلق حَقِيقَة على الْمُتَكَلّم بالخاص، ومجازا على الْكَلَام الْخَاص الْمُبين للمراد بِالْعَام، وَيَنْبَغِي أَن يعلم الْفرق بَين التَّخْصِيص والنسخ وَهُوَ من وُجُوه:

Particularization has two definitions: To clarify the intent behind a [general] term. (i) To clarify that some things indicated by the term do not carry the ruling of the rest. For example, Allah the Exalted states: **{And permissible for you in marriage are chaste believing women as well as chaste**

women of those given the Scripture before you.} [Qur'ān 5:5] This verse particularizes another verse, namely: **{Do not marry polytheistic women until they believe.}** [Qur'ān 2:221] Therefore, according to the first definition, it clarifies that the meaning of [the general phrase] "polytheistic women," is actually non-inclusive of women of the scriptures. According to the second definition, it means that something indicated by [the general phrase] "polytheistic women" does not carry the ruling of the rest, namely, women of the scripture. The term "particularized" is used literally to refer to the one speaking and particularizing something, and is used metaphorically to refer to particular speech that clarifies the intent of general speech. It is very important to understand the difference between particularization and abrogation. There are a number of differences:

مِنْهَا: إن التَّخْصِيص لَا يكون إِلَّا لبَعض الْأَفْرَاد، والنسخ يكون لَهَا كلهَا.

One. Particularization only applies to some instances, while abrogation applies to all instances.

وَمِنْهَا: أن النّسخ يتطَرّق إِلَى كل حكم، سَوَاء كَانَ ثَابتا فِي حق شخص وَاحِد أو أشخاص كَثِيرَة، والتخصيص لَا يتطَرق إِلَّا إِلَى الأول.

Two. Abrogation touches on all rulings, regardless if they apply to one person or to multiple people. Particularization only touches on rulings that apply to individual instances.

وَمِنْهَا: أَنَّه يجوز تَأْخِير النّسخ عَن وَقت الْعَمَل بالمنسوخ، وَلَا يجوز تَأْخِير التَّخْصِيص عَن وَقت الْعَمَل بالمخصوص.

Three. Abrogation can come after the abrogated action has already been implemented. However, particularization cannot come after the particularized ruling has been acted on.[275]

---

275 [T] For example, the Qiblah of the Muslims was initially Jerusalem. People acted on that ruling and prayed in that direction. Then, it was abrogated, and people prayed towards the Ka'bah in Makkah. Therefore, the abrogated ruling was already implemented.

In the other case that al-Shaykh Ibn Badrān mentions, consider the example of particularization that he mentioned. One cannot have acted on the particularized ruling of marrying Christian or Jewish women before that particularization was actually instated, as that would simply be an unlawful action.

وَمِنْهَا: أنَّه يجوز نسخ شَرِيعَة بشريعة أُخْرى، وَلَا يجوز التَّخْصِيص.

Four. An entire legislation can be abrogated by another legislation. However, an entire legislation cannot be particularized by another legislation.

وَمِنْهَا: أن النّسخ رفع الحكم بعد ثُبُوته، بِخِلَاف التَّخْصِيص، فَإِنَّهُ بَيَان المُرَاد بِاللَّفْظِ الْعَام.

Five. Abrogation lifts the ruling after it was once established. Particularization only clarifies the meaning of the general wording.

وَمِنْهَا: أَن التَّخْصِيص بَيَان مَا أُرِيد بِالْعُمُومِ، والنسخ بَيَان مَا لم يرد بالمنسوخ.

Six. Particularization clarifies what was intended by the general ruling. Abrogation clarifies what was not wanted in the abrogated ruling.

وَمِنْهَا: أن النّسخ لَا يكون إِلَّا بقول وخطاب، والتخصيص قد يكون بأدلة الْعقل والقرائن وَسَائِر أَدِلَّة السّمع.

Seven. Abrogation can only occur via a statement, while particularization can occur through rational evidences, contextual evidences, and, of course, all divine textual evidences.

وَمِنْهَا: أن التَّخْصِيص يجوز أَن يكون بِالْإِجْمَاع، والنسخ لَا يجوز أَن يكون بِهِ.

Eight. Particularization can occur via consensus, but abrogation cannot occur via consensus.[276]

وَمِنْهَا: أن التَّخْصِيص لَا يدْخل فِي غير الْعَام، بِخِلَاف النّسخ فَإِنَّهُ يرفع حكم الْعَام وَالْخَاص.

Nine. Particularization can only pertain to general statements, while abrogation can pertain to both general and particular rulings.

وَمِنْهَا: أن التَّخْصِيص يكون فِي الْأَخْبَار وَالْأَحْكَام، والنسخ يخْتَص بِالْأَحْكَامِ

276 [T] Meaning, if the entire Ummah unanimously agreed that prayer is no longer obligatory, it is weightless and meaningless, as they do not have the authority to abrogate the obligation of prayer.

الشَّرْعِيَّة.

Ten. Particularization can occur to both statements and rulings. Abrogation is specific to religious rulings.

وَمِنْهَا: جَوَاز اقتران التَّخْصِيص بِالْعَام، وتقدمه عَلَيْهِ، وتأخره عَنهُ، مَعَ وجوب تَأَخّر النَّاسِخ عَن الْمَنْسُوخ إِلَى غير ذَلِك.

A particularized ruling can occur at the same time, before, or after the general ruling. However, an abrogating ruling must occur after the abrogated ruling.

وَقد سردنا هَذِه الفروق بَيَانا لَا تَحْقِيقا. ثمَّ اعْلَم أَن المخصصات حصرها أَصْحَابنَا فِي تسع:

I have mentioned these differences to clarify, not to exhaustively list and discuss each difference. Further, our *aṣḥāb* have stated that there are nine types of particularizations:

أَولهَا: الْحس، ومثلوا لَهُ بقوله تَعَالَى فِي صفة الرّيح الْعَقِيم: ﴿**تدمر كل شَيْء بِأَمْر رَبهَا**﴾ [الْأَحْقَاف: ٢٥]، قَالُوا: فَإنَّا علمنَا بالحس أَنَّهَا لم تدمر السَّمَاء وَالْأَرْض مَعَ أَشْيَاء كَثِيرَة، فَكَانَ الْحس مُخَصّصا لذَلِك، وَعند التَّحْقِيق تَجِد الْآيَة خَاصَّة، أُرِيد بهَا الْخَاص، وَذَلِكَ لِأَنَّهَا جَاءَت فِي مَوضِع آخر مُقَيّدَة بِمَا يمْنَع الِاسْتِدْلَال بهَا على الْمُدَّعِي، وَهُوَ قَوْله عز وَجل: ﴿**وَفِي عَادٍ إِذْ أَرْسَلْنَا عَلَيْهِمُ الرِّيحَ الْعَقِيمَ مَا تَذَرُ مِنْ شَيْءٍ أَتَتْ عَلَيْهِ إِلَّا جعلته كالرميم**﴾ [الذاريات: ٤١-٤٢]، والقصة وَاحِدَة فَدلَّ على أَن قَوْله ﴿**تُدَمِّرُ كُلَّ شَيْء**﴾ مُقَيّد بِمَا أَتَت عَلَيْهِ، كَأَنَّهُ سُبْحَانَهُ قَالَ: تدمر كل شَيْء أَتَت عَلَيْهِ، وَحِينَئِذٍ يكون التدمير مُخْتَصًّا بذلك، فَتكون الْآيَة خَاصَّة أُرِيد بهَا الْخَاص.

First: The Senses: They gave the example of the barren wind that blew, where Allah the Exalted states: **{It destroyed everything by the command of its Lord.}** [Qur'ān 46:25] They stated that, by our senses, we know that the wind did not destroy the heavens and the earth, and did not destroy many other things. As such, sensory perception was used to particularize the generality of the wording of the verse. This verse, however, is a specific one that is used to intend something very specific. In another verse, Allah the Exalted mentioned the story very specifically to show that it cannot be used as evidence.[277] Allah the Exalted said: **{There is another sign in the ʿĀd: We sent the life-destroying wind against them. There was nothing it came upon that it did not reduce to ashes.}** [Qurʾān 51:41-42] These verses are referring to a single story. It shows that when Allah the Exalted states: **{It destroyed everything by the command of its Lord}** it is particularized by, **{There was nothing it came upon.}** It is as though Allah the Exalted is saying, "It destroyed everything it touched." As such, the destruction is particularized. The verse, then, is specific, intending something specific.[278]

ثَانِيهَا: الْعقل، وَبِه خص من لَا يفهم من عُمُوم النَّص، نَحْو: ﴿وَلِلَّهِ عَلَى النَّاسِ حِجُّ الْبَيْتِ﴾ [آل عمرَان: ٩٧]، ﴿يَا أَيُّهَا النَّاسُ اعْبُدُوا رَبَّكُمُ﴾ [الْبَقَرَة: ٢١] فَإِن هَذَا الْخطاب يتَنَاوَل بِعُمُومِهِ من لَا يفهم من النَّاس، كَالصَّبِيِّ وَالْمَجْنُون، لكنه خرج بِدَلِيل الْعقل، فَكَانَ مُخَصّصا للْعُمُوم الَّذِي بِهِ.

Second: Intellection: For example, those who are not capable of understanding are not included when Allah the Exalted states: **{Pilgrimage to this House is an obligation by Allah.}** [Qurʾān 3:97] Also: **{O humanity! Worship your Lord.}** [Qurʾān 2:21] These two instructions, when taken at their general face value, include people who are not capable of understanding, such as children and clinically insane people. However, rationally speaking, that cannot be the case. As such, both children and insane people were excluded from this instruction, and intellection particularized the generality.[279]

---

277 [T] Meaning, it cannot be used as an example to show sensory particularization of a general text.

278 [T] This was the argument of al-Ṭūfī in his *Sharḥ Mukhtaṣar al-Rawḍah* (2/551-552). A better example was mentioned by al-Qāḍī ʿAlāʾ al-Dīn al-Mardāwī: **{She was given of all things.}** [Qurʾān 27:23] He then said, "We know through observation that there were many things not given to the Queen of Sheba, such as the kingdom of Sulaymān." Refer to *al-Taḥbir Sharḥ al-Taḥrīr* (6/2638).

279 [T] This example is one al-Qāḍī al-Mardāwī referred to as, "Theoretical intellect." He also mentioned another example that is perhaps more suited, which he referred to as, "Necessary intellect." He stated, "An example is where Allah the Exalted states: **{Allah is the Creator of all things.}** [Qurʾān 13:16] Intellect has dictated that by necessity, Allah the Exalted has not created His Honourable Self, nor His Attributes."

ثَالِثهَا: الْإِجْمَاع، لِأَنَّهُ نَص قَاطع شَرْعِي، وَالْعَام ظَاهر، لِأَنَّهُ يدل على ثُبُوت الحكم لكل فَرد من أَفْرَاده بطرِيق الظهُور لَا بطرِيق الْقطع، وَإِذا اجْتمع الْقَاطِع وَالظَّاهِر كَانَ الْقَاطِع مُتَقَدما، وَالْحق أَن التَّخْصِيص يكون بِدَلِيل الْإِجْمَاع لَا بِالْإِجْمَاع نَفسه، وَجعل الصَّيْرَفِي من أمثلته: ﴿يَا أَيُّهَا الَّذِينَ آمَنُوا إِذَا نُودِيَ لِلصَّلَاةِ مِنْ يَوْمِ الْجُمُعَةِ فَاسْعَوْا إِلَى ذِكْرِ اللَّهِ﴾ [الْجُمُعَة: ٩] قَالَ: وَأَجْمعُوا على أَنه لَا جُمُعَة على عبد وَلَا امْرَأَة.

Third: Consensus: The reason is that [consensus] is a definitive religious evidence, and general texts are *ẓāhir*, which is to state that they indicate that the ruling is established for each and every instance and does so apparently, though not definitively. If a definitive evidence and a *ẓāhir* evidence conflict, the definitive one must be given preference. The truth is that particularization occurs through the evidence of the consensus, not the consensus itself. Al-Ṣayrafī mentioned an example of Allah's statement: **{O believers! When the call to prayer is made on Friday, then proceed [diligently] to the remembrance of Allah.}** [Qur'ān 62:9] He mentioned that the scholars have unanimously agreed that the Friday prayer is not an obligation on slaves nor women.

رَابِعهَا: النَّص الْخَاص كتخصيص قَوْله عَلَيْهِ السَّلَام «لَا قطع إِلَّا فِي ربع دِينَار» لعُمُوم قَوْله تَعَالَى ﴿وَالسَّارِقُ وَالسَّارِقَةُ فَاقْطَعُوا أَيْدِيَهُمَا﴾ [الْمَائِدَة: ٣٨]، فَإِن هَذَا يَقْتَضِي عُمُوم الْقطع فِي الْقَلِيل وَالْكثير، فَخص بِالْحَدِيثِ مَا دون ربع دِينَار، فَلَا قطع بِهِ.

Fourth: A Particularized Univocal Text: For example, the Prophet ﷺ said, **"There is no cutting [of the hand] except [for stealing] a quarter of a dinar [or more]."**[280] This ḥadīth clarifies the particulars of the verse where Allah the Exalted states: **{As for male and female thieves, cut off their hands ...}** [Qur'ān 5:38] The verse indicates that the penalty of cutting the hand should be applied irrespective of the value of the stolen goods. However, it was clarified by the ḥadīth, which stated that if the stolen goods are not equal in value to a quarter of a dinar, the perpetrator's hand should not

---

Refer to *al-Taḥbīr Sharḥ al-Taḥrīr* (6/2640).

280 Reported by al-Bukhārī (12/89) and Muslim (1684).

be cut.[281]

وَسَوَاء كَانَ الْعَام كتابا أَو سنة مُتَقَدّمَة أَو مُتَأَخِّرَة لقُوَّة الْخَاص، وَهُوَ قَول الشَّافِعِيَّة. وَعَن أَحْمد رَحمَه الله تَعَالَى: يقدم الْمُتَأَخر من النصين عَاما كَانَ أَو خَاصّا، وَهُوَ قَول الْحَنَفِيَّة لقَوْل ابْن عَبَّاس: **«كُنا نَأْخُذ بالأحدث فالأحدث من أَمر رَسُول الله صلى الله عَلَيْهِ وَسلم»** فَإِن جهل التَّارِيخ فَكَذَلِك يقدم الْخَاص على الْعَام عندنَا، وَعند الْحَنَفِيَّة يتعارضان، وَهُوَ قِيَاس رِوَايَة أَحْمد.

Further, the general text could be from the Qur'ān or the Sunnah and it could be an early text or a later text, because of the strength of particularized texts. This was the view of the Shāfiʿī scholars. As for Aḥmad ﷺ, he said, "The latter of the two texts should be given priority, irrespective if it is general or particularized." This, too, is the view of the Ḥanafī scholars. Their evidence was the statement of Ibn ʿAbbās, "We would follow the latest of the commandments of Allah's Messenger ﷺ."[282] However, according to [Ḥanbalī scholars], if the date is not known, the particularized text should be preferred over the general one. According to Ḥanafī scholars, they are considered conflicting.[283] This view can also be extrapolated from the narration of Aḥmad.

وَقَالَ بعض الشَّافِعِيَّة: لَا يخص عُمُوم السّنة بِالْكتاب، وخرجه ابْن حَامِد قولا، أَي: رِوَايَة لنا. وَالصَّحِيح التَّخْصِيص.

Some Shāfiʿī scholars said that the general texts of the Sunnah are not partic-

281 [T] To understand the value of a quarter of a dinar, consider the following: the minimum wealth one must have in order to be responsible for paying *zakāt* is 20 dinars, which is equal to approximately 85 grams of gold. Each dinar, therefore, is 4.25 grams of gold. A quarter of that is 1.0625 grams of gold. As I calculate that today, it is worth 74.00 USD approximately.

282 Reported by Mālik in his *Muwaṭṭa* (654) and Muslim (1113).

283 [T] In this case, according to Ḥanafī scholars, neither text should be implemented. Al-Ṭūfī offered the reasoning, "Because it is possible that the general text is later, and as such, it abrogates the particularized text. It is also possible that the general text is earlier, and if it is, it would be particularized by the particular text. In this case, there is no way to determine which is corrected. As such, one should abstain, so as to not prefer one over the other arbitrarily." Al-Ṭūfī then disagrees and affirms his position as being in line with the majority of Ḥanbalī scholars. Refer to *Sharḥ Mukhtaṣar al-Rawḍah* (2/561).

ularized by verses from the Qur'ān. Ibn Ḥāmid extrapolated that view as a viable one within our *madhhab*. However, the truth is that [verses from the Qur'ān can] particularize.

خَامِسهَا: الْمَفْهُوم، فَإِن كل مَفْهُوم مُوَافقَة كَانَ مُخَصّصا اتِّفَاقًا، وَإِن كَانَ مَفْهُوم مُخَالفَة، فَإِنَّهُ يكون مُخَصّصا عِنْد الْقَائِل بِهِ، وَخَالف القَاضِي أَبُو يعلى، وَأَبُو الْخطاب أَيْضا، والمالكية، وَابْن حزم.

Fifth: Implications and Referents: If the implication is *a fortiori*,[284] it particularizes the general text, according to the agreement of scholars. However, if the implication is its inverse,[285] it can act as a particularizing text only, according to those scholars who believe in such implications carrying weight as evidence. Al-Qāḍī Abu Ya'lā, Abu 'l-Khaṭṭāb, the Māliki scholars, and Ibn Ḥazm disagreed.

مِثَال الأول: قَوْله عَلَيْهِ السَّلَام «**فِي أَرْبَعِينَ شَاة شَاة**» فَإِنَّهُ يعم كل أَرْبَعِينَ من الشَّاء، سَوَاء كَانَت سَائِمَة أَو غَيرهَا، وَلكنه خص بقوله: «**فِي سَائِمَة الْغنم الزَّكَاة**» فَإِن مَفْهُومه يَقْتَضِي أَن غير السَّائِمَة لَا زَكَاة فِيهَا.

An example[286] of the former is when the Prophet ﷺ said, **"For every forty sheep, a sheep is due [in *zakāt*]."**[287] This is inclusive of all sheep and goats, regardless if they graze or not. However, this was particularized when the Prophet ﷺ said, **"*Zakāt* applies to grazing goats."**[288] The implied meaning here is that the ruling is that there is no *zakāt* to be paid on the

284 [T] Meaning, the implied ruling is equivalent to the expressly stated ruling. This is known as *mafhūm al-muwāfaqah* (an *a fortiori* implication).

285 [T] Meaning, the implied ruling is the inverse of the expressly stated ruling. This is known as *mafhūm al-mukhālafah* (implication of inverse relationships). The inverse of a proposition is its negation. If a proposition goes, if A then B, then the inverse is, if not A, then not B.

286 [T] Note that the two examples al-Shaykh Ibn Badrān will mention are actually both examples of inverse implications. Therefore, to supplement what he said, I will mention the example al-Imām Najm al-Dīn al-Ṭūfī mentioned in his *Sharḥ Mukhtaṣar al-Rawḍah* (2/714), "An example of an *a fortiori* argument is understanding that hitting [the parents] is unlawful, since the text states that grumbling in the face of the parents is *ḥarām*, when Allah the Exalted said: **{Never say to them [even] '*ugh*.'}** [Qur'ān 17:23]"

287 Reported by al-Bukhārī (3/251).

288 Reported by al-Bukhārī (3/253).

non-grazing.

وَمِثَال الثَّانِي قَوْله صلى الله عَلَيْهِ وَسلم «**خلق المَاء طهُورا لَا يُنجسهُ إِلَّا مَا غير لَونه أَو طعمه أَو رِيحه**»، فَإِنَّهُ عَام وخصص بِمَفْهُوم قَوْله: «**إِذا بلغ المَاء قُلَّتَيْنِ لم يحمل خبثا**».

An example of the latter is when the Prophet ﷺ said, **"Water was created pure and purifying. The only time it is impure is when [impurity] changes its colour, taste, or odour."**[289] This ḥadīth was particularized by the implication of another ḥadīth, **"If water reaches the amount of two *qullah*,[290] it does not carry impurity."**[291 292]

سادسها: فعل النَّبِي صلى الله عَلَيْهِ وَسلم كتخصيص قَوْله عز وَجل فِي الْحيض: ﴿**وَلا تَقْرَبُوهُنَّ حَتَّى يَطْهُرْنَ**﴾ [الْبَقَرَة: ٢٢٢]، بِكَوْنِهِ عَلَيْهِ السَّلَام كَانَ يُبَاشر الْحَائِض دون الْفرج متزرة فَإِن الْآيَة اقْتَضَت عُمُوم عدم القربان فِي الْفرج وَغَيره، وَفعله عَلَيْهِ السَّلَام خص النَّهْي بالفرج، وأباح القربان لما سواهُ، وَيُمكن حمل القربان على معنى: لَا تطؤوهن فِي الفرج، وَيكون القربان كِنَايَة ظَاهِرَة عَن ذَلِك، فَلَا عُمُوم.

Sixth: Actions of the Prophet ﷺ: For example, the Prophet ﷺ particularized the statement of Allah the Exalted: **{Do not approach them until they are cleansed.}** [Qur'ān 2:222] The Prophet ﷺ used to enjoy intimacy with his menstruating wives while avoiding their private areas, while his wives would be wearing a lower garment.[293] The verse indicates that inti-

289 Reported by al-Shāfiʿī (1/20), Aḥmad (3/15), Abu Dāwūd (66), al-Tirmidhī (66) and al-Nasāʾī (1/174).
290 [T] A *qullah* is an archaic measurement the Arabs used. It is 500 Iraqi *ritl*. A *ritl* is 382 grams, and therefore, 500 x 382 = 191, 000 grams of water. A kilogram and a liter are equivalent when the liquid is water or has its same density, and therefore, it is 191 liters of water. For the amount of the *ritl*, refer to *Naẓm al-Maqādir* by Dr. Amir Bahjat.
291 Reported by Aḥmad (4605), Abu Dāwūd (63), al-Tirmidhī (67), Ibn Mājah (517), and al-Nasāʾī (1/46).
292 [T] The implication of the ḥadīth is that if the water is less than two *qullah*, it becomes impure in any of the three ways mentioned in the other ḥadīth.
293 Reported by al-Bukhārī (300) and Muslim (293).

macy with a menstruating woman, in general, is prohibited, regardless if the intimacy occurs in the private areas or not. However, the action of the Prophet ﷺ shows that the ruling is particular and specific to the private areas, and his action allowed intimacy in other ways. In the case of this verse, however, some have stated that "Approach them" means, "Do not have intercourse with them in their private areas," making the use of "Approach" metonymic. In that case, the verse is not general at all.

سابعها: تَقْرِير النَّبِي صلى الله عَلَيْهِ وَسلم على خلاف الْعُمُوم، مَعَ قدرته على الْمَنْع من خِلَافه، لِأَن إِقْرَاره كصريح إِذْنه، إِذْ لَا يجوز لَهُ الْإِقْرَار على الْخَطَأ لعصمته. ومثاله على سَبِيل الْفَرْض أَن النَّهْي عَن شرب الْخمر إِنَّمَا هُوَ عَام قطعا، فَلَو فرض أَنه رأى أحدا يشرب مِقْدَارًا يَسِيرا مِنْهَا، وَأقرهُ عَلَيْهِ، كَانَ إِقْرَاره تَخْصِيصًا للْعُمُوم.

Seventh: Acknowledgement of the Prophet ﷺ: This, of course, is if his acknowledgement conflicts with the generality, and when the Prophet ﷺ had ability to prevent conflicting [with the generality of the text]. This is because the silent acknowledgement of the Prophet ﷺ is tantamount to his express permission. The Prophet ﷺ cannot acknowledge a person's error, since he is infallible. If we were to suppose a hypothetical example, it would be that the prohibition of drinking alcohol is general. If we were to suppose that the Prophet ﷺ saw someone drinking a small amount of alcohol and acknowledged it, it would serve as a particularization of the general ruling of drinking alcohol.

ثامنها: قَول الصَّحَابِيّ، لِأَنَّهُ حجَّة، يقدم على الْقيَاس، فَيكون مُخَصّصا.

Eighth: Statements of the Companions: They are evidences and are preferable to analogies. As such, they can be used to particularize a generality.

تاسعها: قِيَاس النَّص الْخَاص يقدم على عُمُوم نَص آخر فيخص بِهِ مِثَاله قَوْله تَعَالَى: ﴿وَأَحَلَّ اللهُ الْبَيْعَ﴾ [الْبَقَرَة: ٢٧٥]، فَهُوَ عَام فِي جَوَاز كل بيع، ثمَّ ورد النَّص بِتَحْرِيم الرِّبَا فِي الْبر بعلة الْكَيْل، وَقِيَاسه تَحْرِيم الرِّبَا فِي الْأرز، فَهُوَ قِيَاس نَص خَاص يخص بِهِ عُمُوم إحلال البيع.

Ninth: Analogy: To be exact, when an analogy is based on a particularized text, it is used to particularize a general text. For example, Allah the Exalted states: **{Allah has permitted trading.}** [Qur'ān 2:275] This verse is general and states that all transactions are lawful. However, there is another text that states that usury in barley is unlawful, and the cause for that is dry measure. By extension of analogy, usury in rice is also unlawful. In this example, an analogy is based on a particularized text, and the subsequent ruling is used to particularize the general text that allows all transactions.

خَاتِمَة: إِذا تعَارض نصان محكمان، فإمَّا أَن يتعارضا من كل وَجه بِحَيْثُ لَا يُمكن الْجمع بَينهمَا بِوَجْه، وَإِمَّا أَن يتعارضا من بعض الْوُجُوه بِحَيْثُ يُمكن الْجمع بَينهمَا بِوَجْه مَا، فَإِن تَعَارضا من كل وَجه فِي الْمَتْن، قدم أَصَحهمَا سندا، فَإِن اسْتَويَا فِيهِ، فَإِن كَانَا صَحِيحَيْنِ صِحَة مُتَساوِيَة، قدم مَا عضده دَلِيل خَارج من نَص أَو إِجْمَاع أَو قِيَاس، فَإِن فقد الدَّلِيل الْخَارِج، فَإِن علم التَّارِيخ، فالمتأخر نَاسخ، وَإِن جهل التَّارِيخ، توقف التَّرْجِيح بَينهمَا على مُرَجّح.

To conclude [these discussions on general and particularized texts]: If there are two definitive texts that conflict, either they conflict in every single possible way, where there is no way to reconcile between them both, or they conflict from some angles, and they can be reconciled in some possible way. If two texts contradict, the text with the more authentic chain of narration should be given preference. If they have the same level of authenticity in the chains of narration, precedence is given to the text that is aided more by external evidences, such as by other texts, consensus, or analogies. If there are no external evidences, if the time the text was stated is known, the later text abrogates the earlier one. If the time-frame of revelation is unknown, however, giving preponderance to one text over the other is contingent on some evidence validating the claim.

وَإِن لم يتعارضا من كل وَجه وَجب الْجمع بَينهمَا بِمَا أمكن من الطّرق، كَمثل أَن يكون أَحدهمَا أخص من الآخر، فَيقدم أخصهما، أَو بِأَن يحمل أَحدهمَا على تَأْوِيل صَحِيح يجمع بِهِ بَين الْحَدِيثين، فَإِن كَانَ كل مِنْهُمَا عَاما من وَجه خَاصّا من وَجه تعادلا، وَطلب الْمُرَجح الْخَارِجِي، وَمن أَمْثِلَة ذَلِك قَوْله عَلَيْهِ السَّلَام: **«من نَام عن صَلَاة أَو نَسِيَهَا فليصلها إِذا ذكرهَا»** مَعَ قَوْله عَلَيْهِ السَّلَام **«لَا**

صَلَاة بعد الْعَصْر» فَالْأول خَاص فِي الْفَائِتَة الْمَكْتُوبَة، عَام فِي الْوَقْت. وَالثَّانِي عَكسه: عَام فِي الصَّلَاة خَاص فِي الْوَقْت، فيتعادلان وَيطْلب الْمُرَجح، وَيجوز تعَارض عمومين من غير مُرَجّح بَينهمَا عقلا لَا وجودا.

If they do not conflict in all ways, they must be reconciled in some possible way, using the various methods of doing so. For example, one text could be more particular than another, and as such, it is given preference. One of the texts could be given a valid interpretation that allows for reconciling between the two aḥadīth. If both are general in some respects, and specific in other respects, they become equivalent in strength, then some external method must be used to give preference to one over the other. For example, the Prophet ﷺ said, **"Whoever sleeps and misses a prayer, or forgets it, should pray it when they remember it."**[294] In another ḥadīth, the Prophet ﷺ said, **"There is no prayer after *'asr*."**[295] The first is specific to missing obligatory prayers, but generalises the time to make the prayer up, and the other is the opposite, meaning, it is general in that it encompasses all prayers, but specific in the time-frame it specifies. As such, they cancel each other out, and some external method of preferring weightier views is taken. Lastly, it is a rational possibility that two general texts conflict without any possible way to determine which should be adopted, though there is no example of such a thing in the religious texts.

فصل

Section

الْمُخَصّص إِمَّا مُنْفَصِل، وَهُوَ المخصصات التسع الَّتِي سبق بَيَانهَا، وَإِمَّا مُتَّصِل، وَهُوَ الِاسْتِثْنَاء، وَالشّرط، والغاية، والصيغة، وَغير ذَلِك مِمَّا سَيَأْتِي.

A particularizing text can either be disjunctive, such as the nine previously mentioned, and can be conjunctive. Conjunctive particularizations are: Exceptions, conditions, prepositions, attributes, and so forth, as follows:

294 Reported by Muslim (684).
295 Reported by al-Bukhārī (2/50).

أما الِاسْتِثْنَاء: فَهُوَ إِخْرَاج بعض الْجُمْلَة بإلا أَو بِمَا قَامَ مقَامهَا، وَهُوَ (غير) وَ(سوى) وَ(عدا)، و(خلا)، و(حاشا)، وَ(لَيْسَ) وَ(لَا يكون). وَالْفرق بَينه وَبَين التَّخْصِيص بالمنفصل بِغَيْر الِاسْتِثْنَاء بِوَجْهَيْنِ:

Exceptions: An exception is to exclude some portion of the sentence by using words such as, "except," or anything that takes its place. Examples are, "save," "other than," "excluding," "aside from," "not," and so forth. The difference between an exception and a disjunctive particularization that is not an exception, is twofold:

أَحدهمَا: أن الِاسْتِثْنَاء يجب اتِّصَاله بالمستثنى مِنْهُ بِخِلَاف التَّخْصِيص بِغَيْر الاستثناء، فَإِنَّهُ يجوز أَن يتراخى، وَذَلِكَ لِأَن صِيغَة الِاسْتِثْنَاء غير مُسْتَقلَّة بِنَفسِهَا، لِأَنهَا تَابِعَة للمستثنى مِنْهُ، بِخِلَاف التَّخْصِيص بغيْرهَا.

An exception must be connected to the text it is excluded from. This is contrary to a particularization without an exception, for it can be later. The reason is that the wording of an exception is one that cannot stand on its own; it follows the text it is excluded from. This is different to particularization.[296]

ثَانِيهَا: أن الِاسْتِثْنَاء يتطَرق إِلَى النَّص، كَقَوْلِه: لَهُ عَليّ عشرة إِلَّا ثَلَاثَة، بِخِلَاف التَّخْصِيص بِغَيْر الِاسْتِثْنَاء، فَإِنَّهُ لَا يَصح فِي النَّص، وَإِنَّمَا يَصح فِي الْعَام، ودلالته ظنية، وَالْفرق بَين الِاسْتِثْنَاء وَبَين النّسخ من وُجُوه:

Two. An exception can apply to a univocal text. One can say, "I owe him ten, except for three." Particularization without an exception does not apply to univocal texts, it applies to general texts, and its indication is presumptive. As for the differences between exceptions and abrogation:

أَولهَا: أَن الِاسْتِثْنَاء يشْتَرط فِيهِ الِاتِّصَال، والنسخ يشْتَرط فِيهِ التَّرَاخِي.

One. An exception must be connected to the text it is excluded from. Abrogation must come after the abrogated text.

ثَانِيهَا: أَن الِاسْتِثْنَاء إِنَّمَا يرفع حكم بعض النَّص، وَلَا يَصح أَن يكون مُسْتَغْرقا،

296 [T] Meaning, "Except Zayd," is a sentence fragment, not a complete sentence. However, a particularizing text is a standalone sentence.

والنسخ يجوز أَن يرد على جَمِيع حكم النَّص، فيرفعه.

Two. An exception lifts the ruling of a part of the text and is not inclusive of all instances the ruling applies to. Abrogation, however, can lift the entire ruling within the text.

ثَالِثهَا: الِاسْتِثْنَاء مَانع لدُخُول الْمُسْتَثْنى تَحت لفظ الْمُسْتَثْنى مِنْهُ، والنسخ يرفع مَا دخل تَحت لفظ الْمَنْسُوخ، وَهَهُنَا مسَائِل:

An exception prevents the excepted thing from falling under the broad spectrum of the thing it was being exempted from. However, an abrogation lifts and removes anything that falls under the wording of the abrogating text. Here, there are a number of useful points to consider:

أَحدهَا: يشْتَرط للاستثناء الِاتِّصَال بِحَيْثُ لَا يفصل بَين الْمُسْتَثْنى والمستثنى مِنْهُ بِكَلَام أَجْنَبِي، وَلَا بسكوت يُمكن التَّكَلُّم فِيهِ كَسَائِر التوابع اللفظية من خبر الْمُبْتَدَأ، وَجَوَاب الشَّرْط، وَالْحَال، والتمييز.

First: A condition for an exception is that it must be connected. There cannot be any pause nor separation between an exception and what it is excluded from, whether in the form of some speech foreign to the discussion or silence wherein speech can be uttered, such as the object of a subject, the apodosis, a circumstantial expression, or a specification.

ثَانِيهَا: يشْتَرط أَن لَا يكون الْمُسْتَثْنى من غير جنس الْمُسْتَثْنى مِنْهُ، فَلَا يَصح أَن يُقَال: قَامَ الْقَوْم إِلَّا حمارا، مَعَ إِرَادَة الْحَقِيقَة، فَإِن أَرَادَ الْمجَاز، صَحَّ هُنَا بِأَن يَجْعَل الْحمار كِنَايَة عَن البليد. وَالْكَلَام هُنَا فِي فن الْأُصُول لَا فِي فن النَّحْو، لِأَن كلامنا فِي التَّخْصِيص وَعَدَمه. والنحاة يَتَكَلَّمُونَ على الْجَوَاز لُغَة لَا شرعا، على أَن أهل الْعَرَبيَّة يسمون الِاسْتِثْنَاء من غير الْجِنْس مُنْقَطِعًا، ويقدرون (إِلَّا) فِيهِ بِمَعْنى (لَكِن) لاشْتِرَاكهمَا فِي معنى الِاسْتِدْرَاك بهَا، فافْتَرقَا.

Second: The excluded thing must be of the same genus of what it is excluded from. One cannot say, "The people stood, except for a donkey," while intending a true donkey. If one intends to use the word "donkey" in a metaphorical sense, it is valid here, if the donkey is used metonymically to refer to a stupid person. However, the current discussion is on legal theories and its specific branch which discusses particularization, or lack thereof, not on language and its syntaxes. Grammarians speak about whether such a sentence is possible from a linguistics perspective, not from the religious perspective. Scholars of the language refer to an exclusion of something unlike the genus of what it is excluded from as a disjunctive exclusion. They treat "except," as "however," since they share in adding additional meaning, therefore separating [between the human and the donkey].

وأما قول الْخرقِيّ فِي (مُخْتَصره): وَمن أقرّ بِشَيْء وَاسْتثنى من غير جنسه، كَانَ اسْتِثْنَاؤُهُ بَاطِلا إِلا أَن يَسْتَثْنِي عينا من ورق، أو وَرقا من عين، فَإِنَّهُ رَاجع إِلَى الِاسْتِثْنَاء من الْجِنْس، غَايَة مَا فِيهِ أَنه اسْتثْنى من الْجِنْس الْبعيد وَهُوَ المَال.

Al-Khiraqī stated in his *Mukhtaṣar*, "If someone admits to something, then makes an exception which is not of the same genus, their exception is invalid, unless they exclude silver from paper money, or vice versa."[297] The reason this is allowed is that it is an exception of the same genus. The worst that can be said is that it belongs to a subaltern genus, namely, money.

ثَالِثهَا: يشْتَرط لصِحَّة الِاسْتِثْنَاء أَن لَا يكون مُسْتَغْرقا، فَإِن كَانَ كَذَلِك نَحْو أَن يَقُول: لَهُ عَليّ عشرَة إِلَّا عشرَة، بَطل إِجْمَاعًا. وَفِي الْأَكْثَر وَالنّصف نَحْو: لَهُ عَليّ عشرَة إِلَّا سِتَّة، أَو إِلَّا خَمْسَة، خلاف. وَاقْتصر قوم على صِحَة الِاسْتِثْنَاء الْأَقَل نَحْو: لَهُ علي عشرَة إِلَّا أَرْبَعَة، وَهُوَ الصَّحِيح من مَذْهَبنَا. قَالَ الشَّيْخ مجد الدّين - من أَصْحَابنَا - فِي كِتَابه (الْمُحَرر): يَصح اسْتِثْنَاء الْأَقَل دون الْأَكْثَر فِي عدد الطَّلَاق والمطلقات والأقارير، نَص عَلَيْهِ، وَفِي النّصْف وَجْهَان، وَقيل: فِي الْأَكْثَر أَيْضا، وَحكى المرداوي فِي (التَّحْرِير) أَنه يَصح اسْتِثْنَاء النّصْف فِي الْأَصَح.

Third: In order for an exception to be valid, it must not be all-encompassing. If one were to say, "I owe ten, except for ten," their exception is invalid, according to consensus. However, if one excludes most or half of the items within their expression, such as saying, "I owe ten, except for six," or, "five," there is a difference of opinion. A number of scholars have sufficed with stat-

297 [T] *Mukhtaṣar al-Khiraqī* (p.76).

ing the validity of excluding the lesser amount of the items, such as, 'I owe ten, except for four.' That is the correct view in our *madhhab*. Al-Shaykh Majd al-Dīn, one of our *aṣḥāb*, stated in *al-Muḥarrar*, "Exclusions of lesser amounts is valid, not the greater amount, in things such as divorce, divorced women, and recognitions, as explicitly stated [by al-Imām Aḥmad]. There are two variants on the topic of [excluding] half, and it was stated so for [excluding] the majority [of items in a set] as well.[298] Further, al-Mardāwī stated in *al-Taḥrīr* that exclusion of half is valid, according to the veracious view.

رَابعهَا: إِذا تعقب الِاسْتِثْنَاء جملا كَقَوْلِه تَعَالَى: ﴿وَالَّذين يَرْمُونَ الْمُحْصَنَاتِ ثُمَّ لَمْ يَأْتُوا بِأَرْبَعَةِ شُهَدَاءَ فَاجْلِدُوهُمْ ثَمَانِينَ جَلْدَةً وَلا تَقْبَلُوا لَهُمْ شَهَادَةً أَبَداً وَأُولَئِكَ هُمُ الْفَاسِقُونَ إِلَّا الَّذِينَ تَابُوا﴾ [النُّور: ٤-٥] عَاد الِاسْتِثْنَاء إِلَى الْكل عندنَا، وَعند الشَّافِعِيَّة، وَإِلَى الْأَخِيرة عِنْد الْحَنَفِيَّة، وَتوقف المرتضى من الشِّيعَة فَقَالَ: يصلح رُجُوعه إِلَى جَمِيع الْجمل، وَإِلَى الْجُمْلَة الْأَخِيرة على جِهَة الِاشْتِرَاك والتساوي، وَلَا رُجْحَان لأَحَدهمَا على الْأُخْرَى.

Fourth: If after an exclusion, there are a number of provisions, such as when Allah states: **{As for those who accuse chaste women of fornication, and then fail to provide four witnesses, strike them eighty times, and reject their testimony ever afterwards: they are the lawbreakers, except those who repent afterwards and mend their ways, then surely Allah is All-Forgiving, Most Merciful.}** [Qur'ān 24:4-5] According to [the Ḥanbalī] and Shāfiʿī scholars, the exclusion applies to all of the provisions. According to the Ḥanafī scholars, it applies to the last-mentioned provision. Al-Murtaḍā, a Shiite, abstained from declaring a view on this matter, saying, "It is possible that it could refer to all of the provisions, and it could also refer to the last provision. These two possibilities are wholly equal and equivalent; none is more favourable than the other."

وَالْقَوْل الْفَصْل: أنه إِن كَانَ فِي الْكَلَام قرينَة معنوية كَقَوْلِه: نساؤه طَوَالِق، وعبيدي أَحْرَار إِلَّا الْحيض، أَو لفظية كَقَوْلِك: أكْرم بني تَمِيم والنحاة البصريون إِلَّا البغدادة، كَانَ الِاسْتِثْنَاء رَاجعا إِلَى الْجُمْلَة الأولى، وَأما فِي الْمِثَال الثَّانِي فالنظر إِلَى الْوَاو، فَإِن ظهر أَنَّهَا للابتداء اخْتصَّ بالأخيرة، وَإِن ترددت بَين الْعَطف

298 [T] *Al-Muḥarrar fi 'l-Fiqh 'alā Madhhab al-Imām Aḥmad ibn Ḥanbal* (2/59).

والابتداء، فالوقف.

The veracious view is that if there is some contextual clue in the meaning, such as someone saying, "My wives are divorced, and my slaves are freed, except for the menstruating ones," or in the wording, such as, "Honour the Tribe of Tamīm and the Baṣran grammarians, but not the Baghdādīs," the exception applies to the first sentence. As for the second example given, one must examine the word "and" to see if it is initiating a new sentence. If it is so, then the exception applies to the last sentence, but if the "and" cannot be determined to be an addition or the start of a new sentence, one must abstain.

تَنْبِيه: حَيْثُ إن الِاسْتِثْنَاء إِذا تعقب جملا عَاد إِلَيْهَا كلهَا على الْمُخْتَار، وَكَانَ الشَّرْط فِي مثل قَول الْقَائِل: وَالله لأَفْعَلَنَّ كَذَا إِن شَاءَ الله، أَو لأصومن ولأتصدقن ولأصلين إِن شَاءَ الله، يعود إِلَى الْجمل كلهَا، سمى الْفُقَهَاء مثل هَذَا اسْتِثْنَاء بِجَامِع افتقار كل مِنْهُمَا إِلَى مَا يتعَلَّق بِهِ، إِذْ الشَّرْط يتعَلَّق بمشروطه، وَلَا يسْتَقلّ بِدُونِهِ، وَالِاسْتِثْنَاء يتعَلَّق بالمستثنى مِنْهُ، وَلَا يسْتَقلّ بِدُونِهِ.

Note: If an exception follows a number of phrases, it applies to them all, according to the chosen view [of the Ḥanbalī scholars]. A condition in statements such as, "By Allah, I will do such-and-such, if Allah Wills," or, "I will fast, give charity, and pray, if Allah the Exalted Wills," applies to all of the provisions. The jurists referred to such things as exclusions on account of the similarity of both [types of exclusions] in that they are contingent on their relational; in other words, a condition is contingent on its conditional, and it cannot exist independently, while an exception is contingent on what it is excepted from, without existing independently.

خَامِسهَا: لَا يَصح الِاسْتِثْنَاء إِلَّا نطقا إِلَّا فِي يَمِين خَائِف بنطقه، وَقيل: قِيَاس مَذْهَب مَالك صِحَّته بِالنيةِ، وَيجوز تَقْدِيمه عِنْد الْكل.

Fifth: An exception can only be verbal, with the exception of the right-hand in the case of a person who is afraid to speak. It was stated that by analogy, the *madhhab* of al-Imām Mālik allows for exceptions via intention. All agree that the exception can precede what it is exempted from.

سادسها: ذهب أَصْحَابنَا والمالكية وَالشَّافِعِيَّة إِلَى أَن الِاسْتِثْنَاء من النَّفْي إِثْبَات، وَمن الْإِثْبَات نفي خلافًا للحنفية فِي الأولى، وَسوى بَعضهم بَينهمَا، وَاسْتثنى الْقَرَافِيّ من الأول الشَّرْط كـ«**لا صَلَاة إِلَّا بِطهُور**».

Sixth: Our *aṣḥāb*, Māliki scholars, and Shāfiʿī scholars agreed that an exception from a negation is an affirmation, and an exception of an affirmation is a negation. The first was disputed by Ḥanafī scholars, and some scholars considered both to be equal. Al-Qarāfī exempted conditions from the first (meaning, an exception after a negation), as in the ḥadīth, **"There is no prayer except with purity."**[299]

سابعها: إِذا وَقع بعد الْمُسْتَثْنى مِنْهُ والمستثنى جملَة تصلح أَن تكون صفة لكل وَاحِد مِنْهُمَا، فَعِنْدَ الشَّافِعِيَّة أَن تِلْكَ الْجُمْلَة ترجع إِلَى الْمُسْتَثْنى مِنْهُ، وَعند الْحَنَفِيَّة إِلَى الْمُسْتَثْنى، وَهَكَذَا إِذا جَاءَ بعد الْجمل ضمير يصلح لكل وَاحِدَة مِنْهُمَا.

Seventh: If there is a sentence after the thing excluded from and after the exception, and that sentence is fit to be an attribute for either [the exception or the excluded from], according to the Shāfiʿī scholars, the sentence refers to the excluded from, but to the Ḥanafī scholars, it refers to the exclusion. The same discussion applies if there is a pronoun that can refer to either.

وَأما التَّخْصِيص بِالشَّرْطِ - وَهُوَ مَا توقف عَلَيْهِ تَأْثِير الْمُؤثر على غير جِهَة السَّبَبِيَّة - ومثاله قَوْله تَعَالَى ﴿**وَإِذَا ضَرَبْتُمْ فِي الْأَرْضِ فَلَيْسَ عَلَيْكُمْ جُنَاحٌ أَنْ تَقْصُرُوا مِنَ الصَّلَاةِ إِنْ خِفْتُمْ أَنْ يَفْتِنَكُمُ الَّذِينَ كَفَرُوا**﴾ [النِّسَاء: ١٠١]، فَإِنَّهُ أجَاز قصر الصَّلَاة بشرطين.

To continue, an example of particularization via a condition, which is defined as what the effect of the cause is contingent on, without being a direct cause, is where Allah the Exalted states: **{When you [believers] are traveling in the land, you will not be blamed for shortening your prayers, if you fear the disbelievers may harm you.}** [Qurʾān 4:101] Allah has allowed for shortening the prayers, and gave two conditions:

---

299 Reported by Muslim (224).

أحدهمَا: الضَّرْب فِي الأَرْض، وَالْآخر خوف فتْنَة الْكفَّار، لَكِن نسخ اعْتِبَار الشَّرْط الثَّانِي بِالرُّخْصَةِ حَتَّى جَازَ الْقصر مَعَ الْأَمْن، وَبَقِي الشَّرْط الأول، وَهُوَ الضَّرْب فِي الأَرْض، فَلَا يجوز الْقصر بِدُونِهِ.

(i) Travelling in the land. (ii) Being fearful of the harm of disbelievers. However, the second condition was abrogated by the concession [given by Allah], making it permissible to shorten the prayer even during times of safety. The first condition remained, however, and it is travelling in the land. As such, it is not permissible to shorten the prayer without that condition.

وينقسم الشَّرْط إِلَى أَرْبَعَة أَقسَام: عَقْلي، كالحياة للْعلم. وشرعي، كالطهارة للصَّلَاة. ولغوي، كالتعليقات نَحْو: إِن قُمْت قُمْت، وعادي، كالسلم لصعود السَّطْح.

Conditions are of four categories: (i) Rational: Such as life being a condition to one having knowledge. (ii) Religious: Such as purity being a condition to the validity of prayer. (iii) Linguistic: Such as making something dependent on another, and an example is saying, "If you stand, I shall stand." (iv) Customary: Such as a ladder being needed to ascend a wall.

وَقد يَتَعَدَّد، وَمَعَ التَّعَدُّد، قد يكون كل وَاحِد شرطا على الْجَمِيع، فَيتَوَقَّف الْمَشْرُوط على حُصُولهَا جَمِيعهَا، وَقد يكون كل وَاحِد شرطا مُسْتقِلا فَيحصل الْمَشْرُوط بِحُصُول أَي وَاحِد مِنْهَا، وَالشّرط كالاستثناء فِي اشْتِرَاط الِاتِّصَال.

A single thing could have multiple conditions. If there are multiple conditions, each individual condition is necessary for the instatement of all of the conditions.[300] One could be an independent condition, however, resulting in the conditional occurring when any of the [independent conditions] occur. A condition resembles an exception in that it must be coupled with the conditional.

---

300 [T] Meaning, if one is nonexistent, the ruling attached to all is nonexistent. For example, if someone says to his wife, "If you enter the home, eat, and drink, you are divorced," the consequent becomes contingent on the existence of all of the conditions. However, if one says, "If you enter the home, eat, or drink, you are divorced," she is divorced if she does any of those three actions. This example was mentioned in *Irshād al-Fuḥūl* (1/377)

وَإِن تعقب جملا متعاطفة كَانَ حكمه رَاجعا إِلَيْهَا كلهَا عِنْد الْأَئِمَّة الْأَرْبَعَة وَغَيرهم. وَحكي إِجْمَاعًا، وَقيل: يخْتَص بِالَّتِي تليه وَلَو كَانَت مُتَأَخِّرَة. وَقَالَ الرَّازِيّ بِالْوَقْفِ، وَيجوز إِخْرَاج الْأَكْثَر بِهِ.

If there are multiple sentences [tied to the condition], it applies to all of the sentences, according to the four *imāms*, and others. It was stated to be a matter of consensus. It was said that [the condition] applies only to the sentence that comes directly after or before it,[301] even if it occurs later. Al-Rāzī abstained from taking a view. Lastly, it is possible for a condition to exclude the majority of items within a set.

وَأما الْغَايَة: فَهِيَ نِهَايَة الشَّيْء الْمُقْتَضِيَة لثُبُوت الحكم قبلهَا وانتفائه بعْدهَا، وَلها لفظان وهما (حَتَّى) وَ(إِلَى) وَكَقَوْلِه تَعَالَى: ﴿وَلَا تَقْرَبُوهُنَّ حَتَّىٰ يَطْهُرْنَ﴾ [الْبَقَرَة: ٢٢٢]، وَقَوله: ﴿وَأَيْدِيَكُمْ إِلَى الْمَرَافِقِ﴾ [الْمَائِدَة: ٦] وَاخْتلفُوا فِي الْغَايَة نَفسهَا، هَل تدخل فِي المغي أم لَا؟ وَالَّذِي صرح بِهِ أَكثر الْأَصْحَاب أَن مَا بعْدهَا مَحْكُوم عَلَيْهِ بنقيض حكم مَا قبلهَا مَا لم يتَقَدَّم على الْغَايَة عُمُوم يشملها، فَإِذا تقدمها ذَلِك نَحْو: قطعت أَصَابِعه كلهَا من الْخِنْصر إِلَى الْإِبْهَام، لم يكن مَا بعْدهَا مُخَالفا لما قبلهَا وَمثله: ﴿سَلَامٌ هِيَ حَتَّىٰ مَطْلَعِ الْفَجْرِ﴾ [الْقدر: ٥]

Prepositions of termination denote the ending of something which necessitated some ruling before and up until [it ended], and the nonexistence of that ruling after it ended. There are two words, "until," and "up to." For example, Allah the Exalted states: **{Do not approach them until they are cleansed.}** [Qur'ān 2:222] Also: **{And your hands up to the elbows.}** [Qur'ān 5:6] Scholars differed on whether "until," or "up to," are inclusive or not. The majority of the *aṣḥāb* have explicitly stated that whatever comes after "until" takes the opposite ruling of whatever the ruling was before it, so long as there is no generality mentioned before it that would encompass it. For example, one could say, "His fingers all got cut off, from his little finger up to his thumb," and in this case, what comes after "up to" does not

301 [T] Meaning, if the condition is the last thing mentioned in a sentence, it applies to the provision immediately before it, and if the condition is the first thing mentioned, it applies to the provision that occurs directly after it. This was an isolated view of some linguists and an early view of al-Sayrafī. Refer to *al-Taḥbir Sharḥ al-Taḥrīr* by al-Qāḍī 'Alā' al-Dīn al-Mardāwī (6/2623).

contradict what comes before it. Another example is when Allah the Exalted said: **{It is all peace until the break of dawn.}** [Qur'ān 97:5]

وَأما الصّفة: فَهِيَ كالاستثناء إِذا وَقعت بعد مُتَعَدد، وَالْمرَاد بِالصّفةِ هُنَا هِيَ المعنوية على مَا حَقَّقَهُ عُلَمَاء الْبَيَان، لَا مُجَرّد النَّعْت الْمَذْكُور فِي علم النَّحْو. قَالَ الْمَازرِيّ: وَلَا خلاف فِي اتِّصَال التوابع، وَهِي النَّعْت، والتوكيد، والعطف، وَالْبدل. وَقَالَ الصفي الْهِنْدِيّ: إِن كَانَت الصِّفَات كَثِيرَة، وَذكرت على الْجمع عقب جملَة، تقيدت بهَا، أَو على الْبَدَل، فلواحدة غير مُعينَة مِنْهَا، وَإِن ذكرت عقب جمل، فَفِي الْعود إِلَى كلهَا أَو إِلَى الْأَخِيرَة خلاف. انْتهى.

Attributes: An attribute is similar to an exception if it occurs after a number of things are mentioned. The meaning of an attribute in this context is a universal descriptor—according to scholars of rhetoric, not the mere adjective that is discussed in grammar.[302] Al-Māzirī stated, "There is no difference of opinion that auxiliary words are connected to the nouns they pertain to." The auxiliary words are adjectives, emphases, syndesis, and appositions. Al-Ṣafī al-Hindī stated, "If there are many attributes mentioned and they are mentioned together after a sentence, they are bound to the sentence. If they are mentioned as appositives, [the sentence] conforms to just one of the attributes, though none in particular. If they are mentioned after a number of sentences, there is a difference of opinion whether they apply to all of them or just the last one."[303]

وَأما إِذا توسطت بَين جمل فَلَا وَجه للْخلاف فِي ذَلِك، فَإِن الصّفة تكون لما قبلهَا لَا لما بعْدهَا، وَقَالَ شيخ الْإِسْلَام أَحْمد ابن تَيْمِية: التوابع المخصصة كالبدل، وَعطف الْبَيَان، والتوكيد، وَنَحْوه كالاستثناء والشروط المعنونة بِحرف الْجَرّ، كَقَوْلِه: على أَنه، أَو بِشَرْط أَنه، أَو بِحرف الْعَطف كَقَوْلِه: وَمن شَرطه كَذَا، فَهِيَ كالشرط اللّغَوِيّ، وَيتَعَلق حرف مُتَأَخّر بِالْفِعْلِ الْمُتَقَدّم. انْتهى.

---

302 [T] The reason is that numbers, adverbs, adjectives, and so forth, are included in the broad spectrum of an "attribute." Therefore, it is more encompassing and is universal. Refer to Shaykh al-ʿAttār's commentary on al-Imām Jalāl al-Dīn al-Maḥallī's explanation of *Jamʿ al-Jawāmiʿ* (1/327).

303 [T] *Al-Fā'iq fī Uṣūl al-Fiqh* (1/327-329).

If attributes appear in the middle of a sentence, there is no legitimacy to any difference of opinion, for it would apply to the sentence before them, and not those after them. Shaykh al-Islām Aḥmad ibn Taymiyyah said, "There are auxiliary words that particularize a sentence, such as appositions, explanatory appositions, emphases, exceptions, and conditions mentioned with [conjunctions,] such as, "provided that [something happens]," "conditioned on," or if it is connected with a syndetic construction, such as by saying, "and its condition is." In the case that these are used, they are similar to linguistic conditionals, and the conjunction relates to the verb that occurs before its usage."[304]

وَالْإِشَارَة بذلك بعد جمل تعود إِلَى الْكل كَقَوْلِه تَعَالَى ﴿وَمن يَفْعَلْ ذَلِكَ يَلْقَ أَثَاماً﴾ [الْفرْقَان: ٦٨]، والتمييز إِذا جَاءَ بعد جمل يعود إِلَى جَمِيع الْجمل الْمُتَقَدّمَة، فَإِذا قَالَ مثلا: لَهُ عَليّ ألف وَخَمْسُونَ درهما، فالجميع دَرَاهِم على الصَّحِيح من الْمَذْهَب، كَمَا قَالَه البعلي فِي قَوَاعِده الْأُصُولِيَّة. وَقَالَ التَّمِيمِي: يرجع فِي تَفْسِير الْألف إِلَيْهِ.

When the phrase, "these things" is used to refer to multiple sentences, it applies to all of the sentences, such as when Allah the Exalted said: **{Whoever does these things will face the penalties.}** [Qur'ān 25:68] When a specification is mentioned after multiple sentences, it also applies to all of the sentences before it. If someone says, for example, "I owe a thousand and fifty dirhams," all of the amount owed is dirhams, according to the correct view in the *madhhab*. This was mentioned by al-Baʿlī in his *Legal Maxims*. Al-Tamīmī stated, "To explain the thousand, the specification [of *dirhams*] is used."

تَنْبِيه: قَوْلنَا: وَالْمرَاد بِالصّفةِ المعنوية مَعْنَاهُ أَنَّهَا تَشْمَل كل مَا أشعر بِمَعْنى يَتَّصِف بِهِ إِفْرَاد الْعَام، سَوَاء كَانَ الْوَصْف نعتا أَو عطف بَيَان أَو حَالا، وَسَوَاء كَانَ ذَلِك مُفردا أَو جملَة أَو شبهها، وَهُوَ الظّرْف وَالْجَار وَالْمَجْرُور. وَلَو كَانَ جَامِدا مؤولا بمشتق، لَكِن يخرج من ذَلِك الْوَصْف الَّذِي خرج مخرج الْغَالِب، كَمَا يَأْتِي فِي المفاهيم، أَو لبَيَان الْوَصْف بمدح أَو ذمّ أَو ترحم أَو توكيد أَو تَفْصِيل، فَلَيْسَ شَيْء

304 [T] *Majmūʿ al-Fatāwā* (31/157).

مِنْ ذَلِكَ مُخَصِّصًا لِلْعُمُومِ.

Note: When I referred to universal descriptors, I was referring to something that encompasses any attribute of the instances falling under a general term. The attribute, of course, could be an adjective, an explanatory apposition, or a circumstantial expression or a phrase. It also applies to singulars, sentences, or anything resembling a sentence, such as an adverb and prepositions with a word governed by the preposition. This also applies if the word is *jāmid mu'awwal bi mushtaq*.[305] However, attributes that are simply descriptions of normative behaviour,[306] or clarify the attributes by praising them,[307] dispraising them,[308] showing mercy,[309] emphasising,[310] or clarifying certain qualities,[311] do not particularize generalities.

---

305 [T] To the best of my knowledge, this has no equivalent terminology in the English language. A *jāmid* word is one that is static; it is not taken from anything else, but it indicates some object or meaning. Examples are, "man," "knowledge (*'ilm*)," etc. A *mushtaq* word is one that is derived from another word, such as, "learned (*'ālīm*)," "known (*ma'lūm*)," "scholarly (*'allām*)," and so forth. All of these words are derived and morphed from the static word, "*'ilm*." As for the concept of *jāmid mu'awwal bi mushtaq*, it is a word that is static but gives a meaning that is derived, examples are "He is an ocean of generosity." The word "ocean," here is static. However, it is being used to refer to a derived meaning, which is, "He is generous," where generous is the equivalent of *karīm* in Arabic, a derived word from, *al-karam*. Refer to *al-Kafāf* by Yūsuf al-Ṣaydāwī and *al-Qawā'id al-Taṭbīqiyyah fi 'l-Lughat al-'Arabiyyah* by Nadīm Da'kūr.

306 [T] For example, Allah the Exalted states: **{O believers! Do not consume interest, multiplying it many times over. And be mindful of Allah, so you may prosper.}** [Qur'ān 3:130] This does not particularize the generality of the verse by stating that if one were to consume small amounts of usury, that it would be allowed. It merely states that the normative usage of usury is in multiplying it many times over, and as such, it has no indication that the inverse ruling is acceptable.

307 [T] For example, when one says, "May Allah have mercy on 'Umar, whose justice was widespread, and whose heart was merciful." This is meant as a praise, not as a particularization. Refer to *Ta'jīl al-Nadā bi Sharḥ Qaṭr al-Nadā* by al-Shaykh 'Abdullah al-Fawzān (p. 246).

308 [T] Such as saying, "I seek refuge in Allah from the accursed Shaytān." Ibid.

309 [T] Such as saying, "O Allah, have mercy on your poor slave." Ibid.

310 [T] Such as when Allah the Exalted said: **{When the Trumpet is sounded a single time.}** [Qur'ān 69:13] Ibid.

311 [T] Such as saying, "A salesman came," or, "Khalid, the author, came." Ibid.

فصل فِي الْمُطلق والمقيد

On Unqualified and Qualified Language

أما الْمُطلق: فَهُوَ مَا تناول وَاحِدًا غير معِين بِاعْتِبَار حَقِيقَة شَامِلَة لجنسه، نَحْو قَوْله عز وَجل: ﴿فَتَحْرِيرُ رَقَبَةٍ﴾ [المجادلة: ٣]، وَقَوله عَلَيْهِ الصَّلَاة وَالسَّلَام: **«لَا نِكَاح إِلَّا بولِي»** فَكل وَاحِد من لفظ الرَّقَبَة وَالْولِيّ قد تناول وَاحِدًا غير معِين من جنس الرقاب والأولياء.

Muṭlaq (unrestricted, unqualified) refers to a term that indicates to an unspecified single instance of something, inasmuch as there is a shared essential nature of the genus. For example, Allah the Exalted states: **{Must free a slave.}**[312] [Qur'ān 58:3] Also, the Prophet ﷺ said, "**There is no marriage without a guardian.**"[313] Therefore, the two terms "a slave" and "a guardian" refer to an unspecified single instance from the genus of slaves and guardians, respectively.

والمقيد: مَا تنَاول معينا نَحْو: أعتق زيدا من العبيد، أَو مَوْصُوفا بِوَصْف زَائِد على حَقِيقَة جنسه نَحْو **﴿وَتَحْرِيرُ رَقَبَةٍ مُؤْمِنَةٍ﴾** [النِّسَاء: ٩٢]، **﴿فَصِيَامُ شَهْرَيْنِ مُتَتَابِعَيْنِ﴾** [النِّسَاء: ٩٢]، وصف الرَّقَبَة بِالْإِيمَان، والشهرين بالتتابع، وَذَلِك وصف زَائِد على حَقِيقَة نفس الرَّقَبَة والشهرين، لِأَن الرَّقَبَة قد تكون مُؤمنَة وكافرة، والشهرين قد يَكُونَا مُتَتَابعين وَغير مُتَتَابعين.

As for the term *muqayyad*, it refers to a single instance. For example, one could say, "Free Zayd from the slaves." Or, it could be an attribute that is an addition to the essential nature of its genus. For example, Allah the Exalted states: **{He must free one Muslim slave.}** [Qur'ān 4:92] Also: **{Must fast for two consecutive months.}** [Qur'ān 4:92] In the first verse, the slave is

312 [T] The description, "a slave," is unrestricted. Therefore, any instance of a slave could be chosen, since any instance of a slave shares in the essential nature of the genus. The essential nature is enslavement.

313 Reported by Aḥmad (4/394), al-Tirmidhī (1101), and Abu Dāwūd (1102).

given the attribute of being a believer, and in the second verse, the months are described as being "consecutive." Those attributes are additions on top of the essential nature of slaves and months, since slaves could be believers or could be disbelievers, and months could be consecutive and could be inconsecutive.

وَالْإِطْلَاق وَالتَّقْيِيد يكونانِ تَارة فِي الْأَمر نَحْو: أعتق رَقبة، وَأعْتق رَقَبَة مُؤمنَة، وَتارة فِي الْخَبَر نَحْو: **«لَا نِكَاح إِلَّا بولي وشاهدين» «لَا نِكَاح إِلَّا بولِي مرشد وشاهدي عدل».**

Unqualified or qualified language sometimes occur in commandments, such as, "Free a slave," and then, "Free a believing slave." At other times, it could occur in declarative sentences, such as, **"There is no marriage without a watchful guardian and two witnesses,"** then, in another narration, **"There is no marriage without a guardian and two upright witnesses."**[314]

وتتفاوت مَرَاتِب الْمُقيد فِي تَقْيِيده بِاعْتِبَار قلَّة الْقُيُود وَكَثْرَتهَا، فَمَا كَانَت قيوده أَكثر كَانَت رتبته فِي التَّقْيِيد أعلى، وَهُوَ فِيهِ أَدخل، فَقَوله سُبْحَانَهُ وَتَعَالَى: **﴿أَنْ يُبْدِلَهُ أَزْوَاجاً خَيْراً مِنْكُنَّ مُسْلِمَاتٍ مُؤْمِنَاتٍ قَانِتَاتٍ تَائِبَاتٍ عَابِدَاتٍ سَائِحَاتٍ ثَيِّبَاتٍ وَأَبْكَاراً﴾** [التَّحْرِيم: ٥] أعلا رُتْبَة فِي التَّقْيِيد من قَوْله: **﴿مُؤْمِنَاتٍ قَانِتَاتٍ﴾** لَا غير.

The levels of a qualified text vary in proportion to how many qualifications there are. If there are more qualifications, its level is higher and it is more qualified. For example, Allah the Exalted states: **{His Lord may well replace you with better wives if the Prophet decides to divorce any of you: wives who are devoted to Allah, true believers, devout, who turn to Him in repentance and worship Him, given to fasting, whether previously married or virgins.}** [Qur'ān 66:5] This is of a higher level of qualification than if the verse were to end with: **{Wives who are devoted to Allah, true believers, devout.}** [Qur'ān 66:5]

وَقد يجْتَمع الْإِطْلَاق وَالتَّقْيِيد فِي لفظ وَاحِد بالجهتين كَقَوْلِه تَعَالَى **﴿فَتَحْرِيرُ رَقَبَةٍ مُؤْمِنَةٍ﴾** [النِّسَاء: ٩٢]، قيدت من حَيْثُ الدّين بِالْإِيمَان، وأطلقت من حَيْثُ

314 Reported by al-Shāfiʿī (2/317) and al-Dāraquṭnī (382).

مَا سواهُ كالصحة والسقم والطول وَالْقصر وَالنّسب والبلد، فَهِيَ مُقيّدَة من جِهَة، مُطلقَة من جِهَة.

A single text could be unqualified and also qualified, both from different perspectives, at the same time. For example, Allah the Exalted states: **{He must free a believing slave.}** [Qur'ān 4:92] This verse is qualified in terms of religion, by the word, "believing." It is also unqualified in other senses, such as health, sickness, height, lineage, and land. Therefore, it is qualified from a perspective, and unqualified from another.

ثمَّ إِنَّه يُقَال هُنَا: إِذا اجْتمع لفظ مُطلق ومقيد، فإمَّا أَن يتحد حكمهمَا أَو يخْتَلف، فَإِن اتَّحد حكمهمَا فإمَّا أَن يتحد سببهما، أَو يخْتَلف، فَهَذِهِ ثَلَاثَة أَقسَام:

Here, it is fit to mention that if an unqualified term is combined with a qualified one, they can either have the same ruling, or different rulings. If their rulings are the same, their cause could be the same, or could differ. These, then, are three categories:

فَإِذا اتَّحد حكمهمَا حمل الْمُطلق على الْمُقيد كَقَوْلِه عَلَيْهِ الصَّلَاة وَالسَّلَام: **«لَا نِكَاح إِلَّا بولِي وشهود»** مَعَ **«إِلَّا بولِي مرشد وشاهدي عدل»**، فَالْأول مُطلق فِي الْوَلِيّ بِالنِّسْبَةِ إِلَى الرشد والغي، وَالشُّهُود بِالنِّسْبَةِ إِلَى الْعَدَالَة وَالْفِسْق. وَالثَّانِي مُقَيّد بِالرشد فِي الْوَلِيّ وَالْعَدَالَة فِي الشُّهُود، وسببهما وَاحِد وَهُوَ النِّكَاح، وحكمهما نَفْيه إِلَّا بولِي وشهود.

One. If they have the same ruling, the unqualified term is understood in light of the qualifications mentioned. For example, the Prophet ﷺ said, **"There is no marriage without a guiding guardian and two witnesses,"** then, in another narration, **"There is no marriage without a watchful guardian and two upright witnesses."**[315] The first ḥadīth is unqualified with regards to the guardian, in that it does not qualify it by mentioning that they must be watchful or in error, nor does it qualify the witnesses by stating whether they must be upright or sinful. The second ḥadīth qualifies the guardian, stating that they must be watchful, offering sound counsel and advice, and that the witnesses must be upright. In this case, the cause of both is one, namely, marriage, and the ruling is that the marriage is void

315 Reported by al-Shāfiʿī (2/317) and al-Dāraquṭnī (382).

without a guardian and witnesses.

وَإِذا اتحدا حكما وَاخْتلفَا سَببا كعتق رَقَبَة مُؤمنَة فِي كَفَّارَة الْقَتْل، ورقبة مُطلقَة فِي كَفَّارَة الظِّهَار، فَعِنْدَ القَاضِي أبي يعلى والمالكية يحمل الْمُطلق على الْمُقَيد، وَنسبه فِي (التَّحْرِير) إِلَى الْأَئِمَّة الْأَرْبَعَة وَغيرهم، وَقَالَ الطوفي فِي (مُخْتَصره): وَخَالف بعض الشَّافِعِيَّة، وَأكْثر الْحَنَفِيَّة، وَأَبُو إِسْحَاق بْن شاقلا من أَصْحَابنَا فَقَالُوا: لَا يحمل الْمُطلق على الْمُقَيد هَاهُنَا، وَقد رُوِيَ عَن أَحْمد مَا يدل على هَذَا أَيْضا. وَقَالَ أَبُو الْخطاب: إِن عضده قِيَاس حمل عَلَيْهِ وَإِلَّا فَلَا.

Two. The scholars differed when they have the same ruling but differ in the cause of the ruling, such as the expiation of murder being to free a believing slave, and the expiation of *ẓihār* being to free a slave without the qualification of being a believer. Al-Qāḍī Abu Ya'lā and the Māliki scholars opined that the unqualified text should be understood in light of the qualifications mentioned in the other. In *Taḥrīr al-Manqūl*, this view was referenced back to the four *imāms* and others. Al-Ṭūfī stated in his *Mukhtaṣar*, "Some scholars of the Shāfiʿī *madhhab* contradicted this view, as did the majority of the Ḥanafī scholars and Abu Isḥāq ibn Shāqillā, who was one of our *aṣḥāb*. They stated that the unqualified text, in this instance, should not be understood in light of the qualifications mentioned elsewhere. There are also some narrations from Aḥmad that indicate as much. Abu 'l-Khaṭṭāb said, 'If it is supported by another analogy, [the restricted text] should be held to [the qualifications mentioned]. Otherwise, it should not.'"[316]

وَإِذا اخْتلف الحكم فَلَا حمل كتقييد صَوْم الْكَفَّارَة بالتتابع، وَإِطْلَاق الْإِطْعَام.

Three. If the ruling differs, the unqualified text should not be interpreted in light of qualifications mentioned in other verses. An example is where fasting for expiation carries the requirement of being consecutive, while feeding of the poor carries no such qualification.[317]

---

316 [T] *Sharḥ Mukhtaṣar al-Rawḍah* (2/639).

317 [T] Allah the Exalted said, **{Even if any of you say to their wives, 'You are to me like my mother's back,' they are not their mothers; their only mothers are those who gave birth to them. What they say is certainly blameworthy and false, but Allah is pardoning and forgiving. Those of you who say such a thing to their wives, then go back on what they have said, must free a slave before the couple may touch one another again—this is what you are commanded to**

وَمَتى اجْتمع مُطلق ومقيدان متضادان حمل الْمُطلق على مَا هُوَ أشبه من المقيدين المتضادين، وَذَلِكَ كَغسْل الْأَيْدِي فِي الْوضُوء، ورد مُقَيّدا بالمرافق، وقطعها فِي السّرقَة، ورد مُقَيّدا بالكوع بِالْإِجْمَاع، ومسحها فِي التَّيَمُّم ورد مُطلقًا فَالْحق بالأشبه بِهِ وَهُوَ الْوضُوء.

Further, whenever an unqualified text has two opposite possible qualifying texts, the unqualified text should be understood in light of the qualifier that is most resembling of its nature. For example, when it comes to washing of the hands in ablution, the verse mentions the hands and qualifies it by saying, **{To the elbows.}** [Qurʾān 5:6] And in terms of the cutting of the wrist for stealing, consensus dictated that its verse is qualified and means, "To the wrist." Therefore, when it comes to *tayammum*, the text is unqualified, and as such, it takes the ruling of the one most similar, namely, ablution.

تَنْبِيه: جَمِيع مَا ذكر فِي التَّخْصِيص للعام وَهُوَ جَار فِي تَقْيِيد الْمُطلق، فَارْجِع إِلَيْهِ.

Lastly, note that anything I mentioned in the section of particularizing general texts is applicable here. As such, review that section.

---

do, and Allah is fully aware of what you do, but anyone who does not have the means should fast continuously for two months before they touch each other, and anyone unable to do this should feed sixty needy people. This is so that you may [truly] have faith in Allah and His Messenger. These are the bounds set by Allah: grievous torment awaits those who ignore them.} [Qurʾān 58:2-4]

In this verse, Allah the Exalted mentions that a person must fast continuously for two months, and then says, "and anyone unable to do this should feed sixty needy people." Since the ruling of feeding needy people differs with the ruling of fasting two consecutive months, the qualification of continuousness does not apply to feeding the needy. As such, one can feed a needy person one day, and not feed another for a few days, and then feed multiple needy people in a single day.

فصل الْمُجْمل

Section on Polysemes

الْمُجْمل لُغَة: مَا جعل جملَة وَاحِدَة لَا ينْفَرد بعض آحادها عَن بعض. وَاصْطِلَاحا: اللَّفْظ المتردد بَين محتملين فَصَاعِدا على السوَاء والإجمال، إِمَّا أَن يَقع فِي اللَّفْظ الْمُفْرد أَو الْمركب، وَالْوَاقِع فِي الْمُفْرد إِمَّا أَن يَقع فِي الْأَسْمَاء أَو الْأَفْعَال أَو الْحُرُوف.

The term *mujmal* (polyseme, obscure) refers linguistically to a sum where its individual parts cannot exist without one another. In religious terminology, it refers to a word that has a meaning with two or more possibilities, all of which are equally viable. Obscurity could define a single word and could define a complex sentence. Obscurity in single words means that it can occur to: Nouns, verbs and particles.

أما وُقُوعه فِي الْأَسْمَاء، فكالعين المترددة بَين مَعَانِيهَا، كالباصرة وَعين المَاء وَالذَّهَب، وَغير هَذَا، والقرء المتردد بَين الْحيض وَالطُّهْر، وكالجون المتردد بَين الْأسود والأبيض، وكالشفق المتردد بَين الْحمرَة وَالْبَيَاض.

An example of when it occurs to nouns is the Arabic word *ʿayn*, which has many meanings depending on the context.[318] For example, it can refer to the physical eye which provides eyesight, a spring of water, gold, etc. The word *qurʾ* also can refer to a menstrual period and to the cessation of a menstrual period. The word *jūn* can refer to white and to black. Lastly, the word *shafaq* can either refer to redness [in the sky] or whiteness.

وَأما وُقُوعه فِي الْأَفْعَال، فنحو: عسعس، فَإِنَّهُ بِمَعْنى أقبل وَأدبر، وَ(بَان) بِمَعْنى غَابَ واختفى.

An example of when it occurs to verbs is the word *ʿasʿasa*, which can mean

318 [T] In the English language, this is referred to as a homonym.

both coming and going. Another example is the word *bānā* [which can refer to two meanings, the first being "it became clear,"] and the second meaning being, "it became hidden."

وَأما فِي الْحُرُوف فنحو: تردد (الْوَاو) بَين الْعَطف والابتداء، وَبَين الْعَطف وَالْحَال، وَنَحْو تردد (من) بَين ابْتِدَاء الْغَايَة والتبعيض.

An example of when it occurs to particles is when the letter *wāw* (و) has various meanings depending on the context. In some cases, it can refer to apposition, in other times, it can refer to commencing. It can also refer to a circumstantial contextual phrase. The word *min* (من) also has various meanings; it can be used as a preposition, and can be used for selecting a portion of something.[319]

وَأما فِي الْمركب، فكقوله تَعَالَى ﴿أَو يَعْفُوَ الَّذِي بِيَدِهِ عُقْدَةُ النِّكَاحِ﴾ [الْبَقَرَة: ٢٣٧]، فَإِنَّهُ مُتَرَدّد بَين الْوَلِيّ وَالزَّوْج، وَالصَّحِيح من مَذْهَب أَحْمد وَالشَّافِعِيّ أَنه الزَّوْج، وَقَالَ مَالك: هُوَ الْوَلِيّ.

Obscurity can also occur in compounded phrases. For example, Allah the Exalted states: **{Or unless the one who holds the marriage tie waives [his right].}** [Qur'ān 2:237] This verse is obscure in its reference to, "The one who holds the marriage tie." Two possibilities that arise are the guardian [of the woman], and her husband. The view correctly attributed to Aḥmad and al-Shāfiʿī states that it is the husband, though Mālik stated that it refers to the guardian.

وَقد وَقع الْإِجْمَال من جِهَة التصريف كالمختار والمحتال، فَإِنَّهُمَا مترددان بَين اعتبارهما اسْم فَاعل أَو اسْم مفعول.

Obscurity can also emanate from the way a word is morphed, where the form of the word is shared between an active participle and an object. Examples include the two words *mukhtār* and *muḥtāl*.[320]

---

319 [T] Meaning, one can say, "I went from (من) Makkah to Madīnah," as an example of the first, and, 'Give me some of (من) your wealth," to indicate just a portion of the wealth, not its entirety.

320 [T] In the case of *mukhtār*, it can either mean someone chosen or someone choosing. In the case of *muḥtāl*, it can refer to someone who was cheated and someone who is doing the cheating.

وَحكم الْمُجْمل التَّوَقُّف على الْبَيَان الْخَارِجِي، لِأَن الله تَعَالَى لم يكلفنا الْعَمَل بِمَا لَا دَلِيل عَلَيْهِ، والمجمل لَا دَلِيل على المُرَاد بِهِ، فَلَا نكلف بِالْعَمَلِ بِهِ. والمجمل وَاقع فِي الْكتاب وَالسّنة فِي الْأَصَح خلافًا لداود الظَّاهِرِيّ، قَالَ بَعضهم: لَا نعلم أحدا قَالَ بِهِ غَيره.

The ruling when there is an obscure text is that one must abstain [from taking a view], until some external evidence disambiguates it. Allah the Exalted did not task us with acting on things without evidence, and obscure texts have no evidence to indicate what is meant, and as such, we are not responsible for acting on them. Obscure texts occur in the Qur'ān and the Sunnah, according to the veracious view. This was not the view of Dāwūd al-Ẓāhirī, though some claimed that he was the only one to hold that view.

تَنْبِيه: ادّعى بعض الْعلمَاء الْإِجْمَال فِي أُمُور، وَلكنهَا غير مجملة لَدَى التَّحْقِيق:

Note: In some instances, scholars have claimed that a text is obscure, when, after investigating, it is not.

مِنْهَا قَوْله تَعَالَى ﴿حُرِّمَتْ عَلَيْكُمُ الْمَيْتَةُ﴾ [الْمَائِدَة: ٣]، ﴿حُرِّمَتْ عَلَيْكُمْ أُمَّهَاتُكُمْ﴾ [النِّسَاء: ٢٣]، ﴿أُحِلَّ لَكُمُ الطَّيِّبَاتُ﴾ [الْمَائِدَة: ٥]، وَغير ذَلِك مِمَّا أضيفت الْأَحْكَام فِيهِ إِلَى الْأَعْيَان، لِأَن المُرَاد: حرم عَلَيْكُم أكل الْميتَة وَوَطْء الْأُمَّهَات، فَالْحكم الْمُضَاف إِلَى الْعين ينْصَرف لُغَة وَعرفا إِلَى مَا أعدت لَهُ، وَهُوَ مَا ذكرْنَاهُ.

For example, Allah the Exalted said: **{Forbidden to you are carrion.}** [Qur'ān 5:3] In another verse, He said: **{Forbidden to you are your mothers.}** [Qur'ān 4:23] Also: **{Today all good things have been made lawful for you.}** [Qur'ān 5:5] In these cases, when a ruling is applied to individuals, the meaning is, "Forbidden to you is *eating* carrion," "Forbidden to you is *intercourse with* your mothers," and so forth. A ruling that is ascribed to an individual refers actually to the action that is applicable to that item.

وَمِنْهَا قَوْله تَعَالَى ﴿وَأَحَلَّ اللَّهُ الْبَيْعَ وَحَرَّمَ الرِّبَا﴾ [الْبَقَرَة: ٢٧٥]، قَالَ الْقَاضِي أَبُو يعلى: هُوَ مُجمل، لِأَن الرِّبَا مَعْنَاهُ لُغَة: الزِّيَادَة كَيْفَمَا كَانَت، وَفِي الشَّرْع: الزِّيَادَة

الْمَخْصُوصَة. وَالصَّحِيح أنه من بَاب الْعَام الْمَخْصُوص.

Another example is when Allah the Exalted said: **{But Allah has permitted trading and forbidden interest.}** [Qur'ān 2:275] Al-Qāḍī Abu Yaʿlā stated that it is obscure, since *riba* (interest), linguistically, refers to any increase, and in the religious sense, it refers to a specific type of increase. The correct view, however, is that it is a particularized general text.

وَمِنْهَا حَدِيث **«لَا صَلَاة إِلَّا بِطهُور»**، **«لَا صِيَام لمن لم يبيت النية»** قَالَ الْحَنَفِيَّة: هُوَ مُجمل، لتردده بَين الْمَعْنى اللّغَوِيّ والشرعي.

Other examples include when the Prophet ﷺ said, **"There is no prayer without purity,"** and when he said, **"There is no fast for the one who does not have their intention the night before."**[321] Ḥanafī scholars took the view that these two narrations are obscure, since they could carry the religious meaning or the linguistic meaning.

وَالْحق أَن كَلَام الشَّارِع يحمل حَقِيقَة على الموضوعات الشَّرْعِيَّة، فالموضوعات اللُّغَوِيَّة فِي مُقَابلَته مجَاز.

The truth is that the polysemes occurring in divine speech are to be understood in their real sense to refer to religious topics. As such, any divine texts that refer to the linguistic meaning of polysemes are metaphorical.

وَمِنْهَا **«إِنَّمَا الْأَعْمَال بِالنياتِ»** قَالُوا: إِن الْأَعْمَال مُبْتَدأ، وبالنيات مُتَعَلق بِمَحْذُوف مُتَرَدّد بَين تَقْدِير الصِّحَّة أَو الْكَمَال، وَالْحق أَنه لَا تردد، لِأَن المُرَاد نفي فَائِدَة الْعَمَل وجدواه بِدُونِ النِّيَّة، فَتبقى صِحَّته متعينة للتقدير، وَقد أشبعنا الْكَلَام عَلَيْهِ فِي شرحنا (عُمْدَة الْأَحْكَام) الحديثية.

Another example is the ḥadīth, **"Actions are but by intentions."** Scholars mentioned that the word "actions" is the subject of a nominal sentence, and "but by intentions" pertains to some omitted word, which should be understood as "validity" or "completeness." However, the reality is that this ḥadīth is not obscure, since the intent of the ḥadīth is to negate the benefit and usefulness of an action without intention. As such, the ḥadīth is refer-

---

321 Reported by Ibn Abi Shaybah (3/31), Abu Dāwūd (2454), al-Nasā'ī (4/196), al-Tirmidhī (730), Ibn Mājah (1700), and Aḥmad (6/287).

ring to validity of actions. I have spoken about this topic at length in my explanation of *ʿUmdat al-Aḥkām*.

وَمِنْهَا قَوْله عَلَيْهِ السَّلَام: **«رفع عَن أمتِي الْخَطَأ، وَالنِّسْيَان، وَمَا اسْتكْرهُوا عَلَيْهِ»** فَإِنَّهُ لَيْسَ الْمُرَاد مِنْهُ رفع الْخَطَأ وَالنِّسْيَان حَتَّى يكون مُجملا، بل الْمُرَاد أَن الْمَرْفُوع حكم الْخَطَأ وَالنِّسْيَان.

Another example is when the Prophet ﷺ said, **"Lifted from my Ummah are mistakes, forgetfulness, and what they were forced to do."**[322] The meaning of this ḥadīth is not that the Ummah is immune from making mistakes or being forgetful; it is not obscure. The meaning is that one is absolved of the rulings [inasmuch as one incurs sin] of mistakes and forgetfulness.

322 Reported by Ibn Mājah (2045).

فصل

Section on Explication

وَأما الْمُبين، فَهُوَ ضد الْمُجْمل، فَيُقَال فِي تَعْرِيفه: هُوَ اللَّفْظ النَّاص على معنى غير مُتَرَدّد متساو، وَقَالَ الْآمِدِيّ: الْمُبين قد يُرَاد بِهِ الْخطاب المستغنى بِنَفسِهِ عَن بَيَان، قد يُرَاد بِهِ مَا يحْتَاج إِلَى الْبَيَان عِنْد وُرُوده عَلَيْهِ كالمجمل وَغَيره.

The term *mubayyan* (explicated, lucid, clear) is the opposite of the *mujmal* category. As such, to define it would be to say it is a term that refers univocally to a single meaning, without any hesitation. Al-Āmidī said, "The *mubayyan* category refers to instructions that do not require clarification. At other times, it refers to the text that requires clarification, similar to a *mujmal* text."[323]

وَهنا أَرْبَعَة أَلْفَاظ: مُجمل وإجمال ومبين وَبَيَان:

Here, there are four terms to discuss: (i) Polysemes (*mujmal*), (ii) polysomy (*ijmāl*), explicated (*mubayyan*), and (iv) explication (*bayān*).

فالمجمل تقدم تَعْرِيفه. والإجمال: إِرَادَة التَّرَدُّد من الْمُتَكَلّم، والنطق بِاللَّفْظِ على وَجه يَقع فِيهِ التَّرَدُّد.

We have already described what a polyseme is. As for the concept of polysomy, it is when a term used is intended to result in hesitation on part of the listener.

والمبين اللَّفْظ الدَّال من غير تردد كَمَا مر آنِفا، يُطلق على فعل الْمُبين، وعَلى الدَّلِيل، وعَلى الْمَدْلُول، وَلذَلِك قَالَ الصَّيْرَفِي: هُوَ إِخْرَاج الشَّيْء من حيّز الْإِشْكَال إِلَى حيّز التجلي والوضوح.

An explicated word or phrase indicates a meaning without any hesitation, as

323 [T] *Al-Ihkām fī Uṣūl al-Aḥkām* (3/26).

has been clarified. As for the term explication, it is used to refer to the action of the one clarifying something. It can also refer to the evidence [being used to explicate an obscure text], and the indication, which is why al-Ṣayrafī said, "It means to take something from a confusing state to a state of being clear and manifest."

وَيَنْبَغِي أَن يُزَاد هَذَا التَّعْرِيف بِالْفِعْلِ أَو بِالْقُوَّةِ؛ لِأَن الْكَلَام قد يرد بَينا بِالْفِعْلِ، وَهُوَ مَعَ ذَلِك مُشكل بِالْقُوَّةِ أَي: قَابل لعروض الْإِشْكَال لَهُ من ذَاته بِتَقْدِير تغير صفته، أَو من خَارج، وَبَيَان ذَلِك بالمثال وَهُوَ: أَن بعض الْحَنَفِيَّة قَالَ: نقل عَن أبي حنيفَة أَنه قَالَ: لَا يدْخل النَّار إِلَّا مُؤمن. وَظَاهر هَذَا مَعَ قَوْله عَلَيْهِ السَّلَام: **«لَا يدْخل الْجنَّة إِلَّا الْمُؤْمِنُونَ»** مُشكل لِأَنهُ يَقْتَضِي أَن أهل الْجنَّة وَالنَّار جَمِيعًا مُؤمنُونَ، وَلَيْسَ كَذَلِك للاتفاق على أَن أهل النَّار كفار، وَأَنه لَا يخلد بهَا إِلَّا كَافِر.

It is best to add here to this definition that explication can be done in actuality or through proximate ability. To clarify: speech can be clear but can also have some proximate level of obscurity, meaning, it is susceptible to being vague in and of itself by change of its description, or due to external factors. To give an example, some Ḥanafī scholars stated that it was reported that Abu Ḥanīfah said, "Only believers will enter hellfire." This phrase is obscure when juxtaposed with the statement of the Prophet ﷺ, **"Only believers will enter paradise."**[324] This would seemingly necessitate that the residents of both hellfire and paradise are all believers. However, this is not true, since there is agreement that the people of hellfire are disbelievers, and that only disbelievers remain in hellfire for eternity.

لَكِن أَبُو حنيفَة ألحق بِكَلَامِهِ بَيَانا بَينه وَأظْهر مَعْنَاهُ المُرَاد لَهُ، بِأَن قَالَ: لَا يدْخل النَّار إِلَّا مُؤمن، لِأَن الْكفَّار حِينَئِذٍ يعاينون مَا كَانُوا يوعدون فيؤمنون بِهِ ويصدقون، لَكِن إِيمَانًا لَا يَنْفَعهُمْ لِأَنهُ اضطراري لَا اخْتِيَاري، وَلقَوْله عز وَجل **﴿فَلم يَكُ يَنْفَعهُمْ إِيمَانهُمْ لَمَّا رَأَوْا بَأْسَنَا﴾** [غَافِر: ٨٥]، وَقَوله عز وَجل لفرعون حِين قَالَ لما أدْركهُ الْغَرق آمَنت: **﴿آلْآنَ وَقَدْ عَصَيْتَ قَبْلُ﴾** [يُونُس: ٩١] فقد حصل من هَذَا أَن كَلَام أبي حنيفَة مُشكل بِالْفِعْلِ، فَاحْتَاجَ إِلَى الْبَيَان.

---

324 Reported by al-Bukhārī (11/436) and Muslim (1142).

However, Abu Ḥanīfah added further explication where he showed the meaning he intended. He said that only believers will enter hellfire, for disbelievers, on that day, will witness firsthand what they were promised of punishment, and at that moment, they become believers and attest to [what they were warned about.] However, their faith does not benefit them on that day, since they were forced to believe on account of their firsthand experience and did not choose faith on their own. The evidence is that Allah the Exalted states: **{But their faith was of no benefit to them when they saw Our torment.}** [Qur'ān 40:85] Also, Allah the Exalted said to Pharaoh, who said that he believed when he was drowning: **{He was told, "Now? But you always disobeyed and were one of the corruptors."}** [Qur'ān 10:91] As such, this speech of Abu Ḥanīfah's was obscure, and it needed to be explicated.

وَأما الْمُبين بِهِ - وَهُوَ مَا يحصل بِهِ الْبَيَان - فَإِنَّهُ يكون بِأُمُور:

There are a number of ways a text can be explicated:

أَحدهَا: القَوْل، بِأَن يَقُول الْمُتَكَلّم، أَو من علم مُرَاد الْمُتَكَلّم: المُرَاد بِهَذَا الْكَلَام كَذَا، كَقَوْلِه تَعَالَى ﴿الْقَارِعَةُ مَا القارعة وَمَا أَدْرَاك مَا القارعة﴾ [القارعة: ١-٣]، فَهَذَا إِجْمَال، ثمَّ بَينه بقوله: ﴿يَوْمَ يَكُونُ النَّاس كَالْفَرَاشِ الْمَبْثُوثِ﴾ [القارعة: ٤]، وَكَذَا الْآيَة بعْدهَا، فَبين أَن القارعة تكون ذَلِك الْيَوْم بِهَذِهِ الصّفة الْعَظِيمَة، ونظائر هَذِه الْآيَة فِي الْقُرْآن الْكَرِيم وَالسّنة النَّبَوِيَّة كَثِيرَة.

First: Statements: The speaker can say something to clarify their intent, or those who know the intent of the speaker can clarify what they meant by that statement. For example, Allah the Exalted states: **{The Striking Disaster! What is the Striking Disaster? And what will make you realize what the Striking Disaster is?}** [Qur'ān 101:1-3] This verse is obscure, but is then explicated by when Allah the Exalted states: **{On a Day when people will be like scattered moths.}** [Qur'ān 101:4] It is also explicated by the verses that occur after. Allah the Exalted clarified that the Striking Disaster is that day which has this profound description. There are many examples of such verses in the Noble Qur'ān and in the Prophetic Sunnah.

وَتَكون السّنة مبينَة لِلْقُرْآنِ كَقَوْلِه تَعَالَى: ﴿وَأَعِدُّوا لَهُمْ مَا اسْتَطَعْتُمْ مِنْ قُوَّةٍ﴾ [الْأَنفَال:

٦٠] فَإِن الْقُوَّة مجملة، وَلَكِن بَينهَا النَّبِي صلى الله عَلَيْهِ وَسلم بقوله: **«أَلا إِن الْقُوة الرَّمْي»** ثمَّ كرر هَذِه الْجُمْلَة تَأْكِيدًا.

The Sunnah can explicate the Qur'ān. For example, Allah the Exalted said: **{Prepare against them what you can of power.}** [Qur'ān 8:60] The strength mentioned here is obscure, but the Prophet ﷺ explicated it when he said, **"Truly, strength is archery."**[325] He then repeated this statement to emphasise his point.

الثَّانِي: الْفِعْل وَيكون بِالْكِتَابَةِ، ككتابة النَّبِي صلى الله عَلَيْهِ وَسلم وَالْخُلَفَاء الرَّاشِدين بعده وَغَيرهم من أهل الولايات إِلَى عمالهم فِي الصَّدقَات وَغَيرهَا من السياسيات، وَيكون بِالْإِشَارَةِ، كَمَا رُوِيَ أَن النَّبِي صلى الله عَلَيْهِ وَسلم آلى من نِسَائِهِ شهرا، فَأَقَامَ فِي مشربَة لَهُ تسعا وَعشْرين، ثمَّ دخل عَلَيْهِنّ، فَقيل لَهُ: إِنَّك آلَيْت شهرا، فَقَالَ: **«الشَّهْر هَكَذَا وَهَكَذَا»**، وَأَشَارَ بأصابعه الْعشْر، وَقبض إبهامه فِي الثَّالِثَة، يَعْنِي تِسْعَة وَعشْرين.

Second: Actions: Actions can occur via writing, such as when the Prophet ﷺ, the Rightly-Guided Caliphs, and other leaders wrote letters to their workers and governors pertaining to *zakāt* and other policy decisions. It can also occur via gesturing. The Prophet ﷺ is reported to have sworn to avoid his wives for a month. He remained in his attic-room for twenty-nine days. Then, he entered the room where they were gathered and it was said to him, "You vowed [that it would be] a month." He replied, **"A month is like this, like this,"** and he gestured with his hands twice with all of his fingers [indicating twenty], and then he gestured a third time with his thumb folded [indicating nine], thereby gesturing to twenty-nine days.[326]

وَجَاء فِي حَدِيث صَحِيح: أَنه قَالَ **«الشَّهْر تسع وَعِشْرُونَ»** هَكَذَا بِلَفْظِهِ، وَهُوَ بَيَان قولي، فقد تضمن هَذَا الحَدِيث نَوْعي الْبَيَان: القولي، والفعلي.

In another narration, the Prophet ﷺ said, **"A month [can be] twenty-nine days."**[327] This ḥadīth is a statement that explicates [what he meant when he said a month.] This discussion, therefore, has encompassed both

325 Reported by Muslim (1917).
326 Reported by al-Bukhārī (9/376).
327 Reported by al-Bukhārī (4/104).

the statement-based and the action-based explications.

وَمن الْبَيَان الْفعْلِيّ قَوْله عَلَيْهِ الصَّلَاة وَالسَّلَام: «**صلوا كَمَا رَأَيْتُمُونِي أُصَلِّي**» «**وخذوا عني مَنَاسِككُم**» أي: انْظُرُوا إِلَى فعلي فِي الصَّلَاة وَالْحج، فافعلوا مثله، فَكَانَ فعله فيهمَا مُبينًا لقَوْله تَعَالَى: ﴿**وَأَقِيمُوا الصَّلَاةَ**﴾ [الْبَقَرَة: ٤٣]، ﴿**وَأَتِمُّوا الْحَجَّ وَالْعُمْرَةَ لِلَّهِ**﴾ [الْبَقَرَة: ١٩٦].

Another example of explication by action is when the Prophet ﷺ said, **"Pray as you have seen me pray."**[328] Also, he said, **"Learn your rituals from me."**[329] Meaning, "watch my actions during prayer and Ḥajj, and do as I do." As such, his actions acted as explication for Allah's statement: **{Establish prayer.}** [Qur'ān 2:43] Also: **{Complete the pilgrimages, major and minor, for the sake of Allah.}** [Qur'ān 2:196]

الثَّالِث: إِقْرَار النَّبِي صلى الله عَلَيْهِ وَسلم على فعل.

Third: Acknowledgements of the Prophet ﷺ.

وَإِن أردْت الْقَاعِدَة العمومية للْبَيَان فَقل: كل مُقَيّد من الشَّرْع بَيَان، ولنذكر بعض أَمْثِلَة لذَلِك تبين المرام.

To give a general rule on the topic of explication, one can say that every qualification mentioned in the religion is considered explication. Let us visit some examples to show the meaning of this statement:

مِنْهَا: أَن يسْتَدلّ الشَّارِع اسْتِدْلَالا عقليا، فيبين بِهِ الْعلَّة، أو مأخذ الحكم، أَو فَائِدَة مَا، كَقَوْلِه تَعَالَى فِي صفة مَاء السَّحَاب: ﴿**فَأَحْيَيْنَا بِهِ الْأَرْضَ بَعْدَ مَوْتِهَا كَذَلِكَ النُّشُورُ**﴾ [فاطر: ٩]، وَفِي مَوضِع آخر: ﴿**كَذَلِكَ الْخُرُوجُ**﴾ [ق: ١١]، فَبين لنا تَعَالَى بذلك طَرِيق الِاسْتِدْلَال على إِمْكَان الْبَعْث والمعاد، وَلَوْلَا هَذَا الطَّرِيق الَّذِي فَتحه الله للْمُؤْمِنين لما اجترأ متكلموهم أَن يستدلوا عَلَيْهِ، وَلَا أَن يتكلموا مَعَ الفلاسفة المنكرين لَهُ فِيهِ. وأمثال هَذِه الْآيَة كثير.

328 Reported by al-Bukhārī (2/93).
329 Reported by Muslim (1297).

For example, the Legislator could use a rational argument and could expound on causality, the source for the argument, or some other benefit. For example, the statement of Allah the Exalted when speaking about water in clouds: **{We drive them to a dead land and with them revive the earth after its death: such will be the Resurrection.}** [Qur'ān 35:9] In another verse, He states: **{This is how the dead will emerge [from their graves].}** [Qur'ān 50:11] In these verses, Allah the Exalted explains rational arguments to show resurrection and gathering on the Day of Judgement. Had Allah the Exalted not shown these examples to the believers, their philosophers would not be able to garner evidence for [resurrection] nor would they have been able to debate with [disbelieving] philosophers who deny resurrection. There are many other examples of this phenomenon.

وَجَمِيع استدلالات الْقُرْآن عقلية، وَهِي مفيدة للْبَيَان:

Note, too, that all of the arguments in the Qur'ān are rational and produce clarification.

وَمِنْهَا: أَن يتْرك عَلَيْهِ السَّلَام فعلا قد أَمر بِهِ، أَو قد سبق مِنْهُ فعله، فَيكون تَركه لَهُ مُبينًا لعدم وجوب. مِثَاله: أَنه قيل لَهُ ﴿وَأَشْهِدُوا إِذَا تَبَايَعْتُمْ﴾ [الْبَقَرَة: ٢٨٢]، ثمَّ إِنَّه اشْترى فرسا من أَعْرَابِي وَلم يشْهد عَلَيْهِ.

For example, the Prophet ﷺ could abandon something he was commanded to do, or which he previously did, showing that it is not obligatory. E.g. it was said to him: **{Have witnesses present whenever you trade with one another.}** [Qur'ān 2:282] Then, the Prophet ﷺ purchased a horse from a Bedouin man and did not have a witness testify to the purchase.[330]

330 The uncle of 'Umarah ibn Khuzaymah, who was a companion himself, reported that the Prophet ﷺ bought a horse from a Bedouin. The Prophet ﷺ took him with him to pay him the price of his horse. The Messenger of Allah ﷺ walked quickly and the Bedouin walked slowly. The people stopped the Bedouin and began to bargain with him for the horse as they did not know that the Prophet ﷺ had bought it. The Bedouin said to the Prophet ﷺ, "If you want this horse, (then buy it), otherwise I shall sell it." The Prophet ﷺ stopped when he heard the call of the Bedouin, and said, **"Have I not bought it from you?"** The Bedouin said, "I swear by Allah, I have not sold it to you." The Prophet ﷺ said, **"Yes, I have bought it from you."** The Bedouin began to say, "Bring a witness." Khuzaymah ibn Thābit then said, "I bear witness that you have bought it." The Prophet ﷺ turned to Khuzaymah and said: **"On what (grounds) do you bear witness?"** He said, "By considering you trustworthy, O Messenger of Allah ﷺ!" The Prophet ﷺ made the witness of Khuzaymah equivalent to the

وَمِنْهَا السُّكُوت بعد السُّؤَال عَن حكم الْوَاقِعَة، فَيعلم أَنه لَا حكم للشَّرْع فِيهَا.
وَهَاهُنَا مسَائِل:

Another example is the Prophet ﷺ remaining silent after being asked about the ruling of some occurrence, which indicates that the religion has no ruling on the matter. Here, it is prudent to discuss some matters:

أَولهَا: الْبَيَان بِالْفِعْلِ أقوى من الْبَيَان بالْقَوْل.

First: Explication via actions is weightier than explication via statements.

ثَانِيهَا: تبين الشَّيْء بأضعف مِنْهُ كالقرآن بِأَحَادِيث الْآحَاد جَائِز.

Second: It is possible to explicate something with a weaker text, such as explicating the Qur'ān using singular reports in the Sunnah.

ثَالِثهَا: تَأْخِير الْبَيَان عَن وَقت الْحَاجة مُمْتَنع، وتأخيره عَن وَقت الْخطاب إِلَى وَقت الْحَاجة جَائِز عِنْد ابْن حَامِد، وَالْقَاضِي ابْن الفراء، وَأَكْثَر الشَّافِعِيَّة، وَبَعض الْحَنَفِيَّة، وَمنعه أَبُو بكر عبد الْعَزِيز وَأَبُو الْحسن التَّمِيمِي والظاهرية والمعتزلة والصيرفي وَأَبُو إِسْحَاق الْمروزِي. وَالْحق الأول لقَوْله تَعَالَى ﴿فَإِذَا قَرَأْنَاهُ فَاتَّبِعْ قُرْآنَهُ ثُمَّ إِنَّ عَلَيْنَا بَيَانَهُ﴾ الْقِيَامَة: [١٨-١٩]، ﴿الر كِتَابٌ أُحْكِمَتْ آيَاتُهُ ثُمَّ فُصِّلَتْ﴾ [هود: ١]، وَ(ثمّ) تفيد التَّرَاخِي.

Third: Postponing explication after it is needed is an impossibility [for the divine texts]. However, if no explanation is needed directly after the statement, it can be postponed up until the moment it is needed, according to Ibn Ḥāmid, al-Qāḍī ibn al-Farrā', the majority of the Shāfi'ī scholars, and some Ḥanafī scholars. However, this latter point was denied by Abu Bakr 'Abd al-'Azīz, Abu 'l-Ḥasan al-Tamīmī, the Ẓāhirī scholars, the Mu'tazilites, al-Ṣayrafī, and Abu Isḥāq al-Marwazī. However, the truth lies in the first view,[331] because Allah the Exalted said: **{When We have recited it, repeat the recitation. Then it is surely upon Us to make it clear.}** [Qur'ān 75:18-19] Also, He said: **{*Alif Lām Rā* [This is] a Scripture whose verses are perfected, then set out clearly.}** [Qur'ān 11:1] The word "then"

witness of two people. This ḥadīth was reported by Abu Dāwūd (3607).

331 [T] Meaning, that a statement can occur and not be explicated until its need arises.

denotes sequencing.

رَابِعهَا: يجوز كَون الْبَيَان أَضْعَف دلَالَة من الْمُبين، وَلَا تعْتَبر مساواته فِي الحكم.

Fourth: The explicating text can be less indicative than the text it is explicating and their equivalence in indicating a ruling does not need to be proportional.[332]

332 [T] The reason is that the slightest indication can serve as explication for an obscure text. A polyseme is one that carries two possible meanings equally. Therefore, if the slightest evidence shows one of the two possibilities to be likelier, it is sufficient. Refer to *al-Taḥbīr Sharḥ al-Taḥrīr* (6/2816).

فصل فِي الْمَنْطُوق وَالْمَفْهُوم
Section on the Pronounced and Implied Meanings

اعْلَم أَن الدَّلِيل الشَّرْعِيّ إِمَّا مَنْقُول، وَإِمَّا مَعْقُول، وَإِمَّا ثَابت بهما، فالمنقول الْكتاب، وَالسّنة، ودلالتهما إِمَّا من مَنْطُوق اللَّفْظ، أَو من غير منطوقه، فَإِن كَانَ من الأول سمي منطوقا كفهم وجوب الزَّكَاة في السَّائِمَة من حَدِيث **«فِي سَائِمَة الْغنم الزَّكَاة»** وكتحريم التأفيف من قَوْله تَعَالَى **﴿فَلا تَقُلْ لَهُمَا أُفٍّ﴾** [الْإِسْرَاء: ٢٣]

You must know that religious evidences are either textual, rational, or a combination of both. Textual evidences comprise of the Qur'ān and the Sunnah, and their significations are either stated clearly or they are not. If they are clearly stated, they are known as *mantūq* (pronounced). An example of a pronounced signification is how we understand that it is obligatory to pay *zakāt* on livestock that graze, because the Prophet ﷺ said, **"*Zakāt* applies to grazing goats."**[333] Also, we learn that it is impermissible to grumble towards the parents in Allah's statement: **{Never say to them [even] *"ugh."*}** [Qur'ān 17:23]

وَالثَّانِي يُسمى مفهوما كفهم عدم وجوب الزَّكَاة فِي المعلوفة من الحَدِيث، وَتَحْرِيم الضَّرْب من الْآيَة. وَهَذَا الْفَصْل مَذْكُور لبَيَان ذَلِك.

[If the signification is not clearly stated,] it is known as *mafhūm* (an implied meaning). For example, we learn from the ḥadīth that it is not obligatory to pay *zakāt* on animals that are stall-fed. From the verse, we learn that hitting the parents is impermissible. This section will expound on these concepts.

والمعقول الْقيَاس لِأَنهُ يُسْتَفَاد بِوَاسِطَة النّظر الْعقلِيّ، وَالثَّابِت بالمنقول والمعقول وَلَيْسَ وَاحِدًا مِنْهُمَا هُوَ الْإِجْمَاع، وَسَيَأْتِي الْكَلَام على الْإِجْمَاع ثمَّ على الْقيَاس.

333 Reported by al-Bukhārī (3/253).

Rational evidences comprise of analogies, since they are deduced based on rational inferences. Evidences that are established through divine texts as well as rational deductions consist of consensus. Both of these will be discussed in the following sections.

إِذا تمهد هَذَا، فَنَقُول: قد علم من هَذَا أَن الْمَنْطُوق: مَا دلّ عَلَيْهِ اللَّفْظ فِي مَحل النُّطْق، وَالْمَفْهُوم: مَا دلّ عَلَيْهِ اللَّفْظ لَا فِي مَحل النُّطْق. ففحوى بِاللَّفْظِ - بِالْحَاء الْمُهْملَة - هُوَ مَا أَفَادَ جِنْسا يتَنَاوَل مَا أَفَادَهُ نطقا وَغير نطق، لَا من صيغته، لِأَنَّهُ لَو كَانَ مِنْهَا، لَكَانَ منطوقا، وَبَيَانه: أَن تَحْرِيم التأفيف علم من صِيغَة اللَّفْظ فَكَانَ منطوقا، وَتَحْرِيم الضَّرْب لم يعلم من الصِّيغَة فَكَانَ مفهوما.

Therefore, a pronounced meaning is one that is signified through the clearly stated text. An implied meaning is one that is not signified through the clearly stated text. The implication of the text is what denotes a non-explicit meaning, though not through its wording. When I said "denotes," that is a genus and includes denoting through the clearly stated text and without using the clearly stated text. The reason why I said, "not from its wording," is because if it were from its wording, it would be pronounced. To clarify further, the prohibition of grumbling towards parents is understood from the wording of the verse, and as such, it is the pronounced meaning. However, the prohibition of hitting the parents was not taken from the wording, and as such, it is an implied meaning.

وَيُقَال لمثله: فحوى الْخطاب، وَيُسمى إِشَارَة، وإيماء، ولحن الْخطاب، إِلَّا أَن الْإِشَارَة مُخْتَصَّة بِالْيَدِ، والإيماء إِشَارَة بِالْيَدِ وَغَيرهَا، فَكل إِشَارَة إِيمَاء وَلَا عكس.

The latter (the implied meaning) is referred to in multiple ways in the Arabic language. It is referred to as, "*faḥwā al-khiṭāb* (the meaning of the instruction)," "*ishārah* (gesturing)," "*īmā* (signal)," and "*laḥn al-khiṭāb* (the tone of the instruction)." However, the term *ishārah* refers to gesturing with the hand, and the word *īmā* refers to signalling with the hand or something else. Therefore, every gesturing is signalling, not vice versa.

وَمن ثمَّ قَالَ الْآمِدِيّ: أما دلَالَة غير الْمَنْطُوق - وَهُوَ مَا دلَالَته غير صَرِيحَة - فَلَا يَخْلُو إِمَّا أَن يكون مَدْلُوله مَقْصُودا للمتكلم أَو لَا، فَإِن كَانَ مَقْصُودا، فَإِن توقف

صدق الْمُتَكَلّم أَو صِحَة الملفوظ بِهِ عَلَيْهِ، فَهِيَ دلَالَة الِاقْتِضَاء، وَإِن لم يتَوَقَّف، فَإِن كَانَ مفهوما فِي مَحل النُّطْق فَهِيَ دلَالَة التَّنْبِيه والإيماء، وَإِلَّا فدلالة الْمَفْهُوم. وَإِن لم يكن مَدْلُوله مَقْصُودا للمتكلم، فَهِيَ دلَالَة الْإِشَارَة. هَذَا كَلَامه. وَأَنت خَبِير، فَإِنَّهُ جعل فرقا بَين دلالتي الْإِشَارَة والإيماء، وَهَذَا هُوَ التَّحْقِيق.

On this note, al-Āmidī stated, "As for the signification of the non-pronounced text, meaning, a non-explicit text, it is either intended by the speaker or not. If it is intended by the speaker: If truthfulness of the speaker[334] or the soundness of their sentence[335] is contingent on [an unmentioned word,] it is a necessitated signification (*dalālat al-iqtiḍā'*[336]). If it is not [contingent on the truthfulness of the speaker or the soundness of their sentence]: (i) If it is tacitly mentioned within the verbiage of the text, it is a signification from indication or signalling (*dalālat al-tanbīh wa 'l-'īmā'*[337]). (ii) If it is

334 [T] Meaning, the truthfulness and validity of their statement. For example, there is a tacit qualification in the ḥadīth where the Prophet ﷺ said, **"Lifted from my Ummah are mistakes, forgetfulness, and what they were forced to do."** Without understanding that there is necessarily an underlying concept being signified, namely, the negation of certain rulings that result from those mistakes, moments of forgetfulness, and actions done by force of coercion, the ḥadīth itself becomes wholly inaccurate and untruthful, since without that necessary signification, the ḥadīth seems to expressly state the nonexistence of those actions, which is not true; they occurred, but they do not result in the incurring of sin. Refer to *al-Iḥkām* by al-Imām Sayf al-Dīn al-Āmidī (3/64).

335 [T] Meaning, without this unmentioned word, the sentence is not sound. An example that can be mentioned here is when Allah the Exalted said: **{Ask the town.}** [Qur'ān 12:82] In order for this sentence to be a rational, proper sentence, there must be some tacit affirmation of the words, "people of," making the sentence, "ask the people of the town," since a town in and of itself is an inanimate thing that can neither be spoken to nor can it respond when addressed.

336 [T] To understand this better, consider the definition provided by al-Imām Najm al-Dīn al-Ṭūfī, "It is an underlying word that is necessary for either the truthfulness of the speaker, such as the word, "valid," in the ḥadīth, **"There is no (valid) action without intention,"** or is needed for the establishment of the religious ruling, such as: **{But whoever of you is ill or on a journey, then [let them fast] an equal number of days.}** [Qur'ān 2:184] Meaning, if you are ill or on a journey and break the fast. Lastly, it is needed rationally, such as: **{Forbidden for you are your mothers.}** [Qur'ān 4:23] The tacit meaning is, 'intercourse with [your mothers].'" Refer to *Sharḥ Mukhtaṣar al-Rawḍah* (2/704).

337[T] Al-Imām al-Ghazālī stated, "The indication and signalling of the cause for the ruling [occurs within the text, though not explicitly], for example, the Prophet ﷺ said, when asked about cats, **'Male and female cats are always roaming around you.'** He

not [tacitly mentioned within the verbiage of the text], it is an implied signification (*dalālat al-mafhūm*). If it is not intended by the speaker, this is known as signification by gesturing (*dalālat al-ishārah*[338])."[339] This is what he said and you are now aware, he differentiated between the signification of *al-'īmā'* and *al-ishārah*, and this is correct.

ثمَّ اعْلَم أَن مَرَاتِب لحن الْخطاب وفحواه تكون مُتَفَاوِتَة، وَذَلِكَ التَّفَاوُت على أضْرب:

Furthermore, note that the levels of the meanings and tones of the instructions are of grades:

أولها: الْمُقْتَضى - بِفَتْح الضَّاد - الَّذِي تَقْتَضِيه صِحَة الْكَلَام وتطلبه، وَهُوَ الْمُضمر الَّذِي تَدْعُو الضَّرُورَة إِلَى اضماره وَتَقْرِيره. وَله وُجُوه.

First: Necessary Implications: Meaning, there are words that necessitate the validity of the speech. This refers to tacit references that are omitted and that, by necessity, must be affirmed and acknowledged. It, too, has various applications:

أَولهَا: مَا تَدْعُو الضَّرُورة إِلَى إضماره لصدق الْمُتَكَلّم نَحْو: لَا عمل إِلَّا بنية، أَي لَا عمل صَحِيح إِلَّا بِالنيةِ، إِذْ لَوْلَا ذَلِك، لم يكن ذَلِك صدقا، لِأَن صُورَة الْأَعْمَال

---

did not say, 'It is because of or due to them constantly being around you,' but rather, he signalled towards the cause for the ruling. Had it not been the cause of the ruling, there would be no point in mentioning the attribute of 'always roaming around you.'" (*Al-Mustaṣfā*, p. 308)

338 [T] An example is when Allah the Exalted said: **{So now you may be intimate with them.}** [Qur'ān 2:187] This verse allows for having intercourse up until *fajr* time, as Allah the Exalted said in the same verse, **{Eat and drink until you see the light of dawn breaking the darkness of night, then complete the fast until nightfall.}** [Qur'ān 2:187] The intention was to clarify that meaning, however, it also suggests that if a person has intercourse at night and started their day in a state of major ritual impurity, their fast is not invalidated, because if someone has intercourse until the ending of the night and the beginning of *fajr*, they will undoubtedly delay their ritual washing until the day has already broken. If that were something that breaks the fast, intercourse would not be allowed in the last portion of the night. Refer to *al-Iḥkām* by al-Āmidī (3/65).

339 [T] *Al-Iḥkām* by al-Imām Sayf al-Dīn al-Āmidī (3/64).

كلها كَالصَّلَاةِ وَالصَّوْمِ وَسَائِرِ الْعِبَادَات، يُمكن وجودهَا بِلَا نِيَّة، فكَانَ إِضْمَار الصِّحَّة من ضَرُورَة صدق الْمُتَكَلّم.

(i) Words that, by necessity, must be considered tacit references to words that, without which, the speaker is untruthful. For example, "There is no action without intention," means, "there is no valid action without intentions." Without that tacit reference to validity, the statement would be untrue, since all actions, such as prayer, fasting, and all other acts of worship can exist without intentions. Tacitly referring to validity, therefore, is a necessary element if the statement of the speaker is to be true.

ثَانِيهَا: وجود الحكم شرعا نَحْو قَوْله تَعَالَى: ﴿فَمَنْ كَانَ مِنْكُمْ مَرِيضاً أَوْ عَلَى سَفَرٍ فَعِدَّةٌ مِنْ أَيَّامٍ أُخَرَ﴾ [الْبَقَرَة: ١٨٤]، تَقْدِيره: أَو على سفر فَأفْطر، فَعَلَيهِ صَوْم عدَّة من أَيَّام أخر، لِأَن قَضَاء الصَّوْم على الْمُسَافِر إِنَّمَا يجب إِذا أفطر فِي سَفَره، أما إِذا صَامَ فِي سَفَره فَلَا مُوجب للقضا، ودليل ذلك ظاهر لغة وشرعا، خلافا لما يحكى عن أهل الظاهر من أن فرض المسافر عدة من أيام أخر، سواء صام في السفر أو أفطر، وهو من جمودهم المعروف.

(ii) Words that establish the religious ruling, such as when Allah the Exalted said: **{Whoever of you is ill or on a journey, then an equal number of other days.}** [Qur'ān 2:184] The implication of this verse is, "or on a journey *and broke their fast*." The reason for fasting an equal number of days is that making up the fast for the one travelling becomes obligatory only if they break their fast while travelling. As for if they travel but do not break their fast, there is no reason to fast those days again. The evidence of this is apparent, both linguistically and religiously. This, of course, differs from the view attributed to Ẓāhirī scholars who claim that it is an obligation on the one who travels while fasting to make those days up, regardless if they broke their fast or not. This is just one example of their unyielding views.

ثالثها: وجود الحكم عقلا نحو قوله تعالى: ﴿حُرِّمَتْ عَلَيْكُمْ أُمَّهَاتُكُمْ﴾ [النساء: ٢٣]، فإن العقل يأبى إضافة التحريم إلى الأعيان، فوجب لذلك إضمار فعل يتعلق به التحريم وهو الوطء، فصار المعنى: حرم عليكم وطء أمهاتكم.

(iii) Words that establish the religious ruling, but do so rationally. For example, Allah the Exalted said: **{Forbidden to you are your mothers.}** [Qurʾān 4:23] Rationally speaking, prohibitions cannot be attributed to a concrete individual. As such, it is necessarily a tacit reference to an action that would relate to the prohibition, and that action is intercourse. Consequently, the meaning of the verse is, "Intercourse with your mothers is unlawful."

الثَّانِي: مِمَّا يتفَاوَت بِهِ لحن الْخطاب وفحواه، تَعْلِيل الحكم بِمَا اقْترب بِهِ من الْوَصْف الْمُنَاسب، كَقَوْلِه ﴿وَالسَّارِقُ وَالسَّارِقَةُ فَاقْطَعُوا أَيْدِيَهُمَا﴾ [الْمَائِدَة: ٣٨]، ﴿الزَّانِيَةُ وَالزَّانِي فَاجْلِدُوا كُلَّ وَاحِدٍ مِنْهُمَا﴾ [النُّور: ٢].

Second: The meanings and tones of the instructions vary in determining causation of rulings based on being coupled with the attribute that has a reasonable relationship [with the ruling]. For example, Allah the Exalted said: **{Cut off the hands of thieves, whether they are man or woman.}** [Qurʾān 5:38] Also, Allah the Exalted said, **{Strike the adulteress and the adulterer one hundred times.}** [Qurʾān 24:2]

أَي: لأجل السّرقَة وَالزِّنَى فَإِن الْمَعْقُول من هَذَا الْكَلَام أَن السّرقَة عِلّة الْقطع، وَالزِّنَى عِلّة الْجلد، لَكِن لَيْسَ هَذَا مفهوما لنا من صَرِيح النُّطْق وَنَصه، بل من فحوى الْكَلَام وَمَعْنَاهُ.

These verses mean, [cut the hand] because of the thievery, and [flog them] because of their fornication. It is understood of the first verse, therefore, that stealing is the cause for the enactment of the penalty of cutting the hand, and fornication is the cause for the enactment of the penalty of flogging. However, this is not understood from the pronounced verbiage of the text, but rather, is understood from the implications and meanings of the verse.

الثَّالِث: فهم الحكم فِي غير مَحل النُّطْق بطرِيق الأولى، وَهُوَ فهم الْمُوَافقَة، كفهم تَحْرِيم الضَّرْب من تَحْرِيم التأفيف من قَوْله تَعَالَى: ﴿فَلَا تَقُلْ لَهُمَا أُفٍّ وَلَا تَنْهَرْهُمَا﴾ [الْإِسْرَاء: ٢٣].

Third: One can infer a ruling, though not from the clearly stated text, but rather, because [the unmentioned ruling carries] greater suitability. This is known as *mafhūm al-muwāfaqah* (*a fortiori* implication[340]). For example,

340 [T] This was explained previously.

we understand it is forbidden to hit the parents because the verse states it is forbidden to grumble towards them. Allah the Exalted said: **{Never say to them [even] *ugh*, nor yell at them.}** [Qur'ān 17:23]

فَإِن مَنْطُوق هَذَا تَحْرِيم التأفيف والانتهار، وَمَفْهُومه - بطرِيق التَّنْبِيه والفحوى - تَحْرِيم الضَّرْب وَغَيره من الإيلامات الزَّائِدَة على التأفيف، والانتهار بطرِيق أولى، وَيُسمى هَذَا مَفْهُوم الْمُوَافقَة، لِأَنهُ يُوَافق الْمَنْطُوق فِي الحكم وَإِن زَاد عَلَيْهِ فِي التَّأْكِيد، بِخِلَاف مَفْهُوم الْمُخَالفَة، فَإِنَّهُ يُخَالف حكم الْمَنْطُوق، كفهم عدم الزَّكَاة فِي المعلوفة من حَدِيث **«فِي سَائِمَة الْغنم الزَّكَاة»**.

The pronounced meaning of this verse is that it is impermissible to grumble towards or berate the parents. The implication indicated in the verse is that hitting, and other forms of abuse that exceed grumbling and berating, *a fortiori* carry the ruling [of prohibition]. This is known as *mafhūm al-muwāfaqah*, since the ruling of the implied action (hitting) is congruous with the ruling of the pronounced action (grumbling and berating), even if [the former] is a more emphasised prohibition. This is the opposite of *mafhūm al-mukhālafah* (implication of inverse relationships[341]), where the unmentioned implied ruling is the opposite of the pronounced ruling. For example, the absence of *zakāt* on stall-fed goat when the Prophet ﷺ said, **"*Zakāt* applies to grazing goats."**[342]

وَحَاصِله: أَن مَفْهُوم الْمُوَافقَة تَنْبِيه بالأدنى على الْأَعْلَى، وَيُسمى فحوى الْخطاب ولحن الْخطاب. وَشَرطه فهم الْمَعْنى فِي مَحل النُّطْق، كالتعظيم فِي قَوْله تَعَالَى: ﴿فَلا تَقُلْ لَهُمَا أُفٍّ﴾ [الْإِسْرَاء: ٢٣]، فَإِنهُ يفهم أَن الْمَعْنى الْمُقْتَضِي لهَذَا النَّهْي هُوَ تَعْظِيم الْوَالِدين، فَلذَلِك فهمنا تَحْرِيم الضَّرْب بطرِيق أولى، حَتَّى لَو لم نفهم من ذَلِك تَعْظِيمًا لما فهمنا تَحْرِيم الضَّرْب أصلا، لكنه لما نفى التأفيف الْأَعَمّ دلّ على نفي الضَّرْب الْأَخَص بطرِيق أولى.

To summarise, *mafhūm al-muwāfaqah* is an *a fortiori* argument. It is referred to as *laḥn al-khiṭāb* and *faḥwā al-khiṭāb*. Its condition is that the meaning is understood from the wording of the text. For example, the

341 [T] This was explained previously.
342 Reported by al-Bukhārī (3/253).

meaning of honouring is understood from when Allah the Exalted said: **{Never say to them [even] *ugh*, nor yell at them.}** [Qur'ān 17:23] It is understood from this verse that the concept that necessitates this prohibition is the honour and respect that the parents are to be given. This is why hitting the parents is *a fortiori* worthier of and more severe in prohibition. If we were not to understand that the verse obligates honouring the parents, we would not have learned that it is prohibited to strike them. However, since grumbling at the parents, which is more inclusive [of types of harm] was prohibited, hitting, which is a more specific [type of harm] is worthier of the prohibition.

وَشَرطه أَيْضا أَن يكون الْمَفْهُوم أولى من الْمَنْطُوق أَو مسَاوٍ لَهُ. وَمِثَال الأول قد تقدم. وَمِثَال الثَّانِي تَحْرِيم إحراق مَال الْيَتِيم الدَّال عَلَيْهِ قَوْله تَعَالَى ﴿إن الَّذين يَأْكُلُون أَمْوَال الْيَتَامَى ظلما﴾ الأية [النِّسَاء: ١٠]، فالإحراق مسَاوٍ للْأكل بِوَاسِطَة الْإِتْلَاف فِي الصُّورَتَيْنِ.

The condition [for *mafhūm al-muwāfaqah*] is that the implied ruling must either be worthier of the ruling, or equally deserving of the ruling. An example of the former (i.e., worthier of the ruling) has already been mentioned. As for an example of the latter (i.e., an equally deserved ruling), it is that it is prohibited to burn the wealth of orphans, as indicated to by the statement of Allah the Exalted: **{Those who consume the property of orphans unjustly ...}** [Qur'ān 4:10] Therefore, burning the wealth of orphans is equal in prohibition to consuming their wealth, since both result in destruction of their wealth.

وَاشْترط لَهُ كثير من أهل الْأُصُول شُرُوطًا فَقَالَ فِي (جمع الْجَوَامِع): وَشَرطه أَن لَا يكون الْمَسْكُوت ترك لخوف وَنَحْوه، كالجهل، وَأَن لَا يكون الْمَذْكُور خرج للْغَالِب خلافًا لِإِمَام الْحَرَمَيْنِ، أَو لسؤال، أَو حَادِثَة، أَو للْجَهْل بِحكمِهِ، أَو غَيره مِمَّا يَقْتَضِي التَّخْصِيص بِالذكر. هَذَا كَلَامه.

Many scholars of *uṣūl* placed other conditions. In *Jamʿ al-Jawāmiʿ* it is stated, "One condition [for inverse implications to be considered valid] is that the intended objects are not omitted out of fear,[343] and so forth (e.g., ig-

343 [T] Shaykh al-Islām Zakariyyā al-Anṣāri stated, "For example, if a new Muslim tells their slave, 'Give this in charity to the Muslims,' but intends non-Muslims, and did not

norance). Also, a condition is that [the unmentioned ruling] is not omitted due to lack of preponderance (*kharaja makhraj al-ghālib*),[344] contrary to Imām al-Ḥarāmayn [al-Juwaynī]. Or, it could be due to a question, an incident, ignorance of its ruling,[345] or other reasons that would necessitate specific mention [of certain qualifications.]"[346][347]

ثمَّ إن مَفْهُوم الْمُوَافقَة قِيَاس جلي فِي الْأَصَح، وَإِلَيْهِ ذهب أَبُو الْحسن الخرزي وَابْن أبي مُوسَى وَأبي الْخطاب والحلواني وَالْفَخْر والطوفي، وَقَالَ مجد الدّين ابْن تَيْمِية: إِن قصد الْأَدْنَى فَقِيَاس، وَإِن قصد التَّنْبِيه فَلَا، وَهُوَ حجَّة عِنْد الْعلمَاء، ودلالته لفظية عِنْد أَحْمد وَالْقَاضِي وَابْن حمدَان وَشَيخ الْإِسْلَام وَابْن عقيل، وَحَكَاهُ عَن أَصْحَابنَا وَالْحَنَفِيَّة والمالكية وَغَيرهم.

Mafhūm al-muwāfaqah is actually an apparent analogy (*qiyās jalī*)[348], according to the correct view. This was opined by Abu 'l-Ḥasan al-Kharzī,

---

say non-Muslims out of fear of being accused of hypocrisy." Refer to *Ḥāshiyat Shaykh al-Islām Zakariyyā al-Anṣāri 'alā Sharḥ Jam' al-Jawāmi'* (p. 87).

344 [T] Examples of this are when Allah the Exalted said: **{O believers! Do not consume interest, multiplying it many times over. And be mindful of Allah, so you may prosper.}** [Qur'ān 3:130] The inverse ruling of this verse is that usury is allowed in small amounts. However, in this case, the overwhelming usage of usury is in great numbers, so the inverse of the ruling does not indicate a ruling at all. Another example is when Allah the Exalted said: **{Forbidden for you are your stepdaughters under your guardianship if you have consummated marriage with their mothers.}** [Qur'ān 4:23] The phrase "under your guardianship," is indicative that usually speaking, they will be in the guardianship of the stepfather. The inverse of this verse is that it is permissible to marry the daughters of one's wife if they did not live with them. This, however, is not the case. When Allah the Exalted said "under your guardianship," He did so because it is rare for daughters of the wife to live elsewhere.

345 [T] Obviously, this refers to when the speech emanates from a fallible being, not when the speech is emanating from a divine source.

346 [T] The example given by Shaykh al-Islām Zakariyyā al-Anṣāri is that Allah the Exalted said: **{The believers should not make the disbelievers their allies rather than other believers.}** [Qur'ān 3:28] He stated that al-Wāḥidī said that this verse was revealed regarding a group of believers who made an alliance with the Jews, thereby forsaking the Muslims. The inverse of this verse is that one can take the disbelievers as allies so long as they also take believers as allies. However, this verse was in the context of rebuking a group of believers, and as such was revealed within a context that does not carry the inverse signification, according to al-Imām Taqī al-Dīn al-Subkī's conditions.

347 [T] *Jam' al-Jawāmi'* (p. 23).

348 [T] Discussions on analogy (*qiyās*) are forthcoming.

Ibn Abi Mūsā, Abu 'l-Khaṭṭāb, al-Ḥalwānī, al-Fakhr [al-Rāzī], and al-Ṭūfī. Majd al-Dīn ibn Taymiyyah said, "If the lesser ruling is intended, it is an analogy, but if it serves to notify,[349] then it is not."[350] It is an evidence according to the scholars. Its implications are based on the actual text [and not an analogy] according to Aḥmad, al-Qāḍī, Ibn Ḥamdān, Shaykh al-Islām [Ibn Taymiyyah], Ibn 'Aqīl, and the majority of our *aṣḥāb*, the Ḥanafī scholars, the Māliki scholars, and others.

ودلالته تكون قَطْعِيَّة كآية التأفيف، وَتكون ظنية كإذا ردَّتْ شَهَادَة فَاسق فكافر أولى، إِذْ الْكفْر فسق وَزِيَادَة، وَوجه كَونه ظنيا أَنه وَاقع فِي الِاجْتِهَاد، إِذ يجوز أَن يكون الْكَافِر عدلا فِي دينه، فيتحرى الصدْق وَالْأَمَانَة.

Sometimes, its indications occur with certainty, such as the verse on grumbling. Sometimes, they are presumptive, such as stating that if the testimony of a sinner is rejected, then so too should the testimony of a disbeliever, since disbelief is sinfulness and more. The reason why it is presumptive is that it is within the scope of scholarly discretion (*ijtihād*), and since it is possible for a disbeliever to be an upright person, adhering to their own religion and actively trying to be honest and trustworthy.

الرَّابِع: دلَالَة تَخْصِيص شَيْء بِحكم يدل على نَفْيه عَمَّا عداهُ، وَهُوَ مَفْهُوم الْمُخَالفَة، سمي بِهِ لمُخَالفته للمنطوق بِهِ، وَذَلِكَ كَقَوْلِه تَعَالَى ﴿**وَمَنْ لَمْ يَسْتَطِعْ مِنكُمْ طَوْلاً أَنْ يَنْكِحَ الْمُحْصَنَاتِ الْمُؤْمِنَاتِ**﴾ [النِّسَاء: ٢٥]، فَإِن تَخْصِيص جَوَاز نِكَاح الْإِمَاء بِعَدَمِ الطول يدل على أَن وَاجِد الطول لَا يجوز لَهُ نِكَاح الْإِمَاء، وَتَخْصِيص الْمُؤْمِنَات بِجَوَاز النكَاح عِنْد عدم الطول يدل على أَن عادم الطول لَا يُبَاح لَهُ نِكَاح الْإِمَاء الكوافر، كَمَا هُوَ أحد الْقَوْلَيْنِ، فَفِي الْآيَة مفهومان:

349 [T] Meaning, to notify of the more emphasised ruling by mention of the lesser ruling. This was al-Majd ibn Taymiyyah's way of referring to *mafhūm al-muwāfaqah*. Refer to *al-Musawwadah* (p. 222) where he explicitly states this.

350 [T] *Al-Musawwadah* (p. 347). Ibn Mufliḥ said, The reason [why implying the more emphasised ruling by mentioning the lesser sin is not an analogy] is because it is intended [by the instruction]. However, if the lesser ruling is intended, it is an analogy. An example is that Aḥmad viewed it impermissible to mortgage a *muṣḥaf* with a *dhimmi* (a non-Muslim with a covenant of peace), and his evidence was that the Prophet ﷺ forbade travelling with the Qur'ān to the lands of the enemies, out of fear that their hands touch it. Refer to *Uṣūl al-Fiqh* by Ibn Mufliḥ (3/1064).

Fourth: Particularizing a ruling indicates that it does not apply to anything else. This is another form of an inverse implication. It was called as such since it is the inverse of the stated text. An example is when Allah the Exalted said: **{If any of you does not have the means to marry a believing free woman, then marry a believing slave.}** [Qur'ān 4:25] Specifying that it is permissible to marry slave-girls only for the one who lacks means shows that those who have the means are not allowed to marry slave-girls. Further, specifying the permissibility of marrying believing slave-girls when one does not have means indicates that those who do not have means cannot marry non-Muslim slave-girls, as is one of the two views on the topic. The verse, therefore, contains two implications:

أَحدهمَا أَنه لَا ينْكح إِلَّا أمة مُؤمنَة.

(i) Only a believing slave-girl may be wed.

وَثَانِيهمَا: أَن وَاجِد الطول لَا يجوز لَهُ نِكَاح الْأمة، وَكَقَوْلِه عَلَيْهِ السَّلَام **«فِي سَائِمَة الْغنم الزَّكَاة»** فَإِن مَفْهُومه يدل على أَن لَا زَكَاة فِي المعلوفة، فتخصيص السّوم بِحكم - وَهُوَ وجوب الزَّكَاة - يدل على نفي ذَلِك الحكم عَن غير السَّائِمَة.

If a person has means, it is not permissible for them to marry a slave girl. This is similar to when the Prophet ﷺ said, **"*Zakāt* applies to grazing goats."**[351] It implies that *zakāt* is not due for owning stall-fed animals. Specifying the ruling to grazing livestock, which is the obligation of *zakāt*, shows that the ruling is not applicable to non-grazing livestock.

وَمَفْهُوم الْمُخَالفَة حجَّة عِنْد الْجُمْهُور. وَقَالَ أَبُو حنيفَة وَبَعض الْمُتَكَلِّمين: لَيْسَ بِحجَّة، وَيُسمى ذَلِك الْمَفْهُوم دَلِيل الْخطاب.

Inverse implications are evidences, according to the majority. Abu Ḥanīfah and some scholars of *kalām* claimed it is not. Another term used to refer to *mafhūm al-mukhālafah* is *mafhūm dalīl al-khiṭāb* (the indication of the instruction).

وَشَرطه أَن لَا تظهر أَوْلَوِيَّة وَلَا مُسَاوَاة فِي الْمَسْكُوت عَنهُ، إِذْ لَو ظهر فِيهِ ذَلِك كَانَ مَفْهُوم مُوَافقَة.

351 Reported by al-Bukhārī (3/253).

One condition for its application is that the tacitly mentioned ruling must not be equal or greater than the expressly mentioned one. If that were the case, it would be considered an *a fortiori* implication (*mafhūm muwāfaqah*).

وَأَن لَا يكون مخرجا مخرج الْغَالِب كَمَا فِي قَوْله تَعَالَى ﴿وَرَبَائِبُكُمُ اللَّاتِي فِي حُجُورِكُمْ﴾ [النِّسَاء: ٢٣]، فَإِن الْغَالِب كَون الربائب فِي حجور الْأَزْوَاج، أَي ترتيبهم.

Another condition is that [the unmentioned ruling] is not omitted due to lack of preponderance (*kharaja makhraj al-ghālib*). For example, Allah the Exalted said: **{The stepdaughters in your care-those born of women with whom you have consummated marriage [are forbidden as wives].}** [Qur'ān 4:23] Usually speaking, daughters of one's wife live with and are raised by the husband.

وَأَن لَا يكون خرج لجواب سُؤَال عَنهُ، أَو حَادِثَة تتَعَلَّق بِهِ، أَو للْجَهْل بِحكمِهِ دون حكم الْمَسْكُوت، كَمَا لَو سُئِلَ صلى الله عَلَيْهِ وَسلم هَل فِي الْغنم السَّائِمَة زَكَاة؟ أَو قيل بِحَضْرَتِهِ: لفُلَان غنم سَائِمَة، أَو خَاطب من جهل حكم الْغنم السَّائِمَة دون المعلوفة فَقَالَ: فِي الْغنم السَّائِمَة زَكَاة.

Another condition is that it must not be in response to a question or related to an incident. The statement must also not emanate out of ignorance of its ruling, though one knows the ruling of the tacitly mentioned omitted thing. For example, if he ﷺ was asked, "Does *zakāt* apply to grazing goats?" Or if someone said in his presence, "So-and-so has grazing goats," or he addresses a person who does not know the ruling of grazing goats, but knows the ruling of non-grazing goats, and says, "*Zakāt* applies to grazing goats."

مثله أَيْضا جَمِيع مَا يَقْتَضِي التَّخْصِيص بِالذكر. كموافقة الْوَاقِع، كَمَا فِي قَوْله تَعَالَى ﴿لَا يَتَّخِذِ الْمُؤْمِنُونَ الْكَافِرِينَ أَوْلِيَاءَ مِنْ دُونِ الْمُؤْمِنِينَ﴾ [آل عمرَان: ٢٨] نزلت - كَمَا قَالَ الواحدي وَغَيره - فِي قوم من الْمُؤمنِينَ والوا الْيَهُود دون الْمُؤمنِينَ، وككون الْكَلَام خرج مخرج التفهيم أَو الامتنان نَحْو ﴿لِتَأْكُلُوا مِنْهُ لَحْماً طَرِيّاً﴾ [النَّحْل: ١٤]، فَإِنَّهُ لَا يدل على منع القديد من لحم مَا يُؤْكَل مِمَّا يخرج من

الْبَحْر كَغَيْرِهِ، وَإِنَّمَا اشترطوا للمفهوم انْتِفَاء الْمَذْكُورَات، لِأنها فَوَائِد ظَاهِرة، وَهُوَ فَائِدَة خُفْيَة فَأخر عَنْهَا.

Another condition is that [the qualifications mentioned] are not given consideration due to some other reasons for mention of the qualifications themselves. For example, the qualifications could be mentioned to tell of some occurrence, such as when Allah the Exalted said: **{The believers should not make the disbelievers their allies rather than other believers.}** [Qurʾān 3:28] Al-Wāḥidī states that this verse was revealed regarding a group of believers who made an alliance with the Jews, thereby forsaking the Muslims. Also, the mentioned specifics do not carry an inverse if the verse is to teach or to show favours. Allah the Exalted said: **{And He is the One Who has subjected the sea, so from it you may eat tender seafood.}** [Qurʾān 16:14] This does not indicate that jerked meat that comes from the sea is prohibited. The reason why the existence of an inverse implication is contingent on the nonexistence of [the previous conditions] mentioned[352] is that there are apparent benefits to mentioning the pronounced rulings, however, the benefits [of the implied rulings] are hidden, and as such, they do not supersede [the pronounced rulings].[353]

ثمَّ إِن دَلِيل الْخطاب بِحَسب الْقُوة والضعف يكون على مَرَاتِب سِتّ.

352 [T] Such as the quality being unmentioned due to fear, and so forth. Refer to al-Banānī's comments on al-Maḥallī's explanation of *Jamʿ al-Jawāmiʿ* (1/392).

353 [T] To summarise this entire concept, the scholars state that in order for a divine text to carry an implication, there must be no intrinsic benefit other than providing an inverse ruling. Whenever there is a benefit, the implied ruling is negated, since it is a hidden benefit and does not supersede the pronounced benefits. Al-Maḥallī stated in his explanation of *Jamʿ al-Jawāmiʿ*, "The point of what was mentioned in all of the previous examples is that they carry no implied inverse ruling." He then said, "As for the verse regarding girls being raised by the husband of the wife, and the verse of alliances with non-believers, [the benefit] is that the prohibition of marrying the daughter of one's wife is so that no aversion or hatred emanates between the wife and the daughter. If it were allowed, and [the husband married his wife's daughter], it would typically occur, regardless if she were raised in his household or not. As for believers showing alliance to non-believers, it was prohibited because the non-believer carries intrinsic enmity [to the believer], and that enmity exists regardless if one shows alliance to believers [along with disbelievers] or not." Refer to *al-Jalīs al-Ṣāliḥ al-Nāfiʿ* by al-Ītyūbī (pp. 75-76). In the example of the ḥadīth, **"*Zakāt* applies to grazing goats,"** there would be no intrinsic benefit to mentioning "grazing goats," other than to imply the negation of the ruling (*zakāt*) to the inverse (stall-fed livestock).

Further, implications of instructions are of six varying levels:

أولها: الحكم إِلَى غَايَة بـ(حتى) أو (إِلَى) وَيُسمى مَفْهُوم الْغَايَة نَحْو ﴿حَتَّىٰ تَنكِحَ زَوْجاً غَيْرَهُ﴾ [الْبَقَرة: ٢٣٠]. ﴿ثمَّ أَتموا الصّيام إِلَى اللَّيْل﴾ [الْبَقَرة: ١٨٧]، فيفيد أن حكم مَا بعد الْغَايَة يُخَالف مَا قبلهَا.

First: Prepositions: These indicate the ruling is enacted up to a certain point. Two such terms that are prepositions are, "until" and "up to the point of." They are referred to as, *mafhūm al-ghāyah*. Examples are when Allah the Exalted said: **{If a husband re-divorces his wife after the second divorce, she will not be lawful for him until she has taken another husband.}** [Qur'ān 2:230] Another example is: **{Then fast until nightfall.}** [Qur'ān 2:187] These verses show that the ruling that occurs after "until" is the opposite of the one that occurs before [those two words].

ثَانِيهَا: تَعْلِيق الحكم على شَرط نَحْو ﴿وَإِنْ كُنَّ أُولاتِ حَمْلٍ فَأَنْفِقُوا عَلَيْهِنَّ﴾ [الطَّلَاق: ٦]، فَإِنَّهُ يُفِيد انْتِفَاء الْإِنْفَاق عِنْد انْتِفَاء الْحمل، وَلَا فرق بَين تَعْلِيقه بِشَرْط أَو شرطين أَو أَكثر.

Second: Conditions: For example: **{If they are pregnant, then maintain them until they deliver.}** [Qur'ān 65:6] This implies that spending is not an obligation if the woman is not pregnant. There is no difference between mentioning just one condition or mentioning many conditions.

ثَالِثهَا: تعقيب ذكر الِاسْم الْعَام بِصفة خَاصَّة فِي معرض الِاسْتِدْرَاك وَالْبَيَان نَحْو: فِي الْغنم السَّائِمَة الزَّكَاة، فالغنم اسْم علم يتَنَاوَل السَّائِمَة والمعلوفة، فاستدرك عُمُومه بِخُصُوص السَّائِمَة، وَبَين أنها الْمُرَاد من عُمُوم الْغنم.

Third: Following a general noun with a particular attribute in the context of clarification. For example, the Prophet ﷺ said, **"*Zakāt* applies to grazing goats."**[354] The word "goats," is general and is inclusive of both stall-fed and pasture fed goats. Its generality was particularised by mention of the attribute, "grazing," and as such, the Prophet ﷺ clarified that out of all goats, he only intended ones that are pasture fed.

354 Reported by al-Bukhārī (3/253).

رَابِعهَا: أَن يعلق الحكم على وصف لَا يسْتَقر، بل يطوى وَيَزُول كالسوم والثيوبة فِي قَوْلنَا: فِي السَّائِمَة وَالزَّكَاة، وَالْبكْر تستأذن، وَالثيب أَحَق بِنَفسِهَا.

Fourth: To tie a ruling to an attribute that is not constant, but rather, comes and goes. For example, the two attributes of "grazing" and "deflowered," in the two statements, "*Zakāt* applies to grazing goats," and "A virgin is to be asked for her permission [before marrying her to someone], and a deflowered woman has more right to herself."

خَامِسهَا: تَخْصِيص نوع من الْعدَد بِحكم نَحْو قَوْله عَلَيْهِ السَّلَام: **«لَا تحرم المصة وَلَا المصتان»** يَعْنِي: فِي الرَّضَاع: وَهَذَا يدل على مُخَالفَة مَا فَوْقه، يَعْنِي تَحْرِيم ثَلَاث رَضعَات، وَبِه قَالَ مَالك وَدَاوُد وَبَعض الشَّافِعِيَّة، خلافًا لأكثرهم وَلأبي حنيفَة.

Fifth: Specifying a type by mentioning a number associated with it, and giving that number a ruling. For example, the Prophet ﷺ said, **"One or two suckles do not make [marriage] prohibited."**[355] This is on the topic of suckling. This shows that anything above that number does prohibit marriage. Meaning, three suckles prohibit marriage. This was the view of Mālik, Dāwūd, and some Shāfiʿī scholars, though going against the majority [of Shāfiʿī scholars], as well as Abu Ḥanīfah.

سادسها: مَفْهُوم اللقب، وَهُوَ تَخْصِيص اسْم بِحكم، وَأنكر الْأَكْثَرُونَ هَذَا الْمَفْهُوم مشتقا كَانَ نَحْو: **«لَا تَبِيعُوا الطعَام إِلا مثلا بِمثل»** فَإِن الطَّعَام مُشْتَقّ من الطّعْم، كالحنطة وَالشعِير وَالتَّمْر وَالْملح وَالذَّهَب وَالْفِضَّة. وَقَالَ الدقاق: مَفْهُوم اللقب حجَّة، وَالضَّابِط فِي بَاب الْمَفْهُوم أَنه مَتى أَفَادَ ظنا. عرف من تصرف الشَّارِع الِالْتِفَات إِلَى مثله خَالِيا عَن معَارض، كَانَ حجَّة يجب الْعَمَل بِهِ.

Sixth: Implications of Titles: This means to specify a ruling and attach the ruling to some title, or name. The majority rejected this implication, even if the title given was derived from another word. For example, the Prophet ﷺ

355 Reported by Muslim (1450). [T] This is referring to a woman breastfeeding a baby. The Prophet ﷺ is saying that a single suck or two does not make it impermissible for the child to marry the woman's son or daughter.

said, **"Do not sell food except like for like."**[356] The title "food (*ṭaʿām*)" is derived from the word *ṭuʿm*, [or is not derived,][357] such as wheat, barley, dates, salt, gold, and silver. Al-Daqqāq stated, "The implications of titles are evidences." The determining factor is if they provide a reasonable probability, the religion has shown to take such things into account as long as there is nothing [stronger] conflicting with it, and in that case, it is an evidence that must be acted on.

والظنون المستفادة من دَلِيل الْخطاب مُتَفَاوِتَة بتفاوت مراتبه، وَمن تدرب بِالنّظرِ فِي اللُّغَة، وَعرف مواقع الْأَلْفَاظ ومقاصد الْمُتَكَلِّمين، سهل عِنْده إِدْرَاك ذَلِك التَّفَاوُت، وَالْفرق بَين تِلْكَ الْمَرَاتِب، وَالله الْموفق.

The probabilities of rulings taken from inverse implications vary inasmuch as their levels vary. If someone trains themselves in the language and knows the intent behind wordings and the meanings behind speech, it becomes easy for them to understand their variances and the differences between the varying levels. And Allah the Exalted is the One that grants divine aid.

356 Reported by Aḥmad (6/400) and Muslim (1592).

357 [T] The phrase between the brackets is not found in the printed version, but exists both in the manuscript and in the original *Sharḥ Mukhtaṣar al-Rawḍah*, where al-Shaykh Ibn Badrān is quoting from.

لمفهوم مشتقا كان نحو لا تبيعوا الطعام الا مثلا بمثل ف
مشتق من الطعم او غير مشتق كالحنطة والشعير والت

الْأَصْل الثَّالِث الْإِجْمَاع

The Third Foundational Principle: Consensus

الْإِجْمَاع لُغَة: الْعَزْم والاتفاق، قَالَ تَعَالَى: ﴿فَأَجْمِعُوا أَمْرَكُمْ﴾ [يُونُس: ٧١]، أَي اعزموا. وَيُقَال: أجمع الْقَوْم على كَذَا أَي اتَّفقُوا عَلَيْهِ.

The word referring to consensus in the Arabic language is *ijmāʿ*, and it refers, linguistically, to decide and agreement. Allah the Exalted said: **{Agree on your course of action.}** [Qurʾān 10:71] Meaning, decide your plan. It is also said that if a people have *ijmāʿ* on something, they have all agreed on it.

وَاصْطِلَاحا: اتِّفَاق الْمُجْتَهدين من هَذِه الْأمة فِي عصر على أَمر، وَمن يرى انْقِرَاض الْعَصْر يزِيد إِلَى انْقِرَاض الْعَصْر، وَمن يرى أن الْإِجْمَاع لَا ينْعَقد مَعَ سبق خلاف مُسْتَقر من حَيّ أَو ميت، جوز وُقُوعه. يزِيد: لم يسْبقهُ خلاف مُجْتَهد مُسْتَقر.

In the terminology of legal theorists, it refers to the agreement of *mujtahid* scholars of this Ummah on a matter during a particular period of time. Those who view that [the establishment of consensus is contingent on] the passing of the generation [of scholars who agreed] must add that qualification to the definition. Those who view that consensus is not established as long as there is previous disagreement, whether the disagreement is on the part of a living person or a person of the past, have agreed that it is a rational possibility, and add, "So long as it was not preceded by established differences among *mujtahid* scholars."

فَقَوله: (اتِّفَاق الْمُجْتَهدين) يخرج المقلدين، لأَنهم من الْعَوام عِنْد أهل الْأُصُول، فَلَا تعْتَبر مُخَالفتهم وَلَا مُوَافقتهم. وَقَوله: (على أَمر) يتَنَاوَل الديني والدنيوي، لَكِن المُرَاد بالدنيوي: مَا يعود إِلَى الدّين كأمر البيع وَالسّلم. وَأما الِاتِّفَاق على أَمر دُنْيَوِيّ مَحْض: كالاتفاق على مصلحَة إِقَامَة متجر أَو حِرْفَة، أَو على أَمر ديني

لكنه لَا يتَعَلَّق بِالدّينِ لذاته بل بِوَاسِطَة، كاتفاقهم على بعض مسَائِل الْعَرَبيَّة، أَو اللُّغَة، أَو الْحساب وَنَحْوه، فَإِن ذَلِك لَيْسَ إِجْمَاعًا شَرْعِيًّا أَو اصطلاحيا، وَإِن كَانَ إِجْمَاعًا شَرْعِيًّا فِي الْحَقِيقَة لتَعَلقه بِالشَّرْعِ وَإِن كَانَ بِوَاسِطَة.

The statement, "Agreement of *mujtahid* scholars," is to exclude blind-followers, since they are considered laypeople in the nomenclature of legal theorists. Their disagreements, therefore, are not valid. The statement, "On a matter," includes religious and worldly matters. However, when I say worldly matters, I mean ones that are tied to the religion, such as matters pertaining to selling and *salam* transactions.[358] Things that are not considered consensus in the religion or in the nomenclature of legal theorists are: (i) Agreements on purely worldly matters, such as agreement on some utility, for example, opening a bartering station or some trade. (ii) Something of the religion that has no intrinsic connection to the religion, but rather, through extrinsic causes, such as their agreement on some issues pertaining to Arabic, linguistics, mathematics, and so forth. However, the second category can be considered a religious consensus, since it does have some relation to the religion, even if it is through an extrinsic way.

وَفِي هَذَا الأَصْل مسَائِل:

There are a number of discussions to be had on the topic of consensus:

أَولهَا: أنكر النظام وَبعض الشِّيعَة جَوَاز الْإِجْمَاع من مجتهدي الْأمة على حكم، وَذَلِكَ رَاجع إِلَى عدم الْجَوَاز من جِهَة الْعقل. وَذهب الْأَكْثَرُونَ إِلَى أَن جَوَازه مَعْلُوم بِالضَّرُورَةِ، لِأَنهُ لَا يلْزم من فرض وُقُوعه محَال لذاته وَلَا لغيره، وَهَذَا هُوَ الْمَعْنى بِالْجَوَازِ الْعقلِيّ، نعم هَؤُلَاءِ استبعدوا وُقُوعه مَعَ كَثْرَة الْعباد، وتباعد الْبِلَاد، وَاخْتِلَاف القرائح، فظنوا الاستبعاد اسْتِحَالَة.

First: Al-Naẓẓām and some Shiites denied the rational possibility of consensus of the *mujtahid* scholars on a ruling. The majority opined that its rational possibility is known by necessary, since if we were to suppose that it did occur, it would not result in any intrinsic nor extrinsic rational impossibili-

358 [T] A *salam* transaction is a contract regarding some described item that will be delivered later, though the payment is made in the contractual meeting. Refer to *Muntahā al-Irādāt* (2/381).

ties. This is what it means for something to be rationally feasible. Sure, some have considered it unlikely to occur, since there are so many slaves of Allah, great distances between lands, and differences in faculties and intelligence. They thought that unlikeliness is tantamount to impossibility.

وَحكى أَصْحَابنَا أَنه رُوِيَ عَن الإِمَام أَحْمد إِنْكَار الْإِجْمَاع، وَاعْتَذَرُوا عَنهُ بِأَنَّهُ مَحْمُول على الْوَرع، أَو على غير عَالم بِالْخِلَافِ، أَو على تعذر معرفَة الْكل، أَو على الْعَام النطقي، إِلَى غير ذَلِك من الاعتذارات.

Our *aṣḥāb* have stated that it is narrated that al-Imām Aḥmad rejected consensus. However, they interpreted his words to mean abstention and carefulness, or that it applies to someone claiming consensus without knowing that there are differences of opinion. Some also interpreted it to mean that it is impossible to know the views of all, and others stated that Aḥmad meant general explicitly stated consensus [by all *mujtahid* scholars]. Others have provided other interpretations, as well.

وَعِنْدِي أَن الإِمَام أَحْمد لم يُوَافق النظام على إِنْكَاره، لِأَن النظام أنكرهُ عقلا، ولإمام صرح بقوله: وَمَا يدريه بِأَنَّهُم اتَّفقُوا فكَأَنَّهُ يَقُول: إِن كثيرا من الْحَوَادِث تقع فِي أقاصي الْمشرق وَالْمغْرب، وَلَا يعلم بوقوعها من بَينهمَا من أهل مصر وَالشَّام وَالْعراق، وَمَا والاهما، فكيف تصح دَعْوَى إِجْمَاع الْكل فِي مثل هَذِه.

My view is that al-Imām Aḥmad did not agree with al-Naẓẓām in denying consensus, because al-Naẓẓām denied it being a rational possibility. However, al-Imām Aḥmad said, "How could one possibly know that [*mujtahid* scholars] have all agreed?" As such, he is effectively stating that there are many things that happen in the East and West and those in Egypt, the Levant, Iraq, and their surrounding areas of which one cannot possibly be aware of them. How, then, can one claim consensus in such matters?

وَإِنَّمَا ثبتَتْ هَذِه بِإِجْمَاع جزئي وَهُوَ إِجْمَاع الإقليم الَّذِي وَقعت فِيهِ. أما إِجْمَاع الأمة قاطبة فمتعذر فِي مثلهَا، وَهَذَا النَّوْع هُوَ الَّذِي نقل إِنْكَاره عَن الإِمَام كَمَا يفهم من قَوْله: وَمَا يدريه بِأَنَّهُم أتفقوا. وَمَا ذَلِك إِلَّا أَن الإِجْمَاع على الْمَسْأَلَة الَّتِي اتّفق جَمِيع مجتهدي الْأمة عَلَيْهَا فرع الْعلم بهَا، والتصديق مَسْبُوق بالتصور،

فَمن لم يعلم مَحل الحكم كَيفَ يتَصَوَّر مِنْهُ الحكم بِنَفْي أَو إِثْبَات؟

Such a consensus has been established via partial *ijmāʿ*, which is the consensus of the region wherein it occurred in. As for the entirety of the Ummah agreeing in such matters, it is impossible. This type of consensus is what has been reportedly rejected by al-Imām Aḥmad, as understood by his statement, "How could one possibly know that [*mujtahid* scholars] have all agreed?" The reason is that consensus on a particular matter, where all *mujtahid* scholars have agreed on a particular ruling, is contingent on knowing about that matter. Assigning truth values or value judgements on issues is contingent on conceptualising the issue beforehand. If someone is wholly unaware of what the ruling applies to, how can it be conceived that they can provide a ruling, whether for or against the issue?

وَهَذَا هُوَ الْحق الَّذِي يلْزم اتِّبَاعه. فَلَا يتوهمن متوهم أَن الإِمَام أنكر الْإِجْمَاع إنكارا عقليا، وَإِنَّمَا أنكر الْعلم بِالْإِجْمَاع على حَادِثَة وَاحِدَة انتشرت فِي جَمِيع الأقطار، وَبَلغت الْأَطْرَاف الشاسعة، ووقف عَلَيْهَا كل مُجْتَهد، ثمَّ أطبق الْكل فِيهَا على قَول وَاحِد، وَبَلغت أَقْوَالهم كلهَا مدعى الْإِجْمَاع عَلَيْهَا: وَأَنت خَبِير بِأَن الْعَادة لَا تساعد على هَذَا كَمَا يُعلمهُ كل منصف تخلى عَن الجمود والتقليد، نعم يُمكن أَن يعلم هَذَا فِي عصر الصَّحَابَة دون مَا بعدهمْ من العصور، لقلَّة الْمُجْتَهدين يَوْمئِذٍ، وتوفر نقل الْمُحدثين على نقل فتاواهم وأرائهم، فَلَا تتهمن أَيهَا الْعَاقِل الإِمَام بإنكار الْإِجْمَاع مُطلقًا فتفترى عَلَيْهِ.

This is the truth that must be adhered to. One should not misconceive the issue and think that the *imām* rejected consensus on a rational basis. He only denied the ability to know of consensus on a single issue that has become widespread in all lands and has reached the furthest of distances, allowing for each *mujtahid* scholar to be aware of it, and then all have the same view on it, and then all of their views reach the person claiming consensus. You know that this is not an ordinary occurrence, and this can be acknowledged by any impartial person that has abandoned rigidity and blind-following. True, this can be known during the time of the Companions, since there were very few *mujtahid* scholars yet there were many scholars of ḥadīth that were transmitting their rulings and views, [but the same cannot be said of the generations that followed.] So, a rational person should not accuse the *imām* of denying consensus altogether, for this would be lying against him.

ثَانِيهَا: الْإِجْمَاع حجَّة قَاطِعَة يجب الْعَمَل بِهِ عِنْد الْجُمْهُور، خلافًا للنظام. وَمعنى كَونه قَاطعا أَنه يقدم على بَاقِي الْأَدِلَّة، وَلَيْسَ الْقَاطِع هُنَا بِمَعْنى الْجَازِم الَّذِي لَا يحْتَمل النقيض، كَقَوْلِنَا: الْوَاحِد نصف الاثْنَي فِي نفس الْأَمر، وَإِلَّا لما اخْتلف فِي تَكْفِير مُنكر حكمه.

Second: Consensus is a definitive evidence that must be acted on, according to the majority. This, too, is contradictory to the position of al-Naẓẓām. The meaning of it being definitive is that it is placed before all other evidences. When I say it is definitive, it does not mean one that is not susceptible to doubt; it is not an axiom as the statement, 'One is half of two,' for example. If it were an axiom, there would be no differences of opinion on whether a person who rejects consensus has left the fold of Islam.

ثَالِثهَا: الْمُعْتَبر فِي الْإِجْمَاع قَول أهل الِاجْتِهَاد لَا الصّبيان والمجانين قطعا، وَلَا يعْتَبر فِيهِ قَول الْعَامَّة، وهم من لَيْسَ بمجتهد وَلَا من عرف الحَدِيث أَو اللُّغَة أَو الْكَلَام وَنَحْوه، وَكَذَا من عرف الْفِقْه أَو أُصُوله عِنْد أَحْمد وَأَصْحَابه، وَكَذَا من فَاتَهُ بعض شُرُوط الِاجْتِهَاد، وَلَا يعْتَبر فِيهِ كَافِر أُصَلِّي مُطلقًا، وَلَا كَافِر بارتكاب بِدعَة عِنْد مكفره، وَلَا فَاسق مُطلقًا سَوَاء كَانَ فسقه من حَيْثُ الِاعْتِقَاد أَو الْأَفْعَال كالاعتزال وَالزِّنَا وَالسَّرِقَة.

Third: Those considered in a claim of consensus are the *mujtahid* scholars, and definitely does not include children or clinically insane people. Also, the views of the laity carry no weight. "Laypeople" here refers to those who are not *mujtahid* scholars. It also does not include scholars who know only ḥadīth, language, *kalām*, and so forth. Likewise, it does not include those who only know jurisprudence or only know legal theories—according to Aḥmad and his disciples; it also does not include those who are missing some preconditions to *ijtihād*. The views of original disbelievers carry no weight. If someone views a heretic to be a disbeliever, the heretic's view also carries no weight. A sinner's view carries no weight, regardless if their sinfulness is in a heresy they espouse, such as the Mu'tazilites, or an action they perform, such as fornicators and thieves.

قَالَ الطوفي فِي (مُخْتَصره): وَالْأَشْبَه اعْتِبَار قَول الأصولي والنحوي فَقَط، لتمكنهما من درس الحكم بِالدَّلِيلِ. وَالْمَسْأَلَة اجتهادية قَالَ: وَيعْتَبر فِي إِجْمَاع كل فن قَول أَهله، إِذْ غيرهم بِالْإِضَافَة إِلَيْهِ عَامَّة. هَذَا كَلَامه، وَهُوَ مَسْلَك جيد، وَلَا يعْتَبر فِي أهل الْإِجْمَاع أَن يبلغُوا عدد التَّوَاتُر.

Al-Ṭūfī stated, "The more veracious view is to consider the views of legal theorists and scholars of grammar, since they [understand][359] the ruling by referring to its evidences, and the matter is one of scholarly discretion. [...] Those whose views are deemed worthy in consensuses in each science are the scholars of those sciences, since others are laymen relative to that science."[360] His approach in this quote is good. Another important matter to mention is that the number needed for recurrence (*tawātur*) is not a precondition to the validity of the consensus.

رَابِعهَا: لَا يخْتَص الْإِجْمَاع بالصحابة، بل إِجْمَاع كل عصر حجَّة، خلافًا لداود الظَّاهِرِيّ.

Fourth: Consensus is not limited to the companions. Rather, the consensus of each generation is evidence. This is contrary to the view of Dāwūd al-Ẓāhirī.

خَامِسهَا: الْجُمْهُور أَن الْإِجْمَاع لَا ينْعَقد بقول الْأَكْثَر دون الْأَقَل حَتَّى يتَّفق الْجَمِيع، قلت: وَمُقْتَضى مَا قدمْنَاهُ عَن الإِمَام أَحْمد أَنه ينْعَقد بقول الْأَكْثَر فِي غير زمن الصَّحَابَة، لتعذر الِاطِّلَاع على اتِّفَاق الْكل فِي غير عصرهم، وَمن ثمَّ قَالَ الطوفي وَغَيره من أَصْحَابنَا بعد ذكر هَذِه الْمَسْأَلَة - خلافًا لِابْنِ جرير - وَعَن أَحْمد رَحمَه الله مثله. انْتهى. وَإِلَيْهِ ذهب أَبُو بكر الرَّازِيّ وَأَبُو الْحُسَيْن الْخياط من الْمُعْتَزلَة، وَابْن حمدَان من أَصْحَابنَا، وَجمع. وَالْحق أَن اتِّفَاق الْأَكْثَر حجَّة يجب الْعَمَل بِهِ على أَهله، لكنه لَيْسَ فِي رُتْبَة الْإِجْمَاع، بل هُوَ فِي رُتْبَة الْقيَاس، وَخبر الْوَاحِد.

359 [T] The portion between the brackets stated, "study," but the printed copy of al-Ṭūfī's *Mukhtaṣar* says, "Understand," as I have placed it.

360 [T] *Sharḥ Mukhtaṣar al-Rawḍah* (3/37).

Fifth: The majority stated that consensus is not established by the majority espousing a view. Rather, all must agree. I say: The previously mentioned statement of al-Imām Aḥmad could necessitate that consensus can occur through the agreement of the majority if it occurs after the companions, since it is impossible to have knowledge of the agreements of all scholars, even those in other generations. After mentioning this issue, al-Ṭūfī and others of the *aṣḥāb* mentioned the opposing view of Ibn Jarir,[361] and then said, "Aḥmad is reported to have a similar view."[362] [363] This was also the view of Abu Bakr al-Rāzī and Abu 'l-Ḥusayn al-Khayyaṭ of the Muʿtazilites, and Ibn Ḥamdān, one our *aṣḥāb*. It was the view reported from a number of other scholars, as well. The truth, though, is that if the majority agree on a view, it is evidence that must be acted on, but is not of the level of consensus. It is of the level of analogies and singular reports.

سادسها: التَّابِعِيّ الْمُجْتَهد المعاصر للصحابة مُعْتَبر مَعَهم فِي الْإِجْمَاع، فَلَا ينْعَقد مَعَ مُخَالفَته، فَإِن صَار مُجْتَهدا بعد انْعِقَاد الْإِجْمَاع، فَمن قَالَ: يشْتَرط فِي الْإِجْمَاع انْقِرَاض الْعَصْر لم يعْتَبر انْعِقَاد الْإِجْمَاع مَعَ مُخَالفَته، وَمن لا يشْتَرط انْقِرَاض الْعَصْر لم يعْتَبره، وَاعْتبر مُوَافقَته أَبُو الْخطاب، وَابْن عقيل، والآمدي. قَالَ المرداوي فِي (التَّحْرِير): وَلَعَل المُرَاد عدم مُخَالفَته، ثمَّ قَالَ: فَائِدَة: تَابع التَّابِعِيّ مَعَ التَّابِعِيّ كَهُوَ مَعَ الصَّحَابِيّ. قَالَه القَاضِي.

Sixth: A *mujtahid* scholar from the generation of the Tābiʿīn, who has lived alongside the companions, is considered with the companions in consensus. Therefore, consensus is not established without his agreement. If he becomes a *mujtahid* after the consensus has been reached, those who said that the generation must end before consensus is established would not consider the consensus to be valid without his approval. Those who do not take the view that the generation must end would not deem his disagreement to be valid. Abu 'l-Khaṭṭāb, Ibn 'Aqīl, and al-Āmidī all considered his agreement to be worthy of consideration. Al-Mardāwī stated in *al-Taḥrīr*, "Perhaps

361 [T] Ibn Jarīr's view, as quoted by al-Ṭūfī, is that consensus is established by the agreement of the majority. Refer to *Sharḥ Mukhtaṣar al-Rawḍah* (3/53).

362 [T] Meaning, one of the reports from al-Imām Aḥmad is that he believed that the only consensus that can be established is that of the companions. Refer to *Sharḥ Mukhtaṣar al-Rawḍah* (3/47).

363 [T] *Sharḥ Mukhtaṣar al-Rawḍah* (3/47).

[al-Āmidī] meant that his lack of disagreement is worthy of consideration."[364] He then said, "It is beneficial to note that the generation after the Tābiʿīn is, to the Tābiʿīn, the same as the Tābiʿīn are to the companions, as stated by al-Qāḍī."[365]

سابعها: الْجُمْهُور لَا يشْتَرط لصِحَّة الْإِجْمَاع انْقِرَاض عصر المجمعين. وَحكى أَصْحَابنَا عَن أَحْمد وَأكْثر أَصْحَابه: أنه يشْتَرط انْقِرَاض الْعَصْر، وَحكى الطوفي الْقَوْل الأول، وَمَال إِلَيْهِ، وَقَالَ: وَقول الإِمَام أَحْمد الْمُوَافق لِلْجُمْهُورِ أَوْمَأَ إِلَيْهِ إيماء انْتهى. قلت: ومعتمد مذْهبه عدم الِاشْتِرَاط.

Seventh: The majority do not consider the death of the generation of scholars who initially agreed to be a precondition to the establishment of the consensus. Our *aṣḥāb* have reported from Aḥmad and the majority of his adherents that the generation of scholars must first pass away. Al-Ṭūfī reported the first view and inclined towards it. He said, "The view of al-Imām Aḥmad is in line with the majority, and he alluded to it subtly."[366] I say: The official view of his *madhhab* is that it is not a condition.[367]

ثامنها: إِذا قَالَ بعض الْأَئِمَّة قولا - سَوَاء كَانَ من الصَّحَابَة أَو مِمَّن بعدهمْ - وَسكت الْبَاقُونَ مَعَ اشتهار ذَلِك القَوْل فيهم، وَكَانَ ذَلِك القَوْل مُتَعَلقا بِأَحْكَام التَّكْلِيف، كَانَ ذَلِك إِجْمَاعًا على الْمُخْتَار، وَيُسمى إِجْمَاعًا سكوتيا. فَلَو لم يشْتَهر القَوْل فيهم، لم يدل سكوتهم على الْمُوَافقَة، وَلَو لم يكن تكليفا لم يكن إِجْمَاعًا وَلَا حجَّة، لِأَن الْإِجْمَاع أَمر ديني، وَمَا لَيْسَ تكليفا لَيْسَ دينيا، بل دنيويا.

Eighth: If some scholars take a view, regardless if those scholars lived during the time of the companions or afterwards, and the rest of the scholars remained silent though the opinion was widespread among them and pertains to rulings of responsibilities (*taklīf*), this is considered consensus, according to the chosen view. This is referred to as a silent consensus (*ijmāʿ sukūtī*). However, if the view is not so popular amongst scholars, their silence does

364 [T] *Taḥrīr al-Manqūl* (p. 147).
365 [T] *Taḥrīr al-Manqūl* (p. 148).
366 [T] *Sharḥ Mukhtaṣar al-Rawḍah* (3/66).
367 [T] Note that the official position of the Ḥanbalī *madhhab* is not what al-Shaykh Ibn Badrān has stated. In the *madhhab*, the death of the generation that had the agreement is a condition. Refer to *Taḥrīr al-Manqūl* (pp. 150-151).

not indicate approval. Also, if the view is not pertaining to responsibilities, it is neither a consensus nor an evidence. Consensus is a religious matter, and if something is not a religious responsibility, it is not a religious matter; rather, it is a worldly matter.

وَلَكِن اخْتِلَاف الزَّمَان أحدث للْإِجْمَاع السكوتي شرطا، وَهُوَ أَنه إِذا أفتى وَاحِد بِحكم على مذْهبه - مَعَ مُخَالفَته لمَذْهَب غَيره - وَسكت الْبَاقُونَ عَنهُ، فَإِن ذَلِك السُّكُوت لَا يعد إِجْمَاعًا، لما تقرر عِنْد أهل الْمذَاهب من عدم إِنْكَار بَعضهم على بعض إِلَّا أَن يُقَال: فرض الْمَسْأَلَة فِي الْأَحْكَام الَّتِي يتداول الْمُجْتَهدُونَ الْبَحْث عَنْهَا، لَا فِي الْأَحْكَام الَّتِي يتداولها المقلدون، لأَنهم لَا فِي العير وَلَا فِي النفير.

The passage of time has dictated another condition for silent consensus, which is: If a scholar gives a *fatwā* according to their own *madhhab*, thereby contradicting other schools of law, and others remain silent, their silence is not to be misconstrued as consensus. The reason is that the adherents to the various schools have agreed that they do not rebuke each other's views except when positing issues in rulings as done by the *mujtahid* scholars when researching. However, this is not applicable to rulings that blind-followers circulate and act on, since they carry no significance in matters of positing and debating issues.

تاسعها: إِذا اخْتلف أهل الْعَصْر على قَوْلَيْنِ، امْتنع على من بعدهمْ إِحْدَاث قَول ثَالِث: وَقَالَ الرَّازِيّ فِي (الْمَحْصُول) والآمدي فِي (مُنْتَهى السول) وتبعهما الطوفي: إِن الْقَوْل الثَّالِث، إِن رفع الْإِجْمَاع الأول على الْقَوْلَيْنِ الْأَوَّلين لم يجز، وَإِن لم يرفعهُ جَازَ، مِثَاله: لَو قَالَ بعض الْأمة بِاعْتِبَار النِّيَّة فِي كل طَهَارَة، وَقَالَ الْبَعْض الآخر باعتبارها فِي بعض الطهارات دون بعض - كَمَا هُوَ قَول أبي حنيفَة - يعْتَبر هَذَا للتيمم دون الْوضُوء، فالنافي اعْتِبَارهَا فِي جَمِيع الْعِبَادَات مُطلقًا يكون رَافعا للْإِجْمَاع الأول.

Ninth: If the scholars of a generation disagree, and that results in two views, it is not allowed for those that come after them to devise a third opinion. Al-Rāzī stated in *al-Maḥṣūl* and al-Āmidī in *Muntahā al-Sūl* respectively, and al-Ṭūfī followed them, that if a third opinion nullifies a prior consensus on two views, it is not allowed. However, if it does not, it is allowed. For example, some scholars state that intentions are necessary for all purification, and others said that intentions are necessary for certain types of purifications, and not others, as is the view of Abu Ḥanīfah, who considered intentions necessary for *tayammum*, but not *wuḍū*. However, if someone were to deny that intentions are necessary for any type of purification, they would be nullifying the previous consensus [of two views].

وَمِثَال مَا لَيْسَ رَافعا للْإِجْمَاع الأول مَا سبق فِي هَذَا الْمِثَال من النَّفْي فِي إِحْدَى الْمَسْأَلَتَيْنِ دون الْأُخْرَى. وكما لَو اخْتلفُوا فِي اعْتِبَار النية فِي الطهارات نفيا وإثباتا، فَالْقَوْل فِي إِثْبَاتهَا فِي الْبَعْض دون الْبَعْض لَا يمْتَنع، لِأَنَّهُ لم يرفع الْإِجْمَاع الأول، بل وَافق كل فريق فِي بعض مَا ذهب إِلَيْهِ، وَرُبمَا كَانَ هَذَا المسلك أولى من الَّذِي قبله.

An example of a view that does not conflict with the previous consensus is an example that has been previously mentioned, on the topic of intentions, where a person denies that intentions are necessary in certain situations, and affirms they are necessary in others. That view would not be considered nullification of the prior consensus; rather, they agree with the views of some who previously held that view. This method of treatment of this issue is better.

عَاشرهَا: إِذا اخْتلف الصَّحَابَة على قَوْلَيْنِ، فاتفق التابعون على أَحدهمَا، كَانَ ذَلِك إِجْمَاعًا، خلافًا للْقَاضِي أبي يعلى وَبَعض الشَّافِعِيَّة.

Tenth: If the companions differ into two views, and the Tābiʿīn agree on one of those two views, this is considered a consensus. This is contrary to the views of al-Qāḍī Abu Yaʿlā and some Shāfiʿī scholars.

حادي عشرهَا: اتِّفَاق الْخُلَفَاء الْأَرْبَعَة بعد رَسُول الله صلى الله عَلَيْهِ وَسلم، مَعَ مُخَالفَة غَيرهم لَهُم، لَيْسَ إِجْمَاعًا، وَإِذا لم يكن اتِّفَاق الْأَرْبَعَة إِجْمَاعًا، فَقَوْل اثْنَيْنِ مِنْهُم أولى بِأَن لَا يكون إِجْمَاعًا. وَنقل عَن الإِمَام أَحْمد: أَن اتِّفَاق الْخُلَفَاء الْأَرْبَعَة حجَّة، وَكَذَا اتِّفَاق أبي بكر وَعمر رَضِي الله عَنْهُمَا لحَدِيث: «**عَلَيْكُم**

بسنتي وَسنة الْخُلَفَاء الرَّاشِدين من بعدِي عضوا عَلَيْهَا بالنواجذ» وَحَدِيث **«اقتدوا بالذين من بعدِي أبي بكر وَعمر»** وَلَو لم تقم الْحجَّة بقَوْلهمْ لما أمرنَا باتبَاعهمْ. وَهَذَا القَوْل هُوَ الْحق.

Eleventh: If the Four Caliphs agree on a view after the Prophet ﷺ while other [companions] disagree with their view, it is not a consensus. Since the agreement of all four is not considered consensus, the agreement of just two of them has all the more reason to not be considered consensus. It was reported from al-Imām Aḥmad that the agreement of the Four Caliphs is an evidence, as is the agreement of Abu Bakr and ʿUmar ﷺ, since the Prophet ﷺ said, **"Follow my Sunnah and that of the Rightly-Guided Caliphs after me. Hold onto it with the molar teeth."**[368] Also, the ḥadīth, **"Follow those who came after me, namely, Abu Bakr and ʿUmar."**[369] If their views do not constitute evidence, we would not have been commanded to follow them. This position is the truth.

ثَانِي عشرهَا: إِجْمَاع أهل الْمَدِينَة من الصَّحَابَة وَالتَّابِعين لَيْسَ بِحجَّة، خلافًا لمَالِك، وَلَا ينْعَقد الْإِجْمَاع بِأَهْل الْبَيْت وحدهم، خلافًا للشعية.

Twelfth: The consensus of the people of Madīnah from the companions and the Tābiʿīn is not evidence. This view is contrary to that held by Mālik. Also, consensus is not established through the views of only the Family of the Prophet ﷺ, contrary to the Shiites.

ثَالِث عَاشرهَا: لَا يكون الْإِجْمَاع إِلَّا عَن دَلِيل، لِأَنَّهُ لَا يكون إِلَّا من الْمُجْتَهدين، والمجتهد لَا يَقُول فِي الدّين بِغَيْر دَلِيل، فَإِن القَوْل بِغَيْر دَلِيل خطأ. وَيجوز كَون الْإِجْمَاع عَن اجْتِهَاد وَقِيَاس، وَقد وَقع كَذَلِك، وَتحرم مُخَالفته.

Thirteenth: Consensus only emanates from an evidence, since it only emanates from *mujtahid* scholars, and *mujtahid* scholars give opinions on the religion based upon evidence. Statements without evidence are mistakes. It is possible for consensus to emanate from scholarly discretion and analogies. This has occurred, and it is impermissible to contradict it.

368 Reported by Aḥmad (17142) and Ibn Mājah (42).
369 Reported by Aḥmad (5/283), al-Tirmidhī (3663), and Ibn Mājah (97).

وَقَالَ ابْن حَامِد وَجمع: يكفر مُنكر حكم الْإِجْمَاع الْقطعِي. وَقَالَ أَبُو الْخطاب وَجمع: لَا يكفر، وَلكنه يفسق. وَقَالَ الطوفي والآمدي وَمن تبعه: يكفر بِنَحْوِ الْعِبَادَات الْخمس، وَهُوَ معنى كَلَام أَصْحَابنَا فِي الْفِقْه.

Ibn Ḥāmid and some other scholars stated that anyone who denies the ruling of a definitive consensus is a disbeliever. Abu 'l-Khaṭṭāb and some others stated that they do not commit disbelief, but they are considered sinners. Al-Ṭūfī, al-Āmidī, and those who followed him opined that they disbelieve by rejecting things such as the five actions of worship. This is the meaning of what our *aṣḥāb* have stated in the books of law.

قَالَ القَاضِي عَلَاء الدّين المرداوي فِي (التَّحْرِير): وَالْحق أَن مُنكر الْإِجماع الضَّرُورِيّ وَالْمَشْهُور الْمَنْصُوص عَلَيْهِ كَافِرًا قطعا، وَكَذَا الْمَشْهُور فَقَط لَا الْخَفي فِي الْأَصَح فيهمَا. هَذَا كَلَامه.

Al-Qāḍī 'Alā' al-Dīn al-Mardāwī stated in his book, *al-Taḥrīr*, "The truth is that if someone rejects a consensus established through necessity and which is also popular and has textual evidences to support it, they are definite disbelievers. The same applies to those who reject well-known consensuses, but it does not apply to those who reject hidden consensuses, according to the stronger view."[370]

وَمِثَال الْخَفي: إِنْكَار اسْتِحْقَاق بنت الابْن السُّدس مَعَ الْبِنْت، وَتَحْرِيم نِكَاح الْمَرْأَة على عَمَّتهَا وخالتها، وَنَحْو ذَلِك. فَهَذَا لَا يكفر منكره لعذر الخفاء، خلافًا لبَعض الْفُقَهَاء فِي قَوْله: إنه يكفر لتكذيب الْأمة. ورد بِأَنَّهُ لم يكذبهم صَرِيحًا إِذا فرض أنه مِمَّا يخفى على مثله، فالإجماع الْخَفي هُوَ مَا كَانَ خافيا على من رده وَلم يعلم بِهِ.

Some examples of hidden consensuses are: Rejecting that the daughter of the son deserves a sixth along with the daughter and the prohibition of marrying a woman along with her maternal or paternal aunt. If someone denies those rulings, they do not fall into disbelief, due to the acceptable excuse of them being unknown. This is contrary to the view of some jurists, who said that they fall into disbelief due to belying the entire Ummah. Their view is

370 [T] *Taḥrīr al-Manqūl wa Tahdhīb 'Ilm al-Uṣūl* (p. 155).

rejected on the basis that they did not outright bely the Ummah, assuming that the consensus is one that is normally not known to [the one who rejects it]. An unknown consensus is one that is unknown to the one denying it.

رَابع عشرهَا: إِذا اسْتدلَّ أهل الْعَصْر بِدَلِيل، أَو أولُوا تَأْوِيلا، فَهَل يجوز لمن بعدهمْ إِحْدَاث دَلِيل آخر أَو تَأْوِيل من غير إِلْغَاء الأول ذهب الْجُمْهُور إِلَى جَوَاز ذَلِك، وَذهب بَعضهم إِلَى الْوَقْف، وَابْن حزم إِلَى التَّفْصِيل بَين النَّص، فَيجوز الِاسْتِدْلَال بِهِ، وَبَين غَيره فَلَا يجوز فِيهِ.

Fourteenth: If the scholars of a generation used an evidence or offered a valid interpretation, is it permissible for those after them to use a different evidence or provide a different valid interpretation, without nullifying the evidences and interpretations of the earlier scholars? The majority stated that it is permissible, and others abstained from giving an answer. Ibn Ḥazm took to a middling view, stating that if the evidence is a text, it is permissible, and if it is not, it is not permissible.

خَامِس عشرهَا: هَل يُمكن وجود دَلِيل لَا معَارض لَهُ اشْترك أهل الْإِجْمَاع فِي عدم الْعلم بِهِ؟ قيل بِالْجَوَازِ إِن كَانَ عمل الأمة مُوَافقا لَهُ، وَعَدَمه إِن كَانَ مُخَالفا لَهُ، وَاخْتَارَهُ الْآمِدِيّ، وَابْن الْحَاجِب، والصفي الْهِنْدِيّ. وَقيل بِالْمَنْعِ مُطلقًا.

Fifteenth: Is it possible for there to be an evidence that does not conflict with any other, and all the scholars within the consensus are unaware of it? It was stated that it is possible only if the Ummah had already been acting in accordance with its implications, and that it is impossible if the Ummah was collectively acting contrary to its implications. This view was taken by al-Āmidī, Ibn al-Ḥājib, and al-Ṣafī al-Hindī. The other view states it is not possible for there to be such evidence that the Ummah collectively is unaware of.

سادس عشرهَا: الْإِجْمَاع الْمَنْقُول بطرِيق الْآحَاد حجَّة، وَقَالَ الْجُمْهُور: يشْترط فِي نَقله عدد التَّوَاتُر، وَقَول الْقَائِل: لَا أعلم خلافًا بَين أهل الْعلم فِي كَذَا، كَمَا يَقُوله صَاحب (الشافي) فِي شرح (الْمقنع) وَغَيره: لَا يكون إِجْمَاعًا لجَوَاز أَن يكون ثمَّة مُخَالف لم يطلع الْقَائِل على خِلَافه، ﴿وَفَوْقَ كُلِّ ذِي عِلْمٍ عَلِيمٌ﴾ وَقد

نص على ذَلِك أَحْمد.

Sixteenth: Consensus that is reported through singular reports is still evidence. The majority stated that it is only evidence if transmitted recurrently. When a scholar says, "I do not know any scholar who disagreed on such-and-such matter," as the author of al-Shāfī, the explanation of *al-Muqni'*,[371] and others said, it does not necessitate a claim of consensus, since there might be some scholar who held a differing view, but the author did not come across it. Allah the Exalted states: **{Above everyone who has knowledge there is the One who is all knowing.}** [Qur'ān 12:76] And Aḥmad explicitly stated such.

سَابِع عشرهَا: لَا يَصح التَّمَسُّك بِالْإِجْمَاع فِيمَا يتَوَقَّف صِحَة الْإِجْمَاع عَلَيْهِ اتفَاقا، كوجود الْبَارِي، وَصِحَّة الرسَالَة، وَدلَالَة المعجزة. وَيصِح فِيمَا لَا يتَوَقَّف وَهُوَ ديني، كالرؤية وَنفي الشّرك وَوُجُوب الْعِبَادَات، أَو عَقْلِي كحدوث الْعَالم خلافًا لأبي الْمَعَالِي مُطلقًا، وللشيرازي فِي كليات أُصُول الدّين، كحدوث الْعَالم، وَإِثْبَات النُّبُوَّة.

Seventeenth: Consensus cannot be used to prove something that is an antecedent to the validity of the consensus in the first place, such as the existence of Allah, the validity of the Message, and the proofs of the miracle. It can be used for something that is not an antecedent, so long as it is a religious matter, such as seeing Allah in the hereafter, negation of polytheism, and the obligation of actions of worship. Also, it can be used in a rational matter, such as the temporal nature of the world. This is contrary to the position held by Abu 'l-Ma'ālī [al-Juwaynī] completely, and al-Shīrāzī, though al-Shīrāzī only held that it was not used for evidence in the universal fundamentals of the religion, such as the temporal nature of the world or establishing prophethood.

أَو دُنْيَوِيّ كرأي فِي حَرْب وَنَحْوه فِي ظَاهر كَلَام القَاضِي وَأبي الْخطاب وَابْن عقيل وَغيرهم. وَاخْتَارَهُ الْآمِدِيّ وَمن تبعه، وَهُوَ أظهر. وَقيل بعد اسْتِقْرَار الرَّأْي؛ وَقيل لَيْسَ بِحجَّة. وَهُوَ ظَاهر (الرَّوْضَة) وَ(الْمقنع) و(مختصر الطوفي) أَو يكون

371 [T] *Al-Shāfī Sharḥ al-Muqni'* is the name of *al-Sharḥ al-Kabīr* by Ibn Abī 'Umar, the nephew of al-Muwaffaq Ibn Qudāmah.

لغويا، وَقيل إِن تعلق بِالدّين.

It can also be used in worldly matters, such as an opinion during war and so forth, according to the apparent view of al-Qāḍī, Abu 'l-Khaṭṭāb, Ibn 'Aqīl, and others. This view was chosen by al-Āmidī and those who followed him, and it is the more apparently veracious view. It was stated that it is evidence after the agreement is made,[372] and some said that it is not an evidence altogether. The last view is the one apparently stated in *al-Rawḍah*, *al-Muqni'*, and *Mukhtaṣar al-Ṭūfī*. If the agreed upon matter is pertaining to language, it is evidence, though some added a caveat, that it only be in linguistic matters pertaining to the religion.

خَاتِمَة: الْإِجْمَاع إِمَّا نطقي أَو سكوتي، وكل وَاحِد مِنْهُمَا إِمَّا أَن يكون متواترا وَإِمَّا أَن يكون آحادا. فالنطقي: مَا كَانَ اتِّفَاق مجتهدي الْأمة جَمِيعهم عَلَيْهِ نطقا، نفيا أَو إِثْبَاتًا. والسكوتي: مَا نطق بِهِ الْبَعْض، وَسكت عَنهُ الْبَعْض الآخر.

To conclude, consensus is either pronounced or silent, and either could be recurrent or could be singular. A pronounced consensus is when the *mujtahid* scholars of the Ummah agree on something verbally, either by affirming or negating. A silent consensus is when some [*mujtahid* scholars] pronounce a ruling, and the rest remain silent [neither affirming or negating the ruling].

وكل وَاحِد من هذَيْن إِمَّا أَن ينْقل أَن جَمِيع الْمُجْتَهدين نطقوا بِهِ نقلا متواترا أَو آحادا، أَو نطق بِهِ الْبَعْض، وَسكت عَنهُ الْبَعْض الآخر تواترا أَو أحادا، وَالْكل حجَّة وَلَكِن تخْتَلف مراتبها، فأقواها النطقي تواترا، ثمَّ آحادا، ثمَّ السكوتي تواترا، ثمَّ آحادا. وَقد سبق الْخلاف فِي أَن الْإِجْمَاع يثبت بِخَبَر الْآحَاد أم لَا. وَالله الْمُوفق.

Both the pronounced and silent types of consensus can be transmitted through recurrent or singular reports. All types are evidence, but their levels vary: (i) The consensus that provides the strongest evidence is the one that has been explicitly pronounced and has been reported through a re-

372 [T] Al-Imām al-Qarāfī stated in *Nafā'is al-Uṣūl fi Sharḥ al-Maḥṣūl*, "This means that before the agreement [in the worldly matter] happens, it is still a matter differed on. As such, it cannot be considered consensus in that matter. Abu 'l-Ḥasan stated in *al-Mu'tamad*, 'An example is unanimous consensus in a matter of war in a particular moment.'" (6/2762)

current chain of narration. (ii) Below it is the one that has been explicitly pronounced and has been reported through a singular chain of narration. (iii) Below it is the one that has been silently affirmed and has been reported through a recurrent chain of narration. (iv) Last is the one that has been silently affirmed and has been reported through a singular chain of narration. I have previously mentioned the difference of opinion on whether consensus can be proven through a singular chain. And Allah is the granter of aid.

الأصل الرابع من الأصول المتفق عليها استصحاب الحال

The Fourth Foundational Principle: Presumption of Continuity

هُوَ استِصْحَاب للنَّفْي الْأَصْلِيّ الْمُقدم ذكره عِنْد ذكر الْأُصُول أَو الْكتاب، وَيعرف: بِأنهُ التَّمَسُّك بِدَلِيل عَقْلِي أَو شَرْعِي لم يظْهر عَنهُ نَاقل مُطلقًا، وَتَحْقِيق مَعْنَاهُ أَن يُقَال: هُوَ اعْتِقَاد كَون الشَّيْء فِي الْمَاضِي أَو الْحَاضِر يُوجب ظن ثُبُوته فِي الْحَال أَو الِاسْتِقْبَال. وتلخيص هَذَا أَن يُقَال: هُوَ ظن دوَام الشَّيْء بِنَاء على ثُبُوت وجوده قبل ذَلِك.

This means to presume the continuity of a previous negation. It is defined as holding fast to a rational or religious evidence that does not appear to have anything that would divert the evidence. However, a more precise definition is: Belief that something in the past or present will have the same ruling in the present or future. To give a summarised definition, it is to state: The presumption that something will remain the same, based on its previous existence.

وَهَذَا الظَّن حجَّة عِنْد الْأَكْثَرين، مِنْهُم مَالك وَأحمد والمزني والصيرفي وَإِمَام الْحَرَمَيْنِ وَالْغزالِيّ وَجَمَاعَة من أَصْحَاب الشَّافِعِي، خلافًا لجمهور الْحَنَفِيَّة وَأبي الْحُسَيْن الْبَصْرِيّ وَجَمَاعَة من الْمُتَكَلِّمين.

This presumption is evidence according to the majority, including Mālik, Aḥmad, al-Muzanī, al-Ṣayrafī, al-Imām al-Ḥaramayn, al-Ghazālī, and a number of Shāfiʿī scholars. Those who opposed the majority were the Ḥanafī scholars, Abu ʿl-Ḥasan al-Basrī, and a number of scholars of *kalām*.

قَالَ الْخَوَارِزْمِيّ فِي (الْكَافِي) استِصْحَاب الْحَال هُوَ آخر مدَار الْفَتْوَى، إِذا لم يجد الْمُفْتِي حكم الْحَادِثَة فِي الْكتاب أَو السّنة أَو الْإِجْمَاع أَو الْقيَاس، أَخذ حكمهَا

من اسْتِصْحَاب الْحَال فِي النَّفْي وَالْإِثْبات، فَإِن كل التَّرَدُّد فِي زَوَاله، فَالْأَصْل بَقَاؤُهُ، وَإِن كَانَ التَّرَدُّد فِي ثُبُوته، فَالْأَصْل عدم ثبوته. انْتهى محصلا.

Al-Khawārizmī stated in *al-Kāfī*, "The presumption of continuity is the last resort in a *fatwā*. If a *muftī* cannot find a ruling for an occurrence in the Qur'ān, Sunnah, consensus, or analogies, they should take the ruling from the presumption of continuity, whether negating [the ruling] or allowing it. If there is doubt about whether the ruling has been lifted, by default the ruling remains the same. If there is doubt about whether the ruling has been established, by default it has not." This has been summarised.

فمثال اسْتِصْحَاب نفي الحكم الشَّرْعِيّ عدم وجوب صَوْم شَوَّال وَغَيره من الشُّهُور سوى رَمَضَان، وَعدم صَلَاة سادسة مَكْتُوبَة، فَإِنَّا لَو فَرضنَا أَن الشَّرْع لم ينص على عدم ذَلِك، لَكَانَ الْعقل دَلِيلا عَلَيْهِ بطرِيق الِاسْتِصْحَاب الْمَذْكُور.

An example of presuming the continuity of a negated ruling is that fasting the month of Shawwāl and other months apart from Ramadan is not an obligation. Also, there is no sixth prayer. If we were to posit that the religion did not explicitly state those things, rational inference would indicate them, based on the presumption of continuity.

وَمِثَال التَّمَسُّك بِدَلِيل شَرْعِي لم يظْهر عَنهُ ناقل: اسْتِصْحَاب الْعُمُوم وَالنَّص حَتَّى يرد مُخَصص أَو نَاسخ، واستصحاب حكم ثَابت كالملك وشغل الذمَّة بِالْإِتْلَاف وَنَحْوه.

An example of holding fast to a religious evidence that has no apparent conflicting evidence is that one presumes the continuity of general wordings in texts, until there is a particularizing or abrogating text. An example of presuming the continuity of an established ruling is ownership[373] and financial liability due to destroying some property.[374]

---

373 [T] Meaning, if someone owns something, they are presumed to retain ownership until there is some evidence to show they do not own the item anymore. Refer to *Sharḥ Mukhtaṣar al-Rawḍah* (3/155).

374 [T] Meaning, if someone is known to owe another person or is known to be liable in destruction of property, they are presumed to continue to owe until there is evidence that shows that they have paid their dues. Ibid.

وَأما اسْتِصْحَاب حَال الْإِجْمَاع فِي مَحل الْخلاف - كالتمسك فِي عدم بطلَان صَلَاة الْمُتَيَمم عِنْد وجود المَاء بِالْإِجْمَاع على صِحَة دُخُوله فِيهَا، فيستصحب حَال تِلْكَ الْمصحَة فالأكثر أَن هَذَا لَيْسَ بِحجَّة، خلافًا للشَّافِعِيّ، وَابْن شاقلا من أَصْحَابنَا.

As for presuming the continuity of consensus in an issue that has differing views, such as holding to consensus to prove that a prayer that has been offered with *tayammum* is still valid after the presence of water, since the consensus is that when they began their prayer, it was valid. The majority did not consider this evidence, contrary to al-Shāfiʿī and Ibn Shāqillā, of our *aṣḥāb*.[375]

وَاعْلَم أَن الْمُسْتَدلّ على نفي الحكم كَقَوْلِه: مَا الْأَمر كَذَا، أَو لَيْسَ الْأَمر كَذَا، يلْزمه أَن يُقيم الدَّلِيل على صِحَة مدعاه، وَلَا يَكْفِيهِ مُجَرّد دَعْوَى النَّفْي.

Know, too, that if a person negates a ruling, such as by saying, "It is not as such," or, "The matter is not as so," they must provide evidence to prove their claim. They cannot merely make a claim of negation.

375 [T] Meaning, there is a difference of opinion on whether one who cannot find water and did *tayammum* may continue their prayer with only *tayammum* after water has been found. Someone may say, "We all agree that when they began their prayer with only *tayammum*, it was a valid entrance into prayer," and use that consensus as evidence to prove that continuing the prayer after the presence of water is valid.

الأصول المختلف فيها

On Disputed Evidences

لما فرغنا من الْكَلَام على الْأُصُول الْمُتَّفق عَلَيْهَا - وَهِي: الْكتاب وَالسّنة وَالْإِجْمَاع، والاستصحاب - أخذنَا فِي الْكَلَام على الْأُصُول الْمُخْتَلف فِيهَا وَهِي أَرْبَعَة: شرع من قبلنَا، وَقَول الصَّحَابِيّ وَالِاسْتِحْسَان والاستصلاح، فَقُلْنَا:

After discussing the evidences that are agreed on by all, namely, the Qur'ān, the Sunnah, consensus, and presumption of continuity, the time has come to discuss disputed evidences, namely: (i) Legislations of religions before ours. (ii) The statements of companions. (iii) Juristic preferences (*istiḥsān*). (iv) Public interests (*istiṣlāḥ*).

أما شرع من قبلنَا، فَإِنَّهُ يجوز أَن يتعبد نَبِي بشريعة نَبِي قبله عقلا، لِأَنهُ لَيْسَ بمحال، وَلَا يلْزم مِنْهُ محَال. وَكَانَ نَبينَا صلى الله عَلَيْهِ وَسلم قبل الْبعْثَة متعبدا فِي الْفُرُوع بشرع من قبله عِنْد القَاضِي والحلواني وَأَوْمَأَ إِلَيْهِ أَحْمد وَاخْتَارَ ابْن عقيل وَالْمجد: أنه كَانَ متعبدا بشريعة إِبْرَاهِيم عَلَيْهِ السَّلَام، وَلم يكن صلى الله عَلَيْهِ وَسلم على مَا كَانَ عَلَيْهِ قومه. قَالَ الإِمَام أَحْمد: من زعم ذَلِك فَقَوله سوء.

As for legislations of religions before ours: It is a rational possibility for a prophet to be tasked with worship according to the legislation of a previous prophet, since it is not impossible nor does it result in impossibilities. Before being sent as a prophet, our Prophet ﷺ was tasked with the laws of the legislations of those who came before him, according to al-Qāḍī and al-Ḥalwānī, and has been indicated to by Aḥmad. Ibn ʿAqīl and al-Majd opined that he was tasked with implementing the religion of Ibrāhīm ﵇ and was not adhering to the religion of his people. Al-Imām Aḥmad said, "Whoever claims such a thing has uttered a terrible statement."

وَبعد الْبعْثَة تعبد بشرع من قبله، وَنقل فِي (التَّحْرِير) هَذَا القَوْل عَن أَحْمد

وَالشَّافِعِيّ وَأَكْثر أصحابهما، وَالْحَنَفِيَّة والمالكية، وَمن ثمَّ كَانَ شرع من قبلنَا شرعا لنا مَا لم ينْسَخ عِنْد أَكثر أَصْحَابنَا وَغَيرهم. قَالَ القَاضِي وَغَيره: بِمَعْنى أَنه مُوَافق لَا متابع انْتهى.

After his despatch, the Prophet ﷺ was enjoined with worship according to previous legislations. In *al-Taḥrīr*, this view is quoted from Aḥmad and al-Shāfiʿī, as well as most of their students and adherents, the Ḥanafī scholars, and the Māliki scholars. Consequently, according to the majority of our *aṣḥāb* and others, the legislations sent to previous nations are also applicable to us, so long as they were not abrogated. Al-Qāḍī and others have stated that if that is the case, the rulings coincide, not that our rulings follow the legislations that occurred before.

لَكِن مَحل ذَلِك إِذا قطع بِأَنَّهُ شرع لمن قبلنَا إِمَّا بِكِتَاب، أَو بِخَبَر الصَّادِق، أَو بِنَقْل متواتر، فَأَما الرُّجُوع إِلَيْهِم أَو إِلَى كتبهمْ، فَلَا. وَقد أَوْمَأَ أَحْمد إِلَى هَذَا، وَمَعْنَاهُ لِابْنِ حمدَان. وَقَالَ الشَّيْخ تَقِيّ الدّين وَغَيره: وَيثبت أَيْضا بأخبار الْآحَاد عَن نبينَا صلى الله عَلَيْهِ وَسلم.

This is all contingent on ascertaining whether it is truly the legislation given to those before us, either through a scripture, an authentic report, or by a recurrent transmission. As for referring to them or their books, it is not allowed, as indicated to by Aḥmad and which has been conveyed by Ibn Ḥamdān. Al-Shaykh Taqī al-Dīn [ibn Taymiyyah] and others stated, "The legislations of those before us are also established through solitary reports from our Prophet ﷺ."[376]

وَأما قَول صَحَابِيّ لم يظْهر لَهُ مُخَالف، فَهُوَ حجَّة أَيْضا، يقدم على الْقيَاس، ويخص بِهِ الْعَام، وَهُوَ قَول مَالك وَبَعض الْحَنَفِيَّة، خلافًا لأبي الْخطاب، وَقَول الشَّافِعِي الْجَدِيد، وَعَن أَحْمد مَا يدل عَلَيْهِ وَهُوَ مَذْهَب الأشاعرة والمعتزلة والكرخي. وَلَا يخفى أَن الْكَلَام فِي قَول الصَّحَابِيّ إِذا كَانَ مَا قَالَه من مسَائِل الِاجْتِهَاد، أما إِذا لم يكن مِنْهَا، وَدلّ دَلِيل على التَّوْقِيف، فَلَيْسَ مِمَّا نَحن بصدده.

As for views of the companions: if there are no objections or divergent views

376 [T] *Al-Musawwadah* (p. 186).

[from other companions], it is evidence and is preferable to analogies. They are used to particularise general texts. This was the view of Mālik and some Ḥanafī scholars, but contrary to that of Abu 'l-Khaṭṭāb and al-Shāfiʿī in his "new *madhhab*." There are reports from Aḥmad that would indicate this, as well. It is also the position of the Ashʿarītes and the Muʿtazilites, as well as al-Karkhī. Obviously, this discussion is regarding the views of the companions if it is in discretionary matters. We are not discussing the case where they are not [discretionary] and there is evidence to suggest the statement they uttered is one that can only emanate from the Prophet ﷺ.[377]

وَالَّذِي يظْهر أَنه الْحق: أن مثل هَذَا لَيْسَ بِحجَّة، فَإِن الله لم يبْعَث إِلَى هَذِه الْأمة إِلَّا نبيها صلى الله عَلَيْهِ وَسلم، وَلَيْسَ لنا إِلَّا رَسُول وَاحِد، وَكتاب وَاحِد، وَجَمِيع الْأمة مأمورة بِاتِّبَاع كِتَابه وَسنة نبيه: وَلَا فرق بَين الصَّحَابَة وَمن بعدهمْ فِي ذَلِك. فَمن قَالَ: إِنَّهَا تقوم الْحجَّة فِي دين الله بِغَيْر كتاب الله وَسنة نبيه وَمَا يرجع إِلَيْهِمَا فقد قَالَ بِمَا لَا يثبت، وَأثبت فِي هَذِه الشَّرِيعَة الإسلامية مَا لم يَأْمر الله بِهِ، وَهَذَا أَمر عَظِيم، وَتقول بَالغ، فَإِن الحكم لفرد أَو أَفْرَاد من عباد الله بِأَن قَوْله أَو أَقْوَالهم حجَّة على الْمُسلمين يجب عَلَيْهِم الْعَمَل بهَا مِمَّا لَا يدان أَن الله عز وَجل بِهِ، وَلَا يحل لمُسلم الركون إِلَيْهِ، فَإِن هَذَا الْمقَام لم يكن إِلَّا لرسل الله لَا لغيرهم، وَلَو بلغ فِي الْعلم وَالدّين وَعظم الْمنزلَة أَي مبلغ.

What appears to be the truth in this issue is that such statements are not proof. Allah the Exalted only sent to this Ummah its Prophet ﷺ and we only have one Messenger and one Book. The entire Ummah is commanded to follow the Book of Allah and the Sunnah of His Prophet. There is no difference between the companions and those after them in this matter. Those who claim that evidence in the religion of Allah can emanate from something other than His Book, the Sunnah of His Prophet ﷺ, or something that draws its legitimacy from one of those two have claimed something that is unproven and has ascribed to this Islamic Religion what Allah has not commanded. This is a grave matter and an emphatic fabrication. To state that the views of an individual or some individual slaves of Allah are

377 [T] Because in the case that there is evidence to suggest that only the Prophet ﷺ could have uttered it, such as it being a matter of the unseen where only a Prophet ﷺ is given knowledge, the statement of the companion is held to be a transmission of a teaching of the Prophet ﷺ, and therefore, evidence.

evidences for other Muslims which they must then act on is something that one cannot take as a religion before Allah the Exalted, and it is not permissible for a Muslim to incline to such a view. Such a station was reserved for the messengers of Allah, and none else, no matter how high one has reached in knowledge, religiosity, and lofty ranks.

وَلَا شكّ أَن مقَام الصُّحْبَة مقَام عَظِيم، وَلَكِن ذَلِك فِي الْفَضِيلَة، وارتفاع الدرجَة، وعظمة الشَّأن، وَهَذَا مُسلم لَا شكّ فِيهِ، وَلَا تلازم بَين هَذَا، وَبَين جعل كل وَاحِد مِنْهُم بِمَنْزِلَة رَسُول الله صلى الله عَلَيْهِ وَسلم فِي حجية قَوْله، وإلزام النَّاس باتباعه، فَإِن ذَلِك مِمَّا لم يَأْذَن الله بِهِ وَلَا ثَبت عَنهُ فِيهِ حرف وَاحِد.

Undoubtedly, the rank of companionship to the Prophet is a lofty, honourable status. That, however, is in terms of lifting their status, raising their stature, and honouring their stations. This fact is undeniable. However, there is no correlation between this fact and giving each of them the status of Allah's Messenger ﷺ in that their views are evidences in and of themselves, and obligating the people to follow them. This is something that Allah the Exalted did not allow, nor is there a single letter from Allah's Book that would prove such a thing.

ثمَّ اعْلَم أَنه إِذا اخْتلف الصَّحَابَة، كَانَ عدم جَوَاز أَخذ الْمُجْتَهد بقول بَعضهم من غير دَلِيل من بَاب أولى.

Further, if the companions differ on a matter, it is all the greater reason to prohibit a *mujtahid* scholar from espousing one of their views without external supporting evidences.

وَأما الِاسْتِحْسَان، وَنسب القَوْل بِهِ إِلَى الْحَنَفِيَّة والحنابلة وَأنْكرهُ غَيرهم حَتَّى قَالَ الشَّافِعِي: من اسْتحْسنَ فقد شرع. قَالَه ابْن الْحَاجِب، ثمَّ قيل فِي تَعْرِيفه: إِنَّه دَلِيل ينقدح فِي نفس الْمُجْتَهد لَا يقدر على التَّعْبِير عَنهُ، وَهُوَ بِهَذَا التَّعْرِيف هوس، لِأَن مَا هَذَا شَأنه لَا يُمكن النّظر فِيهِ لتستبان صِحَّته. وَقَالَ فِي (التَّحْرِير): هُوَ الْعُدُول بِحكم الْمَسْأَلَة عَن نظائرها لدَلِيل شَرْعِي خَاص. وَكَلَام أَحْمد يَقْتَضِي أَنه: عدُول عَن مُوجب قِيَاس لدَلِيل أقوى. وَاخْتَارَ هَذَا أَبُو الْوَفَاء بن عقيل.

As for *istiḥsān*[378]: It has been attributed to Ḥanafī and Ḥanbalī scholars, but other scholars have rejected the concept altogether, to the point that al-Shāfiʿī stated, "Whoever performs *istiḥsān* has indeed legislated." This was stated by Ibn al-Ḥājib, and it was defined as, "An evidence that is embedded in the mind of the *mujtahid*, but they cannot express it." However, according to this definition, *istiḥsān* is madness, because it is something that cannot be researched to verify if it is accurate. In *al-Taḥrīr*, it defines *istiḥsān* as, "A ruling on an issue that departs from its equivalents due to a specific evidence."[379] The quotes from Aḥmad necessitate that it is a departure from the necessary ruling derived of an analogy, in favour of a stronger evidence. This definition was chosen by Abu 'l-Wafā ibn ʿAqīl.

وَعند الْحَنَفِيَّة يثبت بالأثر كالسلم وَبَقَاء صَوْم النَّاسِي وبالإجماع وبالضرورة. وَسموا مَا ضعف أَثَره قِيَاسا، وَالْقَوِي اسْتِحْسَانًا.

According to the Ḥanafī scholars, it is established through texts, as in the ruling of *salam* transactions[380] and the continuance of the fast of a forgetful person.[381] It is also established through consensus and necessity (*ḍarūrah*). If the effect of its cause is weak they referred to it as an analogy, and if it was strong, they referred to it as *istiḥsān*.

وَمَا ذكره فِي (التَّحْرِير) هُوَ أَجود مَا قيل فِيهِ، ومثاله قَول أبي الْخطاب فِي مَسْأَلَة الْعينَة: وَإِذا اشْترى مَا بَاعَ بِأَقَلّ مِمَّا بَاعَ قبل نقد الثّمن الأول لم يجز اسْتِحْسَانًا، وَجَاز قِيَاسا. فَالْحكم فِي نَظَائِر هَذِه الْمَسْأَلَة من الربويات الْجَوَاز، وَهُوَ الْقيَاس، لَكِن عدل بهَا عَن نظائرها بطرِيق الِاسْتِحْسَان، فمنعت. وَحَاصِل هَذَا يرجع إِلَى تَخْصِيص الدَّلِيل بِدَلِيل أقوى مِنْهُ فِي نظر الْمُجْتَهد.

---

378 [T] Note that the word, *istiḥsān*, comes from the root word, *ḥasan*, which means something good.

379 [T] *Taḥrīr al-Manqūl* (p. 327).

380 Ibn ʿAbbās reported that when the Prophet ﷺ came to Madīnah, they were paying one and two years in advance for fruits. So, the Prophet ﷺ said: "Those who paid in advance for fruits must do so for a specified measurement and weight, and for a specified time." This was reported by al-Bukhārī (4/355) and Muslim (1604).

381 Abu Hurayrah reported that the Prophet ﷺ said, **"If someone forgets and eats or drinks, he should continue his fast, for Allah the Exalted is the One who gave him the food or the drink."** Reported by al-Bukhārī (4/134) and Muslim (1155).

The definition mentioned in *al-Taḥrīr* is the most precise. An example of it is what Abu 'l-Khaṭṭāb stated on the topic of *ʿīnah* transactions, where he said, "If someone purchases what they sold for a lesser price than they sold it for, before receiving the amount of their first sale, it is not permissible, out of *istiḥsān*, though it is permissible through analogy." The ruling in such issues pertaining to usury is that they are permissible, based on *qiyās*. However, he departed from its equivalent rulings through use of *istiḥsān*, and thereby prohibited it. The summary of this entire concept is that *istiḥsān* is to particularize an evidence through use of a stronger evidence in the eyes of the *mujtahid* scholar.

وَقَالَ ابْن المعمار البغدادي: وَمِثَال الِاسْتِحْسَان مَا قَالَه أَحْمد رَضِي الله عَنهُ، أَنه يتَيَمَّم لكل صَلَاة اسْتِحْسَانًا، وَالْقِيَاس: إنه بِمَنْزِلَة المَاء حَتَّى يحدث.

Ibn al-Miʿmār al-Baghdādī stated, "An example of *istiḥsān* is when Aḥmad ﷺ said, 'One should perform ablution for each prayer, out of *istiḥsān*.' However, according to *qiyās*, a single *tayammum* should last one until they nullify their state of purity."[382]

وَقَالَ: يجوز شِرَاء أَرض السوَاد وَلَا يجوز بيعهَا، قيل لَهُ: فَكيف يشترى مِمَّن لَا يملك البيع؟ فَقَالَ: الْقيَاس هَكَذَا، وَإِنَّمَا هُوَ اسْتِحْسَان، وَلذَلِك يمْنَع من بيع الْمُصحف، وَيُؤمر بِشِرَائِهِ اسْتِحْسَانًا.

In another narration, he said, "It is permissible to purchase land of al-Sawād region,[383] but not permissible to sell it." It was said to him, "How can someone buy from a person who does not have the license to sell?" He replied, "That would be the analogue; however, this is *istiḥsān*." He also forbade selling of the *muṣḥaf* on the same grounds, but allowed for it to be purchased due to *istiḥsān*.[384]

وَأنت إِذا تَأَمَّلت الِاسْتِحْسَان الْمَنْسُوب إِلَى الإِمَام أَحْمد ترى مَعْنَاهُ: تَقْدِيم الدَّلِيل الشَّرْعِيّ أَو الْعقلِيّ لحسنه، وَمثل هَذَا يجب الْعَمَل بِهِ، لِأَن الْحسن مَا حسنه

382 [T] Refer to *al-Jāmiʿ li ʿUlūm al-Imām Aḥmad* (5/112).

383 [T] Regarding the Sawad region, Abu ʿUbayd stated, "It refers to the area between Mosul and Abadan in longitude and between the small river of al-Qādisiyyah and Halwan in latitude." Refer to *ʿAwn al-Maʿbūd* (8/194).

384 [T] Refer to *al-Jāmiʿ li ʿUlūm al-Imām Aḥmad* (5/112).

الشَّرْع، والقبيح مَا قبحه الشَّرْع، وَأمَا كَونه أَن يكون على مُخَالفَة الدَّلِيل - مثل أَن يكون الشَّيْء مَحْظُورًا بِدَلِيل شَرْعِي وَفِي عادات النَّاس الْعَمَل بِهِ - فَهَذَا لم يقل بِهِ أَحْمد وَلَا غيره، بل يحرم القَوْل بِهِ، وَيجب اتِّبَاع الدَّلِيل وَترك الْعَادة والرأي، سَوَاء كَانَ الدَّلِيل نصا أَو إِجْمَاعًا أَو قِيَاسا.

If you were to reflect on what *istiḥsān* meant to al-Imām Aḥmad, you would find that it is a preference of a religious or rational argument due its being recognised as good. Such evidences must be acted on, since the goodness of a thing is assigned by the legislation, and reprehensibility is also assigned by the legislation. As for *istiḥsān* being contrary to evidences, such as something being impermissible via religious evidences, but people still act on it as their customs, that is not what Aḥmad stated, nor did others provide such a view. Rather, such a view is impermissible. One must follow the evidences, be they divine texts, consensuses, or analogies, and must abandon all customs and outright rationalization.

وَأما الاستصلاح: فَهُوَ اتِّبَاع الْمصلحَة الْمُرْسلَة، فَإِن الشَّرْع أَو الْمُجْتَهد يطْلب صَلَاح الْمُكَلّفين بِاتِّبَاع الْمصلحَة الْمَذْكُورَة ومراعاتها، والمصلحة جلب نفع، أَو دفع ضَرَر. وَهِي متنوعة إِلَى ثَلَاثَة أَنْوَاع:

As for the concept of *istiṣlāḥ*, it means to follow undefined public interests, since the religion, and *mujtahid* scholars by extension, desire what is best for responsible humans by adhering and catering to public interests. The term *maṣlaḥah* refers to garnering some utility or repelling some harm. It is of three types:

أَولهَا: مَا شهد الشَّرْع بِاعْتِبَارِهِ، كاستفادة الحكم، وتحصيله من مَعْقُول دَلِيل شَرْعِي كالنص وَالْإِجْمَاع، وَيُسمى قِيَاسا كاستفادتنا تَحْرِيم شَحم الْخِنْزِير من تَحْرِيم لَحْمه الْمَنْصُوص عَلَيْهِ بِالْكتاب، واستفادتنا تَحْرِيم النَّبِيذ الْمُسكر من تَحْرِيم الْمَنْصُوص عَلَيْهِ بِالْكتاب وَالسّنة، مَعَ أَن النَّبِيذ مَنْصُوص على تَحْرِيمه مَعَ غَيره، بقوله عَلَيْهِ الصَّلَاة وَالسَّلَام: **«كل مُسكر خمر»** وَأَشْبَاه ذَلِك.

The first type: Those that the religion has certified and validated. This includes understanding of rulings and deducing them rationally from a religious evidence, such as a divine text or consensus. This type is known as *qiyās*. For example, we learn that the fat of a pig is prohibited because of the prohibition of its meat, which is mentioned in the Qur'ān. We also learn that intoxicating *nabīdh* is prohibited from the prohibition of other intoxicants in the Qur'ān and the Sunnah, though *nabīdh* in specific falls under the text which prohibits intoxicants, where the Prophet ﷺ said, **"Every intoxicant is alcohol,"**[385] and other similar issues.

ثَانِيهَا: مَا شهد الشَّرْع بِبُطْلَانِهِ من المصلح وَلم يعتبره، كَقَوْل من يَقُول: إِن الْمُوسر كالملك وَنَحْوه يتَعَيَّن عَلَيْهِ الصَّوْم فِي كَفَّارَة الوطء فِي رَمَضَان، وَلَا يُخَيّر بَينه وَبَين الْعتْق وَالْإِطْعَام، لِأَن فَائِدَة الْكَفَّارَة الزّجر عَن الْجِنَايَة على الْعِبَادَة، وَمثل هَذَا لَا يزجره الْعتْق وَالْإِطْعَام لِكَثْرَة مَالَهُ، فيسهل عَلَيْهِ أن يعْتق رقابا فِي قَضَاء شَهْوَته، وَقد لَا يسهل عَلَيْهِ صَوْم سَاعَة، فَيكون الصَّوْم أزْجر لَهُ. فَهَذَا وَأَمْثَاله ملغى غير مُعْتَبر، لِأَنهُ تَغْيِير للشَّرْع بِالرَّأْيِ، وَهُوَ غير جَائِز، وَلَو أَرَادَ الشَّرْع ذَلِك، لبينه أَو نبه عَلَيْهِ فِي حَدِيث الْأَعرَابِي أَو غَيره، إِذْ تَأْخِير الْبَيَان عَن وَقت الْحَاجة لَا يجوز.

The second type: Those that the religion has invalidated and has not deemed worthy of consideration. For example, some say that if a rich person—such as a king—has intercourse during the day in Ramadan while fasting and must expiate, he is only allowed to fast, and is not given the choice between fasting, freeing a slave, and feeding the poor. They claim that the purpose of the expiation is to deter them from their transgression against the worship of fasting, and a rich person is not deterred by freeing a slave or feeding the poor, due to his excess wealth. Consequently, it is quite easy for them to free slaves to expiate their lust, but it is possibly not easy for them to fast for an hour, and as such, fasting is more of a deterrent for them. This, and other similar rationalisations, are null and void, because it is an alteration to the religion with mere rationalisation, and that is impermissible. If the religion wanted to instate such differentiations, it would have indicated it in the ḥadīth of the Bedouin man[386] or in other texts, since it is not possible

---

385 Reported by Muslim (2003).

386 He is referring to the ḥadīth which Abu Hurairah reported, where a man came to the Prophet ﷺ and said, "O Messenger of Allah, I have been destroyed." The Prophet ﷺ responded, **"What has happened to you?"** He said, "I have had intercourse with my wife while fasting." The Prophet ﷺ said, **"Do you have a slave you can free?"** The man said, "No." The Prophet ﷺ said, **"Can you fast two straight months?"**

for necessary clarifications to be delayed beyond the time they are needed.

ثَالِثِهَا: مَا لم يشْهد لَهُ الشَّرْع بِبُطْلَان وَلَا بِاعْتِبَار معِين، وَهَذَا النَّوْع يتنوع إِلَى ثَلَاثَة أَقسَام:

The third type: Those that the religion has neither invalidated nor approved in specific. This, too, is categorised into three types:

أَولهَا: التحسين الْوَاقِع موقع التحسين والتزيين، ورعاية حسن المناهج فِي الْعِبَادَات والمعاملات، وَحسن الْأَدَب فِي السِّيرَة بَين النَّاس، كصيانة الْمَرْأَة عَن مُبَاشرَة عقد نِكَاحهَا بِإِقَامَة الْوَلِيّ مباشرا لذَلِك، لِأَن الْمَرْأَة لَو باشرت عقد نِكَاحهَا لَكَانَ ذَلِك مِنْهَا مشعرا بِمَا لَا يَلِيق بالمروءة من غَلَبَة القحبة، وَقلة الْحيَاء، وتوقان نَفسهَا إِلَى الرِّجَال، فمنعت من ذَلِك حملا لِلْخلقِ على أحسن المناهج وأجمل السّير.

First[387]: Complementary interests that simply serve to complete and beautify something, such as having good conduct in worship and transactions and good treatment of others. Examples of this type are protecting women from directly overseeing their own marriage contracts by giving her a guardian that can do it for her. The reason is that if a woman formulates her own marriage contract, that could show a lack of womanly behaviour such as the preponderance of shamelessness, lack of modesty, and a yearning for men. As such, she was prevented from overseeing her contract in order to encourage her to maintain the best of conduct and most beautiful of behaviour.

The man said, "No." The Prophet ﷺ said, **"Can you feed sixty poor people?"** The man said, "No." The Prophet ﷺ kept silent and while we were in that state, a big basket full of dates was brought to him. He asked, "Where is the questioner?" He replied, "I (am here)." The Prophet ﷺ said, **"Take this (basket of dates) and give it in charity."** The man said, "Should I give it to a person poorer than I? By Allah; there is no family between its (i.e. Madīnah's) two mountains poorer than mine." The Prophet ﷺ smiled till his canine teeth became visible and then said, **"Feed your family with it."** Reported by al-Bukhārī (4/141) and Muslim (1111).

387 [T] This first type is known as, *taḥsīniyyāt*, pl. of *taḥsīni*. *Taḥsīn* means to beautify and complement something. As such, these are things that are not necessarily needed and definitely not necessities, but if one has them, his overall quality of life improves. Refer to *Sharḥ Mukhtaṣar al-Rawḍah* (3/206), *al-Taḥbīr Sharḥ al-Taḥrīr* (7/3387), and *Maqāṣid al-Sharī'ah al-Islāmiyyah* by al-Imām al-Ṭāhir ibn 'Āshūr (3/243).

ثَانِيهَا: الحاجي، وَهُوَ الَّذِي تَدْعُو إِلَيْهِ الْحَاجة، كتسليط الْوَلِيّ على نِكَاح الصَّغِيرَة لحَاجَة تَقْيِيد الكفء خشيَة أَن يفوت، فَإِن ذَلِك مِمَّا يحْتَاج إِلَيْهِ، وَيحصل بحصوله نفع، وَيلْحق بفواته ضَرَر، وَإِن لم يكن ضَرُورِيًّا قَاطعا، وَنسبَة الأول إِلَى هَذَا كنسبة الزِّينَة من الطِّبّ إِلَى بَاقِي كتبه على مَا عرف فِيهِ.

Second: These are referred to as *ḥājīyyāt*, which mean things that are needed. Examples are guardians who are tasked to marry their young daughters off; they are needed to choose suitable husbands, so as not to lose that important interest. This is something needed; its presence results in benefit and its loss results in harm. These things are not dire necessities. The relation of the first category to this one is like the relation between beautification and medicine.

وَلَا يجوز للمجتهد التَّمَسُّك بِمُجَرَّد هذَيْن الْقسمَيْنِ الْمَذْكُورين، وهما التحسيني والحاجي، بل لَا بُد لَهُ من شَاهد من جِنْسهَا يشْهد لَهُ بِاعْتِبَار أحكامهما، لِئَلا يكون ذَلِك وضعا للشَّرْع بِالرَّأْيِ، وَلِأَن اعتبارهما بِدُونِ شَاهد يُؤَدِّي إِلَى الِاسْتِغْنَاء عَن بعث الرُّسُل، ويجر النَّاس إِلَى دين البراهمة الْقَائِلين: لَا حَاجَة لنا إِلَى الرُّسُل، لِأَن الْعقل كَاف لنا فِي التَّأْدِيب وَمَعْرِفَة الْأَحْكَام، إِذا مَا حسنه الْعقل أتيناه، وَمَا قبحه اجتنبناه، وَمَا لم يقْض فِيهِ بِحسن وَلَا قبح فعلنَا مِنْهُ الضَّرُورِيّ، وَتركنَا الْبَاقِي احْتِيَاطًا. والتمسك بِهَذَيْنِ الْقسمَيْنِ من الْمَصَالح من غير شَاهد لَهما بِالِاعْتِبَارِ يُؤَدِّي إِلَى مثل ذَلِك وَنَحْوه فَيكون بَاطِلا.

It is not permissible for the *mujtahid* scholar to only grasp onto the two previous notions, namely, the *taḥsīnī* and the *ḥājī*. Rather, there must be evidence of the same genus that would testify to the validity of their rulings. Otherwise, one would legislate through mere rationalisation. Believing in [*taḥsīnīyyāt* and *ḥājīyyāt*] without evidence would lead to self-sufficiency and the redundancy of sending messengers. It would lead people to the religion of Brāhmins who state that they have no need for messengers, since mere rationalisation is enough to regulate one's actions and to learn rulings. They claim that anything the intellect finds good is allowed, and whatever the intellect finds reprehensible, they avoid. If the mind cannot discern between the inherent goodness or reprehensibility, they only do it inasmuch as it is necessary, and the rest is abandoned out of caution. Adhering to the two previous types of *maṣāliḥ* without evidence that would grant them legitimacy leads to such beliefs, making it invalid and falsehood.

الْقسم الثَّالِث: مَا كَانَ من ضَرُورِيَّة سياسة الْعلم وبقائه وانتظام أَحْوَاله، وَهُوَ مَا عرف الْتِفَات الشَّرْع إِلَيْهِ، والعناية بِهِ، كالضروريات الْخمس؛ وَهُوَ حفظ الدّين بقتل الْمُرْتَد، والداعية إِلَى الردة، وعقوبة المبتدع الدَّاعِي إِلَى الْبِدْعَة، وَحفظ الْعقل بِحَدّ السكر، وَحفظ النَّفس بِالْقصاصِ، وَحفظ النّسَب بِحَدّ الزِّنَى المفضي إِلَى تضييع الْأَنْسَاب باختلاط الْمِيَاه، وَحفظ الْعرض بِحَدّ الْقَذْف، وَحفظ المَال بِقطع يَد السَّارِق.

Third: Things that are necessary for the function, continuance, and organisation of society. These are things that are known to have been given attention by legislation. Examples are the [Six] Universals[388]: (i) Protection of religion. Examples include capital punishment for apostates and promoters of apostasy, and punishments of heretics who promote their heresies. (ii) Protection of intellect. An example is the penalty for drinking alcohol. (iii) Protection of life. An example is the law of retribution. (iv) Protection of lineage. An example is the penalty for fornication and adultery, which lead to the loss of lineages by the mixture of seminal fluids. (v) Protection of reputation. An example is the penalty for slander. (vi) Protection of wealth. An example is the penalty of cutting the thief's hand.

هَذَا وَاخْتلف فِي حجية الْمصَالح الْمُرْسلَة فَذهب أَصْحَابنَا إِلَى اعْتِبَارهَا على مَا أسلفناه، وَقَالَ مَالك باعتبارها، وَعرفهَا ابْن الْحَاجِب الْمَالِكِي وَغيره بِأَنَّهَا: مصَالح لَا يشْهد لَهَا أصل بِالِاعْتِبَارِ فِي الشَّرْع وَإِن كَانَت على سنَن الْمصَالح، وتلقتها الْعُقُول بِالْقبُولِ. وَالْحق مَا سلكه أَصْحَابنَا.

Note, too, that the scholars have differed on whether undefined public interests (*maṣlaḥah mursalah*) are evidence. Our *aṣḥāb* have deemed them worthy of consideration, as previously stated. Mālik also considered them evidence. Ibn al-Ḥājib, the Māliki scholar, and others defined them as, "Public interests not specifically outlined within legislation, though they

388 [T] The *shaykh* said, "Five universals," but then proceeded to enumerate six universals.

are consistent with the interests [preserved in religion], and intellects receive them with acceptance."[389] The truth is what our *aṣḥāb* have stated.

تَنْبِيه: فرق الْقَائِلُونَ بالمصالح الْمُرْسلَة بَينهَا وَبَين الْقيَاس بِأَن الْقيَاس يرجع إِلَى أصل معِين، وَهَذِه لَا ترجع إِلَى أصل معِين، قَالُوا: رَأينَا الشَّارِع اعتبرها فِي مَوَاضِع من الشَّرِيعَة، فاعتبرناها حَيْثُ وجدت، لعلمنا أَن جِنْسهَا مَقْصُود لَهُ، وَقَالَ الطوفي: الرَّاجِح الْمُخْتَار اعْتِبَار الْمصلحَة الْمُرْسلَة. وَفصل هَذَا النَّوْع فِي شَرحه على (مُخْتَصر الرَّوْضَة) تَفْصِيلًا حسنا.

Note: Those who affirmed *maṣlaḥah mursalah* have differentiated between it and analogies by stating that analogies are based on a particular foundational evidence. *Maṣāliḥ*, however, are not. Scholars stated that they found the Legislator has given consideration to [these public interests] at various times in legislation. As such, scholars have given consideration to them whenever they exist, since the genus [of public interests] is found to be a purpose of legislation. Al-Ṭūfī stated, "The veracious view, and the one chosen, is that undefined public interests are worthy of consideration."[390] He explained this concept in depth and very nicely in his explanation of his own summation of *Rawḍat al-Nāẓir*.

خَاتِمَة لهَذِهِ الْأُصُول يذكر فِيهَا أصولا مُخْتَلفا فِيهَا زِيَادَة على الْأُصُول الْأَرْبَعَة الْمُتَقَدّمَة:

To conclude this section, there are a number of other evidences that have been differed on, in addition to the four ones previously mentioned:

أَولهَا: سد الذرائع، وَهُوَ قَول مَالك وأصحابنا، وَهُوَ مَا ظَاهره مُبَاح ويتوصل بِهِ إِلَى محرم، وأباحه أَبُو حنيفَة وَالشَّافِعِيّ. وَمَعْنَاهُ عِنْد الْقَائِل بِهِ يرجع إِلَى إِبْطَال الْحِيَل، وَلذَلِك أنكر الْمُتَأَخّرُونَ من الْحَنَابِلَة على أبي الْخطاب وَمن تَابعه عقد بَاب فِي كتاب الطَّلَاق يتَضَمَّن الْحِيلَة على تَخْلِيص الْحَالِف من يَمِينه فِي بعض الصُّور، وجعلوه من بَاب الْحِيَل الْبَاطِلَة.

389 [T] Refer to *Sharḥ Mukhtaṣar al-Muntahā* (2/273).
390 [T] *Sharḥ Mukhtaṣar al-Rawḍah* (3/211).

First: *Sādd al-dharā'iʿ* (obstruction of means): This is believed to be evidence according to Mālik and our *aṣḥāb*. It is defined as something apparently lawful but which leads to prohibited things. Abu Ḥanīfah and al-Shāfiʿī allowed for them. To those who believe in this concept, it goes back to negation of ploys and stratagems intended to legalise otherwise unlawful things. This is why the later-day Ḥanbalī jurists censured Abu 'l-Khaṭṭāb and those who followed him for placing a section within the Chapter of Divorce consisting of stratagems that can be used to absolve a person who gave a right-hand oath from having to fulfill it in some scenarios. The later-day Ḥanbalī jurists considered them to be invalid ploys.

قَالَ نجم الدّين الطوفي في (شرح مُخْتَصر الرَّوْضَة): وَقد صنف شَيخنَا تَقِيّ الدّين أَبُو الْعَبَّاس أَحْمد ابن تَيْمِية رَحْمَة الله عَلَيْهِ كتابا بناه على بطلَان نِكَاح الْمُحَلّل، وأدرج فِيهِ جمع قَوَاعِد الْحِيَل، وَبَين بُطْلَانهَا على وَجه لَا مزِيد عَلَيْهِ. انْتهى.

Najm al-Dīn al-Ṭūfī stated in *Sharḥ Mukhtaṣar al-Rawḍah*, "Our teacher, Taqī al-Dīn Abu 'l-ʿAbbās Aḥmad ibn Taymiyyah authored a book to invalidate the *taḥlīl* marriages[391] wherein he mentioned all maxims pertaining to legal ploys, clarifying they are invalid, and did so in the utmost fashion."[392]

قلت: وَقد سلك مسلكه صَاحبه شمس الدّين مُحَمَّد ابْن قيم الجوزية فِي كِتَابه (إعْلَام الموقعين) فشن الْغَارة على الْحِيَل وَأَهْلهَا، وحذا بذلك حَذْو شَيْخه، فرحم الله من يصدع بِالْحَقِّ.

His student, Shams al-Dīn Muḥammad ibn Qayyim al-Jawzīyyah took a similar route in his book *Iʿlām al-Muwaqqiʿīn*, launching an attack on legal ploys and those who employ them. In doing so, he emulated his teacher. May Allah the Exalted have mercy on those who utter the truth strongly.

وَقَالَ موفق الدّين الْمَقْدِسِي فِي (الْمُغنِي): والحيل كلهَا مُحرمَة لَا تجوز فِي شَيْء من الدّين، وَهِي أَن يظهر اعتقادا مُبَاحا يُرِيد بِهِ محرما، مخادعة وتوصلا

391 [T] A *taḥlīl* marriage is one where a ploy is used, so that a husband who is regretful of divorcing his wife thrice agrees with another man to marry his wife, then divorce her thrice so that she may be lawful for him once more, after her waiting period is over. The Prophet ﷺ cursed the one performing the *taḥlīl* marriage and the one who it is performed for. Refer to *Sharḥ al-Muntahā* (2/667).
392 [T] *Sharḥ Mukhtaṣar al-Rawḍah* (3/214).

إِلَى فعل مَا حرم الله، واستباحة محظوراته، أَو إِسْقَاط وَاجِب، أَو دفع حق. قَالَ أيوب السّخْتِيَانِيّ: إنهم ليخادعون الله كَمَا يخادعون صَبيا. ثمَّ قَالَ الْمُوفق: إِن الله سُبْحَانَهُ وَتَعَالَى عذب أمة بحيلة احتالوها، فمسخهم قردة وَخَنَازِير، وَسَمَّاهُمْ معتدين، وَجعل ذَلِك نكالا وموعظة لِلْمُتقين، ليتعظوا بهم، ويمتنعوا من فعل أمثالهم.

Muwaffaq al-Dīn al-Maqdisī stated in *al-Mughnī*, "All legal ploys are forbidden and may not be used in any religious matters. A legal ploy is when someone forms a contract[393] that is apparently lawful, but intends to use it for an unlawful matter. By doing so, they are attempting to deceive and use that to perform an action made unlawful by Allah, to legalise what He made illegal, to absolve themselves of an obligation, or to emancipate themselves from fulfilling some right. Ayyūb al-Sikhtiyānī stated, 'They attempt to deceive Allah, as though they are deceiving a child!' [...] Allah punished an entire nation for their ploys, disfiguring them by making them into monkeys and pigs. He referred to them as being transgressors, and made their punishment exemplary and an admonishment to the pious, that they may take heed from their outcome and avoid emulating them.[394]

ثَانِيهَا: الإلهام، اخْتَارَهُ جمَاعَة من الْأُصُولِيِّينَ الْمُتَأَخِّرين، مِنْهُم الفخر الرازي فِي تَفْسِيره عِنْد كَلَامه على أَدِلَّة الْقبْلَة، وَابْن الصّلاح فِي فَتَاوَاهُ قَالَ: وَمن علامته أن ينشرح لَهُ الصَّدْر وَلَا يُعَارضهُ معَارض آخر. وَقَالَ: إلهام خاطر الْحق من الْحق. انْتهى.

Second: Inspiration: Some later-day legal theorists believed inspiration to be evidence, and among them was Fakhr al-Dīn al-Razi in his exegesis when speaking about the evidences for the *Qiblah*. Ibn al-Ṣalāḥ stated in his rulings, "One of its signs is that the chest feels ease and there are no other evidences that conflict with it." He also said, "Inspiration given to a true conscience is truth."[395]

---

393 [T] This is (اعتقادا) in the text, but I have based the translation on the wording from *al-Mughnī* (4/43) as (عقدا).

394 [T] *Al-Mughnī* (4/43). Note that the printed version of *al-Madkhal* has some scribal errors when comparing to the printed copy of *al-Mughnī*. Where there are discrepancies, I gave preference to the printed version of *al-Mughnī*.

395 [T] *Fatāwā Ibn al-Ṣalāḥ* (1/196).

قلت: وَهَذَا المسلك سرى للْقَوْم من جِهَة المتصوفة، وَلَو فتح بَابه، لَأَدَّى إِلَى مفاسد كَثِيرَة، ولكان للمتدلسين مدْخل لإفساد أَكثر الشَّرْع. فَالصَّوَاب أَن لَا يلْتَفت إِلَيْهِ، وإلا لادعى كثير مِنْهُم إِثْبَات مَا يلذ لَهُم بالإلهام والكشف، فكَانَ وَحيا زَائِدا على مَا أُوحِي إِلَى مُحَمَّد صلى الله عَلَيْهِ وَسلم، ولادعى المخرفون شركته فِي رسَالَته.

I say: A number of Ṣūfīs have taken this path, and if its door were opened, it would lead to many negative results, including giving an opportunity for frauds to corrupt most of the religion. The truth is that inspiration should not be given any attention. Otherwise, many would claim to establish things in the religion according to what pleases them, and use inspiration as evidence, making it an additional revelation to what was sent to Muḥammad ﷺ. Also, many believers in superstitions would claim partnership [with Muḥammad ﷺ] in his message.

ثَالِثهَا: ذكر جمَاعَة من أهل الْعلم - مِنْهُم أَبُو إِسْحَاق الإسْفِرَايِينِيّ - أَن من رأى النَّبِي صلى الله عَلَيْهِ وَسلم فِي الْمَنَام وَأمره بِأَمْر يلْزمه الْعَمَل بِهِ، وَيكون قَوْله حجَّة. وَقَالَ الْجُمْهُور: لَا يكون حجَّة، وَلَا يثبت بِهِ حكم شَرْعِي، وَإِن كَانَت رُؤْيَته صلى الله عَلَيْهِ وَسلم حَقًا، والشيطان لَا يتَمَثَّل بِهِ، لَكِن النَّائِم لَيْسَ من أهل التَّحَمُّل للرواية لعدم حفظه. وقيل: إِنَّه يعْمل بِهِ مَا لم يُخَالف شرعا ثَابتا، وَهَذَا القَوْل هُوَ والعدم سَوَاء، لِأَن الْعَمَل يكون بِمَا ثَبت من الشَّرْع لَا بِهِ.

Third: Seeing the Prophet ﷺ in a dream: A number of scholars, including Abu Isḥāq al-Isfarāyīnī, claimed that if someone sees the Prophet ﷺ in a dream and the Prophet ﷺ commands them to do something, it is an obligation to fulfill the commandment, and it is evidence. The majority said that it is not evidence nor does it establish a religious ruling, despite one's seeing of the Prophet ﷺ in a dream being truth, since the devil cannot take his form. However, a sleeping person is not one fit to receive narrations due to lack of memory. It was also stated that anything that does not contradict an established religious ruling should be acted on. However, this last opinion might as well not exist, since if one acts on it, they would be acting on something established through religious evidences, not through the dream.

ثمَّ لَا يخفاك أَن الشَّرْع الَّذِي شَرعه الله لنا على لِسَان نبينَا، قد كمله الله لنا وَقَالَ: ﴿الْيَوْمَ أَكْمَلْتُ لَكُمْ دِينَكُمْ﴾ [الْمَائِدَة: ٣].

Further, it is not unknown to you that the religion that Allah the Exalted legislated via our Prophet is complete. Allah the Exalted completed it, and said: **{Today I have perfected your faith for you.}** [Qur'ān 5:3]

وَلم يأت دَلِيل على أَن رُؤْيَته صلى الله عَلَيْهِ وَسلم فِي النّوم بعد مَوته، إِذا قَالَ فِيهَا بقول، أَو فعل فِيهَا فعلا يكون دَلِيلا وَحجَّة، بل قَبضه الله إِلَيْهِ بعد أَن كمل لهَذِهِ الْأمة مَا شَرعه لَهَا على لِسَانه، وَلم يبْق بعد ذَلِك حَاجَة للأمة فِي أَمر دينهَا، وَقد انْقَطَعت الْبعْثَة لتبليغ الشَّرَائِع وتبيينها بِالْمَوْتِ، وَإِن كَانَ رَسُولا حَيا وَمَيتًا صلى الله عَلَيْهِ وَسلم وَبِهَذَا تعلم أَنا لَو قدرنَا ضبط النَّائِم لم يكن مَا رَآهُ من قَوْله صلى الله عَلَيْهِ وَسلم أَو فعله - حجَّة عَلَيْهِ، وَلَا على غَيره من الْأمة.

There is no evidence in the religion that would suggest that if a person sees the Prophet ﷺ after his death and he says or does something, that it constitutes evidence and proof. Rather, Allah the Exalted took the life of Muḥammad after He finalised the legislation for the Ummah through him. After that, there is nothing more needed by the Ummah in matters of their religion. The sending of Muḥammad ﷺ, which was meant for instruction of legislations, has ended with his death, even though he is a messenger in his life and remains so after his death. As such, it becomes clear that even if we were to suppose the sleeping person precisely memorised the statements or actions of the Prophet ﷺ in the dream, it would be evidence for that one person, not for the entirety of the Ummah.

تَتِمَّة فِي قَوَاعِد عَامَّة ذكرهَا تَقِيّ الدّين الفتوحي فِي (أُصُوله).

Note: There are a number of general legal maxims mentioned by Taqī al-Dīn al-Futūḥī in his book on legal theories that are worthy of discussion.

لَا يرفع الْيَقِين بِالشَّكِّ، فَلَو شكّ فِي امْرَأَة هَل تزَوجهَا أم لَا؟ لم يكن لَهُ وَطْؤُهَا استصحابا لحكم التَّحْرِيم إِلَى أَن يتَحَقَّق تزَوجه بهَا، قلت: وَهَذَا من فروع الِاسْتِصْحَاب.

Certainty is not eliminated through doubt. If a person was doubtful if he married a woman, he may not have intercourse with her due to the continuity of the default prohibition, until he ascertains whether he married her. This is an issue that branches off the discussions on the presumption of continuity.

الضَّرَر لَا يَزُول بِضَرَر آخر.

Harms are not removed through other harms.

الضرورات تبيح الْمَحْظُورَات.

Necessities grant allowance to prohibited matters.

الْمَشَقَّة تجلب التَّيْسِير.

Difficulty results in ease.

دَرْء الْمَفَاسِد أولى من جلب الْمصَالح.

Prevention of harm is preferable to garnering utility.

ودرء الْمفْسدَة الْعليا أولى من دَرْء غَيرهَا.

Prevention of the more harmful thing is preferable to prevention of other [less harmful] things.

وَمن الْقَوَاعِد الْفِقْهِيَّة أَيْضا: الْعَادة محكمَة، وَهَذَا معنى قَول الْأُصُولِيِّينَ: الْوَصْف الْمُعَلل بِهِ قد يكون من مقتضيات الْعرف، وَمِنْه فِي بَاب التَّخْصِيص: تَخْصِيص الْعُمُوم بِالْعَادَةِ، وَحَاصِله أَنه كل فعل رتب عَلَيْهِ الحكم، وَلَا ضَابِط لَهُ فِي الشَّرْع، وَلَا فِي اللُّغَة، كإحياء الْموَات، والحرز فِي السّرقَة، وَالأكل من بَيت الصّديق، وَمَا يعد قبضا وإيداعا وَإِعْطَاء وهدية وغصبا، وَالْمَعْرُوف فِي المعاشرة، وانتفاع الْمُسْتَأْجر بِمَا جرت بِهِ الْعَادة وأمثال ذَلِك مِمَّا هُوَ كثير.

Customs are authoritative. This is what the legal theorists mean when they refer to an attribute that is described as the cause [for the ruling] being an outcome of customs. It is also used in particularization in cases where generalities are qualified by customs. In summary, this rule refers to every action that has a ruling but no specific outline in religion or language. Examples include cultivating wastelands, containers in laws pertaining to thievery, eating at a friend's house, and what is considered collecting money, entrusting others with money, giving gifts, usurpation, as well as what constitutes good conduct in marital relationships and the customary ways a renter is allowed to use the property. There are many such examples.

وَمن الْقَوَاعِد: جعل الْمَعْدُوم كالموجود احْتِيَاطًا كالمقتول تورث عَنهُ الدِّيَة، وَإِنَّمَا تجب بِمَوْتِهِ، وَلَا تورث عَنهُ إِلَّا إِذا دخلت دُخُولهَا فِي ملك، فَيقدر وجودهَا قبل مَوته.

A nonexistent thing is treated like an existing thing out of caution. For example, if a person is murdered, the wergild that is offered in expiation for the murder is inheritable by their offspring. However, the wergild only becomes an obligation for the murderer in the case that the person murdered actually dies, and if that is the case, only things that were within the ownership of the deceased can be inherited. To circumvent this, the wergild was treated as though it existed prior to the person's death [so that the inheritors can receive the amount].

وَمِنْهَا إدارة الْأُمُور فِي الْأَحْكَام على قَصدهَا، كَالصَّلَاةِ لَا تصح إِلَّا بقصدها، بنيتها وَغَيرهَا من الْأَحْكَام كَذَلِك هَذَا.

In determining rulings, things are judged by the intent behind them. For example, a prayer is invalid without its proper intention. There are many other rulings to elucidate this maxim.

وَلما أنجزنا القَوْل فِي الْكتاب وَالسّنة وَالْإِجْمَاع، ولواحقها وَالْأُصُول الْمُخْتَلف بهَا سوى الْقيَاس، شرعنا بِذكرِهِ فَقُلْنَا.

Since we have concluded discussions on Qur'ān, Sunnah, and consensus, as well as the ancillary evidences that pertain to them, and those differed on except for analogy, it is without further ado that we discuss it:

الأَصْل الخَامِس القِيَاس

The Fifth Foundational Principle: Analogy

الْقيَاس فِي اللُّغَة: التَّقْدِير، نَحْو: قست الثَّوْب بالذراع، أَي: قدرته بِهِ. وَفِي الِاصْطِلَاح: مُسَاوَاة فرع الأَصْل فِي عِلّة حكمه، فَشَمَلَ هَذَا التَّعْرِيف الأَصْل وَالْفرع وَالْعلَّة وَالْحكم.

Linguistically, the term *qiyās* refers to estimation. For example, one can say that they estimated the length of a garment by using a cubit measurement. In religious terminology, it is when a subsidiary matter shares equivalence with its basis[396] in the cause for the ruling. This definition encompasses the original ruling, the new case, the cause of the ruling, and the ruling itself.

وَنبهَ على أَن الْمُرَاد بالفرع مَحل الحكم الْمَطْلُوب إِثْبَاته فِيهِ، وبالأصل مَحل الحكم الْمَعْلُوم، وَبِذَلِك انْتَفَى اعْتِرَاض من يزْعم أَن هَذَا التَّعْرِيف دوري. نعم يلْزم الدّور لَو أُرِيد بالفرع الْمَقِيس، وبالأصل الْمَقِيس عَلَيْهِ. وتحقيقه: أَن الْمُرَاد بهما ذَات الأَصْل وَالْفرع، وَالْمَوْقُوف على الْقيَاس وَصفا الفرعية والأصلية.

The meaning of "the new case" is the thing that requires a ruling. The meaning of "the original ruling" is the ruling that is already known. By understanding those two clauses, it becomes clear that the objection to this definition which claims it is circular is invalid. However, it is only circular if "the subsidiary matter" is referring to the actual issue the analogy is being applied to, and if "the precedent" is what it is analogous to. Therefore, the intentions behind the two expressions are the actual subsidiary matter and the actual precedent, both of which derive the descriptions of being "the subsidiary matter" and "the precedent" from the actual analogy that is being made.

396 [T] The precedent here being the original text that the subsidiary shares with. Namely, Qur'ān, Sunnah, and consensus.

وللعلماء فِي تَعْرِيف الْقيَاس عِبَارَات كَثِيرة، وحاصلها يرجع إِلَى أنه اعْتِبَار الْفَرْع بِالْأَصْلِ. وَعرف أَبُو الْعَبَّاس أَحْمد ابن تَيْمِية فِي بعض رسائله الْقيَاس بقوله: هُوَ الْجمع بَين المتماثلين وَالْفرق بَين الْمُخْتَلفين: الأول قِيَاس الطَّرْد وَالثَّانِي: قِيَاس الْعَكْس. انْتهى.

The scholars have many ways of defining *qiyās*, though all of them lead to consideration of the subsidiary case in light of the original ruling. Abu 'l-'Abbās Aḥmad ibn Taymiyyah defined it in his writings as, "It is to gather between two equivalent things and to differentiate between two inequivalent things. The first is known as analogy by co-extension (*qiyās al-ṭard*) and the other is known as analogy by co-exclusion (*qiyās al-'aks*)."[397]

وَاعْلَم أَن الْقيَاس يَنْقَسِم أقساما باعتبارات:

Qiyās can be categorised in various ways.

أَحدهَا: يَنْقَسِم إِلَى جلي وخفي، فالجلي: مَا كَانَت الْعلَّة الجامعة فِيهِ بَين الأَصْل وَالْفرع منصوصة، أَو مجمعا عَلَيْهَا، أَو مَا قطع فِيهِ بِنَفْي الْفَارِق كإلحاق الْأمة بِالْعَبدِ فِي تَقْوِيم النَّصِيب. والخفي: وَهُوَ مَا كَانَت الْعلَّة فِيهِ مستنبطة.

One way it can be categorised is into obvious and subtle analogies: An obvious analogy (*al-qiyās al-jalī*) is where the *ratio legis* that gathers the precedent and the new case is plainly stated in the divine text, is agreed on via consensus, or the differentia between the two cases can categorically be denied, such as in the case of the equivalence of a male and female slave in determining the share a partner has. A subtle analogy (*al-qiyās al-khafī*) is one where the *ratio legis* is deduced.

ثَانِيهَا: يَنْقَسِم إِلَى مُؤثر وَإِلَى ملائم، فَالْأول: مَا كَانَت فِيهِ الْعلَّة الجامعة ثَابِتَة بِنَصّ أَو بِإِجْمَاع، أَو كَانَ الْوَصْف الْجَامِع فِيهِ قد أثر عينه فِي عين الحكم، أَي فِي جنسه، أَو جنسه فِي جنس الحكم. وَالثَّانِي: مَا أثر جنس الْعلَّة فِيهِ فِي جنس الحكم.

It can also be categorised into effective (*mu'athir*) and appropriate

397 [T] *Majmū' al-Fatāwā* (9/239).

(*mulā'im*): (i) An effective analogy (*al-qiyās al-mu'athir*) is one where the *ratio legis* that equivalates is established via a divine text or a consensus and where the equivalating attribute in particular has directly affected the individual instance[398] or genus[399] of the ruling. Or, the genus [of the equivalating attribute] has directly affected the genus of the ruling. (ii) An appropriate analogy (*al-qiyās al-mulā'im*) is one where the genus of the *ratio legis* has affected the genus of the ruling.[400]

ثَالِثهَا: أَن الْقيَاس إِمَّا أَن يُصَرح فِيهِ بِالْعِلَّةِ، أَو بِمَا يلازمها، أَو لم يُصَرح بهَا فِيهِ، فَالْأول قِيَاس الْعلَّة، وَالثَّانِي قِيَاس الدّلَالَة، وَالثَّالِث الْقيَاس فِي معنى الأَصْل: وَهُوَ مَا جمع فِيهِ بَين الأَصْل وَالْفرع بِنَفْي الْفَارِق.

A third categorisation of *qiyās* is: An analogy is either: (i) An analogy by *ratio legis* (*qiyās al-'illah*), where a *ratio legis* is explicitly stated. (ii) An analogy by signification (*qiyās al-dalālah*), where a concomitant attribute is explicitly stated. (iii) An analogy by equivalence (*qiyās fī ma'nā 'l-aṣl*), where the subsidiary and the precedent are declared equivalent by showing a lack of relevant differentiation between the two.

رَابِعهَا: أَن طَرِيق إِثْبات الْعلَّة المستنبطة، إما الْمُنَاسبَة، أَو الشّبَه، أَو السبر

398 [T] An example is that touching the privates is the cause for invalidation of ritual purity in the ḥadīth, **"Whoever touches their privates must perform ablution."** In this case, the particular attribute (touching the privates) has directly affected the ruling (breakage of ritual purity). Refer to *Sharḥ al-Kawkab al-Munir* (4/173).

399 [T] An example where the equivalating attribute in particular has directly affected the individual genus of the ruling is that a brother who shares both parents is given preference when determining inheritance over a brother who only shares the father. This attribute (sharing of parents) has been used to formulate an analogy which gives preference to a brother who shares both parents in guardianship in marriage and other such rulings. Although the religion did not give consideration to this fact in other rulings directly, it was given consideration in the genus, which is preference in general. Refer to *Sharḥ al-Kawkab al-Munir* (4/174).

400 [T] Other scholars, such as al-Imām Ibn Qudāmah, defined it as, "When the affect of the genus is present in the particular ruling." He then gives an example of the genus of difficulty being the cause for the menstruating woman being absolved of the obligation of prayer. Refer to *Rawḍat al-Nāẓir* (2/212). There is a significant amount of difference of opinion on defining these matters. Although naming conventions are important, understanding the concepts irrespective of the terminologies used to define them is what is important. Refer to *Sharḥ Mukhtaṣar al-Rawḍah* (3/398-400) to read an overview of the differences.

والتَّقْسِيم، أَو الطَّرْد، والْعَكْس، فَالْأول يُسمى قِيَاس الإخالة، وَمَعْنَاهُ: أَن الْمُجْتَهد يتخيل لَهُ مُنَاسبَة الْوَصْف للْحكم فيعلقه بِهِ، وَالثَّانِي: قِيَاس الشّبَه، وَالثَّالِث: قِيَاس السبر، وَالرَّابِع: قِيَاس الطَّرْد.

The ways that a derived *ratio legis* is derived are: (i) Suitability and relevance (*munāsabah*). This is known as analogy by appearance (*qiyās al-ikhālah*). It means that the *mujtahid* scholar sees the appearance of the attribute being relevant to the ruling, and thereby ties the ruling to it. (ii) Resemblance (*shabah*). This is known as analogy by resemblance (*qiyās al-shabah*). (iii) Classification and elimination (*al-sabr wa al-taqsīm*). This is referred to as analogy by classification (*qiyās al-sabr*). (iv) Co-extension (*al-ṭard*) and co-exclusion (*al-ʿaks*). This is known as analogy by co-extension (*qiyās al-ṭard*).

وَحَيْثُ أَتَيْنَا على تَقْسِيم الْقيَاس إِجْمَالا فلنذكر ذَلِك مفصلا، وَرُبمَا ذكر مَعَه مَا لم يذكر هُنَا فَنَقُول:

Since we have just mentioned the categorisations of analogy in a summarised fashion, it is now time to discuss those concepts in depth, and possibly mention further classifications that have not been mentioned in this summation. Thus, we state:

فصل

Section: [The Pillars of Legal Analogy]

أَرْكَان الْقيَاس أَرْبَعَة: أصل وَفرع وَعلة وَحكم.

There are four pillars of a legal analogy: (i) The precedent (*al-aṣl*), (ii) the new case (*al-farʿ*), (iii) the *ratio legis* (*al-ʿillah*), and (iv) the ruling (*al-ḥukm*).

فَالْأَصْل عِنْد الْفُقَهَاء مَحل الحكم الْمُشبه بِهِ، كَقَوْلِنَا: النَّبِيذ مُسكر، وكل مُسكر حرَام، فالمقيس عَلَيْهِ الْمُشبه بِهِ هُوَ الْخمر، والمشبه النَّبِيذ، وَالْعلَّة الجامعة بَينهمَا الْإِسْكَار، وَالْحكم التَّحْرِيم.

The precedent, according to the jurists, is the receptacle containing the ruling that will be used to draw similarities. For example, one can say, "*Nabīdh* is intoxicating, and every intoxicant is unlawful." In this case, the precedent which has a ruling and is being used to draw similarities is wine, and the new case which is being shown to be similar to the precedent is *nabīdh*. The *ratio legis* that encompasses them both is intoxication, and the ruling is prohibition.

وَمن ثمَّ قَالَ الشَّيْخ تَقِيّ الدّين أَحْمد ابن تَيْمِية: الأَصْل مَحل الحكم الْمُشبه بِهِ، وَدَلِيل مَحل الحكم. وَقَالَ ابْن عقيل: هُوَ الحكم وَالْعلَّة.

As such, when defining the precedent, al-Shaykh Taqi al-Dīn Aḥmad ibn Taymiyyah stated, "The precedent is the receptacle containing the ruling that will be used to draw similarities, and it is the evidence of the placement of the ruling."[401] Ibn ʿAqīl stated, "It is the ruling and the cause."[402]

وَالْفرع: الْمحل الْمُشبه عِنْد الْفُقَهَاء وَعند الْمُتَكَلّمين، وَابْن قَاضِي الجبل حكمه.

According to the jurists, the definition of the new case is that it is the thing

401 [T] *Majmūʿ al-Fatāwā* (9/120).
402 [T] *Al-Wāḍiḥ* (1/133).

being compared. According to the scholars of *kalām*, as well as Ibn Qāḍī al-Jabal, it is its ruling.[403]

وَالْحكم: هُوَ الْمُعَلل لَا الْمَحْكُوم بِهِ، خلافًا لأبي عَليّ الطَّبَرِيّ الشَّافِعِي.

The ruling is what the *ratio legis* designates; it is not the thing being assigned a ruling, contrary to the position held by Abu ʿAlī al-Ṭabarī al-Shāfiʿī.[404]

وَالْعلَّة فرع للْأَصْل، أصل للفرع، أما كَونهَا فرعا للْأَصْل فَلِأَنها مستنبطة من حكمه، فَإِن الشَّارِع لما حرم الْخمر، استنبطنا مِنْهُ أَن عِلّة تَحْرِيمهَا الْإِسْكَار الْمُفسد للعقول، إِذْ لَا مُنَاسِب للتَّحْرِيم فِيهَا سواهُ. وَأما كَونهَا أصلا للفرع، فَلِأَنها إِذا تحققت فِيهِ ترَتّب عَلَيْهَا إِثْبَات حكم الأَصْل، كالإسكار لما تحقق فِي النَّبِيذ ترَتّب عَلَيْهِ التَّحْرِيم، فالعلة مستخرجة من حكم الأَصْل، والمستخرج فرع على الْمُسْتَخْرج مِنْهُ.

The *ratio legis* is a subsidiary when juxtaposed with the precedent, and the precedent when juxtaposed to the new case. As for why it is a subsidiary of the precedent, it is because it is derived of the ruling of the precedent. When the Legislator prohibited wine, we have deduced from that prohibition that the *ratio legis* is intoxication, which muddles the mind, since there is no relevant description of alcohol that would lead to its prohibition other than its intoxicating nature. Also, it is the precedent of the new case because if the *ratio legis* actualises, it results in applying the ruling of the precedent. For example, when intoxication actualises in *nabīdh*, it results in applying the ruling of prohibition. The *ratio legis* has been extracted from the ruling of the precedent, and what has been extracted is a subsidiary of what it has been extracted from.

---

403 [T] Meaning, the ruling of the thing it is being compared to, and in the previous case of intoxication in wine and *nabīdh*, the ruling is prohibition. Refer to *al-Taḥbīr Sharh al-Taḥrīr* (7/3140).

404 [T] Al-Qāḍī Abu Yaʿlā stated, "The ruling is what the *ratio legis* has determined, or what it has necessitated, inasmuch as it results in prohibition, lawfulness, validity, invalidity, obligation, non-obligation, and so forth." (*Al-ʿUddah* 1/176). The position of Abu ʿAlī al-Ṭabarī al-Shāfiʿī being referenced was quoted by the editor of *Mukhtaṣar al-Taḥrīr Sharḥ al-Kawkab al-Munir*, "Abu ʿAlī al-Ṭabarī stated, "It is the thing being assigned a ruling; it refers to the particulars that are associated with rulings." Refer to *Mukhtaṣar al-Taḥrīr Sharḥ al-Kawkab al-Munir* by Ibn al-Najjār al-Futūḥi (4/16).

ثمَّ إن الِاجْتِهَاد فِي الْعلَّة إِمَّا بِبَيَان مُقْتَضى الْقَاعِدَة الْكُلية الْمُتَّفق عَلَيْهَا فِي الْفَرْع، أَو بِبَيَان وجود الْعلَّة فِيهِ.

To continue, [there are various ways to use *ijtihād* reasoning to establish a *ratio legis*[405]: First: Determining the Presence of the Attribute (*tahqīq al-manat*), this of two types:] (i) To show the implications of a universal maxim, one that is agreed on, in the new case, or (ii) to show the existence of the *ratio legis* in the new case.

مِثَال النَّوْع الأول: أَن يُقَال فِي حمَار الْوَحْش إِذا قَتله الْمحرم مثله، وَفِي الضبع أَيْضا يقْتُلهَا الْمحرم مثلهَا لقَوْله تَعَالَى: ﴿وَمن قَتَلَهُ مِنْكُمْ مُتَعَمِّداً فَجَزَاءٌ مِثْلُ مَا قَتَلَ مِنَ النَّعَمِ﴾ [الْمَائِدَة: ٩٥] وَالْبَقَرَة مثل حمَار الْوَحْش، والكبش مثل الضبع، فَيجب أَن يكون هُوَ الْجَزَاء. فوجوب الْمثل مُتَّفق عَلَيْهِ، ثَابت بِالنَّصِّ الْمَذْكُور.

An example of the first type is that the ruling for someone killing an onager whilst in the state of ritual sanctification is that they must offer a sacrifice that is similar. The same goes for killing a hyena during a state of ritual sanctification, because Allah the Exalted said: **{Whoever kills game intentionally the penalty is an offering of a domestic animal brought to the Ka'bah.}** [Qur'ān 5:95] A cow is similar to an onager, and a goat is similar to a hyena. Therefore, those must be the sacrifices offered, respectively. The obligation of offering a similar livestock animal is agreed on and is established in the verse mentioned.

وَمِثَال النَّوْع الثَّانِي: أَن يُقَال: الطّواف عِلّة لطهارة الْهِرة، بِنَاء على قَوْله عَلَيْهِ السَّلَام: «**إِنَّهَا لَيست بِنَجس، إِنَّهَا من الطوافين عَلَيْكُم والطوافات**» وَالطّواف مَوْجُود فِي الْفَأْرَة وَنَحْوهَا من صغَار الحشرات.

An example of the second type is that the reason that cats are pure is that they are always roaming around humans. The evidence is that the Prophet ﷺ said, **"It is not impure; it is from the male and female roamers around you."**[406] The constant roaming is also present in mice and other

405 [T] What is between the brackets has been added to clarify the topic of discussion, from *Rawḍat al-Nāẓir* by al-Imām al-Muwaffaq Ibn Qudāmah (2/145).

406 Reported by Mālik (1/23), Aḥmad (5/303), Abu Dāwūd (75), al-Tirmidhī (92), al-Nasā'ī (1/55) and Ibn Mājah (367).

small insects.

وَلَكِن هَذَا النَّوْع الثَّانِي دون الَّذِي قبله، وهما متغايران، لِأَن الأول لَيْسَ بِقِيَاس، وَالثَّانِي قِيَاس، وَكِلَاهُمَا يُسمى تَحْقِيق المناط، لِأَن مَعْنَاهُ: إِثْبَات عِلّة حكم الأَصْل فِي الْفَرْع، أَو إِثْبَات معنى مَعْلُوم فِي مَحل خَفِي فِيهِ ثُبُوت ذَلِك الْمَعْنى. وَهُوَ مَوْجُود فِي النَّوْعَيْنِ وَإِن اخْتلفَا فِي أَن أَحدهمَا قِيَاس دون الآخر. فتحقيق المناط أَعم من الْقيَاس، وَهَذَا هُوَ النَّوْع الأول من أَنْوَاع الِاجْتِهَاد فِي الْعلَّة الشَّرْعِيَّة.

These two types are different, however. The first is not an analogy, while the second is, though both are referred to as *taḥqīq al-manāṭ*, since in essence it means to establish the *ratio legis* of the ruling of the precedent in the new case, or to establish a known concept in a place where the concept is not clear to be existent. This is present in both cases mentioned above, even if they differ in that one is an analogy, and the other is not. *Taḥqīq al-manāṭ*, is more general than analogy, and it is the first method of *ijtihād* in a religious *ratio legis*.

وَالنَّوْع الثَّانِي يُسمى تَنْقِيح المناط، وَهُوَ إِلْغَاء بعض الْأَوْصَاف الَّتِي أَضَاف الشَّارِع الحكم إِلَيْهَا لعدم صلاحيتها للاعتبار فِي الْعلَّة، كجعل عِلّة وجوب كَفَّارَة رَمَضَان وقاع إِنْسَان مُكَلّف أَعْرَابِي لاطم فِي صَدره فِي ذَلِك الشَّهْر بِعَيْنِه، فَيلْحق بِهِ من لَيْسَ أَعْرَابِيًا وَلَا لاطما. وَالزَّانِي وَمن وطئ فِي رَمَضَان آخر.

Second: Refining the underlying *ratio legis* (*tanqīḥ al-manāṭ*): This is to disqualify some of the attributes that the Legislator has mentioned along with the ruling but are not fit to be considered in a *ratio legis*. Without this tool, we would state that the cause that obligates the expiation of Ramadan is when a person who is responsible, Bedouin, and is hitting himself in his chest in that particular month, and by extension, we state that it also applies to non-Bedouins, those who are not hitting themselves in the chest, and a fornicator and one who has had intercourse in a different Ramadan.

وَمعنى هَذَا مَا روى أَبُو هُرَيْرَة قَالَ: جَاءَ رجل إِلَى النَّبِي صلى الله عَلَيْهِ وَسلم فَقَالَ «هَلَكت يَا رَسُول الله قَالَ: **وَمَا أهْلكك؟** قَالَ: وَقعت على امْرَأَتي فِي رَمَضَان،

قَالَ: **هَل تَجِد مَا تعْتق رَقَبَة؟** قَالَ: لَا، قَالَ: **فَهَل تَجِد مَا تطعم سِتِّين مِسْكينا؟** قَالَ: لَا» الحَدِيث. وَهُوَ صَحِيح، وعوام الْفُقَهَاء يذكرُونَ أَن هَذَا الرجل كَانَ أَعْرَابِيًا، وَأَنه جَاءَ يلطم وَجهه وصدره، وينعي نَفسه، فَإِن لم يكن جَاءَ بِهَذِهِ الْأَوْصَاف أثر، فلعلهم أخذوها من قَوْله: وَفِي بعض الرِّوَايَات (وأهلكت) لَكِن قَالَ الْخطابِيّ: لَفْظَة (أهلكت) لَيست مَوْجُودَة فِي شَيْء من رِوَايَات هَذَا الحَدِيث. وَأَصْحَاب سُفْيَان لم يرووها عَنهُ. إِنَّمَا ذكرُوا قَوْله (هَلَكت) فَحسب. انْتهى.

This meaning was reported by Abu Hurayrah where a man came to the Prophet ﷺ and said, "O Messenger of Allah, I have been destroyed." The Prophet ﷺ responded, **"What has happened to you?"** He said, "I have had intercourse with my wife while fasting." The Prophet ﷺ said, **"Do you have a slave you can free?"** The man said, "No." The Prophet ﷺ said, **"Can you feed sixty poor people?"** The man said, "No." [...] to the end of the narration, which is authentic. The majority of jurists mention that the man was a Bedouin, and that when he approached the Prophet ﷺ he was slapping his face and chest, and lamenting for himself. Though there might be no narration that mentions these qualities explicitly, they might have understood it from other narrations when he said, "I have destroyed." However, al-Khaṭṭābi stated that the phrase, "I have destroyed," is nonexistent in all narrations of the ḥadīth, and the companions of Sufyan did not report it from him; they only mentioned, "I have been destroyed."

لَكِن فِيمَا رَوَاهُ الشَّافِعِي من مَرَاسِيل سعيد بن الْمسيب قَالَ: «أَتَى أَعْرَابِي إِلَى النَّبِي صلى الله عَلَيْهِ وَسلم ينتف شعره، وَيضْرب نَحره، وَيَقُول: هلك الْأَبْعَد» وعَلى كل، فلسنا الْآن بصدد بَيَان اخْتِلَاف الْأَلْفَاظ فِي الحَدِيث، بل غَايَة الْأَمر إِنَّمَا هُوَ التَّمْثِيل وَبَيَان أَن مَجِيء الْأَعرَابِي على لصِّفَات الْمَذْكُورَة رُبمَا يخيل للسامع أَن مجموعها مَعَ الوقاع فِي رَمَضَان هِيَ مناط وجوب الْكَفَّارَة وعلته.

With that said, al-Shāfi'ī reported from the *mursal* narrations of Sa'īd ibn al-Musayyib, who said, "A Bedouin man came to the Prophet ﷺ pulling at his hair and hitting his chest, saying, 'The furthest person has been destoyed!'" Regardless, we are not in the midst of discussing the variances in the wording of the ḥadīth. The point is to illustrate that the Bedouin man came to the Prophet ﷺ and was described using various characteristics.

Someone might be misled by the mention of these characteristics and think that the totality of these characteristics are the *ratio legis* for the obligation of expiation for intercourse during the day in Ramadan.

لَكِن من جُمْلَتهَا مَا لَيْسَ مناسبا لِأن يكون عِلّة وَلَا جُزْء عِلّة. فاحتيج إِلَى إلغائه، وتنقيح الْعلَّة، وتخليصها بالسبر والتقسيم، فَيُقَال: كَون هَذَا الرجل أَعْرَابِيًا لَا أثر لَهُ، فيلْحق بِهِ من لم يكن أَعْرَابِيًا كالتركي والعجمي وَغَيرهمَا من أَصْنَاف النَّاس، وَكَونه لاطما صَدره وَوَجهه لَا أثر لَهُ، فَيلْحق بِهِ من جَاءَ بسكينة ووقار وثبات، وَكَون الْوَطْء فِي زَوْجَة لَا أثر لَهُ، فَيلْحق بِهِ الْوَطْء فِي ذكر أَو أُنْثَى أَو أمة أَو أَجْنَبِيَّة أَو بَهِيمَة فِي قبل أَو دبر اعْتِبَارا لصورة الوقاع، وَكَونه فِي ذَلِك الشَّهْر الْمعِين لَا أثر لَهُ، فَيلْحق بِهِ من وطئ فِي رَمَضَان آخر.

However, some of the descriptions mentioned are not relevant, making them the *ratio legis* or a part thereof. As such, there is a need for refining the qualities to extract the true *ratio legis*. This is done by the process of examination and elimination. To do so, one would state that the fact that the man was a Bedouin has no effect on the ruling. As such, those who are not Bedouins, such as Turks, non-Arabs, or others are also included in the original ruling. Also, the fact that he was hitting his chest and face has no effect on the ruling. As such, those who approach with solemnity, calmness, and dignity are also included within the original ruling. The fact that he had intercourse with his wife has no effect on the ruling. As such, if someone were to have intercourse with a male, female, slave-girl, an unrelated woman, or animal, whether vaginally or anally, it would all be included within the original ruling. Lastly, the fact that it occurred in that particular Ramadan has no effect, and as such, the ruling applies to a person who has intercourse in any given Ramadan.

وَإِنَّمَا كَانَت هَذِه الْأَوْصَاف لَا أثر لَهَا، لعدم مناسبتها، إِذْ الْوَصْف الَّذِي تظهر مناسبته كَونه وقاع مُكَلّف هتكت بِهِ حُرْمَة عبَادَة الصَّوْم الْمَفْرُوض أَدَاء، وَمَا سوى ذَلِك من التعيينات والأوصاف، فَإِنَّهُ ملغى لَا اعْتِبَار لَهُ.

The attributes mentioned have no effect on the ruling, since they are not relevant. The attribute that is considered relevant, therefore, is that a *mukallaf* person had intercourse [while fasting in Ramadan], thereby violating the sanctity of the worship of obligatory fasting. All other descriptions and attributes are null and void; they are not worthy of consideration.

وَقد يخْتَلف المجتهدون فِي بعض الْأَوْصَاف نَحْو مَا اعْتَبرهُ أَحْمد وَالشَّافِعِيّ فِي كَون عِلّة الْكَفَّارَة إِنَّمَا هِيَ الْجِمَاع فِي رَمَضَان، وَمَا عدا ذَلِك ملغى، فَقَالَا: لَا تجب الْكَفَّارَة إِلَّا بِهِ فِي ذَلِك الشَّهْر.

Mujtahid scholars may differ in judging certain attributes. For example, Aḥmad and al-Shāfiʿī considered the *ratio legis* for the obligation of expiation to be intercourse during Ramadan, and considered all other attributes to be irrelevant. They stated that the expiation is only obligatory if one has intercourse during the day in the month of Ramadan.

وَقَالَ أَبُو حنيفَة وَمَالك: الْعلَّة إِفْسَاد الصَّوْم، وَهُوَ وصف عَام، فَتجب الْكَفَّارَة فِي إفساده بِالْوَطْءِ وبالأكل وَالشرب.

Abu Ḥanīfah and Mālik, however, stated that the *ratio legis* is the invalidation of one's fast, which is a general description. According to them, the expiation is obligatory for any invalidation of one's fast, whether through intercourse, eating, or drinking.

النَّوْع الثَّالِث من الْأَنْوَاع الْمَذْكُورَة: تَخْرِيج المناط، وَهُوَ إِضَافَة حكم لم يتَعَرَّض الشَّرْع لعلته إِلَى وصف يُنَاسب فِي نظر الْمُجْتَهد بالسبر والتقسيم، وَمَعْنَاهُ: أَنا إِذا رَأينَا الشَّارِع قد نَص على حكم وَلم يتَعَرَّض لعلته قُلْنَا: هَذَا الحكم حَادث لَا بُد لَهُ بِحَق الأَصْل من سَبَب حَادث، فيجتهد الْمُجْتَهد فِي اسْتِخْرَاج ذَلِك السَّبَب من مَحل الحكم، فَإِذا ظفر بِوَصْف مُنَاسِب لَهُ، واجتهد وَلم يجد غَيره، غلب على ظَنه أَن ذَلِك الْوَصْف هُوَ سَبَب الحكم.

Third: Extracting the *ratio legis* (*takhrīj al-manāṭ*): This means to ascribe a ruling to a relevant attribute where the *ratio legis* has not been clarified by the Legislator. This process is performed by a *mujtahid* scholar by way of the process *al-sabr wa 'l-taqsīm*. This means that if we find that the Legislator has given a ruling in a divine text, and has not mentioned its *ratio legis*, the ruling is new and by default must have emanated from a new cause. As such, the *mujtahid* scholar uses legal discretion to extract that cause from the cause of the ruling. If they can successfully determine the relevant attribute and, after much thought, cannot find any other possible relevant attribute, it becomes highly possible to them that the attribute they discovered is the cause for the ruling.

مِثَاله أَن يُقَال: حرم الرِّبَا فِي الْبر، لِأَنهُ مَكِيل جنس أَو مطعوم جنس، فالأرز مثله لِأَنهُ كَذَلِك. أَو يُقَال: وَجب الْعشْر فِي زَكَاة الْبر لكَونه قوتا، فتلحق بِهِ الأقوات، أَو لكَونه نَبَات الأَرْض، وفائدتها: فتلحق بِهِ الخضراوات وأنواع النبات.

For example, in the case of the prohibition of usury in barley, one can say that the relevant attribute is its being dry measured or that it is used as a source of food. This ruling would extend to rice, since it shares in either of those qualities. Or, it can be said that a tenth of the produce of barley is due in *zakāt* since it is a basic food item, and as such, all other food items must be included within the ruling. Or, *zakāt* is due because of it being a vegetation, and as such, all other vegetables and vegetation are included within the ruling.[407]

وَقد أجَاز أَصْحَابنَا التعبد بِهَذَا النَّوْع عقلا وَشرعا، وسموه الِاجْتِهَاد القياسي. وَبِه قَالَ عَامَّة الْفُقَهَاء والمتكلمين خلافًا للظاهرية والنظام، وَقد أَوْمَأ إِلَيْهِ أَحْمد، وَحمله أَصْحَابه على قِيَاس قد خَالف نصا. وَقَالَ أَصْحَابنَا وَالشَّافِعِيَّة وَطَائِفَة من الْمُتَكَلِّمين: التَّعَبُّد الْقيَاس وَاجِب شرعا.

Our *aṣḥāb* have ruled it permissible to worship according to [*qiyās*], both rationally and religiously. They referred to it as, "analogous discretion." This type was also espoused by the majority of jurists and scholars of *kalām*, contrary to the Ẓāhirī scholars and al-Naẓẓām; Aḥmad also alluded to this view, and his disciples held his statement to refer to an analogy that contradicts a divine text. Our *aṣḥāb*, the Shāfiʿī scholars, and a number of scholars of *kalām* have stated that it is an obligation to worship in accordance with the rulings emanating of legal analogies.

وَاعْلَم أَن هَذِه الْمَسْأَلَة كثر الْكَلَام فِيهَا كَثْرَة قرب الْمُسَافِر فِي بيدائها أَن يرجع

407 [T] Meaning, these causes for the ruling are extracted by the *mujtahid* scholar after thorough investigation into the divine texts.

بِلَا طائل. وَالْحق أَن الَّذين نفوا الْقيَاس لم يَقُولُوا بإهدار كل مَا يُسمى قِيَاسا، وَإِن كَانَ مَنْصُوصا على علته أَو مَقْطُوعًا فِيهِ بِنَفْي الْفَارِق، وَمَا كَانَ من بَاب فحوى الْخطاب أَو لحنه على اصْطِلَاح من يُسمى ذَلِك قِيَاسا، بل جعلُوا هَذَا النَّوْع من الْقيَاس مدلولا عَلَيْهِ بِدَلِيل الأَصْل، مشمولا بِهِ، مندرجا تَحْتَهُ. وَكَلَام أَحْمد فِي مَنعه يرجع إِلَى هَذَا، فَلَا حَاجَة لما تأوله أَصْحَابه.

This issue has been discussed thoroughly many times, but to no avail. The truth is that those who denied analogy did not categorically reject everything referred to as an 'analogy,' thereby encompassing analogies where the *ratio legis* is mentioned in the divine text or can be definitively stated by negating any relevant differentia. They also did not negate indications as part of *faḥwā al-khiṭāb* (the meaning of the instruction) or *laḥn al-khiṭāb* (the tone of the instruction), if they are considered to be analogies. They considered those two types of implications to be signified and encompassed by the textual evidence itself. When Aḥmad denied analogy, his prohibition was referring to this concept. As such, there was no need for the *aṣḥāb* to present interpretations of what he said.

وَمِنْه تعلم أَن الْخلاف فِي هَذَا النَّوْع لَفْظِي، وَهُوَ من حَيْثُ الْمَعْنى مُتَّفق على الْأَخْذ بِهِ، وَالْعَمَل عَلَيْهِ. وَاخْتِلَاف طَرِيقَة الْعَمَل لَا يلْزم مِنْهُ الِاخْتِلَاف الْمَعْنَوِيّ لَا عقلا وَلَا شرعا وَلَا عرفا، على أَنه لَا يخفى على كل ذِي لب أَن فِي عمومات الْكتاب وَالسّنة ومطلقاتهما وخصوص نصوصهما مَا يَفِي بكل حَادِثَة تحدث، وَيقوم بِبَيَان كل نازلة تنزل، عرف ذَلِك من عرفه، وجهله من جَهله، فَاجْعَلْ هَذِه الْقَاعِدَة نصب عَيْنَيْك، واستغن بهَا عَمَّا أَطَالَ بِهِ أولو الْفضل من الْأَخْذ وَالرد فِي هَذَا الْمقَام.

As such, you learn that differences of opinion on analogy are semantics. As a concept, all agree it is to be accepted and adhered to. The differences in how it is used does not necessitate a fundamental contrast; such a conclusion is not supported by any rational, religious, nor customary reasoning. It is also not hidden to anyone with a heart that the Qur'ān and Sunnah contain generalities, unqualified texts, and particularizations that provide a ruling for every single occurrence that may happen and they clarify every novel issue that may occur. Those who know that, know it, and those who do not, do not. Make this maxim one of your central focuses and refer to it in favour of the lengthy discussions that occur on this topic.

فصل فِي شَرَائِط أرْكَان الْقِيَاس ومصححاتها

Section: On the Preconditions and Requirements of *Qiyās*

تقدم أَن أَرْكَان النَّاس أَرْبَعَة: الأَصْل وَالْفرع الْعلَّة وَالْحكم. وَلها شُرُوط.

Previously, it was mentioned that there are four conditions to *qiyās*: (i) The precedent (*al-aṣl*), (ii) the new case (*al-farʿ*), (iii) the *ratio legis* (*al-ʿillah*), and (iv) the ruling (*al-ḥukm*). These things have preconditions.

فَأَما شَرط الأَصْل - وَهُوَ الحكم فِي مَحل النَّص - فأمور:

The preconditions of the precedent is the ruling in the form of a divine text. It has a number of preconditions:

أَحدهَا: أَن يكون الحكم الَّذِي أُرِيد تعديته إِلَى الْفَرْع ثَابتا فِي الأَصْل، هَذَا من جِهَة الْأُصُول، وَأما من حَيْثُ الجدل، فالخصمان إِمَّا أَن يتَّفقَا على حكم الأَصْل أَو يختلفا، فَإِن اتفقَا، كَانَ ثَابتا بِالنَّصِّ والاتفاق، وَإِن اخْتلفَا فالنص واف بإثباته، وَكَانَ حجَّة لمن قَالَ بِهِ على خَصمه.

First: The ruling that one wishes to extend to the new case must be established in the precedent. This is from the perspective of the legal theory. From the perspective of the science of disputation, the two interlocutors can either agree on the ruling of the precedent, or could disagree. If they agree, the ruling is established via legal theory and agreement. If they disagree, the text sufficiently proves its ruling and is evidence for the one using it against their interlocutor.

الثَّانِي: أَن يكون الحكم الثَّابِت فِي الأَصْل شَرْعِيًّا لَا عقليا وَلَا لغويا، كقياس تَسْمِيَة اللائط زَانيا، والنباش سَارِقا.

Second: The ruling that is established in the precedent must be a religious one, not a rational or linguistic one. Examples [of a linguistic syllogism] are claiming that a person who has engaged in homosexual intercourse as being a fornicator, and referring to a gravedigger as a thief.[408]

الثَّالِث: أَن يكون الطَّرِيق إِلَى مَعْرفَته السّمع.

Third: The method of learning it must be through transmitted knowledge.

الرَّابِع: أَن يكون الحكم ثَابتا بِالنَّصِّ، وَهُوَ الْكتاب أَو السّنة. وَهل يجوز الْقيَاس على الحكم الثَّابِت بِمَفْهُوم الْمُوَافقَة أَو الْمُخَالفَة؟ فَالظَّاهِر أَنه يجوز عَلَيْهِمَا عِنْد من أثبتهما، وَأما مَا ثَبت بِالْإِجْمَاع فَفِيهِ وَجْهَان أَصَحهمَا: الْجَوَاز. وَالثَّانِي عدم الْجَوَاز، وَهَذَا لَيْسَ بِصَحِيح.

Fourth: The ruling must be established in a divine text, namely, the Qur'ān and Sunnah. As for whether it is permissible to use *qiyās* if the ruling is established by use of *mafhūm al-muwāfaqah* (*a fortiori* implication) or *mafhūm al-mukhālafah* (implication of inverse relationships), the more veracious view is that it is permissible according to those who view those implications to be valid evidences. As for if the ruling is established via consensus, there are two views, and the more veracious view is allowance. The second view states that one cannot use a ruling based on consensus as an analogue to establish a ruling in a new case, though this is incorrect.

الْخَامِس: أَن لَا يكون الأَصْل الْمَقِيس عَلَيْهِ فرعا لأصل آخر، وَإِلَيْهِ ذهب الْجُمْهُور، وَهُوَ ظَاهر كَلَام أَحْمد، وَقَالَ القَاضِي أَبُو يعلى: يجوز أَن يستنبط من الْفَرْع الْمُتَوَسّط عِلّة لَيست فِي الأَصْل، وَيُقَاس عَلَيْهِ. وَقَالَ أَيْضا: يجوز كَون الشَّيْء أصلا لغيره فِي حكم، وفرعا لغيره فِي حكم آخر. وَجوزهُ الْفَخر وَأَبُو الْخطاب، وَمنعه أَيْضا، وَقَالَ أَيْضا - هُوَ وابْن عقيل والبصري وَبَعض الشَّافِعِيَّة - يُقَاس عَلَيْهِ بِغَيْر الْعلَّة الَّتِي ثَبت بهَا، وَحكي عَن أَصْحَابنَا، وَمنعه الْمُوفق وَالْمجد والطوفي وَغَيرهم مُطلقًا إِلَّا بِاتِّفَاق الْخَصْمَيْنِ، وَجوزهُ تَقِيّ الدّين أَحْمد ابن تَيمِية فِي قِيَاس

408 [T] Al-Imām Ibn al-Najjār al-Futūḥī stated, "Although rational and linguistic syllogisms are used to reach a religious ruling, such as referring to a person who has engaged in homosexual intercourse as being a fornicator, a gravedigger as a thief, and *nabīdh* as being wine, in order to establish the religious penalty, cutting of the hand, and the prohibition." (*Mukhtaṣar al-Taḥrīr Sharḥ al-Kawkab al-Munīr* 4/18).

الْعلَّة فقَط.

Fifth: The precedent of the original case must not be a subsidiary of any other precedent. This is the view of the majority and is the apparent view of Aḥmad. Al-Qāḍī Abu Ya'lā stated, "It is permissible to deduce a cause from the middle subsidiary[409] that is not found in the precedent, and that cause is used as an analogue."[410] He also said, "It is possible for something to be a precedent for something else in ruling, and a subsidiary for another thing in another ruling."[411] This was also allowed by al-Fakhr and Abu 'l-Khaṭṭāb, though in another instance, the latter also denied it. Abu 'l-Khaṭṭāb, Ibn 'Aqīl, al-Baṣrī, and some Shāfi'ī scholars stated that it can be used as an analogue only if the *ratio legis* that has been used to establish the precedent is different.[412] It was also reported from our *aṣḥāb*. Al-Muwaffaq, al-Majd, al-Ṭūfī and others all disallowed it in all instances, unless both interlocutors agree to it. Taqi al-Dīn Aḥmad ibn Taymiyyah allowed it in an analogy by *ratio legis* (*qiyās al-'illah*) only.

السَّادِس: أَن لَا يكون دَلِيل حكم الأَصْل شَامِلًا لحكم الْفَرْع، إِذْ لَو كَانَ كَذَلِك لم يكن جعل أَحدهمَا بِعَيْنِه أصلا وَالْآخر فرعا أولى من الْعَكْس.

Sixth: The evidence provided for the precedent must not encompass the new case in the first place. If it were, making one in particular the precedent

409 [T] Meaning, the one that has a precedent above it, and a subsidiary below it.
410 [T] *Al-'Uddah fi Uṣūl al-Fiqh* (4/1322).
411 [T] Ibid.
412 [T] For example, if we state that rice is a product that is susceptible to interest rulings because it is a dry-measured product, and then we state that raisins are analogous to rice since they, too, are a dry-measured product, and use that analogy to state that raisins are also susceptible to interest rulings, it would be rejected. Rice, in this example, is a new case, since it is not mentioned in the famous ḥadīth of usury, where the Prophet ﷺ said, **"Gold is to be paid for with gold, silver with silver, wheat with wheat, barley with barley, dates with dates, and salt with salt, same quantity for same quantity and equal for equal, hand to hand. If these classes differ, sell as you wish as long as payment is made on the spot. Gold is to be paid for with gold, silver with silver, wheat with wheat, barley with barley, dates with dates, and salt with salt, same quantity for same quantity and equal for equal, hand to hand. If these classes differ, sell as you wish as long as payment is made on the spot."** (Reported by Muslim, 1584) In this case, a jurist should state that raisins are a new case and are analogous to, say, wheat, since both are dry-measured. According to the scholars listed, such as Abu 'l-Khaṭṭāb, Ibn 'Aqīl, and so forth, this analogy would be rejected. Refer to *al-Musawwadah* (p. 397).

and the other the new case would not be preferable to doing the opposite.[413]

السَّابِع: أَن يكون الحكم فِي الأَصْل مُتَّفقا عَلَيْهِ عِنْد الْخَصْمَيْنِ فَقَط، لنضبط فَائِدَة المناظرة، وَقيل: عِنْد الأمة. وَالصَّحِيح الأول.

Seventh: The ruling stated in the precedent must be agreed on by the two interlocutors, only, in order to preserve the benefit in the debate. Some have stated that it must be agreed on by the entirety of the Ummah, but the first view is correct.

الثَّامِن: أَن لَا يكون حكم الأَصْل ذَا قِيَاس مركب، وَهُوَ مَا اتّفق عَلَيْهِ الخصمان لعلتين مختلفتين، كَقَوْل الْحَنْبَلِيّ فِيمَا إِذا قتل الْحر عبدا: الْمَقْتُول عبد، فَلَا يقتل بِهِ الْحر، كَالْمكَاتبِ إِذا قتل وَترك وَفَاء ووإرثا مَعَ الْمولى، فَإِن أَبَا حنيفَة يَقُول هُنَا: إِنَّه لَا قصاص يلْحق العبدية هُنَا بِجَامِع الرق، فَلَا يحْتَاج الْحَنْبَلِيّ فِيهِ إِلَى إِقَامَة دَلِيل على عدم الْقصاص فِي هَذِه الصُّورَة لموافقة خَصمه، فَيَقُول الْحَنَفِيّ فِي منع ذَلِك: إِن الْعلَّة إِنَّمَا هِيَ جَهَالَة الْمُسْتَحق من السَّيِّد وَالْوَرَثَة لَا الرق.

Eighth: The ruling provided from the precedent must not be a compounded analogy, i.e., when two interlocutors agree on a single ruling but each provide a unique *ratio legis*. For example, a Ḥanbalī could state that when a free person kills a slave, since the one who was killed is a slave, the free person should not receive the capital punishment, similar to if a self-manumitted slave were killed and were to leave behind both the remaining fees due for manumission as well as inheritors, along with his owner. Abu Ḥanīfah in this instance also agrees that there should be no retribution. In this case, a slave is similar to a self-manumitted slave, and their resemblance lies in both being slaves. In this situation, a Ḥanbalī does not need to show evidence to indicate that the free person is not to receive the capital punishment, since they already agree with their interlocutor. A Ḥanafī would say in response that the *ratio legis* is not knowing to whom belongs the right [of retribution]: Is it to the master or to the inheritors, and as such, the reason is not slavery.

---

413 [T] Meaning, stating that the ruling that is encompassed by the evidence for the precedent is the actual precedent.

لِأَن السَّيِّد وَالْوَارِث وَإِن اجْتمعَا على طلب الْقصاص - فَإِن الِاشْتِبَاه لَا يَزُول لاخْتِلَاف الصَّحَابَة [في مكاتب مات عن وفاء، قال بعضهم: يموت عبدا، وتبطل الكتابة. وقال بعضهم: تؤدى الكتابة من أكسابه، يحكم يعتقه في آخر جزء من أجزائه، فقد اشتبه الولي مع هذا الاختلاف، فامتنع القصاص. فإن اعترض عليهم بأنكم لا بد أن تحكموا في هذه الحالة بأحد هذين القولين، أو بموته عبدا أو حرا، وأيا ما كان، فالمستحق معلوم، فيقول الحنفي: نحن نحكم بموته حرا أنه يورث، لا بمعنى وجوب القصاص على قاتله الحر، لأن حكمنا بموته حرا ظن، لاختلاف الصحابة]. وَالْقصاص يَنْتَفِي بِالشُّبْهَةِ، فَهَذِهِ جَهَالَة تصلح لدرء الْقصاص، وَلَا يمْنَع علمنَا بمستحق الْإِرْث.

The point of view of the Ḥanafī in this case is that the master and the inheritor, even if they both demanded retribution, the doubt remains, since companions have differed on how a *mukātab* person, if he is deceased and has the money to pay for his complete manumission, should be treated. Some stated that they die as a slave, and their manumission contract is invalidated. Some stated that their manumission should be completely paid off by the money they left, and the remaining parts of them that are slaves should be judged as free. In this case, the person demanding the retribution is doubted, and due to this, retribution is nullified. One could say in response, "You must judge in the case based off one of the two views; either they died a slave or they died a free person. Regardless of what the outcome is, the person deserving the right is known." The Ḥanafī would respond, "If we were to judge that they are free, it means their wealth should be inherited, not that it is an obligation to establish capital punishment in retribution against the free killer, since our judgement that they died free is conjecture and a mere likely possibility, since the companions differed." Retribution is nullified unless the case is proven beyond a shadow of doubt. The ambiguity of the case is sufficient to nullify capital punishment, though it does not prevent one from knowing who the inheritors are.

وَمن هَذَا النَّوْع مَا يسمونه مركب الْوَصْف، وَهُوَ مَا إِذا كَانَ الْخصم مُوَافقا على الْعلَّة، لَكِن يمْنَع وجودهَا فِي الأَصْل كَأَن يَقُول فِي تَعْلِيق الطَّلَاق قبل النِّكَاح: فُلَانَة الَّتِي أَتزَوَّجهَا طَالِق، فَيَقُول الْحَنَفِيّ: الْعلَّة الَّتِي هِيَ كَونه تَعْلِيقا مفقودة فِي

الأَصْل، فَإِن قَوْله: فُلَانَة الَّتِي أَتزَوَّجهَا طَالِق، تَنْجِيز لَا تَعْلِيق، فَإِن صَحَّ هَذَا، بَطل إِلْحَاق التَّعْلِيق بِهِ لعدم الْجَامِع، وَإِن منع حكم الأَصْل وَهُوَ عدم الْوُقُوع فِي قَوْله: فُلَانَة كَذَا، لِأَنهُ إِنَّمَا منع الْوُقُوع، لِأَنهُ تَنْجِيز، وَلَو كَانَ تَعْلِيقا بِهِ.

Another type of compounded analogy is one that is compounded in its description. This occurs when the interlocutor agrees on a *ratio legis*, but denies its existence in the precedent. For example, in the case of a conditional divorce given before the establishment of the marriage, ["this is a conditional divorce, so it is not valid"][414], where one says, "This woman whom I am to marry is divorced." A Ḥanafī would state that the *ratio legis* which provides that it is a conditional marriage is non-existent in the precedent. When he says, "This woman whom I am to marry is divorced," he is not offering a condition, but rather an effectuation of a divorce. In this case, the rulings of conditional divorces cannot be given the same ruling, since there is no relevant similarity. Otherwise, the ruling of the precedent is negated in that the divorce does not occur [when one says, "This woman whom I am to marry is divorced,"] since it is effectuation, even if it is conditioned on [completion of the marriage].[415]

قلت: وَلنَا فِي هَذِه الْمَسْأَلَة رِسَالَة مُسْتَقلَّة مُشْتَمِلَة على الْأَدِلَّة والبراهين وَبَيَان الْخلاف فِيهَا، وَلَيْسَ كل من الْقسمَيْنِ حجَّة عندنَا وَعند الْأَكْثَر، وَجوزهُ الْأُسْتَاذ أَبُو إِسْحَاق، وَالْقَاضِي أَبُو يعلى، وَابْن عقيل وَجمع.

I have personally written a small booklet on this issue which comprises of the evidences and proofs, and which clarifies the differences of opinion. Neither of the two previously mentioned compounded analogies are evidences according to Ḥanbalī scholars and the majority. They were allowed by al-Ustādh Abu Isḥāq, al-Qāḍī Abu Ya'lā, Ibn 'Aqīl, and a number of other scholars.

---

414 [T] The portion between the brackets is missing from this quotation, which is actually a quote from *Mukhtaṣar al-Taḥrīr Sharḥ al-Kawkab al-Munīr* (4/36).

415 [T] The view of the Ḥanbalī scholars is that a conditional divorce prior to effectuation of the marriage is invalid, while the Ḥanafī scholars argue that it is valid and denies that the statement is a conditional, but rather that it is effectuated immediately on completion of the marriage contract. For the Ḥanbalī view, refer to *al-Rawḍ al-Murbi'* (3/204) and for the Ḥanafī view refer to *al-'Ināyah Sharḥ al-Hidāyah* (4/116).

التَّاسِع: أَن لَا نَكُون متعبدين بِحكم الأَصْل بِالْقطعِ، وَهَذَا النَّوْع فِيهِ خلاف للأصوليين. وَقَالَ الْآمِدِيّ فِي جدله من كِتَابه (الْمُنْتَهى): مِمَّا يرجع إِلَى حكم الأَصْل من شُرُوطه أَن لَا يكون متعبدا بِهِ بِالْعلمِ، لِأَن الْقيَاس لَا يُفِيد إِلَّا الظَّن، وَحِينَئِذٍ يتَعَذَّر الْقيَاس. وَمنع الطوفي من أَصْحَابنَا هَذَا الشَّرْط فِي شَرحه مُخْتَصره، ثمَّ قَالَ: وَالصَّحِيح فِي هَذَا مَا قَالَه الإِمَام فَخر الدّين: إِذا كَانَ تَعْلِيل الأَصْل قَطْعِيا، وَوُجُود الْعلَّة فِي الْفَرْع قَطْعِيا، كَانَ الْقيَاس قَطْعِيا، مُتَّفقا عَلَيْهِ. قَالَ الطوفي: قلت: وَإِذا جَازَ ذَلِك، جَازَ وُرُود التَّعَبُّد بِالْقِيَاسِ بِالْقطعِ، وَحِينَئِذٍ لَا يكون مَا ذكره الْآمِدِيّ شرطا.

Ninth: That we are not told to worship in accordance with the ruling of the precedent in a definitive way, although legal theorists have differed in this precondition. Al-Āmidī stated in his section on disputation in his book *al-Muntahā*, "Another precondition that applies to the precedent is that it is not a definitive instruction of worship, since analogy only establishes probability. In such a case, *qiyās* is not a possibility."[416] Of our *aṣḥāb*, al-Ṭūfī denied this precondition in his *Sharḥ al-Mukhtaṣar*, stating, "The truth in this case is what al-Imām Fakhr al-Dīn stated, 'If the *ratio legis* stated in the precedent is definitive, and its presence in the new case is also definitive, the analogy is definitive and agreed on.'" Al-Ṭūfī then commented, "If this is possible, it is possible to also worship according to a definitive analogy, and as such, the precondition mentioned by al-Āmidī is not correct."[417]

الْعَاشِر: أَن لَا يكون معدولا بِهِ عَن سنَن الْقيَاس، إِذْ الْقيَاس عَلَيْهِ غير مُمكن، وَذَلِكَ على ضَرْبَيْنِ:

Tenth: It must not be a case that does not follow the typical conventions of *qiyās*, since in such scenarios, *qiyās* is not possible. These are of two types:

أَحدهمَا: مَا ورد غير مَعْقُول الْمَعْنى، سَوَاء كَانَ مُسْتَثْنى عَن قَاعِدَة عَامَّة، كتخصيص خُزَيْمَة بِقِيَام شَهَادَته وَحده مقَام نِصَاب الشَّهَادَة، أَو كَانَ مُبْتَدأ بِهِ من غير اسْتِثْنَاء، كالمقدرات من الْحُدُود وَالْكَفَّارَات، وَنصب الزكوات وأعداد

416 [T] *Al-Iḥkām* (7/117).
417 [T] *Sharḥ Mukhtaṣar al-Rawḍah* (3/304).

الرَّكْعَات.

One. Things that have been mentioned but have no meaning that can be rationalised. It might be an exception from a general rule, such as when the Prophet ﷺ gave Khuzaymah the exception by stating that his testimony is that of two men. Or, if the ruling was initiated without being an exception [from a general rule], such as the rulings of penalties, expiations, *zakāt*, and the number of units of prayer.

الضَّرْب الثَّانِي: مَا ورد الشَّرْع بِهِ وَلَا نَظِير لَهُ، معقولا أَو غير مَعْقُول كاللعان، والقسامة، وَضرب الدِّيَة على الْعَاقِلَة، وَجَوَاز الْمسْح على الْخُفَّيْنِ، فهذان الضربان لَا يُمكن الْقيَاس عَلَيْهِمَا لعدم فهم الْعلَّة، أَو لعدم النظير. هَذَا مَا ذكره الْآمِدِيّ وَتَبعهُ ابْن مُفْلِح، وَبِه قَالَ ابْن الْحَاجِب وَغَيره.

Two. Things mentioned in the religion that have no likeness that can be rationalised or otherwise. For example, the rulings on *li'ān*,[418] *qisāmah*,[419] obligating the male relatives of a person convicted of manslaughter to pay the blood money, and the permissibility of wiping over the two *khuffs*. These two types cannot be used in analogies, since the *ratio legis* is not understood, or there is no likeness to the cases. This is what al-Āmidī mentioned, and Ibn Mufliḥ concurred, and is also the view of Ibn al-Ḥājib and others.

وَقَالَ الْبرمَاوِيّ: فِي جعل الْقسَامَة غير معقولة الْمَعْنى، وَهُوَ خَفِي بِخِلَاف شَهَادَة خُزَيْمَة. ومقادير الْحُدُود نظر ظَاهر. انْتهى. وَذَلِكَ النّظر أنهَا متساويات، فَالْفرق بَينهَا غير مَعْقُول.

Al-Barmāwī stated, "Stating that the rules of *qisāmah* are understood, though hidden, and thereby considering it contrasted with things like the testimony of Khuzaymah and the extent of punishments, is obviously de-

418 [T] The rulings of *li'ān* are mentioned in the verse where Allah the Exalted states: **{As for those who accuse their own wives of adultery, but have no other witnesses, let each one four times call Allah to witness that he is telling the truth, and, the fifth time, call Allah to reject him if he is lying; punishment shall be averted from his wife if she in turn four times calls Allah to witness that her husband is lying and, the fifth time, calls Allah to reject her if he is telling the truth.}** [Qur'ān 24:6-9]

419 [T] Meaning, "Repeated right-hand oaths claiming the murder of a protected individual." Refer to *Sharḥ Muntahā al-Irādāt* (3/329).

batable."[420] The reason it is debatable is because they are all equivalent, and as such, the differences between them are not understood.

الْحَادِي عشر: أَن لَا يكون حكم الأَصْل مغلظا، وَفِي هَذَا الشَّرْط خلاف.

Eleventh: The ruling of the precedent must not have emanated out of giving a severe punishment. However, there is a difference of opinion in this precondition.

الثَّانِي عشر: أَن لَا يكون الحكم فِي الْفَرْع ثَابتا قبل الأَصْل، فَلَو تقدم لزم اجْتِمَاع النقيضين أَو الضدين وَهُوَ محَال.

Twelfth: The ruling of the "new case" must not be present before the existence of the ruling in the precedent. If it were, it would necessitate a contradiction in that two opposites would have to occur at the same time, and that is impossible.

الثَّالِث عشر: قَالَ أَصْحَابنَا وَغَيرهم: شَرط حكم الأَصْل أَن لَا يكون مَنْسُوخا، لِأَن الْمَنْسُوخ لم يبْق لَهُ وجود فِي الشَّرْع، فلا تلحق بِهِ الْأَحْكَام بِقِيَاس وَلَا غيره.

Thirteenth: Our *aṣḥāb* and others have stated that the ruling of the precedent must not be abrogated, since an abrogated ruling has no existence in legislation [after its abrogation]. As such, no ruling can be analogous to it.

---

420 [T] In the printed copy, it says, "Saying they are not understood." However, what I have placed is found in *al-Fawā'id al-Saniyyah fī Sharḥ al-Alfiyyah* (4/422) authored by al-Barmāwī himself.

فصل

Subsection: On the Preconditions of the Ruling of the New Case

وَأما حكم الْفَرْع فَلهُ شَرْطَانِ:

The ruling of the new case must have fulfilled two preconditions:

أَحدهمَا: أَن يكون حكمه مُسَاوِيا لحكم الأَصْل، كقياس البيع على النكَاح فِي الصِّحَّة كَقَوْلِنَا فِي بيع الْغَائِب: عقد على غَائِب، فصح قِيَاسا على النِّكَاح، وكقياس الزِّنَى على الشّرْب فِي التَّحْرِيم، وكقياس الصَّوْم على الصَّلَاة فِي الْوُجُوب.

First: Its ruling must be tantamount and equal to the ruling of the precedent. For example, one can state that a business transaction is analogous to a marriage contract in its validity if one of the parties is absent. One can state then, that a transaction occurring with one of the parties being absent is valid, since the same can be said about a marriage [where a contract is valid even if one of the parties is absent.] Also, one can state that fornication is analogous to drinking alcohol in the severity of prohibition, and can state that fasting is analogous to prayer in the imperativeness of its obligation.

الثَّانِي: أَن يكون حكم الْفَرْع حكما شَرْعِيًّا فرعيا لَا عقليا وَلَا أصوليا، وَأَن لا يطْلب فِيهِ الْعلم، لِأَن ذَلِك قَطْعِيّ، وَالْقِيَاس إِنَّمَا يُفِيد الظَّن، والقاطع لَا يثبت بالظني. هَذَا مَا ذكره أَكثر أَصْحَابنَا، وَمِنْهُم الشَّيْخ موفق الدّين فِي (الرَّوْضَة) وَذكر كثير من الأُصُولِيِّينَ شُرُوطًا أخر:

Second: The ruling of the new case must be a religious subsidiary ruling. It must not be a rational ruling or one pertaining to foundational principles, [whether legal or theological] and must not be one where absolute certainty is sought, all of which would make [the ruling] definitive. *Qiyās* provides probability, and definitive things are not established via probable ones. This is what the majority of our *aṣḥāb* have mentioned, including al-Shaykh Muwaffaq al-Dīn in *al-Rawḍah*. And a number of legal theorists have mentioned other preconditions, as well. For example:

مِنْهَا: أَن لَا يُمكن الِاسْتِدْلَال على حكم الْفَرْع بِالنَّصِّ، إِذْ يكون إثْباته بِالْقِيَاسِ حِينَئِذٍ من بَاب فَسَاد الْوَضع، كَمَا يُقَال فِي عدم إِجْزَاء عتق الرَّقَبَة الْكَافِرَة فِي كَفَّارَة الظهَار: تَحْرِير فِي تَكْفِير، فَلَا يَجْزِي فِيهِ كافرة قِيَاسا على كَفَّارَة الْقَتْل، وَهَذَا إِذا تأملته تَجدهُ رَاجعا إِلَى تَقْيِيد الْمُطلق مَعَ اخْتِلَاف السَّبَب، وَلَيْسَ مِمَّا نَحن فِيهِ.

Some have stated that [another precondition for the new case] is that it must not be provable through use of a divine text. If it is, using an analogy would constitute a type of *fasād al-waḍ'*.[421] For example, one can argue that a non-Muslim slave does not fulfill the requirement of 'freeing a slave' when expiating the sin of *ẓihār*. The argument goes, 'since the text mentions freeing a slave to expiate a sin, a non-Muslim slave does not fulfill the requirement, making it analogous to the expiation of killing [where there is also a ruling of freeing a slave to expiate a sin, and where a non-Muslim slave does not fulfill the requirement of expiation]. However, the text [about *ẓihār*] mentions to free a slave, without offering further qualifications. As such, the text is sufficient.[422] This issue, therefore, belongs in discussions on

421 [T] The concept of *fasād al-waḍ'* is quite broad, and al-Shaykh Ibn Badrān will discuss it in detail, however, to give a brief look into its workings, its usage here is not the conventional one offered by al-Muwaffaq ﷺ but rather, a broader usage of the term. Al-Ṭūfī mentioned, "Al-Nili mentions that [*fasād al-waḍ'*] refers to when an analogy conflicts with a textual evidence." He then said, "He also stated that conventional usage of *fasād al-waḍ'* is when the supposed *ratio legis* is used to prove the opposite of what it actually signifies." Refer to *Sharḥ Mukhtaṣar al-Rawḍah* (3/473).

The conventional usage, al-Ṭūfī states, is to consider it similar to a negative conclusion from affirmative premises, which is a syllogistic fallacy. It goes: (i) All A is B. (ii) All B is C. (iii) Therefore, no A is C. The example given by al-Muwaffaq Ibn Qudāmah in *Rawḍat al-Nāẓir* is, "Such as when speaking of the term, 'I bestow on you,' in the context of marriage, 'The term, 'I bestow on you,' can be used in non-marriage related things, and as such, it cannot be used in marriage related things.'" Refer to *Rawḍat al-Nāẓir wa Junnat al-Munāẓir* (2/304). This is equivalent to saying: (i) The term 'I bestow on you,' effectuates contracts. (ii) Marriage is a contract. (iii) Therefore, the term 'I bestow on you,' cannot be used to effectuate a marriage contract.

422 [T] Meaning, there is no need to consider the expiation of *ẓihār* an analogue to the expiation of killing, but rather, one should consider it a qualification and treat it as they would qualified and unqualified divine texts. This paragraph was almost entirely quoted from al-Ṭūfī in *Sharḥ Mukhtaṣar al-Rawḍah*, and where there are discrepen-

qualifying unqualified texts when the causes for the rulings differ, not in discussions on *qiyās*.

وَمِنْهَا أَن يرد النَّص بِحكم الْفَرْع فِي الْجُمْلَة، وَهَذَا الشَّرْط فَاسد لَا اعْتِبَار لَهُ، لِأَن الْعلمَاء قاسوا قَوْله: أَنْت عَليّ حرَام على الظهَار وَالطَّلَاق وَالْيَمِين، وَلم يرد فِيهِ حكم جملَة وَلَا تَفْصِيلًا، وَإِنَّمَا حكم الأَصْل يتَعَدَّى بتعدي الْعلَّة كَيفَ مَا كَانَ.

Another precondition is that the text must state the ruling of the new case in a general sense. This precondition is invalid and is not worthy of consideration, because the scholars stated that the phrase, "You are unlawful for me," is analogous to phrases indicating *ẓihār*, divorce, and a right-hand oath. No ruling in the texts has been mentioned for it, neither in general nor in specific. Rather, the truth is that the ruling of the precedent is transitive inasmuch as its *ratio legis* is transitive.

---

cies, I chose to use the wording of al-Ṭūfī, as it is clearer and expresses the meaning better. Refer to *Sharḥ Mukhtaṣar al-Rawḍah* (3/312).

فصل

Subsection: On the Preconditions of a New Case

وَأما الْفَرْع، فشرطه وجود عِلّة الأَصْل فِيهِ، وَلَا يشْتَرط أَن يكون وجودها فِيهِ مَقْطُوعًا بِهِ، بل تَكْفِي غَلَبَة الظَّن، وَالْحق أَنه إِنَّمَا يشْتَرط تقدم ثُبُوت الأَصْل على الْفَرْع قِيَاس الْعلَّة دون قِيَاس الدّلَالَة، فَإِن الْعَالم دَلِيل على الصَّانِع الْقَدِيم، وَهُوَ مُتَأَخّر عَن صانعه قطعا.

As for the new case, the following statements apply: (i) The *ratio legis* of the precedent must be present. (ii) It is not a precondition for the *ratio legis* to be definitively present in the new case, but rather, likely probability is sufficient. (iii) It is a precondition for the precedent to have antecedence over the new case in an analogy based on a cause, but not in an analogy by signification (*qiyās al-dalālah*). For example, the existence of the universe is evidence showing the existence of the Eternal Creator, and the universe definitively came after its Creator.[423]

423 [T] This example is an analogy by cause (*qiyās al-ʿillah*). Where before, *qiyās al-ʿil-lah* was defined as "analogy by *ratio legis*" here I used the term "cause" since it is not speaking within a specific legal framework, but rather, using the term *ʿillah* to refer to a logical cause.

فصل

Subsection: On the *Ratio Legis*

وَأما الْعلَّة الشَّرْعِيَّة: فلهَا أسام كَثِيرَة ذكرهَا الْبَزْدَوِيّ فِي (المقترح) فَقَالَ: هِيَ السَّبَب والأمارة والداعي والمستدعي والباعث وَالْحَامِل والمناط وَالدَّلِيل والمقتضى والموجب والمؤثر. وَقَالَ فِي (التَّحْرِير) هِيَ الْعَلامَة والمعرف عِنْد أَصْحَابنَا وَالْأَكْثَر، لَا الْمُؤثر فِيهِ. وَقَالَ الفتوحي فِي (مُخْتَصر التَّحْرِير): هِيَ مُجَرّد أَمارة وعلامة نصبها الشَّارِع دَلِيلا على الحكم. انْتهى.

As for a religious *ratio legis* (*ʿillah*), it is referred to by use of many different terminologies. These variances were mentioned by al-Bazdawī in his book, *al-Muqtaraḥ*, where he said, "It is referred to as a cause, sign, motive, eliciting factor, reason, condition, evidence, necessitation, and effectual." In *al-Taḥrīr*, it is defined as, "A sign, and indicator, according to our *aṣḥāb* and the majority. It does not refer to the thing being affected."[424] Al-Futūḥī stated in *Mukhtaṣar al-Taḥrīr*, "It is merely a sign and indication that the legislation has erected as evidence for a ruling."[425]

وَمن شَرطهَا أَن تكون متعدية من مَحل النَّص إِلَى غَيره، كالإسكار والكيل وَالْوَزْن والطعم فَلَا عِبْرَة بالقاصرة وَهِي: مَا لَا تُوجد فِي غير مَحل النَّص كالثمينة فِي النَّقْدَيْنِ، فَإِن هَذَا مُخْتَصّ بهما، قَاصِر عَلَيْهِمَا.

One of its conditions is that it must be transitive, from the place of the text to other rulings. For example, intoxication, dry-measuring, weight, nature of being a food, and so forth. As such, restricted causes are not taken into consideration. A restricted cause is one that only exists in the area of the text, such as the currency attribute present in gold and silver. That attribute is specific and restricted to [gold and silver.]

---

424 [T] *Taḥrīr al-Manqūl* (p. 274).
425 [T] *Mukhtaṣar al-Taḥrīr Sharḥ al-Kawkab al-Munīr* (4/39).

إِذا علم هَذَا، فَليعلم أَن الحكم قد يتَخَلَّف عَن الْعلَّة، وتخلفه عَنْهُمَا يعود إِلَى أَقسَام:

Know, too, that sometimes, the ruling could be absent from the *ratio legis*. This is due to a number of factors:

أَحدهَا: مَا يعلم اسْتِثْنَاؤُهُ عَن قَاعِدَة الْقيَاس، كإيجاب الدِّيَة فِي قتل الْخَطَأ على الْعَاقِلَة، مَعَ الْعلم باختصاص كل امرئ بِضَمَان جِنَايَة نَفسه، لقَوْله تَعَالَى ﴿وَلَا تَزِرُ وَازِرَةٌ وِزْرَ أُخْرَى﴾ [فاطر: ١٨]

First: A ruling could be known to be excepted from the rulings of analogy. For example, the obligation of the family of the father's side being responsible for blood-money in manslaughter, when considering that in other cases, a person is only responsible for their own crimes. Allah the Exalted states: **{No burdened soul will bear the burden of another.}** [Qur'ān 35:18]

وَكَذَا إِيجَاب صَاع تمر فِي الْمُصراة عَن اللَّبن المحتلب هَاهُنَا مَعَ أَن تماثل الْأَجْزَاء عِلّة إِيجَاب الْمثل فِي ضَمَان الْمِثْلِيَّات، فَكَانَ يَقْتَضِي ذَلِك أَن يضمن لبن الْمُصراة بِمثلِهِ، فَهَذَا لَا تبطل بِهِ عِلّة الْقيَاس لثُبُوته قطعا بِنَصّ الشَّارِع ومناسبة الْعقل.

Likewise, it is obligatory to pay a *ṣā'* of dates in a transaction when the udders of livestock are tied (*muṣārrāh*). Analogy would dictate that liability is equal to the item, as have divine texts and consensus.[426] Analogy would dictate that they must return the same amount of what has been milked. This ruling is not used to nullify the *ratio legis* in an analogy, since the text of legislation has stated the ruling, and there is rational precedent for its acceptance.

وَلَا يلْزم المستبدل الِاحْتِرَاز عَنهُ بتعليله بِأَن يَقُول: كل امرئ مُخْتَصّ بِضَمَان جِنَايَة

---

426 [T] The Prophet ﷺ said, **"Do not tie the udders of camel and goats [to give the false impression that they have large amounts of milk]. Whoever buys such an animal has two options: they may choose to keep [the animal], or, they can return [the animal] and supplement [the return] with a *ṣā'* of dates."** Reported by al-Bukhārī (4/361) and Muslim (5/165-167).

نَفسه إِلَّا فِي دِيَة الْخَطَأ. وتماثل الْأَجْزَاء عِلّة إِيجَاب الْمثل فِي ضَمَان الْمِثْلِيَّات إِلَّا فِي المصراة، لِأنهُ إِنَّمَا يجب الِاحْتِرَاز عَمَّا ورد نقضا، وَهَذَا لَيْسَ كَذَلِك، وَإِن كَانَت الْعلَّة مظنونة كورود الْعَرَايَا على عِلّة الرِّبَا على كل قَول وكل مَذْهَب، فَلَا تنقض، وَلَا تَخْصِيص الْعلَّة، بل على المناظر بَيَان وُرُودهَا على مَذْهَب خَصمه أَيْضا.

Further, in such excepted cases, the person seeking to provide evidence does not have to qualify their argument, such as by saying, "Everyone is liable to pay for damages incurred by their crimes, unless it is manslaughter," or, "Similarities of the appendages of the animal is the *ratio legis* for paying damages for similar animals, unless the animal is *muṣarrāh*." Qualifications are only necessary if the exception would otherwise nullify the argument, and this does not do so. If the *ratio legis* is probable, such as when an *ʿarāyā* being sold is susceptible to being within the ruling of usury according to every *madhhab*, this does not negate the *ratio legis*, nor does it particularize it. Rather, an interlocutor must prove that it is an exception in the *madhhab* of their opponent in debate.

وَاعْلَم أَن قَول الْفُقَهَاء: هَذَا الحكم مُسْتَثْنى من قَاعِدَة الْقيَاس، أَو خَارج عَن الْقيَاس، أَو ثَبت على خلاف الْقيَاس، لَيْسَ المُرَاد بِهِ أَنه تجرد عَن مُرَاعَاة الْمصلحَة حَتَّى خَالف الْقيَاس، وَإِنَّمَا المُرَاد بِهِ أَنه عدل بِهِ عَن نَظَائِره لمصْلحَة أكمل وأخص من مَصَالح نَظَائِره على جِهَة الِاسْتِحْسَان الشَّرْعِيّ، فَمن ذَلِك أَن الْقيَاس يَقْتَضِي عدم بيع الْمَعْدُوم، وَجَاز ذَلِك فِي السّلم وَالْإِجَارَة توسعة وتيسيرا على الْمُكَلّفين. وَمِنْه أَن الْقيَاس أَن كل وَاحِد يضمن جِنَايَة نَفسه، وخولف فِي دِيَة الْخَطَأ رفقا بالجاني وتخفيفا عَنهُ لِكَثْرَة وُقُوع الْخَطَأ من الجناة.

Note: When jurists state that a ruling is an exception from the maxim of the analogy, is outside the analogy, or the ruling is contrary to what an analogy would otherwise dictate, it does not mean that it is stripped of its utility so as to contradict the analogy; rather, it means that it was excepted from similar cases in order to provide a more complete and specific benefit than those provided by the similar cases. This is a type of *istiḥsān*. An example is that analogy dictates not selling a nonexistent item. However, that was made permissible in cases of *salam* transactions and rental agreements. These allowances were to give ease and latitude to responsible people. Another example is that each person is liable for the damages caused by their own selves, but in manslaughter, that rule was exempted to show leniency to the perpetrator, since many times, perpetrators commit their crimes out of a mistake.

ثَانِيهَا: النَّقْض التقديري. وَهُوَ تخلف الْعلَّة لَا لخلل فِيهَا بل لمعارضة علّة أُخْرَى أخص كَأَن يُقَال: رق الْأُم عِلّة رق الْوَلَد، فينتقض عَلَيْهِ بولد الْمَغْرُور بِأمِّهِ، وَهُوَ من تزوج امْرَأَة على أَنَّهَا حرة فَبَانَت أمة، فَهَذَا الْوَلَد حر مَعَ أَن أمه أمة، فقد تخلف حكم الْعلَّة عَنْهَا، فَيَقُول الْمُسْتَدلّ: هَذَا الْوَلَد وَإِن كَانَ حرا حكما فَهُوَ رَقِيق فِي التَّقْدِير بِدَلِيل وجوب قِيمَته على أَبِيه لسَيِّد أمته. وَلَو أَن الرق فِيهِ حَاصِل تَقْديرا، لما وَجَبت قِيمَته، إِذْ الْحر لَا يضمن بِالْقيمَةِ.

Second: A relative invalidation occurs when the *ratio legis* is inapplicable, not because it is invalid or lacks cogency, but rather because there is another, more particular, *ratio legis* that it conflicts with. For example, one can claim that slavery of the mother is the cause for the child being born a slave. This *ratio legis*, however, is invalidated in the case when a man marries a woman with the assumption that she is free, but she is actually a slave. If they have a child, it is free, although its mother is a slave. In this case, the *ratio legis* has been invalidated. Someone could respond and state that, although the child is free in its ruling, it is still relatively a slave, because it is still an obligation on the father to pay the master of the slave-girl. [Had it not been][427] that the child is relatively a slave, the fee would not have been made obligatory, since a fee to cover liability does not apply to a free child.[428]

427 [T] What is between the brackets is a correction of the text. Here, al-Shaykh Ibn Badrān has quoted from *Sharḥ Mukhtaṣar al-Rawḍah* of al-Imām al-Ṭūfī. However, he stated, "Had it been," instead of, "Had it not been." Refer to *Sharḥ Mukhtaṣar al-Rawḍah* (3/330).

428 [T] This child is susceptible to being considered within two different rulings. The first is that the child is a slave, because the mother is a slave, and the second is that the child is free, because the father believed the mother was free when the child was born. Because of this, the child is a de facto free child, but relative to certain rulings of the law, is still a slave. This was done to compensate the master of the mother, because the child's freedom has become a loss of wealth. The father must pay restitution to the master because his belief of the freedom of the mother is the cause of the loss of wealth,

وَفِي وُرُود هَذَا النَّوْع نقضا خلاف بَين أَصْحَابنَا، فَذهب القَاضِي أَبُو يعلى، وَأَبُو الْخطاب، وَأَكْثر أَصْحَابنَا إِلَى أَنه لَا يقْدَح مُطلقًا وَيكون حجَّة فِي غير مَا خص. وَذهب ابْن حَامِد وَصَاحبه أَبُو يعلى إِلَى أَنه يقْدَح مُطلقًا. وَقَالَ المُوفق: يقْدَح فِي عِلّة مستنبطة إلا لمَانع أَو فَوَات شَرط، وَلَا يقْدَح فِي المنصوصة، قَالَ الطوفي فِي (مُخْتَصره): الْأَشْبَه أَنه لَا يقْدَح اعْتِبَارا بالتحقيق لَا التَّقْدِير.

The *aṣḥāb* have differed on using this type to invalidate a *ratio legis*. Al-Qāḍī Abu Ya'lā, Abu 'l-Khaṭṭāb, and the majority of our *aṣḥāb* have stated that it does not absolutely nullify the *ratio legis*, and it is evidence in non-particularized cases.[429] Ibn Ḥāmid, and his student Abu Ya'lā,[430] have said that it invalidates the *ratio legis* altogether. Al-Muwaffaq stated, "It invalidates in a derived *ratio legis*[431] unless there is something to prevent it, or the nonexistence of a precondition. It does not invalidate if the *ratio legis* is explicitly stated in the text."[432] [433] Al-Ṭūfī stated in his *Mukhtaṣar*, "The clearer view to me is that it does not invalidate it in establishing de facto rulings, though in some relative ways, it could."[434]

ثَالِثهَا: تخلف الحكم لفَوَات مَحل أَو شَرط لَا لخلل في ركن الْعلَّة كَقَوْلِنَا: البيع

---

and as such, he is financially liable. Refer to *Sharḥ Mukhtaṣar al-Rawḍah* (3/331).

429 [T] Meaning, it is like a general ruling, applying to all cases where the *ratio legis* exists, except the one that has been particularized. This opinion is also prevalent amongst Ḥanafī scholars, who referred to it as a sort of particularization of the *ratio legis*. Refer to *al-Taḥbīr Sharḥ al-Taḥrīr* (7/3215-3216).

430 [T] In this case, al-Qāḍī has expressed two views on the topic. Refer to *Mukhtaṣar al-Taḥrīr* (4/58).

431 [T] For example, the *ratio legis* of retribution in murder is, "a purposeful killing done out of aggression." However, the ruling does not apply to the case where a father kills his son; in such a case, the father does not receive capital punishment in retribution. Refer to *Mukhtaṣar al-Taḥrīr* (4/59).

432 [T] An example is when the Prophet ﷺ said, **"That is simply a vein."** Reported by al-Bukhārī (327) and Muslim (334). This ruling is not invalidated by excretion of impure substances from a place other than the private areas. Refer to *Sharḥ al-Kawkab al-Munīr* (4/59).

433 [T] *Rawḍat al-Nāẓir* (p. 324).

434 [T] Al-Imām al-Ṭūfī states, "The reason it does not invalidate it in all cases is that the ruling dictated by the *ratio legis* is applicable and consistent across all other scenarios, but does not apply in certain cases due to conflicting causes, and as such, it submits to it." Refer to *Sharḥ Mukhtaṣar al-Rawḍah* (3/331).

عِلّة الْملك. وَقد وَقع، فليثبت الْملك فِي زمن الْخِيَار، فينتقض ببيع الْمَوْقُوف والمرهون وَأم الْوَلَد. فقد حصل البيع فِيهِ، وَلم يفد الْملك، فَيُقَال: لم تتخلف إِفَادَة البيع الْملك لكَونه لَيْسَ عِلّة لإفادته، بل لكَونه لم يُصَادف محلا، وكقولنا: السّرقَة عِلّة الْقطع، وَقد وجدت فِي النباش، فينتقض بِسَرِقَة الصَّبِي، أَو سَرقَة دون النّصاب، أَو السّرقَة من غير حرز، فَإِنَّهَا لم توجب الْقطع، فَيُقَال: لَيْسَ ذَلِك لكَون السّرقَة لَيست عِلّة، بل لفَوَات أَهْلِيَّة الْقطع فِي الصَّبِي، وفوات شَرطه فِي دون النّصاب، وَمن غير الْحِرْز.

Third: The nonexistence of a receptacle or a precondition: This is not due to an inconsistency in the *ratio legis*. For example, one can state that selling is the cause for ownership, and since a sale has occurred, ownership should transfer during the opt-out period. However, transfer of ownership does not occur in the case of selling an endowment, a mortgage, or the mother of one's child. Although a sale has occurred, it did not result in a transfer of ownership. In this case, the transfer of ownership did not occur, not because the sale is not the cause for its transfer, but because it did not occur to a valid item of sale. In another example, it can be stated that stealing is the cause for cutting of the hand. The concept of stealing is found in a gravedigger. However, the cause is invalidated in a few different cases, such as if a child stole, if what was stolen was below the minimum amount, or if it was not stolen from a secure place. In that case, the hand is not to be cut, and not because stealing is not the cause of cutting of the hand, but because the competence required in stealing is not found in the child, or because the preconditions of it being above the minimum amount and in a secure place are not found.

فَهَذَا وَأَمْثَاله لَا يفْسد الْعلَّة، لِأَن تَأْثِير الْعلَّة يتَوَقَّف على وجود شُرُوطهَا وَانْتِفَاء موانعها، وَهَذَا مِنْهُ.

Such things do not invalidate the *ratio legis*, because the effect of the *ratio legis* is contingent on the presence of its preconditions and the nonexistence of its impediments. In the cases above, there are impediments.

وَهل يُكَلف الْمُعَلل والمستدل على ثُبوت الحكم بِوُجُود علية الِاحْتِرَاز من هَذَا، كَأَن يَقُول مثلا: بيع صدر من أَهله، وصادف مَحَله، أَو استجمع شُرُوطه، فَأَفَاد

الْملك. أَو الْمُكَلف سرق نِصَابا كَامِلا من حرز مثله لَا شُبْهَة لَهُ فِيهِ، فَوَجَبَ قطعه، هَذَا فِيهِ خلاف بَين عُلَمَاء فن الجدل سهل الْخطب، وَالْأولَى الِاحْتِرَاز عَنهُ، لِأَنهُ أجمع للْكَلَام، وأنفى لنشره وتبدده، وَأَمْنَع لَهُ من أَن يصير مشاغبة، وَمَا سوى ذَلِك من تخلف حكم الْعلَّة فِي الْأَقْسَام الثَّلَاثَة، فَهُوَ نَاقض لِلْعِلَّةِ.

The scholars of disputation have disagreed on whether it is a responsibility of the one establishing the *ratio legis*, in other words: the claimant, to use language that would cater to such exceptions, such as saying, "This is a sale that has occurred from a legitimate party and has occurred to a valid item of sale, while fulfilling the conditions, and as such, it results in a transfer of ownership." Or, "The legally responsible person has stolen the minimum amount from a secure place, and there is no possibility of a misunderstanding, and as such, cutting of the hand is now obligatory." The difference in this issue is minor. With that said, it is best to use language that takes such preconditions into account, since it results in more comprehensive speech and prevents dispersed and unqualified language. It also prevents the discussion from becoming disorderly. Any time the ruling and the *ratio legis* do not conform, and it does not fall under the previous three types, it invalidates the *ratio legis*.

وَأما المعدول بِهِ عَن الْقيَاس، فَلَا يَخْلُو من أَن تفهم علته أَولا.

As for an analogy that does not follow the typical conventions of *qiyās*, there are two possibilities, either the *ratio legis* is understood or not.

فَإِن فهمت الْعلَّة فِيهِ ألحق بِهِ مَا فِي مَعْنَاهُ، كقياس عرية الْعِنَب على عرية الرطب فِيمَا دون خَمْسَة أوسق، إِذْ الْعلَّة مفهومة، وَهِي الرُّخْصَة للنَّاس، والتوسعة عَلَيْهِم إِذا احتاجوا إِلَيْهِ، وكقياس أكل بَقِيَّة الْمُحرمَات على أكل الْميتَة للضَّرُورة بِجَامِع استبْقَاء النَّفس بذلك. وَيُقَاس عَلَيْهِ الْمُكْره على أكلهَا، لِأَنَّهُ فِي معنى الْمُضْطَر إِلَى التغذي بهَا بالجامع الْمَذْكُور.

First: The *ratio legis* could be understood. If the *ratio legis* is understood, similar cases are appended to the ruling. For example, one could state that the ruling of selling *'arayyah* applies to grapes, just as it applies to fresh dates, so long as it is under five *wasq.*[435] In this case, the *ratio legis* is understood, which is the providing of a legal concession and ease to people if needed. Another example is the permissibility of eating other unlawful foods, based on the ruling of the permissibility of eating a dead carcass, because the *ratio legis* is preserving one's life by doing so. Also included are those coerced into eating such foods, since that is the same concept as eating the foods in the previous case.[436]

وَإِن لم تفهم عِلّة المعدول عَن الْقيَاس لم يلْحق بِهِ غَيره، وَذَلِكَ كتخصيص أبي بردة بِأَنهُ ذبح جَذَعَة من الْمعز فِي الْأَضْحِية، فَقَالَ لَهُ رَسُول الله صلى الله عَلَيْهِ وَسلم: **«هِيَ خير نسيكتيك، وَلَا تجزي جَذَعَة، لأحد بعْدك»**، والْحَدِيث فِي (الصَّحِيحَيْنِ) وَرَوَاهُ أَبُو دَاوُد وَالنَّسَائِيّ وَالتِّرْمِذِيّ وَصَححهُ. وكشهادة خُزَيْمَة حَيْثُ اشْترى رَسُول الله صلى الله عَلَيْهِ وَسلم فرسا من أَعْرَابِي وَلم يكن بَينهمَا أحد، ثمَّ جحد الْأَعرَابِي البيع، فَشهد بِهِ خُزَيْمَة بن ثَابت وَحده، فَأجَاز رَسُول الله صلى الله عَلَيْهِ وَسلم شَهَادَته، فَجعل شَهَادَته بشهادتين، فَهَذِهِ التخصيصات مِمَّا لَا يفهم مَعْنَاهَا، فَلَا يلْحق بهَا غير من خص بهَا، وَكَذَا التَّفْرِيق بَين بَوْل الْغُلَام وَالْجَارِيَة، لما لم يعقل الْفرق بَينهمَا، لم يلْحق بهما ذُكُور صغَار الْبَهَائِم وإناثها.

Second: If the *ratio legis* is not understood, no other cases can be appended to the ruling. For example, the Prophet ﷺ gave Abu Burdah an exception to slaughter a goat that was less than a year old, saying, **"It is the better of your two sacrifices; a goat under a year will not suffice for anyone after you."**[437] The ḥadīth was reported in al-Bukhārī and Muslim, as well as by Abu Dāwūd, al-Nasā'ī, and al-Tirmidhī, who ruled it to be authentic. Another example is the testimony of Khuzaymah when Allah's Messenger purchased a horse from a Bedouin man without a witness, then the Bedouin man denied the sale. Khuzaymah ibn Thābit testified to the sale alone, and Allah's Messenger ﷺ allowed his testimony and made it worth that of two men. These special scenarios do not have an understandable *ratio legis*, and

---

435 [T] A *wasq* is an old Arab measurement, equal to 60 *ṣāʿ*. A *ṣāʿ* is an old measurement, and its equivalent in modern standards of weight is 2036 grams, or 2.036 kilograms (refer to *Naẓm al-Maqādir al-Sharʿiyyah* by Dr. ʿAmir Bahjat). Therefore, a *wasq* is (2.036 x 60)5 = 610.8 kg.

436 [T] Meaning, preservation of life.

437 Reported by al-Bukhārī (2/380).

as such, no other cases should be appended to them. Another example is the differentiation between the urine of a baby boy and a baby girl.[438] Since the *ratio legis* is not understood, the ruling is not applied to, say, the urine of male baby livestock and female baby livestock.

۞۞۞

فصل

Section

لَا يشْتَرط أَن تكون الْعلَّة أمرا ثبوتيا، بل يجوز أَن تكون أمرا عدميا، وَهِي كَونهَا صفة أَو اسْما أَو حكما، كَقَوْلِنَا: لَيْسَ بمكيل وَلَا بموزون فَلَا يحرم فِيهِ التَّفَاضُل. وَهَذَا لَا يجوز بيعه، فلا يجوز رَهنه، وَنَحْو ذَلِك خلافًا لبَعض الشَّافِعِيَّة حَيْثُ قَالُوا: لَا يجوز، وَيجوز تَعْلِيل الحكم بعلتين مَعًا، فَلَا يمْتَنع أَن يَجْعَل اللَّمْس وَالْبَوْل عِلَّتَانِ لنقض الْوضُوء.

To continue, the *ratio legis* does not have to be affirmative, but can be privative as well. This can occur by attribute, name, or ruling. For example, one can say, "This item is not dry-measured or weighed, and as such, disparity between them is not prohibited." One can also say, "This item may not be sold, and by extension, it cannot be mortgaged." This is contrary to the view of some Shāfiʿī scholars who stated that it is not permissible to state a privative proposition in defining a *ratio legis*. Further, it is permissible to give a particular ruling two *ratione legis*, thus touching of the privates and urine can both be simultaneous causes for the nullification of ablution.

وَهنا قد تمّ الْكَلَام على شُرُوط الْعلَّة، وَبِه تمّ الْكَلَام على شُرُوط أَرْكَان الْقيَاس الْأَرْبَعَة. ولنشرع فِي بَيَان مَا يفْسد الْقيَاس حسب الْإِمْكَان فَنَقُول:

At this interval, we have concluded our discussions on the preconditions of a *ratio legis*, and by extension, we have concluded discussions on the four pillars of *qiyās*. In the next section, we shall begin discussing things that nullify an analogy, to the best of our ability.

---

438 The Prophet ﷺ said, **"The urine of a baby girl should be washed, but the urine of a baby boy should only be sprinkled."** Reported by Abu Dāwūd (376), Ibn Mājah (526), and al-Nasāʾī (1/158).

فصل
Subsection: The Invalidators of *al-Qiyās*

مفسدات الْقيَاس وُجوه:

There are a number of invalidators of an analogy:

أَحدهَا: أَن لَا يكون الحكم مُعَللا فِي نفس الْأَمر، فَيكون القائس قد علل بِمَا لَيْسَ بمعلل، كمن زعم أَن عِلّة الانتقاض بِلَحْم الجزور، وَهُوَ أَنه لشدَّة حرارته ودسمه مرخ للجوف، وَالصَّحِيح الْمَشْهُور أَن ذَلِك تعبد.

First: The ruling is not one that has a *ratio legis* in and of itself. As such, a person engaging in a legal analogy would use a *ratio legis* to establish a ruling that is not contingent on one. An example is someone claiming that the reason why eating the meat of a camel breaks one's ablution is because it is very hot and fat, and is heavy on the stomach. However, the truth and well-known answer is that the ruling of eating camel meat breaking ablution is a devotional ruling (*ta'abbudi*).[439]

الثَّانِي: أَن يخطئ الْقيَاس عِلّة الحكم عِنْد الله فِي الأَصْل، مثل أَن يعْتَقد أَن عِلّة الرِّبَا فِي الْبر الطّعْم، فَيلْحق بِهِ الخضراوات وَسَائِر المطعومات، وَتَكون علته فِي نفس الْأَمر الْكَيْل أَو الاقتيات أَو الْعَكْس.

Second: The analogy could be tied to a *ratio legis* that is not the true cause for the ruling in the sight of Allah the Exalted. For example, one could believe that the reason why there is usury in barley is that it is a food substance,

439 [T] Typically, scholars state that rulings are of two types. The first is a *ta'līlī* ruling, which means one that has either an obvious or a derived *ratio legis*, and the second are *ta'abbudi*, which are legal rulings where the slaves cannot discern a wisdom for them other than mere devotion to Allah. Refer to *Maqāṣid al-Sharī'ah al-Islamiyyah* by al-Imām Ṭāhir ibn 'Āshūr (3/150). Note, too, that the ruling of eating camel meat breaking *wuḍū* is one of the *mufradāt*, which are the unique and singular views that al-Imām Aḥmad held, contrary to Abu Ḥanīfah, Mālik, and al-Shāfi'ī, may Allah be pleased with them all. Refer to *al-Inṣāf* by al-Mardāwī (1/216).

and as such, include vegetables and all other food substances. However, the true reason why Allah the Exalted might have made barley susceptible to usury is that it is weighed, or that it is a basic food item, or vice versa.

الثَّالِث: أَن يزِيد فِي أَوْصَاف الْعلَّة، أَو ينقص مِنْهَا، مثل أَن يُعلل الْحَنْبَلِيّ بِأَنَّهُ قتل عمد عدوان فَأوجب الْقود، فَيَقُول الْحَنَفِيّ: نقصت من أَوْصَاف الْعلَّة وَصفا، وَهُوَ الْآلَة الصَّالِحَة السارية فِي الْبدن، فَلَا يَصح إِلْحَاق الْمثقل بِهِ، أَو يُعلل الْحَنَفِيّ بذلك فَيَقُول الْخصم: زِدْت فِي أَوْصَاف الْعلَّة وَصفا لَيْسَ مِنْهَا وَهُوَ صَلَاحِية الْآلَة، وَإِنَّمَا الْعلَّة هِيَ الْقَتْل الْعمد الْعدوان فَقَط، فَيلْحق بِهِ الْمثقل.

Third: To add to or remove from attributes crucial to the *ratio legis*. For example, a Ḥanbalī could state the cause for capital punishment as retribution is a purposeful killing that transgresses. The Ḥanafī might respond by saying, "You have removed a crucial attribute, namely, use of a tool that can be used to pierce the body. As such, a heavy item cannot be analogous [to a piercing tool]." The interlocutor could respond by saying, "You have added an attribute that is not a part of the *ratio legis*, namely, a suitable weapon. The *ratio legis* is a purposeful killing that transgresses. As such, the heavy item is analogous."

الرَّابِع: أَن يتَوَهَّم وجود الْعلَّة فِي الْفَرْع وَلَيْسَت فِيهِ، مثل أَن يظنّ أَن الْخِيَار وَنَحْوه مَكِيلًا، فيلحقه فِي تَحْرِيم الرِّبَا أَو بِالْعَكْسِ، مثل أَن يظنّ أَن الْأُرز مَوْزُون، فيلحقه بالخضراوات فِي عدم تَحْرِيم الرِّبَا بِجَامِع أَنه لَيْسَ بمكيل.

Fourth: To mistakenly consider the *ratio legis* to exist in the new case, when in reality it does not. For example, one could consider cucumbers, and so forth, a dry-weighted item, and as such, consider it prohibited by cause of usury. Or, the opposite could occur: one could consider that rice is a weighted item and, as such, consider it analogous to vegetables in that usury does not apply to it, considering it is not a dry-weighted item.

الْخَامِس: أَن يسْتَدلّ على تَصْحِيح الْعلَّة بِمَا لَيْسَ بِدَلِيل فَلَا يَصح، فَلَا يحل لَهُ الْقيَاس، وَإِن أصَاب، كَمَا لَو أصَاب بِمُجَرَّد الْوَهم والحدس، أَو أصَاب الْقبْلَة عِنْد اشتباهها بِدُونِ اجْتِهَاد. ذكر هَذَا الْغَزالِيّ.

Fifth: To attempt to prove the veracity of the *ratio legis* by use of something that is not evidence, thereby invalidating the *qiyās*. *Qiyās* is not allowed in such a case, even if the person has actually reached a sound conclusion. Examples are when a person reaches a conclusion through mere intuition and conjecture, or when a person prays in the correct direction without applying effort in attempting to determine the correct *qiblah*. This was mentioned by al-Ghazālī.

تَنْبِيه: قد تقدم أَن فَائِدَة الْقيَاس إِلْحَاق الْمَسْكُوت عَنهُ بالمنطوق، وَذَلِكَ الْإِلْحَاق على ضَرْبَيْنِ: مَقْطُوع بِهِ، ومظنون.

Note that the purpose of *qiyās* is to extend a pronounced ruling to an unstated one. Such an extension is of two types: (i) Definitive and (ii) probable. Definitive extensions are of two types:

وَالْأول ضَرْبَان: أَحدهمَا: أَن يكون الْمَسْكُوت عَنهُ أولى بالحكم، وَهُوَ فحوى الْخطاب، وَمَفْهُوم الْمُوَافقَة، وَشَرطه مَا سبق فِي مَوْضِعه، نَحْو: إِن قبلت شَهَادَة اثْنَيْنِ، فَثَلَاثَة أولى، وَإِذا لم تصح الْأُضْحِيَة بالعوراء، فالعمياء أولى، وَهُوَ بِخِلَاف قَوْلنَا: إِذا ردَّتْ شَهَادَة الْفَاسِق فشهادة الْكَافِر أولى بِالرَّدِّ، وَإِذا وَجَبت الْكَفَّارَة فِي قتل الْخَطَأ، فَفِي الْعمد لَو أولى فَإِنَّهُ مظنون لِإِمْكَان الْفرق إِذْ بَينهمَا.

First: When the unstated ruling is more deserving of the ruling. This is known as *faḥwā al-khiṭāb*, or an *a fortiori* argument. This has preconditions which have been discussed in the relevant portion of the book. An example is, if the testimony of two witnesses are accepted, three should be even more worthy of acceptance. Another example is if a lame animal is not fit for ritual slaughter, a blind one is even less fit. This, however, is not applicable in certain cases. For example, it is not a given that since the testimony of a sinner is rejected, the testimony of a disbeliever is even more worthy of rejection. It is also not a given that if expiation is an obligation in manslaughter, that it is more of an obligation in murder. This is probable since there is still the possibility of some differentia between the cases.[440]

---

440 [T] Al-Imām Ibn Qudāmah stated, "Murder is different from manslaughter, and as such, an expiation might not be sufficient to lift its burden. Also, a disbeliever might avoid lying out of adherence to their religion, although a sinner is already under scrutiny in their religion." Refer to *Rawḍat al-Nāẓir wa Junnat al-Munāẓir* (2/255).

وَالثَّانِي: أَن يَسْتَوِي الأَصْل وَالْفرع فِي استحقاقهما ومناسبتهما لَهُ، كَقَوْلِنَا: سرى الْعتْق فِي العَبْد، فالأمة مثله، إِذْ لَا تَأْثِير للذكورة وَالْأُنوثَة فِي هَذَا الحكم وَنَحْوه فِي عرف الشَّرْع وتصرفه، إِذْ هما وصفان طرديان كالسواد وَالْبَيَاض، وَإِن كَانَ للذكورية والأنوثية تَأْثِير فِي الْفرق فِي بعض الْأَحْكَام، كولاية النكَاح وَالْقَضَاء وَالشَّهَادَة.

Second: When the precedent and the new case both share equally in suitability and relevance to the *ratio legis*. For example, one could state that since emancipation can be effectuated in male slaves, it can also be effectuated in female slaves, because maleness or femaleness play no part in this ruling in the conventions and actions of the legislation, since they are coincidental attributes, similar to whiteness or blackness. With that said, sex does play a part in differentiating between some rulings, such as in guardianship for marriage, holding positions of a judge, and testimony.

وكقولنا: موت الْحَيَوَان فِي السّمن يُنجسهُ، وَالزَّيْت مثله، وَلَا أثر للفارق، يكون هَذَا سمنا وَهَذَا زيتا، لِأَنهُ فرق لَفْظِي غير مُنَاسِب، وَطَرِيق الْإِلْحَاق فِيهِ من وَجْهَيْن:

Another example is stating that if an animal dies in cooking fat, it renders it impure. The same ruling applies to if it were to die in oil. The difference in the substance has no effect on the ruling. The difference between the two in the ruling is semantics: this is fat, and that is oil. There is no relevance in that differentiation inasmuch as it pertains to the ruling. There are two ways to extend the ruling:

أَحدهمَا: أَن يُقَال: لَا فَارق بَين مَحل النزاع وَمحل الِاحْتِجَاج إِلَّا كَذَا، وَهُوَ لَا أثر لَهُ، فَيجب استواؤهما فِي الحكم كَأَن يُقَال: لَا فَارق بَين العَبْد وَالْأمة فِي سرَايَة الْعتْق وتنصيف الْحَد إِلَّا الذكورية، وَلَا أثر لَهَا، فَيجب استواؤهما فِي ذَلِك الْوَجْه.

One. To state that there is no difference between the disputed case and the case used as precedence except in some attribute that bears no effect on the ruling. As such, they must share equivalency in ruling. For example, one can state that there is no difference between a male slave and a female slave inasmuch as emancipation is effectuated and that half of the penalties are applied, except sex, which has no effect on the ruling, and as such, they share equivalency in that respect.

الثَّانِي: أَن يبين الْجَامِع الَّذِي هُوَ مناط الحكم فِي الأَصْل مَا هُوَ، وَيبين وجوده فِي الفَرْع، فَيثبت الحكم مثل أَن يَقُول: الْعلَّة فِي الأَصْل كَذَا، وَهِي متحققة فِي الْفَرْع، فَيجب استواؤهما فِي الحكم. وَهَذَا النَّوْع مُتَّفق على تَسْمِيَته قِيَاسا، وَفِيمَا قبله خلاف.

Two. To clarify the uniting similarity, which is the thing that the ruling hinges on, in the precedent, and then to show its existence in the new case, thereby establishing the ruling. For example, one can say, "*The ratio legis* of the precedent is such-and-such, and it also exists in the new case, and as such, they must share equivalency in ruling." This way is unanimously referred to as an analogy (*qiyās*), although there is a difference of opinion on whether the first one is an analogy.

وَمن أَمْثِلَة الثَّانِي أَن يُقَال: السكر عِلّة التَّحْرِيم، وَهِي مَوْجُودَة فِي النَّبِيذ، فَينبت التَّحْرِيم فِيهِ. وَإِثْبَات الْمُقدمَة الأولى بِالشَّرْع فَقَط، إِذْ هِيَ وضعية. وَالثَّانيَة بِالْعقلِ وَالْعرْف وَالشَّرْع، وَمَا عدا مَا ذَكرْنَاهُ من الْإِلحَاق بطرِيق الأولى، وَالْقِيَاس فِي معنى الأَصْل، فَهُوَ مظنون كالأقيسة الشبهية.

An example of the second method [of extending the ruling] is to state, "Intoxication is the *ratio legis* for prohibition, and it exists in *nabīdh*, as such, it is prohibited." Establishing the first premise is done only through the religion, since it is declarative. The second premise can be established through rational, customary, or religious reasoning. Anything other than what we mentioned, namely, an extension by an *a fortiori* argument and an analogy by equivalence (*qiyās fī maʿnā al-aṣl*) are probable. Examples are analogies that rely on resemblance.

وَهنا انْتهى بَيَان أَصْنَاف الْإِلْحَاق القياسي قطعا أَو ظنا، ولنتكلم على أَدِلَّة الشَّرْع الَّتِي تثبت بهَا الْعلَّة الشَّرْعِيَّة فَنقُول:

Since we have concluded discussions on how to extend rulings via analogies, whether definitive or probable, let us begin speaking on the religious evidences that can establish the religious *ratio legis*:

مرجع أَدِلَّة الشَّرْع إِلَى نَص أَو إِجْمَاع أَو استنباط، وَتثبت الْعلَّة بِكُل مِنْهَا على

سَبِيل الْبَدَل، فَإِن ثبتَتْ بِالنَّصِّ الَّذِي هُوَ الْكتاب وَالسّنة عمل بهَا، وَإِلَّا ثبتت بِالْإِجْمَاع، فَإِن لم يُوجد، فَفِي الاستنباط. فَأَما إِثْبَاتهَا بِالنَّصِّ - وَهُوَ الدَّلِيل النقلي - فعلى نَوْعَيْنِ:

The evidences of religion emanate out of: (i) Divine texts, (ii) consensus, (iii) deduction. A *ratio legis* can be established through any of those evidences interchangeably. If it is established through divine texts, namely, the Qur'ān and the Sunnah, it is acted on. Otherwise, it is established through consensus, and if there is no consensus, it is deduced. As for establishing a *ratio legis* through divine texts, there are two ways of doing so:

أَحدهمَا: أَن تكون الْعلَّة مُصَرحًا بهَا بِأَن يكون اللَّفْظ مَوْضُوعا للتَّعْلِيل، أَو مَشْهُورا فِيهِ فِي عرف اللغة، كَقَوْلِه تَعَالَى: ﴿**مَا أَفَاءَ اللَّهُ عَلَى رَسُولِهِ مِنْ أَهْلِ الْقُرَى فَلِلَّهِ وَلِلرَّسُولِ وَلِذِي الْقُرْبَى وَالْيَتَامَى وَالْمَسَاكِينِ وَابْنِ السَّبِيلِ كيلَا يكون دولة بَين الْأَغْنِيَاء مِنْكُم**﴾ [الْحَشْر: ٧]، أَي: إِنَّا جعلنَا مصرف الْفَيْء هَذِه الْجِهَات لِئَلَّا يتداوله الْأَغْنِيَاء قوما بعد قوم، فتفوت نَفَقَة تِلْكَ الْجِهَات المحتاجة إِلَيْهِ، وَلَا يَقع من الْأَغْنِيَاء موقع ضَرُورَة.

First: The *ratio legis* could be stated explicitly, where there is a word placed to indicate it or the word is known in conventional linguistic usage to indicate causation. For example, Allah's statement: **{Whatever gains Allah has turned over to His Messenger from the inhabitants of the villages belong to Allah, the Messenger, kinsfolk, orphans, the needy, the traveler in need, this is so that they do not just circulate among those of you who are rich.}** [Qur'ān 59:7] Meaning, Allah has placed these ways of spending war spoils in these various avenues so as to avoid the rich monopolising wealth generationally, resulting in the [benefit][441] not reaching those various categories that need the wealth, while also not fulfilling any necessity that the rich have.

وَقس على ذَلِك أَمْثَاله من الْكتاب وَالسّنة، كَقَوْلِه تَعَالَى ﴿**فأثابكم غماً بِغَمٍّ لِكَيْلا**

441 [T] This paragraph is quoted from al-Imām al-Ṭūfī, and what I have placed is found in *Sharḥ Mukhtaṣar al-Rawḍah* (3/357). Shaykh Ibn Badrān substituted this word for, "spending," which also makes sense in this context.

تَحْزَنُوا عَلَى مَا فَاتَكُمْ﴾ [آل عمران: ١٥٣] أي من الْغَنِيمَة.

This is analogous to various verses in the Qur'ān and the Sunnah. For example: **{Allah rewarded you with sorrow for sorrow. [He has now forgiven you] so that you may not grieve for what you missed.}** [Qur'ān 3:153] Meaning, the spoils.

﴿وَمَا جَعَلْنَا الْقِبْلَةَ الَّتِي كُنتَ عَلَيْهَا إِلَّا لِنَعْلَمَ مَنْ يَتَّبِعُ الرَّسُولَ﴾ [الْبَقَرة: ١٤٣] أي: ليمتحنهم بالانقياد للانتقال من قبْلَة إِلَى قبْلَة.

And: **{We only made the direction the one you used to face [O Prophet] in order to distinguish those who follow the Messenger.}** [Qur'ān 2:143] Meaning, to test you by seeing who will obey in turning from one *qiblah* to another.

فَإِن أضيف الْفِعْل الْمَذْكُور إِلَى مَا لَا يصلح أَن يكون عِلّة فَهُوَ مجَاز، وَيعرف ذَلِك بِعَدَمِ الدَّلِيل على عدم صلاحيته عِلّة مثل أَن يُقَال للْفَاعِل: لم فعلت؟ فَيَقُول: لِأَني أردْت. فالإرادة هُنَا لَا تصلح للتَّعْلِيل، لِأَن الْعلَّة إِنَّمَا هِيَ الْمُقْتَضى الْخَارِجِي للْفِعْل. والإرادة لَيست معنى خَارِجا عَن الْفِعْل، فَكَانَ اسْتِعْمَالهَا هُنَا اسْتِعْمَالا للفظ فِي غير مَحَله فَكَانَت مجَازًا.

If a word indicating causation is joined to something that is not fit to be a true cause, it is a metaphor. This is known by [establishing][442] evidence showing that the stated cause is not an appropriate cause in context. For example, one can say to a person, "Why did you do that?" To which they may respond, "Because I wanted to." Wanting here is not an appropriate cause. A cause is outside of the action and necessitates bringing about the action. Wanting to do something is not a concrete concept existing externally from the action.[443] As such, its usage as a cause is not accurate, making it a metaphor.

---

442 [T] This quotation is taken from *Mukhtaṣar al-Taḥrīr* (4/124), who quoted it erroneously from *Sharḥ Mukhtaṣar al-Rawḍah* (3/359). The erroneous word is, "lack of," which I have replaced with the original in al-Ṭūfī's work, as it otherwise has no discernible meaning in this context.

443 [T] Wanting to do something can necessitate existence of an action, but is not its true cause, which must reside outside of the scope of the action or the actioner. Refer to *Sharḥ Mukhtaṣar al-Rawḍah* (3/360).

فأمَّا مثل قَوْله عَلَيْهِ السَّلَام فِي الْمحرم الَّذِي مَاتَ «**لَا تقربوه طيبا فَإِنَّهُ يبْعَث يَوْم الْقِيَامَة ملبيا**» وَقَوله فِي الروثة لما جِيءَ بهَا ليستجمر بهَا «**أَنَّهَا رِجْس**» وَمثل هَذَا، فَقَالَ أَبُو الْخطاب: هَذَا كُله صَرِيح فِي التَّعْلِيل خُصُوصا فِيمَا لحقته الْفَاء نَحْو: «**فَإِنَّهُ يبْعَث ملبيا**» وَقَالَ غَيره: هُوَ من بَاب التَّنْبِيه والإيماء. وَالْخلاف لَفْظِي، لِأَن أَبَا الْخطاب يَقُول: إِن التَّعْلِيل بِهِ صَرِيح، لِأَنهُ تبادر مِنْهُ إِلَى الذِّهْن بِغَيْر توقف فِي عرف اللُّغَة وَغَيره، يَعْنِي بِكَوْنِهِ لَيْسَ بِصَرِيح أَن حرف (أن) لَيست مَوْضُوعَة للتَّعْلِيل فِي اللُّغَة.

There are statements of the Prophet ﷺ such as when he spoke of a person in a state of ritual sanctity who passes away, **"Do not apply perfume to him, for he will be resurrected on the Day of Judgement saying the *talbiyah*."**[444] Also, when he was brought faeces in order to perform cleaning of the privates with it, he said, **"Indeed, it is impurity."**[445] On these statements, Abu 'l-Khaṭṭāb said, "These are explicit references to causation, especially when connected to the preposition, such as when he said, **'for he will be resurrected on the Day of Judgement saying the *talbiyah*.'**" Others stated that it is just a mention and reference to the quality. The difference of opinion here is mere semantics, because Abu 'l-Khaṭṭāb is stating that there is explicit pronouncement of causation, since it immediately crosses one's mind, without any hesitation, in the customary usage of language and so forth. Meaning, there is no explicit evidence to indicate that prepositions are not to show causation.

الثَّانِي: من إِثْبَات الْعلَّة بِالدَّلِيلِ النقلي الْإِيمَاء. وَالْفرق بَينه وَبَين الأول أَن النَّص يدل على الْعلَّة بوصفه لَهَا، والإيماء يدل عَلَيْهَا بطرِيق الِالْتِزَام، وَهُوَ أَنْوَاع:

Second: Another way to establish a *ratio legis* through a divine text is to deduce it by allusion. The difference between this way and the first way is that in the first way, the text indicates the *ratio legis* by describing it. In this way, the allusion indicates the *ratio legis* by use of implicative signification. It is of varying types:

أَحدهمَا: ذكر الحكم عقيب الْوَصْف بِالْفَاءِ كَقَوْلِه تَعَالَى: ﴿وَيَسْأَلُونَكَ عَنِ

444 Reported by al-Bukhārī (4/55) and Muslim (1206).
445 Reported by al-Bukhārī (1/224).

الْمَحِيضِ قُلْ هُوَ أَذىً فاعتزلوا النِّسَاء فِي الْمَحِيض﴾ [الْبَقَرة: ٢٢٢]، ﴿وَالسَّارِقُ وَالسَّارِقَةُ فَاقْطَعُوا﴾ [الْمَائِدَة: ٣٨]، وَقوله عَلَيْهِ السَّلَام: «من أَحْيَا أَرضًا فَهِيَ لَهُ».

The first type: Mention of the ruling after an attribute, by using, the letter *fā* (meaning: "then," "therefore," or, "so,"), such as in the statement of Allah: **{And they ask you about menstruation. Say, "It is harm, so keep away from wives during menstruation. And do not approach them until they are pure."}** [Qur'ān 2:222] Also: **{Cut off the hands of thieves, whether they are male or female.}** [Qur'ān 5:38] Also, in the Prophet's ﷺ statement, **"If someone revives a dead land, it then belongs to them."**[446]

فَهَذِهِ أَحْكَام ذكرت عقيب أَوْصَاف كاعتزال النِّسَاء عقيب الْمَحِيض، وَقطع السَّارِق عقيب السّرقَة، وَملك الأَرْض بعد الْإِحْيَاء، وَهُوَ يُفِيد أَن الْوَصْف الَّذِي قبل الحكم عِلّة وَسبب لثُبُوته، إِذْ الْفَاء للتعقيب، فتفيد تعقيب الحكم الْوَصْف، وَأَنه سَببه، إِذا السَّبَب مَا ثَبت الحكم عَقِيبه.

These rulings were mentioned after particular attributes or descriptions; avoidance of women was mentioned after menstruation, cutting of the hand of the thief was mentioned after the crime of theft, and ownership of land was mentioned after reviving it. This implies that the attribute that occurred before the ruling is the *ratio legis* and the reason for its establishment. The conjunction *fā* ("then," "therefore," "so," and so forth) indicates succession, and as such, shows that the rulings are successive to the attributes, with the attribute being the cause for the ruling. A cause is what causes a successive ruling.

ثَانِيهَا: تَرْتِيب الحكم على الْوَصْف بِصِيغَة الْجَزَاء كَقَوْلِه تَعَالَى: ﴿وَمن يتق لله يَجْعَلْ لَهُ مَخْرَجاً﴾ [الطَّلَاق: ٢] ﴿وَمَنْ يَتَوَكَّلْ عَلَى اللهِ فَهُوَ حَسْبُهُ﴾ [الطَّلَاق: ٣]، أَي لتقواه وتوكله لتعقيب الْجَزَاء وَالشّرط.

The second type: Showing a ruling to emanate from an attribute by use of wording that shows it is recompense. For example, Allah the Exalted states:

446 Reported by Abu Dāwūd (3073).

{Allah will find a way out for those who are mindful of Him.} [Qur'ān 65:2] Also: **{Allah will be enough for those who put their trust in Him.}** [Qur'ān 65:3] Meaning, due to their mindfulness and trust. This was stated by use of the wording of an apodosis and its condition.

ثَالِثهَا: ذكر الحكم جَوَابا لسؤال يُفِيد أَن السُّؤَال الْمَذْكُور أَو مضمونه عِلّة الْجَواب، كَقَوْلِه عَلَيْهِ الصَّلَاة وَالسَّلَام فِي جَوَاب قَول الْأَعرَابِي: واقعت أَهلِي فِي نَهَار رَمَضَان: أعتق رَقَبَة، لِأَن ذَلِك فِي معنى قَوْله: حَيْثُ واقعت أهلك فَأعتق رَقَبَة.

The third type: Mentioning the ruling as an answer to a question, showing that the question asked, or its contents, are the *ratio legis* of the answer. For example, the Prophet ﷺ was asked by a Bedouin man what he should do if he had intercourse with his wife during the day in Ramadan, and the Prophet ﷺ said, **"Free a slave."** This is equivalent to the Prophet ﷺ saying, "Since you had intercourse with your wife during the day in Ramadan, free a slave."

رَابِعهَا: أَن يذكر الشَّارِع مَعَ الحكم سَببا لَو لم يُعلل الحكم بِهِ، لَكَانَ ذكره لاغيا، فَيجب تَعْلِيل الحكم بذلك الشَّيْء الْمَذْكُور مَعَه لصيانة كَلَام الشَّارِع عَن اللَّغْو. وَهَذَا النَّوْع قِسْمَانِ:

The fourth type: The Legislator mentions, along with the ruling, a cause that, if it were not the *ratio legis*, it would be superfluous. This necessitates considering that cause as the *ratio legis* of the ruling, to refrain from attributing superfluous speech to the Legislator. This type has two additional subtypes:

أَحدهمَا: أَن يسْأَل فِي الْوَاقِعَة عَن أَمر ظَاهر، ثمَّ يذكر الحكم عَقِيبه، فَيدل على التَّعْلِيل، كَقَوْلِه عَلَيْهِ السَّلَام لما سُئِلَ عَن بيع الرطب بِالتَّمْرِ قَالَ: **«أينقص الرطب إِذا يبس؟»** قَالُوا: نعم، قَالَ: **«فَلَا إِذن»**، فَهَذَا اسْتِفْهَام على جِهَة التَّقْرِير لكَونه ينقص إِذا يبس. وَلَيْسَ هَذَا من بَاب الاستعلام، إِذْ الْمَعْلُوم لكل عَاقل أَن الرطب ينقص إِذا يبس لزوَال الرُّطُوبَة الْمُوجبَة لزيادته وَثقله.

One. When a situation occurs, and a question arises of some obvious matter, and then the ruling is mentioned directly after it, it shows it is the *ratio legis*. For example, when the Prophet ﷺ was asked about trading fresh dates for older dates, **"Do dates diminish if they become dry?"** They responded, "Yes." To which he said, **"Then no."**[447] The rhetorical question the Prophet ﷺ posed was to establish that dates do diminish if they become dry. This is not an interrogative sentence, since it is known to everyone with sound intellect that a fresh date diminishes in size when it becomes dry, since the attribute of moistness is what provides an increase in size and weight.

ثَانِيهمَا: أَن يعدل فِي الْجَواب إِلَى نَظِير مَحل السُّؤَال، كَقَوْل عمر رَضِي الله عَنهُ للنَّبِي صلى الله عَلَيْهِ وَسلم إِنِّي قبلت وَأَنا صَائِم، فَقَالَ لَهُ: **«أَرَأَيْت لَو تمضمضت»** فَإِن ذَلِك يدل على التَّعْلِيل بِالْمَعْنَى الْمُشْترك بَين الصُّورَتَيْنِ: المسؤول عَنْهَا، والمعدول إِلَيْهَا بطرِيق الْقيَاس، إِذْ لَو لم يكن كَذَلِك، لخلا السُّؤَال عَن جَوَاب، فَكَأَنَّهُ قَالَ لعمر: إِن الْقبْلَة لَا تضر، وَلَا تفْسد صومك، لِأَنَّهَا مُقَدّمَة شَهْوَة الْفرج، كَمَا أَن الْمَضْمَضَة مُقَدّمَة شَهْوَة الْبَطن.

Two. When the answer to the question is redirected to something equivalent to the topic of the question. For example, 'Umar ﷺ asked the Prophet ﷺ about him kissing his wife while fasting, to which the Prophet ﷺ said, **"Consider it the same as though you have rinsed your mouth [while fasting]."**[448] This answer indicates that the *ratio legis* lies within the shared underlying concept that applies to both the case that was asked about and the case that was alluded to through use of analogy. Had it not been so, the question would have no discernible answer. Therefore, it is as though the Prophet ﷺ said to 'Umar, "A kiss does not harm nor invalidate your fast, since it is simply the beginning to the desires of the privates, just as rinsing the mouth is the beginning to the desires of the stomach."

خَامِسهَا: أَن يذكر عقيب الْكَلَام، أَو فِي سِيَاقه، أَو فِي ضمنه شَيْئا لَو لم يُعلل بِهِ الحكم الْمَذْكُور، لم يكن الْكَلَام منتظما كَقَوْلِه تَعَالَى: ﴿**إِذَا نُودِيَ لِلصَّلَاةِ مِنْ يَوْمِ الْجُمُعَةِ فَاسْعَوْا إِلَى ذِكْرِ اللَّهِ وَذَرُوا الْبَيْعَ**﴾ [الْجُمُعَة: ٩]، وَقَوله عَلَيْهِ السَّلَام: **«لَا**

447 Reported by Mālik (2/624), Abu Dāwūd (3359), al-Tirmidhī (1225), al-Nasā'ī (7/268), and Ibn Mājah (2264).
448 Reported by Aḥmad (138) and Abu Dāwūd (2385).

يقْضِي الْقَاضِي وَهُوَ غَضْبَان».

Fifth: Mentioning something after, during, or within a sentence that, if it were not the *ratio legis*, the speech would not be orderly. For example, Allah the Exalted states: **{When the call to prayer is made on the day of congregation, hurry towards the reminder of Allah and leave off your trading.}** [Qur'ān 62:9] Also, the Prophet ﷺ said, **"A judge must not offer a ruling while angry."**[449]

فَلَو لم يُعلل النَّهْي عَن البيع حِينَئِذٍ بِكَوْنِهِ مَانِعا أَو شاغلا عَن السَّعْي، لَكَانَ ذكره لاغيا، وَكَذَا لَو لم يُعلل النَّهْي عَن الْقَضَاء عِنْد الْغَضَب بِكَوْنِهِ يتَضَمَّن اضْطِرَاب المزاج الْمُوجب لاضطراب الفكرة الْمُوجب غَالِبا للخطأ فِي الحكم، لَكَانَ ذكره لاغيا، إِذْ البيع وَالْقَضَاء لَا يمنعان مُطلقًا، فَلَا بُد إِذن من مَانع، وَلَيْسَ الْمَانِع إِلَّا مَا فهم من سِيَاق النَّص ومضمونه.

In the first text, it would be superfluous to mention hurrying if the *ratio legis* of prohibition of selling [during Friday prayers] was not that it is a preventative from going [to the prayer.] Likewise, it would be superfluous to mention anger as the *ratio legis* if anger did not result in a change in disposition, which in turn results in a disrupted thought process and usually to incorrect judgement. Sales and judgements are not absolutely forbidden, and as such, there must be some impediment to their validity. The impediment is only what was understood from the context and contents of the text.

سادسها: اقتران الحكم بِوَصْف مُنَاسِب نَحْو: أكْرم الْعلمَاء، وأهن الْجُهَّال، ثمَّ إِن الْوَصْف فِي هَذِه الْمَوَاضِع مُعْتَبر فِي تَعْرِيف الحكم أَو تَأْثِيره ووجوده، غير أَنه يحْتَمل أَن الْوَصْف عِلّة بِنَفسِهِ، كالإحياء الْمُقْتَضى لملك الْموَات، وَيحْتَمل أَن الْعلَّة مَا تضمنه واشتمل عَلَيْهِ، كالشغل عَن الْجُمُعَة الَّذِي اشْتَمَل عَلَيْهِ البيع.

Sixth: Coupling the ruling with a relevant and suitable attribute, such as, "Honour the scholars," and "Dishonour ignoramuses." The attribute is worthy of consideration when defining the ruling or in its effectuation and existence. It also can be a *ratio legis* in and of itself. For example, bringing the land to life necessitates ownership of it. It is possible that the *ratio legis*

449 Reported by al-Bukhārī (13/120) and Muslim (1717).

is an implied meaning contained within that attribute, such as the concept of busying one from the Friday prayers contained within selling during prayers.

فصل
Section: [Establishing a *Ratio Legis* Through Consensus]

وَأما إِثْبات الْعلَّة بِالْإِجْمَاع، فكالصغر للولاية، واشتغال قلب القَاضِي بِالْغَضَبِ عَن اسْتِيفَاء النّظر، فَيلْحق بِهِ اشْتِغاله بِالْجُوعِ أَو الْعَطش أَو الْخَوْف أَو الْأَلَم بِالْقِيَاسِ، وككون تلف المَال تَحت الْيَد العادية عِلّة للضَّمان على الْغَضب إِجْمَاعًا، فَيلْحق بِهِ تلف الْعين بيد السَّارِق، وَإِن قطع بهَا لِأَن يَده عَادِية فضمن مَا تلف فِيهَا كَالْغَاصِبِ لاشْتِرَاكهمَا فِي الْوَصْف الْجَامِع، وَهُوَ التّلف تَحت الْيَد العادية. وَكَذَلِكَ الْإِخْوَة من الْأَبَوَيْنِ أثرت فِي التَّقْدِيم فِي الْإِرْث إِجْمَاعًا، فَكَذَا فِي النكَاح، والصغر أثر فِي ثُبُوت الْوَلَايَة على الْبكر، فَكَذَا على الثيب.

As for establishing a *ratio legis* through consensus, there are some examples to mention: (i) Young age being the *ratio legis* for guardianship. (ii) The heart of the judge being busied with anger, causing them to not offer a thorough investigation into the case they are judging in [being the *ratio legis* for the prohibition of offering a judgement while angry]. In this case, being busied with hunger, thirst, fear, or pain are all analogous to anger. (iii) The concept of destruction of property under a force of aggression being the *ratio legis* for the obligation of restitution and liability in cases of usurpation is established by consensus. Analogous to this case is destruction of a particular item by a thief, even if they receive the punishment of having their hand cut off, because they have aggressively stolen, and as such, they must pay restitution for anything they destroyed, similar to the usurper, since they share in the attribute of "destruction of property under a force of aggression." (iv) Sharing two parents plays an effect on priority when receiving inheritance, according to consensus. Likewise, this ruling applies to marriage. (v) Young age has an effect in establishment of guardianship for a virgin, and likewise, the same applies to a previously-married woman.

ثمَّ اعْلَم أَنه إِذا قَاس الْمُسْتَدلّ على عِلّة إجماعية، فَلَيْسَ للمعترض الْمُطَالبَة بتأثير تِلْكَ الْعلَّة فِي الأَصْل وَلَا فِي الْفَرْع، لِأَن تأثيرها فِي الأَصْل ثَابت بِالْإِجْمَاع، وَفِي

الْفَرْع لاطرادها فِي كل قِيَاس، فينشر الْكَلَام، إِذْ مَا من قِيَاس إِلَّا وَيتَّجه عَلَيْهِ سُؤال الْمُطَالبَة بتأثير الْوَصْف فِي الْفَرْع.

If a person wishing to establish evidences uses a *ratio legis* defined through consensus, the interlocutor may not question the effect of the *ratio legis* in the precedent nor in the new case. The reason is that its effect in the precedent is established through consensus and it is extended to the new case since it is consistent in each analogy. If the interlocutor does, it disrupts the discussion, as it results in every analogy being questioned on the basis of what effect the attribute has on the new case.

۞۞۞

فصل

Section: [Establishing a *Ratio Legis* Through Deduction]

وَأما إِثْبَات الْعلَّة بالاستنباط فَهُوَ على أَنْوَاع:

Establishing a *ratio legis* through deduction is of varying types:

أَولهَا: إِثْبَاتهَا بالمناسبة وَهِي أَن يقْتَرن بالحكم وصف مُنَاسِب، وَتسَمى أَيْضا بالإخالة. واستخراجها يُسمى تَخْرِيج المناط، وَقد سبق مِثَاله فِي غير مَوضِع.

First: Establishing the *ratio legis* through suitability and relevance. This occurs when the ruling is coupled with a relevant attribute. This is also known as analogy by appearance (*qiyās al-ikhālah*). Extracting the relevant attribute is known as *takhrij al-manāṭ*. Examples of this have been shown numerous times before.

قَالَ الْعَلامَة نجم الدّين الطوفي رَحمَه الله تَعَالَى: قلت: قد اخْتلف فِي تَعْرِيف الْمُنَاسب، واستقصاء الْقَوْل فِيهِ من الْمُهِمَّات، لِأَن عَلَيْهِ مدَار الشَّرِيعَة، بل مدَار الْوُجُود، إِذْ لَا مَوْجُود إِلَّا وَهُوَ على وفْق الْمُنَاسبَة الْعَقْلِيَّة، لَكِن أَنْوَاع الْمُنَاسبَة تتفَاوَت فِي الْعُمُوم وَالْخُصُوص والخفاء والظهور، فَمَا خفيت مناسبته سمي مُعَللا. فقولنا - يَعْنِي فِي (مُخْتَصره): الْمُنَاسب مَا تتَوَقَّع الْمصلحَة عَقِيبه أَي: مَا إِذا وجد أَو سمع، أدْرك الْعقل السَّلِيم كَون ذَلِك الْوَصْف سَببا مفضيا إِلَى مصلحَة من الْمَصَالح لرابط من الروابط الْعَقْلِيَّة بَين تِلْكَ الْمصلحَة وَذَلِكَ الْوَصْف.

Al-ʿAllāmah Najm al-Dīn al-Ṭūfī said, "Scholars have differed on how to define a 'relevant and suitable attribute,' making the exploration of this topic an important matter, since the legislation revolves around it; rather, existence is contingent on this concept, since there is no existent matter but that it concurs with some rationally suitable and relevant attribute. The types of relevance and suitability differ in their general or particular nature, as well as in their obviousness or obscurity. When the relevance is obscure, it is referred to as [devotional (*taʿabbudi*), and when the relevance is apparent, it is referred to as explainable by cause (*muʿallal*)][450]. Previously, I stated that suitability and relevance are when there is expected utility. This means that when relevance and suitability are found or heard, a sound intellect understands that the attribute is a cause leading to some utility, based on a rational connection between the utility itself and the attribute being mentioned.

قَالَ: ومثاله: أنه إِذا قيل: الْمُسكر حرَام. أدْرك الْعقل أَن تَحْرِيم الْمُسكر مفض إِلَى مصلحَة، وَهِي حفظ الْعُقُول من الِاضْطِرَاب. وَإِذا قيل: الْقصاص مَشْرُوع، أدْرك الْعقل أَن شَرْعِيَّة الْقصاص سَبَب مفض إِلَى مصلحَة، وَهِي حفظ النُّفُوس: وأمثلة كَثِيرَة ظَاهِرَة.

For example, when it is stated, "Intoxicants are unlawful," an intellect would understand that the prohibition of intoxicants leads to some utility or benefit, namely, preservation of intellects from disarray. Further, if one states that retribution is legislated, an intellect would understand that the legality of retribution is a cause leading to a benefit, which is preservation of lives. There are many other clear cases to illustrate this fact.

وَإِنَّمَا قلت: مَا تتَوَقَّع الْمصلحَة عَقِيبه لرابط عَقْلِي أخذا من السَّبَب الَّذِي هُوَ الْقَرَابَة، فَإِن الْمُنَاسب هَاهُنَا مستعار ومشتق من ذَلِك. وَلَا شكّ أَن المتناسبين فِي بَاب النّسَب كالأخوين وَابْني الْعم وَنَحْو ذَلِك، إِنَّمَا كَانَا متناسبين لِمَعْنى رابط بَينهمَا وَهُوَ الْقَرَابَة، فَكَذَلِك الْوَصْف الْمُنَاسب هَهُنَا لَا بُد أَن يكون بَينه وَبَين مَا يُنَاسِبه من الْمصلحَة رابط عَقْلِي، وَهُوَ كَون الْوَصْف صَالحا للإفضاء إِلَى تِلْكَ الْمصلحَة عقلا. ا. ه.

I stated that there is expected utility to follow due to a logical connection taken from the cause, which indicates close proximity. Relevance and suitability, in this context, is used metaphorically to refer to that concept. There is no doubt that two people that share a relevance to one another in genealogy, such as two brothers, two cousins, and so forth, share that relevance due to some connection between them, which is family ties, in this case. Similarly, a relevant and suitable attribute in this case must share some logi-

---

450 [T] What falls between the brackets is found in the printed copy of *Sharḥ Mukhtaṣar al-Rawḍah*, and not al-Shaykh Ibn Badrān's quotation. Refer to *Sharḥ Mukhtaṣar al-Rawḍah* (3/382).

cal connection to the utility it serves, which is that the attribute is fit to lead logically to that utility and benefit."[451] **[End]**

فقد علم أَن الْوَصْف الْمُنَاسب: هُوَ مَا تتَوَقَّع الْمصلحَة عَقِيبه لرابط عَقْلِي، وَلَا يعْتَبر كَونه منشأ للحكمة كَقَوْلِنَا: السّفر منشأ الْمَشَقَّة المبيحة للترخص، وَالْقَتْل منشأ الْمفْسدَة، وَهِي تَفْوِيت النُّفُوس، وَالزِّنَى منشأ الْمفْسدَة، وَهُوَ تَضْييع الْأَنْسَاب، وإلحاق الْعَار، فَهَذِهِ الأوصاف ينشأ عَنْهَا الحكم الَّتِي ثبتت الْأَوْصَاف لأَجلهَا.

Therefore, we have learned that a relevant and suitable attribute (*al-waṣf al-munāsib*) is something where there is expected utility to follow due to a logical connection. This does not take the wisdoms behind the initiation of certain rulings into consideration. For example, we state that travel initiates difficulty, and that leads to a legal concession; killing initiates a vice, which is loss of life; fornication initiates another vice, namely, the loss of genealogy and bringing of shame. These attributes serve to initiate the rulings for which attributes are established.

بل الِاعْتِبَار الْأَعَمّ من ذَلِك سَوَاء كَانَ منشأ للحكمة كَمَا تقدم، أَو كَانَ الْوَصْف مُعرفا للحكمة ودليلا عَلَيْهَا، كَقَوْلِنَا: النِّكَاح أَو البيع الصَّادِر من الْأَهْل فِي الْمحل يُنَاسب الصِّحَّة، أَي: يدل على أَن الِانْتِفَاع بِالْمَبِيعِ وَالْحَاجة اقْتَضَت جعل البيع سَببا لتَحْصِيل الِانْتِفَاع بِوَاسِطَة الصِّحَّة.

What is taken into consideration is much more encompassing. It can include the initiation of some wisdom, as in the previous examples, as well as an attribute that tells of the wisdom and indicates its presence. For example, stating that a marriage or a sale that occurs on part of a qualified person in the correct context is relevant to its validity, which means that it indicates that there is a need that necessitates that sales transactions is a cause to acquire benefit [in the sold item], and that occurs through its validity.

أَو كَانَ يظْهر عِنْد الْوَصْف، وَلم ينشأ عَنهُ، وَلم يدل عَلَيْهِ، كشكر النِّعْمَة الْمُنَاسبَة للزِّيَادَة مِنْهَا، فالشكر: هُوَ الْوَصْف الْمُنَاسب، وَزِيَادَة النِّعْمَة هِيَ الْحِكْمَة، وَوُجُوب

451 [T] *Sharḥ Mukhtaṣar al-Rawḍah* (3/382-383).

الشُّكْر هُوَ الحكم. وَهَذِه الْأَمْثِلَة تقريبية. وَبِالْجُمْلَةِ: مَتى أفْضى الحكم إِلَى مصلحَة علل بِالْوَصْفِ الْمُشْتَمل عَلَيْهَا.

Sometimes, this concept appears when describing something, though it did not initiate because of it nor was it indicated. An example is thankfulness for favours that Allah the Exalted has bestowed, which is relevant to the increase of more favours. Thankfulness is the *waṣf al-munāsib* in this case, the increase of favours is the wisdom behind it, and the obligation of thankfulness is the ruling. These examples are merely meant to explain the concept. To summarise, whenever a ruling leads to some utility, its *ratio legis* is the attribute that it comprises of.

ثمَّ إِنَّه بِاعْتِبَار تَأْثِيره - وَهُوَ اقتضاؤه لحكم الْمُنَاسبَة لترتب الحكم عَلَيْهِ - يَنْقَسِم إِلَى أَقسَام:

To continue, in respect to the effect it plays, meaning, how it necessitates the ruling implied by the relationship between them, it is categorised into types:

أَحدهَا: الْمُؤثر، وَهُوَ مَا ظهر تَأْثِير عينه فِي عين الحكم أَو جنسه بِنَصّ أَو إِجْمَاع، كَقَوْلِنَا: سَقَطت الصَّلَاة عَن الْحرَّة الْحَائِض بِالنَّصِّ وَالْإِجْمَاع لمَشَقَّة التّكْرَار، لِأَن الصَّلَاة تَتَكَرَّر، فَلَو وَجب قَضَاؤُهَا، لشق عَلَيْهَا ذَلِك، فقد ظهر تأثر الْمَشَقَّة الْمَذْكُورَة فِي إِسْقَاط الصَّلَاة بِالْإِجْمَاع، وكتعليل الْحَدث بِمَسّ الذّكر بِالنَّصِّ.

First: Effective (*mu'athir*): This is where the attribute in particular has directly affected the individual instance or genus of the ruling, through a text or consensus. For example, we state that prayer is not an obligation on a menstruating free woman, and the divine texts or consensus is the evidence. The reason for the ruling is the difficulty of repeating those prayers, since prayers repeat often. It would be quite strenuous for her to make those prayers up. Therefore, the attribute of "difficulty" has been shown to apparently affect the ruling in that it lifts the obligation of making-up the prayers, according to consensus. Another example is that the divine texts indicate that touching of the private parts invalidates one's ritual purity.

وَلَا يضر هَذَا الْقسم ظُهُور مُؤثر آخر مَعَه فِي الأَصْل فيعلل بِالْكُلِّ، وَذَلِكَ كالمعتدة وَالْحَائِض والمرتدة يُعلل امْتنَاع وَطئهَا بالأسباب الثَّلَاثَة: الْحيض وَالْعدة وَالردة فَلَو

أردنَا أَن نقيس الْأمة على الْحرة فِي ذَلِك بِأحد الْأَوْصَاف الْمَذْكُورة صَحَّ، وَكَانَ من بَاب الْمُنَاسب الْمُؤثر بِتَقْدِير أَن لَا يكون النَّص شَامِلًا لَهَا.

This type is not disqualified if there appears another effective attribute in the precedent, for if it exists, all of the effective attributes are the *ratio legis*. An example is when a woman who is during her post-divorce waiting period is menstruating, and has apostatised. In this case, the ruling is that it is impermissible to have intercourse with her, on three grounds, namely, her menstruation, her waiting period, and her apostasy. If we wished to analogize a slave-girl to the free woman in establishing this same ruling, and were to use one of those attributes, it would be a perfectly correct analogy. As such, it makes it relevant and effective, when assuming that the divine text is not inclusive [of the new case].

الثَّانِي: الملائم، وَهُوَ مَا ظهر تَأْثِير عينه فِي جنس الحكم، كَقَوْلِنَا: الْأَخ من الْأَبَوَيْنِ مقدم فِي ولَايَة النكَاح، قِيَاسا على تَقْدِيمه فِي الْإِرْث، فالوصف - الَّذِي هُوَ الْأُخوة فِي الأَصْل وَالْفرع - مُتحد بالنوع. وَالْحكم - الَّذِي هُوَ الْوَلَايَة فِي الْإِرْث - مُتحد بِالْجِنْس لَا بالنوع. فَهَذَا وصف أثر عينه فِي جنس الحكم، وَهُوَ جنس التَّقْدِيم، فعين الْأُخوة أثرت فِي جنس التَّقْدِيم.

Second: Appropriate (*mulā'im*): This is where the individual instance of the *ratio legis* has affected the genus of the ruling. For example, we state that a brother who shares both parents is more preferred in guardianship of marriage, because that is analogous to inheritance. The attribute, namely, siblingship in both the precedent and the new case, share in their species. The ruling, which is guardianship and inheritance,[452] share in the genus, not the species. As such, in this ruling, the individual instance has affected the genus of the ruling, which is the genus of preference altogether. The individual instance in this case is siblingship, and it has affected the ruling in the genus of "preference."

452 [T] In the printed copy, it states, "guardianship in inheritance," but that is an incorrect reading of the manuscript.

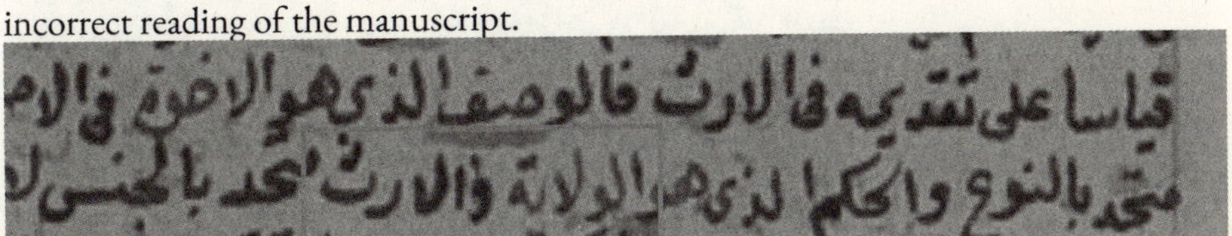
قياسا على تقديمه في الارث فالوصف الذي هو الاخوة في الاص
متحد بالنوع والحكم الذي هو الولاية والارث متحد بالجنس لا

وَمن هَذَا النَّوْع عكس مَا تقدم، وَهُوَ مَا أثر جنسه فِي عين الحكم، كَقَوْلِنَا: سَقَطت الصَّلَاة عَن الْحَائِض لأجل الْمَشَقَّة، قِيَاسا على الْمُسَافِر. فقد أثر جنس الْمَشقَّة فِي عين السُّقُوط.

Another example of this type is the opposite of what has been mentioned, namely, when the genus of a ruling affects an individual instance of a ruling. For example, we state that prayer is not obligatory on a menstruating woman, due to hardship, which is analogous with a traveling person. As such, the genus of hardship has affected the individual instance of non-obligation.

وَمِنْه أَيْضا مَا ظهر تَأْثِير جنسه فِي جنس الحكم كإلحاق بعض الْأَحْكَام بِبَعْض بِجَامِع الْمُنَاسبَة للْمصْلحَة الْمُطلقَة، كإلحاق شَارِب الْخمر بالقاذف فِي جلده ثَمَانِينَ كَمَا قَالَ عَليّ رَضِي الله عَنهُ: «أرَاهُ إِذا سكر هذى، وَإِذا هذى افترى فأرى عَلَيْهِ حد المفتري» فَأخذ مُطلق الْمُنَاسبَة وَمُطلق المظنة.

Another example is where the genus affects the genus of the ruling. For example, some rulings could be analogous to others with the unifying appropriate attribute being utility in and of itself. For example, a person who drinks alcohol could be analogous to a slanderer in the ruling where they are lashed eighty times. ʿAlī ﷺ said, "I find that when he is intoxicated, he speaks deliriously, and when he speaks deliriously, he slanders others. As such, I find that he should be given the penalty of a slanderer."[453] In this case, ʿAlī considered the attribute as is and applied it to a likely area of impact.

وَهَذَا النَّوْع سَمَّاهُ بعض الْأُصُولِيِّينَ الملائم، وَسَماهُ بعضهم بالغريب، وقيل: هذا هو الملائم، وما سواه مؤثر. وقال المرداوي في (التحرير): إن اعْتبر بترتب الحكم على الْوَصْف فَقَط إِن ثبت بِنَصّ أَو إِجْمَاع اعْتِبَار عينه فِي جنس الحكم، أَو بِالْعَكْسِ، أَو جنسه فِي جنس الحكم، فالملائم وَهُوَ حجَّة عِنْد الْمُعظم، وَإِلَّا فالغريب وَهُوَ حجَّة. وَمنعه أَبُو الْخطاب وَالْحَنَفِيَّة. انْتهى.

Some scholars refer to this last case as *mulā'im*, while others referred to it as, "unique (*gharīb*)." Some said that this is *mulā'im* and other cases are

---

453 Reported by Mālik (2/842).

mu'athir. Al-Mardāwī stated in *al-Taḥrīr*, "It is 'appropriate (*mulā'im*),' if it is considered that the ruling is contingent only on the attribute, in the case that [the attribute] is established through a divine text or consensus. Also, the effect of the individual instance must affect the genus of the ruling, or the opposite (the genus affects the individual instance), or if the genus affects the genus of the ruling. A *mula'im* is evidence according to the majority. If it does not fall under the previous description, it is known as *gharib*,[454] and it, too, is evidence.[455] However, Abu 'l-Khaṭṭāb and the Ḥanafī scholars have denied it as evidence." **[End]**[456]

فَفرق بَينهمَا ثمَّ قَالَ: وَإِن اعْتبر الشَّارِع جنسه الْبعيد فِي جنس الحكم، فمرسل ملائم، وَإِلَّا فمرسل غَرِيب مَنعه الْجُمْهُور، أَو مُرْسل ثَبت إلغاؤه كإيجاب الصَّوْم على واطئ قَادر فِي رَمَضَان، وَهُوَ مَرْدُود اتِّفَاقًا. والمرسل الملائم لَيْسَ حجَّة عِنْد الْأَكْثَر، وَقيل: فِي الْعِبَادَات، وَقَالَ مَالك: حجَّة، وَأنْكرهُ أَصْحَابه. وَقَالَ الْغَزالِيّ: بِشَرْط كَون الْمصلحَة ضَرُورِيَّة قَطْعِيَّة، كتترس كفار بِمُسلم، وَلَيْسَ هَذَا مِنْهُ لاعتباره، فَهُوَ حق قطعا. وَمعنى كَلَام الْموفق، وَالْفَخْر، والطوفي: أَن غير الملغي حجَّة. وَقيل: لَا يشْتَرط فِي الْمُؤثر كَونه مناسبا. انْتهى.

As can be seen, he has differentiated between the two. In another instance, al-Mardāwī stated, "If the Legislator considers the subaltern genus [of the attribute] affecting the genus of the ruling, it is known as a "free[457] appropriate description (*mursal mulā'im*)."[458] If He does not,[459] it is referred to as a

454 [T] It is referred to as *gharīb* because the only thing that testifies to its validity is the precedent. Refer to *al-Taḥbīr Sharḥ al-Taḥrīr* (7/3404).

455 [T] An example is the attribute of intoxication being the *ratio legis* for analogizing *nabīdh* to wine. This is based on the fact that there is no divine text that refers to the *ratio legis* of intoxication. Refer to *al-Taḥbīr Sharḥ al-Taḥrīr* (7/3404).

456 [T] *Taḥrīr al-Manqūl wa Tahdhīb 'Ilm al-Uṣūl* (p. 291).

457 [T] It is known as free-reign because it is not known that the legislation affirms nor denies the attribute. Refer to *Tashnīf al-Masāmi'* (3/299).

458 [T] An example of a *mursal mulā'im* is stating that the *ratio legis* of prohibiting a small amount of wine is that it leads to consumption of a greater amount of wine. In this case, the subaltern genus is considered inasmuch as its effect on the genus of the ruling. Another example is stating that since seclusion with women leads to fornication, it is, too, prohibited. Refer to *al-Taḥbir Sharḥ al-Taḥrīr* (7/3405).

459 [T] Meaning, if the Legislator does not consider the subaltern genus of an attribute to affect the genus of the ruling.

"free unique attribute (*mursal gharīb*)."[460] The majority deny it as evidence. Another type is a free attribute whose effect is nullified, such as obligating fasting on a person who is easily able to free a slave if they had intercourse in Ramadan. This is rejected, according to all scholars. The "free appropriate description" (*mursal mulā'im*) is not evidence according to the majority. Others stated it is not evidence in matters of worship, and Mālik stated it is evidence, though his adherents have rejected that. Al-Ghazālī stated, "It must contain a necessary and definitive utility, such as shielding Muslims with non-Muslims." This, however, is not an example. As such, it is definitively correct [to not consider this type to be evidence.] The meaning of what al-Muwaffaq, al-Fakhr, and al-Ṭūfī stated is that the non-negated attributes are evidence. Some have stated that an effective attribute does not have to be appropriate.[461]

ثمَّ اعْلَم أَن للجنسية مَرَاتِب، فأعمها فِي الْوَصْف: كَونه وَصفا، ثمَّ مناطا، ثمَّ مصلحَة خاصَّة. وَفِي الحكم: كَونه حكما، ثمَّ وَاجِبا وَنَحْوه، ثمَّ عبَادَة، ثمَّ صَلَاة، ثمَّ ظهرا.

Genera are of varying levels, from most general to most particular: (i) the description (*al-wasf*),[462] the conditional (*al-manāṭ*),[463] the particular utility

460 [T] An example of a *mursal gharīb* is analogizing a woman who is divorced thrice when her husband is on the death bed to a person who has killed someone they are to inherit from, in the sense that the opposite of their intent would occur. In the case of the woman who was divorced thrice, she would still receive inheritance, and in the case of the murderer, they would not receive any inheritance. Refer to *Bayān al-Mukhtaṣar Sharḥ Mukhtaṣar Ibn al-Ḥājib* (3/129) and *Mukhtaṣar al-Taḥrīr* (4/179).

461 [T] *Taḥrīr al-Manqūl wa Tahdhīb 'Ilm al-Uṣūl* (p. 292).

462 [T] It is too general to be considered a conditional attribute for the ruling. Every conditional is a description, but not every description is a conditional. Refer to *Sharḥ Mukhtaṣar al-Rawḍah* (3/396).

463 [T] This is more general than the particular utility. Every particular utility is a conditional attribute, but not vice versa, since it is possible for a conditional attribute to be devotional (*ta'abbudi*) where the utility in the ruling is unknown. This, of course is in reference to utility as an observable phenomenon. As for in reality, the rulings within legislation always contain some benefit. Ibid.

(*maṣlaḥah khāṣṣah*).[464] When it comes to rulings, it is also of levels[465]: (i) the ruling (*al-ḥukm*), (ii) the obligation (*al-wājib*) etc, (iii) worship (*al-ʿibādah*), (iv) prayer (*al-salat*), (v) and the *ẓuhr* prayer.

وتأثير الْأَخَص فِي الْأَخَص أقوى، وتأثير الْأَعَمّ فِي الْأَعَمّ يُقَابله، وتأثير الْأَخَص فِي الْأَعَمّ وَعَكسه واسطتان، وَبِهَذَا الطَّرِيق تظهر الْأَجْنَاس الْعَالِيَة المتوسطة، والأنواع السافلة للْأَحْكَام والأوصاف من الْمُنَاسب وَغيره، فالإسكار مثلا نوع من الْمفْسدَة، والمفسدة جنس لَهُ، وَالإِخْوَة نوع من الْأَوْصَاف، والتقديم فِي الْمِيرَاث نوع من الْأَحْكَام، فَهُوَ تَأْثِير نوع فِي نوع.

The effect of the most particular ruling in the most particular genus is the strongest. The effect of the most general ruling in the most general genus is the weakest. The effects of the more particular in the more general, and vice versa, are middling levels.[466] As such, the differences between subaltern and proximate genera are known, as well as infima species of rulings and descriptions, by understanding what is relevant and suitable, and so forth. Intoxication, for example, is a species of "evil," and "evil," is its genus. As a description, brotherhood is a species, and as a ruling, preference in inheri-

464 [T] The reason it was referred to as a particular utility is to avoid referring to general utilities, which are things that generally bring about utility. Defining it as a particular utility means that it is referring to necessities (*ḍarūrāt*), needs (*ḥājiyyāt*) and complementary things (*tahsiniyyāt*). Ibid.

465 [T] Here, he is to define the genera of a ruling. The fact that it is a "ruling," is most general, since it does not indicate any species, such as being obligatory. Obligatory is a genus in that it does not indicate a species, such as worship, transaction, behaviour, and so forth. A worship is a genus in that it does not define a species, such as fasting, prayer, and so forth. A prayer is a genus in that it does not specify which prayer: *ẓuhr*, *ʿasr*, *maghrib*, *ʿishā*, *fajr*, or a prayer made obligatory by oath. Lastly, the most particular of this tree is the *ẓuhr* prayer.

Note that al-Qarāfī stated, "The most general genera of rulings are that it first is a ruling. Then, it is particularized by the fact that it is an obligation or a choice-based action. Then, it is particularized by being a prohibition or an obligation. Then, it is particularized by being a prohibition, say, of wine or an obligation of, say, a prayer." Refer to *Sharḥ Mukhtaṣar al-Rawḍah* (3/397).

466 [T] This means that where there is an effect in, say, an obligatory prayer, it is more particular than if the effect is just to an act of worship, if there is an effect on all actions of worship, it is more particular than if the effect was just, say, to obligations, and lastly, if there is an effect on obligations, it is more particular than if there is an effect on rulings as a genus. Ibid.

tance is a species. When they coincide, the species [of the latter] affects the species [of the former].

النَّوْع الثَّانِي: من أَنْوَاع إِثْبَات الْعلَّة بالاستنباط إِثْبَاتهَا بالسبر والتقسيم. فَالْأول: إِبْطَال كل عِلّة علل بهَا الحكم بِالْإِجْمَاع إِلَّا وَاحِدَة فتتعين، وَمعنى ذَلِك أَن الْمُسْتَدلّ بِالْقِيَاسِ إِذا أَرَادَ أَن يبين عِلّة الأَصْل الْمَقِيس عَلَيْهِ كَذَا ليلحق بِهِ الْفَرْع الْمَقِيس، وَأَرَادَ تَبيين الْعلَّة بالسبر والتقسيم، ذكر كل عِلّة علل بهَا حكم الأَصْل، ثمَّ يبطل الْجَمِيع إِلَّا الْعلَّة الَّتِي يختارها، فَيتَعَيَّن التَّعْلِيل، فَيثبت الحكم فِي الْفَرْع بواسطتها، مثل أَن يَقُول: عِلّة الرِّبَا فِي الْبر وَنَحْوه إِمَّا الْكَيْل، وَإِمَّا الطّعْم، وَإِمَّا الْقُوت.

The second of the types of establishing a *ratio legis* is via elimination and classification. Elimination (*al-sabr*) refers to nullifying all possible *ratione legis* of a ruling, where there is consensus that the ruling has a *ratio legis*. This continues until there is just one *ratio legis*, making it the chosen one. This means that the person wishing to establish evidence—when wishing to clarify the *ratio legis* of the precedent that is being used in an analogy to extend a ruling to a new case, and wishes to clarify the *ratio legis* via elimination and classification—he mentions each *ratio legis* that is mentioned for the ruling of the precedent. Then, they proceed to invalidate all of them, keeping one that they choose, making it the *ratio legis* by process of elimination. As such, the ruling extends to the new case by way of the *ratio legis*. For example, one can state that, for the prohibition of usury in barley, there are these possible *ratione legis*: (i) Dry-measuring, (ii) it being a food item, (iii) it being a necessary provision.

وَهَذِه الْعِلَل كلهَا بَاطِلَة إِلَّا الأولى مثلا وَهِي الْكَيْل إِن كَانَ حنبليا أَو حنفيا، أَو إِلَّا الطّعْم إِن كَانَ شافعيا، أَو إِلَّا الْقُوت إِن كَانَ مالكيا، فَيتَعَيَّن للتَّعْلِيل، وَيلْحق الأرز الذّرة وَنَحْو ذَلِك بِجَامِع الْكَيْل. وَيُقِيم الدَّلِيل على بطلَان مَا أبطلهُ إِمَّا بانتقاضة انتقاضا مؤثرا، أَو بِعَدَم مناسبته، أَو غير ذَلِك بِحَسب الْإِمْكَان والاتفاق.

Then, they can state that all of these *ratione legis* are invalidated, except for the first, if they are Ḥanafī or Ḥanbalī. Or, they can state that the second is the *ratio legis*, if they were Shāfiʿī, or the third if they were Māliki. As such, the remaining *ratio legis* is the chosen one to use to extend rulings. In the first case, rice, seeds, and so forth, are encompassed by the *ratio legis* of them being dry-measured. Then, the interlocutor can establish evidences to nullify the other descriptions, either by showing they are not effective or not appropriate, or through other means, so much as they are able.

وَيشْتَرط لصِحَّة السبر أمور:

There are a number of preconditions that regulate the validity of the process of elimination:

أَحدهَا: أَن يكون الحكم فِي الأَصْل مُعَللا، إِذْ لَو كَانَ تعبدا، لامتنع الْقيَاس عَلَيْهِ.

First: The ruling of the precedent must have a discernible *ratio legis*. If it were a devotional action, extending it by analogy would not be possible.

الثَّانِي: أَن يكون مجمعا على تَعْلِيله كَمَا قَالَه أَبُو الْخطاب، إِذْ بِتَقْدِير أَن يكون مُخْتَلفا فِي تَعْلِيله، فللخصم الْتِزَامه التَّعَبُّد فِيهِ، فَيبْطل الْقيَاس. وَقَالَ غَيره: هَذَا الشَّرْط بِالنِّسْبَةِ إِلَى الْمُجْتَهد، لِأَنهُ لَا حجر عَلَيْهِ إِلَّا بإجْمَاع الْأمة، إِذْ بِدُونِهِ لَهُ أَن يلْتَزم التَّعَبُّد فِي الأَصْل، وَيفْسد كل عِلّة علل بهَا خَصمه، بِخِلَاف مَا إِذا كَانَ الْمُسْتَدلّ مناظرا، أَو خَصمه منتميا، إِلَى مَذْهَب ذِي مَذْهَب، فَإِنَّهُ حِينَئِذٍ تكفيه مُوَافقَة الْخصم على التَّعْلِيل، وَلم يعْتَبر الْإِجْمَاع عَلَيْهِ من الْأمة لِأَنهُ لَيْسَ بصدد استنباط الْأَحْكَام.

Second: There must be consensus that the ruling has a discernible *ratio legis*. This was the view of Abu 'l-Khaṭṭāb. The reason is that if there was a difference of opinion on whether it had a *ratio legis*, the opponent in a discussion could state that it is a devotional ruling, and thereby nullify the analogy. Others have stated that this precondition only applies to a *mujtahid* scholar, since they have no qualms in establishing such rulings unless the entirety of the Ummah disagrees with them. Without consensus, if the *mujtahid* scholar wished to take the view that the precedent is a devotional ruling, they may do so, and thereby nullify all *ratione legis* mentioned. However, if the person is merely in a debate or the interlocutor ascribes to a particular *madhhab*, it is only necessary for them both to agree that the ruling has a *ratio legis*. In this case, consensus is not a requirement, since they are not in the midst of deducing rulings.

الثَّالِث: أَن يكون سبره حاصرا لجَمِيع الْعِلَل، إِذْ لَو لم يكن حاصرا لجَاز أَن يبْقى وصف هُوَ الْعلَّة فِي نفس الْأَمر لم يذكرهُ، فَيَقَع الْخَطَأ فِي الْقيَاس، وَلَا يَصح السبر.

Third: Their elimination must comprehensively mention all possible attributes. If it does not, it leaves the possibility that there is an unmentioned attribute that, in reality, is the *ratio legis*. As such, the analogy becomes faulty, and the process of elimination is invalidated.

وَطَرِيق ثُبُوت حصر السبر من وَجْهَيْن:

There are two scenarios to confirm that the process of elimination is all-encompassing:

أَحدهمَا: مُوَافقَة الْخصم على انحصار الْعلَّة فِيمَا ذكره الْمُسْتَدلّ.

First: The opponent can agree that all possible *ratione legis* are confined to what the claimant has mentioned.

الثَّانِي: أَن يعجز الْخصم عَن إِظْهَار وصف زَائِد على مَا ذكره الْمُسْتَدلّ.

Second: The opponent can fail to mention any additional *ratione legis*.

فَإِذا تمّ أحد الْأَمريْنِ وَجب على الْخصم الْمُعْتَرض إِمَّا تَسْلِيم الْحصْر فَيحصل مَقْصُود الْمُسْتَدلّ، أَو إِظْهَار مَا عِنْد الْمُعْتَرض من الْأَوْصَاف الزَّائِدَة على مَا ذكره الْمُسْتَدلّ لينْظر فِيهِ فيفسده، وَلَا يسمع قَول الْمُعْتَرض: عِنْدِي وصف زَائِد لكني لَا أذكرهُ، لِأَنهُ حِينَئِذٍ إِمَّا صَادِق فَيكون كَاتِما لعلم دعت الْحَاجة إِلَيْهِ فيفسق بذلك، أَو كَاذِب فَلَا يعول على قَوْله، وَيلْزمهُ الْحصْر.

If either scenario occurs, the opposing interlocutor must either accept the enumeration of the *ratione legis*, and, if that occurs, the purpose of the claimant is realised. If the opposing interlocutor can mention additional attributes that were not mentioned by the first interlocutor, the latter can investigate them and attempt to nullify them. The claimant must not pay heed to their opponent if they state, "I have an additional attribute, but I will not mention it," because in that case, either they are telling the truth and are hiding some needed knowledge, thereby becoming sinners, or are lying, and if that is the case, what they said has no impact and they must accept the enumeration.

وَإِذا أبرز الْخصم الْمُعْتَرض وَصفا زَائِدا على مَا ذكره الْمُسْتَدلّ لزم صَاحب الِاسْتِدْلَال أَن ينظر فِي ذَلِك الْوَصْف فيفسده وَيبين عدم اعْتِبَاره، وَله إِلَى ذَلِك طَرِيقَانِ:

If the opposing interlocutor can mention an additional attribute, the claimant must investigate the attribute and attempt to invalidate it, showing that it is not worthy of consideration in the case. They can do so in one of two ways:

أَحدهمَا: أَن يبين بَقَاء الحكم مَعَ عَدمه فِي بعض الصُّور مثل أَن يَقُول الْحَنْبَلِيّ أَو الشَّافِعِي: يَصح أَمَان العَبْد، لِأَنهُ أَمَان وجد من عَاقل مُسلم غير مُتَّهم، فَيصح قِيَاسا على الْحر، فَيَقُول الْحَنَفِيّ: إِن مَا ذكرت أَوْصَاف الْعلَّة فِي الأَصْل فَقَط، وَتركت وَصفا آخر - وَهُوَ الْحُرِية - هُوَ مَفْقُود فِي العَبْد، وَحِينَئِذٍ لَا يَصح الْقيَاس، فَيَقُول الْمُسْتَدلّ: وصف الْحُرِّيَّة ملغي بالْعَبدِ الْمَأْذُون لَهُ، فَإِن أَمَانه يَصح بِاتِّفَاق مَعَ عدم الْحُرية، فَصَارَ وَصفا لاغيا لَا تَأْثِير لَهُ فِي الْعلَّة.

First: They can show that the ruling remains though the attribute is nonexistent in some scenarios. For example, a Ḥanbalī or Shāfiʿī might state that an offering of peace made by a slave is valid, since it is an offering of peace made by a Muslim of sound intellect whose upstanding nature is not in question, making them analogous to a free Muslim. A Ḥanafī could respond and state that [they do not agree that those are the only attributes of the precedent,][467] and that there is a missing attribute, namely, freedom, which is nonexistent in the slave. As such, the Ḥanafī will state that the analogy is invalid. The claimant could respond by saying that the attribute of freedom is inconsequential in the slave that has been given permission to do so, for in that case, their offering of peace is valid according to all schol-

467 [T] What is between the brackets was missed from al-Shaykh Ibn Badrān's quotation from *Sharḥ Mukhtaṣar al-Rawḍah* (3/407).

ars, and that is despite them being slaves. As such, the attribute of slavery is inconsequential and plays no part in the *ratio legis*.

الثَّانِي: أَن يبين كَون الْوَصْف الزَّائِد وَصفا طرديا أَي: لم يلْتَفت الشَّرْع إِلَيْهِ فِيمَا عهد من تصرفه، كالطول وَالْقصر، والذكورة وَالْأنوثة، مِثَاله: مَا لَو قَالَ الْمُسْتَدلّ: يسري الْعتْق فِي الْأمة قِيَاسا على العَبْد بِجَامِع الرق، إِذْ لَا عِلّة غَيره عملا بالسبر فَقَالَ الْمُعْتَرض: الذكورية وصف زَائِد مُعْتَبر فِي الأَصْل، لِأَن العَبْد إِذا كمل عتقه بِالسِّرَايَةِ حصل مِنْهُ مَا لَا يحصل من الْأمة من تأهله للْحكم والإمامة وأنواع الولايات، وَلَا يلْزم من ثبوت السَّرَايَة فِي الْأَكْمَل ثبوته فِي غَيره.

Second: They can show that the additional attribute is irrelevant in that the legislation has not given it consideration. Examples are tallness and shortness, maleness and femaleness. For example, a person could state that emancipation can occur to a female slave, because a female slave is analogous to a male slave in that they are both slaves. By process of elimination, we determine that there are no other *ratione legis*. The interlocutor can state that maleness is a further attribute and is worthy of consideration in the precedent, since if a slave's freedom is effectuated, they have privileges that are not given to slave-girls, such as the right to rulership, leading prayer, and other government posts. The fact that emancipation is effectuated in the more complete does not necessitate it is also effectuated in other things.

فَيَقُول الْمُسْتَدلّ: مَا ذكرت من الْفرق مُنَاسِب، غير أَنا لم نر الشَّرْع اعْتبر الذكورية والأنوثية فِي بَاب الْعتْق فَيكون ذَلِك على خلاف مَعْهُود تصرفه، فَيكون وَصفا طرديا فِي ظَاهر الْأَمر.

To respond to this objection, the first interlocutor can state that although the differences mentioned are appropriate, we have not found that the legislation has given consideration to maleness or femaleness in its rulings on emancipation. As such, to consider it in this scenario would be to contravene with what we know of its usual rulings in this regard. As such, [maleness and femaleness] are apparently irrelevant.

وَلَا يَكْفِي الْمُسْتَدلّ فِي إفْسَاد الْوَصْف الَّذِي أبرزه الْمُعْتَرض أَن يبين كَونه منتقضا،

بل يُوجد بِدُونِ الحكم، لِأَن الْوَصْف الْمَذْكُور يجوز أَن يكون جُزْء الْعلَّة، أَو شرطا لَهَا، فَلَا يسْتَقل بالحكم، وَلَا يلْزم من عدم استقلاله صِحَة عِلّة الْمُسْتَدلّ بِدُونِهِ.

Further, it is not sufficient for the first interlocutor, if they wish to invalidate the attribute mentioned by their opponent, to show that it is invalid. Rather, in this scenario, they must show that the attribute exists in some other scenario without the ruling. The reason is that the attribute mentioned might be a part or precondition of a *ratio legis*, and therefore not independently establish a ruling. It is not necessary that, if it cannot independently establish a ruling, the *ratio legis* of the first interlocutor is automatically valid.

فَلَو قَالَ الْمُسْتَدلّ: عِلّة الرِّبَا فِي الْبر الْكَيْل، فعارضه الْمُعْتَرض بالطعم، فنقضه الْمُسْتَدلّ بِالْمَاءِ أَو غَيره مِمَّا يطعم وَلَا رِبًّا فِيهِ، لم يكفه ذَلِك فِي بطلَان كَون الطّعْم عِلّة لجَوَاز أن يكون جُزْء عِلّة الرِّبَا بِأَن تكون الْعلَّة مَجْمُوع الْكَيْل والطعم أَو شرطا فِيهَا، فَتكون عِلّة الرِّبَا الْكَيْل بِشَرْط أَن يكون الْمكيل مطعوما، وَحِينَئِذٍ لَا يلْزم من بطلَان كَون الطّعْم عِلّة مُسْتَقلَّة أَن يكون الْكَيْل عِلّة صَحِيحَة، لجَوَاز أَن يكون الطّعْم جزءها أَو شَرطهَا.

For example, if they state that the *ratio legis* of the prohibition of usury in barley is that it is dry-weighted, and their opponent contradicts them, asserting that it is instead that it is a food product, and the first interlocutor invalidates their *ratio legis* with the example of water, or any other food source that is not susceptible to the rulings of usury, this is not sufficient to invalidate the possible *ratio legis* of it being a food source, since it is possible that the *ratio legis* is the combination of it being dry-measured as well as it being a food source. Or, it being a food source could be a precondition, making the *ratio legis* of the prohibition of usury in barley the fact that it is dry-measured, but with the precondition that it is an edible dry-measured product. As such, it is not necessarily the case that, just because being a food source is not an independent *ratio legis*, the correct *ratio legis* is thus the fact that it is dry-measured, since it being a food source might be a part or precondition of that *ratio legis*.

وَالْفرق بَين النَّقْض وَبَين بَقَاء الحكم مَعَ صدق الْوَصْف حَيْثُ كَانَ مُبْطلًا لَهُ دون

النَّقْض: هُوَ أَن بَقَاء الحكم مَعَ عدم الْوَصْف يدل على أَنه غير مُؤثر، وَلَا يعْتَبر فِي الحكم عِلّة وَلَا جُزْء عِلّة وَلَا شرطا، إِذْ لَو اعْتبر فِيهِ بِأحد هَذِه الْوُجُوه، لما وجد بِدُونِهِ أصلا، بِخِلَاف وجود الْوَصْف بِدُونِ الحكم، فَإِنَّهُ لَا يدل على عدم اعْتِبَاره فِي الحكم بِوَجْه من الْوُجُوه.

Therefore, there is a difference between the two concepts of, first, invalidation, and second, the ruling remaining with the [nonexistence][468] of the attribute, where it negates but does not necessarily invalidate. The difference is that, where the ruling remained though the attribute was nonexistent, it showed that the attribute was not effective and is irrelevant in that it is not considered in the ruling; it is not its *ratio legis*, nor is it a part or precondition of its *ratio legis*. If it were relevant in [being a part, precondition, or the *ratio legis* itself,] the ruling would never exist without its presence. This is contrary to a scenario where the attribute is present, but the ruling is not, because that does not, in any way, indicate that the attribute is wholly irrelevant in the ruling.[469]

وَأَيْضًا لَا يفْسد الْوَصْف الَّذِي أبداه الْمُعْتَرض بقول الْمُسْتَدلّ: إِنِّي لم أعثر بعد الْبَحْث على مُنَاسبَة علتك أَيهَا الْمُسْتَدلّ، فيتعارض الكلامان، وَيقف الْمُسْتَدلّ.

Also, if an opponent mentions a further attribute, and the first interlocutor states, "After investigation, I cannot find how the attribute you mentioned is relevant and suitable." In this case, their speech is contradictory, and the first interlocutor must abstain.

---

468 [T] What is between the brackets was mistakenly quoted as, "With the remaining ruling," but I have corrected it based on what is in *Sharḥ Mukhtaṣar al-Rawḍah* (3/409).

469 [T] Meaning, in a conditional statement 'if p then q,' and p being the ruling with q being the attribute, q can logically exist without p, but p cannot exist without q. In that case, either p is not conditioned on q, or the statement is altogether illogical. As an example, the statement, 'if it is raining (p), then the ground is wet (q).' In this case, the ground can be wet without it having rained. This, then, is the last scenario as described by al-Shaykh Ibn Badrān, where the attribute exists but the ruling does not. However, the statement, 'it is raining, although it is not wet outside,' is a logical fallacy. This is equivalent to saying, 'the ruling exists (p), however, the attribute does not (not q),' and is the example that al-Shaykh Ibn Badrān is attempting to illustrate by mentioning maleness and femaleness vis-à-vis emancipation.

وَإِذا أتفق خصمان على فَسَاد عِلّة غَيرهمَا فِي الحكم الْمُتَنَازع فيهِ، ثمَّ أفسد أَحدهمَا عِلّة الآخر، مثل أَن يتَّفق الْحَنْبَلِيّ وَالشَّافِعِيّ على أَن مَا عدا الْكَيْل والطعم عِلّة فَاسِدَة، ثمَّ نقض الشَّافِعِي عِلّة الْكَيْل بِالْمَاءِ، إِذْ هُوَ مَكِيل وَلَا رَبا فِيهِ، فَفِي كَون ذَلِك مصححا لعلة الناقض قولَانِ، فَقَالَ بعض الْمُتَكَلِّمين :يكون ذَلِك مصححا، وَصحح فِي (الرَّوْضَة) وَغَيرهَا خلاف هَذَا.

If the two interlocutors agree that the *ratio legis* for a ruling expressed by other scholars is invalid, and then one of them invalidates the *ratio legis* of the other, some scholars of *kalām* have stated that it establishes the *ratio legis* of the person who invalidated the attribute of the other, and in *al-Rawḍah*, al-Muwaffaq has stated that it does not establish it. An example is that a Ḥanbalī and a Shāfiʿī both agree that anything other than the attributes of being dry-measured and food items are invalid. Then, the Shāfiʿī invalidates the attribute the Ḥanbalī considers the *ratio legis*, by saying that water is measured in the same way, and it is not susceptible to rulings of usury.[470]

النَّوْع الثَّالِث: من أَنْوَاع إِثْبَات الْعلَّة بالاستنباط إِثْبَاتهَا بالدوران، وَهُوَ ترَتّب حكم على وصف وجودا وعدما، ويفيد الْعلَّة ظنا عِنْد جُمْهُور أَصْحَابنَا وَالشَّافِعِيَّة والمالكية وَبعض الْحَنَفِيَّة، وَقيل: قطعا.

The third way to establish a *ratio legis* through deduction is to do so by showing inseparability, which means that the ruling and the *ratio legis* exist concomitantly. In this case, the *ratio legis* is probable, according to the majority of our *aṣḥāb*, the Shāfiʿī scholars, the Māliki scholars, and some Ḥanafī scholars. Some said that the *ratio legis* is definitive.

---

470 [T] In this case, the scholars of *kalām* would argue by stating that both interlocutors agree that a *ratio legis* not expressed by either of them is invalid, and then the *ratio legis* of the other interlocutor is invalidated by their opponent, and by elimination, the third *ratio legis* is the valid one. Others disagreed, stating that it is not evidence that the remaining *ratio legis* is the valid one, since when they agreed to invalidate the other *ratio legis*, it does not mean it is truly invalidated, but rather, that it is invalid only to the two interlocutors. Their belief on the validity, or lack thereof, of the *ratio legis* is irrelevant to others, since others, such as Māliki scholars, would state that the *ratio legis* of both interlocutors are invalid. However, this might be considered valid in the debate, not when performing *ijtihād*. Refer to *Sharḥ Mukhtaṣar al-Rawḍah* (3/410).

ثمَّ إنَّه قد يكون فِي مَحل وَاحِد كالإسكار فِي الْعصير، فَإِن الْعصير قبل أَن يُوجد الْإِسْكَار كَانَ حَلَالا، فَلَمَّا حدث الْإِسْكَار حرم، فَلَمَّا زَالَ الْإِسْكَار وَصَارَ خلا، صَار حَلَالا، فدار التَّحْرِيم مَعَ الْإِسْكَار وجودا وعدما.

The concept of inseparability can exist in a single receptacle, such as the attribute of intoxication and its relationship to juice. Before it became an intoxicant, juice was lawful, when it became an intoxicant, it became unlawful, and when the attribute of intoxication came to an end when it was made into vinegar, it became lawful again. As such, prohibition is inseparable from the attribute of intoxication; where there is intoxication, there is prohibition, and when there is no intoxication, there is no prohibition.

أو فِي محلين كالطعم فِي تَحْرِيم الرِّبَا، فَإِنَّهُ لما وجد الطّعْم فِي التفاح كَانَ ربويا وَلما لم يُوجد فِي الْحَرِير، مثلا، لم يكن ربويا، فدار جَرَيَان الرِّبَا مَعَ الطّعْم. وَهَذَا الْمِثَال إِنَّمَا يجْرِي على قَول من يَقُول: إِن عِلّة الرِّبَا الطّعْم.

The concept can also exist in multiple receptacles, such as the prohibition of usury in an apple due to it being a food source. Since the attribute of it being a food source is not found in, say, silk, it means that silk is not susceptible to rulings of usury. As such, the existence of the rulings of usury were inseparable from the attribute of being a food source. This example, of course, is applicable to those who state that the *ratio legis* for the prohibition of usury is the attribute of being a food product.

وكقولهم فِي وجوب الزَّكَاة فِي حلي الِاسْتِعْمَال الْمُبَاح: الْعلَّة الْمُوجبَة لِلزَّكَاةِ فِي كل من النَّقْدَيْنِ كَونه أحد الحجرين، لِأَن وجوب الزَّكَاة دَار مَعَ كَونه أحد الحجرين، وَلَا زَكَاة فِيهِ.

Another example given is on the obligation of *zakāt* in lawfully owned jewelry that is in use by its owner. They state that the *ratio legis* that makes *zakāt* obligatory in gold and silver coins (as a currency) is that they are gold or silver [and as such, when either of these two attributes exist, so does the ruling, and when they both are nonexistent, so too is the ruling. As for when it exists, an example is coinage, which can be gold or silver, and *zakāt* is obligatory on coins, and as for when it is nonexistent, an example is real estate: since it is not gold or silver, *zakāt* is not obligatory.][471]

قَالَ الطوفي: لَكِن الدوران فِي صُورَة أقوى مِنْهُ فِي صُورتينِ على مَا هُوَ مدرك ضَرُورَة أَو نظرا ظَاهرا. انْتهى.

Al-Ṭūfī said, "Inseparability in a single concept is stronger than if it affects two different concepts, as is known either by necessity or is clear through research."[472]

وَالْفرق بَينه وَبَين الطَّرْد: أَن الطَّرْد عبارَة عَن الْمُقَارنَة فِي الْوُجُود دون الْعَدَم، والدوران: عبارَة عَن الْمُقَارنَة فِي الْوُجُود والعدم، وَلما بَينا الطرق الدَّالَّة على صِحَة الْعلَّة، أَخذنَا نبين الطّرق الْفَاسِدَة الَّتِي لَا تدل على صِحَّتهَا، وَذَلِكَ فِي أُمُور.

The difference between inseparability and co-extension (*al-ṭard*) is that co-extension is only predicated on concomitance in existence (and not in non-existence). Inseparability is predicated on the coupling of the attribute and ruling both in existence and in non-existence. Since I have clarified the ways that indicate the validity of a proposed *ratio legis*, let us now discuss some invalid ways that do not show the validity of a *ratio legis*:

أَولهَا: اطراد الْعلَّة لَا يدل على صِحَّتهَا، لِأَن معنى اطرادها سلامتها عَن النَّقْص، وَهُوَ بعض مفسداتها، أَو سلامتها عَن مُفسد وَاحِد لَا يَنْبَغِي بُطْلَانهَا بمفسد آخر، ككونها قَاصِرَة أَو عدمية أَو طردية غير مُنَاسبَة عِنْد من لَا يرى التَّعْلِيل بذلك.

First: Co-extension of a *ratio legis* does not show its validity, because the

471 [T] What is between the brackets is from *Sharḥ Tanqīḥ al-Fuṣūl* by al-Imām al-Qarāfī, whom I believe al-Imām al-Ṭūfī is quoting from. In the copy of al-Ṭūfī's *Sharḥ Mukhtaṣar al-Rawḍah*, he says, "The obligation of *zakāt* is inseparable from its being gold or silver, and no *zakāt* is due on it." This, however, seems to be a misquotation of al-Imām al-Qarāfī. As such, I placed what al-Qarāfī stated, as it accurately depicts the concept that al-Ṭūfī, and by extension, al-Shaykh Ibn Badrān, is attempting to explain. Refer to *Sharḥ Tanqīḥ al-Fuṣūl* (p. 396) and *Sharḥ Mukhtaṣar al-Rawḍah* (3/413). Note that the view of Ḥanafī scholars is that *zakāt* is due on gold and silver jewellery owned lawfully, and their evidence is *al-dawarān*. The Ḥanbalī view is that it is not obligatory. Refer to *al-Ghurrat al-Manīfat fi Taḥqīq Ba'ḍ Masā'il al-Imām Abī Ḥanīfah* (p. 55) for the Ḥanafī view and *Sharḥ Muntahā al-Irādāt* (1/431) for the Ḥanbalī view.

472 [T] *Sharḥ Mukhtaṣar al-Rawḍah* (3/413).

only thing implied by it being coexistent is that it is safe from the attribute existing without the ruling,[473] which is only one invalidator of a *ratio legis*. Being safe of just one invalidator does not negate it being void, because that can be proven through another invalidator.[474] For example, it could be intransitive, predicated on nonexistence of something else, or irrelevant, for those who find that such things cannot be used to prove a *ratio legis*.

ثَانِيهَا: الِاسْتِدْلَال على صِحَّتهَا باقتران الحكم، وَهَذَا فَاسد أَيْضا، لِأَن الحكم يقْتَرن بِمَا يلازم الْعلَّة وَلَيْسَ بعلة، كاقتران تَحْرِيم الْخمر بلونها وطعمها وريحها، وَإِنَّمَا الْعلَّة الْإِسْكَار.

Second: Using its being coupled with a ruling to show its validity as a *ratio legis* is an invalid way of showing its validity. Sometimes, rulings are coupled with factors that cling to the *ratio legis* but are not a part of it. For example, the ruling of prohibition of wine is coupled to the colour, taste, and smell of wine. However, the true *ratio legis* is intoxication.

ثَالِثهَا: مَا ذكره الْغَزالِيّ، وَهُوَ اطرادها وانعكاسها، وَهَذَا مَبْنِيّ على أَن الدوران لَا يُفِيد الْعلية، وَهَذَا مَمْنُوع إِذْ التَّحْقِيق أَنه يُفِيد الْعلية.

Third: Al-Ghazālī mentioned that attempting to prove a *ratio legis* through co-extension and co-exclusion is invalid. This is based on the concept of inseparability not being a legitimate method of deducing a *ratio legis*. This, however, is untrue, since after thorough investigation, the truth is that it is a valid method of deducing a *ratio legis*.

خَاتِمَة: إِذا كَانَ الْوَصْف المصلحي الْمُنَاسب يسْتَلْزم أَو يتَضَمَّن مفْسدَة مُسَاوِيَة لمصلحته أَو راجحة عَلَيْهَا، فَقَالَ الْمُوفق، وَالْفَخْر، وَالْمجد، وَابْن الْجَوْزِيّ، والرازي، والبيضاوي: لم تنخرم مناسبته. وَقَالَ الْآمِدِيّ وَأَتْبَاعه: تنخرم.

473 [T] Meaning, it is a logical biconditional.

474 [T] In the printed copy, this entire sentence was mistaken. What I have placed matches what is in the manuscript.

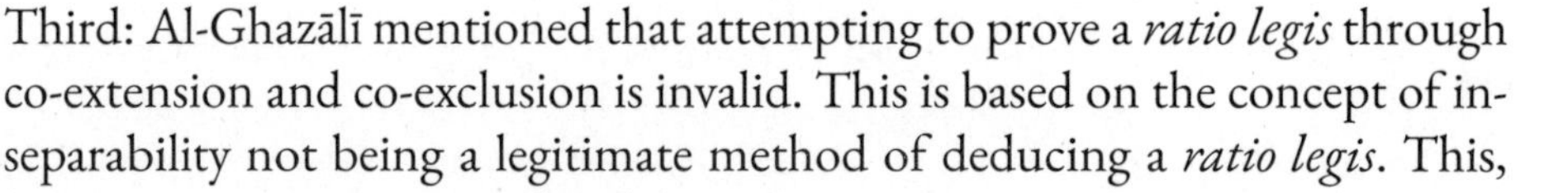
سلامتها عن النقض وهو بعض مفسداتها وسلامتها عن مفسد
واحد لا ينفي بطلانها بمفسد آخر ككونها قاصرة او عدمية او طردية

To conclude, if the appropriate attribute is one based on an undefined public interest and benefit, but also necessitates an equal or worse harm, al-Muwaffaq, al-Fakhr, al-Majd, Ibn al-Jawzī, and al-Bayḍāwī all stated that it is still appropriate (retaining its quality of *munāsabah*). However, al-Āmidī and those who agreed with his view stated that it no longer keeps its quality of appropriateness.

وَالْمُخْتَار الأول لِأَن مُعَارضَة ضد الشَّيْء لَهُ لَا تبطل حَقِيقَته، وَكَذَلِكَ الْمفْسدَة إِذا عارضت الْمصلحَة لَا تبطل حَقِيقَتهَا، نعم قد يخفى أَثَرهَا، وَيمْنَع اعْتِبَارهَا بِالْعرضِ إِذا ساوتها أَو رجحت عَلَيْهَا كَمَا تقدم في مبَاحث الاستصلاح والمصلحة الْمُرْسلَة، وَمن أَمْثِلَة ذَلِك أَن يُقَال فِي الْقمَار: لَهُ نفع، وَهُوَ تَكْثِير المَال، وَله مفْسدَة، وَهِي أكل مَال الْغَيْر بِالْبَاطِلِ، وَهُوَ تِجَارة مُحرمَة كالربا، فَإِن مثل هَذَا تتبع فِيهِ الْمصلحَة.

The first view is more veracious, however, because when something conflicts with its opposite, it does not negate its reality. Likewise, when a harm conflicts with a public benefit, it does not nullify that it is indeed a public benefit. True, its effects may disappear and, by accident, if a harm is equivalent to or greater than its benefit, that might prevent its consideration. This has been discussed earlier, when discussing *maṣlaḥah*. An example is gambling. It contains a utility, which is increasing one's wealth, but also contains harm, which is consuming the wealth of others falsely and it is a prohibited transaction, similar to usury. In this case, the *maṣlaḥah* is adhered to.

فصل

Subsection: [On Various Types of Analogy]

وَأما قِيَاس الشّبَه، وَسَماهُ كثير من أَصْحَابنَا بإِثْبات الْعلَّة بالشبه، وَهُوَ من جملَة مسالك الْعلَّة، وعرفوه: بِأَنَّهُ تردد فرع بَين أصلين شبهه بِأَحَدِهِمَا فِي الْأَوْصَاف أَكثر من الآخر. فإلحاق الْفَرْع بِأحد الْأَصْلَيْنِ الَّذِي شبهه بِهِ أَكثر هُوَ قِيَاس الشّبَه.

Analogy by resemblance (*qiyās al-shabah*) is often referred to by our *aṣḥāb* as: Establishing a *ratio legis* through showing resemblance. It is one method used when defining the *ratio legis*. The scholars have defined it as a new case that fluctuates between two precedents but its qualities bear a greater resemblance to one precedent over the other. In this case, when the new case is appended to the precedent it most resembles, it is referred to as "analogy by resemblance (*qiyās al-shabah*)."

وَلَا يكونَانِ أصلين لهَذَا الْفَرْع حَتَّى يكون فِيهِ مناط كل مِنْهُمَا، مِثَال ذَلِك الْمَذْي، فَإِنَّهُ مُتَرَدّد بَين الْبَوْل والمني، فَمن قَالَ بنَجَاسَتِهِ، قَالَ: هُوَ خَارج من الْفرج، لَا يخلق مِنْهُ الْوَلَد، وَلَا يجب الْغسْل بِهِ، أشبه الْبَوْل. وَمن قَالَ بِطَهَارَتِهِ قَالَ: هُوَ خَارج تخللته الشَّهْوَة، وَخرج أمامها، فَأشبه الْمَنِيّ.

In order for a new case to fluctuate between two precedents, the respective *ratio legis* of each precedent must exist to some extent in the new case. An example is pre-seminal fluid, which fluctuates between urine and sperm. Those who claim it is impure stated that it exits from the privates, does not result in creation of a child, and does not result in a major ritual impurity. In these qualities, it mostly resembles urine. Those who claim it is pure stated that it exits from the privates out of sexual arousal. As such, they stated it is more resembling of sperm.

واعْلَم أنك إِذا تفقدت مواقع الْخلاف من الْأَحْكَام الشَّرْعِيَّة، وَجدتهَا نازعة إِلَى قَاعِدَة قِيَاس الشّبَه، إِذْ أن مسَائِل الْخلاف تَجِد غالبها وَاسِطَة بَين طرفين، تنْزع

إِلَى كل وَاحِد مِنْهُمَا بِضَرْب من الشّبه، فيجذبها أقوى الشبهين إِلَيْهِ، فَإِن وَقع فِي ذَلِك نزاع، فَلَيْسَ فِي هَذِه الْقَاعِدَة، بل فِي أَي الطَّرفَيْنِ أشبه بهَا حَتَّى يلْحق بِهِ.

If one were to inspect the areas of differing in religious rulings, they would find that they tend to be contingent on *qiyās al-shabah*, since most religious rulings fluctuate between two ends of the spectrum, resembling each end in certain ways. In such cases, the ruling gravitates to whichever end of the spectrum it resembles most. If there is difference of opinion, it is not on the veracity of this maxim, but rather, on which ruling the new case most resembles, so that it can be appended to the ruling.

وَيصِح التَّمَسُّك بِقِيَاس الشّبه، لِأَنهُ يثير الظَّن. وَذهب القَاضِي أَبُو يعلى إِلَى أَنه لَا يَصح التَّمَسُّك بِهِ، وَإِذا صَحَّ ذَلِك، فَالْمُعْتَبر فِيهِ الشّبه الْحكمِي، كَأَن يُقَال: شبه العَبْد بالبهيمة فِي كَونهمَا مملوكين، وَالْملك أَمر حكمي. وَلَا يعْتَبر على الصَّحِيح الشّبه الْحَقِيقِيّ، كَأَن يُقَال: شبه العَبْد بِالْحرِّ فِي كَونهمَا آدميين، وَهُوَ وصف حَقِيقِي.

Adhering to *qiyās al-shabah* is valid, since it provides probability. Al-Qāḍī Abu Ya'lā opined that adhering to it is not valid. If adhering to *qiyās al-shabah* is valid, know that the resemblance that is relevant is the resemblance in ruling. For example, one can state that a slave resembles livestock in that both are owned. Ownership is a ruling. According to the more veracious view, essential resemblance is not relevant. For example, it would not be valid to state that a slave resembles a free person in that both are humans. Humanity is a description of a particular essence.

وَلَا ينظر أَيْضا إِلَى مَا يغلب على الظَّن أَنه مناط الحكم مِنْهُمَا، كَأَن يُقَال: إننا نَنْظُر فِي الْبِنْت المخلوقة من الزِّنَى فنجدها من حَيْثُ الْحَقِيقَة ابْنَته، لِأَنهَا خلقت من مَائه، وَمن حَيْثُ الحكم أَجْنَبِيَّة مِنْهُ، لكَونهَا لَا ترثه وَلَا يَرِثهَا، وَلَا يتولاها فِي نِكَاح وَلَا مَال، وَيحد بقذفها، وَيقتل بهَا، وَيقطع بِسَرِقَة مَالهَا. فَنحْن ألحقناها بِبِنْتِهِ فِي النِّكَاح فِي تَحْرِيم نِكَاحهَا عَلَيْهِ، نظرا إِلَى الْمَعْنى الْحَقِيقِيّ، وَهُوَ كَونهَا من مائه. وَالشَّافِعِيّ ألحقها بالأجنبية فِي إباحتها لَهُ، نظرا إِلَى الْمَعْنى الْحكمِي، وَهُوَ انْتِفَاء آثَار الْوَلَد بَينهمَا شرعا. فقد صَار كل من الْفَرِيقَيْنِ إِلَى اعْتِبَار الْوَصْف

الَّذِي غلب على ظَنه أَنه مناط الحكم فِي الأَصْل.

Some have opined that one should not look at the two resembling precedents and consider that one is more probably the *ratio legis*. For example, some state that they have examined a daughter born out of wedlock, and in reality is the daughter of the man, since she was created of his sperm. However, in regards to the rulings, she is not his daughter, since he does not inherit from her nor she from him; he is also not to be her guardian in marriage or wealth and he receives the penalty if he were to accuse her of fornication. Also, he can receive capital punishment in retribution for murdering her and his hand is to be cut for stealing her wealth. We consider her to have the same rulings as his legitimate daughter in that he may not marry her, based on the reality of her being of his progeny. Al-Shāfiʿī, though, considered her closer to a non-related woman in that she is lawful for him, bearing in mind the rulings associated with her situation, namely, that the religious effects that follow a legitimate birth are nonexistent in her regard. Both considered various attributes that they thought were probably the *ratio legis* in the precedent.

وَالْحق أَن هَذَا النَّوْع مُعْتَبر، لِأَن الظَّن وَاجِب الِاتباع، وَهُوَ غير لَازم أبدا للشبه حكما، وَلَا للشبه حَقِيقَة، بل يخْتَلف باخْتلَاف نظر الْمُجْتَهدين، فَيلْزم كل وَاحِد مِنْهُمَا تَارَة، وَلَا يلْزمه تَارَة أُخْرَى، لَكِن لَا يُصَار إِلَى قِيَاس الشّبَه مَعَ إِمْكَان قِيَاس الْعلَّة اتِّفَاقًا وَحَكَاهُ ابْن الباقلاني فِي (التَّقْرِيب) إِجْمَاعًا، فَإِن عدم إِمْكَان قِيَاس الْعلَّة، كَانَ قِيَاس الشّبَه حجَّة عندنَا وَعند الشَّافِعِيَّة.

The truth is that this is worthy of consideration, since it is obligatory to follow probabilities. In this case, it neither is inseparable from a resemblance in essence or in ruling; perspectives would vary inasmuch as the conceptualization of the *mujtahid* scholar differs. The resemblance leans to one precedent at times, and to another at other times. However, an analogy by resemblance should never be used so long as an analogy by *ratio legis* is possible, according to all scholars. This was mentioned by Ibn al-Bāqillānī in *al-Taqrīb*, and he said there is consensus on this point. If there is no possibility of an analogy by *ratio legis*, an analogy by resemblance is evidence according to Ḥanbalī and Shāfiʿī scholars.

فصل
Section

اعْلَم أَن الْقيَاس - من حَيْثُ التَّأْثِير والمناسبة وَعدمهَا - يَنْقَسِم إِلَى الْمُنَاسب والشبهي والطردي كَمَا سبق، وَمن حَيْثُ التَّصْرِيح بِالْعِلَّةِ وَعدمهَا يَنْقَسِم إِلَى قِيَاس الْعلَّة وَقِيَاس الدّلَالَة، وَالْقِيَاس فِي معنى الأَصْل.

Qiyās, in terms of its effectiveness, relevance, and so forth, can be categorised into appropriate, resembling, and coextensive. In terms of how pronounced the *ratio legis* is, it can be categorised into analogy by *ratio legis*, analogy by signification, and analogy by equivalence.

فَقِيَاس الْعلَّة: هُوَ الْجمع بَين الأَصْل وَالْفرع بعلته، كالجمع بَين النَّبِيذ وَالْخمر بعلة الْإِسْكَار.

Analogy by *ratio legis*: Where the precedent and the new case are coupled due to the *ratio legis*. For example, *nabīdh* and wine are coupled based on the *ratio legis* of intoxication.

وَالْقِيَاس فِي معنى الأَصْل هُوَ مَا لَا فَارق فِيهِ بَين الأَصْل وَالْفرع، أَو كَانَ بَينهمَا فَارق لَا أثر لَهُ.

Analogy by equivalence: This is of two types:

مِثَال الأول: قِيَاس المَاء الَّذِي صب فِيهِ الْبَوْل من إِنَاء على المَاء الَّذِي بَال فِيهِ شخص.

First type: Where there is no difference between the precedent and the new case. An example is water that has urine poured into it being analogous to water that one urinated directly in:

وَمِثَال الثَّانِي: قِيَاس الْأمة على العَبْد فِي سرَايَة الْعتق وإلغاء فَارق الذكورية.

Second type: Where there exists a difference that has no effect on the ruling. An example is that a female slave is analogous to a male slave in that emancipation can be effectuated. Maleness is a difference that is rendered inconsequential.

ثمَّ إن هَذَا الْقيَاس يَنْقَسِم إِلَى قَطْعِيّ - كَمَا ذكرْنَاهُ - وَإِلَى ظَنِي، كقياس إِضَافَة الطلَاق إِلَى جُزْء معِين على إِضَافَته إِلَى جُزْء شَائِع، كقياس قَوْله: يدك طَالِق على قَوْله: نصفك أَو ثلثك أَو ربعك طَالِق، لِأَن هَذَا جُزْء وَهَذَا جُزْء، إِذْ الْفرق فِي هَذَا يحْتَمل التَّأْثِير بِأَن الْجُزْء الشَّائِع جعل محلا للْحكم الشَّرْعِيّ كَالْبيع وَالرَّهْن، فَلَا يبعد أَن يكون محلا للطَّلَاق، بِخِلَاف الْمعِين بِخِلَاف الفرق فِي الْقسم الأول، فَإِن تَأْثِيره لَا يظْهر.

As previously mentioned, this *qiyās* is also categorised into definitive—as above—and probable. An example of a probable *qiyās* is that ascribing divorce to a part of the body is analogous to ascribing divorce to a portion of the body. For example, if one says, "Your hand is divorced," it is analogous to saying, "Half, a third, or a fourth of you is divorced." Both are just divisions of the body. The difference between the two statements can possibly be effective, since a portion has a ruling, such as in selling and mortgaging. It is not far-fetched to claim that it also effects divorce. This is different to naming a part of the body in the first section, for its effect does not show [in other cases].

وَأما قِيَاس الدّلَالَة: فَإِنَّهُ الْجمع بَين الأَصْل وَالْفرع بِدَلِيل الْعلَّة، كَقَوْلِنَا فِي إِجْبَار الْبكر: جَازَ تَزْوِيجهَا ساكتة، فَجَاز تَزْوِيجهَا ساخطة كالصغيرة، لِأَن جَوَاز تَزْوِيجهَا ساكتة يدل على عدم اعْتِبَار رِضَاهَا، إِذا لَو اعْتبر رِضَاهَا، لاعتبر نطقها الدَّال عَلَيْهِ، لَكِن نطقها لم يعْتَبر، فَدلَّ على أن رِضَاهَا لَا يعْتَبر، وَإِذا لم يعْتَبر رِضَاهَا، جَازَ تَزْوِيجهَا وَإِن سخطت، إِذْ من لم يعْتَبر رضاه فِي أَمر لَا فرق بَين وُقُوع الْأَمر على وفْق اخْتِيَاره أَو خِلَافه، كَالْمَرْأَةِ لما لم يعْتَبر رِضَاهَا فِي الطَّلَاق، جَازَ عَدمه فِي حَقّهَا باستمرارها على النِّكَاح، ووجوده بِقطع نِكَاحهَا بِهِ.

Analogy by signification: Where the precedent and the new case are coupled based on the evidence of the *ratio legis*. For example, as it pertains to marrying off a virgin: it is permissible to marry her off if she remains silent, and as such, it is permissible to marry her off while she is discontented, similar to a young girl. The permissibility of marrying her off while she remains silent shows that her contentment is not considered. If it were considered, her statement that shows contentment would have to be considered. However, her pronounced statement is not considered, and as such, it shows that her contentment is not considered. If her contentment is not considered, it means that it is permissible to authorise a marriage where she is discontented, since if someone's contentment is not considered in a matter, there is no difference if it occurs according to their choice or not. Another example is a woman whose discontentment plays no part in divorce, and as such, it is allowed to continue a marriage when she is also discontented. Also, it is possible that she is contented but her husband can still divorce her.

فقد جمع فِي هَذَا الْقيَاس بَين الصَّغِيرة وَالْبكْر الْكَبِيرة، بِدَلِيل عدم اعْتِبَار رضاهما، وَهُوَ تزويجهما ساكتتين، فَهُوَ قِيَاس دلَالَة لذَلِك. وَهَذَا النَّوْع يُقَال لَهُ: الِاسْتِدْلَال بالحكم على الْعلَّة.

In this analogy, a young girl, a virgin, and an older woman are all joined in these rulings, and the evidence is that in all cases, their contentment was inconsequential in that they can be married while silent. This is known as analogy by signification, and it is also referred to as using the ruling as evidence to prove the *ratio legis*.

ولقياس الدّلَالَة نوع آخر، وَهُوَ الِاسْتِدْلَال بِأحد أثري الْمُؤثر على الآخر، كَقَوْلِنَا: الْقطع وَالْغُرْم يَجْتَمِعَانِ على السَّارِق إِذا سرق عينا فَبَانَت فِي يَده قطع بهَا، وَغرم قيمتهَا لِأَنَّهَا عين يجب ردهَا مَعَ بَقَائِهَا، فَوَجَبَ ضَمَانهَا مَعَ فَوَاتهَا، كالمغصوب، لِأَن وجوب ردهَا مَعَ بَقَائِهَا دل على وجود عِلّة وجوب الرَّد، إِذْ الْوَاجِب لَا بُد لَهُ من عِلّة، وَالضَّمان عِنْد التّلف رد لَهَا من حَيْثُ الْمَعْنى، وَتلك الْعلَّة تناسبه، وَقد ظهر اعْتِبَارهَا فِي الأَصْل وَهُوَ الْمَغْصُوب، وَالْعلَّة فِي ذَلِك كله إِقَامَة الْعدْل برد الْحق أَو بدله إِلَى مُسْتَحقّه.

There is a second type to the analogy by signification, which is when a ruling has two effects, using one of the two to prove the other. For example, cutting of the hand and a fine are both rulings that apply to a person who has stolen an item and it [disappears][475] in their possession. In this case, their hand is to be cut, and they are fined its worth. The reason is that it is an individual item that must be returned, if it still exists, and as such, restitution

475 [T] What is between the brackets is the correct word as found in *Sharḥ Mukhtaṣar al-Rawḍah* (3/438).

must be paid if it does not exist. This is similar to a usurped item in that it must be returned if it still exists. This indicates to the *ratio legis* that obligates returning the item if it still exists, since an obligatory action must have a *ratio legis*. Paying restitution when destroying an item is, in essence, a way of returning the item. The *ratio legis* in this case is appropriate and is considered in the precedent, which is the usurped item. The *ratio legis* in all of these cases is the establishment of justice by returning items, or restitution, to their rightful owners.

وَبِالْجُمْلَةِ إن قِياس الدّلَالَة تَارة يكون اسْتِدْلَالا بأثر الْعلَّة الْمُفْرد عَلَيْهَا بِلَا وَاسِطَة كَمَا فِي الْقسم الأول، وَتارَة يسْتَدلّ بِأحد أثريها عَلَيْهَا بِوَاسِطَة الْأَثر الآخر.

To summarise, sometimes, analogy by signification occurs by using the effect the individual *ratio legis* has on the ruling without any medium—as in the first category, and at other times, one of its effects is used as evidence to prove the ruling by way of the other effective *ratio legis*.

تَنْبِيه: لما كَانَت الْعلَّة الشَّرْعِيَّة أَمارة، جَازَ أَن تكون وَصفا عارضا، كالشدة فِي الْخمر هِيَ عِلّة التَّحْرِيم، وَهِي وصف عَارض، لِأنهُ عرض للعصير بعد أَن لم يكن، وَجَاز أَن تكون وَصفا لَازما، كالنقدية فِي الذَّهَب وَالْفِضَّة، وكالصغر، وَأَن تكون فعلا، كَالْقَتْلِ وَالسَّرِقَة فِي تَعْلِيل الْقصاص وَالْقطع، وَأَن تكون حكما شَرْعِيًّا نَحْو: تحريم الْخمر، فَلَا يَصح بيعهَا كالميتة، فالعلة الجامعة بَينهمَا التَّحْرِيم، وَهُوَ حكم شَرْعِي علل بِهِ حكم شَرْعِي وَهُوَ فَسَاد البيع.

Note: Since the religious *ratio legis* is tantamount to an indication, it is possible for it to be an accidental[476] property. An example is fermentation in wine being the *ratio legis* of its prohibition. Fermentation is an accidental property that can occur to juice. The *ratio legis* can also be a necessary attribute, such as gold and silver being currencies, as well as being under-aged. It can also be an action, such as killing and stealing that necessitate the penalties of retribution and cutting of the hand, respectively. It can also be anoth-

476 [T] *The Stanford Encyclopedia of Philosophy* states, "The distinction between essential versus accidental properties has been characterized in various ways, but it is currently most commonly understood in modal terms: an essential property of an object is a property that it must have, while an accidental property of an object is one that it happens to have but that it could lack."

er religious ruling, such as stating that wine is prohibited to consume, and as such, it is impermissible to sell, similar to a carcass, since the *ratio legis* that couples them is the prohibition. In this case, a religious ruling was used as a *ratio legis* to prove another ruling, namely, the invalidity of the sale.

وَأَن تكون وَصفا مُفردا كَقَوْلِنَا فِي اللواط: زنى فَأوجب الْحَد كَوَطْء الْمَرْأَة.

A *ratio legis* can also be a singular attribute, such as in the case of homosexuality: It is fornication, and as such, requires that the penalty be enacted, just as if one were to fornicate with a woman.

وَأَن تكون وَصفا مركبا، كَقَوْلِنَا: قتل عمد عدوان، فَأوجب الْقصاص كالمثقل. فالعلة مركبة من ثَلَاثَة أَوْصَاف.

A *ratio legis* can also be a compounded attribute, such as saying that purposeful killing that occurs out of transgression, such as with a heavy item thrown on top of a person, results in the penalty of retribution. The *ratio legis* here is comprised of three attributes.

وَأَن تكون وَصفا مناسبا، كَالْقَتْلِ وَالسَّرِقَة وَالْقَذْف وَالردة وَالسكر لأحكامها، ووصفا غير مُنَاسِب، كالردة، وَأكل لحم الْجَزُور، وَمَسّ الْفرج مَعَ عدم الشَّهْوَة لنقض الْوضُوء.

It can also be a suitable and relevant attribute, such as saying that killing, stealing, slander, apostasy, and intoxication are all the *ratione legis* for their respective rulings.[477] Further, it can be a non-relevant attribute, such as apostasy, eating meat of camels, and touching of the privates without desire all nullifying one's ablution.

ووصفا وجوديا كَقَوْلِنَا: جَازَ بَيْعه، فَجَاز رَهنه. ووصفا عدميا كَقَوْلِنَا: لَا يجوز بَيْعه، فَلَا يجوز رَهنه. وَجَاز أَن تكون الْعلَّة فِي غير مَحل حكمهَا، كتحريم نِكَاح الْأمة لعِلَّة رق الْولَد، فَإِن رق الْولَد وصف قَائِم بِهِ أَو معنى إضافي بَينه وَبَين سَيّده،

477 [T] Meaning, in the texts that establish those rulings, those attributes are mentioned, and they are relevant and suitable descriptions fitting to be the *ratio legis* for those rulings. For example, Allah the Exalted said: **{As for male and female thieves, cut off their hands for what they have done—a deterrent from Allah.}** [Qur'ān 5:38]

وَتَحْرِيم نِكَاح الْأمة وصف قَائِم بِالنكَاحِ أَو معنى إضافي إِلَيْهِ.

The *ratio legis* can be an affirmative, such as stating that something is permissible to sell, therefore permissible to mortgage, and can be a privative, such as stating that something cannot be sold, and therefore, cannot be mortgaged. A *ratio legis* can exist outside of the ruling it affects, such as stating that the prohibition of marrying a slave-girl is due to the child born of the marriage being a slave. The concept of the slavery of the child is an attribute that is consistent, or a concept that is relative between the child and its master. The prohibition of marrying a slave-girl is an attribute consistent to the marriage, or a concept relative to it.

وَيجوز تَعْلِيل الحكم بمحله، كتعليل تَحْرِيم الْخمر بِكَوْنِهِ خمرًا، وتعليل الرِّبَا فِي الْبر بِكَوْنِهِ برا.

It is also allowed to state that the *ratio legis* of a ruling is the receptacle of the ruling. For example, one can state that the prohibition of wine is because it is wine, and the prohibition of usury in barley being that it is barley.

وَالْحَاصِل أَن الْعلَّة يجوز أَن تكون مركبة من أَوْصَاف لَا تَنْحَصِر، خلافًا لمن حصرها فِي خَمْسَة أَو سَبْعَة.

To summarise, it is possible for a *ratio legis* to be compounded of various attributes that cannot be enumerated, contrary to the views of those who attempted to limit them to five or seven.

وَاعْلَم أَن الْقيَاس يجْرِي فِي الْأَسْبَاب وَالْكَفَّارَات وَالْحُدُود، كإثبات كَون اللواط سَببا للحد قِيَاسا على الزِّنَى.

Qiyās also applies to causes, expiations, and penalties. For example, homosexual intercourse is the cause for the punishment, because it is analogous to fornication.

ثمَّ اعْلَم أَن النَّفْي على قسمَيْن:

In continuation: negation is of two types:

أُصَلِّي، وَهُوَ مَا لم يتقدمه ثبوت، كنفي صَلَاة سادسة، وَنفي صَوْم شهر غير

رَمَضَان، فَهَذَا يجْرِي فِيهِ قِيَاس الدلَالَة، وَهُوَ الِاسْتِدْلَال بِانْتِفَاء حكم شَيْء على انتفائه عَن مثله، وَلَا يجْرِي فِيهِ قِيَاس الْعلَّة.

First: Original, which is when something never existed. An example is the negation of a sixth prayer and fasting of a month other than Ramadan. Analogy by deduction is applicable to this type. To do so, one can state that since a ruling is not applicable to a case, it is also not applicable to its analogue. However, analogy by *ratio legis* does not apply to this type.

وَالثَّانِي النَّفْي الطارئ كبراءة الذِّمَّة من الدّين بعد ثبوته فِيهَا، فَهَذَا يجْرِي فِيهِ القياسان: قِيَاس الِاسْتِدْلَال، وَقِيَاس الْعلَّة. فمثال الأول أَن يُقَال: من خَواص بَرَاءَة الذمة من الدّين أَن لَا يُطَالب بعد أَدَائِهِ، وَلَا يرْتَفع إِلَى الْحَاكِم، وَلَا يحبس بِهِ، وكل هَذِه الْخَواص مَوْجُودَة، فَدلَّ على وجود بَرَاءَة الذمَّة، وَمِثَال الثَّانِي أَن يُقَال: عِلّة بَرَاءَة الذمَّة من دين الْآدَمِيّ أَدَاؤُهُ، والعبادات هِيَ دين لله عز وَجل فَلْيَكُن أَدَاؤُهَا عِلّة الْبَرَاءَة مِنْهَا.

Second: Incidental, for example, one can be free of debt after they previously were accountable for a debt. Two types of analogy apply to this type of negation: (i) Analogy by signification. An example is to state that some of the qualities of one paying their debt is that they are not demanded to pay after they have fulfilled all payments, they are not taken to court, and are not imprisoned. All of these qualities exist and they signify that one is free of any liability. (ii) Analogy by *ratio legis*. An example is to state that the *ratio legis* for release of liability of a debt to a person is to pay the debt. Actions of worship are debts to Allah the Exalted. As such, performing the actions of worship release one of the liabilities associated with abandoning them.

فصل

Subsection: On the Objections to *Qiyās*

الأسئلة فِي هَذَا الْمقَام يُرَاد بهَا أحد شَيْئَيْن:

Either of two intents are behind these objections:

أَحدهمَا: كَونهَا من مستفيد يقْصد معرفَة الحكم خَالِصا مِمَّا يرد عَلَيْهِ.

First: They could emanate from a person wishing to benefit by learning a ruling free of any objections that might occur.

وَالثَّانِي: كَونهَا من معاند يقْصد قطع خَصمه ورده إِلَيْهِ.

Second: Or they could emanate from an obstinate person wishing to win in an argument against their opponent.

وَأكْثر المصنفين فِي أصُول الْفِقْه لم يذكرُوا هَذِه الأسئلة فِي كتبهمْ، ثمَّ إِن مِنْهُم من اعتذر عَن تَركهَا بِأنهَا لَيست من مبَاحث الْأُصُول، وَإِنَّمَا هِيَ كالعلاوة عَلَيْهِ، وَإِن مَوضِع ذكرهَا فن الجدل، وَهَذَا اعتذار الْغَزالِيّ فِي (الْمُسْتَصْفى).

Most authors on the subject of Islamic legal theories did not mention these objections in their books. Some apologised for not mentioning them, stating that they are not discussions on legal theory, but are additions to the topic. They state that these objections are best discussed in books on argumentation. This is how al-Ghazālī apologised in his book *al-Mustaṣfā*.

وَمِنْهُم من ذكرهَا، لِأَنهَا من مكملات الْقيَاس الَّذِي هُوَ من أصُول الْفِقْه، ومكمل الشَّيْء من ذَلِك الشَّيْء.

Other authors mentioned these discussions, since collectively they complete the discussion on *qiyās*, which is a discussion within the realm of legal theories. If something completes another thing, it is a part of it.

ولهذه الشُّبْهَة أَكثر قوم من ذكر الْمنطق والعربية وَالْأَحْكَام الكلامية، لِأَنها من مواده ومكملاته. وَنحن نذكرها هُنَا إتماما للفائدة، وتكميلا للمقصود فَنَقُول:

Due to this ambiguity, many authors mention formal logic, Arabic, and issues pertaining to *kalām*, since they are also relevant to and complete the topic of Islamic legal theories. We will mention a number of objections in order to complete the benefit and to fulfill the purpose of the book. Thus, we say:

اخْتلف فِي عدد هَذِه الأسئلة الْمعبر عَنْهَا بالقوادح، فَقَالَ موفق الدّين الْمَقْدِسِي فِي كِتَابه (رَوْضَة النَّاظر وجنة المناظر) قَالَ بعض أهل الْعلم: يتَوَجَّه على الْقياس اثْنَا عشر سؤالا. هَذَا كَلَامه. وعدها ابْن مُفْلِح فِي أُصُوله وَابْن الْحَاجِب خَمْسَة وَعشْرين. وَنحن نسلك فِي كتَابنَا هُنَا مَسْلَك موفق الدّين، وَالْأَكْثَر فِي عَددهَا، وَإِلَيْك الْبَيَان:

Scholars have differed on how many objections there are. They refer to these objections as being detractions. Muwaffaq al-Dīn al-Maqdisī stated in his book *Rawḍat al-Nāẓir wa Junnat al-Munāẓir*, "Some scholars mentioned that there are twelve objections that can be raised against an analogy."[478] Ibn Mufliḥ in his book *Uṣūl al-Fiqh*, and Ibn al-Ḥājib both mentioned twenty-five objections. In this discussion, we shall take the route of Muwaffaq al-Dīn and the majority in enumerating them.

أَولهَا: الاستفسار، وَهُوَ طَلِيعَة للقوادح كطليعة الْجَيْش، لِأَنَّهُ الْمُقدم على كل اعْتِرَاض، وَحَقِيقَته: طلب معنى لفظ الْمُسْتَدلّ لإجماله أَو غرابته، لِأَنهُ لَا يسمع إِذا كَانَ فِي ذَلِك اللَّفْظ إِجْمَال أَو غرابة، وَإِلَّا فَهُوَ تعنت مفوت لفائدة المناظرة، إِذْ يَأْتِي فِي كل لفظ يُفَسر بِهِ لفظ، ويتسلسل.

First. Inquiry: This is the first objection one can raise, and it is similar to the vanguard of an army. Its reality is that one seeks the meaning of the word used by a person wishing to establish a case. The word could be general or could be simply unknown. The objection [is considered valid][479] if the word

478 [T] *Rawḍat al-Nāẓir wa Junnat al-Munāẓir* (2/301).

479 [T] This appears to be a quotation from *Mukhtaṣar al-Taḥrīr*. In the printed version of *al-Madkhal*, al-Shaykh Ibn Badrān states, "It is not valid," although this is

is indeed general or not commonly used. If this is not the case, it is simply obstinacy that defeats the purpose of the debate, since every term can be explained by another word, and if that continues, it will go without end.

وعَلى الْمُعْتَرض بيَان إجماله. مِثَاله: أَن يَقُول الْمُسْتَدلّ: الْمُطلقَة تَعْتَد بالأقراء فَيقَال لَهُ: الْأقرَاء لفظ مُجمل يحْتَمل الْحيض وَالطُّهْر، فَأَي الْمَعْنيين تَعْنِي؟ فَإِذا قَالَ: أعنِي الْحيض، أَو أَعنِي الطُّهْر، أُجِيب حِينَئِذٍ بِحَسب ذَلِك من تَسْلِيم أَو منع أَو بيَان غرابته.

When the question is valid, the objector must clarify the general word. For example, the first interlocutor can state, "A divorced woman must be in the waiting period for three *qur'*." The second interlocutor can state, "The term *qur'* is one that is vague and can possibly carry the meanings of a menstrual period, or the purity that occurs after the menstrual period. Which do you mean?" The first interlocutor can say, "I mean a menstrual period," or, "I mean the purity after a menstrual period." The one raising the objection can then submit to the argument or refute it.

أما من حَيْثُ الْوَضع، فمثاله فِي الْكَلْب الْمعلم يَأْكُل من صَيْده أَن يُقَال: أيل لم يرض فَلَا تحل فريسته، كالسبد أَي: الذِّئْب، فَيقَال: مَا الأيل، مَا معنى لم يرض، وَمَا الفريسة، وَمَا السَّيِّد؟

The other inquiry can be made about the meaning of an unknown or archaic word. For example, a trained dog that eats of the game, it is said, "It is an *ayl*, which has not been trained, so its prey is unlawful, similar to a *sibd* (wolf)." In response, the one raising the objections can say, "What is an *ayl*? What does 'not been trained,' mean? What does prey mean? What is a *sibd*?'

وَأما من حَيْثُ الِاصْطِلَاح، كَأَن يذكر فِي القياسات الْفِقْهِيَّة لفظ الدّور أَو التسلسل أَو الهيولى أَو الْمَادَّة أَو المبدأ أَو الْغَايَة، نَحْو أَن يُقَال فِي شُهُود الْقَتْل، إِذا رجعُوا عَن الشَّهَادَة: لَا يجب الْقصاص، لِأَن وُجُوده تجرد مبدؤه عن غَايَة مَقْصُودة، فَوَجَبَ أَن لَا يثبت، وَمَا أشبه ذَلِك من اصْطِلَاح الْمُتَكَلِّمين. وَإِنَّمَا يكون ذَلِك مَا لم يعرف من حَال خَصمه أَنه يعرف ذَلِك.

---

clearly a slip of the pen. Refer to *Mukhtaṣar al-Taḥrīr* (4/231).

Some inquiries are on nomenclature, such as, when discussing legal analogies, one mentions words such as: "Circular," "infinite regress," "prime matter," "matter," "first principle," "finality," e.g. when discussing witnesses who recant their testimonies to a murder: "Retribution is not obligatory, since its first principle is stripped of any intended finality, and as such, it is incumbent that the ruling not be established." In this and other similar cases, where the terminologies of scholars of *kalām* are used, the inquiry is valid as long as the claimant is not aware that their interlocutor actually knows the meanings of those terminologies.

أما إِذا كَانَ خَصمه عَارِفًا بِهَذِهِ الاصطلاحات، فَلَا غرابة حِينَئِذٍ بِالنِّسْبَةِ إِلَيْهِ، لِأَن الغرابة أَمر نسبي لَا أَمر حَقِيقِي.

If the objector is aware of these terminologies, they are not considered unknown to them, since whether a term is unknown or not is relative, not absolute.

وَلَا يلْزم الْمُعْتَرض إِذا بَين كَون اللَّفْظ مُحْتملا بَيَان تَسَاوِي الِاحْتِمَالَات، فَلَو الْتزمهُ تبرعا وَقَالَ: وهما متساويان لِأَن التَّفَاوُت يَسْتَدْعِي تَرْجِيحا بِأَمْر، وَالْأَصْل عدم الْمُرَجح، لَكَانَ جيدا وَفَاء بِمَا الْتزمهُ أَولا.

When one is objecting and showing that the word being used is vague, they need not clarify that the possibilities of the word are equal. However, if they do so voluntarily, and state, "The word has two equally likely meanings, because a word having multiple possibilities means there must be some factor that makes one meaning more likely than the other, and by default, there is no such factor,' it would be a good gesture and consistent with their initial commitment.

وَجَوَاب الْمُسْتَدلّ عَن الاستفسار، إِمَّا بِمَنْع احْتِمَاله للإجمال، أَو ببيان ظُهُور اللَّفْظ فِي مَقْصُوده، بِنَقْل من اللُّغَة، أَو عرف، أَو قرينَة، أَو تَفْسِيره إِن تعذر إبْطَال غرابته. وَلَو قَالَ الْمُسْتَدلّ: يلْزم ظُهُوره فِي أحد الْمَعْنيين، دفعا للإجمال، وَفِيمَا قصدته بِهِ بعدم ظُهُوره فِي الآخر اتِّفَاقًا مني ومنك، كفى فِي الْأَصَح وَلَا يعْتد بتفسيره بِمَا لَا يحْتَملهُ اللَّفْظ لُغَة.

If the one building their case responds, it can either be by rejecting that the word is general, or by clarifying the apparency of the word in their intent. They can do so by quoting some linguistic source, customary usage, a contextual clue, or just explaining the word if they cannot deny it is archaic or unknown. If the first interlocutor were to say, "One of the two meanings must necessarily be more likely. Thereby, we avoid usage of vague terms, since the other meaning is not relevant to the discussion, based on our agreement," it would be sufficient,[480] according to the more veracious view. If they were to define the word in a way that is not acceptable in the language, their definition would be considered void.

فَائِدَة: نقل الطوفي عَن صَاحب كتاب (الإفصاح) فِي خلق الْإِنْسَان مِثَالا لطيفا لهَذَا النَّوْع، فَقَالَ: كَمَا حكي عَن الْيَهُود أَنهم سَأَلوا النَّبِي صلى الله عَلَيْهِ وَسلم عَن الرّوح وَهُوَ لفظ مُشْتَرك بَين الْقُرْآن، وَجِبْرِيل، وَعِيسَى، وَملك يُقَال لَهُ: الرّوح، وروح الإنْسَان الَّذِي فِي بدنه، ليغلطوه بذلك يَعْنِي إِن قَالَ لَهُم: الرّوح ملك، قَالوا لَهُ: بل هُوَ روح الْإنْسَان، أَو قَالَ: روح الإِنْسَان، قَالُوا: بل هُوَ ملك أَو غَيره من مسميات الرّوح، فَعلم الله مَكْرهمْ، فأجابهم بِجَوَاب مُجمل، كسؤالهم بقوله تَعَالَى ﴿قُلِ الرُّوحُ مِنْ أَمْرِ رَبِّي﴾ [الْإِسْرَاء: ٨٥].

Benefit: Al-Ṭūfī quoted the author of *al-Ifṣāḥ*, who quoted a very pleasant parable to show this type. He said: "It is reported that the Jews asked the Prophet ﷺ about the word *al-rūḥ*, which is a homonym used to refer to the Qur'ān, Jibrīl, 'Īsā, an angel called *al-Rūḥ*, and the human soul which resides in the body. They did so in order to find fault in him. Meaning, if he were to respond and say, 'The *rūḥ* is an angel,' they would respond with, 'Actually, it is the soul of a human.' If he were to say, 'It is the soul of humans,' they would respond, 'Actually, it is an angel,' or mention any of its other meanings. Allah the Exalted knew their plot and gave them a general answer to match their vague question. He said: **{Say, "The Spirit is part of my Lord's domain."}** [Qur'ān 17:85]

وَهُوَ يتنَاوَل المسميات الْخَمْسَة وَغيرهَا، وَهَذَا هُوَ سَبَب الْإِجْمَال فِي مُسَمّى الرّوح، لَا كَون حَقِيقَتهَا غير مَعْلُومَة للبشر. إِذْ قد دلّت قواطع الشَّرْع على

480 [T] This is based on the assumption that the word is not widely used. If the word is widely used, the objector must be reproached. Refer to *al-Taḥbīr Sharḥ al-Taḥrīr* (7/3552).

جسميتها.

In this verse, it is inclusive of all five meanings mentioned, as well as more. This is the reason for the vague mention of the word *rūḥ,* not that its essence is unknown to humans, since the definitive religious texts have shown it is a body.[481]

وَالْحَاصِل: أَن سُؤال الْيَهُود عَن الرّوح كَانَ على سَبِيل المغالطة لَا على سَبِيل الِاحْتِيَاط.

Therefore, their question to the Prophet ﷺ was a fallacy and was not born out of prudence.

ثَانِيهَا: فَسَاد الِاعْتِبَار، وَهُوَ أَن يكون الْقيَاس مُخَالفا للنَّص أَو الْإِجْمَاع، وَسمي بِهَذَا الِاسْم، لِأَن اعْتِبَار الْقيَاس مَعَ النَّص أَو الْإِجْمَاع اعْتِبَار لَهُ مَعَ دَلِيل أقوى مِنْهُ، وَهُوَ اعْتِبَار فَاسد وظلم، لِأَنهُ وضع لَهُ فِي غير مَوْضِعه.

Second. False consideration: This means when the analogy contradicts a divine text or a consensus. It was given this name because to deem analogy worthy of consideration when it stands against a divine text or a consensus is to give it consideration where there are stronger evidences. Such a consideration is false and unjust, since it is to use analogy in a place where it is not fitting.

مِثَال مَا خَالف الْكتاب نصا: قَوْلنَا: يشْتَرط تبييت النية لرمضان لِأَنهُ مَفْرُوض، وَلَا يَصح تبييته من النَّهَار كالقضاء، فَيُقَال: هَذَا فَاسد الِاعْتِبَار لمُخَالفَته نَص الْكتاب، وَهُوَ قَوْله تَعَالَى: ﴿**وَالصَّائِمِينَ وَالصَّائِمَاتِ وَالْحَافِظِينَ فُرُوجَهُمْ وَالْحَافِظَاتِ وَالذَّاكِرِينَ اللَّهَ كَثِيرًا وَالذَّاكِرَاتِ أَعَدَّ اللَّهُ لَهُم مَّغْفِرَةً وَأَجْرًا عَظِيمًا**﴾ [الْأَحْزَاب: ٣٥] فَإِنَّهُ يدل على أَن كل من صَامَ يحصل لَهُ الْأجر الْعَظِيم، وَذَلِكَ مُسْتَلْزم للصِّحَّة، وَهَذَا قد صَامَ فَيكون صَوْمه صَحِيحا.

An example of an analogy that contradicts an univocal text of the Qur'ān is to state that it is a condition to have the intention to fast Ramadan the night prior, since it is an obligatory fast. As such, similar to fasting a missed

481 [T] *Sharḥ Mukhtaṣar al-Rawḍah* (3/461).

day, it is not valid if the intention was from the day. To respond to this, one should say, "This is a false consideration, since it contradicts the Qur'ān." This is referring to when Allah the Exalted states: **{Fasting men and women, chaste men and women, men and women who remember Allah often - Allah has prepared forgiveness and a rich reward.}** [Qur'ān 33:35] This verse indicates that everyone who fasts will earn a great reward, and that necessitates validity. Such a person has fasted, and as such, their fast is valid.

وَمِثَال مَا خَالف السّنة: قَوْلنَا: لَا يَصح السّلم فِي الْحَيَوَان، لِأَنهُ عقد مُشْتَمل على الْغرَر. فَلَا يَصح كالسلم فِي المختلطات، فيقال: هَذَا فَاسد الِاعْتِبَار لمُخَالفَته مَا رُوِيَ عَن النَّبِي صلى الله عَلَيْهِ وَسلم أَنه رخص فِي السّلم.

An example of an analogy that contradicts the Sunnah is to state that a *salam* transaction[482] is not permissible when applied to animals, since it is a contract comprising of uncertainty and risk, similar to mixed items.[483] To respond to this, one would say that this is a false consideration, since it contradicts the ḥadīth where the Prophet ﷺ allowed for *salam* transactions.

وَمِثَال مَا خَالف الْإِجْمَاع: أَن يُقَال: لَا يجوز أَن يغسل الزَّوْج زَوجته، لِأَنهُ يحرم النّظر إِلَيْهَا، فَحرم غسلهَا كالأجنبية، فَيُقَال لَهُ: هَذَا فَاسد الِاعْتِبَار لمُخَالفَته الْإِجْمَاع السكوتي، وَهُوَ أَن عليا غسل فَاطِمَة، وَلم يُنكر عَلَيْهِ، والقضية فِي مَظَنَّة الشهْرَة، فَكَانَ ذَلِك إِجْمَاعًا.

An example of an analogy that contradicts consensus is to state that it is not permissible for a man to wash the body of his dead wife, since he cannot look at her, and as such, he cannot wash her body, similar to a non-related woman. To respond, one would state that this is a false consideration, because it contradicts a silent consensus, which is that ʿAlī washed the body of

482 [T] A *salam* transaction is a contract regarding some described item that will be delivered later, though the payment is made in the contractual meeting. Refer to *Muntahā al-Irādāt* (2/381).

483 [T] This ruling is explained by the Shāfiʿī scholars in their books, where they categorise *salam* transactions into four categories. The category being referenced here is the one where the items are mixed and one cannot definitively estimate its amounts nor descriptions. Examples given are kneaded items. *Salam* in this category is forbidden. Refer to *Rawḍat al-Ṭālibin* (4/16).

Fāṭimah and none of the companions rebuked him for that. This incident is likely to be highly widespread, and as such, it is a consensus.

فَإِذا أَرَادَ الْمُسْتَدلّ الْجَواب عَن فَسَاد الِاعْتِبَار إِمَّا بالطعن بِالنَّصّ كَأَن يَقُول فِي الصَّوْم: لَا نسلم أَن الْآيَة تدل على صِحَة الصَّوْم بِدُونِ تبييت النية لِأَنهَا مُطلقَة وقيدناها بِحَدِيث **«لَا صِيَام لمن لم يبيت الصّيام من اللَيْل»** أَو يَقُول: إِنَّهَا دلّت على أَن الصّيام يُثَاب عَلَيْهِ، وَأَنا أَقُول بِهِ، لَكِنَّهَا لَا تدل على أَنه لَا يلْزمه الْقَضَاء والنزاع فِيهِ، أَو يَقُول: إِنَّهَا دلّت على ثَوَاب الصَّائِم، وَأَنا لَا أسلم أَن الممسك بِدُونِ تبييت النية صَائِم.

If a person wishes to refute the claim that an analogy is being given false consideration, they can critically examine the text itself. In the example of fasting, they can respond by saying, "I do not agree that fasting without having intention during the prior night is valid, because the verse is unrestricted and has been qualified by the ḥadīth, **'There is no fast for the one who does not have their intention the night before.'**"[484] Or, they can respond by saying, "The verse indicates they will receive reward. I agree; however, the verse does not indicate that they do not have to make the day up. The latter is the point of contention." Or, they can say, "The verse shows that the fasting person earns reward. However, I do not agree that a person who refrains from eating and drinking without having the intention the night before fits the description of 'fasting.'"

وَكَأَن يَقُول فِي مَسْأَلة السّلم: لَا نسلم صِحَة التَّرَخُّص فِي السّلم، وَإِن سلمنَا فَلَا نسلم أَن اللَّام للاستغراق فَلَا يتَنَاوَل الْحَيَوَان، وَإِن صَحَّ السّلم فِي غَيره.

In the issue of the *salam* transaction, they can say, "I do not agree that there was a concession given in *salam* transactions, and even if I did, I do not agree that the ruling encompasses all items. As such, animals are not included, even if the *salam* transaction is lawful in other scenarios."

وَكَأَن يُقَال فِي غسل الزَّوْجَة: إِنِّي أمنع صِحَة ذَلِك عَن عَليّ، وَإِن سلم، فَلَا أسلم أَن ذَلِك اشْتهر، وَإِن سلم، فَلَا أسلم أَن الْإِجْمَاع السكوتي حجَّة، وَإِن

484 Reported by Ibn Abi Shaybah (3/31), Abu Dāwūd (2454), al-Nasā'ī (4/196), al-Tirmidhī (730), Ibn Mājah (1700), and Aḥmad (6/287).

سلم فَالْفرق بَين عَليّ وَغَيره أَن فَاطِمَة كَانَت زَوجته فِي الدُّنْيَا وَالْآخِرَة، فالموت لم يقطع النكَاح بَينهمَا بإخْبَار الصَّادِق بِخِلَاف غَيرهمَا فَإِن الْمَوْت يقطع بَينهمَا.

In the issue of washing of the deceased wife, one can respond, "I deny that the narration is authentically attributed to ʿAlī. Even if it is authentic, I do not agree that it was a widespread occurrence. Even if it were widespread, I do not agree that silent consensus is evidence. Even if silent consensus is evidence, the difference between ʿAlī and others is that Fāṭimah is his wife in the worldly life and in the hereafter. Her death did not sever their marriage, as told to us by the Prophet ﷺ.[485] This is contrary to others whose death severs their marriage."

وَإِمَّا أَن يكون الْجَواب بِأَن يبين الْمُسْتَدلّ أَن مَا ذكره من الْقيَاس يسْتَحق التقْدِيم على ذَلِك النَّص، لكَونه حنفيا يرى تَقْدِيم الْقيَاس على النَّص الَّذِي أبداه الْمُعْتَرض، إِمَّا لكَون النَّص ضَعِيفا فَيكون الْقيَاس أولى مِنْهُ، أَو لكَون النَّص عَاما فَيكون الْقيَاس مُخَصّصا لَهُ جمعا بَين الدَّلِيلَيْنِ، أَو لكَون مَذْهَب الْمُسْتَدلّ يقْتَضِي تَقْدِيم الْقيَاس على الْخَبَر إِذا خَالف الْأُصُول، أَو فِيمَا تعم بِهِ الْبلوى، ومالك يرى تَقْدِيم الْقيَاس على الْخَبَر إِذا خَالفه خبر الْوَاحِد.

Another response to these objections is that the one building their case can clarify that the analogy mentioned deserves to be given priority over the text. For example, they could be a Ḥanafī who views that the analogy is given priority over the divine text that their objector mentioned, either by showing that the ḥadīth is weak, and therefore, analogy is preferable to it. Or, the text is general and the analogy particularises it, thereby reconciling between both evidences. Or, the school of thought of the one building the case could necessitate that analogy is given priority over a report if it contradicts the legal theories, or where it contradicts popular behaviour. Mālik viewed that analogies are preferable to singular narrations that they conflict with.

وَبِالْجُمْلَةِ للمستدل الِاعْتِرَاض على النَّص الَّذِي يبديه الْمُعْتَرض بِجَمِيع مَا يعْتَرض بِهِ على النُّصُوص سندا ومتنا.

---

485 [T] I could not find a reference to any such statement of the Prophet ﷺ about ʿAlī and Fāṭimah
رضي الله عنهما.

Generally speaking, the one building the case has the right to use all the various methods to respond to the text that the objector is raising, whether by critiquing its chain of narration or its textual indications.

ثَالِثهَا: فَسَاد الْوَضع؛ وَهُوَ اقتضاء الْعلَّة نقيض مَا علق بهَا، وَإِنَّمَا سمي هَذَا فَسَاد الْوَضع، لِأَن وضع الشَّيْء جعله فِي مَحل على هَيْئَة أَو كَيْفيَّة مَا، فَإِذا كَانَ ذَلِك الْمحل أَو تِلْكَ الهَيْئَة لَا تناسبه، كَانَ وَضعه على خلاف الْحِكْمَة، وَمَا كَانَ على خلاف الْحِكْمَة يكون فَاسِدا، فَيقَال هَاهُنَا: إِن الْعلَّة إِذا اقْتَضَت نقيض الحكم الْمُدعى أَو خِلَافه، كَانَ ذَلِك مُخَالفا للْحكم، إِذْ من شَأْن الْعلَّة أَن تناسب معلولها، لَا أَنَّهَا تخَالفه، فَكَانَ ذَلِك فَاسد الْوَضع بِهَذَا الِاعْتِبَار. فَمَا علق فِيهِ على الْعلَّة ضد مَا تَقْتَضِيه: قَوْلنَا فِي النكَاح بِلَفْظ الهِبَة: لفظ ينْعَقد بِهِ غير النِّكَاح، فَلَا ينْعَقد بِهِ النكَاح، كَلَفْظِ الإجَارة.

Third. Affirming a negative conclusion from affirmative premises: This occurs when the *ratio legis* necessitates the opposite of the ruling associated with it. The Arabic terminology is *fasād al-waḍ'*, which literally means invalid placement, because when placing something in a receptacle or in a manner that does not suit it, its placement contradicts wisdom, and anything that contradicts wisdom is invalid. In this case, one can state that if the *ratio legis* necessitates the opposite of the alleged ruling, or it necessitates a contrary ruling, that it contradicts the ruling. A *ratio legis* must be suitably relevant to the ruling it is attempting to prove; it must not contradict it. One example is when speaking of the term, "I bestow on you," in the context of a marriage contract, the term, "I bestow on you," can be used to establish non-marriage related contracts, and as such, it cannot be used in marriage related contracts, similar to the phrase, "I rent to you."

فَيَقُول الْحَنَفِيّ: هَذَا فَاسد الْوَضع، لِأَن انْعِقَاد غير النكَاح بِلَفْظ الْهِبَة يَقْتَضِي ويناسب انْعِقَاد النكَاح بِهِ، لَكِن تَأْثِيره فِي انْعِقَاد غير النكَاح بِهِ - وَهُوَ الْهِبَة - دَلِيل على أَن لَهُ حظا من التَّأْثِير فِي انْعِقَاد الْعُقُود، وَالنِّكَاح عقد، فلينعقد بِهِ كَالْهِبَةِ، ويلتزم عَلَيْهِ الْإِجَارة، أَو يفرق بَينهمَا وَبَين الهِبَة وَالنكَاح إِن أمكن.

A Ḥanafī might respond by saying, "This is affirming a negative conclusion from an affirmative premise, because if non-marriage contracts are effectuated by the phrase, 'I bestow on you,' it necessitates and relates to marriage contracts effectuated by the same phrase. However, its effect on effectuating non-marriage contracts shows that it plays a part in effectuating all contracts. Marriage is a contract, and therefore, it is effectuated by the phrase, 'I bestow on you,' just as a gift is effectuated." Then, one can contravene their evidence by mentioning the phrase, "I rent to you," or can differentiate between renting, gift-giving, and marriage, if they are able.

وَمن أمثلته أَن يَقُول شَافِعِيّ فِي تكْرَار مسح الرَّأْس مسح، فَيسنّ فِيهِ التّكْرَار كالمسح فِي الِاسْتِجْمَار، فَيُقَال: قياسك هَذَا فَاسد الْوَضع، لِأَن كَونه مسحا مشْعر بِالتَّخْفِيفِ ومناسب لَهُ، والتكرار منَاف لَهُ.

Another example is that a Shāfiʿī could argue, when discussing repetitive wiping on the head (during ablution): It is a wiping, and as such, it is recommended to do so repetitively, like wiping in *istijmār*.[486] To respond, one can say that they have attempted to establish the opposite of the ruling implied by the *ratio legis*, since the fact that it is a wiping indicates that it is intended to give ease, and ease is a suitable and relevant *ratio legis*. Repetitive wiping of the head contradicts ease.

وَالْجَوَاب عَن هَذَا النَّوْع يكون بِأحد أَمريْن: إِمَّا بِأَن يمْنَع الْمُسْتَدل كون علته تَقْتَضِي نقيض مَا علق بهَا، أَو بِأَن يسلم ذَلِك، لَكِن يبين أَن اقتضاءها للمعنى الَّذِي ذكره أرجح من الْمَعْنى الآخر، فَيقدم رجحانه.

There are two ways to respond to an objection raised on *fasād al-waḍʿ*: (i) The one attempting to build the case can refute that their *ratio legis* is opposite to the ruling it is attached to. (ii) To agree that the *ratio legis* is opposite to the ruling it is attached to, but to then clarify that it necessitates the concept they are attempting to prove more than the other concept, and as such, their position is more veracious.

مِثَاله: أَن يَقُول فِي مَسْأَلَة النكَاح بِلَفْظ الْهِبَة: لَا نسلم أَن انْعِقَاد الْهِبَة بلفظها، أَو كَون لفظ الْهِبَة ينْعَقد بِهِ غير النِّكَاح يَقْتَضِي انْعِقَاد النِّكَاح بِهِ، قَوْلكُم: انْعِقَاد

486 [T] *Istijmār* is to use three or more rocks or three different parts of a large enough single rock to purify the private area after urinating or defecating.

غير النكَاح يدل على قوته وتأثيره فِي الْعُقُود، قُلْنَا: إِنَّمَا يدل على تَأْثِيره فِيمَا وضع لَهُ - وَهُوَ الْهِبَة - أما غَيره، فَلَا وَذَلِكَ لوجوه:

For example, when it comes to marriage by use of the phrase, "I bestow on you," one can state that they do not agree that giving a gift is effectuated through use of that particular phrase. Or, they can state that although the phrase, "I bestow on you," effectuates other contracts, it does not necessarily mean that it effectuates marriage contracts. So, when the one presenting the objection says, "Its effect on effectuating non-marriage contracts shows that it plays a part in effectuating all contracts," one can respond by saying that it only shows that it plays a part in effectuating the concept intended by the phrase, namely, gift-giving. As for other things, it plays no part. There are a number of reasons why:

أَولهَا: أَن تَأْثِيره إِنَّمَا يُنَاسب أَن يكون مُسْتَعْملا فِيمَا وضع لَهُ لإشعاره بخواصه ودلالته عَلَيْهَا بِحكم الْوَضع، وَالنكَاح وَالْبيع وَالْإِجَارَة لَهَا خَواص لَا يشْعر بهَا لفظ الْهِبَة، فيضعف عَن إفادتها والتأثير فِي انْعِقَادهَا بِهِ.

One. It is suitable that the effect of a phrase relates to the concept it is used for, since when used conventionally, this is what it indicates to in specific. Marriage, sales, and renting all have particular underlying concepts that the phrase, "I bestow on you," simply does not indicate. As such, it weakens the signification and effect it plays in effectuating [those other contracts].

ثَانِيهَا: أن اسْتِعْمَال اللَّفْظ فِي غير مَوْضُوعه مجَاز، وَهُوَ ضَعِيف بِالنِّسْبَةِ إِلَى الْحَقِيقَة، وَالْأَصْل عدم التَّجَوُّز.

Two. Using a phrase in a non-conventional usage is a metaphor. Metaphors, when juxtaposed with literal usages, are weaker. By default, phrases are not to be understood metaphorically.

ثَالِثهَا: أن قُوَّة اللَّفْظ وسلطانه وَظُهُور دلَالَته إِنَّمَا تكون إِذا اسْتعْمل فِي مَوْضُوعه، فاستعماله في غير مَا وضع لَهُ تَفْرِيق لقُوته، فَهُوَ كالتغريب لَهُ عَن مواطنه، فيضعف بذلك عَن التأْثِير.

Three. The strength, authority, and clear signification of a phrase apply when used in its subject matter. If it is used in a non-conventional way, it scatters its strength. It is similar to proverbially banishing the word from its homeland. Due to that, the effect it plays in non-conventional usages is weakened.

سلمنَا أَن انْعِقَاد غير النكَاح بِلَفْظ الْهِبَة يَقْتَضِي انْعِقَاد النِّكَاح بِهِ، لَكِن اقتضاؤه لعدم انْعِقَاده أقوى من اقتضائه لانعقاده، لِأَن انْعِقَاد النكَاح بِلَفْظ الْهِبَة يَقْتَضِي أَن اللَّفْظ مُشْتَرك بَينهمَا، أَو مجَاز فِي النكَاح عَن الْهِبَة، وَالمجَاز والاشتراك خلاف الأَصْل، وَمَا ذَكَرْنَاهُ يَقْتَضِي نفيهما وَتَخْصِيص كل عقد بِلَفْظ هُوَ وفْق الأَصْل، وَمَا وَافق الأَصْل يكون أولى مِمَّا خَالفه، وعَلى هَذَا النمط يكون الْجَواب فِي غير هَذَا الْمِثَال.

One can submit that other contracts are effectuated by use of the phrase, "I bestow on you," and this necessitates that marriage contracts can be effectuated by the same phrase. However, the fact that it does not effectuate a marriage is stronger than stating that it does effectuate a marriage, since effectuating the marriage by use of the phrase, "I bestow on you," necessitates that the phrase is a homonym, or that the phrase is used metaphorically, in the sense that a gift represents a marriage. Both homonymous and metaphorical usage of words is not the default, and what I mentioned previously would indicate that these two concepts must be negated. Each contract should be effectuated by using the specific verbiage that would indicate them, as is the default. Anything that complies with the default usage is preferable. As such, one can respond to this objection, and in this same way, other objections.

وَاعْلَم أَن بعض الْأُصُولِيِّينَ توهم أَن فَسَاد الْوَضع نقض خَاص، وَلَيْسَ الْأَمر كَذَلِك. وَالتَّحْقِيق أَن فَسَاد الْوَضع يشْتَبه بِأُمُور ويخالفها بِوُجُوه.

Note that some legal theorists mistakenly thought that *fasād al-waḍʿ* means to show that the *ratio legis* exists without its associated ruling, which is referred to as *naqḍ*. This is not the case, however, as after careful investigation, it appears that it is similar to it in some ways and different in other ways.

فَمِنْهُ: أنه يشبه النَّقْض من حَيْثُ إِنَّه بَين فِيهِ ثبوت نقيض الحكم مَعَ الْوَصْف إِلَّا

أَن فِيهِ زِيَادَة، وَهُوَ أَن الْوَصْف هُوَ الَّذِي يثبت النقيض، وَفِي النَّقْض لَا يتَعَرَّض لذَلِك، بل يقنع فِيهِ بِثبوت نقيض الحكم مَعَ الْوَصْف، فَلَو قصد بِهِ ذَلِك، لَكَانَ هُوَ النَّقْض.

For example, it resembles *naqḍ* in that it is clear that the opposite ruling is established through use of the attribute. However, there is an additional factor that *fasād al-waḍʿ* entails, which is that the attribute itself is what proves the opposite ruling. In *naqḍ*, this is not the case; rather, it is sufficient in *naqḍ* that the opposite ruling is established though the *ratio legis* of a supposed ruling exists. If that is intended by *fasād al-waḍʿ*, then it is also *naqḍ*.

وَمِنْه: أَنه يشبه الْقلب من حَيْثُ إِنَّه إِثْبَات نقيض الحكم بعلة الْمُسْتَدلّ إِلَّا أَنه يُفَارِقهُ بِشَيْء، وَهُوَ أَن فِي الْقلب يثبت نقيض الحكم بِأَصْل الْمُسْتَدلّ، وَهَذَا يثبت بِأَصْل آخر، فَلَو ذكره بِأَصْلِهِ، لَكَانَ هُوَ الْقلب.

It also resembles a concept known as *qalb* (reversal)[487] in that it establishes the opposite of the ruling by using the same exact *ratio legis* mentioned by the claimant. However, it is different in that it establishes the opposite ruling with the same *ratio legis*, while in *fasād al-waḍʿ*, the opposite ruling is established through another precedent. If the precedent were mentioned, it would be considered a reversal.

وَمِنْه: أَنه يشبه الْقدح فِي الْمُنَاسبَة من حَيْثُ يَنْفِي مُنَاسبَة الْوَصْف للْحكم لمناسبته لنقيضه، إِلَّا أَنه لَا نقصد هَاهُنَا بَيَان عدم مُنَاسبَة الْوَصْف للْحكم، بل بِنَاء نقيض الحكم عَلَيْهِ فِي أصل آخر، فَلَو بَين مناسبته لنقيض الحكم بِلَا أصل كَانَ قدحا فِي الْمُنَاسبَة.

Also, it resembles invalidation of its suitability and relevance to the ruling at hand, since the *ratio legis* or attribute is actually suitable and relevant to the opposite ruling. However, in *fasād al-waḍʿ*, the point is not to clarify that the attribute is unsuitable to the ruling, but rather, to build the case for the opposite ruling by use of a different precedent. If it were just to clarify

487 [T] Which is defined as, "Stating the opposite ruling mentioned by the claimant is contingent on the same *ratio legis* in particular." Refer to *Sharḥ Mukhtaṣar al-Rawḍah* (3/519). An example would be to state that the *ratio legis* for an action is x, but the same *ratio legis* establishes y, which is the exact opposite of x.

that the attribute is suitable and relevant to the opposite ruling, it would be considered an invalidation.

وَاعْلَم أَنه إِنَّمَا يعْتَبر الْقدح فِي الْمُنَاسبَة إِذا كَانَ مناسبته للنقيض وللحكم من وَجه وَاحِد، وَأما إِن اخْتلف الْوَجْهَانِ فَلَا، لِأَن الْوَصْف قد يكون لَهُ جهتان يُنَاسب بِأَحَدِهِمَا الحكم، وبالأخرى نقيضه.

On that note, invalidation of the suitability and relevance to the ruling is only considered if the suitability and relevance to both the opposite ruling, as well as the ruling at hand, is from only a single standpoint. If they differ where there are multiple manifestations, it is not worthy of consideration. This is because an attribute can have multiple manifestations, with one being suitable and relevant to a ruling, and another being suitable and relevant to its opposite.

مِثَاله: كَون الْمحل مشتهى يُنَاسب إِبَاحَة النكَاح لإراحة الخاطر، ويناسب التَّحْرِيم لإراحة الطمع.

For example, a receptacle of a ruling could be desirable. The attribute of desirability is relevant to the lawfulness of marriage, so that one can clear their mind of desires. It also manifests in the prohibition, which severs one of their longing for unlawful pleasure.

وَمِثَال آخر من العرفيات: الْملك إِذا ظفر بعدوه، فَإِنهُ مُنَاسِب لقَتله نفيا لعاديته، وللإبقاء عَلَيْهِ، وَالرَّدّ إِلَى ولَايَته، إِظْهَارًا للقدرة، وَعدم المبالاة بِمثلِهِ. وَكِلَاهُمَا مِمَّا يقْصِدهُ الْعُقَلَاء.

Another example of this concept in something customary is that if a king captures their enemy, it is suitable for them to kill them, in order to neutralise their hostility. The king can also choose to spare their life and even give them their post back to show their strength and that their enemies are irrelevant in the broader scheme of things. Both objectives are sought by rational people.

وَقد تلخص مِمَّا ذكرنَا أَن ثُبُوت النقيض مَعَ الْوَصْف نقض، فَإِن زيد ثُبُوته بِهِ ففساد الْوَضع، وَإِن زيد كَونه بِهِ وبأصل الْمُسْتَدلّ فقلب، وَبِدُون ثبوته مَعَه، فالمناسبة من

جِهَة وَاحِدَة قدح فِيهَا، وَمن جِهَتَيْنِ لَا يعْتَبر.

To summarise what was previously mentioned: Establishing the opposite ruling with the same attribute is *naqḍ*. If the opposite ruling is established through the same attribute, it is *fasād al-waḍ*ʿ. If an additional qualification is added, namely, that the opposite ruling is established with the same precedent being used by the one building their case, it is a reversal. If the opposite ruling is not established with the attribute, it is an invalidation of its suitability and the relevance. Showing suitability to an opposite from one manifestation of the attribute is invalidation, but if shown from two different manifestations, it is not worthy of consideration.

رَابِعهَا: الْمَنْع، وَهُوَ على أَرْبَعَة أضْرب: أَولهَا منع حكم الأَصْل، الثَّانِي منع وجود الْوَصْف الَّذِي ادعى الْمُسْتَدلّ أَنه الْعلَّة فِي الأَصْل، الثَّالِث منع كَونه عِلّة فِي الأَصْل، الرَّابِع منع وجوده فِي الْفَرْع.

Fourth. Denial: This is of four types: (i) Denying the ruling of the precedent. (ii) Denying the presence of the attribute that the interlocutor is claiming is the *ratio legis* in the precedent. (iii) Denying that an attribute is the *ratio legis* of the ruling of the precedent. (iv) Denying the presence of the attribute in the new case.

وَمِثَال ذَلِك فِيمَا إِذا قُلْنَا: النَّبِيذ مُسكر، فَكَانَ حَرَامًا، قِيَاسا على الْخمر.

To use a previously illustrated example: *Nabīdh*, if intoxicating, is unlawful, since it is analogous to wine.

فَقَالَ الْمُعْتَرض: لَا نسلم تَحْرِيم الْخمر إِمَّا جهلا بالحكم، أَو عنادا، فَهَذَا منع حكم الأَصْل.

[i] Someone might object and state they do not submit to wine being unlawful, either out of ignorance in the ruling or out of obstinance. This is an example of denying the ruling of the precedent.

وَلَو قَالَ: لَا أسلم وجود الْإِسْكَار فِي الْخمر، لَكَانَ هَذَا منع وجود الْمُدَّعِي عِلّة فِي الأَصْل.

[ii] Or, they can say that they do not agree that wine has the attribute of be-

ing intoxicating. This is an example of denying the presence of the attribute that one is claiming is the *ratio legis* in the precedent.

وَلَو قَالَ: لَا أسلم أَن الْإِسْكَار عِلّة التَّحْرِيم، لَكَانَ هَذَا منع علية الْوَصْف فِي الأَصْل.

[iii] If one were to say that they do not submit that intoxication is the *ratio legis* of the prohibition, this would be denying that an attribute is the *ratio legis* of the ruling of the precedent.

وَلَو قَالَ: لَا أسلم وجود الْإِسْكَار فِي النَّبِيذ، لَكَانَ منع وجود الْعلَّة فِي الْفَرْع.

[iv] Lastly, if someone were to claim that the attribute of intoxication is not present in the *nabīdh*, this is denying the presence of the attribute in the new case.

فَفِي الأَصْل ثَلَاثَة مَمْنُوع، وَفِي الْفَرْع منع وَاحِد.

The precedent has three deniable qualities, while the new case has one deniable quality.

وَاعْلَم أَن الْمُسْتَدلّ لَا يَنْقَطِع بِمَنْع حكم الأَصْل على الصَّحِيح، وَإِنَّمَا يَنْقَطِع إِذا ظهر عَجزه عَن إِثْبَاته بِالدَّلِيلِ.

Know that denying the ruling of the precedent does not invalidate the analogy, according to the veracious view. However, it does invalidate the analogy if the claimant is unable to prove the ruling through use of evidences.

خَامِسهَا: التَّقْسِيم، هُوَ احْتِمَال لفظ الْمُسْتَدلّ لأمرين فَأكْثر على السوَاء، بَعْضهَا مَمْنُوع، وَذَلِكَ الْمَمْنُوع هُوَ الَّذِي يحصل بِهِ الْمَقْصُود، وَإِلَّا لم يكن للتقسيم معنى فيمنعه، إِمَّا مع السُّكُوت عَن الآخر، لِأَنهُ لَا يضرهُ، أَو مَعَ التَّعَرُّض لتسليمه، أَو لِأَنهُ لَا يضرّهُ.

Fifth: Categorisation: This occurs when a word used by the claimant has two or more possible, and equally likely, meanings, where some of the meanings are denied, and one of the denied meanings is the one that is used to prove the case. Otherwise, the categorisation would have no point. The objector can either refuse to mention the other possibilities, since they do not harm their argument. Or, they can submit that the other possibilities are valid [by clarifying that][488] they do not harm.

وَهَذَا السُّؤَال لَا يخص الأَصْل، بل كَمَا يجْرِي فِيهِ يجْرِي فِي جَمِيع الْمُقدمَات التِي تقبل الْمَنْع. وَقد منع قوم من قبُول هَذَا السُّؤَال، وَهُوَ وَارِد عندنَا وَعند الْأَكْثَر، لَكِن بِشَرْط، وَهُوَ أَن يكون منعا لما يلْزم الْمُسْتَدلّ بَيَانه.

This objection is not only applicable to the precedent. Rather, it is a valid objection to all premises that can be denied (as shown above). Some have rejected this objection. However, it is valid according to Ḥanbalī scholars and the majority, with the condition that it must be a denial of what the claimant must clarify.

مِثَاله: فِي الصَّحِيح الْحَاضِر إِذا فقد المَاء، وجد سَبَب وجود التَّيَمُّم، وَهُوَ تعذر المَاء، فيجوز التَّيَمُّم، فَيَقُول الْمُعْتَرض: مَا الْمُرَاد بتعذر المَاء؟ أردْت أَن تعذر المَاء مُطلقًا سَبَب، أَو أَن تعذر المَاء فِي السّفر أَو الْمَرَض سَبَب؟ الأول مَمْنُوع، وَحَاصِله أَنه منع بعد تَقْسِيم، فَيَأْتِي فِيهِ مَا تقدم فِي صَرِيح الْمَنْع من الأبحاث، من كَونه مَقْبُولا قطعا وَكَيْفِيَّة الْجَواب عَنهُ.

An example is a healthy person within their hometown but without water. As such, they have the cause for the presence of *tayammum*, which is predicated on the nonexistence of water. This allows them to perform *tayammum*. The objector might say, "What is meant by 'without water?' Does it mean that the impossibility of getting water is a precondition in all situations, or does that only apply during travel and sickness? The first option is denied." The point is, they rejected one of the options after categorising the statement into various options. As such, they mention the options that are definitively denied and differentiate between them and those that are definitively accepted, as well as how to respond to it.

مِثَال آخر لَا يشْتَمل على شَرط الْقبُول، وَهُوَ أَن يَقُول فِي مَسْأَلَة الْقَتْل الْعمد والعدوان: سَبَب الْقصاص، فَيَقُول الْمُعْتَرض: مَتى هُوَ سَبَب، أمع مَانع الالتجاء

488 [T] What is between the brackets is a misquotation from *Fuṣūl al-Badāʾiʿ* by al-Imām Shams al-Dīn al-Fanārī (2/389).

إِلَى الْحَرَام أَو دونه؟ الأول مَمْنوع، وَإِنَّمَا لم يقبل، لِأَن حَاصله أَن الالتجاء إِلَى الْحرم مَانع من الْقصاص. فَكَانَ مُطَالبَته بِبَيَان عدم كَونه مَانِعا، والمستدل لَا يلْزمه بَيَان عدم الْمَانِع، فَإِن الدَّلِيل مَا لو جرد النّظر إِلَيْهِ أَفَادَ الظَّن، إِنَّمَا بَيَان كَونه مَانِعا على الْمُعْترض. وَيَكْفِي الْمُسْتَدلّ أَن يَقُول: إِن الأَصْل عدم الْمَانِع.

Another example that does not consist of the condition of this objection's validity is on the topic of a purposeful killing that occurs out of transgression, which is a cause for retribution. An objector can say, "When is the cause enacted? Is it enacted even if the impediment of fleeing to the *ḥaram* occurs, or not? The first is denied."[489] This objection is not accepted. The point of this objection is that fleeing to the *ḥaram* is an impediment to retribution, and as such, the objector is demanding that it be shown to not be an impediment in this case. However, the claimant does not need to do so, since if this evidence is looked at independently, it provides probability. Clarifying such an impediment is the job of the objector. The claimant must only say, "By default, there are no impediments."[490]

وَاشْترط الطوفي وَغَيره لقبُول التَّقْسِيم شُرُوطًا ثَلَاثَة:

---

489 [T] In the Ḥanafī *madhhab*, retribution is not to be enacted in the *ḥaram*, contrary to the Shāfiʿīs. Refer to *Badāʾiʿ al-Ṣanāʾiʿ fī Tartīb al-Sharāʾiʿ* by al-Imām ʿAlā al-Dīn al-Kasānī al-Ḥanafī (7/114) for the Ḥanafī view, and *Rafʿ al-Ḥājib ʿan Mukhtaṣar Ibn al-Ḥājib* by al-Imām Tāj al-Dīn al-Subkī (4/429) for the Shāfiʿī view.

490 [T] In possibly clearer terms, the reason why this objection is rejected is that for this to be a valid objection, the word used must be equally applicable to two different concepts. In this case, there is no such confusion, since by default, there are no impediments. If the objector wishes to mention an impediment, that is their prerogative. Refer to *Rafʿ al-Ḥājib ʿan Mukhtaṣar Ibn al-Ḥājib* by al-Imām Tāj al-Dīn al-Subkī (4/429) and *Uṣūl al-Fiqh* by al-Imām Shams al-Dīn ibn Mufliḥ (3/1358).

Further, al-Imām Shams al-Dīn al-Aṣfahānī states, "There is an impediment in the conceptualised case where they are disagreeing. This is not a categorisation, since the term does not carry two meanings, one of which can be the true cause, and the other is not a cause. Killing purposely out of aggression is a cause for effectuation of capital punishment as retribution, regardless if fleeing to the *ḥaram* is an impediment or not. Categorisation occurs when the term used has two possible meanings, where one is the cause, and the other is not. The purport of these remarks goes back to [the objector] demanding that the impediment be negated, and it is not obligatory on the claimant to negate impediments. Rather, the objector must clarify the impediments. As such, this question is not relevant. (*Bayān al-Mukhtaṣar Sharḥ Mukhtaṣar Ibn al-Ḥājib* (3/192-193).

Al-Ṭūfī and others stated that there are three conditions to accepting categorisation:

أَحدهَا: أَن يكون مَا ذكره الْمُسْتَدل مِمَّا يَصح انقسامه إِلَى مَا يجوز مَنعه وتسليمه، مِثَاله أَن يَقُول الْمُسْتَدل فِي نذر صَوْم النَّحْر: إنه نذر مَعْصِية، فَلَا ينْعَقد قِيَاسا على سَائِر الْمعاصِي، فَيَقُول الْمُعْتَرض: هُوَ مَعْصِيّة لعَينه أَو لغيره، الأول مَمْنُوع لِأَن الصَّوْم لعَينه قربَة وَعبادَة، فَكيف يكون مَعْصِيّة؟ وَالثَّانِي مُسلم، لَكِن لَا يَقْتَضِي الْبطلَان، بِخِلَاف سَائِر الْمعاصِي.

First. What the person proving their case mentioned must be a concept that can be categorised into two parts: (i) Something that can be denied and (ii) something that can be accepted. For example, a person proving a case can speak about an oath to fast on Eid al-Adha: it is an oath to commit a sin, and as such, it is invalid, since it is analogous to all other sins. An objector can state, "Is it a sin in and of itself, or is it a sin due to exterior causes? The first is denied because fasting in and of itself is an action that garners closeness to Allah and is worship. How, then, can it be a sin in and of itself? The second is accepted, but it does not necessitate that the oath is invalid, contrary to other sins."

ثَانِيهَا: أَن يكون التَّقْسِيم حاصرا لجَمِيع الْأَقْسَام الَّتِي يحتملها لفظ الْمُسْتَدلّ، كَمَا ذكر من انحصار الْمعْصِيَة فِي كَونهَا لعينها أَو لغَيْرهَا، وانحصار الصَّلَاة فِي كَونهَا فرضا أَو نفلا، فَإِن لم يكن التَّقْسِيم حاصرا، لم يَصح، لجَوَاز أَن ينْهض الْقسم الْبَاقِي الْخَارِج عَن الْأَقْسَام الَّتِي ذكرهَا الْمُعْتَرض بغرض الْمُسْتَدلّ، وَحِينَئِذٍ يَنْقَطِع الْمُعْتَرض.

Second: The categorisation must have fully enumerated all possibilities of the phrase or word used by the one proving their case. In the previous example, the objector enumerated all possibilities, namely, that it can be a sin in and of itself or for exterior causes. In other cases, prayer, for example, can be categorised into obligatory and voluntary. However, if the categorisation does not enumerate all possibilities, it is an invalid objection, since the unmentioned category might fulfil the purpose of the one proving their case, thereby refuting the objector.

ومثاله أَن يُقَال: الْوتر لَيْس بِفَرْض، لِأَنهُ إِمَّا فرض أَو نفل، فَالْأول بَاطِل، فَتعين الثَّانِي. فَيَقُول الْمُعْتَرض: لَا فرض، وَلَا نفل، بل وَاجِب.

As an example, one can state that the *witr* prayer is not obligatory, since prayer is of two categories: obligatory, and voluntary. Since the first (obligatory) is rejected, it must be the second (voluntary).' [A Ḥanafī][491] can respond, "It is not a *farḍ* or a voluntary prayer; it is *wājib*.'

ثَالِثهَا: أَن لَا يُورد الْمُعْتَرض فِي التَّقْسِيم زِيَادَة على مَا ذكره الْمُسْتَدلّ فِي دَلِيله، فَإِن زَاد فِي التَّقْسِيم على مَا ذكره الْمُسْتَدلّ، لم يَصح، لِأَنهُ حِينَئِذٍ يكون مناظرا لنَفسِهِ لَا للمستدل، حَيْثُ ذكر مَا لم يذكرهُ الْمُسْتَدلّ، وَجعل يتَكَلَّم عَلَيْهِ، وَإِنَّمَا وَظِيفَة الْمُعْتَرض هدم مَا بَينه لَا بِنَاء زِيَادَة عَلَيْهِ.

Third. When categorising, the objector must not add to what the claimant mentioned in their evidence. If they add to it, it is invalid, since they would then be debating themselves, not the interlocutor, as they have mentioned things the claimant has not and began addressing those unmentioned things. The objector's duty is to dismantle what the interlocutor [builds,][492] not to add to their argument.

مِثَاله: أَن يَقُول الْحَنَفِيّ فِي قتل الْحر بِالْعَبدِ: قتل عمد عدوان، فَأوجب الْقصاص، قِيَاسا على الْحر بِالْحرِّ، فَيُقَال لَهُ: قتل عمد عدوان فِي رَقِيق أَو غير رَقِيق، فَهَذَا تَقْسِيم مَرْدُود، لِأَن دَلِيل الْمُسْتَدلّ لم يتَعَرَّض للرقيق.

For example, in the case of a free person receiving capital punishment in retribution for murder of a slave, a Ḥanafī can state, "This is a purposeful killing occurring out of transgression, and as such, it requires capital

491 [T] This was omitted from al-Shaykh Ibn Badrān's quotation from *Sharḥ Mukhtaṣar al-Rawḍah* (3/495). I thought that including it provided additional context, as the Ḥanafī scholars are the only ones who are known to consistently differentiate between *farḍ*, which is an obligation established via definitive sources, and *wājib* which is an obligation established via probable sources. Refer to *al-Iḥkām* by al-Imām al-Āmidī (1/99).

492 [T] In the printed version and the manuscript, it states, "What occurs between them." Both of which have accurate meanings, but since al-Shaykh Ibn Badrān is quoting from al-Ṭūfī, his wording is preferable. Refer to *Sharḥ Mukhtaṣar al-Rawḍah* (3/495).

punishment; it is analogous to when a free person kills a free person." If someone responds by saying, "It is murder of a slave, or a non-slave?" Their categorisation is rejected, since the evidence quoted by the first interlocutor did not discuss the issue of slavery.

سادسها: سُؤال الْمُطَالبَة: وَهُوَ أَن يطْلب الْمُعْتَرض من الْمُسْتَدلّ الدَّلِيل على أَن الْوَصْف الَّذِي جعله جَامعا بَين الأَصْل وَالْفرع عِلّة، وَهُوَ من أعظم الأسئلة العمومية فِي الأقيسة وتشعب مسالكه، وَالْمُخْتَار: قبوله، وَإِلَّا لأدى إِلَى التَّمَسُّك بِكُل طرد، فيؤدِّي إِلَى اللّعب، فيضيع الْقيَاس، إِذْ لَا يُفِيد ظنا وَتَكون المناظرة عَبثا.

Sixth. Posing of questions: This occurs when the objector requests that the claimant provides evidence that the attribute that they consider to couple between the precedent and the new case is indeed the *ratio legis*. This is one of the greatest of questions, due to its comprehensive usage [to question any attribute claimed to be the *ratio legis*][493] and branching of ways [to establish it as the *ratio legis*][494] that can emanate of it. The chosen view is that it is an acceptable objection. Otherwise, every coexisting attribute must be adhered to, thereby leading to folly and the dismissal of *qiyās* altogether. In that case, *qiyās* would not prove probability of a ruling, and the debate would be rendered a joke.

مِثَاله: أَن يَقُول: مُسكر، فَكَانَ حَرَامًا كَالْخمرِ، أَو مَكِيل، فَحرم فِيهِ التَّفَاضُل كالبر، لم قلت: إِن الْإِسْكَار عِلّة التَّحْرِيم، وَإِن الْكَيْل عِلّة الرِّبَا؟ وَلم قلت: إِن التبديل عِلّة الْقَتْل فِيمَا إِذا قَالَ: إِنْسَان بدل دينه فَقتل كَالرّجلِ.

For example, one can state, "It is intoxicating, and therefore is forbidden, similar to wine." Or, one can say, "It is dry-measured, and therefore disparity is impermissible, similar to barley." The objector can respond by saying, "Why did you say that intoxication is the *ratio legis* of the prohibition, and why did you say that an item being dry-measured is the *ratio legis* of the prohibition of usury?" In the case of capital punishment for apostasy, they can ask, "Why do you claim changing of religion is the *ratio legis* for receiving

---

493 [T] This clarifying bracket was added from *Bayān al-Mukhtaṣar* by al-Imām Shams al-Dīn al-Asfahani (3/194).
494 [T] Ibid.

capital punishment?"

وَهَذَا النَّوْع يتَضَمَّن تَسْلِيم الحكم، لِأَن الْعلَّة فرع الحكم فِي الأَصْل لاستنباطها مِنْهُ، وَالْحكم أصل لَهَا. فمنازعته الْمُعْتَرض فِي الْفَرْع الَّذِي هُوَ الْعلَّة يشْعر بِتَسْلِيم الأَصْل الَّذِي هُوَ الحكم، ويتضمن تَسْلِيم الْوَصْف فِي الْفَرْع وَالْأَصْل، لِأَنهُ يسْأَل عَن كَونه عِلّة وَذَلِكَ فرع على الْوَصْف فِي نَفسه فِي الأَصْل وَالفرع، إِذْ لَو لم يكن ذَلِك، لكَانَ مَنعه وجود الْوَصْف أولى بِهِ وأجدى عَلَيْهِ.

This type requires submitting to the ruling, since the *ratio legis* is a subsidiary of the ruling of the precedent, as it is deduced from it. The ruling is the basis for the *ratio legis*. Disputing the *ratio legis* means submitting that its foundational ruling is accepted. It also means that the attribute exists in both the precedent and the new case, because the question posed in this case is whether that attribute is the *ratio legis*, which is a subsidiary of the attribute existing in both the precedent and the new case. Had it not been so, a better argument would have been to deny the existence of the attribute altogether.

ثمَّ إِن هَذَا النَّوْع ثَالِث المنوع الْمُتَقَدّمَة، وَذَلِكَ أَن قَوْلنَا مثلا: النَّبِيذ مُسكر، فَكَانَ حَرَامًا كَالْخمرِ، يرد عَلَيْهِ أَرْبَعَة منوع، منع حكم الأَصْل بِأَن يُقَال: لَا نسلم تَحْرِيم الْخمر. ثمَّ منع وجود الْوَصْف، كَأَن يُقَال فِيهِ: لَا نسلم وجود الْإِسْكَار فِيهِ. ثمَّ منع كَونه عِلّة بِأَن يُقَال: لَا نسلم كَونه عِلّة، ثمَّ منع وجوده فِي الْفَرْع بِأَن يُقَال: لَا نسلم وجود الْإِسْكَار فِي النَّبِيذ.

This type is the third type of denial. This occurs when we say, for example: "*Nabīdh* is intoxicating, and therefore is forbidden, similar to wine." There are four ways to deny this statement: (i) Denying the ruling of the precedent, by saying, "I do not agree that wine is forbidden." (ii) Denying the presence of the attribute that the interlocutor is claiming is the *ratio legis* in the precedent, such as by saying, "I do not agree that the attribute of intoxication is present in wine." (iii) Denying that an attribute is the *ratio legis* of the ruling of the precedent, by saying, "I do not agree that intoxication is the *ratio legis*." (iv) Denying the presence of the attribute in the new case, by saying, "I do not agree that the attribute of intoxication exists in *nabīdh*."

وَاعْلَم أَن الْعَادة بَين عُلَمَاء الجدل أَن الْمُعْتَرض يبتدئ بالمنوع على التَّرْتِيب الَّذِي ذَكرْنَاهُ فَلَا ينْقل إِلَى منع إِلَّا وَقد سلم الَّذِي قبله انْقِطَاعًا أَو تنزلا.

Keep in mind that it is customary among scholars of argumentation to present the denials in the exact order mentioned. As such, one should not go to the next denial until the one before it either refutes the argument or is relinquished.

سابعها: النَّقْض، وَهُوَ ثُبوت الْعلَّة، وَهِي الْوَصْف فِي صُورة مَعَ عدم الحكم فِيهَا، كَأَن يُقَال فِي النباش: سرق نِصَابا كَامِلا من حرز مثله، فَيجب عَلَيْهِ الْقطع كسارق مَال الْحَيّ، فَيُقَال: هَذَا ينْتَقض بالوالد يسرق مَال وَالِده، وَصَاحب الدّين يسرق مَال مدينه، فَإِن الْوَصْف مَوْجُود فيهمَا، وَلَا يقْطَعَانِ.

Seventh. Contradiction: This occurs when the *ratio legis* exists in a scenario but its supposed corresponding ruling does not exist. For example, in the case of a gravedigger, it can be stated that they stole the entire minimum amount requiring cutting of the hand, and stole it from an enclosed treasury. As such, their hand must be cut, similar to the one who stole the wealth of a living person. To respond, one can state that this is contradictory in the case of a father who steals their son's money, or the creditor stealing from the debtor. The attribute is present in both, but in neither case is the hand to be cut.

وَاخْتلف فِي بطلَان الْعلَّة بِالنَّقْضِ، والأرجح عدم الْبطلَان. وَيجب احْتِرَاز الْمُسْتَدلّ فِي دَلِيله عَن صُورة النَّقْض على الْأَصَح، كَأَن يَقُول فِي الْمِثَال الْمَذْكُور: سرق نِصَابا كَامِلا من حرز مثله وَلَيْسَ أَبَا وَلَا مدينا للمسروق مِنْهُ، فَيلْزمهُ الْقطع، وَلَا نزاع فِي اسْتِحْبَاب هَذَا الِاحْتِرَاز، وَإِنَّمَا النزاع فِي وُجُوبه وَدفعه، إِمَّا بِمَنْع وجود الْعلَّة، أو الحكم فِي صورته.

Scholars have differed on whether showing a contradiction in a *ratio legis* invalidates it, and the stronger view is that it does not. With that said, when establishing their evidence, the claimant must account for the scenario where the contradiction occurs. In the example mentioned, they can state, "They stole the entire minimum amount requiring cutting of the hand, and stole it from an enclosed treasury, and the one stealing was not their father nor their debtor. As such, their hand must be cut." There is no doubt that it is recommended to account for the exceptions in this matter, and the difference of opinion occurred on whether this is obligatory. There are two ways to respond to a supposed contradiction: (i) To deny the existence of the *ratio legis*.[495] (ii) To deny the ruling in the scenario.

مِثَال الأول: أَن يَقُول الْحَنَفِيّ فِي قتل الْمُسلم بالذمي: قتل عمد عدوان، فَيجب الْقصاص، كَمَا فِي الْمُسلم بِالْمُسلمِ، فيُقَال لَهُ: ينْتَقض بقتل الْمعَاهد، فَإِنَّهُ قتل عمد عدوان، وَلَا يقتل بِهِ الْمُسلم، فَيَقُول: لَا أسلم أَنه عدوان، فيندفع النقض بذلك إِن ثَبت لَهُ.

An example of the first response: In the case of a Muslim receiving capital punishment in retribution for killing a *dhimmī*,[496] a Ḥanafī could argue that it is a purposeful killing done out of transgression, and as such, capital punishment in retribution is obligatory, similar to if a Muslim killed another Muslim. To respond, one can state, "This is contradictory in the case that a *muʿāhad*[497] is killed. In that case, it is a purposeful killing done out of transgression, but the Muslim does not receive capital punishment in retribution." To respond, they can state, "I do not agree that it is done out of transgression." In that fashion, the Ḥanafī refutes the claim of contradiction, if indeed their response is true.

وَمِثَال الثَّانِي: أَن يُقَال فِي الْمِثَال الْمَذْكُور: لَا أسلم الحكم فِي الْمعَاهد، فَإِن عِنْدِي يجب الْقصاص بقتْله، وَيَكْفِي الْمُسْتَدلّ قَوْله: لَا أعرف الرِّوَايَة فِيهَا. وَلَيْسَ للمعترض أَن يدل على ثُبُوت الْعلَّة أَو الحكم إِذا منعهما الْمُسْتَدلّ فِي صُورَة النَّقْض، لِأَنهُ انْتِقَال عَن مَحل النّظر، وغصب لمنصب الْمُسْتَدلّ، حَيْثُ يَنْقَلِب الْمُعْتَرض مستدلا.

495 [T] Meaning, in the case where the contradiction occurs. The contradiction occurs when the *ratio legis* exists without its corresponding ruling. If the *ratio legis* is denied, then, the contradiction is denied. Refer to *Sharḥ Mukhtaṣar al-Rawḍah* (3/503).

496 [T] A *dhimmī* person is one that has *dhimmah*, which is when a disbeliever is allowed to keep their religion but must pay the *jizyah* fee and adhere to the rulings of the religion. This ruling applies to a person of scripture (i.e. a Jew or Christian), or those who resemble them in having a scripture. Refer to *Sharḥ Muntahā al-Irādāt* (1/658).

497 [T] A *muʿāhad* is a non-Muslim person who has a treaty with Muslims. Refer to *Ḥāshiyat al-Rawḍ al-Murbiʿ* by al-Shaykh ʿAbd al-Raḥmān ibn Qāsim (4/302).

An example of the second response, in the same scenario, is to say, "I do not agree that is the ruling on the *muʿāhad*; in my view, the murderer should receive capital punishment in that case, as well." The claimant, in that moment, can state that they do not know of a narration that would support that proposition. The objector does not have the right to attempt to prove the *ratio legis* or ruling if the first interlocutor denies it in the contradiction, since it is an altogether different discussion. If the objector attempts to do that, they usurp the role of the first interlocutor, since they go from being an objector to a claimant.

وَلَيْسَ لَهُ أَيْضا أَن يبين فِي صُورَة النَّقْض وجود مَانع أَو انْتِفَاء شَرط تخلف الحكم لأَجله فِي صُورَة النَّقْض، كَمَا إِذا أورد الْمُعْتَرض قتل الوَلَد وَالِده على عِلّة الْقَتْل الْعمد الْعدوان، فَقَالَ الْمُسْتَدلّ: تخلف الحكم لمَانع الأُبُوَّة.

Also, the [claimant][498] may show that in the case of the contradictory ruling, there is an impediment or lack of a precondition causing the ruling to not occur in the case of the contradictory ruling. For example, if the objector mentions the case where a father murders their son as a supposed contradiction of the *ratio legis* of purposeful killing out of transgression, the claimant can respond, "The ruling did not apply because of the impediment of fatherhood."

وَمِثَال انْتِفَاء الشَّرْط: مَا إِذا قَالَ الْمُسْتَدلّ: سرق نِصَابا كَامِلا وَلَا شُبْهَة لَهُ فِيهِ فَقطع، فأورد الْمُعْتَرض السّرقَة من غير حرز، فَقَالَ الْمُسْتَدلّ، لانْتِفَاء شَرط وَهُوَ الْحِرْز.

An example of a precondition not existing is where the claimant states, "They have stolen the entire minimum amount required for cutting of the hand, and there is no doubt, and as such, their hand should be cut." The objector can mention a theft that does not occur from a treasury, and the claimant can respond, "The ruling did not apply because the precondition did not exist; namely, they did not steal from a treasury."

وَيسمع من الْمُعْتَرض نقض أصلي خَصمه، فَيلْزمهُ الْعذر عَنهُ، لَا أصل نَفسه،

498 [T] In the original text of *al-Madkhal*, al-Shaykh Ibn Badrān quotes this as, "They do not have the right," which is a misquotation of *Sharḥ Mukhtaṣar al-Rawḍah* (3/505).

نَحْو: هَذَا الْوَصْف لَا يطرد على أُصَلِّي فكيف يلْزَمنِي! كَمَا إِذا قَالَ الْحَنَفِيّ فِي قتل الْمُسلم بالذمي: إِنَّه قتل عمد عدوان، يُوجب الْقصاص قِيَاسا على الْمُسلم بِالْمُسلمِ، فَيَقُول الْحَنْبَلِيّ: هَذَا ينْتَقض على أصلك بِمَا إِذا قَتله بالمثقل، فَإِن الْأَوْصَاف مَوْجُودَة، وَالْقصاص مُنْتَفٍ عنْدك، فَلهُ أَن يعْتَذر عَنهُ بِأَدْنَى عذر يَلِيق بمذهبه، وَلَا يعْتَرض عَلَيْهِ فِيهِ، لِأَنَّهُ أعرف بمأخذه، كَأَن يَقُول: لَيْسَ ذَلِك قتلا، وَلَيْسَ عمدا، أَو مَا شَاءَ من كَلَامهم.

The objector can only claim contradiction to the precedent of their opponent, forcing them to respond to it. They may not claim contradiction to their own precedent. For example, they may not state, "This attribute is not consistent with my precedent; how, then can I accept it?" For example, on a Muslim receiving capital punishment in retribution for killing a *dhimmī*, a Ḥanafī could state, "It is a purposeful killing emanating from transgression, and as such, capital punishment is obligatory, since this case is analogous to when a Muslim person murders a Muslim." A Ḥanbalī could respond and say, "This contradicts your precedent in the case that a person is killed with a heavy object. The attributes you mentioned are present but capital punishment is not the ruling, according to you." They can respond by mentioning anything that would defend this view, according to their *madhhab*. The objector cannot object to those defenses, since [the Ḥanafī] would be more aware of the workings of their *madhhab*. For example, the Ḥanafī can respond by saying it was not a murder, was not purposeful, or by providing other responses within the Ḥanafī *madhhab*.

وَإِن كَانَ النَّقْض مُتَوَجها من الْمُعْتَرض إِلَى أصل نَفسه لم يقْدَح فِي عِلّة الْمُسْتَدلّ، وَلم يلْزمه الْعذر عَنهُ، وَذَلِكَ كَمَا إِذا قَالَ الْحَنْبَلِيّ: لَا يقتل الْمُسلم بالذمي لِأَنهُ كَافِر، وَلَا يقتل بِهِ الْمُسلم قِيَاسا على الْحَرْبِيّ، فَقَالَ الْحَنَفِيّ: هَذَا الْوَصْف لَا يطرد على أَصلِّي، إِذْ هُوَ بَاطِل بالمعاهد. فَإِنَّهُ كَافِر، وَيقتل بِهِ الْمُسلم عِنْدِي. وَإِذا كَانَ وصفك - أَيهَا الْمُسْتَدلّ - غير مطرد عِنْدِي، فَكيف يلْزَمنِي؟ فَهَذَا لَا يسمع مِنْهُ على الصَّحِيح.

If the contradiction shown by the objector affects their own precedent, it does not negate the *ratio legis* provided by the first interlocutor and they do not have to respond to it. For example, if a Ḥanbalī states, "A Muslim does not receive capital punishment for murder of a *dhimmī*, since the latter is a disbeliever, making them analogous to a warring disbeliever." The Ḥanafī could respond, "This is not consistent with my precedent, since there is a contradiction in the case of a *muʿāhad*, who is a disbeliever and should receive capital punishment in my view. If your attribute is not consistent to me, how can it be imposed on me?" Such an objection does not need to be given any heed, according to the correct view.[499]

وَمن الْأَجْوِبَة عَن النَّقْض أَن يبين الْمُسْتَدلّ أَن صُورة النَّقْض وَارِدَة على مذْهبه وَمذهب خَصمه، كَمَا إِذا قَالَ الْمُسْتَدلّ: مَكِيل فَحرم فِيهِ التَّفَاضُل، فأورد الْمُعْتَرض الْعَرَايَا إِذْ هِيَ مَكِيل، وَقد جَازَ فِيهِ التَّفَاضُل بَينه وَبَين الثّمن الْمَبِيع بِهِ على وَجه الأَرْض، فَيَقُول الْمُسْتَدلّ: هَذَا وَارِد عَليّ وَعَلَيْك جَمِيعًا، فَلَيْسَ بطلَان مذهبي بِهِ أولى من بطلَان مذهبك.

Another response to an allegation of a contradiction is that the claimant may show that the scenario where the contradiction is supposedly proven is plausible both in their own *madhhab* and that of their opponent. For example, if the first interlocutor states, "It is dry-measured, and therefore, disparity in trade is impermissible," and the second interlocutor says, 'However, *ʿarāyā* are dry-measured, and disparity was allowed between it and the price of the item that has fallen on the ground." The first interlocutor can state, "This exception is legitimate in both of our *madhhabs*; it does not invalid my position any more than it invalidates yours."

وَإِذا نقض الْمُعْتَرض عِلّة الْمُسْتَدلّ بِصُورة، فَأجَاب الْمُسْتَدلّ عَن ذَلِك بِأحد الْأَجْوِبَة الْمُتَقَدّمَة إِمَّا منع الْعلَّة أَو الحكم فِي صُورَة النَّقْض، أَو يُورد النَّقْض على الْمذهبين أَو غير ذَلِك فَقَالَ الْمُعْتَرض: الدَّلِيل الَّذِي دلّ على أَن وصفك الَّذِي عللت بِهِ فِي مَحل النزاع عِلّة مَوْجُودَة فِي صُورَة النَّقْض، فيلزمك الْإِقْرَار بِثُبُوت الحكم فِيهَا، عملا بِوُجُود الْوَصْف الْمُقْتَضِي لَهُ، لكنك لم تقل بِهِ، فيلزمك

499 [T] The reason why is that the attribute that necessitates the ruling, namely, disbelief, is the exact evidence of the one proving the case that a Muslim does not receive capital punishment for murder of a *dhimmī*. Refer to *Sharḥ Mukhtaṣar al-Rawḍah* (3/506).

النَّقْض.

The objector can provide a scenario where there is a contradiction in the *ratio legis* of the first interlocutor, and the first interlocutor responds in one of the ways previously mentioned, such as denying the existence of the *ratio legis* or the ruling in the scenario that is supposedly contradictory, or by showing that the contradiction exists in both of their *madhhabs*. At that, the objector can state, "The evidence that you used to prove that the attribute you claim is the *ratio legis* in the disputed scenario also exists in the contradictory scenario. Therefore, you must either admit that the ruling applies [in the other scenario] in order to act on the attribute that necessitates the ruling. However, you have not done so; as such, you must deny it."

ومثاله: قَول الْحَنَفِيّ فِي قتل الْمُسلم بالذمي: قتل عمد عدوان، فَأوجب الْقصاص، كَقَتل الْمُسلم، فَيَقُول الْحَنْبَلِيّ، لَا أسلم أَن قتل الذِّمِّيّ عدوان، فَيَقُول الْحَنَفِيّ: الدَّلِيل عَلَيْهِ أَنه مَعْصُوم بِعَهْد الْإِسْلَام، فَيَقُول الْمُعْتَرض: دَلِيل العدوانية فِي قتل الذِّمِّيّ مَوْجُود فِي قتل الْمعَاهد، فَلْيَكُن عُدْوانًا يجب بِهِ الْقصاص على الْمُسلم، فَهَذَا نقض لدَلِيل الْعلَّة لَا لنَفس الْعلَّة، فَلَا يسمع لِأَنهُ انْتِقَال، وَيَكْفِي الْمُسْتَدل فِي رده أدنى دَلِيل يَلِيق بِأَصْلِهِ، كَأَن يَقُول: إِنَّمَا لم أحكم بالعدوانية فِي الْمِثَال الْمُتَقَدّم لمعارض لي فِي مذهبي، وَهُوَ أَن الْحَرْبِيّ الْمعَاهد مفوت للْعهد، فالمقتضي لانْتِفَاء الْقصاص فِيهِ قوي مُوَافق للْأَصْل، والمقتضي لإثباته ضَعِيف، بِخِلَاف الذِّمِّي، فَإِن الْمُقْتَضِي لقتل الْمُسلم بِهِ قوي لنابذ عَهده وذمته، فَصَار كَالْمُسلمِ أَو غير ذَلِك من الْأَعْذَار.

For example, a Ḥanafī might discuss a Muslim receiving capital punishment as retribution for killing a *dhimmī* and say, "It is a purposeful killing done out of transgression, and therefore, capital punishment is warranted, since it is analogous to the killing of a Muslim." A Ḥanbalī would respond, "I do not believe that killing a *dhimmī* is transgression." The Ḥanafī would respond, "The evidence that it is transgression is that their blood is protected by the treaty of Islam." An objector would say, "The evidence of transgression by killing a *dhimmī* occurs in the murder of a *muʿāhad*. If it is so, the latter case should also be considered transgression, and a Muslim should receive capital punishment." However, this is a denial of the evidence of the *ratio legis*, not of the actual *ratio legis* itself. Therefore, it is not worthy of consideration, since it is a diversion. To respond to this, the claimant would need the slightest evidence to prove their precedent. For example, they can say, "I did not consider it transgression in [the example of a Muslim not receiving capital punishment for the murder of a disbeliever with a treaty] because of an objection within my *madhhab*, namely, that a nonbeliever who has a treaty has a [temporary][500] treaty. The necessitating factor that leads to not exacting capital punishment is strong, and the necessitating factor that leads to establishing it is weaker. This is contrary to a *dhimmī*: the necessitating factor that leads to establishing capital punishment is strong, because of the permanent status of their treaty and protection, making them similar to a Muslim in that regard." Or, they can mention any other factor that causes them to not accept the contradiction in the case.

ثامنها: الْكسر، وَهُوَ نقض الْمَعْنى، وَحَاصِله: وجود الْمَعْنى فِي صُورة مَعَ عدم الحكم فِيهِ.

Eighth. Breakage: This occurs when the concept is denied, where the concept exists in a scenario but no corresponding ruling follows.

مِثَاله: قَول الْحَنَفِيّ فِي العَاصِي بِسَفَرِهِ: يترخص لِأَنهُ مُسَافر، فيترخص كالمسافر سفرا مُبَاحا، فَإِذا قيل لَهُ: لم قلت إِنَّه يترخص، قَالَ: لِأَنهُ يجد مشقة فِي سَفَره، فنَاسَبَ التَّرَخُّص، وَقد شهد لَهُ الأَصْل الْمَذْكُور بِالِاعْتِبَارِ، فَيَقُول: هَذَا ينكسر المكاري والفيج وَنَحْوهمَا مِمَّن دأبه السّفر. يجد الْمَشَقَّة وَلَا يترخص.

An example is, when discussing a person who is sinful in their travel, a Ḥanafī could state, "Since they are travellers, they may use concessions, similar to a person traveling lawfully." Someone might respond, "Why did you state that they may use concessions?" The Ḥanafī would respond, "Because they find the difficulties of travel, and that is appropriate cause for using the concessions. The precedent would take such scenarios into account." The objector might respond, "This reasoning is broken when considering a person who rents animals to carry the belongings of others, and foot-messengers, whose job it is to travel. They find difficulty, but they do not take

500 [T] Al-Shaykh Ibn Badrān quoted it as, "Has nullified their treaty." Refer to *Sharḥ Mukhtaṣar al-Rawḍah* (3/509).

the concessions."[501]

وَحكم الْكسر أَنه غير وَارِد نقضا على الْعلَّة على الصَّحِيح عِنْد الْأُصولِيِّينَ.

With that said, breakage is not a true invalidation of the *ratio legis*, according to the correct view addressed by legal theorists.

تاسعها: الْقلب، وَهُوَ تَعْلِيق نقيض حكم الْمُسْتَدلّ على علته بِعَينهَا، وَهُوَ أَنْوَاع:

Ninth. Reversal: This occurs when the exact opposite of the ruling attempted to be proven is established through the same exact *ratio legis*. This is of a number of types:

أَولهَا: أَن يكون مَقْصُود الْمُعْتَرض بقلب الدَّلِيل تَصْحِيح مَذْهَب نَفسه بِأَن يَقُول الْحَنَفِيّ فِي اشْتِرَاط الصَّوْم للاعتكاف: الِاعْتِكَاف لبث مَحْض، فَلَا يكون بِمُجَرَّدِهِ قربَة، كالوقوف بِعَرَفَة. فَيَقُول الْمُعْتَرض الشَّافِعِي أَو الْحَنْبَلِيّ: الِاعْتِكَاف لبث مَحْض، فَلَا يعْتَبر الصَّوْم فِي كَونه قربَة، كالوقوف بِعَرَفَة، فَكَمَا أَن الْوُقُوف الْمَذْكُور لَا يشْتَرط لصِحَّته الصَّوْم، فَكَذَلِك الِاعْتِكَاف. وَهَذَا النَّوْع لَا تعرض فِيهِ لإبطال مَذْهَب الْغَيْر.

One. By reversing the evidence, the objector wishes to prove their own position. For example, when discussing fasting being a precondition to *iʿtikāf*, a Ḥanafī could say, "*Iʿtikāf* is just a sojourn, and alone, is not an action that garners closeness to Allah the Exalted, similar to standing at *ʿArafah*." A Shāfiʿī or Ḥanbalī objector could respond, "*Iʿtikāf* is simply a sojourn, and as such, fasting plays no part in it being an action that garners closeness, similar to standing at *ʿArafah*. Just as fasting is not a precondition for the validity of standing at *ʿArafah*, it is not a precondition to the validity of *iʿtikāf*.'

[This is predicated on applying the attribute mentioned, namely, that it is a mere sojourn. If it is proven that the attribute mentioned by the first interlocutor is relevant and suitable to both the alleged ruling and its opposite,

501 [T] According to the *madhhab*, a person who rents out their animals to carry the goods of others in travel, and mailmen, do not take the concessions of travel, such as shortening the prayers, and so forth. This is the explicitly stated view of al-Imām Aḥmad and the view of the majority of the *aṣḥāb*. It is one of the singular views within the *madhhab*. Refer to *al-Inṣāf fī Maʿrifah al-Rājiḥ min al-Khilāf* by al-Qāḍī ʿAlāʾ al-Dīn al-Mardāwī (2/334).

neither is more deserving of the ruling than the other. As such, it succumbs as evidence, as it becomes judging one view more veracious without any valid cause. Here, when reversing the evidence, the objector sought to prove their own position, which is that fasting is not a precondition for *iʿtikāf*, as well as to invalidate the view of their opponent in debate.][502]

ثانيهَا: قلب لإبطال مَذْهَب خَصمه من غير تعرض لتصحيح مَذْهَب نَفسه، سَوَاء كَانَ الْإِبْطَال صَرِيحًا بِأَن يَقُول: الرَّأس مَمْسُوح، فَلَا يجب استيعابه كالخف، فَيَقُول الْمُعْتَرض: دليلك هَذَا يَقْتَضِي أَن لَا يتَقَدَّر مسح الرَّأْس بِالربع كالخف. فَفِي هَذَا الِاعْتِرَاض نفي مَذْهَب الْمُسْتَدلّ صَرِيحًا، وَلم يثبت مذْهبه، لاحْتِمَال أَن يكون الْحق فِي غير ذَلِك، وَهُوَ الِاسْتِيعَاب، كَمَا هُوَ قَول أَحْمد وَمَالك.

Two. In the second type, the objector intends on invalidating the view of their opponent in debate, without attempting to prove their own position. The invalidation can be explicit, such as when the claim is made, "The head is a wiped portion during ablution, and therefore, its entirety does not need to be wiped, similar to the *khuff*." The objector could respond, "Your evidence would suggest that there is no minimum to wipe a fourth of the head, similar to a *khuff*."[503] In this objection, the view of the first interlocutor is invalidated explicitly, although the objector did not attempt to prove their own view, since the truth might lie in a third opinion, which is that wiping must be of the entire head, as is the view of Aḥmad and Mālik.

أَو كَانَ الْإِبْطَال بطرِيق الِالْتِزَام، بِأَن يَقُول الْحَنَفِيّ فِي بيع الْغَائِب مثلا: عقد مُعَاوضَة، فَينْعَقد مَعَ جهل الْعِوَض، أَو مَعَ الْجَهْل بالمعوض كَالنِّكَاحِ، فَإِنَّهُ يَصح مَعَ جهل الزَّوْج بِصُورَة الزَّوْجَة وَكَونه لم يرهَا، فَكَذَلِك فِي البيع بِجَامِع كَونهمَا عقد مُعَاوضَة.

---

502 [T] This entire paragraph was missed by al-Shaykh Ibn Badrān. Instead, he stated, "This type does not seek to invalidate the view of the opponent." What I have placed between the brackets is the full quotation from al-Imām Najm al-Dīn al-Ṭūfī in *Sharḥ Mukhtaṣar al-Rawḍah* (3/520).

503 [T] This argument is essentially: If the Ḥanafī alleges that since the head is analogous to the *khuff* in that it is wiped, only a portion must be wiped. However, if it is analogous to the *khuff*, there is no way to state that the minimum to be wiped is a fourth of the head, as is the position of al-Imām Abu Ḥanīfah. Refer to *Sharḥ Mukhtaṣar al-Rawḍah* (3/521).

Invalidation can also occur by showing the logical outcome of the view. For example, a Ḥanafī could say on the topic of selling a non-present item, "It is an exchange contract, and as such, it is valid with the value of the exchange being unknown, or with the item being exchanged for, such as in a marriage contract, which is also valid even if the man never sees his to-be wife. The same applies to sales contracts, since they share in that they are contracts predicated on exchange."

فَيَقُول الْخصم: هَذَا الدَّلِيل يَنْقَلِب، بِأَن يُقَال: عقد مُعَاوضَة، فَلَا يعْتَبر فِيهِ خِيَار الرُّؤْيَة كَالنِّكَاحِ، فَإِن الزَّوْج إِذا رأى الزَّوْجَة وَلم تعجبه لم يجز لَهُ فسخ النِّكَاح، فَكَذَلِك الْمُشْتَرِي لَا يكون خِيَار إِذا رأى الْمَبِيع فِي بيع الْغَائِب بِمُقْتَضى الْجَامِع الْمَذْكُور.

To respond, the objector can state that this evidence can be reversed by saying that since it is an exchange contract, the choice of invalidating the contract after seeing the item is not a condition, as shown by the example of a marriage. If a man sees his prospective wife and is not pleased with her looks, he may not annul the marriage. Likewise, the buyer should not have the choice to invalidate the contract after seeing the items they are sold, based on the analogy that couples both rulings.

فالمستدل لم يُصَرح هَاهُنَا بطلَان مَذْهَب الْمُسْتَدلّ، لكنه دلّ على بُطْلَانه بِبُطْلَان لَازمه، لِأَن ثُبُوت خِيَار الرُّؤْيَة لَازم لصِحَّة بيع الْغَائِب عِنْدهم، وَحَيْثُ كَانَ الْأَمر كَذَلِك، فَإِذا انْتَفَى اللَّازِم انْتَفَى الْمَلْزُوم.

In this case, the objector did not explicitly state that the view of the first interlocutor is false, but rather, indicated its invalidity by showing its invalid logical conclusion, since the choice to invalidate the contract after seeing the item is a condition to the validity of selling the non-present item, according to Abu Ḥanīfah. If that is the case, the conditional is not present, and therefore, its contingent also is not present. [If this condition is invalidated by his using marriage as an analogy, its contingent, which is the validity of the contract, is also invalidated.][504]

ثَالِثهَا: قلب الْمُسَاوَاة، كَقَوْل الْمُسْتَدلّ: الْخلّ مَائِع، طَاهِر، مزيل للخبث كَالْمَاءِ،

504 [T] *Sharḥ Mukhtaṣar al-Rawḍah* (3/522).

فَيَقُول الْمُعْتَرض حِينَئِذٍ: يَسْتَوِي فِيهِ الْحَدث والخبث.

Three. Reversing a comparison. For example, the first interlocutor can state, "Vinegar is a pure liquid, and as such, it removes impurities." The objector can state, "If that is the case, it should also be allowed to be used for lifting ritual impurity, just as it can cleanse tangible impurities."

رَابِعهَا: جعل الْمَعْلُول عِلّة، وَالْعلَّة معلولا من غير إِفْسَاد لَهَا، كَقَوْل أَصْحَابنَا فِي ظِهَار الذِّمِّيّ، من صَحَّ طَلَاقه، صَحَّ ظِهَاره، وَعَكسه، فَالسَّابِق مِنْهُمَا عِلّة للثَّانِي، فَيَقُول الْحَنَفِيّ: اجْعَل الْمَعْلُول عِلّة، وَالْعلَّة معلولا.

Four. Making the effect (the ruling) into the cause (the *ratio legis*), and vice versa, without invalidating the *ratio legis*. For example, on the topic of the *ẓihār* of a *dhimmī*, our *aṣḥāb* state, "If someone can pronounce a valid divorce, they can pronounce a valid statement of *ẓihār*, and vice versa." In this case, the first proposition is the *ratio legis* for the second proposition. A Ḥanafī could respond, "Have you made the cause into the effect, and vice versa?"[505]

خَامِسهَا: قلب الاستبعاد، مِثَاله: لَو ادّعى اللَّقِيط اثْنَان، فَأكْثر للبينة، وَلم تُوجد قافة. وَقُلْنَا: إِنَّه يتْرك حَتَّى يبلغ، فينتسب إِلَى من شَاءَ مِمَّن ادَّعَاهُ، فيعترض بِأَن يُقَال: تحكيم الْوَلَد فِي النّسَب تحكم بِلَا دَلِيل. فَيُقَال، تحكيم الْقَائِف أَيْضا تحكم بِلَا دَلِيل.

Five. Reversal by elimination. For example, if two or more claim a lost child whose lineage is unknown, and there is no expert on determining lineage by facial characteristics, we state that they should be cared for until they reach puberty, and then they may ascribe themselves to whomever they wish. An objector might state, "Giving the child domain over their own lineage is arbitrary," and the response would be, "Giving an expert on facial characteristics domain over the lineage is also arbitrary."[506]

505 [T] The objection of the Ḥanafī in this case is that by doing so, the Ḥanbalī engages in circular logic, where one is predicated on the other. However, the Ḥanbalī would respond by saying that it only invalidates the rational cause and effect relationship, not the religious ruling to *ratio legis* relationship, since a single ruling can have many *ratione legis*. Refer to *Mukhtaṣar al-Taḥrīr Sharḥ al-Kawkab al-Munīr* (4/336).

506 [T] This was an old practice of Muslims. In the modern era, DNA testing can be

سادسها: قلب الدَّلِيل على وَجه يكون مَا ذكره الْمُسْتَدلّ يدل عَلَيْهِ لَا لَهُ، كَأَن يسْتَدلّ بِحَدِيث «**الْخَال وَارِث من لَا وَارِث لَهُ**» فَيُقَال: يدل على أَنه لَا يَرث بطرِيق أبلغ، لِأَنهُ نفي عَام مثل: الْجُوع زَاد من لَا زَاد له، وَالصَّبْر حِيلَة من لَا حِيلَة لَهُ. وَلَيْسَ الْجُوع زادا وَلَا الصَّبْر حِيلَة.

Six. Reversing an evidence, making it proof against the claim of the first interlocutor, not for them. For example, someone could use the ḥadīth, **"The maternal uncle is an inheritor of those who have no inheritors,"**[507] and state that this ḥadīth emphasises that the maternal uncle does not inherit, since it is a general negation. For example, one can say, "Hunger is the provision for those who have no provisions," and "Patience is the solution for those with no solutions." Hunger is not a provision, and patience is not a solution.

عَاشرهَا الْمُعَارضَة وَهِي على قسمَيْنِ: مُعَارضَة فِي الأَصْل، ومعارضة فِي الْفَرْع.

Ten. Objection: This occurs in two ways: (i) Objection to the precedent and (ii) objection to the new case.

أما الأولى فَهِيَ أَن يُبْدِي الْمُعْتَرض معنى آخر يصلح للعلية مُسْتقِلّا أَو غير مُسْتَقل، بل جُزْءا، أما المستقل فَيحْتَمل أَن يكون عِلّة مُسْتَقلَّة دون الأول وَأَن يكون جُزْء عِلّة فَهُوَ مَعَ الأول عِلّة مُسْتَقلَّة، وعَلى التَّقْدِيرَيْنِ فَلَا يحصل الحكم بِالْأولِ وَحده.

(i) As for the first, the objection to the precedent occurs when the objector shows another attribute that can possibly be the *ratio legis*, whether independently or in part. In the case that it is independent, it can be an independent *ratio legis*, taking the place of the attribute alleged by the first interlocu-

more conclusive than such measures. Note, too, that there were stringent conditions for the word of an expert on lineage by facial characteristics to be accepted. For example, they must be upright in their religiosity and must be known to usually be accurate. One way they would test such a person is to take a child, and place the child with ten other men, none of which claim the child. The men are shown to the supposed expert, and if he says that the child belongs to any of those men, their judgement is rendered invalid, as proven by their mistake. Then, the same is done with twenty men, except this time, the one claiming to be the father is among them. If he correctly ascribes the child to the claimant, the child is to be given to the custody of the man. Refer to *al-Inṣāf* by al-Qāḍī ʿAlāʾ al-Dīn al-Mardāwī (16/353).

507 Reported by Abu Dāwūd (2900) and Ibn Mājah (2634).

tor. Or, it can be a part of a *ratio legis*, and in combination with the attribute mentioned by the first interlocutor, is an independent *ratio legis*. In either situation, the alleged *ratio legis* alone does not establish the ruling.[508]

مِثَاله: أَن يُعلل حُرْمَة الرِّبَا بالطعم، فيعارضه بالقوت أَو بِالْكَيْلِ.

An example is to state that the *ratio legis* of the prohibition of usury is that the item is a food-item. The objector can respond by either stating that it is because it is an item of sustenance, or that it is a dry-weighed item.

وَأما غير المستقلة فَيحْتَمل أَن يكون جُزْء الْعلَّة فينفي اسْتِقْلَال الأول. مِثَاله: أَن يُعلل الْقصاص فِي المحدد بِكَوْنِهِ قتلا عمدا عُدْوانًا، فيعارضه بِكَوْنِهِ بالجارح، فَإِنَّهُ لما جَازَ أَن تكون الْعلَّة الْأَوْصَاف الْمَذْكُورة - مَعَ قيد كَونه بالجارح - لم يَتَعَد إِلَى المثقل.

As for [the objector] mentioning a non-independent *ratio legis* as an objection, it could be a part of the *ratio legis*, thus nullifying the independence of the *ratio legis* mentioned by the first interlocutor. An example is that, to establish the ruling of retribution by capital punishment when someone is murdered with a sharp item, one states that the *ratio legis* is that it is a purposeful killing out of transgression. To object, one could bring up that it must be with something that pierces, since although the *ratio legis* could be all of those attributes, as well as piercing, it does not apply to a heavy object.

وَالْحق أَن هَذِه الْمُعَارضَة مَقْبُولَة، وَهل يلْزم الْمُعْتَرض بَيَان أَن الْوَصْف الَّذِي أبديته مُنْتَفٍ فِي الْفَرْع أَولا؟ وَالْمُخْتَار أَنه إِن تعرض لعدمه فِي الْفَرْع صَرِيحًا لزمَه بَيَانه، وَإِلَّا فَلَا.

The truth is that this objection is acceptable. However, there is disagreement on whether the objector must clarify that the attribute is nullified in the new case. The correct view is that if they attempted to prove its nonexistence in the new case explicitly, they must show how the attribute is nonexistent. Otherwise, they do not.

---

508 [T] Meaning, if the other attribute is independent and replaces the attribute mentioned by the first interlocutor, it is not fit to be the *ratio legis* for the ruling. In the case that the attributed mentioned in the objection is just part of a *ratio legis*, the attribute mentioned by the first interlocutor is still not fit to act alone as a *ratio legis*.

وَجَوَاب الْمُعَارضَة من وُجُوه:

There are a number of ways to respond to such an objection:

مِنْهَا: منع وجود الْوَصْف، مثل أَن يُعَارض الْقُوت بِالْكَيْلِ فَيَقُول: لَا نسلم أَنه مَكِيل، لِأَن الْعبْرَة بعادة زمن الرَّسُول صلى الله عَلَيْهِ وَسلم وَكَانَ حِينَئِذٍ مَوْزُونا.

[•] Denying the presence of the attribute. For example, the attribute of food-items could be objected to with the attribute of dry-measuring. The response would be, "I do not submit that it is dry-measured, since the conventions used during the time of the Prophet ﷺ are consequential, and during those times, this food item was weighed."

وَمِنْهَا المطالبة بِكَوْن وصف الْمعَارض مؤثرا، بِأَن يُقَال: وَلم قلت: إِن الْكَيْل مُؤثر؟ وَهَذَا إِنَّمَا يسمع من الْمُسْتَدلّ إِذا كَانَ مثبتا لِلْعِلَّةِ بالمناسبة أَو الشّبَه، حَتَّى يحْتَاج الْمعَارض فِي معارضته إِلَى بَيَان مُنَاسبَة أَو شبه، بِخِلَاف مَا إِذا أثْبته بالسبر، فَإِن الْوَصْف يدْخل فِي السبر بِدُونِ ثبوت الْمُنَاسبَة بِمُجَرَّد الِاحْتِمَال.

[•] Demanding the objector to show why the attribute is effective. For example, they can say, "Why did you say that being dry-measured is effective?" This response to the objection is only worthy of consideration on part of the first interlocutor if they chose to prove their *ratio legis* using suitability and relevance (*munāsabah*), or similarity (*shabah*). In that case, the objector would need to show the suitability or similarity of their own *ratio legis*. The case would be different if [the first interlocutor] attempted to prove their case through classification (*sabr*). The attribute is within the classification without establishing suitability by mere possibility.

وَمِنْهَا: بَيَان خفائه.

[•] Showing that the attribute is hidden.

وَمِنْهَا: عدم انضباطه.

[•] Showing that the attribute is not consistent.

وَمِنْهَا: منع ظُهُوره.

[•] Denying the attribute's apparency.

وَمِنْهَا: منع انضباطه.

[•] Denying the attribute's consistency.

وَمِنْهَا: بَيَان أَن الْوَصْف عدم معَارض فِي الْفَرْع، مِثَاله: أَن يقيس الْمُكْره على الْمُخْتَار فِي الْقصاص بِجَامِع الْقَتْل، فَيَقُول الْمُعْتَرض: معَارض بالطواعية، فَإِن الْعلَّة هِيَ الْقَتْل مَعَ الطواعية، فيجيب الْمُسْتَدلّ بِأَن الطواعية عدم الْإِكْرَاه الْمُنَاسب لنقيض الحكم، وَهُوَ عدم الْقصاص، فحاصلة عدم معَارض، وَعدم الْمعَارض طرد لَا يصلح للتَّعْلِيل، لِأَنهُ لَيْسَ من الْبَاعِث فِي شَيْء.

[•] Showing that the attribute is not objectionable in that it still establishes the ruling in the new case. For example, the case can be made to show that a person coerced into murdering someone is analogous to a person choosing to commit a murder. The unifying attribute is that they murdered someone. An objector could state, "This is objected to, on the basis of freewill. The *ratio legis* is killing with freewill." The first interlocutor can respond by saying, "Freewill is the lack of coercion, which should appropriately prove the opposite ruling, namely, not enacting capital punishment. In this case, the argument is lack of an objection, and the lack of an objection is a coincidence,[509] and no action emanates from the lack of an objection on its own."

وَمِنْهَا: أَن يبين كَون وصف الْمعَارض ملغي، إِذْ قد تبين اسْتِقْلَال الْبَاقِي بالعلية فِي صُورَة مَا بِظَاهِر نَص أَو إِجْمَاع.

[•] To show that the attribute mentioned by the objector is null and void, since the remaining attribute has been shown to be an independent *ratio legis* in some scenario, as shown by a text or consensus.

509 [T] In this case, when the objector responds, it should be noted that lack of freewill is not a portion of a *ratio legis*. The most that can be said about freewill is that it is the lack of an objection in the new case. Freewill means lack of coercion, and coercion is a suitable attribute that can impede the obligation of retribution which is the opposite of the obligation of retribution. As such, coercion is an objection to the new case, namely, the person who was coerced, since it is a suitable attribute that can impede the obligation of retribution, which is the opposite of the ruling. As such, lack of coercion in this case is just coincidental. Refer to *Bayān al-Mukhtaṣar Sharḥ Mukhtaṣar Ibn al-Ḥājib* (3/219).

مِثَاله: إذا عَارض فِي الرِّبَا الطّعْم بِالْكَيْلِ، فيجيب بِأَن النَّص دلّ على اعْتِبَار الطّعْم فِي صُورة مَا، وَهُوَ قَوْله **«لَا تَبِيعُوا الطعَام بِالطعَامِ إلا سَوَاء بِسَوَاء»** هَذَا إذا لم يتَعَرَّض للتعميم، فَلَو عمم، وَقَالَ: فَثَبت ربوية كل مطعوم، لم يسمع، لِأَن ذَلِك إثْبَات للْحكم دون الْقيَاس، لَا تتميم الْقيَاس بالإلغاء، وَالْمَقْصُود ذَلِك.

For example, if a person wishes to establish that being a food source is the *ratio legis* in usury, and then the opponent wishes to object to that, saying that the *ratio legis* is that it is dry-measured. They would respond by saying, "The text has shown that the attribute of being food has been given consideration in a scenario, namely, when the Prophet ﷺ said, **'Do not trade food for food unless it is equal.'**"[510] This is the case if the first interlocutor is not attempting to prove through the generality of the text. If they use the generality of the text and say, "All food is susceptible to usury," their argument is not worthy of consideration, since it is establishment of a ruling without analogy, as opposed to establishing the analogy by virtue of elimination, which is the point.

وَلَا يَكْفِي إثْبَات الحكم فِي صُورة دون وصف الْمعَارض، وَذَلِك لجَوَاز وجود عِلّة أخْرى، وَلأجل ذَلِك لَو أبدى فِي صُورة عدم وصف الْمُعَارضَة وَصفا آخر يخلفه، لِئَلَّا يكون الْبَاقِي مُسْتقِلّا، وَيُسمى تعدد الْوَضع لتَعَدد أَصْلهَا.

It is also not sufficient to establish the ruling in a scenario without the attribute of the objector, since there might be another *ratio legis*. Because of this, if the objector mentions another attribute that could replace the one negated by the first interlocutor by showing that the ruling exists without [the attribute], the negation is invalidated. It is referred to as "multiplicity of conditionality," since it is conditioned on multiple precedents.

مِثَاله: أن يُقَال فِي مَسْأَلَة أَمَان العَبْد للحربي: أَمَان من مُسلم عَاقل فَيقبل كَالْحرِّ، لِأنهمَا مظنتان لإِظْهَار مصَالح الْإِيمَان، فيعترض بِالْحُريةِ، فَإِنَّهَا مَظَنَّة الْفَرَاغ للنَّظَر، فَيكون أكمل، فيلغيها بالمأذون لَهُ فِي الْقِتَال، فَيَقُول: خلف الْإِذن الْحُرية فَإِنَّهَا مَظَنَّة لبذل الوسع، أَو لعلم السَّيِّد بصلاحيته. وَجَوَابه الإلغاء إِلَى أَن يقف أَحدهمَا.

510 Reported by Muslim (1592).

An example of this concept is shown in the issue of a slave giving a promise of safety to a combatant. One could claim, "It is a promise of safety from a Muslim of sound mental faculties, and as such it is accepted, as it would be from a free man, since both one's Islam and mental faculties are likely causes to render giving peace to be valid." Someone could object with freedom, since it is a likely cause for one to be able to give due thought to the granting of peace, making their decision making more complete. The first interlocutor can negate the attribute based on the slave that is given the choice to fight in battle by their master.[511] The objector can respond, "The permission granted by the master replaces the condition of freedom, since the situation is one that calls for generosity, or the master knows that their slave is fit for battle." In this manner, the responses are that each interlocutor continuously negates the argument of the other until one of them cannot respond any further.

وَلَا يُفِيد الإلغاء إِذا كَانَ الْمَعْنى ضَعِيفا إِذا سلم وجود المظنة المتضمنة لذَلِك الْمَعْنى.

If the attribute that is being used as an objection is weak, it does not negate the attribute mentioned by the first interlocutor, so long as there is no likeliness for the attribute to be worthy of consideration.

مِثَاله: أَن يَقُول: الرِّدَّة عِلّة الْقَتْل، فَيَقُول الْمُعْتَرض: بل مَعَ الرجولية، لِأَنَّهُ مَظَنَّة الْإِقْدَام على قتال الْمُسلمين إِذْ يعْتَاد ذَلِك من الرِّجَال دون النِّسَاء، فيجيب الْمُسْتَدل: بِأَن الرجولية وَكَونهَا مَظَنَّة الْإِقْدَام لَا تعْتَبر، وَإِلَّا لم يقتل مَقْطُوع الْيَدَيْنِ، لِأَن احْتِمَال الْإِقْدَام فِيهِ ضَعِيف، بل أَضْعَف من احْتِمَاله فِي النِّسَاء، وَهَذَا لَا يقبل مِنْهُ حَيْثُ سلم أَن الرجولية مَظَنَّة اعتبرها الشَّارِع.

For example, one can say that apostasy is the *ratio legis* for capital punishment. To object, one can say, "Actually, this only applies to men, since it is likely for one to proceed in attacking Muslims afterwards, as that is normal behavior for men, not women." The first interlocutor can respond, 'Manhood and the fact that it makes one likely to fight against Muslims is

511 [T] Meaning, Islam and sound intellect independently act as a *ratio legis* for the lawfulness of a slave fighting in battle if given license by their master. If that is the case, they should be independently sufficient in granting peace. Refer to *al-Taḥbīr Sharḥ al-Taḥrīr* (7/3634).

not worthy of consideration. If it were, the person who has no arms would receive the punishment, though the likeliness of them fighting is even less than that of a woman." This is not acceptable by the first interlocutor, since they admit that manhood is a viable reason for likeliness that is considered by the religion.[512]

وَذَلِكَ كترفه الْملك فِي السّفر لَا يمْنَع رخص السّفر فِي حَقه، لقلَّة الْمَشَقَّة، إِذْ الْمُعْتَبر المظنة، وَقد وجدت، لَا مِقْدَار الْحِكْمَة لعدم انضباطها.

Another example is when a king travels luxuriously. In this case, it does not prevent the application of the concessions associated with travel, just because they experience little hardships. The thing that is worthy of consideration is the likeliness of it occurring, and it exists in this case. The extent of the wisdom of the ruling is not worthy of consideration, since it cannot be quantified nor considered consistent.

وَلَا يَكْفِي أَيْضا أَن يكون الْمعِين راجحا، وَلَا كَونه مُتَعَدِّيا.

Also, when responding to an objection, it is not sufficient for the particular attribute to be preponderant over the attribute mentioned by the objector,[513] nor does it have to be transitive.[514]

مِثَال الأول: أَن يَقُول الْمُسْتَدل فِي جَوَاب الْمُعَارضَة: مَا عنيته من الْوَصْف رَاجِح على مَا عارضت بِهِ، ثمَّ يظْهر وَجها من وُجُوه التَّرْجِيح.

512 [T] Meaning, the ruling can be inseparable to this attribute without attention being given to the wisdom behind it. Refer to *al-Taqrīr wa 'l-Taḥbīr 'alā Taḥrīr al-Kamāl ibn al-Humām* by al-Imām Ibn Amīr al-Ḥāj (3/273).

513 [T] Because there can be two *ratione legis* for a single ruling. Refer to *Tashnīf al-Masami'* (3/254). Also, the preponderance of an attribute does not mean it can act independently as a *ratio legis*, since some parts of a single *ratio legis* can be preponderant over the other parts. In the example of murder, the *ratio legis* for capital punishment is a purposeful killing out of aggression. Of those parts, killing is the most preponderant. Refer to *Bayān al-Mukhtaṣar Sharḥ Mukhtaṣar ibn al-Ḥājib* (3/224).

514 [T] Because the transitive nature of an attribute does not necessitate it is an independent *ratio legis*, since a transitive attribute being preponderant over a non-transitive one is not a given. A transitive attribute is preponderant in that it applies to a vaster scope, but a non-transitive one is more preponderant in that it is more closely aligned with the precedent. Refer to *Bayān al-Mukhtaṣar Sharḥ Mukhtaṣar ibn al-Ḥājib* (3/224).

An example of the former is where the first interlocutor says in response to the objection, "The attribute I mentioned is preponderant over the one you used in your objection," and then mention how it is preponderant.

وَالثَّانِي: أَن يَقُول فِي جَوَاب الْمُعَارضَة: إِن مَا عينته أَنا مُتَعَدٍّ، وَمَا عينته أَنْت قَاصِر، فَهَذَا غير كَاف فِي جَوَاب الْمُعَارضَة، إِذْ مرجعه التَّرْجِيح بذلك، فَيَجِيء التحكم.

An example of the latter would be to say in response to the objection, "The attribute I mentioned is transitive, and the one you mentioned is non-transitive." This is not sufficient to respond to an objection, since declaring preponderance with such concepts is arbitrary.

وَهل يجب على الْمُسْتَدلّ الِاكْتِفَاء بِأَصْل وَاحِد - إِذْ مَقْصُوده الظَّن وَهُوَ يحصل بِهِ - فَيلْغُو مَا زَاد عَلَيْهِ أم لَا؟ وَالصَّحِيح: الأول، لِأَن الظن يقوى بِهِ. وَفِي جَوَاز اقْتِصَار الْمُعَارضَة على أصل وَاحِد قَولَانِ، وعَلى الْجَمِيع فِي جَوَاز اقْتِصَار الْمُسْتَدلّ على أصل وَاحِد قَولَانِ.

Is it obligatory on the first interlocutor to only mention a single precedent, since they are only attempting to establish probability, and that occurs with a single precedent, and thereby negate all additional ones? The correct view is that it is not obligatory, since adding additional precedents strengthens the probability. There are two views on whether an objector may use only one precedent. And when the first interlocutor uses multiple precedents, and they are all objected to by the second interlocutor, there are two views on whether the first interlocutor must respond to all objections.

فصل

Section: [Objection to the New Case]

وَأما الْمُعَارضَة فِي الْفَرْع، فَهِيَ بِمَا يَقْتَضِي نقيض الحكم فِيهِ، بِأَن يَقُول: مَا ذكرته من الْوَصْف، وَإِن اقْتضى ثُبُوت الحكم فِي الْفَرْع، فعندي وصف آخر يَقْتَضِي نقيضه، فَيتَوَقَّف دليلك عَلَيْهِ، وَهَذَا هُوَ الْمَعْنى بالمعارضة إِذا أطلقت.

If the objection is to the new case, it necessitates the opposite of the ruling in that case. For example, they can state, "Though the attribute that you mentioned necessitates the ruling in the new case, I can present another attribute that necessitates its polar opposite. Your evidence is, therefore, halted." This is what is intended by the term, "objection," when it is used.

وَلَا بُد من بنائِهِ على أصل بِجَامِع تثبت عليته، وَله الِاسْتِدْلَال فِي إِثْبَات عليته بِأَيّ مَسْلَك من مسالكها شَاءَ، على نَحْو طرق إِثْبَات الْمُسْتَدلّ للعلية سَوَاء. فَيصير هُوَ مستدلا آنِفا، والمستدل مُعْتَرضًا، فتنقلب الوظيفتان. وَالْمُخْتَار قبُول هَذَا النَّوْع لِئَلَّا تختل فَائِدَة المناظرة، وَهُوَ ثبوت الحكم، لِأَنهُ لَا يتَحَقَّق بِمُجَرَّد الدَّلِيل مَا لم يعلم عدم الْمعَارض.

The attribute being used to establish the opposite ruling must be based on a precedent which must share with the new case in the attribute, proving that it is the *ratio legis*. One can choose to prove their *ratio legis* in any method they wish, following the same ways that the first interlocutor used to prove their *ratio legis*. In such a case, the claimant becomes the objector, and vice versa; their objectives switch. The chosen view is that such an objection is accepted, as otherwise, the purpose of the debate, which is to establish a ruling, would become unsound. This does not mean that the ruling becomes established through evidence so long as one does not know of any objections.

وَجَوَابه بِمَا يعْتَرض بِهِ الْمُعْتَرض ابْتِدَاء، إِذْ الْجَواب هُوَ الْجَواب.

The response to this type of objection is by using the same methods used to object to an argument made by a claimant initially.[515] The response in this case is the same response used by the initial objector.

وَيقبل تَرْجِيح أَحدهمَا بِأَيّ وَجه كَانَ من وُجُوه التَّرْجِيح الْمَذْكُورَة فِي بَابه عِنْد أَصْحَابنَا وَجمع من الْعلمَاء، مِنْهُم الْآمِدِي وَابْن الْحَاجِب، فيتَعَيَّن الْعَمَل بِهِ، وَهُوَ الْمَقْصُود. وَلَا يلْزم الْمُسْتَدلّ الْإِيمَاء إِلَى التَّرْجِيح فِي متن دَلِيله، بِأَن يَقُول فِي

515 [T] Because in this case, the objector becomes the claimant. Therefore, to respond to the objector, the initial claimant must take the role of an objector. Refer to *Bayān al-Mukhtaṣar Sharḥ Mukhtaṣar Ibn al-Ḥājib* (3/230).

أَمَان العَبْد أَمَان من مُسلم عَاقل، وَهُوَ مُوَافق للبراءة الْأَصْلِيَّة.

According to our *aṣḥāb* and other scholars, such as al-Āmidī and Ibn al-Ḥājib, either of the interlocutors can claim preponderance of their view over the other, by using the various methods outlined in its respective chapter. In that case, one must adhere to the preponderant view, as that is the point.[516] The claimant does not need to allude to their reasoning for ruling one view preponderant in their line of argument, such as saying, when speaking about the grants of safety given by a slave, "It is a granting of safety occurring from a rational Muslim, and allowing it is in accordance with the presumption of continuity."

حادي عشرهَا: عدم التَّأْثِير. اعْلَم أَن التَّأْثِير هُوَ إِفَادَة الْوَصْف أَثَره، فَإِذا لم يفده، فَهُوَ عدم التَّأْثِير، وَهُوَ ذكر مَا يَسْتَغْنِي عَنهُ الدَّلِيل فِي ثُبُوت حكم الأَصْل، وَذَلِكَ إِمَّا:

Eleventh. Ineffectiveness: Effectiveness (*taʾthīr*) is when the attribute in question provides an effect. If it does not provide an effect, it is ineffective. An ineffective attribute is one the ruling can do without when it is being established in the precedent. [There are four types:]

لكَون ذَلِك الْوَصْف طرديا لَا يُنَاسب ترَتّب الحكم عَلَيْهِ، كَقَوْل الْمُسْتَدلّ فِي صَلَاة الصُّبْح: صَلَاة لَا تقصر، فَلَا يقدم أذانها على وَقتهَا كالمغرب. فَعدم الْقصر هُنَا بِالنِّسْبَةِ لعدم تَقْدِيم الأذان طردي، فَكَأَنَّهُ قَالَ: لَا يقدم أَذَان الْفجْر عَلَيْهَا لِأَنَّهَا لَا تقصر. وَأطْرد ذَلِك فِي الْمغرب، لكنه لم ينعكس فِي بَقِيَّة الصَّلَوَات، إِذْ مُقْتَضى هَذَا الْقيَاس أَن مَا يقصر من الصَّلَاة يجوز تَقْدِيم أذانه على وقته من حَيْثُ انعكاس الْعلَّة، فَيرجع حَاصله إِلَى سُؤال الْمُطَالبَة.

(i) Ineffectiveness in the attribute: This sometimes occurs because the attribute is coincidental and does not suitably result in a ruling. As an example, when it pertains to the *fajr* prayer, a claimant can say, "It is a prayer that cannot be shortened, and therefore, its *adhān* should not be before its appropriate time, similar to the *maghrib* prayer.' The relationship between the

---

516 [T] Meaning, the point of a debate is to find the preponderant view and to adhere to it.

prayer not being shortened and the *adhān* not being done before its time is coincidental. It occurs in the *maghrib* prayer as well, but does not apply to the other prayers. This analogy necessitates that if a prayer is not shortened, that it is permissible to perform the *adhān* before its time, if we considered the reversibility of the *ratio legis*.

وَإِمَّا لكَون الحكم ثبت بِدُونِهِ، كَأَن يُقَال فِي مَبِيع الْغَائِب: مَبِيع لم يره الْعَاقِد، فَلَا يَصح بَيْعه، كالطير فِي الْهَوَاء. فيعترض بِأَن الْعلَّة الْعَجز عَن التَّسْلِيم، وَهُوَ كَاف فِي الْبطلَان.

[ii] Nonexistence in the precedent: In effect, this resorts to the posing of a question. Either the ruling is established without the *ratio legis*, such as, when speaking on selling a non-present item, claiming, "It is a sold item that was not seen by the person in the contract, and as such, the sales transaction is not valid, similar to a bird in the sky." The objection would state that the *ratio legis* in the latter case is the inability to hand over the merchandise, which is sufficient to invalidate a sale.

وَعدم التَّأْثِير هُنَا جِهَة الْعَكْس، لِأَن تَعْلِيل عدم صِحَة بيع الْغَائِب بِكَوْنِهِ غير مرئي تَقْتَضِي أَن كل مرئي يجوز بَيْعه.

The ineffectiveness in the attribute is also proven in this case by co-exclusion, since if one were to state that the invalidity of a sales transaction of some non-present item is invalid due to it not being visible, it would necessitate that all visible items may be sold.

فهذان قِسْمَانِ من أَقسَام أَرْبَعَة لهَذَا النَّوْع، أَولهمَا يُقَال لَهُ: عدم التأثير فِي الْوَصْف، وَالثَّانِي عَدمه فِي الأَصْل، وَأما الثَّالِث، فَهُوَ عدم التَّأْثِير فِي الحكم.

These are two of the four categories of this type, [...] and the third is termed as ineffectiveness in the ruling:

ومثاله فِي الْمُرْتَدين: مشركون أتلفوا مَالا فِي دَار الْحَرْب، فَلَا ضَمَان عَلَيْهِم كالحربي، فَيَقُول الْمُعْتَرض: دَار الْحَرْب لَا تَأْثِير لَهُ عنْدك أَيهَا الْمُسْتَدل ضَرُورَة اسْتِوَاء الإِتْلَاف فِي دَار الْحَرْب، وَدَار الْإِسْلَام فِي إيجَاب الضَّمَان عنْدك. ومرجع

هَذَا إِلَى مُطَالَبَة تَأْثِير كَونه فِي دَار الْحَرْب فَهُوَ كَالأول.

[(iii): Ineffectiveness in the ruling:] For example, on the topic of apostates, one can state, "They are polytheists who destroyed wealth in a warring land, and as such, they do not have to pay restitution, similar to a combatant."[517] The objector could state, "The fact that it is a warring land has no effect, since the ruling applies to both when it occurs in a warring land or in a Muslim land, in the obligation of restitution." This goes back to raising a question about the effectiveness in a warring land. In that sense, it is similar to the first type.

وَأما الرَّابِع: فَهُوَ أَن يكون الْوَصْف الْمَذْكُور لَا يطرد فِي جَمِيع صور النزاع، وَإِن كَانَ مناسبا يُسمى عدم التَّأْثِير فِي الْفَرْع.

(iv): Inconsistency of the attribute: This occurs when the inconsistency occurs in all scenarios in dispute. If the attribute is suitable and relevant, this type is known as, "Lack of effectiveness in the new case."

مِثَاله: أَن يُقَال فِي تَزْوِيج الْمَرْأَة نَفسهَا: زوجت نَفسهَا بِغَيْر إِذن وَليهَا، فَلَا يَصح، كَمَا لَو زوجت بِغَيْر كُفْء. فَيَقُول الْمُعْتَرض: كَونه غير كفء لَا أثر لَهُ، فَإِن النزاع وَاقع فِيمَا زوجت من كُفْء وَمن غير كُفْء، وحكمهما سَوَاء، فَلَا أثر لَهُ. ومرجع هَذَا النَّوْع إِلَى الْمُعَارضَة بِوَصْف آخر، وَهُوَ تَزْوِيج فَقَط، فَهُوَ كالثاني.

For example, when discussing a woman that marries herself off, one can say, "She married herself off without the permission of her guardian. As such, the marriage is invalid, similar to if she married someone who is not suitable for her." The objector can state, "The fact that he is not suited for her has no effect. The dispute occurs whether she marries herself to a suitable suitor or not. In both cases, the ruling is the same. As such, it has no effect.' This is an

---

517 [T] In this case, a Ḥanafī would argue that apostates who destroy our wealth in a warring land do not have to pay restitution for the property that they destroyed. Their evidence is: They are polytheists who destroyed our wealth in a warring land, making them similar to a combatant who destroys our wealth. In this case, the attribute of, "a warring land," is coincidental, providing no benefit when mentioned. The scholars who obligated restitution obligated it even if it is not in a warring land. Likewise, those who negate the obligation negate it regardless if it occurs in a warring land or a Muslim land. Refer to the explanation of Jalāl al-Dīn al-Maḥallī on *Jamʿ al-Jawāmiʿ*, with the commentaries of al-ʿAṭṭār (2/354).

objection by mention of another attribute, which is the marriage without any qualifications. In that sense, it resembles the second type.

وَاعْلَم أَن حَاصِل مَا ذكر أَن الْأَقْسَام الْأَرْبَعَة: الأول وَالثَّالِث مِنْهَا يرجعان إِلَى منع الْعلَّة، وَالثَّانِي وَالرَّابِع إِلَى الْمُعَارضَة فِي الأَصْل بإبداء عِلّة أُخْرى، فَلَيْسَ هُوَ سُؤالا بِرَأْسِهِ.

To summarise all four types, the first and third are ways of disproving the *ratio legis*, while the second and fourth are objections to the precedent by showing another *ratio legis*. As such, they are not unique objections.

ثَانِي عشرهَا: تركيب الْقيَاس من مذهبي الْمُسْتَدل والمعترض، وَهُوَ الْقيَاس الْمركب الْمَار ذكره عِنْد ذكر شُرُوط حكم الأَصْل.

Twelve. Compounding the analogy: This occurs when the analogy is compounded from the views taken by the claimant as well as that of the objector. This is a compounded analogy that has been mentioned previously when discussing the ruling of the precedent.

مِثَاله: أَن يَقُول الْحَنبلي فِي الْمَرْأَة الْبَالِغَة: أُنْثَى، فَلَا تزوج نَفسهَا بِغَيْر ولي كابنة خمس عشرَة سنة، فالخصم - وَهُوَ الْحَنَفِي - يمْنَع تزوج بنت خمس عشرة سنة لصغرها، لَا لكَونهَا أُنْثَى فاختلفت الْعلَّة فِي الأَصْل، وَإِنَّمَا اتّفق صِحَة هَذَا الْقيَاس لِاجْتِمَاع عِلّة الْخَصْمَيْنِ فِيهِ، فتركب مِنْهُمَا.

An example is for a Ḥanbalī to state, when speaking about a woman who has reached the age of puberty, "She is a woman, and as such, she should not marry herself off without her guardian, similar to a fifteen year old girl." The opponent, in this case, a Ḥanafī, would deny that a fifteen year old girl can marry herself off, because of her young age, not because she is a woman. The *ratio legis* in the precedent is different, but both parties agree that this analogy is valid because both *ratione legis* exist. As such, it becomes compounded of them.

وَتَحْقِيق التَّرْكِيب هَاهُنَا: هُوَ أَن يتَّفق الخصمان على حكم الأَصْل، ويختلفان فِي علته، فَإِذا ألحق أَحدهمَا بذلك الأَصْل فرعا يعْتَبر عِلّة صَاحبه، فَالقِيَاس مُنْتَظم،

لكِن بِنَاء على تركيب حكم الأَصْل من علتين، وَذَلِكَ كَمَا فِي الْمِثَال الْمُتَقَدّم. فَإِن أَحْمد وَالشَّافِعِيّ يعْتَقدان أَن بنت خمس عشرَة لَا تزوج نَفسهَا لأنوثتها، وَأَبُو حنيفَة يعْتَقد أَنهَا لَا تزوج نَفسهَا لصغرها، إِذْ الْجَارِيَة إِنَّمَا تبلغ عِنْده لتسْع عشرَة، وَفِي رِوَايَة لثماني عشرَة كالغلام. فالعلتان مَوْجُودَتَانِ فِيهَا، وَالْحكم مُتَّفق عَلَيْهِ بِنَاء على ذَلِك، فَإِذا قَالَ الْحَنْبَلِي فِي الْبَالِغَة: أُنْثَى فَلَا تزوج نَفسهَا كَبِنْت خمس عشرَة، انتظم الْقيَاس بِنَاء على مَا ذَكَرْنَاهُ من تركب حكم الأَصْل بَين الْخَصْمَيْنِ من العلتين، واستناده عِنْد كل مِنْهُمَا إِلَى علته.

The reality of the compounded nature in this instance is where both interlocutors agree on the ruling in the precedent, but differ on the *ratio legis*. The analogy is cogent, but is based on the ruling being based on two *ratione legis*, as in the previous example. Aḥmad and al-Shāfiʿī opine that a fifteen year old girl cannot marry herself off because of her femaleness, while Abu Ḥanīfah opined that she cannot marry herself off because she is too young to do so, since a girl only reaches puberty, according to him, when she turns nineteen, and in another narration, eighteen, similar to a boy. As such, both *ratione legis* exist, and the ruling is agreed on by both interlocutors based on that. The Ḥanbalī argues that a woman who has reached the age of puberty may not marry herself off, just as a girl who is fifteen years old cannot. In that case, the analogy is cogent because of the ruling in the precedent being compounded of the two *ratione legis*, and both interlocutors using their *ratio legis* to prove the ruling.

وَلِهَذَا جَازَ لأَحَدهمَا منع صِحَة الْقيَاس لاخْتِلَاف الْعلَّة فِي الْفَرْع وَالْأَصْل، مثل أَن يَقُول الْحَنَفِي هَاهُنَا للمستدل: أَنْت عللت الْمَنْع فِي الْبَالِغَة بالأنوثة، وَالْمَنْع فِي بنت خمس عشرَة عِنْدِي مُعَلل بالصغر: فَمَا اتفقت عِلّة الأَصْل وَالْفرع، فَلَا يَصح الْإِلْحَاق.

Either of them can object to the validity of the analogy, since the *ratio legis* differs in the new case and the precedent. For example, the *Ḥanafī* can state to the claimant, "In the case of the woman who reached puberty, you stated that the *ratio legis* is her femaleness. To me, the prohibition for a fifteen year old to marry herself off is her young age. The *ratio legis* of the precedent and the new case do not correspond, and as such, they are not to be coupled in ruling."

وَهَذَا النَّوْع تمسك بِهِ قوم، ونفاه آخَرُونَ، وَالْمُخْتَار إثْباته، وبصحته قَالَ الطوفي والمرداوي من أَصْحَابنَا، لِأَن حَاصله يرجع إِلَى النزاع فِي الأَصْل، وَقد سبق أَن الْقيَاس يجوز على أصل مُخْتَلف فيه، فَإِذا مَنعه الْمُعْتَرض أثْبته الْمُسْتَدل بطريقه، وَصَحَّ قِيَاسه، فهاهنا كَذَلِك يثبت الْمُسْتَدل أَن الْعلَّة فِي بنت خمس عشرَة هِيَ الْأنوثَة، ويحققها فِي الْفَرْع وَهِي الْبَالِغَة، وَيبْطل مَأْخَذ الْخصم وَهُوَ تَعْلِيله فِي الْبِنْت الْمَذْكُورَة بالصغر. وَقد ثَبت مدعاه، وَصَحَّ قِيَاسه، وَهُوَ أَن الْبَالِغَة أُنْثَى، فَلَا تزوج نَفسهَا كَبِنْت خمس عشرَة.

Some scholars adhered to this type, but others denied its plausibility. The chosen view is that it is established. Of our *aṣḥāb*, al-Ṭūfī and al-Mardāwī both stated that it is valid, since in essence, it is an objection to the precedent. It was previously stated that analogies based on precedents that are differed on are allowed, and when the objector refutes them, the claimant can argue to establish it in their own ways, making their analogy valid. In this case, the claimant can attempt to prove that the *ratio legis* for the fifteen year old girl is femaleness, and can establish its presence in the new case, which is the woman who is of the age of puberty. They can then attempt to invalidate the argument of their opponent, which is that the girl that is fifteen years old cannot marry herself off due to her young age. As such, they prove their case, and their analogy is valid, namely, that since a woman above the age of puberty is a female, she may not marry herself off, just as a girl who is fifteen years old cannot.

ثَالِث عشرهَا: القَوْل بِالْمُوجبِ، بِفَتْح الْجِيم أَي: القَوْل بِمَا أوجبه دَلِيل الْمُسْتَدل. أما الْمُوجب بِكَسْرِهَا، فَهُوَ الدَّلِيل الْمُقْتَضِي للْحكم، وَهَذَا النَّوْع لَا يخْتَص بِالْقِيَاسِ، بل يَجِيء فِي كل دَلِيل. وَحَاصِله: تَسْلِيم مَدْلُول الدَّلِيل مَعَ بَقَاء النزاع، وَذَلِكَ دَعْوَى نصب الدَّلِيل فِي غير مَحل النزاع، وَيَقَع على وُجُوه ثَلَاثَة.

Thirteen. Argument from commitment: Meaning, affirming the necessary outcome contingent on the evidence of the claimant, as proven by the necessitating evidence for the ruling. This is not specific to *qiyās*, but rather, applies to all evidences. Its essence is to affirm the outcome of the evidence while still disagreeing. This is where the objector claims that the claimant has used evidence to prove something outside of the scope of debate. This occurs in three ways:

الْوَجْه الأول: أَن يستنتج من الدَّلِيل مَا يتوَهَّم أَنه مَحل النزاع أَو ملازمه، وَلَا يكون كَذَلِك مِثَاله: أَن يَقُول الشَّافِعِي فِي الْقَتْل بالمثقل: قتل بِمَا يقتل غَالِبا، فَلَا يُنَافِي الْقصاص، كَالْقَتْلِ بالحرق. فَيرد القَوْل بِالْمُوجبِ، فَيَقُول: عدم الْمُنَافَاة لَيْسَ مَحل النزاع، لِأَن مَحل النزاع هُوَ وجوب الْقَتْل، وَلَا يَقْتَضِي أَيْضا مَحل النزاع، إِذْ لَا يلْزم من عدم منافاته للْوُجُوب أَن يجب.

First. Extracting something from the evidence thinking that it is within the scope of the debate, or is close in proximity to the contentious issue, while in reality it is not. For example, a Shāfiʿī could say, on the topic of murder with a heavy item, "This person has committed murder using an item that usually kills, and as such, it does not conflict with the ruling of capital punishment, similar to if one murdered another with fire." The objector can refute this argument by what it necessitates, saying, "Lack of conflict [with the ruling of capital punishment] is not the point of contention. The point of disagreement is whether or not capital punishment [in this case] is obligatory." Also [even if we were to state that it does not conflict], it (meaning, the lack of conflict) does not necessitate the point of disagreement [namely, the obligation of capital punishment], since just because something does not conflict with the obligation, it does not mean it becomes obligatory.[518]

الْوَجْه الثَّانِي: أَن يستنتج من الدَّلِيل إِبْطَال أَمر يتوَهَّم أَنه مَأْخَذ الْخصم ومبني مذهبه من الْمَسْأَلَة، وَهُوَ يمْنَع كَونه مأخذا لمذهبه، فَلَا يلْزم من إِبْطَاله إبطَال مذْهبه. مِثَاله: أَن يَقُول الشَّافِعِي فِي الْمِثَال الْمُتَقَدّم - وَهُوَ مَسْأَلَة الْقَتْل بالمثقل - التَّفَاوُت فِي الْوَسِيلَة لَا يمْنَع الْقصاص، كالمتوسل إِلَيْهِ. وَهُوَ أَنْوَاع الْجِرَاحَات القاتلة، فَيرد القَوْل بِالْمُوجبِ، فَيَقُول الْحَنَفِيّ: الحكم لَا يثبت إِلَّا بارتفاع جَمِيع الْمَوَانِع، وَوُجُود الشَّرَائِط بعد قيام الْمُقْتَضِي، وَهَذَا غَايَته عدم مَانع خَاص، وَلَا

518 [T] For example, one can state that being tall does not conflict with being overweight. This does not logically necessitate that the person is overweight. Two things can be non-conflicting yet have no concomitance.

يسْتَلْزم انْتِفَاء الْمَوَانِع، وَلَا وجود الشَّرَائِط، وَلَا وجود الْمُقْتَضِي، فَلَا يلْزم ثُبُوت الحكم.

Second: When the claimant extracts something from the evidence that invalidates what they erroneously believe to be the view of their opponent in the issue, which their opponent denies is their view. If the claimant does this, they have not truly invalidated the view of the opponent. For example, a Shāfiʿī would say, as in the previous example of murder with a heavy item, "Differences in tools used for murder do not prevent capital punishment, just as differences in the types of piercing injuries used to kill do not prevent capital punishment." In this case, they reject the view by assuming its logical conclusion. A Ḥanafī would say, "The ruling is not established without removing all impediments and the presence of all preconditions, after the necessitating factor to establish the ruling. What you have mentioned is the nonexistence of a particular impediment, but does not necessitate the nonexistence of all impediments, the existence of the preconditions, nor the presence of the necessitating factor. As such, the ruling is not necessarily established."

وَقد اخْتلف الجدليون فِي أَن الْمُعْتَرض إِذا قَالَ: لَيْسَ هَذَا مأخذي: هَل يصدق أَو لَا؟ فَقيل: لَا يصدق إِلا بِبَيَان مَأخَذ آخر، إِذْ رُبمَا كَانَ مأخذه ذَلِك، لكنه يعاند، وَاخْتَارَ هَذَا جمع من أَصْحَابنَا، مِنْهُم الْفَخر، وَقَالَ: فَإِن أبْطلهُ الْمُسْتَدل وَإِلَّا انْقَطع. وَقَالَ ابْن الْحَاجِب: وَالصَّحِيح أَنه مُصدق فِي مذْهبه. انْتهى. أَي: لِأَنهُ أعرف بمذهبه وَمذهب إِمَامه، وَلِأَنهُ رُبمَا لَا يعرف، فيدعي احْتِمَال أَن لمقلده مَأخَذ آخر.

If the objector responds by saying, "This is not my position," the scholars of argumentation have disagreed on whether they should be believed or not. Some said that their claim should not be believed unless they clarify another position, since the claimant could have accurately presented their view, but they are being obstinate. This was the view of a number of our *aṣḥāb*, as well as al-Fakhr, who said, "If the claimant negates it, it is negated. Otherwise, their argument subsides." Ibn al-Ḥājib stated, "The correct view is that they should be believed in the view they claim to hold."[519] The reason is that they are most aware of their own views and those of their *imām*. Also, they may

519 [T] Refer to *Bayān al-Mukhtaṣar* (3/242).

not know, and as such, they can claim that other followers of the *imām* have other views.

وَاعْلَم أَن أَكثر القَوْل بِالْمُوجبِ من هَذَا الْقَبِيل، وَهُوَ مَا يقع لاشتباه المأخذ، لخفاء مَأخَذ الْأَحْكَام، وقلما يقع الأول، وَهُوَ اشْتِبَاه مَحل الْخلاف، لشهرته، ولتقدم التَّحْرِير غَالِبا، كَمَا صرح بذلك عضد الدّين فِي (شرح مُخْتَصر ابْن الْحَاجِب) الأصولي.

Most of the arguments from commitment are of this nature. They occur because of ambiguity in the premises of one's argument and when the premise is hidden. The first type, which is a confusion of the area of contention, rarely happens, since usually it is known and has been spoken of at length. This was explicitly stated by ʿAḍud al-Dīn in his explanation of *Mukhtaṣar Ibn al-Ḥājib*, a text on legal theories.

الْوَجْه الثَّالِث: أَن يسكت فِي دَلِيله عَن صغري قِيَاسه، وَلَيْسَت تِلْكَ الصُّغْرى مَشْهُورة.

Third: To fail to mention the minor premise, which, in this particular debate, is not as well-known.

مِثَاله فِي الْوضُوء: مَا ثَبت قربَة، فشرطه النِّيَّة كَالصَّلَاةِ، ويسكت عَن الصُّغْرى فَلَا يَقُول: الْوضُوء ثَبت قربة، فَيرد القَوْل بِالْمُوجبِ، فَيَقُول الْمُعْتَرض: مُسلم وَمن أَيْن يلْزم أَن يكون الْوضُوء شَرطه النِّيَّة؟ فَهَذَا يرد إِذا سكت عَن الصُّغْرى، وَأما إِذا كَانَت الصُّغْرى مَذْكُورة، فَلَا يرد إِلَّا منع الصُّغْرى بِأَن يَقُول: لَا نسلم أَن الْوضُوء ثَبت قربَة، وَيكون حِينَئِذٍ منعا للصغرى لَا قولا بِالْمُوجبِ.

For example, regarding ablution, one can say, "If something is established to be a way of garnering closeness to Allah, it must be predicated on intention, similar to prayer." In that case, they fail to mention the minor premise, which is, "Ablution is established as a way of garnering closeness to Allah."[520]

520 [T] A valid syllogism must have a major premise, a minor premise, and a conclusion. In this argument, the major premise is, "If something is established to be a way of garnering closeness to Allah, it must have a precondition of intention," the minor premise should be, "ablution is established as a way of garnering closeness to Allah,"

As such, they reject the argument based on commitment. An objector can state, "That is conceded; however, what dictates that ablution must have the precondition of intention?" This is a valid response if the claimant fails to mention the minor premise. If they did mention it, they can respond by denying the minor premise, such as saying, "I do not concede that ablution is established as a way of garnering closeness to Allah." By using this argument, they are refuting the minor premise, not arguing from commitment.

قَالَ الجدليون: القَوْل بِالْمُوجبِ فيهِ انْقِطَاع أحد المتناظرين، إِذْ لَو بَين الْمُسْتَدلّ أَن الْمُثبت مدعاه أَو ملزومه، أَو الْمُبْطل مَأخَذ الْخصم، أَو الصُّغْرى حق، انْقطع الْمُعْتَرِض، إِذْ لم يبْق بعده إِلَّا التَّسْلِيم للمطلوب، وَإِلَّا انْقَطع الْمُسْتَدل، إِذْ قد ظهر عدم إفضاء دَلِيله إِلَى مَطْلُوبه.

Scholars of argumentation have stated that arguing from commitment interrupts either of the two interlocutors. If the claimant can prove that their view or its necessary conclusion is established, or if they can prove that the view of their opponent is invalidated or that the minor premise is true, they successfully refute the objector, since the only remaining option would be to submit to the view. If they cannot do so, they lose their footing and are refuted, since it would necessitate that their evidence does not lead to their conclusion.

قَالَ ابْن الْحَاجِب: وَقَوْلهمْ فِيهِ انْقِطَاع أَحدهمَا بعيد فِي الثَّالِث لاخْتِلَاف المرادين. وَجَوَاب الأول: بِأنهُ مَحل النزاع أَو مستلزمه، كَمَا لَو قَالَ: لَا يجوز قتل الْمُسلم بالذمي، فيقال بِالْمُوجبِ، لِأَنهُ يجب، فَيَقُول: الْمَعْنى بِلَا يجوز تَحْرِيمه، وَيلْزم نفي الْوُجُوب. وَعَن الثَّانِي: أَنه المأخذ أَي: لاشتهاره بَين النظار بِالنَّقْلِ عَن أَئِمَّة مَذْهَبهم، وَعَن الثَّالِث: بِأَن الْحَذف سَائِغ.

Ibn al-Ḥājib stated, "Their statement that one of the interlocutors becomes refuted by [negating the minor premise] in this third example is far-fetched, since both the interlocutor and the objector have different objectives.[521] The

and the conclusion would be, 'therefore, it must be predicated on intention.'

521 [T] The objective of the claimant is to prove that the minor premise, though not explicitly mentioned, is presumed. The objective of the objector is that since the major premise alone does not provide a reasonable argument, they object. Refer to *al-Taḥbīr Sharḥ al-Taḥrīr* (7/3680).

response to the first type is to prove it is within the scope of contention or is in close proximity to it. For example, one can say, 'A Muslim cannot receive capital punishment for killing a *dhimmī*,' and when the objector responds with commitment, they say, 'It is actually obligatory.' The claimant can respond, 'When I said it is not permissible, it means it is prohibited, which necessitates it is not obligatory.' The response to the second type is to prove it is the view of their *madhhab* as it is shown to be a popular view among its ideologues, and to proceed to quote from their scholars. The response to the third is to state that removing the minor premise is allowed."[522]

هَذَا وَقد أَطَالَ الْقَوْم فِي تعداد هَذِه الْأَنْوَاع، وَاخْتلفُوا فِي عدهَا اخْتِلَافا كثيرا فَذكر الْبَزْدَوِيّ فِي (المقترح) أنهَا خَمْسَة عشر سؤالا. وعدها النيلي فِي (شرح جدل الشريف) أَرْبَعَة عشر. وعدها الْآمِدِي فِي (الْمُنْتَهى) خَمْسَة وَعشْرين، وَفِي كتاب (الجدل) لَهُ إِحْدَى وَعشْرين.

Scholars have discussed these various types at length, and have disagreed considerably in enumerating them. Al-Bazdawī in *al-Muqtaraḥ* mentions that there are fifteen possible objections. Al-Nīlī in *Sharḥ Jadal al-Sharīf* mentions fourteen. Al-Āmidī in *al-Muntahā* enumerates twenty-five, and in *al-Jadal*, he enumerated twenty-one.

وَعند التَّحْقِيق أَنَّهَا لَا تَنْحَصِر فِي عدد، بل كل مَا قدح فِي الدَّلِيل اتجه إِيرَاده، كَمَا أَن كل سلَاح صلح للتأثير فِي الْعَدو يَنْبَغِي استصحابه. وَجَمِيع مَا ذكره الأصوليون والجدليون يقْدَح فِي الدَّلِيل، فَيَنْبَغِي إيراده، وَلَا يضر تدَاخل الأسئلة وَرُجُوع بَعْضهَا إِلَى بعض، لِأَن صناعَة الجدل اصطلاحية. وَقد اصْطلحَ الْفُضَلَاء على إِيرَاد هَذِه الْمَسْأَلَة، فَهِيَ - وَإِن تداخلت أَو رَجَعَ بَعْضهَا إِلَى بعض - جديرة بِحُصُول الْفَائِدَة من إفحام الخصم، وتهذيب الخواطر، وتمرين الأفهام على فهم السُّؤَال، واستحضار الْجَواب، وتكررها المعنوي لَا يضر، كَمَا لَو رمى الْقَاتِل بِسَهْم وَاحِد مرَّتَيْنِ أَو أَكثر. وَالله الْمُوفق.

In reality, after careful examination, it becomes clear that they cannot be enumerated, since anything that would serve to refute an evidence can be

522 [T] Refer to *Bayān al-Mukhtaṣar* (3/242).

used in discussion, just as every weapon that can be used to affect the enemy should be used. Everything mentioned by the legal theorists and the scholars of argumentation can be used to refute an evidence, and as such, should be used in debate. There is no harm in the objections overlapping to some degree, since the science of argumentation is one that is based on nomenclature, and the virtuous scholars have agreed to use such terminologies to refer to certain concepts. Even if they overlap, they still provide the benefit of refuting one's opponent, perfecting their thought process, and training their minds to understand objections and prepare responses. If the concepts repeat, it does not harm, just as if a fighter were to shoot the same arrow twice or thrice. And Allah is the One that grants divine aid.

وَقد نجز بِحَمْد الله الْكَلَام على الْآلة، وَهَذَا حِين الشُّرُوع فِي بَيَان أَحْكَام الْمُسْتَدلّ وَمَا يتَعَلَّق بِهِ من بَيَان الِاجْتِهَاد والمجتهد، والتقليد والمقلد، ومسائل ذَلِك إِن شَاءَ الله تعالَى.

With praises due to Allah, we have completed the discussions on this tool (analogy). Now, we shall discuss rulings pertaining to the one deducing rulings and issues proximate to their role, namely, scholarly exertion and who the *mujtahid* scholar is, blind-following and blind-followers, and issues pertaining to such matters, if Allah the Exalted Wills.

عقد نضيد في الاِجْتهَاد والتقليد
An Addendum on Scholarly Exertion (*ijtihād*) and Blind-Following (*taqlīd*)

الِاجْتِهَاد فِي اللُّغَة: بذل الْجهد - يَعْنِي الطَّاقَة - فِي عمل شاق، وَإِنَّمَا قيد الْعَمَل بِكَوْنِهِ شاقا، لِأَن الِاجْتِهَاد مُخْتَص بِهِ فِي عرف اللغة، إِذْ يقَال: اجْتهد الرجل فِي حمل الرَّحَى وَنَحْوهَا من الْأَشْيَاء الثَّقِيلَة، وَلَا يُقَال: اجْتهد فِي حمل خردلة وَنَحْوهَا من الْأَشْيَاء الْخَفِيفَة.

Ijtihād, linguistically, refers to exertion of one's effort in a strenuous, difficult task. The reason why the qualifications of, "strenuous," and "difficult," were mentioned is that the term *ijtihād*, as it is used linguistically, purely relates to them. It is said, "A man exerted effort to carry a quern," or other such heavy items. It is not said that one exerted effort in carrying a seed, or other such lightweight items.

وَهُوَ في الِاصْطِلَاح: استفراغ الوسع فِي طلب الظَّن بِشَيْء من الْأَحْكَام الشَّرْعِيَّة على وَجه يحس من النَّفس الْعَجز عَن الْمَزِيد عَلَيْهِ.

In religious terminology, *ijtihād* refers to exertion of the fullest effort in seeking probability in a conclusion regarding a religious ruling. The one engaging in *ijtihād* should feel that they are incapable of doing anything further.

وَقسم الْعلمَاء الِاجْتِهَاد إِلَى قسمَيْنِ: نَاقص وتام.

Scholars have stated that *ijtihād* is of two types: (i) deficient and (ii) complete.

فالناقص: هُوَ النّظر الْمُطلق فِي تعرف الحكم، وتختلف مراتبه بِحَسب الْأَحْوَال.

(i) Deficient: This refers to research to determine a ruling, without any other qualifications. Its levels vary depending on the situation.

والتام: هُوَ استفراغ الْقُوة النظرية حَتَّى يحس النَّاظر من نَفسه الْعَجز عَن مزِيد طلب.

(ii) Complete: This occurs when a person uses the utmost of their intellectual capacity, so that they feel that they cannot exert any further effort in seeking the ruling.

ومثاله: مِثَال من ضَاعَ مِنْهُ دِرْهَم فِي التُّرَاب، فقلبه بِرجلِهِ، فَلم يجد شَيْئا، فَتَركه وَرَاح. وَآخر إِذا جرى لَهُ ذَلِك، جَاءَ بغربال فغربل التراب حَتَّى يجد الدِّرْهَم، أَو يغلب على ظَنّه أَنه مَا عَاد يلقاه. فَالْأول اجْتِهَاد قَاصِر، وَالثَّانِي تَام.

An example of a deficient *ijtihād* is someone who has lost some money in the dirt. To find it, they begin tossing the dirt with their foot, but cannot find it. As such, they simply abandon the money and leave. An example of a complete *ijtihād* is someone who, when they lose their money, bring a shovel and begin to dig until they find their money, or until they think it is improbable that they will find it.

وَعلم من التَّعْرِيف وَمِمَّا سبق أول الْكتاب أَن استفراغ الْجهد إِنَّمَا هُوَ للفقيه، وَهُوَ الْمُجْتَهد، فَلَا عِبْرَة باستفراغ جهد غير الْمُجْتَهد.

It is known, based on the definition provided, as well as the discussions that occurred at the beginning of the book, that the role of *ijtihād* belongs to jurists. The one who engages in *ijtihād* is referred to as a *mujtahid* scholar. There is no consideration to the exertion of effort in research if the person is not a *mujtahid*.

وَقَوْلنَا فِي طلب ظن، يُشِير إِلَى أَنه لَا اجْتِهَاد فِي القطعيات.

In the definition, I said, "Seeking probability," because *ijtihād* does not pertain to definitive matters.

وَقَوْلنَا: بِشَيْء من الْأَحْكَام الشَّرْعِيَّة. يخرج مَا لَو استفرغ جهده فِي طلب شَيْء من الحسيات والعقليات، فَإِنَّهُ بمعزل عَن مقصودنا.

Also, I said, "regarding a religious ruling," to exclude exertion of effort in research in matters pertaining to perceptible or rational things. Those discussions are outside of the scope of our purpose.

والمجتهد: من اتّصف بِصفة الِاجْتِهَاد وَحصل أَهْلِيَّته، وَقد ذكر الْعلمَاء لَهُ شُرُوطًا، وَذَلِكَ أَنه لما لم يكن لَا بُد أَن يكون عَاقِلا بَالغا قد ثبتَتْ لَهُ ملكة يقتدر بهَا على اسْتِخْرَاج الْأَحْكَام من مأخذها، وَلَا يتَمَكَّن من ذَلِك إِلَّا باتصافه بِأُمُور لَا جرم جعلُوا تِلْكَ الْأُمُور شُرُوطًا وَهِي:

A *mujtahid* is a scholar who performs *ijtihād* and is qualified to do so. The scholars have mentioned a number of prerequisites for *ijtihād*. Undoubtedly, one must be above the age of puberty and have sound mental faculties. They must also have a talent for extracting rulings from their sources. They cannot do so unless they have a number of qualities. These qualities are the prerequisites:

أَن الْوَاجِب عَلَيْهِ أَن يعرف من الْكتاب مَا يتَعَلَّق بِالْأَحْكَامِ، وَهُوَ قدر خَمْس مئة آيَة. قَالَه الْغَزالِيّ وَغَيره. وَلَيْسَ هَذَا القَوْل بسديد، وَلَيْسَ هَذَا التَّقْدِير بمعتبر، وَإِن مِقْدَار أَدِلَّة الْأَحْكَام فِي ذَلِك غير منحصرة، فَإِن أَحْكَام الشَّرْع كَمَا تستنبط من الْأَوَامِر والنواهي، كَذَلِك تستنبط من الأقاصيص والمواعظ وَنَحْوهَا، فَقل أَن يُوجد فِي الْقُرْآن الْكَرِيم آيَة إِلَّا ويستنبط مِنْهَا شَيْء. وَقد سلك هَذَا المسلك الشَّيْخ عز الدين بن عبد السَّلَام، فألف كِتَابه (أَدِلَّة الْأَحْكَام) لبَيَان ذَلِك.

They must know the parts of the Qur'ān that pertain to rulings, and there are five-hundred verses of them, as al-Ghazālī and others stated. However, this view is not accurate nor is their enumeration worthy of consideration. The number of verses that pertain to rulings are innumerable, for just as rulings of legislation are deduced from orders and prohibitions, they are also deduced from tales, admonishments, and so forth. Rarely is there a verse in the Qur'ān but that there is something to deduce from it. This was opined by al-Shaykh 'Iz al-Dīn ibn 'Abd al-Salām, who authored his book *Adillat al-Aḥkām* to explain this.

وَكَأن هَؤُلَاءِ الَّذين حصروها فِي خَمْس مِئَة آيَة إِنَّمَا نظرُوا إِلَى مَا قصد مِنْهُ بَيَان الْأَحْكَام دون مَا استفيدت مِنْهُ، وَلم يلتفتوا إِلَى مَا قصد بِهِ بَيَانهَا.

It seems that when those scholars numerated them and stated that there are five-hundred, they were referring to the verses that were meant to clarify rulings, not ones that discussed other subjects but where rulings were deduced from them. As such, they did not take into consideration the indirect objectives of the verses.

وَهل يشْتَرط حفظ الْآيَات عَن ظهر قلب أَو يَكْفِيهِ أَن يكون مستحضرا لَهَا؟ وَالصَّحِيح: الثَّانِي، وَأَنه يَكْفِيهِ أَن يعرف مواقع الحكم من مظانه ليحتج بِهِ عِنْد الْحَاجة إِلَيْهِ، لِأَن مَقْصُود الِاجْتِهَاد هُوَ إِثْبَات الحكم بِدَلِيل يخْتَص بِهِ.

Scholars differed on whether one must memorise the verses by heart, or if it is sufficient to recollect them. The correct view is the second one (they must be able to recall them). The *mujtahid* must know the sources of the rulings, so that they may use them as evidence when needed. The point of *ijtihād* is to establish a ruling by using an evidence that specifically proves it.

وَيشْتَرط أَن يعرف من السّنة مَا يَكْفِيهِ لاستنباط الْأَحْكَام، وَلَا يتَعَيَّن ذَلِك بِبَعْض السّنة دون بعض، خلافًا لمن حصرها فِي خَمْس مئة حَدِيث، لِأَنهُ قل حَدِيث يَخْلُو عَن الدّلَالَة على حكم شَرْعِي. وَمن نظر فِي كَلَام الْعلمَاء على دواوين الحَدِيث كَالْقَاضِي عِيَاض، والنووي على صَحِيح مُسلم، والخطابي والحافظ ابْن حجر على صَحِيح البُخَارِي، وَفِي شرح سنَن أبي دَاوُد وَغَيرهَا، عرف ذَلِك.

The *mujtahid* must also know enough of the Sunnah to be able to deduce rulings. This precondition does not apply to certain *aḥadīth* above others, contrary to those who limited the *aḥadīth* pertaining to rulings to just five-hundred. Rarely is there a ḥadīth that does not signify a religious ruling. If one were to read the words of scholars who explained compendiums of ḥadīth, such as al-Qāḍī ʿIyyāḍ and al-Nawawī in explanation of *Ṣaḥīḥ Muslim*, al-Khaṭṭābi and al-Ḥāfiẓ Ibn Ḥajar in explanation of *Ṣaḥīḥ al-Bukhārī*, the explanations of *Sunan Abī Dāwūd*, and so forth, they would realise my point.

نعم أَحَادِيث السّنة - وَإِن كثرت - محصورة فِي الدَّوَاوِين، والمعول عَلَيْهِ مِنْهَا مَشْهُور كـ(الصحيحين) وَبَقِيَّة السّنَن السِّتَّة، وَمَا أشبههَا. وَقد قرب النَّاس ذَلِك

بتصنيف كتب الْأَحْكَام ككتابي الْحفاظ عبد الْغَنِيّ بن سرُور الْمَقْدِسِي، وَكتب الْحَافِظ عبد الْحق المغربي، وَكتاب الْأَحْكَام لمجد الدين عبد السَّلَام بن تَيْمِية جد شيخ الْإِسْلَام وَنَحْوهَا، وَأجْمع هَذِه الْكتب كتاب (الْأَحْكَام) لمحب الدّين الطَبرِي. وَبِذَلِك صَار الْوُقُوف على مَا احْتِيجَ إِلَيْهِ سهل المرام، قريب المأخذ.

True, the *aḥadīth* in the Sunnah, though they are abundant, are limited to the compendiums that gather them. The books that are relied on are well-known, such as *The Two Ṣaḥīḥs*, as well as the rest of the *Six Books of Sunnah*[523] and other similar works. This corpus has been made accessible to people by the writing of books dedicated to rulings, such as the two works of al-Ḥāfiẓ ʿAbd al-Ghanī al-Maqdisī, the books of al-Ḥāfiẓ ʿAbd al-Haqq al-Maghribi, the book on *aḥadīth* pertaining to rulings by Majd al-Dīn ʿAbd al-Salām ibn Taymiyyah, the grandfather of Shaykh al-Islām, and so forth. The most comprehensive of these works is *al-Aḥkām* by Muḥib al-Dīn al-Ṭabarī. As such, accessibility to the *aḥadīth* one needs is quite easy.

فَإِن قيل فَمَا تَقول فِيمَا رَوَاهُ أَبُو عَليّ الضَّرِير، أَنه قَالَ: قلت لِأَحْمَد بن حَنْبَل: كم يَكْفِي الرجل من الحَدِيث، يَكْفِيهِ مئة ألف؟ قَالَ: لَا، قلت: مِئَتَا ألف؟ قَالَ: لَا، قلت: ثَلَاثَة مئة ألف؟ قَالَ: لَا، قلت: أَرْبَع مئة ألف؟ قَالَ: لَا، قلت: خَمْس مئة ألف؟ قَالَ: أَرْجُو.

Some may question this, based on what was reported from Abu ʿAlī al-Ḍarīr, where he said, "I asked Aḥmad ibn Ḥanbal, 'How many *aḥadīth* does a person need to know? Is one hundred thousand sufficient?' He responded, 'No.' I said, 'What about two hundred thousand?' He said, 'No.' I said, 'What about three hundred thousand?' He said, 'No.' I said, 'What about four hundred thousand?' He said, 'No.' I said, 'What about five hundred thousand?' He said, 'I would hope so.'"[524]

وروى عَنهُ الْحُسَيْن بن إِسْمَاعِيل مثل هَذَا وروى مثله عَن يحيى بن معِين.

Also, al-Ḥusayn ibn Ismāʿīl reported a similar quotation from al-Imām Aḥmad, and Yaḥyā ibn Maʿīn is quoted to have said something similar.

---

523 [T] Namely, Abu Dāwūd, al-Nasāʾī, Ibn Mājah, and al-Tirmidhī.
524 [T] Mentioned in *al-Musawwadah* (p. 514).

وَقَالَ أَحْمد بن عَبدُوس: قَالَ أَحْمد بن حَنْبَل: من لم يجمع علم الحَدِيث وَكَثْرَة طرقه واختلافه لَا يحل لَهُ الحكم على الحَدِيث وَلَا الْفتيا بِهِ. وَقَالَ أَحْمد بن منيع: مر بِنَا أَحْمد بن حَنْبَل جائيا من الْكُوفَة، وَبِيَدِهِ خريطة فِيهَا كتب، فَأخذت بِيَدِهِ، فَقلت: مرة إِلَى الْكُوفَة، وَمرة إِلَى الْبَصْرة إِلَى مَتى؟ إِذا كتب الرجل ثَلَاثِينَ ألف حَدِيث ألم يكفه؟ فَسكت، قلت: فستين ألفا؟ فَسكت، فَقلت: فمئة ألف؟ قَالَ: فَحِينَئِذٍ يعرف شَيْئا، فَنَظَرْنَا، فَإِذا أَحْمد قد كتب عَن بهز - وَأَظنهُ قَالَ: وَعَن روح بن عبَادَة - ثَلَاث مئة ألف حَدِيث إِلَى غير ذَلِك مِمَّا رَوَاهُ عَنهُ أَصْحَابه فِي هَذَا الْمَعْنى.

Aḥmad ibn ʿAbdūs said, "Aḥmad ibn Ḥanbal said, 'If someone does not know the science of ḥadīth, its various routes, and its differences, it is not permissible for them to give rulings on a ḥadīth, nor to give edicts according to it.'"[525] Aḥmad ibn Manīʿ said, "Aḥmad ibn Ḥanbal passed by us while on his way back from Kūfah. He had a map with books on it. I took his hand and said, 'Once to Kūfah, and once to Baṣrah; until when? If a person has written 30,000 *aḥadīth*, is it not sufficient for them?' He remained silent. I said, 'What about 60,000?' He remained silent. I said, 'What about 100,000?' He said, 'At that time, they will know something.' We checked and found that he reported from Bahz (he might have said: and Rawḥ ibn ʿUbādah), 300,000 *aḥadīth*."[526] There are other similar reports that his students reported from him.

قُلْنَا فِي الْجَواب: إِن أَصْحَاب الإِمَام أَحْمد حملُوا كَلَامه هَذَا على الِاحْتِيَاط، والتغليظ فِي الْفتيا، أَو على أَن يكون أَرَادَ وصف أكمل الْفُقَهَاء، حكى هَذَا القَاضِي أَبُو يعلى فِي (الْعدة).

The answer to this is to state that the disciples of al-Imām Aḥmad held these reports to mean that one should be cautious and should be warned against passing *fatwa*. Another way they understood it is that Aḥmad meant to describe the most complete of jurists. This was stated by al-Qāḍī Abu Yaʿlā in *al-ʿUddah*.

525 [T] Ibid.
526 [T] Ibid.

فَأَما الَّذِي لَا بُد مِنْهُ، وَدلّ عَلَيْهِ كَلَام أَحْمد إِن الْأُصُول الَّتِي يَدُور عَلَيْهَا الْعلم عَن النَّبِي صلى الله عَلَيْهِ وَسلم يَنْبَغِي أَن تكون ألفا، أَو ألفا وَمِئتين. انْتهى.

As for the aḥadīth that are truly indispensable, Aḥmad stated that the foundational *aḥadīth* around which knowledge from the Prophet ﷺ revolves are approximately one-to-two thousand.

وَلَا يخفاك أَن لفظ الحَدِيث عِنْد السّلف أَعم مِمَّا رُوِيَ عَن النَّبِي صلى الله عَلَيْهِ وَسلم وَمن آثار الصَّحَابَة وَالتَّابِعِينَ وطرق الْمُتُون، وَإِلا فالأحاديث المروية لا تصل إِلَى عشر هَذَا الْعدَد. وَغَايَة مَا جمعه الإِمَام أَحْمد فِي مُسْنده الَّذِي أحَاط بالأحاديث ثَلَاثونَ ألفا، وَغَايَة مَا ضمه إِلَيْهِ ابْنه عبد الله عشرة آلاف حَدِيث، فكَانَ مَجْمُوعه أَرْبَعِينَ ألفا، فتنبه لذَلِك.

Surely, it is not a secret that the term *ḥadīth,* when used by the Salaf is broader than just things that have been reported from the Prophet ﷺ or the reports from the companions, their successors, or the routes of various texts. The number of *aḥadīth* reported does not reach a tenth of those figures mentioned. The largest compendium of *ḥadīth* collected by al-Imām Aḥmad is his *Musnad*, which encompasses most of the *aḥadīth*, comprises of 30,000 narrations. The amount that his son 'Abdullāh added was approximately 10,000 narrations, making them a total of 40,000 narrations. This is noteworthy.

وَيشْتَرط للمجتهد مَعَ مَعْرفَته بِأَحَادِيث الْأَحْكَام معرفَة صِحَة الحَدِيث، ومعرفته بذلك إِمَّا بِالِاجْتِهَادِ فِيهِ بِأَن يكون لَهُ من الْأَهْلِيَّة وَالْقُوة فِي علم الحَدِيث مَا يعرف بِهِ صِحَة مخرج الحَدِيث أَي: طَرِيقه الَّذِي ثَبت بِهِ، وَمن رِوَايَة أَي الْبِلَاد هُوَ، أَو أَي التراجم، وَيعلم عَدَالَة رُوَاته وضبطهم، وَبِالْجُمْلَةِ يعلم من حَاله وجود شُرُوط قبُوله وَانْتِفَاء موانعه وموجبات رده.

Along with knowing the *aḥadīth* pertaining to rulings, a *mujtahid* must also know the authenticity of a *ḥadīth*. To know the authenticity of a *ḥadīth*, they can either perform *ijtihād* to reach a conclusion. They can do so if they are qualified and are knowledgeable enough in the sciences of *ḥadīth*, where they can become acquainted with the chain of narration, the land of origin of its narrators, their biographies, uprightness, and reliability. Generally speaking, they must be aware of the status of the narration in terms of the presence of the preconditions for its acceptance and the lack of impediments that would necessitate rejecting it.

وَإِمَّا بطرِيق التَّقْلِيد بِأَن يَنْقُلهُ من كتاب صَحِيح ارتضى الْأَئِمَّة رُوَاته كـ(الصحيحين) وَ(سنَن أبي دَاوُد) وَنَحْوهَا، لِأَن ظن الصِّحَّة يحصل بذلك، وَإِن كَانَ الأول أَعلَى رُتْبَة من الثَّانِي.

Another way to know the authenticity of a ḥadīth is to blind-follow, by quoting the ḥadīth from a *Ṣaḥīḥ* collection consisting of narrators that the scholars have accepted. Examples are the *Two Ṣaḥīḥs*, *Sunan Abī Dāwūd*, and others. If they quote from such works, there is a probability of them being authentic. However, the first way [of knowing an authentic ḥadīth] is superior to the second way.

وَأَن يعرف النَّاسِخ والمنسوخ من الْكتاب وَالسّنة، لِأَن الْمَنْسُوخ بَطل حكمه، وَصَارَ الْعَمَل على النَّاسِخ، فَإِن لم يعرف النَّاسِخ من الْمَنْسُوخ، أفْضى إِلَى إِثْبَات الْمَنْفِي وَنفي الْمُثبت، ويكفيه أَن يعرف أَن دَلِيل هَذَا الحكم لَيْسَ بمنسوخ، فَلَا يشْتَرط عَلَيْهِ أَن يعرف جَمِيع الْأَحَادِيث المنسوخة من الناسخة، وَمَعَ هَذَا فالإحاطة بِمَعْرِفَة ذَلِك أيسر من غَيره، لقلَّة الْمَنْسُوخ بِالنِّسْبَةِ إِلَى الْمُحكم من الْكتاب وَالسّنة.

The *mujtahid* must also be aware of the abrogated and abrogating texts in the Qurʾān and Sunnah. The reason is that abrogated rulings are invalidated, and one must act in adherence to the abrogating text. If they cannot differentiate between the abrogating and the abrogated, this will lead them to establishing a nullified ruling and nullifying an established ruling. It is sufficient for them to know that the evidence for the ruling is not abrogated. It is not a precondition, therefore, that they know all of the *aḥadīth* that are abrogated and the ones that are abrogating. With that said, comprehensive knowledge of all of those narrations is easier than mastering other aspects, because there are few abrogated texts relative to the established texts of the Qurʾān and Sunnah.

وَقد صنف فِي نَاسخ الْقُرْآن ومنسوخه جمَاعَة، مِنْهُم: أَبُو جَعْفَر النّحاس، وَالْقَاضِي أَبُو بكر وَابْن الْعَرَبِي، ومكي صَاحب الْإِعْرَاب، وَمن الْمُتَقَدِّمين: هبة الله بن سَلامَة، وَمن الْمُتَأَخِّرين: ابْن الزاغواني وَابْن الْجَوْزِي وَغَيرهم.

A number of scholars have authored works on abrogation in the Qur'ān. Among them are Abu Ja'far al-Naḥḥās, al-Qāḍī Abu Bakr ibn al-'Arabī, and Makkī, the author of the book on grammar. Among the early scholars who authored on the subject was Hibatullāh ibn Salāmah. Among the latter-day scholars were Ibn al-Zāghūnī, Ibn al-Jawzī, and others.

وَألف فِي نَاسخ الحَدِيث ومنسوخه جمَاعَة مِنْهُم: الشَّافِعِي وَابْن قُتَيْبَة وَابْن شاهين وَابْن الْجَوْزِيّ وَغَيرهم.

Further, a number of scholars have written on abrogation in the ḥadīth, such as al-Shāfi'ī, Ibn Qutaybah, Ibn Shāhīn, Ibn al-Jawzī, and others.

وَيعرف ذَلِك معرفَة جَيِّدَة من تفاسير الْقُرْآن والْحَدِيث البسيطة، كتفسير الْقُرْطبِي وشروح (الصَّحِيحَيْنِ) لَكِن يجب على الْمُجْتَهد أَن يَجْعَل تِلْكَ الْكتب دَالَّة لَهُ على الْقَوْل بالنسخ، وَلَا يَأْخُذ قَول أَصْحَابهَا قَضِيَّة مسلمة، لِأَن كثيرا مَا تراهم يردون نَاسِخا ومنسوخا تعصبا لمذهبهم، ويطلقون النّسخ من غير تمحيص، فعلى النَّاظر أَن يطْرَح التعصب، وَينظر بِعَين الْإِنْصَاف كَيْلا يقَع فِي التَّقْلِيد.

Abrogation can be learned quite well by reading the compendiums of exegesis of the Qur'ān and ḥadīth, such as *Tafsīr al-Qurṭubī*, the explanations of the *Two Ṣaḥīḥs*, and so forth. However, it is obligatory for the *mujtahid* to use those books to discover texts that might be abrogated. They must not accept their claims blindly, since many times, you find them rejecting an abrogation based on staunch adherence to their *madhhab*. Other times, they are liberal in declaring abrogation. A researcher should abandon all loyalties to their *madhhab* and must investigate using justice, so that they do not fall into blind-following.

وَلَقَد سلكنا فِي تفسيرنا للْكتاب الْعَزِيز هَذَا المسلك، وَبينا فِيهِ خطأ كثيرين ادعوا نسخ بعض الْآيَات، وَلَا دَلِيل لَهُم إِلَّا التعصب لمذهبهم.

In explaining the Qur'ān, I have taken this route, and have clarified that many have erroneously claimed abrogation of some verses, and they have no evidence; they claimed it out of staunch adherence to their *madhhab*.

وَمن شُرُوط الْمُجْتَهد أَن يعرف من الْإِجْمَاع مَا تقدم فِي بَابه من هَذَا الْكتاب وَغيره، مثل أَن يعلم أَن الْإِجْمَاع حجَّة، وَأَن الْمُعْتَبر فِيهِ اتِّفَاق الْمُجْتَهدين، وَأَنه لَا يخْتَص بِاتِّفَاق بلد دون بلد وَنَحْو ذَلِك. ويكفيه أَن يعلم أَن هَذِه الْمَسْأَلة مِمَّا أجمع عَلَيْهِ، أَو مِمَّا اخْتلف فِيهِ، هَذَا إِذا كَانَ قَائِلا بِالْإِجْمَاع. وَيجب عَلَيْهِ أَن يتثبت فِي هَذَا النَّوْع، لِأَنهُ كم من مَسْأَلَة يرى القَوْل بِالْإِجْمَاع فِيهَا وَيكون مُرَاد الْقَائِل إِجْمَاع أهل مذْهبه، أَو إِجْمَاع الْأَئِمَّة الْأَرْبَعَة، أَو إِجْمَاع أهل الْمَدِينَة. فليتنبه لذَلِك.

Another precondition for a *mujtahid* is that they must be aware of the issues pertaining to consensus, many of which have been discussed, both in this book and other works. For example, they must be aware that consensus is evidence, and that the consensus which is given consideration is that of the *mujtahid* scholars. They must know that it is not applicable to agreement of a single land, and so forth. It is sufficient for them to know that the issue they are discussing is one of consensus or differing, if they are claiming consensus. They must ascertain these matters. Many times, there are claims to consensus, but the one claiming the consensus means that there is consensus among the adherents to their own *madhhab*, the four *imāms*, or the residents of Madīnah. A *mujtahid* should be keenly aware of such things.

وَأَن يعرف من النَّحْو واللغة مَا يَكْفِيهِ فِي معرفَة مَا يتَعَلَّق بِالْكتاب وَالسّنة، من نَص ظَاهر ومجمل، وَحَقِيقَة ومجاز، وعام وخاص، وَمُطلق ومقيد، وَدَلِيل خطاب وَنَحْوه.

Further, a *mujtahid* must know enough grammar to understand things that pertain to the Qur'ān and Sunnah. They should be aware of when a text is univocal, apparent, obscure, literal, metaphorical, general, particular, unqualified, qualified, an indication of the instruction, and so forth.

وَلَا يشْتَرط فِي حَقه أَن يعرف تفاريع الْفِقْه الَّتِي يعْنى بتحقيقها الْفُقَهَاء، لِأَن ذَلِك

من فروع الِاجْتِهَاد الَّتِي وَلَدهَا المجتهدون بعد حِيَازَة منصبه، فَلَو اشْترطت مَعْرفَتهَا فِي الِاجْتِهَاد، لزم الدّور، لتوقف الأَصْل الَّذِي هُوَ الِاجْتِهَاد على الْفَرْع الَّذِي هُوَ تفاريع الْفِقْه.

They need not be aware of all the subsidiary matters that are investigated by the jurists, since they are subsidiaries of *ijtihād* that are borne of *mujtahid* scholars after earning its qualifications. If *ijtihād* is predicated on knowing them, it would necessitate circular knowledge, since *ijtihād*, which is the foundation, would be predicated on knowing its applications in subsidiary matters.

وَكَذَلِكَ لَا يشْتَرط معرفَة دقائق الْعَرَبيَّة والتصريف حَتَّى يكون كسيبويه والأخفش والمازني والمبرد والفارسي وَابْن جني وَنَحْوهم، لِأَن الْمُحْتَاج إِلَيْهِ مِنْهَا فِي الْفِقْه دون ذَلِك.

Likewise, they do not need to be aware of the intricate discussions on Arabic grammar and morphology; in other words, they do not need to be similar to Sībawayh, al-Akhfash, al-Māzinī, al-Mubarrid, al-Fārisī, Ibn Jinnī, and so forth. They only need to know the parts of the Arabic language that pertain to law, not the other intricacies.

وَيشْتَرط للمجتهد أَن يعرف تَقْرِير الْأَدِلَّة، وَمَا يتقوم ويتحقق بِهِ كَيْفيَّة نصب الدَّلِيل وَوجه دلَالَته على الْمَطْلُوب.

The *mujtahid* must know how to establish evidences in order to erect proofs and show their significations to indicate what they are attempting to prove.

وَلَا بَأْس أَن يكون عَالما بِشَيْء من فن الْمنطق، لَا أَن يكون متوغلا فِيهِ، لِأَنَّهُ يعين على تَرْتِيب الْأَدِلة، وَيحْتَاج إِلَيْهِ فِي الْقيَاس احتياجا كثيرا.

There is nothing wrong with gaining some understanding of formal logic, but they must not be overly immersed in it. Formal logic helps to organise evidences, and when using *qiyās*, they will be in great need of it.

وَأَقُول: إِنَّه يشْتَرط فِي حَقه معرفَة فني الْمعَانِي وَالْبَيَان، وَلَا يخفى احْتِيَاج النَّاظر فِي

الْأَحْكَام إِلَيْهِمَا. والمجتهدون المتقدمون كَانُوا يعْرفُونَ الْمنطق بالسليقة والطبع، وَكَذَلِكَ تَقول فِيمَن ساعده طبعه على صَوَاب الْكَلَام وَاجْتنَاب اللّحن فِيهِ: لم يشْتَرط لَهُ علم الْعَرَبيَّة.

They must also be aware of rhetoric and eloquence. The need for the researcher into rulings to be aware of such topics is not a hidden matter. The early *mujtahid* scholars were logical by nature and instinct. The same can be said about the Arabic language: If a person's nature and instincts assist them in speaking correctly without grammatical errors, they do not need to study the Arabic language formally.

وَالْحَاصِل أَن الْمُشْترط فِي الِاجْتِهَاد معرفَة مَا يتَوَقَّف عَلَيْهِ حُصُول ظن الحكم الشَّرْعِيّ، سَوَاء انحصر ذَلِك فِي جَمِيع مَا ذكر، أَو خرج عَنهُ شَيْء لم يذكر، فمعرفته مُعْتَبرَة.

To summarise, the preconditions for a *mujtahid* are the concepts that acquiring probability in a religious ruling are predicated on. They could be restricted to what was mentioned, or there could be some additional unmentioned things that are important. Knowledge of all said things are worthy of consideration.

وَعِنْدِي أَنه يشْتَرط فِي الْمُجْتَهد أَن تُوجد فِيهِ ملكة الاستنباط، وَأَن يكون ذكي الْفُؤَاد، متوقد الذِّهْن، لِأَنهُ كم مِمَّن قَرَأَ فنون الْعَرَبيَّة والعلوم الَّتِي تهيئ لِلِاجْتِهَاد، ثمَّترَاهُ جَامِدا خامل الْفِكر لَا يعلم إِلا مَا يلقى إِلَيْهِ؟ فَإِذا خاطبته وجدت ذهنه متحجرا، تكَلمه شرقا، فيكلمك غربا، فَمثل هَذَا لَا يعول عَلَيْهِ، وَلَا يركن إِلَيْهِ.

To me, a *mujtahid* must have a talent for deduction. They must be intelligent at heart, with a lively mind. Many study sciences of Arabic and other sciences that prepare one for *ijtihād*, but then you find them rigid and lazy, unaware of anything outside of what was dictated to them. If you speak to them, you find their minds resemble rocks; you speak to them about something in the east, and they reply with something in the west. Such people are not to be relied on nor are they to be inclined to.

تَنْبِيه: إِن هَذِه الشُّرُوط الْمَذْكُورة كلهَا إِنَّمَا تشْترط للمجتهد الْمُطلق الَّذِي يُفْتِي

فِي جَمِيع الشَّرْع، أما من أفتى فِي فن وَاحِد، أو فِي مَسْأَلَة وَاحِدَة، وَوجدت فِيهِ شُرُوط الِاجْتِهَاد بِالنِّسْبَةِ إِلَى ذَلِك الْفَنّ أَو تِلْكَ الْمَسْأَلَة، فَلَا يشْتَرط لَهُ ذَلِك، وَجَاز لَهُ أَن يجْتَهد فِيمَا حصل شُرُوط الِاجْتِهَاد فِيهِ، وَإِن لم تتوفر فِيهِ الشُّرُوط فِي غَيرهَا.

Note: All of the previously-mentioned preconditions apply to the absolute *mujtahid*, who is defined as someone who can give edicts on all matters of religion. If they can only give edicts on a single science, or on a single issue, and they have the preconditions of *ijtihād* respective to that science or that issue, they do not need to possess all of those preconditions. They can make *ijtihād* in matters where they are qualified, even if they do not possess the qualities of *ijtihād* in other issues.

وَخَالف قوم فِي هَذَا، وَهَذَا مَبْنِيّ على أنه: هَل يجوز تجزي الِاجْتِهَاد أم لَا يجوز؟ وَالْحق أَنه يتَجَزَّأ، لِأَن كثيرا من أَئِمَّة السّلف الصَّحَابَة وَغَيرهم كَانُوا يسْأَلُون عَن بعض مسَائِل الْأَحْكَام، فَيَقُولُونَ: لَا نَدْرِي؟ حَتَّى إِن مَالِكًا رَضِي الله عَنهُ قَالَ: لَا أَدْرِي، فِي سِتّ وَثَلَاثِينَ مَسْأَلَة من ثَمَانِي وَأَرْبَعين مَسْأَلَة. وَقد توقف الشَّافِعِي وَأحمد، بل الصَّحَابَة والتابعون، فِي الْفَتَاوَى كثيرا، فَلَو كَانَ الِاجْتِهَاد الْمُطلق فِي جَمِيع الْأَحْكَام شرطا فِي الِاجْتِهَاد فِي كل مَسْأَلَة على حدتها، لما كَانَ هَؤُلَاءِ الْأَئِمَّة مجتهدين، لكنه خلاف الْإِجْمَاع، فَدلَّ على أَن ذَلِك لَا يشْتَرط.

Some disagreed with this concept, and the disagreement emanates from whether *ijtihād* is indivisible. The truth is that it is divisible. Many scholars of the Salaf and the companions were asked about issues pertaining to rulings, and would reply with, "I do not know." Once, Mālik ﷺ responded with, "I do not know," in thirty-six out of forty-eight issues. Al-Shāfiʿī and Aḥmad, and actually, the companions and their successors, are all known to have abstained from offering edicts at one time or another. If absolute *ijtihād* in all rulings is a precondition to *ijtihād* in any issue, those scholars would not be considered *mujtahid* scholars. This view, however, goes against consensus. As such, it shows that [possessing the qualities for absolute *ijtihād*] is not a precondition.

وَلَا يشْتَرط عَدَالَة الْمُجْتَهد فِي اجْتِهَاده، لَكِنَّهَا مشترطة فِي قبُول فتياه وَخَبره،

هَذَا مَا يذكرهُ عُلَمَاء الْأُصُول فِي الْمُجْتَهد الْمُطلق، وَيُسمى عِنْدهم بالمجتهد المستقل، ويعرفونه بِأنهُ: الذِي يسْتَقل بإدْرَاك الْأَحْكَام الشَّرْعِيَّة من الْأَدِلة الشَّرْعِيَّة، من غير تَقْلِيد وَلَا تَقْيِيد بِمذهب معِين.

A *mujtahid* does not need to be upright when offering *ijtihād*. However, in order to accept their edict or reports, uprightness is a precondition. This is what scholars of legal theories have mentioned on the topic of the absolute *mujtahid*, whom some of them refer to as the independent *mujtahid*, and they define this as the one who is independent in obtaining religious rulings from religious evidences, without blind-following or adhering to a single *madhhab*.

فصل [أقسام الْمُجْتَهدين]

Section: [On the Categories of *Mujtahid* Scholars]

جعل بعض الْمُتَأَخِّرين أَقسَام الْمُجْتَهدين على خَمْسَ مَرَاتِب، وَمِمَّنْ علمناه جنح إِلَى هَذَا التَّقْسِيم أبو عَمْرو بن الصّلاح، وَابْن حمدَان - من أَصْحَابنَا - فِي كِتَابه (أدب الْمُفْتِي) وتلاهما شيخ الْإِسْلَام أَحْمد بن تَيْمِية، فَإِنَّهُ نقل فِي (مسودة الْأُصُول) كَلَام ابْن الصّلاح، وَلم يتعقبه، وتبعهم الْعَلامَة الفتوحي فِي آخر كِتَابه (شرح الْمُنْتهى) الفقهي، وَنحن نلخص كَلَامهم هُنَا فَنَقُول:

Some latter-day scholars have categorised *mujtahid* scholars into five ranks. Of the scholars that I know who had this view was Abu ʿAmr ibn al-Ṣalāḥ, Ibn Ḥamdān (one of our *aṣḥāb*), in his book *Adab al-Muftī*, and they were followed by Shaykh al-Islām Aḥmad ibn Taymiyyah, who quoted Ibn al-Ṣalāḥ's view in his book, *al-Musawwadah*, without objecting to it. They were also followed by the great scholar, al-Futūḥī, in the ending of his book, *Muntahā al-Irādāt*,[527] on substantive law. I will summarise what they said here.

ذَهَبُوا إِلَى أَن الْمُفْتِي - يَعْنِي الْمُجْتَهد - يَنْقَسِم إِلَى مُسْتَقل وَغير مُسْتَقل، فالمستقل: هُوَ الْمُجْتَهد الْمُطلق، وَقد مر بَيَانه، وَأما غير المستقل، فقد قال ابْن الصّلاح: وَمن دهر طَوِيل طوى بِسَاط الْمُفْتِي المستقل، والمجتهد الْمُطلق، وأفضى أَمر الْفتيا إِلَى الْفُقَهَاء المنتسبين لأئمة الْمذَاهب المتنوعة. انْتهى. وَلَا يلْزم من طي الْبسَاط عدم الْوُجُود، فَإِن فضل الله لَا ينْحَصر فِي زمَان، وَلَا فِي مَكَان. كما سنبينه فِيمَا بعد إِن شَاءَ الله تَعَالَى.

They stated that a *mufti*, meaning, a *mujtahid* scholar, can be categorised into independent and non-independent. An independent scholar is the absolute *mujtahid*, whose definition has already been clarified. As for a

527 [T] Note that al-Shaykh Ibn Badrān said, *"Sharḥ al-Muntahā,"* but that is a minor slip of the pen.

non-independent scholar, Ibn al-Ṣalāḥ stated, "For a long time, the proverbial carpet of the independent *mufti* and the absolute *mujtahid* has been folded. Edicts, now, are given by jurists who adhere to *imāms* of the schools of law that are followed."[528] His statement that the proverbial carpet has been folded does not necessitate that they do not exist. The favours of Allah the Exalted are not specific to a single time-frame nor to a single place, as we will clarify in an upcoming discussion, Allah willing.

ثمَّ إِن للمفتي المنتسب إِلَى أحد الْمذَاهب أَربع أَحْوَال:

Furthermore, a *mufti* that ascribes to one of the schools of law can be one of four categories:

أَحدهَا: أَن لَا يكون مُقلدًا لإمامه لَا فِي مذْهبه وَلَا فِي دَليله، لكنه سلك طَرِيقه فِي الِاجْتِهَاد وَالْفَتْوى، ودعا إِلَى مذْهبه، وَقَرَأَ كثيرا مِنْهُ على أَهله فَوَجَدَهُ صَوَابا، وَأولى من غَيره، وَأَشد مُوَافقَة فِيهِ وَفِي طَرِيقه. وَإِلَى هَذَا أَشرنَا أول الْكتاب، حَيْثُ بَينا لأي شَيْء اخْتَار كبار أَصْحَاب أَحْمد مذهبه على مَذْهَب غَيره، وَيُؤْخَذ هَذَا من كَلَام ابْن الصّلاح أَيْضا، فَإِنَّهُ قَالَ: ذكر عَن أبي إِسْحَاق الإسفراييني أَنه حكى عَن أَصْحَاب مَالك وَأحمد وَدَاوُد وَأكْثر أَصْحَاب أبي حنيفَة أَنهُم صَارُوا إِلَى مَذاهب أئمتهم تقليدا لَهُم، قَالَ ابْن الصّلاح: وَالصَّحِيح الَّذِي ذهب إِلَيْهِ الْمُحَقِّقُونَ مَا ذهب إِلَيْهِ أَصْحَابنَا، وَهُوَ أَنهم صَارُوا إِلَى مَذْهَب الشَّافِعِي لَا على جِهَة التَّقْلِيد لَهُ، لَكِن لأَنهم وجدوا طَرِيقه فِي الِاجْتِهَاد والفتاوى أَسد الطرق.

First. They do not blindly follow their *imām* in his *madhhab* nor in the evidences he cites, however, they follow the *imām's* method of *ijtihād* and *fatwa*, invite others to his school of thought, and have studied a good amount of it from its people, where they found it to be veracious and better than others schools. They usually concord in their conclusions to their *imām's* school of law. This is what I referred to at the outset of the book, where I clarified why the major disciples of Aḥmad chose his *madhhab* over that of other schools. This can also be understood from Ibn al-Ṣalāḥ's statement, as well. He said, "It was mentioned that Abu Isḥāq al-Isfarāyīnī (a Shāfiʿī) reported that the adherents of Mālik, Aḥmad, Dāwūd, and most adherents of Abu Ḥanīfah chose the views within the *madhhab* of their *imāms* out of

528 [T] *Adab al-Muftī wa 'l-Mustaftī* (p. 91).

blind following. [...] However, what is correct is that the deep researchers trod the same path as our companions (the Shāfiʿī scholars), who chose the *madhhab* of al-Shāfiʿī not out of blind following, but rather, they found his method of *ijtihād* and *fatwa* to be the most veracious of ways."

قَالَ أَبُو عَمْرو: وَدَعوى انْتِفَاء التقْلِيد مُطلقًا من كل وَجه لَا يَسْتَقِيم إِلَّا أَن يَكُونُوا قد أحاطوا بعلوم الِاجْتِهَاد الْمُطلق، وَذَلِكَ لَا يلائم الْمَعْلُوم من أَحْوَالهم أَو أَحْوَال أَكْثَرهم. وَذهب بعض الْأُصُولِيِّينَ من أَصْحَابنَا إِلَى أَنه لم يُوجد بعد عصر الصَّحَابَة مُجْتَهد مُسْتَقل، وَحكى اخْتِلَافا بَين الْحَنَفِيَّة وَالشَّافِعِيَّة فِي أبي يُوسُف وَمُحَمّد والمزني وَابْن سُرَيج: هَل كَانُوا مستقلين أم لَا؟ قَالَ: وَلَا تستنكر دَعْوى ذَلِك فيهم فِي فن من فنون الْفِقْه بِنَاء على جَوَاز تجزي منصب الِاجْتِهَاد. وَيبعد جَرَيَان الْخلاف فِي حق هَؤُلَاءِ المتبحرين الَّذين عَم نظرهم الْأَبْوَاب كلهَا، وفتوى المنتسبين فِي هَذِه الْحَال فِي حكم فَتْوى الْمُجْتَهد المستقل الْمُطلق يعْمل بهَا، ويعتد بهَا فِي الْإِجْمَاع وَالْخلاف.

And Ibn al-Ṣalāḥ said, "The claim that someone can be free of blind following absolutely and in all situations is one that cannot be correct, unless a person has gained comprehensive knowledge of all the sciences needed to make one an absolute *mujtahid*. That, however, does not fit what is known to the situation of many. Some scholars of legal theory of our companions have opined that after the era of the companions, there is no independent *mujtahid*. There was stated to be a difference of opinion between the Ḥanafī and Shāfiʿī scholars regarding Abu Yūsuf, Muḥammad [ibn al-Ḥasan al-Shaybānī], al-Muzanī, and Ibn Surayj, on whether they were independent or not. The reality is that this claim cannot be denied in some sciences of law, based on the possibility of the divisibility of the status of *ijtihād*. It is difficult to imagine differences of opinion on scholars of such vast knowledge who have researched all chapters of law. The edicts given by scholars in this rank are considered the edicts of an independent and absolute *mujtahid*. It can be adhered to and is given consideration in matters of consensus and differences of opinion."[529]

ثَانِيهَا: أَن يكون مُجْتَهدا مُقَيّدا فِي مَذْهَب إِمَامه، يسْتَقلّ بتقرير مذْهبه بِالدَّلِيلِ،

529 [T] Adapted from *Adab al-Muftī wa 'l-Mustaftī* (pp. 91-94).

غير أَنه لَا يتجَاوَز فِي أدلته أصُول إِمَامه، وَلَا بُد أَن يكون عَالما بأصول الْفِقْه، لكنه قد أخل بِبَعْض الأدوات كالحديث واللغة. وَإِذا اسْتدلَّ بِدَلِيل إِمَامه لَا يبْحَث عَن معَارض لَهُ، وَلَا يَسْتَوْفِي النّظر فِي شُرُوطه، وَقد اتخذ نُصُوص إِمَامه أصولا يستنبط مِنْهَا، كَمَا يفعل الْمُجْتَهد المستقل بنصوص الشَّارِع. وَالْعَامِل بفُتْيَا هَذَا مقلد لإمامه. قَالَ: وَمثل هَذَا يتأَدَّى بِهِ فرض الْكِفَايَة فِي الْفَتْوَى، وَلَا يتأَدَّى بِهِ فِي إحْيَاء الْعُلُوم الَّتِي مِنْهَا استمداد الْفَتْوَى، لِأَنهُ قَائِم مقَام الْمُطلق.

Second. A *mujtahid* that is limited to the *madhhab* of their *imām*. They can independently state their *madhhab* with evidence. However, when providing their evidence, they do not go beyond the legal theories of their *imām*. They must be scholars of legal theories, but might have deficiencies in other sciences, such as ḥadīth or language. If they state the evidence of their *imām*, they do not search for any conflicting views, nor do they investigate its preconditions deeply. The texts of their *imām* are their foundations, from which they deduce rulings, just as the independent *mujtahid* does with the divine texts. If a person acts according to this edict, they have adhered to their *imām*. This level causes one to have achieved the communal responsibility of *fatwa*. However, they do not contribute to reviving the sciences from which the *fatwa* emanates, for that is the job of the absolute *mujtahid*.

ثَالِثهَا: أَن لَا يبلغ رُتْبَة أَئِمَّة الْمَذْهَب أَصْحَاب الْوُجُوه والطرق، غير أَنه فَقِيه النَّفس، حَافظ مَذْهَب إِمَامه، عَارِف بأدلته، قَائِم بتقريره ونصرته، يصور وَيُحَرر، ويمهد ويقرر، ويزيف ويرجح، لكنه قصر عَن دَرَجَة أُولَئِكَ، إِمَّا لكَونه لَا يبلغ فِي حفظ الْمَذْهَب مبلغهم، وَإِمَّا لكَونه غير متبحر فِي أُصُول الْفِقْه وَنَحْوه، غير أَنه لَا يَخْلُو مثله فِي ضمن مَا يحفظه من الْفِقْه، ويعرفه من أدلته، عَن أَطْرَاف من قَوَاعِد أُصُول الْفِقْه وَنَحْوه.

Third. They do not reach the level of the *imāms* of the *madhhab*, namely, those who have viable interpretations and methods of deduction within the *madhhab*. However, this individual is a "jurist of the soul" (i.e. it is ingrained within him); they have amassed knowledge of the *madhhab* of their *imām*, are aware of its evidences, and can establish and defend it. They can conceptualise and deeply conceive its rulings, and can lay the framework to establish its conclusions. They can falsify any falsities and can discern between its views. With that said, they are below the previous level, either because they have not amassed the same amount of knowledge of the *madhhab*, or because they are not proficient in legal theories, and so forth. However, falling under the knowledge they have amassed of substantive law and its evidences is some understanding and awareness of the maxims of legal theory, and so forth.

وَإِمَّا لكَونه مقصرا فِي غير ذَلِك من الْعُلُوم الَّتِي هِيَ أدوات الِاجْتِهَاد الْحَاصِلَة لأَصْحَاب الِاجْتِهَاد بالوجوه والطرق. قَالَ ابْن الصّلاح: وَهَذِه هِيَ مرتبة المصنفين إِلَى أَوَاخِر الْمِئَة الْخَامِسَة، وَقد قصروا عَن الْأَوَّلين فِي تمهيد الْمَذْهَب، وَأما فِي الْفَتْوى، فبسطوا بسط أولَئِكَ، وقاسوا على الْمَنْقُول والمسطور، غير مقصرين على الْقياس الْجَلِي، وإلغاء الْفَارِق.

Another reason they could be of such a level is that they are deficient in other sciences that are considered tools for *ijtihād*, which are amassed by the scholars who perform *ijtihād* by mention of variants and deductions [within their own *madhhab*]. Ibn al-Ṣalāḥ said, "This level comprises of authors until the end of the 5th century. They fell short in laying the framework for the *madhhab* in the way their predecessors did. As for their edicts, they elucidated similarly to their predecessors, engaged in textual analogies and were not limited to obvious analogies nor analogies based on denying differentia."[530]

رَابِعهَا: أَن يحفظ الْمَذْهَب ويفهمه فِي واضحات الْمسَائِل ومشكلاتها، غير أَنه مقصر فِي تَقْرِير أدلته، فَهَذَا يعْتَمد نَقله وفتواه في نُصُوص إِمَامه وتفريعات أَصْحَابه الْمُجْتَهدين فِي مذْهبه، وَمَا لم يجده مَنْقُولًا، فَإِن وجد فِي الْمَنْقُول مَا يعلم أَنه مثله - من غير فضل - فكر وَتَأمل أَنه لَا فَارق بَينهمَا، كَمَا فِي الْأمة بِالنِّسْبَةِ إِلَى العَبْد الْمَنْصُوص عَلَيْهِ فِي إِعْتَاق الشَّرِيك، جَازَ لَهُ إِلْحَاقه بِهِ، وَالْفَتْوى بِهِ.

Fourth. They amass knowledge of the *madhhab* and understand its clear cases and the contentious. However, they are deficient in establishing its evidences. When transmitting the *madhhab* and giving edicts, this person

530 [T] Ibid. (p. 99)

relies on the texts of their *imām* and the branching discussions of the *mujtahid* adherents to the *madhhab*. If there is no explicit text, they search for a similar issue, and if they find one, they reflect on it to discover that there is no difference between [the unmentioned case and the mentioned one]. An example is the female slave in comparison to the male slave, who is explicitly mentioned in discussions on when a slave is shared between two owners, and one of the partners frees their share. The member of this category would find no difference between a female slave owned between multiple shareholders and a male one. As such, they extend the ruling to the female slave and give the edict according to that.

وَكَذَلِكَ مَا يعلم اندراجه تَحت ضَابِط مَنْقُول ممهد فِي الْمَذْهَب، فَإِنَّهُ يجوز لَهُ إِلْحَاقه بِهِ، وَالْفَتْوى بِهِ، وَمَا لم يكن كَذَلِك فَعَلَيهِ الْإِمْسَاك عَن الْفَتْوَى بِهِ. قَالَ ابْن الصّلاح: ويندر عدم ذَلِك، كَمَا قَالَ أَبُو الْمَعَالِي: يبعد أَن تقع وَاقعَة لم ينص على حكمهَا فِي الْمَذْهَب، وَلَا هِيَ فِي معنى شَيْء من الْمَنْصُوص فِيهِ من غير فرق، وَلَا هِيَ مندرجة تَحت شَيْء من ضوابطه.

Likewise, if they are aware that the case at hand falls under a known, well-researched maxim in the *madhhab*, they may extend the ruling and offer an edict on that accord. However, if it falls outside of the scope of those examples, they must abstain from offering an edict in the case. Ibn al-Ṣalāḥ said, "The inability to do so is quite rare. Abu al-Maʿālī said, 'It is far-fetched to think that an occurrence happens that does not have a ruling in the *madhhab*, nor is it similar to any textually explicit rulings, and also does not fall under any maxims.'"[531]

وَلَا بُد فِي صَاحب هَذِه الْمرتبة أَن يكون فَقِيه النَّفس، لِأَن تصور الْمسَائِل على وَجههَا، وَنقل أَحْكَامهَا لَا يقوم بِهِ إِلَّا فَقِيه النَّفس. قَالَ ابْن حمدَان: ويكفيه أَن يستحضر أَكثر الْمَذْهَب مَعَ قدرته على مطالعة بَقِيَّته. انْتهى.

The member of this level must be a jurist of the soul, because conceptualising cases accurately and then transmitting their rulings is something that can only be undertaken by a jurist of the soul. Ibn Ḥamdān stated, "It is sufficient for them to recollect the majority of the *madhhab* while retaining

531 [T] Ibid. (p. 100).

the ability to research and refer to the rest."[532]

قَالَ ابْن الصّلاح: وَلَا تجوز الْفَتْوَى لغير هَؤُلَاءِ الْأَصْنَاف الْخَمْسَة، يَعْنِي الْمُجْتَهد الْمُطلق، والطبقات الْأَرْبَع بعده، كَمَا قطع بِهِ أَبُو الْمَعَالِي فِي الأصولي الماهر الْمُتَصَرف في الْفِقْه أَنه يجب عَلَيْهِ الاستفتاء. قَالَ ابْن الصّلاح: وَكَذَا الْمُتَصَرف النظار البحاث فِي الْفِقْه، هَذَا كَلَامه وَكَلَام غيره فِي طَبَقَات الْفُقَهَاء.

Ibn al-Ṣalāḥ stated, "It is not permissible for anyone outside of the five categories mentioned, namely, the absolute *mujtahid*, and then the four levels below them, to pass an edict, as Abu al-Maʿālī concluded on a bright legal theorist who can navigate the law: They must seek an edict from elsewhere. [Ibn al-Ṣalāḥ said:] The same applies to those who research deeply into the law."[533] This is his view and the view of other scholars who spoke on the levels and ranks of the jurists.

ثمَّ اعْلَم أَن هَاهُنَا مسَائِل يوردها الأصوليون فِي هَذَا الْمقَام:

There are a number of important cases that legal theorists discuss on this topic:

الأولى: يجوز التعبد بِالِاجْتِهَادِ فِي زمن النَّبِي صلى الله عَلَيْهِ وَسلم للْغَائِب عَنهُ وللحاضر، بِإِذْنِهِ وبدونه.

One. It is permissible to worship Allah the Exalted according to an *ijtihād* during the time of the Prophet ﷺ, for those distant from him or close to him, with his permission or without it.

الثَّانِيَة: يجوز أَن يكون عَلَيْهِ السَّلَام متعبدا بِالِاجْتِهَادِ فِيمَا لَا نَص فِيهِ.

Two. The Prophet ﷺ may be tasked with worshipping Allah the Exalted where there is no divine text.

الثَّالِثَة: قَالَ أَصْحَابنَا: الْحق فِي قَول وَاحِد من الْمُجْتَهدين معِين فِي فروع الدّين وأصوله، وَمن عداهُ مخطئ، ثمَّ إِن كَانَ خطأ المخطئ فِي فروع الدين، وَلَيْسَ

532 [T] *Sifat al-Fatwā* (p. 23).
533 [T] *Adab al-Muftī wa 'l-Mustaftī* (p. 101).

هُنَاكَ دَلِيل قَاطع عَلَيْهِ، فَهُوَ مَعْذور فِي خطئه، مثاب على اجْتِهَاده، وَهُوَ قَول بعض الْحَنَفِيَّة وَالشَّافِعِيَّة. نعم إِذا كَانَت الْمَسْأَلة فقهية ظنية، فَإِن كَانَ فِيهَا نَص، وَقصر الْمُجْتَهد فِي طلبه، فَهُوَ مخطئ آثم.

Three. Our *aṣḥāb* have stated: The truth lies within the view of a single particular *mujtahid*, both in subsidiary and fundamentals of the religion. Anyone else is mistaken.[534] If the mistake is in a subsidiary issue of the religion, and there is no definitive evidence to suggest its inaccuracy, they are excused for their mistake and are actually rewarded for their *ijtihād*. This is the view of some Ḥanafī and Shāfiʿī scholars. This is the case if the matter is a speculative jurisprudential issue. However, if there is a univocal text affirming a particular ruling, and the *mujtahid* has engaged in deficient research to seek the ruling, they are mistaken and sinful.

وَإِن لم يكن فِيهَا نَص، أَو كَانَ فِيهَا نَص، وَلم يقصر فِي طلبه انْتَفَى عَنهُ الْإِثْم، وَهَذِه الْمَسْأَلَة تعرف بِمَسْأَلة تصويب الْمُجْتَهد. وَالْكَلَام فِيهَا كثير، وَالْحق مَا ذكرْنَاهُ لقَوْله تَعَالَى: ﴿فَفَهَّمْنَاهَا سُلَيْمَانَ﴾ [الْأنبِيَاء: ٧٩].

If the ruling has or does not have a definitive text that would indicate it, and the *mujtahid* has not been neglectful in seeking it, the sin is waived in their case. This issue is known as that of "correctness of the *mujtahid*." There is much discussion on the topic. The truth is what we mentioned, because Allah the Exalted said: **{We made Solomon understand the case.}** [Qurʾān 21:79]

وَلَوْلَا أَن الْحق فِي جِهَة بِعَينهَا لما خص سُلَيْمَان بالتفهيم، إِذْ كَانَ يكون تَرْجِيحا بِلَا مُرَجّح، وَلَوْلَا سُقُوط الْإِثْم عَن المخطئ، لما مدح دَاوُد بقوله: ﴿وَكُلًّا آتَيْنَا حُكْماً وَعِلْماً﴾ [الْأَنْبِيَاء: ٧٩]، لِأَن المخطئ لَا يمدح، فَدلَّ على أَن الْحق فِي قَول مُجْتَهد معِين، وَأَن المخطئ فِي الْفُرُوع غير آثم، وَلِلْحَدِيثِ الثَّابِت فِي (الصَّحِيح) من طرق «**إِن الْحَاكِم إِذا اجْتَهد فأصَاب، فَلهُ أَجْرَانِ، وَإِن اجْتَهد فأخْطَأَ، فَلهُ أجر**».

534 [T] Meaning, the *aṣḥāb* do not take the view of relative truth. The truth to Allah is absolute, but a person who does due diligence to reach a valid conclusion is excused for their error.

Had the truth not been in either of the two views, Allah would not have mentioned that He gave the understanding to Sulaymān specifically, since that would be arbitrary. Likewise, had it not been that the sin is waived for the mistaken *mujtahid*, Allah the Exalted would not have praised Dāwūd with the statement: **{Though We gave sound judgement and knowledge to both of them.}** [Qur'ān 21:79] A mistaken person is not praised. This shows that the truth in a particular case is the view of just a single of the *mujtahid* scholars, but the one who is mistaken in subsidiary matters is not sinful. Also, it states in the report in *al-Ṣaḥīḥ* established from various routes, **"When a judge performs *ijtihād* and reaches a sound conclusion, he earns two rewards, but when he performs *ijtihād* and reaches an unsound conclusion, he earns one reward."**[535]

الرَّابِعَة: إِذا تعَارض دليلان عِنْد الْمُجْتَهد، وَلم يترَجَّح أَحدهمَا، لزمَه التَّوَقُّف حَتَّى يظْهر الْمُرَجح.

Four. When two evidences conflict for a *mujtahid*, and they cannot discern which is stronger, they must abstain from offering a ruling until they can discern which is stronger.

الْخَامِسَة: لَيْسَ للمجتهد أَن يَقُول فِي مَسْأَلَة قَوْلَيْنِ فِي وَقت وَاحِد عِنْد الْجُمْهُور، وَقد فعله الشَّافِعِي فِي مَوَاضِع.

Five. A single *mujtahid* cannot hold two opinions on the same issue at the same time, according to the majority. However, this was practically done by al-Shāfiʿī at times.

مِنْهَا قَوْله فِي المسترسل من اللِّحْيَة قَولَانِ: وجوب الْغسْل، وَعَدَمه. وَنقل الْآمِدِي وَغَيره أن ذَلِك وَقع مِنْهُ فِي سبع عشرة مَسْأَلَة.

An example is the long hairs that flow from the beard and extend beyond the face. He has two views on the topic, the first being that it is obligatory to wash it, and the other being that it is not obligatory. Al-Āmidī and others have stated that it occurs in seventeen issues.

قَالَ الطوفي: قلت: وَوَقع ذَلِك من أَحْمد رَضِي الله عَنهُ. قَالَ أَبُو بكر فِي (زَاد

535 Reported by al-Bukhārī (13/268) and Muslim (1716).

الْمُسَافِر) قَالَ - يَعْنِي أَحْمد - فِي رِوَايَة أبي الْحَارِث: إِذا أخرت الْمَرْأَة الصَّلَاة إِلَى آخر وَقتهَا، فَحَاضَت قبل خُرُوج الْوَقْت، فَفِيهِ قَولَانِ، أحد الْقَوْلَيْنِ: لَا قَضَاء عَلَيْهَا، لِأَن لَهَا أَن تُؤخر إِلَى آخر الْوَقْت، وَالْقَوْل الآخر: أن الصَّلَاة قد وَجَبت عَلَيْهَا بِدُخُول الْوَقْت، فعلَيْهَا الْقَضَاء، وَهُوَ أعجب الْقَوْلَيْنِ إِلَي. انْتهى. قَالَ عبد الْعَزِيز: وَبِهَذَا أَقُول. انْتهى كَلَام الطوفي.

Al-Ṭūfī said, "That also occurred on the part of Aḥmad ﷺ. Abu Bakr said in *Zād al-Musāfir*, 'Aḥmad said, in the narration of Abu 'l-Ḥārith, 'If a woman delays her prayer to the ending of its time, and menstruates before the time ends, there are two views. The first view is that she does not have to make the prayer up, because she was allowed to delay the prayer to that time. The other view is that the prayer became obligatory when its designated time began. As such, she must make the prayer up. The latter is more appealing to me.' 'Abd al-'Azīz said, 'This is also my view.'"[536]

قلت: مَا ذكره لَيْسَ منافيا للقاعدة، لِأَن مَعْنَاهُ: لَيْسَ للمجتهد أَن يَقُول فِي مَسْأَلَة وَاحِدَة قَوْلَيْنِ فِي وَقت وَاحِد، ويطلقهما بِلَا تَرْجِيح أَحدهمَا على الآخر، أما لَو قَالَ قَوْلَيْنِ كل مِنْهُمَا لَهُ دَلِيل قوي، ثمَّ رجح أَحدهمَا على الآخر - كَمَا فعل الإِمَام أَحْمد فَقَالَ: وَهُوَ أعجب الْقَوْلَيْنِ إِلَي - فَذَلِك مِمَّا تَقْتَضِيه صناعَة الِاجْتِهَاد، ويقبله الْفَهم الثاقب وَالْعقل السَّلِيم.

I say: What al-Ṭūfī mentioned does not conflict with the principle, because the meaning is that a *mujtahid* cannot hold two differing views on the same issue at a single time, and mention them without preferring one over the other. As for if he mentions two views, both of which have a strong evidence, then prefers and chooses one over the other, as al-Imām Aḥmad did when he said, "The latter is more appealing to me," this is what the process of *ijtihād* dictates. A sharp mind and sound intellect would accept such a statement.

فَإِن قَالَ الْمُجْتَهد قَوْلَيْنِ فِي وَقْتَيْنِ، وَجهل أسبقهما، فمذهبه أقربهما من الْأَدِلَّة، أَو أقربهما من قَوَاعِده عِنْد الْأَصْحَاب، وَفِي (الرَّوْضَة) أَيْضا هما كخبرين تَعَارضا.

536 [T] *Sharḥ Mukhtaṣar al-Rawḍah* (3/621-622).

وَمنع الْآمِدِي من الْعَمَل بِأَحَدِهِمَا، وَإِن علم أسبقهما فَالثَّانِي مذْهبه، وَهُوَ نَاسخ عِنْد الْأَكْثَر.

If a *mujtahid* pronounces two views on a single topic at two times, and it is unknown which came first, their *madhhab* is the one closest to the evidences, or it is the one closest to the maxims he adhered to, according to the *aṣḥāb*. In *al-Rawḍah*, Ibn Qudāmah mentions that they should be considered similar to two narrations that conflict. Al-Āmidī forbade acting on one of them. If it is known which was pronounced first, the second view he pronounced is his *madhhab*. According to the majority, it abrogates the first view.

وَقَالَ ابْن حَامِد: مَذْهَب الأول مَا لم يُصَرح بِالرُّجُوعِ عَنهُ. وَقيل مذْهبه الأول وَلَو رَجَعَ عَنهُ. قَالَ الْمجد ابْن تَيْمِية: هُوَ مُقْتَضى كَلَامهم. انْتهى. وَالْمُخْتَار الأول.

Ibn Ḥāmid said, "His *madhhab* is his first view, so long as he does not explicitly state that he has retracted it. It was also said that his first view is the *madhhab*, even if he retracts it. Al-Majd ibn Taymiyyah said, 'That is the necessary outcome of their discussions on the topic.'" The chosen view is the first one (i.e. that if the date of the first view is known, the second view is his *madhhab*).

تَنْبِيه: هَاهُنَا مَسْأَلَة مهمة يَنْبَغِي التَّنْبِيه عَلَيْهَا، وَهِي - وَإِن كَانَت مَعْلُومَة إِجْمَالا مِمَّا سبق أَوَائِل الْكتاب - لَكِن كَانَ لَهَا من مزِيد الْفَائِدَة مَا يَنْبَغِي الِالْتِفَات إِلَيْهِ يُقَال فِيهَا: المكرر أحلى، وخصوصا تعلق المهم لموضوع كتابنَا يُشِير إِلَى بَيَانهَا، وَمَا هِيَ إِلَّا أَن الْعَلامَة نجم الدّين الطوفي قَالَ فِي شَرحه (مُخْتَصر الرَّوْضَة) الْأُصُولِيَّة.

In this moment, there is a very important issue that must be given attention. It is generally well-known from the earlier parts of the book, but there are more beneficial points that must be alluded to, where one can say, "The repeated phrases are sweeter." It has a very important connection to the topic of our book and it clarifies it. The beneficial point is that the great scholar, Najm al-Dīn al-Ṭūfī, stated in his explanation of his summation of *al-Rawḍah*:

إن قيل: إذا كَانَ الْقَوْل الْقَدِيم المرجوع عَنهُ لَا يعد من الشَّرِيعَة بعد الرُّجُوع عَنهُ، فَمَا الْفَائِدَة فِي تدوين الْفُقَهَاء للأقوال الْقَدِيمَة عَن أئمتهم؟ حَتَّى رُبمَا نقل عَن أحدهم فِي الْمَسْأَلَة الْوَاحِدَة الْقَوْلَانِ وَالثَّلَاثَة كثيرا وَالْأَرْبَعَة، كَمَا فِي مَسْأَلَة الدَّاخِل وَالْخَارِج عَن أَحْمد، والستة، كَمَا فِي مَسْأَلَة مَتْرُوك التَّسْمِيَة عَنهُ. وَنقل عَنهُ أَكثر من ذَلِك.

If it is stated: If the older view that has been retracted is not considered a part of the legislation after it has been retracted, what is the point of the jurists mentioning the older views of their *imāms*? Sometimes, a single *imām* could have two, three, or even four views reported on a single issue. An example of this is the issue of "the inside and the outside,"[537] with Aḥmad, and sometimes there are as many as six reported views, such as those reported from Aḥmad regarding a person who forgot to utter the *tasmiyah* (*bismillah*). Even more were reported from him.

قيل: كَانَ الْقيَاس أَن لَا تدون تِلْكَ الْأَقْوَال، وَهُوَ أقرب إِلَى ضبط الشَّرْع، إِذْ مَا لَا عمل عَلَيْهِ لَا حَاجَة إِلَيْهِ، فتدوينه تَعب مَحْض، لَكِنَّهَا دونت لفائدة أُخْرَى وَهِي: التَّنْبِيه على مدارك الْأَحْكَام، وَاخْتِلَاف القرائح والآراء، وَأَن تِلْكَ الْأَقْوَال قد أدى إِلَيْهَا اجْتِهَاد الْمُجْتَهدين فِي وَقت من الْأَوْقَات وَذَلِكَ مُؤثر فِي تقريب الترقي إِلَى رُتْبَة الِاجْتِهَاد الْمُطلق، أَو الْمُقيد، فَإِن الْمُتَأَخر إِذا نظر إِلَى مَأْخَذ الْمُتَقَدِّمين نظر فِيهَا، وقابل بَينهَا، فاستخرج مِنْهَا فَوَائِد، وَرُبمَا ظهر لَهُ من مجموعها تَرْجِيح بَعْضهَا. وَذَلِكَ من المطالب المهمة، فَهَذِهِ فَائِدَة تدوين الْأَقْوَال الْقَدِيمَة عَن الْأَئِمَّة، وَهِي عَامَّة.

It was stated that by analogy, those views should not have been written, which is more ideal for preservation of legislation, since if something is not

537 [T] This is an issue where two individuals claim to own a particular item that is in the possession of one of the two. Each presents their evidence that would indicate it belongs to them. The 'inside,' person is the one who the item is inside their hand, and the outside person is the one who does not possess the item. Al-Imām Aḥmad has two views on the topic. The first is that the claim of the one who does not possess the item should be given preference, and the other is that the one who possesses the item is given preference. Refer to *Sharḥ Mukhtaṣar al-Rawḍah* (3/703).

acted on, there is no need for it. They concluded, as such, that writing those views is just pure tiring labour. However, these views were written for another benefit, namely, that they contain insights into rulings and the differences of nature and views. Those views were the conclusions of *mujtahid* scholars at some points in time, and this affects how we understand how scholars ascended to levels of absolute or restricted *ijtihād*. An individual in later times could read the reasonings of the early scholar and compare them, extracting beneficial points along the way. By their accumulated readings, preference of one view over the other might become apparent to the latter-day scholar. That is an important quest. Hence, this is the benefit of writing the older views of the scholars, and it is general.

وَثمّ فَائِدَة خَاصَّة بِمذهب أَحْمد وَمَا كَانَ مثله، وَذَلِكَ أَن بعض الْأَئِمَّة، كالشافعي وَنَحْوه، نصوا على الصَّحِيح من مَذْهَبهم، إِذْ الْعَمَل من مَذْهَب الشَّافِعِي على الْقَوْل الْجَدِيد، وَهُوَ الَّذِي قَالَه بِمصْر، وصنف فِيهِ الْكتب ك(الأم) وَنَحْوه، وَيُقَال: إِنَّه لم يبْق من مذْهبه شَيْء لم ينص على الصَّحِيح مِنْهُ إِلَّا سبع عشرَة مَسْأَلَة، تَعَارَضَت فِيهَا الْأَدِلَّة، واخترم قبل أَن يُحَقّق النّظر فيها.

There is also another benefit that pertains to the *madhhab* of Aḥmad and those similar to him. Some scholars, such as al-Shāfiʿī and others, explicitly stated what was the correct view as per their way of thought. Action in the Shāfiʿī *madhhab* is based on the "*New Madhhab*," which is the one he pronounced in Egypt, where he authored his books, such as *al-Umm* and others. It was stated that there were only seventeen issues where he did not explicitly mention what the correct view was, and they were issues where the evidences conflicted. He passed away before he could look deeply into them.

بخِلَاف الإِمام أَحْمد وَنَحْوه، فَإِنَّهُ كَانَ لَا يرى تدوين الرَّأي، بل همه الحَدِيث، وَجمعه، وَمَا يتَعَلَّق بِهِ. وَإِنَّمَا نقل الْمَنْصُوص عَنهُ أَصْحَابه تلقيا مِّن فِيهِ، من أجوبته فِي سؤالاته وفتاويه، فكل من روى مِنْهُم عَنهُ شَيْئا دونه وَعرف بِهِ، كمسائل أبي دَاوُد، وَحرب الْكرْمَانِي، ومسائل حَنْبَل وابنيه صَالح وَعبد الله، وَإِسْحَاق بن مَنْصُور، والمروزي، وَغَيرهم مِمَّن ذكرهم أَبُو بكر فِي أول (زَاد الْمُسَافِر) وهم كثير. وَرُوِيَ عَنهُ أَكثر مِنْهُم.

This was contrary to al-Imām Aḥmad, who did not believe in compiling opinions. Rather, his goal was ḥadīth: gathering it, and anything associated with it. The texts reported from Aḥmad are the ones his students reported from his verbal expressions, his answers to questions, and his edicts. Therefore, all of his students that reported from him compiled the statements and were known to have done so, such as the *Masā'il* collections of Abī Dāwūd, Ḥarb al-Kirmānī, Ḥanbal, his two sons, Ṣāliḥ and 'Abdullāh, Isḥāq ibn Manṣūr, al-Marwazī, and others mentioned by Abu Bakr in the outset of *Zād al-Musāfir*. He mentioned many, and the amount of people that reported from him were even more [than those mentioned in *Zād al-Musāfir*].

ثمَّ انتدب لجمع ذَلِك أَبُو بكر الْخلال فِي (جَامعة الْكَبِير) ثمَّ تِلْمِيذه أَبُو بكر فِي (زَاد الْمُسَافِر) فحوى الكتابان علما جما من علم الإِمَام أَحْمد رَضِي الله عَنهُ، من غير أَن يعلم مِنْهُ فِي آخر حَيَاته الْإِخْبَار بِصَحِيح مذْهبه فِي تِلْكَ الْفُرُوع، غير أَن الْخلال يَقُول فِي بعض الْمسَائِل: هَذَا قَول قديم لِأَحْمَد، رَجَعَ عَنهُ، لَكِن ذَلِك يسير بِالنِّسْبَةِ إِلَى مَا لم يعلم حَاله مِنْهَا، وَنحن لَا يَصح لنا أَن نجزم بِمذهب إِمَام حَتَّى نعلم أَنه آخر مَا دونه من تصانيفه وَمَات عَنهُ، أَو أَنه نَص عَلَيْهِ سَاعَة مَوته، وَلَا سَبِيل لنا إِلَى ذَلِك فِي مَذْهَب أَحْمد، والتصحيح الَّذِي فِيهِ إِنَّمَا هُوَ من اجْتِهَاد أَصْحَابه بعده، كَابْن حَامِد، وَالْقَاضِي، وَأَصْحَابه، وَمن الْمُتَأَخِّرين الشَّيْخ أَبُو مُحَمَّد الْمَقْدِسِي رَحْمَة الله عَلَيْهِم أَجْمَعِينَ.

Abu Bakr al-Khallāl took to gathering those reports in his large compendium, known as *al-Jāmi'at al-Kabīr*. Then, his student, Abu Bakr, did the same in his book *Zād al-Musāfir*. The two books gathered an immense amount of the knowledge of al-Imām Aḥmad ﵁. It was not known that al-Imām Aḥmad stated the correct view as per his *madhhab* in those subsidiary matters at the end of his life. Sometimes, al-Khallāl would comment on certain issues, saying, "This is the older view of Aḥmad; he recanted this view." However, the number of issues where this occurs is small relative to the ones where there is no clear indication. We cannot definitively state the *madhhab* of a scholar until we know that the view is the last view he wrote on the issue, and he died espousing the view, or that he explicitly stated it as his view at the time of his death. That is not possible when it comes to the *madhhab* of Aḥmad. The corrections that occur within the *madhhab* are the scholarly exertions performed by his *aṣḥāb* after his death, such as those by Ibn Ḥāmid, al-Qāḍī and his students, and of the later scholars, al-Shaykh Abu Muḥammad [Ibn Qudāmah] al-Maqdisī.

لَكِن هَؤُلَاءِ - بالغين مَا بلغُوا - لَا يحصل الوثوق من تصحيحهم لمَذْهَب أَحْمد كَمَا يحصل من تَصْحِيحه هُوَ لمذهبه قطعا، فَمن فرضناه جَاءَ بعد هَؤُلَاءِ، وَبلغ من الْعلم درجتهم أَو قاربهم، جَازَ لَهُ أَن يتَصَرف فِي الْأَقْوَال المنقولة عَن صَاحب الْمَذْهَب كتصرفهم، ويصحح مِنْهَا مَا أدى اجْتِهَاده إِلَيْهِ، وافقهم أَو خالفهم، وَعمل بذلك وَأفْتى.

Despite the achievements of those scholars, one cannot be as confident in their corrections of the *madhhab* as one would be of the corrections of al-Imām Aḥmad to his own *madhhab*. If we presume that someone lived after those scholars and reached their level in knowledge, or at least came close to it, he may also proceed independently in analysing the views that were reported from the originator of the *madhhab*, just as those before him did. They may correct and sanction certain views, as per their *ijtihād*, regardless if their conclusions coincide or contradict those before them. They may act on and give rulings according to their conclusions.

وَفِي عصرنا من هَذَا الْقَبِيل: شَيخنَا الإِمَام الْعَالم الْعَلامَة تَقِيّ الدّين أَبُو الْعَبَّاس أَحْمد بن تَيمِية الْحَرَّانِي - حرسه الله تَعَالَى - فَإِنَّهُ لَا يتوقف فِي الْفتيا على مَا صَححهُ الْأَصْحَاب من الْمَذْهَب، بل يعْمل ويفتي بِمَا قَامَ عَلَيْهِ الدَّلِيل عِنْده، فَتكون هَذِه فَائِدَة خَاصَّة بِمذهب أَحْمد، وَمَا كَانَ مثله لتدوين نصوصه، ونقلها، وَالله تَعَالَى أعلم بِالصَّوَابِ. هَذَا كَلَام الطوفي، نَقَلْنَاهُ برمتِهِ لنفاسته.

From our generation, there are individuals who fit this description, including our *shaykh*, the great *imām* and erudite scholar, Taqī al-Dīn Abu 'l-'Abbās Aḥmad ibn Taymiyyah al-Ḥarrānī, may Allah protect him. He does not depend solely on what the *aṣḥāb* have ruled is the correct view of the *madhhab*. He acted on and gave rulings according to conclusions that he felt the evidences strengthened. Therefore, this was a benefit that was specific to the *madhhab* of Aḥmad and those similar to him, in terms of why their texts were compiled and transmitted. Allah the Exalted is Most Knowledgeable of what is right.[538] **[End.]** That is what al-Ṭūfī stated. I quoted it in its entirety due to its precious and valuable contents.

السَّادِسَة: يجوز للعامي تَقْلِيد الْمُجْتَهد بالِاتِّفَاقِ، وَلَا يجوز ذَلِك لمجتهد اجْتهد وَغلب على ظَنّه أَن الحكم كَذَا بالِاتِّفَاقِ أَيْضا. أما من لم يجْتَهد فِي الحكم بعد، وَهُوَ مُتَمَكن من مَعْرفَته بِنَفسِهِ بِالْقُوَّةِ الْقَرِيبَة من الْفِعْل، لكَونه أَهلا لِلِاجْتِهَاد، فَلَا يجوز لَهُ تَقْلِيد غَيره أَيْضا مُطلقًا، لَا لأَعْلم مِنْهُ وَلَا لغيره، لَا من الصَّحَابَة رَضِي الله عَنْهُم وَلَا من غَيرهم، لَا للفتيا وَلَا للْعَمَل، لَا مَعَ ضيق الْوَقْت وَلَا مَعَ سعته، هَذَا مَا اقْتَضَاهُ مَسْلَك الْمُحَقِّقين من الْأُصُولِيِّينَ.

Six. It is permissible for a layperson to blindly follow a *mujtahid*, according to the agreement of all scholars. It is not permissible for a *mujtahid* who performs *ijtihād* in an issue and believes there is probability that it is the correct ruling to blindly follow another *mujtahid*, also according to the agreement of scholars. If a scholar has not yet performed *ijtihād* on a ruling, but is able to gain knowledge of the ruling on their own through proximate ability, being that they are qualified for *ijtihād*, they, too, absolutely may not blindly follow others. It does not matter if the person they are blindly following is more knowledgeable than them, or otherwise. They also may not blindly follow the companions ﷺ nor anyone else, and this applies to their own actions as well as giving edicts to others. Shortage of time and abundance of time are also not valid excuses. This is what the legal theorists who engaged in deep research have concluded.

وَقيل يجوز لَهُ التَّقْلِيد مَعَ ضيق الْوَقْت وَقيل يجوز لَهُ ليعْمَل لَا ليفتي وَقيل لمن هُوَ أعلم مِنْهُ من الصَّحَابَة وَالْمُخْتَار مَا قدمْنَاهُ نعم لَهُ أَن ينقل وَقيل مَذْهَب غَيره للمستفتي وَلَا يُفْتِي هُوَ بتقليد أحد.

Some others have stated it is permissible for them to blindly follow others if there is a shortage of time, and others stated they may do so in order to act on it themselves, not to give an edict according to it. It was also stated that they may blindly follow those more knowledgeable than them, of the companions. However, the view that was mentioned at the outset of this discussion is the one chosen. Yes, they may quote the views of others to a

538 [T] *Sharḥ Mukhtaṣar al-Rawḍah* (3/626-628).

person seeking an edict, but they may not give an edict based on blindly-following anyone.

السَّابِعَة: إِذا نَص الْمُجْتَهد على حكم فِي مَسْأَلَة لعِلَّة بَينهَا، فمذهبه فِي كل مَسْأَلَة وجدت فِيهَا تِلْكَ الْعلَّة كمذهبه فِي الْمَسْأَلَة الْمَنْصُوص عَلَيْهَا، لِأَن الحكم يتبع الْعلَّة، فيوجد حَيْثُ وجدت، وَإِن لم يبين الْعلَّة، فَلَا يحكم بِحكم تِلْكَ الْمَسْألة فِي غَيرهَا من الْمسَائِل، وَإِن شبهتها - وَلَو نَص فِي مَسْأَلَتَيْنِ مشتبهتين على حكمين مُخْتَلفين - لم يجز أن يَجْعَل فيهمَا رِوَايَتَانِ بِالنَّقْلِ والتخريج، كَمَا لَو سكت عَن إِحْدَاهمَا وَأولى، وَالْأولَى جَوَاز ذَلِك بعد الْجد والبحث فِيهِ من أَهله، إِذْ خَفَاء الْفرق مَعَ ذَلِك - وَإِن دق - مُمْتَنع عَادَة.

Seven. If a *mujtahid* offers a ruling in an issue while clarifying its *ratio legis*, his *madhhab* is the same ruling in any other issue that has the same *ratio legis*. The reason is that rulings coexist with their *ratio legis*; existing where they exist, and not existing where they are nonexistent. If they did not clarify their rationale, the same ruling cannot be applied to other issues, even if they resemble one another. If he offered two different rulings on two similar issues, it is not permissible to state they are two different opinions [on the same issue] by extending and extrapolating [his words]. The same applies *a fortiori* to if he offers a view on one of the issues, but not the other. With that said, it is best to consider [extrapolating one of the two similar issues to be a variant of the other similar issue, and vice versa] possible after strenuous research by capable scholars, since even if the differences [between the two issues] are quite subtle, it is usually impossible for them to be wholly indiscoverable.

وَقد وَقع النَّقْل والتخريج فِي مَذْهَبنَا، فَقَالَ فِي (الْمُحَرر) من كتب أَصْحَابنَا: وَمن لم يجد إِلَّا ثوابًا نجسا صلى فِيهِ وَأَعَاد، نَص عَلَيْهِ، وَنَصّ فِيمَن حبس فِي مَوضِع نجس فصلى أنه لَا يُعِيد، فيتخرج فيهمَا رِوَايَتَانِ، وَذَلِكَ لِأَن طَهَارَة الثَّوْب وَالْبدن كِلَاهُمَا شَرط فِي الصَّلَاة. وَهَذَا وَجه الشّبَه بَين الْمَسْأَلَتَيْنِ، وَقد نَص فِي الثَّوْب النَّجس أَنه يُعِيد، فينقل حكمه إِلَى الْمَكَان، وَيتَخَرَّج فِيهِ مثله، وَنَصّ فِي الْموضع النَّجس على أَنه لَا يُعِيد؛ فينقل إِلَى الثوب النَّجس، فيتخرج فِيهِ مثله،

فَلَا جرم صَار فِي كل وَاحِد من الْمَسْأَلتَيْنِ رِوَايَتَانِ: إِحْدَاهمَا بِالنَّصِّ، وَالْأُخْرَى بِالنَّقْلِ. وَذكر مثل ذَلِك فِي الْوَصَايَا وَالْقَذف، وَمثل مَا حكيناه عَن مَذْهَبنَا من النَّقْل والتخريج وَقع كثيرا فِي مَذْهَب الشَّافِعِي.

This has occurred in our *madhhab*. In *al-Muḥarrar* [by al-Majd ibn Taymiyyah] (one of the books of our *aṣḥāb*) it states, "If someone can only find an impure garment, they should pray in it, but then repeat the prayer. This was explicitly stated by Aḥmad. Likewise, he explicitly stated that if someone is imprisoned in an impure area and prayed there, they should not repeat the prayer. This results in two separate narrations. This is because purity of the garment and the place of prayer are both conditions for the prayer. This is the similarity between the two issues. On the issue of the impure garment, he stated that the prayer does have to be repeated. As such, that ruling can be applied to the [impure] place, resulting in the same view. On the topic of the impure place, he stated that one does not have to repeat the prayer, and that view can be applied to the impure garment, resulting in the same view. There is no doubt that each of the two issues has two different opinions: one occurred through an explicit text and the other through extrapolation. He mentioned the same about wills and defamation. There are also many examples of this in the Shāfiʿī *madhhab*.

وَإِذا نَص على حكمين مُخْتَلفين فِي مَسْأَلَة، فمذهبه آخرهما إِن علم التَّارِيخ، وَإِلَّا فأشبههما بأصوله وقواعد مذْهبه، وأقربهما إِلَى الدَّلِيل الشَّرْعِيّ.

If a *mujtahid* scholar gives two different rulings on a single issue, his *madhhab* should be considered the later of the two views, if the chronology is known. If the date is not known, the view that is most aligned with [the scholar's] legal theory, the maxims of his *madhhab*, and the closest to the religious evidence should be considered his *madhhab*.

تَتِمَّة: الْفرق بَين النَّقْل والتخريج: أَن النَّقْل يكون من نَص الإِمَام، بِأَن ينْقل عَن مَحل إِلَى غَيره بالجامع الْمُشْتَرك، والتخريج: يكون من قَوَاعِده الْكُلية، فَهُوَ أَعم من النَّقْل، لِأَنهُ يكون من الْقَوَاعِد الْكُلية للْإِمَام أَو الشَّرْع أَو الْعقل، لِأَن حَاصله أَنه: بِنَاء فرع على أصل بِجَامِع مُشْتَرك، كتخريجنا على قَاعِدَة تَفْرِيق الصَّفْقَة فروعا كَثِيرَة، وعَلى قَاعِدَة تَكْلِيف مَا لَا يُطَاق أَيْضا فروعا كَثِيرَة فِي أصُول الْفِقْه وفروعه.

وَأما النَّقْل والتخريج مَعًا فَهُوَ مُخْتَصّ بنصوص الإِمَام.

[There are two terminologies that are similar. The first is *al-naql*, which means, "to extend and extrapolate," and the other is *al-takhrīj*, which means to extrapolate.][539] The difference is that *al-naql* refers to extrapolating from the texts of the *imām* by extending [a ruling] from one to another on account of the similarities between the two rulings. *Al-takhrīj* means to extrapolate based on the universal maxims. Therefore, it is more general than *naql*, since it can occur from the universal maxims of the *imām*, the legislation, or rationality. To summarise, it is a method of building a new case on a precedent on account of some similarities between them. For example, the legal maxim pertaining to partitioning transactions is the basis for many subsidiary matters of substantive law. Likewise, the concept of tasking people with things they cannot bear results in many branching matters, both in the scope of legal theory and substantive law. As for the term *al-naql wa 'l-takhrīj*, it specifically refers to the texts of the *imām*.

الثَّامِنَة: لَا ينْقض حكم حَاكم فِي مَسْأَلَة اجتهادية عِنْد الْأَئِمَّة الْأَرْبَعَة وَمن وافقهم، وَهُوَ معنى قَول الْفُقَهَاء فِي الْفُرُوع: لَا ينْقض الِاجْتِهَاد بِالِاجْتِهَادِ، وَهَذَا مَبْنِيّ على أَن الْحق مُتَعَدد.

Eight. The rulings of judges are not nullified in matters that are subject to juristic reasoning, according to the Four Imāms and those who espouse their view. This is what scholars mean when they say, in matters of substantive law, "An *ijtihād* does not nullify another *ijtihād*." This is based on the belief that there are multiple truths.

وينقض بِنَاء على أَن الْمُصِيب وَاحِد، وينقض أَيْضا بمخالفة نَص كتاب أَو سنة، وَلَو كَانَ نَص السّنة آحادا، وَخَالف القَاضِي أَبُو يعلى فِي الْآحَاد، وينقض أَيْضا بمخالفته إِجْمَاعًا قَطْعِيا لَا ظنيا فِي الْأَصَح، وَلَا ينْقض بمخالفته الْقيَاس، سَوَاء كَانَ جليا أَو خفيا، خلافًا لمَالِك وَالشَّافِعِيّ وَابْن حمدَان فِي الْجَلِيّ، وَزَاد مَالك ينْقض بمخالفة الْقَوَاعِد الشَّرْعِيَّة. وَلَا يعْتَبر لنقضه طلب صَاحب الْحق على الصَّحِيح من الْمَذْهَب. وَقَالَ القَاضِي فِي (الْمُجَرّد) والموفق فِي (الْمُغنِي)

539 [T] What is between the brackets was added by the translator for context.

وَالشَّارِح وَابْن رزين: لَا ينْقض إِلَّا بمطالبة صَاحبه. وَقَالَ دَاوُد وَأَبُو ثَوْر: ينْقض مَا بَان خطأ. قلت: وَهَذَا هُوَ الْحق الَّذِي لَا محيد عَنهُ. وَجوز ابْن الْقَاسِم نقض اجْتِهَاد تبين أَن غَيره أصوب مِنْهُ.

However, rulings are negated by the fact that only one view is the truth. Also, they are negated by contradiction to the univocal texts of the Qur'ān or Sunnah, and regardless if the Sunnah was a singular narration, though al-Qāḍī Abu Ya'lā disagreed on its application when there is a singular narration. They also are negated when they contradict definitive matters of consensus, as opposed to probable ones, according to the truer view. An *ijtihād* is not nullified by conflicting with *qiyās*, regardless if the *qiyās* was obvious or obscure, contrary to Mālik, al-Shāfi'ī, and Ibn Ḥamdān in obvious analogies. Mālik added that it is negated when it conflicts with the maxims of legislation. The request of a person whose right has been infringed on is not given consideration on the topic of negating a ruling, according to the correct view of the *madhhab*. However, al-Qāḍī in *al-Mujarrad*, al-Muwaffaq in *al-Mughnī*, al-Shāriḥ[540], and Ibn Razīn all stated that the ruling is only negated at the request of the owner of the right. Dāwūd and Abu Thawr opined that it is negated if a mistake is unearthed. I say: This is the truth, from which there can be no deviation. Ibn al-Qāsim took to the view that one may invalidate an *ijtihād* if it becomes clear that a different *ijtihād* is more veracious than it.

وَحكم الْحَاكِم بِخِلَاف اجْتِهَاده بَاطِل، وَلَو قلد غَيره فِي الحكم، عِنْد الْأَئِمَّة الْأَرْبَعَة وَمن وافقهم. وَقَالَ فِي (الْإِرْشَاد) لَا يبطل حكمه، وَلكنه يَأْثَم. وَمن قضى بِرَأْي يُخَالف رَأْيه نَاسِيا لَهُ نفذ حكمه وَلَا إِثْم عَلَيْهِ، وَبِهَذَا قَالَ أَبُو حنيفَة. وَقَالَ أَبُو يُوسُف والمالكية وَالشَّافِعِيَّة يرجع عَنهُ وينقضه. وَنقل أَبُو طَالب عَن الإِمَام أَحْمد: إِذا أَخطَأ بِلَا تَأْوِيل فليرده وَيطلب صَاحبه، فَيَقْضِي بِحَق.

If a judge gives a ruling contrary to the conclusion they reached via their *ijtihād*, their judgement is invalid, even if they blindly-followed another scholar in their judgement. This is according to the Four Imāms and those who agree with them. In *al-Irshād*, it states that their judgement is not invalidated, but that the judge bears sinfulness for doing so. If someone for-

---

540 [T] Meaning, 'Abd al-Raḥmān ibn Qudāmah, the nephew of al-Muwaffaq Ibn Qudāmah. He authored an explanation of *al-Muqni'*.

getfully gives a judgement according to a different view than the view they hold, their judgement must be adhered to, and he bears no sin. This was also the view of Abu Ḥanīfah. However, Abu Yūsuf, the Māliki scholars and the Shāfiʿī scholars all said that they must retract their view and negate it. Abu Ṭālib reported that al-Imām Aḥmad said, "If the judge makes a mistake without any valid excuse for reinterpretation, they must reject their ruling, seek the person to whom the right belongs, and give a correct judgement."[541]

وَإِن حكم مقلد بِحكم بِخِلَاف مَا قَالَه إِمَامه فعلى قَول من يرى صِحَة حكم الْمُقَلّد يَصح حكمه، وعَلى قَول من يرى أن الْمُقَلّد لَا يجوز لَهُ تَقْلِيد غير إِمَامه لم يَصح حكمه، صرح بِهَذَا الْآمِدِيّ وَابْن حمدَان. وَقَالَ ابْن حمدَان أَيْضا: مُخَالفَة الْمُفْتِي نَص إِمَامه كمخالفة نَص الشَّارِع.

If a blind-follower gives a ruling contrary to that of the *imām* they blindly-follow, according to those who view that the rulings and judgements offered by blind-followers are valid, their judgement is valid. According to the scholars who do not believe that a blind-follower may follow anyone but their *imām*, their ruling is not valid. This was mentioned explicitly by al-Āmidī and Ibn Ḥamdān. Ibn Ḥamdān also said, "When a *mufti* contradicts the texts of their *imām*, it is similar to contradicting the texts of legislation."[542]

وَقَالَ ابْن هُبَيرَة: عمله بقول الْأَكْثَر أولى، وَلَو اجْتهد فَتزَوج بِلَا ولي ثمَّ تغير اجْتِهَاده حرمت عَلَيْهِ امْرَأَته فِي الْأَصَح. وَقَالَ القَاضِي، والموفق، وَابْن حمدَان، والطوفي، والآمدي: تحرم عَلَيْهِ إِن لم يكن حكم بِصِحَّة النِّكَاح حَاكم.

Ibn Hubayrah said, "It is best to act in accordance with the majority view. If someone marries without a guardian [for the woman], and then changes their *ijtihād* [believing that it is an invalid marriage,] their wife becomes unlawful for them, according to the veracious view."[543] Al-Qāḍī, al-Muwaffaq, Ibn Ḥamdān, al-Ṭūfī, and al-Āmidī all opined that she becomes unlawful for him if their marriage was not officiated and ruled valid by a judge.

---

541 [T] Mentioned by Ibn Mufliḥ in *Uṣūl al-Fiqh* (4/1512).
542 [T] *Sifat al-Fatwā* (p. 31).
543 [T] *Ifṣāḥ ʿan Maʿānī al-Ṣiḥāḥ* (2/344).

وأما الْمُقَلّد فَقَالَ أَبُو الْخطاب والموفق والطوفي: لَا تحرم عَلَيْهِ لتغير اجْتِهَاد من قلّدهُ. وَقَالَ الشَّافِعِيَّة وَابْن حمدَان: تحرم. قَالَ المرداوي فِي (التَّحْرِير): وَهُوَ مُتَّجه كالتقليد فِي الْقبْلَة، وَإِذا لم يعْمل الْمُقَلّد بفتوى من قلّدهُ حَتَّى تغير اجْتِهَاده مفتية، لزم الْمُفْتِي إِعْلَام الْمُقَلّد لَهُ، فَلَو مَاتَ الْمُفْتِي قبل إِعْلَام الْعَامِيّ بتغيُّر اجْتِهَاده اسْتمرّ على مَا أفتى بِهِ فِي الْأَصَح. قَالَ فِي (شرح التَّحْرِير): وَهُوَ الْمُعْتَمد، وَقيل: يمْتَنع.

As for a blind-follower, Abu 'l-Khaṭṭāb, al-Muwaffaq, and al-Ṭūfī all stated that his wife does not become unlawful for him due to the changing in the conclusion of the scholar he followed. The Shāfiʿī scholars and Ibn Ḥamdān opined that she does become unlawful. Al-Mardāwī stated in his book *al-Taḥrīr*, "That is a fair view, similar to blindly following in the direction of the *qiblah*."[544] If a blind-follower was given an edict, and did not act in accordance with it before the *muftī* changed their view, the *muftī* must inform them of their change their view. If the *muftī* dies before informing the layperson of their change in *ijtihād*, the layperson should continue to act according to the ruling they were aware of, according to the veracious view. In *Sharḥ al-Taḥrīr*, it says, "This is the official view [of the Ḥanbalī *madhhab*]."[545] Others said that they should refrain.

وَاعْلَم أَن الْأُصُولِيِّينَ اخْتلفُوا فِي تَقْلِيد الْعَامِيّ لمجتهد ميت، فَقَالَ جُمْهُور الْعلمَاء: لَا فرق بَين تَقْلِيد الْمَيِّت وتقليد الْحَي، لِأَن قَوْله بَاقٍ فِي الْإِجْمَاع، وَلذَلِك قَالَ الشَّافِعِي: الْمذَاهب لَا تَمُوت بِمَوْت أَرْبَابهَا، وَقيل: لَيْسَ للعامي تَقْلِيد الْمَيِّت إِن وجد مُجْتَهدا حَيا، وَإِلَّا جَازَ. وَقيل: لَا يجوز تَقْلِيد الْمَيِّت مُطلقًا. قَالَ الفتوحي فِي (شرح مُخْتَصر التَّحْرِير) وَهُوَ وَجه لَهَا وللشافعية.

Legal theorists have differed on the topic of blindly-following a dead *mujtahid*. The majority of scholars said that there is no difference between blindly following someone who is dead or alive, since the view of the *mujtahid* remains when it comes to consensus. That is why al-Shāfiʿī said, "Ways of law do not die with the deaths of their founders." It was said that a layperson cannot follow a dead scholar if there is a *mujtahid* that is still alive, and if

---

544 [T] *Taḥrīr al-Manqūl* (p. 336).
545 [T] *Al-Taḥbīr Sharḥ al-Taḥrīr* (8/3981).

there is no *mujtahid* alive, they may follow the dead one. Others said that one may not follow a dead *mujtahid* in any circumstance. Al-Futūḥī said in *Sharḥ Mukhtaṣar al-Taḥrīr*, "It is a view within our *madhhab* and according to the Shāfi'ī scholars."[546]

وَمن بلغ رتبة الِاجْتِهَاد، حرم عَلَيْهِ تَقْلِيد غَيره اتفاقًا، سَوَاء اجْتهد أَو لم يجْتَهد، وَإِلَيْهِ ذهب أَحْمد وَمَالك وَالشَّافِعِيّ، وَلأبي حنيفَة رِوَايَتَانِ.

If a person reaches the level of *ijtihād*, it is forbidden for them to blindly-follow anyone else, according to the agreement of scholars. This is regardless if they do *ijtihād* or do not. Aḥmad, Mālik, al-Shāfi'ī took to this view, and Abu Ḥanīfah has two views on the topic.

وَقيل: يجوز تَقْلِيده إِن لم يجْتَهد مُطلقًا قَالَ أَبُو الْفرج، وَحكي عَن أَحْمد وَإِسْحَاق وَالثَّوْرِي. وللمجتهد أَن يجْتَهد ويدع غَيره، والتوقف من الْمُجْتَهد فِي مَسْأَلَة نحوية أَو فِي حَدِيث - بِحَيْثُ يحْتَاج إِلَى مُرَاجعَة أهل النَّحْو أَو أهل الحَدِيث - يَجعله فِي رُتْبَة الْعَاميّ فِيمَا توقف فِيهِ، عِنْد أبي الْخطاب والموفق والآمدي وَغَيرهم، والعامي يلْزمه التَّقْلِيد مُطلقًا.

Others said that it is allowed for them to blindly-follow if they did not use *ijtihād* to come to a conclusion. This was the view of Abu 'l-Faraj [ibn al-Jawzī], and is reported from Aḥmad, Isḥāq, and al-Thawrī. A *mujtahid* may perform *ijtihād* and avoid all others. When a *mujtahid* abstains from offering a view on an issue pertaining to language or ḥadīth, in order to refer the issue to scholars of language or ḥadīth, it makes them a layperson in the field they abstained from giving an answer on. This was stated by Abu 'l-Khaṭṭāb, al-Muwaffaq, al-Āmidī, and others. Commoners must always blind-follow a scholar.

لتَّاسِعَة: هَل يجوز خلو الْعَصْر عَن الْمُجْتَهدين أَو لَا؟ ذهب أَصْحَابنَا إِلَى أَنه لَا يجوز خلو الْعَصْر عَن مُجْتَهد، وَإِلَى ذَلِك ذهب طوائف، وَلم يذكر ابْن عقيل خلاف هَذَا إِلَّا عَن بعض الْمُحدثين، وَاخْتَارَهُ القَاضِي عبد الْوَهَّاب الْمَالِكِي وَجمع من الْمَالِكِيَّة وَمن غَيرهم، وَصرح بِهِ ابْن بطال فِي (شرح البُخَارِيّ) وَاخْتَارَهُ

546 [T] *Mukhtaṣar al-Taḥrīr Sharḥ al-Kawkab al-Munīr* (4/514).

ابْن دَقِيق الْعِيد فِي (شرح العنوان).

Nine. Is it possible for an era to not have any *mujtahid* scholars? Our *aṣḥāb* took the view that it is not possible for an era to have no *mujtahid* scholars. This was also the view held by some other scholars. Ibn ʿAqīl did not mention any differing views on this topic, except some that are held by a number of scholars of ḥadīth. This was also the view of al-Qāḍī ʿAbd al-Wahhāb al-Māliki and a number of Māliki scholars and others. It was explicitly stated by Ibn Baṭṭāl in his explanation of *Ṣaḥīḥ al-Bukhārī*, and it was also the view chosen by Ibn Daqiq al-ʿĪd in *Sharh al-ʿUnwān*.

وَقَالَ ابْن حمدَان من أَصْحَابنَا: وَمن زمن طَوِيل عدم الْمُجْتَهد الْمُطلق، مَعَ أَنه الْآن أيسر مِنْهُ فِي الزَّمن الأول، وَأطَال فِي بَيَان أَنه متيسر الْآن. وَحكى مثله النَّوَوِيّ فِي (شرح الْمُهَذّب) وَقَالَ الرَّافِعِيّ: النَّاس الْيَوْم كالمجمعين على أَنه لَا مُجْتَهد الْيَوْم. وَنقل ابْن مُفْلِح كِلَاهُمَا، ثمَّ ذيله بقوله: وَفِيه نظر. قَالَ فِي (شرح التَّحْرِير): وَهُوَ كَمَا قَالَ، فَإِنَّهُ وجد من الْمُجْتَهدين بعد ذَلِك جمَاعَة، مِنْهُم الشَّيْخ تَقِيّ الدّين ابْن تَيْمِية، انْتهى.

Ibn Ḥamdān, one of our *aṣḥāb*, stated, "It has been a long time since an absolute *mujtahid* existed, although nowadays, it is easier to achieve that status than it was before."[547] He spoke at length clarifying that it is easier during these times. Al-Nawawī said something similar in *Sharḥ al-Muhadhab*, and al-Rāfiʿī said, "People nowadays, it seems they agree unanimously that there are no *mujtahid* scholars alive." Ibn Mufliḥ quoted them both, then said, "This is contentious." In *Sharḥ al-Taḥrīr*, it states, "It is as [Ibn Mufliḥ] stated, since there were *mujtahid* scholars that emerged after that group of scholars, among them al-Shaykh Taqī al-Dīn ibn Taymiyyah."[548]

وَقد أَطَالَ عُلَمَاء النَّفس فِي هَذَا الْمَوْضُوع، وَأورد كل من الْفَرِيقَيْنِ حججًا وأدلة، وَكَأن الْقَائِلين بِجَوَاز خلو عصر عَن مُجْتَهد قاسوا جَمِيع عُلَمَاء الْأمة على أنفسهم، وخيلوا لَهَا أَنه لَا أحد يبلغ أَكثر من مبلغهم من الْعلم، ثمَّ رازوا أنفسهم، فوجدوها سَاقِطَة فِي الدَّرك الْأَسْفَل من التَّقْلِيد، فمنعوا فضل الله تَعَالَى وَقَالُوا: لَا

547 [T] *Sifat al-Fatwā* (p. 17).
548 [T] *Mukhtaṣar al-Taḥrīr Sharḥ al-Kawkab al-Munīr* (4/570).

يُمكن وجود مُجْتَهد فِي عصرنا أَلْبَتَّة، بل غلا أَكْثَرهم فَقَالَ: لَا مُجْتَهد بعد الأربع مئة من الْهِجْرَة. وينحل كَلَامهم هَذَا إِلَى أَن فضل الله تَعَالَى كَانَ مدرارا على أهل العصور الْأَرْبَعَة، ثمَّ إِنَّه نضب، فَلم يبْق مِنْهُ قَطْرَة، تنزل على الْمُتَأَخِّرين، مَعَ أَن فضل الله تَعَالَى لَا ينضب، وعطاؤه ومدده لَا يقفان عِنْد الْحَد الَّذِي حَده أُولَئِكَ.

Scholars have spoken at length on this topic, with each camp of scholars quoting their evidences and proofs. It seems that the scholars who stated it is possible for an era to not have a single *mujtahid* considered all scholars of the Ummah analogous to themselves. They felt that no one can reach higher levels than their own knowledge. Then, they analysed themselves and found themselves falling to the lowest levels of blind-following. As such, they prevented the proliferation of Allah's favours, stating that there is no possible way for there to be a *mujtahid* scholar in our times. Many of them were even more extreme, saying that there are no *mujtahid* scholars after four hundred years post *hijrah*. Their view is invalidated because it means that the favours of Allah the Exalted were flowing copiously for those of the first four centuries, and then became depleted, leaving not a single drop that could befall the latter-generations. However, the truth is that the favours of Allah the Exalted never deplete, and His favours and aid never stop at the limits that were set by those individuals.

فبعيشك قل لي: هَل وزن الْقَائِل بِانْقِطَاع الِاجْتِهَاد علم جَمِيع عُلَمَاء عصره فِي جَمِيع الأقطار حَتَّى علم أَن وَاحِدًا مِنْهُم لم يبلغ دَرَجَة الِاجْتِهَاد، ثمَّ حكم بِهَذَا الحكم الْجَائِز؟ على أَنه رُبمَا خَفِي عَلَيْهِ علم كثير من عُلَمَاء بَلَده، بل رُبمَا لم يعرفهُمْ. وَمَا أَتَى هَذَا الغبي إِلَّا من دَاء الجمود الْمُوجب للخلود فِي حضيض الْجَهْل المركب. أَلا يرى هَذَا أَن الْأَئِمَّة الْمُتَقَدِّمين كَانَ الْوَاحِد مِنْهُم يجوب أقطار الأَرْض لكتابة الحَدِيث وَأَخذه عَن أئمته، حَتَّى ليستنزف مَا عِنْد غيره؟ ثمَّ قَامَ الجهابذة النقاد فدونوا الحَدِيث، ودونوا فنونه، ونقحوها، وهذبوها، وَوَضَعُوا كتب أَسمَاء الرِّجَال، وبينوا الصَّحِيح من غَيره، وسهلوا تناول البغية وَالْمَطْلُوب أَيّمَا تسهيل، بِحَيْثُ تيَسّر لمن بعدهمْ قطوف ثمراته الدانية، واستطلاع شموس فَوَائده من بروجها، وهم قَارون فِي بلدانهم، مستريحون فِي بُيُوتهم، لَا يَحْتَاجُونَ إِلَّا إِلَى

المطالعة والتنقيب.

By your life, tell me something: Did the person who claimed that *ijtihād* has been severed weigh all scholars of their times in all lands to know that not a single one has reached the level of *ijtihād*, and then afterwards, uttered this unjust statement? They might not be aware of many scholars from their own lands, and maybe do not even know them. What does this stupidity emanate from, except the disease of stagnation, which dictates perpetually roaming within the depths of compound ignorance? Does this person not see that the early scholars would travel the various parts of the world just to write a ḥadīth and learn it from its scholars, and deplete what others knew? Then, the erudite critics of ḥadīth authored the compendiums of ḥadīth; they authored its sciences, perfected them, refined them, and authored the books on the names of narrators. They clarified the authentic aḥadīth, differentiating between them and other categories of ḥadīth. They made seeking one's goals to be very facilitated. They made it easy for those after them to reap its fruits, which hang low, and to explore the radiant lights emanating from its benefits from its towering castles. They facilitated these things for people who can remain in their own lands and relax in their own homes, who need only to read and explore.

ثمَّ إن من تقدم كَانُوا يتعبون فِي نسخ كتب الحَدِيث وَغيرهَا، ويبذلون الْأَمْوَال فِي طلبَهَا، حَتَّى أنشئت المطابع فأغنتهم عَن تَعب النّسخ والتجول للتفتيش على الْكتب، وَلم يزل انتشار كتب الْعلم فِي ازدياد، فَلم يبْق لصَاحب الهمة فَقِيه النَّفس عذر يعْتَذر بِهِ، فيالله الْعجب مِمَّن يتحكم على الله، وَيحكم على فَضله بِمَا تزينه لَهُ نَفسه.

The early scholars used to exhaust themselves in copying the books of ḥadīth and other books. They spent vast wealth in seeking to purchase books. When the printing press was invented, it served as a substitute for that laborious work of copying, travelling, and looking for books. Books are becoming increasingly available. As such, a person who has resolve and determination and is a jurist of the soul has no excuse that he could possibly contrive. So, by Allah, how strange is the person who thinks they can control Allah and judge His favours in ways that their soul beautifies for them!

على أننا نقُول لمن قطع بخلو الْعَصْر من مُجْتَهد: إن هَذِه الْمَسْأَلة الَّتِي حكمت

بهَا اجتهادية مَحْضَة، فَإِن كَانَ الحكم مِنْك عَلَيْهَا بِاجْتِهَاد مِنْك، فقد أكذبت نَفسك، حَيْثُ اجتهدت أَن لَا اجْتِهَاد، وَأمسى كلامك سَاقِطا، وَإِن كنت حكمت بذلك تقليدا لغيرك، قُلْنَا لَك: الْمُقَلّد لَا يجوز لَهُ أَن يحكم بِشَيْء مُقلدًا لمن غلط بِاجْتِهَادِهِ وَذَلِكَ أَن الَّذِي قلدته إِمَّا أَن يكون مُجْتَهدا، فنعيد عَلَيْهِ الكرة بالاحتجاج السَّابِق، وَإِن كَانَ مُقلدًا، خاطبناه بِمَا خاطبناك بِهِ، ثمَّ ينتقل الْكَلَام إِلَى الثَّانِي وَالثَّالِث وَمَا قبلهمَا، فيتسلسل الْأَمر أَو يَدُور، والدور والتسلسل باطلان.

Lastly, we say to those who brazenly claim that certain eras lack *mujtahid* scholars: this issue is one that is subject to scholarly discretion. If you have offered a judgement on the issue, you have used *ijtihād*! As such, you have belied yourself; you made *ijtihād* to state that there is no *ijtihād*, making your speech invalid. If you have made that claim blindly following others, we say to you: a blind follower cannot offer judgements on things while blindly following someone whose *ijtihād* was erroneous, because either the one you have followed is a *mujtahid*, and if so, we repeat the same argument against them, or is a blind-follower themselves, and we offer them this same monologue. This argument repeats to the second and third person in the chain, and it results in an infinite regress, which is a logical fallacy.

وقصارى أَمر هَؤُلَاءِ المعاندين أَنهم سوفسطائية، يُنكرُونَ الْحَقَائِق إِمَّا جهلا مركبا، وَإِمَّا كبرا وعنادا، فَلذَا يجب ترك المشاغبة مَعَهم، وَيُقَال: لَا يجوز خلو عصر عَن مُجْتَهد رَضِيتُمْ أم سخطتم، فدعوا العناد، وخوضوا بَحر الجمود إِلَى يَوْم الدّين.

In brief, these obstinate individuals are sophists: they reject realities, either out of compounded ignorance or out of arrogance and obstinacy. That is why it is obligatory on one to avoid disputing with them and to just say to them: it is not possible for there to be no *mujtahid* scholars in any given era, whether that pleases you or angers you. Therefore, abandon all obstinacy, or delve deeply into the ocean of rigidity until the Day of Judgement.

فصل [التقْلِيد]

Subsection: [On Blind-Following (*taqlīd*)]

وَأما التَّقْلِيد: فَهُوَ فِي اللغَة: جعل شَيْء فِي عنق الدَّابَّة وَغَيره محيطا، قَالَ فِي (النِّهَايَة) فِي حَدِيث: **«قلدوا الْخَيل وَلا تقلدوها الأوتار»** أَي لَا تجْعَلُوا فِي أعناقها الأوتار فتختنق، لِأَن الْخَيل رُبمَا رعت الْأَشْجَار، فنشبت الأوتار بِبَعْض شعبها، فخنقتها.

The term *taqlīd* linguistically refers to tying something around the neck of a livestock, or something else, to encompass it. In *al-Nihāyah*, when discussing the ḥadīth, **"Tie horses (*qallidū*), but do not tie them with strings."**[549] [He said:] This ḥadīth means that one should not tie horses with strings, otherwise, they will choke, because a horse could be grazing from trees, and the strings might tangle to its branches, causing the horse to choke.

وَشرعا: قبُول قَول الْغَيْر من غير حجَّة، اسْتِعَارة من الْمَعْنى اللّغَوِيّ، كَأَن الْمُقلّد يطوق الْمُجْتَهد إِثْم مَا غشه بِهِ فِي دينه، وكتمه عَنهُ من علمه.

In religious terminology, it refers to acceptance of the view or statement of another person without evidence. It is a metaphorical usage of the linguistic meaning. A person who does *taqlīd* (referred to as a *muqallid*), ties the sin of being cheated in religious matters and having knowledge hidden from them to the *mujtahid*.

وَهَهُنَا مسَائِل:

There are a number of important issues to discuss here:

أولهَا: لَيْسَ قبُول قَول النَّبِي صلى الله عَلَيْهِ وَسلم تقليدا، لِأَنهُ هُوَ حجَّة فِي نَفسه، وَقَالَ الشَّيْخ تَقِي الدّين ابْن تَيمِية فِي (المسودة) التَّقْلِيد: قبول قَول الْغَيْر بِغَيْر

549 Reported by Abu Dāwūd (2553), Aḥmad (4/345), and al-Nasā'ī (6/218).

دَلِيل، فَلَيْسَ المصير إِلَى الإِجْمَاع تقليدا، لِأَن الْإِجْمَاع دَلِيل، وَلذَلِك يقبل قَول النَّبِي صلى الله عَلَيْهِ وَسلم، وَلَا يُقَال: هُوَ تَقْلِيد: بِخِلَاف فتيا الْفَقِيه. وَذكر فِي ضمن مَسْأَلَة التَّقْلِيد أَن الرُّجُوع إِلَى قَول الصَّحَابَة لَيْسَ بتقليد، لِأَنهُ حجَّة. وَقَالَ أَيْضا: لما جَازَ تَقْلِيد الصَّحَابَة، لزمَه ذَلِك، وَلم يجز لَهُ مُخَالفَته، بِخِلَاف الأعلم. وَقد قَالَ أَحْمد فِي رِوَايَة أبي الْحَارِث: من قلد الْخَبَر، رَجَوْت أَن يسلم إِن شَاءَ الله. فقد أطلق التَّقْلِيد على من صَار إِلَى الْخَبَر، وَإِن كَانَ حجَّة فِي نَفسه.

First: Acceptance of the statement of the Prophet ﷺ is not considered blind-following, because the Prophet ﷺ is proof in and of himself. Al-Shaykh Taqī al-Dīn stated in *al-Musawwadah*, "Blind following means to accept the statements of others without evidence. As such, acceptance of consensus is not blind following, since consensus is an evidence. Also due to this, the statement of the Prophet ﷺ is accepted, and it is not to be said that it is blind following, contrary to when a jurist offers an edict."[550] In the midst of his discussions on this issue, he also mentioned that referring to the statement of a companion is also not blind following, since their views are evidence. He also said, "When one has the possibility to blindly follow the companions, they are obliged to do so, and may not contradict them, contrary to the more knowledgeable scholar."[551] Aḥmad said, in the narration of Abu 'l-Ḥārith, "Whoever blindly-follows narrations, I hope that they are safe, if Allah Wills." He used the term *taqlīd* to refer to a person resorting to narrations, even though the narrations are proofs in and of themselves.

ثَانِيهَا: يحرم التَّقْلِيد فِي معرفَة الله تَعَالَى والتوحيد والرسالة عِنْد الإِمَام أَحْمد وَأَصْحَابه، وَهُوَ الْحق. وَيحرم أَيْضا فِي أَرْكَان الْإِسْلَام الْخمسة وَنَحْوهَا مِمَّا تَوَاتر واشتهر. وَحكي ذَلِك إِجْمَاعًا. وَأما التَّقْلِيد فِي الْفُرُوع فَهُوَ جَائِز إِجْمَاعًا لغير الْمُجْتَهد.

Second: It is forbidden to blindly follow in matters pertaining to knowledge of Allah, monotheism, and the message, according to Aḥmad and his adherents. This is the truth. It is also impermissible to blindly follow anyone

550 [T] *Al-Musawwadah* (p. 462).
551 [T] *Al-Musawwadah* (p. 462). What he means by, "contrary to the more knowledgeable scholar," is that the view of a more knowledgeable scholar may be left in favour of the view of the less knowledgeable *mujtahid* scholar.

regarding the five pillars of Islam, and other such issues that have become widespread and recurrent. It was stated that this point is a matter of consensus. As for blind following in matters of substantive law, it is allowed for a non-*mujtahid* to do so, according to the consensus of all scholars.

ثَالِثهَا: إِن الْعَامِيّ - وَهُوَ الَّذِي لَيْسَ بمجتهد - عَلَيْهِ أَن يسْأَل الْعَالم، وَحِينَئِذٍ لَا يَخْلُو حَاله من أنه إِمَّا أَن يعلم، أَو يظنّ أَن المسؤول أهل للفتيا، أَو يعلم أَنه جَاهِل لَا يصلح لذَلِك، أو يجهل حَاله، فَلَا يعلم أَهْلِيَّته وَلَا عدمهَا.

Third: A layperson, defined here as a person who is not a *mujtahid*, must ask a scholar. In the case that they ask a scholar, three things might happen: (i) He knows or thinks that the one being asked has competency in giving edicts. (ii) He knows him to be ignorant and not fit for such a task. (iii) He is ignorant of his level, not knowing if he has competence or not.

فَالْأول: لَهُ أَن يستفتيه باتفاقهم، وَعلمه بأهليته إِمَّا بإِخْبَار عدل عَنهُ بذلك، أَو باشتهاره بَين النَّاس بالفتيا، أَو بانتصابه لَهَا، وانقياد النَّاس للأخذ عَنهُ، أَو نَحْو ذَلِك من الطرق. وَالظن يقوم مقَام الْعلم فِي ذَلِك.

(i) They know or think that the one being asked is a scholar. In this case, they may ask them for an edict, according to the agreement of all scholars. There are a number of ways they can learn that a person has competence, such as, but not limited to: (a) When informed by an upright person that the scholar is qualified to give rulings. (b) When the scholar is well-known as a person of edicts. (c) When the scholar is appointed to give rulings. (d) When people yield to learning from them. Probability takes the place of definitive knowledge in this case.

وَالثَّانِي: وَهُوَ من علم أَو ظن جَهله، لَا يجوز لَهُ أَن يستفتيه، لِأَنهُ تَضْيِيع لأحكام الشَّرِيعَة، فَهُوَ كالعالم يُفْتِي بِغَيْر دَلِيل.

(ii) They know or think that they are ignorant and not fit to be questioned. In this case, it is not permissible to ask them for an edict, because that would lead to squandering the laws of legislation. They resemble a scholar that gives an edict with no evidence.

أما إِذا جهل حَاله، فَلَا يقلده أَيْضا عِند الْأَكْثَر خلافًا لقوم.

(iii) They do not know the status of the person and whether they are fit to answer the question or not. In this case, they should not be blindly followed, according to the majority, while a minority stated that they may be followed.

رَابِعهَا: يَكْفِي الْمُقلّد سُؤال من يَشَاء من مجتهدي الْبَلَد، وَلَا يلْزمه سُؤال جَمِيعهم، وَهل يجب عَلَيْهِ أَن يتَخَيَّر الْأَفْضَل من الْمُجْتَهدين فيستفتيه؟ فِيهِ قَولَانِ بِالنفْي وَالْإِثْبَات. وَالْحق أَنه لَا يلْزمه استفتاء أفضل الْمُجْتَهدين مُطلقًا، فَإِن هَذَا يسد بَاب التَّقْلِيد، أما إِذا قيدنا ذَلِك بمجتهدي الْبَلَد، فَإِنَّهُ يلْزمه حِينَئِذٍ تحري الْأَفْضَل، لِأَن الْفضل فِي كل بلد مَعْرُوف مَشْهُور، فَإِن سَأَلَ المستفتي مجتهدين فَأَكْثَر، فَاخْتَلَفُوا عَلَيْهِ فِي الْجَواب فَقَوْلَانِ، أظهرهمَا: وجوب مُتَابعَة الْأَفْضَل.

Fourth: It is sufficient for a blind follower to ask any *mujtahid* of the land. They do not need to ask them all. However, there are two views on whether a person must choose the most virtuous of the *mujtahid* scholars available to ask them for an edict. Some said that they must, while others denied that responsibility. The truth is that they do not need to ask the absolute most virtuous *mujtahid*, because that would close the door of blind-following. However, if we were to qualify the statement by referring only to the *mujtahid* scholars of the land, in that case it is necessary for the one seeking an edict to search for the most virtuous. Virtuousness is known to the residents of each land. And if someone asks two or more *mujtahid* scholars, the scholars differed on what they are to do with the answers, but the view most apparently correct is that they must follow the more virtuous scholar.

فَإِن قيل: الْعَاميّ لَيْسَ أَهلا لمعْرِفَة الْفَاضِل من الْمَفْضُول، وقصارى أمره أَن يغتر بظواهر هَيْئَة حَسَنَة، وعمامة كَبِيرَة، وجبة وَاسِعَة الأكمام، فَرُبمَا اعْتقد الْمَفْضُول فَاضلا. قُلْنَا: هَذَا لَيْسَ بِعُذْر، فعَلَيهِ أَن يتَكَلَّف فِي الِاخْتِيَار وَسعه.

Some might respond and say, "A commoner cannot discern between the more virtuous and the less virtuous scholar. In the end they will be deceived by the apparent good looks, large turban, and cloak with wide sleeves. As such, they might think that the less virtuous scholar is more virtuous." The response is that this is not an excuse; they must spend their utmost effort in choosing whom to ask.

قَالَ في (الرَّوْضَة) وَتَبعهُ الطوفي: وَيعرف الْأَفْضَل بالإخبار، وإذعان الْمَفْضُول لَهُ. وتقديمه على نَفسه فِي الْأُمُور الدِّينِيَّة، كالتلميذ مَعَ شَيْخه لِأَنهُ يفِيد الْقطع بهَا عَادَة، أَو بأمارات غير ذَلِك مِمَّا يُفِيد الْقطع أَو الظن. انْتهى.

Ibn Qudāmah stated a view in his *Rawḍah*, which was then concurred by al-Ṭūfī, where he said, "The more virtuous scholar is known by transmission of news and when the less virtuous scholar yields to their views, preferring them over their own selves in matters related to religion, just as a student does with their teacher. Usually, that provides definitive insight. There are also other ways to discern who is more virtuous that provide one with definitive or probable knowledge."[552]

قلت: رحم الله الْمُوفق، والطوفي، فَإِنَّهُمَا تكلما على زمانهما، حَيْثُ النَّاس نَاس يعْرفُونَ الفضل ويقرون بِهِ، وَأما الْيَوْم، فالتقديم بالغنى وَقلة الْحيَاء وَالْجهل الْمركب، يعْتَقد الْجَاهِل فِي نَفسه أَنه أعلم الْعلمَاء، فيزاحم أهل الفضل، وَلَا يقر لأحد، وَلَو ألقيت عَلَيْهِ أقل مَسْأَلَة، وجم وَسكت، وقابلك بالسفاهة والحمق، وَلَو قلت لَهُ: هَذَا حَدِيث مَوْضُوع، لقَالَ لَك: أَنْت تكذب النَّبِي صلى الله عَلَيْهِ وَسلم، وَعلا صَوته، وَانْتفَخَتْ أوداجه، وَجمع عَلَيْك الْعَامَّة، وَرُبمَا آذوك بِالضَّرْبِ، والشتم والإخراج عَن الدّين.

I say: May Allah have mercy on al-Muwaffaq and al-Ṭūfī. They were speaking about their time, a time when people knew virtuousness and would acknowledge it in others. As for today, preference is given to those with wealth, who lack shame, and have compounded ignorance. An ignoramus believes themselves to be the most knowledgeable of scholars. They compete with people of virtue and do not acknowledge anyone but themselves. If they are presented with the smallest of issues, they remain silent and speechless, responding in turn with foolishness and idiocy. If you tell them, "This is a fabricated ḥadīth," they respond, "So you are saying the Prophet ﷺ is lying?" Then raise their voice, become haughty, and gather the commoners against you, who might harm you by attacking or cursing you, and even sometimes declare you outside of the religion.

552 [T] *Rawḍat al-Nāẓir* (2/387).

وَمِمَّا ابتدع فِي زَمَانِنَا أَنهم يجمعُونَ أهل العمائم، فينتخبون مفتيا، ويسمونه رَئِيس الْعلمَاء، ثمَّ تقرره الْحُكُومَة مفتيا، ويحصرون الْفَتْوى فِيهِ، فكثيرا مَا ينَال هَذَا المنصب الْجَاهِل الْغمر الَّذِي لَو عرضت عَلَيْهِ عبارَة بعض كتب الْفُرُوع مَا عرف لَهَا قبيلا من دبير، فنسأل الله حسن الْعَاقِبَة.

Another innovated thing done nowadays is that they gather those with large turbans and choose a *muftī*, referring to him as, "the leader of the scholars." The government then declares him as the *muftī* and makes edicts limited to him. Many times, an unskilled ignoramus takes such roles. If they are presented with phrases from some books of substantive law, they would not know its front from its back! We ask Allah the Exalted for a good ending.

على أَن اخْتِصَاص وَاحِد بِمنْصب الْإِفْتَاء - لَا يقبل الْحَاكِم الْفَتْوى إِلَّا مِنْهُ - لم يكن مَعْرُوفا فِي الْقُرُون الأولى، وَإِنَّمَا كَانَ الْإِفْتَاء موكولا إِلَى الْعلمَاء الْأَعْلَام، وَاسْتمر ذَلِك إِلَى أَن دخل السُّلْطَان سليم العثماني دمشق سنة اثْنَتَيْنِ وَعشْرين وَتِسْع مِئَة من الْهِجْرَة، وامتلكها، فَرَأى كَثْرَة المشاغبات بَين المدعين للْعلم، خصص إِفْتَاء كل مَذْهَب بِرَجُل من علمائه الأفاضل قطعا للمشاغبات، ثمَّ طَال الزَّمن، فَتَوَلّى هَذَا المنصب الْجَلِيل كثير مِمَّن لَا يدْرِي مَا هِيَ الْأُصُول وَمَا هِيَ الْفُرُوع، فوسد الْأَمر إِلَى غير أَهله، وَأعْطى الْقوس غير باريها.

Note, too, that assigning the role of giving edicts to just one person, where the ruler only accepts edicts from them, was not something known in the early generations. Granting of edicts was a role of the great scholars. That was the case until the Ottoman Sultan Selim I entered Damascus, in the year 922 *hijri*, after conquering it. After he saw the number of disputes between claimants of knowledge, he appointed *muftīs* of each school of law, comprising of virtuous scholars, in order to quell the disputes. Then, as time passed, this lofty status was held by people who know neither the fundamentals nor the subsidiary matters. Matters were put in the control of undeserving individuals, and the arrow was given to someone who did not configure it.

هَذَا فَإِن اسْتَوى الْمُجْتَهد عِنْد المستفتي فِي الْفَضِيلَة، وَاخْتلفَا عَلَيْهِ فِي الْجَواب، اخْتَار الأشد مِنْهُمَا، لما روى التِّرْمِذِي من حَدِيث عَائِشَة قَالَت: قَالَ رَسُول الله

صلى الله عَلَيْهِ وَسلم: «**مَا خير عمار بَين أَمريْن إلا اخْتَار أشدهما**» وَفِي لفظ «**أرشدهما**» قَالَ التِّرْمِذِي: هَذَا حَدِيث حسن غَرِيب، رَوَاهُ أَيْضا النَّسَائِي، وَابْن مَاجَه، فَثبت بِهَذَيْنِ اللَّفْظَيْنِ للْحَدِيث أَن الرشد فِي الْأَخْذ بالأشد، وَالْأولَى أَن يعْتَبر الْقَوْلَيْنِ ساقطين لتعارضهما، وَيرجع إِلَى استفتاء آخر.

With that said, if there are two *mujtahid* scholars who are equal in virtue in the eyes of the one seeking the edict, and they give two different answers, they should act on the more stringent of the two, because al-Tirmidhī reported that ʿĀ'ishah said, "Allah's Messenger ﷺ said, **'Whenever ʿAmmār is given the choice between two options, he chooses the more stringent.'**"[553] In another wording, he said, **"He chose the one with more guidance in it."** Al-Tirmidhī said, "This ḥadīth is *ḥasan gharīb*." It was also narrated by al-Nasā'ī and Ibn Mājah. Taking these two wordings into account, we learn that guidance lies in choosing the stringent option. It is best to consider both statements to cancel each other out and to ask someone else.

خَامِسهَا: قَالَ أَكثر أَصْحَابنَا وَغَيرهم: لَا يُفْتِي إِلَّا مُجْتَهد، وَمَعْنَاهُ عَن الإِمَام أَحْمد. وَجوز فِي (التَّرْغِيب) وَ(التَّلْخِيص) الإِفْتاء لمجتهد فِي مَذْهَب إِمَامه للضَّرُورة. وَقَالَ فِي (التَّحْرِير) الْحَنْبَلِي: وَيمْنَع عندنَا وَعند الْأَكْثَر من الإِفْتاء من لم يعرف بِعلم. أَو كَانَ حَاله مَجْهُولا، وَيلْزم ولي الْأَمر مَنعه. قَالَ ربيعَة: بعض من يُفْتِي أَحَق بالسجن من السراق.

Fifth: The majority of our *aṣḥāb* have stated that only a *mujtahid* should give an edict. This concept has also been reported from al-Imām Aḥmad. In *al-Targhīb* and *al-Talkhīṣ*, they state that it is allowed to ask a *mujtahid* within a *madhhab* out of necessity. In *al-Taḥrīr*, on Ḥanbalī legal theory, it states, "It is prohibited, according to us and the majority, to ask someone who is not known to be knowledgeable, or whose status is unknown. It is required for leadership to prevent them."[554] Rabīʿah said, "Some who give edicts are more fit for prison than thieves are."

وَحكى شيخ الْإِسْلَام ابْن تَيْمِية فِي (المسودة) عَن ابْن حمدَان من أَصْحَابنَا أَنه

553 Reported by Aḥmad (6/113) and al-Tirmidhī (3800).
554 [T] *Taḥrīr al-Manqūl* (p. 340).

قَالَ:

Shaykh al-Islam ibn Taymiyyah said in *al-Musawwadah* that Ibn Ḥamdān, one of our *aṣḥāb*, said:

من اجْتهد فِي مَذْهَب إِمَامه، فَلم يقلده فِي حكمه وَدَلِيله، ففتياه بِهِ عَن نَفسه لَا عَن إِمَامه، فَهُوَ مُوَافق لَهُ فِيهِ، لَا متابع لَهُ، فَإِن قوي عِنْده مَذْهَب غَيره، أفتى بِهِ، وَأعلم السَّائِل مَذْهَب إِمَامه، وَلم يفته بِغَيْرِه، وَإِن قوي عِنْده وَلَا بِهِ حَيْثُ لم يقو عِنْده، فَإِن قلد إِمَامه فِي حكمه - فِي دَلِيله أَو دون دَلِيله - ففتياه بِهِ عَن إِمَامه إِن جَازَ تَقْلِيده، وَإِلا فَعَن نَفسه إِن قدر على التَّحْرِير والتقرير والتصوير وَالتَّعْلِيل والتفريع والتخريج وَالْجمع وَالْفرق، كَالَّذي لم يُقَلّد فيهمَا، فَإِن عجز عَن ذَلِك أَو بعضه، ففتياه عَن إِمَامه لَا عَن نَفسه.

If someone is a *mujtahid* in the *madhhab* of their *imām* and does not blindly-follow their *imām* in their rulings nor the evidences they used, their edict represents themselves, not their *imām*. As such, their view coincides with the opinion of their *imām* in that issue, instead of following him. If the view of some other *madhhab* appears to be more veracious to him, he can give the edict according to the other view but must tell the questioner what the view of their own *imām* is, and that he did not give the ruling according to that *madhhab*. If the point of the questioner is to follow the *madhhab* of the *imām* of the scholar they are asking, they must not offer them another ruling, even if it is stronger to them. The reason is, even if the view is not strong, if they follow their *imām* in their ruling and evidence, or just their ruling, the edict is transmitted from their *imām*, if it is permissible to follow a dead *mujtahid*. Otherwise, the edict is from themselves, if they are able to discern, research, conceptualise, prove, ramify, extrapolate, show similarities, and show differentia, and as such, their edict resembles that of a person who did not follow anyone in the ruling or the evidence. If they are unable to do all or any of those actions, their edict is considered from their *imam*, not themselves.

وَكَذَا الْمُجْتَهد فِي نوع علم أَو مَسْأَلَة مِنْهُ، وَمنعه فيهمَا أظهر. وَقيل: من عرف الْمَذْهَب دون دَلِيله جَازَ تَقْلِيده فِيهِ. إِن لم يجد فِي بَلَده وَلَا بِقُرْبِهِ مفتيا غَيره،

وَعجز عَن السّفر إِلَى مفت فِي مَوضِع بعيد، فَإِن عَدمه فِي بَلَده وَغَيره فَلهُ حكم مَا قبل الشَّرْع من إِبَاحَة وحظر ووقف.

Similarly, if a person is a *mujtahid* in a subject of knowledge or an issue within that subject, prohibition of *ijtihād* is the more apparently veracious view.[555] It was said that when a person knows a *madhhab*, but not its evidences, they may blindly follow them. A caveat mentioned by others is that there must be no other *muftī* in the land or close-by and they are unable to travel to a *muftī* in a far land. If there is no *muftī* in their land, they can judge based on the rulings of those things before legislation in terms of what was allowed, prohibited, and which have no rulings.[556]

وَمن أفتى بِحكم، أَو سَمعه من مفت، فَلهُ الْعَمَل بِهِ لَا فَتوى غَيره، لِأَنهُ حِكَايَة فَتوَى غَيره، وَإِنَّمَا سُئِلَ عَمَّا عِنْده. هَذَا كَلَامه.

Further, whoever gives an edict according to some ruling, or hears it from a *muftī*, they may act on it, and no other edict, because in that case, they would be telling the edict of someone else, and they were asked about their own edict. **[End.]**[557]

وَاعْلَم أَن أَمثَال هَذِه المباحث يكثر من ذكرهَا الْفُقَهَاء فِي كتب الْفُرُوع فِي بَاب آدَاب الْقَاضِي والمفتي، فَلَا نطيل بهَا هُنَا، وَقد أوسع المجال فِي هَذَا الْمقَال

555 [T] Note that the view that Ibn Ḥamdān mentions is, "If someone knows *qiyās* and its preconditions, they can give an edict based on issues that are subject to *qiyās* that have nothing to do with ḥadīth. If someone knows inheritance, they can offer *fatwa* on that subject, even if they are ignorant of the *aḥadīth* about marriage, and so forth. It was said that they may offer a *fatwa* on inheritance, nothing else. Some others said that both are disallowed. However, that view is farfetched." Refer to *Ṣifat al-Muftī* (p. 171). Therefore, there is a misquotation of al-Imām Ibn Ḥamdān, where he speaks about a person not being allowed to perform *ijtihād* in the subjects they have mastered.

556 [T] Meaning, the things that were lawful before legislation are lawful, the things prohibited before legislation are prohibited, and the things unmentioned before legislation remain without a ruling.

557 [T] *Al-Musawwadah* (p. 523). Note that both al-Shaykh Ibn Badrān's quotation of *al-Musawwadah* and Shaykh al-Islam's quotation of Ibn Ḥamdān's *Ṣifat al-Muftī* contain errors. I have corrected Ibn Badrān's misquotations by referring to the original *al-Musawwadah*, and as shown in the footnote before the last, I have corrected Ibn Taymiyyah's misquotation by referring to Ibn Ḥamdān's *Ṣifat al-Muftī*.

الإِمَام شمس الدّين مُحَمَّد ابن قيم الجوزية فِي كِتَابه (إِعْلَام الموقعين عَن رب الْعَالمين) بِمَا لَا مزِيد عَلَيْهِ، فليراجعه من أَرَادَ استطلاع الْحق من بروجه، فجزاه الله خيرا.

Know that these types of discussions are mentioned frequently by jurists in the books of substantive law, in the chapters of the manners of a judge and a *muftī*. As such, we shall not speak at length about them. Al-Imām Shams al-Dīn Muḥammad ibn Qayyim al-Jawzīyyah has spoken broadly on these topics in his book *I'lām al-Muwaqqi'īn 'an Rab al-'Ālamin*. Nothing can be added to his discussions. Those who want to seek the truth from its sources should go there. May Allah reward him.

عقد نفيس في ترتيب الأدلة والترجيح

Valuable Discussions on Categorising Evidences and Discovering Preponderance

اعْلَم أَن هَذَا العقد من مَوْضُوع نظر الْمُجْتَهد وضروراته، لِأَن الْأَدِلَّة الشَّرْعِيَّة مُتَفَاوِتَة فِي مَرَاتِب الْقُوة، فَيحْتَاج الْمُجْتَهد إِلَى معرفَة مَا يقدم مِنْهَا وَمَا يُؤَخر، لِئَلَّا يَأْخُذ بالأضعف مِنْهَا مَعَ وجود الْأَقْوى، فَيكون كالمتيم مَعَ وجود المَاء. وَقد يعرض للأدلة التَّعَارُض والتكافؤ، فَتصِير بذلك كالمعدومة، فَيحْتَاج إِلَى إِظْهَار بَعْضهَا بالترجيح ليعْمَل بِهِ، وَإِلَّا تعطلت الْأَدِلَّة وَالْأَحْكَام. فَهَذَا العقد مِمَّا يتَوَقَّف عَلَيْهِ الِاجْتِهَاد توقف الشَّيْء على جزئه أَو شَرطه.

The contents of this section pertain to the research and necessities needed by a *mujtahid* scholar. Religious evidences vary in their level of strength. A *mujtahid*, therefore, must be aware of which to give preference to, and which to put off, so that they do not take the weaker evidence while the stronger evidence is present. If they do so, they would resemble a person who does dry ablution with the existence of water. Evidences could conflict and could be equivalent, thereby cancelling each other out. As such, one of the evidences must be shown to be weightier and preponderant, so that it is enacted. Without this process, evidences and rulings would be lost. *Ijtihād* is predicated on this section just as a whole item is predicated on the existence of its parts.

إذا تقرر هَذَا، فَاعْلَم أَن التَّرْتِيب هُوَ جعل كل وَاحِد من شَيْئَيْنِ فَأكْثر فِي رتبته الَّتِي يَسْتَحِقهَا بِوَجْه مَا.

Categorisation means to place two or more items in their due order, based on some criteria.

فالإجماع مقدم على بَاقِي أَدِلَّة الشَّرْع، لكَونه قَاطعا مَعْصُوما عَن الْخَطَأ بِشَهَادَة الْمَعْصُوم بذلك، وَيقدم مِنْهُ الْإِجْمَاع الْقطعِي الْمُتَوَاتر، ثمَّ الْإِجْمَاع النطقي

الثَّابِت بالآحاد، ثمَّ يَلِيهِ الْإِجْمَاع السكوتي الْمُتَوَاتر، ثمَّ الْإِجْمَاع السكوتي الثَّابِت بالآحاد.

(i) Consensus is given priority over all other evidences of the religion, since it is definitive and infallible, as testified to by the infallible. Consensus is then categorised as follows: (a) Recurrent and definitive consensuses are given priority. (b) Then an uttered consensus that is established through singular reports. (c) Then silent consensus that is recurrent. (d) Then silent consensuses that are established through singular reports.

ثمَّ يقدم فِي الدّلَالَة بعد الْإِجْمَاع بأنواعه الْكتاب، ويساويه فِي ذَلِك متواتر السّنة، لِأَنهُمَا جَمِيعًا قاطعان من جِهَة الْمَتْن، وَلذَلِك جَازَ نسخ كل وَاحِد مِنْهُمَا بِالْآخرِ.

(ii) Qur'ān and recurrent Sunnah are considered next, after all types of consensus, because they are both definitive in their texts, which is also why they can abrogate one another.

ثمَّ خبر الْوَاحِد.

(iii) Singular reports are considered next.

ثمَّ الْقيَاس.

(iv) Analogy is considered after singular reports.

هَكَذَا قَالَ فِي (الرَّوْضَة) و(مختصرها).

This was the order given in *Rawḍat al-Nāẓir* and its summation, *Mukhtaṣar al-Rawḍah*.

وَقَالَ المرداوي فِي (التَّحْرِير) وَتَبعهُ الفتوحي فِي (مُخْتَصره): يقدم بعد خبر الْآحَاد قَول صَحَابِيّ، فَالقِيَاس. فَجعلَا قَول الصَّحَابِي مقدما على الْقيَاس، وَهُوَ الْحق.

Al-Mardāwī stated in *al-Taḥrīr*, as was confirmed by al-Futūḥī in his summation, "After singular reports come the statements of the companions, and then analogy."[558] They both considered the statements of companions to be preferable to analogy, and their view is the truth.

558 [T] *Taḥrīr al-Manqūl* (p. 347).

وَأما التَّصرف فِي الْأَدِلَّة - من حَيْثُ الْعُمُوم وَالْخُصُوص، وَالْإِطْلَاق وَالتقْيِيد وَنَحْوه من حمل الْمُجْمل على الْمُبين وَأَشْبَاه ذَلِك - فقد سبق فِي بَابه.

As for dealing with the evidences inasmuch as generality, particularization, qualified and unqualified language, and so forth, such as explaining obscure texts by using clarified texts, and so forth, such things have been discussed in their relevant chapter.

فصل
Section

وَأما التَّرْجِيح: فَهُوَ: تَقْدِيم أحد طريقي الحكم لاختصاصه بِقُوة الدّلَالَة، ورجحان الدليل عبارة عَن كَون الظن الْمُسْتَفَاد مِنْهُ أقوى، وَاسْتِعْمَال الرجحان - حَقِيقَة - إِنَّمَا هُوَ فِي الْأَعْيَان الجوهرية، والأجسام، تقول: هَذا الدِّينَار، أَو الدِّرْهَم رَاجِح على هَذَا، لِأن الرجحان من آثار النَّقْل والاعتماد، وَهُوَ من خَواص الْجَوَاهِر، ثمَّ اسْتعْمل فِي الْمعَانِي مجَازًا نَحْو: هَذَا الدَّلِيل أَو الْمَذْهَب رَاجِح على هَذَا، وَهَذَا الرَّأي أرجح من ذَلِك.

As for determining preponderance (*tarjīḥ*), it means to prefer either of the two means that lead to a ruling over another because of their particular strength in signification. The strength of evidence means that the probability it provides is stronger. The term comes from the word *rujḥān*, which is a scale used to weigh substances and matter. One can say, "This dinar or dirham weighs more than that one," because that pertains to their weight, a quality of substances. These terms are used metaphorically, when saying, "This evidence or view is weightier (*rājiḥ*) than this other view."

وَقَالَ ابْن الباقلاني: لَا يرجح بعض الْأَدِلَّة على بعض، كَمَا لَا يرجح بعض الْبَيِّنَات على بعض. وَكَلَامه هَذَا لَيْسَ بِشَيْء، ومورد التَّرْجِيح إِنَّمَا هُوَ الأدِلة الظنية، من الألفَاظ المسموعة، والمعاني المعقولة، كنصوص الكتاب وَالسّنة وظواهرهما، وكأنواع الأقيسة والتنبيهات المستفادة من النُّصُوص، فَلَا مدْخل لَهُ فِي الْمذَاهب من غير تمسك بِدَلِيل، فَلَا يُقَال: مَذْهَب الشَّافِعِي مثلا أرجح من مَذهَب أبي

حنيفَة أَو غَيرهمَا أَو بِالْعَكْسِ، لَكِن هَذَا بِاعْتِبَار مَجْمُوع مَذْهَب على مَجْمُوع مَذْهَب آخر. وَأما من حَيْثُ الْأَدِلة على الْمسَائِل فالترجيح ثَابت، وَلَا مدْخل للترجيح أَيْضا فِي القطعيات، لِأنهُ لَا غَايَة وَرَاء الْقطعِي.

Ibn al-Bāqillānī said, "Evidences are not weighed over one another, just as testimonies are not weighed over another." His view has no weight. The concept of preponderance applies to probable evidences, namely, the words that are heard and the meanings that are understood, such as the univocal and apparent texts of the Qur'ān and Sunnah, and such as the different types of analogies and indications provided by the texts. As such, preponderance is not something that can be assigned to the various *madhhabs* without there being evidence to suggest it. As such, one cannot say, for example, "The *madhhab* of al-Shāfi'ī is preponderant over that of Abu Ḥanīfah," or the opposite. However, this is when the judgement is given to a *madhhab* as a whole over another *madhhab* as a whole. As for the evidences in the issues, one can commit to discovering preponderance. Further, preponderance does not apply to definitive matters, since there would be no point.[559]

وَقَوْلنَا: من الْأَلْفَاظ المسموعة. أردنَا بِهِ نُصُوص الْكتاب وَالسّنة، فيدخلها التَّرْجِيح، فَإِذا تعَارض نصان، فَأَما أَن يجهل تاريخهما، أَو يعلم، فَإِن جهل، قدمنَا الْأَرْجَح مِنْهَا بِبَعْض وُجُوه التَّرْجِيح، وَإِن علم تاريخهما، فإمَّا أَن يُمكن الْجمع بَينهمَا بِوَجْه من وُجُوه الْجمع أَو لَا، فَإِن أمكن جمع بَينهمَا من حَيْثُ يَصح الجمع، إِذْ الوَاجِب اعْتِبَار أَدِلَّة الشَّرْع جَمِيعهَا مَا أمكن، وَإِن لم يُمكن الْجمع، فَالثَّانِي نَاسخ إِن صَحَّ سندهما، أَو أحدهمَا كذب إِن لم يَصح سَنَده، إِذْ لَا تنَاقض بَين دَلِيلين شرعيين، لِأَن الشَّارِع حَكِيم، والتناقض يُنَافِي الْحِكْمَة، فأحد المتناقضين يكون بَاطِلا إِمَّا لكَونه مَنْسُوخا، أَو لكذب نَاقله، أَو لخطئه بِوَجْه مَا من وُجُوه تصفح أُمُورهم فِي النقليات، أَو لخطأ النَّاظر فِي العقليات، كالإخلال بشكل الْقيَاس أَو شَرطه وَنَحْو ذَلِك.

---

559 [T] The purpose of finding preponderance is to discover which view is most probably the truth. In the case of definitive matters, the fact is known and definite, and as such, there is no point to finding which is weightier. Refer to *Sharḥ Mukhtaṣar al-Rawḍah* (3/687).

When I said, "the words that are heard," I was referring to the texts of the Qur'ān and Sunnah. These texts are disposed to be given preponderance over one another. If two texts conflict, either the date is known or it is unknown. If the date is unknown, we use various methods of finding the preponderant view to give priority to one evidence over the other. If the date is known, there might either be a way to reconcile between them or not. If they can be reconciled, that should be done in a valid, cogent way, since the obligation is to take all evidences of the religion into account, so long as one is able. However, if they cannot be reconciled, the later text abrogates the earlier one, if both chains of narration of the texts are authentic. If one of the chains of narration is weak, it is a lie, since no two religious evidences can be wholly contradictory, because the religion is coherent and contradiction negates coherence. Therefore, one of the two contradictory texts is invalid, either because it is abrogated, is a lie, or is a mistake in some way pertaining to transmitted texts. Or, it could be because of a mistake in conceptualising a rational matter, such as mistakenly applying *qiyās* or its precondition, or something else.

وَقد يخْتَلف اجْتِهَاد الْمُجْتَهدين فِي النُّصُوص إِذا تَعَارَضَت، فَمنهمْ من يسْلك طرق التَّرْجِيح، وَمِنْهُم من يسْلك طَرِيق الْجمع، وَالصَّوَاب تَقْدِيم الْجمع على التَّرْجِيح مَا أمكن إِلا أَن يُفْضِي الْجمع إِلَى تكلف يغلب على الظن بَرَاءَة الشَّرْع مِنْهُ، وَيبعد أَنه قَصده، فيتَعَيَّن التَّرْجِيح ابْتِدَاء.

Mujtahid scholars may differ in their conclusions on how to treat conflicting texts. Some take the route of discovering preponderance, and others take the route of reconciling. The correct method is, so long as one is able, to give priority to reconciliation over discovering preponderance, unless the reconciliation leads to far-fetched conclusions that the legislation is most probably free of and did not intend. In that case, one should begin with finding preponderance of one text over the other.

إِذا علم هَذَا، فَاعْلَم أَن التَّرْجِيح الْوَاقِع فِي الْأَلْفَاظ إِمَّا أَن يكون من جِهَة الْمَتْن، أَو السَّنَد، أَو الْقَرِينَة.

Inasmuch as the discovery process of preponderance pertains to expressions and words, sometimes it is applicable to the text, sometimes to the chain of narration, and sometimes to an inference:

أما من جِهَة السَّنَد: فَيقدم الْمُتَوَاتر على الْآحَاد القطعية، وَالْأَكْثَر رُوَاة على الْأَقَل، وَيقدم المسند على الْمُرْسل، لِأَنهُ مُخْتَلف فِي كَونه حجَّة، وَالْمَرْفُوع على الْمَوْقُوف، والمتصل على الْمُنْقَطع، والمتفق عَلَيْهِ فِي ذَلِك على الْمُخْتَلف فِيهِ، وَرِوَايَة المتقن والأتقن، وَالضَّابِط والأضبط، والعالم والأعلم، والورع والأورع، والتقي والأتقى على غَيرهم، وَصَاحب الْقِصَّة والملابس لَهَا على غَيره لاختصاصه بمزيد علم يُوجب إِصَابَته.

First: As it pertains to the chain of narration, the recurrent narrations should be given preference over the definitive singular narrations. Narrations that have more reporters should be given preference over narrations that have less reporters. A narration with a connected chain of narration to the Prophet ﷺ is given priority over one with a *mursal* chain, since there is disagreement on whether the latter is considered evidence. Further, a ḥadīth raised to the Prophet ﷺ is given priority over one ascribed to the companion. A connected chain of narration is preferable to a disconnected one. A ḥadīth that is agreed on is preferable to one that is disagreed on. The precise, trustworthy, scholarly, abstinent, and pious person, respectively, should be given priority. Also, in the case where there are two of each, the one who is more precise, more trustworthy, more scholarly, more abstinent, and more pious should be given priority in their respective narrations. The one to whom the situation affected and the one who was in attendance is given preference over others, because they have additional contextual knowledge that would necessitate that their versions of narrations are true.

مِثَال رِوَايَة صَاحب الْقِصَّة حَدِيث مَيْمُونَة رَضِي الله عَنْهَا: تزَوجنِي رَسُول الله صلى الله عَلَيْهِ وَسلم وَهُوَ حَلَال، فحديثها يقدم على حَدِيث ابْن عَبَّاس: أَنه تزَوجهَا وَهُوَ محرم.

An example of a narration of the person affected in the story is that of Maymūnah ﷺ where she said, "Allah's Messenger ﷺ married me while he was outside of the state of ritual sanctity."[560] Her narration is given priority over that of Ibn ʿAbbās, who reported, "He married her while in the state of ritual sanctity."[561]

---

560 Reported by Muslim (1411), Abu Dāwūd (1843) and Ibn Mājah (1964).
561 Reported by al-Bukhārī (4/45) and Muslim (1410).

وَمِثَال حَدِيث الملابس - يَعْنِي الْمُبَاشر للقصة - حَدِيث أبي رَافع: تزوج رَسُول الله صلى الله عَلَيْهِ وَسلم مَيْمُونَة وَهُوَ حَلَال، وَكنت السفير بَينهمَا، فَإِنهُ يقدم على حَدِيث ابْن عَبَّاس.

An example of someone who was in attendance is the narration of Abu Rāfiʿ, who said, "Allah's Messenger ﷺ married Maymūnah while he was outside of the state of ritual sanctity, and I was the messenger between them."[562] This narration, therefore, should be given priority in acceptance over that of Ibn ʿAbbās.

وَتقدم الرِّوَايَة المتسقة المنتظمة على الرِّوَايَة المضطربة، والمتأخرة على الْمُتَقَدّمَة. وَمعنى اتساق الرِّوَايَة: انتظامها، وَهُوَ ارتباط بعض ألفاظها بِبَعْض، ووفاء الْأَلْفَاظ بِالْمَعْنَى من غير نقص مخل، وَلَا زِيَادَة مخلة. واضطرابها: تنافر ألفاظها، واختلافها بالزِّيَادَةِ وَالنَّقْص.

A coherent narration is given preference over a confused one, and the later narration should be given preference over the earlier one. The meaning of a coherent narration is one that does not have a deficiency nor addition that violates its sequence. The meaning of a confused narration is one where its wordings are disharmonious or where the wordings of the narration differ, with some adding words and others subtracting them.

وَمِثَال الْمُتَأَخِّرَة الحَدِيث الصَّحِيح: كَانَ آخر الْأَمريْنِ من رَسُول الله صلى الله عَلَيْهِ وَسلم ترك الْوضُوء مِمَّا مست النَّار.

An example of a later ḥadīth is, "The last of the two injunctions from Allah's Messenger ﷺ was to not perform ablution after eating something cooked over fire."[563]

وَأما تَقْدِيم رِوَايَة مُتَقَدم الْإِسْلَام على متأخره، فَفِيهِ خلاف، اخْتَار القَاضِي، وَالْمجد، والطوفي: أَنَّهُمَا سَوَاء، وَقَالَ ابْن عقيل، وَالْأَكْثَر: ترجح رِوَايَة مُتَأَخر الْإِسْلَام على متقدمه. قلت: وَهُوَ الصَّوَاب، لِأَنهُ يحفظ آخر الْأَمريْنِ عَن رَسُول

562 Reported by Aḥmad (6/393) and al-Tirmidhī (841).
563 Reported by Abu Dāwūd (192) and al-Nasāʾī (1/108).

الله صلى الله عَلَيْهِ وَسلم، وَعَلِيهِ عمل أَصْحَابنَا فِي الْفُرُوع.

The scholars have differed on whether the narrations of those who were earlier in acceptance of Islam are preferable to those of companions who accepted Islam later. Al-Qāḍī, al-Majd, and al-Ṭūfī all stated that their narrations are equal. Ibn ʿAqīl and the majority said that the narrations of those who were later in acceptance of Islam are weightier than those of companions who accepted Islam earlier. My view coincides with the latter view, because the one who accepted Islam later would know the latest of the commandments of Allah's Messenger ﷺ. This was enacted by our *aṣḥāb* in their determination of substantive law.

وَفِي تَقْدِيم رِوَايَة الْخُلَفَاء الْأَرْبَعَة خلاف أَيْضا. وَاخْتَارَ تقديمهم الْفَخر والطوفي، وتبعهما المرداوي فِي (التَّحْرِير) والفتوحي فِي (مُخْتَصره). قَالَ الطوفي: وَالأشبه تَرْجِيح رِوَايَة الأكابر - يَعْنِي من الصَّحَابَة رضوَان الله عَلَيْهِم - انْتهى. قلت: وَهُوَ الْحق.

There has also been a disagreement on whether the narrations of the Four Caliphs are to be given priority. Al-Fakhr and al-Ṭūfī viewed that they should be given priority. Al-Mardāwī in *al-Taḥrīr* and al-Futūḥī in its summation both concurred. Al-Ṭūfī went on to say, "The more veracious view is that the narrations of the senior companions are preferable."[564] The view he stated is the truth.

وَأما التَّرْجِيح اللَّفْظِيّ من جِهَة الْمَتْن، فَهُوَ مَبْنِيّ على تفَاوت دلالات الْعبارَات فِي أَنْفسهَا، فيرجح الأدل مِنْهَا، فالأدل، فالنص مقدم على الظَّاهِر، وللظاهر مَرَاتِب بِاعْتِبَار لَفظه أَو قرينته، فَيقدم الْأَقْوَى مِنْهَا فالأقوى بِحَسب قُوَّة دلَالَته وضعفها.

Second: As it pertains to discovering preponderance between the texts of the narrations, it is based on the levels of the meanings signified by the phrases of the texts themselves. The most explicit in signification must be given preponderance. Therefore, a univocal text is given preference over an apparent text. Apparent texts vary in levels depending on their wording or any inferences that can be made. The stronger should be given priority; this is all in proportion to its strength or lack thereof.

---

564 [T] *Sharḥ Mukhtaṣar al-Rawḍah* (3/697).

وَيقدم الْخبَر الْمُخْتَلف فِي اللَّفْظ فَقَط على مَا اتَّحد لَفظه وَلم يخْتَلف، لدلَالَة اخْتِلَاف أَلْفَاظه على اشتهاره. وَاخْتَارَ قوم تَقْدِيم مَا اتَّحد لَفظه على غَيره. وَلكُل من الْقَوْلَيْنِ مُرَجّح، فَهِيَ مَسْأَلة اجتهادية.

A text whose wording is differed on is preferred over a text that has only a single wording, because the fact that there are numerous wordings indicates it is more popular in consumption among scholars. Other scholars took the view that the narration with a single wording is preferable. Both views have evidences that might lead one to view it as more veracious, making it an issue of scholarly discretion.

وَالصَّوَاب أَن اخْتِلَاف الْأَلفَاظ - إِن كَانَ مِمَّا يخْتَلف بِهِ الْمَعْنى وَلَو أدنى اخْتِلَاف أَو تغير انتظام الرِّوَايَة واتساقها - قدم المتحد لفظا، وَإِلا فالمختلف، أَو يتعارضان.

The correct view is that when the wordings differ and this leads to differences in meaning or cohesion of the narration, the narration that has a single wording should be given priority. If not, the one that has differing wordings should be given priority. Or, they should be considered contradictory, and neither given preference.

وَأما الْمُخْتَلف معنى فَإِنَّهُ لَا يُعَارض المتحد معنى، قولا وَاحِدًا، وَيقدم ذُو الزِّيَادَة على مَا لَا زِيَادَة فِيهِ والمثبت على النَّافِي، إِلَّا أَن يسند النَّفْي إِلَى علم بِالْعدمِ، كَقَوْلِه: اعْلَم أَن فلَانا فعل كَذَا. لَا عدم الْعلم، كَأَن يَقُول: لم أعلم أَن فلَانا فعل كَذَا. فَإِن اسْتَندَ الحديثان إِلَى عدم الْعلم، اسْتَويَا.

Narrations that differ in meaning do not contradict narrations that have a single meaning, according to all scholars. The narration that has additional information should be given preference to those that do not have those additions. Also, the narrations of those affirming something are given preference to those denying it, unless the denial is relating to knowledge that something did not exist, for example, if someone says, "I know that someone did not do that action." If the denial is based on lack of knowledge, such as when one says, "I do not know that this person has done this action," it is not given preference. If two aḥadīth are based on lack of knowledge that an occurrence happened, they are equal.

وَيقدم مَا اشْتَمل على حظر أَو وَعِيد على غَيره احْتِيَاطًا. وَهَذِه طَرِيقَة القَاضِي أبي يعلى. وَقيل: لَا يرجح بذلك، ويرجح النَّاقِل عَن حكم الأَصْل على غَيره، مثل أَن يلْتَزم أَن الأَصْل فِي الْأَشْيَاء الإِبَاحَة، ثمَّ نجد دَلِيلين، أَحدهمَا: حَاكم بِالْإِبَاحَةِ، وَالثَّانِي بالحظر.

A narration that consists of a prohibition or a promise of punishment should be given preference over other narrations, out of caution. This was the view of al-Qadī Abu Ya'lā. It was stated that such things are not factors in preponderance. A narration that changes the ruling from its default ruling is given preference. For example, one can state that the default ruling on things is legality. As such, there would be two evidences, the first being the default ruling of lawfulness, and the other would be the prohibition.

وَإِذا تعَارض دليلان أَحدهمَا مسْقط للحد، وَالْآخر يُوجِبهُ، أَو أَحدهمَا يُوجب الجِزْيَة، وَالْآخر يمْنَعهَا، لم يرجح مسْقط الْحَد، وَمُوجب الْجِزْيَة على مقابلهما، إِذْ لَا تَأْثِير لذَلِك فِي صدق الرَّاوِي. وَقيل: بلَى لموافقتهما الأَصْل.

If two evidences conflict, and one of them waives a penalty and the other obligates it, or one waives [freedom][565] and another obligates it, the one that waives the penalty and the one that obligates [freedom] are not given preponderance over the other narration, since that has no effect on the truthfulness of its narrator. Another view stated was that the narration waving the penalty and nullifying slavery should be given preference, because they concur with the default ruling.[566]

وَيقدم قَوْله عَلَيْهِ الصَّلَاة وَالسَّلَام على فعله، لِأَن القَوْل لَهُ صِيغَة دلَالَة، بِخِلَاف الْفِعْل، فَإِنَّهُ لَا صِيغَة لَهُ تدل بِنَفسِهَا، وَإِنَّمَا دلَالَة الْفِعْل لأمر خَارج، وَهُوَ كَونه عَلَيْهِ السَّلَام وَاجِب الِاتِّبَاع، فَكَانَ القَوْل أقوى، فيرجح لذَلِك.

The statements of the Prophet ﷺ are given priority over his actions, because the statements have a wording, and that wording has a signification, contrary to the action, which has no signification in and of itself. The sig-

565 [T] Al-Shaykh Ibn Badrān quotes this as "*jizyah* (الجزية)," whereas in *Sharḥ Mukhtaṣar al-Rawḍah* (where he is quoting from) it states, "freedom (الحرية)." Refer to *Sharḥ Mukhtaṣar al-Rawḍah* (3/703).

566 [T] The default ruling being that penalties are not applied and that a person is free.

nification of an action is external, which is that it is obligatory to follow the Prophet ﷺ. As such, his statement is weightier, and is given preponderance.

وَأما التَّرْجِيح من جِهَة الْقَرِينَة، فَإِذا تعَارض عامان: أَحدهمَا بَاقٍ على عُمُومه، وَالْآخر قد خص بِصُورَة فَأكثر، رجح الْبَاقِي على عُمُومه على الْمَخْصُوص، وَكَذَلِكَ يقدم مَا خص بِصُورَة على مَا خص بصورتين، وَهَكَذَا فِيمَا بعد ذَلِك. وَحَاصِله: أَنه يقدم الْأَقَل تَخْصِيصًا على الْأَكْثَر.

Third: As for the discovery process of preponderance as it pertains to inferences, when two general texts conflict, and one keeps its generality and the other is particularized in one or more scenarios, the one that retains its generality is considered preponderant over the particularized one. Likewise, a text that is particularized in a single scenario is given preference over one that is particularized in two scenarios, and so forth. To summarise: the text that has been particularized less is given priority over the one that has been particularized more.

وَيقدم من النصين مَا تَلقاهُ الْعلمَاء بِالْقبُولِ، وَلم يلْحقهُ إِنْكَار من أحد مِنْهُم، على مَا فِيهِ الْإِنْكَار من بَعضهم. وَهَذِه الْقَاعِدَة تقضي بِتَقْدِيم مَا رُوِيَ فِي (الصَّحِيحَيْنِ) أَو أَحدهمَا على مَا لم يرو فيهمَا، لتلقي الْأمة لَهما بِالْقبُولِ.

The text that scholars have received with acceptance and without objection is given priority over those that have been rejected by some. This necessitates that the aḥadīth that are in the *Two Ṣaḥīḥs*, or either of them, are given priority to those that are not reported in those collections, since the Ummah has received those two books with acceptance.

وَيقدم مَا أنكرهُ وَاحِد على مَا أنكرهُ اثْنَان، وَهَكَذَا فِي اثْنَيْنِ وَثَلَاثَة.

The narration that is denied by a single scholar is given preference to one that is denied by two or more.

ويرجح مَا عضده عُمُوم كتاب، أَو سنة، أَو قِيَاس شَرْعِي، أَو معنى عَقْلِي، على مَا لم يعضده بِشَيْء من ذَلِك، فَإِن عضد أحد النصين قُرْآن وَالْآخر سنة، فَفِيهِ رِوَايَتَانِ: أَحدهمَا: يقدم مَا عضده الْقُرْآن، وَهُوَ الْمُخْتَار. وَثَانِيهمَا: يقدم مَا

عضده الحَدِيث، وَالضَّابِط أَنه يرجح مَا تخيل فِيهِ زِيَادَة قُوَّة كَائِنا من ذَلِك مَا كَانَ، وَقد تتخيل زِيَادَة الْقُوَّة مَعَ اتِّحَاد النَّوْع واختلافه.

Any narration that is strengthened by the generalities of the Qur'ān or Sunnah, or any legal analogy or rational concept, is given preference over narrations that have none of those supporting evidences. If one narration is supported with a verse from the Qur'ān and the other narration is supported with a Sunnah, there are two views: (i) The one that is supported by the Qur'ān is given preference. This is the chosen view. (ii) The one that is supported by the ḥadīth is given preference. The factor considered in these scenarios is that if an additional strengthening element is envisaged, it is given priority, irrespective of what that element is. The element that is envisaged to increase the strength could be of the same type of evidence or could be a different type of evidence.

ويرجح مَا ورد ابْتِدَاء على غير سَبَب على مَا ورد على سَبَب، لاحْتِمَال اخْتِصَاصه بِسَبَبِهِ، وَمَا عمل بِهِ الْخُلَفَاء الراشدون على غَيره على القَوْل الْمُخْتَار.

If something is initiated without any prior cause, it is preferred over texts initiated due to a cause, since there is the possibility that the ruling entailed in the latter is specific to the cause. If the Rightly-Guided Caliphs act on some ruling, it is given priority over other views, according to the chosen view.

تَنْبِيه: قَالَ الطوفي فِي شرح (مُخْتَصره): إِذا وجدنَا فتيا صَحَابِيّ مَشْهُور بِالْعلمِ وَالْفِقْه على خلاف نَص، لا يجوز لنا أَن نجزم بخطئه الْخَطَأ الاجتهادي، لاحْتِمَال ظُهُور الصَّحَابِيّ على نَص أو دَلِيل رَاجِح أفْتِي بِهِ، فَإِن الصَّحَابَة رَضِي الله عَنْهُم أقرب إِلَى معرفَة النُّصُوص منا، لمعاصرتهم للنَّبِي صلى الله عَلَيْهِ وَسلم. وَكم من نَص نبوي كَانَ عِنْد الصَّحَابَة - رَضِي الله عَنْهُم - ثمَّ دثر فَلم يبلغنَا، وَذَلِكَ كفتيا عَليّ وَابْن عَبَّاس رَضِي الله عَنْهُمَا: أن الْمُتَوفى عَنْهَا زَوجهَا تَعْتَد بأطول الأَجلَيْنِ، وَنَحْوهَا من الْمسَائِل الَّتِي نقم بعض النَّاس على عَليّ فِيهَا لمُخَالفته للنَّص، وخطئه بذلك. انْتهى.

Note: Al-Ṭūfī stated in his book *Sharḥ Mukhtaṣar al-Rawḍah*, "If we find the edict of a companion who is known to have knowledge and understanding of the law, and it contradicts a text, we cannot definitively state that they made a mistake in their scholarly discretion, due to the possibility of the companion knowing another text or evidence that is preponderant, and giving an edict according to it. The reason is that the companions ﷺ are likelier to know the texts than we are, since they lived in the same age of the Prophet ﷺ. Many a time, a prophetic text would exist amongst the companions, and then fall into oblivion without reaching us. Examples are the edicts given by ʿAlī and Ibn ʿAbbās ﷺ that the woman whose husband has died should adhere to the longer of the two waiting times,[567] and other similar issues that were the causes for people to harbour malice against ʿAlī for contradicting a text, and declaring him wrong for doing so."[568]

وَإِذا تعَارض خبران، أَحدهمَا قد نقل عَن رِوَايَة خِلَافه قولا أَو فعلا، وَالْآخر لم ينْقل عَن رِوَايَة خِلَافه، قدم الثَّانِي.

If two reports conflict, and the narrator of one report has been reported to have contradicted the narration, either in statement or action, and the narrator of the other report is not known to have contradicted their narration, the second is given priority.

وَلَا تَرْجِيح بقول أهل الْمَدِينَة، خلافًا لبَعض الشَّافِعِيَّة، وَلَا بقول أهل الْكُوفَة، خلافًا لبَعض الْحَنَفِيَّة.

The views of the people of Madīnah bear no weight in declaring preponderance, contrary to some Shāfiʿī scholars[569], nor are the views of the residents of Kufah, contrary to some Ḥanafī scholars.

567 Reported by al-Bukhārī (8/500) and Muslim (1485). Abu Salamah ibn ʿAbd al-Raḥmān and Ibn ʿAbbās once gathered with Abu Hurayrah and were discussing a woman who gave birth a few nights after her husband passed away. Ibn ʿAbbās opined that her waiting period is the longer of the two waiting times, meaning, the waiting time of death, which is four months and ten days, and the waiting period of post-delivery. Abu Salamah stated that she has ended her waiting period when she gave birth, and they disputed on the matter. Abu Hurayrah stated that he agreed with Abu Salamah, and they sent Kurayb, the servant of Ibn ʿAbbās to Umm Salamah to ask her about that issue. He told them that Umm Salamah said, "Subayʿah al-Aslamiyyah gave birth a few nights after her husband passed away, and she mentioned that to the Prophet ﷺ and he commanded her to remarry."

568 [T] *Sharḥ Mukhtaṣar al-Rawḍah* (3/709).

569 [T] Perhaps he means Mālikī scholars.

وَإِذا كَانَ الْخَبَر يحْتَمل وُجُوهًا، وتتجه لَهُ محامل، ففسره الرَّاوِي على بَعْضهَا، كَانَ مَا فسره الرَّاوِي عَلَيْهِ مقدما على بَاقِيهَا، وَكَذَلِكَ إِن ترجح بعض الِاحْتِمَالَات الْمَذْكُورَة بِوَجْه من وُجُوه التَّرْجِيح، كَانَ مقدما على غَيره، مَا لم يتَرَجَّح بذلك.

If a narration has many potential meanings, and its narrator explains it according to one of those potential meanings, the explanation of the narrator is given preference over the other potential meanings. Likewise, if one of those potential meanings appears to be preponderant in some way, it is preferable over other narrations that do not have such strengthening factors.

وَأما التَّرْجِيح من جِهَة الْقيَاس، فَهُوَ إِمَّا من جِهَة أَصله، أَو علته، أَو قرينَة تقترن بِأحد القياسين تعضده، فيترجح على الآخر.

As for preponderance of an analogy, it can occur either in the precedent, the *ratio legis*, or some other inferential evidence that would support either of the two analogies, making it weightier than the other.

أما الأول فَمن وُجُوه:

Preponderance of the precedent can occur in a number of ways:

أَحدهَا: إِذا أمكن قِيَاس الْفَرْع على أصلين - حكم أَحدهمَا ثَابت بِالْإِجْمَاع، وَالْآخر ثَابت بِالنَّصِّ - كَانَ الْقيَاس على الأَصْل الثَّابِت بِالْإِجْمَاع مقدما على مَا ثبت بِالنَّصِّ.

First. If a new case can be analogised to two precedents, and the ruling of one of the precedents is established via consensus and the other is established via a text, the analogy that extends from the precedent established via consensus is given priority over the one established via a text.

ثَانِيهَا: حكم الأَصْل الثَّابِت بِمُطلق النَّص رَاجِح على حكم الأَصْل الثَّابِت بِالْقِيَاسِ.

Second. The ruling of the precedent that is established via any text is prioritised over the ruling of the precedent that is established via analogy.

ثَالِثهَا: حكم الأَصْل الثَّابت بِالْقُرْآنِ الْكَرِيم، أَو بِالسنةِ المتوترة رَاجِح على حكم الأَصْل الثَّابِت بآحاد السّنة.

Third. The ruling of the precedent that is established via the Qur'ān or recurrent Sunnah is prioritised over the ruling of the precedent established via a singular narration.

رَابِعهَا: الحكم الْمَقِيس على أُصُول أَكثر رَاجِح على غَيره.

Fourth. The ruling that is analogized to multiple precedents is prioritised over a ruling that is analogized to less precedents.

خَامِسهَا: الْمَقِيس على أصل لم يخص رَاجِح على الْمَقِيس على أصل مَخْصُوص.

Fifth: The case that is analogized to an un-particularised precedent is weightier than the one that is analogized to a particularised precedent.

وَبِالْجُمْلَةِ إِن حكم أصل الْقيَاس حكم مُسْتَنده الَّذِي ثَبت بِهِ، فَمَا قدم من المستندات قدم مَا ثَبت بِهِ من أُصُول الأقيسة.

Generally speaking, the ruling of the precedent of the analogy is that of its reference from which it was established. Wherever the reference for the ruling of the precedent is given priority, so too is the ruling established, which is then used as a precedent for an analogy.

وَأما الثَّانِي: وَهُوَ تَرْجِيح الْقيَاس من جِهَة علته - فَمن وُجُوه أَيْضا.

As for discovering preponderance from the perspective of its *ratio legis*, it occurs in a number of ways:

أَولهَا: ترجح الْعلَّة الْمجمع عَلَيْهَا على الْعلَّة الَّتِي لَيْسَ بمجمع عَلَيْهَا.

First. The *ratio legis* that is established via consensus is prioritised over the one where there is no consensus.

ثَانِيهَا: ترجح الْعلَّة المنصوصة على المستنبطة.

Second. The *ratio legis* that is stated in the text is prioritised over the one that is deduced.

ثَالِثهَا: ترجح الْعلَّة الَّتِي تثبت عليتها بالتواتر على الَّتِي تثبتت عليتها بالآحاد.

Third. The *ratio legis* that is established through recurrence is prioritised over the one that is established through singular ways.

رَابِعهَا: ترجح الْعلَّة الْمُنَاسبَة على غَيرهَا. لَكِن هَذَا فِي العلتين المنصوصتين أَو المستنبطين، أما إِذا كَانَت إِحْدَاهمَا منصوصة، فَهِيَ الراجحة، سَوَاء كَانَت مُنَاسبَة أَو أَشد مُنَاسبَة أَو لَا.

Fourth: A *ratio legis* that is relevant and suitable is prioritised over other *ratione legis*. However, this is applicable if the two *ratione legis* are textually stated or are deduced. As for when one is textual, it is preponderant, regardless if it is relevant and suitable, more relevant and suitable than the other *ratio legis*, or none of those options.

خَامِسهَا: ترجح الْعلَّة الناقلة عَن حكم الأَصْل على الْعلَّة المقررة عَلَيْهِ.

Fifth. The *ratio legis* that establishes a ruling that goes against the default ruling is prioritised over the one that retains it.

سادسها: ترجح الْعلَّة الَّتِي توجب الْحَظْر على الَّتِي توجب الْإِبَاحَة.

Sixth. The *ratio legis* that necessitates impermissibility is prioritised over the one that necessitates lawfulness.

سابعها: ترجح الْعلَّة المسقطة للحد على موجبته، وموجبة الْعتْق على ناقيته، وَالَّتِي هِيَ أخف حكما على الَّتِي هِيَ أثقل حكما، لَكِن هَذَا كُله فِي المنصوصتين، وَفِي المستنبطتين، أما فِي المنصوصة والمستنبطة، فالمنصوصة وَاجِبَة التَّقْدِيم فِي كل حَال.

Seventh. The *ratio legis* that waives the penalty is given priority over the one that obligates it, and the one that necessitates freedom is preferable over the one that negates it. The one that necessitates the easier ruling is prioritised over the one that establishes the more difficult one. However, this all applies in the case where the *ratione legis* are both textually stated or are deduced. As for when one is textually stated and the other is deduced, the textually stated one must be prioritised in every situation.

ثامنها: ترجع الْعلَّة الَّتِي هِيَ وصف على الَّتِي هِيَ اسْم، لِأَن التَّعْلِيل بالأوصاف مُتَّفق عَلَيْهِ. بِخِلَاف العليل بالأسماء، فتعليل الربا فِي الذَّهَب بِكَوْنِهِ مَوْزُونا يقدم على التَّعْلِيل بِكَوْنِهِ ذَهَبا.

Eighth. The *ratio legis* that is an attribute is prioritised over the one that is a name, because establishing a *ratio legis* through attributes is agreed on. The same cannot be said about establishing a *ratio legis* through names. For example, establishing that usury applies to gold because it is weighed is preponderant over stating that it applies to gold because it is gold.

تاسعها: تقدم الْعلَّة الْمَرْدُودَة إِلَى أصل قَاس الشَّارِع عَلَيْهِ على غَيرهَا، كقياس النَّبِي صلى الله عَلَيْهِ وَسلم الْقبْلَة فِي الصّيام على الْمَضْمَضَة.

Ninth. The *ratio legis* that is referenced to a precedent that the legislator has used as a precedent for an analogy is preferable to other *ratione legis*. An example is that the Prophet ﷺ analogized kissing while fasting to rinsing the mouth.

عَاشرهَا: ترجح الْعلَّة المطردة على غير المطردة إِن قيل بِصِحَّتِهَا.

Tenth. The *ratio legis* that is consistent is given preference to the one that is not consistent, if it is even stated to be valid at all.

حَادي عشرهَا: الْعلَّة المنعكسة راجحة على غير المنعكسة، على الْقَوْل بِاشْتِرَاط الْعَكْس فِي الْعِلَل. نعم إِن الْعلَّة القاصرة لَا يُمكن الْقيَاس عَلَيْهَا، وَلَيْسَ فَائِدَة هَذَا تَرْجِيح أحد القياسين على الآخر، بل فَائِدَته أَنا إِذا رجحنا المتعدية أمكن الْقيَاس.

Eleventh. The co-exclusive *ratio legis* is given priority over the one that is not co-exclusive, according to the view that states that a *ratio legis* must be co-exclusive. An intransitive *ratio legis* cannot be used in an analogy. Although there is no point in determining which analogy is preferable over the other in the case of a transitive and intransitive *ratio legis*. The point of mentioning this here is that if we were to state that the transitive *ratio legis* is preponderant, we can state that an analogy can be made based on it.

وَيقدم الحكم الشَّرْعِيّ واليقيني على الْوَصْف الْحسي والإثباتي عِنْد قوم، ويرجح

الْمُؤثر على الملائم، والملائم على الْغَرِيب، وَقد سبقت حقائقها وأحكامها وصفاتها ومراتبها عِنْد الْكَلَام على طَرِيق إِثْبات الْعلَّة عِنْد ذكر أَقسَام الْمُنَاسب.

Religious and definitive rulings are given priority over perceptible and probative attributes, according to some scholars. Effective attributes are given priority over appropriate ones, and appropriate ones are given priority over unique ones. Their realities, rulings, attributes, and varying levels have all been previously discussed when speaking about how to establish a *ratio legis*, when the categories of suitability and relevance were discussed.

وَإِذا دارت عِلّة الْقيَاس بَين وصف مُنَاسِب وشبهي قدم الْمُنَاسب، لِأَنهُ مُتَّفق عَلَيْهِ، والمصلحة فِيهِ ظَاهِرة، بِخِلَاف الشبهي فيهمَا.

If the *ratio legis* of an analogy revolves between either being a suitable and relevant attribute as opposed to a resembling attribute, the suitable and relevant attribute is given priority, since it is agreed on and the utility in doing so is obvious, contrary to the resembling attribute.

وَاعْلَم أَن تفاصيل التَّرْجِيح لم تَنْحَصِر فِيمَا ذَكرْنَاهُ، وَقد ذكر فِي كتب الْأُصُول المطولة أَكثر مِنْهَا، وَالْقَاعِدَة الْكُلية فِي التَّرْجِيح أَنه مَتى اقْترن بِأحد الدَّلِيلَيْنِ المتعارضين أَمر نقلي كآية أَو خبر، أَو اصطلاحي كعرف أَو عَادَة، عَاما كَانَ الْأَمر أَو خَاصًّا، أَو قرينَة عقلية، أَو لفظية، أَو حَالية وَأَفَاد ذَلِك زِيَادَة ظن، رجح بِهِ. وَقد حصل بِهَذَا بَيَان الرجحان من جِهَة الْقَرَائِن، فَلَا حَاجَة إِلَى ذكر مَا وعدنا بِهِ من الْقسم الثَّالِث الَّذِي هُوَ التَّرْجِيح بالقرائن مفصلا.

Know, too, that the details of discovering preponderance are not limited to what we mentioned. In the compendiums of legal theory, more details are mentioned. The universal principle on the topic of preponderance is that whenever the two conflicting evidences are coupled with something transmitted, such as a verse or a ḥadīth, something conventional, such as customs or habits, regardless if it is general or particular, or some rational, textual, or situational inference, and that increases the probability, the one whose probability has increased is declared preponderant. With that statement, we have clarified what it means for one evidence to be preponderant based on inference, and as such, there is no need for further detailed discussions on the third type, namely, deciphering preponderance through use of inferences.

وَوجه الرجحان فِي أَكثر هَذِه الترجيحات ظَاهر لمن تفطن وأعمل مَا وهبه الله تَعَالَى من الْفِكر السَّلِيم وَالْعقل الْمُسْتَقيم.

The manifest nature of preponderance in many of these cases is obvious to someone who notices and uses the sound thinking and upright intellect that Allah the Exalted has given them.

وَاعْلَم أَنِّي حِينمَا تَكَلَّمت على هَذَا النَّوْع كنت أَسْتَمدّ من:

When speaking about these topics, I drew from various books, such as:

(الرَّوْضَة) للْإِمَام موفق الدّين عبد الله الْمَقْدِسِي صَاحب (الْمُغنِي) وَغيره.

Al-Rawḍah by al-Imām Muwaffaq al-Dīn ʿAbdullāh al-Maqdisī, the author of *al-Mughnī* and other works.

وَمن (مُخْتَصر الرَّوْضَة) وَشَرحهَا للعلامة نجم الدّين الطوفي.

Mukhtaṣar al-Rawḍah and its commentary, both authored by the great scholar Najm al-Dīn al-Ṭūfī.

وَمن (التَّحْرِير) للعلامة عَلَاء الدّين المرداوي، وَمن (مُخْتَصره) وَشَرحه، كليهمَا للعلامة أَحْمد الفتوحي صَاحب كتاب (مُنْتَهى الإرادات).

Al-Taḥrīr by the great scholar ʿAlā' al-Dīn al-Mardāwī, as well its summary and the summary's commentary, the latter two by the great scholar, Aḥmad al-Futūḥī, who also authored *Muntahā al-Irādāt*.

وَمن (مُخْتَصر ابْن الْحَاجِب)، وَشَرحه للعلامة عضد الدّين الإيجي.

Mukhtaṣar Ibn al-Ḥājib by al-Imām Ibn al-Ḥājib, as well as its explanation by the great scholar ʿAḍud al-Dīn al-Ījī.

فَهَؤُلَاءِ أُصُول كتابي هُنَا، وَكنت كثيرا مَا أراجع.

Those books are the foundation of my book. Also, of the books that I reviewed are:

(مسودة الْأُصُول) لمجد الدين وَابْنه عبد السَّلَام وحفيده شيخ الْإِسْلَام، وهم بَنو تَيمِية.

Musawwadat al-Uṣūl by Majd al-Dīn, his son ʿAbd al-Salām, and his grandson, Shaykh al-Islām, all of whom were from the family of Taymiyyah.

وَ(حُصُول المأمول من علم الْأُصُول) لصديق حسن خَان.

Ḥuṣūl al-Mảmūl min ʿIlm al-Uṣūl by Ṣiddīq Ḥasan Khān.

مَعَ الْتِقَاط فَوَائِد كَثِيرَة من:

I also gained many useful and beneficial points from:

(الْمُسْتَصْفى) للغزالي.

Al-Mustaṣfā by al-Ghazālī.

و(منتهى السول) للآمدي.

Muntahā al-Sūl by al-Āmidī.

وَ(جمع الْجَوَامِع) لِابْنِ السُّبْكِيّ، وَشَرحه للمحلى.

Jamʿ al-Jawāmiʿ by Ibn al-Subkī and its explanation by al-Maḥallī.

و(التنقيح)، وَشَرحه (التَّوْضِيح) لصدر الشَّرِيعَة، وحاشيته (التلويح) لسعد الدين التَّفْتَازَانِيّ.

Al-Tanqīḥ and its explanation *al-Tawḍīḥ* by Ṣadr al-Sharīʿah, as well as its commentary *al-Talwīḥ* by Ṣaʿd al-Dīn al-Taftāzānī.

و(المنهاج) للبيضاوي، وَشَرحه للأسنوي.

Al-Minhāj al-Wuṣūl ilā ʿIlm al-Uṣūl by al-Bayḍāwī, as well as its explanation by al-Isnawī.

و(التمهيد) لأبي الْخطاب.

Al-Tamhīd fi Uṣūl al-Fiqh by Abu ʿl-Khaṭṭāb.

و(الواضح) لِابْنِ عقيل.

Al-Wāḍiḥ fi Uṣūl al-Fiqh by Ibn ʿAqīl.

و(آداب الْمُفْتِي) لِابْنِ حمدَان.

Ādāb al-Muftī by Ibn Ḥamdān.

فأسأله تَعَالَى أَن يوفقنا لكل خير وينفع بِنَا، وينفعنا، ويجعلنا أَهلا لخدمة هَذِه الشَّرِيعَة آمين.

I ask Allah the Exalted to grant us divine aid to reach every goodness, to allow others to benefit from us, to allow us to benefit, and to make us worthy of servicing this religion. *Āmīn.*

العقد السَّادِس

Chapter Six

فِيمَا اصْطلحَ عَلَيْهِ المؤلفون فِي فقه الإِمَام أَحْمد مِمَّا يحْتَاج إِلَيْهِ الْمُبْتَدِي وأبرز الْأَسْمَاء الَّتِي تذكر فِي مصنفاتهم

On the Terminologies Beginners Need to Know Used by Authors Who Wrote About the Jurisprudence of al-Imām Aḥmad, and Their Most Important Works

قد غلب على الْفُقَهَاء من أَصْحَابنَا وَغَيرهم، أَنهم يكتفون فِي الألقاب بِالنِّسْبَةِ إِلَى صناعَة أَو محلّة أَو قبيلَة أَو قَرْيَة، فَيَقُولُونَ مثلا: الْخرقِيّ نِسْبَة إِلَى بيع الْخرق، والخلال وَالطيَالِسِي، وَالْحَرْبِيّ نِسْبَة إِلَى بَاب حَرْب - محلة فِي بَغْدَاد - كالزهري والتميمي وكاليونيني والبعلي والصاغاني والحراني وأمثال ذلك.

A common practice of the jurists of the Ḥanbalī *madhhab*, and other schools of thought, is that, when giving nicknames, they refer to a person based on their vocation, area of living, tribe, or town. As an example, al-Khiraqī is referred to as such because he would sell *khiraq* (cloth). The same can be said about al-Khallāl (making of *khal* which is vinegar) and al-Ṭayālisī (maker of *ṭayālis*, which are palliums). Al-Ḥarbī is a reference to *Bab Ḥarb*, which is a place in Baghdad, and it can be applied to others, such as al-Zuhrī, al-Tamīmī, al-Yūnīnī, al-Baʿli, al-Ṣaghānī, al-Ḥarrānī, and so forth.

فيطلقون تِلْكَ الْأَسْمَاء بِلَا تَعْظِيم، وَكَانَت هَذِه عَادَة الْمُتَقَدِّمين، ثمَّ جَاءَ من بعدهمْ فَأَكْثرُوا الغلو فِي الألقاب الَّتِي تَقْتَضِي التَّزْكِيَة وَالثنَاء، فَقَالُوا علم الدّين، ومحيي الدّين ومجد الدين وشهاب الدّين إِلَى غير ذَلِك من الألقاب الضخمة، وَعم ذَلِك بِلَاد الْعَرَب والعجم، وَلم يرتض هَذَا غَالب الْعلمَاء، فقد نقل فِي (الْفُرُوع) عَن القَاضِي أبي يعلى أَنه قَالَ: وَتكره التَّسْمِيَة بِكُل اسْم فِيهِ تفخيم

أَو تَعْظِيم، وَاحْتج بِهَذَا على معنى التسمي بِالْملكِ، لقَوْله تعالى ﴿لَهُ الْملك﴾ [التغابن: ١] وَأجَاب بِأَن الله إِنَّمَا ذكره إِخْبَارًا عَن الْغَيْر، وللتعريف، فَإِنَّهُ كَانَ مَعْرُوفا عِنْدهم بِهِ، وَلِأَن الْملك من أَسمَاء الله المختصة، بِخِلَاف حَاكم الْحُكَّام، وقاضي الْقُضَاة، لعدم التَّوْقِيف، وَبِخِلَاف الأوحد فَإِنَّهُ يكون فِي الْخَيْر وَالشَّر، وَلِأَن الْملك هُوَ الْمُسْتَحق لمَالِك. وَحَقِيقَته: إِمَّا التَّصَرُّف التَّام وَإِمَّا التَّصَرُّف الدَّائِم، وَلَا يصحان إِلَّا لله.

They use those words without venerating them. This was the practice of the early scholars. Afterwards, [people] were very extravagant when giving nicknames that implied purity and praise. For example, they would say, *'Alam al-Dīn* (the Sign of the Religion), *Muḥyī al-Dīn* (the Reviver of the Religion), *Majd al-Dīn* (the Honour of the Religion), *Shihāb al-Dīn* (the Shooting Star of the Religion), and other grand titles. That became a practice in the lands of the Arabs and non-Arabs alike. The majority of scholars did not like this practice. In *al-Furū'*, there is a quotation of al-Qāḍī Abu Ya'lā, who said, "It is disliked to give a name that indicates grandness or veneration."[570] He[571] used this to prove the prohibition[572] of calling oneself a king, because Allah the Exalted said: **{The kingdom is His.}** [Qur'ān 64:1] He responded by saying that Allah the Exalted mentioned that quality when informing about others and to define people, because some people are known as kings to their people. Otherwise, the word "King" is one of Allah's Names, specific to Him, contrary to "the Ruler of Rulers," and "the Judge of Judges," neither of which is mentioned in the scriptures. The term "the singular," can be used for good and bad meanings. A king, though, is deserving of kingship, and it refers to having absolute control or everlasting control, both of which are descriptions belonging only to Allah.

وَفِي (الصَّحِيحَيْنِ) بِلَفْظِهِ أَو دلَالَة حَال، وَأبي دَاوُد «وأخنا الْأَسْمَاء يَوْم الْقِيَامَة وأخبثه رجل كَانَ سمي ملك الْأَمْلَاك لَا ملك إِلا الله».

Al-Bukhārī, Muslim, either in wording or in spirit, and Abu Dāwūd re-

570 [T] *Al-Furū' wa Taṣḥīḥ al-Furū'* (6/105).
571 [T] Meaning al-Qāḍī Abu Ya'lā.
572 [T] In the printed version of *al-Madkhal*, it states, "meaning," but what I placed is more accurate, as per the published version of *al-Furū'* (6/105), which is where al-Shaykh Ibn Badrān is quoting from here.

ported that the Prophet ﷺ said, **"One of the most obscene and wicked names on the Day of Resurrection is that belonging to a man who was called 'the king of kings.' There is no king but Allah."**[573]

وروى الإمَام أَحْمد **«اشْتَدَّ غضب الله على رجل تسمى ملك الأَمْلَاك، لَا ملك إِلا الله»**.

Al-Imām Aḥmad reported, **"The anger of Allah is severe against a man who takes the name, 'the king of kings.' There is no king but Allah."**[574]

وَأفْتى أَبُو عبد الله الصَّيْمَرِيّ الْحَنَفِيّ، وَأَبُو الطّيب الطَّبَرِي، والتميمي الْحَنْبَلِي بِالْجَوَاز. وَالْمَاوَرْدِيّ بِعَدَمِه، وَجزم بِهِ فِي شرح مُسلم. قَالَ ابْن الْجَوْزِيّ فِي تَارِيخه: قَول الْأَكْثَر هُوَ الْقيَاس إِذا أُرِيد مُلُوك الدنْيَا، وَقَول الْمَاوَرْدِي أولى للْخَبَر.

Abu 'Abdullāh al-Ṣaymarī al-Ḥanafī, Abu 'l-Ṭayyib al-Ṭabarī, and al-Tamīmī al-Ḥanbalī all said that it is permissible. After them, al-Māwardī stated that it is impermissible, stating that authoritatively in his explanation of Muslim. Ibn al-Jawzī stated in his book on history, "The position of the majority is due to analogy, if a person intends [king of] kings of the worldly life. However, the position of al-Māwardī is preferred, because of [its alignment with] the texts."

وَأنكر بعض الْحَنابِلَة على بَعضهم فِي الخطبَة قَوْله: الْملك الْعَادِل ابْن أيوب، وَاعْتذر الْحَنْبَلِيّ بقوله عَلَيْهِ السَّلَام: **«ولدت فِي زمن الْملك الْعَادِل»** وَقد قَالَ الْحَاكِم فِي (تَارِيخه): الحَدِيث الذِي روته الْعَامَّة **«ولدت فِي زمن الملك الْعَادِل»** بَاطِل، لَيْسَ لَهُ أصل بإِسْنَاد صَحِيح، وَلَا سقيم.

Some Ḥanbalī scholars rejected that some other [Ḥanbalī scholars] were referring to a ruler in their speech, saying, "The just king, the son of Ayyūb." The Ḥanbalī scholar [that did this] defended himself by quoting the statement of the Messenger ﷺ **"I was born in the age of the just king."** Al-Ḥākim said in his book on history, "This ḥadīth that the commoners report, which is, **'I was born in the age of the just king,'** is invalid; it cannot be traced to any authentic nor inauthentic chain of narration."

---

573 Reported by al-Bukhārī (10/486) and Abu Dāwūd (4961).
574 Reported by Aḥmad (2/492).

قلت: أورد فِي (الْفُرُوع) هَذِه الْحِكَايَة مُبْهمَة، وَهِي إِنَّمَا كَانَت من الشَّيْخ أبي عمر الْمَقْدِسِي، فَإِنهُ هُوَ الَّذِي قَالَ: وانصر الْملك العَادِل، فَرد عَلَيْهِ اليونيني، فاحتج أَبُو عمر بِالْحَدِيثِ، فَأنكرهُ اليونيني، وَبَين بُطْلَانه، قَالَ فِي (الْفُرُوع): وَلم يمْنَع جمَاعَة التَّسْمِيَة بِالْملكِ. انْتهى.

I say: This story was mentioned in *al-Furūʿ*, but without explicit mention of its details, though it was al-Shaykh Abu ʿUmar al-Maqdisī who said, "Come to the aid of the just king," and al-Yūnīnī rejected his statement, to which Abu ʿUmar quoted the alleged ḥadīth, and al-Yūnīnī repudiated it, clarifying its falsehood. In *al-Furūʿ*, it is stated, "A group [of scholars] did not forbid calling someone 'the king.'"[575]

وَمنع أَبُو عبد الله الْقُرْطُبِيّ فِي كِتَابه (شرح الْأَسْمَاء الْحسنى) من النعوت الَّتِي تَقْتَضِي التَّزْكِيَة وَالثنَاء، كزكي الدّين، ومحيي الدّين، وَعلم الدّين، وَشبه ذَلِك.

Abu ʿAbdullāh al-Qurtubī, in his book *Sharḥ al-Asmāʾ al-Ḥusnā*, prohibited such descriptions that necessitate praise and extolling, such as "the Purifier of the Religion (*Zakī al-Dīn*)," "the Reviver of the Religion (*Muhyī al-Dīn*)," and 'the Sign of the Religion (*ʿAlam al-Dīn*),' and so forth.

وَقَالَ أَحْمد بن النّحاس الدمياطي الْحَنَفِيّ، ثمَّ الشَّافِعِي فِي كِتَابه (تَنْبِيه الغافلين) عِنْد ذكر الْمُنْكَرَات: فَمِنْهَا: مَا عَمت بِهِ الْبلوى فِي الدّين من الْكَذِب الْجَارِي على الألسن، وَهُوَ مَا ابتدعوه من الألقاب، كمحيي الدّين، وَنور الدّين، وعضد الدّين، وغياث الدّين، ومعين الدّين، وناصر الدّين، وَنَحْوهَا من الْكَذِب الَّذِي يتَكَرَّر على الْأَلْسِنَة حَال النداء والتعريف والحكاية، وكل هَذَا بدعَة فِي الدّين ومنكر. انْتهى.

Aḥmad ibn al-Naḥḥās al-Dimyātī, the Ḥanafī turned Shāfiʿī scholar, said, in his book, *Tanbīh al-Ghāfilīn*, when mentioning some reprehensible actions, "One example is what has become so widespread in this religion, namely, a form of lying with the tongues: the innovated titles, such as "the Reviver of the Religion (*Muhyī al-Dīn*)," "the Light of the Religion (*Nūr al-Dīn*)," "the Support of the Religion (*ʿAḍud al-Dīn*)," "the Helper of the

575 [T] *Al-Furūʿ wa Taṣḥīḥ al-Furūʿ* (6/106).

Religion (*Ghiyāth al-Dīn*)," "the Assister of the Religion (*Mu'īn al-Dīn*)," "the Aider of the Religion (*Nāṣir al-Dīn*)," and so forth. These are lies that are oft-repeated by people when calling, describing, and telling stories of [scholars]. This is an innovation in the religion and is reprehensible."[576]

وَقَالَ ابْن الْقيم: وَقد كَانَ جمَاعَة من أهل الدّين يتورعون عَن إِطْلَاق قَاضِي الْقُضَاة، وحاكم الْحُكَّام، قَالَ: وَكَذَلِكَ تحرم التَّسْمِيَة بِسَيِّد النَّاس، وَسيد الْكل، كَمَا يحرم بِسَيِّد ولد آدم. انْتهى. أَي: لأنهُ لَا يَلِيق إِلا بِهِ صلى الله عَلَيْهِ وَسلم.

Ibn al-Qayyim said, "A group of people of religion abstained from using the term, 'the Judge of Judges (*Qāḍī al-Quḍāh*),' and 'the Ruler of Rulers (*Ḥākim al-Ḥukkām*).' Similarly, it is forbidden to use, as a title, 'the Chief of People (*Sayyid al-Nās*),' 'the Chief of all (*Sayyid al-Kull*),' and 'the Chief of the Children of Adam (*Sayyid Walad Ādam*).'"[577] I.e. because it is not suitable except for the Prophet ﷺ.

وَقد توَسط الحجاوي فِي (إقناعه) فَقَالَ: وَمن لقب بِمَا يصدق فعله للقبه، جَازَ، وَيحرم مَا لم يَقع على مخرج صَحِيح، على أَن التَّأْوِيل فِي كَمَال الدّين وَشرف الدّين، أن الدين كمله وشرفه، قَالَه ابْن هُبَيْرَة. هَذَا كَلَامه.

Al-Ḥajjāwī took a moderate view in his book, *al-Iqna'*, where he stated, "Whoever is given a title that coincides with their actions, it is permissible, but it is not permissible to use titles that do not have a permissible interpretation. With that said, the two terms, 'the Perfection of Religion (*Kamāl al-Dīn*),' and 'the Honour of Religion (*Sharaf al-Dīn*),' have been interpreted as, the religion has perfected and honoured the person, as stated by Ibn Hubayrah."[578]

وَمن اصْطِلَاح الْفُقَهَاء التَّسْمِيَة بشيخ الْإِسْلَام، وَكَانَ الْعرف فيما سلف أَن هَذَا اللَّفْظ، يُطلق على من تصدر للإفتاء، وَحل المشكلات فِيمَا شجر بَين النَّاس من النزاع وَالْخِصَام، من الْفُقَهَاء الْعِظَام، والفضلاء الفخام، كشيخ الْإِسْلَام أَحْمد

576 [T] *Tanbīh al-Ghāfilīn 'an A'māl al-Jāhilīn wa Tahdhīr al-Sālikīn min Af'āl al-Jahilīn* (p. 509).
577 [T] *Tuhfat al-Mawlūd* (p.115).
578 [T] *Al-Iqnā'* (1/410).

بن تَيْمِية الْحَرَّانِي، وَصَاحب (الْمُغنِي) وَغَيرهمَا.

A common practice is for jurists to use the term, "the Teacher of Islam (*Shaykh al-Islām*)." Among the Salaf, it was customary to use this title to refer to a person who passes rulings and mediates between people amidst disputes and differences. It was used to refer to the great jurists and the honorable noblemen, such as Shaykh al-Islām Aḥmad ibn Taymiyyah al-Ḥarrānī, the author of *al-Mughnī* [Muwaffaq al-Dīn Ibn Qudāmah], and others.

وَقَالَ السخاوي فِي كتاب لَهُ سَمَّاهُ (الْجَوَاهِر) كَانَ السّلف يطلقون شيخ الْإِسْلَام على المتبع لكتاب الله وَسنة رَسُوله، مَعَ التبحر فِي الْعُلُوم من الْمَعْقُول وَالْمَنْقُول. قَالَ: وقد يُوصف بِهِ من طَال عمره فِي الْإِسْلَام، فَدخل فِي عداد **«من شَاب فِي الْإِسْلَام، كَانَت لَهُ نورا»** وَلم تكن هَذِه اللَّفْظَة مَشْهُورَة بَين القدماء بعد الشَّيْخَيْنِ: الصّديق والفاروق، فَإِنَّهُ ورد وصفهما بذلك، ثمَّ اشْتهر بِهِ جمَاعَة من عُلَمَاء السّلف، حَتَّى ابتذلت على رَأس الْمِئَة الثَّامِنَة، فوصف بهَا من لَا يُحْصى، وَصَارَت لقبا لمن ولي الْقَضَاء الأكبر، وَلَو عري عَن الْعلم وَالسّن. هَذَا كَلَامه.

Al-Sakhāwī said in his book *al-Jawāhir*, "The Salaf would use the title *Shaykh al-Islām* to refer to a person who follows the Book of Allah and the Sunnah of His Messenger, while also having encyclopedic knowledge in rational and textual sciences. The title can also be used for those who live long lives as Muslims, thereby being indirectly mentioned within those mentioned, **"Whoever becomes old as a Muslim, it will be, for them, a light."**[579] This term was not popular among the early Muslims after the two *shaykhs*, [Abu Bakr] al-Ṣiddīq and [ʿUmar ibn al-Khaṭṭāb] al-Fārūq. There are some narrations that show they were described as such, then it became more popular with a group of the scholars of the Salaf, until its worth became devalued in the 8th century, where innumerable amounts of people were given the title. At that time, it was given to those who were appointed to be major judges, even if they were stripped of any knowledge or mature age."[580]

ثمَّ صَارَت الْآن لقبا لمن تولى منصب الْفَتْوَى وَإِن عري عَن الدّين وَالتَّقوى،

579 Reported by Aḥmad (4/535-536), al-Tirmidhī (1643) and al-Nasāʾī (6/27).
580 [T] *Al-Jawāhir wa 'l-Durar fī Tarjamat Shaykh al-Islām Ibn Ḥajar* (1/65).

بل صَارَت الألقاب الضخمة للباس والزي، والعمائم والكبار، والأكمام الواسعة، وَالْعلم عِنْد الله.

[I say:] nowadays, it has become a title given to those who pass rulings, even if they have no religiosity nor piety. Actually, the grand titles are now for adornment and fashion, as are large turbans and wide sleeves. Knowledge belongs to Allah.

وَحَيْثُ أفضى بِنَا الْمقَال إِلَى هَذَا الْبَحْث، فلنذكر المبهمات مِمَّن أطلق فِي كتب الْفِقْه:

Since we have led to this discussion, let us mention some obscure names mentioned without clarification in the books of law:

فَنَقُول: إِن أَصْحَابنَا مُنْذُ عصر القَاضِي أبي يعلى إِلَى أثْنَاء الْمِئَة الثَّامِنَة يطلقون لفظ (القَاضِي) ويريدون بِهِ عَلامَة زَمَانه محَمَّد بن الْحُسَيْن بن مُحَمَّد بن خلف بن أَحْمد بن الْفراء، الملقب بِأبي يعلى، وَكَذَا إِذا قَالُوا: أَبُو يعلى وأطلقوه. وَإِذا قَالُوا: أَبُو يعلى الصَّغِير، فَالْمُرَاد بِهِ وَلَده مُحَمَّد صَاحب الطَّبَقَات.

Since the time of al-Qāḍī Abu Ya'lā until approximately the 8th century, our *aṣḥāb* have used the term *al-Qāḍī* to refer to the great scholar of his time, Muḥammad ibn al-Ḥusayn ibn Khalaf ibn Aḥmad ibn al-Farrā', whose title was Abu Ya'lā. Likewise, they referred to him if they just said "Abu Ya'lā" without qualification. If they said, "Abu Ya'lā al-Ṣaghīr (the Junior)," they are referring to his son, Muḥammad, the author of *Ṭabaqāt [al-Ḥanābilah]*.

وَأما الْمُتَأَخّرُونَ كصاحب (الْإِقْنَاع) و(المنتهى) وَمن بعدهمَا، فيطلقون لفظ (القَاضِي) ويريدون بِهِ القَاضِي عَلَاء الدّين عَليّ بن سُلَيْمَان السَّعْدِيّ المرداوي ثمَّ الصَّالِحِي، وَكَذَلِكَ يلقبونه بالمنقح لِأَنهُ نقح (الْمقنع) فِي كِتَابه (التَّنْقِيح المشبع) وَكَانَت وَفَاته سنة خمس وَثَمَانِينَ وَثَمَان مِئَة، ويسمونه الْمُجْتَهد فِي تَصْحِيح الْمَذْهَب.

As for the later scholars, such as the authors of *al-Iqnā'* and *al-Muntahā* and those after them, they use the term *al-Qāḍī* to refer to al-Qāḍī 'Alā' al-

Dīn ʿAlī ibn Sulaymān al-Siʿdī al-Mardāwī, later to be known as, al-Ṣāliḥi. They also refer to him as '*Al-Munaqqiḥ* (the Reviser),' since he revised the text known as *al-Muqniʿ* in his work *al-Tanqīḥ al-Mushbiʿ*. He passed away in the year 885. They refer to him as being a *mujtahid* in that he verified many positions in the *madhhab*.

وَقَالَ الشَّيْخ مَنْصُور البهوتي الْحَنْبَلِيّ فِي (شرح الإِقْنَاع): إِذا أطلق الْمُتَأَخّرُونَ - كصاحب (الْفُرُوع) وَ(الْفَائِق)، و(الاختيارات) وَغَيرهم - (الشَّيْخ) أَرَادوا بِهِ الشَّيْخ الْعَلامَة موفق الدّين أَبَا مُحَمَّد عبد الله بن قدامَة الْمَقْدِسِي. وَإِذا قيل الشَّيْخَانِ فالموفق وَالْمجد - يَعْنِي مجد الدّين عبد السَّلَام ابْن تَيمِية - وَإِذا قيل: (الشَّارِح) فَهُوَ الشَّيْخ شمس الدّين عبد الرَّحْمَن ابْن الشَّيْخ أبي عمر الْقُدسِي، وَهُوَ ابْن أخي موفق الدّين وتلميذه، وَإِذا أطلق (القَاضِي) فَالْمُرَاد بِهِ القَاضِي أَبُو يعلى مُحَمَّد بن الْحُسَيْن بن مُحَمَّد بن خلف بن أَحْمد الْفراء. وَإِذا قيل: وَ(عنهُ) يَعْنِي عَن الإِمَام أَحْمد رَحمَه الله. وَقَوْلهمْ: (نصا) مَعْنَاهُ: لنسبته إِلَى الإِمَام أَحْمد أَيْضا. هَذَا كَلَامه.

Al-Shaykh Manṣūr al-Buhūtī al-Ḥanbalī stated in his book *Sharḥ al-Iqnāʿ*, "When the later scholars, such as the respective authors of *al-Furūʿ*, *al-Fāʾiq*, and *al-Ikhtiyārāt* use the term '*shaykh*,' they are referring to the *shaykh* and grand scholar, Muwaffaq al-Dīn, Abu Muḥammad ʿAbdullāh ibn Qudāmah al-Maqdisī. When they say, 'The two *shaykhs*,' they are referring to al-Muwaffaq and al-Majd (meaning, Majd al-Dīn ʿAbd al-Salām ibn Taymiyyah). When they say, 'the Explainer (*al-shāriḥ*),' they are referring to al-Shaykh Shams al-Dīn ʿAbd al-Raḥmān, the son of al-Shaykh Abu ʿUmar al-Maqdisī, and the nephew and student of Muwaffaq al-Dīn Ibn Qudāmah. With the unqualified term 'the Judge (*al-qāḍī*),' they refer to al-Qāḍī Abu Yaʿlā Muḥammad ibn al-Ḥusayn ibn Muḥammad ibn Aḥmad al-Farrāʾ. When they say, 'And from him (*wa ʿanhu*),' they mean [a narration] from al-Imām Aḥmad ﷬. When they say, 'Textually (*naṣṣan*),' they mean it is a text attributed to al-Imām Aḥmad, as well."[581]

قلت: وَإِذا أطْلقُوا (الشَّرْح) أَرَادوا بِهِ شرح (الْمقنع) الْمُسَمّى بـ(الشافي) لِابْنِ أبي

581 [T] *Kashāf al-Qināʿ ʿan Matn al-Iqnāʿ* (1/20).

عمر الْمُتَقَدّم، وَهَذَا اصْطِلَاح خَاص، وَإِلَّا فالقاعدة أَن شَارِح متن مَتى أطلق الشَّرْح أَو الشَّارِح أَرَادَ بِهِ أول شَارِح لذَلِك الْمَتْن، لَكِن لما كَانَ كتاب (الْمقنع) أصلا لمتون المُتَأَخِّرين، وَكَانَ شمس الدّين أول شَارِح لَهُ، لَا جرم استعملوا هَذَا الِاصْطِلَاح، وَلَا مشاحة فيه.

I say: When they refer to a book by calling it *al-Sharḥ*, they are referring to the explanation of *al-Muqni'* called *al-Shāfī*, written by Ibn Abi 'Umar, who was previously mentioned. This is a specific terminology. Otherwise, the general rule is that when a scholar explaining a text says, "The explanation/explainer," they are referring to the earliest commentator on that particular text. However, considering that *al-Muqni'* was the foundational work on which the texts of the latter-day scholars relied, and Shams al-Dīn was the first one to explain it, there is no doubt they used this terminology, and there is nothing wrong with it.

وَكَثِيرًا مَا يُطلق الْمُتَأَخّرُونَ (الشَّيْخ) ويريدون بِهِ شيخ الْإِسْلَام ابْن تَيْمِية، وَمِنْهُم ابْن قندس فِي حَوَاشِي (الْفُرُوع).

Often times, latter-day scholars used the term '*shaykh*," to refer to Shaykh al-Islam Ibn Taymiyyah. An example of someone who does this is Ibn Qandas in his commentaries on *al-Furū'*.

وَإِذا أطلق الإِمَام عَليّ بن عقيل وَأَبُو الْخطاب (شَيخنَا) أَرَادوا بِهِ القَاضِي أَبَا يعلى، وَإِذا أطلقهُ ابْن الْقيم وَابْن مُفلِح - صَاحب (الْفُرُوع) - أَرَادَا بِهِ شيخ الْإِسْلَام. وَقَالَ صَاحب (الْإِقْنَاع) ومرادي بالشيخ يَعْنِي حَيْثُ أطلق شيخ الْإِسْلَام بَحر الْعُلُوم أبو العباس أَحْمد ابن تَيْمِية. انْتهى. وَقد سلك طَرِيقَته من جَاءَ بعده.

If al-Imām 'Alī ibn 'Aqīl or Abu 'l-Khaṭṭāb use the term, "Our *shaykh*," they are referring to al-Qāḍī Abu Ya'lā. If Ibn al-Qayyim or Ibn Mufliḥ (the author of *al-Furū'*) use the term, they are referring to Shaykh al-Islām. The author of *al-Iqnā'* said, "When I say, '*shaykh*,' (meaning, without other qualifiers), I am referring to Shaykh al-Islām, the ocean of knowledge, Abu 'l-'Abbās Aḥmad ibn Taymiyyah."[582] Scholars who lived after [al-Ḥajjawi] also took the same approach.

---

582 [T] *Al-Iqnā'* (1/3).

ثمَّ اعْلَم أن الْأَصْحَاب فِي مصنفاتهم كثيرا مَا يستعملون المبهمات في الْأَسْمَاء والكتب، فيبقى ذَلِك مغلقا على من لَا اطلَاع لَهُ على كتب الطَّبَقَات والتاريخ. فَمن ثمَّ خطر لي أَن أبين بعض ذَلِك، خدمَة للمبتدئين، وَتَذْكِرَة لغَيرهم فَأَقُول:

Many times, in their authorships, the *aṣḥāb* will use obscure names to refer to people or books. This would be a source of confusion for someone who is not aware of the books that detail the lives of scholars or books of history. As such, I decided to clarify some of those obscurities, to serve beginners and to remind those who are not beginners:

ابْن الْمُنَادِي: هُوَ أَحْمد بن جَعْفَر بن مُحَمَّد بن عبد الله، توفّي سنة سِتّ وَثَلَاثِينَ وثلاث مئة.

Ibn al-Munādī: Aḥmad ibn Jaʿfar ibn Muḥammad ibn ʿAbdullāh, he died in the year 336.

ابْن قَاضِي الْجَبَل: أَحْمد بن الْحسن بن عبد الله بن أبي عمر الْمَقْدِسِي، من بني قدامَة، من تلامذة شيخ الْإِسْلَام ابن تَيْمِية، صَاحب كتاب (الْفَائِق)، توفّي سنة إِحْدَى وَسبعين وَسَبْع مئة، وَله اختيارات فِي الْمَذْهَب.

Ibn Qāḍī al-Jabal: Aḥmad ibn al-Ḥasan ibn ʿAbdullāh ibn Abi ʿAmr al-Maqdisī, from the tribe of Qudāmah. He was a student of Shaykh al-Islām Ibn Taymiyyah, and the author of a book known as *al-Fā'iq*. He died in the year 771, and he has his own opinions on matters within the *madhhab*.

ابْن حمدَان: أَحْمد بن حمدَان بن شبيب بن حمدَان بن شبيب بن حمدَان النميري الْحَرَّانِي؛ الْفَقِيه الأصولي، لَهُ (الرِّعَايَة الصُّغْرى) و(الكبرى) وفيهَا نقُول كَثِيرَة جدا، وَبَعضهَا غير مُحَرر، توفي سنة خمس وَتِسْعين وست مِئَة.

Ibn Ḥamdān: Aḥmad ibn Ḥamdān ibn Shabīb ibn Ḥamdān ibn Shabīb ibn Ḥamdān al-Numayrī al-Ḥarrānī. He was a jurist and a scholar of legal theory. He wrote *al-Riʿāyat al-Sughra*, and *[al-Riʿāyat] al-Kubrā*. They have many quotations within them, but some are not well studied or explored. He died in the year 695.

أَبُو بكر النجاد: أَحْمد بن سُلَيْمَان بن الْحسن بن إِسْرَائِيل بن يُونُس، الْمُحدث، توفّي سنة ثَمَان وَأَرْبَعين وثلاث مئة.

Abu Bakr al-Najjād: Aḥmad ibn Salmān ibn al-Ḥasan ibn Isrāʾīl ibn Yūnus. He was a scholar of ḥadīth who died in the year 348.

لأَثْرَم: أَحْمد بن مُحَمَّد بن هانئ الطَّائِي، الإِمَام الْجَلِيل: الْحَافِظ، مَاتَ بعد السِّتين وَمِئَتَيْن، وَكَانَ عِنْده تيقظ عَجِيب أثنى عَلَيْهِ يحيى بن معِين، وَقَالَ إِبْرَاهِيم ابن الْأَصْفَهَانِي: هُوَ أحفظ من أبي زرْعَة الرَّازِي، وأتقن، روى عَنهُ النَّسَائِيّ وَجَمَاعَة. وَقَالَ في (تذهيب الْكَمَال): أَبُو بكر الْأَثْرم الْخُرَاسَانِي الْبَغْدَادِيّ الإسكاف الْفَقِيه الْحَافِظ، أحد الْأَعْلَام، صَاحب السّنَن، عَن أَحْمد بن حَنْبَل، وَأبي نعيم، وَعَفَّان والقعنبي وَخلق. روى عَنهُ النَّسَائِيّ. قَالَ ابْن حبان: كَانَ من خِيَار عباد الله. انْتهى. وَهُوَ أحد الناقلين رِوَايَات الإِمَام أَحْمد. وَأكْثر أَصْحَابنَا الْمُتَقَدّمين يَقُولُونَ عَن أَحَادِيث: رَوَاهُ الْأَثْرَم.

Al-Athram: Aḥmad ibn Muḥammad ibn Hāniʾ al-Ṭāʾī, the lofty *imām*. He died in the year 260, and he possessed an immense level of memory. Yaḥyā ibn Maʿīn praised him, and Ibrāḥīm ibn al-Aṣfahānī stated, "He memorised more and was more precise than Abu Zurʿah al-Rāzī." Al-Nasāʾī and others reported from him. In *Tahdhīb al-Kamāl*, it states, "Abu Bakr al-Athram al-Khurāsānī al-Baghdādī. He was a shoemaker and was a jurist and a scholar of ḥadīth. He was a noteworthy individual and authored his *Sunan*, reporting from Aḥmad ibn Ḥanbal, Abu Nuʿaym, ʿAffān, al-Qaʿnabī, and others. Al-Nasāʾī reported from him. Ibn Ḥibbān said, 'He was one of the best of the slaves of Allah.'"[583] He was one of those who reported the narrations of al-Imām Aḥmad. Most of the early *aṣḥāb* often would say, when quoting aḥadīth, "It was reported by al-Athram."

الْخلال: أَحْمد بن مُحَمَّد بن هَارُون أَبُو بكر، سمع الحَدِيث من ابْن عَرَفَة وَغَيره، صَاحب (الْجَامِع) و(العلل) وَ(السّنة) و(الطبقات) وَ(تَفْسِير الْغَرِيب) وَ(الْأَدب)، وَهُوَ الَّذِي جمع فِي كِتَابه الرِّوَايَات عَن الإِمَام أَحْمد كَمَا أسلفنا ذَلِك، توفّي سنة

583 [T] *Tahdhīb al-Kamāl* (1/476-479).

إِحْدَى عشرَة وثلاث مئة.

Al-Khallāl: Aḥmad ibn Muḥammad ibn Hārūn, Abu Bakr. He heard ḥadīth from Ibn ʿArafah and others. He wrote *al-Jāmiʿ*, *al-ʿIlal*, *al-Sunnah*, *al-Ṭabaqāt*, *Tafsīr al-Gharīb*, and *al-Adab*. He is the one who gathered the narrations from al-Imām Aḥmad in his book, which we previously discussed. He passed away in the year 311.

ابْن نصر الله: أَحْمد بن نصر الله بن أَحْمد بن مُحَمَّد بن عمر، شيخ الْمَذْهَب، ومفتي الديار المصرية، الْبَغْدَادِيّ الأَصْل، ثمَّ الْمصْرِيّ، صَاحب حَوَاشِي (الْمُحَرر) وَ(الْفُرُوع)، توفّي سنة أَربع وَأَرْبَعين وَثَمَان مِئَة.

Ibn Nasrullāh: Aḥmad ibn Nasrullāh ibn Aḥmad ibn Muḥammad ibn ʿUmar. He was the *shaykh* of the *Madhhab* and the *muftī* of Egypt. He was originally from Baghdad, but then settled in Egypt. He wrote commentaries on *al-Muḥarrar* and *al-Furūʿ*. He passed away in the year 844.

الْحَرْبِيّ: اسْمه إِبْرَاهِيم بن إِسْحَاق بن إِبْرَاهِيم، صَاحب (غَرِيب الحَدِيث) وَ(دَلَائِل النُّبُوَّة)، توفّي سنة خمس وَثَمَانِينَ وَمِئَتَيْنِ، وَهُوَ أحد الناقلين مَذْهَب أَحْمد عَنهُ. قَالَه فِي (المطلع). وَقَالَ: هَكَذَا قيدناه عَن بعض شُيُوخنَا، وَكَذَا سمعته من غير وَاحِد مِنْهُم.

Al-Ḥarbī: His name was Ibrāḥīm ibn Isḥāq ibn Ibrāḥīm. He wrote *Gharīb al-Ḥadīth* and *Dalāʾil al-Nubuwwah*. He died in the year 285. He was one of the transmitters of the *madhhab* of Aḥmad, from [Aḥmad], as stated in *al-Muṭliʿ*. He said, "This is what we noted from some of our teachers, and that is what I heard from more than one [teacher]."

ابْن شاقلا: بِسُكُون الْقَاف وَفتح اللَّام: هُوَ إِبْرَاهِيم بن أَحْمد بن عمر بن حمدَان ابْن شاقلا، الْفَقِيه الأصولي، توفّي سنة تسع وَسِتِّينَ وثلاث مئة.

Ibn Shāqillā: Ibrāḥīm ibn Aḥmad ibn ʿUmar ibn Ḥamdān ibn Shāqillā. He was a jurist and a scholar of legal theory. He passed away in the year 369.

ابْن الْبَنَّاء: الْحسن بن أَحْمد بن عبد الله بن الْبَنَّاء الْبَغْدَادِيّ، الإِمَام الْفَقِيه الْمقري

الْمُحدث الْوَاعِظ، لَهُ نَحْو من خَمْس مِئَة مُصَنف، وَهُوَ صَاحب كتاب (الْمُجَرّد) فِي الْفِقْه وَ(شرح الْخرقِيّ) توفّي سنة إِحْدَى وَسبعين وَأَرْبَع مِئَة.

Ibn al-Bannā': Al-Ḥasan ibn Aḥmad ibn 'Abdullāh ibn al-Bannā' al-Baghdādī. He was an *imām*, jurist, teacher of Qur'ān, scholar of ḥadīth, and preacher. He wrote approximately five-hundred works, and he wrote a book called *al-Mujarrad* on law, and explained al-Khiraqī's [text]. He died in the year 471.

ابْن حَامِد: الْحسن بن حَامِد بن عَليّ بن مَرْوَان الْبَغْدَادِيّ، إِمَام الْحَنَابِلَة فِي زَمَنه، ومؤدبهم ومعلمهم، وأستاذ القَاضِي أبي يعلى، لَهُ (الْجَامِع فِي الْمَذْهَب) وَ(شرح الْخرقِيّ)، توفّي سنة ثَلَاث وَأَرْبَع مِئَة.

Ibn Ḥāmid: Al-Ḥasan ibn Ḥāmid ibn 'Alī ibn Marwān al-Baghdādī. He was the *imām* of the Ḥanābilah in his time, taught them mannerisms, and was their teacher. He was the teacher of al-Qāḍī Abu Ya'lā. He wrote a book called *al-Jāmi' fi 'l-Madhhab*, and explained *al-Khiraqī*. He died in the year 403.

صَاحب الْبلْغَة فِي الْفِقْه: الْحُسَيْن بن الْمُبَارك بن مُحَمَّد بن يحيى بن مُسلم الربعِي الْبَغْدَادِيّ، توفّي سنة إِحْدَى وَثَلَاثِينَ وست مِئَة.

The Author of *al-Bulghah fi 'l-Fiqh*: Al-Ḥusayn ibn al-Mubārak ibn Muḥammad ibn Yaḥyā ibn Muslim al-Rib'ī al-Baghdādī. He died in the year 631.

صَاحب الْوَجِيز: الْحسن بن يُوسُف بن مُحَمَّد بن أبي السّري الدجيلي ثمَّ الْبَغْدَادِيّ، الإِمَام الْفَقِيه المفنن، ألف (الْوَجِيز) فِي الْفِقْه، وكتابا فِي أصُول الدّين، و(نزهة الناظرين) و(تنبيه الغافلين) وَله قصيدة لامية فِي الْفَرَائِض. توفّي سنة اثْنَتَيْنِ وَثَلَاثِينَ وَسَبْع مئة.

The Author of *al-Wajīz*: Al-Ḥusayn ibn Yūsuf ibn Muḥammad ibn Abī al-Sarrī al-Dujaylī, who later resided in Baghdad. He was an *imām*, jurist, and was knowledgeable in various sciences. He wrote his book *al-Wajīz* on the topic of law, and wrote a book about the fundamentals of religion.[584] He

584 [T] Meaning, a book on beliefs.

also wrote *Nuzhat al-Nāẓirīn* and *Tanbīh al-Ghāfilīn*. He wrote a poem, wherein each couplet ends in the letter *lām* (ل), on the topic of inheritance. He died in the year 732.

حَرْب الْكرْمَانِي: حَرْب بن إِسْمَاعِيل بن خلف الْحَنْظَلِي الْكرْمَانِي، مِمَّن روى مسَائِل عَن الإِمَام أَحْمد.

Ḥarb al-Kirmānī: Ḥarb ibn Ismāʿīl ibn Khalaf al-Ḥanẓalī al-Kirmānī. He was one of the narrators of the questions posed to al-Imām Aḥmad [and his subsequent answers to them].

ابْن شيخ السلامية: حَمْزَة بن مُوسَى بن أَحْمد بن الْحُسَيْن بن بدران، شرح بعض الْأَحْكَام لمجد الدّين ابْن تَيْمِية، وَهُوَ من المنتصرين لشيخ الْإِسْلَام ابْن تَيْمِية، والعارفين بفتاواه، توفي سنة تسع وَسِتِّينَ وَسَبْع مئة.

Ibn Shaykh al-Salāmiyyah: Ḥamzah ibn Mūsā ibn Aḥmad ibn al-Ḥusayn ibn Badrān. He explained some of Majd al-Dīn ibn Taymiyyah's book on aḥadīth pertaining to law. He was a supporter of Shaykh al-Islām Ibn Taymiyyah and was well aware of his edicts. He died in the year 769.

حَنْبَل بن إِسْحَاق بن حَنْبَل الشَّيْبَانِيّ: ابْن عَم الإِمَام أَحْمد، كَانَ ثِقَة ثبتا، وَثَّقَهُ الدَّارَقُطْنِي، قَالَ حَنْبَل: جَمعنَا عمي وَأَوْلَاده، وَقَرَأَ علينا (الْمسند) وَمَا سَمعه مِنْهُ - يَعْنِي تَاما - غيرنَا، وَقَالَ لنا: إِن هَذَا الْكتاب قد جمعته وانتقيته من أَكثر من سَبْع مِئة ألف وخسمين ألفا، فَمَا اخْتلف النَّاس فِيهِ من حَدِيث رَسُول الله فأرجعوه إِلَيْهِ، فَإِن وجدتموه فِيهِ وَإِلَّا فَلَيْسَ بحجَّة. توفي سنة ثَلَاث وَسبعين وَمِئَتَيْنِ.

Ḥanbal ibn Isḥāq ibn Ḥanbal al-Shaybānī: The cousin of al-Imām Aḥmad. He was a solid, trustworthy narrator. Al-Dāraquṭnī declared him to be trustworthy. Ḥanbal said, "My uncle [al-Imām Aḥmad] gathered us and his own children and read the *Musnad* to us. None but us heard it from him (meaning, in its entirety). He said to us, 'This book, I have collected it and selected [its narrations] from 750,000 [narrations]. If people differ about the aḥadīth of Allah's Messenger, refer back to it. If it is present [succumb to it], but otherwise, it is not evidence.'" He died in the year 273.

الطوفي: سُلَيْمَان بن عبد الْقوي بن عبد الْكَرِيم بن سعيد الطوفي ثمَّ الْبَغْدَادِيّ، الْفَقِيه الأصولي المفنن، صَاحب (مُخْتَصر الرَّوْضَة) الْأُصُولِيَّة، وَشَرحهَا شرحا متقنا عجيبا، وَشرح الْخرقِيّ، توفّي سنة عشر وَسبْع مئة.

Al-Ṭūfī: Sulaymān ibn ʿAbd al-Qawī ibn ʿAbd al-Karīm ibn Saʿīd al-Ṭūfī, who later resided in Baghdad. He was a jurist, legal theorist, and scholar of various sciences. He wrote a summation of *al-Rawḍah* on the topic of legal theories. He also explained it masterfully and amazingly. He also explained *al-Khiraqī*. He died in the year 716.

صَالح بن الإِمَام أَحْمد: كَانَ أكبر أَوْلَاده، وَكَانَ أَبوهُ يُحِبهُ ويكرمه، وَنقل عَن أَبِيه مسَائِل كَثِيرَة. توفّي سنة سِتّ وَسِتِّينَ وَمِئَتَيْنِ.

Ṣāliḥ, the son of al-Imām Aḥmad: He was the oldest of his children. His father loved and honoured him. He reported many answers to questions from his father. He died in the year 266.

عبد الله ابْن الإِمَام أَحْمد: كَانَ ثبتا فهما ثِقَة حَافِظًا، وَثَّقَهُ ابْن الْخَطِيب وَغَيره. توفّي سنة تسعين وَمِئَتَيْن.

ʿAbdullāh, the son of al-Imām Aḥmad: He was trustworthy, possessed understanding, was reliable, and was a memoriser of ḥadīth. He was ruled as trustworthy by Ibn al-Khaṭīb and others. He died in the year 290.

موفق الدّين: عبد الله بن مُحَمَّد بن أَحْمد بن مُحَمَّد بن قدامَة الْمَقْدِسِي الأَصْل، ثمَّ الدِّمَشْقِي الصَّالِحِي. قَالَ ابْن غنيمَة: مَا أعرف أحدا فِي زmننا أدْرك دَرَجَة الِاجْتِهَاد إِلَّا الْمُوفق. انْتهى. وَهُوَ مؤلف (الْمُغنِي) وَ(الْكَافِي) وَ(الْمقنع) و(العمدة) و(مختصر الْهِدَايَة) فِي الْفِقْه. توفّي سنة عشْرين وست مِئَة.

Muwaffaq al-Dīn [al-Maqdisī[585]]: ʿAbdullāh ibn Muḥammad ibn Aḥmad ibn Muḥammad ibn Qudāmah, originally from Jerusalem, but later residing in Damascus, in al-Ṣāliḥiyyah. Ibn Ghanīmah said, "I do not know of anyone in our age who has reached the level of *ijtihād*, except for al-Muwaffaq." He was the author of *al-Mughnī*, *al-Kāfī*, *al-Muqniʿ*, *al-ʿUmdah*, and *Mukhtaṣar al-Hidāyah*, all on jurisprudence. He died in the year 620.

585 [T] This is in the manuscript, but not the printed version (see next page):

الْمهم شرح الْخرقِيّ: تأليف الْفَقِيه الزَّاهِد عبد الله بن أبي بكر بن أبي الْبَدْر الْحَرْبِيّ الْبَغْدَادِيّ. توفّي سنة إِحْدَى وَثَمَانِينَ وست مِئَة.

***Al-Muhimm Sharḥ al-Khiraqī*:** It is the authorship of the jurist and ascetic, ʿAbdullāh ibn Abī Bakr ibn Abī al-Badr al-Ḥarbī al-Baghdādī. He died in the year 681.

الْوَجِيز: تأليف عبد الله بن مُحَمَّد بن أبي بكر بن إِسْمَاعِيل بن أبي البركات الزريراني الْبَغْدَادِي، فَقِيه الْعِرَاق ومفتي الْآفَاق، حُكي عَنهُ فِي (الْمَقْصد الأرشد) أَنه طالع (الْمُغنِي) للموفق ثَلَاثًا وَعشْرين مرة، وعلق عَلَيْهِ حَوَاشِي. توفي سنة تسع وَعشْرين وَسبْع مئة.

***Al-Wajīz*:** It is the authorship of ʿAbdullāh ibn Muḥammad ibn Abī Bakr ibn Ismāʿīl ibn Abī al-Barakāt al-Zarīrānī al-Baghdādī. He was the jurist of Iraq and the *muftī* of the horizons. In *al-Maqṣad al-Arshad*, it is stated that he read *al-Mughnī* of al-Muwaffaq twenty-three times, and wrote marginalia on it. He passed away in the year 729.

الْقَوَاعِد: تصنيف الْعلامَة الْحَافِظ، شيخ الْحَنَابِلَة فِي وقته، عبد الرَّحْمَن بن أَحْمد بن رَجَب الْبَغْدَادِي ثمَّ الدِّمَشْقِي. توفي سنة خمس وَتِسْعين وَسبْع مئة.

***Al-Qawāʿid*:** The authorship of the erudite scholar and preserver [of ḥadīth], the *shaykh* of the Ḥanbalīs of his time, ʿAbd al-Raḥmān ibn Aḥmad ibn Rajab, who resided first in Baghdad and then relocated to Damascus. He died in the year 795.

ابْن رزين: عبد الرَّحْمَن بن رزين بن عبد الله بن نصر بن عبيد الغساني الحوراني ثمَّ الدِّمَشْقِي، كَانَ فَقِيها فَاضلا، اختصر (الْمُغنِي) فِي مجلدين، وسمى مَا

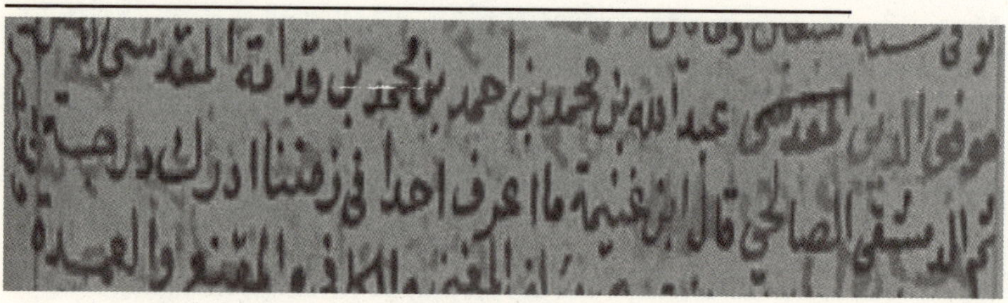

اخْتَصَرَهُ (التَّهْذِيب) توفّي سنة سِت وَخمسين وسِت مِئَة.

Ibn Razīn: ʿAbd al-Raḥmān ibn Razīn ibn ʿAbdullāh ibn Naṣr ibn ʿUbayd al-Ghassānī al-Ḥūrānī, who later resided in Damascus. He was a virtuous jurist. He wrote a summation of *al-Mughnī* in two volumes, and called it, *al-Tahdhīb*. He died in the year 656.

الْحَاوِي: تصنيف الْفَقِيه عبد الرَّحْمَن بن عمر بن أبي الْقَاسِم بن عَلي الضَّرِير الْبَصْرِي، حفظ كتاب (الْهِدَايَة) لأبي الْخطاب. توفي سنة أَربع وَثَمَانِينَ وسِت مِئَة.

Al-Ḥāwī: It is the authorship of the jurist, ʿAbd al-Raḥmān ibn ʿUmar ibn Abi ʾl-Qāsim ibn ʿAlī al-Ḍarīr al-Baṣrī. He memorised Abu ʾl-Khaṭṭāb's *Hidāyah*. He died in the year 684.

الشَّارِح وَصَاحب الشَّرْح: عبد الرَّحْمَن بن مُحَمَّد بن أَحْمد بن قدامَة الْمَقْدِسِي ثمَّ الصَّالِحِي، الإِمَام الْفَقِيه الزَّاهِد شرح (الْمقنع) فِي عشر مجلدات مستمدا من الْمُغنِي، وَمَتى قَالَ الْأَصْحَاب: قَالَ فِي الشَّرْح، كَانَ المُرَاد هَذَا الْكتاب. وَمَتى قَالُوا: الشَّارِح، أَرَادوا مُؤَلفه. توفّي سنة اثْنَتَيْنِ وَثَمَانِينَ وسِت مِئَة.

***Al-Shāriḥ* and *Ṣāḥib al-Sharḥ*:** ʿAbd al-Raḥmān ibn Muḥammad ibn Aḥmad ibn Qudāmah, originally from Jerusalem and then resided in al-Ṣāliḥiyyah. He was an *imām*, a jurist, and an ascetic. He wrote an explanation of *al-Muqniʿ* in ten volumes, taking from *al-Mughnī* along the way. Whenever the *aṣḥāb* say, "He said in *al-Sharḥ*," they are referring to this book, and whenever they say, "*Al-Shāriḥ* (the explainer)," they are referring to its author. He died in the year 682.

غُلَام الْخلال: عبد الْعَزِيز بن جَعْفَر بن أَحْمد بن دَارا، الإِمَام الْمُحدث الْفَقِيه، يكنى بِأبي بكر، لَهُ (الشافي) و(التنبيه) وَ(الْمقنع) وَ(زَاد الْمُسَافِر) فِي الْفِقْه. وَكثِيرًا مَا يَقُول أَصْحَابنَا: قَالَه أَبُو بكر عبد الْعَزِيز فِي (الشافي) وَنَحْو هَذِه الْعبارَة. توفّي سنة ثَلَاث وَسِتِّينَ وثلاث مئة.

Ghulām al-Khallāl: ʿAbd al-ʿAzīz ibn Jaʿfar ibn Aḥmad ibn Dārā. He was an *imām*, scholar of ḥadīth, and jurist. His nickname was Abu Bakr. He wrote *al-Shāfī*, *al-Tanbīh*, *al-Muqni'*, and *Zād al-Musāfir*, all on jurisprudence. Many times, our *aṣḥāb* will say, "As stated by Abu Bakr 'Abd al-'Azīz in *al-Shāfī*," and other similar expressions. He died in the year 363.

الرسعني: عبد الرزاق بن رزق الله بن أبي بكر بن خلف بن أبي الهيجاء، الْفَقِيه الْمُحدث الْمُفَسّر، لم أر لَهُ ذكرا فِي كتب الْفُقَهَاء، على أني وجدت بِخَط مُحَمَّد بن كنان الصَّالِحِي أَنه رأى لَهُ شرحا على الْخرقِي مزجا فِي مجلدين. قلت: وَرَأَيْت لَهُ تَفْسِيرا لِلْقُرْآنِ، سَمَّاهُ (رموز الْكُنُوز) وَهُوَ تَفْسِير جليل فِي أَربع مجلدات، يذكر فِيهِ أَحَادِيث يَرْوِيهَا بالسند، ويناقش الزَّمَخْشَرِيّ فِي (كشافه) وَيذكر فروع الْفِقْه على الْخلاف بِدُونِ دَلِيل. وَبِالْجُمْلَةِ هُوَ تَفْسِير مُفِيد جدا لمن طالعه. توفي سنة سِتِّينَ وست مِئَة.

Al-Rasa'ni: 'Abd al-Razzaq ibn Rizqullāh ibn Abī Bakr ibn Khalaf ibn Abī al-Hayjā'. He was a jurist, scholar of ḥadīth, and an exegete. I did not find his mention in the books of the jurists. However, I did find in the handwriting of Muḥammad ibn Kinān al-Ṣāliḥi that he saw a two-volume commentary of his on al-Khiraqī. I, myself, saw a book on exegesis of the Qur'ān, called *Rumūz al-Kunūz*. It is a valuable exegesis, comprised of four volumes. He mentioned aḥadīth with their chains of narration and engaged al-Zamakhsharī's *Kashāf*. He mentioned subsidiary matters of law by explaining differences of opinion, though without mentioning evidences. Generally speaking, it is very beneficial for anyone who reads it. He died in the year 660.

الشريف أَبُو جَعْفَر: الْهَاشِمِي العباسي، لَهُ ذكر فِي كتب أَصْحَابنَا، وَهُوَ عبد الْخَالِق بن عِيسَى، يتَّصل نسبه بِالْعَبَّاسِ بن عبد المطلب رَضِي الله عَنهُ، كَانَ مُخْتَصر الْكَلَام، مليح التدريس، جيد الْكَلَام فِي المناظرة، عَالما بالفرائض وَأَحْكَام الْقُرْآن وَالْأُصُول، لَهُ مقامات فِي منع الْبدع عِنْد الْخُلَفَاء. توفّي سنة سبعين وَأَرْبَع مِئَة.

Al-Sharīf Abu Ja'far: He was a Hashemite of the offspring of al-'Abbās. He is mentioned in the books of our *aṣḥāb*. His name was 'Abd al-Khāliq ibn 'Īsā. His genealogy is traced back to al-'Abbās ibn 'Abd al-Muṭṭalib ﷺ. His speech was concise, his lessons were pleasant, and he was an excellent debater. He was a scholar of inheritance, the rulings of Qur'ān, and legal theories. He has many instances where he prevented innovations in the presence of caliphs. He died in the year 470.

الْمُنْتَخب: تصنيف عبد الْوَهَّاب بن عبد الْوَاحِد بن مُحَمَّد بن عَلي الشِّيرَازِيّ ثمَّ الدِّمَشْقِي، الْفَقِيه الْوَاعِظ، لَهُ (الْمُنْتَخب) فِي الْفِقْه مجلدان، و(المفردات) و(البرهان) فِي أصُول الدّين. توفّي سنة سِتّ وَثَلَاثِينَ وَخمْس مِئة.

***Al-Muntakhab*:** It is the authorship of 'Abd al-Wahhāb ibn 'Abd al-Wāḥid ibn Muḥammad ibn 'Alī al-Shīrāzī, who resided later in Damascus. He was a jurist and a preacher. He authored *al-Muntakhab* on law, in two volumes. He also authored *al-Mufradāt*, and on beliefs, he authored *al-Burhān*. He died in the year 536.

الغنية: تأليف شيخ الْعَصْر وقدوة العارفين، عبد الْقَادِر بن أبي صَالح عبد الله بن جنكي دوست الجيلي الْبَغْدَادِيّ الْمَشْهُور.

***Al-Ghunyah*:** It is the authorship of the *shaykh* of his generation, and the role-model of the knowers, the well-known 'Abd al-Qādir ibn Abī Ṣāliḥ 'Abdullāh ibn Jankī Dost al-Jīlī al-Baghdādī.[586]

الْمجد: عبد السَّلَام بن عبد الله بن أبي الْقَاسِم الْخضر بن مُحَمَّد بن عَليّ ابْن تَيْمِية الْحَرَّانِي، الْفَقِيه المفنن الْمقرئ، الملقب بمجد الدّين، جد شيخ الْإِسْلَام أَحْمد ابْن تَيْمِية، صَاحب (الْمُنْتَقى) وَ(الْمُحَرر) فِي الْفِقْه و(مسودة مُنْتَهى الْغَايَة فِي شرح الْهِدَايَة) بيض بعض الشَّرْح، وَله (مسودة) فِي أصُول الْفِقْه، زَاد فِيهَا وَلَده عبد الْحَلِيم، ثمَّ حفيده شيخ الْإِسْلَام، وَله كتاب أَحَادِيث التَّفْسِير. توفّي سنة اثْنَتَيْنِ وَخمسين وست مِئَة.

Al-Majd: 'Abd al-Salām ibn 'Abdullāh ibn Abī al-Qāsim al-Khaḍir ibn Muḥammad ibn 'Alī ibn Taymiyyah al-Ḥarrānī. He was a jurist, scholar of various sciences, and teacher of the Qur'ān. His title is Majd al-Dīn. He was the grandfather of Shaykh al-Islām Aḥmad ibn Taymiyyah. He wrote *al-Muntaqā* and *al-Muḥarrar*, both on law, and wrote *Musawwadat Muntahā 'l-Ghayat fī Sharḥ al-Hidāyah*, where he wrote parts of its ex-

586 [T] Also known as al-Jīlānī, as in, the famous 'Abd al-Qādir al-Jīlānī.

planation. He also wrote *al-Musawwadah*, on legal theories. Then, his son ʿAbd al-Ḥalīm added to it, and afterwards, his grandson, Shaykh al-Islām, also added to it. He wrote a book on aḥadīth pertaining to exegesis. He died in the year 652.

ابْن الزغواني: عَلي بن عبد الله بن نصر بن السّري الزَّاغُونِيّ الْبَغْدَادِيّ، الْفَقِيه الْمُحدث الْوَاعِظ، أحد أَعْيَان الْمَذْهَب، صنف (الْإِقْنَاع) و(الواضح) وَ(الْخلاف الْكَبِير) و(المفردات) وَ(التَّلْخِيص) فِي الْفَرَائِض. توفّي سنة سبع وَعشْرين وَخَمْس مئة.

Ibn al-Zāghūnī: ʿAlī ibn ʿAbdullah ibn Naṣr ibn al-Sarī al-Zāghūnī al-Baghdādī. He was a jurist, scholar of ḥadīth, and preacher. He is a noteworthy person in the *madhhab*. He wrote *al-Iqnāʿ*, *al-Wāḍiḥ*, *al-Khilāf al-Kabīr*, and *al-Mufradāt*, and on inheritance, he wrote *al-Talkhīṣ*. He died in the year 527.

ابْن عَبدُوس: عَليّ بن عمر بن أَحْمد بن عمار بن أَحْمد بن عَلي بن عَبدُوس الْحَرَّانِي، الْفَقِيه الوَاعِظ، لَهُ كتاب (الْمَذْهَب فِي الْمَذْهَب)، وَله تَفْسِير كَبِير. توفّي سنة تسع وَخمسين وَخَمْس مِئة.

Ibn ʿAbdūs: ʿAlī ibn ʿUmar ibn Aḥmad ibn ʿAmmār ibn Aḥmad ibn ʿAlī ibn ʿAbdūs al-Ḥarrānī. He was a jurist and preacher. He wrote a book called *al-Madhhab fi ʾl-Madhhab*. He also has a large exegesis. He died in the year 559.

ابْن عقيل: عَلي بن مُحَمَّد بن عقيل الْبَغْدَادِي، الإِمَام الْفَقِيه الأصولي الْمقرئ الْوَاعِظ، أوحد الْمُجْتَهدين، صَاحب المؤلفات، وَسَتَأْتِي تَرْجَمته فِي تراجم الْكِبَار، من أَصْحَاب أَحْمد، وَله كتاب (الْفُصُول) و(التذكرة) و(كفاية الْمُفْتِي) سبع مجلدات كبار و(رؤوس الْمسَائِل) وَغير ذَلِك فِي الْفِقْه. توفي سنة ثَلَاث عشرَة وَخَمْس مِئة.

Ibn ʿAqīl: ʿAlī ibn Muḥammad ibn ʿAqīl al-Baghdādī. He was an *imām*, a jurist, legal theorist, teacher of Qurʾān, and preacher. He was a unique *mujtahid*, and had many authorships. His biography will be mentioned among the biographies of the major *aṣḥāb* of Aḥmad.[587] He authored *al-Fuṣūl*, *al-Tadhkirah*, *Kifāyat al-Muftī* in seven large volumes, *Ru'ūs al-Masā'il*, and other works on law. He died in the year 513.

الْخرقِيّ: عمر بن الْحُسَيْن بن عبد الله بن أَحْمد الْخرقِي، بِكَسْر الْخَاء الْمُعْجَمَة وَفتح الرَّاء الْمُهْملَة، نِسْبَة إِلَى بيع الْخرق، ذكره السَّمْعَانِي. هُوَ صَاحب (الْمُخْتَصر الْمَشْهُور. توفّي سنة أَربع وَثَلَاثِينَ وثلاث مئة.

Al-Khiraqī: ʿUmar ibn al-Ḥusayn ibn ʿAbdullāh ibn Aḥmad al-Khiraqī. The word *khiraqī* means that he was a cloth seller, as mentioned by al-Samʿānī. He authored the famous *Mukhtaṣar*. He died in the year 334.

البوشنجي: مُحَمَّد بن إِبْرَاهِيم بن سعيد بن مُوسَى، أحد الناقلين الرِّوَايَات عَن الإِمَام أَحْمد. توفّي سنة تسعين وَمِئَتَيْنِ.

Al-Būshinjī: Muḥammad ibn Ibrāḥīm ibn Saʿīd ibn Mūsā. He was a transmitter of the narrations from al-Imām Aḥmad. He died in the year 290.

ابْن أبي مُوسَى: مُحَمَّد بن أَحْمد بن أبي مُوسَى الْهَاشِمِي، صَاحب (الْإِرْشَاد) توفّي سنة ثَمَان وَعشْرين وَأَرْبع مِئَة.

Ibn Abī Mūsā: Muḥammad ibn Aḥmad ibn Abī Mūsā al-Hāshimī. He authored *al-Irshād*. He died in the year 428.

ابْن تَمِيم: مُحَمَّد بن تَمِيم الْحَرَّانِي، الْفَقِيه. لَهُ (الْمُخْتَصر) الْمَشْهُور فِي الْفِقْه، وصل فِيهِ إِلَى أَثْنَاء كتاب الزَّكَاة. توفّي قَرِيبا من سنة خمس وَسبعين وست مِئَة.

Ibn Tamīm: Muḥammad ibn Tamīm al-Ḥarrānī. He was a jurist and authored a book called *al-Mukhtaṣar*. It was a noteworthy book on jurisprudence, but he only completed until the Chapter of *Zakāt*. He died in approximately 675.

الْآجُرِيّ: بِمد الْهمزَة وَضم الْجِيم. وَتَشْدِيد الرَّاء الْمُهْملَة، مُحَمَّد بن الْحسن بن عبد الله، لَهُ مصنفات مِنْهَا كتاب (النَّصِيحَة) فِي الْفِقْه، وعادته فِيهِ أَنه لَا يذكر

587 No mention of his biography, nor the biographies of other notable *aṣḥāb* of al-Imām Aḥmad were made. Perhaps the author intended to do so but forgot.

إِلَّا اختيارات الْأَصْحَاب. توفّي سنة سِتِّينَ وثلاث مئة.

Al-Ājurrī: Muḥammad ibn al-Ḥasan ibn ʿAbdullāh. He wrote many books, among them was *al-Naṣīḥah* on law. Usually, he would only mention the choice opinions of the *aṣḥāb*. He died in the year 360.

أَبُو يعلى: مُحَمَّد بن الْحُسَيْن بن مُحَمَّد بن خلف بن أَحْمد ابن الْفراء، عَلامَة الزَّمَان قَاضِي الْقُضَاة مُجْتَهد الْمَذْهَب بل الْمُجْتَهد الْمُطلق، لَهُ (الْخلاف الْكَبِير) وَ(الْأَحْكَام السُّلْطَانِيَّة) وَ(شرح الْخرقِي) وَسَتَأْتِي تَرْجَمته. توفّي سنة ثَمَان وَخمسين وَأَرْبَع مِئَة.

Abu Yaʿlā: Muḥammad ibn al-Ḥusayn ibn Muḥammad ibn Khalaf ibn Aḥmad ibn al-Farrāʾ. He was the great scholar of his time, the judge of judges, and the *mujtahid* within the *madhhab*; rather, he was an absolute *mujtahid*. He authored *al-Khilāf al-Kabīr*, *al-Aḥkām al-Sulṭāniyyah*, and *Sharḥ al-Khiraqī*. His biography is forthcoming. He died in the year 458.

الْبلْغَة: تصنيف مُحَمَّد بن الْخضر بن مُحَمَّد بن الْخضر بن عَليّ بن عبد الله ابْن تَيْمِية الْحَرَّانِي، الْفَقِيه الْمُفَسّر فَخر الدّين، وَله فِي الْفِقْه (التَّرْغِيب) وَ(التَّلْخِيص) وَ(الْبُلْغَة) وَهُوَ أصغرهما وَ(شرح الْهِدَايَة) لأبي الْخطاب، وَلم يتمه. وهو ابن عَم مجد الدّين. توفّي سنة اثْنَتَيْنِ وَعشْرين وسِت مئَة.

***Al-Bulghah*:** It is the authorship of Muḥammad ibn al-Khaḍir ibn ʿAlī ibn ʿAbdullāh ibn Taymiyyah al-Ḥarrānī. He was a jurist and exegete. He was nicknamed *Fakhr al-Dīn* (the pride of Islam), and wrote books on law, including *al-Targhīb*, *al-Talkhīṣ*, *al-Bulghah*, which is the shortest one, and explained *al-Hidāyah*, the book of Abu ʿl-Khaṭṭāb, but did not complete it. He is the cousin of Majd al-Dīn. He died in the year 622.

(الْمُسْتَوْعب): بِكَسْر الْعين، تأليف مُحَمَّد بن عبد الله بن الْحُسَيْن السامري بِضَم الْمِيم وَتَشْدِيد الرَّاء، نِسْبَة إِلَى مَدِينَة سر من رأى بِضَم السِّين. لَهُ فِي الْفِقْه (الْمُسْتَوْعب) و(الفروق) وَكتاب (الْبُسْتَان) فِي الْفَرَائِض، وَغير ذَلِك. توفّي سنة عشر وسِت مِئَة.

***Al-Mustawʿib*:** It is the authorship of Muḥammad ibn ʿAbdullāh ibn al-Ḥusayn al-Sāmurrī, a description that signified his origin from *Surr man Rảa* (Samarra). On jurisprudence, he authored *al-Mustawʿib*, and *al-Furūq*. He authored *al-Bustān*, on inheritance, and other works. He died in the year 610.

النَّاظِم: مُحَمَّد بن عبد الْقوي بن بدران الْمَقْدِسِي، الْفَقِيه الْمُحدث، لَهُ (منظومة الْآدَاب) صغرى وكبرى، و(الفرائد) تبلغ خَمْسَة آلاف بَيت، وَكتاب (النِّعْمَة) جزءان، و(نظم الْمُفْردَات)، وَكلهَا على رُوِيَ الدَّال. توفّي سنة تسع وَتِسْعين وسِت مئة.

***Al-Nāẓim*:** Muḥammad ibn ʿAbd al-Qawī ibn Badrān al-Maqdisī. He was a jurist and scholar of ḥadīth. He authored two poems on mannerisms; one was small and one was large. He also wrote *al-Farāʾid*, which comprised of five thousand couplets. He has a book called *al-Niʾmah,* which is of two volumes. He also wrote *Naẓm al-Mufradāt*, a poem that ends each couplet with a *dāl* (د). He died in the year 699.

الْحلْوانِي: مُحَمَّد بن عَليّ بن مُحَمَّد بن عُثْمَان بن مراق الْحلْوانِي، لَهُ (كِفَايَة الْمُبْتَدِي) فِي الْفِقْه، مُجَلد. وَكتاب فِي أُصُول الْفِقْه مجلدان. توفي سنة خمس وَخَمْس مِئة.

Al-Ḥulwānī: Muḥammad ibn ʿAlī ibn Muḥammad ibn ʿUthmān ibn Marāq al-Ḥulwānī. He has *Kifāyat al-Mubtadī* in law, consisting of one volume. He has a book in legal theory in two volumes. He died in the year 505.

(الْمُفْرِدَات) اسْم لمؤلفات مُتعَدِّدَة فِي هَذَا النَّوْع، أشهرها عِنْد الْمُتَأَخِّرين، الألفية المسمات ب(النظم الْمُفِيد الأحمد في مُفْرَدَات الإِمَام أَحْمد) للْقَاضِي مُحَمَّد بن عَليّ بن عبد الرَّحْمَن بن مُحَمَّد الْخَطِيب. توفّي سنة عشْرين وَثَمَان مئة.

***Al-Mufradāt*:** It is a name referring to a number of books on the same genre, the most famous of which, among the latter-day scholars, is the thousand-line poem called, *al-Naẓm al-Mufīd al-Aḥmad fī Mufradāt al-Imām Aḥmad*, written by al-Qāḍī Muḥammad ibn ʿAlī ibn ʿAbd al-Raḥmān ibn Muḥammad al-Khaṭīb. He died in the year 820.

(المطلع): تصنيف مُحَمَّد بن أبي الْفَتْح بن أبي الْفضل، الْفَقِيه الْمُحدث النَّحْوِيّ اللّغَوِي، وَقد سمى كِتَابه هَذَا (المطلع على أَبْوَاب الْمقنع) فسر فِيهِ الْكَلِمَات الغريبة الْوَاقِعَة فِي الْمقنع، على نمط (الْمغرب) للحنفية و(المصباح) للشَّافِعِيَّة، غير أَنه رتبه على أَبْوَاب الْكتاب لَا على حُرُوف المعجم، ثمَّ أتبعه بتراجم الْأَعْلَام الْمَذْكُورين فِي (الْمقنع) فَصَارَ كشرح مُخْتَصر، توفّي سنة تسع وَسَبْع مئة.

Al-Muṭli: It is the authorship of Muḥammad ibn Abi ʿl-Fatḥ ibn Abi ʿl-Faḍl. He was a jurist, scholar of ḥadīth, and scholar of syntax and language. He called the book *al-Muṭliʿ ʿala Abwāb al-Muqniʿ*. In it, he explained the ambiguous words occurring in *al-Muqniʿ*. It resembles *al-Maghrib*, [a book on the same genre] in the Ḥanafī [*Madhhab*], and *al-Miṣbāḥ* to the Shāfiʿīs. However, he organised it according to the chapters of the book, not alphabetically. Then, he appended biographies of the noteworthy people mentioned in *al-Muqniʿ*. As such, it became like a summarised explanation. He died in the year 790.

أَبُو يعلى الصَّغِير: مُحَمَّد بن مُحَمَّد بن الْحُسَيْن بن مُحَمَّد بن خلف بن أَحْمد بن الْفراء - هُوَ ابْن أبي يعلى الْمُتَقَدّم. توفي سنة سِتِّينَ وَخمْس مِئَة.

Abu Yaʿlā al-Ṣaghīr: Muḥammad ibn Muḥammad ibn al-Ḥusayn ibn Muḥammad ibn Khalaf ibn Aḥmad ibn al-Farrāʾ. He is the son of Abu Yaʿlā, who was previously mentioned. He died in the year 560.

الْفُرُوع: تصنيف مُحَمَّد بن مُفْلِح بن مُحَمَّد بن مفرج الْمَقْدِسِي ثمَّ الصَّالِحِي الراميني، شيخ الْحَنَابِلَة فِي وقته، وَأحد الْمُجْتَهدين فِي الْمَذْهَب. توفّي سنة ثَلَاث وَسِتِّينَ وَسبع مئة.

Al-Furūʿ: It is the authorship of Muḥammad ibn Mufliḥ ibn Muḥammad ibn Mufrij, born in the Ṣāliḥiyyah district of Damascus, but originally from Ramīn, Palestine, and residing later in Jerusalem. He was the *shaykh* of the Ḥanbalīs of his time and one of the *mujtahids* in the *madhbab*. He died in the year 763.

الزَّرْكَشِيّ: مُحَمَّد بن عبد الله بن مُحَمَّد الزَّرْكَشِيّ الْمصْرِيّ، شرح الْخرقِيّ شرحا لم يسْبق إِلَى مثله، وَكَلَامه فِيهِ يدل على فقه نفس وَتصرف فِي كَلَام الْأَصْحَاب،

وَله شرح على الْخرقِيّ مُخْتَصر، وصل فِيهِ إِلَى أَثْنَاء بَاب الْأَضَاحِي، وَله غير ذَلِك مِمَّا لم يكمل. توفّي سنة أَربع وَسبعين وَسَبْع مئة.

Al-Zarkashī: Muḥammad ibn ʿAbdullāh ibn Muḥammad al-Zarkashī al-Miṣrī. He explained *al-Khiraqī* in an unprecedented way. His words show he had understanding of the soul and was able to interpret the speech of the *aṣḥāb*. He has a shorter explanation of *al-Khiraqī*, where he reached the Chapter on Sacrifices. He also has other unfinished works. He died in the year 774.

أَبُو الْخطاب: مَحْفُوظ بن أَحْمد بن الْحسن بن أَحْمد الكلوذاني الْبَغْدَادِي، أحد الْمُجْتَهدين فِي الْمَذْهَب، لَهُ فِي الْفِقْه (الْهِدَايَة) و(الانتصار) وَهُوَ الْخلاف الْكَبِير، وَله الْخلاف الصَّغِير سَمَّاهُ (رُؤُوس الْمسَائِل) وَله كتاب (التَّمْهِيد) فِي أُصُول الْفِقْه. توفّي سنة عشر وَخَمْس مِئَة.

Abu 'l-Khaṭṭāb: Maḥfūẓ ibn Aḥmad ibn al-Ḥasan ibn Aḥmad al-Kalwadhānī al-Baghdādī. He was one of the *mujtahids* of the *madhhab*. On law, he wrote *al-Hidāyah*, *al-Intiṣār*, which comprises of inter-*madhhab* differences, and also discussed intra-*madhhab* differences, which he called, *Ru'ūs al-Masā'il*. He also wrote *al-Tamhīd*, on legal theories. He died in the year 510.

ابْن المنجا: منجا بن عُثْمَان بن أسعد بن المنجا التنوخي، الْفَقِيه الأصولي الْمُفَسّر النَّحْوِي، لَهُ (الممتع شرح الْمقنع). توفّي سنة خمس وَتِسْعين وسِت مِئَة.

Ibn al-Munajjā: Munajjā ibn ʿUthmān ibn Asʿad ibn al-Munajjā al-Tanūkhī. He was a jurist, legal theorist, exegete, and scholar of syntax. He wrote *al-Mumtiʿ Sharḥ al-Muqniʿ*. He died in the year 695.

الْمروزِي: هيدام بن قُتيبَة، أحد الناقلين مَذْهَب أَحْمد عَنهُ. توفّي سنة أَربع وَسبعين وَمِئتيْنِ.

Al-Marwazī: Haydām ibn Qutaybah. He was a transmitter of the *madhhab* of Aḥmad, from [Aḥmad]. He died in the year 274.

ابْن الصَّيْرفِي: يحيى بن أبي مَنْصُور بن أبي الْفَتْح بن رَافع بن عَليّ الْحَرَّانِي،

الْفَقِيه الْمُحدث، المعمر بِفَتْح الْمِيم الْمُشَدّدَة، أحد مَشَايِخ شيخ الإِسْلَام ابْن تَيْمِية، نقل عَنهُ صَاحب (الْفُرُوع) فِي كتاب الْجَنَائِز فِي بَاب: عِيَادَة الْمَرِيض. توفّي سنة ثَمَان وَسبعين وست مِئَة.

Ibn al-Ṣayrafī: Yaḥyā ibn Abī Manṣūr ibn Abī 'l-Fatḥ ibn Rāfiʿ ibn ʿAlī al-Ḥarrānī. He was a jurist, scholar of ḥadīth, and lived a long life. He was one of the teachers of Shaykh al-Islam Ibn Taymiyyah. The author of *al-Furūʿ* quoted him in the Chapter on Funerals, under the Section: Visiting the Sick. He died in the year 678.

ابْن هُبَيْرَة: يحيى بن مُحَمَّد بن هُبَيْرَة الدوري ثمَّ الْبَغْدَادِيّ، الْوَزير عون الدّين، شرح (الصَّحِيحَيْنِ) فِي عدَّة مجلدات وَسَماهُ (الإفصاح عَن مَعَاني الصِّحَاح) وَلما بلغ فِيهِ إِلَى شرح **«من يرد الله بِهِ خيرا يفقهه فِي الدّين»** شرح الحَدِيث، وَتكلم على الفِقه وَذكر الْمسَائِل الْمُتَّفق عَلَيْهَا والمختلف فِيهَا بَين الأَئِمَّة الْأَرْبَعَة. وَقد أفرده النَّاس من الْكتاب، وجعلوه مُسْتقِلّا فِي مُجَلد لطيف، وَقد اطلَعت عَلَيْهِ، فَوَجَدته كتابا نَافِعًا. وَهَذَا الشَّرْح صنفه فِي ولَايَته الوزارة، وَجمع النَّاس عَلَيْهِ من الْمذَاهب، حَتَّى قدمُوا من الْبِلَاد الشاسعة، وَأنْفق عَلَيْهِ نَحْو مئة ألف دِينَار وَثَلَاثَة عشر ألف. وَحدث بِهِ، وَاجْتمعَ الْخلق الْعَظِيم لسماعه عَلَيْهِ.

Ibn Hubayrah: Yaḥyā ibn Muḥammad ibn Hubayrah al-Dūrī, later residing in Baghdad. He was known as al-Wazīr ʿAwn al-Dīn. He authored an explanation of *al-Bukhārī* and *Muslim*, calling it, *al-Ifṣāḥ ʿan Maʿānī al-Ṣiḥāḥ*. When he reached the ḥadīth, **"Whomever Allah wants good for, He gives them understanding of the religion,"**[588] he explained the ḥadīth, and then spoke about jurisprudence, mentioning the issues that are agreed on and disagreed on amongst the four *imāms*. People have published it into its own pleasant volume. I read it, and found it beneficial. This explanation was written when he was a minister. People of various schools of thought united around him, and even travelled from far lands [to learn it from him]. He spent approximately 113,000 dirhams on it. He then taught it, and many people gathered to hear him teach it.

قلت: سقى الله تِلْكَ الْأَيام الَّتِي كَانَ بهَا الاعتناء بِالْعلمِ، ثمَّ ولت واضمحلت،

588 Reported by al-Bukhārī (1/150-151) and Muslim (1037).

حَتَّى لم يبْق فِي أيامنا وَفِي بِلَادنَا للْعلم رسم وَلَا ظلّ. توفي سنة سِتِّين وَخَمْس مِئة.

I say: Oh, how we have nostalgia for those days where there was care and concern for knowledge. Then, those days passed and withered away, leaving us in a time and place where knowledge has no semblance nor shade.[589] He died in the year 560.

الأزجي: يحيى بن يحيى الْأَزجي، الْفَقِيه، صَاحب (نِهَايَة الْمطلب فِي علم الْمَذْهَب) قَالَ برهَان الدّين بن مُفْلِح فِي (الْمَقْصد الأرشد): هُوَ كتاب كَبِير جدا، حذا فِيهِ حَذو (نِهَايَة الْمطلب) لإِمَام الْحَرَمَيْنِ، وَأَكْثر استمداده من (الْمُجَرد) للْقَاضِي أبي يعلى و(الفصول) لِابْن عقيل، وَفِيه أَشْيَاء سَاقِطَة لَا تَحْقِيق فِيهَا. قَالَ ابْن رَجَب: ويغلب على ظني أَنه توفي بعد الست مئة بِقَلِيل.

Al-Azjī: Yaḥyā ibn Yaḥyā al-Azjī. He was a jurist and authored *Nihāyat al-Maṭlab fī ʿIlm al-Madhhab*. Burhān al-Dīn ibn Mufliḥ said, in *al-Maqṣad al-Arshad*, "It is a very large book, wherein he emulated the style of *Nihāyat al-Maṭlab* of Imām al-Ḥaramayn. He often referenced *al-Mujarrad* by al-Qāḍī Abu Yaʿlā, and *al-Fuṣūl* of Ibn ʿAqīl. It contains some blunders that lack precision." Ibn Rajab said, "I am confident that he passed away a short time after the year 600."

ابْن قندس: أَبُو بكر بن إِبْرَاهِيم بن قندس تَقِيّ الدّين البعلي، صَاحب (حَوَاشِي الْفُرُوع) و(حواشي الْمُحَرر). توفّي سنة إِحْدَى وَسِتِّين وَثَمَان مِئَة.

Ibn Qundus: Abu Bakr ibn Ibrāhīm ibn Qundus, also known as Taqī al-Dīn al-Baʿli. He authored commentaries on *al-Furūʿ* and *al-Muḥarrar*. He died in the year 861.

الْمُبْدع: شرح الْمقنع، تأليف إِبْرَاهِيم بن مُحَمَّد بن الْأَكْمَل بن عبد الله بن مُحَمَّد بن مُفْلِح الْمَقْدِسِي الصَّالِحِي، وَكتابه (الْمُبْدع) فِي أَربع مجلدات، وَهُوَ شرح حافل ممزوج مَعَ الْمَتْن، حذا فِيهِ حَذو المحلى الشَّافِعِي فِي شرح (الْمِنْهَاج) الفرعي، وَفِيه من الْفَوَائِد والنقول مَا لَا يُوجد فِي غَيره. وصنف فِي

589 [T] What can be said of the year 2021?

الْأُصُول كتابا سَمَّاهُ (مرقاة الْوُصُول إِلَى علم الْأُصُول) وَله (الْمَقْصد الأرشد فِي ذكر أَصْحَاب الإِمَام أَحْمد) توفي سنة أربع وَثَمَانِينَ وَثَمَان مِئَة.

***Al-Mubdi*ʿ:** An explanation of *al-Muqni*ʿ. It is the authorship of Ibrāḥīm ibn Muḥammad al-Akmal ibn ʿAbdullāh ibn Muḥammad ibn Mufliḥ al-Maqdisī al-Ṣāliḥi. It is comprised of four volumes. It is a copious work that blends seamlessly with the original text. He emulated al-Maḥallī, the Shāfiʿī scholar, in his explanation of *al-Minhāj* by al-Farʿī. It contains useful points of benefit and quotations that cannot be found elsewhere. On legal theory, he authored *Murqāt al-Wuṣūl ilā ʿIlm al-Uṣūl*. He also wrote, *al-Maqṣad al-Arshad fī Dhikr Aṣḥāb al-Imām Aḥmad*. He died in the year 884.

وَهنا انْتهى بِنَا الْمقَال فِي بيان جل المبهمات الَّتِي يذكرهَا الْأَصْحَاب، وَأَرْجُو الله أَن يكون ذَلِك الْبيان وافيا بِالْمَقْصُودِ، ومفيدا للمشتغلين فَائِدَة تبذل لي الْأجر وَالثَّوَاب من الله الْكَرِيم الْوَهَّاب بمنه وَكَرمه. هَذَا ولنختم هَذَا العقد بفوائد:

Here is where we conclude our clarification of obscure words mentioned by the *aṣḥāb*. I ask Allah the Exalted that my clarifications fulfil the purpose and benefit those who busy themselves [with learning] in a way that produces rewards and recompense for me from Allah the Generous and Giver. This, of course, is due to His Favors and Generosity. To conclude, there are a number of points of benefit that I shall mention:

الأولى: لا بد ايها النَّاظر فِي كتابي هَذَا أَن يكون قد طرق سَمعك لَفْظَة (أهل الرأي) وَحِينَئِذٍ فَاعْلَم أَن أَصْحَاب الرَّأْي عِنْد الْفُقَهَاء هم أهل الْقيَاس والتأويل، كأصحاب أبي حنيفَة النُّعْمَان، وَأبي الْحسن الْأَشْعَرِي، والتأويل: علم مَا يؤول إِلَيْهِ الْكَلَام من الْخَطَأ وَالصَّوَاب. ويقابلهم (أهل الظاهِر)، وهم مثل دَاوُد الظَّاهِرِيّ، وَابْن حزم، وَمن نحا نَحْوهمَا.

First. When reading this book, you have undoubtedly come across the term, Ahl al-Ray (People of Intellectualism). When reading it, be aware that the People of Ray, according to the jurists, are people of analogies and interpretation, such as the students of Abu Ḥanīfah al-Nuʿmān and Abu ʿl-Ḥasan al-Ashʿarī. Interpretation means to deduce the implications of words, whether right or wrong. They are contrasted by Ahl al-Ẓāhir (People of Literalism), such as Dāwūd al-Ẓāhirī, Ibn Ḥazm, and those who treaded their ways.

الثَّانِيَة: الْمُرَاد بِمذهب السّلف مَا كَانَ عَلَيْهِ الصَّحَابَة الْكِرَام، وأعيان التَّابِعين، وأتباعهم، وأئمة الدّين مِمَّن شهد لَهُ بِالْإِمَامَةِ، دون من رمي ببدعة، أَو شهر بلقب غير مرضِي، كالخوارج وَالرَّوَافِض والقدرية والمرجئة والجبرية والجهمية والمعتزلة والكرامية وَنَحْوهم.

Second. When using the phrase, "The way of the Salaf," it means what the Companion and noteworthy Followers espoused, as well as those who followed them, including the *imāms* of the religion whose scholarship is attested to. It does not include those accused of innovations or those famous with titles that are dispraise worthy, such as Khārijites, Rāfiḍites, Qadarites, Murjiʿites, Jabrites, Jahmites, Muʿtazilites, Karrāmites, and so forth.

ثمَّ غلب ذَلِك اللقب على الإِمَام أَحْمد وَأَتْبَاعه على اعْتِقَاده، من أَي مَذْهَب كَانُوا، فَقيل لَهُم فِي فن التَّوْحِيد: عُلَمَاء السّلف. هَذَا مَا اصْطلحَ عَلَيْهِ أَصْحَابنَا والمحدثون. وَقَالَ ابْن حجر الْفَقِيه فِي رسَالَته (شن الْغَارة): الصَّدْر الأول لَا يُقَال إِلا على السّلف، وهم أهل الْقُرُون الثَّلَاثَة الأول، الَّذين شهد لَهُم النَّبِي صلى الله عَلَيْهِ وَسلم بِأنهُم خير الْقُرُون. وَأما من بعدهمْ، فَلَا يُقَال فِي حَقهم ذَلِك.

The term then became standard usage for referring to al-Imām Aḥmad and his followers who espouse his creed, irrespective of the school of law they adhered to. When discussing creed, they are referred to as the scholars of the Salaf. This is what our *aṣḥāb* and the scholars of ḥadīth have used as verbiage. Ibn Ḥajar, the jurist, said in his book *Shan al-Ghārah*, "The phrase, 'The first generations,' can only be used to refer to the Salaf, i.e. those living in the first three generations, whom the Prophet ﷺ attested to as being the best of generations. As for those after them, they cannot be referred to in such a manner."

الثَّالِثَة: مَتى قَالَ فقهاؤنا: وَلَو كَانَ كَذَا وَنَحْوه، كَانَ إِشَارَة إِلَى الْخلاف، وَذَلِكَ كَقَوْل صَاحب (الْإِقْنَاع) وَغَيره فِي بَاب الآذان: ويكرهان - يَعْنِي الأذان وَالْإِقَامَة - للنِّسَاء، وَلَو بِلَا رفع صَوت. فَإِنَّهُم أشاروا بـ(لو) إِلَى الْخلاف فِي الْمَسْأَلَة، فَفِي

(الْفُرُوع) وَفِي كراهتهما - يَعْنِي الأذان وَالْإِقَامَة - للنِّسَاء بِلَا رفع صَوت. وَقيل: مُطلقًا، رِوَايَتَان. وَعنهُ: يسن لَهُنَّ الْإِقَامَة وفَاقا للشَّافِعِيّ لَا الأذان، خلافًا لمَالِك. انْتهى. فَقَوله: وَلَو بِلَا رفع صَوت، إِشَارَة إِلَى الرِّوَايَة الثَّانِية.

Third. When our jurists say, "If this were as such," and other similar phrases, they are indicating that the issue is one of difference of opinion. For example, the author of *al-Iqnāʿ* stated in the *Chapter on Adhān*, "They (meaning the *adhān* and *iqāmah*) are disliked for women, even without raising the voice."[590] When he says, "even without," he is referring to the difference of opinion on the issue. *Al-Furūʿ* mentions, "On the topic of its undesirability (meaning, *adhān* and *iqāmah*) for women, even if their voices are not raised or, as stated, absolutely [without the qualification of raising the voice], there are two narrations. From him [Aḥmad]: It is the Sunnah for [women] to do the *iqāmah*, thereby agreeing with al-Shāfiʿī; however, [it is not Sunnah] to perform the *adhān*, contrary to Mālik."[591] Therefore, when he says, "Even without raising the voice," he is referring to the difference of opinion on this matter.

وَقَالُوا أَيْضا: وَلَا يكره مَاء الْحمام وَلَو سخن بِنَجس، وَفِي هَذِه الْمَسْأَلَة خلاف أَيْضا، فقد قَالَ فِي (الْفُرُوع): وَعنهُ: يكره مَاء الْحمام لعدم تحري من يدْخلهُ. فاحفظ هَذِه الْقَاعِدَة، فَإِنَّهَا مهمة جدا.

Further, they stated, "Water of bathhouses is not undesirable, even if it is heated with an impure substance."[592] This issue is one where there is difference of opinion, as well. In *al-Furūʿ*, it states, "From him: It is disliked to use bathhouse water, because one cannot be sure who entered [the bathhouse]."[593] Therefore, keep this principle in your recollection, as it is extremely important.

---

590 [T] *Al-Iqnāʿ* (1/75).
591 [T] *Al-Furūʿ* (2/8).
592 [T] *Mukhtaṣar al-Ifādāt* by Ibn Balban (p. 32).
593 [T] *Al-Furūʿ* (1/64).

العقد السَّابِع
Chapter Seven

فِي ذكر الْكتب الْمَشْهُورَة فِي الْمَذْهَب وَبَيَان طَرِيقَة بَعْضهَا وَمَا عَلَيْهِ من التعليقات والحواشي حسب الْإِمْكَان

On Famous Texts Written on the *Madhhab*, Their Styles, and Their Commentaries and Explanations, to the Best of My Abilities

تعلم أَيهَا الْفَاضِل الألمعي أَن الْخَوْض فِي هَذَا الْبَحْر الزاخر صَعب المسلك، بعيد المرمى، خُصُوصا فِي هَذَا الزَّمَان المعاند للْعلم وَأَهله، حَتَّى رماهم فِي سوق الكساد، ونادى عَلَيْهِم بالحرمان، فَأنى لمثلي أَن يجول فِي هَذَا الميدان، ويناضل أُولَئِكَ الفرسان؟ مَعَ أنه تمْضِي عَليّ الشُّهُور بل الأعوام، وَلَا أرى أحدا يسألني عَن مَسْأَلَة فِي مَذهَب الإِمَام أَحْمد، لانقراض أَهله فِي بِلَادنَا، وتقلص ظله مِنْهَا، فَلذَلِك أصبح اشتغالي بِغَيْر الْفِقْه من الْعُلُوم، وَإِن اشتغلت بِهِ، فاشتغالي إِمَّا على طَرِيقَة الاستنباط، وَإِمَّا بمراجعة كتب الْأَئِمَّة على اخْتِلَاف مذاهبهم. وَلَوْلَا أملي بنفع سكان جَزِيرَة الْعَرَب من الْحَنَابِلَة لما حركت - فِيمَا رَأَيْت من الْفَوَائِد - قلما، وَلَا خاطبت رسما مِنْهَا وَلَا طللا، وَلَكِن إِنَّمَا الْأَعْمَال بِالْبيناتِ، وَالله مطلع على السرائر.

You are aware, O virtuous, brilliant individual, that delving into this rich ocean is a difficult endeavour, and a distant target, especially during these unyielding times, both for knowledge and its people, which have cast them into the markets of stagnation and proclaimed deprivation against them. How, then, can someone like me roam in this domain and contend with those horsemen? Sometimes, months and even years pass, and I find not a single person asks me about an issue in the *madhhab* of al-Imām Aḥmad, because its people have died off in our lands and so its shade has shrunk in this era. Due to these reasons, I find myself preoccupied with sciences other than law. If I do occupy myself with [jurisprudence], it is either to deduce [some rulings] or to review the books of the *imāms*, irrespective of their *madhhab*. Had it not been that I hoped that the Ḥanbalī residents of the Arabian Peninsula would benefit, I would not have moved my pen to write any beneficial point that you have seen, nor would I have engaged in any description or addressed its ruins. However, actions are but by intentions, and Allah the Exalted is aware of the secrets.

نعم إن كثيرا من سكان الجزيرة وخصوصا أهل نجد - أكثر الله من أمثالهم - يبذلون الْآن النفيس والنفيس بطبع كتب هَذَا الْمَذْهَب، ويحيون رفاة الْكتب المندرسة مِنْهُ، فَأَحْبَبْت مشاركتهم فِي هَذَا الْأجر، وأقدمت على ذكر الْكتب الْمَشْهُورَة، ليتنبه أهل الْخَيْر إِلَيْهَا، فيبرزونها مطبوعة طبعا حسنا، لينْتَفع بهَا أهل هَذَا الْمَذْهَب وَغَيرهم، كَمَا هِيَ عَادَتهم فِي عمل الْخَيْر. فَقلت مستعينا بِاللَّه تَعَالَى.

Yes, many residents of the Arabian Peninsula, and especially Najd, may Allah increase their like, spend their valuables to print the books of this *madhhab*, and they revive the remains of its extinct works. Therefore, I loved that I could partake with them in the reward, and began writing about its famous books, so that people of goodness can be aware of them and publish them in new, proficient editions, in order for the people of this *madhhab*, and others, to benefit. That is their custom in doing good actions. Therefore, I state, while relying on Allah:

لقد كَانَت دمشق فِيمَا مضى أَكثر بِلَاد الْإِسْلَام مدارس، وكل مدرسة كَانَ بهَا خزانَة كتب تضم مَا يحْتَاج إِلَيْهِ أهل الْمدرسَة، وَكَانَ فِي مدارس الْحَنَابِلَة من كتبهمْ مَا يبهر الْعُقُول، وخصوصا الْمدرسَة العمرية الشيخية الَّتِي بالصالحية، فَإِنَّهَا كَانَ بهَا من خزائِن الْكتب مَا لَا يُوجد فِي غَيرهَا، ثمَّ تلاعبت أَيدي المختلسين فِي تِلْكَ الخزائن، حَتَّى تركوها وَمَا بهَا ورقة وَاحِدَة، وَلم يبْق بَين أَيدي النَّاس إِلَا مَا نبا عَنهُ طوفان الْجَهْل، وَسلم من أَفْوَاه الأرضة، وَمَعَ هَذَا فَإنَّك ترى تِلْكَ الْبَقِيَّة الْبَاقِيَة تكَاد أَن لَا يكمل مِنْهَا كتاب، وليت هَذِه الْبَقِيَّة من سفر من أسفار أَو جُزْء من أَجزَاء مبذولة لمن ينْتَفع بهَا، وَلَكِن الزَّمَان قضى عَلَيْهَا أَن تكون فِي

خزَائِن الْجَاهِلين الَّذين لَا يَنْتَفِعُونَ بهَا وَلَا ينفعون، وَتلك البلية عَمت فَإِنَّا لله وَإِنَّا إِلَيْهِ رَاجِعُون. فَلم يبْق لنا إِلَّا أَن نذْكر مِنْهَا بَعْضًا مِمَّا اطَّلَعْنَا عَلَيْهِ عَسى أَن ينْتَفع بصنعنا من يطلع على كتَابنَا، أَو يسْتَدرك عَلَيْهِ مُسْتَدْرك فَيكون لنا أجر السَّبق.

Once upon a time, Damascus had the most schools out of any other land of Islam. Each school had a library that contained books needed by those in the school. In the Ḥanbalī schools, some of their books were mind-dazzling, especially in the school known as *al-Madrasat al-ʿUmariyyah al-Shaykhiyyah*, in the Ṣāliḥiyyah district. It had an unparalleled library. Then, thieves began toying with those bookcases, until not a single paper remained on them. Nothing remained in the hands of people, save the remnants of what the flood of ignorance missed and what was saved from the mouths of termites. With that said, you find that the remnants rarely comprise of the entirety of a book. If only those remnant tomes or volumes are put into use for those who would benefit from them. Alas though, the times have done away with those books, leaving them in the collections of ignoramuses that neither benefit nor allow others to benefit. This was the disaster that became widespread, and indeed, to Allah we belong and to Him we shall return. The only thing I can do is mention some of those books which I was able to read. Perhaps there is some benefit in this exercise for those who read my book, or, someone can add missed books onto them, and as such, I can earn the rewards of precedence.

الْمُغنِي ومختصر الخرقي
Al-Mughnī and *Mukhtaṣar al-Khiraqī*

اشْتهر فِي مَذْهَب الإِمَام أَحْمد عِنْد الْمُتَقَدِّمين والمتوسطين مُخْتَصر الْخرقِي، وَلم يخْدم كتاب فِي الْمَذْهَب مثل مَا خدم هَذَا الْمُخْتَصر، وَلَا اعتني بِكِتَاب مثل مَا اعتني بِهِ، حَتَّى قَالَ الْعَلامَة يُوسُف بن عبد الْهَادِي فِي كِتَابه (الدر النقي فِي شرح أَلْفَاظ الْخرقِي): قَالَ شَيخنَا عز الدين الْمصْرِي: ضبطت للخرقي ثَلَاث مِئَة شرح، وَقد اطلعْنَا لَهُ على مَا يقرب من عشْرين شرحا. وَسمعت من شُيُوخنَا وَغَيرهم: أن من قَرَأَهُ حصل لَهُ إِحدى ثَلَاث خِصَال: إِمَّا أَن يملك مئة دِينَار، أَو يَلِي الْقَضَاء، أَو يصير صَالحا. هَذَا كَلَامه.

Mukhtaṣar al-Khiraqī became widespread among the scholars of the early and middle periods of the development of the *madhhab* of Aḥmad.[594] No book was shown as much service as was this *mukhtaṣar*, nor was any book given the same level of attention as it was. The great scholar, Yūsuf ibn ʿAbd al-Hādī, stated in his book *al-Durr al-Naqī fī Sharḥ Alfaẓ al-Khiraqī*, "Our *shaykh*, ʿIzz al-Dīn al-Miṣrī, stated, 'I have enumerated three hundred explanations of *al-Khiraqī*, and I have personally read almost twenty explanations. I heard from my teachers, and others, that whoever reads it will gain one of three qualities: either they will own one hundred dinars, or they will become judges, or they will become righteous.''[595]

وَقَالَ في (الْمَقْصد الأرشد) قَالَ أَبُو إِسْحَاق الْبَرْمَكِي: عدد مسَائِل الْخرقِي أَلْفَانِ وثلاث مئة مَسْأَلَة، فَمَا ظَنك بِكِتَاب ولع مثل أبي إِسْحَاق فِي عد مسَائِله؟ وَمَا ذَلِك إِلَّا لمزيد الاعتناء بِهِ.

In *al-Maqṣad al-Arshad*, its author stated, "Abu Isḥāq al-Barmakī said, 'There are two thousand, three hundred issues discussed in al-Khiraqī.'[596] What, then are your thoughts of a book that enamored someone like Abu Isḥāq to sit and count the issues it discusses? Indeed, this shows the great keenness shown to this book."

---

594 [T] There are three phases of the *Ḥanbalī* scholars. al-Shaykh Bakr Abu Zayd lists them as follows:

First: The Early Scholars: They begin with al-Imām Aḥmad and end at al-Imām al-Ḥasan ibn Ḥāmid (d. 403 AH).

Second: The Middle Scholars: They begin with al-Qāḍī Abu Yaʿlā and end with al-Imām al-Burhān ibn Mufliḥ (d. 884 AH).

Third: The Late Scholars: They begin with al-Qāḍī ʿAlāʾ al-Dīn al-Mardāwī and continue till this day.

Refer to *al-Madkhal al-Mufaṣṣal* (1/455).

However, al-Shaykh Ibn Qāsim lists them as follows:

First: The Early Scholars: They begin with al-Imām Aḥmad and end with al-Qāḍī Abu Yaʿlā.

Second: The Middle Scholars: From al-Qāḍī Abu Yaʿlā's time until al-Muwaffaq Ibn Qudāmah al-Maqdisī.

Third: The Late Scholars: From al-Muwaffaq's time until now.

Refer to *Hashiyat al-Rawḍ al-Murbiʿ* (1/93). It is likely that al-Shaykh Ibn Qāsim's remarks were quoted from al-Shaykh Ibn Ḥumayd who held the same view, as in his commentaries on *al-Rawḍ al-Murbiʿ* (p. 161).

595 [T] *Al-Durr al-Naqī* (3/873).

596 [T] *Al-Maqṣad al-Arshad* (2/298).

وَكتب أَبُو بكر عبد الْعَزِيز على نسخته مُخْتَصر الْخرقِي: خالفني الْخرقِي فِي مُخْتَصره فِي سِتِّين مَسْأَلَة، وَلم يسمهَا.

Abu Bakr ʿAbd al-ʿAzīz wrote in his copy of *Mukhtaṣar al-Khiraqī*, "Al-Khiraqī disagreed with me on sixty issues." However, he did not name them.

وَقَالَ الْقَاضِي أَبُو الْحُسَيْن ابْن الْفراء: تتبعها فَوَجَدتهَا ثَمَانِي وَتِسْعين مَسْأَلَة. انْتهى.

Al-Qāḍī Abu 'l-Ḥusayn ibn al-Farrāʾ stated, "I studied those issues, and found that [they actually disagreed in] eighty nine issues."

وَبِالْجُمْلَةِ فَهُوَ مُخْتَصر بديع، لم يشْتَهر متن عِنْد الْمُتَقَدِّمين اشتهاره، وَأعظم شروحه وأشهرها (الْمُغنِي) للْإِمَام موفق الدّين الْمَقْدِسِي، وَقد كَانَ فِي تسع مجلدات ضخام بِخَطِهِ، وأغلب نسخه الْآن فِي ثَلَاثَة عشر مجلدا.

To summarise, it is a marvellous summation, and no text was as popular among the early scholars as it was. Its most important, and most famous explanation is *al-Mughnī* by al-Imām Muwaffaq al-Dīn al-Maqdisī. It was explained in nine large volumes, written in his own handwriting. Most copies nowadays consist of thirteen volumes.[597]

وطريقته فِي هَذَا الشَّرْح أَن يكْتب الْمَسْأَلَة من الْخرقِي، ويجعلها كالترجمة، ثمَّ يَأْتِي على شرحها وتبيينها، وببيان مَا دلّت عَلَيْهِ بمنطوقها ومفهومها ومضمونها، ثمَّ يتبع ذَلِك مَا يشبهها مِمَّا لَيْسَ بمذكور فِي الْكتاب، فَتحصل الْمسَائِل كتراجم الْأَبْوَاب.

The method in this explanation is that he would write the issue discussed by al-Khiraqī, and would make it an introductory heading, then would explain and clarify it. He would explain what it refers to literally, its connotations, and what it comprises of. Then, he would mention other similar issues that are not mentioned in [*Mukhtaṣar al-Khiraqī*.] Therefore, the issues become headings to the chapters.

---

597 [T] In the year 2021, the most popular copy is that of Dr. ʿAbdullah al-Turki, the editor of this *Introduction to the Madhhab of al-Imām Aḥmad*, and it comprises of fifteen volumes, though the last volume consists of the indexes.

وَيبين فِي كثير من الْمسَائِل مَا اخْتلف فِيهِ مِمَّا أجمع عَلَيْهِ، وَيذكر لكل إِمَام مَا ذهب إِلَيْهِ، وَيُشِير إِلَى دَلِيل بعض أَقْوَالهم، ويعزو الْأَخْبَار إِلَى كتب الْأَئِمَّة من أهل الحَدِيث، ليحصل التفقه بمدلولها، والتمييز بَين صحيحها ومعلولها، فيعتمد النَّاظر على معروفها، ويعرض عَن مجهولها.

He also clarified many issues where there are differences of opinion and where there are consensuses. He would mention the views of each major scholar, and would refer to the evidences of some of their views. He referenced the narrations back to the books of the scholars of ḥadīth, so that one can gain understanding of the law by referring to those books and so that he could differentiate between authentic and defective aḥadīth. As such, a reader can base their views on the authentic ones and disregard the unknown ones.

وَالْحَاصِل أَنه يذكر الْمَسْأَلَة من الْخرقِيّ، وَيبين غَالِبا رِوَايَات الإِمَام بهَا، ويتصل الْبَيَان بِذكر الْأَئِمَّة من أَصْحَاب الْمذَاهب الْأَرْبَع وَغَيرهم من مجتهدي الصَّحَابَة وَالتَّابِعِينَ وتابعيهم، وَمَا لَهُم من الدَّلِيل وَالتَّعْلِيل، ثمَّ يرجع قولا من أُولَئِكَ الْأَقْوَال، على طَرِيقَة فن الْخلاف والجدل، ويتوسع فِي فروع الْمَسْأَلة. فَأصْبح كِتَابه مُفِيدا للعُلَمَاء كَافة على اخْتِلَاف مذاهبهم، وأضحى المطلع عَلَيْهِ ذَا معرفَة بِالْإِجْمَاع والوفاق وَالْخلاف والمذاهب المتروكة، بِحَيْثُ تتضح لَهُ مسالك الِاجْتِهَاد، فيرتفع من حضيض التَّقْلِيد إِلَى ذرْوَة الْحق الْمُبين، ويمرح فِي روض التَّحْقِيق.

In summary, he mentions an issue from al-Khiraqī, usually clarifies the reports from the *imām* about it, and then mentions what was stated by the scholars of the four *madhhabs*, and other scholars, such as the *mujtahid* scholars among the Companions, their students and those who followed them. He also mentions their evidences and the reasons they chose their views, and then would give preference to one of those views. He would do so using the art of disputation and argumentation. He would also elaborate on the various subsidiaries of the issue. Because of these reasons, his book was very beneficial to scholars irrespective of their schools of thought. A reader of [*al-Mughnī*] would leave knowing the points of consensus, agreement, disagreement, and the views that have been abandoned, providing a clear understanding of the methods of *ijtihād*. It would lift a person from the depths of blind-following to the pinnacle of the clear truth, allowing them to frolic in the garden of precision and criticalness.

قَالَ ابْن مُفْلِح فِي (الْمَقْصد الأرشد): اشْتغل الْمُوفق بتأليف (الْمُغنِي) أحد كتب الْإِسْلَام، فَبلغ الأمل فِي إنهائه. وَهُوَ كتاب بليغ فِي الْمَذْهَب، تَعب فِيهِ، وأجاد فِيهِ، وجمل بِهِ الْمَذْهَب، وقرأه عَلَيْهِ جمَاعَة، وَأثْنى ابْن غنيمَة على مُؤَلفه فَقَالَ: مَا أعرف أحدا فِي زَمَاننَا أدْرك دَرَجَة الِاجْتِهَاد إِلَّا الْمُوفق.

Ibn Mufliḥ stated in *al-Maqṣad al-Arshad*, "Al-Muwaffaq busied himself with authoring *al-Mughnī*, one of the books of Islam, and reached his wish of completing it. It is a marvelous book in the *madhhab*. He tired himself in research, doing so excellently. He beautified the *madhhab* by authoring it. A group read it to him, and Ibn Ghunaymah praised its author, saying, 'I am not aware of anyone in our time who has reached the level of *ijtihād* except for al-Muwaffaq.'"[598]

وَقَالَ الشَّيْخ عز الدين بن عبد السَّلَام: مَا رَأَيْت فِي كتب الْإِسْلَام مثل (الْمحلى) و(المجلى) لابْنِ حزم، وَكتاب (الْمُغنِي) للشَّيْخ موفق الدّين، فِي جودتهما، وَتَحْقِيق مَا فيهمَا. وَنقل عَنهُ أَنه قَالَ: لم تطب نَفسِي بالإفتاء حَتَّى صَارَت عِنْدِي نُسْخَة (الْمُغنِي) نقل ذَلِك ابْن مُفْلِح.

Al-Shaykh 'Izz al-Dīn ibn 'Abd al-Salam said, "Of the books authored on Islam, I have not seen anything like *al-Muḥallā* and *al-Mujallā*, both by Ibn Ḥazm, and *al-Mughnī* by al-Shaykh Muwaffaq al-Dīn, in their quality and the precision of their contents."[599] He is also reported to have said, "I did not feel confident in giving edicts until I had a copy of *al-Mughnī*." This last portion was transmitted by Ibn Mufliḥ.[600]

وَحكى أَيْضا فِي تَرْجَمَة الزريراني صَاحب (الْوَجِيز) أَنه طالع (الْمُغنِي) ثَلَاثًا وَعشْرين مرة، وعلق عَلَيْهِ حَوَاشِي.

[Ibn Mufliḥ] also reported, in the biography of al-Zarīrānī (the author of *al-Wajīz*), that he read *al-Mughnī* twenty-three times, and wrote margina-

598 [T] *Al-Maqṣad al-Arshad* (2/16).
599 [T] This was mentioned by al-Dhahabī in *Siyar A'lām al-Nubalā'* (18/193).
600 [T] Ibid

lia on it.

وَحكي أَيْضا فِي تَرْجَمَة ابْن رزين أَنه اختصر (الْمُغنِي) فِي مجلدين، وَسَماهُ (التَّهْذِيب)، وَحكي أَيْضا فِي تَرْجَمَة عبد الْعَزِيز بن عَليّ بن الْعِزّ بن عبد الْعَزِيز الْبَغْدَادِي ثمَّ الْمَقْدِسِي، الْمُتوفى سنة سِت وَأَرْبَعين وَثَمَان مِئَة: أَنه اختصر (الْمُغنِي).

In the biography of Ibn Razīn, [Ibn Mufliḥ] also stated that he summarised it into two volumes, and called it, *al-Tahdhīb*. He said, in the biography of ʿAbd al-ʿAzīz ibn ʿAlī ibn al-ʿIzz ibn ʿAbd al-ʿAzīz al-Baghdādī, who was later a resident of Jerusalem and died in the year 846, that he summarised the book.

وَمِمَّا اطَّلَعْنَا عَلَيْهِ من شُرُوح الْخرقِيّ شرح القَاضِي أبي يعلى مُحَمَّد ابن الْحُسَيْن ابْن الْفراء الْبَغْدَادِي، وَهُوَ فِي مجلدين ضخمين، وَبَعض نسخه فِي أَربع مجلدات وطريقته: أَنه يذكر الْمَسْأَلَة من الْخرقِي، ثمَّ يذكر من خَالف فِيهَا، ثمَّ يَقُول: وَدَلِيلنَا فيفيض فِي إِقَامَة الدَّلِيل من الْكتاب وَالسّنة وَالْقِيَاس على طَرِيقَة الجدل.

Of the books that I have seen that explain al-Khiraqī are: The explanation of al-Qāḍī Muḥammad ibn al-Ḥusayn ibn al-Farrāʾ al-Baghdādī, occurring in two large volumes, and some even in four. His method of explaining is that he would mention the issue mentioned by al-Khiraqī, then would discuss those who disagreed, and would say, "Our evidence is," and would then delve deeply into the evidences from the Qurʾān, Sunnah, and analogies, by use of argumentation.

مِثَاله: أَنه يَقُول: مَسْأَلَة، قَالَ أَبُو الْقَاسِم: وَلَا ينْعَقد النِّكَاح إِلَّا بولِي وشاهدين من الْمُسلمين. أما قَوْله: لَا ينْعَقد إِلَّا بولي، فَهُوَ خلاف لأبي حنيفَة فِي قَوْله: الْوَلِيّ لَيْسَ بِشَرْط فِي نِكَاح الْبَالِغَة. دليلنا: فيذكر دَلِيل الْمَسْأَلَة سالكا مَسْلَك فن الْخلاف، ثمَّ يَقُول: وَقَوله بِشَاهِدين من الْمُسلمين، خلافًا لمَالِك وَدَاوُد فِي قَوْلهمَا: الشَّهَادَة لَيست بِشَرْط فِي انْعِقَاد النِّكَاح، وَخِلَافًا لأبي حنيفَة فِي قَوْله: ينْعَقد بِشَاهِد وَامْرَأَتَيْنِ، وينْعَقد نِكَاح الْمسلمَة والكتابية بِشَهَادَة كَافِرين. ثمَّ

يَقُول: دليلنا على مَالك وَدَاوُد: كَذَا وَكَذَا، وعَلى أبي حنيفَة كَذَا وَكَذَا.

For example, he said, "Issue: Abu 'l-Qāsim said, 'A marriage is not effectuated without a guardian and two Muslim witnesses.' As for his statement, 'It is not effectuated without a guardian,' it is contrary to [the view of] Abu Ḥanīfah, who opined that a guardian is not a precondition to [the validity of] the marriage of a girl above the age of puberty. Our evidence is [...]" Then, he mentioned the evidences of the issue, doing so while adhering to the rules of disputation. He then said, "His statement, 'And two Muslim witnesses,' is contrary to Mālik and Dāwūd, both of whom stated, 'Witnesses are not a precondition to effectuation of marriage.' Also, it is contrary to Abu Ḥanīfah, who stated that a marriage may be effectuated with one [male] witness and two women, and the marriage of a Muslim woman and a Christian or Jewish woman with the testimony of two disbelieving witnesses." Then, he would state, "Our evidence against Mālik and Dāwūd is such-and-such, and against Abu Ḥanīfah it is such-and-such."

وَالْفرق بَين هَذَا الشَّرْح وَبَين (الْمُغنِي) أَن (الْمُغنِي) يسْلك قَرِيبا من هَذَا المسلك، وَيكثر من ذكر الْفُرُوع زِيَادَة على مَا فِي الْمَتْن، فَلذَلِك صَار كتابا جَامعا لمسائل الْمَذْهَب، وَأما أَبُو يعلى فَإِنَّهُ لَا يذكر شَيْئا زَائِدا على مَا فِي الْمَتْن، وَلكنه يُحَقّق مسَائِله، وَيذكر أدلتها، ومذاهب الْمُخَالفين لَهَا، فَإِذا طبع (الْمُغنِي) مَعَ شرح القَاضِي قرب النَّاظر فيهمَا من أن يُحِيط بِالْمذهبِ، دَلَائِل وفروعا، وحصلت لَهُ معرفَة بِبَقِيَّة الْمذَاهب، وَتلك غَايَة قصوى يحتاجها كل مُحَقّق.

The difference between [the] explanation [of Abu Ya'lā] and *al-Mughnī* is that the latter closely resembles the method of authorship of [Abu Ya'lā's explanation], but mentions a lot of subsidiary matters not mentioned in the text. Consequently, it is a comprehensive book, comprising of a large sum of the issues discussed in the *madhhab*. As for Abu Ya'lā, he does not mention anything beyond what is mentioned in the text. What he does, however, is scrutinise its issues, mention its evidences and the views of those who disagreed. If *al-Mughnī* were to be printed with the explanation of al-Qāḍī, it would be easy for a reader to grasp the entirety of the *madhhab*, in its evidences and the issues it comprises of, and they would also learn about the other schools of thought, which is a superior aim and goal that every scrutinising and diligent scholar needs.

وَقد نظم الْخرقِي الْفَقِيه الأديب اللّغَوِي الزَّاهِد الشَّاعِر المفلق، يحيى بن يُوسُف بن يحيى بن مَنْصُور بن المعمر بِفَتْح الْمِيم الْمُشَدّدَة - بن عبد السَّلَام الْأَنْصَارِيّ الصرصري الزريراني الضَّرِير، صَاحب الدِّيوَان الْمَشْهُور فِي مدح النَّبِي صلى الله عَلَيْهِ وَسلم الْمُتَوفى سنة سِتّ وَخمسين وست مِئَة شَهِيدا قَتله التتار. وَقد نظم الْخرقِي نظما صَدره بِخطْبَة نثرا، قَالَ فِيهَا: جعلت أَكثر تعويلي فِي نظمي هَذَا على مُخْتَصر الخرقي فِيمَا نقلته، إِذْ كَانَ فِي نَفسِي أوثق من تابعته، وسمى نظمه (الدرة الْيَتِيمَة والمحجة المستقيمة) ثمَّ ذكر أنه كَانَ قد عزم على نظم ربع الْعِبَادَات، ثمَّ شرح الله صَدره لإكمال الْكتاب فَفعل، ونظمه من بَحر الطوِيل، وحرف الروي الدَّال.

Al-Khiraqī was made into a poem by the author, linguist, ascetic, and great poet, Yaḥyā ibn Yūsuf ibn Yaḥyā ibn Manṣūr ibn al-Muʿammar ibn ʿAbd al-Salām al-Anṣārī al-Ṣarṣarī al-Zarīrānī, the blind. He wrote a famous poem praising the Prophet ﷺ. He died in the year 656 as a martyr after being killed by the Tatars. He made al-Khiraqī into poetic form, which he prefaced with an introduction in prose. He said, "I made the majority of my reliance, in this poem, on *Mukhtaṣar al-Khiraqī* in my quotations [of issues], since I believed within myself that it is the most trustworthy source that I have followed." He named his poem *al-Durrat al-Yatīmah wa 'l-Maḥajjah al-Mustaqīmah*. He then mentioned that he wanted to just create a poem of the quarter of worship,[601] but then Allah the Exalted opened his heart to completing the entire book, which he did. He wrote it in the long meter,[602] and the final letter of each line [that is heard] is a *dāl* (د).

قَالَ فِي أَوَائِل النّظم

He said at the outset of his poem:

يَا طَالبا للْعلم وَالْعَمَل اسْتمع　　مَا قلت مَخْصُوصًا بِمذهب أَحْمد

إِن من اخْتَار الإِمَام ابْن حَنْبَل　　إِمَامًا لَهُ فِي وَاضح الشَّرْح يَهْتَدِي

601 [T] *Fiqh* studies fall into four categories: (i) Actions of worship (*al-ʿIbādāt*), (ii) Dealings and transactions (*al-Muʿāamalāt*), (iii) Marriage and divorce (*al-Nikāḥ wa 'l-Ṭalāq*) and (iv) Criminal law (*al-Jināʾiyāt*).

602 [T] This is a reference to *al-Baḥr al-Ṭawīl*, which is a poetic meter used by Arabs.

فاشرع فِي ذكر الطَّهَارَة أَولا   وَهل عَالم إِلَّا بذلك يبتدي

O seeker of knowledge and action listen,
To what I say, specific to the madhhab of Aḥmad.
Indeed, the one who chooses al-Imām Aḥmad,
As a leader, in the clarity of exposition he will be guided.
I commence with mention of purification first,
As one can ask: Is there a scholar except that he commenced with that?

وَقَالَ فِي آخر النّظم

And he stated at the end of the poem:

أَلفَيْنِ فاعددها وَسبعا مئاتها   وَسبعين بَيْتا ثمَّ أَرْبَعَة زد

بعد المئين السِّت والأربع الَّتِي   تلتها الثَّلَاثُونَ استتمت فقيد

بصرصر فِي أَيَّام أشرف مَالك   أُمُور الورى الْمُسْتَنْصر بن مُحَمَّد

وناظمها يحيى بن يُوسُف أفقر الْأَ   نَام إِلَى غفران رب ممجد

Such were two-thousand—count them—and seven-hundreds,
As well as seventy four more lines.
In the year 634, this was completed—so write.
In Ṣarṣar, during the days of the noblest disposer,
Of people's matters: al-Muṣtansir ibn Muḥammad,
Authored by Yaḥyā ibn Yūsuf, the neediest of people,
Of forgiveness from a Lord, most Honourable.

ثمَّ إِن الصرصري نظم (زَوَائِد الْكَافِي) على الْخرقِيّ فِي كتاب مُسْتَقل، وَالنُّسْخَة الَّتِي رَأَيْتهَا وجدت أَولهَا مخروما، إِلَى بَاب الْمسْح على الْخُفَّيْنِ، فَلم أدر شَرطه فِيهَا. وَالنّظم من بَحر الطوِيل على رُوِيَ الدَّال أَيْضا. وَقَالَ فِي آخرهَا:

Al-Ṣarṣarī also authored *Zawā'id al-Kāfī*, which is a poem of al-Khiraqī, but published as an independent book. The first part of the copy that I found was destroyed, all the way to the chapter on wiping over leather socks. As such, I did not learn what his method was. However, I did find that it is in the long meter and ended each line with the sound of the *dāl* (د) letter, as well. He stated at its ending:

فَخذهَا هداك الله أَخذ موفق   لغر الْمعَانِي حَافظ متسدد
مسَائِل فقه واضحات لناشد   بِأَبْيَات شعر رائقات لِمُنْشِد
وعدتها أَلفَانِ كن خير ألف   لَهَا تحمد الْآثار مِنْهَا وتحمد
تخيرتها مِمَّا حوى ابْن قدامَة ال   مُوفق فِي الْكَافِي تخير مقتد
هما لقنا صدق لَهُ ولجمعه   بتوفيقه تَكْفِي الضلال وتهتدي
وأسندت منظومي إِلَيْهِ تبركا   بألفاظه الْحسنى تبرك أرشد
فهذي وَمَا ألفت من قبلهَا إِذا   حفظتهما حفظ اللبيب المجود
وطارحت أهل الْبَحْث من فقهائنا   بِمَا حوت الثنتان ترشد وترشد

Learn them, may Allah guide you, as someone aided,
To its honourable meanings; memorise them as one guided.
Matters of law, clear to the seeker,
By couplets of poetry, finely made by a bard.
They number two thousand, be quite accustomed to them,
Its effects will be praiseworthy – as shall you.
I selected them from the yield of Ibn Qudāmah,
Al-Muwaffaq in al-Kāfī, opting for emulation.
Both thousands are in fealty to it, and in its authorship,
With Divine Aid you will be delivered from heresy; guided.
I attributed my poem to him so as to attain blessings,
And to his beautiful words, seeking blessings and guidance.
So this, and what I have written before, if you,
Memorise them as an intelligent, proficient person does,
And if you exchanged with our diligent jurists,
You will be guided and guide others with these two-thousand [lines].

وَألف فِي لُغَات الْخرقِيّ وَشرح مفرداتها يُوسُف بن حسن بن عبد الْهَادِي كتابا

سَمَّاهُ (الدّر النقي فِي شرح أَلفَاظ الْخرقِيّ) وَهُوَ فِي مُجَلد، حذا فِيهِ حَذْو صَاحب (المطلع)، ورتبه على أَبْوَاب الْكتاب. وَقد رَأَيْته بِخَطِّهِ فِي خزانَة الْكتب الدمشقية المودعة فِي قبة الْملك الظَّاهِر بيبرس، وَحكى فِي آخِره أَنه فرغ من تأليفه سنة سِتّ وَسبعين وَثَمَان مئة، وَبِالْجُمْلَةِ فَهُوَ كتاب نَافِع فِي بَابه.

On the language and terminology of al-Khiraqī, Yūsuf ibn Ḥasan ibn ʿAbd al-Hādī authored a book called *al-Durr al-Naqī fī Sharh Alfaẓ al-Khiraqī*, in one volume. He emulated the author of *al-Muṭliʿ* and also organised it according to the chapters of the book. I saw a manuscript in his own handwriting in the library of Damascus which is near the school of King al-Ẓāhir Bibars. At the end of the book, he mentioned that he finished writing it in the year 876. Generally, it is a beneficial book on the subject.

هَذَا مَا أمكنني الِاطِّلَاع عَلَيْهِ من مواد مُخْتَصر الخرقِي.

These were the books I was able to read on the topic of *Mukhtaṣar al-Khiraqī*.

الْمُسْتَوْعب

Al-Mustawʿib

بِكَسْر الْعين الْمُهْملَة، تأليف الْعلامَة مُجْتَهد الْمَذْهَب مُحَمَّد بن عبد الله بن الْحُسَيْن بن مُحَمَّد بن قَاسم بن إِدْرِيس السامري - بِضَم الْمِيم وَكسر الرَّاء مُشَدّدَة - الْمُتَقَدّم ذكره. وَهُوَ كتاب مُخْتَصر الْأَلفَاظ، كثير الْفَوَائِد والمعاني، ذكر مُؤَلفه فِي خطبَته أَنه جمع فِيهِ (مُخْتَصر الْخرقِي) و(التنبيه) للخلال، و(الإرشاد) لِابْنِ أبي مُوسَى، وَ(الْجَامِع الصَّغِير) و(الخصال) للْقَاضِي أبي يعلى، و(الخصال) لِابْنِ الْبنا، وَكتاب (الْهِدَايَة) لأبي الْخطاب، و(التذكرة) لِابْنِ عقيل، ثمَّ قَالَ: فَمن حصل كتابي هَذَا، أغناه عَن جَمِيع هَذِه الكتب الْمَذْكُورة، إِذْ لم أخل بِمَسْأَلَة مِنْهَا إِلَّا وَقد ضمنته حكمهَا وَمَا فِيهَا من الرِّوَايَات وأقاويل أَصْحَابنَا الَّتِي تضمنتها هَذِه الْكتب، اللَّهُمَّ إِلَّا أَن يكون فِي بعض نسخهَا نُقْصَان. وَلَقَد تحريت أصح مَا قدرت عَلَيْهِ مِنْهَا، ثمَّ زِدْت على ذَلِك مسَائِل وَرِوَايَات لم تذكر فِي هَذِه الْكتب،

نقلتها من (الشافي) لغلام الْخلال، وَمن (الْمُجَرّد)، وَمن (كِفَايَة الْمُفْتِي)، وَمن غَيرهمَا من كتب أَصْحَابنَا. هَذَا كَلَامه.

It is the authorship of the great scholar and *mujtahid* of the *madhhab*, Muḥammad ibn ʿAbdullāh ibn al-Ḥusayn ibn Muḥammad ibn Qāsim ibn Idrīs al-Sāmurrī, who was previously mentioned. This book is concise in its wording, but rich in benefit and information. In the introduction, the author mentioned that he combined *Mukhtaṣar al-Khiraqī*, *al-Tanbīh* by al-Khallāl, *al-Irshād* by Ibn Abī Mūsā, *al-Jāmiʿ al-Saghīr* and *al-Khiṣāl* by al-Qāḍī Abu Yaʿlā, *al-Khiṣāl* by Ibn al-Bannā, *al-Hidāyah* by Abu ʿl-Khaṭṭāb, and *al-Tadhkirah* by Ibn ʿAqīl. Then, he said, "Whoever reads this book, it will suffice him from all of the mentioned texts, since I did not neglect a single issue, but that I added its ruling and the narrations [from al-Imām Aḥmad], and positions of our *aṣḥāb*, as stated in those books. Save, of course, if the copies of those texts had some deficiencies or lost pages. I attempted to extract the most correct speech from them, and then I added issues and reports to them that were not mentioned in those books, but which I quoted from *al-Shāfī* by Ghulām al-Khallāl, *al-Mujarrad*, *Kifāyat al-Mufti*, and other books authored by our *aṣḥāb*."

وَبِالْجُمْلَةِ فَهُوَ كتاب أحسن متن صنف فِي مَذْهَب الإِمَام أَحْمد وأجمعه، وَقَالَ فِي كِتَابه: إنه لم يتَعَرَّض فِيهِ لشَيْء من أُصُول الدّين، وَلَا من أُصُول الْفِقْه، وَيكثر فِيهِ من ذكر الْآدَاب الْفِقْهِيَّة. انْتهى. وَهُوَ فِي مجلدين ضخمين. وَقد حذا حذوه الشَّيْخ مُوسَى الحجاوي فِي كِتَابه (الإِقنَاع لطَالب الِانْتِفَاع) وَجعله مَادَّة كِتَابه، وَإِن لم يذكر ذَلِك فِي خطبَته، لكنه عِنْد تَأمل الْكِتَابَيْنِ يتَبَيَّن ذَلِك. رحمهمَا الله تَعَالَى.

Generally, it is the best and most comprehensive text authored on the *madhhab* of al-Imām Aḥmad. He said, "I did not discuss anything pertaining to theology or legal theories, but I did mention mannerisms pertaining to jurisprudence." The book comprises of two large volumes. al-Shaykh Mūsā al-Ḥajjāwī, in his book *al-Iqnāʾ li Ṭālib al-Intifāʿ*, emulated this work, and based his book off of it. Though he did not explicitly say so in his introduction, when reflecting on the two books, it is clear that he did so. May Allah have mercy on both.

الْكَافِي
Al-Kāfī

هُوَ فِي مجلدين، للشَّيْخ موفق الدّين الْمَقْدِسِي صَاحب (الْمُغنِي) يذكر فِيهِ الْفُرُوع الْفِقْهِيَّة، وَلَا يَخْلُو من ذكر الْأَدِلَّة وَالرِّوَايَات. قَالَ مُصَنفه فِي خطبَته: توسطت فِيهِ بَين الإطالة والاختصار، وأومأت إِلَى أَدِلَّة مسَائِل مَعَ الِاقْتِصَار، وغزوت أَحَادِيثه إِلَى كتب أَئِمَّة الْأَمْصَار، وَرَأَيْت كتابا لطيفا لِلْحَافِظِ الْكَبِير صَاحب الْأَحَادِيث المختارة مُحَمَّد بن عبد الْوَاحِد بن أَحْمد بن عبد الرَّحْمَن بن إِسْمَاعِيل بن مَنْصُور السَّعْدِيّ الْمَقْدِسِي الملقب بالضيا فِي تَخْرِيج أَحَادِيث الْكَافِي، وَقد توفّي الْحَافِظ سنة ثَلَاث وَأَرْبَعين وست مِئَة.

It is a two-volume book authored by Muwaffaq al-Dīn al-Maqdisī, the author of *al-Mughnī*. In this book, he mentions subsidiary matters of law, and mentions evidences and narrations. The author stated in the introduction, "I wrote this as an intermediate text, not too long, and not too short. I also referred to evidences of the issues, in a concise way, and referenced the aḥadīth to the books of the *imāms* of the various lands." I also saw a very nice book authored by the major ḥadīth master, the author of *al-Aḥādīth al-Mukhtārah*, Muḥammad ibn ʿAbd al-Wāḥid ibn Aḥmad ibn ʿAbd al-Raḥmān ibn Ismāʿīl ibn Manṣūr al-Siʿdī al-Maqdisī, also known as al-Ḍiyā, where he referenced the aḥadīth of *al-Kāfī*. Al-Ḥāfiẓ [al-Ḍiyā] died in the year 643.

الْعُمْدَة
Al-ʿUmdah

كتاب مُخْتَصر فِي الْفِقْه، لصَاحب (الْمُغنِي) جرى فِيهِ على قَول وَاحِد مِمَّا اخْتَارَهُ، وَهُوَ سهل الْعبارَة، يصلح للمبتدئين. وطريقته فِيهِ أَنه يصدر الْبَاب بِحَدِيث من الصِّحَاح، ثمَّ يذكر من الْفُرُوع مَا إِذا أدققت النّظر، وَجدتهَا مستنبطة من ذَلِك الحَدِيث، فترتقي همة مطالعه إِلَى طلب الحَدِيث، ثمَّ يرتقي إِلَى مرتبَة الاستنباط وَالِاجْتِهَاد فِي الْأَحْكَام.

It is a short, summarised book on *fiqh*, authored by the author of *al-Mughnī*. In this book, he chose to mention only one opinion, the one he chose [as the correct representation of the *madhhab*.] Its phrasing is easy to understand, making it suitable for beginners. His method in the book is that he would begin the chapter by mentioning an authentic ḥadīth, and then would mention the subsidiary matters that, after careful inspection, one would find are deduced from that ḥadīth. This raises a person's incentive to study ḥadīth and be able to deduce and perform *ijtihād* in rulings.

ولنفاسته ولطف مسلكه شَرحه الإِمَام بَحر الْعُلُوم النقلية والعقلية أَحْمد بن تَيْمِية الملقب بشيخ الْإِسْلَام، فزينه بمسالكه الْمَعْرُوفَة، وأفرغ عَلَيْهِ من لِبَاس الإجادة صنوفه، وكساه حلل الدَّلِيل، وحلاه بحلى جَوَاهِر الْخلاف، وزينه بِالْحَقِّ والإنصاف، فَرضِي الله عَنْهُمَا. وَلَقَد رَأَيْت مِنْهُ المجلد الأول: أَوله أول الْكتاب، وَآخره بَاب الآذان.

Due to its preciousness and pleasant style, it was explained by the *imām* and the ocean of knowledge in scriptural and rational sciences, Aḥmad ibn Taymiyyah, also known as Shaykh al-Islām. He beautified it with his known style of authoring, and poured various types of excellence on it, by beautifying it with the adornments of evidence, decorating it with the jewels of discussions on differences of opinion, and adorned it with the truth and impartiality. May Allah be pleased with both. I have seen the first volume, which begins with the outset of the book and ends at the Chapter of *Adhān*.

مُخْتَصر ابْن تَمِيم

Mukhtaṣar Ibn Tamīm

مُؤَلفه ابْن تَمِيم الْمُتَقَدّم، يذكر فِيهِ الرِّوَايَات عَن الإِمَام أَحْمد وَخلاف الْأَصْحَاب، وَيذْهب فِيهِ تَارَة مَذْهَب التفريع، وآونة إِلَى التَّرْجِيح. وَهُوَ كتاب نَافِع جدا لمن يُرِيد الِاطِّلَاع على اختيارات الأَصْحَاب، لكنه لم يكمل، بل وصل فِيهِ مُؤَلفه إِلَى أَثْنَاء كتاب الزَّكَاة، إِلَى قَوْله: فصل: وَمن غرم لإِصْلَاح ذَات الْبَين، أَي: فَإِنَّهُ يُعْطى من الزَّكَاة.

The author, Ibn Tamīm, was previously mentioned. In this book, he mentioned the narrations from al-Imām Aḥmad, and the differences occurring among the *aṣḥāb*. Sometimes, he takes the route of exploring deductions and subsidiary matters, and sometimes, he takes the route of preferring one view over the other. It is a very useful and beneficial book for anyone who wishes to explore the positions taken by the *aṣḥāb*. However, he did not complete the book; the author only reached the Chapter of *Zakāt*, specifically, to his statement, "Section: Whoever shoulders the responsibilities associated with reconciliation, they are given of *zakāt*."

وطريقته فِيهِ أنه إِذا قَالَ: شَيخنَا، يكون المُرَاد بِهِ نَاصح الدّين أَبُو الْفرج ابْن أبي الْفَهم، وَظن بَعضهم أنه يُرِيد بِهِ أَبَا الْفرج الشيرازِي، وَهُوَ غلط.

In this book, when he says, "Our teacher," he is referring to Nāṣiḥ al-Dīn Abu 'l-Faraj ibn Abi 'l-Fahm. Some thought it refers to Abu 'l-Faraj al-Shīrāzī, which is a mistake.

رُؤُوس الْمسَائِل
Ru'ūs al-Masā'il

للشريف الإِمَام الأوحد عبد الْخَالِق بن عِيسَى بن أَحْمد بن أبي مُوسَى الْهَاشِمِي الْمُتَقدّم. وطريقته فِيهِ أنه يذكر الْمسَائِل الَّتِي خَالف فِيهَا الإِمَام أحمد وَاحِدًا من الْأَئِمَّة أَو أَكثر، ثمَّ يذكر الْأَدِلَّة منتصرا للْإِمَام، وَيذكر الْمُوَافق لَهُ فِي تِلْكَ الْمَسْأَلَة، بِحَيْثُ أَن من تَأمل كِتَابه وجده مصححا للمذاهب، وذاهبا من أقوالها الْمَذْهَب الْمُخْتَار. فجزاه الله خيرا.

Authored by the Sharif[603] and unique *imām*, 'Abd al-Khāliq ibn 'Īsā ibn Aḥmad ibn Abī Mūsā al-Hāshimī, who was previously mentioned. His style is that he would mention the issues that al-Imām Aḥmad disagreed with another *imām* or more than one. Then, he would mention the evidences to support the view of the *imām*, and would mention those who concurred with that view. As such, those who deeply reflect on the contents of the book will find that it corrects the views of other *madhhabs*, and chooses the choice view of their opinions. May Allah reward him.

603 [T] A 'Sharīf' refers to someone being a direct descendant of the Prophet ﷺ.

الْهِدَايَة

Al-Hidāyah

لأبي الْخطاب الكلوذاني، مُجَلد ضخم جليل، يذكر فِيهِ الْمسَائِل الْفِقْهِيَّة، وَالرِّوَايَات عَن الإِمَام أَحْمد بهَا: فَتَارَة يَجْعَلهَا مُرْسلَة، وَتارَة يبين اخْتِيَاره، وَإِذا قَالَ فِيهِ: قَالَ شَيخنَا أَو عِنْد شَيخنَا، فمراده بِهِ القَاضِي أَبُو يعلى ابْن الْفرا.

Authored by Abu ʿl-Khaṭṭāb al-Kalwadhānī, it is a large, magnificent volume. He mentioned issues pertaining to law and the narrations of al-Imām Aḥmad pertaining to them. Sometimes, he leaves them as is, without commentary, but at other times, he clarifies his position. In this book, when he says, "Our *shaykh* said," or, "According to our *shaykh*," he is referring al-Qāḍī Abu Yaʿlā ibn al-Farrāʾ.

وَبِالْجُمْلَةِ فَإِنَّهُ حذا فِيهِ حَذْو الْمُجْتَهدين فِي الْمَذْهَب، لِلصَّحِحَيْنِ لروايات الإِمَام. وَسَمعنَا أَن الشَّيْخ مجد الدّين عبد السَّلَام ابْن تَيْمِية وضع عَلَيْهِ شرحا سَمَّاهُ (مُنْتَهى الْغَايَة فِي شرح الْهِدَايَة) لكنه بيض بعضه وَبَقِي مسودة. وَكَثِيرًا مَا رَأينَا الْأَصْحَاب ينقلون عَن تِلْكَ المسودة، وَرَأَيْت مِنْهَا فصولا على هوامش بعض الْكتب.

In summary, he treaded the way of the *mujtahid* scholars of the *madhhab* who validated the narrations of the *imām*. I have heard that Majd al-Dīn ʿAbd al-Salām ibn Taymiyyah authored an explanation, which he called, *Muntahā al-Ghāyat fī Sharḥ al-Hidāyah*. However, he authored some of it, but the rest was kept as a draft. Many of the *aṣḥāb*, though, quote that draft copy, and I have seen portions of it in the margins of some books, acting as commentary.

التَّذْكِرة

Al-Tadhkirah

للْإِمَام أبي الْوَفَاء عَلي بن عقيل الْبَغْدَادِي، جعلهَا على قَول وَاحِد فِي الْمَذْهَب، مِمَّا صَححهُ وَاخْتَارَهُ، وَهِي وَإِن كَانَت متْنا متوسطا لَا تَخْلُو من سرد الْأَدِلَّة فِي

بعض الْأَحَايين، كَمَا هِيَ طَرِيقَة الْمُتَقَدِّمين من أَصْحَابنَا.

It is the authorship of Abu 'l-Wafā' 'Alī ibn 'Aqīl al-Baghdādī. He wrote it only to quote one view in the *madhhab*, which he preferred and chose. Although it is an intermediate text, it mentions evidences occasionally, as was the norm with the earlier *aṣḥāb*.

الْمُحَرر
Al-Muḥarrar

كتاب فِي الْفِقْه، للْإِمَام مجد الدين عبد السَّلَام ابن تَيمِية الْحَرَّانِي، حذا فِيهِ حَذْو (الْهِدَايَة) لأبي الْخطاب، يذكر الرِّوَايَات: فَتَارَة يرسلها، وَتارَة يبين اخْتِيَاره فِيهَا. وَقد شَرحه الفَقِيه الفرضي المفنن عبد الْمُؤمن بن عبد الْحق بن عبد الله بن عَلي بن مَسْعُود الْقطيعِي الأَصْل الْبَغْدَادِي، الملقب بصفي الدين، الْمُتَوفَّى سنة تسع وَثَلَاثِينَ وَسَبْع مئة، شرحا سَمَّاهُ (تَحْرِير الْمُقَرّر فِي شرح الْمُحَرر) قَالَ فِي خطبَته: لم أذكر فِيهِ سوى مَا هُوَ فِي الْكتاب من الرِّوَايَات وَالْوُجُوه التِي ذكرهَا غَيره، لخُرُوج ذَلِك عَن المَقْصُود، إِنَّمَا أنا بصدد بيَان مَا أودع من ذَلِك لَا غير. انْتهى.

It is a book on law, authored by al-Imām Majd al-Dīn 'Abd al-Salam ibn Taymiyyah al-Ḥarrānī. In this book, he imitated the style of *al-Hidāyah*, authored by Abu 'l-Khaṭṭāb. He mentioned various quotations [from al-Imām Aḥmad], and would sometimes leave them without commentary, but at other times, would choose one as the choice view. It was explained by the jurist, scholar of inheritance and various sciences, 'Abd al-Mu'min ibn 'Abd al-Ḥaqq ibn 'Abdullah ibn 'Alī ibn Mas'ūd al-Qaṭī'ī, who was originally from Baghdad. His title was Ṣafī al-Dīn, and he died in the year 739. His explanation was entitled, *Taḥrīr al-Muqarrar fi Sharḥ al-Muḥarrar*. In the introduction, he said, "I did not mention, in this book, anything besides the narrations and possibilities that were already present in [*al-Muḥarrar*], and I avoided any [narrations and possibilities] mentioned by anyone else, because that is not the purpose of the book. I am in the midst of explaining what he has written in this book, nothing else."

وطريقته فِيهِ: أنه يذكر الْمَسْأَلَة من الْكتاب، ثمَّ يشرع فِي شرحها بِبَيَان مقاصدها، وَيبين منطوقها ومفهومها وَمَا تنطوي عَلَيْهِ من المباحث، وَلَا يخل مَعَ ذَلِك بِذكر الدَّلِيل وَالتَّعْلِيل وَالتَّحْقِيق، فَهُوَ من الْكتب الَّتِي يَلِيق الاعتناء بهَا.

His method in authoring this book is that he would mention an issue from the book, and then would engage in explaining it by detailing its purpose, discussing its explicit meanings and its indirect connotations, as well as issues that it comprises of. Along with that, he did not fail to mention evidences, causes for the rulings, and attempt to precisely analyse the text. It is a book worthy of being shown attention.

ولتقي الدّين بن قندس حَاشِيَة على (الْمُحَرر) وَلابْن نصر الله حَوَاشِي عَلَيْهِ حَسَنَة، وَللْإِمَام ابْن مُفْلِح حَاشِيَة على (الْمُحَرر) سَمَّاهَا (النكت والفوائد السّنيَّة) على (الْمُحَرر) لمجد الدّين ابْن تَيْمِية، مَوْجُودة فِي خزانَة الْكتب الخديوية بِمصْر.

Taqi al-Dīn ibn Qundus also wrote a commentary on *al-Muḥarrar*, and Ibn Nasrullāh wrote some useful commentaries on it. Likewise, al-Imām Ibn Mufliḥ authored commentaries on *al-Muḥarrar*, calling it *al-Nukat wa 'l-Fawā'id al-Saniyyah 'ala 'l-Muḥarrar li Majd al-Dīn Ibn Taymiyyah*. It is present in the library of al-Khadyawiyyah in Egypt.

الْمقنع
Al-Muqni'

هُوَ فِي مُجَلد، تأليف الإِمَام موفق الدّين الْمَقْدِسِي. وَقَالَ فِي خطبَته: اجتهدت فِي جمعه وترتيبه، وإيجازه وتقريبه، وسطا بَين القصير والطويل، وجامعا لأَكْثَر الأَحْكَام عرية عَن الدَّلِيل وَالتَّعْلِيل. انْتهى.

It comprises of a single volume, authored by al-Imām Muwaffaq al-Dīn al-Maqdisī. He stated in the introduction, "I put my full effort into compiling and arranging it, making it concise and easy to grasp. It is an intermediately large work, neither short nor long, and it comprises of most rulings, though without mentioning evidences nor causes for the rulings."

وَذَلِكَ أَن موفق الدّين رَاعى فِي مؤلفاته أَربع طَبَقَات، فصنف (الْعُمْدَة) للمبتدئين،

ثمَّ ألف (الْمقنع) لمن ارْتقى عَن درجتهم وَلم يصل إِلَى دَرَجَة المتوسطين، فَلذَلِك جعله عريا عَن الدَّلِيل وَالتَّعْلِيل، غير أنه يذكر الرِّوَايَات عَن الإِمَام، ليجعل لقارئه مجالا إِلَى كد ذهنه، ليتمرن على التَّصْحِيح، ثمَّ صنف المتوسطين (الْكَافِي) وَذكر فِيهِ كثيرا من الْأَدِلَّة، لتسمو نفس قارئه إِلَى دَرَجَة الِاجْتِهَاد فِي الْمَذْهَب حينما يرى الْأَدِلَّة، وترتفع نَفسه إِلَى مناقشتها، وَلم يَجْعَلهَا قَضِيَّة مسلمة. ثمَّ ألف (الْمُغنِي) لمن ارْتقى دَرَجَة عَن المتوسطين، وَهُنَاكَ يطلع قارئه على الرِّوَايَات، وعَلى خلاف الْأَئِمَّة، وعَلى كثير من أدلتهم، وعَلى مَا لَهُم وَمَا عَلَيْهِم من الْأَخْذ وَالرَّد، فَمن كَانَ فَقِيه النَّفس حِينَئِذٍ مرن نَفسه على السمو إِلَى الِاجْتِهَاد الْمُطلق إِن كَانَ أَهلا لذَلِك، وتوفرت فِيهِ شُرُوطه وَإِلَّا بَقِي على أَخذه بالتقليد.

Muwaffaq al-Dīn, in his authorships, catered to four levels and ranges of study: (i) He authored *al-ʿUmdah* to cater to beginners. (ii) Then *al-Muqniʿ* for one who advanced beyond the beginner stages but is not yet an intermediate student. Because of that reason, he authored it without mentioning evidences nor causes for rulings. However, he did mention narrations from the *imām*, so that the reader can have the opportunity to engage in deep thought and practice authentication of views. (iii) Then, he authored *al-Kāfī* for intermediate students, wherein he mentioned many evidences. The purpose was for the student to advance to a level of *ijtihād* in the *madhhab* by learning of the evidences, and to progress to the level of disputing evidences, no longer regarding matters as being simply unquestionable. (iv) Then, he authored *al-Mughnī* for those who surpassed the levels of intermediate students. In [*al-Mughnī*], the reader can read about the narrations, and the differences of opinion occurring with the other scholars, as well as many of their evidences. Also, [the reader can discover] the points of strength and the points of contention in their arguments. At that level, a jurist at heart can train themselves to ascend to the level of absolute *ijtihād*, if they are capable and possess its requisite attributes. Otherwise, they can continue to follow via *taqlīd*.

فَهَذِهِ هِيَ مَقَاصِد ذَلِك الإِمَام فِي مؤلفاته الْأَربعَة، وَذَلِكَ ظَاهر من مسالكه لمن تدبرها، بل هِيَ مَقَاصِد أَئِمَّتنَا الْكِبَار كَأبي يعلى وَابْن عقيل وَابْن حَامِد وَغَيرهم قدس الله أَرْوَاحهم.

Therefore, these are the motives of that *imām* in his four authorships. His motives are clear to those who think deeply about [his books]. Actually, they are the same motives shared by our great scholars, such as Abu Yaʿlā, Ibn ʿAqīl, Ibn Ḥāmid, and others, may Allah sanctify their souls.

وَاعْلَم أن لِأَصْحَابِنَا ثَلَاثَة متون حازت اشتهارا أَيمَا اشتهار. أَولهَا: (مُخْتَصر الْخرقِي) فَإِن شهرته عِنْد الْمُتَقَدمين سَارَتْ مشرقا ومغربا إِلَى أَن ألف الْمُوفق كِتَابه (الْمقنع) فاشتهر عِنْد عُلَمَاء الْمَذْهَب قَرِيبا من اشتهار الْخرقِي إِلَى عصر التسْع مئة، حَيْثُ ألف الْقَاضِي علاء الدين المرداوي (التنقِيح المشبع) ثمَّ جَاءَ بعده تَقِي الدين أَحْمد ابْن النجار الشهير بالفتوحي، فَجمع الْمقنع مَعَ التَّنْقِيح فِي كتاب سَمَّاهُ (مُنْتَهى الإرادات فِي جمع الْمقنع مَعَ التَّنْقِيح وزيادات) فعكف النَّاس عَلَيْهِ، وهجروا مَا سواهُ من كتب الْمُتَقَدِّمين، كسلا مِنْهُم ونسيانا لمقاصد عُلَمَاء هَذَا الْمَذْهَب التِي ذكرنَاهَا آنِفا.

Be aware that our *aṣḥāb* have three texts that have become extremely famous and widespread. The first is *Mukhtaṣar al-Khiraqī*. Its popularity among the early scholars spread from the east to the west, until al-Muwaffaq authored *al-Muqniʿ*, which then became almost as popular as that of al-Khiraqī, until the 9th century. Then, al-Qāḍī ʿAlā al-Dīn al-Mardāwī authored *al-Tanqīḥ al-Mushbiʿ*, and afterwards, Taqī al-Dīn Aḥmad ibn al-Najjār, known more widely as al-Futūḥī, consolidated *al-Muqniʿ* with *al-Tanqīḥ*, in a book he called *Muntahā al-Irādāt fī Jamʿ al-Muqniʿ maʿ al-Tanqīḥ wa Ziyādāt*. People then began to dedicate themselves to it and abandoned other books written by the early scholars, out of laziness and forgetfulness of the intents of the scholars of this *madhhab*, which we have previously clarified.

وَكَذَلِكَ الشَّيْخ مُوسَى الحجاوي ألف كِتَابه: (الْإِقْنَاع) وحذا بِهِ حَذْو صَاحب (الْمُسْتَوْعب) بل أَخذ مُعظم كِتَابه مِنْه وَمن (الْمُحَرر) وَ(الْفُرُوع) وَ(الْمقنع) وَجعله على قَول وَاحِد، فَصَارَ معول الْمُتَأَخرين على هذَيْن الْكِتَابيْنِ وَعلى شرحيهما.

Likewise, al-Shaykh Mūsā al-Ḥajjawī authored his book *al-Iqnāʿ*, and emulated the style of the author of *al-Mustawʿab*. Actually, he took the majority of his book from [*al-Mustawʿab*], *al-Muḥarrar*, *al-Furūʿ*, and *al-Muqniʿ*,

but only mentioned one view. The latter-day scholars relied on these two books and their explanations.

وَلما عكف النَّاس على (الْمقنع) أَخذ الْعلمَاء فِي شَرحه، فَأول شَارح لَهُ الإِمَام عبد الرَّحْمَن ابْن الإِمَام أبي عمر مُحَمَّد بن أَحْمد بن قدامَة الْمَقْدِسِي، فَإِنَّهُ شَرحه شرحا وافيا سَمَّاهُ بـ(الشافي)، وَقَالَ فِي خطبَته: اعتمدت فِي جمعه على كتاب (الْمُغنِي) وَذكرت فِيهِ من غَيره مَا لم أجِدهُ فِيهِ من الْفُرُوع وَالْوُجُوه وَالرِّوَايَات، وَلم أترك من كتاب (الْمُغنِي) إِلَّا شَيْئا يَسِيرا من الْأَدِلَّة، وعزوت من الْأَحَادِيث مَا لم يعز مِمَّا أمكنني عزوه. هَذَا كَلَامه.

When people dedicated their time to studying *al-Muqni'*, scholars began explaining it. The first to explain it was al-Imām 'Abd al-Raḥmān, the son of al-Imām Abu 'Umar Muḥammad ibn Aḥmad ibn Qudāmah al-Maqdisī. He explained it thoroughly, calling it *al-Shāfī*. He stated in its introduction, "In compiling this book, I relied on *al-Mughnī*, though I also mentioned other subsidiary matters, possible interpretations, and narrations mentioned in other books and not found in [*al-Mughnī*]. I only left a small amount of evidences mentioned in *al-Mughnī* out. Also, I referenced the aḥadīth that were not referenced [in *al-Mughnī*], so much as I was able."

وَبِالْجُمْلَةِ فطريقته فِيهِ: أَنه يذكر الْمَسْأَلَة من (الْمقنع) فيجعلها كالترجمة، ثمَّ يذكر مَذْهَب الْمُوَافق فِيهَا والمخالف لَهَا، وَيذكر مَا لكل من دَلِيله، ثمَّ يسْتَدلّ ويعلل للمختار، ويزيف دَلِيل الْمُخَالف، فمسلكه مَسْلَك الِاجْتِهَاد إِلا أَنه اجْتِهَاد مُقَيّد فِي مَذْهَب أَحْمد.

Generally speaking, his method was that he would mention the issue from *al-Muqni'* as a title, and then would mention the position of al-Muwaffaq on the topic, and those who contradicted [his view]. He would then mention the evidences cited by each camp, and would himself use evidences to declare the preferred view, while also weakening the evidences of those who hold other views. His style is that of *ijtihād*, though it is limited to the *madhhab* of Aḥmad.

ثمَّ شَرحه القَاضِي برهَان الدّين إِبْرَاهِيم بن مُحَمَّد الْأَكْمَل بن عبد الله بن مُحَمَّد

بن مُفْلِح، الْمُتَوفى سنة أَربع وَثَمَانِينَ وَثَمَان مئة، وَشَرحه فِي أَربع مجلدات ضخام، مزج الْمَتْن بالشرح، وَلم يتَعَرَّض بِهِ لمذاهب الْمُخَالفين، إِلا نَادرا، وَمَال فِيهِ إِلَى التَّحْقِيق وَضم الْفرُوع، سالكا مَسْلَك الْمُجْتَهدين فِي الْمَذْهَب، فَهُوَ أَنْفَع شُرُوح (الْمقنع) للمتوسطين. وعَلى طَرِيقَته سرى شَارِح (الإقناع) وَمِنْه يستمد.

Then, it was explained by al-Qāḍī Burhān al-Dīn Ibrāḥīm ibn Muḥammad al-Akmal ibn ʿAbdullah ibn Muḥammad ibn Mufliḥ, who died in the year 884. He explained it in four large volumes, and seamlessly transitioned between the text and its explanation. He rarely discussed the differing positions held by others. In this text, he leaned to precision and gathering subsidiary matters, taking a style of *ijtihād* in the *madhhab*. As such, it is one of the most beneficial explanations of *al-Muqni*ʿ for intermediate students. The explainer of *al-Iqnā*ʿ emulated its style, and drew from its contents.

وَرَأَيْت من شروحه أَيْضا (الممتع شرح الْمقنع) لسيف الدّين أبي البركات ابْن المنجا، الْمُتَقَدم ذكره، قَالَ فِي خطبَته: أَحْبَبْت أَن أشرح (المقنع) وَأبين مُرَاده وأوضحه، وأذكر دَلِيل كل حكم وأصححه.

I saw another explanation called *al-Mumti*ʿ *Sharḥ al-Muqni*ʿ, authored by Sayf al-Dīn Abu ʾl-Barakāt ibn al-Munajjā, who was previously mentioned. He said in its introduction, "I wanted to commentate on *al-Muqni*ʿ to explain and clarify its intents, then mention the evidences of each ruling and correct it." His method in this book is that he would mention an issue from *al-Mughnī* and would clarify its evidence, then would research its related issues and the narrations. He did not discuss anything but the *madhhab* of the *imām*.

وطريقته: أَنه يذكر الْمَسْأَلَة من (الْمُغنِي) وَيبين دليلها، ويحقق الْمسَائِل وَالرِّوَايَات، وَلم يتَعَرَّض لغير مَذْهَب الإِمَام. ثمَّ لما انحطت الهمم عَن طلب الدَّلِيل، وغاض نهر الِاشْتِغَال بِالْخِلَافِ، وأكب النَّاس على التَّقْلِيد البحت، وكادت كتب الْمُتَقَدِّمين ومسالكهم أَن تذْهب أدراج الرياح، انتصب لنصرة هَذَا الْمَذْهَب وَضم شَمله الْعَلامَة الْفَاضِل الْقَاضِي علاء الدين عَليّ بن سُلَيْمَان السَّعْدِي المرداوي ثمَّ الصَّالِحِي، فَوجدَ أهل زَمَنه قد أَكَبوا على (المقنع) فألف عَلَيْهِ شبه شرح سَمَاء

بـ(الإنصاف فِي معرفَة الرَّاجِح من الْخلاف) وطريقته فِيهِ: أَنه يذكر فِي الْمَسْأَلَة أَقْوَال الْأَصْحَاب، ثمَّ يَجْعَل الْمُخْتَار مَا قَالَه الْأَكْثَر مِنْهُم، سالكا فِي ذَلِك مَسْلَك ابْن قَاضِي عجلون فِي تَصْحِيحه لمنهاج النَّوَوِيّ وَغَيره من كتب التَّصْحِيح، فَصَارَ كِتَابه مغنيا للمقلد عَن سَائِر كتب الْمَذْهَب.

When people's resolve to seek evidences weakened, the river of engaging in differences of opinion diminished, people engaged in unadulterated blind-following, and the books of the early scholars almost were considered unfruitful, a great and virtuous scholar, al-Qāḍī 'Alā' al-Dīn 'Alī ibn Sulaymān al-Si'dī al-Mardāwī, who later settled in al-Ṣāliḥiyyah and was known as al-Ṣāliḥi, stood to come to the service of the *madhhab* and reassembled it. He found that people during his time were showing a great level of attention to *al-Muqni'*, so he authored a book that was almost an explanation of it, called *al-Inṣāf fī Ma'rifat al-Rājiḥ min al-Khilāf*. His style of authorship was that he would mention the views of the *aṣḥāb* pertaining to an issue, then would choose, of those views, the one that was stated by the majority. His style emulated that of Ibn Qāḍī 'Ajlūn in his corrections on *Minhāj* of al-Nawawi, and other books that sought to correct [their original texts]. [*Al-Inṣāf*] became a book sufficient for any *muqallid*, making them not need any other book in the *madhhab*.

ثمَّ اقتضب مِنْهُ كِتَابه الْمُسَمّى بـ(التنقيح المشبع فِي تَحْرِير أَحْكَام الْمقنع) فصحح فِيهِ الرِّوَايَات الْمُطلقَة فِي (الْمقنع) وَمَا أطلق فِيهِ من الْوَجْهَيْنِ أَو الْأَوْجه، وَقيد مَا أخل بِهِ من الشُّرُوط، وَفسر مَا أبهم فِيهِ من حكم أَو لفظ، وَاسْتثنى من عُمُومه مَا هُوَ مُسْتَثْنى على الْمَذْهَب حَتَّى خَصَائِص النَّبِي صلى الله عَلَيْهِ وَسلم، وَقيد مَا يحْتَاج إِلَيْهِ مِمَّا فِيهِ إِطْلَاقه وَيحمل على بعض فروعه مَا هُوَ مُرْتَبِط بهَا، وَزَاد مسَائِل محررة مصححة، فَصَارَ كِتَابه تَصْحِيحا لغالب كتب الْمَذْهَب.

Afterwards, he abridged it in another book, which he called *al-Tanqīḥ al-Mushbi' fī Taḥrīr Aḥkām al-Muqni'*, where he would correct the unqualified narrations in *al-Muqni'*, and the unqualified views that he mentioned consisted of two or more possibilities. He also qualified the preconditions mentioned and explained the obscure rulings and terminologies. He also mentioned exceptions to general rules, as opined by the *madhhab*, including the rulings that apply only to the Prophet ﷺ. He restricted the statements that were left without restrictions, and also synthesised the various connected branching rulings. He also added other issues after scrutinising them and correcting them. As such, the book became a method of correcting the majority of the books of the *madhhab*.

وَبِالْجُمْلَةِ فَهَذَا الْفَاضِل يَلِيق بِأَن يُطلق عَلَيْهِ مُجَدد مَذْهَب أَحْمد فِي الْأُصُول وَالْفُرُوع.

Generally speaking, this virtuous man deserves to be referred to as the reviver of the *madhhab* of Aḥmad, both in its legal theories and its subsidiary branches of law.

وَقد انتدب لشرح لُغَات (الْمقنع) الْعَلامَة اللّغَوِيّ مُحَمَّد بن أبي الْفَتْح البعلي، فألف فِي هَذَا النَّوْع كِتَابه (المطلع على أَبْوَاب الْمقنع) فأجاد فِي مبَاحث اللغَة، وَنقل فِي كِتَابه فَوَائِد مِنْهَا دلت على رسوخ قدمه فِي اللغَة وَالْأَدب، وَكَثِيرًا مَا يذكر فِيهِ مقَالا لشيخه الإِمَام مُحَمَّد ابن مَالك الْمَشْهُور. ورتب كِتَابه على أَبْوَاب (الْمقنع) ثمَّ ذيله بتراجم مَا ذكر فِي (الْمقنع) من الأَعْلَام. فجَاء كِتَابه غَايَة فِي الْجَوْدَة، وَوَقع فِي طرة نُسْخَة الْمقنع المطبوعة بِمصْر أن (المطلع) شرح (الْمقنع) وَهُوَ سَهْو. وَالْحق أَنه شرح للغاته، فدرجته كدرجة (الْمغرب) للحنفية، و(المصباح) للشَّافِعِيَّة.

The great scholar and grammarian, Muḥammad ibn Abi 'l-Fatḥ al-Baʿli, sought to explain the language and verbiage used in *al-Muqniʿ*, causing him to author a work in the genre, which he called *al-Muṭliʿ ʿalā Abwāb al- Muqniʿ*. He did well in his discussions on language, and he mentioned some useful points that showed his deep-rooted knowledge in language and literature. Often times, he would mention statements which he attributed to his teacher al-Imām Muḥammad ibn Mālik, who is well-known. He arranged his book in accordance to the chapters of *al-Muqniʿ*, and added an appendix giving biographies of the authorities mentioned in *al-Muqniʿ*. The outcome was that he produced a very high-quality work. In the margins of the version of *al-Muqniʿ* printed in Egypt, it is mentioned that *al-Muṭliʿ* is an explanation of *al-Muqniʿ*, which is a mistake. The truth is, it is an explanation of its terminology and its verbiage, making it resemble *al-Maghrib*, a book authored on the Ḥanafī *madhhab* and *al-Miṣbāḥ* in the

Shāfiʿī *madhhab*.

وَاخْتصرَ (الْمقنع) الشَّيْخ مُوسَى الحجاوي كَمَا سَيأْتِي.

Al-Muqniʿ was summarised by al-Shaykh Mūsā al-Ḥajjawi, as will be mentioned in the upcoming discussions.

الْفُرُوع
Al-Furūʿ

قَالَ فِي (كشف الظنون) هُوَ فِي مجلدين، للشَّيْخ شمس الدّين أبي عبد الله مُحَمَّد بن مُفْلِح الْحَنْبَلِي، الْمُتَوفَّى سنة ثَلَاث وَسِتِّينَ وَسَبْع مئة، أَجَاد فِيهِ وَأحسن على مذْهبه، وَشَرحه الشيْخ الإِمَام أَحْمد بن أبي بكر مُحَمَّد بن الْعِمَاد الْحَمَوِي، سَمَّاهُ (الْمَقْصد المنجح لفروع ابْن مُفْلِح) انْتهى. قلت: وَهُوَ عِنْدِي فِي مُجَلد وَاحِد ضخم. وَهَذَا الكتاب قل أن يُوجد نَظِيره.

In *Kashf al-Ẓunūn*, it states, "It is two volumes, authored by al-Shaykh Shams al-Dīn Abī ʿAbdillāh Muḥammad ibn Mufliḥ al-Ḥanbalī, who died in the year 763. He authored a high-quality and well-written work on his *madhhab*. It was explained by al-Shaykh, al-Imām Aḥmad ibn Abī Bakr Muḥammad ibn al-ʿImād al-Ḥamawī, in a book he called *al-Maqṣad al-Munjiḥ li Furūʿ Ibn Mufliḥ*."[604] I say: My copy of it is a single large volume. There is almost no parallel for this book.

وَقد مدحه الْحَافِظ ابْن حجر فِي (الدُّرَر الكامنة) فَقَالَ: صنف - يَعْنِي ابْن مُفْلِح - الْفُرُوع فِي مجلدين، أَجَاد فيهمَا إِلَى الْغَايَة، وَأورد فِيهِ من الْفُرُوع الغريبة مَا بهر بِهِ الْعلمَاء.

It was praised by al-Ḥāfiẓ Ibn Ḥajar in *al-Durar al-Kāminah*, where he said, "He authored *al-Furūʿ* in two volumes, and he did so proficiently and excellently. He mentioned unknown subsidiary matters of law that dazzled the scholars."[605]

---

604 [T] *Kashf al-Ẓunūn ʿan Asāmī al-Kutub wa ʾl-Funūn* by al-Shaykh Ḥājī Khalīfah (2/1256).
605 [T] *Al-Durar al-Kamīnah* (6/14).

وَقَالَ ابْن كثير: كَانَ مُؤَلفه بارعا، فَاضلا، متفننا فِي عُلُوم كَثِيرَة، وَلَا سِيمَا علم الْفُرُوع، وَله على (الْمقنع) نَحْو ثَلَاثِينَ مجلدة، وعلق على كتاب (الْمُنْتَقى) للمجد ابْن تَيْمِية. انْتهى.

Ibn Kathīr mentioned, "Its author was brilliant, virtuous, and knowledgeable in many sciences, especially subsidiary matters of law. He also explained *al-Muqniʿ* in approximately thirty volumes, and commented on *al-Muntaqā* of al-Majd Ibn Taymiyyah."[606]

وطريقته فِي هَذَا الْكتاب: أَنه جرده من دَلِيله وتعليله، وَيقدم الرَّاجِح فِي الْمَذْهَب، فَإِن اخْتلف التَّرْجِيح أطلق الْخلاف، وَإِذا قَالَ: فِي الْأَصَح، فمراده أصح الرِّوَايَتَيْنِ.

His style in this book is that he removed any mention of evidences from the book, and removed any causes for rulings. He would prefer the most veracious position in the *madhhab*. If there was a difference of opinion on which view is more preferred, he would mention the difference of opinion without choosing or preferring one over another. If he says, "According to the most correct view," he means, the most correct of the two narrations on the topic.

وَبِالْجُمْلَةِ فقد ذكر اصْطِلَاحه فِي أول كِتَابه، وَلَا يقْتَصر على مَذْهَب أَحْمد، بل يذكر الْمجمع عَلَيْهِ، والمتفق مَعَ الإِمَام أَحْمد فِي الْمَسْأَلة، والمخالف لَهُ فِيهَا من الْأَئِمَّة الثَّلَاثَة وَغَيرهم. وَيُشِير إِلَى ذَلِك بالرمز، ويطيل النَّفس فِي بعض المباحث، وَأَحْيَانا يتطرق إِلَى ذكر الْأَدِلَة، وَيذكر من النفائس مَا يَنْبَغِي للفاضل أَن يطلع عَلَيْهِ، بِحَيْثُ أَن كِتَابه يَسْتَفِيد مِنْهُ أَتبَاع كل مَذْهَب. فرحم الله مُؤَلفه.

To summarise, he mentioned his terminology in the outset of his book. His discussions are not limited to just the *madhhab* of Aḥmad, but rather, he mentions issues of consensus, as well as whom from the other three *imāms* (and others) agreed or disagreed with al-Imām Aḥmad in some of his views. He would refer to them with symbols. In some discussions, he would elaborate deeply, and at other times, he would only mention evidences. Sometimes, he mentioned useful points of benefit that virtuous people should be aware of. As such, his book is a source of benefit for followers of all *madh-*

606 [T] *Al-Bidāyah wa 'l-Nihāyah* (14/294).

habs. May Allah the Exalted have mercy on its author.

وَقد شَرحه الْعَلامَة شيخ الْمَذْهَب، مفتي الديار المصرية، محب الدّين أَحْمد بن نصر الله بن أَحْمد بن مُحَمَّد بن عمر الْبَغْدَادِي الأَصْل ثمَّ الْمصْرِي، الْمُتوفى سنة أَربع وَأَرْبَعين وَثَمَان مِئَة. وَشَرحه هَذَا أشبه بالحواشي مِنْهُ بالشروح، وَكتب على الْفُرُوع حَاشِيَة العَلامَة ذُو الْفُنُون تَقِي الدين أَبُو بكر بن إِبْرَاهِيم بن قندس، الْمُتَوفى سنة إِحْدَى وَسِتِّينَ وَثَمَان مِئَة. وَهَذِه الْحَاشِيَة فِي مُجَلد، وَبهَا من التَّحْقِيق والفوائد مَا لَا يُوجد فِي غَيرهَا.

It was explained by the great scholar and *shaykh* of the *madhhab*, the *Muftī* of Egypt, Muḥib al-Dīn Aḥmad ibn Naṣrullāh ibn Aḥmad ibn Muḥammad ibn ʿUmar al-Baghdādī, who was originally of Egyptian heritage, and who died in the year 844. His explanation is more resembling a marginalia. Another individual who wrote marginalia on *al-Furūʿ* is the great scholar of various sciences, Taqī al-Dīn Abu Bakr ibn Ibrāḥīm ibn Qundus, who died in the year 861. His work occurs in a single volume, and it contains precision and benefits that are not present in other works.

مغنى ذَوي الأفهام عَن الْكتب الْكَثِيرَة فِي الْأَحْكَام

Mughnī Dhawi ʿl-Afhām ʿan al-Kutub al-Kathīrah fi ʿl-Aḥkām

تأليف الْعَلامَة الْمُحدث يُوسُف بن حسن بن أَحْمد بن عبد الْهَادِي، الشهير بِابْن المبرد الصَّالِحِي، أَخذ الْفِقْه عَن القَاضِي علاء الدين المرداوي وَعَن تَقِي الدين ابْن قندس الْمُتَوفى سنة تسع وَتِسْع مئة.

It is the authorship of the great scholar and scholar of ḥadīth, Yūsuf ibn Ḥasan ibn Aḥmad ibn ʿAbd al-Hadi, known more commonly as Ibn al-Mibrad al-Ṣāliḥi. He learned *fiqh* from ʿAlāʾ al-Dīn al-Mardāwī and Taqī al-Dīn Ibn Qundus. He died in the year 909.

وَهَذَا الْكتاب فِي مُجَلد لطيف، صَدره بفن أصُول الديانات - يَعْنِي التَّوْحِيد - ثمَّ بِبَاب معرفَة الْأَعْرَاب، ثمَّ بأصول الْفِقْه، ثمَّ بِمَا يسْتَعْمل من الْأَدَب، ثمَّ أتبعه بِبَعْض اصْطِلَاحَات فِي الْمَذْهَب، ثمَّ استرسل فِي الْفِقْه على نمط وجيز، ثمَّ

خَتمه بقواعد كُلية يَتَرَتَّب عَلَيْهَا مسَائِل جزئية.

This book is in a single volume, and is a pleasant read. He began his book with the science of the foundation of the religion, i.e. *al-tawḥīd*, and then discussed grammar, legal theories, and manners. He followed this with the mention of some nomenclature of the *madhhab*, and then elaborated on *fiqh* in a concise manner, concluding his book with universal maxims that many particular issues stem from.

لكن مَا ذكره من الْفُنُون فِي صَدره لَا يُفِيد إِلَّا فَائِدَة قَليلَة جدا. وسلك فِي الْفِقْه مسلكا غَرِيبا فَقَالَ فِي أول كِتَابه: كتبت فِيهِ القَوْل الْمُخْتَار، وأشير إِلَى الْمَسْأَلَة الْمجمع عَلَيْهَا بِأَن أجعَل حكمهَا اسْم فَاعل أَو مفعول، وَمَعَ ذَلِك (ع) وَمَا اتفق عَلَيْهِ الْأَئِمَّة الْأَرْبَعَة بِصِيغَة الْمُضَارع، وَرُبمَا وَقع ذَلِك لنا فِيمَا اتفق فِيهِ أَبُو حنيفَة وَالشَّافِعِي فِي بعض مسَائِل لم نعلم فِيهَا مَذهَب الإِمَام مَالك، أَو لَهُ فِيهَا أَو فِي مذْهبه ثمَّ قَول غير الْمَشْهُور. فَإِن كَانَ لَا خلاف عندنَا فِي الْمَسْأَلَة فب(الباء) وَأَيْضًا (وَاو) وَإِن كَانَ فِيهِ خلاف عندنَا فب(التاء) وَأَيْضًا (وَاو) وَإِن كَانَ فِيهِ خلاف عندنَا فب(التاء) وَأَيْضًا (وَر) ووفاق الشَّافِعِي فَقَط ب(الْهَمْزَة) وَأَيْضًا (وس) وَأبي حنيفية فَقَط ب(النُّون)، وَأَيْضًا رقم (ح) وَلَا أكرر فِيهِ مَسْأَلَة فِي علم وَاحِد إِلا لزِيَادَة فَائِدَة، وَلَا يمْتَنع تكرارها فِي علمين لِأَن كل علم تجْرِي فِيهِ على أَصله، فَرُبمَا اخْتلف حكمهَا فِي العلمين، وَرُبمَا اتّفق. هَذَا كَلَامه.

With that said, the discussions he presents at the outset of the book contain very little benefit. He also had a very strange style when writing on *fiqh*, which he explained himself by saying, "I wrote the chosen view, and I refer to issues that have consensus, by writing its ruling in the subject or the object form, and placing an *ʿayn* (ع) letter besides it. When the Four Imāms agree on something, I write it in the present tense. Sometimes, that occurs when Abu Ḥanīfah and al-Shāfiʿī agree on issues but I am not aware of the position of al-Imām Mālik, or if he or his *madhhab* espoused an unpopular view. If there is no difference of opinion to us, I placed the *bā* (ب) letter, and the *wāw* (و) letter. If there is a difference of opinion, I placed the *tā* (ت) letter and the combination of *wāw* and *rā* (ور). When only al-Shāfiʿī agrees, I placed a *hamza* (ء), and a combination of *wāw* and *sīn* (وس). When only

Abu Ḥanīfah agrees, I played a *nūn* (ن), and a *hā* (ح). Whenever I repeat an issue in a single subject, it is to increase the benefit. That does not necessitate that I do not repeat it in two subjects, since each subject is treated independently. Sometimes, the rulings coincide, and sometimes, they do not."

وَرَأَيْت بِخَط مُؤَلفه هذَيْن الْبَيْتَيْنِ على ظهر الْكتاب:

I saw the following two couplets written on the back of the book in the author's handwriting:

هَذَا كتاب قد سما فِي حصره   أوراقه من لطفه مُتعَدِّدَة

جمع الْعُلُوم بِلُطْفِهِ فبجمعه   يُغْنِيك عَن عشْرين ألف مجلدة

This is a book exalted in its summation,
Its pages, from its pleasantness, are numerous.
It has compiled many sciences pleasantly, and thereby,
Is sufficient for you instead of twenty-thousand volumes.

وقرظه ابْن قَاضِي أذرعات بقوله:

Ibn Qāḍī praised it abundantly in his words:

يَا كتابا أزرى بِكُل كتاب   هُوَ فِي الأَرْض لوحنا المحظوظ

زَاد رَبِي منشيه علما وفضلا   ثمَّ لَا زَالَ سعده الْمَحْفُوظ

O book which puts all books to shame,
It is on the earth similar to our own preserved tablet.
My Lord proliferated knowledge and virtue in its author,
And subsequently, his blessings remained preserved.

مُنْتَهى الإرادات فِي جمع الْمقنع مَعَ التَّنْقِيح وزيادات
Muntahā al-Irādāt fi Jamʿ al-Muqniʿ maʿ 'l-Tanqīḥ wa Ziyādāt

هُوَ كتاب مَشْهُور، عُمْدَة الْمُتَأَخِّرين فِي الْمَذْهَب، وَعَلِيهِ الْفَتْوى فِيمَا بَينهم، تأليف الْعَلامَة تَقِي الدّين مُحَمَّد ابن العَلامَة أَحْمد بن عبد الْعَزِيز بن عَلي بن

إِبْرَاهِيم الفتوحي الْمصْرِي، الشهير بِابْن النجار. رَحل إِلَى الشَّام فالف بهَا كِتَابه (الْمُنتَهى) ثمَّ عَاد إِلَى مصر بعد أَن حرر مسَائِله على الرَّاجِح من الْمَذْهَب، واشتغل بِهِ عَامَّة الطلبَة فِي عصره، واقتصروا عَلَيْهِ، ثمَّ شَرحه شرحا مُفِيدا فِي ثَلَاث مجلدات ضخام، وغالب استمداده فِيهِ من كتاب (الْفُرُوع) لِابْنِ مُفْلِح. وَبِالْجُمْلَةِ فقد كَانَ مُنْفَردا فِي علم الْمَذْهَب. توفي سنة اثْنَتَيْنِ وَسبعين وَتِسْع مئة.

It is a popular book and is the relied-on book to the latter-day scholars. They use it for *fatwā* amongst themselves. It is the authorship of the great scholar, Taqī al-Dīn Muḥammad, the son of the great scholar Aḥmad ibn ʿAbd al-ʿAzīz ibn ʿAlī ibn Ibrāḥīm al-Futūḥī, the Egyptian. His famous title was Ibn al-Najjār. He travelled to the Levant and, while there, wrote *al-Muntahā*, then returned to Egypt after engaging in deep critique and study of its issues, according to the more correct opinion in the *madhhab*. The majority of students busied themselves with it during his time, resorting only to it. Then, he wrote a very useful and beneficial explanation of it in three large volumes. Mostly, his source in it was *al-Furūʿ* by Ibn Mufliḥ. In summary, he was unique in his knowledge of the *madhhab*. He died in the year 972.

وقرأت فِي (طَبَقَات الْحَنَابِلَة) لكَمَال الدّين الْغَزي الشَّافِعِي نقلا عَن ابْن طولون: أَن الْعَلامَة الْمُحَقق أَحْمد بن عبد الله بن أَحْمد العسكري صنف كتابا جمع فِيهِ بَين (الْمقنع) و(التنقيح) فاخترمته الْمنية قبل إكماله قَالَ: وَقد بَلغنِي أَن صاحبنا أَحْمد الشويكاني تِلْمِيذه شرع فِي تكملته. توفي العسكري سنة عشر وَتِسْع مِئَة.

I read a quote transmitted from Ibn Ṭūlūn in *Ṭabaqāt al-Ḥanābilah* by Kamal al-Dīn al-Ghizzī al-Shāfiʿī, “The great scholar and researcher, Aḥmad ibn ʿAbdullāh ibn Aḥmad al-ʿAskarī authored a book where he joined *al-Muqniʿ* and *al-Tanqīḥ* but he died before completing it. I was told, though, that one of our *aṣḥāb*, Aḥmad al-Shuwaykānī, his student, took to completing it. Al-ʿAskarī died in the year 910.

وَقَالَ الْغزي فِي تَرْجَمَة أَحْمد بن مُحَمَّد بن أَحْمد بن عمر بن أَحْمد ابن أبي بكر الشويكي النابلسي ثمَّ الدِّمَشْقِي الصَّالِحِي الْمُتَوفى سنة تسع وَثَلَاثِينَ وَتِسْع مِئَة: إنه جاور فِي الْمَدِينَة المنورة، وَجمع كتاب (التَّوْضِيح) جمع فِيهِ بَين (الْمقنع)

للشَّيْخ موفق الدّين بن قدامَة و(التنقيح) لعلاء الدين المرداوي، وَزَاد عَلَيْهِمَا أَشْيَاء مهمة. قَالَ ابْن طولون: وَسَبقه إِلَى ذَلِك شَيْخه الشهَاب العسكري، لكنه مَاتَ قبل إِتْمَامه، وَلم يصل فِيهِ إِلَّا إِلَى بَاب الْوَصَايَا. وعاصره أَبُو الْفضل ابْن النجار، فَجمع كِتَابه الْمَشْهُور بـ(المنتهى) لكنه عقد عباراته. انْتهى.

Al-Ghizzī said, in the biography of Aḥmad ibn Muḥammad ibn Aḥmad ibn ʿUmar ibn Aḥmad ibn Abī Bakr al-Shuwaykī, who was from Nāblus but then settled in the Ṣāliḥiyyah district of Damascus, and who died in the year 939, "He lived in *al-Madīnat al-Munawwarah*. He compiled *al-Tawḍīḥ*, a book where he combined the contents of *al-Muqniʿ* by al-Shaykh Muwaffaq al-Dīn Ibn Qudāmah, and *al-Tanqīḥ* by ʿAlāʾ al-Dīn al-Mardāwī, and added some important discussions. Ibn Ṭūlūn said, 'He was preceded to the task by his teacher, al-Shihāb al-ʿAskarī, but he died before completing the book, only reaching to the chapter of wills and testaments. Abu 'l-Faḍl ibn al-Najjār was a contemporary, and he authored his famous book *al-Muntahā*, but complicated the verbiage."

وَشرح (مُنْتَهى الإرادات) الْعَلامَة مَنْصُور بن يُونُس بن صَلَاح الدّين بن حسن بن أَحْمد بن عَليّ بن إِدْرِيس البهوتي، شيخ الْحَنَابِلَة فِي عصره، الْمُتوفى سنة إِحْدَى وَخمسين وَألف. وَشَرحه فِي ثَلَاث مجلدات، جمعه من شرح مؤلف (الْمُنْتَهى) لكتابه، وَمن شَرحه نَفسه على (الْإِقْنَاع) وَهُوَ شرح مَشْهُور مطبوع.

Muntahā al-Irādāt was explained by the great scholar, Manṣūr ibn Yunus ibn Ṣalāḥ al-Dīn ibn Ḥasan ibn Aḥmad ibn ʿAlī ibn Idrīs al-Buhūtī, the scholar of the Ḥanbalīs of his time, who died in the year 1051. His explanation consists of three volumes, which he compiled from the author of *al-Muntahā*, [Ibn al-Najjar's] explanation of his own book, and his (al-Buhūtī's) own explanation of *al-Iqnāʿ*. It is a popular, published work.

وَلَقَد كنت فِي حُدُود أَربع عشرة وثلاث مئة بعد الْألف أَقمت مُدَّة فِي قَصَبَة دَوْمًا دمشق، فأقرأت هَذَا الشَّرْح، وكتبت عَلَيْهِ حَاشِيَة وَضعتهَا أثْنَاء الْقِرَاءَة، وصلت فِيهَا إِلَى بَاب السّلم فِي مُجَلد ضخم، ثمَّ خرجت من دَوْمًا إِلَى دمشق، وهنالك لم أجد أحدا يطْلب الْعلم من الْحَنَابِلَة، بل ينْدر وجود حنبلي بهَا، ففترت همتي

عَن إتْمَامها، وَبقيت على مَا هِيَ عَلَيْهِ.

In the year 1314, I lived for a period in the town of Dūmā, a district of Damascus. I taught this explanation, and wrote a commentary on it as it was being read. I reached the chapter of advanced payments, and it was a large volume. Then, I left Dūmā, heading for Damascus, where I did not find a single person seeking knowledge from Ḥanbalīs; rather, Ḥanbalīs themselves were quite rare to find. Because of that, my determination subsided, causing me to not complete it. It remained in that state.

وللشيخ مَنْصُور حَاشِيَة على الْمَتْن. وَكتب الشَّيْخ مُحَمَّد بن أَحْمد بن عَليّ البهوتي الشهير بالخلوتي الْمصْرِي تحريرات على هَامِش نسخته متن (الْمُنتَهى) فجردت بعد مَوته فبلغت أَرْبَعِينَ كراسا. وَكَانَ من الملازمين للشَّيْخ مَنْصُور، توفي سنة ثَمَان وَثَمَانِينَ وَألف.

Al-Shaykh Manṣūr [al-Buhūtī] also has a commentary on the text, and al-Shaykh Muḥammad ibn Aḥmad ibn ʿAlī al-Buhūtī, more famously known as al-Khalwatī, the Egyptian, wrote some useful commentary and research in margins of his copy of *al-Muntahā*. After he passed away, they were transcribed, and they reached about forty notebooks. He was a close student of al-Shaykh Manṣūr, and died in the year 1088.

وعَلى الْمَتْن حَاشِيَة أَيْضا للشَّيْخ عُثْمَان بن أَحْمد النجدي صَاحب (شرح الْعُمْدَة للشَّيْخ مَنْصُور البهوتي المتوفى سنة [...] وَهِي حَاشِيَة نافعة تميل إِلَى التَّحْقِيق والتدقيق.

Al-Shaykh ʿUthmān ibn Aḥmad al-Najdī, the author of *Sharḥ al-ʿUmdah* (*ʿUmdat [al-Ṭālib]* being a text authored by al-Shaykh Manṣūr al-Buhūtī), also wrote a commentary on [*al-Muntahā*]. He died in the year [...],[607] and it is a very beneficial commentary, leaning towards precision and thoroughness.

الْإِقْنَاع لطَالب الِانْتِفَاع

Al-Iqnāʿ li Ṭālib al-Intifāʿ

607 The original manuscript has a blank spot at the area of the year, but after searching, I found that he died in the year 1097.

مُجَلد ضخم، كثير الْفَوَائِد، جم الْمَنَافِع، للعلامة الْمُحَقق مُوسَى ابن أَحْمد بن مُوسَى بن سَالم بن عِيسَى بن سَالم الحجاوي الْمَقْدِسِي، ثمَّ الدِّمَشْقِي الصَّالِحِي، بَقِيَّة الْمُجْتَهدين، والمعول عَلَيْهِ فِي مَذْهَب أَحْمد فِي الديار الشامية، تَرْجمهُ الكَمَال الْغزي فِي (النَّعْت الأَكْمَل) وَلم يذكر سنة وَفَاته، وَنجم الدّين الْغزي فِي (الْكَوَاكِب السائرة).

It is a large volume comprising of many useful points and is of immense benefit. It is an authorship of the great scholar and researcher, Mūsā ibn Aḥmad ibn Mūsā ibn Sālim ibn ʿĪsā ibn Sālim al-Ḥajjāwī al-Maqdisī. He was originally from Jerusalem, but then settled in the Ṣāliḥiyyah district of Damascus. He was a remnant of the *mujtahid* scholars, and is the relied upon scholar in the *madhhab* of Aḥmad in the Levant. Al-Kamāl al-Ghizzī wrote a biography of him in *al-Naʿt al-Akmal*, but did not mention his year of death. Najm al-Dīn al-Ghizzī also wrote about him in *al-Kawākib al-Sāʾirah*.

وَبِالْجُمْلَةِ فَهُوَ من أساطين الْعلمَاء وأجلهم، توفي سنة ثَمَان وَسِتِّينَ وَتسع مِئَة. وَقد شرح كِتَابه (الْإِقْنَاع) الشَّيْخ مَنْصُور البهوتي شرحا مُفِيدا فِي أَربع مجلدات، وَكتب الشَّيْخ مُحَمَّد الخلوتي عَلَيْهِ تعليقات، جردت بعد مَوته فبلغت اثْنَي عشر كراسا بالخط الدَّقِيق. وللشيخ مَنْصُور عَلَيْهِ حَاشِيَة، ولصاحبه كتاب فِي شرح غَرِيب لغاته.

To summarise, he was a luminary and an authoritative scholar. He died in the year 968. Al-Shaykh Manṣūr al-Buhūtī explained his book *al-Iqnāʿ* in a most beneficial way, comprising of four volumes. Al-Shaykh Muḥammad al-Khalwatī authored some notes on [the explanation]. They were transcribed after [al-Khalwati's] death, and they were approximately twelve notebooks of small handwriting. Al-Shaykh Manṣūr also has a short commentary on it. The author [al-Ḥajjāwī] also has a book explaining the obscure or unknown words in his text.

دَلِيل الطَّالِب
Dalīl al-Ṭālib

متن مُخْتَصر مَشْهُور، تأليف الْعَلامَة بَقِيَّة الْمُجْتَهدين، مرعي بن يُوسُف بن أبي بكر بن أَحْمد بن أبي بكر بن يُوسُف بن أَحْمد الكرمي - نِسْبَة لطور كرم قَرْيَة بِقرب نابلس - ثمَّ الْمَقْدِسِي، أحد أكَابِر عُلَمَاء هَذَا الْمَذْهَب بِمصْر، الْمُتوفى سنة ثَلَاث وَثَلَاثِينَ وَألف، وَكتابه هَذَا أشهر من أَن يذكر، وللعلامة أَحْمد بن عوض بن مُحَمَّد المرداوي الْمَقْدِسِي تلميذ الشَّيْخ عُثْمَان النجدي وَكَانَ مَوْجُودا سنة وَاحِد وَمِئَة وَألف حَاشِيَة عَلَيْهِ فِي مجلدين.

It is a popular summation, authored by the great scholar and the remnant of the *mujtahids*, Marʿī ibn Yūsuf ibn Abī Bakr ibn Aḥmad ibn Abī Bakr ibn Yūsuf ibn Aḥmad al-Karmī. Al-Karmī is a reference to Ṭūlkarm, a town near Nablus [in Palestine]. He later moved to Jerusalem. He was one of the greatest scholars of this *madhhab* in Egypt. He died in the year 1033. The book we are referring to is too popular than to even discuss. However, the great scholar Aḥmad ibn ʿIwaḍ ibn Muḥammad al-Mardāwī al-Maqdisī, the student of al-Shaykh ʿUthmān al-Najdi, who was alive in the year 1101, authored a marginalia on it, comprising of two volumes.

وقرأت فِي بعض المجاميع أَن الْعَلامَة الْفَاضِل الشَّيْخ مصطفى الدومي الْمَعْرُوف بالدوماني ثمَّ الصَّالِحِي، ثمَّ مفتي رواق الْحَنابِلَة فِي مصر، لَهُ حَاشِيَة لَطِيفَة على (دَلِيل الطالِب). وَرَأَيْت لَهُ كتابا سَمَّاهُ (ضوء النيرين لفهم تَفْسِير الجلالين) وشرحا على (الْكَافِي فِي الْعرُوض والقوافي) وَلم أعلم سنة وَفَاته، غير أَن مترجمه قَالَ: رَحل إِلَى الْقُسْطَنْطِينِيَّة وَتُوفِي بهَا فِي خلَافَة السُّلْطَان عبد الحميد - يَعْنِي الأول - وَكَانَت سلطنته من سنة ثَمَان وَسبعين وَمِئَة وَألف إِلَى سنة ثَلَاثة وَمِئَتَيْنِ وَألف.

Further, I read in some encyclopedias that the great and virtuous scholar, al-Shaykh Muṣṭafā al-Dūmī, also known as al-Dūmānī, who later resided in the Ṣāliḥiyyah district and would later become the *muftī* of the Ḥanbalī corridor in Egypt, authored a pleasant marginalia on *Dalil al-Ṭālib*. I also saw that he wrote a book called *Ḍaw' al-Nayyirayn li Fahm Tafsīr al-Jalalayn*, and also saw that he wrote an explanation on *al-Kāfi fi 'l-ʿUrūḍ wa 'l-Qawāfi*. I was unaware of the date of his death, though. However, his biographer stated, "He traveled to Constantinople and died there during the caliphate of Sultan ʿAbd al-Ḥāmid (the First).” His sultanate lasted from 1178 to 1203.

وَشرح هَذَا الْكتاب الشَّيْخ عبد الْقَادِر بن عمر بن عبد الْقَادِر بن عمر بن أبي تغلب بن سَالم التغلبي الشَّيْبَانِي الصُّوفِي الدِّمَشْقِي، وَرَأَيْت فِي بعض المجاميع نِسْبَة إِلَى دَوْمًا دمشق، الْفَقِيه الفرضي الْمُتَوفَّى سنة خمس وَثَلَاثِينَ وَمِئَة وَألف. وَشَرحه هَذَا متداول مطبوع لكنه غير مُحَرر وَلَيْسَ بواف بمقصود الْمَتْن.

Moreover, *[Dalīl al-Ṭālib]* was explained by al-Shaykh ʿAbd al-Qādir ibn ʿUmar ibn ʿAbd al-Qādir ibn Abī Taghlib ibn Sālim al-Taghlibī al-Shaybānī, the Ṣūfī from Damascus, who some encyclopedias list as being from Dūmā, in Damascus. He was a jurist and scholar of inheritance who died in the year 1135. His explanation is in circulation and in print, but it is not well-researched nor does it fulfil the purpose of the text.

وَشَرحه فِي مجلدين الْعَلامَة إِسْمَاعِيل بن عبد الْكَرِيم بن محيي الدّين الدِّمَشْقِي الشهير بالجراعي وَكَانَت وَفَاته سنة اثْنَتَيْنِ وَمِئَتَيْنِ وَألف، وَلم يتم الْكتاب.

It was also explained in two volumes by the great scholar Ismāʿīl ibn ʿAbd al-Karīm ibn Muḥyī al-Dīn al-Dimashqī, more commonly known as al-Jarāʿī. He died in the year 1202, and did not complete the book.

وَرَأَيْت فِي تَرْجَمَة الشَّيْخ مُحَمَّد بن أَحْمد السفاريني أَن لَهُ شرحا على (دَلِيل الطالِب) وَلم نره، وَلم نجد من أخبرنَا أَنه رَآهُ.

Lastly, when reading the biography of al-Shaykh Muḥammad ibn Aḥmad al-Saffārīnī, I noted that it was mentioned that he has an explanation of *Dalīl al-Ṭālib*. However, I have not seen it, nor have I met anyone who has informed me that they have seen it.

غَايَة الْمُنْتَهى

Ghāyat al-Muntahā

كتاب جليل للشَّيْخ مرعي الكرمي، جمع فِيهِ بَين (الإِقْنَاع) و(المنتهى) وسلك فِيهِ مسالك الْمُجْتَهدين، فأورد فِيهِ اتجاهات لَهُ كَثِيرَة، يعنونها بِلَفْظ: وَيتَّجه، وَلكنه

جَاءَ مُتَأخرًا على حِين فَتْرَة من عُلَمَاء هَذَا الْمَذْهَب، وَتمكن التَّقْلِيد من أفكارهم، فَلم ينتشر انتشار غَيره.

It is a remarkable book authored by al-Shaykh Marʿī al-Karmī. In it, he combined between *al-Iqnāʿ* and *al-Muntahā*, taking the route of the *mujtahid imāms*. He mentioned many of his own personal views, and would begin mentioning them by saying, "It is possible." However, since he came at a later stage, after a period of scholars of this *madhhab*, blind-following overtook their minds, and because of that, he was not as popular as others were.

وَقد تصدى لشرحه الْعَلامَة الْفَقِيه الأديب أَبُو الْفَلاح عبد الْحَيّ ابن مُحَمَّد بن الْعِمَاد، فشرحه شرحا لطيفا، دلّ على فقهه وجودة قلمه، لكنه لم يتمه، ثمَّ ذيل على شَرحه هَذَا الْعَلامَة الجراعي، فوصل فِيهِ إِلَى بَاب (الْوكَالَة) ثمَّ اخترمته الْمنية.

His book was explained by the great scholar, jurist, and linguist, Abu 'l-Falāḥ ʿAbd al-Ḥayy ibn Muḥammad ibn al-ʿImād. He wrote a beautiful explanation that showed his juristic capabilities and the quality of his literary abilities. However, he did not complete the book. The great scholar, al-Jarāʿī, authored an addendum to his explanation, reaching the chapter of power of attorney, but then he passed away.

ثمَّ تلاهما الْعَلامَة الْفَقِيه الشَّيْخ مصطفى بن سعد بن عَبده السُّيُوطِي الرحيباني مولدا ثمَّ الدِّمَشْقِي. الْعَلامَة الفَقِيه الفرضي الْمُحَقق، مولده سنة خمس وَسِتِّين وَمِئَة وَألف، وَتُوفِّي سنة ثَلَاث وَأَرْبَعين وَمِئَتَيْنِ وَألف، فابتدأ بشرح الْكتاب من أوله حَتَّى أتمه فِي خمس مجلدات بِخَطِهِ، لكنه فِي شَرحه هَذَا يَأتِي إِلَى الْمَسْأَلَة من الْمُنْتَهى، فينقل عبارة شرحها للشَّيْخ مَنْصُور، إِلَى الْمَسْأَلَة من (الإِقنَاع) فينقل عبارة شَرحه أَيْضا، فَكَأَنهُ جمع بَين الشرحين من غير تصرف، فَإِذا وصل إِلَى إتجاه لم يحققه، بل قصارى أمره أنه يَقُول: لم أَجِدهُ لأحد من الأَصْحَاب.

They were succeeded by the great scholar and jurist, al-Shaykh Muṣṭafā ibn Ṣaʿd ibn ʿAbdah al-Suyūṭī al-Ruḥaybānī, who later resided in Damascus. He was a great scholar, jurist, expert in inheritance, and researcher. He was born in the year 1165 and died in the year 1243. He began explaining the book from the beginning onward, and completed it. The final product was five volumes that were authored with his own handwriting. However, in his explanation, he would mention an issue from *al-Muntahā* and would quote its explanation by al-Shaykh Manṣūr, and then would mention an issue from *al-Iqnāʿ*, and would quote [al-Shaykh Manṣūr's] explanation as well. Therefore, he combined the two explanations without annotating the text. If he discussed a view [of al-Shaykh Marʿī] he had not deeply researched, he would say, "I have not found this mentioned by any of the *aṣḥāb*."

ثمَّ تلاه تِلْمِيذه شيخ مَشَايِخنَا الْعَلامَة الأوحد الشَّيْخ حسن بن عمر بن مَعْرُوف بن عبد الله ابن مصطفى ابْن الشَّيْخ شطي المتوفي سنة [...] فَأخذ فِي مَوَاضِع الاتجاه من الْغَايَة وَالشَّرْح، وانتصر للشَّيْخ مرعي وَبَين صَوَاب تِلْكَ الاتجاهات، وَمن قَالَ بهَا غَيره من الْعلمَاء، وَذكر فِي غُضُون ذَلِك مباحث رائقة وفوائد لَا يسْتَغْنى عَنْهَا، فجَاء كِتَابه هَذَا فِي أَرْبَعِينَ كراسا بِخَطِّهِ الدَّقِيق، فَلَو ضم هَذَا الْكتاب إِلَى الشَّرْح وطبع لجاء مِنْهُ كتاب فريد فِي بَابه، وَلَا سِيمَا إِذا ضم إِلَيْهِمَا مَا كتبه العِمَاد والجراعي. فاللهم ارْفَعْ لِوَاء هَذَا المَذهَب، وَأكْثر من علمائه.

He was succeeded by his student, the teacher of our teachers, the unique and great scholar, al-Shaykh Ḥasan ibn ʿUmar ibn Maʿrūf ibn ʿAbdullāh ibn Muṣṭafā ibn al-Shaykh al-Shaṭṭī, who died in the year ....[608] He mentioned the views [of al-Shaykh Marʿī] mentioned both in *al-Ghāyah* and then in the explanation, and would support the views of al-Shaykh Marʿi and clarify their veracity and the views of other scholars that support them. In the course of those discussions, he mentioned beneficial and useful points that are indispensable. His book consisted of forty notebooks with his small handwriting. If his book were to be combined with the explanation and published altogether, it would be quite the unique work on its subject matter, especially if the commentaries of al-ʿImād and al-Jarāʿī were added. Allah, raise the flag of this *madhhab* and increase the numbers of its scholars.

عُمْدَة الرَّاغِب

ʿUmdat al-Rāghib (al-Ṭālib)[609]

608 There was a white space in the area where his death date was supposed to be. After researching, it was found that he died in the year 1274.

609 [T] It seems as though the author mixed up between the name of the text and its commentary in this section. The text is named *ʿUmdat al-Ṭālib*, whilst the commen-

مُخْتَصر لطيف، للشَّيْخ مَنْصُور البهوتي، وَضعه للمبتدئين، وَشَرحه الْعَلامَة الشَّيْخ عُثْمَان بن أَحْمد النجدي شرحا لطيفا مُفِيدا مسبوكا سبكا حسنا ونظمها الشَّيْخ صَالح بن حسن البهوتي من عُلَمَاء الْقرن الْحَادِي عشر بمنظومة أولهَا:

It is a pleasant summation authored by al-Shaykh Manṣūr al-Buhūtī. It was authored for beginners and explained by the great scholar, al-Shaykh ʿUthmān ibn Aḥmad al-Najdi. He authored a beautiful, beneficial, and well-formulated explanation. It was also made into a poem by al-Shaykh Ṣāliḥ ibn Ḥasan al-Buhūtī, a scholar of the 11th century. It states at its beginning:

يَقُول راجي عَفْو ربه العلى   أَبُو الْهدى صَالح نجل الْحَنْبَلِي

It is stated by the one hopeful of the forgiveness of His Lord, the High.
Abu ʾl-Hudā Ṣālih Najl al-Ḥanbalī.

وَسمي نظمه (وَسِيلَة الرَّاغِب لعمدة الرَّاغِب).

He called it *Wasīlat al-Rāghib li ʿUmdat al-Rāghib*.

كَافِي الْمُبْتَدِي وأخصر المختصرات ومختصر الإفادات

Kāfī al-Mubtadī, Akhṣar al-Mukhtaṣarāt, and *Mukhtaṣar al-Ifādāt*

هَذِه الْمُتُون الثَّلَاثَة للفقيه الْمُحدث الصَّالح مُحَمَّد بن بدر الدين ابن بلبان البلباني البعلي الأَصْل ثمَّ الدِّمَشْقِي الصَّالِحِي، كَانَ يقْرَأ الْفِقْه لطلاب الْمذَاهب الْأَرْبَعَة، توفي سنة ثَلَاث وَثَمَانِينَ وَألف، وَقد اعتنى من بعده بكتبه.

These three books were authored by the jurist and righteous scholar of ḥadīth, Muḥammad ibn Badr al-Dīn ibn Balbān al-Balbānī al-Baʿlī, who later settled in Damascus in the Ṣāliḥiyyah district. He would teach jurisprudence to students of all four *madhhabs*. He died in the year 1083. Those who lived after him showed great devotion to his books.

---

tary is *Hidāyat al-Rāghib*, written by al-Shaykh ʿUthmān ibn Aḥmad. al-Shaykh ibn Badrān merged the two and stated, "*ʿUmdat al-Rāghib*." It is a minor slip of the pen.

فَأَما (كَافِي الْمُبْتَدِي) فقد شَرحه الْوَرع الْفَقِيه الأصولي الفرضي أَحْمد بن عبد الله بن أَحْمد بن مُحَمَّد بن أَحْمد بن أحمد بن مصطفى الْحلَبِي الأَصْل البعلي الدِّمَشْقِي شرحا لطيفا محررا، توفي سنة تسع وَثَمَانِينَ وَمِئَة بعد الْألف، وَسمي شَرحه (الرَّوْض الندي شرح كَافِي الْمُبْتَدِي) وَله (شرح عُمْدَة كل فارض) فِي الْفَرَائِض، وَله (الذخر الحَرِير شرح مُخْتَصر التَّحْرِير) فِي الْأُصُول، وَله غير ذَلِك من التعليقات فِي الْحساب والفرائض وَالْفِقْه.

As for *Kāfī al-Mubtadī*, it was explained by the pious jurist, legal theorist, and expert on inheritance, Aḥmad ibn ʿAbdullāh ibn Aḥmad ibn Muḥammad ibn Aḥmad ibn Aḥmad ibn Muṣṭafā, who was originally from Aleppo, but then was resettled in Damascus and known as al-Baʿlī. He wrote a pleasant and well-researched explanation. He died in the year 1189. The name of his explanation was *al-Rawḍ al-Nadī Sharḥ Kāfī al-Mubtadī*. He also wrote *Sharḥ ʿUmdat Kul Fāriḍ* on inheritance and *al-Dhikhr al-Ḥarīr Sharḥ Mukhtaṣar al-Taḥrīr* on legal theories. He also has other commentaries on mathematics, inheritance, and law.

وَأما (أخصر المختصرات) فَهُوَ متن مُخْتَصر جدا، اختصر فِيهِ كَافِي (الْمُبْتَدِي)، وَقد شَرحه الْعَلامَة عبد الرَّحْمَن بن عبد الله بن أَحْمد بن مُحَمَّد البعلي الدِّمَشْقِي نزيل حلب، وَكَانَ فَقِيها متفننا أديبا شَاعِرًا، توفّي سنة اثْنَتَيْنِ وَتِسْعين وَمِئَة بعد الْألف، وَشَرحه هَذَا مُحَرر منقح، كثير النَّفْع للمبتدئين.

As for *Akhṣar al-Mukhtaṣarāt*, it is a very concise text wherein he summarised *Kāfī al-Mubtadī*. It was explained by the great scholar, ʿAbd al-Raḥmān ibn ʿAbdullāh ibn Aḥmad ibn Muḥammad al-Baʿlī al-Dimashqī, who lived in Aleppo. He was a jurist with scholastic abilities in various sciences, and was a linguist and a poet. He died in the year 1192. His explanation is very well-written and precise, containing much benefit for beginners.

وَأما (مُخْتَصر الإفادات) فقد صَدره أَولا بربع الْعِبَادَات، فَجعل الْكَلَام عَلَيْهِ وسطا بَين الإسهاب والإيجاز، مستمدا من (الْإِقْنَاع) ثمَّ ذكر أَحْكَام البيع والربا، ثمَّ أتبعه بقوله: كتاب الْآدَاب، وفصله فصولا، ثمَّ أتبعه بِفضل الصَّلَاة على النَّبِي صلى الله عَلَيْهِ وَسلم، وَفصل ذكر الله تَعَالَى، وَالْأَمر بِالْمَعْرُوفِ وَالنَّهْي عَن

الْمُنكر، وَالْإِخْلَاص، ثمَّ أتبع ذَلِك بعقيدته الَّتِي اختصر بهَا (نِهَايَة المبتدئين) لِابْنِ حمدَان، ثمَّ ختم الْكتاب بِوَصِيَّة نافعة. وَبِالْجُمْلَةِ فَهَذَا الْكتاب كَاف وواف للمتعبدين، وَلَقَد كنت قَرَأت هَذَا الْكتاب على شَيخنَا الْعَلامَة الشَّيْخ مُحَمَّد بن عُثْمَان الْمَشْهُور بخطيب دَوْمًا، وعلقت على هوامشه تعليقات انتخبتها أَيَّام بدايتي فِي الطّلب.

As for *Mukhtaṣar al-Ifādāt*, it began with the quarter of worship.[610] His style in this book was intermediate; it was not too long nor too short. It was derived from *al-Iqnāʿ*. He then mentioned the rulings of transactions and usury, and followed that with his statement, "The Chapter of Mannerisms," and included many sections. Then, he followed with mentioning the virtues of sending blessings on the Prophet ﷺ and the virtues of remembering Allah the Exalted, commanding good, forbidding evil, and being sincere. He then mentioned his beliefs, which was actually a summation of *Nihāyat al-Mubtadiʾīn* by Ibn Ḥamdān. He then concluded his book with a very useful and beneficial admonishment. Overall, this book is sufficient and ample for the worshipper. I read this book to my *shaykh*, the great scholar al-Shaykh Muḥammad ibn ʿUthmān, more commonly known as the Orator of Dūmā. I placed some comments in the margins of the book which I selected from my early days in studying.

الرعايتان

Al-Riʿāyatān **(The Two *Riʿāyah*)**

كِلَاهُمَا لِابْنِ حمدَان، قد كنت رَأَيْتهمَا ثمَّ غابا عني. قَالَ فِي (كشف الظنون) رِعَايَة فِي فروع الحنبلية للشَّيْخ نجم الدّين ابْن حمدَان الْحَرَّانِي، الْمُتَوفَّى سنة خمس وَتِسْعين وست مِئَة، كبرى وصغرى، وحشاهما بالروايات الغريبة الَّتِي لا

610 [T] In the printed text, Dr. al-Turki expresses some confusion over the wording, as what was in the first edition indicates some missing words. Indeed, that is the case. What I have placed is corroborated by the manuscript.

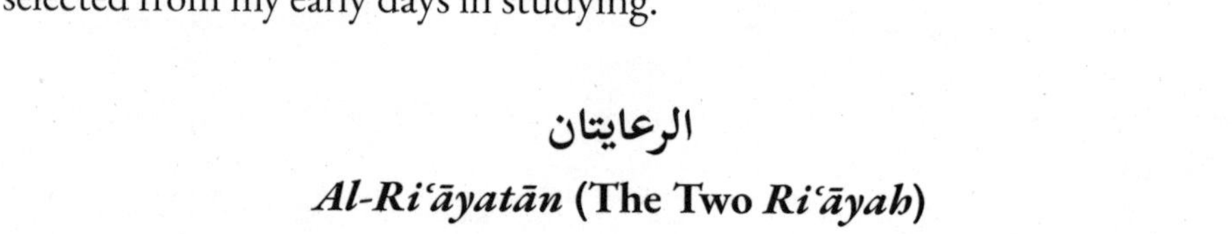

هذا المحرر منقح كثير النفع للمبتدئين واما مختصر الافادات فقد صدره اولا بربع العبادات فجعل الكلام عليه وسطا بين الاسهاب والايجاز مستمدا

تكاد تُوجد فِي الْكتب الْكَثِيرَة، أَولهَا الْحَمد لله قبل كل مقَال، وَأمَام كل رَغْبَة وسؤال، إِلَى آخِره. وَهِي على ثَمَانِيَة أَجزَاء فِي مُجَلد، شرحها الشَّيْخ شمس الدّين مُحَمَّد بن الإِمَام شرف الدّين هبة الله بن عبد الرَّحِيم الْبَارِزِي، الْمُتَوفَّى سنة ثَمَان وَثَلَاثِينَ وَسَبْع مئة، وَسمى شَرحه (الدِّرَايَة لأحكام الرِّعَايَة) و(مختصر الرِّعَايَة) للشَّيْخ عز الدين بن عبد السَّلَام. انْتهى.

Both of them are authored by Ibn Ḥamdān. I saw them, but then I could not find them thereafter. In *Kashf al-Ẓunūn*, it states, "A *Riʿāyah* on subsidiary matters of law through the Ḥanbalī perspective, authored by al-Shaykh Najm al-Dīn ibn Ḥamdān al-Ḥarrānī, who died in the year 695. It comprises of a larger one and a smaller one. He filled them with some strange narrations that cannot be found in many books, the first of which stated, 'All praise is due to Allah before every statement and before every wish and ask,' to the end of the quotation. It occurs in eight sections in a single volume. It was explained by al-Shaykh Shams al-Dīn Muḥammad, the son of al-Imām Sharaf al-Dīn Hibatullāh ibn ʿAbd al-Raḥīm al-Bārizī, who died in the year 738. He called his explanation *al-Dirāyat li Aḥkām al-Riʿāyah*. Also, there is another book called *Mukhtaṣar al-Riʿāyah* by al-Shaykh ʿIz al-Dīn ibn ʿAbd al-Salām."[611]

وَقَالَ ابْن مُفْلِح فِي بَاب زَكَاة الثَّمر وَالزَّرْع من كِتَابه (الْفُرُوع) عِنْد الْكَلَام على زَكَاة الزَّرْع والثمرات: وَلَا يسْتَقر الْوُجُوب إِلا بجعله فِي الجرين والبيدر، وَعنهُ: بتمكنه من الآدَاء، كَمَا سبق فِي كتاب الزَّكَاة، للُزُوم الإِخْرَاج إِذن وفَاقا، فَإِنَّهُ يلْزم إِخْرَاج زَكَاة الْحبّ مصفى، وَالثَّمر يَابسا وفَاقا. وَفِي (الرِّعَايَة) وَقيل: يَجْزِي رطبه، وَقيل: فِيمَا لَا يتمر وَلَا يزبب، كَذَا قَالَ. وَهَذَا وَأَمْثَاله لَا عِبْرَة بِهِ، وَإِنَّمَا يُؤْخَذ مِنْهُمَا أَي من (الرِّعَايَتَيْنِ) بِمَا انْفَرد بِهِ التَّصْرِيح، وَكَذَا يقدم - يَعْنِي ابْن حمدَان - فِي مَوضِع الإِطْلَاق، وَيُطلق فِي موضِع التَّقْدِيم، وَيُسَوِّي بَين شَيْئَيْنِ الْمَعْرُوف التَّفْرِقَة بَينهمَا، وَعَكسه، فلهَذَا وَأَمْثَاله حصل الْخَوْف من كِتَابيه، وَعدم، الاِعْتِمَاد عَلَيْهِمَا. انْتهى.

Ibn Mufliḥ said, in his section on *zakāt* paid for fruits and vegetation, in his

611 [T] *Kashf al-Ẓunūn* (1/908).

book *al-Furūʿ*, "The obligation is not in effect until one places [the fruits or vegetables] on a threshing floor.[612] From [al-Imām Aḥmad]: [The obligation is in effect] when one is able to pay, as previously was mentioned in the chapter of *zakāt*. As such, it is due to the ability to pay at that time, in agreement with the other *madhhabs*. Further, it is necessary to pay the *zakāt* as refined grains, and the fruits must be dried, according to [Aḥmad] in agreement with the other three *madhhabs*. In *al-Riʿāyah*, it states, 'It was said that fresh fruits fulfil the requirement, and others said that [fresh fruits fulfil the requirement] if the fruit cannot be dried or made into raisins.' That is what he said. This quotation, and other similar ones, are not taken into account. [The two *Riʿāyah* books] should be taken from when he explicitly states that he is solitary in the view. Sometimes, [Ibn Ḥamdān] restricts[613] when there are no restrictions, and removes restrictions when there are restrictions. He sometimes equates issues that are known to be different, and vice versa. Due to this reason, and other similar reasons, one is fearful from taking from his two books and does not rely on them."[614]

وَبِالْجُمْلَةِ: فهذان الكتابان غير محررين.

Therefore, in summary, the two books [that have both been authored by Ibn Ḥamdān] are not well-researched.

مُخْتَصر الشَّرْح الْكَبِير والإنصاف

Mukhtaṣar*[615] *al-Sharh al-Kabir* and *al-Inṣāf

612 [T] Two terms were used in this instance by al-Imām Ibn Mufliḥ, but both mean the same thing. The first term is *al-jarīn*, and the second is *al-baydar*. Al-Imām al-Mardāwī said, "The term *jarīn* is used in Egypt and Iraq, while *baydar* is used in the east and in the Levant." (*Al-Inṣāf*, 3/102)

613 [T] Note that the printed version of *al-Madkhal* says, "يقدم," which has no real meaning in this context. In the printed version of *al-Furūʿ*, it correctly states, "يقيد," which means, "restricts," as I have placed in the text.

614 [T] *Al-Furūʿ* (4/92).

615 [T] This word is missing in the printed version but found in the manuscript.

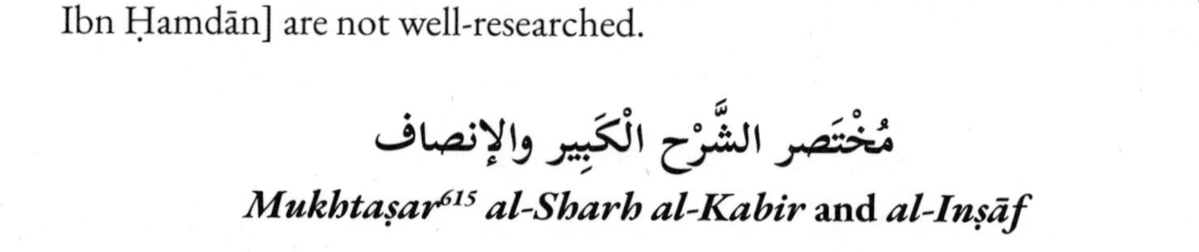

تأليف الْعَالم الأثري، وَالْإِمَام الْكَبِير، مُحَمَّد بن عبد الْوَهَّاب بن سُلَيْمَان بن عَلي، يتَّصل نِسْبَتَة بِعَبْد مَنَاة بن تَمِيم التَّمِيمِي، ولد سنة خمس عشرة وَمِئَة وَألف. وَقد رَحل إِلَى الْبَصْرَة والحجاز لطلب الْعلم، وَأخذ عَن الشَّيْخ عَليّ أَفَنْدِي الداغسطاني، وَعَن الْمُحدث الشَّيْخ إِسْمَاعِيل العجلوني، وَغَيرهمَا من الْعلمَاء، وَأَجَازَهُ محدثو الْعَصْر بكتب الحَدِيث وَغَيرهَا على اصْطِلَاح أهل الحَدِيث من الْمُتَأَخرِّين.

They are the authorships of the scholar who followed narrations and the great *imām*, Muḥammad ibn ʿAbd al-Wahhāb ibn Sulaymān ibn ʿAlī. His genealogy is traced to ʿAbd Manāt ibn Tamīm al-Tamīmī. He was born in the year 1115. He travelled to al-Baṣrah and the Hejaz to learn knowledge. He studied with al-Shaykh ʿAlī Afandī al-Dāghasṭānī, as well as the scholar of ḥadīth, al-Shaykh Ismāʿīl al-ʿAjlūni, and other scholars. The scholars of ḥadīth of his era gave him permission to transmit the books of ḥadīth, and other books, as was the norm among latter day scholars of ḥadīth.

وَلما امْتَلَأَ وطابه من الْآثَار وَعلم السّنة، وبرع فِي مَذْهَب أَحْمد، أَخذ ينصر الحق، ويحارب الْبدع، ويقاوم مَا أدخلهُ الجاهلون فِي هَذَا الدّين الْحَنَفِيّ والشريعة السمحاء. وأعانه قوم، أَخْلصُوا الْعِبَادَة لله وَحده على طَرِيقَته التِي هِيَ إِقَامَة التَّوْحِيد الْخَالِص، والدعاية إِلَيْهِ وإخلاص الوحدانية وَالْعِبَادَة كلهَا بِسَائِر أَنْوَاعهَا لخالق الْخلق وَحده، فحبا إِلَى معارضته أَقوام ألفوا الجمود على مَا كَانَ عَلَيْهِ الْآبَاء، وتدرعوا بِالْكَسَلِ عَن طلب الْحق، وهم لَا يزالون إِلَى الْيَوْم يضْربُونَ على ذَلِك الْوتر، وجنود الْحق تكافحهم فَلَا تبقي مِنْهُم وَلَا تذر. وَمَا أحقهم بقول الْقَائِل:

When he learned about the narrations, learned the Sunnah, and became proficient in the *madhhab* of Aḥmad, he began supporting the truth, fighting innovations, and resisting what ignoramuses have made a part of this monotheistic religion and easygoing legislation. Some people supported him and made their worship solely for the sake of Allah the Exalted, following his path, which was to establish pure monotheism and call to it. For surely, sincerity in monotheism and worship, in all of its forms, belongs only to the Creator of creation, alone. Some people resisted him; they were used to rigidity in following what their forefathers did, and they armoured themselves with laziness instead of seeking the truth. To this day, they play to this same tune, while the armies of truth oppose them, leaving none of them remaining. And how apt is the following couplet for them:

كناطح صَخْرَة يَوْمًا ليوهنها فَلم يَضرهَا وأعيا قرنه الوعل

It is like a day spent banging a rock so as to soften it,
And no effect is made while the billy-goat weakened its horns.

وَلم يزل مثابرا على الدعْوة إِلَى دين الله تَعَالَى حَتَّى توفاه الله تَعَالَى سنة سِت وَمِئَتَيْنِ وَألف. وطريقته فِي هَذَا الْمُخْتَصر: أَنه يصدر الْبَاب مِنْهُ بمسائل الشَّرْح، ثمَّ يزيل ذَلِك بِكَلَام (الْإِنْصَاف) وَهُوَ كتاب فِي مُجَلد.

He continued in calling to the religion of Allah the Exalted until he died in the year 1206. In this summation, he began chapters by mentioning the issues of the explanation, and then would add to them quotations from *al-Inṣāf*. It is a book consisting of one volume.

هَذَا بَيَان مَا اطَّلَعت عَلَيْهِ من كتب هَذَا الْمَذْهَب الْجَلِيل، مِمَّا بعضه مَوْجُود عِنْدِي، وَبَعضه قد أودع فِي خزانَة الْكتب الدمشقية فِي مدرسة الْملك الظَّاهِر بيبرس، وَشَيْء يسير يُوجد فِي خزانَة الْكتب الخديوية بِمصْر، وَلم أقصد بذلك تأليفا مثل (كشف الظنون)، بل الْقَصْد التَّنْبِيه على مَا يُمكن وجوده مِمَّا إِذا طبع وانتشر انْتفع أهل الْعلم بِهِ أَيّمَا انْتِفَاع، وَإِلَّا فكتب الْمَذْهَب كَثِيرَة لَا تكَاد تدخل تَحت حصر، فحذرا أيهَا الْمطَالع من الانتقاد على مَا كَانَ مني من الِاخْتِصَار، وَالله يتَوَلَّى الصَّالِحين.

This brings me to the conclusion of this description of the books I have seen which speak about this honourable *madhhab*. Some of these books are present with me, and some have been placed in the Damascene Library in the School of King Ẓāhir Bibars. Some are also in the library in al-Khadyūwiyyah, in Egypt. I did not intend to author a book similar to *Kashf al-Ẓūnūn*, but rather, my intent was to bring awareness to some books that can possibly be found, and if published, can benefit people of knowledge in the greatest way. Otherwise, the books of the *madhhab* are plenty and almost innumerable. Reader, beware of criticising me for my short summation. Allah the Exalted protects the righteous.

العقد الثَّامِن
Chapter Eight

فِي أَقسَام الْفِقْه عِنْد أَصْحَابنَا وَمَا ألف فِي هَذَا النَّوْع
On the Categories of Jurisprudence According to Our *Aṣḥāb* and Authorships About This Topic

وَفِي هَذَا العقد دُرَر. اعْلَم أَن أَصْحَابنَا تفننوا فِي علومهم الْفِقْهِيَّة فنونا، وَجعلُوا لشجرتها المثمرة بأنواع الثمرات غصونا، وشعبوا من نهرها جداول تروي الصادي ويحمد سَيرهَا الساري فِي سَبِيل الْهدى وَطَرِيق الِاقْتِدَاء، ففرعوا الْفِقْه إِلَى الْمسَائِل الفرعية، وألفوا فِيهَا كتبا قد اطَّلَعت على بعض مِنْهَا.

This chapter contains numerous benefits. Know that our *aṣḥāb* diversified their knowledge of jurisprudence. To service its fruitful tree, they created branches that also diversified the types of fruits it would bear. They created forks in its river, some to quench the thirst of the dehydrated, and some would be praised by traversers on the path of guidance and the route of adherence. Therefore, they divided jurisprudence to subsidiary matters, and authored books, some of which I have read.

ثمَّ أفردوا لما فِيهِ خلاف لأحد الْأَئِمَّة فنًّا، وسموه بفن الْخلاف، وَتارَة يطلقون عَلَيْهِ (الْمُفْردَات)، وضموا المتناسبات فألحقوها بأصول استنبطوها من فن أُصُول الْفِقْه، وَسموا فنها بالقواعد، وَجعلُوا للمسائل المشتبهة صُورة الْمُخْتَلفَة حكما ودليلا وَعلة فَنا سموهُ بالفروق، وعمدوا إِلَى الْأَحْكَام الَّتِي تَتَغَير بِتَغَير الْأَزْمَان مِمَّا ينطبق على قَاعِدَة الْمصَالح الْمُرْسلَة فأسسوها وسموها بـ(الْأَحْكَامِ السُّلْطَانِيَّة)، وَأتوا على مَا اختلقه الْعَوام وأرباب التَّدْلِيس فَسَموهُ بالبدع، وعَلى مَا هُوَ من الْأَخْلَاق مِمَّا هُوَ للتأديب والتربية ووسموه بفن الْآدَاب.

They wrote separate works on differences of opinion belonging to one of the *imāms*, calling it, "The Art of Disputation," and referring to it sometimes as *al-mufradāt* (the singular views of Aḥmad). They also assembled the issues that have similar attributes and attached them to some deduced principles of legal theory, calling the science "The Science of Legal Maxims *(al-Qawāʿid)*." On issues that resemble one another in likeness and differ in ruling, evidence, and cause of ruling, they delved into a science called "The Art of Differentia *(al-Furūq)*." They discussed rulings that differ based on time which the concept of *al-Maṣlaḥah al-Mursalah* can be applied to, and called it, "Rulings of Governance *(al-Aḥkām al-Sulṭāniyyah)*." They wrote about the innovations brought about by the laity and the heads of deception, entitling the works "*al-Bidʿah* (innovation)." They discussed matters pertaining to mannerisms and etiquette, calling it, "The Art of Mannerisms *(al-Adāb)*."

وَلما كَانَت كتبهمْ لَا تَخْلُو عَن الِاسْتِدْلَال بِالْكتاب وَالسّنة وَالْقِيَاس صنفوا كغيرهم فِي أصُول الْفِقْه، ثمَّ فِي تَخْرِيج أَحَادِيث الْكتب المصنفة فِي الْفُرُوع، ثمَّ عَمدُوا إِلَى جمع الْأَحَادِيث الَّتِي يَصح الِاسْتِدْلَال بهَا، فجمعوها ورتبوها على أَبْوَاب كتب فقههم، وَسموا ذَلِك فن الأحْكَام، وألفوا كغيرهم كتب الْفَرَائِض مُفْردَة، وَكتب الْحساب والجبر والمقابلة، وأفردوا كتب التَّوْحِيد عَن كتب المتأولين، وَأَكْثرُوا فِيهَا إِقَامَة الدَّلَائِل انتصارا لمَذْهَب السّلف. فجزاهم الله خيرا. وَيحسن بِنَا هُنَا أَن نذْكر بعض مَا ألف فِي كل فن من تِلْكَ الْفُنُون انتقاء للأجود مِنْهَا فَنَقُول:

Their books are filled with evidences from the Qur'ān, Sunnah, and analogies. They authored, as did other scholars, on topics pertaining to legal theories, then referencing the aḥadīth mentioned in books of subsidiary aspects of law. Then, they took to gathering aḥadīth that can be used as evidence. They gathered them and organised them according to the chaptering of their books of law, calling it "The Science of Rulings (*Aḥkām*)." Like other scholars, they authored on inheritance, mathematics, algebra, and balancing. They wrote individual books about monotheism, different to those who reinterpret [the Attributes of Allah], establishing many evidences to support the way of the Salaf. May Allah reward them. Here, it is appropriate to mention some of the highest quality books of those mentioned that have been authored in the various sciences.

[فن الْخلاف]

[The Science of Disputation *(al-Jadal)*]

أما فن الْخلاف: فَهُوَ علم يعرف بِهِ كَيْفيَّة إِيرَاد الْحجَج الشَّرْعِيَّة، وَدفع الشُّبْهَة وقوادح الْأَدِلَّة الخلافية، بإيراد الْبَرَاهِين القطعية، وَهُوَ الجدل الَّذِي هُوَ قسم من أَقسَام الْمنطق، إِلَّا أَنه خص بالمقاصد الدِّينيَّة، وَقد يعرف بِأَنهُ علم يقتدر بِهِ على حفظ أَي وضع وَهدم أَي وضع كَانَ بِقدر الْإِمْكَان، وَلِهَذَا قيل: الجدلي إِمَّا مُجيب يحفظ وضعا، أَو سَائل يهدم وضعا.

It is a science through which one learns how to present religious evidences and rebut doubts. It is a means to learn ways to invalidate evidences on issues of difference of opinion, by presenting conclusive proofs. It is called the science of disputation, and is a branch of formal logic. However, it is specific to religious purposes. It can also be defined as a knowledge that can be used to preserve any convention or position, or to dismantle any convention or position. It was said: a debater is either providing an answer to preserve a convention, or is questioning to dismantle a convention.

وَقد علمت مِمَّا سبق فِي أَوَاخِر فن الْأُصُول هَذِه المسالك، لَكِن مَا تقدم لَك عَام للمجتهدين وَغَيرهم، وَمَا نَحن بصدده الْآن خَاص بالمقلدين الَّذين يجمدون على قَول إِمَامهمْ، أَو على مَا صَحَّ لديهم من رواياته، ثمَّ يسلكون مَسْلَك فن الجدل فِي نصْرَة مَا قلدوه وَهدم مَا لم يقلدوه.

Based on what has previously been presented in the final sections of the chapter on legal theories, you have already learned some of these techniques. However, what has been previously mentioned is something general, fit for *mujtahids* and others alike. However, what we are in the midst of mentioning now is specific to blind-followers who follow closely what their *imām* stated or the authentic narrations from [that *imām*]. Then, they take the route of disputation to aid the view they follow and dismantle the other views.

وَأجْمع مَا رَأَيْته لِأَصْحَابِنَا فِي هَذَا النَّوْع (الْخلاف الْكَبِير) للْقَاضِي أبي يعلى، وَهُوَ فِي مجلدات لم أطلع مِنْهُ إِلَّا على المجلد الثَّالِث، وَهُوَ ضخم. أَوله: كتاب

الْحَج، وَآخره: بَاب السّلم. وَقد سلك فِيهِ مسلكا وَاسِعًا، وتفنن فِي هدم كَلَام الْخصم تفننا لم أره فِي غَيره، وَاسْتدلَّ بِأَحَادِيث كَثِيرَة، لَكِن تعقبه فِي أَحَادِيثه الْحَافِظ أَبُو الْفرج عبد الرَّحْمَن بن عَلي، الْمَعْرُوف بـ(ابْن الْجَوْزِي) الصديقي الْقرشِي الْبكْرِي، الْمُتَوفَّى سنة سبع وَتِسْعين وَخمْس مئة، وَسمي كِتَابه هَذَا (التَّحْقِيق فِي مسَائِل التَّعْلِيق) قَالَ فِي أوله: هَذَا كتاب نذْكر فِيهِ مَذْهَبنَا فِي مسَائِل الْخلاف وَمذهب الْمُخَالف، ونكشف عَن دَلِيل المذهبين من النَّقْل كشف مناصف، لَا نَمِيل لنا وَلَا علينا فِيمَا نقُول وَلَا نجازف، وسيحمدنا المطلع عَلَيْهِ إِن كَانَ منصفا والواقف، وَيعلم أننا أولى بِالصَّحِيحِ من جَمِيع الطوائف.

The most comprehensive authorship I saw on the subject was *al-Khilāf al-Kabīr*[616] by al-Qāḍī Abu Yaʿlā. It consists of multiple volumes, and I have only seen the third volume, which is large. [The third volume] begins with the Chapter of Ḥajj, and ends with the Chapter of Advanced Payments. He took a very comprehensive approach and used various methods of dismantling the positions of interlocutors, in a way I have not seen anyone else do. He used many aḥadīth as evidence. However, with that said, many of the aḥadīth he used were critiqued by al-Ḥāfiẓ Abu ʿl-Faraj ʿAbd al-Raḥmān ibn ʿAlī, more commonly known as Ibn al-Jawzī, al-Ṣiddīq al-Qurashī al-Bakrī, who died in the year 597. He named his book *al-Taḥqīq fī Masāʾil al-Taʿlīq*. He said at its outset, "This is a book wherein we mention our way of thought pertaining to issues of difference of opinion, as well as the viewpoints of those who disagree [with us]. We will mention the evidences of both camps equally, without being biased to what is for us nor against us, and without being reckless. Those who read and peruse this book will thank us, if they are impartial, and will know that we are more worthy of correct viewpoints than all other schools of law."

ثمَّ قَالَ:

Then he said:

كَانَ سَبَب إثارة الْعَزْم لتصنيف هَذَا الْكتاب أَن جمَاعَة من إخْوَانِي ومشايخي فِي

616 [T] The name of the book is *al-Taʿliq al-Kabīr fī ʾl-Masāʾil al-Khilāfiyyah bayn al-Aʾimmah*. It has been published in four volumes.

الْفِقْه كَانُوا يَسْأَلُونِي فِي زمن الصِّبَا جمع أَحَادِيث التَّعْلِيق وَمَا صَحَّ مِنْهَا وَمَا طعن فِيهِ، وَكنت أتوانى عَن هَذَا لسببين:

The purpose for my motivation in my decision to author this book is that a group of my brethren and teachers in *fiqh* would ask me, when I was younger, to gather the aḥadīth found in *al-Taʿliq*, and [to clarify] the authentic ones to discern them from the inauthentic ones. I refrained from doing so for two reasons:

أَحدهمَا: اشتغالي بِالطَّلَبِ.

Firstly: I was busy with studying.

وَالثَّانِي: ظَنِّي أَن مَا فِي التَّعَالِيق من ذَلِك يَكْفِي. فَلَمَّا نظرت فِي التَّعَالِيق رَأَيْت بضَاعَة أَكثر الْفُقَهَاء فِي الحَدِيث مزجاة، يعول أَكْثَرهم على أَحَادِيث لَا تصح، ويعرض عَن الصِّحَاح، ويقلد بَعضهم بَعْضًا فِيمَا ينْقل.

Secondly: I thought that the commentaries written were sufficient. However, when I looked at the commentaries, I found that the jurists had little merchandise in terms of their knowledge of ḥadīth. Most of them rely on aḥadīth that are inauthentic, and ignore the authentic narrations. They blindly follow one another in their quotations.

ثمَّ قد انقسم الْمُتَأَخّرُونَ ثَلَاثَة أَقسَام:

The latter-day scholars have differed into three camps:

الْقسم الأول: قوم غلب عَلَيْهِم الكسل، وَرَأَوا أَن فِي الْبَحْث تعبا وكلفة، فتعجلوا الرَّاحَة، واقتنعوا بِمَا سطره غَيرهم.

First. Those who were overcome with laziness and thought that deep study and research was tiresome and discomforting. They were hasty in order to not be inconvenienced and were convinced by the writings of others.

وَالْقسم الثَّانِي: قوم لم يهتدوا إِلَى أمكنة الْأَحَادِيث، وَعَلمُوا أَنه لَا بُد من سُؤال من يعلم هَذَا، فاستنكفوا عَن ذَلِك.

Second. Those who were unaware of the sources of ḥadīth. They knew that they must ask those who know this, but abstained from doing so.

وَالْقسم الثَّالِث: قوم مقصودهم التَّوَسُّع فِي الْكَلَام طلبا للتقدم والرياسة، واشتغالهم بالجدل وَالْقِيَاس، وَلَا الْتِفَات لَهُم إِلَى الحَدِيث، لَا إِلَى تَصْحِيحه وَلَا إِلَى الطعْن فِيهِ، وَلَيْسَ هَذَا شَأن من استظهر لدينِهِ، وَطلب الْوَثِيقَة فِي أمره.

Third. Those who wanted to write comprehensive authorships in order to show superiority and to garner positions of authority. They became engulfed in disputation and syllogisms, never taking ḥadīth into consideration; they neither sought to authenticate nor engage in criticism of the aḥadīth. This is not the case of those who seek assistance in their religion and yearn to have trustworthy information.

وَلَقَد رَأَيْت بعض الأكابر من الْفُقَهَاء يَقُول فِي تصنيفه عَن أَلْفَاظ قد أخرجت فِي الصِّحَاح: لَا يجوز أَن يكون رَسُول الله صلى الله عَلَيْهِ وَسلم قَالَ هَذِه الْأَلْفَاظ، وَيرد الحَدِيث الصَّحِيح، وَيَقُول: هَذَا لَا يعرف، وَإِنَّمَا هُوَ لَا يعرفهُ. ثمَّ رَأَيْته قد اسْتدلَّ بِحَدِيث زعم أن البُخَارِي أخرجه وَلَيْسَ كَذَلِك، ثمَّ نَقله عَن مُصَنف آخر كَمَا قَالَ تقليدا لَهُ، ثمَّ اسْتدل فِي مَسْأَلَة فَقَالَ: دليلنا مَا روى بَعضهم أَن النَّبِي صلى الله عَلَيْهِ وَسلم قَالَ كَذَا، وَرَأَيْت جُمْهُور مَشَايِخنَا يَقُولُونَ فِي تصانيفهم: دليلنا مَا روى أَبُو بكر الْخلال بِإِسْنَادِهِ عَن رَسُول الله صلى الله عَلَيْهِ وَسلم، وَدَلِيلنَا مَا روى أَبُو بكر عبد الْعَزِيز بِإِسْنَادِهِ، وَدَلِيلنَا مَا روى ابْن بطة بِإِسْنَادِهِ. وَجُمْهُور تِلْكَ الْأَحَادِيث فِي الصِّحَاح وَفِي الْمسند وفي السنن، عير أن السبب في اقتناعهم بهذا التكاسل عن البحث. والعجب ممن ليس له شغل سوى مسائل الْخلاف، ثمَّ قد اقْتصر مِنْهَا فِي المناظرة على خمسين مَسْأَلَة، وَجُمْهُور هَذِه الْخمسين لَا يسْتَدل فِيهَا بِحَدِيث، فَمَا قدر الْبَاقِي حَتَّى يتكاسل عَن الْمُبَالغَة فِي مَعْرفَته.

I have seen one from the senior jurists say, when writing about wordings [of aḥadīth] written in the authentic books [which gather ḥadīth], "The Messenger of Allah ﷺ could not have said such words," and thereby reject an authentic ḥadīth, saying, "This is unknown." The reality is that he does not know it. Then, I saw that same jurist using a ḥadīth as evidence while claiming that al-Bukhārī reported it, which simply was not true. He also quoted a different compendium [of ḥadīth], simply blind-following [the author of the compendium]. In another instance, he attempted to provide evidence for an issue, stating, "Our evidence is that some reported that the Prophet ﷺ said such-and-such." However, I personally found that the majority of our teachers have stated in their works, "Our evidence is what Abu Bakr al-Khallāl reported with his chain of narration from the Messenger of Allah ﷺ," or, "Our evidence is what Abu Bakr 'Abd al-'Azīz reported with his chain of narration," or, "Our evidence is what Ibn Baṭṭah reported with his chain of narration." However, the majority of those aḥadīth are in the authentic books of transmission, in the *Musnad* [of al-Imām Aḥmad], and in the books of *Sunan*. The reason they were content with [reporting it as such] was simply laziness in research. It is strange to find a person who has no purpose but to engage in issues of differences of opinion, then debate fifty issues, and the majority of which are not evinced by a ḥadīth, so imagine the state of the rest of the issues that he cannot even be bothered to make a false show of knowing. **[End]**

ثمَّ قَالَ: فصل: وألزم عِنْدِي مِمَّن قد لمته من الْفُقَهَاء وَجَمَاعَة من كبار الْمُحدثين عرفُوا صَحِيح النَّقْل وسقيمه، وصنفوا فِي ذَلِك، فَإِذا جَاءَ حَدِيث ضَعِيف يُخَالف مَذْهَبهم بينوا وَجه الطعْن فِيهِ، وَإِن كَانَ مُوَافقا لمذهبهم سكتوا عَن الطعْن فِيهِ، وَهَذَا ينبئ عَن قلَّة دين، وَغَلَبَة هوى.

Then he said, "Section: More blameworthy[617] to me than the jurists I have censured, are a group of major scholars of ḥadīth who are aware of authentic and inauthentic narrations, and even have written books on the topic. However, when a weak ḥadīth is discussed, and it contradicts their *madhhab*, they clarify its weakness. However, if it is in agreement with their *madhhab*, they remain silent, never clarifying its weakness. This shows a lack of religiosity and a predominance of desires."

ثمَّ روى بِإِسْنَادِهِ إِلَى وَكِيع أَنه قَالَ: أهل الْعلم يَكْتُبُونَ مَا لَهُم وَمَا عَلَيْهِم، وَأهل الْأَهْوَاء لَا يَكْتُبُونَ إِلَّا مَا لَهُم.

Then he reported with his chain of narration to Wakīʿ that he said, "The

617 [T] The printed and manuscript versions say (وألزم) but the printed version of Ibn al-Jawzī's book states, (وألوَم), so that is what I placed.

people of knowledge quote all that supports them and all that contradicts them. The people of desires only quote what supports them."[618]

ثمَّ إِن ابْن الْجَوْزِي أَخذ فِي تَخْرِيج أَحَادِيث التَّعْلِيق بإِسْنَادِهِ على شَرط ذكره هُوَ فَقَالَ: وَهَذَا حِين شروعنا فِيمَا انتدبنا لَهُ من ذكر الْأَحَادِيث، معرضين عَن العصبية الَّتِي نعتقدها فِي مثل هَذَا حَرَامًا.

After this introduction, Ibn al-Jawzī began referencing the aḥadīth of *al-Ta'līq* [by Abu Ya'lā], with their chains of narrations, with a condition that he mentioned when he said, "This is the time I shall begin what I have charged myself with doing, namely, mentioning the aḥadīth, disregarding all partisanship and impartiality, which I believe is unlawful in such circumstances."

هَذَا وَمَوْضِع كِتَابه أَنه يذكر الْمَسْأَلَة فَيَقُول مثلا: مَسْأَلَة الطّهُور: هُوَ الطَّاهِر فِي نَفسه، المطهر لغيره، ثمَّ يفِيض فِي بَيَان الحَدِيث، فيذكره أَولا بِإِسْنَادِهِ، ثمَّ يتَكَلَّم عَلَيْهِ بِكَلَام كَاف شاف.

In this instance, he began mentioning issues, and would say, for example, "The issue of *ṭahūr* water, which is water that is pure in and of itself, as well as purifying to other things." He would then write extensively about the ḥadīth, mentioning it first with its chain of narration, then speaking about it comprehensively.

وَقد ألمع الْفَاضِل كَاتب جلبي فِي كِتَابه (كشف الظنون) إِلَى كتاب ابْن الْجَوْزِي فَقَالَ: التَّحْقِيق فِي أَحَادِيث الْخلاف لأبي الْفرج عبد الرَّحْمَان بن عَلي ابْن الْجَوْزِي الْبَغْدَادِي الْحَنْبَلِي، الْمُتَوفَّى سنة سبع وَتِسْعين وَخَمْس مِئَة. ومختصره للبرهان إِبْرَاهِيم بن عَليّ بن عبد الْحق، الْمُتَوفَّى سنة أَربع وَأَرْبَعين وَسَبْع مئة. انْتهى.

The virtuous author, Kâtip Çelebi[619] alluded to the book of Ibn al-Jawzī, in

618 [T] *Al-Taḥqīq fī Aḥadīth al-Khilāf* (1/22-24).

619 [T] This title refers to al-Shaykh Ḥājī Khalīfah, the author of *Kashf al-Ẓunūn*, and an Ottoman polymath and scholar. In Turkish, it means something along the lines of, "the well-mannered and Godly clerk."

his book *Kashf al-Ẓunūn*, where he stated, "*Al-Taḥqīq fī Aḥadīth al-Khilāf*, written by Abu 'l-Faraj ʿAbd al-Raḥmān ibn ʿAlī ibn al-Jawzī al-Baghdādī, the Ḥanbalī scholar. He died in the year 597. This book was summarised by al-Burhān Ibrāḥīm ibn ʿAlī ibn ʿAbd al-Ḥaqq, who died in the year 744."[620]

ثمَّ تلاه الإِمَام الْحَافِظ مُحَمَّد بن أَحْمد بن عبد الْهَادِي بن عبد الحميد بن عبد الْهَادِي بن يُوسُف بن مُحَمَّد بن قدامَة الجماعيلي الأَصْل الصَّالِحِي، ولد سنة أَربع وَسَبْع مئة، وَتُوفي سنة أَربع وَأَرْبَعين وَسَبْع مئة، وَكَانَ من أَصْحَاب شيخ الْإِسْلَام ابْن تَيْمِية، فنقح التَّعْلِيق لِابْنِ الْجَوْزِي، وَحذف أَسَانِيده، وَنسب أَحَادِيثه إِلَى من خرجها من الْأَئِمَّة الْأَعْلَام، وَتكلم عَلَيْهَا بِمَا يَلِيق بهَا، وسمى كِتَابه (التَّحْقِيق فِي أَحَادِيث التَّعْلِيق) وَهُوَ فِي مجلدين.

Afterwards, he was followed by the *imām* and scholar of ḥadīth, Muḥammad ibn Aḥmad ibn ʿAbd al-Hādī ibn ʿAbd al-Ḥāmid ibn ʿAbd al-Hādī ibn Yūsuf ibn Muḥammad ibn Qudāmah al-Jammāʿīlī al-Ṣāliḥi, who was born in the year 704 and died in the year 744. He was a student of Shaykh al-Islām Ibn Taymiyyah. He revised *al-Taḥqīq* of Ibn al-Jawzī, removed his chains of narration, and referenced the aḥadīth to whomever from the great *imāms* narrated them, discussing them appropriately. He called his book, *al-Taḥqīq fī Aḥadīth al-Taʿlīq.*[621] It consists of two volumes.

وَالْكَلَام على الْمسَائِل قد شحنت كتب الْحَنَابِلَة المطولة بِهِ، وَلَا سِيمَا شُرُوح الْمُتَقَدِّمين.

The compendiums of the Ḥanābilah have been filled with discussions on issues [of law], especially the explanations of the early scholars.

[الْمُفْرَدَات]

The Singular Views of al-Imām Aḥmad *(al-Mufradāt)*

وَأما الْمُفْرَدَات: فَهِيَ من جنس الْخلاف، وَالَّذِي رَأَيْنَاهُ وسم بِهَذَا الِاسْم

620 [T] *Kashf al-Ẓunūn* (p. 379).
621 [T] The name of the book authored by al-Imām Ibn ʿAbd al-Hādī is *Tanqīḥ al-Taḥqīq fī Aḥadīth al-Taʿlīq*. It has been published in five volumes.

(الْمُفْرَدَات) للْقَاضِي أبي يعلى الصَّغِير. و(المفردات) لأبي الْخطاب مَحْفُوظ الكلوذاني، وَقد سمى كِتَابه ب(الانتصار فِي الْمَسَائِل الْكِبَار) وَكِلَاهُمَا يذكران أَفْرَاد الْمسَائِل الْكِبَار من الْخلاف بَين الْأَئِمَّة، وينتصران لمَذهَب الإِمَام أَحْمد، مَعَ ذكر مَا اسْتدلَّ بِهِ أَصْحَاب كل إِمَام لنصرة إِمَامه وهدمه. ومفردات الإِمَام أبي الوَفَاء عَلي ابن عقيل الْبَغْدَادِي من هَذَا النَّوْع.

It is a science that is of the same category as discussions on differences of opinion. The first person I have seen use this term *mufradāt* was the junior Qāḍī Abu Ya'lā, as well as Abu 'l-Khaṭṭāb Maḥfūẓ al-Kalwadhānī, who named his book *al-Intiṣār fi 'l-Masā'il al-Kibār*. Both of them mentioned the major issues where there are differences between the scholars, and would support the views of al-Imām Aḥmad, while also mentioning, and refuting the evidences used by the students of the scholars when defending their views. The *Mufradāt* of al-Imām Abu 'l-Wafā' 'Alī ibn 'Aqīl is also of this category.

وَاعْلَم أَنك مَتى رَأَيْت فِي كتب أَصْحَابنَا الإطالة فِي الدَّلِيل، فَاعْلَم أَن هُنَالك خلافًا حَتَّى فِي شرحي (الإِقنَاع) و(المنتهى).

Be aware, too, that whenever you see lengthy discussions on evidences in the books of our *aṣḥāb*, it means that there is a difference of opinion on the issue. This is even the case in the respective explanations of *al-Iqnā'* and *al-Muntahā*.

وَآخر من علمناه صنف فِي نوع الْمُفْردَات الْعَلامَة مُحَمَّد بن عَلي بن عبد الرَّحْمَن بن مُحَمَّد بن سُلَيْمَان بن حَمْزَة بن أَحْمد بن عمر ابْن الشَّيْخ أبي عمر بن قدامَة، الْمُتَوفَّى سنة عشْرين وَثَمَان مِئَة. فَإِنَّهُ نظم الْمسَائِل الملقبة ب(المفردات) فِي ألفية من بَحر الرجز.

The last person from our luminaries that I am aware of who authored on the topic of *mufradāt* is the great scholar, Muḥammad ibn 'Alī ibn 'Abd al-Raḥmān ibn Muḥammad ibn Sulaymān ibn Ḥamzah ibn Aḥmad ibn 'Umar, the son of al-Shaykh Abu 'Umar ibn Qudāmah. He died in the year 820. He authored a poem of a thousand lines on the topic of *Mufradāt*, and did so in the *rajaz* meter.

قَالَ فِي خطبتها:

He said in its opening:

وَهَذِه مسَائِل فقهية　　　أرجوزة وجيزة ألفية
أذكر فِيهَا مَا بِهِ قد انْفَرد　　　إمامنا فِي سلك أَبْيَات تعد
وَهُوَ الإِمَام أَحْمد الشَّيْبَانِي　　　الْعلم الحبر التقي الرباني
عَن مَذْهَب النُّعْمَان ثمَّ ابْن أنس　　　وَالشَّافِعِيّ كلهم يَحْكِي القبس
فَفِي فروع الْفِقْه حَيْثُ اخْتلفُوا　　　أذكر مَا عَسى عَلَيْهِ أَقف
وَكل ما قد جَاءَ من أَقْوَاله　　　مُنْفَردا بِذَاكَ عَن أَمْثَاله
فَمثله إِمَّا عَن الرَّسُول　　　أَو صَاحب أَو تَابع مَقْبُول
مصداق ذَا إِن شِئْت يَا إمامي　　　وَانْظُر وطالع كتب الْإِسْلَام
وَاعْلَم بِأَن أَصْحَابنَا قد صنفوا　　　فِي الْمُفْردَات جملا وألفوا
لكِنهمْ لم يقصدوا هَذَا النمط　　　بل قصدُوا الرَّد على الكيا فَقَط
فَإِنَّهُ - أَعنِي كيا - قد صنفا　　　فِي مُفْردَات أَحْمد مصنفا
وَقصد الرَّد عَلَيْهِ فِيهَا　　　وَكَانَ فِيمَا قد عَنى سَفِيهَا
غَالب مَا قَالَ بِأَنَّهُ انْفَرد　　　فَإِنَّهُ سَهْو ووهم فليرد
فَإِنَّهُ لم يعْتَبر بِالْأَشْهرِ　　　وَلَا خلاف مَالك فِي النّظر
وَإِنَّمَا يقْصد فِيمَا ألفا　　　إِذا رأى قولا وَلَو مزيفا
لِأَحْمَد قد خَالف النعمانا　　　وَالشَّافِعِيّ نصب البرهانا
فصحح الْأَصْحَاب مَا قد صَحا　　　مِنْهَا وَمَا كَانَ إِلَيْهِ ينحى
وبينوا أغلاطه ووهمه　　　وناقشوه لَفظه وَكَلمه
فَابْن عقيل مِنْهُم وَالْقَاضِي　　　سبط أبي يعلى بعزم ماضي
كَذَلِك الْجَوْزِي والزاغوني　　　وَغَيرهم بالجد لَا بالهون

أَكْثَرهم ردا عَلَيْهِ اقتصروا ونصبوا أَدِلَّة وانتصروا

وَابْن عقيل زادنا مسائلا مَشْهُورة وناصبا دلائلا

لكنه حذا كَمَا تقدما ينصر غير أشهر قد قدما

أَو مَا يكون مَالك قد وافقا إمامنا فِيمَا لَهُ قد حققا

فَتلك إِذْ قد حررت تقل والمفردات أَصْلهَا يجل

إِذْ قد أخلوا بالكثير مِنْهَا وأدخلوا المنفى قطعا عَنْهَا

أَحْبَبْت أَن أسبر مَا قد ذكرُوا وأنظم الصَّحِيح إِذْ يحرر

وأنف مَا لَا يسلم التفريد فِيهِ وَمَا يسر لي أَزِيد

بنيتها على الصَّحِيح الْأَشْهر عِنْد أَكثر الْأَصْحَاب أهل النّظر

وَهَكَذَا فسائر الْمذَاهب وَالْخلف ذكرا لَيْسَ من مطالبي

إِلَّا إِذا مَا اخْتلف التَّصْحِيح فَذكره حِينَئِذٍ تلميح

أَو أن يكن قَائِل ذَاك الحكم مفصلا كَمَا ترى فِي النّظم

These are jurisprudential issues,
Expressed in the rajaz poetic form, summarised in a thousand [couplets].
I mentioned in them issues wherein there was solitude,
Of our leader, utilising the method of a set number of couplets.
He is al-Imām Aḥmad al-Shaybānī,
The eminent, scholarly master, the pious and nurturer,
[Solitude] from the madhhabs of al-Nuʿmān, Ibn Anas,
And al-Shāfiʿī, though all of them can be followed as illuminating lights.
So, in subsidiary jurisprudential issues wherein they differed,
I mentioned what I hope is sufficient.
Also, everything reported from his statements,
Isolated in this from his peers,
It either emanates from the Messenger,
A Companion, or an accepted Follower.
Confirm that if you wish my liege,

Look and go through the Islamic literary corpus.
And know that our aṣḥāb have authored,
Numerous works on the singular views.
However, they did not attempt the same style,
Rather, they only sought to refute Ilkiyā.
For he—i.e. Ilkiyā—authored,
In the singular views of Aḥmad a work,
With the intention of refuting him through this,
However, he was foolish in what he mentioned,
As most of what he cited as singular views,
Were forgetfulness, fanciful and so rejected.
Indeed, he did not give consideration to the more well-known view,
Nor was the variance of Mālik given attention.
His goal in his authorship,
Was that when he saw a statement—even if unauthoritative,
Of Aḥmad wherein he differed with al-Nuʿmān,
And al-Shāfiʿī, he sought to cite evidence against it.
Thus, the aṣḥāb authenticated what was authentic,
From it and what was attributed to him.
And they clarified his mistakes and misinterpretations,
And they debated him, taking to task his wordings and speech.
From them were Ibn ʿAqīl, and al-Qāḍī,
The child of Abī Yaʿlā, who did so diligently.
Likewise, al-Jawzī and al-Zāghūnī,
And other than them, working assiduously and not lackadaisically.
Most of them were restricted to refuting him,
And establishing evidences and aiding [Aḥmad].
And Ibn ʿAqīl increased on it in issues,
Which were well-known and established evidences.
However, he trod the path we mentioned above,
Attempting to argue for that which was not the well-known view as mentioned,
Or that wherein Mālik concurred,
With our imām, where this fact was duly scrutinised.

And these issues [mentioned by Ilkiya] if you examined them, are in fact few,
Though the singular views, in fact, are far more.
As they did not mention many from the singular views,
And included issues which are absolutely outside of them.
I wished that I could select from what they wrote,
And compose the authentic as was scrutinised [as Aḥmad's view].
And omit that which is not singular,
In it, and whatever I was facilitated to add, I did.
I based it on the authentic and well-known views,
According to the majority of the scholars of insight amongst our aṣḥāb.
And this is the case for all of the madhhabs,
And the mention of divergences is not my purpose.
Except wherein authentication is differed over,
Mention of which, then, serves as an indication,
Or if the one stating that ruling,
Provides detail, as you will see in my poem.

ثمَّ إن النَّاظِم استرسل فِي مَوْضُوعه، وَإِنَّمَا رقمت مَا رَأَيْت من هَذَا النّظم لما بِهِ من الْفَائِدَة الْمُتَعَلّقَة بموضوعنا.

The author spoke at great length on the topic. I numbered whatever I could of this poem, because it contains some benefit that is pertinent to our present discussion.

وَأما (الكيا) فَهُوَ بِكَسْر الْهمزَة، وَاللَّام سَاكِنة، وَالْكَاف مَكْسُورَة، بعْدهَا مثناة تحتية، فَمَعْنَاه بالعجمية الْكَبِير. وَيُقَال لَهُ: الكيا الهراسي، وَهُوَ عَلي بن مُحَمَّد بن عَلي، إِمَام أَصْحَاب الشَّافِعِي فِي زَمَانه، والمناظر عَنْهُم، برع فِي الْفِقْه وَالْأُصُول وَالْخلاف.

He makes mention of an individual known as Ilkiyā, which is a Persian word for "large." He is known as Ilkiyā al-Harāsī, and his full name was ʿAlī ibn Muḥammad ibn ʿAlī. He was the *imām* of the Shāfiʿīs of his time, and was their main defender in debates. He was astonishing in jurisprudence and differences of opinion.

وَولي تدريس النظامية بِبَغْدَاد، تَرْجَمَة الشَّيْخ عبد الْوَهَّاب السُّبْكِي فِي (طَبَقَات الشَّافِعِيَّة) وعد من مؤلفاته (أَحْكَام الْقُرْآن) و(شفاء المسترسلين فِي مبَاحث الْمُجْتَهدين) وَ(نقض مُفْرَدَات أَحْمد) وَله كِتَابَانِ فِي أصُول الْفِقْه. وَكَانَ عبد الغافر الشَّافِعِي يَقُول عَنهُ: كَانَ ثَانِي الْغَزالِي، بل أَمْلَح وَأطيب فِي النّظر وَالصَّوْت، وَأبين فِي الْعبارَة والتقرير مِنْهُ، وَإِن كَانَ الغَزالِي أحد وأصوب خاطر، أَو أَسْرع بَيَانا وَعبارَة مِنْهُ. ولد سنة خمسين وَأَرْبَع مِئَة، وَتُوفِي سنة أَربع وَخَمْس مِئة.

He taught in the Niẓamiyyah School in Baghdad. Al-Shaykh ʿAbd al-Wahhāb al-Subkī authored a biography of him, in his book known as *Ṭabaqāt al-Shāfiʿīyyah*. He was the author of *Aḥkām al-Qur'ān*, *Shifā' al-Mustarsilīn fī Mabāḥith al-Mujtahidīn*, and *Naqḍ Mufradāt Aḥmad*. He also authored two books on *Uṣūl al-Fiqh*. ʿAbd al-Ghāfir al-Shāfiʿī used to say of him, "He was the second coming of al-Ghazālī, except more handsome, with a more beautiful voice, and clearer in speech. Though, al-Ghazālī was sharper and a greater intellectual, being faster in clarifying and composing than he was." He was born in the year 450 and died in the year 504.

وَكَانَت بَينه وَبَين الزَّيْنَبِي والدامغاني الحنفيين منافسه. وَحكى ابْن رَجَب وَابْن مُفْلِح فِي طبقاتهما: أَن أَبَا الوَفَاء عَلي بن عقيل البَغْدَادِي كَانَ كثير المناظرة للكيا الهراسي، فكَانَ الكيا ينشده:

Between himself and al-Zaynabī and al-Damighānī (both of whom were Ḥanafī scholars) was a fierce rivalry. Ibn Rajab and Ibn Mufliḥ mentioned in their books on biographies that Abu al-Wafā' ʿAlī ibn ʿAqīl al-Baghdādī was in constant debates with Ilkiyā al-Harrāsī, so Ilkiyā would recite the following monostich:

ارْفُقْ بعبدك إن فِيهِ فهاهة　　جبلية وَلَك الْعرَاق وماؤها

Be gentle on your servant: He's mute, like a mountaineer,
While you have Iraq – it's waters too.

قَالَ السلفي: مَا رَأَتْ عَيْنَايَ مثل الشَّيْخ أبي الْوَفَاء بن عقيل، مَا كَانَ أحد يقدر أَن يتَكَلَّم مَعَه، لغزارة علمه، وَحسن إِيرَاده، وبلاغة كَلَامه. وَقُوَّة حجَّته. وَلَقَد

تكلم يَوْمًا مَعَ شَيخنَا أبي الْحسن إلكيا الهراسي فِي مَسْأَلَة فَقَالَ شَيخنَا: لَيْسَ هَذَا مذهبك. فَقَالَ لَهُ أَبُو الْوَفَاء: أَنا لي اجْتِهَاد، مَتى مَا طالبني خصمي بِحجَّة كَانَ عِنْدِي مَا أدفع بِهِ عَن نَفسِي وأقوم لَهُ بحجتي، فَقَالَ لَهُ شَيخنَا: كَذَلِك الظَّن بك.

Al-Silafī stated, "My eyes have never gazed on someone similar to al-Shaykh Abu 'l-Wafā' ibn 'Aqīl. None could match him in a discussion, due to the breadth of his knowledge, the proficiency of his citations, the eloquence of his speech, and the strength of his arguments. One day, he spoke to our *shaykh*, Abu 'l-Ḥasan Ilkiyā al-Harrāsī on an issue, and our *shaykh* said, 'This is not your viewpoint,' to which Abu 'l-Wafā' responded, 'I have my own *ijtihād*. Whenever my interlocutor demands evidence, I have whatever I can use to defend myself and stand forth with my evidence.' Our *shaykh* [Ilkiyā] said, 'That is exactly what I expect of you.'"

[الْقَوَاعِد]

The Science of Legal Maxims *(Al-Qawā'id al-Fiqhiyyah)*

وَأما الْقَوَاعِد، وَهِي أَن تُؤْخَذ الْقَاعِدَة الْأُصُولِيَّة، ثمَّ يفرع عَنْهَا مَا يَلِيق بهَا من الْفُرُوع. وَقد رَأينَا كتابا فِي خزانَة الكتب العمومية فِي دمشق، بِخَط مُؤَلفه، وعَلى ظَهره بِخَط يُوسُف بن عبد الْهَادِي مَا لَفظه: يُقَال: إِنَّه لِابْنِ قَاضِي الْجَبَل.

It is a science where a legal maxim is discussed, and its appropriate subsidiary and branching issues are then clarified. I have found a book in this genre in the library of al-'Amūmiyyah in Damascus, in the handwriting of its author. On the back, there was a statement written in the handwriting of Yūsuf ibn 'Abd al-Hādī, "It is said that this is the authorship of Ibn Qāḍī al-Jabal."

وَطَرِيقَة هَذَا الْكتاب: ذكر الْقَاعِدَة أَولا. مِثَاله: أَن يَقُول الْجَائِز وَاللَّازِم، ثمَّ يفرع على هَذِه الْقَاعِدَة بقوله: الْوكَالَة تصرف بِالْإِذْنِ، وَمن الْمَعْلُوم أَنه لَيْسَ لَازِما، لَا من طرف الْآذِن وَلَا من طرف الْمَأْذُون لَهُ، بل لكل وَاحِد مِنْهُمَا أَن يفعل وَأَن لَا يفعل ابْتِدَاء واستدامة، وَقد يكون فِي بعض الْمَوَاضِع فِي الْخُرُوج عَن الْوكَالَة ضَرَر، فَيخرج خلاف، كَمَا لَو وَكله فِي بيع الرَّهْن لَيْسَ لَهُ عَزله فِي قَول، وَفِي الْوَصِيَّة لَيْسَ لِلْمُوصى عزل نَفسه بعد موت الْمُوصي فِي قَول، فَهُوَ يشبه من وَجه الْعُقُود

اللَّازِمَة، يُخَيّر فِي ابتدائها وَلَا يُخَيّر بعد انْعِقَادهَا ولزومها.

The methodology of this book is that he would first mention a legal maxim. For example, he discussed the maxim of contracts that are permissible and ones that are binding. Then, he discussed the issues that branch off this maxim, saying, "The power of attorney is to act [on someone's behalf] with their permission. It is not binding, neither on part of the principal nor the attorney-in-fact. Both have full choice to adhere to the initiation, or after initiation, the continuation, of [the power of attorney] or to not adhere to it. In some cases, relinquishing the power of attorney results in harm, resulting in differences of opinion. For example, if a person gives power of attorney to an individual to sell a mortgaged item, they cannot withdraw [the power of attorney], according to one view. In the case of wills, the heir cannot dismiss themselves after the death of the testator, according to one view. As such, it resembles a binding contract. They are given the choice initially, but after [the power of attorney] is granted and made legally binding, they no longer have a choice [whether to opt out or to retain the responsibility]."

ثمَّ إِنَّه يَقُول: مَا ثَبت للضَّرُورَة وَالْحَاجة وَيقدر الحكم بِقَدرِهَا. ثمَّ يفرع عَن هَذِه الْقَاعِدَة قَوْله: من وَجب عَلَيْهِ أَمر لدفع ضَرَر إِذا زَالَ الضَّرَر لم يلْزمه عوض مثل نَفَقَة الْقَرِيب إِذا مضى الزَّمَان. وَمثل الْمضَارب إِذا فعل مَا عَلَيْهِ فعله ليَأْخُذ أجرته، لِأَن دفع الأُجْرَة إِنَّمَا كَانَ لتَحْصِيل الْمَقْصُود، وَقد حصل، فَلَا عوض. انْتهى.

Then, in another instance, he mentions, "Anything that is established due to necessity or need, the ruling should be sufficiently proportional [to the necessity and need posed]." Then, he mentions some subsidiary and branching matters that are based on this legal maxim, stating, "If something is obligated on someone to repel harm, when the harm is lifted, they are not responsible for paying restitution. An example is spending on the family after a long time has passed.[622] Another is if a shareholder hires someone to

622 [T] This issue goes: If a person does not pay their responsibilities towards their family for such a long time, are they responsible to pay past due responsibilities? In the example Ibn al-Laḥḥām is stating, he does not, since the harm endured because of lack of payment has ended. Note, too, that the Ḥanbalī scholars differentiate between whose responsibilities were shirked. If it is the wife, he must pay his obligations to her, as stated in *Sharḥ al-Muntahā* (3/230). However, they do not need to pay it for other relatives. Al-Shaykh Manṣūr al-Buhūtī stated, "Whoever abstains from obligatory payments for a period does not have to repay it. This was mentioned without any qualifications by the majority. Their reasoning is that spending on relatives is an obligation to

do some work, but then decides to do it themselves. The payment was done to fulfil the responsibility, and since the responsibility was done, they are due no compensation."[623]

وَبِذَلِك قد علمت مَسْلَك كتب الْقَوَاعِد. وَللْإِمَام سُلَيْمَان بن عبد الْقوي الطوفي الْحَنْبَلِي. الْمُتوفَّى سنة عشر وَسبع مئة كِتَابَانِ فِي هَذَا النَّوْع: أَحدهمَا (الْقَوَاعِد الْكُبْرى) وَالثَّانِي (الْقَوَاعِد الصُّغْرى) وللحافظ زين الدّين عبد الرَّحْمَن بن أَحْمد بن رَجَب الْبَغْدَادِي ثمَّ الدِّمَشْقِي، الْمُتوفى سنة خمس وَتِسْعين وَسبع مئة كتاب فِي الْقَوَاعِد يدل على معرفَة تَامَّة بِالْمذهبِ. قَالَ فِي (كشف الظنون) وَهُوَ كتاب نَافِع من عجائب الدَّهْر حَتَّى إِنَّه استكثر عَلَيْهِ. وَزعم بَعضهم أَن ابْن رَجَب وجد قَوَاعِد مبددة لشيخ الْإِسْلَام ابْن تَيْمِية فجمعها، وَلَيْسَ الْأَمر كَذَلِك، بل كَانَ - رَحمَه الله - فَوق ذَلِك. انْتهى.

As such, you have now learned the methodology of the books on legal maxims. Al-Imām Sulaymān ibn ʿAbd al-Qawi al-Ṭūfī al-Ḥanbalī, who died in the year 710, has two books authored on the subject. The first is called *al-Qawāʿid al-Kubrā*, and the other is *al-Qawāʿid al-Ṣughrā*. Further, al-Ḥāfiẓ Zayn al-Dīn ʿAbd al-Raḥmān ibn Aḥmad ibn Rajab, who was originally from Baghdad but then settled in Damascus, and who died in the year 795, authored a book that shows his thorough knowledge of the *madhhab*. In *Kashf al-Ẓunūn* it states, "It is a beneficial book and is a marvel of history. Some were very insolent towards him, claiming that Ibn Rajab found some dispersed maxims mentioned by Shaykh al-Islām Ibn Taymiyyah and simply gathered them into a single work. This is not true; he, may Allah have mercy

---

fulfil their needs and maintain their lives. However, they were able to survive without the financial assistance. A number of scholars mentioned that is the case unless the judge rules that they must pay it, and it becomes obligatory by their judgement, making it tantamount to spending on the wife." Refer to *Kashāf al-Qināʿ* (5/484).

623 [T] In this case, there are two partners. Each is required to fulfil their responsibilities as dictated by the norm. If one of the shareholders decides to hire someone to fulfil their responsibility, they are solely responsible for the payments. However, if that same person fulfils the responsibility of the person they hired, and then attempts to take payment for the work, they are not to be compensated unless they stipulate that in the contract. Refer to *al-Furūʿ* along with *Taṣḥīḥ al-Furūʿ* (7/91). Another way they can be paid is if their partner hires them for the work, as stated by Al-Shaykh Ibn Qāsim in his commentary on *al-Rawḍ al-Murbiʿ* (5/252).

on him, was far above that."[624]

وَمن هَذَا النَّوْع الْقَوَاعِد لعلاء الدين عَلي بن عَبَّاس البعلي الْحَنْبَلِي، الْمَعْرُوف بـ(ابْن اللحام) الْمُتوفى سنة ثَلَاث وَثَمَان مِئَة، وَهِي قَوَاعِد مختصرة مفيدة جدا، وَفِي أَوله نَحْو تسع وَرَقَات، تشْتَمل على كشف مسَائِل هَذَا الْكتاب، مرتبة على أَبْوَاب الْفِقْه، رؤيت فِي خزانَة الْكتب العمومية فِي دمشق.

Another book on the topic is *al-Qawāʿid*, authored by ʿAlāʾ al-Dīn ʿAlī ibn ʿAbbās al-Baʿlī al-Ḥanbalī, known as Ibn al-Laḥḥām, who died in the year 803. It is a concise presentation of maxims but is very useful. It begins with approximately nine pages detailing the issues of the book, arranged the same way the chapters of *fiqh* are arranged. It was seen in the Library of ʿAmūmiyyah in Damascus.

[الفروق]

The Science of Differentia *(al-Furūq)*

وَأما الفروق: فقد ذكر الإسنوي الشَّافِعِي فِي كِتَابه (مطالع الدقائق) أَن المطارحة بالمسائل ذَوَات المآخذ المؤتلفة المتفقة، والأجوبة الْمُخْتَلفَة المفترقة من مآثر أفكار الْعلمَاء انْتهى. وَهَذَا النَّوْع كثيرا مَا يُوجد فِي كتب الْفُرُوع وشروح الْمُتُون، وَقد أفرد بالتأليف.

Al-Isnawī al-Shāfiʿī mentioned in his book *Maṭāliʿ al-Daqāʾiq* that: "Engaging issues that are similar and resemble one another, and providing answers on issues that are different and vary are achievements reached only by the intellects of scholars."[625] This is often found in books of jurisprudence and explanations of texts, though it also has dedicated works on the topic.

وَقد اطَّلَعْنَا على كتاب فِي هَذَا المسلك لأبي عبد الله السامري - بِضَم الْمِيم وَكسر الرَّاء مُشَدّدَة - مُسَمّى بـ(الفروق) وَذكر فِيهِ الْمسَائِل المشتبهة صُورَة، الْمُخْتَلفَة أَحْكَامهَا وأدلتها وعللها، بِأَن يَقُول مثلا: خُرُوج النَّجَاسَات من غير

624 [T] *Kashf al-Ẓunūn* (2/1359).
625 [T] *Maṭāliʿ al-Daqāʾiq fī Taḥrīr al-Jawāmiʿ wa ʾl-Fawāriq* (2/7).

السَّبِيلَيْنِ ينْقض الْوضُوء كثيرها، وَلَا ينْقض يسيرها، وَالْفرق بَينهمَا مَا روى الدارَقُطنِي عَن أبي هُرَيْرَة أَن النَّبِي صلى الله عَلَيْهِ وَسلم قَالَ: **«لَيْسَ فِي القطرة وَلَا فِي القطرين من الدَّم وضوء، وَإِنمَا الْوضُوء من كل دم سَائل»** وَهَذَا نَص قَاطع فِي الفرق. ثمَّ إِنَّه يسترسل فِي هَذَا المهيع، فَتَارَة يَجْعَل الْفرق من الحَدِيث كَمَا علمت، وَتارَة من جِهَة الْقَوَاعِد الْأُصُولِيَّة. وَهُوَ كتاب نَافِع جدا.

I have read a book that engages the topic in this way, written by Abu ʿAbdullāh al-Sāmurrī, called, *al-Furūq*. He mentioned issues that appear to resemble one another in appearance, but differ in their rulings, evidences, and causes. For example, he said, "When impurities leave the body through anywhere besides the two routes[626], if a lot leaves the body, one's state of purity is nullified, but not if a small amount leaves." Then, he mentioned the ḥadīth reported by al-Dāraquṭnī from Abu Hurayrah who reported that the Prophet ﷺ said, **"One or two drops of blood does not necessitate ablution; rather, ablution must be performed due to flowing blood."**[627] This is an explicit text indicating the difference. He would then continue clarifying in this manner. Sometimes, he would show the differentia via the ḥadīth, as you have seen, and at other times, would use legal maxims to do so. It is a very beneficial book.

[الْأَحْكَام السُّلْطَانِيَّة]

Rulings of Governance *(al-Aḥkām al-Sulṭāniyyah)*

وَأما الْأَحْكَام السُّلْطَانِيَّة: فقد اطَّلَعت على ثَلَاث مؤلفات فِي هَذَا النَّوْع لِأَصْحَابِنَا:

I have read three authorships on the topic, written by our *aṣḥāb*:

أَولهَا: الْأَحْكَام السُّلْطَانِيَّة، مُجَلد مُفِيد جدا، لِلْإِمَام أبي يعلى مُحَمَّد بن الْحُسَيْن ابن الْفراء.

One. *Al-Aḥkām al-Sulṭāniyyah*: It is a very useful volume authored by al-Imām Abu Yaʿlā Muhamamd ibn al-Ḥusayn ibn al-Farrāʾ.

---

626 [T] Meaning, the urinal tract or the rectum.

627 Reported by al-Dāraquṭnī (1/157).

وَالثَّانِي: لشيخ الْإِسْلَام تَقِي الدّين الإِمَام أَحْمد بن تَيمِية.

Two. An authorship belonging to Shaykh al-Islām Taqī al-Dīn, the Imām Aḥmad ibn Taymiyyah.

وَالثَّالِث: للْإِمَام شمس الدّين مُحَمَّد ابْن الْقيم.

Three. An authorship by al-Imām Shams al-Dīn Muḥammad ibn al-Qayyim.

والأخيران مطبوعان.

The last two mentioned are published.

[مناهضة الْبدع]

Opposing Innovations

وَأما مناهضة الْبدع. فأجمع كتاب رَأَيْته لِأَصْحَابِنَا كتاب (تلبيس إبْليس) لِلْحَافِظِ أبي الْفرج عبد الرحمن ابْن الْجَوْزِي، رتبه على أَبْوَاب الْفِقْه، وَقَالَ فِيهِ: الْأَنْبِيَاء جاؤوا بِالْبَيَانِ الْكَافِي، فَأقبل الشَّيْطَان يخلط بِالْبَيَانِ شبها، فَرَأَيْت أَن أحذر من مكائده، وقسمته ثَلَاثَة عشر بَابا، ينْكَشف بمجموعها تلبيسه وتدليسه.

The most comprehensive one that I have seen by our *aṣḥāb* is *Talbīs Iblīs*, authored by al-Ḥāfiẓ Abu 'l-Faraj 'Abd al-Raḥmān ibn al-Jawzī. He organised the book according to the chapters of *fiqh*. He said, "The prophets arrived with sufficient clarification, but the devil sought to infuse clarity with doubts. I thought then to warn of his plots. I organised this book into thirteen chapters, through all of which, the deception and lies [of the devil] are exposed."[628]

وَهُوَ كتاب فِي مُجَلد نَافِع جدا، وَلَا يَسْتَغْنِي عَنهُ طَالب الْحق، وَلَا الْفَقِيه وَلَا المتعبد.

It is a single volume and is extremely beneficial. It is indispensable to a seeker of the truth, a jurist, and a worshipper.

628 [T] *Talbīs Iblīs* (p. 4).

وللشيخ موفق الدّين الْمَقْدِسِي رِسَالَة فِي ذمّ الموسوسين، أَجَاد فِيهَا وَأَفَاد، وَقد علقت عَلَيْهَا حَاشِيَة نفيسة. وَكتب فِي هَذَا النَّوْع لغير أَصْحَابنَا كَثِيرَة جدا، فجزى الله الْكل خيرا.

Al-Shaykh Muwaffaq al-Dīn al-Maqdisī authored a treatise on the topic of dispraise of those affected by whisperings [of the devil], wherein he wrote excellently and beneficially. I have made some useful comments on his treatise. Books on this topic authored by those outside of our *madhhab* are quite numerous, so may Allah reward all.

[فن الْآدَاب]

Mannerisms *(al-Ādāb)*

وَأما فن الْآدَاب: فَإِنَّهُ فن شرِيف. وَقد يذكر مفرقا فِي كتب الْفِقْه كـ(المستوعب) و(الإقناع) و(مختصر الإفادات) وَغَيرها. وَقد أفرده كثير من الْأَصْحَاب بالتأليف كَابْن أبي مُوسَى وَغَيره. وَأجْمع، مَا رَأَيْنَاهُ صنف فِي هَذَا النَّوْع كتاب (الْآدَاب الشَّرْعِيَّة والمصالح المرعية) لشمس الدّين مُحَمَّد بن مُفْلِح صَاحب (الْفُرُوع) فَإِنَّهُ جمع فِيهِ كثيرا من كتب من تقدمه فِي هَذَا النمط، وسرد أسماءها فِي خطبَة كِتَابه وَقَالَ فِي أَوله: أما بعد: فَهَذَا كتاب يشْتَمل على جمل كَثِيرَة من الآدَاب الشَّرْعِيَّة، والمصالح المرعية، يحْتَاج إِلَى مَعْرفَته ... إِلَى آخر مَا قَالَه. وَهُوَ فِي مجلدين، أَجَاد فيهمَا وَأَفَاد، ووفى بالمراد. وَله أَيْضا (الآدَاب الصُّغْرى) فِي مُجَلد.

It is a noble science. Sometimes, it is scattered in the books of law, such as *al-Mustawʿab*, *al-Iqnāʿ*, *Mukhtaṣar al-Ifādāt*, and other books. Many of the *aṣḥāb* have authored individual works on the topic, such as Ibn Abi Mūsā, and others. The most comprehensive work that I have seen, though, is *al-Ādāb al-Sharʿiyyah wa ʾl-Maṣāliḥ al-Marʿiyyah*, written by Shams al-Dīn Muḥammad ibn Mufliḥ, the author of *al-Furūʿ*. In it, he compiled much of what was written by scholars before him on the topic. He mentioned his sources in the introduction to his book, and then stated, "As to what follows: this is a book comprising on a large portion of religious mannerisms and benefits that must be conformed to, many need to know it ..."[629] It comprises of two volumes, wherein he offers much useful commentary and writes excellently, giving the purpose of the book its due. He also wrote *al-Ādāb al-Ṣughrā*, which comprises of a single volume.

وَللْإِمَام الْفَقِيه الْمُحدث مُحَمَّد بن عبد الْقوي بن بدران الْمَقْدِسِي، الْمُتوفَّى سنة تسع وَتِسْعين وَتِسْع مِئَة منظومتان فِي هَذَا النَّوْع، من بَحر الطوِيل، والروي دَال، أَحدهمَا: صغرى، وَقد شرحها الشَّيْخ شرف مُحَمَّد الحجاوي. وَالثَّانِيَة: ألفية، وَقد شرحها الشَّيْخ عَلَاء الدّين المرداوي، ثمَّ الشَّيْخ مُحَمَّد السفاريني الْحَنْبَلِيّ، وسمى شَرحه (غذَاء الْأَلبَاب بشرح منظومة الْآدَاب)، فجَاء شرحا نفيسا فِي مجلدين، وَقد طبع فَلَا حَاجَة إِلَى التَّرْجَمَة عَنهُ.

The *imām*, jurist, and scholar of ḥadīth, Muḥammad ibn ʿAbd al-Qawi ibn Badrān al-Maqdisī, who died in the year 999, wrote two poems in this genre. One is in long form *(al-baḥr al-ṭawīl)*, and the ending of each couplet is with the letter *dāl* (د). The first of which was smaller, though, and was explained by al-Shaykh Sharaf Muḥammad al-Ḥajjāwī. The second was a thousand-line poem, explained by al-Shaykh ʿAlāʾ al-Dīn al-Mardāwī, then al-Shaykh Muḥammad al-Saffārīnī al-Ḥanbalī. [The latter] named his explanation *Ghidhāʾ al-Albāb bi Sharḥ Manẓūmah al-Ādāb*. It is a highly exemplary explanation, authored in two volumes. It has been published, and as such, does not require much definition.

وَلابْن عبد الْقوي ولع كثير فِي الْآدَاب، فَإِنَّهُ كثر مَا ضمن مؤلفاته الْمَنْظُومَة مِنْهُ ككتابه (النِّعْمَة) وَهُوَ جزءان، و(الفرائد) يبلغ خَمْسَة آلاف بَيت، وَكلهَا على رُوِيَ الدَّال. فرحم الله الْجَمِيع.

Further, Ibn ʿAbd al-Qawī had a passion for authoring on mannerisms. Many of his poems have such discussions, such as *al-Niʿmah*, which is in two volumes, and *al-Farāʾid*, which is of five-thousand lines and ends with the *dāl* (د) letter. So, may Allah have mercy on [them] all.

[فن الْأُصُول]

629 [T] *Al-Ādāb al-Sharīʿiyyah* (1/2).

Legal Theories *(Uṣūl al-Fiqh)*

وَأما فن الْأُصُول: فقد تقدم لَك بَيَانه، وَالْقَصْد هُنَا ذكر مَا اطَّلَعْنَا عَلَيْهِ مِمَّا ألف فِيهِ، وَانْتِقَاء الأنفع مِنْهَا للمشتغل بِهَذَا الْفَنّ، ولنقسم ذَلِك إِلَى قسمَيْنِ، أولهَا: الْمُتُون المختصرة. وَإِلَيْك بَيَانهَا:

Clarification of *Uṣūl al-Fiqh* has already been mentioned. However, here, I would like to mention the books I have seen and read on the topic, and pick the most useful of these books for those studying this science. Let us categorise the books on this topic into two categories, the first of which is: summations.

(قَوَاعِد الأَصُول ومعاقد الْفُصُول) لصفي الدّين عبد الْمُؤمن بن عبد الْحَيّ بن عبد الله بن عَلي بن مَسْعُود الْقطيعِي الأَصْل الْبَغْدَادِي، الفَقِيه الفرضي المفنن، الْمُتَوفى سنة تسع وَثَلَاثِينَ وَسَبْع مئة. وَهَذَا الْمُخْتَصر فِي نَحْو سبع وَعشْرين ورقة، اخْتَصَرَهُ من كتاب لَهُ سَمَّاهُ (تَحْقِيق الأمل)، وجرده عَن الدَّلَائِل. وَهُوَ مُخْتَصر مُفِيد.

Qawāʿid al-Uṣūl wa Maʿāqid al-Fuṣūl: Authored by Ṣafī al-Dīn ʿAbd al-Mu'min ibn ʿAbd al-Ḥaqq[630] ibn ʿAbdullāh ibn ʿAlī ibn Masʿūd al-Qaṭīʿī, who would later reside in Baghdad. He was a jurist, scholar of inheritance, and proficient in numerous sciences. He died in the year 739. This summation is approximately twenty-seven pages. He wrote it as a summation of another book he wrote, called *Taḥqīq al-Amal*, but removed any of the evidences. *[Qawāʿid al-Uṣūl wa Maʿāqid al-Fuṣūl]* is a very beneficial summation.

مُخْتَصر فِي الْأُصُول لعَلي بن عَبَّاس البعلي الْحَنْبَلِيّ الْمَعْرُوف بـ(ابْن اللحام) جعله مَحْذُوف التَّعْلِيل والدلائل، وَأَشَارَ فِيهِ إِلَى الْخلاف والوفاق فِي غَالب الْمسَائِل، وَهُوَ فِي نَحْو خمس وَأَرْبَعين ورقة.

Mukhtaṣar[631] *fi 'l-Uṣūl*: authored by ʿAlī ibn ʿAbbās al-Baʿlī al-Ḥanbalī,

630 [T] Both the printed and manuscript versions mention that his name was ʿAbd al-Ḥayy, but this is incorrect. What I have placed is the accurate name of his father.
631 [T] There is a mistake in the printed editions, where the term '*Mukhtaṣar*,' is miss-

known better by Ibn al-Laḥḥām. He removed any causes for rulings and evidences, and made note of differences of opinions and agreements in most issues. It comprises of approximately forty five pages.

(مُخْتَصر الرَّوْضَة القدامية) للعلامة سُلَيْمَان الطوفي، مُشْتَمل على الدَّلَائِل، مَعَ التَّحْقِيق والتدقيق، وَالتَّرْتِيب والتهذيب، ينخرط مَعَ مُخْتَصر ابْن الْحَاجِب فِي سلك وَاحِد، وَقد شَرحه مُؤَلفه فِي مجلدين، حقق فيهمَا فن الْأُصُول وَأَبَان فِيهِ عَن بَاع وَاسع فِي هَذَا الْفَن، واطلاع وافر. وَبِالْجُمْلَةِ: فَهُوَ أحسن مَا صنف فِي هَذَا الْفَنّ وأجمعه وأنفعه، مَعَ سهولة الْعبارَة وسبكها فِي قالب يدْخل الْقُلُوب بِلَا اسْتِئْذَان، وَقد شرح الْمَتْن أَيْضا الشَّيْخ علاء الدين الْعَسْقَلَانِي الْكِنَانِي فِي مُجَلد، وَلم أره، لَكِن رَأَيْت عَلَاء الدّين المرداوي ذكره.

Mukhtaṣar Rawḍat al-Nāẓir[632]*:* Authored by the great scholar, Sulaymān al-Ṭūfī. It consists of evidences, with precision and close scrutiny of the issues. It is well-organised and a very refined, polished work. It is closely associated with the style of the *Mukhtaṣar of Ibn al-Ḥājib*. The author himself (al-Ṭūfī) has explained the book in two volumes, wherein he precisely scrutinised the science of legal theories, showing a copious understanding and vast readership of this science. Generally, it is the best and most comprehensive work on the topic and is comprised of ease in its prose; it is authored in a way that allows the information to enter the hearts without asking permission. It was also explained by Shaykh ʿAlā' al-Dīn al-ʿAsqalānī al-Kinānī in a single volume, though I have not seen it.[633] I became aware of it because ʿAlā'

ing. The manuscript version has this word, which is why I added it.

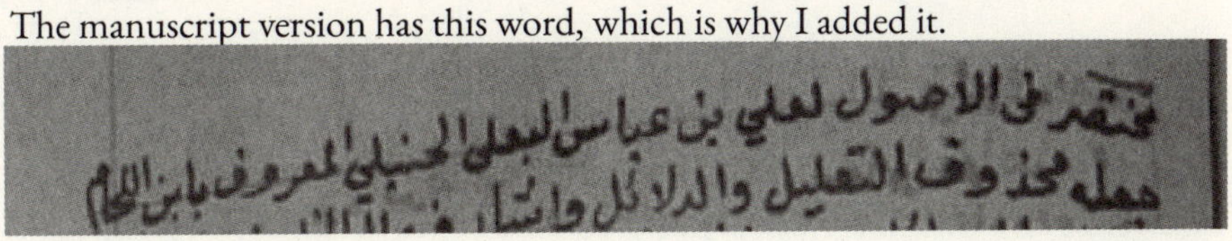

632 [T] The title given to it by al-Shaykh Ibn Badrān was a common nickname used for the book, where he said, *"Al-Rawḍat al-Qudāmiyyah,"* which means, "The *Rawḍah* of [Ibn] Qudāmah." However, I have placed the original title of the book, in the hopes it helps someone seeking to find it.

633 The book is present in manuscript form, and I think it is in the Ẓāhirīyyah Library. As for the explanation of *Mukhtaṣar al-Rawḍah* by al-Ṭūfī, I hope it sees the light soon, so that people can benefit from this most precious work of the Ḥanābilah.

[T] All praise is due to Allah, al-Ṭūfī's explanation has been printed by the same editor of this book, Dr. ʿAbdullah al-Turki, in the year 2014. May Allah reward him

al-Dīn al-Mardāwī mentioned it.

(مُخْتَصر التَّحْرِير) للعلامة الْفَقِيه الأصولي النَّحْوِي مُحَمَّد بن الْعَلامَة شهَاب الدّين أَحْمد بن عبد الْعَزِيز بن عَلي الفتوحي الشهير بابْن النجار صَاحب (الْمُنْتَهى) ذكر أَنه اختصر فِيهِ كتاب (تَحْرِير الْمَنْقُول من علم الْأُصُول) لعلاء الدّين المرداوي، وَأَنه محتو على مسَائِل مِمَّا قدمه المرداوي، أَو كَانَ عَلَيْهِ الْأَكْثَر من الْأَصْحَاب، دون بَقِيَّة الْأَقْوَال، خَال من قَول ثَان إِلَّا لفائدة تزيد على معرفَة الْخلاف، من عزو مقَال إِلَى من إِيَّاه قَالَ.

Mukhtaṣar al-Taḥrīr: By the great scholar, jurist, legal theorist, and grammarian, Muḥammad, the son of the great scholar Shihāb al-Dīn Aḥmad ibn ʿAbd al-ʿAzīz ibn ʿAlī al-Futūḥī, known better as Ibn al-Najjār. He authored *al-Muntahā*. He mentioned that he summarised *Taḥrīr al-Manqūl min ʿIlm al-Uṣūl* of ʿAlāʾ al-Dīn al-Mardāwī, and that [his summation] comprised of the views that al-Mardāwī preferred or which are held by the majority of the *aṣḥāb*, omitting the rest [that did not fit those criteria], and also omitting any other opinions, unless there is some discernible utility gained by knowing the existence of the differences, such as which views are held by whom.

ثمَّ قَالَ: وَمَتى قلت: فِي وَجه، فالمقدم غَيره. أَو فِي قَول أَو على قَول، كَانَ إِذا قوي الْخلاف أَو اخْتلف التَّرْجِيح. مَعَ إِطْلَاق الْقَوْلَيْنِ أَو الْأَقْوَال إِذا لم أطلع على مُصَرح بالتصحيح.

He said, "Whenever I have said, 'In a varying view (*wajh*),' the opposite view is considered preferred and given priority. If I say, 'In a view,' or 'According to a view,' it means there is either (a) a significant difference of opinion, (b) differences in which a view is preferred, or (c) unqualified views have been mentioned[634] on the topic[635] and I did not come cross anyone explicitly stating one is preferred over the other."[636]

---

for his efforts.

634 [T] Meaning, by al-Mardāwī in the original text.

635 [T] This means views that have been mentioned without providing any preference. As in, X scholar had one view, Y scholar had the other view, without mentioning any preference to one view over the other.

636 [T] *Mukhtaṣar al-Taḥrīr* (p. 11).

ثمَّ إن مُصَنفه شَرحه فِي مُجلد وَسَماهُ (الْكَوْكَب الْمُنِير فِي شرح مُخْتَصر التَّحْرِير)، ثمَّ شَرحه الشَّيْخ أَحْمد البعلي وَسَماهُ (الذخر الْحَرِير شرح مُخْتَصر التَّحْرِير) وَهَذَانِ الشرحان يفيدان الْمُتَوَسّط فِي هَذَا الْفَنّ.

The author himself wrote an explanation on the text, calling it *al-Kawkab al-Munīr fī Sharḥ Mukhtaṣar al-Taḥrīr*. Then, al-Shaykh Aḥmad al-Baʿlī explained it, and called his text *al-Dhikhr al-Ḥarīr Sharḥ Mukhtaṣar al-Taḥrīr*. These two explanations are suitable for intermediate students of this science.

(تَحْرِير الْمَنْقُول وتهذيب علم الْأُصُول) للْقَاضِي علاء الدين عَلي بن سُلَيْمَان بن أَحْمد ابْن مُحَمَّد الْمَقْدِسِي المرداوي السَّعْدِي، مُحَرر أُصُول الْمَذْهَب وفروعه، صَاحب (التَّنْقِيح) و(الإنصاف) استمد فِي وَضعه من غَالب كتب هَذَا الْفَن، وَقَالَ فِي أَوله: هَذَا مُخْتَصر فِي أصُول الْفِقْه، جَامع لمعظم أَحْكَامه، حاو لقواعده وضوابطه وأقسامه، مُشْتَمل على مَذَاهِب الْأَئِمَّة الأَرْبَعَة الأَعْلَام وأتباعهم وَغَيرهم، لَكِن على سَبِيل الأَعْلَام اجتهدت فِي تَحْرِير نقُوله وتهذيب أُصُوله.

Taḥrīr al-Manqūl wa Tahdhīb ʿIlm al-Uṣūl: Written by al-Qāḍī ʿAlāʾ al-Dīn ʿAlī ibn Sulaymān ibn Aḥmad ibn Muḥammad al-Maqdisī al-Mardāwī al-Siʿdī. He is the scrutiniser and deep researcher into the legal theories and substantive law of the *madhhab* of Aḥmad. He authored *al-Tanqīḥ* and *al-Inṣāf*. In [*Taḥrīr al-Manqul*], he relied in his writings on the majority of the books of this science. He said in its introduction, "This is a summation on the topic of legal theories, comprising of most of its rulings and gathering its maxims, principles, and categories. It also comprises of the views of the Four Notable *Imāms* and their followers, as well as others, as additional information. I have put the utmost work into accurately portraying its quotations and refining its theories.[637]

وَقَالَ الفتوحي فِي شرح مُخْتَصره: وَإِنَّمَا وَقع اخْتِيَاري على اخْتِصَار هَذَا الْكتاب دون بَقِيَّة كتب هَذَا الْفَنّ، لِأَنهُ جَامع لأَكْثَر أَحْكَامه، حاو لقواعده وضوابطه وأقسامه. انْتهى.

637 [T] *Taḥrīr al-Manqūl* (p. 55).

Al-Futūḥī said in the explanation of his own summation, "I chose to summarise this book over others on the topic because it comprises of most of its rulings and gathers its maxims, principles, and categories."[638]

وَقد شَرحه مُؤَلفه فِي مجلدين، أَجَاد فيهمَا وَأَفَاد.

It was explained in two volumes, where he did so excellently and beneficially.

الْقسم الثَّانِي: الْكتب المطولة فِي هَذَا الْفَنّ وَإِلَيْك بَيَان بَعْضهَا:

The second category [of books on legal theories] consists of the compendiums on the topic. Here are some of them:

(الْوَاضِح) لِابْنِ عقيل، وَهُوَ كتاب كَبِير فِي ثَلَاث مجلدات، أبان فِيهِ عَن علم كالبحر الزاخر، وَفضل يفحم من فِي فَضله يكابر، وَهُوَ أعظم كتاب فِي هَذَا الْفَنّ، حذا فِيهِ حَذْو الْمُجْتَهدين.

Al-Wāḍiḥ by Ibn ʿAqīl: It is a large book comprised of three volumes. In it, he shows knowledge similar to an abundant ocean and virtues that are undeniable even by the obstinate. This is the greatest book on this science. In it, he followed the method and style of *mujtahid* scholars.

(التَّمْهِيد فِي أصُول الْفِقْه) لأبي الْخطاب، مَحْفُوظ الكلوذاني، مُجَلد ضخم، سلك فِيهِ مسالك الْمُتَقَدِّمين، وَأكْثر من ذكر الدَّلِيل وَالتَّعْلِيل.

Al-Tamhīd fī Uṣūl al-Fiqh: Authored by Abu 'l-Khaṭṭāb Mahfūẓ al-Kalwadhānī. It is a large volume authored in the style of the early scholars. He mentioned many evidences and causes.

(رَوْضَة النَّاظر وجنة المناظر) - بِضَم الْجِيم وَتَشْدِيد النُّون الْمَفْتُوحَة - للْإِمَام الْمُجْتَهد، موفق الدّين الْمَقْدِسِي، صَاحب (الْمُغنِي) وَ(الْكَافِي) وَ(الْمقنع) و(العمدة) وَهُوَ كتاب فِي مُجَلد متوسط، رتبه على ثَمَانِيَة أَبْوَاب، عدد أَبْوَاب الْجنَّة، وترتيبها هَكَذَا: حَقِيقَة الحكم وأقسامه، ثمَّ تَفْصِيل الأُصُول الْأَرْبَعَة، ثمَّ بَيَان الأُصُول الْمُخْتَلف فِيهَا، ثمَّ تقاسيم الْأَسْمَاء ثمَّ الْأَمر وَالنَّهْي، والعموم

638 [T] *Mukhtaṣar al-Taḥrīr Sharḥ al-Kawkab al-Munīr* (1/29).

وَالْخُصُوص، وَالِاسْتِثْنَاء وَالشّرط، وَدَلِيل الْخطاب وَنَحْوه، ثمَّ الْقيَاس، ثمَّ حكم الْمُجْتَهد، ثمَّ التَّرْجِيح.

Rawḍat al-Nāẓir wa Junnat al-Munāẓir: Authored by the *imām* and *mujtahid*, Muwaffaq al-Dīn al-Maqdisī, the author of *al-Mughnī*, *al-Kāfī*, *al-Muqni'*, and *al-'Umdah*. It is a moderately sized volume comprised of eight chapters, to match the gates of paradise. They are: (i) The reality and categories of rulings. (ii) Defining the four fundamentals. (iii) Clarifying the fundamentals that are differed on. (iv) The categories of names. (v) Orders and prohibitions, generality and specificity, exceptions and preconditions, the evidences of instructions, and so forth. (vi) Analogy. (vii) The rulings of the *mujtahid*. (viii) Discovering preponderance (*tarjih*).

وَقد تبع فِي كِتَابه هَذَا الشَّيْخ أَبَا حَامِد الْغَزالِي فِي (الْمُسْتَصْفى) حَتَّى فِي إِثْبَات الْمُقدمَة المنطقية فِي أَوله، وَحَتَّى قَالَ أَصْحَابنَا وَغَيرهم مِمَّن رأى الْكِتَابَيْنِ: إن (الرَّوْضَة) مُخْتَصر (المستصفى). وَيظْهر ذَلِك قطعا فِي إِثْبَات الْمُقدمَة المنطقية، مَعَ أَنه خلاف عَادَة الْأُصُولِيِّينَ من أَصْحَابنَا وَكثير من غَيرهم، وَمن مُتَابَعَته على ذكر كثير من نُصُوص أَلْفَاظ الشَّيْخ أبي حَامِد. قَالَ الطوفي فِي أَوَائِل شَرحه (مُخْتَصر الرَّوْضَة) له:

He followed the style of al-Shaykh Abu Ḥāmid al-Ghazālī in his book, *al-Mustaṣfā*, even going as far as to write an introduction to formal logic at the beginning of the book. Our *aṣḥāb*, and others who saw both books, said that *Rawḍah* is actually a summation of *al-Mustaṣfā*. This is evident and clear, especially in the fact that [Ibn Qudāmah] wrote his introduction to formal logic, which, normally, is not something done by those of our *aṣḥāb* who are legal theorists, and many other [authors on the genre.] He also used the same terminology and texts that al-Shaykh Abu Ḥāmid stated. Al-Ṭūfī stated in the outset to his explanation of the summation of *al-Rawḍah*:

أَقُول: إن الشَّيْخ أَبَا مُحَمَّد الْتقط أَبْوَاب (الْمُسْتَصْفى)، فتصرف فِيهَا بِحَسب رَأيه، وأثبتها، وَبنى كِتَابه عَلَيْهَا، وَلم ير الْحَاجة ماسة إِلَى مَا اعتنى بِهِ الشَّيْخ أَبُو حَامِد من درج الْأَبْوَاب تَحت أقطاب الْكتاب، أَو أنه أحب ظُهُور الامتياز بَين الْكِتابيْن، باخْتلَاف التَّرْتِيب، لِئَلَّا يصير مُخْتَصر الْكتاب وَهُوَ إِنَّمَا يصنع كتابا

مُسْتقِلا فِي غير الْمَذْهَب الَّذِي وضع فِيهِ أَبُو حَامِد كِتَابه، لِأَن أَبَا حَامِد أشعري شَافِعِي، وَأَبُو مُحَمَّد أثري حنبلي.

Al-Shaykh Abu Muḥammad [ibn Qudāmah] gathered the chapters of *al-Mustaṣfā* and then adapted them as he saw fitting. Then, he placed those chapters in his book and based his book off them. He did not see a major need to do what al-Shaykh Abu Ḥāmid did, namely, sectioning the book. Or, he wanted to differentiate between the two books, to show that [although there were similarities,] the book was arranged differently and so people did not think it was a summation, but a new authorship written according to a different *madhhab* than the one Abu Ḥāmid's book was based on. For Abu Ḥāmid was an Ashʿarī Shāfiʿī, and Abu Muḥammad [ibn Qudāmah] was an Atharī Ḥanbalī scholar.

وَهِي طَرِيقَة الْحُكَمَاء الْأَوَائِل وَغَيرهم، لَا تكَاد تَجِد لَهُم كتابا فِي طب أَو فلسفة إِلا وَقد ضبطت مقالاته وأبوابه فِي أَوله، بِحَيْثُ يقف النَّاظر الذكي من مُقَدّمَة الْكتاب على مَا فِي أَثْنَائِهِ، وَقد نهج أَبُو حَامِد هَذَا الْمنْهَج فِي (المستصفي). هَذَا كَلَامه.

It is the method of the logicians of yore, and others, that when writing books about medicine, philosophy, and so forth, they arrange its propositions and chapters in the outset, so that the intelligent reader can infer from the introduction what the book will be comprised of. Abu Ḥāmid followed a similar route in *al-Mustaṣfā*. **[End]**[639]

ثمَّ اعْلَم إِن الشَّيْخ أَبَا مُحَمَّد أثبت فِي أَوَائِل (الرَّوْضَة) مُقَدّمَة تَضَمَّنت مسَائِل من فن الْمنطق، كَمَا فعل مثل ذَلِك الْغَزالِي، ثمَّ ابْن الْحَاجِب، فَمن أجل ذَلِك تبين أَنه كَانَ تَابعا للغزالي، لِأَن أَبَا مُحَمَّد لم يكن متكلما وَلَا منطقيا، حَتَّى يُقَال غلب عَلَيْهِ علمه المألوف. وَقد قَالَ الثِّقَات: إِن إِسْحَاق العلثي لما اطلع على (الرَّوْضَة) وَرَأى فِيهَا الْمُقدمَة المنطقية، عَاتب الشيخ أَبَا مُحَمَّد فِي إِلْحَاقه هَذِه الْمُقدمَة فِي كِتَابه، وَأنكر عَلَيْهِ ذَلِك، فأسقطها من (الرَّوْضَة) بعد أَن انتشرت بَين النَّاس، فَلهَذَا تُوجد فِي نُسْخَة دون نُسْخَة.

639 [T] *Sharḥ Mukhtaṣar al-Rawḍah* (1/98).

Note, too, that in the beginning of *al-Rawḍah*, al-Shaykh Abu Muḥammad [ibn Qudāmah] authored an introduction, comprising of various discussions in formal logic, just as al-Ghazālī, and afterwards, Ibn al-Ḥājib did. As such, it shows he was following al-Ghazālī by doing so, because Abu Muḥammad was neither a scholar of *kalām* nor was he a logician where one could make the argument that the more familiar science to him was very influential in authoring his book. Reliable scholars have claimed that when Isḥāq al-ʿAlthī read *al-Rawḍah*, and saw its introduction to formal logic, he censured al-Shaykh Abu Muḥammad for placing it in the introduction to his book and repudiated it, causing [Ibn Qudāmah] to remove it from later editions of the book, though this was after the book had become popular among people. This is why [the formal logic sections] are found in some editions, but not in others.

وَلما اختصر الطوفي الْكتاب أسقط الْمُقدمَة وَاعْتذر بأعذار: مِنْهَا: وَهُوَ الَّذِي عول عَلَيْهِ - أَنه لَا تَحْقِيق لَهُ فِي فن الْمنطق، وَلَا أَبُو مُحَمَّد لَهُ تَحْقِيق بِهِ أَيْضا. فَلَو اختصرها لظهر بَيَان التَّكْلِيف عَلَيْهَا من الْجِهَتَيْنِ، فَلَا يتَحَقَّق الِانْتِفَاع بهَا للطَّالِب، وَيقطع عَلَيْهِ الْوَقْت.

Further, when al-Ṭūfī summarised the book, he removed the introduction [to formal logic] altogether, and presented some excuses for doing so, the first of which was that neither he nor Abu Muḥammad [ibn Qudāmah] were experts in formal logic. Therefore, if he were to summarise it, it would have been burdensome in two ways, [the first being] that students will not fully benefit from it, [and the second being] that it would waste his time.

وَأما إِسْحَاق العلثي - بالثاء الْمُثَلَّثَة - فَهُوَ إِسْحَاق بن أَحْمد بن مُحَمَّد بن عَلي بن غَانِم العلثي الْحَنْبَلِي، الإِمَام الزَّاهِد القدوَة، كَانَ فَقِيها عَالما أمارا بِالْمَعْرُوفِ نهاءا عَن الْمُنكر، لَا يخَاف أحدا إِلَّا الله، وَلَا تَأْخُذهُ فِي الله لومة لائم. أنكر على الْخَلِيفَة النَّاصِر فَمن دونه، وواجه الْخَلِيفَة وصدعه بِالْحَقِّ، قَالَ بَعضهم: هُوَ شيخ الْعرَاق، والقائم بالإنكار على الْفُقَهَاء والفقراء وَغَيرهم فِيمَا ترخصوا فِيهِ. وَقَالَ الحَافِظ الْمُنْذِرِي: قيل: إِنَّه لم يكن فِي زَمَانه مثله، أَكثر إنكارا للْمُنكر مِنْهُ، وَحبس على ذَلِك مُدَّة، وَله رسائل كَثِيرَة إِلَى الأَعْيَان بالإنكار عَلَيْهِم والنصح

لَهُم. توفي سنة أَربع وَثَلَاثِينَ وست مِئَة بِبَلَدِهِ (العلث). هَكَذَا تَرْجمهُ الْحَافِظ ابْن رَجَب، وبرهان الدين بن مُفْلِح.

As for Isḥāq al-ʿAlthī [who was previously mentioned,] he is Isḥāq ibn Aḥmad ibn Muḥammad ibn ʿAlī ibn Ghanim al-ʿAlthī al-Ḥanbalī. He was an *imām*, an ascetic, and a role model. He was also a jurist, a scholar, an enjoiner of good, and a prohibiter of evil who feared none but Allah the Exalted and who feared no blame when acting for the sake of Allah the Exalted. He rejected some practices of the caliph al-Nāṣir, as well as his subordinates, and confronted the caliph, declaring the truth unequivocally. Some said he was the *shaykh* of Iraq and the person most upholding censure of jurists, the destitute and others in things they took for granted. Al-Ḥāfiẓ al-Mundhirī said, "It was said that none repudiated and rejected falsehoods more than him, and he was imprisoned for his efforts, for a period. He has many letters which he sent to the luminaries in repudiation and as advice to them. He died in the year 634 in the town of ʿAlth."[640] Similarly, al-Ḥāfiẓ Ibn Rajab and Burhān al-Dīn ibn Mufliḥ wrote biographies of him.

ولنرجع إِلَى الْكَلَام على (الرَّوْضَة) فَنقُول: إِنَّه أَنْفَع كتاب لمن يُرِيد تعَاطِي الْأُصُول من أَصْحَابنَا، فمقام هَذَا الْكتاب بَين كتب الأُصُول مقَام (الْمقنع) بَين كتب الْفُرُوع. وَلَقَد ابتدأت فِي شَرحه على وَجه يُوضح مَنَاره، ويكشف أستاره وَللَّه الْحَمد.

Back to our discussions on *al-Rawḍah*: It is truly one of the most beneficial books for those who want to study legal theories according to our *aṣḥāb*. The stature of this book, among other books of legal theory, is similar to the standing of *al-Muqni*ʿ among other books of substantive law. I have begun explaining it in a way that clarifies its radiant theories and shows its hidden benefits, and praise belongs to Allah.

ولأصحابنا فِي فن الْأُصُول كتب كَثِيرَة، مِنْهَا:

Our *aṣḥāb* have authored many works on legal theories, such as:

---

640 [T] *Al-Takmilah li Wafayāt al-Naqalah* (3/441) In the printed version, it states, "his times had no one like him." However, I placed the correct quotation of al-Mundhirī in the main text.

(الكافية) وَ(الْمُعْتَمد) وَ(الْعدة) الْجَمِيع للْقَاضِي أبي يعلى.

Al-Kāfiyah, al-Muʿtamad, and *ʿUddah,* all of which are by al-Qāḍī Abu Yaʿlā.

وَمِنْهَا (مسودة بني تَيمِية) وهم الشَّيْخ مجد الدين، وَولده الشَّيْخ عبد الْحَلِيم، وحفيده شيخ الإِسْلَام الشَّيْخ تَقِي الدين.

Al-Musawwadah of the Family of Taymiyyah, authored by al-Shaykh Majd al-Dīn, his son al-Shaykh ʿAbd al-Halim, and his grandson Shaykh al-Islām Shaykh Taqī al-Dīn.

وَمِنْهَا (الْمقنع) لِابْنِ حمدَان.

Al-Muqniʿ by Ibn Ḥamdān.

وَمِنْهَا (الْإِيضَاح فِي الجدل) للشَّيْخ أبي مُحَمَّد ابْن الشَّيْخ الإِمَام الْحَافِظ عبد الرَّحْمَن ابْن الْجَوْزِي.

Al-Īḍāḥ fi 'l-Jadal by al-Shaykh Abu Muḥammad, son of the *shaykh* and scholar of ḥadīth, ʿAbd al-Raḥmān ibn al-Jawzī.

وَمِنْهَا (مُخْتَصر الْمقنع) لِابْنِ حمدَان وَشَرحه، كِلَاهُمَا لأبي عبد الله مُحَمَّد بن أَحْمد الْحَرَّانِي الْمَعْرُوف بِابْن الحبال أحد من شرح الْخرقِي، الْمُتَوفى سنة تسع وَأَرْبَعين وَسَبْع مئة.

A summation of *al-Muqniʿ* by Ibn Ḥamdān, as well as its explanation, both authored by Abu ʿAbdullāh Muḥammad ibn Aḥmad al-Ḥarrānī, known as Ibn al-Ḥabbāl, one of the scholars who explained al-Khiraqī. He died in the year 749.

وَمِنْهَا مُجَلد كَبِير للعلامة ابْن مُفْلِح صَاحب (الْفُرُوع) قَالَ الشَّيْخ عَلَاء الدين المرداوي: وَهُوَ أصل كتابنا - يَعْنِي تَحْرِير الْمَنْقُول - فَإِن غَالب استمدادنا مِنْهُ.

[Uṣūl al-Fiqh], a large volume written by the great scholar Ibn Mufliḥ, the author of *al-Furūʿ*. Al-Shaykh ʿAlā al-Dīn al-Mardāwī said, "It is the foundation of my book (meaning, *Taḥrīr al-Manqūl*), and the book we most

derived from."[641]

وَمِنْهَا أُصُول الشَّيْخ عبد الْمُؤمن، وَهُوَ فِي مُجَلد كَبِير.

[Qawāʿid al-Uṣūl wa Maʿāqid al-Fuṣūl] by al-Shaykh ʿAbd al-Muʾmin, which is a large volume.

وَمِنْهَا مُجَلد فِي الْأُصُول لعَلي بن عَبَّاس البعلي.

[Al-Mukhtaṣar fī Uṣūl al-Fiqh] by ʿAlī ibn [Muḥammad] ibn ʿAbbās al-Baʿlī.

وَمِنْهَا (التَّذكِرة فِي الأصُول) لِابْنِ الْحَافِظ عبد الْغَنِي.

Al-Tadhkirah fī 'l-Uṣūl by the son of al-Ḥāfiẓ ʿAbd al-Ghanī [al-Maqdisī].

وَمِنْهَا (مُخْتَصر الْحَاصِل) و(مختصر المَحْصُول) و(معراج الْوُصُول إِلَى فن الْأُصُول) وَالْكل للطوفي.

Mukhtaṣar al-Ḥāṣil and *Mukhtaṣar al-Maḥṣūl*, and *Miʿrāj al-Wuṣūl ilā Fan al-Uṣūl*, all of which are by al-Ṭūfī.

وَمِنْهَا عير ذَلِك مِمَّا يطول ذكره.

If we were to mention more, the discussion would be too lengthy.

تَخْرِيج أَحَادِيث الْكتب المصنفة وَكتب الْأَحْكَام

Referencing of al-Aḥadīth and Aḥadīth on Rulings (*Aḥadīth al-Aḥkām*)

وَأما تَخْرِيج أَحَادِيث الْكتب المصنفة وَكتب الْأَحْكَام:

As for books on referencing the aḥadīth mentioned in the authored works and books that collect aḥadīth on rulings:

فَأَما الأول: فَإِنِّي لم أطلع مِنْهُ إِلَّا على تَخْرِيج أَحَادِيث الْكَافِي فِي الْفِقْه للْإِمَام الْحَافِظ ضِيَاء الدين مُحَمَّد بن عبد الوَاحِد بن أَحْمد بن عبد الرَّحْمَن السَّعْدِي

641 [T] *Taḥrīr al-Manqūl* (p. 362).

الْمَقْدِسِي الْحَافِظ الْكَبِير، لَكِن هَذَا التَّخْرِيج مُخْتَصر جدا، لم يشف غليلا، وَلِهَذَا الحَافِظ كتاب (الأحَادِيث المختارة) وَهِي الأحَادِيث التِي تصلح أَن يحْتَج بهَا سوى مَا فِي (الصَّحِيحَيْن) خرجها من مسموعاته. قَالَ بَعضهم: هِيَ خير من صَحِيح الْحَاكِم انْتهى. قلت: وَقد اطلَعت مِنْهَا على مجلدات بِخَطه. قَالَ فِي (كشف الظنون) نقلا عَن كتاب (الشواذ الفياح) التزم فِيهِ الصِّحَّة، فصحح فِيهِ أحَادِيث لم يسْبق إِلَى تصحيحها. قَالَ ابْن كثير: وَهَذَا الْكتاب لم يتم، وَكَانَ بعض الْحفاظ من مَشَايِخنَا يرجحه على (مُسْتَدْرك الحَاكِم) توفّي الضياء سنة ثَلَاث وَأَرْبَعين وسِت مِئَة.

As for the first category [on referencing aḥadīth mentioned in the authored works], I have only come across referencing of the aḥadīth of *al-Kāfī fi 'l-Fiqh* by the *imām* and ḥadīth master, Ḍiyā' al-Dīn Muḥammad ibn 'Abd al-Wāḥid ibn Aḥmad ibn 'Abd al-Raḥmān al-Si'dī al-Maqdisī, the great ḥadīth master. However, his references are very brief, not satisfying the need in that regard. The same scholar has a book called *al-Aḥadīth al-Mukhtārah*, which comprises of aḥadīth that are fit to be used as evidence but that are not within the two *Ṣaḥīḥ* collections [of al-Bukhārī and Muslim.] He referenced them based on the aḥadīth that he narrated himself. Some even said it is better than the *Ṣaḥīḥ* collection of al-Ḥākim. I have come across a volume of it, in his own handwriting. In *Kashf al-Ẓunūn*, there is a quote from a book called *al-Shawādh al-Fayyāḥ*, where [al-Ḍiyā' al-Maqdisī] took it on himself to only reference authentic aḥadīth, authenticating aḥadīth that none before him did. Ibn Kathīr said, "This book is incomplete and some of my teachers used to prefer it over the *Mustadrak of al-Ḥākim*."[642] [Al-Ḍiyā'] died in the year 643.

وَأما كتب الْأَحْكَام: فأجلها وأوسعها وأنفعها كتاب (منتقى الْأَحْكَام) للْإِمَام مجد الدين عبد السَّلَام ابْن تَيْمِية، فَإِنَّهُ جمع فِيهِ الْأَحَادِيث الَّتِي يعْتَمد عَلَيْهَا عُلَمَاء الْإِسْلَام فِي الْأَحْكَام، انتقاها من الكتب السَّبْعَة: صحيحي البُخَارِي وَمُسلم، ومسند الإِمَام أَحْمد بن حَنْبَل، وجامع التِّرْمِذِي، وَسنَن النَّسَائِي، وَسنَن أبي دَاوُد، وَسنَن ابْن مَاجَه، وَتارة يذكر أَحَادِيث من سنَن الدَّارَقُطنِيّ وَغَيره.

642 [T] *Al-Bā'ith al-Hathīth* (p. 29).

As for books on aḥadīth of rulings, the best, most comprehensive, and most beneficial is *Muntaqā al-Aḥkām*, authored by al-Imām Majd al-Dīn 'Abd al-Salām ibn Taymiyyah. He gathered the aḥadīth that the scholars of Islam rely on in deriving rulings, which he selected from seven books: *Ṣaḥīḥ al-Bukhārī*, *Ṣaḥīḥ Muslim*, *Musnad of al-Imām Aḥmad ibn Ḥanbal*, *Jāmi' al-Tirmidhī*, *Sunan al-Nasā'ī*, *Sunan Abi Dāwūd* and *Sunan Ibn Mājah*. Sometimes, he also mentioned aḥadīth from the *Sunan of al-Dāraquṭnī*, and other sources.

ورتب أَحَادِيثه على تَرْتِيب أَبْوَاب كتب الْفِقْه، ورتب لَهُ أبوابا بِبَعْض مَا دلت عَلَيْهِ أَحَادِيثه من الْفَوَائِد، وَبِالْجُمْلَةِ فَهُوَ كتاب كَاف للمجتهد. وَقد اعتنى المحدثون بِهَذَا الْكتاب اعتناء تَاما، واشتهر عِنْدهم اشتهارا وَأي اشتهار، فشرحه سراج الدّين عمر ابْن الملقن الشَّافِعِي الْمُتَوفى سنة أَربع وَثَمَان مِئَة، لكنه لم يكلمهُ، بل كتب قِطْعَة، وَقَالَ فِي كِتَابه (الْبَدْر الْمُنِير).

He arranged his book according to the way books of *fiqh* are arranged, and also arranged the chapters in ways to show some beneficial points mentioned in the aḥadīth. In general, it is a sufficient book for a *mujtahid*. The scholars of ḥadīth have shown a great interest in this book and it became very popular among them. For example, Sirāj al-Dīn 'Umar ibn al-Mulaqqin, a Shāfi'ī scholar who died in the year 804, explained the book, though he did not complete it. He only wrote a portion of it. He said in his book *al-Badr al-Munīr*:

أَحْكَام الْحَافِظ مجد الدين عبد السَّلَام ابْن تَيْمِية الْمُسَمى ب(المنتقى) هُوَ كاسمه، لَوْلَا إِطْلَاقه فِي كثير من الْأَحَادِيث الْعَزْو إِلَى كتب الْأَئِمَّة دون التحسين والتضعيف، يَقُول مثلا: رَوَاهُ أَحْمد، رَوَاهُ الدَّارَقُطْنِي، رَوَاهُ أَبُو دَاوُد، وَيكون الحَدِيث ضَعِيفا. وَأَشد من ذَلِك كَون الحَدِيث فِي جَامع التِّرْمِذِي مُبينًا ضعفه فيعزيه إِلَيْهِ من غير بَيَان ضعفه.

The book on aḥadīth pertaining to rulings authored by al-Ḥāfiẓ Majd al-Dīn 'Abd al-Salām ibn Taymiyyah, which was called *al-Muntaqā*,[643] its title is indicative of its contents. [What a rich book it is,][644] were it not for his

643 [T] The word *al-Muntaqā* means "choice selections."

644 [T] What is between the brackets is found in the original book *al-Badr al-Munīr*,

referencing aḥadīth to the books of the scholars without authenticating or weakening [the narrations.] For example, he says, "Aḥmad reported it," "al-Dāraquṭnī reported it," or, "Abu Dāwūd reported it," though the ḥadīth is weak. Worse than that is when the narration is in *Jāmiʿ al-Tirmidhī* and [al-Tirmidhī] has clarified its weakness, and [al-Majd] references the ḥadīth to [al-Tirmidhī] without also clarifying its weakness.

فَيَنْبَغِي لِلْحَافِظِ جمع هَذِه الْمَوَاضِع وكتبها على حَوَاشِي هَذَا الْكتاب، أَو جمعهَا فِي مُصَنف لتكمل فَائِدَة الْكتاب. وَقد شرعت فِي كتب ذَلِك على حَوَاشِي نُسْخَتي، وَأَرْجُو إِتْمَامه. هَذَا كَلَامه.

It would be [more] appropriate for [such] a master of ḥadīth to gather instances of these happenings and to make note of them in the margins of the book, or gather them in an independent work of its own, so that the benefit of *[al-Muntaqā]* is complete. I have begun doing so in the margins of my copy of the book. I hope to finish it. **[End]**[645]

ولمحمد بن أَحْمد بن عبد الْهَادِي صَاحب (تَنْقِيح التَّحْقِيق) تَعْلِيقه على (الْمُنْتَقى) أَيْضا لم تكمل.

Muḥammad ibn Aḥmad ibn ʿAbd al-Hādī, the author of *Tanqīḥ al-Taḥqīq*, authored a commentary on *al-Muntaqā*, though he, too, did not complete it.

ثمَّ لم يزل هَذَا الْكتاب بكرا يتجول فِي الأقطار حَتَّى حط ركابه فِي الْبِلَاد اليمانية، فاشتهر هُنَاكَ وَلَا كَالشَّمْسِ فِي رَابِعَة النَّهَار، فتصدى لشرحه مُجْتَهد الْقطر الْيَمَانِي، مُحَمَّد بن عَلي بن عبد الله الشَّوْكَانِي - بِفَتْح الشين وَسُكُون الْوَاو، نِسْبَة إِلَى قَرْيَة من قرى السحامية إِحْدَى قبائل خولان، بَينهَا وَبَين صنعاء دون مَسَافَة يَوْم - ثمَّ الصَّنْعَانِي الْيَمَانِي، وَكَانَت وِلَادَته سنة اثْنَتَيْنِ وَسبعين وَمِئَة وَألف، وَتُوفِي سنة خمسين وَمِئَتَيْنِ وَألف، فيسر الله لَهُ إِتْمَام شَرحه فِي ثَمَان مجلدات، وَسَماهُ (نيل الأوطار من أسرار منتقى الأَخْبَار) وَهُوَ - على اختصاره -

but was not mentioned by al-Shaykh Ibn Badrān.

645 [T] *Al-Badr al-Munīr* by Ibn al-Mulaqqin (1/276).

واف بالمرام، قد جرده عَن كثير من التفريعات والمباحث، خُصُوصا فِي المقامات التِي يقل فِيهَا الِاخْتِلَاف، وَأطَال فِي المواطن التِي يحتدم فِيهَا الْجِدَال، وَبَين مَذَاهِب الأئِمَّة حَتَّى مَذْهَب أهل البَيْت، وَلم يتعصب فِيهِ لمَذْهَب بل دَار مَعَ الدَّلِيل كَيْفَمَا دَار. وَهَذَا الشَّرْح قد طبع فِي مصر، وتداوله كل ذِي ذهن وقاد، وفكر يسمو إِلَى مدارك الِاجْتِهَاد، وغض الطرف عَنهُ كل حسود مكابر، على ذام التَّقْلِيد مطبوع وَعَن غَيره زاجر، فنسأل الله السَّلامَة من شُؤْم التَّقْلِيد الأعْمَى، ولؤم التعصب الذميم، وشيطانه الرَّجِيم.

This book (*al-Muntaqā*) remained similar to a camel, traversing in the various lands, until it landed in Yemen, becoming as popular as the sun in midday. Its explanation was undertaken by the *mujtahid* of Yemen, Muḥammad ibn ʿAlī ibn ʿAbdullāh al-Shawkānī, whose last name is an ascription to one of the towns of al-Suḥāmiyyah, belonging to one of the tribes of Khawlān. Between it and Ṣanʿāʾ, there is fewer than the distance of a day's travel. [Al-Shawkānī] then resided in Ṣanʿāʾ. He was born in the year 1172 and died in the year 1250. Allah the Exalted facilitated for him the completion of its explanation in eight volumes. He called his book *Nayl al-Awṭār min Asrār Muntaqā al-Akhbār*.[646] Although it is quite summarised, it fulfills its purpose. He removed discussions of many subsidiary matters and discussions, especially where there is little difference of opinion. At other times, he spoke at length on issues where disagreements flared up. He clarified the positions of the scholars, even the scholars of Ahl al-Bayt. He was not bigoted towards any one school; rather, he went wherever the evidence took him. This explanation has been published in Egypt, and has been in circulation among anyone possessing a lively intellect and thought that uplifts them to the subjects of *ijtihād*, while ignoring all envious, obstinate people. It is impressed on those who censure blind-following, and it rejects the practices of all others. We ask Allah the Exalted safety from the misfortune of blind-following, the ignobility of dispraised bigotry, and from the devil who has been cast away.

وَمِمَّا اطَّلَعْنَا عَلَيْهِ من كتب الْأَحْكَام لِأَصْحَابِنَا كتاب (الْمطَالع) وَيُقَال لَهُ: مطالع ابْن عُبَيْدَان، جمع وتأليف الشَّيْخ عبد الرَّحْمَن بن مَحْمُود بن عُبَيْدَان البعلبكي الْحَنْبَلِي، ولد سنة خمس وَسبعين وست مِئَة، وَتُوفي سنة أَرْبَعِينَ وَسَبْع مئة، وَكَانَ

646 The published book is called *Nayl al-Awṭār Sharḥ Muntaqā al-Akhbār*.

عَارِفًا بالفقه وغوامضه وَالْأُصُول، والْحَدِيث، والعربية، ولازم شيخ الإِسْلَام ابْن تَيْمِية رَضِي الله عَنهُ، لكنه مَال فِي آخر أمره إِلَى الْقَوْل بوحدة الْوُجُود، واختل عقله حَتَّى توفاه الله تَعَالَى. وَكتابه هَذَا فِي مُجَلد، جمعه من الْكتب السِّتَّة، ورمز فِيهِ إِلَى الحَدِيث الصَّحِيح وَالْحسن، ورتبه على أَبْوَاب (الْمقنع).

Another book on the topic of *aḥadīth al-aḥkām* authored by one of our *aṣḥāb* is *al-Maṭāli*ʿ, which is more commonly known as *Maṭāli*ʿ *Ibn ʿUbaydān*. It was authored by al-Shaykh ʿAbd al-Raḥmān ibn Maḥmūd ibn ʿUbaydān al-Baʿalbakī al-Ḥanbalī. He was born in the year 675 and died in the year 740. He was well-aware of jurisprudence and its obscurities, as well as legal theories, ḥadīth, and the Arabic language. He accompanied Shaykh al-Islām Ibn Taymiyyah ﵁ but inclined, towards the end of his life, to pantheism, and his mind became deranged, until Allah the Exalted took his life. This book, though, consists of a single volume. He compiled it from the Six Books, and indicated which aḥadīth were authentic and which were acceptable. He arranged the book according to the chaptering of *al-Muqni*ʿ.

وَمِنْهَا (الْأَحْكَام الْكُبْرى) الْمرتبَة على أَحْكَام ضِيَاء الدين الْمَقْدِسِي لِلْحَافِظِ مُحَمَّد بن أَحْمد الْمَعْرُوف بِابْن عبد الْهَادِي صَاحب (تَنْقِيح التَّحْقِيق) لكنه لم يكمل بل تمّ مِنْهَا سبع مجلدات.

Another is called *al-Aḥkām al-Kubrā*, which is arranged exactly as Ḍiyāʾ al-Dīn al-Maqdisī arranged his collection. It was authored by al-Ḥāfiẓ Muḥammad ibn Aḥmad, known better as Ibn ʿAbd al-Hādī, the author of *Tanqīḥ al-Tahqīq*. However, he did not complete it; he was only able to complete seven volumes.

وَمِنْهَا (عُمْدَة الْأَحْكَام الْكُبْرى)، لِلْإِمَام الْحَافِظ عبد الْغَنِيّ بن عبد الْوَاحِد بن عَلي بن سرُور الجماعيلي الْمَقْدِسِي الْحَنْبَلِي، الْمُتوفى سنة سِتّ مئة، وَهُوَ كتاب فِي ثَلَاث مجلدات، عز نَظِيره، قَالَ فِي خطبَته: حصرت الْكَلَام فِي خَمْسَة أَقسَام. الأول: التَّعْرِيف بِمن ذكر من رُوَاة الحَدِيث إِجْمَالا، وَله أَسمَاء رجالها فِي مُجَلد. قَالَ: أفردت هَذِه بِكِتَاب سميته (الْعدة). الثَّانِي: فِي أَحَادِيثه. الثَّالِث: بِبَيَان مَا وَقع فِيهِ من المبهمات. الرَّابِع: فِي ضبط لَفظه.

Another is called *'Umdat al-Aḥkām al-Kubrā*, by the *imām* and ḥadīth master, 'Abd al-Ghanī ibn 'Abd al-Wāḥid ibn 'Alī ibn Surūr al-Jamā'īlī al-Maqdisī al-Ḥanbalī. He died in the year 600. The book consists of three volumes. Its parallel is rare. He said in its introduction, "I have limited discussions to five topics: (i) A general overview of the narrators of ḥadīth mentioned. I have made this into its own unique work, called *al-'Uddah*. (ii) On its aḥadīth. (iii) Clarifying its ambiguous wording. (iv) Critiquing its wording. (v) [Indicating some things that can be derived."[647]

[...] ذكر هَذَا صَاحب (كشف الظنون).

It was explained by Abu 'Abdullāh Muḥammad ibn Aḥmad ibn Marzuq al-Tilmisānī al-Māliki, who died in the year 781, in five volumes.][648] This was mentioned by the author of *Kashf al-Ẓunūn*.[649]

وللحافظ الْمَذْكُور كتاب (عُمْدَة الْأَحْكَام) أَيْضا وَهِي الصُّغْرى. قَالَ فِي أولهَا: أما بعد: فَإِن بعض إخْوَانِي سَأَلَني اخْتِصَار جملَة من أَحَادِيث الْأَحْكَام، مِمَّا اتفق عَلَيْهِ الإمامان: الإِمَام أَبُو عبد الله مُحَمَّد بن إِسْمَاعِيل بن إِبْرَاهِيم البُخَارِي، وَمُسلم بن الحجَّاج، فأجبته إِلَى سُؤَاله. وَقد بلغ هَذَا الْكتاب خَمْس مِئَة حَدِيث. وَقد اعتنى الْعلمَاء بِهَذَا الْكتاب فشرحه.

The same Ḥāfiẓ ['Abd al-Ghani al-Maqdisī] also wrote *'Umdat al-Aḥkam*, which is a summarised version. He said in its introduction, "One of my brethren have asked me to summarise some of the aḥadīth pertaining to rulings, which have been agreed on between the two *imāms*: Al-Imām Abu 'Abdillāh Muḥammad ibn Ismā'īl ibn Ibrāḥīm al-Bukhārī and Muslim ibn al-Ḥajjaj. Therefore, I fulfilled his request."[650] This book consists of over five hundred aḥadīth and has been shown incredible care by the scholars. As such, it was explained by the following scholars:

أَبُو عبد الله مُحَمَّد بن أَحْمد بن مَرْزُوق التلمساني الْمَالِكِي، الْمُتوفى سنة إِحْدَى

647 [T] *Kashf al-Ẓunūn* (2/1164).

648 [T] The words between the brackets are not found in the printed version, but are found in the manuscript.

649 Ibid

650 *'Umdat al-Aḥkām* (p. 3).

وثمانين وَسَبْع مئة فِي خمس مجلدات شرحا جَمع فِيهِ بَين كَلَام ابْن دَقِيق الْعِيد، وَابْن الْعَطار، والفاكهاني، وَغَيرهم. وَشَرحه سراج الدين عمر ابْن الملقن الشَّافِعِي، الْمُتَوفَّى سنة أَربع وَثَمَان مِئَة، سَمَّاهُ بـ(الإعلام)، وَهُوَ من أحسن مصنفاته.

Abu 'Abdullāh Muḥammad ibn Aḥmad ibn Marzūq al-Tilmisānī al-Māliki, who died in the year 781, in five volumes, where he combined the explanations of Ibn Daqiq al-'Īd, Ibn al-'Aṭṭār, al-Fākihānī, and others. It was also explained by Sirāj al-Dīn 'Umar ibn al-Mulaqqin al-Shāfi'ī, who died in the year 804. He called it *al-I'lām*, and it is one of his best authorships.

وَشَرحه صَاحب (الْقَامُوس) مجد الدين مُحَمَّد بن يَعْقُوب الفيروزأبادي الشِّيرَازِي، وَسَماهُ (عدَّة الْحُكَّام فِي شرح عُمْدَة الْأَحْكَام) وَهُوَ مجلدان، وَكَانَت وَفَاة المجد سنة سبع عشرة وَثَمَان مِئَة.

It was also explained by the author of al-Qāmūs, whose name was Majd al-Dīn Muḥammad ibn Ya'qūb al-Fayrūzabādī al-Shīrāzī. He called his book *'Uddat al-Ḥukkām fī Sharḥ 'Umdaṭ al-Aḥkām*. It consists of two volumes. Al-Majd died in the year 817.

وَشَرحه السَّيِّد تَاج الدّين عبد الْوَهَّاب بن مُحَمَّد بن حسن بن أبي الْوَفَاء الْعلوِي، الْمُتوفى سنة خمس وَسبعين وَثَمَان مِئَة، وَسَماهُ (عدَّة الحُكام).

It was also explained by al-Sayyid Tāj al-Dīn 'Abd al-Wahhāb ibn Muḥammad ibn Ḥasan ibn Abi 'l-Wafā' al-'Alawī, who died in the year 875. He called it *'Uddat al-Ḥukkām*.

وَشَرحه عبد الرَّحْمَن بن عَلي بن خلف الشَّيْخ زين الدين أبي الْمَعَالِي الفارسكوري الشَّافِعِي شرحا دلّ على كَثْرَة فَضله، وَتُوفي سنة ثَمَان وَثَمَان مِئَة، قَالَه فِي (كشف الظنون) ثمَّ قَالَ: وَلَعَلَّ هَذَا (عُمْدَة الْفِقْه).

It was also explained by 'Abd al-Raḥmān ibn 'Alī ibn Khalaf al-Shaykh Zayn al-Dīn Abi 'l-Ma'ālī al-Fārskūrī al-Shāfi'ī. His explanation showed his immense virtue. He died in the year 808, as the author of *Kashf al-Ẓunūn* stated, who then said, "It is possibly called *'Umdat al-Fiqh*."[651]

---

651 [T] *Kashf al-Ẓunūn* (2/1164).

وَشَرحه الشَّيْخ عماد الدين إِسْمَاعِيل بن أَحْمد بن سعيد بن مُحَمَّد بن الْأَثِير الْحلَبِي الشَّافِعِي، ذكر فِيهِ أنه قَرَأَ هَذَا الْكتاب على ابْن دَقِيق الْعِيد، فشرحه لَهُ على طَرِيقَة الإِمْلَاء، وَسَماهُ (أَحْكَام الْأَحْكَام) قلت: وَهَذَا الشَّرْح مطبوع ومشهور بِأنهُ لِابْنِ دَقِيق الْعِيد، وَقد رَأيْته وطالعته.

It was also explained by al-Shaykh ʿImād al-Dīn Ismāʿīl ibn Aḥmad ibn Saʿīd ibn Muḥammad ibn al-Athīr al-Ḥalabī al-Shāfiʿī. He mentioned that he read this book to Ibn Daqīq al-ʿĪd, and he explained it to him verbally. He called it *Iḥkām al-Aḥkām*. This explanation is published and it is well-known to be an authorship of Ibn Daqīq al-ʿĪd. I have seen and read it.

وَشَرحه أَيْضا الْبرمَاوِي الشَّافِعِ.

It was also explained by al-Burmāwī al-Shāfiʿī.

وَشَرحه أَيْضا الشَّيْخ أَحْمد بن عبد الله الْغزِّي ثمَّ الدِّمَشْقِي شرحا وصل فِيهِ إِلَى بَاب الصَدَاق، وَمَات عَنهُ، فأتمه الشَّيْخ رَضِي الدّين الْغزِّي الشَّافِعِي الدِّمَشْقِ.

It was also explained by al-Shaykh Aḥmad ibn ʿAbdullāh al-Ghizzī, who resided later in his life in Damascus. He reached the Chapter of Bride's Gifts but then death reached him, and it was completed by al-Shaykh Raḍī al-Dīn al-Ghizzī al-Shāfiʿī al-Dimashqī.

وَشَرحه الْعَلامَة الشَّيْخ مُحَمَّد بن أَحْمد السفاريني الْحَنْبَلِي فِي مجلدين، وَقد كنت طالعته قَدِيما أثْنَاء الطّلب.

It was also explained by the great scholar al-Shaykh Muḥammad ibn Aḥmad al-Saffārīnī al-Ḥanbalī in two volumes. I read it long ago, when I was early in my pursuit of knowledge.

ثمَّ إِنِّي كنت مِمَّن ولع فِي هَذَا الْكتاب، وقرأته درسا فِي جَامع بني أُميَّة تَحت قبة النسْر، ثمَّ شرحته فِي مجلدين، وسميته (موارد الأفهام على سلسبيل عُمْدَة الْأَحْكَام) سَائِلًا مِنْهُ تَعَالَى أَن ينفع بِهِ من يطالعه بمنه وَكَرمه.

To add to this, I became enamoured by this book, and I read and taught it in the Umayyad Mosque, under the dome of al-Nasr. Then, I explained it in two volumes, and called it *Mawārid al-Afhām ʿalā Salsabīl ʿUmdat al-Aḥkām*. I ask Allah the Exalted to allow it to benefit those who read it, by His Favour and Grace.

وَاعْلَم أَيهَا الطَّالِب للحق أَن الْبَحْر الزاخر فِي هَذَا الْمَوْضُوع، والمورد العذب، والوابل الصيب إِنَّمَا هُوَ مُسْند الإِمَام أَحْمد بن مُحَمَّد بن حَنْبَل رَضِي الله عَنهُ وأرضاه، وَجعل الْجنَّة منقلبه ومثواه، وَإِنَّمَا منع الِاشْتِغَال بِهِ اشتغالا كالاشتغال بالسنن أُمُور:

In continuation, know, O seeker of truth, that in this subject, the copious ocean, the sweet spring, and the abundant downpour [of knowledge] emanates from the *Musnad* of al-Imām Aḥmad ibn Muḥammad ibn Ḥanbal ﵁, and make paradise his place of resort and abode. The reasons why [the *Musnad*] is not given the same care and attention as the *Sunan* collections of ḥadīth are:

أَحدهَا: كَونه مُرَتبا على أَحَادِيث الصَّحَابَة، وَهَذَا التَّرْتِيب أصبح غير مألوف عِنْد المتوسطين والمتأخرين، فَصَارَ بِحَيْثُ لَو أَرَادَ مُحدث أن يجمع أَحَادِيث بَاب مِنْهُ احْتَاجَ إِلَى مطالعته من أوله إِلَى آخِره، وَهَذَا أَمر عسير جدا.

One. The *Musnad* is arranged according to the aḥadīth of the companions. This arrangement is not customary to the [ḥadīth] scholars of the middle periods and later periods. Therefore, if a scholar of ḥadīth wished to gather all aḥadīth on a topic, he would have to read the book in its entirety, which is extremely difficult.

ثَانِيهَا: عزة وجوده لطوله، فَإِنَّهُ قد ضم ثَلَاثِينَ ألف حَدِيث، وَزَاد عَلَيْهِ وَلَده الإِمَام عبد الله عشرة آلَاف حَدِيث فَصَارَ أَرْبَعِينَ ألفا وَقد بلغنَا أَن الْحفاظ الْكِبَار كَانُوا يعْجبُونَ إِذا ظفروا بأجزاء مِنْهُ، وَلم يطلع عَلَيْهِ بِتَمَامِهِ إِلا النَّادِر، وَلَقَد كنت سَمِعت من بعض مَشَايِخنَا الْحَنَابِلَة مِمَّن لَهُم إِلْمَام بِالْحَدِيثِ، يَزْعمُونَ أَن (الْمسند) قد غرق فِي دجلة بَغْدَاد وينكر وجوده، فَكنت أفند مزاعمه وَأَقُول لَهُ: إِنِّي اطَّلَعت على معظمه فِي خزانَة الْكتب العمومية بِدِمَشْق، فيصر على مَا زَعمه وَيَقُول: هَذَا مُسْند عبد الله. ثمَّ إِن الْكتاب طبع وتجلى للعيان.

Two. It was scarce, due to its length. It comprised of thirty thousand aḥadīth, and his son, al-Imām ʿAbdullāh, added another ten thousand aḥadīth, making it a total of forty thousand. It has reached us that the great scholars of ḥadīth would become happy if they came across chapters and volumes of it. Very few people read it in its entirety. I heard one of my Ḥanbalī teachers, who has knowledge of ḥadīth, claim that the *Musnad* was washed away in the Tigris in Baghdad, and denied its very existence. I would refute his claim by stating that I came across it in the library of al-ʿAmūmiyyah, in Damascus. He was insistent on his claim, though, and said, "That is the *Musnad* of ʿAbdullāh." Later, the book would be published and become visible for all to see.

ثَالِثهَا: أَن عزة وجوده كَانَت سَببا لعدم خدمته كَمَا خدمت السّنَن، وَغَيرهَا من كتب الحَدِيث، وَمَعَ هَذَا فَلم يعْدم معتنيا بِهِ.

Three. Its scarcity was a factor in the lack of attention it received, in contrast to the attention and service shown to the other *Sunan* and other books of ḥadīth. However, with that said, [the *Musnad*] was never fully abandoned, where none busied themselves with it.

وَقد وَقع لَهُ فِيهِ من الثلاثيات مَا ينوف عَن ثَلَاث مِئَة حَدِيث ثلاثية الإِسْنَاد، وَقد كنت رَأَيْت شرحا لَهَا للعلامة مُحَمَّد بن أَحْمد السفاريني الْحَنْبَلِي، ثمَّ غَابَ عني. وَقد طلب مني أحد أفاضل النجديين شرحها فابتدأت بِهِ وَأَنا أسأل الله تَعَالَى أَن يمن بإتمامه وطبعه.

[The *Musnad*] contains more than three hundred aḥadīth that have three people [between al-Imām Aḥmad and the Prophet ﷺ.] I saw an explanation of them, written by the great scholar, Muḥammad ibn Aḥmad al-Saffārīnī al-Ḥanbalī, but then I lost it. A virtuous person from Najd asked me to explain them, which I began doing. I ask Allah the Exalted to allow me to complete and publish it.

وَقد حكى الْحفاظ أَن الإِمَام أَحْمد اشْترط أَن لَا يخرج فِي مُسْنده إِلَّا حَدِيثا صَحِيحا عِنْده. قلت: وَهَذَا صَحِيح بِالنِّسْبَةِ إِلَى أَحَادِيث الأَحْكَام. وَقد رُوِيَ عَنهُ أَنه قَالَ: إِذا كَانَ الحَدِيث فِي الحَلَال وَالحرَام شددنا، وَإِذا كَانَ فِي غَيره

تساهلنا.

Scholars of ḥadīth have mentioned that al-Imām Aḥmad placed a condition that he only narrates aḥadīth in his *Musnad* that he considered authentic. My perspective is: This is true if we constrict this qualification to aḥadīth of rulings. It was reported that he said, "If the ḥadīth is concerning the lawful or the unlawful, I was stricter, but if it is on other topics, I was more lenient."

وَحكى البقاعي عَن أبي مُوسَى الْمَدِينِي أَنه قَالَ: إِن فِيهِ أَحَادِيث مَوْضُوعَة كَذَا قَالَ، وَتَبعهُ الْحَافِظ ابْن الْجَوْزِي فِي كِتَابه (الموضوعات) فأورد فِيهِ أَحَادِيث من مُسْند الإِمَام أَحْمد، وانتصر لَهُ الْحَافِظ أَحْمد بن حجر الْعَسْقَلَانِي فِي كِتَابه (الْقَوْل المسدد في الذب عَن مُسْند أَحْمد) وَبَين خطأ ابْن الْجَوْزِي، ورد عَلَيْهِ أحسن الرَّد. وأبلغ من ذَلِك أَن مِنْهَا حَدِيثا مخرجا فِي صَحِيح مُسلم حَتَّى قَالَ ابْن حجر: هَذِه غَفلَة شَدِيدَة من ابْن الْجَوْزِي، حَيْثُ حكم على هَذَا الحَدِيث بِالْوَضْع.

Al-Biqā'ī mentioned that Abu Mūsā al-Madīnī said, "It contains fabricated aḥadīth," and this position was also held by al-Ḥāfiẓ Ibn al-Jawzī in his book *al-Mawḍū'āt*. He mentioned some reports from the *Musnad of al-Imām Aḥmad*. However, [the *Musnad*] was defended by al-Ḥāfiẓ Aḥmad ibn Ḥajar al-'Asqalānī in his book *al-Qawl al-Musaddad fi 'l-Dhabb 'an Musnad Aḥmad*, wherein he clarified the mistake of Ibn al-Jawzī excellently. More indicative is that one of [those aḥadīth mentioned by Ibn al-Jawzī] is a ḥadīth that is reported in *Ṣaḥīḥ Muslim*. Ibn Ḥajar said, "This is a severe blunder on [Ibn al-Jawzī's] part,"[652] in reference to judging that ḥadīth as being fabricated.

وَمهما تعصب الْقَوْم فَإِن أَحَادِيث الْمسند كلهَا يَصح الِاحْتِجَاج بهَا، وَهِي صَحِيحَة على طَرِيقَته الَّتِي استقام عَلَيْهَا، كَمَا أَشَرنَا إِلَى بعض ذَلِك عِنْد الْكَلَام على أُصُوله. وَلَعَل الَّذين قَالُوا بِضعْف أَحَادِيث من مُسْنده جَاءَتْهُم من طرق ضَعِيفَة غير طَرِيقَته، فضعفوها بِاعْتِبَار مَا جَاءَهُم من طرقها، وَكَثِيرًا مَا يذهب إِلَى

652 [T] *Al-Qawl al-Musaddad* by Ibn Ḥajar (p. 31).

مثل هَذَا أَصْحَاب الحَدِيث مِمَّن لَا يُحِيط علما بالطرق، فتَأمل هَذَا، واحفظه، وَاعْتبر بِهِ كتب الحَدِيث، فَإنَّك تَجِد الْأَمر وَاضحا.

Irrespective of the biases and bigotry of people, it remains that all of the aḥadīth of the *Musnad* are viable evidences, and are authentic, in accordance with the methodology [al-Imām Aḥmad] held himself to, some of which we referred to when speaking about his legal theories. Perhaps those who held that some of the aḥadīth of the *Musnad* are inauthentic were judging those aḥadīth based on other weak chains of narration instead of those of [al-Imām Aḥmad], and judged the aḥadīth to be inauthentic based on routes of the ḥadīth they had. Many times, the people of ḥadīth do such things when they do not have comprehensive knowledge of the routes of ḥadīth. Therefore, reflect on this point and recollect it when considering the books of ḥadīth, and you will find the matter to be clear.

هَذَا وَقد جمع غَرِيب (الْمسند) أَبُو عمر مُحَمَّد بن عبد الْوَاحِد، الْمَعْرُوف بِغُلَام ثَعْلَب فِي كتاب ذكر فِيهِ مَا فِي أَحَادِيث المسند من اللُّغَات الغريبة، وَكَانَ حنبليا، رُوِيَ عَنهُ أَنه أمْلى من حفظه ثَلَاثِينَ ألف ورقة فِيمَا نقل وَجَمِيع كتبه الَّتِي بأيدي النَّاس إِنَّمَا أملاها بِغَيْر تصنيف، قَالَه ابْن مُفْلِح فِي (الْمَقْصد الأرشد) وَتُوفي سنة خمس وَأَرْبَعين وثلاث مئة.

The ambiguous terminologies [in the aḥadīth reported in] *al-Musnad* were gathered by Abu ʿUmar Muḥammad ibn ʿAbd al-Wāḥid, known as Ghulām Thaʿlab, in a book he authored where he mentions the ambiguous wordings used in the *Musnad*. He was a Ḥanbalī, as well, who is reported to have dictated 30,000 pages filled with his own narrations. All of the books [of Ghulam Thaʿlab] that are in the possession of people are of his dictation; he authored none of them by hand. Ibn Mufliḥ said in *al-Maqṣad al-Arshad*, "He died in the year 345."[653]

وَاخْتصرَ الْمسند الشَّيْخ الإِمَام سراج الدين عمر بن عَلي، الْمَعْرُوف بِابْن الملقن الشَّافِعِي الْمُتوفَّى سنة خمس وَثَمَان مئة، وَعَلَيهِ تعليقة للسيوطي فِي إعرابه، سَمَّاهَا (عُقُود الزبرجد).

653 [T] *Al-Maqṣad al-Arshad* (2/443).

The *Musnad* was summarised by the *shaykh* and *imām* Sirāj al-Dīn ʿUmar ibn ʿAlī, known as Ibn al-Mulaqqin, a Shāfiʿī scholar. He died in the year 805. His summary has a syntaxial commentary by al-Suyūṭī, called *ʿUqūd al-Zabarjad*.

وَقد شرح الْمسند أَبُو الْحسن مُحَمَّد بن عبد الْهَادِي السندي، نزيل الْمَدِينَة المنورة، الْمُتَوفَّى سنة تسع وَثَلَاثِينَ وَمِئَة وَألف، وَقيل: سنة ثَمَان وَثَلَاثِينَ، وَهُوَ شرح مُخْتَصر مُفِيد، كَمَا أَخْبرنِي من اطلع عَلَيْهِ فِي خَزَائِن الْكتب بِالْمَدِينَةِ، وَهُوَ فِي نَحْو خمسين كراسة كبار، حذا فِيهِ حَذْو حَوَاشِيه على الْكتب السِّتَّة.

The *Musnad* was also explained by Abu ʿl-Ḥasan Muḥammad ibn ʿAbd al-Hādī al-Sindī, a resident of Madīnah who died in the year 1139, or the year 1138, as some stated. It is a concise, yet beneficial, commentary, as I was told by people who read it in the library where it is located, in Madīnah. It is approximately fifty large volumes, where he explained it as he did the Six Books.

وَاخْتَصَرَهُ الشَّيْخ زين الدّين عمر بن أَحْمد الشماع الْحلَبِي، وَسَماهُ (در المنتقد من مَذْهَب أَحْمد) وَرَأَيْت فِي خزانَة الْكتب العمومية بِدِمَشْق كتابا فِي تراجم رجال الْمسند، تأليف الإِمَام الْحَافِظ مُحَمَّد بن مُحَمَّد بن مُحَمَّد بن عَلي بن يُوسُف الْجزرِي، سَمَّاهُ (الْمَقْصد الأحمد فِي رجال أَحْمد) وَله أَيْضا (الْمسند الأحمد فِيمَا يتَعَلَّق بِمُسْنَد أَحْمد) و(المصعد الأحمد فِي ختم مسانيد أَحْمد) وَتُوفِي سنة أَربع وَثَلَاثِينَ وَثَمَان مئة.

It was also summarised by al-Shaykh Zayn al-Dīn ʿUmar ibn Aḥmad al-Shammāʾ al-Ḥalabī. He called it *al-Durr al-Muntaqad min Madhhab Aḥmad*. I saw in the Library of ʿAmūmiyyah, in Damascus, a book about the biographies of the narrators contained in the *Musnad*, authored by the *imām* and ḥadīth scholar, Muḥammad ibn Muḥammad ibn ʿAlī ibn Yūsuf al-Jazarī. He called it *al-Maqṣad al-Aḥmad fī Rijāl Aḥmad*. He also wrote, *al-Musnad al-Aḥmad fī mā Yataʿallaq bī Musnad Aḥmad*, and *al-Maṣʿad al-Aḥmad fi Khatm Masānīd Aḥmad*. He died in the year 834.

وَمِمَّنْ رتب الْمسند على الْأَبْوَاب عَلي بن حُسَيْن بن عُرْوَة - كَذَا ذكره السخاوي

فِي (الضَّوْء اللامع) وَقَالَ فِي (الْمَقْصد الأرشد) عَلي بن عُرْوَة قلت وَهَكَذَا رَأَيْته بِخَطِهِ - المشرقي ثمَّ الدمَشْقِي الْحَنْبَلِي الْمَعْرُوف بِابْن زكنون فَإِنَّهُ رتبه فِي كتاب سَمَّاهُ (الكواكب الدراري فِي تَرْتِيب مُسْند أَحْمد على صَحِيح البُخَارِي) وَهَذَا الْكتاب من تعاجيب الْكتب، وَقد وَصفه السخاوي فِي (الضَّوْء) فَقَالَ: هَذَا الْكتاب رتب فِيهِ (الْمسند) وَشَرحه فِي مئة وَعشْرين مجلدا. طَرِيقَته فِيهِ أَنه إِذا جَاءَ حَدِيث الْإِفْك - مثلا - يَأْخُذ نُسْخَة من شَرحه للْقَاضِي عِيَاض، فَيَضَعهَا بِتَمَامِهَا. وَإِذا مرت بِهِ مَسْأَلَة فِيهَا تصنيف مُفْرد لِابْنِ الْقيم أَو شَيْخه ابْن تَيمِية أَو غَيرهمَا وَضعه بِتَمَامِهِ، ويستوفي ذَلِك الْبَاب من الْمُغنِي لِابْنِ قدامَة وَنَحْوه، وكل ذَلِك مَعَ الزّهْد والورع. هَذَا كَلَامه.

Among the scholars who organised the *Musnad* according to the chapters [of *fiqh*] is ʿAlī ibn Ḥusayn ibn ʿUrwah al-Mashriqī al-Dimashqī. This was his name according to al-Sakhāwī in *al-Ḍaw' al-Lāmi'*, though in *al-Maqṣad al-Arshad*, it is stated that his name is ʿAlī ibn ʿUrwah. My view is the latter, because I saw him write his name in his own handwriting. He was a Ḥanbalī scholar known as Ibn Zaknūn. He arranged [the *Musnad*,] and called his rearrangement *al-Kawākib al-Darārī fi Tartīb Musnad Aḥmad ʿalā Ṣaḥīḥ al-Bukhārī*. This book is a marvellous work. Al-Sakhāwī described it in *al-Ḍaw' al-Lāmi'*, stating, "This book rearranged and explained the *Musnad* in approximately one hundred and twenty volumes. The way he did so is that when he wished to explain the ḥadīth of the slander [of ʿĀ'ishah,] for example, he would place the entirety of the explanation of al-Qāḍī ʿIyyāḍ. If an issue came up that had some independent work of Ibn al-Qayyim, his teacher Ibn Taymiyyah, or others, he would place their entire discussion. He would then fulfill the chapter by adding from *al-Mughnī* of Ibn Qudāmah, and other such books. This is in addition to his asceticism and abstinence."[654]

قلت: وَقد رَأَيْت من هَذَا الْكتاب أَرْبَعَة وَأَرْبَعين مجلدا، فَرَأَيْت مجلداته تَارَة مفتتحة بتفسير الْقُرْآن، فَإِذا جَاءَت آيَة فِيهَا، أَو إِشَارَة إِلَى مؤلف، وَضعه بِتَمَامِهِ، وَتارَة مفتتحا بترتيب المسند، فَيكون على نمط مَا ذكره السخاوي، حَتَّى إِن فِيهِ شرح البُخَارِي لِابْنِ رَجَب الَّذِي وصل فِيهِ إِلَى بَاب صَلَاة الْعِيدَيْنِ.

654 [T] *Al-Ḍaw' al-Lāmi'* (5/214).

My commentary: I have seen forty-four volumes of this work. Sometimes, its volumes begin with explanation of Qur'ān, and when he discusses a verse or alludes to an author, he quotes the entire discussion, sometimes by first arranging the *Musnad*, as al-Sakhāwī stated. It even contains the explanation of al-Bukhārī written by Ibn Rajab, wherein [Ibn Rajab] reached the Chapter of the Two Eid Prayers.

وغالب مصنفات شيخ الْإِسْلَام ابْن تَيمِية نسخت من هَذَا الْكتاب وطبعت، حَيْثُ فِيهِ كثير من كتبه ورسائله، وَالنَّاس يظنون أَن مَا فِيهِ من التَّفْسِير لِابْنِ تَيْمِية، وَهَذَا غلط وَاضح. نعم رَأَيْت فِيمَا رَأَيْت مِنْهُ مجلدين خاصين بترتيب الْمسند.

Most of the works of Shaykh al-Islām Ibn Taymiyyah were copied from this book and were printed, since it contains many of his books and treatises. People think that the *tafsīr* in the book, however, belongs to Ibn Taymiyyah, but that is an obvious mistake. In this book, I did find that there were two volumes dedicated to the arrangement of the *Musnad*.

ولنذكر تَرْجَمَة هَذَا الرجل لغرابة أمره وَأمر كِتَابه فَنَقُول: تَرْجَمَة السخاوي فَقَالَ:

We should discuss the biography of this man, due to his and his book's amazing nature. Al-Sakhāwī provided a biographical account, saying:

ولد قبل السِّتين وَسَبْع مئة، وَنَشَأ فِي ابْتِدَائه جمالا، ثمَّ أعرض عَن ذَلِك، وَحفظ الْقُرْآن، وتفقه وبرع، وَسمع من عُلَمَاء زَمَنه الحَدِيث، وسرد السخاوي مشايخه ثمَّ قَالَ: وَانْقطع إِلَى الله تَعَالَى فِي مَسْجِد الْقدَم بآخر أَرض القبيبات بِدِمَشْق، يُؤَدب الأَطْفَال احتسابا.

He was born before the year 760, and he began as a porter, though he later abandoned that vocation and memorised the Qur'ān. Afterwards, he learned jurisprudence, and was quite skilled. He heard ḥadīth from the scholars of his time. (Al-Sakhāwī then mentioned some of his teachers). He secluded himself for Allah the Exalted in Masjid al-Qidam, in the furthest end of the Qabībāt district of Damascus, where he would teach children, only seeking reward.

مَعَ اعتنائه بتحصيل نفائس الْكتب وَجمعهَا، وكل ذَلِك مَعَ الزهد والورع اللَّذين

صَار فيهمَا مُنْقَطع النظير، والتبتل لِلْعِبَادَةِ، ومزيد الإقبال عَلَيْهَا، والتقلل من الدُّنْيَا وسد رمقه بِمَا تكتسبه يَدَاهُ فِي نسج العبي، والاقتصار على عباءة يلبسهَا، والإقبال على مَا يعنيه، حَتَّى صَار قدوة، وَحدث، سمع مِنْهُ الْفُضَلَاء، وقرئ عَلَيْهِ كِتَابه (الْكَوَاكِب) أَو أَكْثَره فِي أَيَّام الْجمع بعد الصَّلَاة بِجَامِع بني أُميَّة.

He was also keen on garnering and collecting useful and precious books, in addition to his asceticism and abstinence, both of which had no parallel, devotion and high amounts of worship, meagre indulgence in the worldly life, and providing for himself with the bare minimum by weaving garments. He only wore a single garment and was always embarking on things that pertained to him. Due to all of this, he became a role-model. He narrated ḥadīth, and many virtuous people learned from him. His book *al-Kawākib*, or at least most of it, was read to him on Fridays after the [Friday] prayer, in the Umayyad Mosque.

وَلم يسلم مَعَ هَذَا كُله من طَاعن فِي علاهُ، ظاعن عَن حماه، حَتَّى حصلت لَهُ شَدَائِد ومحن كَثِيرَة، كلهَا فِي الله، وَهُوَ صابر محتسب، حَتَّى مَاتَ سنة سبع وَثَلَاثِينَ وَثَمَان مِئَة فِي مَسْجده بالقدم.

Despite all of these [virtues], he was not safe from the attacks on his lofty status nor abandonment from people who no longer wished to support him. Because of this, he endured many hardships and suffered much distress, but it was all for Allah; he remained patient, seeking rewards, until he died in the year 837 in his mosque in Qidam. **[End]**[655]

وترجمه الْحَافِظ ابْن حجر فِي (أنباء الْغمر) بِنَحْوِ مَا تقدم، وَقَالَ: كَانَ لَا يقبل من أحد شَيْئا، وثار بَينه وَبَين الشَّافِعِيَّة شَرّ كبير بِسَبَب الِاعْتِقَاد. وَذكره الْبُرْهَان ابْن مُفلح فِي (الْمَقْصد الأرشد) وَقَالَ: رتب مُسْند الإِمَام أَحْمد رَضِي الله عَنهُ على الأَبْوَاب، وَزَاد فِيهِ أنواعا كَثِيرَة من الْعلم، وَقد نُوقِشَ فِي ذَلِك، وَكَانَ مِمَّن جبله الله تَعَالَى على حب الشَّيْخ تَقِي الدين ابْن تَيمِية، وَكَانَ النَّاس يعظمونه، ويعتقدون فِيهِ الصلاح وَالْخَيْر، ويتباركون بِهِ وبدعائه، ويقصدونه من كل نَاحيَة،

655 Ibid (5/214-215).

وَكَانَ منجمعا عَن النَّاس فِي منزله، وَهُوَ على طَرِيق السّلف الصَّالح. انْتهى.

Al-Ḥāfiẓ Ibn Ḥajar also mentioned his biography in *Inbā' al-Ghumar*, mentioning similar things as [al-Sakhāwī mentioned.] He said, "He would never accept a thing from anyone. He had many evil encounters with the Shāfiʿīs because of matters of theology."[656] Al-Burhān Ibn Mufliḥ mentioned him in *al-Maqṣad al-Arshad*, stating, "He arranged the *Musnad* of al-Imām Aḥmad ﵁ according to the chapters [of *fiqh* works], and added many aspects of knowledge to it, for which he was questioned. He was someone whom Allah the Exalted gave love of al-Shaykh Taqī al-Dīn ibn Taymiyyah. People honoured him and believed him to be righteous and goodly. They would seek blessings by his supplication, and would seek him from all directions. He would withdraw himself from people, instead choosing to remain at home. He followed the ways of the pious predecessors."[657]

وَمِمَّنْ جمع كتابا فِي الْأَحْكَام الْعَلامَة الصَّالح، يُوسُف بن مُحَمَّد بن التقي عبد الله بن مُحَمَّد بن مَحْمُود جمال الدين المرداوي، ذكره الذهَبِيّ فِي (المعجم الْمُخْتَص) وَقَالَ فِي حَقه الإِمَام الْمُفْتِي الصَّالح أَبُو الْفضل: شَاب، خير إِمَام فِي الْمَذْهَب - يَعْنِي الْحَنْبَلِي - وَله اعتناء بِالْمَتْنِ والإسناد. وَقَالَ ابْن حجي: كَانَ عَارِفًا بِالْمذهبِ، لم يكن فيهم مثله، مَعَ فهم وَكَلَام جيد فِي الْبَحْث وَالنَّظَر، ومشاركة فِي أُصُول وعربية، وَجمع كتابا فِي أَحَادِيث الْأَحْكَام. قَالَ الْبُرْهَان ابْن مُفْلِح فِي (المَقصد): وَكتابه هَذَا سَمَّاهُ (الِانْتِصَار) وبوبه على أَبْوَاب (الْمقنع) فِي الْفِقْه، وَهُوَ محفوظنا. توفي سنة تسع وَسِتِّينَ وَسَبْع مئة.

Another individual who authored on [aḥadīth about] rulings is the great and righteous scholar, Yūsuf ibn Muḥammad ibn al-Taqī ʿAbdullāh ibn Muḥammad ibn Maḥmūd Jamāl al-Dīn al-Mardāwī. He was mentioned by al-Dhahabī in *al-Muʿjam al-Mukhtaṣ*, where he said about him, "He was the righteous *imām* and *muftī*, Abu 'l-Faḍl. He was a young man, and was a great scholar of the (Ḥanbalī) *madhhab*. He also was keen on texts and chains of narration."[658] Ibn Ḥijjī said, "He was well-aware of the *madhhab*; there was no one among the [Ḥanbalīs] similar to him. He also had

656 [T] *Inbā' al-Ghumar* (3/528-528).
657 [T] *Al-Maqṣad al-Arshad* (1/83).
658 [T] *Al-Muʿjam al-Mukhtaṣ bi 'l-Muḥaddithīn* (p. 301).

understanding, and excellent verbal skills when debating and arguing and had contributions to jurisprudence and the Arabic language. He authored a book on aḥadīth pertaining to rulings." Al-Burhān ibn Mufliḥ said in *al-Maqṣad*, "His book was called *al-Intiṣār*, and he arranged it according to the chapters of *al-Muqni' fi 'l-Fiqh*. It has been preserved by myself. He died in the year 769."[659]

فصل [كتب التَّفْسِير لِأَصْحَابنَا]

Exegesis *(Tafsīr)*

وَأما مَا اتَّصل بِنَا خَبره من كتب التَّفْسِير لِأَصْحَابِنَا، فـ(زَاد المسير فِي علم التَّفْسِير) وَهُوَ فِي أَرْبَعَة أَجزَاء، لِلْحَافِظِ أبي الْفرج عبد الرَّحْمَن بن عَلي الْمَعْرُوف بـ(ابْن الْجَوْزِي) الْبَغْدَادِي، الْمُتوفى سنة سبع وَتِسْعين وَخَمْس مِئة، وَقد كنت اطلَعت على المجلد الأخير مِنْهُ.

As far as books that have reached us on the topic of exegesis authored by our *aṣḥāb*, the most popular is *Zād al-Masīr fī 'Ilm al-Tafsīr*, which consists of four volumes, authored by al-Ḥāfiẓ Abu 'l-Faraj 'Abd al-Raḥmān ibn 'Alī, more commonly known as Ibn al-Jawzī. He was from Baghdad, and he died in the year 597. I read the last volume [of his exegesis].

وَمِنْهَا: تَفْسِير أبي الْبَقاء عبد الله بن الْحُسَيْن بن عبد الله بن الْحُسَيْن العكبري الْحَنْبَلِي ثمَّ البَغْدَادِي، الْفَقِيه الْمقري الْمُفَسّر النَّحْوِي، الضَّرِير، الْمُتوفى سنة سِت عشرَة وست مِئَة، وَتَفْسِيره هَذَا غير تَفْسِيره الَّذِي هُوَ إِعْرَاب الْقُرْآن وَهُوَ مطبوع مَشْهُور.

Another is that of Abu 'l-Baqā' 'Abdullāh ibn al-Ḥusayn ibn 'Abdullāh ibn al-Ḥusayn al-'Ukbarī al-Ḥanbalī, who resided in Baghdad. He was a jurist, a teacher of Qur'ān, an exegete, a linguist, and also, blind. He died in the year 616. The exegesis I am referencing is not the same as his other exegesis, which is a syntactical analysis of the Qur'ān. The latter is published and popular.

وَمِنْهَا: مَا ذكره فِي (كشف الظنون) قَالَ: تَفْسِير الْخرقِي هُوَ الإِمَام أَبُو الْقَاسِم

659 [T] *Al-Maqṣad al-Arshad* (3/147).

عمر بن الْحُسَيْن الدِّمَشْقِي الْحَنْبَلِي، الْمُتَوفى سنة أَربع وَثَلَاثِين وثلاث مئة.

Another was mentioned in *Kashf al-Ẓunūn*, when [the author] said, "*Tafsīr al-Khiraqī*: It was authored by al-Imām Abu 'l-Qāsim 'Umar ibn al-Ḥusayn al-Dimashqī al-Ḥanbalī. He died in the year 334."[660]

وَمِنْهَا: تَفْسِير الْفَاتِحَة، للشَّيْخ أبي إِسْحَاق إِبْرَاهِيم بن أَحْمد الرقي الْحَنْبَلِي الْوَاعِظ، الْمُتَوفى سنة ثَلَاث وَسَبْع مئة، قَالَ الذهَبِيّ فِي (العبر): كَانَ من أَوْلِيَاء الله تَعَالَى، وَمن كبار المذكرين. وَقَالَ الْحَافِظ ابْن رَجَب فِي طبقاته: صنف تَفْسِير الْقُرْآن، وَلَا أعلم هَل أكمله أم لَا.

Yet another is *Tafsīr al-Fātiḥah*, authored by al-Shaykh Abu Isḥāq Ibrāḥīm ibn Aḥmad al-Raqqi al-Ḥanbalī, who was also a preacher. He died in the year 703. Al-Dhahabī said in his book *al-'Ibar*, "He was a *walī* of Allah the Exalted and one of the major admonishers and preachers."[661] Ibn Rajab said in his book, *[Dhayl] Ṭabaqāt [al-Ḥanābilah]*, "He authored an exegesis of the Qur'ān, but I do not know if he completed it or not."

وَمِنْهَا: تَفْسِير الْمَقْدِسِي، وَهُوَ شهَاب الدّين أَحْمد بن مُحَمَّد ابن الْحَنْبَلِي، الْمُتَوفى سنة ثَمَان وَعشْرين وَسَبْع مئة.

Another is the exegesis of al-Maqdisī, whose full name was Shihāb al-Dīn Aḥmad ibn Muḥammad ibn al-Ḥanbalī, who died in the year 728.

وَمِنْهَا: تَفْسِير الْعَلامَة عبد الرَّحْمَن ابن الشَّيْخ مُحَمَّد ابْن الشَّيْخ زين الدين أبي هُرَيْرة عبد الرَّحْمَن ابن الشَّيْخ مُحَمَّد الْعمري العليمي، المتوفى سنة [...]، وقد رَأَيْته فِي مُجَلد، يُفَسر تَفْسِيرا متوسطا، وَيذكر الْقرَاءَات، وَإِذا جَاءَت مَسْأَلَة فرعية ذكر أَقْوَال الأَئِمَّة الأَرْبَعَة بهَا، وَفِيه فَوَائِد لَطِيفَة.

Another is the exegesis of the great scholar, 'Abd al-Raḥmān, the son of al-Shaykh Muḥammad, the son of al-Shaykh Zayn al-Dīn Abu Hurayrah 'Abd al-Raḥmān, the son of al-Shaykh Muḥammad al-'Umarī al-'Alīmī, who died in the year [...][662]. I saw it consist of a single volume. It is an intermediate

660 [T] Ibid (3/147).

661 [T] *Al-'Ibar fī Akhbar man Ghabar* (4/8).

662 In the published version, it states, "There is a blank area." Al-'Alīmī died in the

exegesis. He mentions the variant readings, and when he comes to a subsidiary matter, he mentions the views of the Four Imāms about it. It contains pleasant beneficial points.

وَأجل هَذِه التفاسير كلهَا وأنفعها تَفْسِير الإِمَام الْحَافِظ عبد الرَّزَّاق بن رزق الله بن أبي بكر بن خلف بن أبي الهيجاء الرسعني، الْفَقِيه الْمُحدث الْحَنْبَلِي، ولد سنة تسع وَثَمَانِينَ وخمس مئة، وَسمع من خلق كثير، مِنْهُم: الشَّيْخ موفق الدّين المَقْدِسِي، وتفقه عَلَيْهِ، وَحفظ كِتَابه (الْمقنع) فِي الْفِقْه. وَذكره الذهَبِي فِي (طَبَقَات الحفاظ) وَتُوفِي سنة سِتِّينَ وست مِئَة، وَتَفْسِيره سَمَّاهُ (رموز الكُنُوز) وَهُوَ فِي أَربع مجلدات، وَفِيه فَوَائِد حَسَنَة، ويروى فِيهِ أَحَادِيث بِإِسْنَادِهِ. وَيذكر الْفُرُوع الْفِقْهِيَّة مُبينًا خلاف الأَئِمَّة فِيهَا، وَله مناقشات مَعَ الزَّمَخْشَرِي. وَلَقَد اطلَعت عَلَيْهِ، وارتويت من مورده العذب الزلَال، وشنفت مسامعي بتحقيقه، وارتويت من كوثر تَدْقِيقه، فرحم الله مُؤَلفه.

The best and most beneficial of these exegeses, though, is that of the *imām* and scholar of ḥadīth, ʿAbd al-Razzaq ibn Rizq-Allah ibn Abī Bakr ibn Khalaf ibn Abi ʾl-Hayjāʾ al-Rasʿanī. He was a Ḥanbalī jurist and a scholar of ḥadīth. He was born in the year 589, and learned from many [teachers], such as al-Shaykh Muwaffaq al-Dīn al-Maqdisī, from whom he learned jurisprudence; he memorised *al-Muqniʿ fi ʾl-Fiqh*. Al-Dhahabī mentioned him in his book *Ṭabaqāt al-Huffaẓ*. He died in the year 660. His exegesis is known as *Rumūz al-Kunūz*, and consists of four volumes. It contains good benefit, and in it, he reports aḥadīth with their chains of narration. He also mentions the subsidiary matters of law and discusses the differences of opinion scholars have in those matters. He also engages al-Zamakhsharī. I have read it and have quenched my thirst of its sweet, fresh spring and delighted my hearing with its detailed discussions; I quenched myself of its pool of precision. May Allah have mercy on its author.

هَذَا مَا اتَّصل بِنَا خَبره أَو رَأَيْنَاهُ من كتب التَّفْسِير لِأَصْحَابِنَا، وأرجوه تَعَالَى أَن يوفقني لإتمام التَّفْسِير الَّذِي أشتغل الْآن بِهِ، وسميته (جَوَاهِر الأفكار ومعادن الأَسْرَار فِي تَفْسِير كَلَام الْعَزِيز الْجَبَّار) وَأَن يمْنَع عني الشواغل عَن إِتْمَامه، مَعَ

year 928.

إتْمَام شرح سنَن النَّسَائِي، فَإِنَّهُ تَعَالَى واهب الْفضل ومفيض الْجُود.

Those are all of the books of exegesis authored by our *aṣḥāb* that I have heard of or seen. I ask Allah the Exalted to give me divine aid in completing the exegesis I am currently writing, which I have named *Jawāhir al-Afkār wa Maʿādin al-Asrār fī Tafsīr Kalām al-ʿAzīz al-Jabbār* (The Gems of Thought and the Mines of Secrets in Explaining the Speech of the Powerful, the Almighty). I also ask Him to halt any distractions that might prevent me from completing it, as well as the explanation of al-Nasāʾī. Truly, He is the giver of favours and the one who grants of His plentiful generosity.

فصل: [كتب الطبقَات]

Biographical Accounts *(Ṭabaqāt*[663]*)*

وَأما مَا اتَّصل بِنَا من كتب الطبقَات الْخَاصَّة بتراجم أَصْحَابنَا فأجلها (الطبقَات) لأبي الْحُسَيْن مُحَمَّد بن مُحَمَّد بن الْحُسَيْن بن مُحَمَّد ابن الْفراء القَاضِي الشَّهِيد، ابْن شيخ الْمَذْهَب، القَاضِي أبي يعلى الْمَقْتُول فِي دَاره لَيْلًا، سنة سِت وَعشْرين وَخَمْس مِئة. وَقد جعل هَذِه الطبقَات على سير الطبقَات الأولى، ثمَّ الثَّانِيَة، وَهَكَذَا مُرتبا كل طبقَة على حُرُوف المعجم، مُرتبا الطبقَات على تَقْدِيم الْعُمر والوفاة. وانْتهى فِيهِ إِلَى سنة اثْنَتَيْ عشرَة وَخَمْس مِئة.

As for books on biographical accounts that are specifically dedicated to giving the biographies of our *aṣḥāb*, the best is *al-Ṭabaqāt* by Abu 'l-Ḥusayn Muḥammad ibn Muḥammad ibn al-Ḥusayn ibn Muḥammad ibn al-Farrāʾ, the judge who died a martyr. He was the son of the *shaykh* of the *madhhab*, al-Qāḍī Abu Yaʿlā. He was killed in his home, at night, in the year 526. He authored his work on *Ṭabaqāt* by arranging them into levels. He would mention the first, then the second, and so forth, and would arrange them [within each level] alphabetically. He then arranged the actual levels in accordance with age and date of death. The last person biographed in his book died in the year 512.

663 [T] The word *ṭabaqāt* is the plural of the word *ṭabaqah*, which literally means a layer. *Ṭabaqāt* works arrange biographical accounts into layers; some do so according to chronology, some according to status and virtue, and so forth.

ثمَّ ذيله الْحَافِظ زين الدين عبد الرَّحْمَن بن أَحْمد الْمَعْرُوف بـ(ابْن رَجَب) فوصل فِي الذيل إِلَى سنة خمسين وَسَبْع مئة، ثمَّ ذيله الْعَلامَة يُوسُف بن حسن بن أَحْمد الحَنْبَلِي الْمَقْدِسِي، مُرتبا على الْحُرُوف، وَفرغ من تأليفه سنة إِحْدَى وَسبعين وَثَمَان مِئَة. قَالَ فِي (كشف الظنون): وذيله أَيْضا الشَّيْخ تَقِي الدّين مُفْلِح. وَلم يزدْ على هَذَا، وَلم أدر من مُفْلِح.

Then, al-Ḥāfiẓ Zayn al-Dīn ʿAbd al-Raḥmān ibn Aḥmad, known more commonly as Ibn Rajab, wrote an addendum [to the *Ṭabaqāt* of Ibn Abī Yaʿlā], reaching the year 750. After him, the great scholar Yūsuf ibn Ḥasan ibn Aḥmad al-Ḥanbalī al-Maqdisī wrote an addendum [to Ibn Rajab's addendum], and arranged it alphabetically. He finished writing in the year 871. In *Kashf al-Ẓunūn*, it states, "Another addendum was authored by al-Shaykh Taqī al-Dīn Mufliḥ."[664] However, he did not add any other details, and I do not know who the "Mufliḥ" referred to is.

وَمِنْهَا (الْمَقْصد الأرشد فِي ذكر أَصْحَاب الإِمَام أَحْمد) للعلامة برهَان الدين إِبْرَاهِيم بن عبد الله بن مُحَمَّد بن مُفْلِح، صَاحب (الْمُبْدع) وَهُوَ كتاب مُسْتَقل فِي مُجَلد، ابْتَدَأَ فِيهِ بترجمة الإِمَام أَحْمد، ثمَّ رتب تراجم الأَصْحَاب على حُرُوف المعجم إِلَى زَمَنه، وَكَانَت وَفَاته - كَمَا تقدم - سنة أَربع وَثَمَانِينَ وَثَمَان مِئَة، غير أَنه مَال فِيهِ إِلَى الِاخْتِصَار، وَإِذا ترْجم من الْأَصْحَاب من لَهُ مؤلفات يذكر أَحْيَانًا كتابا من مؤلفاته، وَأَحْيَانا لَا يذكر مِنْهَا شَيْئا. وَقد كنت عزمت على جمع ذيل لَهُ أثْنَاء الطّلب، فسودت مِنْهُ جانبا، ثمَّ بعد ذَلِك فترت همتي لعدم اشتهار الكتاب، فصممت أَن أجعَل مَا سودته ذيلا على طَبَقَات الْحَافِظ ابْن رَجَب، لكَونه يَسْتَوْفِي أَسمَاء مؤلفات المترجم، وَيذكر مَا لأَصْحَاب الاختيارات كثيرا من اختياراتهم، ولكونها أشهر من الْمَقْصد وأغزر فَائِدَة.

Another book [in the *Ṭabaqāt* genre] is *al-Maqṣad al-Arshad fī Dhikr Aṣḥāb al-Imām Aḥmad*, authored by the great scholar Burhān al-Dīn Ibrāḥīm ibn ʿAbdullāh ibn Muḥammad ibn Mufliḥ, the author of *al-Mubdiʿ*. It is an independent work, consisting of a single volume. He began with mentioning the biography of al-Imām Aḥmad, and then arranged the biographies of the

664 [T] *Kashf al-Ẓunūn* (2/1098).

aṣḥāb alphabetically. He wrote [about scholars who lived] up until his time. As mentioned previously, he died in the year 884. In this book, though, he was more inclined to conciseness. When he wrote a biography of one of the *aṣḥāb* who authored works, he would sometimes mention just one of their authorships, and sometimes not mention any of them at all. When I was still studying, I intended to write an addendum to it. I wrote a draft of a portion of it, but after that, my determination waned, because *[al-Maqṣad al-Arshad]* was not a very popular book. Instead, I decided to make my draft an addendum to the *Ṭabaqāt of al-Ḥāfiẓ Ibn Rajab*, since he mentioned the authorships of the person he was biographing as well as the individual views of those of the *aṣḥāb* who were fit to have independent views. Also, it is more popular and beneficial than *al-Maqṣad [al-Arshad]*.

وَمِنْهَا طَبقَات الْعَلامَة عبد الرَّحْمَن بن مُحَمَّد بن عبد الرَّحْمَن العليمي الْمَقْدِسِي، وَاسْمهَا (الْمنْهَج الأحمد فِي تراجم أَصْحَاب الإِمَام أَحْمد).

Another is the *Ṭabaqāt* of the great scholar ʿAbd al-Raḥmān ibn Muḥammad ibn ʿAbd al-Raḥmān al-ʿAlīmī al-Maqdisī. His book is called *al-Manhaj al-Aḥmad fī Tarājim Aṣḥāb al-Imām Aḥmad*.

وَمِنْهَا (الرياض اليانعة فِي أَعْيَان الْمائَة التَّاسِعَة) وَكتاب (التَّبيين فِي طَبَقَات الْمُحدثين الْمُتَقَدِّمين والمتأخرين) كِلَاهُمَا ليوسف ابْن عبد الْهَادِي.

Others are called *al-Riyāḍ al-Yāniʿah fī Aʿyān al-Māʾih al-Tāsiʿah* and *al-Tabyīn fī Ṭabaqāt al-Muḥaddithīn al-Mutaqaddimīn wa ʾl-Mutáakhirīn*, both of which are by Yūsuf ibn ʿAbd al-Hādī.

وَمِنْهَا (النَّعْت الْأَكْمَل لأَصْحَاب الإِمَام أَحْمد بن حَنْبَل) للفاضل الأديب مُحَمَّد كَمَال الدّين بن مُحَمَّد بن مُحَمَّد بن عبد الرَّحْمَن الدِّمَشْقِي الشهير ب(الغزي) الشَّافِعِي، وَهِي طَبَقَات لَطِيفَة، جمع فِيهَا مَا كَانَ فِي الْقرن التَّاسِع والعاشر من عُلَمَاء الْمَذهَب، وَقد طالعته بِتَمَامِهِ.

Another is called *al-Naʿt al-Akmal li Aṣḥāb al-Imām Aḥmad ibn Ḥanbal*, authored by the virtuous linguist, Muḥammad Kamāl al-Dīn ibn Muḥammad ibn Muḥammad ibn ʿAbd al-Raḥmān al-Dimashqī, known better as al-Ghizzī. He was a Shāfiʿī scholar. His *Ṭabaqāt* is quite pleasant, and in it, he mentions the biographies of the scholars of the *madhhab* who lived in the ninth and tenth centuries. I have read it in its entirety.

فرائد فوائد

Unique and Beneficial Points [On Other Ancillary Important Sciences a Student Should Learn][665]

من اللَّازِم على من يُرِيد التفقه على مَذْهَب من مَذَاهِب الْأَئِمَّة أَن يعرف أمورا:

It is incumbent on a person wishing to learn jurisprudence according to one of the *madhāhib* of the scholars to learn some other important sciences:

الْأَمر الأول: أَن يعرف فن الْحساب، وَهُوَ الْعلم بقواعد يعرف بهَا طرق اسْتِخْرَاج المجهولات العددية من المعلومات العددية الْمَخْصُوصَة، وَالْمرَاد من الاستخراج معرفَة كمياتها، وموضوعه الْعدَد، إِذْ يبْحَث فِيهِ عَن عوارضه الذاتية، وَالْعدَد هُوَ الكمية المتألفة من الوحدات، فالوحدة مقومة للعدد.

One. Mathematics: One must know mathematics, which is knowledge of the principles by which a person can learn how to extract numerical unknowns from specific numerical knowns. The meaning of "extract" is to know its quantities. Mathematics discusses numbers; the one engaging in mathematics looks to find the accidents affecting the essential nature of numbers. Numbers are quantities composed of individual units. A unit, therefore, is a formative element of a number.

وَأما الْوَاحِد: فَلَيْسَ بِعَدَد، وَلَا مقوم لَهُ، وَقد يُقَال لكل مَا يَقع تَحت الْعد، فَيَقع على الْوَاحِد.

As for "one," it is not a number, nor is it a formative element. "A number," can be used to describe each element being counted, and as such, encompass the number "one."

وَإِنَّمَا جعلنَا فن الْحساب مِمَّا يلْزم المتفقه أَن يُعلمهُ، لِأَنَّهُ يدْخل فِي كثير من

665 [T] The text between the brackets in the heading has been added by the translator for clarity in organising the book and is not from the words of al-Shaykh Ibn Badrān.

أَبْوَاب الْفِقْه، فَيحْتَاج إِلَيْهِ فِيهَا، وَذَلِكَ كضبط الْمُعَامَلَات، وَحفظ الْأَمْوَال فِي الشركَة وَالْمُضَاربَة، وَقَضَاء الدُّيُون، وَقِسْمَة التركات، وَغير ذَلِك. وَمَا من علم من الْعُلُوم إِلا وَيحْتَاج إِلَيْهِ، فيقبح بالمتفقه أَن يكون جَاهِلا بِهِ، عَارِيا عَنهُ، وخصوصا فِي فن الْفَرَائِض، فَإِن مَدَاره على الْحساب، وَلَا يَسْتَغْنِي عَنهُ أبدا.

I designated mathematics as a science that the student of *fiqh* should learn because it is relevant and needed in various chapters of law. For example, it is needed to precisely monitor transactions, protect wealth when engaging in partnership *(sharikah)* and speculation *(muḍārabah)*, repaying of debts, dividing estates, and so forth. Every science is in need of [mathematics], and as such, it is quite abominable for a student of law to be ignorant and devoid of its workings. This is especially true when considering the science of inheritance, which revolves and is reliant entirely on mathematics.

وَمن ثمَّ قَالَت الْحُكَمَاء: الْأَحْسَن الِابْتِدَاء عِنْد التَّعْلِيم بفن الْحساب، لِأَنهُ معارف منضجة، وبراهينه منتظمة، فينشأ عَنهُ فِي الْغَالِب عقل يدل على الصَّوَاب. وَقد يُقَال: إِن من أَخذ نَفسه بتَعَلُّم الحساب أول أمره يغلب عَلَيْهِ الصدْق، لما فِي الحساب من صِحَة المباني، ومناقشة النَّفس، فَيصير لَهُ ذَلِك خلقا، ويتعود الصدْق ويلازمه مذهبا.

Some philosophers said, "It is best to start with teaching mathematics, since it consists of fully developed and mature knowledge and organised proofs. As such, usually it results in an intellect that can direct to veracious information." Some could say that if one learns mathematics at an early age, they are likelier to be truthful, since mathematics consists of sound premises and self-discussions, both of which become a part of one's moral fabric. As such, truthfulness becomes their nature and way of behaviour at all times.

وَمن فروع علم الْحساب علم الْجَبْر والمقابلة، وَإِنَّمَا كَانَ من فروعه لِأَنهُ علم يعرف بِهِ اسْتِخرَاج مجهولات عددية من مَعْلُومَات مَخْصُوصَة على وَجه مَخْصُوص. وَمعنى الْجَبْر: زِيَادَة قدر مَا نقص من الْجُمْلَة المعادلة بالِاسْتثنَاءِ فِي الْجُمْلَة الْأُخْرى ليتعادلا. وَمعنى الْمُقَابلَة: إِسْقَاط الزَّائِد من إِحْدَى الجملتين للتعادل، وَقد كَانَ لكثير من أَصْحَابنَا الْمُتَقَدمين والمتأخرين ولع بفني الْحساب والجبر،

وَلَهُم فيهمَا مؤلفات.

A subsidiary of mathematics is algebra. It is a subsidiary of mathematics because it is defined as a science with which one learns how to extract numerical unknowns from specific knowns in a specific manner. The meaning of *al-jabr* is completion, [and as such, algebra means completing] a quantity of a thing possessing deficiency in one side of an equation by excluding from the other side of the equation in order to make them equal. The meaning of *al-muqābalah* is to balance, which is to remove the extra components of one side of the equation so that they are equal on both sides. There was significant fondness amongst our *aṣḥāb*—the early and the later—in studying these two sciences, and they have books written on the topic.

وَقيل: إِن أول من ألف فِي فن الْجَبْر الأُسْتَاذ أَبُو عبد الله مُحَمَّد بن مُوسَى الخوارزمي، وَقد كَانَ كِتَابه فِيهِ مَعْرُوفا مَشْهُورا، وصنف فِيهِ بعده أَبُو كَامِل شُجَاع بن أسلم كِتَابه (الشَّامِل)، وَهُوَ من أحسن الكتب فِيهِ، وَمن أحسن شروحه شرح الْقرشِي.

It was stated that the first to author about algebra was al-Ustādh Abu ʿAbdullāh Muḥammad ibn Mūsā al-Khawārizmī. His book was quite known and popular. After him, Abu Kāmil Shujāʿ ibn Aslam authored *al-Shāmil*, on the same topic. It is one of the best books [on algebra]. One of its best explanations is that of al-Qurashī.

وللمسلمين مؤلفات لَا تحصى فِي هذَيْن الفنين، ثمَّ إِن الفرنجة أخذُوا هذَيْن الفنين وهذبوهما، ونقحوهما، واختاروا أقرب الطرق، وأدخلوهما فِي مدارسهما، ثمَّ إِن عُلَمَاء الْمُسلمين أخذُوا كتب الفرنجة، وترجموها إِلَى لغاتهم، وسلكوا فيها طريقهم، فانتشر انتشارا باهرا، وهجرت كتب المُسلمين في هذَيْن الفنين حَتَّى صَار المشتغلون بفن الجَبْر يَعْتَقِدُونَ أَن هَذَا الْفَنّ من مخترعات عُلَمَاء أوروبا، وَمن حقق الْأَمر وجده من مخترعات عُلَمَاء الْإِسْلَام.

Muslims have written an unquantifiable number of authorships on these two topics (mathematics and algebra). Then, Europeans learned those two sciences and refined and polished them, seeking the most efficient ways. They then began teaching these sciences in their schools. Afterwards, the

Muslim scholars took the books of the Europeans and translated them to their own languages, and they became extremely popular. The early works of the Muslims on these two sciences were then abandoned, and those studying algebra began to think it was of the inventions of the scholars of Europe. Those who search deeply, though, will find that it was borne of Muslim scholars.

وَذَلِكَ أنه عَن لبَعض حكمائهم تَحْلِيل الْمُقدمَة التِي استعملها أرشميدس فِي الرَّابِع من الثَّانِيَة من الكرة والإسطوانة بالجبر، فتأدى حلهَا إِلَى كعاب وأموال وأعداد متعادلة، فَلم يتَّفق لَهُ حلهَا بعد أَن فكر فِيهَا مَلِيًّا، فَجزم بِأَنهُ مُمْتَنع، حَتَّى تبعه أَبُو جَعْفَر الخازن وحلها بالقطوع المخروطية، ثمَّ افْتقر بعده جمَاعَة من المهندسين إِلَى عدَّة أَصْنَاف مِنْهَا، فبعض تِلْكَ الْأَصْنَاف حل الْبَعْض الآخر.

One reason [for the development of algebra] was that a philosopher[666] attempted to solve Archimedes' fourth proposition of the second chapter of his book, *On the Sphere and Cylinder*[667] by using algebra. His efforts led to an equation involving cubes, squares and numbers, but ultimately, he

666 [T] The philosopher in reference is Muḥammad ibn 'Īsā al-Mahānī, a 3rd century *hijri* scholar and mathematician. George Sarton remarks in his *Introduction to the History of Science* (1/597-598), "He wrote commentaries on Euclid and Archimedes, and improved Ishaq ibn Hunain's translation of Menelaos's spherics."

667 [T] The proposition goes, "Proposition 4. (Problem) To cut a given sphere by a plane so that the volumes of the segments are to one another in a given ratio." (*The Works of Archimedes*, pp. 62-79)

Sarton remarks here, "He tried vainly to solve an Archimedean problem: to divide a sphere by means of a plane into two segments being in a given ratio. That problem led to a cubic equation, $x^3 + c^2b = cx^2$, which Muslim writers called al-Mahānī's equation. [...] His failure to solve the Archimedian problem is quoted by 'Umar al-Khayyam." (*Introduction to the History of Science*, 1/597-598)

Sarton is referring to Ghiyāth al-Dīn 'Umar ibn Ibrāḥīm al-Khayyam al-Naysabūrī, a 5th century *hijri* scholar and mathematician. In relation to this discussion, in *The Development of Arabic Mathematics: Between Arithmetic and Algebra*, (1/44) R. Rashed quotes al-Khayyam as saying, "Al-Mahānī was one of the modern authors who conceived the idea of solving the auxiliary theorem used by Archimedes in the fourth proposition of the second book of his treatise on the sphere and the cylinder algebraically. However, he was led to an equation involving cubes, squares and numbers which he failed to solve after giving it lengthy meditation. Therefore, this solution was declared impossible until the appearance of Abu Ja'far al-Khāzin who solved the equation with the help of conic sections."

was unable to solve the problem, even after thinking about it for a period of time. He felt strongly that a solution to the equation was an impossibility. Later, Abu Jaʿfar al-Khāzin solved it with conic sections. Afterwards, scholars of mathematics were in need of various types [of mathematics], and some of those types are in need of other types for solutions to the problems.

الْأَمر الثَّانِي: فن المساحة الَّذِي هُوَ فن من فنون الهندسة، وَهُوَ فن يحْتَاج إِلَيْهِ فِي مسح الأَرْض. وَمَعْنَاهُ: اسْتِخْرَاج مِقْدَار الأَرْض الْمَعْلُومَة بِنِسْبَة شبر أو ذِرَاع أَو غيرهمَا، أو نِسْبَة أرض من أرض إذا قويست بِمثل ذَلِك، وَهَذَا الْفَن يحْتَاج إِلَيْهِ المتفقه فِي مَسْأَلة المَاء: هَل يبلغ قلتَيْنِ أم لَا؟ على قَول الشَّافِعِي وَأحمد فِيمَا إِذا كَانَ مَكَان المَاء مدورا أَو مثلثا أو مستطيلا، أَو كَانَ على وضع من أوضاع أشكال الهندسة، وَفِي مَسْألة: هَل يبلغ سطح المَاء عشرا فِي عشر؟ على قَول الْمُتَأَخِّرين من الْحَنَفِيَّة فِيمَا إذا كَانَ مَحل المَاء على وضع من الأوضاع الْمَذْكُورة. وَيحْتَاج إِلَيْهِ فِي قسْمَة الأَرْض الْمُشْتَركَة الْمُتَنَازع فِيهَا بَين الشركَاء، وَيحْتَاج إِلَيْهِ أَيْضا فِي توظيف الْخراج على الْمزَارِع والفدن وبساتين الغراسة، وَفِي قسْمَة الحوائط والأراضي بَين الشركَاء أَو الْوَرَثَة، وأمثال ذَلِك. وَبِالْجُمْلَةِ فَهُوَ فن لَا يَسْتَغْنِي النَّاس عَنهُ، ويقبح بالمتفقه جَهله.

Two. Geometry: It is a branch of mathematics. It is a science needed to know to survey land. It means to extract the area of known land in measurements of a *shibr*,[668] cubits, and so forth, or by comparing it relative to another piece of land that has been measured with *[shibr* and *dhirāʿ]*. This science is needed by the student of *fiqh* in issues pertaining to water. For example, a jurist might ask, has this water reached *qullatayn* or not? In respect to the *madhhabs* of al-Shāfiʿī and Aḥmad, it is dependent on whether the thing carrying the water is circular, triangular, or rectangular, or if it possesses some other geometric shapes. Another issue of particular relevance to latter-day Ḥanafīs is their discussions on if the surface of the water reached ten cubits by ten cubits [and as such, can be considered a "large" amount of water]. Likewise, [a jurist needs geometry] to [judge in cases on] partition-

668 [T] The term *shibr* refers to an approximate measurement used by Arabs. It is measured as the distance between the tip of the pinkie finger and the thumb when the hand is extended. Refer to *al-Ṣiḥāḥ* (2/692)

ing disputed land that is shared between various stakeholders. Further, it is needed when extracting the necessary land charity in farms, feddans, and gardens fit for cultivation. Also, when dividing land between stakeholders or inheritors. Generally speaking, it is a science that is needed by all people, and it is shameful for a student of law to be unaware of it.

الْأَمر الثَّالِث: فن الْمِيقَات: إِذْ بِهِ تعرف جِهَة الْقبْلَة للصلوات، وتعرف بِهِ الْأَوْقَات وَتَصْحِيح السَّاعَات المخترعة لمعْرِفَة الْأَوْقَات، وَهَذَا يعرف بالاسطرلاب، وللعمل بِهِ رسائل وَكتب كَثِيرَة، وبالربعين الْمُجيب والمقنطر، وَلَهُمَا أَيْضا رسائل، وبآلات أخر مَشْهُورَة. وَأَن يعرف من النجُوم مَا بِهِ يعرف القبْلَة، وَكَانَ للفقهاء اعتناء زَائِد بِهَذَا. وَهَذَا موفق الدين الْمَقْدِسِي كَانَ من العارفين بِهَذَا الشَّأْن، وَقد ذكر فِي كِتَابه (المُغنِي) لمعْرِفَة الْقبْلَة عدَّة قَوَاعِد تدل على تمكنه من هَذَا الْفَن. فاللازم على المتفقه أن لَا يهمله.

Three. Geography: With geography, one can know the direction of the *qiblah*, to offer prayers. Also, one can know the time, and can even fix invented clocks to determine time. Such a tool is known as an astrolabe. There are many books and treatises on how to use them. Also, these discussions take one to concepts such as the sine and astrolabe quadrants, both of which have manuals on how to use them. Also, there are other tools that can be used in this regard. One must also know enough astronomy to learn the direction of the *qiblah*. The jurists showed heightened interest in such matters. For example, Muwaffaq al-Dīn al-Maqdisī (Ibn Qudāmah) was well-aware of these issues. In his book, *al-Mughnī*, he mentioned how to determine the *qiblah* by mentioning a number of fundamentals that show his grasp of this science. Therefore, a learner of *fiqh* should not neglect this.

الْأَمر الرَّابع: معرفَة تراجم عُلَمَاء مذْهبه، وَمَا لَهُم من المؤلفات، وَأَن يعرف طبقاتهم، وَإِلَّا فقد يمر بِهِ اسْم وَاحِد من الْحَنَابِلَة فيظنه حنفيا، أَو من الْحَنَفِيَّة فيظنه شافعيا، أَو من الْمُتَقَدمين فيظنه مُتَأَخِّرًا، أَو من أَرْبَاب الْأَقْوَال وَالْوُجُوه فِي مذْهبه فيظنه مُقَلدًا بحتا، وَمثل هَذَا يقبح بالمتفقه، وينادي على انحطاطه عَن ذرْوَة الْكَمَال. وَالله يتَوَلَّى الصَّالِحين.

Four. Biographies of the Scholars of One's *Madhhab:* One should also be aware of their writings and their ranks and the epoch they lived in. Otherwise, one might come across a single name of a Ḥanbalī, and think he was a Ḥanafī, or a Ḥanafī, and think he was a Shāfiʿī. Or, they could come across an early scholar and think he was a latter-day scholar, or the views of a scholar in the *madhhab* whose views, opinions, and variants carry weight, but instead think he was a mere blind-follower. [Ignorance of] such things are shameful for a learner of *fiqh*, and speaks to their decline below the pinnacles of completeness. May Allah attend to the righteous.

الْأَمر الْخَامِس: أَن يكون لَهُ إِلْمَام بفن الْعرُوض والقوافي، وَذَلِكَ أَن كل مَذْهَب لَا يَخْلُو من كتاب فِيهِ منظوم، وَقد يذكر الْفُقَهَاء كثيرا من الشرُوط، أَو الْوَاجِبَات. أَو السنَن، أَو الْآدَاب، أَو الْمسَائِل الْفِقْهِيَّة منظومة، وَلم يذكروها كَذَلِك إِلَّا ترغيبا للطالِب فِي حفظهَا، فَإِذا كَانَ المريد لحفظها جَاهِلا بفني الْعرُوض والقوافي حفظهَا مختلة الْوَزْن غير مُسْتَقِيمَة. وَربُمَا كَانَ بِحَيْثُ لَا يفرق بَين المنظوم والمنثور، وَلَا سِيمَا إِذا كَانَ النَّاسِخ جَاهِلا فكتب النظم ككتابته للنثر، فهناك يفوت الْمَقْصُود، ويعد ذَلِك من الجَهْل. وَقد أدْركْت من عُلَمَاء بلدنا الْكِبَار من إِذا قَرَأَ نظما قَرَأَهُ كقراءته للنثر بِلَا فرق، وَربُمَا لحن فِيهِ لحنا فَاحِشا، وَمَا ذَلِك إِلَّا لعدم مزاولته هَذَا الْفَن، فاللائق بالمتفقه أَن يُعلمهُ، لِئَلا يكون جَاهِلا بِهِ.

Five. Prosodies and Rhythmic Structures: The importance of this science lies in the fact that each *madhhab* has poems. Many times, jurists will mention many conditions, obligations, recommendations, mannerisms, or other aspects of law, in poetic form. The reason they do so is to encourage students to memorise them. If the one memorising these poems is unaware of the two sciences of prosodies and rhythmic structures, they will memorise [the poems] without accurately articulating its meters. Sometimes, they cannot differentiate between prose and poetry, especially if the copyist [of the work] is an ignoramus, and wrote the poem in the manner that prose is written. At that, the point [of the poem] is lost, and this becomes considered ignorance. I have seen from the major scholars of our city (Damascus) the reading of poetry as though it is prose, without differentiating between them. Sometimes, he reads it while erring horrendously in the syntax. The reason for this is that he does not practice this art. It is, therefore, appropriate for a student of law to learn it, so that they are not wholly unaware of its workings.

الْأَمر السَّادِس: أَن يعلم من مُفْرَدَات اللغَة مَا بِهِ يَسْتَعِين على فهم الكتاب الَّذِي يطالع فِيهِ، وَإِلَى هَذَا وَجه الْفُقَهَاء أنظار الطلبَة، فقد ألف (الْمِصْبَاح الْمُنِير) للغات (الشَّرْح الكَبِير) على (الْوَجِيز) للرافعي، وَألف (الْمغرب) للحنفية لهَذِهِ الْغَايَة أَيْضا، ولمثلها ألف (المطلع) على أَبْوَاب المقنع الْحَنْبَلِي (والدر النقي لشرح أَلْفَاظ الْخرقِي)، وَألف الحجاوي كتابا فِي بَيَان غَرِيب كِتَابه (الْإِقْنَاع)، فَيَنْبَغِي للمتفقه أَن لَا يكون خلوا من معرفَة اللغَة، فَإِن هَذَا يشينه ويعيبه.

Six. Vocabulary: One must know enough vocabulary to understand the book they are reading. This is something jurists often guided the attention of their students to. For example, *al-Miṣbaḥ al-Munīr* was written to explain the verbiage used within *al-Sharḥ al-Kabīr ʿala ʾl-Wajiz* of al-Rāfiʿī. A Ḥanafī scholar authored *al-Maghrib* to fulfil this same purpose, as well. *Al-Muṭliʿ ʿalā Abwāb al-Muqniʿ* was authored for Ḥanbalī law. *Al-Durr al-Naqī li Sharḥ Alfāẓ al-Khiraqī*, was also written, and al-Ḥajjāwī wrote a book explaining the unique terminologies used in his book *al-Iqnāʿ*. Therefore, a student of law should not be unaware of language. If he is, it truly dishonours and shames them.

الْأَمر السَّابِع: أَن يتَعَلَّم من فن التجويد مَا يعرف مِنْهُ مخارج الْحُرُوف، وَمَا لَا بُد للقارئ أَن يُعلمهُ، فَإِن جهل مثل ذَلِك رُبمَا أخل بِصَلَاتِهِ، وخصوصا فَإِن لهَذَا مدخلًا فِي بَاب الْإِمَامَة، حَيْثُ يَقُول الْفُقَهَاء، يقدم الأقرأ فالأقرأ، وَمن لم يكن عَارِفًا بفن التجويد كَيفَ يُمَيز بَين القارئ والأقرأ؟ وَكم رَأينَا من المتصدرين لإقراء الْفِقْه وللإمامة ثمَّ إِنَّهُم إِذا قرؤوا فِي الصَّلَاة كَانَت قِرَاءَة الأعجمي أحسن حَالا من قراءتهم، وَرُبمَا لم يفرقُوا بَين السِّين وَبَين الثَّاء الْمُثَلَّثَة الفوْقية، وَيزِيدُونَ فِي الْكَلِمَات حروفا لَيست مِنْهَا وهم لَا يَشْعُرُونَ، وَمثل هَذَا يعاب بِهِ الْعَامي فضلا عَن المتفقه.

Seven. Pronunciation *(Tajwīd):* One must know the exit points of letters and other basics that a reader [of the Qurʾān] must know. If they do not, it is possible they breach [some integral parts of] their prayer. This topic has a relevance to the Chapter of Leadership of Prayer, where jurists state that the most read person should be put to lead the prayer. If someone does not know *tajwīd,* how else can one differentiate between a mere reader [of Qur'ān] as opposed to the most read? We have seen many who are put forward to teach *fiqh* and to lead the prayers, though when they lead, the recitation of foreigners is better than theirs. Sometimes, they cannot differentiate between the *sīn* (س) letter and *thā* (ث) letters. They inadvertently add letters to words that were otherwise not there. This is something that is shameful for a commoner, let alone a student of law.

لطائف قوَاعِد

Subtleties and Foundations [On How a Student Should Learn][669]

اعْلَم أَن كثيرا من النَّاس يقضون السنين الطوَال فِي تعلم الْعلم، بل فِي علم وَاحِد، وَلَا يحصلون مِنْهُ على طائل، وَرُبمَا قضوا أعمارهم، وَلم يرتقوا عَن دَرَجَة المبتدئين، وَإِنَّمَا يكون ذَلِك لأحد أَمريْن:

Be aware that many people spend long years learning knowledge, or even, learning a single branch of knowledge, but do not gain any benefit from it. Sometimes, they spend their lives without ever transcending the level of a beginner. This happens for one of two reasons:

أَحدهمَا: عدم الذكاء الفطري، وَانْتِفَاء الْإِدْرَاك التصوري، وَهَذَا لَا كَلَام لنا فِيهِ وَلَا فِي علاجه.

First: Lack of natural intelligence and inability to conceptually understand things. This is not part of the discussion at hand, and neither is its cure.

وَالثَّانِي: الْجَهْل بطرق التَّعْلِيم، وَهَذَا قد وَقع فِيهِ غَالب المعلمين، فتراهم يَأْتِي إِلَيْهِم الطالِب المبتدئ ليتعلم النَّحْو مثلا فيشغلونه بالكلَام على البَسْمَلَة، ثمَّ على الحمدلة، أيامًا بل شهورا، ليوهموه سَعَة مداركهم، وغزارة علمهم، ثمَّ إِذا قدر لَهُ الخَلَاص من ذَلِك أخذوا يلقنونه متنا أَو شرحا بحواشيه وحواشي حَوَاشِيه، ويحشرون لَهُ خلاف العلمَاء، ويشغلونه بِكَلَام من رد على القَائِل، وَمَا أُجِيب بِهِ عَن الرَّد وَلَا يزالون يضْربُونَ لَهُ على ذَلِك الوتر، حَتَّى يرتكز فِي ذهنه أن نوال هَذَا الْفَن من قبيل الصعب الَّذِي لَا يصل إِلَيْهِ إِلا من أوتِيَ الْوَلَايَة، وَحضر مجْلِس

669 [T] The text between the brackets in the heading has been added by the translator for clarity in organising the book and is not from the words of al-Shaykh Ibn Badrān ﷺ.

الْقرب والاختصاص. هَذَا إِذا كَانَ الملقن يفهم ظَاهرا من عِبَارَات المصنفين.

Second: Ignorance on the ways of learning. This is something most teachers fall into. You see them: When a beginner student comes to them to learn syntax, for example, they busy [the student] with discussions on the *basmalah* (i.e. *Bismillahi 'l-Raḥmāni 'l-Raḥīm*), then the *ḥamdalah* (i.e. *al-Ḥamdu lillāh*), for days; rather, for months, to give the impression to the student of their own broad mental faculties and breadth of knowledge. Then, if they are able to complete that stage, they teach the student a text, or an explanation of a text, while including its commentaries, and its commentary's commentaries. They mention the differences of opinions of the scholars and busy them with the speech of those that refuted the claim of the author [of the text], and what the response is to that refutation. They continue to harp on that topic until the student begins to believe that understanding this science is difficult, and only those who are *awliyā'* of Allah or attend special gatherings can understand it. This is, of course, if the teacher can understand the apparent phrases of the authors.

وَأما إِذا كَانَ من أهل الشغف بالرسوم أُشير إِلَيْهِ بِأنهُ عَالم، فموه على النَّاس، وَأنزل نَفسه منزلَة الْعلمَاء الْمُحَققين، وَجلسَ للتعليم، فيأتيه الطالِب بِكِتَاب مطول أَو مُخْتَصر، فيتلقاه مِنْهُ سردا، لَا يفتح لَهُ مِنْهُ مغلقا، وَلَا يحل لَهُ طلسما فَإِذا سَألهُ ذَلِك الطالِب المِسْكِين عَن حل مُشكل، انتفخ أَنفه، وورم، وقابله بالسب والشتم، وَنسبه إِلَى الْبَهَائِم، ورماه بالزندقة، وأشاع عَنهُ أَنه يطْلب الِاجْتِهَاد.

However, if the teacher is one that is obsessed with emitting an external image which displays him to possess scholarship, causing him to disguise himself before people, place himself in the position of erudite scholars, and sit to teach others, when a student approaches with a book, whether long or short, [the student] learns the book in a narrative tone; the teacher does not explain any difficult wording nor solve any of its ambiguous phrases. If the poor student asks [the teacher] to explain some difficult phrase, he huffs and puffs, curses the student, ascribes them to livestock, accuses them of heresy, and spreads rumours that they are merely seeking to become *mujtahid* scholars.

وَمن أُولَئِكَ من لَا يروم الحماقة، لكنه يَقُول: إننا نَقْرَأ الكتب للتبرك بمصنفيها،

وَأكْثر هَؤُلَاءِ هم الَّذين يتصدرون لإقراء كتب المتصوفة، فَإنَّهُم يصرحون بِأَن كتبهمْ لَا يفهمها إِلا أهلهَا، وَأنهُمْ إِنَّمَا يشغلون أوقاتهم بهَا تبركا. ولعمري لَو تبرك هَؤُلَاءِ بِكِتَاب الله الْمنزل لَكَانَ خيرا لَهُم من ذَلِك الفضول. وَهَؤُلَاء كـ(المنبت لَا أَرضًا قطع، وَلَا ظهرا أبقى).

Some of them do not seek to be stupid, but they say, "We only read books to gain the blessings of their author." This is prevalent among people who take the initiative in teaching books of the Ṣūfīs. They state explicitly that their books can only be understood by those capable, and that they busy themselves with reading said books to garner blessings. By my life,[670] if they busied their time with the revealed Book of Allah, it would be better for them than such vanities. Such people resemble those who travel long distances, only to overdo themselves and become stuck in a remote land, neither having reached their destination nor taken care of their vehicle.

وَمِنْهُم من يكون داريا بالمسائل وَحل الْعبارَات، وَلكنه متعاظم فِي نَفسه، فَإِذا جَاءَهُ طَالب علم الفِقْه أَحَالهُ على شرح (مُنْتَهى الإرادات) إِن كَانَ حنبليا، وعَلى (الهِدَايَة) إِن كَانَ حنفيا وعَلى (التُّحْفَة) إِن كَانَ شافعيا وعَلى (شرح مُخْتَصر خَلِيل) للحطاب إِن كَانَ مالكيا. ثمَّ إِن كَانَ مبتدئا صَاح قَائِلا: إِلَى المُلتقى يَوْم الدّين. وَإِن كَانَ مِمَّن زاول العَرَبِيَّة وَأخذ طرفا من فن أُصُول الفِقْه انْتفع انتفاعا نسبيا لَا حَقِيقِيًّا.

Some [teachers] might be aware of the issues and are able to explain complex phrases, but they view themselves too highly. When a student of *fiqh* comes to them, they refer them to the explanation of *Muntahā al-Irādāt*, if they are Ḥanbalī, *al-Hidāyah*, if they are Ḥanafī, *al-Tuḥfah*, if they are Shāfiʿī, and *Sharḥ Mukhtaṣar al-Khalil* by al-Ḥaṭṭāb, if they are Māliki. Then, if

---

670 [T] Al-Imām ʿAbd al-Razzāq reported a narration from ʿAṭāʾ who said, "Khālid ibn al-ʿĀṣ and Shaybah ibn ʿUthmān used to say, when swearing, 'By my father.' Abu Hurayrah then stopped them from that; he stopped them from swearing by their fathers.' Shaybah stopped, and instead used to say, 'By my life.'" This occurred when ʿAṭāʾ was asked about saying, "By my life." ʿAbd al-Razzaq then said, "My view is that as long as it is not a swearing by something other than Allah, there is nothing wrong with it. As such, the statement, 'By my life,' is not an oath." Refer to *Muṣannaf ʿAbd al-Razzāq* (15933).

they are beginners they say, "We will meet on the Day of Judgement." If they previously have engaged in some studies of Arabic or some legal theories, they benefit relatively, though without anything genuine.

وَقد تفطن فلاسفة المُسلمين لهَذَا الدَّاء فألف أَبُو نصر الفارابي رسَالَة فِي كَيْفيَّة المدْخل إِلَى كتب أرسطاليس الفلسفية، وحذا حذوه قوم من عُلَمَاء الشَّرْع، فأثبتوا نتفا من الكَلَام فِي هَذَا الْمَوْضُوع، إِذْ غَايَة أَمرهم أَنهم يَتَكَلَّمُونَ على الْفُنُون، فيذكرُونَ الكتب المختصرة فِي الفَنّ، والمتوسطة والمطولة. وَرُبمَا كَانَ مَا ذكرُوهُ مَشْهُورا فِي أيامهم، ثمَّ عز وجوده وَانْقطع خَبره، ثمَّ إِنَّه بعد الألف من الهِجْرَة ألف الفَاضِل المُحدث الشَّيْخ أَحْمد المنيني الدِّمَشْقِي كتابا لطيفا سَمَّاهُ (الفرائد السّنيَّة فِي الفَوَائِد النحوية) وَأَشَارَ فِيهِ إِلَى طرف من آدَاب المطالعة، وَقد لخصت ذَلِك الطرف فِي رِسَالَة، وزدت عَلَيْهِ أَشْيَاء استفدتها بالتجربة، وَسميت تِلْكَ الرسَالَة (آدَاب المطالعة) وَذكرت أَيْضا جملَة كَافِيَة فِي مُقَدّمَة كتابي (إِيضَاح المعالم من شرح العَلامَة ابْن النَّاظِم) الَّذِي هُوَ شرح (ألفية ابن مَالك) فِي النَّحْو.

The Muslim philosophers have been very cognisant of this sickness. To respond, Abu Naṣr al-Fārābī authored a primer on how to approach Aristotle's works on philosophy. This was done by other scholars of the religion, where they engage in some short discussions on this topic. Their goal is that they wish to speak about the sciences and mention the summarised, intermediate, and voluminous works on the topic. Sometimes, the books they mention were very popular during their days, but they became rare and unknown afterwards. After 1,000 *hijri*, the virtuous scholar of ḥadīth, al-Shaykh Aḥmad al-Manīnī al-Dimashqī authored a pleasant primer, which he called *al-Farā'id al-Saniyyah fi 'l-Fawā'id al-Naḥwiyyah*. In it, he refers to a number of etiquettes of reading. I have summarised his short discussions and have added some concepts I learned through experience. I called my summation and addendum *Ādāb al-Muṭāla'ah*. I also mentioned a sufficient amount in the introduction to my book *Īḍāḥ al-Ma'ālīm min Sharḥ al-'Allāmah Ibn al-Nāẓim*, which is an explanation of Ibn Mālik's thousand-line poem on Arabic grammar.

وَحَيْثُ إِن كتابي هَذَا مدْخل لعلم الْفِقْه أَحْبَبْت أَن أذكر من النصائح مَا يتَعَلَّق

بذلك الْعلم فَأَقُول: لَا جرم أَن النَّصِيحَة كالفرض، وخصوصا على الْعلمَاء، فَالْوَاجِب الديني على الْمعلم - إِذا أَرَادَ إقراء المبتدئين - أَن يُقْرِئهُمْ أَولا كتاب (أخصر المختصرات) أَو (الْعُمْدَة) للشَّيْخ مَنْصُور متْنا إِن كَانَ حنبليا، أَو (الغَايَة) لأبي شُجَاع إِن كَانَ شافعيا، (العشماوية) إِن كَانَ مالكيا، أَو (منية الْمُصَلي) أَو (نور الإِيضَاح) إِن كَانَ حنفيا. وَيجب عَلَيْهِ أَن يشْرَح لَهُ الْمَتْن بِلَا زِيَادَة وَلَا نُقْصَان، بِحَيْثُ يفهم مَا اشْتَمَل عَلَيْهِ ويأمره أَن يصور مسَائِله فِي ذهنه، وَلَا يشْغلهُ بما زَاد على ذَلِك.

Considering that this book of mine is an introduction to the science of law, I wished to mention some useful points that pertain to that science. Undoubtedly, advice is similar to an obligation, especially for scholars. The religious duty of a teacher who wishes to teach beginners is that they first teach them *Akhsar al-Mukhtaṣarāt* [by Ibn Balbān], or *al-ʿUmdah* by al-Shaykh Manṣūr [al-Buhūtī], if they are Ḥanbalī. If they are Shāfiʿī, they should begin with *al-Ghāyah* by Abu Shujāʿ. If they are Māliki, they should begin with *al-ʿAshmāwiyyah*. If they are Ḥanafī, they should begin with *Munyat al-Mūsāllī* or *Nūr al-Īḍāḥ*. The teacher must explain the text without adding or subtracting from it, so as to help the student understand the issues it contains. He must command the student to conceptualise its issues in their mind, and should not busy them with anything additional.

وَقد كَانَت هَذِه طَرِيقَة شَيخنَا الْعَلامَة الشَّيْخ مُحَمَّد بن عُثْمَان الْحَنْبَلِي، الْمَشْهُور ب(خطيب دَوْمًا) الْمُتَوفى بالمَدينة المنورة سنة ثَمان وثلاث مئة بعد الألف، وَكَانَ رَحمَه الله يَقُول لنا: لَا يَنبغي لمن يقْرَأ كتابا أَن يتَصَوَّر أَنه يُرِيد قِرَاءَته مرة ثَانِيَة، لِأَن هَذَا التَّصَوُّر يمنعهُ عَن فهم جَمِيع الْكتاب، بل يتَصَوَّر أَنه لَا يعود إِلَيْهِ مرة ثَانيَة أبدا، وَكَانَ يَقُول: كل كتاب يشْتَمل على مسَائِل مَا دونه وَزِيَادَة، فحقق مسَائِل مَا دونه لتوفر جدك على فهم الزِّيَادَة. انْتهى. وَلما أخذت نصيحته مَأْخَذ الْقبُول لم أحتج فِي الْقِرَاءَة على الأساتذة الْعُلُوم والفنون إِلَى أَكثر من ست سِنين، فجزاه الله خيرا، وَأَسْكَنَهُ فراديس جنانه.

This was the way of our teacher, the great scholar al-Shaykh Muḥammad ibn ʿUthmān al-Ḥanbalī, more commonly known as the Orator of Dūmā, who died in the year 1308. He ﷺ used to say, "It is not appropriate for someone who reads a book to fathom ever reading it a second time; this concept prevents [the reader] from understanding the book in its entirety. Rather, they should feel that they will never read it a second time." He also said, "Every book comprises of information presented in lower level texts, and some additions. Understand the items from the earlier text so that you can put full effort into understanding the additions." When I took his advice and acted on it, I needed to spend only six years reading and studying sciences with teachers. Therefore, may Allah reward him and allow him to dwell in the Firdaws area of paradise.

فَإِذا فرغ الطَّالِب من فهم تِلْكَ الْمُتُون، نَقله الْحَنْبَلِي إِلَى (دَلِيل الطَّالِب)، وَالشَّافِعِي إِلَى (شرح الغَايَة)، والحنفي إِلَى (ملتقى الأبحر)، والمالكي إِلَى (مُخْتَصر خَلِيل) وليشرح لَهُ تِلْكَ الكتب على النمط الذِي أسلفناه. فَلَا يتعداه إِلَى غَيره، لِأَن ذهن الطالِب لم يزل كليلا، ووهمه لم يزل عَنهُ بِالكُلية. وَالأولَى عِنْدِي للحنبلي أَن يُبدل (دَلِيل الطالِب) بـ(عمدة) موفق الدين المَقْدِسِي إِن ظفر بهَا، ليأنس الطالِب بالحَدِيثِ، ويتعود على الِاسْتِدْلَال بِهِ، فَلَا يبْقى جَامِدا.

When the student completely understands those [beginner] texts, the Ḥanbalī should teach *Dalīl al-Ṭālib* next. The Shāfiʿī, *Sharḥ al-Ghāyah*, the Ḥanafī, *Multaqā al-Abḥur*, and the Māliki, *Mukhtaṣar al-Khalīl*. The teacher should explain those books in the same way as previously mentioned: They should not add anything to [the text]. The student's mind, at this point, is still feeble, and their false impressions have yet to depart. To me, it is ideal for the Ḥanbalī to substitute *Dalīl al-Ṭālib* with *ʿUmdat [al-Fiqh]*, authored by Muwaffaq al-Dīn Ibn Qudāmah al-Maqdisī, if they can get a hold of a copy. That way, the student can become familiarised with ḥadīth and become accustomed to using the ḥadīth as evidence, no longer being inflexible.

ثمَّ إِذا شرح لَهُ تِلْكَ الْكتب، وَكَانَ قد اشْتغل، بفن الْعَرَبيَّة على النمط الْمُتَقدم، أوفقه هُنَالك، وأشغله بشرح أدنى مُخْتَصر فِي مذهبه من فن أصُول الْفِقْه، كالورقات لإِمَام الْحَرَمَيْنِ، وَشَرحهَا للمحلي، دون مَالهَا من شرح الشَّرْح لابنِ قَاسم العَبَّادِي، والحواشي التِي على شرحها. فَإِذا أتمهَا نَقله إِلَى (مُخْتَصر التَّحْرِير)

إن كَانَ حنبليا مثلا، وَيتَخَيَّر لَهُ من أصُول مذهبه مَا هُوَ أَعلَى من الورقات وَشرحهَا.

Afterwards, if the teacher has explained the previously-mentioned books, and the student has studied Arabic, in the same way as previously outlined, the teacher should stop them there and busy them with a most beginner text on the legal theories of their *madhhab*. For example, *al-Waraqāt* by Imām al-Ḥaramayn [al-Juwaynī] and its explanation by al-Maḥallī, without adding from the explanation of the explanation by Ibn Qāsim al-ʿAbbādī, and the commentaries on his explanation. When the student completes this stage, the teacher should teach them *Mukhtaṣar al-Taḥrīr*, for example, if they are Ḥanbalī. They should choose a text on the legal theories of their *madhhab*, so long as it is of a higher level than *al-Waraqāt* and its explanation.

فَإِذا أتم شرح ذَلِك، أقرأه الْحَنْبَلِي (الرَّوْض المربع بشرح زَاد المستنقع)، والحنفي (شرح الكَنْز) للطائي، والمالكي أحد شُرُوح متن خَلِيل المختصرة، وَالشَّافِعِي شرح الْخَطِيب الشربيني للغاية. وَلَا يتَجَاوَز الشرُوح إِلَى حواشيها، وَلَا يقرئها إِيَّاه إِلَّا بعد اطلَاعه على طرف من فن أصُول الْفِقْه.

When they complete that book, the Ḥanbalī should teach their student *al-Rawḍ al-Murbiʿ Sharḥ Zād al-Mustaqniʿ*, the Ḥanafī, *Sharḥ al-Kanz* by al-Ṭāʾī, the Māliki, one of the explanations of the text *Khalīl*, and the Shāfiʿī, al-Khaṭīb al-Shirbīnī's explanation of *al-Ghāyah*. The teacher should not go beyond the commentary and discuss its marginalia, and they should not teach these books without the student having studied some portion of *Uṣūl al-Fiqh*.

وَاعْلَم أَنه لَا يُمكن للطَّالِب أَن يصير متفقها مَا لم تكن لَهُ دراية بالأصول، وَلَو قَرَأَ الفِقْه سنينا وأعواما، وَمن ادعى غير ذَلِك كَانَ كَلَامه إِمَّا جهلا وَإِمَّا مُكَابرَة.

Know, too, that it is impossible for a student to become a student of *fiqh* until they know legal theories, even if they were to read books on substantive law for years and years. Anyone who claims otherwise is either an ignoramus or is obstinate.

فَإِذا انْتهى من هَذِه الْكتب وَشَرحهَا شرح من يفهم الْعبارَات، وَيدْرك بعض

الإشارات، نَقله الْحَنْبَلِي إِلَى (شرح المُنتهى) للشَّيْخ مَنْصُور. و(روضة النَّاظر وجنة المناظر) فِي الْأُصُول، وَالشَّافِعِي إِلَى (التُّحْفَة) فِي الْفِقْه وَ(شرح الإِسْنَوِي على منهاج البَيْضَاوِي) فِي الأُصُول. والمالكي إِلَى (شرح مُخْتَصر ابْن الحَاجِب) الأصولي وَ(شرح أقرب المسالك لمَذْهَب مَالك)، والحنفي إِلَى (الهِدَايَة) وَ(شرح المنَار) فِي الأُصُول، فَإِذا فرغ من هَذِه الكتب وَشَرحهَا بفهم واتقان، قَرَأَ مَا شَاءَ، وطالع مَا أَرَادَ، فَلَا حجر عَلَيْهِ بعد هَذَا.

After completing explanation of these books in a way which allows for their phrases to be understood and some of their allusions to be conceptualised, the Ḥanbalī should then teach *Sharḥ al-Muntahā* by al-Shaykh Manṣūr and *Rawḍat al-Nāẓir wa Junnat al-Munāẓir* on legal theories. The Shāfiʿī should proceed to *al-Tuhfah* on substantive law and *Sharḥ al-Isnawī ʿalā Minhāj al-Bayḍāwī* on legal theories. The Māliki to *Sharḥ Mukhtaṣar Ibn al-Ḥājib*, on legal theories, and *Sharḥ Aqrab al-Maṣālik li Madhhab Mālik* [on substantive law]. The Ḥanafī should proceed to *al-Hidāyah*, and *Sharḥ al-Manār* on legal theories. When the student has completed and understood these texts with mastery, they can read whatever they wish and read whatever they want; there is nothing to hold them back at that point.

وَاعْلَم أَن للمطالعة وللتعليم طرقا ذكرهَا الْعلمَاء، وإننا نثبت هُنَا مَا أخذناه بالتجربة، ثمَّ نذكر بَعْضًا من طرقهم، لئَلا يَخْلُو كتابنَا هَذَا من هَذِه الْفَوَائِد.

Know, too, that reading and teaching have methods; the scholars mentioned them. I will mention some concepts I learned through experience, and then mention some ways of the scholars, so that this book is not void of such benefit.

إِذا تمهد هَذَا فَاعْلَم أننا اهتدينا - بفضله تَعَالَى - أَثْنَاء الطلب إِلَى قَاعِدَة، وَهِي أننا كُنَّا نأتي إِلَى الْمَتْن أَولا، فنأخذ مِنْهُ جملَة كَافِيَة للدرس، ثمَّ نشتغل بِحل تِلْكَ الجُمْلَة من غير نظر إِلَى شرحها، ونزاولها حَتَّى نظن أننا فهمناها، ثمَّ نقبل على الشَّرْح فنطالعه المطالعة الأولى امتحانا لفهمنا، فَإِن وجدنَا فِيمَا فهمناه غَلطا صححناه، ثمَّ أَقبلنَا على تفهم الشَّرْح على نمط مَا فَعَلْنَاهُ فِي الْمَتْن، ثمَّ إِذا ظننا أننا فهمناه راجعنا حَاشِيَته - إِن كَانَ لَهُ حَاشِيَة - مُرَاجعَة امتحان لفكرنا، فَإِذا

علمنَا أننا فهمنا الدَّرْس تركنَا الكتاب وَاشْتَغَلْنَا بتصوير مَسْأَلَة فِي ذهننا، فحفظناه حفظ فهم وتصور، لَا حفظ تراكيب وألفاظ. ثمَّ نجتهد على أَدَاء مَعْنَاهُ بعبارات من عندنَا، غير ملتزمين تراكيب المُؤلف، ثمَّ نَذهَب إِلَى الأسْتَاذ للْقِرَاءَة، وهنالك نمتحن فكرنا فِي حل الدَّرْس، ونقوم مَا عساه أَن يكون بِهِ من اعوجاج، ونوفر الهمة على مَا يُورِدهُ الأسْتَاذ مِمَّا هُوَ زَائِد على المَتْن وَالشَّرْح.

By the Grace of Allah, while I was still a student, I learned a principle, which was that I would first read enough of the text in preparation for the class, and I would spend time attempting to decipher its phrases, without reading its explanation. I would engage in this process until I felt I understood it, and then would read the explanation for the first time to test my understanding. If I found I understood it wrongly, I would correct my understanding. Then, I would engage the explanation in an attempt to understand it, in the same way I approached the text. When I felt I understood [the explanation], I would refer to its commentaries, if it had any, to retest my understanding. After I felt I understood the portion of the text meant for the class, I would leave the book and begin to busy myself with conceptualising its rulings in my mind. As such, I memorised the text with understanding and conceptualisation. I did not simply memorise it as an assembled portion of words. Afterwards, I would spend effort in rendering and vocalising the meanings [of what I learned] in my own words, without adhering to the wording of the author. After all of that, I would go to the teacher to read to him, which is where I truly tested the thought process I followed to understand the portion of the text meant for class, would correct any possible faults, and would spend my energy in learning the additions the teacher added to the text and explanation.

وَكُنَّا نرى أَن من قَرَأَ كتابا وَاحِدًا من فن على هَذِه الطَرِيقَة سهل عَلَيْهِ جَمِيع كتب هَذَا الفن، مختصراتها ومطولاتها، وَثبتت قَوَاعِده فِي ذهنه، وَكَانَ الأمر على ذَلِك.

I found that people who read a single book on a science in this way find it easier to read all books on that particular science, irrespective of its length, and its principles become deeply embedded in their mind.

ثمَّ إِن الأولى فِي تَعْلِيم المبتدئ أَن يجنبه أستاذه عَن إقرائه الكتب الشَّدِيدَة

الِاخْتِصَار، العسرة على الفَهم، كـ(مختصر الأصُول) لابنِ الحَاجِب، و(الكافية) لَهُ فِي النَّحْو، لِأن الِاشْتِغَال بِمثل هذَيْن الكِتَابَيْنِ المختصرين إخلال بالتحصيل، لما فيهمَا وَفِي أمثالهما من التَّخْلِيط على المبتدئ، بإلقاء الغايات من العلم عَلَيْهِ، وَهُوَ لم يستعد لقبولها بعد، وَهُوَ من سوء التَّعْلِيم، ثمَّ فِيهِ مَعَ ذَلِك شغل كَبِير على المتعلم بتتبع أَلْفَاظ الاخْتِصَار العويصة للفهم، بتزاحم المعانِي عَلَيْهَا، وصعوبة اسْتِخرَاج المسَائِل من بَينهَا، لِأن أَلْفَاظ المختصرات تجدها - لأجل ذَلِك - صعبة عويصة، فَينقَطِع فِي فهمها حَظ صَالح عَن الوَقْت، كَمَا أَشَارَ إِلَى ذَلِك ابْن خلدون فِي مقدمته ثمَّ قَالَ:

Further, it is ideal, when teaching beginners, that the teacher keeps the student away from reading books that are extremely concise and difficult to understand, such as *Mukhtaṣar al-Uṣūl* by Ibn al-Ḥājib, or his *Kāfiyah*, on syntax. Busying oneself with such concise books defeats the purpose of learning. They confuse things for beginners by teaching them the outcomes of knowledge without them being ready to learn them yet. This is a bad way of teaching. Also, the learner spends a lot of effort in attempting to follow the phrasing of the summation, which makes it difficult to understand and extract the issues. The phrasing of summations, you find, are extremely difficult. To understand them, you must spend a decent amount of time. This was alluded to by Ibn Khaldun in his *Muqaddimah*, where he said:

وَبعد ذَلِك فالملكة الْحَاصِلَة من التَّعْلِيم فِي تِلْكَ المختصرات إِذا تمّ على سداده، وَلم تعقبه آفة، فَهِيَ ملكة قَاصِرة عَن الملكات التِي تحصل من الموضوعات البسيطة المطولة، بِكَثْرَة مَا يَقع فِي تِلْكَ من التّكْرَار والإحالة المفيدين لحُصُول الملكة التَّامَّة. وَإِذا اقْتصر على التكرَار قصرت الملكة لقلته، كشأن هَذِه الموضوعات المختصرة، فقصدوا إِلَى تسهيل الحِفظ على المتعلمين، فأركبوهم صعبا يقطعهم عَن تَحْصِيل الملكات النافعة وتمكنها. هَذَا كَلَامه.

Moreover, after all these (difficulties), the (scholarly) habit that results from receiving instruction from brief handbooks, (even) when (such instruction) is at its best and is not accompanied by any flaw, is inferior to the habits resulting from (the study of) more extensive and lengthy works. The latter contain a great amount of repetition and lengthiness, but both are useful for the acquisition of complete aptitude. When there is little repetition, inferior aptitude is the result. This is the case with the abridgments. The intention was to make it easy for students to memorise (scholarly subjects), but the result is that it has become (more) difficult for them, because they are prevented from acquiring useful and firmly established habits. **[End]**[671]

وَاعْلَم أَنَّك إِذا قابلت بَين من قَرَأَ (الكافية) وَبَين من قَرَأَ ابْن عقيل شرح ألفية ابْن مَالك، وجدت الأول جَامِدا غير متسع الصَّدْر فِي ذَلِك الفَن، وَوجدت الثَّانِي أغزر مَادَّة، منفسحا لَهُ المجال.

Know, too, that if you compare a person who read *al-Kāfiyah* and a person who read Ibn 'Aqīl's explanation of the *Alfiyyah* of Ibn Mālik, you find the first is rigid, not open-minded about the science, and you find the second having more copious content with a broad-minded approach.

وَحَاصِل الْأَمر أَن الأسْتَاذ يَنْبَغِي أَن يكون حكيما، يتَصَرَّف فِي طرق التَّعْلِيم بِحَسب مَا يرَاهُ مُوَافقا لاستعداد المتعلم، وَإِلَّا ضَاعَ الْوَقْت بِقَلِيل من الفَائِدَة، وَرُبمَا لم تُوجد الفَائِدَة أصلا.

As such, the teacher must be wise and must mold their teaching style with what they find most appropriate considering the student's abilities to learn. Otherwise, much time will be lost without much benefit to show for it, if there was any benefit at all.

وطرق التَّعْلِيم أمر ذوقي، وَأَمَانَة مودعة عِنْد الأساتذة، فَمن أَدَّاهَا أثيب على أَدَائِهَا، وَمن جَحدهَا كَانَ مطالبا بهَا. وَقد أودع ابْن خلدون فِي مُقَدّمَة تَارِيخه نفائس من هَذِه المباحث، كالمقدمات، ومطالعتها تهدي النتيجة لصَادِق الهمة، مُطلق من قيد التَّقْلِيد.

Teaching styles are a matter of inclination and style. It is a trust consigned within a teacher. Whoever fulfills the trust adequately will be rewarded for their performance, and whoever negates the right will be held accountable

---

671 [T] *The Muqaddimah: An Introduction to History*, by Ibn Khaldūn, translated by Franz Rosenthal (3/291).

for it. In his *Muqaddimah*, Ibn Khaldūn mentioned many valuable insights relevant to these discussions, to introduce these concepts. Reading them will result in results for those who have honest and sincere resolve that is unchained by the bonds of blind-following.

وَللَّه در ابْن عَرَفَة الْمَالِكِي حَيْثُ قَالَ:

How excellent was Ibn ʿArafah al-Mālikī when he said:

إِذا لم يكن فِي مجْلِس الدَّرْس نُكْتَة   وَتَقْرِير إِيضَاح لمشكل صُورة
وعزو غَرِيب النَّقْل أَو حل مقفل   أَو إِشْكَال أبدته نتيجة فكرة
فدع سَعْيه وَانْظُر لنَفسك واجتهد   وَلَا تتركن فالترك أقبح خلة

If, in the class, there is no useful point,
Or establishing some clarity for a contentious point
Or offering citation to an ambiguous quote, or unlocking a locked phrase,
Or offering of a contention as result of deep thought,
Abandon pursuing it, research for yourself and put effort,
But do not cease, for giving up is the worst of behaviors.

وَهنا وقف بِنَا جواد الْقَلَم عَن المجال فِي هَذَا الميدان على سَبِيل الِاخْتِصَار، وَلَو ركبنَا متن الإسهاب لطال الكتاب، والهمم قَاصِرة، والإقبال فِي عصرنا على الْعلم قد صَار رَوْضَة كالهشيم تَذْرُوهُ الريَاح، وغضونه ذابلة، وجداوله تشتاق إِلَى المَاء، فنسأله تَعَالَى أن يرفع لَهُ منارا، ويجدد شوقا لأهله على الإقبال عَلَيْهِ بمنه وَكَرمه.

At this point, the pen no longer has anything to write on this topic, in an effort to be concise. If we were to write at length, the book would become too long. Resolves are insufficient, and undertaking knowledge during our times has become like a garden turned to dry remnants, quickly blown away by the winds; its branches have withered, and its irrigation channels long for water. We ask Him, the Exalted, to raise its light-post once more and to revive a longing within people, causing them to embark on learning. This, by His Favours and Generosity.

رد العجز على الصدر

Rectifying the Deficiency of the Earlier Chapters [On Studying Creed][672]

لَا يخفاك - أَيهَا الفَاضِل - أننا صدرنا كتَابنَا وزيناه بِمَا نَقَلْنَاهُ عَن إِمَام أهل السنة والأثر أَحْمد بن مُحَمَّد بن حَنْبَل - رَضِي الله عَنهُ - من رسائله التِي نقلت عَنهُ فِي أُصُول الدين، مِمَّا فِيهِ كِفَايَة لمن كَانَ سلفيا، وَعَن لنا الآن أَن نختم كتَابنَا بِذكر شَيْء مِمَّا أَلفه عُلَمَاء مَذهَب السّلف، ليَكُون البدء مُوَافقا للختام، رَجَاء مِنْهُ تَعَالَى أَنه كَمَا وفقنا للتوحيد، وَجَعَلنَا من أَهله أَن تكون الخاتمة على توحيده تعالى الخَالِص من الزيغ والإلحاد بمنه تَعَالَى وَكَرمه، فَنَقُول:

It is not hidden to you, O virtuous person, that we began our book and beautified it by quoting from the *imām* of the people of Sunnah and narrations, Aḥmad ibn Muḥammad Ḥanbal ﷺ from his treatises which have been reported from him, which discuss theology. Those were sufficient for someone who follows the pious predecessors. Now, it has occurred to me to close this book by mentioning some books authored by the scholars who adhere to the way of thought of the Salaf, so that the beginning matches the end. This, while hoping that Allah the Exalted, just as He has granted us divine aid to acceptance of monotheism and made us of its people, that our endings are also while we adhere to pure monotheism, free of any deviance or heresies. This, of course, is by His Grace and Generosity. So, we say:

إِن الكتب الْمُؤَلّفَة فِي هَذَا الْعلم لَيست محصورة بمؤلفات أَصْحَاب الإِمَام أَحْمد، بل جَمِيع عُلَمَاء القُرُون الثَّلَاثَة، وعلماء الحَدِيث بأجمعهم على مُعْتَقد السّلف، لَا يشذ مِنْهُم عَن ذَلِك إِلَّا من جعل الفلسفة طَرِيقه الَّتِي يعول عَلَيْهَا،

672 [T] The text between the brackets in the heading has been added by the translator for clarity in organising the book and is not from the words of al-Shaykh Ibn Badrān ﷺ.

وأساسه الَّذِي يَبْنِي عَلَيْهِ، غير ملتفت إِلَى مَا كَانَ عَلَيْهِ الصَّحَابَة والتابعون وتابعوهم بِإِحْسَان.

Books authored on this science are not limited to the authorships of the *aṣḥāb* of al-Imām Aḥmad; rather, it encompasses all scholars of the third century, and all scholars of ḥadīth who followed the way of the Salaf. None diverged from [the path of the Salaf], except those who made philosophy their point of reliance and foundation, on which they built [their creed], without paying heed to what the companions, their successors, and their followers in goodness believed.

فأعظم كتاب فِي هَذَا النَّوْع كتاب الله تَعَالَى الَّذِي لَا يَأْتِيهِ البَاطِل من بَين يَدَيْهِ وَلَا من خَلفه، ثمَّ مَا ورد وَصَحَّ عَن نبيه المُصْطَفى صلى الله عَلَيْهِ وَسلم فهما الشفَاء من الدَّاء العضال، وَالهَدْي فِي بيداء الحيرة والضلال، فَلَا يحْتَاج بعدهمَا إِلَى تأليف وَلَا إِلَى تنميق وترصيف تصنيف، وَلَكِن لما ترجمت كتب الحُكَمَاء، وَظَهرت الْفرق وَتبع أَهلهَا مقالات أرسطو وأفلاطون، وَسموا مَا بنوه على ذَلِك بِالْعلمِ الإلهي، احْتَاجَ عُلَمَاء السّلف لتأليف الكتب وتصنيفها للرَّد عَلَيْهِم، ولدلالة النَّاس على الصِّرَاط المُسْتَقيم.

The greatest book on [creed] is the Book of Allah the Exalted, which cannot be proven false from any angle. Next, the authentic narrations from His Prophet, al-Muṣṭafā ﷺ. Those two sources contain sufficiency from the chronic disease, and guidance in the midst of confusion and misguidance. As such, one is not in need of any authorships, compositions, writings, or compilations. However, when the books of the philosophers were translated, the sects appeared, and their adherents followed the categorisations of Aristotle and Plato. They called the knowledge based on [the works of those two philosophers], "theology." The scholars of the Salaf needed to author books and compilations to respond to them and to guide people to the straight path.

وَتكلم الأئِمَّة بِالرد على من حاد عَن الطَّرِيقَة المثلى، فَكثر الشغب، وتفاقم الأمر، وَثَبت اتبَاع الإِمَام أَحْمد على سَبِيل الكتاب وَالسنة، وناضلوا عَنهُ أَشد النضال، وألفوا فِي ذَلِك كتبا مختصرة ومطولة، وَلم يتعدوا عَمَّا كَانَ عَلَيْهِ الصَّحَابَة

والتابعون، وَالأئِمَّة الموثوق بهم كَأبي حنيفَة، وسُفيَان الثَّوْري، وسُفيَان بن عُيَيْنَة، وَمَالك، وَالشَّافِعِي، وَأحمد، وَأبي عبيد، وَدَاوُد، وأمثالهم قدما، وَلم يثنهم عَن عزمهم طلاقة لِسَان مخادع، وَلَا سفسطة متأول، وَلَا بهرجة ملحد، وَلَا زخرفة متفلسف.

The *imāms* spoke about individuals who veered from the ideal path, and as such, caused many disturbances and exacerbated matters. The followers of al-Imām Aḥmad held fast to the path of the Book and the Sunnah, defending it fiercely. They wrote both short and long authorships on the topic, never bypassing what the companions, Tābi'īn, and the great, trustworthy scholars believed, such as Abu Ḥanīfah, Sufyān al-Thawrī, Sufyān ibn 'Uyaynah, Mālik, al-Shāfi'ī, Aḥmad, Abu 'Ubayd, Dāwūd, and others who are of the same footing. The eloquence of speech of tricksters did not dissuade them, nor did the sophistry of those who indulge in false interpretations, the empty, sham splendors of heretics, or the false adornments of philosophers.

وَكلما انْقَضتْ طبقَة مِنْهُم أنشأ الله تَعَالَى طبقَة غَيرهَا على سَبِيل من قبلهَا، فهم الأبدال والأخيار والأنجاب، كَيفَ لَا وَقد أخبر عَنْهُم الصَّادِق الأمين فِيمَا رويناهُ من سنَن ابْن مَاجَه عَن أبي عنبَة الخولَانِي - وَكَانَ قد صلى إِلَى القبْلتَيْنِ مَعَ رَسُول الله صلى الله عَلَيْهِ وَسلم قَالَ: سَمِعت رَسُول الله صلى الله عَلَيْهِ وَسلم يَقُول: **«لَا يزَال الله يغرس فِي هَذَا الدين غرسا يستعملهم فِي طَاعَته»** وحصلت الإِشَارة إِلَيْه أَيْضا فِي الحَدِيث المَشْهُور المَرْوِي بطرق كَثِيرة عَن أبي هُرَيْرَة وَغَيره: أَن النَّبِي صلى الله عَلَيْهِ وَسلم قَالَ: **«لَا تزَال طَائِفَة من أمتِي قَوَّامَة على أَمر الله لَا يَضرهَا من خالفها»** وَقَالَ ابْن مُفْلِح فِي (الآدَاب الشَّرْعِيَّة): نقل نعيم بن طريف عَن الإِمَام أَحْمد أَنه قَالَ فِي حَدِيث: **«لَا يزَال الله يغْرس»** إِلَى آخِره: هم أَصْحَاب الحَدِيث وَنَص أَحْمد على أَن لله أبدالا فِي الأَرْض. وَقَالَ أَيْضا عَنْهُم: إِن يَكُونُوا هَؤُلَاءِ النَّاس - يَعْنِي أهل الحَدِيث - فَلَا أَدْرِي من النَّاس.

Whenever a generation of such scholars passed away, Allah the Exalted commenced another generation that followed the path of the one before it.

They are the *abdāl,*[673] the *akhyār,*[674] the *anjāb.*[675] How are they not, when the Truthful and Trustworthy one [Muḥammad ﷺ,] said of them, in the ḥadīth reported in *Sunan Ibn Mājah*, from Abu ʿAnabah al-Khawlānī who had prayed towards both Qiblah (Jerusalem and Makkah) with Allah's Messenger ﷺ. He said, "I heard Allah's Messenger ﷺ, say, **'Allah will continuously plant in this religion individuals whom He will use for His obedience.'"**[676] This was also indicated in the famous ḥadīth that has been reported through many routes from Abu Hurayrah and others, who said that the Prophet ﷺ said, **"There will always remain a group from my Ummah who are upholding the order of Allah. None who oppose them will harm them."**[677] Ibn Mufliḥ said in his book *al-Adāb al-Sharʿiyyah*, "Nuʿaym ibn Ṭurayf reported that al-Imām Aḥmad said of the ḥadīth, **'Allah will continuously plant...'** 'They are the people of ḥadīth.' Further, Aḥmad explicitly stated that Allah the Exalted has *abdāl* on the earth, saying, 'If they are not those people (meaning, the people of ḥadīth), then I have no idea who they are.'"[678]

ثمَّ اعْلَم أَن أجل كتب اعْتِقَاد السّلف مَا نَقله الأَئِمَّة الموثوق بهم، وَرُوَاهُ الثقَات عَن أبي حنيفَة وَمَالك وَالشَّافِعِي وَأحمد، فَإِنَّهُم أَكْثرُوا من القَوْل فِي الِاعْتِقَاد

673 [T] In Ṣūfī terminology, the *Abdāl* are very righteous men who achieved the levels of dissolving into Allah the Exalted in the sense that they only view Allah the Exalted, and the rest of creation is meaningless to them. They are called *Abdāl* from the word *badal*, which means replacement. The meaning is that they are replaced time and time again by Allah the Exalted. Refer to *Mawsūʿat Muṣṭalaḥāt al-Ṣūfiyyah*, p. 2)

674 [T] In Ṣūfī terminology, *Akhyār* refers to "Those who have insight and are the epitome of resolve and resoluteness. As such, they saw the paths of the heavens, caring not for the mediums on earth. They held fast to the rope of Allah, without paying heed to their relationships with creation. They were certain about the signs of Allah and saw his path, without turning to the whisperings of the devil, the creation, or the soul. If they hear whisperings from the devil, the soul, or another human, they engage in repelling and contradiction [of the whisperings], until creation leaves them alone, the devil abandons them, their soul obeys them, and they follow the upright path." Ibid. p. 34)

675 [T] In Ṣūfī terminology, the *Anjāb*, or *Nujabāʾ*, refer to forty individuals who are tasked with reforming people's situations and withstanding their difficulties, because they have a merciful disposition. However, they can only help others, not themselves. (Refer to *Mawsūʿat Muṣṭalaḥāt al-Ṣūfiyyah* by Dr. ʿAbd al-Karim al-Ḥafnī) Al-Shaykh Ibn Badrān is making a play at words, stating that those who follow the Salaf are those who should be considered as reformers.

676 Reported by Ibn Mājah (8).

677 Reported by Ibn Mājah (7).

678 [T] *Al-Ādāb al-Sharʿiyyah* (1/211).

الصَّحِيح، وَلم تختلف كلمتهم فِيهِ. وَقد بنى أَبُو جَعْفَر الطَّحَاوِي عقيدته على مَا رَوَاهُ عَن أبي حنيفَة النُّعْمَان بن ثَابت، وَأبي يُوسُف يَعْقُوب بن إِبْرَاهِيم، وَأبي عبد الله مُحَمَّد بن الْحسن الشَّيْبَانِي، وَصرح بِأَنَّهُ نقل عَنْهُم مَا يَعْتَقِدُونَ من أُصُول الدين، ويدينون بِهِ رب الْعَالمين. وعقيدته هَذِه سلفية مَحْضَة، وليت الحَنَفِيَّة من بعده جعلُوا هَذِه العقيدة أساس معتقدهم.

Further, be aware that the best books on the creed of the Salaf are those that have been transmitted by trustworthy scholars from Abu Ḥanīfah, Mālik, al-Shāfiʿī, and Aḥmad. They have an abundance of statements wherein they explain the correct creed; they did not differ in those matters. Abu Jaʿfar al-Ṭaḥāwī based his entire creed on what has been reported from Abu Ḥanīfah al-Nu'mān ibn Thābit, Abu Yūsuf Yaʿqūb ibn Ibrāḥīm, and Abu ʿAbdullāh Muḥammad ibn al-Ḥasan al-Shaybānī. He explicitly stated that he quoted their beliefs on the foundational axiomatic creedal matters of the religion, and what they considered correct religion to worship Allah the Exalted. The *Creed of [al-Ṭaḥāwī]* is purely that of the Salaf. If only Ḥanafīs after him would adhere to it, and make it the foundation of their beliefs.

وَأكْثر من روى عَنهُ من هَذَا الشَّأن الإِمَام أَحْمد بن حَنْبَل، لِأَن زَمَنه كَانَ زمن القَوْل بِخلق الْقُرْآن، وَالقِيَام بتشييد البدع، وامتحن على ذَلِك، فَأكْثر من القَوْل فِيهِ، بِحَيْثُ أن مَا نقل عَنهُ من الرسائل فِي هَذَا السَّبِيل كَاف لمتبع سَبِيل السلف.

One of the most often quoted scholars on these matters is al-Imām Aḥmad ibn Ḥanbal. His era witnessed the belief of the Qur'ān being created and where innovations were often being erected and publicised. He faced an inquisition due to these matters. As such, he spoke often about these issues. The treatises he wrote on the topic are sufficient for those who wish to follow the Salaf.

وَهَذَا سَبِيل جَمِيع الأَئِمَّة الْمُجْتَهدين وعلماء الحَدِيث، دع عَنْك أُولَئِكَ الَّذين يسمون أنفسهم بالخلف، ويستندون فِي مقالاتهم إِلَى دَلَائِل التقطوها من مقالات الفلاسفة، فَإِنَّهُم مهما جالوا واستطالوا، كَانَ قصارى أمرهم إِلَى الحيرة. والموفق مِنْهُم من رَجَعَ آخر أمره إِلَى التَّسْلِيم والتفويض، وَقدم مَذْهَب سلف الأَئِمَّة على

من انتحله.

Such was the path of all *mujtahid* scholars and scholars of ḥadīth. Ignore those who call themselves "the latter-day" individuals. They base their theology on evidences taken from the categorisations of the philosophers. No matter how much they occupy one's mind and act audaciously, their final status will lead to confusion. Those who have been given divine aid among them return to submission and consigning, preferring the *madhhab* of the scholars of the Salaf over any other beliefs.

وَلَا يغرنك انتساب أولَئِكَ إِلَى الإِمَام أبي الْحسن الْأَشْعَرِي - رَحمَه الله تَعَالَى - فَإِنَّهُم عِنْد التَّحْقِيق لم يسلكوا مسلكه، وَلم يفهموا مرامه، لأن هَذَا الإِمَام تصدى أولا للرد على المُعْتَزلَة بعد أَن كَانَ مِنْهُم، وَصَاحب البَيْت أدرى بِالَّذِي فِيهِ يكون، فسلك فِي الرد عَلَيْهِم مَسْلَك فن الجدل، وَأخذ يقطع عَلَيْهِم الطَرِيق بِأي وَجه كَانَ، ويزيف مقالاتهم بِأَي وَاسِطَة كَانَت، كَمَا هُوَ شَأن فن الجدل الذِي قصارى أمره غَلَبَة الخصم بِأَي وَجه وَبِأَيِّ طَرِيقَة كَانَت. وَكَثِيرًا مَا يحْتَاج المجادل فِي غَلَبَة خَصمه إِلَى السفسطة، بل إِلَى إبراز المستحيل فِي صُورة الجَائِز، والجائز فِي صُورة الوَاجِب.

Do not be confused by people who ascribe themselves to al-Imām Abu 'l-Ḥasan al-Ash'arī ﷺ. When carefully examining, one finds that they did not follow his path, nor did they understand his intents. This *imām* set out, first, to respond to Mu'tazilites, after he was previously one of their adherents. The owner of the house is most aware of what the house contains. Therefore, he responded to them using tools provided in the science of argumentation. He closed off all possibilities they could use [to prove their case]. He falsified their statements in any way possible, as occurs in the science of argumentation, the point of which is to refute the interlocutor by any means necessary. Many times, people who engage in debate resort to sophistry, or present impossibilities in the form of possibilities, and possibilities in the form of necessaries.

ثمَّ إِنَّه فِي آخر أمره ألف كِتَابه الْمُسَمّى بـ(الإبانة) فأبان بهَا مَذْهَب أهل الْحق، وباح باعتقاده. وَلما كَانَت خصومه من الدهاء والفطنة بِدَرَجَة لَا تنكر، وَكَانَ

لَهُم فِي دولتهم مكانة، وَلم يطيقوا مدافعة الإِمَام، عَمدُوا من بعده إِلَى كتبه، فالتقطوا مِنْهَا مَا قَالَه فِي مقَام المدافعة، وَلم تكن من عقيدته مِمَّا يقرب من نحلتهم، ودونوا ذَلِك وجعلوه مذهبا مَنْسُوبا إِلَيْهِ، ثمَّ أخذوا يثبتون مَا ادعوا أنه من معتقده، بِمَا ألفوه من أدلتهم. ثمَّ أَتَى من بعدهمْ فَدس فِيهِ قَوَاعِد الفلاسفة، وقواها بأدلتهم، حَتى أصبح مَا نسب إِلَيْهِ من جنس مَا يذكر فِي العلم المُسَمى عِنْد أولَئِكَ بالإلهي، لَا فرق بَينه وَبَينه.

Towards the end of his life, he authored *al-Ibānah*, wherein he clarified the path of the people of the truth, and openly revealed his creed. Since his opponents were shrewd and clever and had positions in the government, they were unable to respond to the *imām*, so those after him took to his books and selected passages wherein he was refuting [the Muʿtazilah,] but did not truly express his creed in validation of their beliefs. They gathered all of these passages and compiled them into a way of thought, attributing it to him. Then, they began espousing what they claimed was his creed, but it was actually authored by them, using their evidences. They were succeeded by those who foisted the principles of the philosophers [onto his creed], and strengthened their positions with their evidences. As a result, whatever has been ascribed to him is of the same genus as theology [of the Greeks]; indeed, there is no difference between the two.

ثمَّ جَاءَ من بعدهمْ مِمَّن شَأْنه التَّقْلِيد الأَعْمَى، والتقليد يبعد عَن الحق ويروج البَاطِل، فَاعْتقد بِأَن تِلكَ النتف وتلك المفتريات هِيَ مَذْهَب الإِمَام الْأَشْعَرِي، فَأَخذهَا قَضِيَّة مسلمة، وتلقى أدلتها بِالقبُولِ. فَمنهمْ من اختصرها، وَمِنْهُم من نظمها، وَمِنْهُم من شرحها، وَلَو أَبْصر الأَشْعَرِي مَا نسبوه إِلَيْهِ، لتبرأ مِنْهُ ولقال لَهُم: أخطأتم المرمى، وَمَا الغي مِنْكُم بِبَعِيد، ألم تروا كتابي (الإِبَانَة) الَّذِي هُوَ آخر مؤلفاتي؟ ألم تعلمُوا مقاصدي فِي مسالكي فِي الرَّد على خصومي؟

Then came individuals whose sole purpose was to blindly follow. Blind-following creates a distance from the truth and promotes falsehood. They began believing that those excerpts and alleged writings were the way of thought of al-Imām al-Ashʿarī, taking it as axiomatic propositions and accepting their evidences wholeheartedly. Some summarised them, some poeticised them, and some explained them. If al-Ashʿarī were to see what they have ascribed to him, he would free himself of them and would state, "You have erred in your goal; transgression is not a far-fetched description of you. Have you not seen my book *al-Ibānah*, which is the last of my authorships? Have you not known my method of debating my interlocutors?"

وَالْحق يُقَال: إن الأَشْعَرِي أجل من أن تنسب تِلْكَ المفتريات إِلَيْهِ، وَلَقَد تنبه لذَلِك جمَاعَة من العلمَاء، فتبعوا مذهبه الحق، وَهُوَ مَا كَانَ عَلَيْهِ السلف. وَلَوْلَا خوف الملَل لذكرتهم وَاحِدًا بعد وَاحِد، وَلَكِن أَقُول: أَجلهم إِمَام الحَرَمَيْنِ، وَمن رأى كَلَامه فِي آخر عمره يعلم يقِينا أنه رَجَعَ عَن جَمِيع مَا كَانَ، حَيْثُ قَالَ: نِهَايَة أقدام الْعُقُول عقال، وَمِمَّنْ صرح بذلك السنوسي صَاحب العقيدة الْمَشْهُورة بَين المدعين بِأنهم أشاعرة، فَإِنَّهُ نَادَى بذلك علنا فِي شرح لَهُ، كَمَا تقدم ذَلِك أول الْكتاب، وَتبع الأَشْعَرِي الحَقِيقِي، لَا الأَشْعَرِي الوهمي الَّذِي لَيْسَ لَهُ وجود فِي الْخَارِج.

The truth be said, al-Ashʿarī is loftier than to be ascribed to such falsities. This was noticed by a group of scholars, and as such, they followed the true creed, namely, the way of the Salaf. Had it not been that I fear to bore the reader, I would have mentioned them, name by name. Alas, though, I state that the loftiest of them was Imām al-Ḥaramayn [al-Juwaynī]. Those who see his speech at the end of his life can be sure that he recanted all of his previous theological viewpoints. He said, "The finality of the audacious pursuits of the mind is fettered."[679] Anther who explicitly mentioned as much was al-Sanūsī, who authored the creed famous among those who claim to be Ashʿarī. He stated such openly, in an explanation he wrote, as I alluded to in the earlier portion of the book. He followed the true path of al-Ashʿarī, not the fancified al-Ashʿarī that has no external presence [outside of the imagination].

وَأنت - أيها الْمُؤَيد بنور الْحق - إِذا رَأَيْت كتب الَّذين يَزْعمُونَ أَنهم أشاعرة رَأَيْتهمْ

679 [T] This quotation is actually ascribed to al-Imām Fakhr al-Dīn al-Rāzī, the great theologian, legal theorist, jurist, and exegete. It is claimed to be found within a manuscript known as *Taqsīm al-Ladhāt*, which means, *The Categories of Pleasures*. It is quoted by many historians, such as al-Imām Shams al-Dīn al-Dhahabī in his *Tārīkh al-Islām* (43/217).

على مَذْهَب أرسطاطاليس وَمن تبعه كَابْن سينا والفارابي، وَرَأَيْت كتبهم عنوانها علم التَّوْحِيد، وباطنها النَّوْع الْمُسَمّى بالإلاهي من الفلسفة. وَإِذا كنت فِي ريب مِمَّا قُلْنَاهُ من الكَلَام فَانْظر (المواقف) لعضد الدّين الايجي، وَشَرحه للسَّيِّد الْجرْجَانِي، وَمَا عَلَيْهِ من الْحَوَاشِي. ثمَّ تَأمل كتاب (الإشارات) وَكتاب (الشفا) لِابْنِ سينا، وشروح الأول، فَإنَّك تَجِد الكل من وَاد وَاحِد، لَا فرق بَينهمَا إِلَّا بالتصريح باسم الْمُعْتَزلَة والجبرية وَغيرهمَا، فَهَل يُؤْخَذ تَوْحِيد من هَذِه الْكتب إِلا بعد الوُقوع بِألف ورطة؟ ثمَّ إِن سلم السالك من هَذِه الطامَّات ظفر بتوحيد من جنس تَوْحِيد الفلاسفة والملاحدة، وَمثل هَذَا حَال المشتغل بالطوالع والمطالع وشروحهما وحواشيهما وَمَا أشبههما.

When you, O person aided with the light of the truth, see the books of those who claim to be Ashʿarī, you simply find them following the ways of Aristotle and his followers, such as Ibn Sīnā (Avicenna) and al-Fārābī. You find their books given titles of *Knowledge of Monotheism*, but its contents are simple philosophical theology. If you are in doubt of what I claim, read *al-Mawāqif* by ʿAdhud al-Dīn al-Ījī, and its explanation by al-Sayyid al-Jurjānī, as well as its commentaries. Then, reflect on *al-Ishārāt* and *al-Shifā*, both by Ibn Sīnā, and read the explanations of the former. You will find that they all emanate from a single valley; there is no difference between the two, except that some explicitly proclaim themselves as Muʿtazilites or Jabrites, and so forth. Is monotheism to be learned from such books, except after falling into a thousand dilemmas? Then, if a seeker is safe from the grave errors, they learn the monotheism of philosophers and heretics. This is the case of those who busy themselves with books such as *Ṭawālīʿ [al-Anwār min Maṭāliʿ al-Anẓār* by al-Bayḍāwī] and *Maṭāliʿ [al-Anwār* by Sirāj al-Dīn al-Urmawī] as well as their explanations and commentaries.

لطالما أشغلنا بِهَذِهِ الكتب فَلم نر فِيهَا إِلَّا أَن أَصْحَابهَا فتحُوا على أنفسهم أَبْوَاب شُبُهَات عجزوا عَن سدها، فَأخذوا فِي إقناع أنفسهم، وَكلما أغلقوا مِنْهَا بَابا انفتحت لَهُم أَبْوَاب، فَأَطَالُوا ذيول الْكَلَام، وَكَتَبُوا المجلدات، ثمَّ ألزموا النَّاس بهَا، وأنفسهم لما ينالوا مِنْهَا هدى فكيف غَيرهم يَهْتَدِي بهَا؟! على أنهم لَو أعْطوا عمر نوح، وملؤوا الدُّنْيَا كتبا يبحثون بهَا عَن الهدى لم يجدوه إِلَّا فِي الكتاب

وَالسّنة، وَالرُّجُوع إِلَى عقيدة السّلف. فكن عَلَيْهَا أيها الناصح لنفسِهِ من أول الأمر، وَلَا تطوح بِنَفسِك فِي تِلكَ الأودية فتهلك، وَإِنِي لَكَ الناصح الْأمين، وَالله يتَوَلى هداك.

Indeed, such books have long busied us, but we only found that their authors opened doors to machinations they were unable to fend off. Afterwards, they took to simply convincing themselves. Every time they closed a door [of doubt], many other doors opened. They spoke at lengths, and wrote compendiums, then forced people to adhere to them. They did not gain guidance from them, so how can others garner guidance from them? If they were to be given lives as lengthy as that of Nūḥ and filled the earth with books to search for guidance, they would not find it in any source but the Qur'ān, Sunnah, and the creed of the Salaf. Therefore, adhere to them from an early stage if you are sincere to yourself. Do not tumble into such depths, lest you perish. I am, to you, a sincere advisor, and Allah the Exalted will provide you guidance.

وَحَيْثُ أفْضى بِنَا الْمقَال إِلَى هَذا الْحَد لزمنا أَن نقُول: قد ألف الْعلمَاء الْأَعْلَام فِي بَيَان مَا كَانَ عَلَيْهِ السلف كتبا لَا تحصى، مُطَولَة ومختصرة، وَأَنا أرشدك إِلَى بَعْضهَا، لِأَن من طالع كتابا مِنْهَا فَكَأَنَّهُ قد طالع الْكل، لاتفاقهم على طَرِيقَة وَاحِدَة.

Since our discussions have brought us to this point, we must say: The great scholars have authored innumerable books to clarify what the Salaf held as beliefs, some of which were short, and others were lengthy. I shall guide you to some of them. If someone reads one of them, it is the same as reading all, since they all emanate from a single path.

فأجل مَا كتب فِي هَذَا الْمَوْضُوع (رسائل الإِمَام أَحْمد)، وَأحسن طَرِيقَة لمن يطْلب التَّحْقِيق والبرهان كتب شيخ الإسْلَام تَقِي الدين أَحْمد ابن تَيمِية الْحَرَّانِي رَضِي الله عَنهُ، فَإِنَّهُ انتصر لمَذهَب السلف انتصارا لَا مزِيد عَلَيْهِ، وأخلص لله تَعَالَى فِي عمله، ونصح لله وَلِرَسُولِهِ ولأئمة الْمُسلمين وعامتهم، وَلَا يهولنك مَا وصمه بِهِ أعداؤه، فَإِن كَلَام الحساد كالزبد يذهب جفَاء. ثمَّ من بعده مصنفات

صَاحبه شمس الدين مُحَمَّد ابن قيم الجوزية، فَإِنَّهُ على طَرِيقَة شَيْخه سلك، وأثره اقتفى، وَحَقِيقَة مؤلفاته بسط مقالات أستاذه، وَذَلِكَ كالصواعق المحرقة، والجيوش الإسلامية والكافية الشافية الْمُسَمَّاة بالنونية.

The best book on the topic is the *Rasā'il* (Treatises) of al-Imām Aḥmad. Also, the best way, for those seeking critical knowledge and evidence, is contained within the works of Shaykh al-Islām Taqī al-Dīn Aḥmad ibn Taymiyyah al-Ḥarrānī ﷺ. He aided the *madhhab* of the Salaf in a way that leaves none to add. He was sincere to Allah the Exalted in his work. He was sincere to Allah, His Messenger, the scholars of the Muslims, and the Muslim commoners. Do not be fearful of the ways his enemies attempted to disgrace him, for the speech of the envious is like froth on the ocean: it is soon cast away. Afterwards, read the books of his student, Shams al-Dīn Muḥammad ibn Qayyim al-Jawziyyah. He followed the path of his teacher and held fast to his remnant path. The reality is that [Ibn al-Qayyim's] authorships are simply explanations of the statements of his teacher. For example, refer to *al-Ṣawā'iq [al-Mursalah]*, *[Ijtimā'] al-Juyūsh al-Islāmiyyah*, and *al-Kāfiyah al-Shāfiyah*, known better as *al-Nūniyyah*.

ثمَّ اعْلَم أَن كتب أُولَئِكَ الْقَوْم تَنْقَسِم إِلَى قسمَيْنِ:

Know, too, that books on creed are of two categories:

الْقسم الأول: مِنْهَا قد تكفل بِذكر نحل الْفرق، ثمَّ مِنْهُم من يذكر ذَلِك سردا، وَلم يتَعَرَّض للرد على أحد مِنْهُم، وَذَلِكَ كَأبي مَنْصُور عبد القاهر بن طَاهِر الْبَغْدَادِي، الْمُتَوفَّى سنة تسع وَعشْرين وَأَرْبع مئة فِي كِتَابه (الفرق بَين الفرق)، وكأبي الْفَتْح مُحَمَّد بن عبد الكَرِيم الشهرستاني، الْمُتَوفَّى سنة ثَمَانِيَة وَأَرْبَعين وَخمْس مِئة. وَهَذَانِ الكتابان مطبوعان ومشهوران. وَمِنْهُم من يذكر الْفرق ويتكفل بِالرَّدِّ عَلَيْهِم، وَذَلِكَ كَأبي مُحَمَّد عَلي بن أَحْمد الْمَعْرُوف ب(ابْن حزم) فِي كِتَابه الفصل - بِكَسْر الفَاء وَفتح الصَّاد - وَهُوَ مطبوع مَشْهُور، وَكَانَت وَفَاة صَاحبه سنة سِت وَخمسين وَأَرْبع مِئَة. وَقد قَالَ عَنهُ الشهرستاني: هُوَ عِنْدِي خير كتاب صنف. وَقد اعْتدى الشَّيْخ عبد الْوَهَّاب ابْن السُّبْكِيّ على الفصل فَقَالَ فِي كِتَابه (الطَّبَقَات): هَذَا من أشهر الْكتب، وَمَا برح الْمُحَقِّقُونَ من أَصْحَابنَا ينهون عَن النظر فِيهِ لما فِيهِ

من الازدراء بِأَهْل السّنة، وَقد أفرط فِي التعصب على أبي الحسن الأشْعَري حَتَّى صرح بنسبته إِلَى الْبِدْعَة، هَذَا كَلَامه.

First: Some take it upon themselves to mention the beliefs of the various sects, though some mention them without responding to them, such as Abu Manṣūr ʿAbd al-Qāhir ibn Ṭāhir al-Baghdādī, who died in the year 429 and authored *al-Farq bayn al-Firaq*. Also, similar to Abu ʿl-Fatḥ Muḥammad ibn ʿAbd al-Karīm al-Shahrastānī, who died in the year 548. Their respective books are both published and popular. Some mention the sects and take it upon themselves to refute them, such as Abu Muḥammad ibn Aḥmad, known better as Ibn Ḥazm, who authored *al-Fiṣal*. It is a popular book whose author died in the year 456. Al-Shahrastānī said of [Ibn Ḥazm's book], "To me, it is the best book authored."[680] Al-Shaykh ʿAbd al-Wahhāb ibn al-Subkī transgressed against *al-Fiṣal*, when he said, in his book *al-Ṭabaqāt*, "This is one of the most popular books. The critical scholars of [the Shāfiʿīs] have continuously prohibited reading it, because it shows contempt to Ahl al-Sunnah, and its author has shown overt bigotry against Abu ʿl-Ḥasan al-Ashʿarī, explicitly ascribing him to innovations."[681]

أَقُول: أَرَادَ بِأَهْل السنة من كَانَ على شاكلته من أَتبَاع الْأَشْعَرِيّ الموهوم، الَّذِي لَا تحقق لَهُ فِي الْخَارِج، وَإِنَّمَا وجوده فِي مخيلة أَصْحَابه، وهم الَّذي افتروا على الْأَشْعَرِي الْحَقِيقِي، فنسبوا إِلَيْهِ مَا هُوَ بَرِيء مِنْهُ، وَابْن حزم كَانَ أندلسيا، فاتصلت بِهِ تِلْكَ المفتريات، فَظن أنهَا من نحلة الأشْعَرِي الْحَقِيقِي، فَرد كَلَامه، فالجرم على المتسبب لَا على الإِمَام الْكَامِل ابْن حزم.

My comment is: When he says, "Ahl al-Sunnah," he means those who conformed to his ways in following the imagined al-Ashʿarī, the one who has no external existence but is merely present in the fantasies of his adherents. They have made false claims against the true al-Ashʿarī, ascribing things to him which he was innocent of. Ibn Ḥazm was an Andalusian, and those false claims reached him, so he thought that it was the true creed of al-Ashʿarī. As such, he refuted those claims. The crime, then, belongs to the causer, not on the complete *imām*, Ibn Ḥazm.

680 [T] This is actually al-Imām Taj al-Dīn al-Subki's description of the book of al-Shahrastānī. Refer to *Ṭabaqāt al-Shāfiʿīyyah al-Kubrā* (6/128).
681 [T] *Ṭabaqāt al-Shāfiʿīyyah al-Kubrā* (1/90).

وَالْقسم الثَّانِي: مِنْهَا مَا هُوَ مَوْضُوع لبَيَان مَذْهَب السلف، وَهِي كَثِيرة جدا كَمَا أسلفناه، لكننا نرشد الطَّالِب هُنَا إِلَى مَا فِيهِ مقنع لَهُ فَنَقُول مِنْهَا:

Second: Books that have been authored to simply elucidate the *madhhab* of the Salaf. They are abundant, as previously mentioned. However, here I shall guide the student to an amount that suffices:

(العقيدة الحموية) وَ(شرح العقيدة الأصفهانية) لشيخ الْإِسْلَام ابْن تَيْمِية وَغَيرهما من رسائله ومصنفاته.

Al-ʿAqīdah al-Ḥamawiyyah and *Sharḥ al-ʿAqīdah al-Aṣfahāniyyah*, by Shaykh al-Islām Ibn Taymiyyah, as well as his other booklets and authorships.

وَمِنْهَا (لمْعَة الِاعتِقَاد الهَادِي إِلَى سَبِيل الرشاد) للْإِمَام موفق الدين عبد الله بن أَحْمد بن مُحَمَّد ابن قدامَة الْمَقْدِسِي، وَهِي كراسة لَطِيفَة.

Lumʿat al-Iʿtiqād al-Hādī ilā Sabīl al-Rashād by al-Imām Muwaffaq al-Dīn ʿAbdullāh ibn Aḥmad ibn Muḥammad ibn Qudāmah al-Maqdisī. It is a pleasant treatise.

وَمِنْهَا (مُخْتَصر نِهَايَة المبتدئين) للشَّيْخ بدر الدين مُحَمد البلباني.

Mukhtaṣar Nihāyat al-Mubtadi'īn by al-Shaykh Badr al-Dīn Muḥammad al-Balbānī.

وَمِنْهَا (الْعين والأثر) للشَّيْخ عبد الْبَاقِي.

Al-ʿAyn wa 'l-Athar by al-Shaykh ʿAbd al-Bāqī.

وَمِنْهَا عقيدة الإِمَام حَافظ الْوَقْت عبد الغَنِي بن سرُور عبد الْوَاحِد ابن عَلي بن سرُور الجماعيلي.

The creed of the *imām* and the ḥadīth scholar of his times, ʿAbd al-Ghanī ibn Surūr ʿAbd al-Wāḥid ibn ʿAlī ibn Surūr al-Jamāʿīlī.

وَمِنْهَا (نجاه الخلف فِي اعْتِقَاد السّلف) للشَّيْخ عُثْمَان بن أَحْمد النجدي.

Najāt al-Khalaf fī I'tiqād al-Salaf by al-Shaykh 'Uthmān ibn Aḥmad al-Najdī.

وَمِنْهَا (الدرية المضية فِي عقيدة أهل الفرْقَة المرضية) وَهِي مِئَتا بَيت وَبضْعَة عشر بَيتا، نظمها الشَّيْخ العَلامَة مُحَمَّد بن أَحْمد السفاريني، ثمَّ شرحها فِي مُجَلد وَسَماهُ (لوامع الأنوَار البهية وسواطع الْأَسْرَار الأثرية لشرح الدرة المرضية) وَهُوَ شرح مُفِيد إِلا أنه جرى فِيهِ مسلكا وسطا بَين أهل الأثر وَبين طريقَة المُتَأخرين، وسلك فِيهِ غير مَسْلَك التَّحْقِيق، وَزَاد فِي آخر النظم وَالشرْح أَشْيَاء لم يرض بذكرها من سلف، وَلم يجعلوها من الاعتِقَاد فِي شَيْء، كذكر المَهْدي وأمثال ذَلِك مِمَّا حَقه أن يذكر فِي كتب الْمَلَاحِم والمواعظ لَا في كتب الاعتِقَاد. وَقد اختصر شيخ مَشَايخنَا الشَيْخ حسن الشطي الحنبَلِي الدمَشْقِي هَذَا الشَّرْح، إِلا أَنه أَخذ كَلَام السفاريني بلَفظِهِ، وَحذف الأقوَال وَالخلاف، فَحق هَذَا المُخْتَصر أَن ينْسب للسفاريني لَا لَهُ. وعَلى كل فَهَذَا الشرح مُفِيد وَقد طبع واشتهر.

Al-Durrat al-Muḍiyyah fī 'Aqīdah Ahl al-Firqah al-Marḍiyyah, which consists of two hundred and some-ought lines of poetry, authored by the *shaykh* and great scholar, Muḥammad ibn Aḥmad al-Saffārīnī. He also explained it in a single volume, naming his explanation *Lawāmi' al-Anwār al-Bahiyyah wa Sawāṭi' al-Asrār al-Athariyyah li Sharḥ al-Durrat al-Marḍiyyah*. Indeed, it is a useful explanation. However, he took a middling path, between that of the followers of narrations and the ways of the latter-day scholars. He did not take the critical route. At the end of his poem and explanation, he mentioned some things that the Salaf were not pleased with uttering and did not consider a part of the creed, such as mention of the Mahdī, and other things that should be mentioned in books on Signs of the Hour or admonishments. The teacher of our teachers, al-Shaykh Ḥasan al-Shaṭṭī al-Ḥanbalī al-Dimashqī, has summarised his explanation. However, he merely quoted al-Saffārīnī verbatim, but omitted any variant views. The summation, therefore, should be considered a work of al-Saffārīnī, not [al-Shaṭṭī]. Despite all of this, it is a very beneficial work, and has been published and become famous.

وَمِنْهَا كتاب (الْمُعْتَمد) ومختصره، كِلَاهُمَا للْقَاضِي أبي يعلى.

Al-Muʿtamad, and its summation, both by al-Qāḍī Abu Yaʿlā.

وَمِنْهَا كتاب (الإِبَانَة عَن شَرِيعَة الفرْقَة النَّاجِية ومجانبة الفرق المذمومة) للإِمَام عبيد الله بن مُحَمَّد بن مُحَمَّد بن حمدَان بن بطة العكبري، أحد شُيُوخ الإِمَام ابْن حَامِد، وَمن مؤلفاته (الإِبَانَة) الكَبِير وَالصَّغِير وَغَيرهمَا من الرسائل. وَقيل: إن مصنفاته تزيد على مئة مُصَنف، توفي سنة سبع وَثَمَانِينَ وثلاث مئة. وبطة - بِفَتْح البَاء والطاء المُشَدّدَة - قَالَه فِي المطلع.

Al-Ibānah ʿan Sharīʿah al-Firqah al-Nājiyah wa Mujānabah al-Firaq al-Madhmūmah, by al-Imām ʿUbaydullāh ibn Muḥammad ibn Muḥammad ibn Ḥamdān ibn Baṭṭāh al-ʿUkbarī, one of the teachers of al-Imām Ibn Ḥāmid. He wrote a larger and a smaller version of *al-Ibānah*, as well as other treatises. It was said that he wrote over one hundred authorships. He died in the year 387.

وَمِنْهَا كتاب التَّوْحِيد، وَمَعْرِفَة أسمَاء الله تَعَالَى وَصِفَاته على الاتفاق والتفرد، للْإِمَام مُحَمَّد بن إِسْحَاق بن مُحَمَّد بن يحيى بن مَنْدَه الأَصْبَهَانِي، وَكَانَ من أَصْحَابنَا، وَحكي عَنهُ فِي (المَقْصد الأرشد) أنه قَالَ: طفت الشرق والغرب مرَّتَيْنِ وَلم أسمع من المبتدعين حَدِيثا، توفي سنة نَيف وَسبعين وَأَرْبَع مِئَة، وَكتابه هَذا فِي سَبْعَة أجزَاء.

Kitāb al-Tawḥīd wa Maʿrifat Asmāʾ Allah Taʿālā wa Ṣifātih ʿala ʾl-Ittifāq wa ʾl-Tafarrud by al-Imām Muḥammad ibn Isḥāq ibn Muḥammad ibn Yaḥyā ibn Mandah al-Aṣbahānī. He was of our *aṣḥāb*. In *al-Maqṣad al-Arshad*, he is quoted as saying, "I travelled the earth from east to west twice, and never learned a ḥadīth from a person of innovation." He died in the year 470-odd. His book is comprised of seven volumes.

وَابْن مَنْدَه اثْنَان، وهما من أَصْحَابنَا. أَولهمَا هَذَا، وَالثَّانِي: الإِمَام الْحَافِظ صَاحب التصانيف الكَثِيرة الَّتِي مِنْهَا (تَارِيخ أَصْبَهَان) و(مناقب الإِمَام أَحْمد) رَضِي الله عَنهُ، وَهُوَ مُجَلد كَبِير، وَفِيه فَوَائِد حَسَنَة. قَالَ فِي أوله:

There are two scholars known as Ibn Mandah, but both are of our *aṣḥāb*. The first is [the author of *Kitāb al-Tawḥīd*], and the second is the *imām* and scholar of ḥadīth, the author of many works, such as *Tārīkh Aṣbahān* and *Manāqib al-Imām Aḥmad* ﵀ which is a large volume with useful points of benefit. He started it by saying:

وَمن أعظم جهالتهم - يَعْنِي المبتدعة - وغلوهم فِي مقالتهم، وقوعهم فِي الإِمَام المرضي إِمَام الأئِمَّة، وكهف الأمة، نَاصِر الإِسْلَام وَالسّنة، وَمن لم تَر عين مثله علما وزهدا وديانة وإمامة، إِمَام أهل الحَدِيث، أبي عبد الله أَحْمد بن مُحَمَّد بن حَنبَل الشَّيبَانِي، قدس الله روحه، وَبرد عَلَيْهِ ضريحه، الإِمَام الذِي لَا يجارى، والفحل الذِي لَا يُبارى، وَمن أجمع أئِمَّة الدين - رضوَان الله عَلَيْهِم وَرَحمته - فِي زَمَانه على تقدمه فِي شَأنه ونبله، وعلو مقَامه ومكانه، وَالذِي لَهُ من المناقب مَا لَا يعد وَلَا يُحْصى، قَامَ لله مقَاما لولاه لجهم النَّاس، ولمشوا على أَعْقَابهم الْقَهْقَرِي، ولضعف الإِسْلَام، واندرس الْعلم. وَلَقَد صدق الإِمَام أَبُو رَجَاء قتيبَة بن سعيد حَيْثُ قَالَ: إِن أَحْمد بن حَنبَل فِي زَمَانه بِمَنْزِلَة أبي بكر وَعمر فِي زمانهما. وَأحسن من قَالَ: لَو كَانَ أَحْمد فِي بني إِسْرَائِيل، لَكَانَ آيَة. أعاشنا الله على عقيدته، وحشرنا يَوْم الْقِيَامَة فِي زمرته.

One of the biggest falsities (i.e. of innovators) and signs of extremism in their views is that they disparage the *imām* that all are pleased with, the *imām* of *imāms*, the cave of knowledge of the Ummah, the supporter of Islam and Sunnah, the one the likes of whom have never been seen in terms of his knowledge, asceticism, religiosity, and scholarship. He was the *imām* of the scholars of ḥadīth, he was Abu 'Abdullāh Aḥmad ibn Muḥammad ibn Ḥanbal al-Shaybānī. May Allah sanctify his soul and make his tomb cool and full of relief. He was the *imām* that none could keep pace with, and the stallion that none could compete with. He was one that the scholars of the religion (may Allah be pleased with and show mercy to them) agreed on his superiority and nobility and lofty status and standing. He had an innumerable amount of virtues. He stood for the sake of Allah the Exalted in moments that, had he not, people would have followed Jahm and would have turned back on their heels, backwards. Islam would have become weak, and knowledge would have been lost. Al-Imām Abu Rajā' Qutaybah ibn Sa'īd told the truth when he said, "Aḥmad ibn Ḥanbal, in his times, was equivalent to Abu Bakr and 'Umar in theirs." Also, one has done good by saying, "Had Aḥmad ibn Ḥanbal lived during the age of the Children of Israel, he would have been a sign from Allah." May Allah allow us to live on his creed and resurrect us in his group on the Day of Resurrection.

وَحين وقفت على سرائر هَؤُلَاءِ، وخبث اعْتِقَادهم فِي هَذَا الإِمَام، قصدت لمجموع نبهت فِيهِ على بعض فضائله، ونبذه من مناقبه، وَذكرت طرفا مِمَّا منحه الله من المنزلَة الرفيعة، والرتبة العلية فِي الإِسْلَام وَالسّنة، مَعَ أني لست أَدْرِي لنفسي أَهْلِيَّة لذَلِك. وَأَن الْمَشَايِخ الماضين - رَحِمهم الله تَعَالَى - قد عنوا بجمعه، فشفوا، لكنني أردْت أَن يبْقى لي بِجمع مناقبه ذكر، وَأَن أكون مشرفا فِيمَا بَين أهل الْعلم من أهل السّنة بانتسابي إِلَيْهِ، ومحلى بمذهبه وطريقته.

When I came across the secretive matters and their malicious beliefs about this *imām*, I sought to compile a book to indicate some of his virtues and to give an excerpt of his outstanding traits. I made mention of some of what Allah the Exalted has given him, in terms of his high status and lofty position in Islam and the Sunnah, though I am not sure if I am deserving of doing so. The teachers who lived before ﵏ took great concern in compiling these matters. They did their job sufficiently. However, I wanted my name to remain inasmuch as I compiled his virtues, and wanted to be honoured among people of knowledge among Ahl al-Sunnah, as I ascribe myself to him and adorn myself with his *madhhab* and way. **[End]**[682]

وهَذَا كَلَامه. توفي سنة إِحْدَى عشرة، وَقيل اثْنَتَا عشرة وَخَمْس مِئة بأصبهان، وَبهَا دفن عِنْد آبَائِهِ رَحمَه الله تَعَالَى.

That is the conclusion of his remarks. He died in the year 511 or 512 in Aṣbahān, and his father was buried there as well. May Allah show him mercy.

وَمِنْهَا كتاب (التَّنْبِيه وَالرَّدّ على أهل الأَهْوَاء والبدع)، للمحدث الكَبِير أَحْمد بن مُحَمَّد المَلْطِي، المَعْرُوف بالطرائفي وَهُوَ كتاب لطيف، يذكر فِيهِ الفرق المبتدعة، وينصر مَذهَب أهل الحَدِيث.

Al-Tanbīh wa 'l-Rad 'alā Ahl al-Ahwā' wa 'l-Bida' by the great scholar of

682 [T] Although this book seems to be lost, this passage was quoted by al-Ḥāfiẓ Ibn Rajab in his *Dhayl Ṭabaqāt al-Ḥanābilah* (1/297).

ḥadīth, Aḥmad ibn Muḥammad al-Malṭī, known as al-Ṭarā'ifī. It is a pleasant book where he mentions innovated sects and evinces for the ways of Ahl al-Ḥadīth.

وَمِنْهَا غير ذَلِك مِمَّا لَا يُحْصى مِمَّا هُوَ مَشْهُور وَأكثر من أَن يذكر، وَلَيْسَ قصدنا استقصاء أَسمَاء الكتب، بل قصدنا التَّنْبِيه، على بعض مَا اطلَعْنَا عَلَيْهِ مِمَّا لَو طبع لأتى بفوائد جمة، تعود على مطالعه بالنفع، وَإِلا فَفِي كتاب (كشف الظنون) مَا فِيهِ مقنع لمن أَرَادَ معرفَة أَسمَاء كتب لَا يُمكن الْحُصُول إِلَّا على أقل الْقَلِيل مِنْهَا. وَالله الهَادِي والموفق.

There are many other books; they cannot be enumerated, and they are also very popular. The goal was not to mention an exhaustive list of books, but rather, to allude to some of the books that I have read, and that, if published, would result in useful benefits for the reader. *Kashf al-Ẓunūn* contains a sufficient number of names of books for those who wish. Only a few of them can be acquired, though. Allah the Exalted is the Guider and the One who provides divine aid.

وَهنا أَلْقى عَصَاهُ، وَاسْتقر بِهِ النَّوى، فَمَا أَجاد بِهِ فَمن فضل الله مفيض الجُود وَالْإِحْسَان وَالْكَرم، وَمَا عساه أَن يكون زل بِهِ أَلتمس عَنهُ عذرا، فَإِن الإِنسَان مَحل الْخَطَأ وَالنِّسْيَان. فنسأله تَعَالَى أَن ينفع بِمَا حررناه، وَأَن يقبل مَا رقمناه وَأَن يَجعله مَقبُولا مُنْتَفعا بِهِ، فَإِنَّمَا الأَعْمَال بِالنيَّاتِ. وحسبنا الله وَنعم الْوَكِيل.

Here, the pen ceases. Anything that has been of quality is from the favours of Allah, the giver of Generosity, Kindness, and Bounty. Everything that might not [be of quality] is a mistake that I seek an excuse for, for humans are mistake-prone and forgetful. I ask Allah the Exalted to benefit others with my compilation and to accept what I have penned. May it be accepted and beneficial. Indeed, actions are but by their intentions, and Allah is sufficient for us; He is the best to entrust to.

وَكَانَ الْفَرَاغ من كِتَابَة هَذِه المسودة فِي جُمَادَى الأول سنة ثَمَان وَثَلَاثِينَ وثلاث مئة وَألف فِي دمشق الزاهرة، فِي مدرسة المرحوم عبد الله باشا العظم، على يَدي، وَأَنا مُؤَلفه الفَقِير عبد القَادِر بن أَحْمد بن مصطفى بن عبد الرحِيم

بن مُحَمَّد الْمَعْرُوف بـ(ابْن بدران) اللَّهُمَّ اغْفِر لي ولوالدي ولمشايخي وَلِجَمِيعِ الْمُسلمين أَجْمَعِينَ آمين.

The completion of the draft of this book occurred in Jumādā al-Awwal in the year 1338, in the brilliant and radiant city of Damascus, in the school of ʿAbdullāh Bāshā al-ʿAẓm ﷺ. This draft was written with my own hand, and I, the author of this book, am the poor slave, ʿAbd al-Qādir ibn Aḥmad ibn Muṣṭafā ibn ʿAbd al-Raḥīm ibn Muḥammad, known better as Ibn Badrān. O Allah, forgive me, my parents, my teachers, and all Muslims. Amen.